Collins Gem

Dicionário
Inglês › Português
Português › Inglês

www.disal.com.br

Collins Gem
An Imprint of HarperCollinsPublishers

first published in this edition 1986
third edition 2000

© William Collins Sons & Co. Ltd 1986
© **HarperCollins Publishers** 1993, **2000**

ISBN 0-00-472409-7

Collins Gem® and Bank of English® are registered trademarks
of HarperCollins Publishers Limited

The Collins Gem website address is
www.collins-gem.com

The HarperCollins USA website address is
www.harpercollins.com

ISBN 0-00-472407-0
www.disal.com.br

contributors/colaboradores
John Whitlam, Victoria Davies, Mike Harland,
Jane Horwood, Lígia Xavier, Gerard Breslin,
Helen Newstead, Laura Neves

editorial staff/redação
Emma Aeppli, Marianne Davidson, Jennifer Baird

computing/informática
Jane Creevy

Typeset by Wordcraft, Glasgow
Printed and bound in Great Britain by Omnia Books Ltd, Glasgow G64

ÍNDICE

CONTENTS

Marcas Registradas

As palavras que acreditamos constituir marcas registradas foram assim denominadas. Todavia, não se deve supor que a presença ou a ausência dessa denominação possa afetar o status legal de qualquer marca.

Note on trademarks

Words which we have reason to believe constitute trademarks have been designated as such. However, neither the presence nor the absence of such designation should be regarded as affecting the legal status of any trademark.

INTRODUÇÃO

Ficamos felizes com a sua decisão de comprar o Dicionário Inglês-Português Collins Gem e esperamos que este lhe seja útil na escola, em casa, de férias ou no trabalho.

Esta introdução fornece algumas sugestões de como utilizar da melhor maneira possível o seu dicionário – não somente a partir da ampla lista de palavras mas também a partir das informações fornecidas em cada verbete. Este dicionário visa ajudá-lo a ler e a entender o inglês moderno assim como a exprimir-se corretamente.

No início do Dicionário Collins Gem aparecem as abreviaturas utilizadas, e a ilustração dos sons através de símbolos fonéticos. Você encontrará quadros de verbos irregulares ingleses na parte final do dicionário, seguidos por uma seção contendo números, expressões de tempo e um pequeno glossário de frases úteis.

COMO UTILIZAR O DICIONÁRIO COLLINS

Um grande número de informações pode ser encontrado neste dicionário. Vários tipos e tamanhos de letras, símbolos, abreviaturas e parênteses foram utilizados. As convenções e símbolos usados são explicados nas seções seguintes.

▶ Verbetes

As palavras que você procurar no dicionário – os verbetes – estão em ordem alfabética. Eles estão impressos **em negrito** para uma rápida identificação. Os dois verbetes que aparecem no topo de cada página indicam a primeira e a última palavras encontradas na página em questão.

Informações sobre a utilização ou forma de certos verbetes são dadas entre parênteses e, em geral, aparecem em forma abreviada e em itálico (*p. ex.:* (*fam*), (*COM*)).

Quando for apropriado, palavras derivadas aparecem agrupadas no mesmo verbete (**abade, abadia; produce, producer**) num formato ligeiramente menor do que o verbete.

As expressões comuns nas quais o verbete aparece estão impressas em um tamanho diferente de negrito romano. O símbolo '**~**' usado nas expressões representa o verbete principal no começo de cada parágrafo. Por exemplo, na entrada '**cold**', a expressão '**to be ~**' equivale a '**to be cold**'.

▶Significados

A tradução para o verbete aparece em letra normal e quando há mais de um significado ou utilização, estes estão separados por um ponto e vírgula. Freqüentemente, você encontrará outras palavras em itálico e entre parênteses antes da tradução, sugerindo contextos nos quais o verbete pode aparecer (*p. ex.*: **rough** *(voice)* ou *(weather)* ou fornecer sinônimos (*p. ex.*: **rough** *(violent)*).

▶Palavras 'chaves'

Atenção especial foi dada a certas palavras em inglês e em português consideradas palavras 'chaves' em cada língua. Elas podem, por exemplo, ser usadas com muita freqüência ou ter muitos tipos de utilização (*p. ex.*: **be, get**). Verbetes destacados com barras e números ajudam a distinguir as categorias gramaticais e diferentes significados. Informações complementares são fornecidas entre parênteses e em itálico na língua relevante para o usuário.

▶Informação gramatical

As categorias gramaticais são dadas em itálico e abreviadas após a ortografia fonética do verbete (*p. ex.*: *vt, adj, vi*)

Os adjetivos aparecem em ambos os gêneros quando forem diferentes (**interno, -a**). Esta distinção também é feita quando os adjetivos têm uma forma irregular no feminino ou no plural (*p. ex.*: **ateu, atéia**). As formas irregulares dos substantivos feminino ou plural também são indicadas (*p. ex.*: **child** (*pl ~ren*)).

INTRODUCTION

We are delighted you have decided to buy the Collins Portuguese Dictionary and hope you will enjoy and benefit from using it at school, at home, on holiday or at work.

This introduction gives you a few tips on how to get the most out of your dictionary – not simply from its comprehensive wordlist but also from the information provided in each entry. This will help you to read and understand modern Portuguese, as well as communicate and express yourself in the language.

The Collins Gem Portuguese Dictionary begins by listing the abbreviations used in the text and illustrating the sounds shown by the phonetic symbols. You will find Portuguese verb tables and English irregular verbs at the back, followed by a final section on numbers, time, dates, and useful phrases.

USING YOUR COLLINS DICTIONARY

A wealth of information is presented in the dictionary, using various typefaces, sizes of type, symbols, abbreviations and brackets. The conventions and symbols used are explained in the following sections.

▶ Headwords

The words you look up in the dictionary – 'headwords' – are listed alphabetically. They are printed in **bold type** for rapid identification. The two headwords appearing at the top of each page indicate the first and last word dealt with on the page in question.

Information about the usage or form of certain headwords is given in brackets after the phonetic spelling. This usually appears in abbreviated form and in italics. (*e.g.*: (*fam*), (*COMM*)).

Where appropriate, words related to headwords are grouped in the same entry (**abade, abadia; produce, producer**) in a slightly smaller bold type than the headword. Common expressions in which the headword appears are shown in a different size of bold roman type. The swung dash, ~, represents the main headword at the start of each entry. For example, in the entry for '**caminho**', the phrase '**pôr-se a ~**' should be read '**pôr-se a caminho**'.

► **Phonetic spellings**

The phonetic spelling of each headword (indicating its pronunciation) is given in square brackets immediately after the headword (*eg.*: **grande** ['grãdʒi]. A list of these spellings is given on page ix.

► **Meanings**

Headword translations are given in ordinary type and, where more than one meaning or usage exists, they are separated by a semicolon. You will often find other words in italics in brackets before the translations. These offer suggested contexts in which the headword might appear (e.g. **intenso** (*emoção*)) or provide synonyms (e.g. **cândido** (*inocente*)).

► **'Key' Words**

Special status is given to certain Portuguese and English words which are considered as 'key' words in each language. They may, for example, occur very frequently or have several types of usage (e.g. **bem, ficar**). A combination of lozenges and numbers helps you to distinguish different parts of speech and different meanings. Further helpful information is provided in brackets and in italics in the relevant language for the user.

► **Grammatical information**

Parts of speech are given in abbreviated form in italics after the phonetic spellings of headwords (e.g. *vt, adj, prep*).

Genders of Portuguese nouns are indicated as follows: *m* for a masculine and *f* for a feminine noun. Feminine and irregular plural forms of nouns are also shown next to the headword (**inglês, -esa; material** (*pl* **-ais**)). Adjectives are given in both masculine and feminine forms where these forms are different (**comilão, -lona**).

The gender of the Portuguese translation also appears in *italics* immediately following the key element of the translation, except where there is a regular masculine singular noun ending in 'o', or a regular feminine singular noun ending in 'a'.

ABREVIATURAS		ABBREVIATIONS
abreviatura	ab(b)r	abbreviation
adjetivo	adj	adjective
administração	ADMIN	administration
advérbio, locução adverbial	adv	adverb, adverbial phrase
aeronáutica	AER	flying, air travel
agricultura	AGR	agriculture
anatomia	ANAT	anatomy
arquitetura	ARQ, ARCH	architecture
artigo definido	art def	definite article
artigo indefinido	art indef	indefinite article
uso atributivo do substantivo	atr	compound element
automobilismo	AUT(O)	the motor car and motoring
auxiliar	aux	auxiliary
aeronáutica	AVIAT	flying, air travel
biologia	BIO	biology
botânica, flores	BOT	botany
português do Brasil	BR	Brazilian Portuguese
inglês britânico	BRIT	British English
química	CHEM	chemistry
linguagem coloquial (!chulo)	col(!)	colloquial (!offensive)
comércio, finanças, bancos	COM(M)	commerce, finance, banking
comparativo	compar	comparative
computação	COMPUT	computing
conjunção	conj	conjunction
construção	CONSTR	building
uso atributivo do substantivo	cpd	compound element
cozinha	CULIN	cookery
artigo definido	def art	definite article
economia	ECON	economics
educação, escola e universidade	EDUC	schooling, schools and universities
eletricidade, eletrônica	ELET, ELEC	electricity, electronics

especialmente	**esp**	especially
exclamação	**excl**	exclamation
feminino	**f**	feminine
ferrovia	**FERRO**	railways
uso figurado	**fig**	figurative use
física	**FÍS**	physics
fotografia	**FOTO**	photography
(verbo inglês) do qual a partícula é inseparável	**fus**	(phrasal verb) where the particle is inseparable
geralmente	**gen**	generally
geografia, geologia	**GEO**	geography, geology
geralmente	**ger**	generally
impessoal	**impess, impers**	impersonal
artigo indefinido	**indef art**	indefinite article
linguagem coloquial (!chulo)	**inf(!)**	colloquial (!offensive)
infinitivo	**infin**	infinitive
invariável	**inv**	invariable
irregular	**irreg**	irregular
jurídico	**JUR**	law
gramática, lingüística	**LING**	grammar, linguistics
masculino	**m**	masculine
matemática	**MAT(H)**	mathematics
medicina	**MED**	medicine
ou masculino ou feminino, dependendo do sexo da pessoa	**m/f**	masculine/feminine
militar, exército	**MIL**	military matters
música	**MÚS, MUS**	music
substantivo	**n**	noun
navegação, náutica	**NÁUT, NAUT**	sailing, navigation
adjetivo ou substantivo numérico	**num**	numeral adjective or noun
	o.s.	oneself
pejorativo	**pej**	pejorative

fotografia	PHOT	photography
física	PHYS	physics
fisiologia	PHYSIO	physiology
plural	pl	plural
política	POL	politics
particípio passado	pp	past participle
preposição	prep	preposition
pronome	pron	pronoun
português de Portugal	PT	European Portuguese
pretérito	pt	past tense
química	QUÍM	chemistry
religião e cultos	REL	religion, church services
	sb	somebody
educação, escola e universidade	SCH	schooling, schools and universities
singular	sg	singular
	sth	something
sujeito (gramatical)	su(b)j	(grammatical) subject
subjuntivo, conjuntivo	sub(jun)	subjunctive
superlativo	superl	superlative
também	tb	also
técnica, tecnologia	TEC(H)	technical term, technology
telecomunicações	TEL	telecommunications
tipografia, imprensa	TIP	typography, printing
televisão	TV	television
tipografia, imprensa	TYP	typography, printing
inglês americano	US	American English
ver	V	see
verbo	vb	verb
verbo intransitivo	vi	intransitive verb
verbo reflexivo	vr	reflexive verb
verbo transitivo	vt	transitive verb
zoologia	ZOOL	zoology
marca registrada	®	registered trademark
equivalente cultural	≃	cultural equivalent

PORTUGUESE PRONUNCIATION

The rules given below refer to Portuguese as spoken in the city and surrounding region of Rio de Janeiro, Brazil.

▶ Consonants

c	[k]	café	c before a, o, u is pronounced as in cat
ce, ci	[s]	cego	c before e or i, as in receive
ç	[s]	raça	ç is pronounced as in receive
ch	[ʃ]	chave	ch is pronounced as in shock
d	[d]	data	as in English EXCEPT
de, di	[dʒ]	difícil	d before an i sound or final unstressed e
		cidade	is pronounced as in judge
g	[g]	gado	g before a, o, u as in gap
ge, gi	[ʒ]	gíria	g before e or i, as s in leisure
h		humano	h is always silent in Portuguese
j	[ʒ]	jogo	j is pronounced as s in leisure
l	[l]	limpo, janela	as in English EXCEPT
	[w]	falta, total	l after a vowel tends to become w
lh	[ʎ]	trabalho	lh is pronounced like the lli in million
m	[m]	animal, massa	as in English EXCEPT
	[ãw]	cantam	m at the end of a syllable preceded by a vowel nasalizes the preceding vowel
	[ĩ]	sim	
n	[n]	nadar, penal	as in English EXCEPT
	[ã]	cansar	n at the end of a syllable, preceded by a vowel and followed by a consonant, nasalizes the preceding vowel
	[ẽ]	alento	
nh	[ɲ]	tamanho	nh is pronounced like the ni in onion
q	[k]	queijo	qu before i or e is pronounced as in kick
q	[kw]	quanto	qu before a or o, or qü before e or i, is pronounced as in queen
		cinqüenta	
-r-	[r]	compra	r preceded by a consonant (except n) and followed by a vowel is pronounced with a single trill
r-, -r-	[x]	rato, arpão	inital r, r followed by a consonant and rr pronounced similar to the Scottish ch in loch
rr	[x]	borracha	
-r	[*]	pintar, dizer	word-final r before a word beginning with a consonant or at the end of a sentence is pronounced [x]; before a word beginning with a vowel it is pronounced [r]. In colloquial speech this variable sound is often not pronounced at all.

s-	[s]	sol	as in English EXCEPT
-s-	[z]	mesa	intervocalic s is pronounced as in rose
-s-	[ʒ]	rasgar, desmaio	s before b, d, g, l, m, n, r, and v, as in leisure
-s-, -s	[ʃ]	escada, livros	s before c, f, p, qu, t and finally, as in sugar
-ss-	[s]	nosso	double s is always pronounced as in boss
t	[t]	todo	as in English EXCEPT
te, ti	[tʃ]	amante tipo	t followed by an i sound or final unstressed e is pronounced as ch in cheer
x-	[ʃ]	xarope explorar	initial x or x before a consonant (except c) is pronounced as in sugar
-xce-, -xci-	[s]	exceto excitar	x before ce or ci is unpronounced
ex-	[z]	exame	x in the prefix ex before a vowel is pronounced as z in squeeze
-x-	[ʃ]	relaxar	x in any other position may be pronounced as in sugar, axe or sail
	[ks]	fixo	
	[s]	auxiliar	
z-, -z-	[z]	zangar	as in English EXCEPT
-z	[ʒ]	cartaz	final z is pronounced as in leisure

b, f, k, p, v, w are pronounced as in English.

▶ Vowels

a, á, à, â	[a]	mata	a is normally pronounced as in father
ã	[ã]	irmã	ã is pronounced approximately as in sung
e	[e]	vejo	unstressed (except final) e is pronounced like e in they, stressed e is pronounced either as in they or as in bet
-e	[i]	fome	final e is pronounced as in money
é	[ɛ]	miséria	é is pronounced as in bet
ê	[e]	pêlo	ê is pronounced as in they
i	[i]	vida	i is pronounced as in mean
o	[o]	locomotiva	unstressed (except final) o is pronounced as in local;
	[ɔ]	loja	stressed o is pronounced either as in local
	[o]	globo	or as in rock
-o	[u]	livro	final o is pronounced as in foot
ó	[ɔ]	óleo	ó is pronounced as in rock
ô	[o]	colônia	ô is pronounced as in local
u	[u]	luva	u is pronounced as in rule; it is silent in gue, gui, que and qui

xii

▶ Diphthongs

ãe	[ãj]	mãe	nasalized, approximately as in flying
ai	[aj]	val	as is ride
ao, au	[aw]	aos, auxílio	as is shout
ão	[ãw]	vão	nasalized, approximately as in round
ei	[ej]	feira	as is they
eu	[ew]	deusa	both elements pronounced
oi	[oj]	boi	as is toy
ou	[o]	cenoura	as is local
õe	[õj]	aviões	nasalized, approximately as in 'boing!'

▶ Stress

The rules of stress in Portuguese are as follows:

(a) when a word ends in *a, e, o, m* (except *im, um* and their plural
 forms) or *s*, the second last syllable is stressed;
 cama*ra*da; cama*ra*das
 *par*te; *par*tem

(b) when a word ends in *i, u, im* (and plural), *um* (and plural), *n* or a
 consonant other than *m* or *s*, the stress falls on the last syllable:
 ven*di*, al*gum*, al*guns*, fa*lar*

(c) when the rules set out in (a) and (b) are not applicable, an acute or
 circumflex accent appears over the stressed vowel:
 *ó*tica, *â*nimo, in*glês*

In the phonetic transcription, the symbol ['] precedes the syllable on which
the stress falls.

PRONÚNCIA INGLESA

▶ Vogais

	Exemplo Inglês	Explicação
[a:]	father	Entre o *a* de pa*d*re e o o de *n*ó; como em fa*d*a
[ʌ]	but, come	Aproximadamente como o primeiro *a* de ca*m*a
[æ]	man, cat	Som entre o *a* de *l*á e o *e* de *p*é
[ə]	father, ago	Som parecido com o *e* final pronunciado em Portugal
[ɔ:]	bird, heard	Entre o *e* aberto e o o fechado
[ɛ]	get, bed	Como em *p*é
[ɪ]	it, big	Mais breve do que em *s*í
[i:]	tea, see	Como em *f*íno
[ɔ]	hot, wash	Como em *p*ó
[ɔ:]	saw, all	Como o o de por*t*e
[u]	put, book	Som breve e mais fechado do que em bur*r*o
[u:]	too, you	Som aberto como em ju*r*o

▶ Ditongos

	Exemplo Inglês	Explicação
[aɪ]	fly, high	Como em ba*í*le
[au]	how, house	Como em c*au*sa
[ɛə]	there, bear	Como o *e* de a*er*oporto
[eɪ]	day, obey	Como o *ei* de *l*ei
[ɪə]	here, hear	Como *ia* de companh*ia*
[əu]	go, note	[ə] seguido de um *u* breve
[ɔɪ]	boy, oil	Como em b*ói*a
[uə]	poor, sure	Como *ua* em s*ua*

xiv

▶ Consoantes

	Exemplo Inglês	Explicação
[d]	mended	Como em *dado*, an*d*ar
[g]	get, big	Como em *g*rande
[dʒ]	gin, judge	Como em i*d*ade
[ŋ]	sing	Como em ci*n*co
[h]	house, he	*h* aspirado
[j]	young, yes	Como em *i*ogurte
[k]	come, mock	Como em *c*ama
[r]	red, tread	*r* como em *para*, mas pronunciado no céu da boca
[s]	sand, yes	Como em *s*ala
[z]	rose, zebra	Como em *z*ebra
[ʃ]	she, machine	Como em *ch*apéu
[tʃ]	chin, rich	Como *t* em *t*imbre
[w]	water, which	Como o *u* em ág*u*a
[ʒ]	vision	Como em *j*á
[θ]	think, myth	Sem equivalente, aproximadamente como um *s* pronunciado entre os dentes
[ð]	this, the	Sem equivalente, aproximadamente como um *z* pronunciado entre os dentes

b, f, l, m, n, p, t, v pronunciam-se como em português.

O signo [*] indica que o r final escrito pronuncia-se apenas em inglês britânico, excepto quando a palavra seguinte começa por uma vogal. O signo ['] indica a sílaba acentuada.

EUROPEAN PORTUGUESE SPELLING

The spelling of European Portuguese differs significantly from that of Brazilian. The differences, which affect consonant groups and accents, follow general patterns but do not on the whole conform to fixed rules. Limited space makes it impossible to cover all European forms in the dictionary text, but major differences in spelling and vocabulary have been included. In addition, the following guide is intended as a broad outline of these differences.

The following changes in spelling are consistent:

- Brazilian *gü* and *qü* become European *gu* and *qu*, e.g. *agüentar* (*BR*), *aguentar* (*PT*); *cinqüenta* (*BR*), *cinquenta* (*PT*).
- Brazilian *-éia* becomes European *-eia*, e.g. *idéia* (*BR*), *ideia* (*PT*).
- European spelling links forms of the verb *haver de* with a hyphen, e.g. *hei de* (*BR*), *hei-de* (*PT*).
- The numbers *dezesseis* (*BR*), *dezessete(BR)*, *dezenove* (*BR*) become *dezasseis* (*PT*), *dezassete* (*PT*), *dezanove* (*PT*).
- Adverbial forms of adjectives ending in *m* take double *m* in European spelling, single *m* in Brazilian, e.g. *comumente* (*BR*), *comummente* (*PT*).
- European spelling adds an acute accent to the final *a* in first person plural preterite forms of irregular *-ar* verbs to distinguish them from the present tense, e.g. *amamos* (*BR*), *amámos* (*PT*).
- Brazilian *conosco* becomes European *connosco*.

The following changes may take place, but are not consistent:

▶ Consonant changes

- Brazilian *c* and *ç* double to *cc* and *cç*, *acionista* (*BR*), *accionista* (*PT*), *seção* (*BR*), *secção* (*PT*).
- Brazilian *t* becomes *ct*, e.g. *elétrico* (*BR*), *eléctrico* (*PT*).
- European spelling adds *b* to certain words, e.g. *súdito* (*BR*), *súbdito* (*PT*), *sutilizar* (*BR*), *subtilizar* (*PT*).
- European spelling changes *ç*, *t* to *pç*, *pt*, e.g. *exceção* (*BR*), *excepção* (*PT*), *ótimo* (*BR*), *óptimo* (*PT*).
- Brazilian *-n-* becomes *-mn-*, e.g. *anistia* (*BR*), *amnistia* (*PT*).
- Brazilian *tr* becomes *t*, e.g. *registro* (*BR*), *registo* (*PT*).

▶ Accentuation changes

- Brazilian *ôo* loses circumflex accent, e.g. *vôo* (*BR*), *voo* (*PT*).
- European spelling changes circumflex accent on *e* and *o* to acute, e.g. *tênis* (*BR*), *ténis* (*PT*), *abdômen* (*BR*), *abdómen* (*PT*).

ENGLISH-PORTUGUESE
INGLÊS-PORTUGUÊS

A

A [eɪ] n (MUS) lá m

> KEYWORD

a [eɪ, ə] indef art (before vowel or silent h: an) **1** um(a); ~ **book/girl** um livro/uma menina; **an apple** uma maçã; **she's** ~ **doctor** ela é médica **2** (instead of the number "one") um(a); ~ **year ago** há um ano, um ano atrás; ~ **hundred/thousand** etc **pounds** cem/mil etc libras **3** (in expressing ratios, prices etc): **3** ~ **day/week** 3 por dia/semana, **10 km an hour** 10 km por hora; **30p** ~ **kilo** 30p o quilo

AA n abbr (= Alcoholics Anonymous) AA m; (BRIT: = Automobile Association) ≈ TCB m (BR), ≈ ACP m (PT)

AAA n abbr (= American Automobile Association) ≈ TCB m (BR), ≈ ACP m (PT)

aback [ə'bæk] adv: **to be taken** ~ ficar surpreendido, sobressaltar-se

abandon [ə'bændən] vt abandonar ♦ n: **with** ~ com desenfreio

abbey ['æbɪ] n abadia, mosteiro

abbot ['æbət] n abade m

abbreviation [əbriːvɪ'eɪʃən] n abreviatura

abdicate ['æbdɪkeɪt] vt abdicar, renunciar a ♦ vi abdicar, renunciar ao trono

abdomen ['æbdəmən] n abdômen m

abduct [æb'dʌkt] vt seqüestrar

ability [ə'bɪlɪtɪ] n habilidade f, capacidade f; (talent) talento

ablaze [ə'bleɪz] adj em chamas

able ['eɪbl] adj capaz; (skilled) hábil,

competente; **to be** ~ **to do sth** poder fazer algo

abnormal [æb'nɔːməl] adj anormal

aboard [ə'bɔːd] adv a bordo ♦ prep a bordo de

abode [ə'bəud] n (LAW): **of no fixed** ~ sem domicílio fixo

abolish [ə'bɔlɪʃ] vt abolir

aborigine [æbə'rɪdʒɪnɪ] n aborígene m/f

abort [ə'bɔːt] vt (MED) abortar; (plan) cancelar; **abortion** n aborto; **to have an abortion** fazer um aborto, abortar; **abortive** [ə'bɔːtɪv] adj fracassado

> KEYWORD

about [ə'baut] adv **1** (approximately) aproximadamente; **it takes** ~ **10 hours** leva mais ou menos 10 horas; **it's just** ~ **finished** está quase terminado **2** (referring to place) por toda parte, por todo lado; **to run/walk** etc ~ correr/andar etc por todos os lados **3**: **to be** ~ **to do sth** estar a ponto de fazer algo ♦ prep **1** (relating to) acerca de, sobre; **what is it** ~? do que se trata?, é sobre o quê?; **what** or **how** ~ **doing this?** que tal se fizermos isso? **2** (place) em redor de, por

above [ə'bʌv] adv em or por cima, acima; (greater) acima ♦ prep acima de, por cima de; (greater than: in rank) acima de; (: in number) mais de; ~ **all** sobretudo; **aboveboard** adj legítimo, limpo

abrasive [ə'breɪzɪv] *adj* abrasivo; (*fig*) cáustico, mordaz

abreast [ə'brest] *adv* lado a lado; **to keep ~ of** (*fig*) estar a par de

abroad [ə'brɔːd] *adv* (*be*) no estrangeiro; (*go*) ao estrangeiro

abrupt [ə'brʌpt] *adj* (*sudden*) brusco; (*curt*) ríspido; **abruptly** *adv* bruscamente

abscess ['æbsɪs] *n* abscesso (*BR*), abcesso (*PT*)

absence ['æbsəns] *n* ausência

absent ['æbsənt] *adj* ausente; **absentee** [æbsən'tiː] *n* ausente *m/f*; **absent-minded** *adj* distraído

absolute ['æbsəluːt] *adj* absoluto; **absolutely** [æbsə'luːtlɪ] *adv* absolutamente

absorb [əb'zɔːb] *vt* absorver; (*business*) incorporar; (*changes*) assimilar; (*information*) digerir; **absorbent cotton** (*us*) *n* algodão *m* hidrófilo

abstain [əb'steɪn] *vi*: **to ~ (from)** abster-se (de)

abstract ['æbstrækt] *adj* abstrato

absurd [əb'sɜːd] *adj* absurdo

abuse [*n* ə'bjuːs, *vb* ə'bjuːz] *n* (*insults*) insultos *mpl*; (*ill-treatment*) maus-tratos *mpl*; (*misuse*) abuso ♦ *vt* insultar; maltratar; abusar de; **abusive** [ə'bjuːsɪv] *adj* ofensivo

abysmal [ə'bɪzməl] *adj* (*ignorance*) profundo, total; (*failure*) péssimo

abyss [ə'bɪs] *n* abismo

AC *abbr* (= *alternating current*) CA

academic [ækə'demɪk] *adj* acadêmico; (*pej: issue*) teórico ♦ *n* universitário(-a)

academy [ə'kædəmɪ] *n* (*learned body*) academia; **~ of music** conservatório

accelerate [æk'seləreɪt] *vt, vi* acelerar; **accelerator** *n* acelerador *m*

accent ['æksənt] *n* (*written*) acento;

(*pronunciation*) sotaque *m*; (*fig: emphasis*) ênfase *f*

accept [ək'sept] *vt* aceitar; (*responsibility*) assumir; **acceptable** *adj* (*offer*) bem-vindo; (*risk*) aceitável; **acceptance** *n* aceitação *f*

access ['æksɛs] *n* acesso; **accessible** [æk'sɛsəbl] *adj* acessível; (*available*) disponível

accessory [æk'sɛsərɪ] *n* acessório; (*LAW*): **~ to** cúmplice *m/f* de

accident ['æksɪdənt] *n* acidente *m*; (*chance*) casualidade *f*; **by ~** (*unintentionally*) sem querer; (*by coincidence*) por acaso; **accidental** [æksɪ'dɛntl] *adj* acidental; **accidentally** [æksɪ'dɛntəlɪ] *adv* sem querer; **accident-prone** *adj* com tendência para sofrer ou causar acidente, desastrado

acclaim [ə'kleɪm] *n* aclamação *f*

accommodate [ə'kɔmədeɪt] *vt* alojar; (*subj: car, hotel, etc*) acomodar; (*oblige, help*) comprazer a; **accommodation** [əkɔmə'deɪʃən] *n* alojamento; **accommodations** (*us*) *npl* = **accommodation**

accompany [ə'kʌmpənɪ] *vt* acompanhar

accomplice [ə'kʌmplɪs] *n* cúmplice *m/f*

accomplish [ə'kʌmplɪʃ] *vt* (*task*) concluir; (*goal*) alcançar; **accomplishment** *n* realização *f*

accord [ə'kɔːd] *n* tratado ♦ *vt* conceder; **of his own ~** por sua iniciativa; **accordance** [ə'kɔːdəns] *n*: **in accordance with** de acordo com; **according**: **according to** *prep* segundo, conforme; **accordingly** *adv* por conseguinte; (*appropriately*) do modo devido

accordion [ə'kɔːdɪən] *n* acordeão *m*

account [ə'kaunt] *n* conta; (*report*)

relato; **~s** npl (*books, department*) contabilidade f; **of no ~** sem importância; **on ~** por conta; **on no ~** de modo nenhum; **on ~ of** por causa de; **to take into ~, take ~ of** levar em conta; **account for** vt fus (*explain*) explicar; (*represent*) representar; **accountancy** n contabilidade f; **accountant** n contador(a) m/f (BR), contabilista m/f (PT); **account number** n número de conta

accumulate [ə'kju:mjuleıt] vt acumular ♦ vi acumular-se

accuracy ['ækjurəsı] n exatidão f, precisão f

accurate ['ækjurıt] adj (*description*) correto; (*person, device*) preciso; **accurately** adv com precisão

accusation [ækju'zeıʃən] n (*act*) incriminação f; (*instance*) acusação f

accuse [ə'kju:z] vt acusar; **accused** n: **the accused** o/a acusado(a)

accustom [ə'kʌstəm] vt acostumar; **accustomed** adj: **accustomed to** acostumado a

ace [eıs] n ás m

ache [eık] n dor f ♦ vi (*yearn*): **to ~ to do sth** ansiar por fazer algo; **my head ~s** dói-me a cabeça

achieve [ə'tʃi:v] vt alcançar; (*victory, success*) obter; **achievement** n realização f; (*success*) proeza f

acid ['æsıd] adj ácido; (*taste*) azedo ♦ n ácido

acknowledge [ək'nɒlıdʒ] vt (*fact*) reconhecer; (*also: ~ receipt of*) acusar o recebimento de (BR) or a recepção de (PT); **acknowledgement** n notificação f de recebimento

acne ['æknı] n acne f

acorn ['eıkɔ:n] n bolota

acoustic [ə'ku:stık] adj acústico; **acoustics** n, npl acústica

acquaint [ə'kweınt] vt: **to ~ sb with sth** pôr alguém ao corrente de algo; **to be ~ed with** conhecer; **acquaintance** n conhecimento; (*person*) conhecido(-a)

acquire [ə'kwaıə*] vt adquirir

acquit [ə'kwıt] vt absolver; **to ~ o.s. well** desempenhar-se bem

acre ['eıkə*] n acre m (= 4047m²)

acrobat ['ækrəbæt] n acrobata m/f

across [ə'krɒs] prep (*on the other side of*) no outro lado de; (*crosswise*) através de ♦ adv: **to go** (*or walk*) **~** atravessar; **the lake is 12km ~** o lago tem 12km de largura; **~ from** em frente de

acrylic [ə'krılık] adj acrílico ♦ n acrílico

act [ækt] n ação f; (THEATRE) ato; (*in show*) número; (LAW) lei f ♦ vi tomar ação; (*behave, have effect, THEATRE*) agir; (*pretend*) fingir ♦ vt (*part*) representar; **in the ~ of** no ato de; **to ~ as** servir de; **acting** adj interino ♦ n: **to do some acting** fazer teatro

action ['ækʃən] n ação f; (MIL) batalha, combate m; (LAW) ação judicial; **out of ~** (*person*) fora de combate; (*thing*) com defeito; **to take ~** tomar atitude; **action replay** n (TV) replay m

activate ['æktıveıt] vt acionar

active ['æktıv] adj ativo; (*volcano*) em atividade; **actively** adv ativamente; **activity** [æk'tıvıtı] n atividade f

actor ['æktə*] n ator m

actress ['æktrıs] n atriz f

actual ['æktjuəl] adj real; (*emphatic use*) em si; **actually** adv realmente; (*in fact*) na verdade; (*even*) mesmo

acute [ə'kju:t] adj agudo; (*person*) perspicaz

ad [æd] n abbr = **advertisement**

adamant ['ædəmənt] adj inflexível
adapt [ə'dæpt] vt adaptar ♦ vi: to ~ (to) adaptar-se (a); **adaptable** adj (device) ajustável; (person) adaptável; **adapter** n (ELEC) adaptador m; **adaptor** = adapter
add [æd] vt acrescentar; (figures: also: ~ up) somar ♦ vi: to ~ to aumentar
addict ['ædɪkt] n viciado(-a); **drug** ~ toxicômano(-a); **addicted** [ə'dɪktɪd] adj: **to be addicted to** ser viciado em; (fig) ser fanático por; **addiction** n dependência; **addictive** adj que causa dependência
addition [ə'dɪʃən] n adição f; (thing added) acréscimo; **in** ~ além disso; **in** ~ **to** além de; **additional** adj adicional
additive ['ædɪtɪv] n aditivo
address [ə'drɛs] n endereço; (speech) discurso ♦ vt (letter) endereçar; (speak to) dirigir-se a, dirigir a palavra a; **to** ~ **(o.s. to)** enfocar
adept ['ædɛpt] adj: ~ **at** hábil ou competente em
adequate ['ædɪkwɪt] adj (enough) suficiente; (satisfactory) satisfatório
adhere [əd'hɪə*] vi: to ~ **to** aderir a; (abide by) ater-se a
adhesive [əd'hi:zɪv] n adesivo
adjective ['ædʒɛktɪv] n adjetivo
adjoining [ə'dʒɔɪnɪŋ] adj adjacente
adjourn [ə'dʒɜːn] vt (session) suspender ♦ vi ser suspenso
adjust [ə'dʒʌst] vt (change) ajustar; (clothes) arrumar; (machine) regular ♦ vi: to ~ **(to)** adaptar-se (a); **adjustment** n ajuste m; (of engine) regulagem f; (of prices, wages) reajuste m; (of person) adaptação f
ad-lib [-lɪb] vi improvisar ♦ adv: **ad lib** à vontade
administer [əd'mɪnɪstə*] vt administrar; (justice) aplicar; (drug) minis-

trar; **administration** [ədmɪnɪs-'treɪʃən] n administração f; (management) gerência; (government) governo; **administrative** [əd-'mɪnɪstrətɪv] adj administrativo
admiral ['ædmərəl] n almirante m
admire [əd'maɪə*] vt (respect) respeitar; (appreciate) admirar
admission [əd'mɪʃən] n (admittance) entrada; (fee) ingresso; (confession) confissão f
admit [əd'mɪt] vt admitir; (accept) aceitar; (confess) confessar; **admit to** vt fus confessar; **admittance** n entrada; **admittedly** adv evidentemente
ado [ə'du:] n: **without (any) more** ~ sem mais cerimônias
adolescent [ædəu'lɛsnt] adj, n adolescente m/f
adopt [ə'dɔpt] vt adotar; **adopted** adj adotivo; **adoption** n adoção f
adore [ə'dɔ:*] vt adorar
Adriatic (Sea) [eɪdrɪ'ætɪk-] n (mar m) Adriático
adrift [ə'drɪft] adv à deriva
adult ['ædʌlt] n adulto(-a) ♦ adj adulto; (literature, education) para adultos
adultery [ə'dʌltərɪ] n adultério
advance [əd'vɑːns] n avanço; (money) adiantamento ♦ adj antecipado ♦ vt (money) adiantar ♦ vi (move) avançar; (progress) progredir; **in** ~ com antecedência; **to make** ~**s to sb** fazer propostas a alguém; **advanced** adj adiantado
advantage [əd'vɑːntɪdʒ] n (gen, TENNIS) vantagem f; (supremacy) supremacia; **to take** ~ **of** aproveitar-se de, levar vantagem de
adventure [əd'vɛntʃə*] n façanha; (excitement in life) aventura
adverb ['ædvɜːb] n advérbio
adverse ['ædvɜːs] adj (effect) con-

trário; (*weather, publicity*) desfavorável

advert ['ædvə:t] *n abbr* = **advertisement**

advertise ['ædvətaız] *vi* anunciar ♦ *vt* (*event, job*) anunciar; (*product*) fazer a propaganda de; **to ~ for** (*staff*) procurar; **advertisement** [əd'və:tısmənt] *n* (*classified*) anúncio; (*display, TV*) propaganda, anúncio; **advertising** *n* publicidade *f*

advice [əd'vaıs] *n* conselhos *mpl*; (*notification*) aviso; **piece of ~** conselho; **to take legal ~** consultar um advogado

advise [əd'vaız] *vt* aconselhar; (*inform*): **to ~ sb of sth** avisar alguém de algo; **to ~ sb against sth/doing sth** desaconselhar algo a alguém/aconselhar alguém a não fazer algo; **adviser** *or* **advisor** *n* conselheiro(-a); (*consultant*) consultor(a) *m/f*; **advisory** *adj* consultivo; **in an advisory capacity** na qualidade de assessor *or* consultor

advocate [*vb* 'ædvəkeıt, *n* 'ædvəkıt] *vt* defender; (*recommend*) advogar ♦ *n* advogado(-a); (*supporter*) defensor(a) *m/f*

Aegean [i:'dʒi:ən] *n*: **the ~ (Sea)** o (mar) Egeu

aerial ['ɛərıəl] *n* antena ♦ *adj* aéreo

aerobics [ɛə'rəubıks] *n* ginástica *f*

aeroplane ['ɛərəpleın] (*BRIT*) *n* avião *m*

aerosol ['ɛərəsɔl] *n* aerossol *m*

aesthetic [i:s'θɛtık] *adj* estético

afar [ə'fɑ:*] *adv*: **from ~** de longe

affair [ə'fɛə*] *n* (*matter*) assunto; (*business*) negócio; (*question*) questão *f*; (*also*: **love ~**) caso

affect [ə'fɛkt] *vt* afetar; (*move*) comover; **affected** *adj* afetado

affection [ə'fɛkʃən] *n* afeto, afeição *f*; **affectionate** *adj* afetuoso

afflict [ə'flıkt] *vt* afligir

affluent ['æfluənt] *adj* rico; **the affluent society** a sociedade de abundância

afford [ə'fɔ:d] *vt* (*provide*) fornecer; (*goods etc*) ter dinheiro suficiente para; (*permit o.s.*): **I can't ~ the time/to take that risk** não tenho tempo/não posso correr esse risco

afloat [ə'fləut] *adv* flutuando

afoot [ə'fut] *adv*: **there is something ~** está acontecendo algo

afraid [ə'freıd] *adj* assustado; **to be ~ of/to** ter medo de; **I am ~ that** lamento que; **I'm ~ so/not** receio que sim/não

Africa ['æfrıkə] *n* África; **African** *adj*, *n* africano(-a)

after ['ɑ:ftə*] *prep* depois de ♦ *adv* depois ♦ *conj* depois que; **a quarter ~ two** (*US*) duas e quinze; **what/who are you ~?** o que você quer?/ quem procura?; **~ having done** tendo feito; **he was named ~ his grandfather** ele recebeu o nome do avô; **to ask ~** perguntar por alguém; **~ all** afinal (de contas); **~ you!** passe primeiro!; **aftermath** *n* consequências *fpl*; **afternoon** *n* tarde *f*; **afters** (*inf*) *n* sobremesa; **after-sales service** (*BRIT*) *n* serviço pós-vendas; **after-shave (lotion)** *n* loção *f* após-barba; **aftersun** *n* loção *f* pós-sol; **afterwards** *adv* depois

again [ə'gɛn] *adv* (*once more*) outra vez; (*repeatedly*) de novo; **to do sth ~** voltar a fazer algo; **not ... ~!** ... de novol; **~ and ~** repetidas vezes

against [ə'gɛnst] *prep* contra; (*compared to*) em contraste com

age [eıdʒ] *n* idade *f*; (*period*) época ♦ *vt*, *vi* envelhecer; **he's 20 years of ~** ele tem 20 anos de idade; **to come of ~** atingir a maioridade; **it's been ~s since I saw him** faz muito

tempo que eu não o vejo; **aged¹**
[eɪdʒd] adj: **aged 10** de 10 anos de
idade; **aged²** [ˈeɪdʒɪd] adj idoso
♦ npl: **the aged** os idosos; **age
group** n faixa etária; **age limit** n
idade f mínima/máxima

agency [ˈeɪdʒənsɪ] n agência;
(government body) órgão m

agenda [əˈdʒendə] n ordem f do dia

agent [ˈeɪdʒənt] n agente m/f

aggravate [ˈæɡrəveɪt] vt agravar;
(annoy) irritar

aggressive [əˈɡresɪv] adj agressivo

agitate [ˈædʒɪteɪt] vt agitar ♦ vi: **to ~
for** fazer agitação a favor de

AGM n abbr (= annual general meeting) AGO f

ago [əˈɡəu] adv: **2 days ~** há 2 dias
(atrás); **not long ~** há pouco tempo;
how long ~? há quanto tempo?

agony [ˈæɡənɪ] n (pain) dor f; **to be
in ~** sofrer dores terríveis

agree [əˈɡriː] vt combinar ♦ vi
(correspond) corresponder; **to ~
(with)** concordar (com); **to ~ to
sth/to do sth** consentir algo/aceitar
fazer algo; **to ~ that** concordar or
admitir que; **agreeable** adj agradável; (willing) disposto; **agreed** adj
combinado, combinado; **agreement** n acordo;
(comm) contrato; **in agreement** de
acordo

agricultural [æɡrɪˈkʌltʃərəl] adj (of
crops) agrícola; (of cows and cattle)
agropecuário

agriculture [ˈæɡrɪkʌltʃəʳ] n (of
crops) agricultura; (of cows and cattle) agropecuária

aground [əˈɡraund] adv: **to run ~**
encalhar

ahead [əˈhed] adv adiante; **go right**
or **straight ~** siga em frente; **go ~!**
(fig) vá em frente!; **~ of** na frente de

aid [eɪd] n ajuda; (device) aparelho
♦ vt ajudar; **in ~ of** em benefício de;

to ~ and **abet** (LAW) ser cúmplice de

AIDS [eɪdz] n abbr (= acquired immune deficiency syndrome) AIDS f
(BR), SIDA f (PT)

aim [eɪm] vt: **to ~ sth (at)** apontar
algo (para); (remark) dirigir algo (a)
♦ vi (also: **take ~**) apontar ♦ n (skill)
pontaria; (objective) objetivo; **to ~ at**
mirar; **to ~ to do** pretender fazer

ain't [eɪnt] (inf) = **am not**; **aren't**;
isn't

air [ɛəʳ] n ar m; (appearance) aparência, aspeto; (tune) melodia ♦ vt arejar; (grievances, ideas) discutir ♦ cpd
aéreo; **to throw sth into the ~** jogar
algo para cima; **by ~** (travel) de
avião; **on the ~** (RADIO, TV) no ar; **air-
bed** (BRIT) n colchão m de ar; **air
conditioning** n ar condicionado;
aircraft n inv aeronave f; **airfield**
n campo de aviação; **Air Force** n
Força Aérea, Aeronáutica; **air
freshener** n perfumador m de ar;
airgun n espingarda de ar comprimido; **air hostess** (BRIT) n aeromoça (BR), hospedeira (PT); **air letter** (BRIT) n aerograma m; **airline** n
linha aérea; **airliner** n avião m de
passageiros; **airmail** n: **by airmail**
por via aérea; **air mile** n milha
aérea; **airplane** (US) n avião m; **airport** n aeroporto; **airsick** adj: **to
be airsick** enjoar (no avião); **air-
tight** adj hermético; **airy** adj
(room) arejado; (manner) leviano

aisle [aɪl] n (of church) nave f (of
theatre etc) corredor m

ajar [əˈdʒɑːʳ] adj entreaberto

alarm [əˈlɑːm] n alarme m; (anxiety)
inquietação f ♦ vt alarmar; **alarm
clock** n despertador m

album [ˈælbəm] n (for stamps etc)
álbum m; (record) elepê m

alcohol [ˈælkəhɔl] n álcool m;
alcohol-free adj sem álcool; **alco-**

holic [ælkə'hɒlɪk] adj alcoólico ♦ n alcoólatra m/f

ale [eɪl] n cerveja

alert [ə'lɜːt] adj atento; (to danger, opportunity) alerta ♦ n alerta ♦ vt alertar; **to be on the ~** estar alerta; (MIL) ficar de prontidão

Algarve [æl'gɑːv] m. **the ~** o Algarve

algebra ['ældʒɪbrə] n álgebra

Algeria [æl'dʒɪərɪə] n Argélia

alias ['eɪlɪəs] adv também chamado ♦ n (of criminal) alcunha; (of writer) pseudônimo

alibi ['ælɪbaɪ] n álibi m

alien ['eɪlɪən] n estrangeiro(-a); (from space) alienígena m/f ♦ adj: ~ **to** alheio a

alight [ə'laɪt] adj em chamas; (eyes) aceso; (expression) intento ♦ vi (passenger) descer (de um veículo); (bird) pousar

alike [ə'laɪk] adj semelhante ♦ adv similarmente, igualmente; **to look ~** parecer-se

alimony ['ælɪmənɪ] n (payment) pensão f alimentícia

alive [ə'laɪv] adj vivo; (lively) alegre

KEYWORD

all [ɔːl] adj (sg) todo(-a); (pl) todos(-as); ~ **day/night** o dia inteiro/a noite inteira; ~ **five came** todos os cinco vieram; ~ **the books/food** todos os livros/toda a comida ♦ pron **1** tudo; ~ **of us/the boys went** todos nós fomos/todos os meninos foram; **is that ~?** é só isso?; (in shop) mais alguma coisa? **2** (in phrases): **above** ~ sobretudo; **after** ~ afinal (de contas); **at** ~: **not at** ~ (in answer to question) em absoluto, absolutamente não; **I'm not at** ~ **tired** não estou nada cansado; **anything at** ~ **will do** qualquer

coisa serve; ~ **in** ao todo ♦ adv todo, completamente; ~ **alone** completamente só; **it's not as hard as** ~ **that** não é tão difícil assim; ~ **the more** ainda mais; ~ **the better** tanto melhor, ainda melhor; ~ **but** quase; **the score is 2** ~ o escore é 2 a 2

allege [ə'ledʒ] vt alegar; **allegedly** [ə'ledʒɪdlɪ] adv segundo dizem

allegiance [ə'liːdʒəns] n lealdade f

allergic [ə'lɜːdʒɪk] adj: ~ **(to)** alérgico (a)

allergy ['ælədʒɪ] n alergia f

alleviate [ə'liːvɪeɪt] vt (pain) aliviar; (difficulty) minorar

alley ['ælɪ] n viela

alliance [ə'laɪəns] n aliança

all-in (BRIT) adj, adv (charge) incluído

all-night adj (café) aberto toda a noite; (party) que dura toda a noite

allocate ['æləkeɪt] vt destinar

allot [ə'lɒt] vt: **to ~** designar para; **allotment** n partilha; (garden) lote m

all-out adj (effort etc) máximo ♦ adv: **all out** com toda a força

allow [ə'lau] vt permitir; (claim, goal) admitir; (sum, time) calcular; (concede): **to ~ that** reconhecer que; **to ~ sb to do** permitir a alguém fazer; **allow for** vt fus levar em conta; **allowance** [ə'lauəns] n ajuda de custo; (welfare payment) pensão f, auxílio; (TAX) abatimento; (pocket money) mesada; **to make allowances for** levar em consideração

all: all right adv (well) bem; (correctly) corretamente; (as answer) está bem!; **all-time** adj de todos os tempos

ally [n 'ælaɪ, vb ə'laɪ] n aliado ♦ vt: **to**

~ o.s. with aliar-se com

almighty [ɔːlˈmaɪtɪ] *adj* onipotente; *(row etc)* a maior

almond [ˈɑːmənd] *n* amêndoa

almost [ˈɔːlməust] *adv* quase

alone [əˈləun] *adj* só, sozinho; *(unaided)* sozinho ♦ *adv* só, somente, sozinho; **to leave sb** ~ deixar alguém em paz; **to leave sth** ~ não tocar em algo; **let** ... ~ ... sem falar em ...

along [əˈlɒŋ] *prep* por, ao longo de ♦ *adv*: **is he coming** ~? ele vem conosco?; **he was hopping/limping** ~ ele ia pulando/coxeando; ~ **with** junto com; **all** ~ o tempo todo; **alongside** *prep* ao lado de ♦ *adv* encostado

aloof [əˈluːf] *adj* afastado, altivo ♦ *adv*: **to stand** ~ afastar-se

aloud [əˈlaud] *adv* em voz alta

alphabet [ˈælfəbɛt] *n* alfabeto

Alps [ælps] *npl*: **the** ~ os Alpes

already [ɔːlˈrɛdɪ] *adv* já

alright [ˈɔːlˈraɪt] *(BRIT) adv* = **all right**

Alsatian [ælˈseɪʃən] *(BRIT) n (dog)* pastor *m* alemão

also [ˈɔːlsəu] *adv* também; *(moreover)* além disso

altar [ˈɔltə*] *n* altar *m*

alter [ˈɔltə*] *vt* alterar ♦ *vi* modificar-se

alternate [*adj* ɔlˈtəːnɪt, *vb* ˈɔltəːneɪt] *adj* alternado; *(US: alternative)* alternativo ♦ *vi* alternar-se; **alternating** *adj*: **alternating current** corrente *f* alternada

alternative [ɔlˈtəːnətɪv] *adj* alternativo ♦ *n* alternativa; **alternatively** *adv*: **alternatively one could** ... por outro lado se podia ...

although [ɔːlˈðəu] *conj* embora; *(given that)* se bem que

altitude [ˈæltɪtjuːd] *n* altitude *f*

alto [ˈæltəu] *n (female)* contralto *f*; *(male)* alto

altogether [ɔːltəˈgɛðə*] *adv* totalmente; *(on the whole)* no total

aluminium [æljuˈmɪnɪəm] *(US* **aluminum)** *n* alumínio

always [ˈɔːlweɪz] *adv* sempre

Alzheimer's disease [ˈæltshaɪməz-] *n* doença de Alzheimer

am [æm] *vb* see **be**

a.m. *adv abbr* (= *ante meridiem*) da manhã

amateur [ˈæmətə*] *adj*, *n* amador(a) *m/f*

amaze [əˈmeɪz] *vt* pasmar; **to be** ~**d (at)** espantar-se (de *or* com); **amazement** *n* pasmo, espanto; **amazing** *adj* surpreendente; *(fantastic)* fantástico

Amazon [ˈæməzən] *n* Amazonas *m*

ambassador [æmˈbæsədə*] *n* embaixador (embaixatriz) *m/f*

amber [ˈæmbə*] *n* âmbar *m*; **at** ~ *(BRIT: AUT)* em amarelo

ambiguous [æmˈbɪgjuəs] *adj* ambíguo

ambition [æmˈbɪʃən] *n* ambição *f*; **ambitious** *adj* ambicioso

ambulance [ˈæmbjuləns] *n* ambulância

ambush [ˈæmbuʃ] *n* emboscada ♦ *vt* emboscar

amend [əˈmɛnd] *vt* emendar; **to make** ~**s (for)** compensar

amenities [əˈmiːnɪtɪz] *npl* atrações *fpl*, comodidades *fpl*

America [əˈmɛrɪkə] *n (continent)* América; *(USA)* Estados Unidos *mpl*; **American** *adj* americano; norte-americano, estadunidense ♦ *n* americano(-a); norte-americano(-a)

amiable [ˈeɪmɪəbl] *adj* amável

amicable [ˈæmɪkəbl] *adj* amigável

amid(st) [əˈmɪd(st)] *prep* em meio a

amiss [əˈmɪs] *adv*: **to take sth** ~ levar algo a mal; **there's something** ~ aí tem coisa

ammunition [æmjʊˈnɪʃən] n munição f

among(st) [əˈmʌŋ(st)] prep entre, no meio de

amount [əˈmaunt] n quantidade f; (of money etc) quantia ♦ vi: **to ~ to** (total) montar a; (be same as) equivaler a, significar

amp(ère) [ˈæmp(ɛə*)] n ampère m

ample [ˈæmpl] adj amplo; (abundant) abundante; (enough) suficiente

amplifier [ˈæmplɪfaɪə*] n amplificador m

amuse [əˈmjuːz] vt divertir; (distract) distrair; **amusement** n diversão f; (pleasure) divertimento; (pastime) passatempo

an [æn, ən, n] indef art see **a**

anaemic [əˈniːmɪk] (US **anemic**) adj anêmico

anaesthetic [ænɪsˈθetɪk] (US **anesthetic**) n anestésico

analyse [ˈænəlaɪz] (US **analyze**) vt analisar; **analysis** [əˈnæləsɪs] (pl **analyses**) n análise f; **analyst** [ˈænəlɪst] n analista m/f; (psychoanalyst) psicanalista m/f

analyze [ˈænəlaɪz] (US) vt = **analyse**

anarchist [ˈænəkɪst] n anarquista m/f

anarchy [ˈænəkɪ] n anarquia f

anatomy [əˈnætəmɪ] n anatomia f

ancestor [ˈænsɪstə*] n antepassado

anchor [ˈæŋkə*] n âncora f ♦ vi (also: **to drop ~**) ancorar, fundear ♦ vt (fig): **to ~ sth to** firmar algo em; **to weigh ~** levantar âncoras

anchovy [ˈæntʃəvɪ] n enchova

ancient [ˈeɪnʃənt] adj antigo; (person, car) velho

ancillary [ænˈsɪlərɪ] adj auxiliar

and [ænd] conj e; **~ so on** e assim por diante; **try ~ come** tente vir; **he talked ~ talked** ele falou sem parar;

better ~ better cada vez melhor

Andes [ˈændiːz] npl: **the ~** os Andes

anemic [əˈniːmɪk] (US) n = **anaemic**

angel [ˈeɪndʒəl] n anjo

anger [ˈæŋgə*] n raiva

angina [ænˈdʒaɪnə] n angina (de peito)

angle [ˈæŋgl] n ângulo; (viewpoint): **from their ~** do ponto de vista deles

Anglican [ˈæŋglɪkən] adj, n anglicano(-a)

angling [ˈæŋglɪŋ] n pesca à vara (BR) or à linha (PT)

Angola [æŋˈgəulə] n Angola (no article)

angry [ˈæŋgrɪ] adj zangado; **to be ~ with sb/at sth** estar zangado com alguém/algo; **to get ~** zangar-se

anguish [ˈæŋgwɪʃ] n (physical) dor f, sofrimento; (mental) angústia

animal [ˈænɪməl] n animal m, bicho ♦ adj animal

animate [ˈænɪmɪt] adj animado; **animated** adj animado

aniseed [ˈænɪsiːd] n erva-doce f, anis f

ankle [ˈæŋkl] n tornozelo

annex [n ˈæneks, vb əˈneks] n (also: BRIT: **annexe**: building) anexo ♦ vt anexar

anniversary [ænɪˈvəːsərɪ] n aniversário

announce [əˈnauns] vt anunciar; **announcement** n anúncio; (official) comunicação f; (in letter etc) aviso; **announcer** n (RADIO, TV) locutor(a) m/f

annoy [əˈnɔɪ] vt aborrecer; **don't get ~ed!** não se aborreça!; **annoyance** n aborrecimento; **annoying** adj irritante

annual [ˈænjuəl] adj anual ♦ n (BOT) anual m; (book) anuário

annul [əˈnʌl] vt anular

anonymous [ə'nɔnɪməs] *adj* anônimo

anorak ['ænəræk] *n* anoraque *m* (BR), anorak *m* (PT)

another [ə'nʌðə*] *adj*: ~ **book** (one more) outro livro, mais um livro; (a different one) um outro livro, um livro diferente ♦ *pron* outro; *see also* **one**

answer ['ɑːnsə*] *n* resposta; (to problem) solução *f* ♦ *vi* responder ♦ *vt* (reply to) responder a; (problem) resolver; **in ~ to your letter** em resposta o respondendo à sua carta; **to ~ the phone** atender o telefone; **to ~ the bell** *or* **the door** atender à porta; **answer back** *vi* replicar, retrucar; **answer for** *vt fus* responder por, responsabilizar-se por; **answer to** *vt fus* (description) corresponder a; **answering machine** *n* secretária eletrônica

ant [ænt] *n* formiga

antagonism [æn'tægənɪzəm] *n* antagonismo

antagonize [æn'tægənaɪz] *vt* contrariar, hostilizar

Antarctic [ænt'ɑːktɪk] *n*: **the ~ o** Antártico

antenatal ['æntɪ'neɪtl] *adj* pré-natal

anthem ['ænθəm] *n*: **national ~** hino nacional

anti... [ænti] *prefix* anti...; **anti-aircraft** *adj* antiaéreo; **antibiotic** ['æntɪbaɪˈɔtɪk] *adj* antibiótico ♦ *n* antibiótico; **antibody** *n* anticorpo

anticipate [æn'tɪsɪpeɪt] *vt* prever; (expect) esperar; (look forward to) aguardar, esperar; **anticipation** *n* expectativa; (eagerness) entusiasmo

anticlimax [æntɪ'klaɪmæks] *n* desapontamento

anticlockwise [æntɪ'klɔkwaɪz] (BRIT) *adv* em sentido anti-horário

antics ['æntɪks] *npl* bobices *fpl*; (of

child) travessuras *fpl*

antidepressant ['æntɪdɪ'presən*] *n* antidepressivo

antifreeze ['æntɪfriːz] *n* anticongelante *m*

antihistamine [æntɪ'hɪstəmiːn] *n* anti-histamínico

antiquated ['æntɪkweɪtɪd] *adj* antiquado

antique [æn'tiːk] *n* antiguidade *f* ♦ *adj* antigo; **antique shop** *n* loja de antiguidades

antiseptic [æntɪ'septɪk] *n* antiséptico

antisocial [æntɪ'səuʃəl] *adj* antisocial

antlers ['æntləz] *npl* esgalhos *mp*, chifres *mpl*

anxiety [æŋ'zaɪətɪ] *n* (worry) inquietude *f*; (MED) ansiedade *f*; (eagerness): ~ **to do** ânsia de fazer

anxious ['æŋkʃəs] *adj* (worried) preocupado; (worrying) angustiante; (keen): ~ **to do** ansioso par fazer; **to be ~ that** desejar que

KEYWORD

any ['enɪ] *adj* **1** (in questions etc algum(a); **have you ~ butter/chi dren?** você tem manteiga/filhos?; **there are ~ tickets left** se houve alguns bilhetes sobrando

2 (with negative) nenhum(a); **haven't ~ money/books** não tenh dinheiro/livros

3 (no matter which) qualquer **choose ~ book you like** escolh qualquer livro que quiser

4 (in phrases): **in ~ case** em todo caso; ~ **day now** qualquer dia des ses; **at ~ moment** a qualquer momento; **at ~ rate** de qualquer modo; ~ **time** a qualquer momen to; (whenever) quando quer que sej ♦ *pron* **1** (in questions etc) algum(a

have you got ~? tem algum?
2 (*with negative*) nenhum(a); **I haven't ~ (of them)** não tenho nenhum (deles)
3 (*no matter which one(s)*): **take ~ of those books (you like)** leve qualquer um desses livros (que você quiser)
♦ *adv* **1** (*in questions etc*) algo; **do you want ~ more soup/sandwiches?** quer mais sopa/sanduíches?; **are you feeling ~ better?** você está se sentindo melhor?
2 (*with negative*) nada; **I can't hear him ~ more** não consigo mais ouvilo

anybody [ˈɛnɪbɔdɪ] *pron* = **anyone**
anyhow [ˈɛnɪhaʊ] *adv* (*at any rate*) de qualquer modo, de qualquer maneira; (*haphazard*) de qualquer jeito; **I shall go ~** eu irei de qualquer jeito; **do it ~ you like** faça do jeito que você quiser; **she leaves things just ~** ela deixa as coisas de qualquer maneira
anyone [ˈɛnɪwʌn] *pron* (*in questions etc*) alguém; (*with negative*) ninguém; (*no matter who*) quem quer que seja; **can you see ~?** você pode ver alguém?; **if ~ should phone ...** se alguém telefonar ...; **could do it** qualquer um(a) poderia fazer isso
anything [ˈɛnɪθɪŋ] *pron* (*in questions etc*) alguma coisa; (*with negative*) nada; (*no matter what*) qualquer coisa; **can you see ~?** você pode ver alguma coisa?
anyway [ˈɛnɪweɪ] *adv* (*at any rate*) de qualquer modo; (*besides*) além disso; **I shall go ~** eu irei de qualquer jeito
anywhere [ˈɛnɪwɛə*] *adv* (*in questions etc*) em algum lugar; (*with*

negative) em parte nenhuma; (*no matter where*) não importa onde, onde quer que seja; **can you see him ~?** você pode vê-lo em algum lugar?; **I can't see him ~** não o vejo em parte nenhuma; **~ in the world** em qualquer lugar do mundo

apart [əˈpɑːt] *adv* à parte, à distância; (*separately*) separado; (*movement*): **to move ~** distanciar-se; (*aside*): ... **~**, ... de lado, além de ...; **10 miles ~** separados por 10 milhas; **to take ~** desmontar; **~ from** com exceção de; (*in addition to*) além de
apartheid [əˈpɑːteɪt] *n* apartheid *m*
apartment [əˈpɑːtmənt] (*US*) *n* apartamento
ape [eɪp] *n* macaco ♦ *vt* macaquear, imitar
aperitif [əˈpɛrɪtɪ] *n* aperitivo
aperture [ˈæpətʃjʊə*] *n* orifício; (*PHOT*) abertura
APEX *n abbr* (= *advance purchase excursion*) tarifa aérea com desconto, adquirida com antecedência
apologetic [əpɔləˈdʒɛtɪk] *adj* cheio de desculpas
apologize [əˈpɔlədʒaɪz] *vi*: **to ~ (for sth to sb)** desculpar-se *or* pedir desculpas (por *or* de algo a alguém); **apology** *n* desculpas *fpl*
apostle [əˈpɔsl] *n* apóstolo
apostrophe [əˈpɔstrəfɪ] *n* apóstrofo
appalling [əˈpɔːlɪŋ] *adj* horrível; (*ignorance*) terrível
apparatus [æpəˈreɪtəs] *n* aparelho; (*in gym*) aparelhos *mpl*; (*organization*) aparato
apparent [əˈpærənt] *adj* aparente; (*obvious*) claro, patente; **apparently** *adv* aparentemente, pelo(s) visto(s)
appeal [əˈpiːl] *vi* (*LAW*) apelar, recorrer ♦ *n* (*LAW*) recurso, apelação *f*; (*request*) pedido; (*plea*) súplica;

(*charm*) atração f; **to ~ (to sb) for sth** (*request*) pedir algo (a alguém); (*plead*) suplicar algo (a alguém); **to ~ to** atrair; **appealing** *adj* atraente

appear [ə'pɪə*] *vi* aparecer; (*LAW*) apresentar-se, comparecer; (*publication*) ser publicado; (*seem*) parecer; **to ~ in "Hamlet"** trabalhar em "Hamlet"; **to ~ on TV** (*person, news item*) sair na televisão; (*programme*) passar na televisão; **appearance** *n* aparecimento; (*presence*) comparecimento; (*look*) aparência

appendicitis [əpɛndɪ'saɪtɪs] *n* apendicite f

appendix [ə'pɛndɪks] (*pl* **appendices**) *n* apêndice *m*

appetite ['æpɪtaɪt] *n* apetite *m*; (*fig*) desejo; **appetizer** *n* (*food*) tira-gosto; (*drink*) aperitivo

applaud [ə'plɔːd] *vi* aplaudir ♦ *vt* aplaudir; (*praise*) admirar; **applause** *n* aplausos *mpl*

apple ['æpl] *n* maçã f; **apple tree** *n* macieira

appliance [ə'plaɪəns] *n* aparelho; **electrical** or **domestic ~s** eletrodomésticos *mpl*

applicant ['æplɪkənt] *n* (*for post*) candidato(-a); (*for benefit etc*) requerente *m/f*

application [æplɪ'keɪʃən] *n* aplicação f; (*for a job, a grant etc*) candidatura, requerimento; (*hard work*) esforço; **application form** *n* formulário de requerimento

apply [ə'plaɪ] *vt* (*paint etc*) usar; (*law etc*) pôr em prática ♦ *vi*: **to ~ to** (*be suitable for*) ser aplicável a; (*be relevant to*) valer para; (*ask*) pedir; **to ~ for** (*permit, grant*) solicitar, pedir; (*job*) candidatar-se a; **to ~ o.s. to** aplicar-se a, dedicar-se a

appoint [ə'pɔɪnt] *vt* (*to post*) nomear; **appointment** *n* (*engage-ment*) encontro marcado, compromisso; (*at doctor's etc*) hora marcada; (*act*) nomeação f; (*post*) cargo **to make an appointment (with sb)** marcar um encontro (com alguém)

appraisal [ə'preɪzl] *n* avaliação f

appreciate [ə'priːʃɪeɪt] *vt* (*like*) apreciar, estimar; (*be grateful for*) agradecer a; (*understand*) compreender ♦ *vi* (*COMM*) valorizar-se **appreciation** *n* apreciação f, estima; (*understanding*) compreensão f (*gratitude*) agradecimento; (*COMM*) valorização f; **appreciative** *adj* (*person*) agradecido; (*comment*) elogioso

apprehensive [æprɪ'hɛnsɪv] *adj* apreensivo, receoso

apprentice [ə'prɛntɪs] *n* aprendiz *m/f*

approach [ə'prəʊtʃ] *vi* aproximar-se ♦ *vt* aproximar-se de; (*ask, apply to*) dirigir-se a; (*subject, passer-by*) abordar ♦ *n* aproximação f; (*access*) acesso; (*to problem, situation*) enfoque *m*; **approachable** *adj* (*person*) tratável; (*place*) acessível

appropriate [*adj* ə'prəʊprɪɪt, ə'prəʊprɪeɪt] *adj* (*apt*) apropriado; (*relevant*) adequado ♦ *vt* apropriar-se de

approval [ə'pruːvəl] *n* aprovação f **on ~** (*COMM*) a contento

approve [ə'pruːv] *vt* (*publication, product*) autorizar; (*motion, decision*) aprovar; **approve of** *vt fus* aprova

approximate [ə'prɒksɪmɪt] *adj* aproximado; **approximately** *adv* aproximadamente

apricot ['eɪprɪkɒt] *n* damasco

April ['eɪprəl] *n* abril *m*

apron ['eɪprən] *n* avental *m*

apt [æpt] *adj* (*suitable*) adequado (*appropriate*) apropriado; (*likely*): **to** do sujeito a fazer

Aquarius [əˈkwɛərɪəs] n Aquário

Arab [ˈærəb] adj, n árabe m/f

Arabian [əˈreɪbɪən] adj árabe

Arabic [ˈærəbɪk] adj árabe; (numerals) arábico ♦ n (LING) árabe m

arbitrary [ˈɑːbɪtrərɪ] adj arbitrário

arbitration [ɑːbɪˈtreɪʃən] n arbitragem f

arcade [ɑːˈkeɪd] n arcos mpl; (passage with shops) galeria

arch [ɑːtʃ] n arco; (of foot) curvatura ♦ vt arquear, curvar

archaeologist [ɑːkɪˈɔlədʒɪst] (US **archeologist**) n arqueólogo(-a)

archaeology [ɑːkɪˈɔlədʒɪ] (US **archeology**) n arqueologia

archbishop [ɑːtʃˈbɪʃəp] n arcebispo

archeology etc [ɑːkɪˈɔlədʒɪ] (US) = **archaeology** etc

archery [ˈɑːtʃərɪ] n tiro de arco

architect [ˈɑːkɪtɛkt] n arquiteto(-a)

architecture n arquitetura

archives [ˈɑːkaɪvz] npl arquivo

Arctic [ˈɑːktɪk] adj ártico ♦ n: **the ~** o Ártico

are [ɑː*] vb see **be**

area [ˈɛərɪə] n (zone) zona, região f; (part of place) região; (in room, of knowledge, experience) área; (MATH) superfície f, extensão f; **area code** (US) n (TEL) código de discagem (BR), indicativo (PT)

aren't [ɑːnt] = **are not**

Argentina [ɑːdʒənˈtiːnə] n Argentina

arguably [ˈɑːgjuəblɪ] adv possivelmente

argue [ˈɑːgjuː] vi (quarrel) discutir; (reason) argumentar; **to ~ that** sustentar que

argument [ˈɑːgjumənt] n (reasons) argumento; (quarrel) briga, discussão f; **argumentative** [ɑːgjuˈmɛntətɪv] adj briguento

Aries [ˈɛərɪz] n Áries m

arise [əˈraɪz] (pt **arose**, pp **arisen**) vi (emerge) surgir

aristocrat [ˈærɪstəkræt] n aristocrata m/f

arithmetic [əˈrɪθmətɪk] n aritmética

ark [ɑːk] n: **Noah's A~** arca de Noé

arm [ɑːm] n braço; (of clothing) manga; (of organization etc) divisão f ♦ vt armar; **~s** npl (weapons) armas fpl; (HERALDRY) brasão m; **~ in ~** de braços dados

armaments [ˈɑːməmənts] npl armamento

armchair [ˈɑːmtʃɛə*] n poltrona

armed [ɑːmd] adj armado

armour [ˈɑːmə*] (US **armor**) n armadura

armpit [ˈɑːmpɪt] n sovaco

armrest [ˈɑːmrɛst] n braço (de poltrona)

army [ˈɑːmɪ] n exército

aroma [əˈrəumə] n aroma; **aromatherapy** n aromaterapia

arose [əˈrəuz] pt of **arise**

around [əˈraund] adv em volta; (in the area) perto ♦ prep em volta de; (near) perto de; (fig: about) cerca de

arouse [əˈrauz] vt despertar; (anger) provocar

arrange [əˈreɪndʒ] vt (organize) organizar; (put in order) arrumar; **to ~ to do sth** combinar em or ficar de fazer algo; **arrangement** n (agreement) acordo; (order, layout) disposição f; **arrangements** npl (plans) planos mpl; (preparations) preparativos mpl; **home deliveries by arrangement** entregas a domicílio por convênio; **I'll make all the necessary arrangements** eu vou tomar todas as providências necessárias

array [əˈreɪ] n: **~ of** variedade f de

arrears [əˈrɪəz] npl atrasos mpl; **to be in ~ with one's rent** atrasar o aluguel

arrest [əˈrest] vt prender, deter; (sb's attention) chamar, prender ♦ n detenção f, prisão f; **under ~** preso

arrival [əˈraɪvl] n chegada; **new ~** recém-chegado; (baby) recém-nascido

arrive [əˈraɪv] vi chegar

arrogant [ˈærəgənt] adj arrogante

arrow [ˈærəu] n flecha; (sign) seta

arse [ɑːs] (BRIT: inf!) n cu m (!)

arson [ˈɑːsn] n incêndio premeditado

art [ɑːt] n arte f; (skill) habilidade f, jeito; **A~s** npl (SCH) letras fpl

artery [ˈɑːtərɪ] n (MED) artéria; (fig) estrada principal

art gallery n museu m de belas artes; (small, private) galeria de arte

arthritis [ɑːˈθraɪtɪs] n artrite f

artichoke [ˈɑːtɪtʃəuk] n (also: globe ~) alcachofra; (also: Jerusalem ~) topinambo

article [ˈɑːtɪkl] n artigo; **~s** npl (BRIT: LAW: training) contrato de aprendizagem; **~s of clothing** peças fpl de vestuário

articulate [adj ɑːˈtɪkjulɪt, vb ɑːˈtɪkjuleɪt] adj (speech) bem articulado; (writing) bem escrito; (person) eloquente ♦ vt expressar; **articulated lorry** (BRIT) n caminhão m (BR) or camião m (PT) articulado, jamanta

artificial [ɑːtɪˈfɪʃl] adj artificial; (manner) afetado

artist [ˈɑːtɪst] n artista m/f; (MUS) intérprete m/f; **artistic** [ɑːˈtɪstɪk] adj artístico

art school n ≈ escola de artes

KEYWORD

as [æz, əz] conj **1** (time) quando; **~ the years went by** no decorrer dos anos; **he came in ~ I was leaving** ele chegou quando eu estava sain-

do; **~ from tomorrow** a partir de amanhã

2 (in comparisons) tão ... (como); tanto(s) ... (como); **~ big ~ tão** grande como; **twice ~ big ~** duas vezes maior que; **~ much/many ~ tanto/tantos como; ~ much money/many books ~** tanto dinheiro quanto/tantos livros quanto; **~ soon ~** logo que, assim que

3 (since, because) como

4 (referring to manner, way) como; **do ~ you wish** faça como quiser

5 (concerning): **~ for** or **to that** quanto a isso

6: **~ if** or **though** como se; **he looked ~ if he was ill** ele parecia doente

♦ prep (in the capacity of): **he works ~ a driver** ele trabalha como motorista; **he gave it to me ~ a present** ele me deu isso de presente; see also **long; such; well**

a.s.a.p. abbr = **as soon as possible**

asbestos [æzˈbestəs] n asbesto, amianto

ascend [əˈsend] vt subir; (throne) ascender

ascertain [æsəˈteɪn] vt averiguar, verificar

ash [æʃ] n cinza; (tree, wood) freixo

ashamed [əˈfeɪmd] adj envergonhado; **to be ~ of** ter vergonha de

ashore [əˈʃɔː] adv em terra; **to go ~** descer à terra, desembarcar

ashtray [ˈæʃtreɪ] n cinzeiro

Asia [ˈeɪʃə] n Ásia; **Asian** adj, n asiático(-a)

aside [əˈsaɪd] adv à parte, de lado ♦ n aparte m

ask [ɑːsk] vt perguntar; (invite) convidar; **to ~ sb sth/to do sth** perguntar algo a alguém/pedir para alguém fazer algo; **to ~ (sb) a ques-**

tion fazer uma pergunta (a alguém); **to ~ sb out to dinner** convidar alguém para jantar; **ask after** vt fus perguntar por; **ask for** vt fus pedir; **it's just ~ing for trouble** é procurar encrenca

asleep [əˈsliːp] adj dormindo; **to fall ~** dormir, adormecer

asparagus [əsˈpærəgəs] n asparago (BR), espargo (PT)

aspect [ˈæspekt] n aspecto; (direction in which a building etc faces) direção f

aspire [əsˈpaɪə*] vi: **to ~ to** aspirar a

aspirin [ˈæsprɪn] n aspirina

ass [æs] n jumento, burro; (inf) imbecil m/f; (us: inf!) cu m (!)

assailant [əˈseɪlənt] n assaltante m/f, atacante m/f

assassinate [əˈsæsɪneɪt] vt assassinar; **assassination** [əsæsɪˈneɪʃən] n assassinato, assassínio

assault [əˈsɔːlt] n (MIL, fig) ataque m ♦ vt assaltar, atacar; (sexually) agredir, violar

assemble [əˈsɛmbl] vt (people) reunir; (objects) juntar; (TECH) montar ♦ vi reunir-se

assembly [əˈsɛmblɪ] n reunião f, (institution) assembléia

assent [əˈsɛnt] n aprovação f

assert [əˈsɜːt] vt afirmar

assess [əˈsɛs] vt avaliar; (tax, damages) calcular; **assessment** n avaliação f, cálculo

asset [ˈæset] n vantagem f, trunfo; **~s** npl (property, funds) bens mpl

assign [əˈsaɪn] vt (date) fixar; **to ~ (to)** (task) designar (a); (resources) destinar a; **assignment** n tarefa

assist [əˈsɪst] vt ajudar; **assistance** n ajuda, auxílio; **assistant** n assistente m/f, auxiliar m/f; (BRIT: also: **shop assistant**) vendedor(a) m/f

associate [adj, n əˈsəʊʃɪt, vb

əˈsəʊʃɪeɪt] adj associado; (professor etc) adjunto ♦ n sócio(-a) ♦ vi: **to ~ with** associar-se com ♦ vt associar; **association** [əsəʊsɪˈeɪʃən] n associação f; (link) ligação f

assorted [əˈsɔːtɪd] adj sortido

assortment [əˈsɔːtmənt] n (of shapes, colours) sortimento; (of books, people) variedade f

assume [əˈsjuːm] vt (suppose) supor, presumir; (responsibilities) assumir; (attitude, name) adotar, tomar; **assumption** [əˈsʌmpʃən] n suposição f, presunção f

assurance [əˈʃʊərəns] n garantia; (confidence) confiança; (insurance) seguro

assure [əˈʃʊə*] vt assegurar; (guarantee) garantir

asthma [ˈæsmə] n asma

astonish [əsˈtɒnɪʃ] vt assombrar, espantar; **astonishment** n assombro, espanto

astound [əsˈtaʊnd] vt pasmar, estarrecer

astray [əˈstreɪ] adv: **to go ~** extraviar-se; **to lead ~** desencaminhar

astrology [əsˈtrɒlədʒɪ] n astrologia

astronaut [ˈæstrənɔːt] n astronauta m/f

astronomy [əsˈtrɒnəmɪ] n astronomia

asylum [əˈsaɪləm] n (refuge) asilo; (hospital) manicômio; **asylum seeker** n requerente m/f de asilo

┌─ KEYWORD ─┐

at [æt] prep **1** (referring to position) em; (referring to direction) a; ~ **the top** em cima; ~ **home** em casa; **to look** ~ **sth** olhar para algo

2 (referring to time): ~ **4 o'clock** às quatro horas; ~ **night** à noite; ~ **Christmas** no Natal; ~ **times** às

vezes
3 (*referring to rates, speed etc*): ~ **£1 a kilo** a uma libra o quilo; **two ~ a time** de dois em dois
4 (*referring to manner*): ~ **a stroke** de um golpe; ~ **peace** em paz
5 (*referring to activity*): **to be ~ work** estar no trabalho; **to play ~ cowboys** brincar de mocinho
6 (*referring to cause*): **to be shocked/surprised/annoyed** ~ sth ficar chocado/surpreso/chateado com algo; **I went ~ his suggestion** eu fui por causa da sugestão dele

ate [eɪt] *pt of* **eat**
atheist [ˈeɪθɪɪst] *n* ateu (atéia) *m/f*
Athens [ˈæθɪnz] *n* Atenas
athlete [ˈæθliːt] *n* atleta *m/f*; **athletic** [æθˈletɪk] *adj* atlético; **athletics** *n* atletismo
Atlantic [ətˈlæntɪk] *adj* atlântico ♦ *n*: **the ~ (Ocean)** o (oceano) Atlântico
atlas [ˈætləs] *n* atlas *m inv*
ATM *n abbr* (= *automated telling machine*) caixa *m* automático
atmosphere [ˈætməsfɪə*] *n* atmosfera; (*of place*) ambiente *m*
atom [ˈætəm] *n* átomo; **atomic** [əˈtɔmɪk] *adj* atômico; **atomizer** *n* atomizador *m*, pulverizador *m*
atone [əˈtəun] *vi*: ~ **for** (*sin*) expiar; (*mistake*) reparar
atrocious [əˈtrəuʃəs] *adj* péssimo
attach [əˈtætʃ] *vt* prender; (*document*) juntar, anexar; (*importance etc*) dar; **to be ~ed to sb/sth** (*like*) ter afeição por alguém/algo
attachment [əˈtætʃmənt] *n* (*tool*) acessório; (*love*): ~ **(to)** afeição *f* (por)
attack [əˈtæk] *vt* atacar; (*subj: criminal*) assaltar; (*task etc*) empreender ♦ *n* ataque *m*; (*on sb's life*) atentado;

heart ~ ataque cardíaco *or* de coração
attain [əˈteɪn] *vt* (*also:* ~ **to**: *happiness, results*) alcançar, atingir; (: *knowledge*) obter
attempt [əˈtempt] *n* tentativa ♦ *vt* tentar; **to make an ~ on sb's life** atentar contra a vida de alguém; **attempted** *adj*: **attempted theft** tentativa de roubo
attend [əˈtend] *vt* (*lectures*) assistir a; (*school*) cursar; (*church*) ir a; (*course*) fazer; (*patient*) tratar; **attend to** *vt fus* (*matter*) encarregar-se de; (*needs, customer*) atender a; (*patient*) tratar de; **attendance** *n* comparecimento; (*people present*) assistência; **attendant** *n* servidor(a) *m/f* ♦ *adj* concomitante
attention [əˈtenʃən] *n* atenção *f*; (*care*) cuidados *mpl* ♦ *excl* (MIL) sentido!; **for the ~ of ...** (ADMIN) atenção ...
attentive [əˈtentɪv] *adj* atento; (*polite*) cortês
attic [ˈætɪk] *n* sótão *m*
attitude [ˈætɪtjuːd] *n* atitude *f*
attorney [əˈtəːnɪ] *n* (US: *lawyer*) advogado(-a)
attract [əˈtrækt] *vt* atrair, chamar; **attraction** *n* atração *f*; **attractive** *adj* atraente; (*idea, offer*) interessante
attribute [*n* ˈætrɪbjuːt, *vb* əˈtrɪbjuːt] *n* atributo ♦ *vt*: **to ~ sth to** atribuir algo a
aubergine [ˈəubəʒiːn] *n* berinjela
auction [ˈɔːkʃən] *n* (*also:* **sale by ~**) leilão *m* ♦ *vt* leiloar
audience [ˈɔːdɪəns] *n* audiência; (*at concert, theatre*) platéia; (*public*) público
audio-visual [ˈɔːdɪəu-] *adj* audiovisual
audit [ˈɔːdɪt] *vt* fazer a auditoria de

audition [ɔːˈdɪʃən] n audição f

August [ˈɔːgəst] n agosto

aunt [ɑːnt] n tia; **auntie** n titia;
aunty n titia

au pair [ˈəuˈpɛə*] n (also: ~ **girl**) au
pair f

Australia [ɔsˈtreɪlɪə] n Austrália;
Australian adj, n australiano(-a)

Austria [ˈɔstrɪə] n Áustria; **Austrian** adj, n austríaco(-a)

authentic [ɔːˈθεntɪk] adj autêntico

author [ˈɔːθə] n autor(a) m/f

authoritarian [ɔːθɔrɪˈtεərɪən] adj
autoritário

authoritative [ɔːˈθɔrɪtətɪv] adj
(account) autorizado; (manner)
autoritário

authority [ɔːˈθɔrɪtɪ] n autoridade f;
(government body) jurisdição f; (permission) autorização f; **the authorities** npl (ruling body) as autoridades

authorize [ˈɔːθəraɪz] vt autorizar

auto [ˈɔːtəu] (US) n carro, automóvel
m

autobiography [ɔːtəbaɪˈɔgrəfɪ] n
autobiografia

autograph [ˈɔːtəgrɑːf] n autógrafo
♦ vt (photo etc) autografar

automatic [ɔːtəˈmætɪk] adj automático ♦ n (gun) pistola automática;
(washing machine) máquina de lavar
roupa automática; (car) carro automático

automobile [ˈɔːtəməbiːl] (US) n
carro, automóvel m

autonomy [ɔːˈtɔnəmɪ] n autonomia

autumn [ˈɔːtəm] n outono

auxiliary [ɔːgˈzɪlɪərɪ] adj, n auxiliar
m/f

available [əˈveɪləbl] adj disponível;
(time) livre

avalanche [ˈævəlɑːnʃ] n avalanche
f

Ave. abbr (= avenue) Av., Avda.

avenge [əˈvεndʒ] vt vingar

avenue [ˈævənjuː] n avenida; (drive)
caminho; (means) solução f

average [ˈævərɪdʒ] n média ♦ adj
(mean) médio; (ordinary) regular
♦ vt alcançar uma média de; **on ~**
em média; **average out** vi: **to ~
out at** dar uma média de

avert [əˈvəːt] vt prevenir; (blow,
one's eyes) desviar

avocado [ævəˈkɑːdəu] n (also: BRIT:
~ pear) abacate m

avoid [əˈvɔɪd] vt evitar

await [əˈweɪt] vt esperar, aguardar

awake [əˈweɪk] (pt awoke or awok-
en, pp ~d) adj acordado ♦ vt, vi
despertar, acordar; **~ to** atento a;
awakening n despertar m

award [əˈwɔːd] n prêmio, condecoração f; (LAW) indenização f ♦ vt
outorgar, conceder; indenizar

aware [əˈwεə*] adj: **~ of** (conscious)
consciente de; (informed) informa-
do de or sobre; **to become ~ of**
reparar em, saber de; **awareness** n
consciência

away [əˈweɪ] adv fora; (far~) muito
longe; **two kilometres ~** a dois
quilômetros de distância; **the holiday was two weeks ~** faltavam
duas semanas para as férias; **he's ~
for a week** está ausente uma sema-
na; **to take ~** levar; **to work** etc **~**
trabalhar sem parar; **to fade ~**
(colour) desbotar; (enthusiasm,
sound) diminuir

awe [ɔː] n temor m respeitoso; **awe-
inspiring** [ˈɔːɪnspaɪərɪŋ] adj imponente

awful [ˈɔːfəl] adj terrível, horrível;
(quantity): **an ~ lot of** um monte de;
awfully adv (very) muito

awkward [ˈɔːkwəd] adj (person,
movement) desajeitado; (shape)
incômodo; (problem) difícil; (situation) embaraçoso, delicado

awning [ˈɔːnɪŋ] n toldo
awoke [əˈwəuk] pt of **awake**
awoken [əˈwəukən] pp of **awake**
axe [æks] (US **ax**) n machado ♦ vt (project etc) abandonar; (jobs) reduzir
axis [ˈæksɪs] (pl **axes**) n eixo
axle [ˈæksl] n (also: ~ **tree**: AUT) eixo
Azores [əˈzɔːz] npl: **the ~** os Açores

B

B [biː] n (MUS) si m
BA n abbr = **Bachelor of Arts**
babble [ˈbæbl] vi balbuciar; (brook) murmurinhar
baby [ˈbeɪbɪ] n neném m/f, bebê m/f, bebê m/f; (US: inf) querido(-a).
baby carriage (US) n carrinho de bebê; **baby food** n comida de bebê; **baby-sit** (irreg) vi tomar conta da(s) criança(s); **baby-sitter** n baby-sitter m/f
bachelor [ˈbætʃələ*] n solteiro; **B~ of Arts/Science** ≈ bacharel m em Letras/Ciências
back [bæk] n (of person) costas fpl; (of animal) lombo; (of hand) dorso; (of car, train) parte f traseira; (of house) fundos mpl; (of chair) encosto; (of page) verso; (of book) lombada; (of crowd) fundo ♦ (FOOTBALL) zagueiro (BR), defesa m (PT) ♦ vt (candidate: also: ~ **up**) apoiar; (horse: at races) apostar em; (car) recuar ♦ vi (car etc: also: ~ **up**) dar marcha-ré (BR), fazer marcha atrás (PT) ♦ cpd (payment) atrasado; (AUT: seats, wheels) de trás ♦ adv (not forward) para trás; (returned): **he's ~** ele voltou; (restitution): **throw the ball ~** devolva a bola; (again): **he called ~** chamou de novo; **he ran ~** recuou correndo; **back down** vi

desistir; **back out** vi (of promise) voltar atrás, recuar; **back up** vt (support) apoiar; (COMPUT) tirar um backup de; **backache** n dor f nas costas; **backbone** n coluna vertebral; (fig) esteio; **backfire** vi (AUT) engasgar; (plan) sair pela culatra; **background** n fundo; (of events) antecedentes mpl; (basic knowledge) bases fpl; (experience) conhecimentos mpl, experiência; **family background** antecedentes mpl familiares; **backhand** n (TENNIS: also: **backhand stroke**) revés m; **backing** n (fig) apoio; **backlog** n: **backlog of work** atrasos mpl; **backpack** n mochila; **back pay** n salário atrasado; **backside** (inf) n traseiro; **backstage** adv nos bastidores; **backstroke** n nado de costas; **backup** adj (train, plane) reserva inv; (COMPUT) de backup ♦ n (support) apoio; (COMPUT: also: **backup file**) backup m; **backward** adj (movement) para trás; (person, country) atrasado; **backwards** adv (move, go) para trás; (read a list) às avessas; (fall) de costas; **backwater** n (fig) lugar m atrasado; **backyard** n quintal m
bacon [ˈbeɪkən] n toucinho, bacon m
bacteria [bækˈtɪərɪə] npl bactéria fpl
bad [bæd] adj mau (má), ruim; (child: levado; (mistake) grave; (food) estragado; **his ~ leg** sua perna machucada; **to go ~** estragar-se
badge [bædʒ] n (of school etc) emblema m; (policeman's) crachá m
badger [ˈbædʒə*] n texugo
badly [ˈbædlɪ] adv mal; **~ wounded** gravemente ferido; **he needs it ~** faz-lhe grande falta; **to be ~ off** (for money) estar com pouco dinheiro

badminton ['bædmɪntən] n badminton m

bad-tempered [-'tɛmp] adj mal humorado; (temporary) de mau humor

baffle ['bæfl] vt (puzzle) deixar perplexo, desconcertar

bag [bæg] n saco, bolsa; (handbag) bolsa; (satchel) sacola; (case) mala; **~s of ...** (inf: lots of) ... de sobra; **baggage** n bagagem f; **baggy** adj folgado, largo; **bagpipes** npl gaita de foles

bail [beɪl] n (payment) fiança; (release) liberdade f sob fiança ♦ vt (prisoner: gen: grant ~ to) libertar sob fiança; (boat: also: ~ out) baldear a água de; **on ~** sob fiança; see also **bale**; **bail out** vt (prisoner) afiançar

bait [beɪt] n isca, engodo; (for criminal etc) atrativo, chamariz m ♦ vt iscar, cevar; (person) apoquentar

bake [beɪk] vt cozinhar ao forno; (TECH: clay etc) cozer ♦ vi assar; **baked beans** npl feijão m cozido com molho de tomate; **baked potato** n batata assada com a casca; **baker** n padeiro(-a); **bakery** n (for bread) padaria; (for cakes) confeitaria; **baking** n (act) cozimento; (batch) fornada ♦ adj (inf: hot) escaldante; **baking powder** n fermento em pó

balance ['bæləns] ♦ n equilíbrio; (scales) balança; (COMM) balanço; (remainder) resto, saldo ♦ vt equilibrar; (budget) nivelar; (account) fazer o balanço de; **~ of trade/payments** balança comercial/balanço de pagamentos; **balanced** adj (report) objetivo; (personality, diet) equilibrado; **balance sheet** n balanço geral

balcony ['bælkənɪ] n varanda; (closed) galeria; (in theatre) balcão m

bald [bɔːld] adj calvo, careca; (tyre) careca

bale [beɪl] n (AGR) fardo; **bale out** vi (of a plane) atirar-se de pára-quedas

ball [bɔːl] n bola; (of wool, string) novelo; (dance) baile m, **to play ~ with sb** jogar bola com alguém; (fig) fazer o jogo de alguém

ballast ['bæləst] n lastro

ballerina [bælə'riːnə] n bailarina

ballet ['bæleɪ] n balé m; **ballet dancer** n bailarino(-a)

balloon [bə'luːn] n balão m

ballot ['bælət] n votação f

ballpoint (pen) ['bɔːlpɔɪnt-] n (caneta) esferográfica

balsamic vinegar [bɔl'sæmɪk-] n vinagre m balsâmico

ban [bæn] n proibição f, interdição f; (suspension) exclusão f ♦ vt proibir, interditar; excluir

banana [bə'nɑːnə] n banana

band [bænd] n (group) orquestra; (MIL) banda; (strip) faixa, cinta; **band together** vi juntar-se, associar-se

bandage ['bændɪdʒ] n atadura (BR), ligadura (PT) ♦ vt enfaixar

bandaid ['bændeɪd] ® (US) n esparadrapo

bang [bæŋ] n estalo; (of door) estrondo; (of gun, exhaust) explosão f; (blow) pancada ♦ excl bum!, bumba! ♦ vt (one's head etc) bater; (door) fechar com violência ♦ vi produzir estrondo; (door) bater; (fireworks) soltar

bangs [bæŋz] (US) npl (fringe) franja

banish ['bænɪʃ] vt banir

banister(s) ['bænɪstə(z)] n(pl) corrimão m

bank [bæŋk] n banco; (of river, lake) margem f; (of earth) rampa, ladeira ♦ vi (AVIAT) ladear-se; **bank on** vt fus contar com, apostar em; **bank**

account n conta bancária; **bank card** n cartão m de garantia de cheques; **banker** n banqueiro(-a); **banker's card** (BRIT) n = bank card; **Bank holiday** (BRIT) n feriado nacional; **banking** n transações fpl bancárias; **banknote** n nota (bancária); **bank rate** n taxa bancária

bankrupt ['bæŋkrʌpt] adj falido, quebrado; **to go ~** falir

bank statement n extrato bancário

banner ['bænə*] n faixa

baptism ['bæptɪzəm] n batismo

bar [bɑː*] n barra; (rod) vara; (of window etc) grade f; (fig: hindrance) obstáculo; (prohibition) impedimento; (pub) bar m; (counter: in pub) balcão m ♦ vt (road) obstruir; (person) excluir; (activity) proibir ♦ prep: **~ none** sem exceção; **behind ~s** (prisoner) atrás das grades; **the B~** (LAW) a advocacia

barbaric [bɑːˈbærɪk] adj bárbaro

barbecue ['bɑːbɪkjuː] n churrasco

barbed wire ['bɑːbd-] n arame m farpado

barber ['bɑːbə*] n barbeiro, cabeleireiro

bar code n código de barras

bare [bɛə*] adj despido; (head) descoberto; (trees) sem vegetação; (minimum) básico ♦ vt mostrar; **barefoot** adj, adv descalço; **barely** adv apenas, mal

bargain ['bɑːgɪn] n negócio; (agreement) acordo; (good buy) pechincha ♦ vi (haggle) regatear; (negotiate) negociar; **to ~ with (sb)** pechinchar (com alguém); **into the ~** ainda por cima; **bargain for** vt fus: **he got more than he ~ed for** ele conseguiu mais do que pediu

barge [bɑːdʒ] n barcaça; **barge in** vi irromper

bark [bɑːk] n (of tree) casca; (of dog) latido ♦ vi latir

barley ['bɑːlɪ] n cevada

barmaid ['bɑːmeɪd] n garçonete f (BR), empregada (de bar) (PT)

barman ['bɑːmən] (irreg) n garçom m (BR), empregado (de bar) (PT)

barn [bɑːn] n celeiro

barometer [bəˈrɒmɪtə*] n barômetro

baron ['bærən] n barão m; (of press, industry) magnata m; **baroness** ['bærənɪs] n baronesa

barracks ['bærəks] npl quartel m, caserna

barrage ['bærɑːʒ] n (MIL) fogo de barragem; (dam) barragem f; (fig): **a ~ of questions** uma saraivada de perguntas

barrel ['bærəl] n barril m; (of gun) cano

barren ['bærən] adj (land) árido

barricade [bærɪˈkeɪd] n barricada

barrier ['bærɪə*] n barreira; (fig: to progress etc) obstáculo

barrister ['bærɪstə*] (BRIT) n advogado(-a), causídico(-a)

barrow ['bærəu] n (wheel~) carrinho (de mão)

bartender ['bɑːtendə*] (US) n garçom m (BR), empregado (de bar) (PT)

barter ['bɑːtə*] vt: **to ~ sth for sth** trocar algo por algo

base [beɪs] n base f ♦ vt (opinion, belief): **to ~ sth on** basear or fundamentar algo em ♦ adj (thoughts) sujo; **baseball** n beisebol m

basement ['beɪsmənt] n porão m

bases[1] ['beɪsiːz] npl of **base**

bases[2] ['beɪsiːz] npl of **basis**

bash [bæʃ] (inf) vt (with fist) dar soco or murro em; (with object) bater em

bashful ['bæʃful] adj tímido,

envergonhado

basic ['beɪsɪk] adj básico; (facilities) mínimo; **basically** adv basicamente; (really) no fundo; **basics** npl: **the basics** o essencial

basin ['beɪsn] n (vessel, GEO) bacia; (also: **wash~**) pia

basis ['beɪsɪs] n (pl bases) n base f; **on a part-time ~** num esquema de meio-expediente; **on a trial ~** em experiência

bask [bɑːsk] vi: **to ~ in the sun** tomar sol

basket ['bɑːskɪt] n cesto; (with handle) cesta; **basketball** n basquete(bol) m

bass [beɪs] n (MUS) baixo

bastard ['bɑːstəd] n bastardo(-a); (inf!) filho-da-puta m (!)

bat [bæt] n (ZOOL) morcego; (for ball games) bastão m; (BRIT: for table tennis) raquete f ♦ vt: **he didn't ~ an eyelid** ele nem pestanejou

batch [bætʃ] n (of bread) fornada; (of papers) monte m

bath [bɑːθ] n banho; (bathtub) banheira ♦ vt banhar; **to have a ~** tomar banho (de banheira); see also **baths**

bathe [beɪð] vi banhar-se; (US: have a bath) tomar um banho ♦ vt (wound) lavar; **bathing** n banho; **bathing costume** (US **bathing suit**) n (woman's) maiô m (BR), fato de banho (PT)

bathrobe ['bɑːθrəub] n roupão m de banho

bathroom ['bɑːθrum] n banheiro (BR), casa de banho (PT)

baths [bɑːðz] npl banhos mpl públicos

baton ['bætən] n (MUS) batuta; (ATHLETICS) bastão m; (truncheon) cassetete m

batter ['bætə*] vt espancar; (subj:

wind, rain) castigar ♦ n massa (mole); **battered** ['bætəd] adj (hat, pan) amassado, surrado

battery ['bætərɪ] n bateria; (of torch) pilha

battle ['bætl] n (also: fig) luta ♦ vi lutar; **battlefield** n campo de batalha; **battleship** n navio de guerra (BR), couraçado (PT)

bawl [bɔːl] vi gritar; (child) berrar

bay [beɪ] n (GEO) baía; **to hold sb at ~** manter alguém à distância; **bay window** n janela saliente

bazaar [bə'zɑː*] n bazar m

B & B n abbr = **bed and breakfast**

BBC n abbr (= British Broadcasting Corporation) companhia britânica de rádio e televisão

B.C. adv abbr (= before Christ) a.C.

┌─────────────┐
│ *KEYWORD* │
└─────────────┘

be [biː] (pt was or were, pp been) aux vb **1** (with present participle: forming continuous tense): estar; **what are you doing?** o que você está fazendo (BR) or a fazer (PT)?; **it is raining** está chovendo (BR) or a chover (PT)?; **I've been waiting for you for hours** há horas que eu espero por você

2 (with pp: forming passives): **to ~ killed** ser morto; **the box had been opened** a caixa tinha sido aberta; **the thief was nowhere to ~ seen** ninguém viu o ladrão

3 (in tag questions): **it was fun, wasn't it?** foi divertido, não foi?; **she's back again, is she?** ela voltou novamente, é?

4 (+ to + infin): **the house is to ~ sold** a casa está à venda; **you're to ~ congratulated for all your work** você devia ser cumprimentado pelo seu trabalho; **he's not to open it** ele não pode abrir isso

♦ *vb + complement* **1** *(gen)*: I'm English sou inglês; I'm tired estou cansado; **2 and 2 are 4** dois e dois são quatro; ~ **careful!** tome cuidado!; ~ **quiet!** fique quieto!, fique calado!; ~ **good!** seja bonzinho! **2** *(of health)* estar; **how are you?** como está?

3 *(of age)*: **how old are you?** quantos anos você tem?; I'm **twenty (years old)** tenho vinte anos

4 *(cost)* ser; **how much was the meal?** quanto foi a refeição?; **that'll ~ £5.75, please** são £5.75, por favor

♦ *vi* **1** *(exist, occur etc)* existir, haver; **the best singer that ever was** o maior cantor de todos os tempos; **is there a God?** Deus existe?; ~ **that as it may ...** de qualquer forma ...; **so ~ it** que seja assim

2 *(referring to place)* estar; I **won't ~ here tomorrow** eu não estarei aqui amanhã; **Edinburgh is in Scotland** Edimburgo é or fica na Escócia

3 *(referring to movement)* ir; **where have you been?** onde você foi?; I've **been in the garden** estava no quintal

♦ *impers vb* **1** *(referring to time)* ser; **it's 8 o'clock** são 8 horas; **it's the 28th of April** é 28 de abril

2 *(referring to distance)* ficar; **it's 10 km to the village** fica a 10 km do lugarejo

3 *(referring to the weather)* estar; **it's too hot/cold** está quente/frio demais

4 *(emphatic)*: **it's only me** sou eu!; **it was Maria who paid the bill** foi Maria quem pagou a conta

beach [biːtʃ] *n* praia ♦ *vt* puxar para a terra *or* praia, encalhar

beacon [ˈbiːkən] *n* *(lighthouse)* farol *m*; *(marker)* baliza

bead [biːd] *n* *(of necklace)* conta; *(of sweat)* gota

beak [biːk] *n* bico

beaker [ˈbiːkə*] *n* copo com bico

beam [biːm] *n* *(ARCH)* viga; *(of light)* raio ♦ *vi* *(smile)* sorrir

bean [biːn] *n* feijão *m*; *(of coffee)* grão *m*; **runner/broad ~** vagem *f*/fava

bear [bɛə*] *n* urso ♦ *vb* *(pt* bore, *pp* borne) *vt* *(carry, support)* arcar com; *(tolerate)* suportar ♦ *vi*: **to ~ right/ left** virar à direita/à esquerda; **bear out** *vt* *(theory, suspicion)* confirmar, corroborar; **bear up** *vi* agüentar, resistir

beard [biəd] *n* barba; **bearded** *adj* barbado, barbudo

bearing [ˈbɛəriŋ] *n* porte *m*, comportamento; *(connection)* relação *f*; **~s** *npl* *(also:* **ball ~s)** rolimã *m*; **to take a ~** fazer marcação

beast [biːst] *n* bicho; *(inf)* fera; **beastly** *adj* horrível

beat [biːt] *n* *(pt* beat, *pp* beaten) *n* *(of heart)* batida; *(MUS)* ritmo, compasso; *(of policeman)* ronda ♦ *vt* *(hit)* bater em; *(eggs)* bater; *(defeat)* vencer, derrotar ♦ *vi* *(heart)* bater; **to ~ it** *(inf)* cair fora; **off the ~en track** fora de mão; **beat off** *vt* repelir; **beat up** *vt* *(inf: person)* espancar; *(eggs)* bater; **beating** *n* *(thrashing)* surra

beautiful [ˈbjuːtiful] *adj* belo, lindo, formoso; **beautifully** *adv* admiravelmente

beauty [ˈbjuːti] *n* beleza; *(person)* beldade *f*, beleza

beaver [ˈbiːvə*] *n* castor *m*

because [biˈkɔz] *conj* porque; ~ **of** por causa de

beckon [ˈbɛkən] *vt* *(also:* ~ **to)** chamar com sinais, acenar para

become [biˈkʌm] *(irreg: like* **come**) *vi* *(+ n)* virar, fazer-se, tornar-se; *(+*

adj tornar-se, ficar

bed [bɛd] *n* cama; (*of flowers*) canteiro; (*of coal, clay*) camada, base *f*; (*of sea, lake*) fundo; (*of river*) leito; **to go to ~** ir dormir, deitar(-se); **bed and breakfast** *n* (*place*) pensão *f*; (*terms*) cama e café da manhã (*BR*) *or* pequeno almoço (*PT*); **bedclothes** *npl* roupa de cama; **bedding** *n* roupa de cama

bedraggled [bɪˈdrægld] *adj* molhado, ensopado

bed: **bedridden** *adj* acamado; **bedroom** *n* quarto, dormitório; **bedside** *n*: **at sb's bedside** à cabeceira de alguém; **bedsit** (*BRIT*) *n* conjugado; *ver quadro*

BEDSIT

Um bedsit é um quarto mobiliado cujo aluguel inclui uso de cozinha e banheiro comuns. Esse sistema de alojamento é muito comum na Grã-Bretanha entre estudantes, jovens profissionais liberais etc.

---

bedspread [ˈbɛdsprɛd] *n* colcha

bedtime [ˈbɛdtaɪm] *n* hora de ir para cama

bee [biː] *n* abelha

beech [biːtʃ] *n* faia

beef [biːf] *n* carne *f* de vaca; **roast ~** rosbife *m*; **beefburger** *n* hambúrguer *m*

beehive [ˈbiːhaɪv] *n* colméia

been [biːn] *pp* of **be**

beer [bɪə*] *n* cerveja

beetle [ˈbiːtl] *n* besouro

beetroot [ˈbiːtruːt] (*BRIT*) *n* beterraba

before [bɪˈfɔː*] *prep* (*of time*) antes de; (*of space*) diante de ♦ *conj* antes que ♦ *adv* antes, anteriormente; à frente, na dianteira; **~ going** antes de sair; **the week ~** a semana anterior; **I've never seen it ~** nunca vi

isso antes; **beforehand** *adv* antes

beg [bɛg] *vi* mendigar, pedir esmola ♦ *vt* (*also:* **~ for**) mendigar; **to ~ sb to do sth** implorar a alguém para fazer algo; *see also* **pardon**

began [bɪˈgæn] *pt* of **begin**

beggar [ˈbɛgə*] *n* mendigo(-a)

begin [bɪˈgɪn] (*pt* **began**, *pp* **begun**) *vt, vi* começar, iniciar; **to ~ doing** *or* **to do sth** começar a fazer algo; **beginner** *n* principiante *m/f*; **beginning** *n* início, começo

behalf [bɪˈhɑːf] *n*: **on** *or* **in** (*US*) **~ of** (*as representative of*) em nome de; (*for benefit of*) no interesse de

behave [bɪˈheɪv] *vi* comportar-se; (*well: also:* **~ o.s.**) comportar-se (bem); **behaviour** (*US* **behavior**) *n* comportamento

behead [bɪˈhɛd] *vt* decapitar, degolar

behind [bɪˈhaɪnd] *prep* atrás de ♦ *adv* atrás; (*move*) para trás ♦ *n* traseiro; **to be ~** (*schedule*) **with sth** estar atrasado *or* com atraso em algo; **~ the scenes** nos bastidores

beige [beɪʒ] *adj* bege

Beijing [beɪˈʒɪŋ] *m* Pequim

being [ˈbiːɪŋ] *n* (*state*) existência; (*entity*) ser *m*

belated [bɪˈleɪtɪd] *adj* atrasado

belch [bɛltʃ] *vi* arrotar ♦ *vt* (*also:* **~ out:** *smoke etc*) vomitar

Belgian [ˈbɛldʒən] *adj, n* belga *m/f*

Belgium [ˈbɛldʒəm] *n* Bélgica

belief [bɪˈliːf] *n* (*opinion*) opinião *f*; (*trust, faith*) fé *f*

believe [bɪˈliːv] *vt*: **to ~ sth/sb** acreditar algo/em alguém ♦ *vi*: **to ~ in** (*God*) crer em; (*method, person*) acreditar em; **believer** *n* (*REL*) crente *m/f*, fiel *m/f*; (*in idea*) partidário(-a)

belittle [bɪˈlɪtl] *vt* diminuir, depreciar

bell [bɛl] *n* sino; (*small, door-*)

campainha

belligerent [bɪ'lɪdʒərənt] *adj* agressivo

bellow ['beləu] *vi* mugir; (*person*) bramar

belly ['belɪ] *n* barriga, ventre *m*

belong [bɪ'lɒŋ] *vi*: **to ~ to** pertencer a; (*club etc*) ser sócio de; **the book ~s here** o livro fica guardado aqui; **belongings** *npl* pertences *mpl*

beloved [bɪ'lʌvɪd] *adj* querido, amado

below [bɪ'ləu] *prep* (*beneath*) embaixo de; (*less than*) abaixo de ♦ *adv* em baixo; **see ~** ver abaixo

belt [belt] *n* cinto; (*of land*) faixa; (*TECH*) correia ♦ *vt* (*thrash*) surrar; **beltway** [US] *n* via circular

bemused [bɪ'mju:zd] *adj* bestificado, estupidificado

bench [bentʃ] *n* banco; (*work ~*) bancada (de carpinteiro); (*BRIT: POL*) assento num Parlamento; **the B~** (*LAW: judge*) o magistrado; (: *judges*) os magistrados, o corpo de magistrados

bend [bend] (*pt, pp* **bent**) *vt* (*leg, arm*) dobrar; (*pipe*) curvar ♦ *vi* dobrar-se, inclinar-se ♦ *n* curva; (*in pipe*) curvatura; **bend down** *vi* abaixar-se; **bend over** *vi* debruçar-se

beneath [bɪ'ni:θ] *prep* abaixo de; (*unworthy of*) indigno de ♦ *adv* em baixo

benefactor ['benɪfæktə*] *n* benfeitor(a) *m/f*

beneficial [benɪ'fɪʃəl] *adj*: **~ (to)** benéfico (a)

benefit ['benɪfɪt] *n* benefício, vantagem *f*; (*money*) subsídio, auxílio ♦ *vt* beneficiar ♦ *vi*: **to ~ from sth** beneficiar-se de algo

benevolent [bɪ'nevələnt] *adj* benévolo

benign [bɪ'naɪn] *adj* (*person, smile*) afável, bondoso; (*MED*) benigno

bent [bent] *pt, pp of* **bend** ♦ *n* inclinação *f* ♦ *adj*: **to be ~ on** estar empenhado em

bereaved [bɪ'ri:vd] *npl*: **the ~** os enlutados

beret ['bereɪ] *n* boina

Berlin [bə:'lɪn] *n* Berlim

berm [bə:m] (*US*) *n* acostamento (*BR*), berma (*PT*)

berry ['berɪ] *n* baga

berserk [bə'sə:k] *adj*: **to go ~** perder as estribeiras

berth [bə:θ] *n* (*bed*) beliche *m*; (*cabin*) cabine *f*; (*on train*) leito; (*for ship*) ancoradouro ♦ *vi* (*in harbour*) atracar, encostar-se; (*at anchor*) ancorar

beside [bɪ'saɪd] *prep* (*next to*) junto de, ao lado de, ao pé de; **to be ~ o.s. (with anger)** estar fora de si; **that's ~ the point** isso não tem nada a ver

besides [bɪ'saɪdz] *adv* além disso; (*in any case*) de qualquer jeito ♦ *prep* (*as well as*) além de

besiege [bɪ'si:dʒ] *vt* (*town*) sitiar, pôr cerco a; (*fig*) assediar

best [best] *adj* melhor ♦ *adv* (o) melhor; **the ~ part of** (*quantity*) a maior parte de; **at ~** na melhor das hipóteses; **to make the ~ of sth** tirar o maior partido possível de algo; **to do one's ~** fazer o possível; **to the ~ of my knowledge** que eu saiba; **to the ~ of my ability** o melhor que eu puder; **best before date** *n* data *f* de validade; **best man** *n* padrinho de casamento

bet [bet] (*pt, pp* **bet** or **~ted**) *n* aposta ♦ *vt, vi* apostar

betray [bɪ'treɪ] *vt* trair; (*denounce*) delatar

better ['betə*] *adj, adv* melhor ♦ *vt*

melhorar; (go above) superar ♦ n: **to get the ~ of** vencer; **you had ~ do it** é melhor você fazer isso; **he thought ~ of it** pensou melhor, mudou de opinião; **to get ~** melhorar; **better off** adj mais rico; (fig): **you'd be better off this way** seria melhor para você assim

betting ['bɛtɪŋ] n jogo; **betting shop** (BRIT) n agência de apostas

between [bɪ'twiːn] prep no meio de, entre ♦ adv no meio

beverage ['bɛvərɪdʒ] n bebida

beware [bɪ'wɛə*] vi: **to ~** (of) precaver-se (de), ter cuidado (com); **"~ of the dog"** "cuidado com o cachorro"

bewildered [bɪ'wɪldəd] adj atordeado; (confused) confuso

beyond [bɪ'jɔnd] prep (in space) além de; (exceeding) acima de, fora de; (date) mais tarde que; (above) acima de ♦ adv além; (in time) mais longe, mais adiante; **~ doubt** fora de qualquer dúvida; **to be ~ repair** não ter conserto

bias ['baɪəs] n (prejudice) preconceito; **bias(s)ed** adj parcial

bib [bɪb] n babadouro, babador m

Bible ['baɪbl] n Bíblia

bicker ['bɪkə*] vi brigar

bicycle ['baɪsɪkl] n bicicleta

bid [bɪd] (pt **bade** or **bid**, pp **bidden** or **bid**) n oferta; (at auction) lance m; (attempt) tentativa ♦ vi fazer lance ♦ vt oferecer; **to ~ sb good day** dar bom dia a alguém

bide [baɪd] vt: **to ~ one's time** esperar o momento adequado

bifocals [baɪ'fəuklz] npl óculos mpl bifocais

big [bɪg] adj grande; (bulky) volumoso; **~ brother/sister** irmão/irmã mais velho/a

bigheaded ['bɪg'hɛdɪd] adj convencido

bike [baɪk] n bicicleta

bikini [bɪ'kiːnɪ] n biquíni m

bilingual [baɪ'lɪŋgwəl] adj bilíngüe

bill [bɪl] n conta; (invoice) fatura; (POL) projeto de lei; (US: banknote) bilhete m, nota; (in restaurant) conta, notinha; (of bird) bico; (THEATRE) cartaz m; **to fit** or **fill the ~** (fig) servir; **billboard** n quadro para cartazes

billfold ['bɪlfəuld] (US) n carteira

billiards ['bɪlɪədz] n bilhar m

billion ['bɪlɪən] (BRIT) n trilhão m; (US) bilhão m

bin [bɪn] n caixa; (BRIT: for rubbish) lata de lixo

bind [baɪnd] (pt, pp **bound**) vt atar, amarrar; (oblige) obrigar; (book) encadernar ♦ n (inf) saco; (nuisance) chatice f

binge [bɪndʒ] (inf) n: **to go on a ~** tomar uma bebedeira

bingo ['bɪŋgəu] n bingo

binoculars [bɪ'nɔkjuləz] npl binóculo

bio... [baɪəu] prefix bio...; **biochemistry** n bioquímica; **biography** n biografia; **biology** n biologia

birch [bɜːtʃ] n bétula

bird [bɜːd] n ave f, pássaro; (BRIT: inf: girl) gatinha

Biro ['baɪərəu] ® n (caneta) esferográfica

birth [bɜːθ] n nascimento; **to give ~ to** dar à luz, parir; **birth certificate** n certidão f de nascimento; **birth control** n controle m de natalidade; (methods) métodos mpl anticoncepcionais; **birthday** n aniversário (BR), dia m de anos (PT) ♦ cpd de aniversário; see also **happy**

biscuit ['bɪskɪt] n (BRIT) bolacha, biscoito; (US) pão m doce

bishop ['bɪʃəp] n bispo; (CHESS) peça

de jogo de xadrez

bit [bɪt] *pt of* **bite ♦** *n* pedaço, bocado; (*of horse*) freio; (*COMPUT*) bit *m*; **a ~ of** (*a little*) um pouco de; **~ by ~** pouco a pouco

bitch [bɪtʃ] *n* (*dog*) cadela, cachorra; (*inf!*) cadela (!), vagabunda (!)

bite [baɪt] (*pt* **bit**, *pp* **bitten**) *vt, vi* morder; (*insect etc*) picar ♦ *n* (*insect ~*) picada; (*mouthful*) bocado; **to ~ one's nails** roer as unhas; **let's have a ~ (to eat)** (*inf*) vamos fazer uma boquinha

bitter ['bɪtə*] *adj* amargo; (*wind, criticism*) cortante, penetrante; (*weather*) horrível ♦ *n* (*BRIT: beer*) cerveja amarga; **bitterness** *n* amargor *m*; (*anger*) rancor *m*

black [blæk] *adj* preto; (*humour*) negro ♦ *n* (*colour*) cor *f* preta; (*person*): **B~** negro(-a), preto(-a) ♦ *vt* (*BRIT: INDUSTRY*) boicotar; **to give sb a ~ eye** esmurrar alguém e deixá-lo de olho roxo; **~ and blue** contuso, contundido; **to be in the ~** (*in credit*) estar com saldo credor; **blackberry** *n* amora silvestre; **blackbird** *n* melro; **blackboard** *n* quadro(-negro); **black coffee** *n* café *m* preto, bica (*PT*); **blackcurrant** *n* groselha negra; **blackmail** *n* chantagem *f* ♦ *vt* fazer chantagem a; **black market** *n* mercado or câmbio negro; **blackout** *n* blecaute *m*; (*fainting*) desmaio; (*of radio signal*) desvanecimento; **Black Sea** *n*: **the Black Sea** o mar Negro; **blacksmith** *n* ferreiro

bladder ['blædə*] *n* bexiga

blade [bleɪd] *n* lâmina; (*of oar*) pá *f*; **a ~ of grass** uma folha de relva

blame [bleɪm] *n* culpa ♦ *vt*: **to ~ sb for sth** culpar alguém por algo; **to be to ~** ter a culpa

bland [blænd] *adj* (*taste*) brando

blank [blæŋk] *adj* em branco; (*look*) sem expressão ♦ *n* (*on form*) espaço em branco; (*cartridge*) bala de festim; (*of memory*): **to go ~** dar um branco

blanket ['blæŋkɪt] *n* cobertor *m*

blare [blεə*] *vi* (*horn, radio*) clangorar

blast [blɑːst] *n* (*of wind*) rajada; (*of explosive*) explosão *f* ♦ *vt* fazer voar; **blast-off** *n* (*SPACE*) lançamento

blatant ['bleɪtənt] *adj* descarado

blaze [bleɪz] *n* (*fire*) fogo; (*in building etc*) incêndio; (*fig: of colour*) esplendor *m*; (: *of glory, publicity*) explosão ♦ *vi* (*fire*) arder; (*guns*) descarregar; (*eyes*) brilhar ♦ *vt*: **to ~ a trail** (*fig*) abrir (um) caminho

blazer ['bleɪzə*] *n* casaco esportivo, blazer *m*

bleach [bliːtʃ] *n* (*also: household ~*) água sanitária ♦ *vt* (*linen*) branquear

bleak [bliːk] *adj* (*countryside*) desolado; (*prospect*) desanimador(a), sombrio; (*weather*) ruim

bleed [bliːd] (*pt, pp* **bled**) *vi* sangrar

bleeper ['bliːpə*] *n* (*of doctor*) bip *m*

blemish ['blɛmɪʃ] *n* mancha; (*on reputation*) mácula

blend [blɛnd] *n* mistura ♦ *vt* misturar ♦ *vi* (*colours etc: also: ~ in*) combinar-se, misturar-se; **blender** *n* liquidificador *m*

bless [blɛs] (*pt, pp* **~ed** *or* **blest**) *vt* abençoar; **~ you!** (*after sneeze*) saúde!; **blessing** *n* bênção *f*; (*godsend*) graça, dádiva; (*approval*) aprovação *f*

blew [bluː] *pt of* **blow**

blind [blaɪnd] *adj* cego ♦ *n* (*for window*) persiana; (: *also:* **Venetian ~**) veneziana ♦ *vt* cegar; (*dazzle*) deslumbrar; **the ~** *npl* (*~ people*) os cegos; **blind alley** *n* beco-sem-saída *m*; **blindfold** *n* venda ♦ *adj*, *adv* com os olhos vendados, às cegas ♦ *vt* vendar os olhos a; **blindness** *n* cegueira; **blind spot** *n* (AUT) local *m* pouco visível; (*fig*) ponto fraco

blink [blɪŋk] *vi* piscar

bliss [blɪs] *n* felicidade *f*

blister ['blɪstə*] *n* (*on skin*) bolha; (*in paint, rubber*) empola ♦ *vi* empolar-se

blizzard ['blɪzəd] *n* nevasca

bloated ['bləutɪd] *adj* (*swollen*) inchado; (*full*) empanturrado

blob [blɔb] *n* (*drop*) gota; (*indistinct shape*) ponto

block [blɔk] *n* (*of wood*) bloco; (*of stone*) laje *f*; (*in pipes*) entupimento; (*of buildings*) quarteirão *m* ♦ *vt* obstruir, bloquear; (*progress*) impedir; **~ of flats** (BRIT) prédio (de apartamentos); **mental ~** bloqueio; **blockade** [blɔ'keɪd] *n* bloqueio; **blockage** *n* obstrução *f*; **blockbuster** *n* grande sucesso

bloke [bləuk] (BRIT: *inf*) *n* cara *m* (BR), gajo (PT)

blond(e) [blɔnd] *adj, n* louro(-a)

blood [blʌd] *n* sangue *m*; **blood donor** *n* doador(a) *m/f* de sangue; **blood group** *n* grupo sanguíneo; **bloodhound** *n* sabujo; **blood poisoning** *n* toxemia; **blood pressure** *n* pressão *f* arterial *or* sangüínea; **bloodshed** *n* matança, carnificina; **bloodshot** *adj* (*eyes*) injetado; **bloodstream** *n* corrente *f* sangüínea; **blood test** *n* exame *m* de sangue; **bloodthirsty** *adj* sangüinário; **blood vessel** *n* vaso sangüíneo; **bloody** *adj* sangrento; (*nose*) ensangüentado; (BRIT: *inf!*): **this bloody ...** essa droga de ..., esse maldito ...; **bloody strong/good** forte/bom pra burro; **bloodyminded** (BRIT: *inf*) *adj* espírito de porco *inv*

bloom [blu:m] *n* flor *f* ♦ *vi* florescer

blossom ['blɔsəm] *n* flor *f* ♦ *vi* florescer; (*fig*): **to ~ into** (*fig*) tornar-se

blot [blɔt] *n* borrão *m*; (*fig*) mancha ♦ *vt* borrar; **blot out** *vt* (*view*) tapar; (*memory*) apagar

blotchy ['blɔtʃɪ] *adj* (*complexion*) cheio de manchas

blotting paper ['blɔtɪŋ-] *n* mataborrão *m*

blouse [blauz] *n* blusa

blow [bləu] (*pt* **blew**, *pp* **blown**) *n* golpe *m*; (*punch*) soco ♦ *vi* soprar ♦ *vt* (*subj: wind*) soprar; (*instrument*) tocar; (*fuse*) queimar; **to ~ one's nose** assoar o nariz; **blow away** *vt* levar, arrancar ♦ *vi* ser levado pelo vento; **blow down** *vt* derrubar; **blow off** *vt* levar; **blow out** *vi* (*candle*) apagar; **blow over** *vi* (*storm, crisis*) passar; **blow up** *vi* explodir ♦ *vt* explodir; (*tyre*) encher; (PHOT) ampliar; **blow-dry** *n* escova; **blow-out** *n* (*of tyre*) furo

blue [blu:] *adj* azul; (*depressed*) deprimido; **~s** *n* (MUS): **the ~s** o blues; **~ film/joke** filme/anedota picante; **out of the ~** (*fig*) de estalo, inesperadamente; **bluebell** *n* campainha; **bluebottle** *n* varejeira azul

bluff [blʌf] *vi* blefar ♦ *n* blefe *m*; **to call sb's ~** pagar para ver alguém

blunder ['blʌndə*] *n* gafe *f* ♦ *vi* cometer *or* fazer uma gafe

blunt [blʌnt] *adj* (*knife*) cego; (*pencil*) rombudo; (*person*) franco, direto

blur [blə:*] *n* borrão *m* ♦ *vt* (*vision*) embaçar; (*distinction*) reduzir, diminuir

blush [blʌʃ] *vi* corar, ruborizar-se ♦ *n* rubor *m*, vermelhidão *f*

boar [bɔ:*] *n* javali *m*

board [bɔ:d] *n* tábua; (*card~*) quadro; (*notice ~*) quadro de avisos; (*for* *chess etc)* tabuleiro; *(committee)* junta, conselho; *(in firm)* diretoria, conselho administrativo; *(NAUT, AVIAT)*: **on ~ a** bordo ♦ *vt* embarcar em; **full ~** *(BRIT)* pensão f completa; **half ~** *(BRIT)* meia-pensão f; **~ and lodging** casa e comida; **to go by the ~** ficar abandonado, dançar *(inf)*; **board up** *vt* entabucar; **boarder** *n* interno(-a); **boarding card** *n* = **boarding pass**; **boarding house** *n* pensão *m*; **boarding pass** *(BRIT)* *n* cartão *m* de embarque; **boarding school** *n* internato

boast [bəust] *vi*: **to ~ (about** or **of)** gabar-se (de), jactar-se (de)

boat [bəut] *n (small)* bote *m*; *(big)* navio

bob [bɔb] *vi* balouçar-se; **bob up** *vi* aparecer, surgir

bobby ['bɔbɪ] *(BRIT: inf)* *n* policial *m/f (BR)*, polícia *m (PT)*

bobsleigh ['bɔbsleɪ] *n* bob *m*, trenó *m* duplo

bodily ['bɔdɪlɪ] *adj* corporal; *(needs)* material ♦ *adv (lift)* em peso

body ['bɔdɪ] *n* corpo; *(corpse)* cadáver *m*; *(of car)* carroceria; *(fig: group)* grupo; *(: organization)* organização f; *(quantity)* conjunto; *(of wine)* corpo; **body-building** *n* musculação f; **bodyguard** *n* guardacostas *m inv*; **bodywork** *n* lataria

bog [bɔg] *n* pântano, atoleiro ♦ *vt*: **to ~ged down** *(fig)* atolar-se

bogus ['bəugəs] *adj* falso

boil [bɔɪl] *vt* ferver; *(CULIN)* cozer, cozinhar ♦ *vi* ferver ♦ *n (MED)* furúnculo; **to come to the** *(BRIT)* or **a** *(US)* **~** começar a ferver; **boil down to** *vt fus (fig)* reduzir-se a; **boil over** *vi* transbordar; **boiled egg** *n* ovo cozido; **boiled potatoes** *npl* batatas *fpl* cozidas; **boiler** *n* caldeira; *(for central heating)* boiler *m*; **boil-**

ing point *n* ponto de ebulição

boisterous ['bɔɪstərəs] *adj (noisy)* barulhento; *(excitable)* agitado; *(crowd)* turbulento

bold [bəuld] *adj* corajoso; *(pej)* atrevido, insolente; *(outline, colour)* forte

Bolivia [bə'lɪvɪə] *n* Bolívia

bollard ['bɔləd] *(BRIT)* *n (AUT)* poste *m* de sinalização

bolt [bəult] *n (lock)* trinco, ferrolho; *(with nut)* parafuso, cavilha ♦ *adv*: **~ upright** direito como um fuso ♦ *vt (door)* fechar a ferrolho, trancar; *(food)* engolir às pressas ♦ *vi* fugir; *(horse)* disparar

bomb [bɔm] *n* bomba ♦ *vt* bombardear

bombshell ['bɔmʃɛl] *n (fig)* bomba

bond [bɔnd] *n (binding promise)* compromisso; *(link)* vínculo, laço; *(FINANCE)* obrigação f; *(COMM)*: **in ~** *(goods)* retido sob caução na alfândega

bone [bəun] *n* osso; *(of fish)* espinha ♦ *vt* desossar; tirar as espinhas de

bonfire ['bɔnfaɪə*] *n* fogueira

bonnet ['bɔnɪt] *n* toucado; *(BRIT: of car)* capô *m*

bonus ['bəunəs] *n (payment)* bônus *m*; *(fig)* gratificação f

bony ['bəunɪ] *adj* ossudo; *(meat)* cheio de ossos; *(fish)* cheio de espinhas

boo [bu:] *vt* vaiar ♦ *excl* ruuh!, bu!

booby trap ['bu:bɪ-] *n* armadilha explosiva

book [buk] *n* livro; *(of stamps, tickets)* talão *m* ♦ *vt* reservar; *(driver)* autuar; *(football player)* mostrar o cartão amarelo a; **~s** *npl (COMM)* contas *fpl*, contabilidade f; **bookcase** *n* estante f (para livros); **booking office** *(BRIT)* *n (RAIL, THEATRE)* bilheteria *(BR)*, bilheteira *(PT)*; **book-keeping** *n* escrituração f, contabilidade f; **booklet** n livrinho, brochura; **bookshop** n, **bookstore** n livraria

boom [bu:m] n (noise) barulho, estrondo; (in sales) aumento rápido ♦ vi retumbar; (business) tomar surto

boon [bu:n] n dádiva, benefício

boost [bu:st] n estímulo ♦ vt estimular

boot [bu:t] n bota; (for football) chuteira; (BRIT: of car) porta-malas m (BR), porta-bagagem m (PT) ♦ vt (COMPUT) dar carga em; to ~ ... (in addition) ainda por cima ...

booth [bu:ð] n (at fair) barraca; (telephone ~, voting ~) cabine f

booze [bu:z] (inf) n bebida alcoólica

border ['bɔːdə*] n margem f; (for flowers) borda; (of a country) fronteira; (on cloth etc) debrum m, remate m ♦ vt (also: ~ on) limitar-se com; **border on** vt fus (fig) chegar às raias de; **borderline** n fronteira; **Borders** n: the Borders a região fronteiriça entre a Escócia e a Inglaterra

bore [bɔː*] pt of bear ♦ vt (hole) abrir; (well) cavar; (person) aborrecer ♦ n (person) chato(-a), maçante m/f; (of gun) calibre m; to be ~d estar entediado; **boredom** n tédio, aborrecimento; **boring** adj chato, maçante

born [bɔːn] adj: to be ~ nascer

borne [bɔːn] pp of bear

borough ['bʌrə] n município

borrow ['bɔrəu] vt: to ~ sth (from sb) pedir algo emprestado (a alguém)

Bosnia (and) Herzegovina ['bɔzniə(ənd)hɜːtsəɡəu'viːnə] n Bósnia e Herzegovina

bosom ['buzəm] n peito

boss [bɔs] n (employer) patrão(-troa) m/f ♦ vt (also: ~ about; ~ around) mandar em; **bossy** adj mandão(-dona)

botch [bɔtʃ] vt (also: ~ up) estropiar, atamancar

both [bəuθ] adj, pron ambos(-as), os dois (as duas) ♦ adv: ~ A and B tanto A como B; ~ of us went, we ~ went nós dois fomos, ambos fomos

bother ['bɔðə*] vt (worry) preocupar; (disturb) atrapalhar ♦ vi (also: ~ o.s.) preocupar-se ♦ n preocupação f; (nuisance) amolação f, inconveniente m

bottle ['bɔtl] n garrafa; (of perfume, medicine) frasco; (baby's) mamadeira (BR), biberão m (PT) ♦ vt engarrafar; **bottle up** vt conter, refrear; **bottle bank** n depósito de vidro para reciclagem, vidrão m (PT); **bottleneck** n (traffic) engarrafamento; (fig) obstáculo, problema m, **bottle-opener** n abridor m (de garrafas) (BR), abre-garrafas m inv (PT)

bottom ['bɔtəm] n fundo; (buttocks) traseiro; (of page, list) pé m; (of class) nível m mais baixo ♦ adj (low) inferior, mais baixo; (last) último

bough [bau] n ramo

bought [bɔːt] pt, pp of buy

boulder ['bəuldə*] n pedregulho, matacão m

bounce [bauns] vi saltar, quicar; (cheque) ser devolvido ♦ vt fazer saltar ♦ n (rebound) salto; **bouncer** (inf) n leão-de-chácara m

bound [baund] pt, pp of bind ♦ n (leap) pulo, salto; (gen pl: limit) limite m ♦ vi (leap) pular, saltar ♦ vt (border) demarcar ♦ adj: ~ by limitado por; to be ~ to sth (obliged) ter a obrigação de fazer algo; (likely) na certa ir fazer algo; ~ for com destino a

boundary ['baundrɪ] n limite m, fronteira

bout [baut] n (of malaria etc) ataque m; (of activity) explosão f; (BOXING *etc*) combate *m*

bow¹ [bəu] *n* (*knot*) laço; (*weapon*, *MUS*) arco

bow² [bau] *n* (*of the body*) reverência; (*of the head*) inclinação *f*; (*NAUT: also: ~s*) proa ♦ *vi* curvar-se, fazer uma reverência; (*yield*): **to ~ to** or **before** ceder ante, submeter-se a

bowels [ˈbauəlz] *npl* intestinos *mpl*, tripas *fpl*; (*fig*) entranhas *fpl*

bowl [bəul] *n* tigela; (*ball*) bola ♦ *vi* (*CRICKET*) arremessar a bola

bowler [ˈbəulə*] *n* (*CRICKET*) lançador *m* (da bola); (*BRIT: also: ~ hat*) chapéu-coco *m*

bowling [ˈbəulɪŋ] *n* (*game*) boliche *m*; **bowling alley** *n* boliche *m*; **bowling green** *n* gramado (*BR*) or relvado (*PT*) para jogo de bolas

bowls [bəulz] *n* jogo de bolas

bow tie [ˈbəu-] *n* gravata-borboleta

box [bɔks] *n* caixa; (*THEATRE*) camarote *m* ♦ *vt* encaixotar; (*SPORT*) boxear contra ♦ *vi* (*SPORT*) boxear, **boxer** *n* (*person*) boxeador *m*, pugilista *m*; **boxer shorts** *npl* samba-canção *m* (*BR*), boxers *mpl* (*PT*); **boxing** *n* (*SPORT*) boxe *m*, pugilismo; **Boxing Day** (*BRIT*) *n* Dia de Santo Estêvão (*26 de dezembro*); **box office** *n* bilheteria (*BR*), bilheteira (*PT*)

boy [bɔɪ] *n* (*young*) menino, garoto; (*older*) moço, rapaz *m*; (*son*) filho

boycott [ˈbɔɪkɔt] *n* boicote *m*, boicotagem *f* ♦ *vt* boicotar

boyfriend [ˈbɔɪfrɛnd] *n* namorado

BR *abbr* = **British Rail**

bra [brɑ:] *n* sutiã *m* (*BR*), soutien *m* (*PT*)

brace [breɪs] *n* (*on teeth*) aparelho; (*tool*) arco de pua ♦ *vt* retesar; **~s** *npl* (*BRIT*) suspensórios *mpl*; **to ~ o.s.** (*also fig*) preparar-se

bracelet [ˈbreɪslɪt] *n* pulseira

bracing [ˈbreɪsɪŋ] *adj* tonificante

bracket [ˈbrækɪt] *n* (*TECH*) suporte *m*; (*group*) classe *f*, categoria; (*range*) faixa, parêntese *m* ♦ *vt* pôr entre parênteses; (*fig*) agrupar

brag [bræg] *vi* gabar-se, contar vantagem

braid [breɪd] *n* (*trimming*) galão *m*; (*of hair*) trança

brain [breɪn] *n* cérebro; **~s** *npl* (*CULIN*) miolos *mpl*; (*intelligence*) inteligência, miolos; **brainwash** *vt* fazer uma lavagem cerebral em; **brainwave** *n* inspiração *f*, idéia luminosa or brilhante; **brainy** *adj* inteligente

braise [breɪz] *vt* assar na panela

brake [breɪk] *n* freio (*BR*), travão *m* (*PT*) ♦ *vt, vi* frear (*BR*), travar (*PT*)

bran [bræn] *n* farelo

branch [brɑ:ntʃ] *n* ramo, galho; (*COMM*) sucursal *f*, filial *f*; **branch out** *vi* (*fig*) diversificar suas atividades; **to ~ out into** estender suas atividades a

brand [brænd] *n* marca; (*fig: type*) tipo ♦ *vt* (*cattle*) marcar com ferro quente

brand-new *adj* novo em folha, novinho

brandy [ˈbrændɪ] *n* conhaque *m*

brash [bræʃ] *adj* descarado

Brasilia [brəˈzɪlɪə] *n* Brasília

brass [brɑ:s] *n* latão *m*; **the ~** (*MUS*) os metais; **brass band** *n* banda de música

brat [bræt] (*pej*) *n* pirralho(-a), fedelho(-a), malcriado(-a)

brave [breɪv] *adj* valente, corajoso ♦ *vt* (*face up to*) desafiar; **bravery** *n* coragem *f*, bravura

brazen [ˈbreɪzn] *adj* descarado ♦ *vt*: **to ~ it out** defender-se descaradamente

Brazil [brəˈzɪl] *n* Brasil *m*; **Brazilian** *adj, n* brasileiro(-a)

breach [briːtʃ] vt abrir brecha em
♦ n (gap) brecha; (breaking): ~ of
contract inadimplência (BR), inadim-
plemento (PT); ~ of the peace perturbação f da ordem pública

bread [bred] n pão m; **bread and
butter** n pão m com manteiga; (fig)
ganha-pão m; **breadbin** (US **bread
box**) n caixa de pão; **breadcrumbs** npl migalhas fpl; (CULIN)
farinha de rosca

breadth [brɛtθ] n largura; (fig)
amplitude f

breadwinner ['brɛdwɪnə*] n arrimo de família

break [breɪk] (pt **broke**, pp **broken**)
vt quebrar (BR), partir (PT); (promise)
quebrar; (law) violar, transgredir;
(record) bater ♦ vi quebrar-se, partir-
se; (storm) começar subitamente;
(weather) mudar; (dawn) amanhecer; (story, news) revelar ♦ n (gap)
abertura; (fracture) fratura; (rest)
descanso; (interval) intervalo; (at
school) recreio; (chance) oportunidade f; to ~ the news to sb dar a
notícia a alguém; to ~ even sair sem
ganhar nem perder; to ~ free or
loose soltar-se; to ~ open (door etc)
arrombar; **break down** vt (figures,
data) analisar ♦ vt (machine, AUT)
enguiçar, pifar (inf); (MED) sofrer
uma crise nervosa; (person: cry)
desatar a chorar; (talks) fracassar;
break in vt (horse etc) domar ♦ vi
(burglar) forçar uma entrada; (interrupt) interromper; **break into** vt fus
(house) arrombar; **break off** vi
(speaker) parar-se, deter-se; (branch)
partir; **break out** vi (war) estourar;
(prisoner) libertar-se; to ~ out in
spots/a rash aparecer coberto de
manchas/brotoejas; **break up** vi
(ship) partir-se; (partnership) acabar;
(marriage) desmanchar-se ♦ vt

(rocks) partir; (biscuit etc) quebrar;
(journey) romper; (fight) intervir em;
breakage n quebradura; **breakdown** n (AUT) enguiço, avaria; (in
communications) interrupção f; (of
marriage) fracasso, término; (MED:
also: **nervous breakdown**) esgotamento nervoso; (of figures) discriminação f, desdobramento

breakfast ['brɛkfəst] n café m da
manhã (BR), pequeno almoço (PT)

break: **break-in** n roubo com
arrombamento; **breakthrough** n
(fig) avanço, novo progresso

breast [brɛst] n (of woman) peito,
seio; (chest, meat) peito; **breast-
feed** (irreg: like **feed**) vt, vi amamentar; **breast-stroke** n nado de
peito

breath [brɛθ] n fôlego, respiração f;
out of ~ ofegante, sem fôlego;
Breathalyser ['brɛθəlaɪzə*] ® n
bafômetro

breathe [briːð] vt, vi respirar;
breathe in vt, vi inspirar; **breathe
out** vt, vi expirar; **breathing** n respiração f

breathless ['brɛθlɪs] adj sem fôlego

breed [briːd] (pt, pp **bred**) vt (animals) criar; (plants) multiplicar ♦ vi
criar, reproduzir ♦ n raça

breeze [briːz] n brisa, aragem f;
breezy adj (person) despreocupado, animado; (weather) ventoso

brew [bruː] vt (tea) fazer; (beer) fermentar ♦ vi (storm, fig) armar-se;
brewery n cervejaria

bribe [braɪb] n suborno ♦ vt subornar; **bribery** n suborno

brick [brɪk] n tijolo; **bricklayer** n
pedreiro

bride [braɪd] n noiva; **bridegroom**
n noivo; **bridesmaid** n dama de
honra

bridge [brɪdʒ] n ponte f; (NAUT)

ponte de comando; (CARDS) bridge
m; (of nose) cavalete m ♦ vt transpor
bridle ['braɪdl] n cabeçada, freio
brief [briːf] adj breve ♦ n (LAW) causa;
(task) tarefa ♦ vt (inform) informar;
~s npl (for men) cueca (BR), cuecas
fpl (PT); (for women) calcinha (BR),
cuecas fpl (PT); **briefcase** n pasta;
briefly adv (glance) rapidamente;
(say) em poucas palavras
bright [braɪt] adj claro, brilhante;
(weather) resplandecente; (person:
clever) inteligente; (: lively) alegre,
animado; (colour) vivo; (future)
promissor(a), favorável; **brighten**
(also: **brighten up**) vt (room) tornar
mais alegre; (event) animar, alegrar
♦ vi (weather) clarear; (person) animar-se, alegrar-se; (face) iluminar-
se; (prospects) tornar-se animado e
favorável
brilliance ['brɪljəns] n brilho, claridade f
brilliant ['brɪljənt] adj brilhante;
(inf: great) sensacional
brim [brɪm] n borda; (of hat) aba
brine [braɪn] n (CULIN) salmoura
bring [brɪŋ] (pt, pp **brought**) vt trazer; **bring about** vt ocasionar, produzir; **bring back** vt restabelecer;
(return) devolver; **bring down** vt
(price) abaixar; (government, plane)
derrubar; **bring forward** vt adiantar; **bring off** vt (plan) levar a
cabo; **bring out** vt (object) tirar;
(meaning) salientar; (book etc)
lançar; **bring round** vt fazer voltar
a si; **bring up** vt (person) educar,
criar; (carry up) subir; (question)
introduzir; (food) vomitar
brisk [brɪsk] adj vigoroso; (tone, person) enérgico; (trade) ativo
bristle ['brɪsl] n (of animal) pêlo rijo;
(of beard) pêlo de barba curta;
(of brush) cerda ♦ vi (in anger)

encolerizar-se
Britain ['brɪtən] n (also: **Great ~**)
Grã-Bretanha
British ['brɪtɪʃ] adj britânico ♦ npl:
the ~ os britânicos; **British Isles**
npl: **the British Isles** as ilhas
Britânicas; **British Rail** n companhia ferroviária britânica
Briton ['brɪtən] n britânico(-a)
brittle ['brɪtl] adj quebradiço, frágil
broach [brəʊtʃ] vt abordar, tocar
em
broad [brɔːd] adj (street, range)
amplo; (shoulders, smile) largo; (distinction) geral; (accent) carregado;
in ~ daylight em plena luz do dia;
broadcast (pt, pp **~cast**) n transmissão f ♦ vt, vi transmitir; **broaden**
vt alargar ♦ vi alargar-se; **to broaden
one's mind** abrir os horizontes;
broadly adv em geral; **broad-
minded** adj tolerante, liberal
broccoli ['brɒkəlɪ] n brócolis mpl
brochure ['brəʊʃjʊə*] n folheto,
brochura
broke [brəʊk] pt of **break** ♦ adj (inf)
sem um vintém, duro; (: company):
to go ~ quebrar
broken ['brəʊkən] pp of **break** ♦ ad,
quebrado; in **~ English** num inglês
mascavado; **broken-hearted** adj
com o coração partido
broker ['brəʊkə*] n corretor(a) m/f
brolly ['brɒlɪ] (BRIT: inf) n guarda-
chuva m
bronchitis [brɒŋ'kaɪtɪs] n bronquite f
bronze [brɒnz] n bronze m
brooch [brəʊtʃ] n broche m
brood [bruːd] n ninhada ♦ vi (person) cismar, remoer
broom [bruːm] n vassoura; (BOT)
giesta-das-vassouras
Bros. abbr (COMM: = brothers) Irmãos
broth [brɒθ] n caldo

brothel ['brɒθl] n bordel m

brother ['brʌðə*] n irmão m; **brother-in-law** n cunhado

brought [brɔːt] pt, pp of **bring**

brow [brau] n (forehead) fronte f, testa; (rare: gen: eye~) sobrancelha; (of hill) cimo, cume m

brown [braun] adj marrom (BR), castanho (PT); (hair) castanho; (tanned) bronzeado, moreno ♦ n (colour) cor f marrom (BR) or castanha (PT) ♦ vt (CULIN) dourar; **brown bread** n pão m integral; **Brownie** n (also: **Brownie Guide**) fadinha de bandeirante; **brownie** (US) n (cake) docinho de chocolate com amêndoas; **brown paper** n papel m pardo; **brown sugar** n açúcar m mascavo

browse [brauz] vi (in shop) dar uma olhada; **to ~ through a book** folhear um livro; **browser** ['brauzə*] n (COMPUT) browser m, navegador m

bruise [bruːz] n hematoma m, contusão f ♦ vt machucar

brunette [bruː'nɛt] n morena

brunt [brʌnt] n: **the ~ of** (greater part) a maior parte de

brush [brʌʃ] n escova; (for painting, shaving) pincel m; (quarrel) bateboca m ♦ vt varrer; (groom) escovar; (also: ~ against) tocar ao passar, roçar; **brush aside** vt afastar, não fazer caso de; **brush up** vt retocar, revisar

Brussels ['brʌslz] n Bruxelas; **Brussels sprout** n couve-de-bruxelas f

brutal ['bruːtl] adj brutal

brute [bruːt] n bruto; (person) animal m ♦ adj: **by ~ force** por força bruta

BSc n abbr = **Bachelor of Science**

BSE n abbr (= bovine spongiform encephalopathy) BSE f

bubble ['bʌbl] n bolha (BR), borbu-

lha (PT) ♦ vi borbulhar; **bubble bath** n banho de espuma; **bubble gum** n chiclete m (de bola) (BR), pastilha elástica (PT)

buck [bʌk] n (rabbit) macho; (deer) cervo; (US) dólar m ♦ vi corcovear; **to pass the ~** fazer o jogo de empurra; **buck up** vi (cheer up) animar-se, cobrar ânimo

bucket ['bʌkɪt] n balde m

buckle ['bʌkl] n fivela ♦ vt afivelar ♦ vi torcer-se, cambar-se

bud [bʌd] n broto; (of flower) botão m ♦ vi brotar, desabrochar

Buddhism ['budɪzəm] n budismo

buddy ['bʌdɪ] (US) n camarada m, companheiro

budge [bʌdʒ] vt mover ♦ vi mexer-se

budgerigar ['bʌdʒərɪɡaː*] n periquito

budget ['bʌdʒɪt] n orçamento ♦ vi: **to ~ for sth** incluir algo no orçamento

budgie ['bʌdʒɪ] n = **budgerigar**

buff [bʌf] adj (colour) cor de camurça ♦ n (inf: enthusiast) aficionado(-a)

buffalo ['bʌfələu] (pl ~ or ~es) n (BRIT) búfalo; (US: bison) bisão m

buffer ['bʌfə*] n (COMPUT) buffer m, memória intermediária

buffet¹ ['bufeɪ] (BRIT) n (in station) bar m; (food) bufê m; **buffet car** (BRIT) n vagão-restaurante m

buffet² ['bʌfɪt] vt fustigar

bug [bʌɡ] n (esp US: insect) bicho; (fig: germ) micróbio; (spy device) microfone m oculto, escuta clandestina; (COMPUT: of program) erro ♦ vt (inf: annoy) apoquentar, incomodar; (room) colocar microfones em; (phone) grampear

bugle ['bjuːɡl] n trompa, corneta

build [bɪld] n (pt, pp **built**) n (of per-

son) talhe *m*, estatura ♦ *vt* construir, edificar; **build up** *vt* acumular; **builder** *n* construtor(a) *m/f*, empreiteiro(-a); **building** *n* (*trade*) construção *f*; (*house, structure*) edifício, prédio; **building society** (*BRIT*) *n* sociedade *f* de crédito imobiliário, financiadora

built [bɪlt] *pt, pp* of **build** ♦ *adj*: **~-in** embutido; **built-up area** ['bɪltʌp-] *n* zona urbanizada

bulb [bʌlb] *n* (*BOT*) bulbo; (*ELEC*) lâmpada

Bulgaria [bʌl'gɛərɪə] *n* Bulgária

bulge [bʌldʒ] *n* bojo, saliência ♦ *vi* inchar-se; (*pocket etc*) fazer bojo

bulk [bʌlk] *n* (*of building, object*) volume *m*; (*of person*) corpanzil *m*; **in ~** (*COMM*) a granel; **the ~ of** a maior parte de; **bulky** *adj* volumoso

bull [bul] *n* touro; **bulldog** *n* buldogue *m*

bulldozer ['buldəuzə*] *n* buldôzer *m*, escavadora

bullet [bulɪt] *n* bala

bulletin ['bulɪtɪn] *n* noticiário; (*journal*) boletim *m*

bulletproof ['bulɪtpruːf] *adj* à prova de bala

bullfight ['bulfaɪt] *n* tourada; **bullfighter** *n* toureiro; **bullfighting** *n* tauromaquia

bullion ['buljən] *n* ouro (*or* prata) em barras

bullock ['bulək] *n* boi *m*, novilho

bullring ['bulrɪŋ] *n* praça de touros

bull's-eye *n* centro do alvo, mosca (do alvo) (*BR*)

bully ['bulɪ] *n* fanfarrão *m*, valentão *m* ♦ *vt* intimidar, tiranizar

bum [bʌm] *n* (*inf*: *backside*) bumbum *m*; (*esp US: tramp*) vagabundo(-a), vadio(-a)

bumblebee ['bʌmblbiː] *n* maman-

gaba

bump [bʌmp] *n* (*in car*) batida; (*jolt*) sacudida; (*on head*) galo; (*on road*) elevação *f* ♦ *vt* bater contra; dar encontrão em ♦ *vi* dar sacudidas; **bump into** *vt fus* chocar-se com *or* contra, colidir com; (*inf: person*) dar com, topar com; **bumper** *n* (*BRIT*) pára-choque *m* ♦ *adj*: **bumper crop** supersafra; **bumper cars** *npl* carros *mpl* de trombada; **bumpy** ['bʌmpɪ] *adj* (*road*) acidentado, cheio de altos e baixos

bun [bʌn] *n* pão *m* doce (*BR*), pãozinho (*PT*); (*in hair*) coque *m*

bunch [bʌntʃ] *n* (*of flowers*) ramo; (*of keys*) molho; (*of bananas*) cacho; (*of people*) grupo; **~es** *npl* (*in hair*) cachos *mpl*

bundle ['bʌndl] *n* trouxa, embrulho; (*of sticks*) feixe *m*; (*of papers*) maço ♦ *vt* (*also*: **~ up**) embrulhar, atar; (*put*): **to ~ sth/sb into** meter *or* enfiar algo/alguém correndo em

bungalow ['bʌŋgələu] *n* bangalô *m*, chalé *m*

bungle ['bʌŋgl] *vt* estropear, estragar

bunion ['bʌnjən] *n* joanete *m*

bunk [bʌŋk] *n* beliche *m*; **bunk beds** *npl* beliche *m*, cama-beliche *f*

bunker ['bʌŋkə*] *n* (*coal store*) carvoeira; (*MIL*) abrigo, casamata; (*GOLF*) bunker *m*

buoy [bɔɪ] *n* bóia; **buoy up** *vt* (*fig*) animar; **buoyant** *adj* flutuante; (*person*) alegre; (*COMM: market*) animado

burden ['bəːdn] *n* responsabilidade *f*, fardo; (*load*) carga ♦ *vt* sobrecarregar; (*trouble*): **to be a ~ to sb** ser um estorvo para alguém

bureau [bjuə'rəu] (*pl* **~x**) *n* (*BRIT: desk*) secretária, escrivaninha; (*US:*

chest of drawers cômoda; (*office*) escritório, agência

bureaucracy [bjuə'rɔkrəsɪ] *n* burocracia

burglar ['bɔ:glə*] *n* ladrão *m/f*; **burglar alarm** *n* alarma de roubo; **burglary** *n* roubo

burial ['berɪəl] *n* enterro

Burma ['bɔ:mə] *n* Birmânia

burn [bɔ:n] (*pt, pp* **~ed** or **burnt**) *vt* queimar; (*house*) incendiar ♦ *vi* queimar-se, arder; (*sting*) arder, picar ♦ *n* queimadura; **burn down** *vt* incendiar; **burner** *n* (*on cooker, heater*) bico de gás, fogo; **burning** *adj* ardente; (*hot: sand etc*) abrasador(a); (*ambition*) grande

burrow ['bʌrəu] *n* toca, lura ♦ *vi* fazer uma toca, cavar; (*rummage*) esquadrinhar

bursary ['bɔ:sərɪ] (*BRIT*) *n* (*SCH*) bolsa

burst [bɔ:st] (*pt, pp* **burst**) *vt* arrebentar; (*banks*) romper ♦ *vi* estourar; (*tyre*) furar ♦ *n* rajada; **to ~ into flames** incendiar-se de repente; **to ~ into tears** desatar a chorar; **to ~ out laughing** cair na gargalhada; **to be ~ing with** (*subj: room, container*) estar abarrotado de; (*: person: emotion*) estar tomado de; **a ~ of energy** uma explosão de energia; **burst into** *vt fus* (*room etc*) irromper em

bury ['berɪ] *vt* enterrar; (*at funeral*) sepultar; **to ~ one's head in one's hands** cobrir o rosto com as mãos; **to ~ one's head in the sand** (*fig*) bancar avestruz; **to ~ the hatchet** (*fig*) fazer as pazes

bus [bʌs] *n* ônibus *m inv* (*BR*), autocarro *m* (*PT*)

bush [buʃ] *n* arbusto, mata; (*scrubland*) sertão *m*; **to beat about the ~** ser evasivo

bushy ['buʃɪ] *adj* (*thick*) espesso

business ['bɪznɪs] *n* negócio; (*trad-*

ing) comércio, negócios *mpl*; (*firm*) empresa; (*occupation*) profissão *f*; **to be away on ~** estar fora a negócios; **it's my ~ to ...** encarrego-me de ...; **it's none of my ~** eu não tenho nada com isto; **he means ~** fala a sério; **businesslike** *adj* eficiente, metódico; **businessman** (*irreg*) *n* homem *m* de negócios; **business trip** *n* viagem *f* de negócios; **businesswoman** (*irreg*) *n* mulher *f* de negócios

busker ['bʌskə*] (*BRIT*) *n* artista *m/f* de rua

bus: bus station *n* estação *f* rodoviária; **bus stop** *n* ponto de ônibus (*BR*), paragem *f* de autocarro (*PT*)

bust [bʌst] *n* (*ANAT*) busto ♦ *adj* (*inf: broken*) quebrado; **to go ~** falir

bustle ['bʌsl] *n* animação *f*, movimento ♦ *vi* apressar-se, andar azafamado; **bustling** *adj* (*town*) animado, movimentado

busy ['bɪzɪ] *adj* (*person*) ocupado, atarefado; (*place*) movimentado; (*US: TEL*) ocupado (*BR*), impedido (*PT*) ♦ *vt*: **to ~ o.s. with** ocupar-se em or de

---

KEYWORD

---

but [bʌt] *conj* **1** (*yet*) mas, porém; **he's tired ~ Paul isn't** ele está cansado mas Paul não; **the trip was enjoyable ~ tiring** a viagem foi agradável porém cansativa

2 (*however*) mas; **I'd love to come, ~ I'm busy** eu adoraria vir, mas estou ocupado

3 (*showing disagreement, surprise etc*) mas; **~ that's far too expensive!** mas isso é caro demais!

♦ *prep* (*apart from, except*) exceto, menos; **he was nothing ~ trouble** ele só deu problema; **no-one ~ him** só ele, ninguém a não ser ele; **~ for**

sem, se não fosse; **(I'll do) anything ~ that** (eu faria) qualquer coisa menos isso
♦ *adv* (*just, only*) apenas; **had I ~ known** se eu soubesse; **I can ~ try** a única coisa que eu posso fazer é tentar; **all ~** quase

butcher ['butʃə*] *n* açougueiro (*BR*), homem *m* do talho (*PT*) ♦ *vt* (*prisoners etc*) chacinar, massacrar; (*cattle etc for meat*) abater e carnear; **butcher's (shop)** *n* açougue *m* (*BR*), talho *m* (*PT*)

butler ['butlə*] *n* mordomo

butt [bʌt] *n* (*cask*) tonel *m*; (*of gun*) coronha; (*of cigarette*) toco (*BR*), ponta (*PT*); (*BRIT: fig: target*) alvo *m*; (*subj: goat*) marrar; (: *person*) dar uma cabeçada em; **butt in** *vi* (*interrupt*) interromper

butter ['bʌtə*] *n* manteiga ♦ *vt* untar com manteiga

butterfly ['bʌtəflaɪ] *n* borboleta; (*SWIMMING: also: ~ stroke*) nado borboleta

buttocks ['bʌtəks] *npl* nádegas *fpl*

button ['bʌtn] *n* botão *m*; (*US: badge*) emblema *m* ♦ *vt* (*also: ~ up*) abotoar ♦ *vi* ter botões

buy [baɪ] (*pt, pp* **bought**) *vt* comprar ♦ *n* compra; **to ~ sb sth/sth from sb** comprar algo para alguém/algo a alguém; **to ~ sb a drink** pagar um drinque para alguém; **buyer** *n* comprador(a) *m/f*

buzz [bʌz] *n* zumbido; (*inf: phone call*) **to give sb a ~** dar uma ligada para alguém ♦ *vi* zumbir; **buzzer** *n* cigarra, vibrador *m*; **buzz word** *n* modismo

by [baɪ] *prep* **1** (*referring to cause, agent*) por, de; **killed ~ lightning**

morto por um raio; **a painting ~ Picasso** um quadro de Picasso
2 (*referring to method, manner, means*) de, com; **~ bus/car/train** de ônibus/carro/trem; **to pay ~ cheque** pagar com cheque; **~ moonlight/ candlelight** sob o luar/à luz de vela; **~ saving hard, he** ... economizando muito, ele ...
3 (*via, through*) por, via; **we came ~ Dover** viemos por or via Dover
4 (*close to*) perto de, ao pé de; **a holiday ~ the sea** férias à beira-mar; **she sat ~ his bed** ela sentou-se ao lado de seu leito
5 (*past*) por; **she rushed ~ me** ela passou por mim correndo
6 (*not later than*): **~ 4 o'clock** antes das quatro; **~ this time tomorrow** esta mesma hora amanhã; **~ the time I got here it was too late** quando eu cheguei aqui, já era tarde demais
7 (*during*): **~ daylight** durante o dia
8 (*amount*) por; **~ the kilometre** por quilômetro
9 (*MATH, measure*) por; **it's broader ~ a metre** tem um metro a mais de largura
10 (*according to*) segundo, de acordo com; **it's all right ~ me** por mim tudo bem
11: (**all**) **~ oneself** *etc* (completamente) só, sozinho; **he did it (all) ~ himself** ele fêz tudo sozinho
12: **~ the way** a propósito
♦ *adv* **1** *see* **go**; **pass** *etc*
2: **~ and ~** logo, mais tarde; **~ and large** em geral

bye(-bye) ['baɪ('baɪ)] *excl* até logo (*BR*), tchau (*BR*), adeus (*PT*)

bypass ['baɪpɑːs] *n* via secundária, desvio; (*MED*) ponte *f* de safena ♦ *vt* evitar

bystander ['baɪstændə*] n circunstante m/f; (observer) espectador(a) m/f

byte [baɪt] n (COMPUT) byte m

C

C [siː] n (MUS) dó m

CA n abbr = **chartered accountant**

cab [kæb] n táxi m; (of truck etc) boléia f; (of train) cabina de maquinista

cabaret ['kæbəreɪ] n cabaré m

cabbage ['kæbɪdʒ] n repolho (BR), couve f (PT)

cabin ['kæbɪn] n cabana; (on ship) camarote m; (on plane) cabina de passageiros; **cabin cruiser** n lancha a motor com cabine

cabinet ['kæbɪnɪt] n (POL) gabinete m; (furniture) armário; (also: **display ~**) armário com vitrina

cable ['keɪbl] n cabo; (telegram) cabograma m ♦ vt enviar cabograma para; **cable-car** n bonde m (BR), teleférico (PT); **cable television** n televisão f a cabo

cache [kæʃ] n esconderijo; **a ~ of arms** etc um depósito secreto de armas etc

cactus ['kæktəs] (pl **cacti**) n cacto

cadge [kædʒ] (inf) vt filar

café ['kæfeɪ] n café m

cage [keɪdʒ] n (bird ~) gaiola; (for large animals) jaula; (of lift) cabina

cagey ['keɪdʒɪ] (inf) adj cuidadoso, reservado, desconfiado

cagoule [kə'ɡuːl] n casaco de náilon

Cairo ['kaɪərəu] n o Cairo

cake [keɪk] n (large) bolo; (small) doce m, bolinho; **~ of soap** sabonete m

calculate ['kælkjuleɪt] vt calcular;

(estimate) avaliar; **calculation** n cálculo; **calculator** n calculador m, calculadora

calendar ['kæləndə*] n calendário; **~ month/year** mês m/ano civil

calf [kɑːf] (pl **calves**) n (of cow) bezerro, vitela; (of other animals) cria; (also: **~skin**) pele f ou couro de bezerro; (ANAT) barriga-da-perna

calibre ['kælɪbə*] (US **caliber**) n (of person) capacidade f, calibre m

call [kɔːl] vt chamar; (label) qualificar, descrever; (TEL) telefonar a, ligar para; (witness) citar; (meeting) convocar ♦ vi chamar; (shout) gritar; (TEL) telefonar; (visit: also: **~ in**; **~ round**) dar um pulo ♦ n (shout) chamada; (also: **telephone ~**) chamada, telefonema m; (of bird) canto; **to be ~ed** chamar-se; **on ~** de plantão; **call back** vi (return) voltar, passar de novo; (TEL) ligar de volta; **call for** vt fus (demand) requerer, exigir; (fetch) ir buscar; **call off** vt (cancel) cancelar; **call on** vt fus (visit) visitar; (appeal to) pedir; **call out** vi gritar, bradar; **call up** vt (MIL) chamar às fileiras; (TEL) dar uma ligada; **callbox** (BRIT) n cabine f telefônica; **call centre** (BRIT: TEL) n central f de chamadas; **caller** n visita m/f; (TEL) chamador(a) m/f; **call girl** n call girl f, prostituta; **calling card** (US) n cartão m de visita

callous ['kæləs] adj cruel, insensível

calm [kɑːm] adj calmo; (peaceful) tranqüilo; (weather) estável ♦ n calma ♦ vt acalmar; (fears, grief) abrandar; **calm down** vi acalmar, tranqüilizar ♦ vt acalmar

Calor gas ['kælə*-] ® n butano

calorie ['kælərɪ] n caloria

calves [kɑːvz] npl of **calf**

Cambodia [kæm'bəudjə] n Camboja

camcorder [ˈkæmkɔːdə*] n filmadora, máquina de filmar

came [keɪm] pt of **come**

camel [ˈkæməl] n camelo

camera [ˈkæmərə] n máquina fotográfica; (CINEMA, TV) câmera; **in ~** (LAW) em câmara

camouflage [ˈkæməflɑːʒ] n camuflagem f ♦ vt camuflar

camp [kæmp] n campo, acampamento; (MIL) acampamento; (for prisoners) campo; (faction) facção f ♦ vi acampar ♦ adj afeminado

campaign [kæmˈpeɪn] n (MIL, POL ETC) campanha ♦ vi fazer campanha

camp bed (BRIT) n cama de campanha

camper [ˈkæmpə*] n campista m/f; (vehicle) reboque m

camping [ˈkæmpɪŋ] n camping m (BR), campismo (PT); **to go ~** acampar

campsite [ˈkæmpsaɪt] n camping m (BR), parque m de campismo (PT)

campus [ˈkæmpəs] n campus m, cidade f universitária

can¹ [kæn] n lata ♦ vt enlatar

KEYWORD

can² [kæn] (negative **cannot** or **can't**, pt, conditional **could**) aux vb
1 (be able to) poder; **you ~ do it if you try** se você tentar, você consegue fazê-lo; **I'll help you all I ~** ajudarei você em tudo que eu puder; **she couldn't sleep that night** ela não conseguiu dormir aquela noite; **~ you hear me?** você está me ouvindo?
2 (know how to) saber; **I ~ swim** sei nadar; **~ you speak Portuguese?** você fala português?
3 (may) **could I have a word with you?** será que eu podia falar com você?
4 (expressing disbelief, puzzlement): **it CAN'T be true!** não pode ser ver-

dade!; **what CAN he want?** o que é que ele quer?
5 (expressing possibility, suggestion etc): **he could be in the library** ele talvez esteja na biblioteca; **they could have forgotten** eles podiam ter esquecido

Canada [ˈkænədə] n Canadá m; **Canadian** [kəˈneɪdɪən] adj, n canadense m/f

canal [kəˈnæl] n canal m

canary [kəˈnɛərɪ] n canário

cancel [ˈkænsəl] vt cancelar; (contract) anular; (cross out) riscar, invalidar; **cancellation** [kænsəˈleɪʃən] n cancelamento

cancer [ˈkænsə*] n câncer m (BR), cancro (PT); **C~** (ASTROLOGY) Câncer m

candid [ˈkændɪd] adj franco, sincero

candidate [ˈkændɪdeɪt] n candidato(-a)

candle [ˈkændl] n vela; (in church) círio; **candlelight** n: **by candlelight** à luz de vela; **candlestick** n (plain) castiçal m; (bigger, ornate) candelabro, lustre m

candour [ˈkændə*] (US **candor**) n franqueza

candy [ˈkændɪ] n (also: **sugar-~**) açúcar m cristalizado; (US) bala (BR), rebuçado (PT); **candy-floss** (BRIT) n algodão-doce m

cane [keɪn] n (BOT) cana; (stick) bengala f ♦ vt (BRIT: SCH) castigar (com bengala)

canister [ˈkænɪstə*] n lata

cannabis [ˈkænəbɪs] n maconha

canned [kænd] adj (food) em lata, enlatado

cannon [ˈkænən] (pl inv or **~s**) n canhão m

cannot [ˈkænɔt] = **can not**

canoe [kəˈnuː] n canoa

can opener n abridor m de latas

(BR), abre-latas *m inv* *(PT)*

canopy ['kænəpɪ] *n* dossel *m*

can't [kɑːnt] = **can not**

canteen [kæn'tiːn] *n* cantina; *(BRIT: of cutlery)* jogo de talheres)

canter ['kæntə*] *vi ir* a meio galope

canvas ['kænvəs] *n (material)* lona; *(for painting)* tela; *(NAUT)* velas *fpl*

canvass ['kænvəs] *vi (POL):* to ~ for fazer campanha por ♦ *vt* sondar

canyon ['kænjən] *n* canhão *m* garganta, desfiladeiro

cap [kæp] *n* gorro; *(of pen, bottle)* tampa; *(contraceptive:* also *~)* diafragma *m* ♦ *vt (outdo)* superar; *(put limit on)* limitar

capable ['keɪpəbl] *adj (of sth)* capaz; *(competent)* competente, hábil

capacity [kə'pæsɪtɪ] *n* capacidade *f*; *(of stadium etc)* lotação *f*; *(role)* condição *f*, posição *f*

cape [keɪp] *n* capa; *(GEO)* cabo

caper ['keɪpə*] *n (CULIN: gen: ~s)* alcaparra; *(prank)* travessura

capital ['kæpɪtl] *n (also: ~ city)* capital *f*; *(money)* capital *m*; *(also: ~ letter)* maiúscula; **capitalism** *n* capitalismo; **capitalist** *adj, n* capitalista *m/f*; **capital punishment** *n* pena de morte

Capitol ['kæpɪtl] *n:* the ~ o Capitólio; *ver quadro*

Capricorn ['kæprɪkɔːn] *n* Capricórnio

capsize [kæp'saɪz] *vt, vi* emborcar, virar

capsule ['kæpsjuːl] *n* cápsula

captain ['kæptɪn] *n* capitão *m*

caption ['kæpʃən] *n* legenda

captive ['kæptɪv] *adj, n* cativo(-a)

capture ['kæptʃə*] *vt* prender, aprisionar; *(person)* capturar; *(place)* tomar; *(attention)* atrair, chamar ♦ *n* captura; *(of place)* tomada

car [kɑː*] *n* carro, automóvel *m*; *(RAIL)* vagão *m*

caramel ['kærəməl] *n (sweet)* caramelo; *(burnt sugar)* caramelado

caravan ['kærəvæn] *n* reboque *m (BR)*, trailer *m (BR)*, rulote *f (PT)*; *(in desert)* caravana

carbohydrate [kɑːbəʊ'haɪdreɪt] *n* hidrato de carbono; *(food)* carboidrato

carbon ['kɑːbən] *n* carbono; **carbon dioxide** [-daɪ'ɒksaɪd] *n* dióxido de carbono; **carbon monoxide** [-mɒn'ɒksaɪd] *n* monóxido de carbono

carburettor [kɑːbju'retə*] *(US* **carburetor**) *n* carburador *m*

card [kɑːd] *n (also:* **playing ~**) carta; *(visiting ~)* cartão *m*; *(thin cardboard)* cartolina; **cardboard** *n* cartão *m*, papelão *m*

cardiac ['kɑːdɪæk] *adj* cardíaco

cardigan ['kɑːdɪgən] *n* casaco de lã, cardigã *m*

cardinal ['kɑːdɪnl] *adj* cardeal; *(MATH)* cardinal ♦ *n (REL)* cardeal *m*

care [kɛə*] *n* cuidado; *(worry)* preocupação *f*; *(charge)* encargo, custódia ♦ *vi:* to ~ about *(person, animal)* preocupar-se com; *(thing, idea)* ter interesse em; ~ of *(on letter)* aos cuidados de; in sb's ~ a cargo de alguém; to take ~ **(to do)** ter o cuidado (de fazer); to take ~ of *(person)* cuidar de; *(situation)* encarregar-se de; I don't ~ não me importa; I couldn't ~ less não dou a mínima; **care for** *vt fus* cuidar de; *(like)* gostar de

career [kə'rɪə*] *n* carreira ♦ *vi (also:*

along) correr a toda velocidade

carefree ['kɛəfriː] *adj* despreocupado

careful ['kɛəful] *adj* (*thorough*) cuidadoso; (*cautious*) cauteloso; (**be**) ~! tenha cuidado!; **carefully** *adv* cuidadosamente; cautelosamente

careless ['kɛəlɪs] *adj* descuidado; (*heedless*) desatento

caress [kə'rɛs] *n* carícia ♦ *vt* acariciar

caretaker ['kɛəteɪkə*] *n* zelador(a) *m/f*

car-ferry *n* barca para carros (*BR*), barco de passagem (*PT*)

cargo ['kɑːgəu] (*pl* **~es**) *n* carga

car hire (*BRIT*) *n* aluguel *m* (*BR*) or aluguer *m* (*PT*) de carros

Caribbean [kærɪ'biːən] *n*: **the ~ (Sea)** o Caribe

caring ['kɛərɪŋ] *adj* (*person*) bondoso; (*society*) humanitário

carnation [kɑː'neɪʃən] *n* cravo

carnival ['kɑːnɪvəl] *n* carnaval *m*; (*US: funfair*) parque *m* de diversões

carol ['kærəl] *n*: **(Christmas) ~** cântico de Natal

carp [kɑːp] *n inv* (*fish*) carpa; **carp at** *vt fus* criticar

car park (*BRIT*) *n* estacionamento *m*

carpenter ['kɑːpɪntə*] *n* carpinteiro

carpet ['kɑːpɪt] *n* tapete *m* ♦ *vt* atapetar

car phone *n* telefone *m* de carro

carriage ['kærɪdʒ] *n* carruagem *f*; (*BRIT: RAIL*) vagão *m*; (*of goods*) transporte *m*; (*: cost*) porte *m*; **carriageway** (*BRIT*) *n* (*part of road*) pista

carrier ['kærɪə*] *n* transportador(a) *m/f*; (*company*) empresa de transportes, transportadora; (*MED*) portador(a) *m/f*; **carrier bag** (*BRIT*) *n* saco, sacola

carrot ['kærət] *n* cenoura

carry ['kærɪ] *vt* levar; (*transport*) transportar; (*involve: responsibilities*

etc) implicar ♦ *vi* (*sound*) projetar-se; **to get carried away** (*fig*) exagerar; **carry on** *vi* seguir, continuar ♦ *vt* prosseguir, continuar; **carry out** *vt* (*orders*) cumprir; (*investigation*) levar a cabo, realizar; **carrycot** (*BRIT*) *n* moisés *m inv*

cart [kɑːt] *n* carroça, carreta ♦ *vt* transportar (em carroça)

carton ['kɑːtən] *n* (*box*) caixa (de papelão); (*of yogurt*) pote *m*; (*of milk*) caixa; (*packet*) pacote *m*

cartoon [kɑː'tuːn] *n* (*drawing*) desenho; (*BRIT: comic strip*) história em quadrinhos (*BR*), banda desenhada (*PT*); (*film*) desenho animado

cartridge ['kɑːtrɪdʒ] *n* cartucho; (*of record player*) cápsula

carve [kɑːv] *vt* (*meat*) trinchar; (*wood, stone*) cinzelar, esculpir; (*initials, design*) gravar; **carve up** *vt* dividir, repartir; **carving** *n* (*object*) escultura; (*design*) talha, entalhe *m*; **carving knife** (*irreg*) *n* trinchante *m*, faca de trinchar

case [keɪs] *n* caso; (*for spectacles etc*) estojo; (*LAW*) causa; (*BRIT: also*: **suit-case**) mala; (*of wine etc*) caixa; **in ~ (of)** em caso (de); (**in) any ~** em todo o caso; **just in ~** (*conj*) se por acaso ♦ *adv* por via das dúvidas

cash [kæʃ] *n* dinheiro (em espécie) ♦ *vt* descontar; **to pay (in) ~** pagar em dinheiro; **~ on delivery** pagamento contra entrega; **cash card** (*BRIT*) *n* cartão *m* de saque; **cash desk** (*BRIT*) *n* caixa; **cash dispenser** *n* caixa automática *or* eletrônica

cashew [kæ'ʃuː] *n* (*also*: **~ nut**) castanha de caju

cashier [kæ'ʃɪə*] *n* caixa *m/f*

cash register *n* caixa registradora

casing ['keɪsɪŋ] *n* invólucro

casino [kə'siːnəu] *n* cassino

casket ['kɑ:skɪt] n cofre m, porta-jóias m inv; (US: coffin) caixão m

casserole ['kæsərəul] n panela de ir ao forno; (food) ensopado (BR) no forno, guisado (PT) no forno

cassette [kæ'set] n fita-cassete f; **cassette player** n toca-fitas m inv; **cassette recorder** n gravador m

cast [kɑ:st] (pt, pp cast) vt (throw) lançar, atirar; (THEATRE): to ~ sb as Hamlet dar a alguém o papel de Hamlet ♦ n (THEATRE) elenco; (also: plaster ~) gesso; to ~ one's vote votar; **cast off** vi (NAUT) soltar o cabo; (KNITTING) rematar os pontos; **cast on** vi montar os pontos

castaway ['kɑ:stəweɪ] n náufrago(-a)

caster sugar ['kɑ:stə*-] (BRIT) n açúcar m branco refinado

cast iron n ferro fundido

castle ['kɑ:sl] n castelo; (CHESS) torre f

castor ['kɑ:stə*] n (wheel) rodízio; **castor oil** n óleo de rícino

casual ['kæʒjul] adj (by chance) fortuito; (work) eventual; (unconcerned) despreocupado; (clothes) descontraído, informal; **casually** adv casualmente; (dress) informalmente

casualty ['kæʒjultɪ] n ferido(-a); (dead) morto(-a); (of situation) vítima; (department) pronto-socorro

cat [kæt] n gato

catalogue ['kætəlɔg] (US catalog) n catálogo ♦ vt catalogar

catalyst ['kætəlɪst] n catalisador m

catapult ['kætəpʌlt] (BRIT) n (sling) atiradeira

catarrh [kə'tɑ:*] n catarro

catastrophe [kə'tæstrəfɪ] n catástrofe f

catch [kætʃ] (pt, pp caught) vt pegar (BR), apanhar (PT); (fish) pes-

car; (arrest) prender, deter; (person: by surprise) flagrar, surpreender; (attention) atrair; (hear) ouvir; (also: ~ up) alcançar ♦ vi (fire) pegar; (in branches etc) ficar preso, prender-se ♦ n (fish) pesca; (game) manha, armadilha, (of lock) trinco, lingüeta; to ~ fire pegar fogo; (building) incendiar-se; to ~ sight of avistar; **catch on** vi (understand) entender (BR), perceber (PT); (grow popular) pegar; **catch up** vi equiparar-se ♦ vt (also: ~ up with) alcançar; **catching** adj (MED) contagioso; **catch phrase** n clichê m, slogan m; **catchy** adj que pega fácil, que gruda no ouvido

category ['kætɪgərɪ] n categoria

cater ['keɪtə*] vi preparar comida; **cater for** vt fus (needs) atender a; (consumers) satisfazer; **catering** n serviço de bufê; (trade) abastecimento

caterpillar ['kætəpɪlə*] n lagarta

cathedral [kə'θi:drəl] n catedral f

catholic ['kæθəlɪk] adj eclético; **Catholic** adj, n (REL) católico(-a)

cattle ['kætl] npl gado

catty ['kætɪ] adj malicioso

caught [kɔ:t] pt, pp of **catch**

cauliflower ['kɔlɪflauə*] n couve-flor f

cause [kɔ:z] n causa; (reason) motivo, razão f ♦ vt causar, provocar

caution ['kɔ:ʃən] n cautela, prudência; (warning) aviso ♦ vt acautelar, avisar

cautious ['kɔ:ʃəs] adj cauteloso, prudente, precavido

cavalry ['kævəlrɪ] n cavalaria

cave [keɪv] n caverna, gruta; **cave in** vi ceder; **caveman** ['keɪvmæn] (irreg) n troglodita m, homem m das cavernas

CB n abbr = **Citizens' Band (Radio)**

CBI n abbr (= Confederation of British Industry) federação de indústria

cc abbr (= cubic centimetre) cc; (on letter etc) = **carbon copy**

CD n abbr = **compact disc; compact disc player; CD-ROM** n abbr (= compact disc read-only memory) CD-ROM m

cease [si:s] vt, vi cessar; **ceasefire** n cessar-fogo m

cedar ['si:də*] n cedro

ceiling ['si:lɪŋ] n (also fig) teto

celebrate ['sɛlɪbreɪt] vt celebrar ♦ vi celebrar; (birthday, anniversary etc) festejar; (REL: mass) rezar; **celebrated** adj célebre; **celebration** [sɛlɪ'breɪʃən] n (party) festa

celery ['sɛlərɪ] n aipo

cell [sɛl] n cela; (BIO) célula; (ELEC) pilha, elemento

cellar ['sɛlə*] n porão m; (for wine) adega

cello ['tʃɛləʊ] n violoncelo

cellphone ['sɛlfəʊn] n telefone m celular

Celt [kɛlt, sɛlt] n celta m/f; **Celtic** adj celta

cement [sə'mɛnt] n cimento; **cement mixer** n betoneira

cemetery ['sɛmɪtrɪ] n cemitério

censor ['sɛnsə*] n censor(a) m/f ♦ vt censurar; **censorship** n censura

census ['sɛnsəs] n censo

cent [sɛnt] n cêntimo; see also **per**

centenary [sɛn'ti:nərɪ] n centenário

center ['sɛntə*] (US) = **centre**

centigrade ['sɛntɪɡreɪd] adj centígrado

centimetre ['sɛntɪmi:tə*] (US centimeter) n centímetro

central ['sɛntrəl] adj central; **Central America** n América Central; **central heating** n aquecimento central

centre ['sɛntə*] (US center) n centro;

(of room, circle etc) meio ♦ vt centrar

century ['sɛntjʊrɪ] n século; **20th ~** século vinte

ceramic [sɪ'ræmɪk] adj cerâmico

cereal ['si:rɪəl] n cereal m

ceremony ['sɛrɪmənɪ] n cerimônia; (ritual) rito; **to stand on ~** fazer cerimônia

certain ['sə:tən] adj (sure) seguro; (person): **a ~ Mr Smith** um certo Sr. Smith; (particular): **~ days/places** certos dias/lugares; (some): **a ~ coldness/pleasure** uma certa frieza/um certo prazer; **for ~** com certeza; **certainly** adv certamente, com certeza; **certainty** n certeza

certificate [sə'tɪfɪkɪt] n certidão f

certified mail ['sə:tɪfaɪd-] (US) n correio registrado

certified public accountant ['sə:tɪfaɪd-] (US) n perito-contador m

certify ['sə:tɪfaɪ] vt certificar

cervical ['sə:vɪkl] adj: **~ cancer** câncer m (BR) or cancro (PT) do colo do útero

cf. abbr (= compare) cf.

CFC n abbr (= chlorofluorocarbon) CFC m

ch. abbr (= chapter) cap.

chafe [tʃeɪf] vt (rub) roçar

chain [tʃeɪn] n corrente f; (of islands) grupo; (of mountains) cordilheira; (of shops) cadeia; (of events) série f ♦ vt (also: ~ up) acorrentar; **chain-smoke** vi fumar um (cigarro) atrás do outro; **chain store** n magazine m (BR), grande armazém f (PT)

chair [tʃɛə*] n cadeira; (armchair) poltrona; (of university) cátedra; (of meeting) presidência, mesa ♦ vt (meeting) presidir; **chairlift** n teleférico; **chairman** (irreg) n presidente m

chalk [tʃɔ:k] n (GEO) greda; (for writing) giz m

challenge ['tʃælɪndʒ] n desafio ♦ vt

desafiar; (*right*) disputar, contestar;
challenging *adj* desafiante; (*tone*)
de desafio

chamber ['tʃeɪmbə*] *n* câmara;
(*BRIT: LAW: gen pl*) sala de audiências;
~ of commerce câmara de comércio; **chambermaid** *n* arrumadeira
(*BR*), empregada (*PT*)

champagne [ʃæm'peɪn] *n* champanhe *m* or *f*

champion ['tʃæmpɪən] *n* campeão(-peã) *m/f*; (*of cause*) defensor(a) *m/f*; **championship** *n*
campeonato

chance [tʃɑːns] *n* (*opportunity*)
oportunidade, ocasião *f*; (*likelihood*)
chance *f*; (*risk*) risco ♦ *vt* arriscar
♦ *adj* fortuito, casual; **to take a ~**
arriscar-se; **by ~** por acaso; **to ~ it**
arriscar-se

chancellor ['tʃɑːnsələ*] *n* chanceler
m; **C~ of the Exchequer** (*BRIT*)
Ministro da Economia (Fazenda e
Planejamento)

chandelier [ʃændə'lɪə*] *n* lustre *m*

change [tʃeɪndʒ] *vt* (*alter*) mudar;
(*wheel, money*) trocar; (*replace*)
substituir; (*clothes, house*) mudar
de, trocar de; (*nappy*) mudar, trocar; (*transform*): **to ~ sb into** transformar alguém em ♦ *vi* mudar(-se);
(*change clothes*) trocar-se; (*trains*)
fazer baldeação (*BR*), mudar (*PT*); (*be
transformed*): **to ~ into** transformarse em ♦ *n* mudança; (*exchange*)
troca; (*difference*) diferença; (*of
clothes*) muda; (*coins*) trocado; **to ~
gear** (*AUT*) trocar de marcha; **to ~
one's mind** mudar de idéia; **for a
~** para variar; **changeable** *adj*
(*weather, mood*) instável; **change
machine** *n* máquina que fornece
trocado; **changeover** *n* mudança

changing ['tʃeɪndʒɪŋ] *adj* variável;
changing room (*BRIT*) *n* (*in shop*)

cabine *f* de provas

channel ['tʃænl] *n* canal *m*; (*of river*)
leito; (*groove*) ranhura; (*fig: medium*)
meio, via ♦ *vt* canalizar; **the
(English) C~** o Canal da Mancha

chant [tʃɑːnt] *n* canto; (*REL*) cântico
♦ *vt* cantar; (*slogan*) entoar

chaos ['keɪɔs] *n* caos *m*

chap [tʃæp] *n* (*BRIT: inf: man*) sujeito
(*BR*), tipo (*PT*)

chapel ['tʃæpl] *n* capela

chaplain ['tʃæplɪn] *n* capelão *m*

chapped [tʃæpt] *adj* ressecado

chapter ['tʃæptə*] *n* capítulo

character ['kærɪktə*] *n* caráter *m*;
(*in novel, film*) personagem *m/f*; (*letter*) letra; **characteristic** [kærɪktə-
'rɪstɪk] *adj* característico

charcoal ['tʃɑːkəʊl] *n* carvão *m* de
lenha; (*ART*) carvão *m*

charge [tʃɑːdʒ] *n* (*LAW*) encargo,
acusação *f*; (*fee*) preço, custo; (*responsibility*) encargo ♦ *vt* (*battery*)
carregar; (*MIL*) atacar; (*customer*)
cobrar dinheiro de; (*LAW*): **to ~ sb
(with)** acusar alguém (de) ♦ *vi*
precipitar-se; **~s** *npl*: **bank ~s** taxas
fpl cobradas pelo banco; **to reverse
the ~s** (*BRIT: TEL*) ligar a cobrar; **how
much do you ~?** quanto você
cobra?; **to ~ an expense (up) to sb's
account** pôr a despesa na conta de
alguém; **to take ~ of** encarregar-se
de, tomar conta de; **to be in ~ of**
estar a cargo de *or* encarregado de;
charge card *n* cartão *m* de crédito
(*emitido por uma loja*)

charity ['tʃærɪtɪ] *n* caridade *f*; (*organization*) obra de caridade; (*kindness*) compaixão *f*; (*gifts*) donativo

charm [tʃɑːm] *n* (*quality*) charme *m*;
(*talisman*) amuleto; (*on bracelet*)
berloque *m* ♦ *vt* encantar, deliciar;
charming *adj* encantador(a)

chart [tʃɑːt] *n* (*graph*) gráfico; (*dia-*

gram) diagrama *m*; (*map*) carta de navegação ♦ *vt* traçar; **~s** *npl* (*MUS*) paradas *fpl* (de sucesso)

charter ['tʃɑːtə*] *vt* fretar ♦ *n* (*document*) carta, alvará *m*; **chartered accountant** (*BRIT*) *n* peritocontador (perita-contadora) *m/f*; **charter flight** *n* vôo charter or fretado

chase [tʃeɪs] *vt* perseguir; (*also*: ~ **away**) enxotar ♦ *n* perseguição *f*, caça

chasm ['kæzəm] *n* abismo

chat [tʃæt] *vi* (*also*: **have a ~**) conversar, bater papo (*BR*), cavaquear (*PT*) ♦ *n* conversa, bate-papo *m* (*BR*), cavaqueira (*PT*); **chat show** (*BRIT*) *n* programa *m* de entrevistas

chatter ['tʃætə*] *vi* (*person*) tagarelar; (*animal*) emitir sons; (*teeth*) tiritar ♦ *n* tagarelice *f*; emissão *f* de sons; (*of birds*) chilro; **chatterbox** *n* tagarela *m/f*

chatty ['tʃætɪ] *adj* (*style*) informal; (*person*) conversador(a)

chauffeur ['ʃəufə*] *n* chofer *m*, motorista *m/f*

chauvinist ['ʃəuvɪnɪst] *n* chauvinista *m/f*; (*also*: **male ~**) machista *m*; (*nationalist*) chauvinista *m/f*

cheap [tʃiːp] *adj* barato; (*poor quality*) barato, de pouca qualidade; (*behaviour*) vulgar; (*joke*) de mau gosto ♦ *adv* barato; **cheaply** *adv* barato, por baixo preço

cheat [tʃiːt] *vi* trapacear; (*at cards*) roubar (*BR*), fazer batota (*PT*); (*in exam*) colar (*BR*), cabular (*PT*) ♦ *vt*: to ~ **sb** (**out of sth**) passar o conto do vigário em alguém ♦ *n* fraude *f*; (*person*) trapaceiro(-a)

check [tʃek] *vt* (*examine*) controlar; (*facts*) verificar; (*halt*) conter, impedir; (*restrain*) parar, refrear ♦ *n* controle *m*, inspeção *f*; (*curb*) freio; (*US*:

bill) conta; (*pattern*: *gen pl*) xadrez *m*; (*US*) = **cheque** ♦ *adj* (*pattern*, *cloth*) xadrez *inv*; **check in** *vi* (*in hotel*) registrar-se; (*in airport*) apresentar-se ♦ *vt* (*luggage*) entregar; **check out** *vi* pagar a conta e sair; **check up** *vi*: to ~ **up on sth** verificar algo; to ~ **up on sb** investigar alguém; **checkers** (*US*) *n* (*jogo de*) damas *fpl*; **check-in** (**desk**) *n* check-in *m*; **checking account** (*US*) *n* conta corrente; **checkout** *n* caixa; **checkpoint** *n* (ponto de) controle *m*; **checkroom** (*US*) *n* depósito de bagagem; **checkup** *n* (*MED*) check-up *m*

cheek [tʃiːk] *n* bochecha; (*impudence*) folga, descaramento; **cheekbone** *n* maçã *f* do rosto; **cheeky** *adj* insolente, descarado

cheer [tʃɪə*] *vt* dar vivas a, aplaudir; (*gladden*) alegrar, animar ♦ *vi* gritar com entusiasmo ♦ *n* (*gen pl*) gritos *mpl* de entusiasmo; **~s** *npl* (*of crowd*) aplausos *mpl*; **~s!** saúde!; **cheer up** *vi* animar-se, alegrar-se ♦ *vt* alegrar, animar; **cheerful** *adj* alegre; **cheerio** (*BRIT*) *excl* tchau (*BR*), adeus (*PT*)

cheese [tʃiːz] *n* queijo; **cheeseboard** *n* (*in restaurant*) sortimento de queijos

cheetah ['tʃiːtə] *n* chitá *m*

chef [ʃef] *n* cozinheiro-chefe (cozinheira-chefe) *m/f*

chemical ['kemɪkəl] *adj* químico ♦ *n* produto químico

chemist ['kemɪst] *n* (*BRIT*: *pharmacist*) farmacêutico(-a); (*scientist*) químico(-a); **chemistry** *n* química; **chemist's (shop)** (*BRIT*) *n* farmácia

cheque [tʃek] (*BRIT*) *n* cheque *m*; **chequebook** *n* talão *m* (*BR*) or livro (*PT*) de cheques; **cheque card** (*BRIT*) *n* cartão *m* (de garantia) de cheques

cherish ['tʃɛrɪʃ] vt (person) tratar com carinho; (memory) lembrar (com prazer)

cherry ['tʃɛrɪ] n cereja; (also: ~ **tree**) cerejeira

chess [tʃɛs] n xadrez m; **chessboard** n tabuleiro de xadrez

chest [tʃɛst] n (ANAT) peito; (box) caixa, cofre m; ~ **of drawers** cômoda

chestnut ['tʃɛsnʌt] n castanha

chew [tʃuː] vt mastigar; **chewing gum** n chiclete m (BR), pastilha elástica (PT)

chic [ʃɪk] adj elegante

chick [tʃɪk] n pinto; (inf: girl) broto

chicken ['tʃɪkɪn] n galinha; (food) galinha, frango; (inf: coward) covarde m/f, galinha; **chicken out** (inf) vi agalinhar-se; **chickenpox** n catapora (BR), varicela (PT)

chief [tʃiːf] n (of tribe) cacique m, morubixaba m; (of organization) chefe m/f ♦ adj principal; **chiefly** adv principalmente

chilblain ['tʃɪlbleɪn] n frieira

child [tʃaɪld] (pl ~**ren**) n criança; (offspring) filho(-a); **childbirth** n parto; **childhood** n infância; **childish** adj infantil; **child minder** (BRIT) n cuidadora de crianças; **children** ['tʃɪldrən] npl of **child**

Chile ['tʃɪlɪ] n Chile m

chill [tʃɪl] n frio, friagem f; (MED) resfriamento ♦ vt (CULIN) semi-congelar; (person) congelar

chilli ['tʃɪlɪ] (US **chili**) n pimentão m picante

chilly ['tʃɪlɪ] adj frio; (person) friorento

chime [tʃaɪm] n (of bell) repique m; (of clock) soar m ♦ vi repicar; soar

chimney ['tʃɪmnɪ] n chaminé f

chimpanzee [tʃɪmpæn'ziː] n chimpanzé m

chin [tʃɪn] n queixo

China ['tʃaɪnə] n China

china ['tʃaɪnə] n porcelana; (crockery) louça fina

Chinese [tʃaɪ'niːz] adj chinês(-esa) ♦ n inv chinês(-esa) m/f; (LING) chinês m

chip [tʃɪp] n (gen pl: CULIN) batata frita; (: US: also: **potato** ~) batatinha frita; (of wood) lasca; (of glass, stone) lasca, pedaço; (COMPUT: also: **micro~**) chip m ♦ vt (cup, plate) lascar; **chip in** (inf) vi interromper; (contribute) compartilhar as despesas

chiropodist [kɪ'rɔpədɪst] (BRIT) n pedicuro(-a)

chirp [tʃəːp] vi chilrar, piar

chisel ['tʃɪzl] n (for wood) formão m, (for stone) cinzel m

chit [tʃɪt] n talão m

chitchat ['tʃɪttʃæt] n conversa fiada

chivalry ['ʃɪvəlrɪ] n cavalheirismo

chives [tʃaɪvz] npl cebolinha

chocolate ['tʃɔklɪt] n chocolate m

choice [tʃɔɪs] n (selection) seleção f; (option) escolha; (preference) preferência ♦ adj seleto, escolhido

choir ['kwaɪə*] n coro

choke [tʃəuk] vi sufocar-se; (on food) engasgar ♦ vt estrangular; (block) obstruir ♦ n (AUT) afogador m (BR), ar m (PT)

cholesterol [kə'lɛstərɔl] n colesterol m

choose [tʃuːz] (pt **chose**, pp **chosen**) vt escolher; **to ~ to do** optar por fazer; **choosy** adj exigente

chop [tʃɔp] vt (wood) cortar, talhar; (CULIN: also: ~ **up**) cortar em pedaços; (meat) picar ♦ n golpe m; (CULIN) costeleta; **~s** npl (inf: jaws) beiços mpl

chopper ['tʃɔpə*] n helicóptero

choppy ['tʃɔpɪ] adj (sea) agitado

chopsticks ['tʃɒpstɪks] *npl* pauzinhos *mpl*, palitos *mpl*

chord [kɔːd] *n* (*MUS*) acorde *m*

chore [tʃɔː*] *n* tarefa; (*routine task*) trabalho de rotina

chorus ['kɔːrəs] *n* (*group*) coro; (*song*) coral *m*; (*refrain*) estribilho

chose [tʃəuz] *pt of* **choose**; **chosen** *pp of* **choose**

Christ [kraɪst] *n* Cristo

christen ['krɪsn] *vt* batizar; (*nickname*) apelidar

Christian ['krɪstɪən] *adj*, *n* cristão(-tã) *m/f*; **Christianity** [krɪstɪ'ænɪtɪ] *n* cristianismo *m*; **Christian name** *n* prenome *m*, nome *m* de batismo

Christmas ['krɪsməs] *n* Natal *m*; **Happy** or **Merry ~**! Feliz Natal!; **Christmas card** *n* cartão *m* de Natal; **Christmas cracker** *n* busca-pé-surpresa *m*; *ver quadro*

CHRISTMAS CRACKER

Um cilindro de papelão que ao ser aberto faz estourar uma bombinha. Contém um presente surpresa e um chapéu de papel que cada convidado coloca na cabeça durante a ceia de Natal.

Christmas: **Christmas Day** *n* dia *m* de Natal; **Christmas Eve** *n* véspera de Natal; **Christmas tree** *n* árvore *f* de Natal

chrome [krəum] *n* = **chromium**

chromium ['krəumɪəm] *n* cromo

chronic ['krɒnɪk] *adj* crônico

chubby ['tʃʌbɪ] *adj* roliço, gorducho

chuck [tʃʌk] *vt* jogar (*BR*), deitar (*PT*); (*BRIT: also*: **~ up**, **~ in**: *job*) largar; (: *person*) acabar com; **chuck out** *vt* (*thing*) jogar (*BR*) or deitar (*PT*) fora; (*person*) expulsar

chuckle ['tʃʌkl] *vi* rir

chum [tʃʌm] *n* camarada *m/f*

chunk [tʃʌŋk] *n* pedaço, naco

church [tʃəːtʃ] *n* igreja; **churchyard** *n* adro, cemitério

churn [tʃəːn] *n* (*for butter*) batedeira; (*also*: **milk ~**) lata, vasilha; **churn out** *vt* produzir em série

chute [ʃuːt] *n* rampa; (*also*: **rubbish ~**) despejador *m*

CIA (*us*) *n abbr* (= *Central Intelligence Agency*) CIA *f*

CID (*BRIT*) *n abbr* = **Criminal Investigation Department**

cider ['saɪdə*] *n* sidra

cigar [sɪ'gɑː*] *n* charuto

cigarette [sɪgə'ret] *n* cigarro; **cigarette case** *n* cigarreira

Cinderella [sɪndə'relə] *n* Gata Borralheira

cine-camera ['sɪnɪ-] (*BRIT*) *n* câmera (cinematográfica)

cinema ['sɪnəmə] *n* cinema *m*

cinnamon ['sɪnəmən] *n* canela

circle ['səːkl] *n* círculo; (*in cinema*) balcão *m* ♦ *vi* dar voltas ♦ *vt* (*surround*) rodear, cercar; (*move round*) dar a volta de

circuit ['səːkɪt] *n* circuito; (*lap*) volta; (*track*) pista

circular ['səːkjulə*] *adj* circular ♦ *n* (carta) circular *f*

circulate ['səːkjuleɪt] *vt*, *vi* circular; **circulation** [səːkju'leɪʃən] *n* circulação *f*; (*of newspaper, book etc*) tiragem *f*

circumstances ['səːkəmstənsɪz] *npl* circunstâncias *fpl*; (*conditions*) condições *fpl*; (*financial condition*) situação *f* econômica

circus ['səːkəs] *n* circo

CIS *n abbr* (= *Commonwealth of Independent States*) CEI *f*

cistern ['sɪstən] *n* tanque *m*; (*in toilet*) caixa d'água

citizen ['sɪtɪzn] *n* (*of country*)

cidadão(-dã) m/f; (of town) habitante m/f; **citizenship** n cidadania

citrus fruit ['sɪtrəs-] n citrino

city ['sɪtɪ] n cidade f; **the C~** centro financeiro de Londres

civic ['sɪvɪk] adj cívico, municipal

civil ['sɪvɪl] adj civil; (polite) delicado, cortês; **civilian** [sɪ'vɪlɪən] adj, n civil m/f

civilized ['sɪvɪlaɪzd] adj civilizado

civil: civil servant n funcionário público (funcionária pública); **Civil Service** n administração f pública; **civil war** n guerra civil

claim [kleɪm] vt exigir, reclamar; (rights etc) reivindicar; (responsibility, credit) assumir; (assert): **to ~ that/to be** afirmar que/ser ♦ vi (for insurance) reclamar ♦ n reclamação f; (assertion) afirmação f; (wage ~ etc) reivindicação f

clam [klæm] n molusco

clammy ['klæmɪ] adj (hands, face) úmido e pegajoso

clamp [klæmp] n grampo ♦ vt (two things together) grampear; (put: one thing on another) prender; **clamp down on** vt fus suprimir, proibir

clan [klæn] n clã m

clap [klæp] vi bater palmas, aplaudir; **clapping** n aplausos mpl, palmas fpl

clarinet [klærɪ'nɛt] n clarinete m

clarity ['klærɪtɪ] n clareza

clash [klæʃ] n (fight) confronto, (disagreement) desavença; (of beliefs) divergência; (of colours, styles) choque m; (of dates) coincidência; (noise) estrondo ♦ vi (gangs, beliefs) chocar-se; (disagree) entrar em conflito, ter uma desavença; (colours) não combinar; (dates) coincidir; (weapons, cymbals etc) estrefitar

clasp [klɑːsp] n fecho; (embrace) abraço ♦ vt prender; abraçar

class [klɑːs] n classe f; (lesson) aula; (type) tipo ♦ vt classificar

classic ['klæsɪk] adj clássico ♦ n clássico; **classical** adj clássico

classified ['klæsɪfaɪd] adj secreto

classmate ['klæsmeɪt] n colega m/f de aula

classroom ['klæsrum] n sala de aula

clatter ['klætə*] n ruído, barulho; (of hooves) tropel m ♦ vi fazer barulho or ruído

clause [klɔːz] n cláusula; (LING) oração f

claw [klɔː] n (of animal) pata; (of bird of prey) garra; (of lobster) pinça; **claw at** vt fus arranhar, (tear) rasgar

clay [kleɪ] n argila

clean [kliːn] adj limpo; (story) inocente ♦ vt limpar; (hands etc) lavar; **clean out** vt limpar; **clean up** vt limpar, assear; **clean-cut** adj alinhado; **cleaner** n faxineiro(-a); (product) limpador m; **cleaner's** n (also: **dry cleaner's**) tinturaria; **cleaning** n limpeza; **cleanliness** ['klɛnlɪnəs] n limpeza

cleanse [klɛnz] vt limpar; (purify) purificar; **cleanser** n (for face) creme m de limpeza

clean-shaven [-'ʃeɪvn] adj sem barba, de cara raspada

clear [klɪə*] adj claro; (footprint, photograph) nítido; (obvious) evidente; (glass, water) transparente; (road, way) limpo, livre; (conscience) tranqüilo; (skin) macio ♦ vt (space) abrir; (room) esvaziar; (LAW: suspect) absolver; (fence) saltar, transpor; (cheque) compensar ♦ vi (weather) abrir; (sky) clarear; (fog etc) dissipar-se ♦ adv: **~ of** a salvo de; **to ~ the table** tirar a mesa; **clear up** vt limpar; (mystery) resolver, esclarecer;

clearance n remoção f; (*permission*) permissão f; **clear-cut** adj bem definido, nítido; **clearing** n (*in wood*) clareira f; **clearly** adv distintamente; (*obviously*) claramente; (*coherently*) coerentemente; **clearway** (*BRIT*) n estrada onde não se pode estacionar

clef [klɛf] n (*MUS*) clave f

clementine ['klɛməntaɪn] n clementina

clench [klɛntʃ] vt apertar, cerrar; (*teeth*) trincar

clergy ['klɜːdʒɪ] n clero; **clergyman** (*irreg*) n clérigo, pastor m

clerical ['klɛrɪkəl] adj de escritório; (*REL*) clerical

clerk [klɑːk, (*US*) klɜːrk] n auxiliar m/f de escritório; (*BRIT*: *sales person*) balconista m/f

clever ['klɛvə*] adj inteligente; (*deft*) hábil; (*arrangement*) engenhoso

click [klɪk] vt (*tongue*) estalar; (*heels*) bater; (*COMPUT*) clicar em ♦ vi (*make sound*) estalar; (*COMPUT*) clicar

client ['klaɪənt] n cliente m/f

cliff [klɪf] n penhasco

climate ['klaɪmɪt] n clima m

climax ['klaɪmæks] n clímax m, ponto culminante; (*sexual*) clímax

climb [klaɪm] vi subir; (*plant*) trepar; (*plane*) ganhar altitude; (*prices etc*) escalar ♦ vt (*stairs*) subir; (*tree*) trepar em; (*hill*) escalar ♦ n subida; (*of prices etc*) escalada; **climber** n alpinista m/f; (*plant*) trepadeira; **climbing** n alpinismo

clinch [klɪntʃ] vt (*deal*) fechar; (*argument*) decidir, resolver

cling [klɪŋ] (*pt, pp* clung) vi: **to ~ to** pegar-se a, aderir a; (*support, idea*) agarrar-se a; (*clothes*) ajustar-se a

clinic ['klɪnɪk] n clínica; **clinical** adj clínico; (*fig*) frio, impessoal

clip [klɪp] n (*for hair*) grampo (*BR*),

gancho (*PT*); (*also:* **paper ~**) mola, clipe m; (*TV, CINEMA*) clipe ♦ vt (*cut*) aparar; (*fasten*) grampear; **clippers** npl (*for gardening*) podadeira; (*also:* **nail clippers**) alicate m de unhas; **clipping** n recorte m

cloak [kləuk] n capa, manto ♦ vt (*fig*) encobrir; **cloakroom** n vestiário; (*BRIT*: *WC*) sanitários mpl (*BR*), lavatórios mpl (*PT*)

clock [klɔk] n relógio; **clock in** or **on** (*BRIT*) vi assinar o ponto na entrada; **clock off** or **out** (*BRIT*) vi assinar o ponto na saída; **clockwise** adv em sentido horário; **clockwork** n mecanismo de relógio ♦ adj de corda

clog [klɔg] n tamanco ♦ vt entupir ♦ vi (*also:* **~ up**) entupir-se

cloister ['klɔɪstə*] n claustro

close¹ [kləus] adj (*near*): **~ (to)** próximo (a); (*friend*) íntimo; (*examination*) minucioso; (*watch*) atento; (*contest*) apertado; (*weather*) abafado ♦ adv perto; **~ to** perto de; **~ by**, **~ at hand** = **~ by**; **to have a ~ shave** (*fig*) livrar-se por um triz

close² [kləuz] vt fechar; (*end*) encerrar ♦ vi fechar; (*end*) concluir-se, terminar-se ♦ n (*end*) fim m, conclusão f, terminação f; **close down** vi fechar definitivamente; **closed** adj fechado

close-knit adj muito unido

closely ['kləuslɪ] adv (*watch*) de perto; (*connected, related*) intimamente; (*resemble*) muito

closet ['klɔzɪt] n (*cupboard*) armário

close-up ['kləus-] n close m, close-up m

closure ['kləuʒə*] n fechamento

clot [klɔt] n (*gen: blood ~*) coágulo; (*inf: idiot*) imbecil m/f ♦ vi coagular-se

cloth [klɔθ] n (*material*) tecido,

fazenda; (rag) pano

clothe [kləuð] vt vestir

clothes [kləuðz] npl roupa; **clothes brush** n escova (para a roupa); **clothes line** n corda (para estender a roupa); **clothes peg** (US **clothes pin**) n pregador m

clothing ['kləuðɪŋ] n = **clothes**

cloud [klaud] n nuvem f; **cloudy** adj nublado; (liquid) turvo

clout [klaut] vt dar uma bofetada em

clove [kləuv] n cravo; ~ **of garlic** dente m de alho

clover ['kləuvə*] n trevo

clown [klaun] n palhaço ♦ vi (also: ~ about; ~ around) fazer palhaçadas

club [klʌb] n (society) clube m; (weapon) cacete m; (also: **golf** ~) taco ♦ vt esbordoar ♦ vi: **to** ~ **together** cotizar-se; ~**s** npl (CARDS) paus mpl

clue [klu:] n indício, pista; (in crossword) definição f; **I haven't a** ~ não faço idéia

clump [klʌmp] n (of trees etc) grupo

clumsy ['klʌmzɪ] adj (person) desajeitado; (movement) deselegante, mal-feito; (attempt) inábil

clung [klʌŋ] pt, pp of **cling**

cluster ['klʌstə*] n grupo; (of flowers) ramo ♦ vi agrupar-se, apinhar-se

clutch [klʌtʃ] n (grip, grasp) garra; (AUT) embreagem f (BR), embraiagem f (PT) ♦ vt empunhar, pegar

clutter ['klʌtə*] vt (also: ~ **up**) abarrotar, encher desordenadamente

CND n abbr = **Campaign for Nuclear Disarmament**

Co. abbr = **company**; (= county) Cia.

c/o abbr (= care of) a/c

coach [kəutʃ] n (bus) ônibus m (BR), autocarro m (PT); (horse-drawn) carruagem f, coche m; (of train) vagão m; (SPORT) treinador(a) m/f, instrutor(a) m/f; (tutor) professor(a) m/f particular ♦ vt (SPORT) treinar;

(student) preparar, ensinar; **coach trip** n passeio de ônibus (BR) or autocarro (PT)

coal [kəul] n carvão m

coalition [kəuə'lɪʃən] n (POL) coalizão f

coalman (irreg) n carvoeiro

coalmine n mina de carvão

coarse [kɔːs] adj grosso, áspero; (vulgar) grosseiro, ordinário

coast [kəust] n costa, litoral m ♦ vi (AUT) ir em ponto morto; **coastal** adj costeiro; **coastguard** n (person) guarda m que policia a costa; (service) guarda costeira; **coastline** n litoral m

coat [kəut] n (overcoat) sobretudo; (of animal) pelo; (of paint) demão f, camada ♦ vt cobrir, revestir; **coat hanger** n cabide m; **coating** n camada

coax [kəuks] vt persuadir com meiguice

cobbles ['kɔblz] (also: **cobblestones**) npl pedras fpl arredondadas

cobweb ['kɔbweb] n teia de aranha

cocaine [kə'keɪn] n cocaína

cock [kɔk] n (rooster) galo; (male bird) macho ♦ vt (gun) engatilhar; **cockerel** n frango, galo pequeno

cockle ['kɔkl] n berbigão m

cockney ['kɔknɪ] n londrino(-a) (nativo dos bairros populares do leste de Londres)

cockpit ['kɔkpɪt] n (in aircraft) cabina; (in car) compartimento do piloto

cockroach ['kɔkrəutʃ] n barata

cocktail ['kɔkteɪl] n coquetel m (BR), cocktail m (PT); **cocktail party** n coquetel (BR), cocktail (BR)

cocoa ['kəukəu] n cacau m; (drink) chocolate m

coconut ['kəukənʌt] n coco

cocoon [kə'ku:n] n casulo

COD abbr = **cash** (BRIT) or **collect** (US)

on delivery
cod [kɔd] n inv bacalhau m
code [kəud] n cifra; (dialling ~, post ~) código; ~ **of practice** deontologia f
coercion [kəu'ɔːʃən] n coerção f
coffee ['kɔfi] n café m; **coffee bar** (BRIT) n café m, lanchonete f; **coffee bean** n grão m de café; **coffeepot** n cafeteira; **coffee table** n mesinha de centro
coffin ['kɔfin] n caixão m
coil [kɔil] n rolo; (ELEC) bobina; (contraceptive) DIU m ♦ vt enrolar
coin [kɔin] n moeda ♦ vt (word) cunhar, criar; **coin box** (BRIT) n telefone m público
coincide [kəuin'said] vi coincidir; **coincidence** [kəu'insidəns] n coincidência
Coke [kəuk] ® n (drink) coca
coke [kəuk] n (coal) coque m
colander ['kɔləndə*] n coador m, passador m
cold [kəuld] adj frio ♦ n frio; (MED) resfriado (BR), constipação f (PT); **it's ~** está frio; **to be** or **feel ~** (person) estar com frio; (object) estar frio; **to catch ~** resfriar-se (BR), apanhar constipação (PT); **to catch a ~** apanhar um resfriado (PT) ou uma constipação (PT); **in ~ blood** a sangue frio; **cold sore** n herpes m labial
coleslaw ['kəulslɔː] n salada de repolho cru
collapse [kə'læps] vi cair, tombar; (building) desabar; (resistance, government) sucumbir; (MED) desmaiar ♦ n desabamento, desmoronamento; (of government) queda; (MED) colapso; **collapsible** adj dobrável
collar ['kɔlə*] n (of shirt) colarinho; (of coat etc) gola; (for dog) coleira; (TECH) aro, colar m; **collarbone** n clavícula

colleague ['kɔliːg] n colega m/f
collect [kə'lekt] vt (as a hobby) colecionar; (gather) recolher; (wages, debts) cobrar; (donations, subscriptions) colher; (mail) coletar; (BRIT: call for) (ir) buscar, vir apanhar ♦ vi (people) reunir-se ♦ adv: **to call ~**; (US: TEL) ligar a cobrar; **collection** [kə'lekʃən] n coleção f; (of people) grupo; (of donations) arrecadação f; (of post, for charity) coleta; (of writings) coletânea; **collector** n colecionador(a) m/f; (of taxes etc) cobrador(a) m/f
college ['kɔlidʒ] n (of university) faculdade f; (of technology, agriculture) escola de nível superior; ver quadro

---

COLLEGE

Além de "universidade", **college** também se refere a um centro de educação superior para jovens que terminaram a educação obrigatória, **secondary school**. Alguns oferecem cursos de especialização em matérias técnicas, artísticas ou comerciais, outros oferecem disciplinas universitárias.

---

collide [kə'laid] vi: **to ~ (with)** colidir (com)
collision [kə'liʒən] n colisão f
Colombia [kə'lɔmbiə] n Colômbia
colon ['kəulən] n (sign) dois pontos; (MED) cólon m
colonel ['kəːnl] n coronel m
colony ['kɔləni] n colônia
colour ['kʌlə*] (US color) n cor f ♦ vt colorir; (with crayons) colorir, pintar; (dye) tingir; (fig: account) falsear ♦ vi (blush) corar; **~s** npl (of party, club) cores f pl; **in ~** (photograph etc) a cores; **colour in** vt (drawing) colorir; **colour-blind** adj daltônico;

coloured adj colorido; (person) de cor; **colour film** n filme m a cores;
colourful adj colorido; (account) vívido; (personality) vivo, animado;
colouring ['kʌlərɪŋ] n colorido; (complexion) tez f; (in food) colorante m; **colour television** n televisão f a cores

colt [kəult] n potro

column ['kɔləm] n coluna; (of smoke) faixa; (of people) fila

coma ['kəumə] n coma

comb [kəum] n pente m; (ornamental) crista ♦ vt pentear; (area) vasculhar

combat ['kɔmbæt] n combate m ♦ vt combater

combination [kɔmbɪ'neɪʃən] n combinação f; (of safe) segredo

combine [vb kəm'baɪn, n 'kɔmbaɪn] vt combinar; (qualities) reunir ♦ vi combinar-se ♦ n (ECON) associação f

KEYWORD

come [kʌm] (pt **came**, pp **come**) vi
1 (movement towards) vir; **~ with me** vem comigo; **to ~ running** vir correndo
2 (arrive) chegar; **she's ~ here to work** ela veio aqui para trabalhar; **to ~ home** chegar em casa
3 (reach): **to ~ to** chegar a; **the bill came to £40** a conta deu £40; **her hair came to her waist** o cabelo dela batia na cintura
4 (occur): **an idea came to me** uma idéia me ocorreu
5 (be, become) ficar; **to ~ loose/undone** soltar-se/desfazer-se; **I've ~ to like him** passei a gostar dele
come about vi suceder, acontecer
come across vt fus (person) topar com; (thing) encontrar
come away vi (leave) ir-se embora; (become detached) desprender-se, soltar-se

come back vi (return) voltar
come by vt fus (acquire) conseguir
come down vi (price) baixar; (tree) cair; (building) desmoronar-se
come forward vi apresentar-se
come from vt fus (subj: person) ser de; (: thing) originar-se de
come in vi entrar; (on deal) participar; (be involved) estar envolvido
come in for vt fus (criticism) merecer
come into vt fus (money) herdar; (fashion) ser; (be involved) estar envolvido em
come off vi (button) desprender-se, soltar-se; (attempt) dar certo
come on vi (pupil, work, project) avançar; (lights, electricity) ser ligado; **~ on!** vamos!, vai!
come out vi (fact) vir à tona; (book) ser publicado; (stain, sun) sair
come round vi voltar a si
come to vi voltar a si
come up vi (sun) nascer; (in conversation) surgir; (event) acontecer
come up against vt fus (resistance, difficulties) tropeçar com, esbarrar em
come up with vt fus (idea) propor, sugerir; (money) contribuir
come upon vt fus encontrar, achar

comedian [kə'miːdɪən] n cômico, humorista m

comedy ['kɔmɪdɪ] n comédia

comfort ['kʌmfət] n (well-being) bem-estar m; (relief) alívio ♦ vt consolar, confortar; **~s** npl (of home etc) conforto; **comfortable** adj confortável; (financially) tranqüilo; (walk, climb etc) fácil; **comfortably** adv confortavelmente; **comfort station** (US) n banheiro (BR), lavatórios mpl (PT)

comic ['kɔmɪk] *adj (also: ~al)* cômico ♦ *n (person)* humorista *m/f; (BRIT: magazine)* revista em quadrinhos *(BR),* revista de banda desenhada *(PT),* gibi *m (BR: inf)*

coming ['kʌmɪŋ] *n* vinda, chegada ♦ *adj* que vem, vindouro

comma ['kɔmə] *n* vírgula

command [kə'mɑːnd] *n* ordem *f,* mandado; *(control)* controle *m; (MIL: authority)* comando; *(mastery)* domínio ♦ *vt* mandar; **commander** *n (MIL)* comandante *m/f*

commemorate [kə'meməreɪt] *vt (with monument)* comemorar; *(with celebration)* celebrar

commence [kə'mens] *vt, vi* começar, iniciar

commend [kə'mend] *vt* elogiar, louvar; *(recommend)* recomendar

comment ['kɔment] *n* comentário ♦ *vi:* **to ~ (on)** comentar (sobre); "**no ~**" "sem comentário"; **commentary** ['kɔməntəri] *n* comentário; **commentator** ['kɔməntəteɪtə*] *n* comentarista *m/f*

commerce ['kɔmə:s] *n* comércio

commercial [kə'mə:ʃl] *adj* comercial ♦ *n* anúncio, comercial *m*

commiserate [kə'mɪzəreɪt] *vi:* **to ~ with** comiserar-se de, condoer-se de

commission [kə'mɪʃn] *n* comissão *f; (order)* empreitada, encomenda ♦ *vt (work of art)* encomendar; **out of ~** com defeito; **commissioner** *n* comissário(-a)

commit [kə'mɪt] *vt* cometer; *(resources)* alocar; *(to sb's care)* entregar; **to ~ o.s. (to do)** comprometer-se (a fazer); **to ~ suicide** suicidar-se; **commitment** *n* compromisso; *(political etc)* engajamento; *(undertaking)* promessa

committee [kə'mɪtɪ] *n* comitê *m*

commodity [kə'mɔdɪtɪ] *n* mercadoria

common ['kɔmən] *adj* comum; *(vulgar)* vulgar ♦ *n* área verde aberta ao público; **C~s** *npl (BRIT: POL):* **the (House of) C~s** a Câmara dos Comuns; **in ~** em comum; **commonly** *adv* geralmente; **Common Market** *n* Mercado Comum; **commonplace** *adj* vulgar; **common sense** *n* bom senso; **Commonwealth** *n:* **the Commonwealth** a Comunidade Britânica

commotion [kə'məuʃən] *n* tumulto, confusão *f*

communal [kə'mju:nl] *adj* comum

commune [*n* 'kɔmju:n, *vb* kə'mju:n] *n (group)* comuna ♦ *vi:* **to ~ with** comunicar-se com

communicate [kə'mju:nɪkeɪt] *vt* comunicar ♦ *vi:* **to ~ (with)** comunicar-se (com); **communication** [kəmju:nɪ'keɪʃən] *n* comunicação *f; (letter, call)* mensagem *f;* **communication cord** *(BRIT) n* sinal *m* de alarme

communion [kə'mju:nɪən] *n (also:* Holy C~) comunhão *f*

communism ['kɔmjunɪzəm] *n* comunismo; **communist** *adj, n* comunista *m/f*

community [kə'mju:nɪtɪ] *n* comunidade *f;* **community centre** *n* centro social

commutation ticket [kɔmju-'teɪʃən-] *(US) n* passe *m,* bilhete *m* de assinatura

commute [kə'mju:t] *vi* viajar diariamente ♦ *vt* comutar; **commuter** *n* viajante *m/f* habitual

compact [*adj* kəm'pækt, *n* 'kɔmpækt] *adj* compacto ♦ *n (also: powder ~)* estojo; **compact disc** *n* disco laser, CD *m;* **compact disc player** *n* som cd *m*

companion [kəmˈpænɪən] *n* companheiro(-a); **companionship** *n* companhia, companheirismo

company [ˈkʌmpənɪ] *n* companhia; (COMM) sociedade *f*, companhia; **to keep sb** ~ fazer companhia a alguém

comparative [kəmˈpærətɪv] *adj* (study) comparativo; (peace, safety) relativo; (stranger) meio; **comparatively** *adj* relativamente

compare [kəmˈpeə*] *vt* comparar ♦ *vi*: **to ~ with** comparar-se com; **comparison** [kəmˈpærɪsn] *n* comparação *f*

compartment [kəmˈpɑːtmənt] *n* compartimento; (of wallet) divisão *f*

compass [ˈkʌmpəs] *n* bússola; **~es** *npl* compasso

compassion [kəmˈpæʃən] *n* com paixão *f*

compatible [kəmˈpætɪbl] *adj* compatível

compel [kəmˈpel] *vt* obrigar

compensate [ˈkɒmpənseɪt] *vt* indenizar ♦ *vi*: **to ~ for** compensar; **compensation** [kɒmpənˈseɪʃən] *n* compensação *f*; (damages) indenização *f*

compete [kəmˈpiːt] *vi* (take part) competir; (vie): **to ~ (with)** competir (com), fazer competição (com)

competent [ˈkɒmpɪtənt] *adj* competente

competition [kɒmpɪˈtɪʃn] *n* (contest) concurso; (ECON) concorrência; (rivalry) competição *f*

competitive [kənˈpetɪtɪv] *adj* competitivo; (person) competidor(a)

competitor [kəmˈpetɪtə*] *n* (rival) competidor(a) *m/f*; (participant, ECON) concorrente *m/f*

complain [kəmˈpleɪn] *vi* queixar-se; **to ~ of** (pain) queixar-se de; **com-**

plaint *n* (objection) objeção *f*; (criticism) queixa; (MED) achaque *m*, doença

complement [ˈkɒmplɪmənt] *n* complemento; (esp ship's crew) tripulação *f* ♦ *vt* complementar

complete [kəmˈpliːt] *adj* completo; (finished) acabado ♦ *vt* (finish: building, task) acabar; (: set, group) completar; (a form) preencher; **completely** *adv* completamente; **completion** *n* conclusão *f*, término; (of contract etc) realização *f*

complex [ˈkɒmpleks] *adj* complexo ♦ *n* complexo; (of buildings) conjunto

complexion [kəmˈplekʃən] *n* (of face) cor *f*, tez *f*

complicate [ˈkɒmplɪkeɪt] *vt* complicar; **complicated** *adj* complicado; **complication** [kɒmplɪˈkeɪʃən] *n* problema *m*; (MED) complicação *f*

compliment [*n* ˈkɒmplɪmənt, *vb* ˈkɒmplɪment] *n* (praise) elogio ♦ *vt* elogiar; **~s** *npl* (regards) cumprimentos *mpl*; **to pay sb a ~** elogiar alguém; **complimentary** [kɒmplɪˈmentərɪ] *adj* lisonjeiro; (free) gratuito

comply [kəmˈplaɪ] *vi*: **to ~ with** cumprir com

component [kəmˈpəunənt] *adj* componente ♦ *n* (part) peça

compose [kəmˈpəuz] *vt* compor; **to be ~d of** compor-se de; **to ~ o.s.** tranqüilizar-se; **composed** *adj* calmo; **composer** *n* (MUS) compositor(a) *m/f*; **composition** [kɒmpəˈzɪʃən] *n* composição *f*

compound [ˈkɒmpaund] *n* (CHEM, LING) composto; (enclosure) recinto ♦ *adj* composto

comprehend [kɒmprɪˈhend] *vt* compreender

comprehensive [kɒmprɪˈhensɪv]

adj abrangente; *(INSURANCE)* total; **comprehensive (school)** *(BRIT) n* escola secundária de amplo programa; *ver* quadro

---

COMPREHENSIVE SCHOOL

Criadas na década de 1960 pelo governo trabalhista da época, as **comprehensive schools** são estabelecimentos de ensino secundário polivalentes concebidos para acolher todos os alunos sem distinção e lhes oferecer oportunidades iguais, em oposição ao sistema seletivo das *grammar schools*. A maioria dos estudantes britânicos freqüenta atualmente uma **comprehensive school**, mas as *grammar schools* não desapareceram de todo.

---

compress [*vb* kəm'prɛs, *n* 'kɒm-prɛs] *vt* comprimir; *(text, information etc)* reduzir ♦ *n* (MED) compressa

comprise [kəm'praiz] *vt* (*also*: **be ~d of**) compreender, constar de; *(constitute)* constituir

compromise ['kɒmprəmaiz] *n* meio-termo ♦ *vt* comprometer ♦ *vi* chegar a um meio-termo

compulsion [kəm'pʌlʃən] *n* compulsão *f*; *(force)* coação *f*, força

compulsive [kəm'pʌlsɪv] *adj* compulsório

compulsory [kəm'pʌlsəri] *adj* obrigatório; *(retirement)* compulsório

computer [kəm'pju:tə*] *n* computador *m*; **computer game** *n* vídeo game *m*; **computerize** *vt* informatizar, computadorizar; **computer progra(m)mer** *n* programador(a) *m/f*; **computer program(m)ing** *n* programação *f*; **computer science** *n* informática *f*; **computing** *n* computação *f*; *(science)*

informática

comrade ['kɒmrid] *n* camarada *m/f*

con [kɒn] *vt* enganar; *(cheat)* trapacear ♦ *n* vigarice *f*

conceal [kən'si:l] *vt* ocultar; *(information)* omitir

conceited [kən'si:tɪd] *adj* vaidoso

conceive [kən'si:v] *vt* conceber ♦ *vi* conceber, engravidar

concentrate ['kɒnsəntreit] *vi* concentrar-se ♦ *vt* concentrar; **concentration** *n* concentração *f*

concept ['kɒnsɛpt] *n* conceito

concern [kən'sə:n] *n* (COMM) empresa; *(anxiety)* preocupação *f* ♦ *vt* preocupar; *(involve)* envolver; *(relate to)* dizer respeito a; **to be ~ed (about)** preocupar-se (com); **concerning** *prep* sobre, a respeito de, acerca de

concert ['kɒnsət] *n* concerto; **concerted** [kən'sə:tɪd] *adj* *(joint)* conjunto

concession [kən'sɛʃən] *n* concessão *f*; **tax ~** redução no imposto

conclude [kən'klu:d] *vt* *(finish)* acabar, concluir; *(treaty etc)* firmar; *(agreement)* chegar a; *(decide)* decidir; **conclusion** [kən'klu:ʒən] *n* conclusão *f*; **conclusive** [kən'klu:sɪv] *adj* conclusivo, decisivo

concoct [kən'kɒkt] *vt* *(excuse)* fabricar; *(plot)* tramar; *(meal)* preparar; **concoction** *n* *(mixture)* mistura

concrete ['kɒnkri:t] *n* concreto (BR), betão *m* (PT) ♦ *adj* concreto

concussion [kən'kʌʃən] *n* (MED) concussão *f* cerebral

condemn [kən'dɛm] *vt* denunciar; *(prisoner, building)* condenar

condensation [kɒndɛn'seiʃən] *n* condensação *f*

condense [kən'dɛns] *vi* condensar-se ♦ *vt* condensar; **condensed milk** *n* leite *m* condensado

condition [kən'dıʃən] n condição f; (MED: illness) doença ♦ vt condicionar; ~s npl (circumstances) circunstâncias fpl; on ~ that com a condição (de) que; **conditioner** n (for hair) condicionador m; (for fabrics) amaciante m

condolences [kən'dəulənsız] npl pêsames mpl

condom ['kɔndɔm] n preservativo, camisinha, camisa-de-Venus f

condominium [kɔndə'mınıəm] (US) n (building) edifício

condone [kən'dəun] vt admitir, aceitar

conducive [kən'dju:sıv] adj: ~ to conducente para or a

conduct [n 'kɔndʌkt, vb kən'dʌkt] n conduta, comportamento ♦ vt (research etc) fazer; (heat, electricity) conduzir; (MUS) reger; **to ~ o.s.** comportar-se; **conducted tour** n viagem f organizada; **conductor** n (of orchestra) regente m/f; (on bus) cobrador(a) m/f; (US: RAIL) revisor(a) m/f; (ELEC) condutor m; **conductress** n cobradora

cone [kəun] n cone m; (BOT) pinha; (for ice-cream) casquinha; (on road) cone colorido para sinalizar obras

confectioner [kən'fekʃənr] n (sweetmeats) doces mpl; (sweets) balas fpl

confer [kən'fə:*] vt: **to ~ sth on** conferir algo a; (advantage) conceder algo a ♦ vi conferenciar

conference ['kɔnfərns] n congresso m

confess [kən'fes] vt confessar ♦ vi (admit) admitir; **confession** n admissão f; (REL) confissão f

confetti [kən'feti] n confete m

confide [kən'faıd] vi: **to ~ in** confiar em, fiar-se em

confidence ['kɔnfıdns] n confiança; (faith) fé f; (secret) confidên-

cia; **in ~** em confidência; **confidence trick** n conto do vigário; **confident** adj confiante, convicto; (positive) seguro; **confidential** [kɔnfı'denʃəl] adj confidencial

confine [kən'faın] vt (shut up) encarcerar; (limit): **to ~ (to)** confinar (a); **confined** adj (space) reduzido; **confines** ['kɔnfaınz] npl confins mpl

confirm [kən'fə:m] vt confirmar; **confirmation** [kɔnfə'meıʃən] n confirmação f; (REL) crisma; **confirmed** adj inveterado

confiscate ['kɔnfıskeıt] vt confiscar

conflict [n 'kɔnflıkt, vb kən'flıkt] n (disagreement) divergência; (of interests, loyalties etc) conflito; (fighting) combate m ♦ vi estar em conflito; (opinions) divergir; **conflicting** [kən'flıktıŋ] adj (reports) divergente; (interests) oposto

conform [kən'fɔ:m] vi conformar-se; **to ~ to** ajustar-se a, acomodar-se a

confound [kən'faund] vt confundir

confront [kən'frʌnt] vt (problems) enfrentar; (enemy, danger) defrontar-se com; **confrontation** [kɔnfrən'teıʃən] n confrontação f

confuse [kən'fju:z] vt (perplex) desconcertar; (mix up) confundir, misturar; (complicate) complicar; **confused** adj confuso; **confusing** adj confuso; **confusion** [kən'fju:ʒən] n (mix-up) mal-entendido; (perplexity) perplexidade f; (disorder) confusão f

congeal [kən'dʒi:l] vi coagular-se

congenial [kən'dʒi:nıəl] adj simpático, agradável

congestion [kən'dʒestʃən] n (MED) congestão f; (traffic) congestionamento

congratulate [kən'grætjuleıt] vt

parabenizar; **congratulations** [kəngrætjʊ'leɪʃənz] *npl* parabéns *mpl*

congregate ['kɔŋgrɪgeɪt] *vi* reunir-se; **congregation** [kɔŋgrɪ'geɪʃən] *n* (*in church*) fiéis *mpl*

congress ['kɔŋgrɛs] *n* congresso; (*US*): **C~** Congresso; *ver quadro*

CONGRESS

O Congresso é o Parlamento dos Estados Unidos. Consiste na *House of Representatives* e no Senado *Senate*. Os representantes e senadores são eleitos por sufrágio universal direto. O Congresso se reúne no *Capitol*, em Washington.

---

congressman (*US*) (*irreg*) *n* deputado

conjunctivitis [kəndʒʌŋktɪ'vaɪtɪs] *n* conjuntivite *f*

conjure ['kʌndʒə*] *vi* fazer truques; **conjure up** *vt* (*ghost, spirit*) fazer aparecer, invocar; (*memories*) evocar; **conjurer** *n* mágico(-a), prestidigitador(a) *m/f*

con man ['kɔn-] (*irreg*) *n* vigarista *m*

connect [kə'nɛkt] *vt* (*ELEC, TEL*) ligar; (*fig: associate*) associar; (*join*) *vt* to ~ **with** (*train*) conectar com; to be ~ed **with** estar relacionado com; **I'm trying to ~ you** (*TEL*) estou tentando completar a ligação; **connection** *n* ligação *f*, (*ELEC, RAIL, fig*) conexão *f*; (*TEL*) ligação *f*

conquer ['kɔŋkə*] *vt* conquistar; (*enemy*) vencer; (*feelings*) superar; **conquest** ['kɔŋkwɛst] *n* conquista

conscience ['kɔnʃəns] *n* consciência

conscientious [kɔnʃɪ'ɛnʃəs] *adj* consciencioso

conscious ['kɔnʃəs] *adj* consciente;

(*deliberate*) intencional; **consciousness** *n* consciência; (*MED*): **to lose/regain consciousness** perder/recuperar os sentidos

conscript ['kɔnskrɪpt] *n* recruta *m/f*

consent [kən'sɛnt] *n* consentimento ♦ *vi*: **to ~ to** consentir em

consequence ['kɔnsɪkwəns] *n* consequência; (*significance*): **of ~** de importância; **consequently** *adv* por conseguinte

conservation [kɔnsə'veɪʃən] *n* conservação *f*; (*of the environment*) preservação *f*

conservative [kən'sə:vətɪv] *adj* conservador(a); (*cautious*) moderado; (*BRIT: POL*): **C~** conservador(a) ♦ *n* (*BRIT: POL*) conservador(a) *m/f*

conservatory [kən'sə:vətrɪ] *n* (*MUS*) conservatório; (*greenhouse*) estufa

conserve [kən'sə:v] *vt* (*preserve*) preservar; (*supplies, energy*) poupar ♦ *n* conserva

consider [kən'sɪdə*] *vt* considerar; (*take into account*) levar em consideração; (*study*) estudar, examinar; **to ~ doing sth** pensar em fazer algo

considerable [kən'sɪdərəbl] *adj* considerável; (*sum*) importante

considerate [kən'sɪdərɪt] *adj* atencioso; **consideration** [kənsɪdə-'reɪʃən] *n* consideração *f*; (*deliberation*) deliberação *f*; (*factor*) fator *m*

considering [kən'sɪdərɪŋ] *prep* em vista de

consign [kən'saɪn] *vt*: **to ~ to** (*place*) relegar para; (*care*) confiar a; **consignment** *n* consignação *f*

consist [kən'sɪst] *vi*: **to ~ of** (*comprise*) consistir em

consistency [kən'sɪstənsɪ] *n* coerência; (*thickness*) consistência

consistent [kən'sɪstənt] *adj* (*person*) coerente, estável; (*idea*) sólido

consolation [kɔnsə'leɪʃən] n conforto

console [vb kən'səul, n 'kɔnsəul] vt confortar ♦ n consolo

consonant ['kɔnsənənt] n consoante f

conspicuous [kən'spɪkjuəs] adj conspícuo

conspiracy [kən'spɪrəsɪ] n conspiração f, trama

constable ['kʌnstəbl] (BRIT) n policial m/f (BR), polícia m/f (PT); **chief ~** chefe m/f de polícia

constant ['kɔnstənt] adj constante

constipated ['kɔnstɪpeɪtəd] adj com prisão de ventre

constipation [kɔnstɪ'peɪʃən] n prisão f de ventre

constituency [kən'stɪtjuənsɪ] n (POL) distrito eleitoral; (people) eleitorado

constitution [kɔnstɪ'tjuːʃən] n constituição f; (health) compleição f

constraint [kən'streɪnt] n coação f, pressão f; (restriction) limitação f

construct [kən'strʌkt] vt construir; **construction** n construção f; (structure) estrutura

consul ['kɔnsl] n cônsul m/f; **consulate** ['kɔnsjulɪt] n consulado

consult [kən'sʌlt] vt consultar; **consultant** n (MED) (médico(-a)) especialista m/f; (other specialist) assessor(a) m/f, consultor(a) m/f; **consulting room** (BRIT) n consultório

consume [kən'sjuːm] vt (eat) comer; (drink) beber; (fire etc, COMM) consumir; **consumer** n consumidor(a) m/f

consumption [kən'sʌmpʃən] n consumação f; (buying, amount) consumo

cont. abbr = **continued**

contact ['kɔntækt] n contato ♦ vt

entrar or pôr-se em contato com; **contact lenses** npl lentes fpl de contato

contagious [kən'teɪdʒəs] adj contagioso; (fig: laughter etc) contagiante

contain [kən'teɪn] vt conter; **to ~ o.s.** conter-se; **container** n recipiente m; (for shipping etc) container m, cofre m de carga

contaminate [kən'tæmɪneɪt] vt contaminar

cont'd abbr = **continued**

contemplate ['kɔntəmpleɪt] vt (idea) considerar; (person etc) contemplar

contemporary [kən'tempərərɪ] adj (account) contemporâneo; (design) moderno ♦ n contemporâneo(-a)

contempt [kən'tempt] n desprezo; **~ of court** (LAW) desacato à autoridade do tribunal; **contemptuous** [kən'temptjuəs] adj desdenhoso

contend [kən'tend] vt (assert): **to ~ that** afirmar que ♦ vi: **to ~ with** (struggle) lutar com; (difficulty) enfrentar; (compete): **to ~ for** competir por; **contender** n contendor(a) m/f

content [adj, vb kən'tent, n 'kɔntent] adj (happy) contente; (satisfied) satisfeito ♦ vt contentar, satisfazer ♦ n conteúdo; (fat ~, moisture ~ etc) quantidade f; (of packet, book) conteúdo; **~s** npl (of packet, book) conteúdo; **contented** adj contente, satisfeito

contest [n 'kɔntest, vb kən'test] n contenda; (competition) concurso ♦ vt (legal case) defender; (POL) ser candidato a; (competition) disputar; **contestant** [kən'testənt] n competidor(a) m/f; (in fight) adversário(-a)

context ['kɔntekst] n contexto

continent ['kɔntɪnənt] n continente *m*; **the C~** (*BRIT*) o continente europeu; **continental** [kɔntɪˈnɛntl] *adj* continental; **continental quilt** (*BRIT*) *n* edredom *m*

contingency [kənˈtɪndʒənsɪ] *n* contingência

continual [kənˈtɪnjuəl] *adj* contínuo

continuation [kəntɪnjuˈeɪʃən] *n* prolongamento

continue [kənˈtɪnjuː] *vi* prosseguir, continuar ♦ *vt* continuar; (*start again*) recomeçar, retomar; **continuous** [kənˈtɪnjuəs] *adj* contínuo; **continuous stationery** (*COMPUT*) formulários *mpl* contínuos

contour [ˈkɔntuə*] *n* contorno; (*also:* ~ **line**) curva de nível

contraband [ˈkɔntrəbænd] *n* contrabando

contraceptive [kɔntrəˈsɛptɪv] *adj* anticoncepcional ♦ *n* anticoncepcional *f*

contract [*n* ˈkɔntrækt, *vb* kənˈtrækt] *n* contrato ♦ *vi* (*become smaller*) contrair-se, encolher-se; (*COMM*): **to ~ to do sth** comprometer-se por contrato a fazer algo ♦ *vt* contrair; **contraction** [kənˈtrækʃən] *n* contração *f*

contradict [kɔntrəˈdɪkt] *vt* contradizer, desmentir

contraption [kənˈtræpʃən] (*pej*) *n* engenhoca, geringonça

contrary¹ [ˈkɔntrərɪ] *adj* contrário ♦ *n* contrário; **on the ~** muito pelo contrário; **unless you hear to the ~** salvo aviso contrário

contrary² [kənˈtrɛərɪ] *adj* teimoso

contrast [*n* ˈkɔntrɑːst, *vb* kənˈtrɑːst] *n* contraste *m* ♦ *vt* comparar; **in ~ to** em contraste com, ao contrário de

contravene [kɔntrəˈviːn] *vt* infringir

contribute [kənˈtrɪbjuːt] *vt* contri-

buir ♦ *vi* dar; **to ~ to** (*charity*) contribuir para; (*newspaper*) escrever para; (*discussion*) participar de; **contribution** [kɔntrɪˈbjuːʃən] *n* (*donation*) doação *f*; (*BRIT: for social security*) contribuição *f*; (*to debate*) intervenção *f*; (*to journal*) colaboração *f*; **contributor** [kənˈtrɪbjutə*] *n* (*to appeal*) contribuinte *m/f*; (*to newspaper*) colaborador(a) *m/f*

contrive [kənˈtraɪv] *vi*: **to ~ to do** chegar a fazer

control [kənˈtrəul] *vt* controlar; (*machinery*) regular; (*temper*) dominar ♦ *n* controle *m*; (*of car*) direção *f* (*BR*), condução *f* (*PT*); (*check*) freio, controle; **~s** *npl* (*of vehicle*) instrumentos *mpl* de controle; (*on radio, television etc*) controle; (*governmental*) medidas *fpl* de controle; **to be in ~ of** ter o controle de; (*in charge of*) ser responsável por

controversial [kɔntrəˈvəːʃl] *adj* controvertido, polêmico

controversy [ˈkɔntrəvəːsɪ] *n* controvérsia, polêmica

convalesce [kɔnvəˈlɛs] *vi* convalescer

convector [kənˈvɛktə*] *n* (*heater*) aquecedor *m* de convecção

convenience [kənˈviːnɪəns] *n* (*easiness*) facilidade *f*; (*suitability*) conveniência; (*advantage*) vantagem *f*, conveniência; **at your ~** quando lhe convier; **all modern ~s** (*also: BRIT: all mod cons*) com todos os confortos

convenient [kənˈviːnɪənt] *adj* conveniente

convent [ˈkɔnvənt] *n* convento

convention [kənˈvɛnʃən] *n* (*custom*) costume *m*; (*agreement*) convenção *f*; (*meeting*) assembléia; **conventional** *adj* convencional

conversation [kɔnvə'seɪʃən] *n* conversação *f*, conversa

converse [*n* 'kɔnvɜːs, *vb* kən'vɜːs] *n* inverso *vi* conversar; **conversely** [kən'vɜːslɪ] *adv* pelo contrário, inversamente

convert [*vb* kən'vɜːt, *n* 'kɔnvɜːt] *vt* converter ♦ *n* convertido(-a); **convertible** [kən'vɜːtəbl] *n* conversível *m*

convey [kən'veɪ] *vt* transportar, levar; (*thanks*) expressar; (*information*) exprimir; **conveyor belt** *n* correia transportadora

convict [*vb* kən'vɪkt, *n* 'kɔnvɪkt] *vt* condenar ♦ *n* presidiário(-a); **conviction** *n* condenação *f*; (*belief*) convicção *f*; (*certainty*) certeza

convince [kən'vɪns] *vt* (*assure*) assegurar; (*persuade*) convencer; **convincing** *adj* convincente

convulse [kən'vʌls] *vt*: **to be ~d with** (*laughter, pain*) morrer de

cook [kuk] *vt* cozinhar; (*meal*) preparar ♦ *vi* cozinhar ♦ *n* cozinheiro(-a); **cookbook** *n* livro de receitas; **cooker** *n* fogão *m*; **cookery** *n* culinária; **cookery book** (*BRIT*) *n* = **cookbook**; **cookie** (*US*) *n* bolacha, biscoito; **cooking** *n* cozinha

cool [kuːl] *adj* fresco; (*calm*) calmo; (*unfriendly*) frio ♦ *vt* resfriar ♦ *vi* esfriar

coop [kuːp] *n* (*for poultry*) galinheiro; (*for rabbits*) capoeira; **coop up** *vt* (*fig*) confinar

cooperate [kəu'ɔpəreɪt] *vi* colaborar; (*assist*) ajudar; **cooperative** [kəu'ɔpərətɪv] *adj* cooperativo ♦ *n* cooperativa

coordinate [*vb* kəu'ɔːdɪneɪt, *n* kəu'ɔːdɪnət] *vt* coordenar ♦ *n* (*MATH*) coordenada; **~s** *npl* (*clothes*) coordenados *mpl*

cop [kɔp] (*inf*) *n* polícia *m/f* (*BR*), poli-

cial *m/f*, tira *m* (*inf*)

cope [kəup] *vi*: **to ~ with** poder com, arcar com; (*problem*) estar à altura de

copper ['kɔpə*] *n* (*metal*) cobre *m*; (*BRIT: inf: policeman/woman*) polícia *m/f*, policial *m/f* (*BR*); **~s** *npl* (*coins*) moedas *fpl* de pouco valor

copy ['kɔpɪ] *n* duplicata; (*of book etc*) exemplar *m* ♦ *vt* copiar; (*imitate*) imitar; **copyright** *n* direitos *mpl* autorais, copirraite *m*

coral ['kɔrəl] *n* coral *m*

cord [kɔːd] *n* corda; (*ELEC*) fio, cabo; (*fabric*) veludo cotelê

cordial ['kɔːdɪəl] *adj* cordial ♦ *n* (*BRIT*) bebida à base de fruta

cordon ['kɔːdn] *n* cordão *m*; **cordon off** *vt* isolar

corduroy ['kɔːdərɔɪ] *n* veludo cotelê

core [kɔː*] *n* centro; (*of fruit*) caroço; (*of problem*) âmago ♦ *vt* descaroçar

cork [kɔːk] *n* rolha; (*tree*) cortiça; **corkscrew** *n* saca-rolhas *m inv*

corn [kɔːn] *n* (*BRIT*) trigo; (*US: maize*) milho; (*on foot*) calo; **~ on the cob** (*CULIN*) espiga de milho

corned beef ['kɔːnd-] *n* carne *f* de boi enlatada

corner ['kɔːnə*] *n* (*outside*) esquina; (*inside*) canto; (*in road*) curva; (*FOOTBALL, BOXING*) córner *m* ♦ *vt* (*trap*) encurralar; (*COMM*) açambarcar, monopolizar ♦ *vi* fazer uma curva

cornet ['kɔːnɪt] *n* (*MUS*) cornetim *m*; (*BRIT: of ice-cream*) casquinha

cornflakes ['kɔːnfleɪks] *npl* flocos *mpl* de milho

cornflour ['kɔːnflauə*] (*BRIT*) *n* farinha de milho, maisena ®

cornstarch ['kɔːnstɑːtʃ] (*US*) *n* = **cornflour**

Cornwall ['kɔːnwəl] *n* Cornualha

corny ['kɔːnɪ] (*inf*) *adj* (*joke*) gasto

coronary ['kɔrənərɪ] *n*: **~** (**throm-**

bosis) trombose f (coronária)

coronation [kɔrə'neɪʃən] n coroação f

coroner ['kɔrənə*] n magistrado que investiga mortes suspeitas

corporal ['kɔ:pərl] n cabo ♦ adj: ~ **punishment** castigo corporal

corporate ['kɔ:pərɪt] adj coletivo; (finance) corporativo; (image) de empresa

corporation [kɔ:pə'reɪʃən] n (of town) município, junta; (COMM) sociedade f

corps [kɔ:*, pl kɔ:z] (pl corps) n (MIL) unidade f; (diplomatic) corpo; **the press ~** a imprensa

corpse [kɔ:ps] n cadáver m

correct [kə'rekt] adj exato; (proper) correto ♦ vt corrigir; **correction** n correção f

correspond [kɔrɪs'pɔnd] vi (write): **to ~ (with)** corresponder-se (com); (be equal to): **to ~ to** corresponder a; (be in accordance): **to ~ (with)** corresponder a; **correspondence** n correspondência f; **correspondent** n correspondente m/f

corridor ['kɔrɪdɔ:*] n corredor m

corrode [kə'rəud] vt corroer ♦ vi corroer-se

corrugated ['kɔrəgeɪtɪd] adj corrugado; **corrugated iron** n chapa ondulada or corrugada

corrupt [kə'rʌpt] adj corrupto; (COMPUT) corrupto, danificado ♦ vt corromper; corromper, danificar; **corruption** n corrupção f; corrupção, danificação f

Corsica ['kɔ:sɪkə] n Córsega f

cosmetic [kɔz'metɪk] n cosmético ♦ adj (fig) simbólico, artificial

cost [kɔst] (pt, pp cost) n (price) preço ♦ vt custar; **~s** npl (COMM: overheads) custos mpl; (LAW) custas fpl; **at all ~s** custe o que custar

co-star [kəu-] n co-estrela m/f

Costa Rica ['kɔstə'ri:kə] n Costa Rica

costly ['kɔstlɪ] adj caro

costume ['kɔstju:m] n traje m; (BRIT: also: **swimming ~: woman's**) maiô m (BR), fato de banho (PT); (: man's) calção m (de banho) (BR), calções mpl de banho (PT); **costume jewellery** n bijuteria

cosy ['kəuzɪ] (US **cozy**) adj aconchegante; (person) confortável

cot [kɔt] n (BRIT) cama (de criança), berço (BR); (US) cama de lona

cottage ['kɔtɪdʒ] n casa de campo; **cottage cheese** n ricota (BR), queijo creme (PT)

cotton ['kɔtn] n algodão m; (thread) fio, linha; **cotton on** (inf) vi: **to ~ on (to sth)** sacar (algo); **cotton candy** (US) n algodão m doce; **cotton wool** (BRIT) n algodão m (hidrófilo)

couch [kautʃ] n sofá m; (doctor's) cama; (psychiatrist's) divã m

couchette [ku:'ʃet] n leito

cough [kɔf] vi tossir ♦ n tosse f

could [kud] pt, conditional of **can²**

couldn't ['kudnt] = **could not**

council ['kaunsl] n conselho; **city or town ~** câmara municipal; **council estate** (BRIT) n conjunto habitacional; **council house** (BRIT) n casa popular; **councillor** n vereador(a) m/f

counsellor ['kaunsələ*] (US **counselor**) n conselheiro(-a); (US: LAW) advogado(-a)

count [kaunt] vt contar; (include) incluir ♦ vi contar ♦ n (of votes etc) contagem f; (of pollen, alcohol) nível m; (nobleman) conde m; **count on** vt fus (expect) esperar; (depend on) contar com; **countdown** n contagem f regressiva

counter ['kauntə*] n (in shop)

balcão m; (in post office etc) guichê m; (in games) ficha ♦ vt contrariar ♦ adv: ~ **to** ao contrário de; **counteract** vt neutralizar

counterfeit ['kauntəfɪt] n falsificação f ♦ vt falsificar ♦ adj falso, falsificado

counterfoil ['kauntəfɔɪl] n canhoto (BR), talão m (PT)

counterpart ['kauntəpɑːt] n (of person) homólogo(-a); (of company etc) equivalente m/f

countess ['kauntɪs] n condessa

countless ['kauntlɪs] adj inumerável

country ['kʌntrɪ] n país m; (nation) nação f; (native land) terra; (as opposed to town) campo; (region) região f, terra; **country dancing** (BRIT) n dança regional; **country house** n casa de campo; **countryman** n (national) compatriota m; (rural) camponês m; **countryside** n campo

county ['kauntɪ] n condado

coup [kuː] n (also: ~ de mestre; (also: ~ **d'état**) golpe (de estado)

couple ['kʌpl] n (of things, people) par m; (married ~) casal m; **a ~ of** um par de; (a few) alguns (algumas)

coupon ['kuːpɔn] n cupom m (BR), cupão m (PT); (voucher) vale m

courage ['kʌrɪdʒ] n coragem f

courier ['kurɪə*] n correio m; (for tourists) guia m/f, agente m/f de turismo

course [kɔːs] n (direction) direção f; (process) desenvolvimento; (of river, SCH) curso; (of ship) rumo; (GOLF) campo; (part of meal) prato; ~ **of treatment** tratamento; **of** ~ naturalmente; (certainly) certamente; **of** ~! claro!, lógico!

court [kɔːt] n (royal) corte f; (LAW) tribunal m; (TENNIS etc) quadra ♦ vt (woman) cortejar, namorar; **to take to** ~ demandar, levar a julgamento

courteous ['kɜːtɪəs] adj cortês(-esa)

courtesy ['kɜːtəsɪ] n cortesia; **(by) ~ of** com permissão de

court-house (US) n palácio de justiça

court martial (pl **courts martial**) n conselho de guerra

courtroom ['kɔːtrum] n sala de tribunal

courtyard ['kɔːtjɑːd] n pátio

cousin ['kʌzn] n primo m/f; **first ~** primo irmão (prima irmã)

cove [kəuv] n angra, enseada

cover ['kʌvə*] vt cobrir; (with lid) tapar; (chairs etc) revestir; (distance) percorrer; (include) abranger; (protect) abrigar; (issues) tratar ♦ n (lid) tampa; (for chair etc) capa; (for bed) cobertor m; (of book, magazine) capa; (shelter) abrigo; (INSURANCE: also: of spy) cobertura; **to take ~** abrigar-se; **under ~** (indoors) abrigado; **under separate ~** (COMM) em separado; **cover up** vi: **to ~ up for sb** cobrir alguém; **coverage** n cobertura; **cover charge** n couvert m; **covering** n cobertura; (of snow, dust etc) camada; **covering letter** (US **cover letter**) n carta de cobertura; **cover note** n nota de cobertura

covert ['kʌvə:t] adj (threat) velado

cover-up n encobrimento (dos fatos)

covet ['kʌvɪt] vt cobiçar

cow [kau] n vaca ♦ vt intimidar

coward ['kauəd] n covarde m/f; **cowardice** n covardia; **cowardly** adj covarde

cowboy ['kaubɔɪ] n vaqueiro

coy [kɔɪ] adj tímido

cozy ['kəuzɪ] (US) adj = **cosy**

CPA (US) n abbr = **certified public accountant**

crab [kræb] n caranguejo

crack [kræk] n rachadura; (gap) brecha; (noise) estalo; (drug) crack m ♦ vt quebrar; (nut) partir, descascar; (wall) rachar; (whip etc) estalar; (joke) soltar; (mystery) resolver; (code) decifrar ♦ adj (expert) de primeira classe; **crack down on** vt fus (crime) ser linha dura com; **crack up** n (PSYCH) sofrer um colapso nervoso; **cracker** n (biscuit) biscoito; (Christmas ~) busca-pé-surpresa m

crackle ['krækl] vi crepitar

cradle ['kreɪdl] n berço

craft [krɑːft] n (skill) arte f; (trade) ofício; (boat: pl inv) barco; (plane: pl inv) avião; **craftsman** (irreg) n artífice m, artesão m; **craftsmanship** n qualidade f; **crafty** adj astuto, esperto

cram [kræm] vt (fill): **to ~ sth with** encher or abarrotar algo de; (put): **to ~ sth into** enfiar algo em ♦ vi (for exams) estudar na última hora

cramp [kræmp] n (MED) cãibra; **cramped** adj apertado, confinado

cranberry ['krænbəri] n oxicoco

crane [kreɪn] n (TECH) guindaste m; (bird) grou m

crank [kræŋk] n manivela; (person) excêntrico(-a)

crash [kræʃ] n (noise) estrondo; (of car) batida; (of plane) desastre m de avião; (COMM) falência, quebra; (STOCK EXCHANGE) craque m ♦ vt (car) colidir; (plane) espatifar ♦ vi bater; cair, espatifar-se; (cars) colidir, bater; (COMM) falir, quebrar; **crash course** n curso intensivo; **crash helmet** n capacete m; **crash landing** n aterrissagem f forçada (BR), aterragem f forçosa (PT)

crate [kreɪt] n caixote m; (for bottles) engradado

crave [kreɪv] vt, vi: **to ~ for** ansiar por

crawl [krɔːl] vi arrastar-se; (child) engatinhar; (insect) andar; (vehicle) arrastar-se a passo de tartaruga ♦ n (SWIMMING) crawl m

crayfish ['kreɪfɪʃ] n inv (freshwater) camarão-d'água-doce m; (saltwater) lagostim m

crayon ['kreɪən] n lápis m de cera, crayon m

craze [kreɪz] n (fashion) moda

crazy ['kreɪzɪ] adj louco, maluco, doido

creak [kriːk] vi chiar, ranger

cream [kriːm] n (of milk) nata; (artificial ~, cosmetic) creme m; (élite): **the ~ of** a fina flor de ♦ adj (colour) creme inv; **cream cake** n bolo de creme; **cream cheese** n ricota (BR), queijo creme (PT); **creamy** adj (colour) creme inv; (taste) cremoso

crease [kriːs] n (fold) dobra, vinco; (in trousers) vinco; (wrinkle) ruga ♦ vt (wrinkle) amassar, amarrotar ♦ vi amassar-se, amarrotar-se

create [kriːˈeɪt] vt criar; (produce) produzir

creature ['kriːtʃə*] n (animal) animal m, bicho; (living thing) criatura

credit ['krɛdɪt] n crédito; (merit) mérito ♦ vt (also: **give ~ to**) acreditar; (COMM) creditar; **~s** npl (CINEMA, TV) crédito; **to ~ sb with sth** (fig) atribuir algo a alguém; **to be in ~** ter fundos; **credit card** n cartão m de crédito; **creditor** n credor(a) m/f

creed [kriːd] n credo

creek [kriːk] n enseada; (US) riacho

creep [kriːp] (pt, pp **crept**) vi (animal) rastejar; (person) deslizar(-se); **creeper** n trepadeira; **creepy** adj horripilante

cremate [krɪˈmeɪt] vt cremar; **crematorium** (pl **crematoria**) n crematório

crept [krɛpt] pt, pp of **creep**

crescent ['krɛsnt] n meia-lua; (street) rua semicircular

cress [krɛs] n agrião m

crest [krɛst] n (of bird) crista; (of hill) cimo, topo; (of coat of arms) timbre m; **crestfallen** adj abatido, cabisbaixo

Crete [kriːt] n Creta

crevice ['krɛvɪs] n fenda; (gap) greta

crew [kruː] n (of ship) tripulação f; (CINEMA) equipe f; **crew-cut** n corte m à escovinha

crib [krɪb] n manjedoira, presépio; (US: cot) berço ♦ vt (inf) colar

cricket ['krɪkɪt] n (insect) grilo; (game) criquete m, cricket m

crime [kraɪm] n (no pl: illegal activities) crime m, (offence) delito; (fig) pecado, maldade f; **criminal** ['krɪmɪnl] n criminoso ♦ adj criminal; (morally wrong) imoral

crimson ['krɪmzn] adj carmesim inv

cringe [krɪndʒ] vi encolher-se

cripple ['krɪpl] n aleijado(-a) ♦ vt aleijar

crisis ['kraɪsɪs] (pl crises) n crise f

crisp [krɪsp] adj fresco; (bacon etc) torrado; (manner) seco; **crisps** (BRIT) npl batatinhas fpl fritas

criss-cross [krɪs-] adj (design) entrecruzado; (pattern) em xadrez; ~ **pattern** (padrão m em) xadrez m

criterion [kraɪˈtɪərɪən] (pl criteria) n critério

critic ['krɪtɪk] n crítico(-a); **critical** adj crítico; (illness) grave; **to be critical of sth/sb** criticar algo/alguém; **critically** adv (examine) criteriosamente; (speak) criticamente; (ill) gravemente; **criticism** ['krɪtɪsɪzəm] n crítica; **criticize** ['krɪtɪsaɪz] vt criticar

croak [krəuk] vi (frog) coaxar; (bird) crocitar; (person) estar rouco

Croatia [krəuˈeɪʃə] n Croácia

crochet ['krəuʃeɪ] n crochê m

crockery ['krɔkərɪ] n louça

crocodile ['krɔkədaɪl] n crocodilo

crocus ['krəukəs] n açafrão-da-primavera m

croft [krɔft] (BRIT) n pequena chácara

crook [kruk] n (inf: criminal) vigarista m/f; (of shepherd) cajado; **crooked** ['krukɪd] adj torto; (dishonest) desonesto

crop [krɔp] n (produce) colheita; (amount produced) safra; (riding ~) chicotinho ♦ vt cortar; **crop up** vi surgir

cross [krɔs] n cruz f; (hybrid) cruzamento ♦ vt cruzar; (street etc) atravessar; (thwart) contrariar ♦ adj zangado, mal-humorado; **cross out** vt riscar; **cross over** vi atravessar; **crossbar** n (SPORT) barra transversal; **cross-examine** vt (LAW) reperguntar; **cross-eyed** adj vesgo; **crossing** n (sea passage) travessia; (also: **pedestrian crossing**) faixa (para pedestres) (BR), passadeira (PT); **cross-reference** n referência remissiva; **crossroads** n cruzamento; **cross section** n (of object) corte m transversal; (of population) grupo representativo; **crosswalk** (US) n faixa (para pedestres) (BR), passadeira (PT); **crossword** n palavras fpl cruzadas

crouch [krautʃ] vi agachar-se

crow [krəu] n (bird) corvo; (of cock) canto, cocoricó m ♦ vi (cock) cantar, cocoricar

crowbar ['krəubɑː*] n pé-de-cabra m

crowd [kraud] n multidão f ♦ vt (fill) apinhar ♦ vi (gather): **to ~ round** reunir-se; (cram): **to ~ in** apinhar-se em; **crowded** adj (full) lotado, (*densely populated*) superlotado

crown [kraun] *n* coroa; (*of head, hill*) topo ♦ *vt* coroar; (*fig*) rematar; **crown jewels** *npl* jóias *fpl* reais

crucial ['kru:ʃl] *adj* (*decision*) vital; (*vote*) decisivo

crucifix ['kru:sɪfɪks] *n* crucifixo

crude [kru:d] *adj* (*materials*) bruto; (*fig: basic*) tosco; (: *vulgar*) grosseiro

cruel ['kruəl] *adj* cruel

cruise [kru:z] *n* cruzeiro ♦ *vi* (*ship*) fazer um cruzeiro; (*car*): **to ~ at ... km/h** ir a ... km por hora; **cruiser** *n* (*motorboat*) barco a motor; (*warship*) cruzador *m*

crumb [krʌm] *n* (*of bread*) migalha; (*of cake*) farelo

crumble ['krʌmbl] *vt* esfarelar ♦ *vi* (*building*) desmoronar-se; (*plaster, earth*) esfacelar-se; (*fig*) desintegrar-se

crumpet ['krʌmpɪt] *n* bolo leve

crumple ['krʌmpl] *vt* (*paper*) amassar; (*material*) amarrotar

crunch [krʌntʃ] *vt* (*food etc*) mastigar; (*underfoot*) esmagar ♦ *n* (*fig*): **the ~** o momento decisivo; **crunchy** *adj* crocante

crusade [kru:'seɪd] *n* (*campaign*) campanha

crush [krʌʃ] *n* (*crowd*) aglomeração *f*; (*love*): **to have a ~ on sb** ter um rabicho por alguém; (*drink*): **lemon ~** limonada ♦ *vt* (*press*) esmagar; (*squeeze*) espremer; (*paper*) amassar; (*cloth*) enrugar; (*army, opposition*) aniquilar; (*hopes*) destruir; (*person*) arrasar

crust [krʌst] *n* (*of bread*) casca; (*of snow*) crosta; (*of earth*) camada

crutch [krʌtʃ] *n* muleta

crux [krʌks] *n* ponto crucial

cry [kraɪ] *vi* chorar; (*shout: also: ~ out*) gritar ♦ *n* grito; (*of bird*) pio; (*of animal*) voz *f*; **cry off** *vi* desistir

cryptic ['krɪptɪk] *adj* enigmático

crystal ['krɪstl] *n* cristal *m*; **crystal-clear** *adj* cristalino, claro

cub [kʌb] *n* filhote *m*; (*also*: **~ scout**) lobinho

Cuba ['kju:bə] *n* Cuba

cube [kju:b] *n* cubo ♦ *vt* (*MATH*) elevar ao cubo; **cubic** *adj* cúbico

cubicle ['kju:bɪkl] *n* cubículo

cuckoo ['kuku:] *n* cuco; **cuckoo clock** *n* relógio de cuco

cucumber ['kju:kʌmbə*] *n* pepino

cuddle ['kʌdl] *vt* abraçar ♦ *vi* abraçar-se

cue [kju:] *n* (*SNOOKER*) taco; (*THEATRE etc*) deixa

cuff [kʌf] *n* (*of shirt, coat etc*) punho; (*US: on trousers*) bainha; (*blow*) bofetada; **off the ~** de improviso; **cuff links** *npl* abotoaduras *fpl*

cul-de-sac ['kʌldəsæk] *n* beco sem saída

cull [kʌl] *vt* (*story, idea*) escolher, selecionar ♦ *n* matança seletiva

culminate ['kʌlmɪneɪt] *vi*: **to ~ in** terminar em

culprit ['kʌlprɪt] *n* culpado(-a)

cult [kʌlt] *n* culto

cultivate ['kʌltɪveɪt] *vt* cultivar; **cultivation** [kʌltɪ'veɪʃən] *n* cultivo

cultural ['kʌltʃərəl] *adj* cultural

culture ['kʌltʃə*] *n* cultura; **cultured** *adj* culto

cumbersome ['kʌmbəsəm] *adj* pesado, desajeitado; (*person*) lente, ineficiente

cunning ['kʌnɪŋ] *n* astúcia ♦ *adj* astuto, malandro; (*device, idea*) engenhoso

cup [kʌp] *n* xícara (*BR*), chávena (*PT*); (*prize, of bra*) taça

cupboard ['kʌbəd] *n* armário

curator [kjuə'reɪtə*] *n* diretor(a) *m/f*

curb [kə:b] *vt* refrear ♦ *n* freio; (*US:*

kerb) meio-fio *(BR)*, borda do passeio *(PT)*

curdle ['kə:dl] *vi* coalhar

cure [kjuə*] *vt* curar ♦ *n* *(MED)* tratamento, cura; *(solution)* remédio

curfew ['kə:fju:] *n* toque *m* de recolher

curious ['kjuəriəs] *adj* curioso; *(nosy)* abelhudo; *(unusual)* estranho

curl [kə:l] *n* *(of hair)* cacho ♦ *vt* *(loosely)* frisar; *(: tightly)* encrespar ♦ *vi* *(hair)* encaracolar; **curl up** *vi* encaracolar-se; **curler** *n* rolo, bobe *m*; **curly** *adj* cacheado, crespo

currant ['kʌrnt] *n* passa de corinto; *(black~, red~)* groselha

currency ['kʌrnsı] *n* moeda; **to gain ~** *(fig)* consagrar-se

current ['kʌrnt] *n* corrente ♦ *adj* corrente; *(present)* atual; **current account** *(BRIT)* nota corrente; **current affairs** *npl* atualidades *fpl*; **currently** *adv* atualmente

curriculum [kə'rıkjuləm] *(pl* **~s** *or* **curricula**) *n* programa *m* de estudos; **curriculum vitae** *n* curriculum vitae *m*, currículo

curry ['kʌrı] *n* caril *m* ♦ *vt*: **to ~ favour with** captar simpatia de

curse [kə:s] *vi* xingar *(BR)*, praguejar *(PT)* ♦ *vt* *(swear at)* xingar *(BR)*; *(bemoan)* amaldiçoar ♦ *n* maldição *f*; *(swearword)* palavrão *m* *(BR)*, baixo calão *m* *(PT)*; *(problem)* castigo

cursor ['kə:sə*] *n* *(COMPUT)* cursor *m*

curt [kə:t] *adj* seco, brusco

curtail [kə:'teıl] *vt* *(freedom, rights)* restringir; *(visit etc)* abreviar, encurtar; *(expenses etc)* reduzir

curtain ['kə:tn] *n* cortina; *(THEATRE)* pano

curts(e)y ['kə:tsı] *vi* fazer reverência

curve [kə:v] *n* curva ♦ *vi* encurvar-se, torcer-se; *(road)* fazer (uma) curva

cushion ['kuʃən] *n* almofada; *(of air)* colchão *m* ♦ *vt* amortecer

custard ['kʌstəd] *n* nata, creme *m*

custody ['kʌstədı] *n* custódia; **to take into ~** deter

custom ['kʌstəm] *n* *(tradition)* tradição *f*; *(convention)* costume *m*; *(habit)* hábito; *(COMM)* clientela; **customary** *adj* costumeiro; **customer** *n* cliente *m/f*; **customized** *adj* *(car etc)* feito sob encomenda

customs ['kʌstəmz] *npl* alfândega; **customs officer** *n* inspetor(a) *m/f* da alfândega, aduaneiro(-a)

cut [kʌt] *(pt, pp* **cut)** *vt* cortar; *(reduce)* reduzir ♦ *vi* cortar ♦ *n* corte *m*; *(in spending)* redução *f*; *(of garment)* talho; **out down** *vt* *(tree)* derrubar; *(consumption)* reduzir; **cut off** *vt* *(piece, TEL)* cortar; *(person, village)* isolar; *(supply)* suspender; **cut out** *vt* *(shape)* recortar; *(activity etc)* suprimir; *(remove)* remover; **cut up** *vt* cortar em pedaços

cute [kju:t] *adj* bonitinho, gracinha

cutlery ['kʌtlərı] *n* talheres *mpl*

cutlet ['kʌtlıt] *n* costeleta; *(vegetable ~, nut ~)* medalhão *m*

cut: cut-price *(US* **cut-rate)** *adj* a preço reduzido; **cutting** *adj* cortante ♦ *n* *(BRIT: from newspaper)* recorte *m*; *(from plant)* muda

CV *n abbr* = **curriculum vitae**

cwt *abbr* = **hundredweight**

cyanide ['saıənaıd] *n* cianeto

cybercafé ['saıbəkæfeı] *n* cibercafé *m*

cyberspace ['saıbəspeıs] *n* ciberespaço

cycle ['saıkl] *n* ciclo; *(bicycle)* bicicleta ♦ *vi* andar de bicicleta; **cycle lane** *or* **path** *n* ciclovia *f*

cycling ['saıklıŋ] *n* ciclismo

cyclist ['saıklıst] *n* ciclista *m/f*

cylinder ['sılındə*] *n* cilindro; *(of*

gas) bujão *m*

cymbals ['sɪmblz] *npl* pratos *mpl*

cynic ['sɪnɪk] *n* cínico(-a); **cynical** *adj* cínico

Cyprus ['saɪprəs] *n* Chipre *f*

cyst [sɪst] *n* cisto; **cystitis** *n* cistite *f*

czar [zɑː*] *n* czar *m*

Czech [tʃɛk] *adj* tcheco ♦ *n* tcheco(-a); (*LING*) tcheco; **Czech Republic** *n*: **the Czech Republic** a República Tcheca

D

D [diː] *n* (*MUS*) ré *m*

dab [dæb] *vt* (*eyes, wound*) tocar (de leve); (*paint, cream*) aplicar de leve

dabble ['dæbl] *vi*: **to ~ in** interessar-se por

dad [dæd] (*inf*) *n* papai *m*

daddy ['dædɪ] *n* = **dad**

daffodil ['dæfədɪl] *n* narciso-dos-prados *m*

daft [dɑːft] *adj* bobo, besta

dagger ['dægə*] *n* punhal *m*, adaga

daily ['deɪlɪ] *adj* diário ♦ *n* (*paper*) jornal *m*, diário ♦ *adv* diariamente

dainty ['deɪntɪ] *adj* delicado

dairy ['dɛərɪ] *n* leiteria; **dairy products** *npl* laticínios *mpl*; **dairy store** (*US*) *n* leiteria

daisy ['deɪzɪ] *n* margarida

dam [dæm] *n* represa, barragem *f* ♦ *vt* represar

damage ['dæmɪdʒ] *n* (*harm*) prejuízo; (*dents etc*) avaria ♦ *vt* danificar; (*harm*) prejudicar; **~s** *npl* (*LAW*) indenização *f* por perdas e danos

damn [dæm] *vt* condenar; (*curse*) maldizer ♦ *n* (*inf*): **I don't give a ~** não dou a mínima, estou me lixando ♦ *adj* (*inf*: *also*: **~ed**) danado, maldito; **~ (it)!** (que) droga!; **damning** *adj* (*evidence*) prejudicial

damp [dæmp] *adj* úmido ♦ *n* umidade *f* ♦ *vt* (*also*: **~en**: *cloth, rag*) umedecer; (: *enthusiasm etc*) jogar água fria em

damson ['dæmzən] *n* ameixa pequena

dance [dɑːns] *n* dança; (*party etc*) baile *m* ♦ *vi* dançar; **dance hall** *n* salão *m* de baile; **dancer** *n* dançarino(-a); (*professional*) bailarino(-a); **dancing** *n* dança

dandelion ['dændɪlaɪən] *n* dente-de-leão *m*

dandruff ['dændrəf] *n* caspa

Dane [deɪn] *n* dinamarquês(-esa) *m/f*

danger ['deɪndʒə*] *n* perigo; (*risk*) risco; **"~!"** (*on sign*) "perigo!"; **to be in ~ of** correr o risco de; **in ~** em perigo; **dangerous** *adj* perigoso

dangle ['dæŋgl] *vt* balançar ♦ *vi* pender balançando

Danish ['deɪnɪʃ] *adj* dinamarquês(-esa) ♦ *n* (*LING*) dinamarquês *m*

dare [dɛə*] *vt*: **to ~ sb to do sth** desafiar alguém a fazer algo ♦ *vi*: **to ~ (to) do sth** atrever-se a fazer algo, ousar fazer algo; **I ~ say** (*I suppose*) acho provável que; **daring** *adj* audacioso; (*bold*) ousado ♦ *n* coragem *f*, destemor *m*

dark [dɑːk] *adj* escuro; (*complexion*) moreno ♦ *n* escuro; **to be in the ~ about** (*fig*) estar no escuro sobre; **after ~** depois de escurecer; **darken** *vt* escurecer; (*colour*) fazer mais escuro ♦ *vi* escurecer-se; **dark glasses** *npl* óculos *mpl* escuros; **darkness** *n* escuridão *f*; **darkroom** *n* câmara escura

darling ['dɑːlɪŋ] *adj*, *n* querido(-a)

darn [dɑːn] *vt* cerzir

dart [dɑːt] *n* dardo; (*in sewing*) alinhavo ♦ *vi* precipitar-se, correr para; **to ~ away/along** ir-se/seguir precipitadamente; **darts** *n* (*game*) jogo de dardos

dash [dæʃ] n (sign) hífen m; (: long) travessão m; (quantity) pontinha ♦ vt arremessar; (hopes) frustrar ♦ vi correr para, ir depressa; **dash away** vi sair apressado; **dash off** vi = **dash away**

dashboard ['dæʃbɔːd] n painel m de instrumentos

data ['deɪtə] npl dados mpl; **database** n banco de dados; **data processing** n processamento de dados

date [deɪt] n data; (with friend) encontro; (fruit) tâmara ♦ vt datar; (person) namorar; **to** ~ até agora; **out of** ~ fora de moda; (expired) desatualizado; **up to** ~ moderno; **dated** ['deɪtɪd] adj antiquado; **date rape** n estupro cometido pelo acompanhante da vítima, geralmente após encontro romântico

daub [dɔːb] vt borrar

daughter ['dɔːtə*] n filha; **daughter-in-law** (pl ~s-in-law) n nora

daunting ['dɔːntɪŋ] adj desanimador(a)

dawdle ['dɔːdl] vi (go slow) vadiar

dawn [dɔːn] n alvorada, amanhecer m; (of period, situation) surgimento, início ♦ vi (day) amanhecer; (fig): it ~ed on him that ... começou a perceber que ...

day [deɪ] n dia m; (working ~) jornada, dia útil; (heyday) apogeu m; **the** ~ **before** a véspera; **the** ~ **before yesterday** anteontem; **the** ~ **after tomorrow** depois de amanhã; **by** ~ de dia; **daybreak** n amanhecer m; **daydream** vi devanear; **daylight** n luz f de dia; **day return** (BRIT) n bilhete m de ida e volta no mesmo dia; **daytime** n dia m; **day-to-day** adj cotidiano

daze [deɪz] vt (stun) aturdir ♦ n: **in a**

~ aturdido

dazzle ['dæzl] vt (bewitch) deslumbrar; (blind) ofuscar

DC abbr (ELEC) = **direct current**

dead [dɛd] adj morto; (numb) dormente; (telephone) cortado; (ELEC) sem corrente ♦ adv completamente; (exactly) absolutamente ♦ npl: **the** ~ os mortos; **to shoot sb** ~ matar alguém a tiro; ~ **tired** morto de cansado; **to stop** ~ estacar; **deaden** vt (blow, sound) amortecer; (pain) anestesiar; **dead end** n beco sem saída; **deadline** n prazo final; **deadlock** n impasse m; **dead loss** (inf) n: **to be a dead loss** não ser de nada; **deadly** adj mortal, fatal; (accuracy, insult) devastador(a); (weapon) mortífero; **deadpan** adj sem expressão

deaf [dɛf] adj surdo; **deafen** vt ensurdecer; **deafness** n surdez f

deal [diːl] (pt, pp **dealt**) n (agreement) acordo ♦ vt (cards, blows) dar; **a good** or **great** ~ (of) bastante, muito; **deal in** vt fus (COMM) negociar em or com; **deal with** vt fus (people) tratar com; (problem) ocupar-se de; (subject) tratar de; **dealer** n negociante m/f; **dealings** npl transações fpl

dean [diːn] n (REL) decano; (SCH: BRIT) reitor(a) m/f; (: US) orientador(a) m/f de estudos

dear [dɪə*] adj querido, caro; (expensive) caro ♦ n: **my** ~ meu querido (minha querida) ♦ excl: ~ **me!** ai, meu Deus!; **D~ Sir/Madam** (in letter) Ilmo. Senhor (Exma. Senhora) (BR), Exmo. Senhor (Exma. Senhora) (PT); **D~ Mr/Mrs X** Caro Sr. X/Cara Sra. X; **dearly** adv (love) ternamente; (pay) caro

death [dɛθ] n morte f; (ADMIN) óbito; **death certificate** n certidão f de óbito; **deathly** adj (colour) pálido; (silence) profundo; **death penalty** n pena de morte

debatable [dɪ'beɪtəbl] adj discutível

debate [dɪ'beɪt] n debate m ♦ vt debater

debit ['debɪt] n débito ♦ vt: **to ~ a sum to sb** or **to sb's account** lançar uma quantia ao débito de alguém or à conta de alguém

debt [dɛt] n dívida; (state) endividamento; **to be in ~** ter dívidas, estar endividado; **debtor** n devedor(a) m/f

decade ['dɛkeɪd] n década

decaff ['diːkæf] (inf) n descafeinado m

decaffeinated [diː'kæfɪneɪtɪd] adj descafeinado

decanter [dɪ'kæntə*] n garrafa ornamental

decay [dɪ'keɪ] n ruína; (also: **tooth ~**) cárie f ♦ vi (rot) apodrecer-se

deceased [dɪ'siːst] n falecido(-a)

deceit [dɪ'siːt] n engano; (duplicity) fraude f; **deceitful** adj enganador(a)

deceive [dɪ'siːv] vt enganar

December [dɪ'sembə*] n dezembro m

decent ['diːsənt] adj (proper) decente; (kind, honest) honesto, amável

deception [dɪ'sepʃən] n engano; (deceitful act) fraude f; **deceptive** adj enganador(a)

decide [dɪ'saɪd] vt (person) convencer; (question) resolver ♦ vi decidir; **to ~ on sth** decidir-se por algo; **decided** adj decidido; (definite) claro, definido; **decidedly** adv claramente; (emphatically) decididamente

decimal ['dɛsɪməl] adj decimal ♦ n decimal m

decision [dɪ'sɪʒən] n (choice) escolha; (act of choosing) decisão f; (decisiveness) resolução f

decisive [dɪ'saɪsɪv] adj (action) decisivo; (person) decidido

deck [dɛk] n (NAUT) convés m; (of bus): **top ~** andar m de cima; (of cards) baralho; **record ~** toca-discos m inv; **deckchair** n cadeira de lona, espreguiçadeira

declare [dɪ'klɛə*] vt (intention) revelar; (result) divulgar; (income, at customs) declarar

decline [dɪ'klaɪn] n declínio; (lessening) diminuição f, baixa ♦ vt recusar ♦ vi diminuir

decorate ['dɛkəreɪt] vt (adorn) adornar; (paint) pintar; (paper) decorar com papel; **decoration** [dɛkə'reɪʃən] n enfeite m; (act) decoração f; (medal) condecoração f; **decorator** n (painter) pintor(a) m/f

decoy ['diːkɔɪ] n (person) armadilha; (object) engodo, chamariz m

decrease [n 'diːkriːs, vb diː'kriːs] n: **~ (in)** diminuição f (de) ♦ vt reduzir ♦ vi diminuir

decree [dɪ'kriː] n decreto

dedicate ['dedɪkeɪt] vt dedicar; **dedication** [dedɪ'keɪʃən] n dedicação f; (in book) dedicatória; (on radio) mensagem f

deduce [dɪ'djuːs] vt deduzir

deduct [dɪ'dʌkt] vt deduzir; **deduction** n (deducting) redução f; (amount) subtração f; (deducing) dedução f

deed [diːd] n feito; (LAW) escritura, título

deep [diːp] adj profundo; (voice) baixo, grave; (breath) fundo; (colour) forte, carregado ♦ adv: **the spectators stood 20 ~** os espectadores formaram-se em 20 fileiras; **to be 4 metres ~** ter 4 metros de profundidade; **deepen** vt aprofundar

♦ vi aumentar; **deepfreeze** n congelador m, freezer m (BR); **deep-fry** vt fritar em recipiente fundo; **deeply** adv fundo; (moved) profundamente; **deep-seated** adj arraigado

deer [dɪə*] n inv veado, cervo

deface [dɪ'feɪs] vt desfigurar

default [dɪ'fɔ:lt] n (COMPUT: also: **~ value**) valor m de default; **by ~** por desistência

defeat [dɪ'fi:t] n derrota; (failure) malogro ♦ vt derrotar, vencer

defect [n 'di:fekt, vb dɪ'fekt] n defeito ♦ vi: **to ~ to the enemy** desertar para se juntar ao inimigo; **defective** [dɪ'fektɪv] adj defeituoso

defence [dɪ'fens] (US **defense**) n defesa, justificação f; **defenceless** adj indefeso

defend [dɪ'fend] vt defender; (LAW) contestar; **defendant** n acusado(-a), (in civil case) réu (ré) m/f; **defender** n defensor(a) m/f; (SPORT) defesa

defer [dɪ'fə:*] vt (postpone) adiar

defiance [dɪ'faɪəns] n desafio, rebeldia; **in ~ of** a despeito de

defiant [dɪ'faɪənt] adj desafiador(a)

deficiency [dɪ'fɪʃənsɪ] n (lack) deficiência, falta; (defect) defeito

deficit ['defɪsɪt] n déficit m

define [dɪ'faɪn] vt definir

definite ['defɪnɪt] adj (fixed) definitivo; (clear, obvious) claro, categórico; (certain) certo; **he was ~ about It** ele foi categórico; **definitely** adv sem dúvida

deflate [di:'fleɪt] vt esvaziar

deflect [dɪ'flekt] vt desviar

defraud [dɪ'frɔ:d] vt: **to ~ sb (of sth)** trapacear alguém (por causa de algo)

defrost [di:'frɔst] vt descongelar

defuse [di:'fju:z] vt tirar o estopim

or a espoleta de; (situation) neutralizar

defy [dɪ'faɪ] vt desafiar; (resist) opor-se a

degenerate [vb dɪ'dʒenəreɪt, adj dɪ'dʒenərɪt] vi degenerar ♦ adj degenerado

degree [dɪ'gri:] n grau m; (SCH) diploma m, título; **in maths** formatura em matemática; **by ~s** (gradually) pouco a pouco; **to some ~, to a certain ~** até certo ponto

dehydrated [di:haɪ'dreɪtɪd] adj desidratado; (eggs, milk) em pó

de-ice vt (windscreen) descongelar

deign [deɪn] vi: **to ~ to do** dignar-se a fazer

dejected [dɪ'dʒektɪd] adj deprimido

delay [dɪ'leɪ] vt (decision etc) retardar, atrasar; (train) atrasar ♦ vi hesitar ♦ n demora; (postponement) adiamento; **to be ~ed** estar atrasado; **without ~** sem demora or atraso

delegate [n 'delɪgɪt, vb 'delɪgeɪt] n delegado(-a) ♦ vt (person) autorizar; (task) delegar

delete [dɪ'li:t] vt eliminar, riscar; (COMPUT) deletar

deliberate [adj dɪ'lɪbərɪt, vb dɪ'lɪbəreɪt] adj (intentional) intencional; (slow) pausado, lento ♦ vi considerar; **deliberately** [dɪ'lɪbərɪtlɪ] adv (on purpose) de propósito

delicacy ['delɪkəsɪ] n delicadeza; (of problem) dificuldade f; (food) iguaria

delicate ['delɪkɪt] adj delicado; (health) frágil

delicatessen [delɪkə'tesn] n delicatessen m

delicious [dɪ'lɪʃəs] adj delicioso; (food) saboroso

delight [dɪ'laɪt] n prazer m, deleite m; (person) encanto; (experience) delícia ♦ vt encantar, deleitar; **to**

take (a) ~ in deleitar-se com;
delighted *adj*: **delighted (at** or
with) encantado (com); **delightful**
adj encantador(a), delicioso
delinquent [dɪˈlɪŋkwənt] *adj, n*
delinqüente *m/f*
delirious [dɪˈlɪrɪəs] *adj* delirante; **to
be ~** delirar
deliver [dɪˈlɪvə*] *vt* (*distribute*) distribuir; (*hand over*) entregar; (*mes-
sage*) comunicar; (*speech*) proferir;
(*MED*) partejar; **delivery** *n* distribuição *f*; (*of speaker*) enunciação *f*;
(*MED*) parto; **to take delivery of**
receber
delude [dɪˈluːd] *vt* iludir, enganar
delusion [dɪˈluːʒən] *n* ilusão *f*
demand [dɪˈmɑːnd] *vt* exigir;
(*rights*) reivindicar, reclamar ♦ *n*
exigência; (*claim*) reivindicação *f*;
(*ECON*) procura; **to be in ~** estar em
demanda; **on ~** à vista; **demanding** *adj* (*boss*) exigente; (*work*)
absorvente
demeanour [dɪˈmiːnə*] (*US* **demean-
or**) *n* conduta, comportamento
demented [dɪˈmentɪd] *adj* demente, doido
demise [dɪˈmaɪz] *n* falecimento
demo [ˈdɛməu] (*inf*) *n* *abbr* (=
demonstration) passeata
democracy [dɪˈmɒkrəsɪ] *n* democracia; **democrat** [ˈdɛməkræt] *n*
democrata *m/f*; **democratic**
[dɛməˈkrætɪk] *adj* democrático
demolish [dɪˈmɒlɪʃ] *vt* demolir,
derrubar; (*argument*) refutar, contestar
demonstrate [ˈdɛmənstreɪt] *vt*
demonstrar ♦ *vi*: **to ~ (for/against)**
manifestar-se (a favor de/contra);
demonstration [dɛmənˈstreɪʃən]
n (*POL*) manifestação *f*; (: *march*)
passeata; (*proof*) demonstração *f*;
(*exhibition*) exibição *f*; **demonstra-**

tor *n* manifestante *m/f*
demote [dɪˈməut] *vt* rebaixar de
posto
den [dɛn] *n* (*of animal*) covil *m*; (*of
thieves*) antro, esconderijo; (*room*)
aposento privado, cantinho
denial [dɪˈnaɪəl] *n* refutação *f*; (*refusal*) negativa
denim [ˈdɛnɪm] *n* brim *m*, zuarte *m*;
~s *npl* jeans *m* (*BR*), jeans *mpl* (*PT*)
Denmark [ˈdɛnmɑːk] *n* Dinamarca
denomination [dɪnɒmɪˈneɪʃən] *n*
valor *m*, denominação *f*; (*REL*) confissão *f*, seita
denounce [dɪˈnauns] *vt* denunciar
dense [dɛns] *adj* denso, espesso;
(*inf*: *stupid*) estúpido, bronco;
densely *adv*: **densely populated**
com grande densidade de população
density [ˈdɛnsɪtɪ] *n* densidade *f*; **sin-
gle/double ~ disk** (*COMPUT*) disco de
densidade simples/dupla
dent [dɛnt] *n* amolgadura, depressão *f* ♦ *vt* amolgar, dentar
dental [ˈdɛntl] *adj* (*treatment*) den-
tário; (*hygiene*) dental
dentist [ˈdɛntɪst] *n* dentista *m/f*
dentures [ˈdɛntʃəz] *npl* dentadura
deny [dɪˈnaɪ] *vt* negar; (*refuse*) recusar
deodorant [diːˈəudərənt] *n* desodorante *m* (*BR*), deodorizante *m* (*PT*)
depart [dɪˈpɑːt] *vi* ir-se, partir; (*train
etc*) sair; **to ~ from** (*fig*: *differ from*)
afastar-se de
department [dɪˈpɑːtmənt] *n* (*SCH*)
departamento; (*COMM*) seção *f*;
(*POL*) repartição *f*; **department
store** *n* magazine *m* (*BR*), grande
armazém *m* (*PT*)
departure [dɪˈpɑːtʃə*] *n* partida,
ida; (*of train etc*) saída; (*of employee*)
saída; **a new ~** uma nova orientação; **departure lounge** *n* sala de

embarque

depend [dɪ'pɛnd] vi: **to ~ (up)on** depender de; (rely on) contar com; **it ~s** depende; **~ing on the result ...**; dependendo do resultado ...; **dependable** adj (person) de confiança, seguro; (car) confiável; **dependant** n dependente m/f; **dependent** adj: **to be dependent (on)** depender (de), ser dependente (de) ♦ n = **dependant**

depict [dɪ'pɪkt] vt (in picture) retratar, representar; (describe) descrever

deport [dɪ'pɔːt] vt deportar

deposit [dɪ'pɔzɪt] n (COMM, GEO) depósito; (CHEM) sedimento; (of ore, oil) jazida; (down payment) sinal m ♦ vt depositar; (luggage) guardar; **deposit account** n conta de depósito a prazo

depot ['dɛpəu] n (storehouse) depósito, armazém m; (for vehicles) garagem f, parque m; (US) estação f

depress [dɪ'prɛs] vt deprimir; (wages) reduzir; (press down) apertar; **depressed** adj deprimido; (area) em depressão; **depressing** adj deprimente; **depression** n depressão f; (hollow) achatamento

deprivation [dɛprɪ'veɪʃən] n privação f

deprive [dɪ'praɪv] vt: **to ~ sb of** privar alguém de; **deprived** adj carente

depth [dɛpθ] n profundidade f; (of feeling) intensidade f; **in the ~s of despair** no auge do desespero; **to be out of one's ~** (BRIT: swimmer) estar sem pé; (fig) estar voando

deputy ['dɛpjutɪ] adj: **~ chairman** vice-presidente(-a) m/f ♦ n (assistant) adjunto(-a); (POL: MP) deputado(-a); **~ head** (BRIT: SCH) diretor adjunto (diretora adjunta)

derail [dɪ'reɪl] vt: **to be ~ed**

descarrilhar

deranged [dɪ'reɪndʒd] adj (person) louco, transtornado

derby [də:bɪ] (US) n chapéu-coco

derelict ['dɛrɪlɪkt] adj abandonado

derive [dɪ'raɪv] vt: **to ~ (from)** obter or tirar (de) ♦ vi: **to ~ from** derivar-se de

derogatory [dɪ'rɔgətərɪ] adj depreciativo

descend [dɪ'sɛnd] vt, vi descer; **to ~ from** descer de; **to ~ to** descambar em; **descent** n descida; (origin) descendência

describe [dɪs'kraɪb] vt descrever; **description** [dɪs'krɪpʃən] n descrição f; (sort) classe f, espécie f

desert [n 'dɛzət, vb dɪ'zəːt] n deserto ♦ vt (place) desertar, (partner, family) abandonar ♦ vi (MIL) desertar; **deserter** [dɪ'zəːtə*] n desertor m; **desert island** n ilha deserta; **deserts** npl: **to get one's just deserts** receber o que merece

deserve [dɪ'zəːv] vt merecer; **deserving** adj (person) merecedor(a), digno; (action, cause) meritório

design [dɪ'zaɪn] n (sketch) desenho, esboço; (layout, shape) plano, projeto; (pattern) desenho, padrão m; (art) design m; (intention) propósito, intenção f ♦ vt (plan) projetar

designer [dɪ'zaɪnə*] n (ART) artista m/f gráfico(-a); (TECH) desenhista m/f, projetista m/f; (fashion ~) estilista m/f

desire [dɪ'zaɪə*] n (sexual) desejo ♦ vt querer, desejar, cobiçar

desk [dɛsk] n (in office) mesa, secretária; (for pupil) carteira f; (at airport) balcão m; (in hotel) recepção f; (BRIT in shop, restaurant) caixa; **desktop publishing** n editoração f eletrônica

desolate ['dɛsəlɪt] *adj* (*place*) deserto; (*person*) desolado

despair [dɪs'pɛə*] *n* desesperança ♦ *vi*: **to ~ of** desesperar-se de

despatch [dɪs'pætʃ] *n*, *vt* = **dispatch**

desperate ['dɛspərɪt] *adj* desesperado; (*situation*) desesperador(a); (*fugitive*) violento; **to be ~ for sth/to do** estar louco por algo/para fazer; **desperately** *adv* desesperadamente; (*very: unhappy*) terrivelmente; (: *ill*) gravemente; **desperation** [dɛspə'reɪʃən] *n* desespero, desesperança; **in (sheer) desperation** desesperado

despise [dɪs'paɪz] *vt* desprezar

despite [dɪs'paɪt] *prep* apesar de, a despeito de

despondent [dɪs'pɔndənt] *adj* abatido, desanimado

dessert [dɪ'zɜ:t] *n* sobremesa

destination [dɛstɪ'neɪʃən] *n* destino

destined ['dɛstɪnd] *adj*: **to be ~ to do sth** estar destinado a fazer algo; **~ for** com destino a

destiny ['dɛstɪnɪ] *n* destino

destitute ['dɛstɪtjuːt] *adj* indigente, necessitado

destroy [dɪs'trɔɪ] *vt* destruir; (*animal*) sacrificar; **destruction** *n* destruição

detach [dɪ'tætʃ] *vt* separar; (*unstick*) desprender; **detached** *adj* (*attitude*) imparcial, objetivo; (*house*) independente, isolado

detail ['diːteɪl] *n* detalhe *m*; (*trifle*) bobagem *f* ♦ *vt* detalhar; **in ~** pormenorizado, em detalhe

detain [dɪ'teɪn] *vt* deter; (*in captivity*) prender; (*in hospital*) hospitalizar

detect [dɪ'tɛkt] *vt* perceber; (MED, POLICE) identificar; (MIL, RADAR, TECH) detectar; **detection** *n* descoberta; **detective** *n* detetive *m/f*; **detective story** *n* romance *m* policial

detention [dɪ'tɛnʃən] *n* detenção *f*, prisão *f*; (SCH) castigo

deter [dɪ'tɜː*] *vt* (*discourage*) desanimar; (*dissuade*) dissuadir

detergent [dɪ'tɜːdʒənt] *n* detergente *m*

deteriorate [dɪ'tɪərɪəreɪt] *vi* deteriorar-se

determine [dɪ'tɜːmɪn] *vt* descobrir; (*limits*) demarcar; **determined** *adj* (*person*) resoluto; **determined to do** decidido a fazer

detour ['diːtuə*] *n* desvio

detract [dɪ'trækt] *vi*: **to ~ from** diminuir

detrimental [dɛtrɪ'mɛntl] *adj*: **~ (to)** prejudicial (a)

devastate ['dɛvəsteɪt] *vt* devastar; (*fig*): **to be ~d by** estar arrasado com

develop [dɪ'vɛləp] *vt* desenvolver; (PHOT) revelar; (*disease*) contrair; (*resources*) explotar ♦ *vi* (*advance*) progredir; (*evolve*) evoluir; (*appear*) aparecer; **developer** [dɪ'vɛləpə*] *n* empresário(-a) de imóveis; **developing country** país *m* em desenvolvimento; **development** [dɪ'vɛləpmənt] *n* desenvolvimento; (*advance*) progresso; (*of land*) urbanização *f*

device [dɪ'vaɪs] *n* aparelho, dispositivo

devil ['dɛvl] *n* diabo

devious ['diːvɪəs] *adj* (*person*) malandro, esperto

devise [dɪ'vaɪz] *vt* (*plan*) criar; (*machine*) inventar

devoid [dɪ'vɔɪd] *adj*: **~ of** destituído de

devote [dɪ'vəut] *vt*: **to ~ sth to** dedicar algo a; **devoted** [dɪ'vəutɪd] *adj* (*friendship*) leal; (*partner*) fiel; **to be**

devoted to estar devotado a; **the book is devoted to politics** o livro trata de política; **devotee** [dɛvəu'tiː] n adepto(-a), entusiasta m/f; (REL) devoto(-a); **devotion** n devoção f; (to duty) dedicação f

devour [dɪ'vauə*] vt devorar

devout [dɪ'vaut] adj devoto

dew [djuː] n orvalho

diabetes [daɪə'biːtiːz] n diabete f

diabolical [daɪə'bɒlɪkl] (inf) adj (dreadful) horrível

diagnosis [daɪəg'nəusɪs] (pl **diagnoses**) n diagnóstico

diagonal [daɪ'ægənl] adj diagonal ♦ n diagonal f

diagram ['daɪəgræm] n diagrama m, esquema m

dial ['daɪəl] n disco ♦ vt (number) discar (BR), marcar (PT)

dialect ['daɪəlɛkt] n dialeto

dialling code ['daɪəlɪŋ-] (US **dial code**) n código de discagem

dialling tone ['daɪəlɪŋ-] (US **dial tone**) n sinal m de discagem (BR) or de marcar (PT)

dialogue ['daɪəlɒg] (US **dialog**) n diálogo; (conversation) conversa

diameter [daɪ'æmɪtə*] n diâmetro

diamond ['daɪəmənd] n diamante m; (shape) losango, rombo; **~s** npl (CARDS) ouros mpl

diaper ['daɪəpə*] (US) n fralda

diaphragm ['daɪəfræm] n diafragma m

diarrhoea [daɪə'riːə] (US **diarrhea**) n diarréia

diary ['daɪərɪ] n (daily account) diário; (engagements book) agenda

dice [daɪs] n inv dado ♦ vt (CULIN) cortar em cubos

dictate [dɪk'teɪt] vt ditar; **dictation** n (of letter) ditado; (of orders) ordem f

dictator [dɪk'teɪtə*] n ditador(a) m/f; **dictatorship** n ditadura

dictionary ['dɪkʃənrɪ] n dicionário

did [dɪd] pt of **do**

didn't ['dɪdnt] = **did not**

die [daɪ] vi morrer; (fig: fade) murchar; **to be dying for sth/to do sth** estar louco por algo/para fazer algo; **die away** vi (sound, light) extinguir-se lentamente; **die down** vi (fire) apagar-se; (wind) abrandar; (excitement) diminuir; **die out** vi desaparecer

diesel ['diːzl] n diesel m; (also: ~ **oil**) óleo diesel

diet ['daɪət] n dieta; (restricted food) regime m ♦ vi (also: **be on a ~**) estar de dieta, fazer regime

differ ['dɪfə*] vi (be different): **to ~ from sth** ser diferente de algo, diferenciar-se de algo; (disagree): **to ~ (about)** discordar (sobre); **difference** n diferença; (disagreement) divergência; **different** adj diferente; **differentiate** [dɪfə'rɛnʃɪeɪt] vi: **to differentiate (between)** distinguir (entre)

difficult ['dɪfɪkəlt] adj difícil; **difficulty** n dificuldade f

dig [dɪg] (pt, pp **dug**) vt cavar ♦ n (prod) pontada; (archaeological) excavação f; (remark) alfinetada; **to ~ one's nails into sth** cravar as unhas em algo; **dig into** vt fus (savings) gastar; **dig up** vt (plant) arrancar; (information) trazer à tona

digest [vb daɪ'dʒɛst, n 'daɪdʒɛst] vt (food) digerir; (facts) assimilar ♦ n sumário; **digestion** [dɪ'dʒɛstʃən] n digestão f

digit ['dɪdʒɪt] n (MATH) dígito; (finger) dedo; **digital** adj digital; **digital camera** n câmara digital; **digital TV** n televisão f digital

dignified ['dɪgnɪfaɪd] adj digno

dignity ['dɪgnɪtɪ] n dignidade f

digress [daɪ'grɛs] vi: **to ~ from**

afastar-se de

digs [dɪgz] (BRIT: inf) npl pensão f, alojamento

dilapidated [dɪˈlæpɪdeɪtɪd] adj arruinado

dilemma [daɪˈlɛmə] n dilema m

diligent [ˈdɪlɪdʒənt] adj (worker) diligente; (research) cuidadoso

dilute [daɪˈluːt] vt diluir

dim [dɪm] adj fraco; (outline) indistinto; (room) escuro; (inf: person) burro ♦ vt diminuir; (US: AUT) baixar

dime [daɪm] (US) n dez centavos

dimension [dɪˈmɛnʃən] n dimensão f; (measurement) medida; (also: ~s: scale, size) tamanho

diminish [dɪˈmɪnɪʃ] vi diminuir

diminutive [dɪˈmɪnjutɪv] adj diminuto ♦ n (LING) diminutivo

dimple [ˈdɪmpl] n covinha

din [dɪn] n zoeira

dine [daɪn] vi jantar; **diner** n comensal m/f; (US: eating place) lanchonete f

dinghy [ˈdɪŋgɪ] n dingue m; (also: rubber ~) bote m; (: also: sailing ~) bote de borracha

dingy [ˈdɪndʒɪ] adj (room) sombrio, lúgubre; (clothes, curtains etc) sujo

dining car [ˈdaɪnɪŋ-] (BRIT) n (RAIL) vagão-restaurante m

dining room [ˈdaɪnɪŋ-] n sala de jantar

dinner [ˈdɪnə*] n (evening meal) jantar m; (lunch) almoço m; (banquet) banquete m; **dinner jacket** n smoking m; **dinner party** n jantar m; **dinner time** n (midday) hora de almoçar; (evening) hora de jantar

dip [dɪp] n (slope) inclinação f; (in sea) mergulho m; (CULIN) pasta para servir com salgadinhos ♦ vt (in water) mergulhar; (ladle) meter; (BRIT: AUT: lights) baixar ♦ vi descer subitamente

diploma [dɪˈpləumə] n diploma m

diplomat [ˈdɪpləmæt] n diplomata m/f

dipstick [ˈdɪpstɪk] (US **diprod**) n (AUT) vareta medidora

dire [daɪə*] adj terrível

direct [daɪˈrɛkt] adj direto; (route) reto; (manner) franco, sincero ♦ vt dirigir; (order): **to ~ sb to do sth** ordenar alguém para fazer algo ♦ adv direto; **can you ~ me to ...?** pode me indicar o caminho a ...?;

direction [dɪˈrɛkʃən] n (way) indicação f; (TV, RADIO, CINEMA) direção f; **directions** npl (instructions) instruções fpl; **directions for use** modo de usar;

directly adv diretamente; (at once) imediatamente; **director** n diretor(a) m/f

directory [dɪˈrɛktərɪ] n (TEL) lista (telefônica); (also: COMM) anuário comercial; (COMPUT) diretório; **directory enquiries** (US **directory assistance**) n informações fpl

dirt [dɜːt] n sujeira (BR), sujidade (PT); **dirty** adj sujo; (joke) indecente ♦ vt sujar; **dirty trick** n golpe m baixo, sujeira

disability [dɪsəˈbɪlɪtɪ] n incapacidade f

disabled [dɪsˈeɪbld] adj deficiente ♦ npl: **the ~ os** deficientes

disadvantage [dɪsədˈvɑːntɪdʒ] n desvantagem f; (prejudice) inconveniente m

disagree [dɪsəˈgriː] vi (differ) diferir; (be against, think otherwise): **to ~ (with)** não concordar (com), discordar (de); **disagreeable** adj desagradável; **disagreement** n desacordo; (quarrel) desavença

disallow [ˈdɪsəˈlau] vt (LAW) vetar, proibir

disappear [dɪsəˈpɪə*] vi desaparecer, sumir; (custom etc) acabar; **disappearance** n desaparecimento, desaparição f

disappoint [dɪsə'pɔɪnt] vt decepcionar; **disappointed** adj desiludido; **disappointment** n decepção f; (cause) desapontamento

disapproval [dɪsə'pruːvəl] n desaprovação f

disapprove [dɪsə'pruːv] vi: **to ~ of** desaprovar

disarmament [dɪs'ɑːməmənt] n desarmamento

disaster [dɪ'zɑːstə*] n (accident) desastre m; (natural) catástrofe f

disbelief [dɪsbə'liːf] n incredulidade f

disc [dɪsk] n disco; (COMPUT) = **disk**

discard [dɪs'kɑːd] vt (old things) desfazer-se de; (fig) descartar

discern [dɪ'sɜːn] vt perceber; (identify) identificar; **discerning** adj perspicaz

discharge [vb dɪs'tʃɑːdʒ, n 'dɪstʃɑːdʒ] vt (duties) cumprir, desempenhar; (patient) dar alta a; (employee) despedir; (soldier) dar baixa em, dispensar; (defendant) pôr em liberdade; (waste etc) descarregar, despejar ♦ n (ELEC, CHEM) descarga; (dismissal) despedida; (of duty) desempenho; (of debt) quitação f; (from hospital) alta; (from army) baixa; (LAW) absolvição f; (MED) secreção f

discipline ['dɪsɪplɪn] n disciplina ♦ vt disciplinar; (punish) punir

disc jockey n (on radio) radialista m/f; (in disco) discotecário(-a)

disclose [dɪs'kləʊz] vt revelar; **disclosure** n revelação f

disco ['dɪskəʊ] n abbr discoteca

discomfort [dɪs'kʌmfət] n (unease) inquietação f; (physical) desconforto

disconcert [dɪskən'sɜːt] vt desconcertar

disconnect [dɪskə'nekt] vt desligar;

(pipe, tap) desmembrar

discontent [dɪskən'tent] n descontentamento; **discontented** adj descontente

discontinue [dɪskən'tɪnjuː] vt interromper; (payments) suspender; **"~d"** (COMM) "fora de linha"

discount [n 'dɪskaʊnt, vb dɪs'kaʊnt] n desconto ♦ vt descontar; (idea) ignorar

discourage [dɪs'kʌrɪdʒ] vt (dishearten) desanimar; (advise against): **to ~ sth/sb from doing** desaconselhar algo/alguém a fazer

discover [dɪs'kʌvə*] vt descobrir; (missing person) encontrar; (mistake) achar; **discovery** n descoberta

discredit [dɪs'kredɪt] vt desacreditar; (claim) desmerecer

discreet [dɪs'kriːt] adj discreto; (careful) cauteloso

discrepancy [dɪ'skrepənsɪ] n diferença

discretion [dɪ'skreʃən] n discrição f; **at the ~ of** ao arbítrio de

discriminate [dɪ'skrɪmɪneɪt] vi: **to ~ between** fazer distinção entre; **to ~ against** discriminar contra; **discriminating** adj criterioso; **discrimination** [dɪskrɪmɪ'neɪʃən] n (discernment) discernimento; (bias) discriminação f

discuss [dɪ'skʌs] vt discutir; (analyse) analisar; **discussion** n discussão f; (debate) debate m

disdain [dɪs'deɪn] n desdém m

disease [dɪ'ziːz] n doença

disembark [dɪsɪm'bɑːk] vt, vi desembarcar

disentangle [dɪsɪn'tæŋgl] vt desvencilhar; (wool, wire) desemaraçar

disfigure [dɪs'fɪgə*] vt (person) desfigurar; (object) estragar, enfear

disgrace [dɪs'greɪs] n ignomínia; (shame) desonra ♦ vt (family) enver-

gonhar; (*name*, *country*) desonrar;
disgraceful *adj* vergonhoso;
(*behaviour*) escandaloso
disgruntled [dɪs'grʌntld] *adj* descontente
disguise [dɪs'gaɪz] *n* disfarce *m* ♦ *vt*:
to ~ (as) disfarçar (de); **in ~** disfarçado
disgust [dɪs'gʌst] *n* repugnância
♦ *vt* repugnar a, dar nojo em; **disgusting** *adj* repugnante; (*unacceptable*) inaceitável
dish [dɪʃ] *n* prato; (*serving ~*) travessa; **to do** *or* **wash the ~es** lavar os pratos *or* a louça; **dish out** *vt* repartir; **dish up** *vt* servir; **dishcloth** *n* pano de prato *or* de louça
dishearten [dɪs'hɑːtn] *vt* desanimar
dishevelled [dɪ'ʃevəld] (*US* **disheveled**) *adj* (*hair*) despenteado; (*clothes*) desalinhado
dishonest [dɪs'ɒnɪst] *adj* (*person*) desonesto; (*means*) fraudulento
dishonour [dɪs'ɒnə*] (*US* **dishonor**) *n* desonra
dishtowel ['dɪʃtauəl] (*US*) *n* pano de prato
dishwasher ['dɪʃwɔʃə*] *n* máquina de lavar louça *or* pratos
disillusion [dɪsɪ'luːʒən] *vt* desiludir
disinfectant [dɪsɪn'fektənt] *n* desinfetante *m*
disintegrate [dɪs'ɪntɪgreɪt] *vi* desintegrar-se
disjointed [dɪs'dʒɔɪntɪd] *adj* desconexo
disk [dɪsk] *n* (*COMPUT*) disco; **single-/double-sided ~** disquete de face simples/dupla; **disk drive** *n* unidade *f* de disco; **diskette** [dɪs'kɛt] (*US*) *n* = **disk**
dislike [dɪs'laɪk] *n* (*feeling*) desagrado; (*gen pl*: *object of ~*) antipatia, aversão *f* ♦ *vt* antipatizar com, não

gostar de
dislocate ['dɪsləkeɪt] *vt* deslocar
dislodge [dɪs'lɒdʒ] *vt* mover, deslocar
disloyal [dɪs'lɔɪəl] *adj* desleal
dismal ['dɪzml] *adj* (*depressing*) deprimente; (*very bad*) horrível
dismantle [dɪs'mæntl] *vt* desmontar, desmantelar
dismay [dɪs'meɪ] *n* consternação *f* ♦ *vt* consternar
dismiss [dɪs'mɪs] *vt* (*worker*) despedir; (*pupils*) dispensar; (*soldiers*) dar baixa a; (*LAW*, *possibility*) rejeitar; **dismissal** *n* demissão *f*
dismount [dɪs'maunt] *vi* (*from horse*) desmontar; (*from bicycle*) descer
disobedient *adj* desobediente
disobey [dɪsə'beɪ] *vt* desobedecer a; (*rules*) transgredir
disorder [dɪs'ɔːdə*] *n* desordem *f*; (*rioting*) distúrbios *mpl*, tumulto; (*MED*) distúrbio; (*untidy*) desarrumado; (*meeting*) tumultuado; (*behaviour*) escandaloso
disown [dɪs'əun] *vt* repudiar; (*child*) rejeitar
disparaging [dɪs'pærɪdʒɪŋ] *adj* depreciativo
dispatch [dɪs'pætʃ] *vt* (*send*: *parcel etc*) expedir; (: *messenger*) enviar ♦ *n* (*sending*) remessa, urgência; (*PRESS*) comunicado; (*MIL*) parte *f*
dispel [dɪs'pel] *vt* dissipar
dispense [dɪs'pens] *vt* (*medicine*) preparar (e vender); **dispense with** *vt fus* prescindir de; **dispenser** *n* (*device*) distribuidor *m* automático
disperse [dɪs'pəːs] *vt* espalhar; (*crowd*) dispersar ♦ *vi* dispersar-se
displace [dɪs'pleɪs] *vt* (*shift*) deslocar
display [dɪs'pleɪ] *n* (*in shop*) mostra;

(exhibition) exposição f; *(COMPUT, TECH: information)* apresentação f visual; *(: device)* display m; *(of feeling)* manifestação f ♦ vt mostrar; *(ostentatiously)* ostentar

displease [dɪsˈpliːz] vt *(offend)* ofender; *(annoy)* aborrecer; **displeased** adj: **displeased with** descontente com; *(disappointed)* aborrecido com; **displeasure** [dɪsˈplɛʒə*] n desgosto

disposable [dɪsˈpəuzəbl] adj descartável; *(income)* disponível

disposal n *(of rubbish)* destruição f; *(of property etc)* venda, traspasse m; **at sb's ~** à disposição de alguém

disposed [dɪsˈpəuzd] adj: **to be ~ to do sth** estar disposto a fazer algo; **to be well ~ towards sb** estar predisposto a favor de alguém

dispose of [dɪsˈpəuz-] vt fus *(unwanted goods)* desfazer-se de; *(problem, task)* lidar; **disposition** [dɪspəˈzɪʃən] n disposição f, *(temperament)* índole f

disprove [dɪsˈpruːv] vt refutar

dispute [dɪsˈpjuːt] n *(domestic)* briga; *(also:* **industrial ~)** conflito, disputa ♦ vt *(fact, statement)* questionar; *(ownership)* contestar

disqualify [dɪsˈkwɔlɪfaɪ] vt *(SPORT)* desclassificar; **to ~ sb for sth/from doing sth** desqualificar alguém para algo/de fazer algo

disregard [dɪsrɪˈgɑːd] vt ignorar

disreputable [dɪsˈrɛpjutəbl] adj *(person)* de má fama; *(behaviour)* vergonhoso

disrupt [dɪsˈrʌpt] vt *(plans)* desfazer; *(conversation)* perturbar, interromper

dissect [dɪˈsɛkt] vt dissecar

dissent [dɪˈsɛnt] n dissensão f

dissertation [dɪsəˈteɪʃən] n *(also:*

SCH) dissertação f, tese f

dissolve [dɪˈzɔlv] vt dissolver ♦ vi dissolver-se; **to ~ in(to) tears** debulhar-se em lágrimas

distance [ˈdɪstns] n distância; **in the ~** ao longe

distant [ˈdɪstnt] adj distante; *(manner)* afastado, reservado

distaste [dɪsˈteɪst] n repugnância; **distasteful** adj repugnante

distil [dɪsˈtɪl] *(US* **distill**) vt destilar; **distillery** n destilaria

distinct [dɪsˈtɪŋkt] adj distinto; *(clear)* claro; *(unmistakable)* nítido; **as ~ from** em oposição a; **distinction** n diferença; *(honour)* honra; *(in exam)* distinção f

distinguish [dɪsˈtɪŋgwɪʃ] vt *(differentiate)* diferenciar; *(identify)* identificar; **to ~ o.s.** distinguir-se; **distinguished** adj *(eminent)* eminente; *(in appearance)* distinto; **distinguishing** adj *(feature)* distintivo

distort [dɪsˈtɔːt] vt distorcer

distract [dɪsˈtrækt] vt distrair; *(attention)* desviar; **distracted** adj distraído; *(anxious)* aturdido; **distraction** n distração f; *(confusion)* aturdimento, perplexidade f; *(amusement)* divertimento

distraught [dɪsˈtrɔːt] adj desesperado

distress [dɪsˈtrɛs] n angústia ♦ vt afligir; **distressing** adj angustiante

distribute [dɪsˈtrɪbjuːt] vt distribuir; *(share out)* repartir, dividir; **distribution** [dɪstrɪˈbjuːʃən] n distribuição f; *(of profits)* repartição f; **distributor** n *(AUT)* distribuidor m; *(COMM)* distribuidor(a) m/f

district [ˈdɪstrɪkt] n *(of country)* região f; *(of town)* zona f; *(ADMIN)* distrito; **district attorney** *(US)* n promotor público *(promotora pública)* m/f

distrust [dɪs'trʌst] n desconfiança
♦ vt desconfiar de

disturb [dɪs'tɜːb] vt (disorganize)
perturbar; (upset) incomodar; (interrupt) atrapalhar; **disturbance** n
(upheaval) convulsão f; (political,
violent) distúrbio; (of mind) transtorno; **disturbed** adj perturbado;
(childhood) infeliz; **to be emotionally disturbed** ter problemas emocionais; **disturbing** adj perturbador(a)

ditch [dɪtʃ] n fosso; (irrigation ~)
rego ♦ vt (inf: partner) abandonar;
(: car, plan etc) desfazer-se de

dither ['dɪðə*] vi vacilar

ditto ['dɪtəu] adv idem

dive [daɪv] n (from board) salto;
(underwater) mergulho ♦ vi mergulhar; **to ~ into** (bag, drawer) enfiar a
mão em; (shop, car) entrar em;
diver n mergulhador(a) m/f

diversion [daɪ'vɜːʃən] n (BRIT: AUT)
desvio; (distraction) diversão f; (of
funds) desvio

divert [daɪ'vɜːt] vt desviar

divide [dɪ'vaɪd] vt (MATH) dividir;
(separate) separar; (share out) repartir ♦ vi dividir-se; (road) bifurcar-se;
divided highway (US) n pista dupla

dividend ['dɪvɪdend] n dividendo;
(fig): **to pay ~s** valer a pena

divine [dɪ'vaɪn] adj (also fig) divino

diving ['daɪvɪŋ] n salto; (underwater)
mergulho; **diving board** n trampolim m

divinity [dɪ'vɪnɪtɪ] n divindade f;
(SCH) teologia

division [dɪ'vɪʒən] n divisão f; (sharing out) repartição f; (disagreement)
discórdia; (FOOTBALL) grupo

divorce [dɪ'vɔːs] n divórcio ♦ vt
divorciar-se de; (dissociate) dissociar;
divorced adj divorciado; **divorcee** n divorciado(-a)

DIY n abbr = **do-it-yourself**

dizzy ['dɪzɪ] adj tonto

DJ n abbr = **disc jockey**

┌─────────────┐
│ KEYWORD │
└─────────────┘

do [duː] (pt **did**, pp **done**) vb aux
1 (in negative constructions): **I don't
understand** eu não compreendo
2 (to form questions): **didn't you
know?** você não sabia?; **what ~ you
think?** o que você acha?
3 (for emphasis, in polite expressions)
she does seem rather late ela está
muito atrasada; **~ sit down/help
yourself** sente-se/sirva-se; **~ take
care!** tome cuidado!
4 (used to avoid repeating vb): **she
swims better than I ~** ela nada melhor que eu; **~ you agree? – yes, I ~/
no, I don't** você concorda? – sim,
concordo/não, não concordo; **she
lives in Glasgow – so ~ I** ela mora
em Glasgow – eu também; **who
broke it? – I did** quem quebrou
isso? – (fui) eu
5 (in question tags): **you like him,
don't you?** você gosta dele, não é?; **he
laughed, didn't he?** ele riu, não foi?
♦ vt **1** (gen: carry out, perform etc)
fazer; **what are you ~ing tonight?** o
que você vai fazer hoje à noite?; **to
~ the washing-up/cooking** lavar a
louça/cozinhar; **to ~ one's teeth/
nails** escovar os dentes/fazer as
unhas; **to ~ one's hair** (comb)
pentear-se; (style) fazer um penteado; **we're ~ing Othello at school**
(studying) nós estamos estudando
Otelo na escola; (performing) nós
vamos encenar Otelo na escola
2 (AUT etc): **the car was ~ing 100** o
carro estava a 100 por hora; **we've
done 200 km already** nós já fizemos
200 km; **he can ~ 100 in that car** ele
consegue dar 100 nesse carro

♦ vi 1 (act, behave) fazer; ~ as I ~ faça como eu faço
2 (get on, fare) ir; how ~ you ~? como você está indo?
3 (suit) servir; will it ~? serve?
4 (be sufficient) bastar; will £10 ~? £10 dá?; that'll ~ é suficiente; that'll ~! (in annoyance) basta!, chegal; to make ~ (with) contentar-se (com)
♦ n (inf: party etc) festa; it was rather a ~ foi uma festança
do away with vt fus (kill) matar; (law etc) abolir; (withdraw) retirar
do up vt (laces) atar; (zip) fechar; (dress, skirt) abotoar; (renovate: room, house) arrumar, renovar
do with vt fus (need): I could ~ with a drink/some help eu bem que gostaria de tomar alguma coisa/ou bem que precisaria de uma ajuda; (be connected) ter a ver com; what has it got to ~ with you? o que é que isso tem a ver com você?
do without vi: if you're late for tea then you'll ~ without se você chegar atrasado ficará sem almoço ♦ vt fus passar sem

dock [dɔk] n (NAUT) doca; (LAW) banco (dos réus) ♦ vi (NAUT: enter ~) entrar no estaleiro; (SPACE) unir-se no espaço; ~s npl docas fpl; **docker** n portuário, estivador m; **dockyard** n estaleiro
doctor ['dɔktə*] n médico(-a); (PhD etc) doutor(a) m/f ♦ vt (drink etc) falsificar
document ['dɔkjumənt] n documento; **documentary** [dɔkju-'mɛntəri] adj documental ♦ n documentário
dodge [dɔdʒ] n (trick) trapaça ♦ vt esquivar-se de, evitar; (tax) sonegar; (blow) furtar-se a
Dodgems ['dɔdʒəmz] ® (BRIT) npl carros mpl de choque
does [dʌz] vb see do; **doesn't** = does not
dog [dɔg] n cachorro, cão m ♦ vt (subj: person) seguir, ir; (: bad luck) perseguir; **dog-eared** adj surrado
dogged ['dɔgid] adj tenaz, persistente
dogsbody ['dɔgzbɔdi] (BRIT: inf) n faz-tudo m/f
doings ['duːiŋz] npl atividades fpl
do-it-yourself n sistema m faça-você-mesmo
dole [dəul] (BRIT) n (payment) subsídio de desemprego; **on the ~** desempregado; **dole out** vt distribuir
doll [dɔl] n boneca; (US: inf: woman) mulher f jovem) è bonita
dollar ['dɔlə*] n dólar m
dolphin ['dɔlfin] n golfinho
dome [dəum] n (ARCH) cúpula
domestic [də'mɛstik] adj doméstico; (national) nacional; **domesticated** adj domesticado; (home-loving) prendado
dominate ['dɔmineit] vt dominar
domineering [dɔmi'niəriŋ] adj dominante, mandão(-dona)
domino ['dɔminəu] (pl ~es) n peça de dominó; ~s npl (game) dominó m
donate [də'neit] vt: to ~ (to) doar (para)
done [dʌn] pp of do
donkey ['dɔŋki] n burro
donor ['dəunə*] n doador(a) m/f; **donor card** n cartão m de doador
don't [dəunt] = do not
doodle ['duːdl] vi rabiscar
doom [duːm] n (fate) destino ♦ vt: to be ~ed to failure estar destinado or fadado ao fracasso
door [dɔː*] n porta; **doorbell** n campainha; **doorman** (irreg) n porteiro; **doormat** n capacho; **door-**

step n degrau m da porta, soleira;
doorway n vão m da porta, entrada
dope [dəup] n (inf: person) imbecil
m/f; (: drug) maconha ♦ vt (horse
etc) dopar
dormitory ['dɔ:mɪtrɪ] n dormitório;
(us) residência universitária
dormouse ['dɔ:maus] (pl dormice)
n rato (de campo)
dose [dəus] n dose f
dot [dɔt] n ponto; (speck) marca
pequena ♦ vt: **~ted with** salpicado
de; **on the ~** em ponto
dote [dəut]: **to ~ on** vt fus adorar,
idolatrar
dotted line ['dɔtɪd-] n linha ponti-
lhada
double ['dʌbl] adj duplo ♦ adv
(twice): **to cost ~ (sth)** custar o
dobro (de algo) ♦ n (person) du-
plo(-a) ♦ vt dobrar ♦ vi dobrar; **at the**
~ (BRIT), **on the ~** em passo acelerado; **double bass** n contrabaixo;
double bed n cama de casal;
double-click vi (COMPUT) dar um
clique duplo; **doublecross** vt
(trick) enganar; (betray) atraiçoar;
doubledecker n ônibus m (BR) or
autocarro (PT) de dois andares;
double room n quarto de casal
doubt [daut] n dúvida ♦ vt duvidar;
(suspect) desconfiar de; **to ~ if** or
whether duvidar que; **doubtful** adj
duvidoso; **doubtless** adv sem dúvida
dough [dəu] n massa; **doughnut**
(us donut) n sonho (BR), bola de
Berlim (PT)
dove [dʌv] n pomba
dowdy ['daudɪ] adj (clothes) desalinhado; (person) deselegante, pouco
elegante
down [daun] n (feathers) penugem f
♦ adv (~wards) para baixo; (on the
ground) por terra ♦ prep (towards

lower level) embaixo de; (movement
along) ao longo de ♦ vt (inf: drink)
tomar de um gole só; **~ with**
X! abaixo X!; **down-and-out** n
(tramp) vagabundo(-a); **down-at-**
heel adj descuidado, desmazelado;
(appearance) deselegante; **down-**
cast adj abatido; **downfall** n
queda, ruína; **downhearted** adj
desanimado; **downhill** adv: **to go**
downhill descer, ir morro abaixo;
(fig: business) degringolar
Downing Street ['daunɪŋ-] (BRIT)
n ver quadro

DOWNING STREET

Downing Street é a rua de
Westminster (Londres) onde estão
localizadas as residências oficiais
do Primeiro-ministro (número 10)
e do Ministro da Fazenda (número 11). O termo **Downing Street**
é freqüentemente utilizado para
designar o governo britânico.

---

down: download |daun'ləud| vt
(COMPUT) fazer o download de,
baixar; **downpour** n aguaceiro;
downright adj (lie) patente; (refusal) categórico; **downstairs** adv
(below) (lá) em baixo; (movements)
para baixo; **downstream** adv água
or rio abaixo; **down-to-earth** adj
prático, realista; **downtown** adv
no centro da cidade; **down under**
adv na Austrália (or Nova Zelândia);
downward adj, adv para baixo;
downwards adv = **downward**
doz. abbr (= dozen) dz.
doze [dəuz] vi dormitar; **doze off** vi
cochilar
dozen ['dʌzn] n dúzia; **a ~ books**
uma dúzia de livros; **~s of** milhares
de
Dr abbr (= doctor) Dr(a) m/f

drab [dræb] *adj* sombrio

draft [drɑːft] *n (first copy)* rascunho; *(POL: of bill)* projeto de lei; *(bank ~)* saque *m*, letra; *(US: call-up)* recrutamento ♦ *vt (plan)* esboçar; *(speech, letter)* rascunhar; *see also* **draught**

drag [dræg] *vt* arrastar; *(river)* dragar ♦ *vi* arrastar-se ♦ *n (inf)* chatice *f (BR)*, maçada *(PT)*, *(women's clothing)*: **in** ~ em travesti; **drag on** *vi* arrastar-se

dragon ['drægən] *n* dragão *m*

dragonfly ['drægənflaɪ] *n* libélula

drain [dreɪn] *n* bueiro; *(source of loss)* sorvedouro ♦ *vt (glass)* esvaziar; *(land, marshes)* drenar; *(vegetables)* coar ♦ *vi (water)* escorrer, escoar-se

drainage *n (act)* drenagem *f*; *(system)* esgoto; **drainpipe** *n* cano de esgoto

drama ['drɑːmə] *n (art)* teatro; *(play)* drama *m*; **dramatic** [drə-'mætɪk] *adj* dramático; *(theatrical)* teatral

drank [dræŋk] *pt of* **drink**

drape [dreɪp] *vt* ornar, cobrir; **drapes** *(US)* *npl* cortinas *fpl*

drastic ['dræstɪk] *adj* drástico

draught [drɑːft] *(US* **draft)** *n (of air)* corrente *f*; *(NAUT)* calado; *(beer)* chope *m*; **on** ~ *(beer)* de barril; **draughts** *(BRIT)* *n (jogo de damas)* *fpl*

draw [drɔː] *(pt* **drew**, *pp* **drawn)** *vt* desenhar; *(cart)* puxar; *(curtain)* fechar; *(gun)* sacar; *(attract)* atrair; *(money)* tirar; *(: from bank)* sacar ♦ *vi* empatar ♦ *n* empate *m*; *(lottery)* sorteio; **to** ~ **near** aproximar-se; **draw out** *vt (money)* sacar; **draw up** *vi (stop)* parar(-se) ♦ *vt (chair etc)* puxar; *(document)* redigir; **drawback** *n* inconveniente *m*, desvantagem *f*; **drawbridge** *n* ponte *f* leva-

diça; **drawer** *n* gaveta; **drawing** *n* desenho; **drawing pin** *(BRIT)* *n* tachinha *(BR)*, pionés *m (PT)*; **drawing room** *n* sala de visitas

drawl [drɔːl] *n* fala arrastada

drawn [drɔːn] *pp of* **draw**

dread [dred] *n* medo, pavor *m* ♦ *vt* temer, recear, ter medo de; **dreadful** *adj* terrível

dream [driːm] *(pt, pp* ~**ed** *or* ~**t)** *n* sonho ♦ *vt, vi* sonhar; **dreamy** *adj* sonhador(a), distraído; *(music)* sentimental

dreary ['drɪərɪ] *adj (talk, time)* monótono; *(weather)* sombrio

dregs [dregz] *npl* lia; *(of humanity)* escória, ralé *f*

drench [drentʃ] *vt* encharcar

dress [dres] *n (vestido)*; *(no pl: clothing)* traje *m* ♦ *vt* vestir; *(wound)* fazer curativo em ♦ *vi* vestir-se; **to get** ~**ed** vestir-se; **dress up** *vi* vestir-se com elegância; *(in fancy dress)* fantasiar-se; **dress circle** *(BRIT)* *n* balcão *m* nobre; **dresser** *n (BRIT: cupboard)* aparador *m*; *(US: chest of drawers)* cômoda de espelho; **dressing** *n (MED)* curativo; *(CULIN)* molho; **dressing gown** *(BRIT)* *n* roupão *m*; *(woman's)* peignoir *m*; **dressing room** *n (THEATRE)* camarim *m*; *(SPORT)* vestiário; **dressing table** *n* penteadeira *(BR)*, toucador *m (PT)*; **dressmaker** *n* costureiro(-a); **dress rehearsal** *n* ensaio geral

drew [druː] *pt of* **draw**

dribble ['drɪbl] *vi (baby)* babar ♦ *vt (ball)* driblar

dried [draɪd] *adj (fruit, beans)* seco; *(eggs, milk)* em pó

drier ['draɪə*] *n* = **dryer**

drift [drɪft] *n (of current etc)* força; *(of snow)* monte *m*; *(meaning)* sentido ♦ *vi (boat)* derivar; *(sand, snow)* amontoar-se

drill [drɪl] n furadeira; (of dentist) broca; (for mining etc) broca, furadeira; (MIL) exercícios mpl militares ♦ vt furar, brocar; (MIL) exercitar ♦ vi (for oil) perfurar

drink [drɪŋk] (pt **drank**, pp **drunk**) n bebida; (sip) gole m ♦ vt, vi beber; a ~ **of water** um copo d'água; **drinker** n bebedor(a) m/f; **drinking water** n água potável

drip [drɪp] n gotejar m; (one ~) gota, pingo; (MED) gota a gota m ♦ vi gotejar; (tap) pingar; **drip-dry** adj de lavar e vestir; **dripping** n gordura

drive [draɪv] (pt **drove**, pp **driven**) n passeio de (automóvel); (journey) trajeto, percurso; (also: **~way**) entrada; (energy) energia, vigor m; (campaign) campanha; (COMPUT: also: **disk ~**) unidade f de disco ♦ vt (car) dirigir (BR), guiar (PT); (push) empurrar; (TECH: motor) acionar; (nail etc) cravar ♦ vi (AUT: at controls) dirigir (BR), guiar (PT); (: travel) ir de carro; **left-/right-hand ~** direção à esquerda/direita; **to ~ sb mad** deixar alguém louco

drivel ['drɪvl] (inf) n bobagem f, besteira

driver ['draɪvə*] n motorista m/f; (RAIL) maquinista m; **driver's license** (US) n carteira de motorista (BR), carta de condução (PT)

driveway ['draɪvweɪ] n entrada

driving ['draɪvɪŋ] n direção f (BR), condução f (PT); **driving instructor** n instrutor(a) m/f de auto-escola (BR) ou de condução (PT); **driving licence** (BRIT) n carteira de motorista (BR), carta de condução (PT); **driving school** n auto-escola f; **driving test** n exame m de motorista

drizzle ['drɪzl] n chuvisco

drool [druːl] vi babar-se

droop [druːp] vi pender

drop [drɔp] n (of water) gota; (lessening) diminuição f; (fall: distance) declive m ♦ vt (allow to fall) deixar cair; (voice, eyes, price) baixar; (set down from car) deixar (saltar/descer); (omit) omitir ♦ vi cair; (wind) parar; **~s** npl (MED) gotas fpl; **drop off** vi (sleep) cochilar ♦ vt (passenger) deixar (saltar/descer); **drop out** vi (withdraw) retirar-se; **drop-out** n pessoa que abandona o trabalho, os estudos etc

drought [draut] n seca

drove [drəuv] pt of **drive**

drown [draun] vt afogar; (also: **~ out**: sound) encobrir ♦ vi afogar-se

drowsy ['drauzɪ] adj sonolento

drug [drʌg] n remédio, medicamento; (narcotic) droga ♦ vt drogar; **to be on ~s** estar viciado em drogas; (MED) estar sob medicação; **drug addict** n toxicômano(-a); **druggist** (US) n farmacêutico(-a); **drugstore** (US) n drogaria

drum [drʌm] n tambor m; (for oil, petrol) tambor, barril m; **~s** npl (kit) bateria; **drummer** n baterista m/f

drunk [drʌŋk] pp of **drink** ♦ adj bêbado ♦ n (also: **~ard**) bêbado(-a); **drunken** adj (laughter) de bêbado; (party) cheio de bêbado; (person) bêbado

dry [draɪ] adj seco; (day) sem chuva; (humour) irônico ♦ vt secar, enxugar; (tears) limpar ♦ vi secar; **dry up** vi secar completamente; **dry-cleaner's** n tinturaria; **dryer** n secador m; (US: spin-dryer) secadora

DSS (BRIT) n abbr (= Department of Social Security) ≈ INAMPS m

DTP n abbr (= desktop publishing) DTP m, editoração f eletrônica

dual ['dju:əl] adj dual, duplo; **dual carriageway** (BRIT) n pista dupla; **dual-purpose** adj de duplo uso

dubbed [dʌbd] adj (CINEMA) dublado

dubious ['dju:bɪəs] adj duvidoso; (reputation, company) suspeitoso

duchess ['dʌtʃɪs] n duquesa

duck [dʌk] n pato ♦ vi abaixar-se repentinamente; **duckling** ['dʌklɪŋ] n patinho

due [dju:] adj (proper) devido; (expected) esperado ♦ n: **to give sb his** (or her) ~ ser justo com alguém ♦ adv: ~ **north** exatamente ao norte; ~**s** npl (for club, union) quota; (in harbour) direitos mpl; **in ~ course** no devido tempo; (eventually) no final; ~ **to** devido a

duet [dju:'et] n dueto

dug [dʌg] pt, pp of **dig**

duke [dju:k] n duque m

dull [dʌl] adj (light) sombrio; (wit) lento; (boring) enfadonho; (sound, pain) surdo; (weather) nublado, carregado ♦ vt (pain) aliviar; (mind, senses) entorpecer

duly ['dju:lɪ] adv devidamente; (on time) no devido tempo

dumb [dʌm] adj mudo; (pej: stupid) estúpido; **dumbfounded** adj pasmado

dummy ['dʌmɪ] n (tailor's model) manequim m; (mock-up) modelo; (BRIT: for baby) chupeta ♦ adj falso

dump [dʌmp] n (also: rubbish ~) depósito de lixo; (inf: place) chiqueiro ♦ vt (put down) depositar, descarregar; (get rid of) desfazer-se de; (COMPUT) tirar um dump de

dumpling ['dʌmplɪŋ] n bolinho cozido

dunce [dʌns] n burro, ignorante m/f

dung [dʌŋ] n estrume m

dungarees [dʌŋgə'ri:z] npl ma-

cacão m (BR), fato macaco (PT)

dungeon ['dʌndʒən] n calabouço

duplex ['dju:pleks] (US) n casa geminada; (also: ~ **apartment**) duplex m

duplicate [n 'dju:plɪkət, vb 'dju:-plɪkeɪt] n (of document) duplicata; (of key) cópia ♦ vt duplicar; (photocopy) multigrafar; (repeat) reproduzir

durable ['djuərəbl] adj durável; (clothes, metal) resistente

during ['djuərɪŋ] prep durante

dusk [dʌsk] n crepúsculo, anoitecer m

dust [dʌst] n pó m, poeira ♦ vt (furniture) tirar o pó de; (cake etc): **to ~ with** polvilhar com; **dustbin** n (BRIT) lata de lixo; **duster** n pano de pó; **dustman** (BRIT) (irreg) n lixeiro, gari m (BR: inf); **dusty** adj empoeirado

Dutch [dʌtʃ] adj holandês(-esa) ♦ n (LING) holandês m ♦ adv: **let's go** ~ (inf) cada um paga o seu, vamos rachar; **the** ~ npl (people) os holandeses; **Dutchman** (irreg) n holandês m; **Dutchwoman** (irreg) n holandesa

duty ['dju:tɪ] n dever m; (tax) taxa; **on** ~ de serviço; **off** ~ de folga; **duty-free** adj livre de impostos

duvet ['du:veɪ] (BRIT) n edredom m (BR), edredão m (PT)

DVD n abbr (= digital versatile or video disc) DVD m

dwarf [dwɔ:f] (pl dwarves) n anão (anã) m/f ♦ vt ananicar

dwindle ['dwɪndl] vi diminuir

dye [daɪ] n tintura, tinta ♦ vt tingir

dynamite ['daɪnəmaɪt] n dinamite f

dyslexia [dɪs'leksɪə] n dislexia

E

E [i:] n (MUS) mi m
each [i:tʃ] adj cada inv ♦ pron cada
um(a); **~ other** um ao outro; **they
hate ~ other** (eles) se odeiam
eager ['i:gə*] adj ávido; **to be ~ for/
to do sth** ansiar por/por fazer algo
eagle ['i:gl] n águia
ear [ɪə*] n (external) orelha; (inner,
fig) ouvido; (of corn) espiga; **ear-
ache** n dor f de ouvidos; **eardrum**
n tímpano
earl [ə:l] (BRIT) n conde m
earlier ['ə:lɪə*] adj mais adiantado;
(edition) anterior ♦ adv mais cedo
early ['ə:lɪ] adv cedo; (before time)
com antecedência ♦ adj cedo;
(sooner than expected) prematuro;
(reply) pronto; (Christians, settlers)
primeiro; (man) primitivo; (life,
work) juvenil; **in the ~ or ~ in the
spring/19th century** no princípio
da primavera/do século dezenove
earmark ['ɪəmɑːk] vt: **to ~ sth for**
reservar or destinar algo para
earn [ə:n] vt ganhar; (COMM: interest)
render; (praise) merecer
earnest ['ə:nɪst] adj intenso;
(manner) sério; **in ~** a sério
earnings ['ə:nɪŋz] npl (personal)
vencimentos mpl salário, ordenado;
(of company) lucro
ear: earphones npl fones mpl de
ouvido; **earring** n brinco; **earshot**
n: **within earshot** ao alcance do
ouvido or da voz
earth [ə:θ] n terra; (BRIT: ELEC) fio
terra ♦ vt (BRIT: ELEC) ligar à terra;
earthenware n louça de barro
♦ adj de barro; **earthquake** n terremoto (BR), terramoto (PT)
ease [i:z] n facilidade f; (relaxed
state) sossego; (comfort) conforto
♦ vt facilitar; (pain, tension) aliviar;

(help pass): **to ~ sth in/out** meter/
tirar algo com cuidado; **at ~!** (MIL.)
descansar!; **ease off** vi acalmar-se;
(wind) baixar; (rain) moderar-se;
ease up vi = ease off
easel ['i:zl] n cavalete m
easily ['i:zɪlɪ] adv facilmente, fácil
(inf)
east [i:st] n leste m ♦ adj (region)
leste; (wind) do leste ♦ adv para o
leste; **the E~** o Oriente; (POL.) o leste
Easter ['i:stə*] n Páscoa; **Easter
egg** n ovo de Páscoa
easterly ['i:stəlɪ] adj (to the east)
para o leste; (from the east) do leste
eastern ['i:stən] adj do leste, oriental
eastward(s) ['i:stwəd(z)] adv ao
leste
easy ['i:zɪ] adj fácil; (comfortable) folgado, cômodo; (relaxed) natural,
complacente; (victim, prey) despro-
tegido ♦ adv: **to take it or things ~**
(not worry) levar as coisas com
calma; (go slowly) ir devagar; (rest)
descansar; **easy chair** n poltrona;
easy-going adj pacato, fácil
eat [i:t] (pt ate, pp eaten) vt, vi
comer; **eat away** vt corroer; **eat
away at** vt fus corroer; **eat into** vt
fus = eat away at
eavesdrop ['i:vzdrɔp] vi: **to ~ (on)**
escutar às escondidas
ebb [eb] n refluxo ♦ vi baixar; (fig:
also: **~ away**) declinar
ebony ['ebənɪ] n ébano
EC n abbr (= European Community)
CE f
ECB n abbr (= European Central
Bank) BCE m, Banco Central Europeu
eccentric [ɪk'sɛntrɪk] adj, n excên-
trico(-a)
echo ['ɛkəu] (pl ~es) n eco ♦ vt
ecoar, repetir ♦ vi ressoar, repetir
eclipse [ɪ'klɪps] n eclipse m

ecology [ɪ'kɔlədʒɪ] n ecologia

e-commerce n abbr (= electronic commerce) comércio eletrônico

economic [i:kə'nɔmɪk] adj econômico; (business etc) rentável; **economical** adj econômico; **economics** n economia ♦ npl aspectos mpl econômicos

economize [ɪ'kɔnɑmaɪz] vi economizar, fazer economia

economy [ɪ'kɔnəmɪ] n economia; **economy class** n (AVIAT) classe f econômica

ecstasy ['ɛkstəsɪ] n êxtase m; **ecstatic** [ɛks'tætɪk] adj extasiado

ECU [eɪkju:] n abbr (= European Currency Unit) ECU m

eczema ['ɛksɪmə] n eczema m

edge [ɛdʒ] n (of knife etc) fio; (of table, chai etc) borda; (of lake etc) margem f ♦ vt (trim) embainhar; **on ~** (fig) = **edgy**; **to ~ away from** afastar-se pouco a pouco de; **edgy** adj nervoso, inquieto

edible ['ɛdɪbl] adj comestível

Edinburgh ['ɛdɪnbərə] n Edimburgo

edit ['ɛdɪt] vt editar; (be editor of) dirigir; (cut) cortar, redigir (COMPUT, TV) editar; (CINEMA) montar; **edition** [ɪ'dɪʃən] n edição f; **editor** n redator(a) m/f; (of newspaper) diretor(a) m/f; (of column) editor(a) m/f; (of book) organizador(a) m/f; **editorial** [ɛdɪ'tɔːrɪəl] adj editorial

educate ['ɛdjukeɪt] vt educar

education [ɛdju'keɪʃən] n educação f; (schooling) ensino; (teaching) pedagogia; **educational** adj (policy, experience) educacional; (toy etc) educativo

eel [i:l] n enguia

eerie ['ɪərɪ] adj (strange) estranho; (mysterious) misterioso

effect [ɪ'fɛkt] n efeito ♦ vt (repairs)

fazer; (savings) efetuar; **to take ~** (law) entrar em vigor; (drug) fazer efeito; **in ~** na realidade; **effective** [ɪ'fɛktɪv] adj eficaz; (actual) efetivo; **effectiveness** n eficácia

efficiency [ɪ'fɪʃənsɪ] n eficiência

efficient [ɪ'fɪʃənt] adj eficiente; (machine) rentável

effort ['ɛfət] n esforço; **effortless** adj fácil

e.g. adv abbr (= exempli gratia) p. ex.

egg [ɛg] n ovo; **hard-boiled/soft-boiled ~** ovo duro/mole; **egg on** vt incitar; **eggcup** n oveiro; **egg-plant** (esp US) n beringela, **eggshell** n casca de ovo

ego ['i:gəu] n ego; **egotism** n egotismo m

Egypt ['i:dʒɪpt] n Egito; **Egyptian** [ɪ'dʒɪpʃən] adj, n egípcio(-a)

eiderdown ['aɪdədaun] n edredom m (BR), edredão m (PT)

eight [eɪt] num oito; **eighteen** [eɪ'ti:n] num dezoito; **eighth** [eɪtθ] num oitavo; **eighty** ['eɪtɪ] num oitenta

Eire ['ɛərə] n (República da) Irlanda

either ['aɪðə*] adj (one or other) um ou outro; (each) cada; (both) ambos ♦ pron: **~ (of them)** qualquer (dos dois) ♦ adv: **no, I don't ~** eu também não ♦ conj: **~ yes or no** ou sim ou não

eject [ɪ'dʒɛkt] vt expulsar

elaborate [adj ɪ'læbərɪt, vb ɪ'læbəreɪt] adj complicado ♦ vt (expand) expandir; (refine) aperfeiçoar ♦ vi: **to ~ on** acrescentar detalhes a

elastic [ɪ'læstɪk] adj elástico; (adaptable) flexível, adaptável ♦ n elástico; **elastic band** (BRIT) n elástico

elated [ɪ'leɪtɪd] adj: **to be ~** rejubilar-se

elbow ['ɛlbəu] n cotovelo

elder ['ɛldə*] *adj* mais velho ♦ *n* (*tree*) sabugueiro; (*person*) o mais velho (a mais velha); **elderly** *adj* idoso, de idade ♦ *npl*: **the elderly** as pessoas de idade, os idosos

eldest ['ɛldɪst] *adj* mais velho ♦ *n* o mais velho (a mais velha)

elect [ɪ'lɛkt] *vt* eleger ♦ *adj*: **the president ~** o presidente eleito; **to ~ to do** (*choose*) optar por fazer; **election** *n* (*voting*) votação f; (*installation*) eleição f; **electioneering** [ɪlɛkʃə'nɪərɪŋ] *n* campanha *or* propaganda eleitoral; **electorate** *n* eleitorado

electric [ɪ'lɛktrɪk] *adj* elétrico; **electrical** *adj* elétrico; **electric fire** *n* lareira elétrica

electrician [ɪlɛk'trɪʃən] *n* eletricista m/f

electricity [ɪlɛk'trɪsɪtɪ] *n* eletricidade f

electrify [ɪ'lɛktrɪfaɪ] *vt* (*fence*, RAIL) eletrificar; (*audience*) eletrizar

electronic [ɪlɛk'trɔnɪk] *adj* eletrônico; **electronic mail** *n* correio eletrônico; **electronics** *n* eletrônica

elegant ['ɛlɪgənt] *adj* (*person*, *building*) elegante; (*idea*) refinado

element ['ɛlɪmənt] *n* elemento; **elementary** [ɛlɪ'mɛntərɪ] *adj* (*gen*) elementar; (*primitive*) rudimentar; **elementary school** (*US*) *n* escola primária; *ver quadro*

ELEMENTARY SCHOOL

Nos Estados Unidos e no Canadá, uma **elementary school** (também chamada de *grade school* ou *grammar school* nos Estados Unidos) é uma escola pública onde os alunos passam de seis a oito dos primeiros anos escolares.

---

elephant ['ɛlɪfənt] *n* elefante(-a) m/f

elevator ['ɛlɪveɪtə*] (*US*) *n* elevador m

eleven [ɪ'lɛvn] *num* onze; **eleventh** *num* décimo-primeiro

elicit [ɪ'lɪsɪt] *vt*: **to ~ (from** (*information*) extrair (de); (*response*, *reaction*) provocar (de)

eligible ['ɛlɪdʒəbl] *adj* elegível, apto; **to be ~ for sth** (*job etc*) ter qualificações para algo

elm [ɛlm] *n* olmo

elongated ['iːlɔŋgeɪtɪd] *adj* alongado

elope [ɪ'ləup] *vi* fugir

eloquent ['ɛləkwənt] *adj* eloqüente

El Salvador [ɛl'sælvədɔ:*] *n* El Salvador

else [ɛls] *adv* outro, mais; **something ~** outra coisa; **nobody ~** spoke ninguém mais falou; **elsewhere** *adv* (*be*) em outro lugar (BR), noutro sítio (PT); (*go*) para outro lugar (BR), a outro sítio (PT)

elusive [ɪ'luːsɪv] *adj* esquivo; (*quality*) indescritível

e-mail [ɪ'meɪl] *n* e-mail m, correio eletrônico ♦ *vt* (*person*) enviar um e-mail a

emancipate [ɪ'mænsɪpeɪt] *vt* libertar; (*women*) emancipar

embankment [ɪm'bæŋkmənt] *n* aterro; (*of river*) dique m

embark [ɪm'bɑːk] *vi* embarcar ♦ *vt* embarcar; **to ~ on** (*fig*) empreender, começar

embarrass [ɪm'bærəs] *vt* constranger; (*politician*) embaraçar; **embarrassed** *adj* descomfortável; **embarrassing** *adj* embaraçoso, constrangedor(a); **embarrassment** *n* embaraço, constrangimento

embassy ['ɛmbəsɪ] *n* embaixada

embellish [ɪm'belɪʃ] vt embelezar; (story) florear

embers ['embəz] npl brasa, borralho, cinzas fpl

embezzle [ɪm'bezl] vt desviar

embitter [ɪm'bɪtə*] vt (person) amargurar; (relations) azedar

embody [ɪm'bɔdɪ] vt (features) incorporar; (ideas) expressar

embrace [ɪm'breɪs] vt abraçar, dar um abraço em; (include) abarcar, abranger ♦ vi abraçar-se ♦ n abraço

embroider [ɪm'brɔɪdə*] vt bordar; **embroidery** n bordado

emerald ['emərəld] n esmeralda

emerge [ɪ'mɜːdʒ] vi sair; (from sleep) acordar; (fact, idea) emergir

emergency [ɪ'mɜːdʒənsɪ] n emergência; **in an ~** em caso de urgência; **emergency cord** (us) n sinal m de alarme; **emergency exit** n saída de emergência; **emergency landing** n aterrissagem f forçada (BR), aterragem f forçosa (PT)

emigrate ['emɪgreɪt] vi emigrar

eminent ['emɪnənt] adj eminente

emit [ɪ'mɪt] vt (smoke) soltar; (smell) exalar; (sound) produzir

emotion [ɪ'məʊʃən] n emoção f; **emotional** adj (needs) emocional; (person) sentimental, emotivo; (scene) comovente; (tone) emocionante

emperor ['empərə*] n imperador m

emphasis ['emfəsɪs] (pl **emphases**) n ênfase f

emphasize ['emfəsaɪz] vt (word, point) enfatizar, acentuar; (feature) salientar

emphatic [em'fætɪk] adj (statement) vigoroso, expressivo; (person) convincente; (manner) enfático

empire ['empaɪə*] n império

employ [ɪm'plɔɪ] vt empregar; (tool) utilizar; **employee** n empre-

gado(-a); **employer** n empregador(a) m/f, patrão(-troa) m/f; **employment** n (gen) emprego; (work) trabalho

empress ['emprɪs] n imperatriz f

emptiness ['emptɪnɪs] n vazio, vácuo

empty ['emptɪ] adj vazio; (place) deserto; (house) desocupado; (threat) vão (vã) ♦ vt esvaziar; (place) evacuar ♦ vi esvaziar-se; (place) ficar deserto; **empty-handed** adj de mãos vazias

EMU n abbr (= economic and monetary union) UEM f, União Econômica e Monetária

emulate ['emjuleɪt] vt emular com

emulsion [ɪ'mʌlʃən] n emulsão f; (also: ~ **paint**) tinta plástica

enable [ɪ'neɪbl] vt: **to ~ sb to do sth** (allow) permitir que alguém faça algo; (make possible) tornar possível que alguém faça algo

enamel [ɪ'næməl] n esmalte m

enchant [ɪn'tʃɑːnt] vt encantar; **enchanting** adj encantador(a)

enc(l). abbr (in letters etc) = **enclosed; enclosure**

enclose [ɪn'kləʊz] vt (land) cercar; (with letter) anexar (BR), enviar junto (PT); **please find ~d** segue junto

enclosure [ɪn'kləʊʒə*] n cercado

encompass [ɪn'kʌmpəs] vt abranger, encerrar

encore [ɔŋ'kɔː*] excl bis!, outra! ♦ n bis m

encounter [ɪn'kaʊntə*] n encontro ♦ vt encontrar, topar com; (difficulty) enfrentar

encourage [ɪn'kʌrɪdʒ] vt (activity) encorajar; (growth) estimular; (person): **to ~ sb to do sth** animar alguém a fazer algo; **encouragement** n estímulo

encroach [ɪn'krəʊtʃ] vi: **to ~ (up)on**

invadir; (*time*) ocupar

encyclop(a)edia [ɛnsaɪkləuˈpiːdɪə] *n* enciclopédia

end [ɛnd] *n* fim *m*; (*of table, rope etc*) ponta; (*of street, town*) final *m* ♦ *vt* acabar, terminar; (*also:* **bring to an ~, put an ~ to**) acabar com, pôr fim a ♦ *vi* terminar, acabar; **in the ~** ao fim, por fim, finalmente; **on ~** na ponta; **to stand on ~** (*hair*) arrepiar-se; **for hours on ~** por horas a fio; **end up** *vi*: **to ~ up in** terminar em; (*place*) ir parar em

endanger [ɪnˈdeɪndʒə*] *vt* pôr em risco

endearing [ɪnˈdɪərɪŋ] *adj* simpático, atrativo

endeavour [ɪnˈdɛvə*] (*US* **endeavor**) *n* esforço; (*attempt*) tentativa ♦ *vi*: **to ~ to** do esforçar-se para fazer; (*try*) tentar fazer

ending [ˈɛndɪŋ] *n* fim *m*, conclusão *f*; (*of book*) desenlace *m*; (*LING*) terminação *f*

endless [ˈɛndlɪs] *adj* interminável; (*possibilities*) infinito

endorse [ɪnˈdɔːs] *vt* (*cheque*) endossar; (*approve*) aprovar; **endorsement** *n* (*BRIT*: *on driving licence*) descrição *f* das multas; (*approval*) aval *m*

endure [ɪnˈdjuə*] *vt* (*bear*) agüentar, suportar ♦ *vi* (*last*) durar

enemy [ˈɛnəmɪ] *adj*, *n* inimigo(-a)

energy [ˈɛnədʒɪ] *n* energia

enforce [ɪnˈfɔːs] *vt* (*LAW*) fazer cumprir

engage [ɪnˈgeɪdʒ] *vt* (*attention*) chamar; (*interest*) atrair; (*lawyer*) contratar; (*clutch*) engrenar ♦ *vi* engrenar; **to ~ in** dedicar-se a, ocupar-se com; **to ~ sb in conversation** travar conversa com alguém; **engaged** *adj* (*BRIT*: *phone*) ocupado (*BR*), impedido (*PT*); (: *toilet*) ocupado;

(*betrothed*) noivo; **to get engaged** ficar noivo; **engaged tone** (*BRIT*) *n* (*TEL*) sinal *m* de ocupado (*BR*) or de impedido (*PT*); **engagement** *n* encontro; (*booking*) contrato; (*to marry*) noivado; **engagement ring** *n* aliança de noivado

engaging [ɪnˈgeɪdʒɪŋ] *adj* atraente, simpático

engine [ˈɛndʒɪn] *n* (*AUT*) motor *m*; (*RAIL*) locomotiva

engineer [ɛndʒɪˈnɪə*] *n* engenheiro(-a); (*US*: *RAIL*) maquinista *m/f*; (*BRIT*: *for repairs*) técnico(-a); (*on ship*) engenheiro(-a) naval; **engineering** *n* engenharia

England [ˈɪŋglənd] *n* Inglaterra

English [ˈɪŋglɪʃ] *adj* inglês (inglesa) ♦ *n* (*LING*) inglês *m*; **the ~** *npl* (*people*) os ingleses; **English Channel** *n*: **the English Channel** o Canal da Mancha; **Englishman/woman** (*irreg*) *n* inglês (inglesa) *m/f*

engraving [ɪnˈgreɪvɪŋ] *n* gravura

engrossed [ɪnˈgrəust] *adj*: **~ in** absorto em

engulf [ɪnˈgʌlf] *vt* (*subj: fire, water*) engolfar, tragar; (: *panic, fear*) tomar conta de

enhance [ɪnˈhɑːns] *vt* (*gen*) ressaltar, salientar; (*enjoyment*) aumentar; (*beauty*) realçar; (*reputation*) melhorar; (*add to*) aumentar

enjoy [ɪnˈdʒɔɪ] *vt* gostar de; (*health, privilege*) desfrutar de; **to ~ o.s.** divertir-se; **enjoyable** *adj* agradável; **enjoyment** *n* prazer *m*

enlarge [ɪnˈlɑːdʒ] *vt* aumentar; (*PHOT*) ampliar ♦ *vi*: **to ~ on** (*subject*) desenvolver, estender-se sobre

enlighten [ɪnˈlaɪtn] *vt* (*inform*) informar, instruir; **enlightened** *adj* sábio; (*cultured*) culto; (*knowledgeable*) bem informado; (*tolerant*) compreensivo; **enlightenment** *n* esclarecimento; (HISTORY): **the Enlightenment** o Século das Luzes

enlist [ɪn'lɪst] vt alistar; (support) conseguir, aliciar ♦ vi alistar-se

enmity ['enmɪtɪ] n inimizade f

enormous [ɪ'nɔːməs] adj enorme

enough [ɪ'nʌf] adj: ~ **time/books** tempo suficiente/livros suficientes ♦ pron: **have you got ~?** você tem o suficiente? ♦ adv: **big ~** suficientemente grande; ~! basta!, chega!; **that's ~, thanks** chega, obrigado; **I've had ~ of him** estou farto dele; **which, funnily or oddly ~** ... o que, por estranho que pareça ...

enquire [ɪn'kwaɪə*] vt, vi = **inquire**

enrage [ɪn'reɪdʒ] vt enfurecer, enraivecer

enrol [ɪn'rəul] (us **enroll**) vt inscrever; (SCH) matricular ♦ vi inscrever-se; matricular-se; **enrolment** n inscrição f; (SCH) matrícula

ensure [ɪn'ʃuə*] vt assegurar

entail [ɪn'teɪl] vt implicar

enter ['entə*] vt entrar em; (club) ficar or fazer-se sócio de; (army) alistar-se em; (competition) inscrever-se em; (sb for a competition) inscrever; (write down) completar; (COMPUT) entrar com ♦ vi entrar; **enter for** vt fus inscrever-se em; **enter into** vt fus estabelecer; (plans) fazer parte de; (debate) entrar em; (agreement) chegar a, firmar

enterprise ['entəpraɪz] n empresa; (undertaking) empreendimento; (initiative) iniciativa; **enterprising** adj empreendedor(a)

entertain [entə'teɪn] vt divertir, entreter; (guest) receber (em casa); (idea) estudar; **entertainer** n artista m/f; **entertaining** adj divertido; **entertainment** n (amusement) entretenimento, diversão f; (show)

espetáculo

enthusiasm [ɪn'θuːzɪæzəm] n entusiasmo

enthusiast [ɪn'θuːzɪæst] n entusiasta m/f; **enthusiastic** [ɪnθuːzɪ-'æstɪk] adj entusiasmado; **to be enthusiastic about** entusiasmar-se por

entire [ɪn'taɪə*] adj inteiro; **entirely** adv totalmente, completamente; **entirety** [ɪn'taɪərətɪ] n: **in its entirety** na sua totalidade

entitle [ɪn'taɪtl] vt: **to ~ sb to sth** dar a alguém direito a algo; **entitled** [ɪn'taɪtld] adj (book etc) intitulado; **to be entitled to do** ter direito de fazer

entrance [n 'entrns, vb ɪn'trɑːns] n entrada; (arrival) chegada ♦ vt encantar, fascinar; **to gain ~ to** (university etc) ser admitido em; **entrance examination** n exame m de admissão; **entrance fee** n jóia

entrant ['entrənt] n participante m/f; (BRIT: in exam) candidato(a)

entrepreneur [ɔntrəprə'nɜː*] n empresário(-a)

entrust [ɪn'trʌst] vt: **to ~ sth to sb** confiar algo a alguém

entry ['entrɪ] n entrada; (in competition) participante m/f; (in register) registro, assentamento; (in account) lançamento; (in dictionary) verbete m; (arrival) chegada; **"no ~"** "entrada proibida"; (AUT) "contramão" (RR), "entrada proibida" (PT); **entry phone** (BRIT) n interfone m (em apartamento)

envelope ['envələup] n envelope m

envious ['envɪəs] adj invejoso; (look) de inveja

environment [ɪn'vaɪərnmənt] n meio ambiente m; **environmental** [ɪnvaɪərn'mentl] adj ambiental; **environmentally friendly** adj (products, industry) não agressivo ao meio ambiente

envisage [ɪn'vɪzɪdʒ] *vt* prever

envoy ['ɛnvɔɪ] *n* enviado(-a)

envy ['ɛnvɪ] *n* inveja ♦ *vt* ter inveja de; **to ~ sb sth** invejar alguém por algo, cobiçar algo de alguém

epic ['ɛpɪk] *n* epopéia ♦ *adj* épico

epidemic [ɛpɪ'dɛmɪk] *n* epidemia

epilepsy ['ɛpɪlɛpsɪ] *n* epilepsia

episode ['ɛpɪsəʊd] *n* episódio

epitomize [ɪ'pɪtəmaɪz] *vt* epitomar, resumir

equal ['iːkwl] *adj* igual; (*treatment*) equitativo, equivalente ♦ *n* igual *m/f* ♦ *vt* ser igual a; **to be ~ to** (*task*) estar à altura de; **equality** [iːˈkwɔlɪtɪ] *n* igualdade *f*; **equalize** *vi* igualar; (*SPORT*) empatar; **equally** *adv* igualmente; (*share etc*) por igual

equate [ɪ'kweɪt] *vt*: **to ~ sth with** equiparar algo com

equator [ɪ'kweɪtə*] *n* equador *m*

equilibrium [iːkwɪ'lɪbrɪəm] *n* equilíbrio

equip [ɪ'kwɪp] *vt* equipar; (*person*) prover, munir; **to be well ~ped** estar bem preparado *or* equipado; **equipment** *n* equipamento; (*machines*) equipamentos *mpl*, aparelhagem *f*

equivalent [ɪ'kwɪvələnt] *adj*: **~ (to)** equivalente (a) ♦ *n* equivalente *m*

era ['ɪərə] *n* era, época

erase [ɪ'reɪz] *vt* apagar; **eraser** *n* borracha (de apagar)

erect [ɪ'rɛkt] *adj* (*posture*) ereto; (*tail, ears*) levantado ♦ *vt* erigir, levantar; (*assemble*) montar; **erection** *n* construção *f*; (*of tent, PHYSIO*) ereção *f*; (*assembly*) montagem *f*

ERM *n abbr* (= *Exchange Rate Mechanism*) SME *m*

erode [ɪ'rəʊd] *vt* (*GEO*) causar erosão em; (*confidence*) minar

erotic [ɪ'rɔtɪk] *adj* erótico

errand ['ɛrnd] *n* recado, mensagem *f*

erratic [ɪ'rætɪk] *adj* imprevisível

error ['ɛrə*] *n* erro

erupt [ɪ'rʌpt] *vi* entrar em erupção; (*fig*) explodir, estourar; **eruption** *n* erupção *f*; explosão *f*

escalate ['ɛskəleɪt] *vi* intensificar-se

escalator ['ɛskəleɪtə*] *n* escada rolante

escapade [ɛskə'peɪd] *n* peripécia

escape [ɪ'skeɪp] *n* fuga; (*of gas*) escapatória ♦ *vi* escapar; (*flee*) fugir, evadir-se; (*leak*) vazar, escapar ♦ *vt* fugir de; (*elude*): **his name ~s me** o nome dele me foge da memória; **to ~ from** (*place*) escapar de; (*person*) escapulir de

escort [*n* 'ɛskɔ:t, *vb* ɪs'kɔ:t] *n* acompanhante *m/f*; (*MIL*) escolta ♦ *vt* acompanhar

Eskimo ['ɛskɪməʊ] *n* esquimó *m/f*

especially [ɪ'spɛʃlɪ] *adv* (*above all*) sobretudo; (*particularly*) em particular

espionage ['ɛspɪənɑːʒ] *n* espionagem *f*

Esquire [ɪ'skwaɪə*] *n* (*abbr Esq.*): **J. Brown, ~ Sr.** J. Brown

essay ['ɛseɪ] *n* ensaio

essence ['ɛsns] *n* essência

essential [ɪ'sɛnʃl] *adj* (*necessary*) indispensável; (*basic*) essencial ♦ *n* elemento essencial

establish [ɪ'stæblɪʃ] *vt* estabelecer; (*facts*) verificar; (*proof*) demonstrar; (*reputation*) firmar; **established** *adj* consagrado; (*business*) estabelecido; **establishment** *n* estabelecimento; **the Establishment** a classe dirigente

estate [ɪ'steɪt] *n* (*land*) fazenda (*BR*), propriedade *f* (*PT*); (*LAW*) herança; (*POL*) estado; (*BRIT: also: housing ~*) conjunto habitacional; **estate agent** (*BRIT*) *n* corretor(a) *m/f* de imóveis (*BR*), agente *m/f* imobiliário(-a) (*PT*); **estate car** (*BRIT*) *n* perua (*BR*), canadiana (*PT*)

esteem [ɪ'stiːm] *n*: **to hold sb in high ~** estimar muito alguém

esthetic [ɪs'θetɪk] (*US*) *adj* = **aesthetic**

estimate [*n* 'estɪmət, *vb* 'estɪmeɪt] *n* (*assessment*) avaliação *f*; (*calculation*) cálculo; (*COMM*) orçamento ♦ *vt* estimar, avaliar, calcular; **estimation** [estɪ'meɪʃən] *n* opinião *f*; cálculo

etc. *abbr* (= *et cetera*) etc.

eternal [ɪ'təːnl] *adj* eterno

eternity [ɪ'təːnɪtɪ] *n* eternidade *f*

ethical ['eθɪkl] *adj* ético

ethics ['eθɪks] *n* ética ♦ *npl* moral *f*

Ethiopia [iːθɪ'əupɪə] *n* Etiópia

ethnic ['eθnɪk] *adj* étnico; (*culture*) folclórico

etiquette ['etɪket] *n* etiqueta

EU *n* *abbr* (= *European Union*) UE *f*

euro ['juərəu] *n* (*currency*) euro *m*

Eurocheque ['juərəutʃek] *n* eurocheque *m*

Europe ['juərəp] *n* Europa; **European** [juərə'piːən] *adj*, *n* europeu (-péia); **European Union** *n*: **the European Union** a União Européia

evacuate [ɪ'vækjueɪt] *vt* evacuar

evade [ɪ'veɪd] *vt* (*person*) evitar; (*question*, *duties*) evadir; (*tax*) sonegar

evaporate [ɪ'væpəreɪt] *vi* evaporar-se

evasion [ɪ'veɪʒən] *n* fuga; (*of tax*) sonegação *f*

eve [iːv] *n*: **on the ~ of** na véspera de

even ['iːvn] *adj* (*level*) plano; (*smooth*) liso; (*equal*) igual; (*number*) par ♦ *adv* até, mesmo; (*showing surprise*) até (mesmo); (*introducing a comparison*) ainda; **~ if** mesmo que; **~ though** mesmo que, embora; **~ more** ainda mais; **~ so** mesmo assim; **not ~** nem; **to get ~ with sb**

ficar quite com alguém; **even out** *vi* nivelar-se

evening ['iːvnɪŋ] *n* (*early*) tarde *f*; (*late*) noite *f*; (*event*) noitada; **in the ~** à noite; **evening class** *n* aula noturna; **evening dress** *n* (*man's*) traje *m* de rigor (*BR*) or de cerimónia (*PT*); (*woman's*) vestido de noite

event [ɪ'vent] *n* acontecimento; (*SPORT*) prova; **in the ~ of** no caso de; **eventful** *adj* movimentado, cheio de acontecimentos; (*game etc*) cheio de emoção, agitado

eventual [ɪ'ventʃuəl] *adj* final; **eventually** *adv* finalmente; (*in time*) por fim

ever ['evə*] *adv* (*always*) sempre; (*at any time*) em qualquer momento; (*in question*): **why ~ not?** por que não?, **the best ~** o melhor que já se viu; **have you ~ seen it?** você alguma vez já viu isto?; **better than ~** melhor que nunca; **~ since** ♦ *adv* desde então ♦ *conj* depois que; **evergreen** *n* sempre-verde *m*; **everlasting** *adj* eterno, perpétuo

┌─────────────────────────┐
│ *KEYWORD* │
└─────────────────────────┘

every ['evrɪ] *adj* **1** (*each*) cada; **~ one of them** cada um deles; **~ shop in the town was closed** todas as lojas da cidade estavam fechadas **2** (*all possible*) todo(-a); **I have ~ confidence in her** tenho absoluta confiança nela; **we wish you ~ success** desejamo-lhe o maior sucesso; **he's ~ bit as clever as his brother** ele é tão inteligente quanto o irmão **3** (*showing recurrence*) todo(-a); **~ other car had been broken into** cada dois carros foram arrombados; **she visits me ~ other/third day** ele me visita cada dois/três dias; **~ now and then** or **every now and then** de vez em quando

everybody ['εvrɪbɔdɪ] *pron* todos, todo mundo (*BR*), toda a gente (*PT*)

everyday ['εvrɪdeɪ] *adj* (*daily*) diário; (*usual*) corrente; (*common*) comum

everyone ['εvrɪwʌn] *pron* = **everybody**

everything ['εvrɪθɪŋ] *pron* tudo

everywhere ['εvrɪwεə*] *adv* (*be*) em todo lugar (*BR*), em toda a parte (*PT*); (*go*) a todo lugar (*BR*), a toda a parte (*PT*); (*wherever*): ~ **you go you meet** ... aonde quer que se vá, encontra-se ...

evict [ɪ'vɪkt] *vt* despejar

evidence ['εvɪdəns] *n* (*proof*) prova(s) *f* (*pl*); (*of witness*) testemunho, depoimento; (*indication*) sinal *m*; **to give** ~ testemunhar, prestar depoimento

evident ['εvɪdənt] *adj* evidente; **evidently** *adv* evidentemente; (*apparently*) aparentemente

evil ['iːvl] *adj* mau (má) ♦ *n* mal *m*, maldade *f*

evoke [ɪ'vəuk] *vt* evocar

evolution [iːvə'luːʃən] *n* evolução *f*; (*development*) desenvolvimento

evolve [ɪ'vɔlv] *vt* desenvolver ♦ *vi* desenvolver-se

ex- [εks] *prefix* ex-

exact [ɪg'zækt] *adj* exato; (*person*) meticuloso ♦ *vt*: **to** ~ **sth (from)** exigir algo (de); **exacting** *adj* exigente; (*conditions*) difícil; **exactly** *adv* exatamente; (*indicating agreement*) isso mesmo

exaggerate [ɪg'zædʒəreɪt] *vt*, *vi* exagerar; **exaggeration** [ɪgzædʒə-'reɪʃən] *n* exagero

exam [ɪg'zæm] *n abbr* = **examination**

examination [ɪgzæmɪ'neɪʃən] *n* exame *m*; (*inquiry*) investigação *f*

examine [ɪg'zæmɪn] *vt* examinar; (*inspect*) inspecionar; **examiner** *n* examinador(a) *m/f*

example [ɪg'zɑːmpl] *n* exemplo; **for** ~ por exemplo

exasperate [ɪg'zɑːspəreɪt] *vt* exasperar, irritar

excavate ['εkskəveɪt] *vt* escavar

exceed [ɪk'siːd] *vt* exceder; (*number*) ser superior a; (*speed limit*) ultrapassar; (*limits*) ir além de; (*powers*) exceder-se em; (*hopes*) superar; **exceedingly** *adv* extremamente

excellent ['εksələnt] *adj* excelente

except [ɪk'sεpt] *prep* (*also*: ~ **for**, ~**ing**) exceto, a não ser ♦ *vt* excluir; ~ **if/when** a menos que, a não ser que; **exception** *n* exceção *f*; **to take exception to** ressentir-se de

excerpt ['εksəːpt] *n* trecho

excess [ɪk'sεs] *n* excesso; **excess baggage** *n* excesso de bagagem; **excess fare** (*BRIT*) *n* (*RAIL*) sobretaxa de excesso; **excessive** *adj* excessivo

exchange [ɪks'tʃeɪndʒ] *n* troca; (*of teachers, students*) intercâmbio; (*also*: **telephone** ~) estação *f* telefônica (*BR*), central *f* telefónica (*PT*) ♦ *vt*: **to** ~ **(for)** trocar (por); **exchange rate** *n* (taxa de) câmbio

Exchequer [ɪks'tʃεkə*] (*BRIT*) *n*: **the** ~ ≈ o Tesouro Nacional

excite [ɪk'saɪt] *vt* excitar; **to get** ~**d** entusiasmar-se; **excitement** *n* emoções *fpl*; (*agitation*) agitação *f*; **exciting** *adj* emocionante, empolgante

exclaim [ɪk'skleɪm] *vi* exclamar; **exclamation** [εksklə'meɪʃən] *n* exclamação *f*; **exclamation mark** *n* ponto de exclamação (*BR*) or de admiração (*PT*)

exclude [ɪkˈskluːd] vt excluir

exclusive [ɪkˈskluːsɪv] adj exclusivo; **~ of tax** sem incluir os impostos

excruciating [ɪkˈskruːʃieɪtɪŋ] adj doloroso, martirizante

excursion [ɪkˈskəːʃən] n excursão f

excuse [n ɪksˈkjuːs, vb əksˈkjuːz] n desculpa ♦ vt desculpar, perdoar; **to ~ sb from doing sth** dispensar alguém de fazer algo; **~ me!** desculpe!; **if you will ~ me ...** com a sua licença ...

ex-directory (BRIT) adj: **~ (phone) number** número que não figura na lista telefônica

execute [ˈeksɪkjuːt] vt (plan) realizar; (order) cumprir; (person, movement) executar; **execution** n realização f; (killing) execução f

executive [ɪgˈzekjutɪv] adj, n executivo(-a)

exempt [ɪgˈzempt] adj isento ♦ vt: **to ~ sb from** dispensar or isentar alguém de

exercise [ˈeksəsaɪz] n exercício ♦ vt exercer; (right) valer-se de; (dog) levar para passear; (mind) ocupar ♦ vi (also: **to take ~**) fazer exercício; **exercise book** n caderno

exert [ɪgˈzəːt] vt exercer; **to ~ o.s.** esforçar-se, empenhar-se; **exertion** n esforço

exhale [eksˈheɪl] vt expirar; (air) exalar; (smoke) emitir ♦ vi expirar

exhaust [ɪgˈzɔːst] n (AUTO: also: **~ pipe**) escape m, exaustor m; (fumes) escapamento (de gás) ♦ vt esgotar; **exhaustion** n exaustão f

exhibit [ɪgˈzɪbɪt] n (ART) obra exposta; (LAW) objeto exposto ♦ vt (courage) manifestar, mostrar; (quality, emotion) demonstrar; (paintings) expor; **exhibition** [eksɪˈbɪʃən] n exposição f; (of talent etc) mostra f

exhilarating [ɪgˈzɪləreɪtɪŋ] adj esti-

mulante, tônico

exile [ˈeksaɪl] n exílio; (person) exilado(-a) ♦ vt desterrar, exilar

exist [ɪgˈzɪst] vi existir; (live) viver; **existence** n existência; vida; **existing** adj atual

exit [ˈeksɪt] n saída ♦ vi (COMPUT, THEATRE) sair

exonerate [ɪgˈzɔnəreɪt] vt: **to ~ from** desobrigar de; (guilt) isentar de

exotic [ɪgˈzɔtɪk] adj exótico

expand [ɪkˈspænd] vt aumentar ♦ vi aumentar; (gas etc) expandir-se; (metal) dilatar-se

expanse [ɪkˈspæns] n extensão f

expansion [ɪkˈspænʃən] n (of town) desenvolvimento; (of trade) expansão f; (of population) aumento

expect [ɪkˈspekt] vt esperar; (suppose) supor; (require) exigir ♦ vi: **to be ~ing** estar grávida; **expectant mother** n gestante f; **expectation** [ekspekˈteɪʃən] n esperança; (belief) expectativa

expedient [ekˈspiːdɪənt] adj conveniente, oportuno ♦ n expediente m, recurso

expedition [ekspəˈdɪʃən] n expedição f

expel [ɪkˈspel] vt expelir; (from place, school) expulsar

expend [ɪkˈspend] vt gastar; **expenditure** [ɪksˈpendɪtʃə*] n gastos mpl; (of energy) consumo

expense [ɪkˈspens] n gasto, despesa; (expenditure) despesas fpl; **~s** npl (costs) despesas fpl; **at the ~ of** à custa de; **expense account** n relatório de despesas

expensive [ɪkˈspensɪv] adj caro

experience [ɪkˈspɪərɪəns] n experiência ♦ vt (situation) enfrentar; (feeling) sentir; **experienced** adj experiente

experiment [ɪk'spɛrɪmənt] n experimento, experiência ♦ vi: **to ~ (with/on)** fazer experiências (com/em)

expert ['ɛkspɔ:t] adj hábil, perito ♦ n especialista m/f; **expertise** [ɛkspɔ:'ti:z] n perícia

expire [ɪk'spaɪə*] vi expirar; (run out) vencer; **expiry** n expiração f, vencimento

explain [ɪk'spleɪn] vt explicar; (clarify) esclarecer; **explanatory** [ɪks'plænətrɪ] adj explicativo

explicit [ɪk'splɪsɪt] adj explícito

explode [ɪk'spləud] vi estourar, explodir

exploit [n 'ɛksplɔɪt, vb ɪks'plɔɪt] n façanha ♦ vt explorar; **exploitation** [ɛksplɔɪ'teɪʃən] n exploração f

explore [ɪk'splɔ:*] vt explorar; (fig) examinar, pesquisar; **explorer** n explorador(a) m/f

explosion [ɪk'spləuʒən] n explosão f

explosive [ɪk'spləusɪv] adj explosivo ♦ n explosivo

export [vb ɛks'pɔ:t, n 'ɛkspɔ:t] vt exportar ♦ n exportação f ♦ cpd de exportação; **exporter** n exportador(a) m/f

expose [ɪk'spəuz] vt expor; (unmask) desmascarar; **exposed** adj (house etc) desabrigado

exposure [ɪk'spəuʒə*] n exposição f; (publicity) publicidade f; (PHOT) revelação f; **to die from ~** (MED) morrer de frio

express [ɪk'sprɛs] adj expresso, explícito; (BRIT: letter etc) urgente ♦ n rápido ♦ vt exprimir, expressar; (quantity) representar; **expression** n expressão f; **expressly** adv expressamente; **expressway** (US) n rodovia (BR), auto-estrada (PT)

exquisite [ɛk'skwɪzɪt] adj requintado

extend [ɪk'stɛnd] vt (visit, street) prolongar; (building) aumentar; (offer) fazer; (hand) estender

extension [ɪk'stɛnʃən] n (ELEC) extensão f; (building) acréscimo, expansão f; (of time) prorrogação f; (of rights) ampliação f; (TEL) ramal m (BR), extensão f (PT); (of deadline) prolongamento, prorrogação f

extensive [ɪk'stɛnsɪv] adj extenso; (damage) considerável; (coverage) amplo; (broad) vasto, amplo; **extensively** adv: **he's travelled extensively** ele já viajou bastante

extent [ɪk'stɛnt] n (breadth) extensão f; (of damage etc) dimensão f; (scope) alcance m; **to some ~** até certo ponto

exterior [ɛk'stɪərɪə*] adj externo ♦ n exterior m; (appearance) aspecto

external [ɛk'stə:nl] adj externo

extinct [ɪk'stɪŋkt] adj extinto

extinguish [ɪk'stɪŋgwɪʃ] vt extinguir

extort [ɪk'stɔ:t] vt extorquir; **extortionate** adj extorsivo, excessivo

extra ['ɛkstrə] adj adicional ♦ adv adicionalmente ♦ n (luxury) luxo; (surcharge) extra m, suplemento; (CINEMA, THEATRE) figurante m/f

extract [vb ɪks'trækt, n 'ɛkstrækt] vt tirar, extrair; (tooth) arrancar; (mineral) extrair; (money) extorquir; (promise) conseguir, obter ♦ n extrato

extradite ['ɛkstrədaɪt] vt (from country) extraditar; (to country) obter a extradição de

extraordinary [ɪk'strɔ:dnrɪ] adj extraordinário; (odd) estranho

extravagance [ɪk'strævəgəns] n extravagância; (no pl: spending) esbanjamento

extravagant [ɪk'strævəgənt] adj

(lavish) extravagante; *(wasteful)* gastador(a), esbanjador(a)

extreme [ɪkˈstriːm] *adj* extremo ♦ *n* extremo; **extremely** *adv* muito, extremamente

extrovert [ˈekstrəvɜːt] *n* extrovertido(-a)

eye [aɪ] *n* olho; *(of needle)* buraco ♦ *vt* olhar, observar; **to keep an** ~ **on** vigiar, ficar de olho em; **eyebrow** *n* sobrancelha; **eyedrops** *npl* gotas *fpl* para os olhos; **eyelash** *n* cílio; **eyelid** *n* pálpebra; **eyeliner** *n* delineador *m*; **eye-opener** *n* revelação *f*, grande surpresa; **eyeshadow** *n* sombra de olhos; **eyesight** *n* vista, visão *f*; **eyesore** *n* monstruosidade *f*; **eye witness** *n* testemunha *m/f* ocular

F

F [ɛf] *n* (MUS) fá *m* ♦ *abbr* = Fahrenheit
fable [ˈfeɪbl] *n* fábula
fabric [ˈfæbrɪk] *n* tecido, pano
face [feɪs] *n* cara, rosto; *(grimace)* careta; *(of clock)* mostrador *m*; *(side)* superfície *f*; *(of building)* frente *f*, fachada ♦ *vt (facts)* enfrentar; *(direction)* dar para; *(card)* virado para baixo; **to lose** ~ perder o prestígio; **to save** ~ salvar as aparências; **to make** *or* **pull a** ~ fazer careta; **in the** ~ **of** diante de, à vista de; **on the** ~ **of it** a julgar pelas aparências, à primeira vista; **face up to** *vt fus* enfrentar; **face cloth** *(BRIT)* *n* toalhinha de rosto; **face cream** *n* creme *m* facial; **face lift** *n* (operação *f*) plástica; *(of façade)* remodelamento; **face powder** *n* pó *m* de arroz; **face value** *n* *(of coin, stamp)* valor *m* nominal; **to take sth at face value** *(fig)* tomar algo em sentido literal

facilities [fəˈsɪlɪtɪz] *npl* facilidades *fpl*, instalações *fpl*; **credit** ~ crediário
facing [ˈfeɪsɪŋ] *prep* de frente para
facsimile [fækˈsɪmɪlɪ] *n* fac-símile *m*
fact [fækt] *n* fato; **in** ~ realmente, na verdade
factor [ˈfæktə*] *n* fator *m*
factory [ˈfæktərɪ] *n* fábrica
factual [ˈfæktjuəl] *adj* real, fatual
faculty [ˈfækəltɪ] *n* faculdade *f*; *(US)* corpo docente
fad [fæd] *(inf)* *n* mania, modismo
fade [feɪd] *vi* desbotar; *(sound, hope)* desvanecer-se; *(light)* apagar-se; *(flower)* murchar
fag [fæg] *(BRIT: inf)* *n* cigarro
fail [feɪl] *vt (candidate)* reprovar; *(exam)* não passar em, ser reprovado em; *(subj: leader)* fracassar; *(: courage)* faltar; **his courage ~ed him** faltou-lhe coragem; *(: memory)* falhar ♦ *vi* fracassar; *(brakes)* falhar; *(health)* deteriorar; *(light)* desaparecer; **to** ~ **to do sth** deixar de fazer algo; *(be unable)* não conseguir fazer algo; **without** ~ sem falta; **failing** *n* defeito ♦ *prep* na *or* à falta de; **failing that** senão; **failure** *n* fracasso; *(mechanical)* falha
faint [feɪnt] *adj* fraco; *(recollection)* vago; *(mark)* indistinto; *(smell)* leve ♦ *n* desmaio ♦ *vi* desmaiar; **to feel** ~ sentir tonteira
fair [fɛə*] *adj* justo; *(hair)* louro; *(complexion)* branco; *(weather)* bom; *(good enough)* razoável; *(sizeable)* considerável ♦ *adv*; **to play** ~ fazer jogo limpo ♦ *n* *(also:* **trade** ~*)* feira; *(BRIT: funfair)* parque *m* de diversões; **fairly** *adv (justly)* com justiça; *(quite)* bastante; **fairness** *n* justiça; *(impartiality)* imparcialidade *f*
fairy [ˈfɛərɪ] *n* fada
faith [feɪθ] *n* fé *f*; *(trust)* confiança;

(*denomination*) seita; **faithful** *adj*
fiel; (*account*) exato; **faithfully** *adv*
fielmente; **yours faithfully** (*BRIT: in
letters*) atenciosamente

fake [feɪk] *n* (*painting etc*) falsificação *f*; (*person*) impostor(a) *m/f*
♦ *adj* falso ♦ *vt* fingir; (*painting etc*)
falsificar

falcon ['fɔːlkən] *n* falcão *m*

fall [fɔːl] (*pt* **fell**, *pp* **fallen**) *n* queda;
(*US: autumn*) outono *m* ♦ *vi* cair; (*price*)
baixar; (*country*) render-se; **~s** *npl*
(*waterfall*) cascata, queda d'água;
to ~ flat cair de cara no chão; (*plan*)
falhar; (*joke*) não agradar; **fall back**
vi retroceder; **fall back on** *vt fus*
recorrer a; **fall behind** *vi* ficar para
trás; **fall down** *vi* (*person*) cair;
(*building*) desabar; **fall for** *vt fus*
(*trick*) cair em; (*person*) enamorar-se
de; **fall in** *vi* ruir; (*MIL*) alinhar-se;
fall off *vi* cair; (*diminish*) declinar,
diminuir; **fall out** *vi* cair; (*friends
etc*) brigar; **fall through** *vi* furar

fallacy ['fæləsɪ] *n* erro; (*misconception*) falácia

fallout ['fɔːlaut] *n* chuva radioativa

false [fɔːls] *adj* falso; **under ~ pre-
tences** por meios fraudulentos;
false teeth (*BRIT*) *npl* dentadura
postiça

falter ['fɔːltə*] *vi* (*engine*) falhar;
(*person*) vacilar

fame [feɪm] *n* fama

familiar [fə'mɪlɪə*] *adj* (*well-known*)
conhecido; (*tone*) familiar, íntimo;
to be ~ with (*subject*) estar familiarizado com

family ['fæmɪlɪ] *n* família

famine ['fæmɪn] *n* fome *f*

famished ['fæmɪʃt] *adj* faminto

famous ['feɪməs] *adj* famoso, célebre

fan [fæn] *n* (*hand-held*) leque *m*;
(*ELEC*) ventilador *m*; (*person*) fã *m/f*

(*BR*), fan *m/f* (*PT*) ♦ *vt* abanar; (*fire,
quarrel*) atiçar; **fan out** *vi* espalhar-
se

fanatic [fə'nætɪk] *n* fanático(-a)

fan belt *n* correia do ventilador (*BR*)
or da ventoinha (*PT*)

fancy ['fænsɪ] *n* capricho; (*imagination*) imaginação *f*; (*fantasy*) fantasia
♦ *adj* ornamental; (*clothes*) extravagante; (*food*) elaborado; (*luxury*)
luxoso ♦ *vt* desejar, querer; (*imagine*)
imaginar; (*think*) acreditar, achar; **to
take a ~ to** tomar gosto por; **he fan-
cies her** (*inf*) ele está a fim dela;
fancy dress *n* fantasia

fang [fæŋ] *n* presa

fantastic [fæn'tæstɪk] *adj* fantástico

fantasy ['fæntəsɪ] *n* (*dream*) sonho;
(*unreality*) fantasia; (*imagination*)
imaginação *f*

far [fɑː*] *adj* (*distant*) distante ♦ *adv*
muito; (*also: ~ away, ~ off*) longe;
at the ~ side/end do lado/extremo
mais afastado; **~ better** muito melhor; **~ from** longe de; **by ~** de
longe; **go as ~ as the farm** vá até a
(*BR*) or à (*PT*) fazenda; **as ~ as I know**
que eu saiba; **how ~?** até onde?;
(*fig*) até que ponto?; **faraway**
['fɑːrəweɪ] *adj* remoto, distante

farce [fɑːs] *n* farsa

fare [feə*] *n* (*on trains, buses*) preço
(da passagem); (*in taxi: cost*) tarifa;
(*food*) comida; **half/full ~** meia/
inteira passagem

Far East *n*: **the ~** o Extremo Oriente

farewell [feə'wel] *excl* adeus ♦ *n*
despedida

farm [fɑːm] *n* fazenda (*BR*), quinta
(*PT*) ♦ *vt* cultivar; **farmer** *n* fazen-
deiro(-a), agricultor *m*; **farmhand**
n lavrador(a) *m/f*, trabalhador(a)
m/f; **farmhouse** *n* casa da fazenda
(*BR*) or da quinta (*PT*); **farming** *n*
agricultura; (*tilling*) cultura; (*of ani-*

mals) criação f; **farmland** n terra de cultivo; **farmyard** n curral m

far-reaching [-'ri:tʃɪŋ] adj de grande alcance, abrangente

fart [fɑːt] *(inf!)* vi soltar um peido (!), peidar (!)

farther ['fɑːðə*] adv mais longe ♦ adj mais distante, mais afastado

farthest ['fɑːðɪst] superl of **far**

fascinate ['fæsɪneɪt] vt fascinar

fascism ['fæʃɪzəm] n fascismo

fashion ['fæʃən] n moda; (~ *industry)* indústria da moda; *(manner)* maneira f ♦ vt modelar, dar feitio a; **in ~** na moda; **fashionable** adj da moda, elegante; **fashion show** n desfile m de modas

fast [fɑːst] adj rápido; *(dye, colour)* firme, permanente; *(clock)*: **to be ~** estar adiantado ♦ adv rápido, rapidamente, depressa; *(stuck, held)* firmemente ♦ n jejum m ♦ vi jejuar; **~ asleep** dormindo profundamente

fasten ['fɑːsn] vt fixar, prender; *(coat)* fechar; *(belt)* apertar ♦ vi prender-se, fixar-se; **fastener** n presilha, fecho; **fastening** n = **fastener**

fast food n fast food f

fat [fæt] adj gordo; *(book)* grosso; *(wallet)* recheado; *(profit)* grande ♦ n gordura; *(lard)* banha, gordura

fatal ['feɪtl] adj fatal; *(injury)* mortal

fate [feɪt] n destino; *(of person)* sorte f; **fateful** adj fatídico

father ['fɑːðə*] n pai m; **father-in-law** n sogro; **fatherly** adj paternal

fathom ['fæðəm] n braça ♦ vt compreender

fatigue [fə'tiːg] n fadiga, cansaço

fatten ['fætn] vt, vi engordar

fatty ['fætɪ] adj *(food)* gorduroso ♦ n *(inf)* gorducho m

faucet ['fɔːsɪt] *(US)* n torneira

fault [fɔːlt] n *(blame)* culpa; *(defect*

mals) criação f; **farmland** n terra

defeito; *(GEO)* falha; *(TENNIS)* falta, bola fora ♦ vt criticar; **to find ~ with** criticar, queixar-se de; **at ~** culpado; **faulty** adj defeituoso

favour ['feɪvə*] *(US* **favor***)* n favor m ♦ vt favorecer; *(assist)* auxiliar; **to do sb a ~** fazer favor a alguém; **to find ~ with** cair nas boas graças de; **in ~ of** em favor de; **favourite** ['feɪvrɪt] adj predileto ♦ n favorito(-a)

fawn [fɔːn] n cervo novo, cervato ♦ adj *(also:* **~-coloured***)* castanho-claro inv ♦ vi: **to ~ (up)on** bajular

fax [fæks] n fax m, fac-símile m ♦ vt enviar por fax ou fac-símile

FBI n abbr (= *Federal Bureau of Investigation)* FBI m

fear [fɪə*] n medo ♦ vt ter medo de, temer; **for ~ of** com medo de; **fearful** adj medonho, temível; *(cowardly)* medroso; *(awful)* terrível

feasible ['fiːzəbl] adj viável

feast [fiːst] n banquete m; *(REL: also:* **~ day)** festa ♦ vi banquetear-se

feat [fiːt] n façanha, feito

feather ['feðə*] n pena, pluma

feature ['fiːtʃə*] n característica; *(article)* reportagem f ♦ vt *(subj: film)* apresentar ♦ vi: **to ~** figurar em; **~s** npl *(of face)* feições fpl; **feature film** n longa-metragem m

February ['februarɪ] n fevereiro

fed [fed] pt, pp of **feed**

federal ['fedərəl] adj federal

fed up adj: **to be ~** estar *(de saco)* cheio *(BR)*, estar farto *(PT)*

fee [fiː] n taxa *(BR)*, propina *(PT)*; *(of school)* matrícula; *(of doctor, lawyer)* honorários mpl

feeble ['fiːbl] adj fraco; *(attempt)* ineficaz

feed [fiːd] *(pt, pp* **fed***)* n *(of baby)* alimento infantil; *(of animal)* ração f; *(of printer)* mecanismo alimentador ♦ vt alimentar; *(baby)* amamen-

tar; (*animal*) dar de comer a; (*data*):
to ~ **into** introduzir em; **feed on** *vt
fus* alimentar-se de; **feedback** *m*
reação *f*

feel [fiːl] (*pt, pp* felt) *n* sensação *f*;
(*sense*) tato; (*impression*) impressão *f*
♦ *vt* tocar, apalpar; (*anger, pain etc*)
sentir; (*think*) achar, acreditar; **to ~
hungry/cold** estar com fome/frio
(*BR*), ter fome/frio (*PT*); **to ~ lonely/
better** sentir-se só/ melhor; **I don't ~
well** não estou me sentindo bem; **it
~s soft** é macio; **to ~ like** querer; **to
~ about** *or* **around** tatear; **feeling** *n*
sensação *f*; (*emotion*) sentimento *f*;
(*impression*) impressão *f*

feet [fiːt] *npl of* **foot**

feign [fem] *vt* fingir

fell [fɛl] *pt of* **fall** ♦ *vt* (*tree*) lançar por
terra, derrubar

fellow ['fɛləu] *n* camarada *m/f*; (*inf:
man*) cara *m* (*BR*), tipo (*PT*); (*of
learned society*) membro ♦ *cpd*: ~
students colegas *m/fpl* de curso;
fellowship *n* amizade *f*; (*grant*)
bolsa de estudo; (*society*) associação
f

felony ['fɛlənɪ] *n* crime *m*

felt [fɛlt] *pt, pp of* **feel** ♦ *n* feltro; **felt-
tip pen** *n* caneta pilot ® (*BR*) or de
feltro (*PT*)

female ['fiːmeɪl] *n* (*ZOOL*) fêmea; (*pej:
woman*) mulher *f* ♦ *adj* fêmeo(-a); (*sex, character*) feminino;
(*vote*) das mulheres; (*child*) do sexo
feminino

feminine ['fɛmɪnɪn] *adj* feminino

feminist ['fɛmɪnɪst] *n* feminista *m/f*

fence [fɛns] *n* cerca ♦ *vt* (*also*: ~ **in**)
cercar ♦ *vi* esgrimir; **fencing** *n*
(*sport*) esgrima

fend [fɛnd] *vi*: **to ~ for o.s.** defender-
se, virar-se; **fend off** *vt* defender-se
de

fender ['fɛndə*] *n* (*of fireplace*)

guarda-fogo *m*; (*on boat*) defesa de
embarcação; (*US: AUT*) pára-lama *m*

ferment [*vb* fə'mɛnt, *n* 'fəːmɛnt] *vi*
fermentar ♦ *n* (*fig*) agitação *f*

fern [fəːn] *n* samambaia (*BR*), feto
(*PT*)

ferocious [fə'rəuʃəs] *adj* feroz

ferret ['fɛrɪt] *n* furão *m*; **ferret out**
vt (*information*) desenterrar, descobrir

ferry ['fɛrɪ] *n* (*small*) barco (de travessia); (*large: also*: ~**boat**) balsa ♦ *vt*
transportar

fertile ['fəːtaɪl] *adj* fértil; (*BIO*) fecun-
do; **fertilizer** ['fəːtɪlaɪzə*] *n* adubo,
fertilizante *m*

fester ['fɛstə*] *vi* inflamar-se

festival ['fɛstɪvəl] *n* (*REL*) festa; (*ART,
MUS*) festival *m*

festive ['fɛstɪv] *adj* festivo; **the ~
season** (*BRIT: Christmas*) a época do
Natal

festivities [fɛs'tɪvɪtɪz] *npl* festas *fpl*,
festividades *fpl*

fetch [fɛtʃ] *vt* ir buscar, trazer; (*sell
for*) alcançar

fête [feɪt] *n* festa

feud [fjuːd] *n* disputa, rixa

fever ['fiːvə*] *n* febre *f*; **feverish** *adj*
febril

few [fjuː] *adj, pron* poucos(-as); **a ~**
... alguns (algumas) ...; **fewer**
['fjuːə*] *adj* menos; **fewest** ['fjuːɪst]
adj o menor número de

fiancé(e) [fɪ'ãːnseɪ] *n* noivo(-a)

fib [fɪb] *n* lorota

fibre ['faɪbə*] (*US* **fiber**) *n* fibra;
fibreglass ['faɪbəglɑːs] *n* fibra de
vidro

fickle ['fɪkl] *adj* inconstante; (*weather*) instável

fiction ['fɪkʃən] *n* ficção *f*; **fictional**
adj de ficção; **fictitious** *adj* fictício

fiddle ['fɪdl] *n* (*MUS*) violino; (*swindle*) trapaça ♦ *vt* (*BRIT: accounts*) falsi-

ficar; **fiddle with** vt fus brincar com

fidget ['fidʒit] vi estar irrequieto, mexer-se

field [fi:ld] n campo; (fig) área, esfera, especialidade f; **fieldwork** n trabalho de campo

fiend [fi:nd] n demônio

fierce [fɪəs] adj feroz; (wind) violento; (heat) intenso

fiery ['faɪərɪ] adj ardente; (temperament) fogoso

fifteen [fɪf'ti:n] num quinze

fifth [fɪfθ] num quinto

fifty ['fɪftɪ] num cinqüenta; **fiftyfifty** adv: **to share** or **go fifty-fifty with sb** dividir meio a meio com alguém, rachar com alguém ♦ adj: **to have a fifty-fifty chance** ter 50% de chance

fig [fɪg] n figo

fight [faɪt] (pt, pp **fought**) n briga; (MIL) combate m; (struggle: against illness etc) luta ♦ vt lutar contra; (cancer, alcoholism) combater; (election) competir ♦ vi lutar, brigar, bater-se; **fighter** n combatente m/f; (plane) caça m; **fighting** n batalha; (brawl) briga

figment ['fɪgmənt] n: **a ~ of the imagination** um produto da imaginação

figurative ['fɪgjʊrətɪv] adj (expression) figurado; (style) figurativo

figure ['fɪgə*] n (DRAWING, MATH) figura, desenho; (number) número, cifra; (outline) forma; (person) personagem m ♦ vt (esp US) imaginar ♦ vi figurar; **figure out** vt compreender

file [faɪl] n (tool) lixa; (dossier) dossiê m, pasta; (folder) pasta; (COMPUT) arquivo; (row) fila, coluna ♦ vt (wood, nails) lixar; (papers) arquivar; (LAW: claim) apresentar, dar entrada em

♦ vi: **to ~ in/out** entrar/sair em fila

filing cabinet n fichário, arquivo

fill [fɪl] vt: **to ~ with** encher com; (vacancy) preencher; (need) satisfazer ♦ n: **to eat one's ~** encher-se or fartar-se de comer; **fill in** vt (form) preencher; (hole) tapar; (time) encher; **fill up** vt encher ♦ vi (AUT) abastecer o carro

fillet ['fɪlɪt] n filete m, filé m; **fillet steak** n filé m

filling ['fɪlɪŋ] n (CULIN) recheio; (for tooth) obturação f (BR), chumbo (PT); **filling station** n posto de gasolina

film [fɪlm] n filme m; (of liquid) camada, veu m ♦ vt rodar, filmar ♦ vi filmar; **film star** n astro/estrela do cinema

filter ['fɪltə*] n filtro ♦ vt filtrar; **filter-tipped** adj filtrado

filth [fɪlθ] n sujeira (BR), sujidade f (PT); **filthy** adj sujo; (language) indecente, obsceno

fin [fɪn] n barbatana

final ['faɪnl] adj final, último; (ultimate) maior; (definitive) definitivo ♦ n (SPORT) final f; **~s** npl (SCH) exames mpl finais; **finale** [fɪ'nɑ:lɪ] n final m; **finalize** vt concluir, completar; **finally** adv finalmente, por fim

finance [faɪ'næns] n fundos mpl; (money management) finanças fpl ♦ vt financiar; **~s** npl (personal ~s) finanças fpl; **financial** [faɪ'nænʃəl] adj financeiro

find [faɪnd] (pt, pp **found**) vt encontrar, achar; (discover) descobrir ♦ n achado, descoberta; **to ~ sb guilty** (LAW) declarar alguém culpado; **find out** vt descobrir; (person) desmascarar ♦ vi: **to ~ out about** (by chance) saber de; **findings** npl (LAW) veredito, decisão f; (of report)

fine 100 **fix**

constatações fpl

fine [faɪn] *adj* fino; (*excellent*) excelente; (*subtle*) sutil ♦ *adv* muito bem ♦ *n* (*LAW*) multa ♦ *vt* (*LAW*) multar; **to be ~** (*person*) estar bem; (*weather*) estar bom; **fine arts** *npl* belas artes *fpl*

finger ['fɪŋgə*] *n* dedo ♦ *vt* manusear; **fingernail** *n* unha; **fingerprint** *n* impressão *f* digital; **fingertip** *n* ponta do dedo

finish ['fɪnɪʃ] *n* fim *m*; (*SPORT*) chegada; (*on wood etc*) acabamento ♦ *vt*, *vi* terminar, acabar; **to ~ doing sth** terminar de fazer algo; **to ~ third** chegar no terceiro lugar; **finish off** *vt* terminar; (*kill*) liquidar; **finish up** *vt* acabar ♦ *vi* ir parar; **finishing line** *n* linha de chegada, meta

Finland ['fɪnlənd] *n* Finlândia

Finn [fɪn] *n* finlandês(-esa) *m/f*; **Finnish** *adj* finlandês(-esa) ♦ *n* (*LING*) finlandês *m*

fir [fə:*] *n* abeto

fire ['faɪə*] *n* fogo; (*accidental*) incêndio; (*gas ~, electric ~*) aquecedor *m* ♦ *vt* (*gun*) disparar; (*arrow*) atirar; (*interest*) estimular; (*dismiss*) despedir ♦ *vi* disparar; **on ~** em chamas; **fire alarm** *n* alarme *m* de incêndio; **firearm** *n* arma de fogo; **fire brigade** (*us* **fire department**) *n* (corpo de) bombeiros *mpl*; **fire engine** *n* carro de bombeiro; **fire escape** *n* escada de incêndio; **fire extinguisher** *n* extintor *m* de incêndio; **fireman** (*irreg*) *n* bombeiro; **fireplace** *n* lareira; **fire station** *n* posto de bombeiros; **firewood** *n* lenha; **fireworks** *npl* fogos *mpl* de artifício

firing squad *n* pelotão *m* de fuzilamento

firm [fə:m] *adj* firme ♦ *n* firma

first [fə:st] *adj* primeiro ♦ *adv* (*before*

others) primeiro; (*listing reasons*) em primeiro lugar ♦ *n* (*in race*) primeiro(-a); (*AUT*) primeira; (*BRIT: SCH*) menção *f* honrosa; **at ~** no início; **~ of all** antes de tudo, antes de mais nada; **first aid** *n* primeiros socorros *mpl*; **first-aid kit** *n* estojo de primeiros socorros; **first-class** *adj* de primeira classe; **first-hand** *adj* de primeira mão; **first lady** (*us*) *n* primeira dama; **firstly** *adv* primeiramente, em primeiro lugar; **first name** *n* primeiro nome *m*; **first-rate** *adj* de primeira categoria

fish [fɪʃ] *n inv* peixe *m* ♦ *vt*, *vi* pescar; **to go ~ing** ir pescar; **fisherman** (*irreg*) *n* pescador *m*; **fish fingers** (*BRIT*) *npl* filezinhos *mpl* de peixe; **fishing boat** *n* barco de pesca; **fishing line** *n* linha de pesca; **fishing rod** *n* vara (de pesca); **fishmonger's (shop)** *n* peixaria; **fish sticks** (*us*) *npl* = **fish fingers**; **fishy** (*inf*) *adj* (*tale*) suspeito

fist [fɪst] *n* punho

fit [fɪt] *adj* em (boa) forma; (*suitable*) adequado, apropriado ♦ *vt* (*subj: clothes*) caber em; (*put in*) colocar; (*equip*) equipar; (*suit*) assentar a ♦ *vi* (*clothes*) servir; (*parts*) ajustar-se; (*in space*) caber ♦ *n* (*MED*) ataque *m*; (*of anger*) acesso; **~ to** bom para; **~ for** adequado para; **by fits and starts** espasmodicamente; **fit in** *vi* encaixar-se; (*person*) dar-se bem (com todos); **fitment** *n* móvel *m*; **fitness** *n* (*MED*) saúde *f*, boa forma; **fitting** *adj* apropriado ♦ *n* (*of dress*) prova; **fittings** *npl* (*in building*) instalações *fpl*, acessórios *mpl*

five [faɪv] *num* cinco; **fiver** (*inf*) *n* (*BRIT*) nota de cinco libras; (*us*) nota de cinco dólares

fix [fɪks] *vt* (*secure*) fixar, colocar; (*arrange*) arranjar; (*mend*) consertar; (*meal, drink*) preparar ♦ *n*: **to be in a ~** estar em apuros; **fix up** *vt* (*meeting*) marcar; **to ~ sb up with sth** arranjar algo para alguém; **fixation** [fɪk'seɪʃən] *n* fixação *f*; **fixed** *adj* (*prices, smile*) fixo; **fixture** *n* (*furniture*) móvel *m* fixo; (*SPORT*) desafio, encontro

fizzy ['fɪzɪ] *adj* com gás, gasoso

flabbergasted ['flæbəgɑːstɪd] *adj* pasmado

flabby ['flæbɪ] *adj* flácido

flag [flæg] *n* bandeira; (*for signalling*) bandeirola; (~*stone*) laje *f* ♦ *vi* acabar-se, descair; **flag down** *vt*: **to ~ sb down** fazer sinais a alguém para que pare

flagpole ['flægpəul] *n* mastro de bandeira

flagship ['flægʃɪp] *n* nau *f* capitânia; (*fig*) carro-chefe *m*

flair [flɛə*] *n* (*talent*) talento; (*style*) habilidade *f*

flake [fleɪk] *n* (*of rust, paint*) lasca; (*of snow, soap powder*) floco ♦ *vi* (*also: ~ off*) lascar, descamar-se

flamboyant [flæm'bɔɪənt] *adj* (*dress*) espalhafatoso; (*person*) extravagante

flame [fleɪm] *n* chama

flammable ['flæməbl] *adj* inflamável

flan [flæn] *n* (*BRIT*) torta

flannel ['flænl] *n* (*BRIT: also: face ~*) toalhinha de rosto; (*fabric*) flanela; **~s** *npl* calça (*BR*) or calças *fpl* (*PT*) de flanela

flap [flæp] *n* (*of pocket*) aba; (*of envelope*) dobra ♦ *vt* (*arms*) oscilar; (*wings*) bater ♦ *vi* (*sail, flag*) ondular; (*inf: also: be in a ~*) estar atarantado

flare [flɛə*] *n* fogacho, chama; (*in skirt etc*) folga; **flare up** *vi* chamejar; (*fig: person*) encolerizar-se; (: *violence*) irromper

flash [flæʃ] *n* (*of lightning*) clarão *m*; (*also: news ~*) notícias *fpl* de última hora; (*PHOT*) flash *m* ♦ *vt* piscar; (*news, message*) transmitir; (*look, smile*) brilhar ♦ *vi* brilhar; (*light on ambulance, eyes etc*) piscar; **in a ~** num instante; **to ~ by** or **past** passar como um raio; **flashlight** *n* lanterna de bolso

flashy ['flæʃɪ] (*pej*) *adj* espalhafatoso

flask [flɑːsk] *n* frasco; (*also: vacuum ~*) garrafa térmica (*BR*), termo (*PT*)

flat [flæt] *adj* plano; (*battery*) descarregado; (*tyre*) vazio; (*beer*) choco; (*denial*) categórico; (*MUS*) abemolado; (: *voice*) desentoado; (*rate*) único; (*fee*) fixo ♦ *n* (*BRIT: apartment*) apartamento; (*MUS*) bemol *m*; (*AUT*) pneu *m* furado; **~ out** (*work*) a toque de caixa; **flatly** *adv* terminantemente; **flatten** *vt* (*also: flatten out*) aplanar; (*demolish*) arrasar

flatter ['flætə*] *vt* lisonjear; **flattering** *adj* lisonjeiro; (*clothes etc*) favorecedor(a); **flattery** *n* bajulação *f*

flaunt [flɔːnt] *vt* ostentar, pavonear

flavour ['fleɪvə*] (*US* **flavor**) *n* sabor *m* ♦ *vt* condimentar, aromatizar; **strawberry-~ed** com sabor de morango; **flavouring** *n* condimento; (*synthetic*) aromatizante *m*

flaw [flɔː] *n* defeito; (*in character*) falha; **flawless** *adj* impecável

flax [flæks] *n* linho

flea [fliː] *n* pulga

fleck [flek] *n* mancha, sinal *m*

flee [fliː] (*pt, pp* **fled**) *vt* fugir de ♦ *vi* fugir

fleece [fliːs] *n* tosão *m*; (*wool*) lã *f*; (*coat*) velo ♦ *vt* (*inf*) espoliar

fleet [fliːt] *n* (*of lorries etc*) frota; (*of ships*) esquadra

fleeting ['fliːtɪŋ] *adj* (*glimpse, happiness*) fugaz; (*visit*) passageiro

Flemish ['flemɪʃ] *adj* flamengo

flesh [fleʃ] *n* carne *f*; (*of fruit*) polpa

flew [fluː] *pt of* **fly**

flex [fleks] *n* fio ♦ *vt* (*muscles*) flexionar; **flexible** *adj* flexível

flick [flɪk] *n* pancada leve; (*with finger*) peteleco, piparote *m*; (*with whip*) chicotada ♦ *vt* dar um peteleco; (*towel*) dar uma lambada; (*whip*) dar uma chicotada; (*switch*) apertar; **flick through** *vt fus* folhear

flicker ['flɪkə*] *vi* tremular; (*eyelids*) tremer

flight [flaɪt] *n* vôo *m*; (*escape*) fuga; (*of steps*) lance *m*; **flight attendant** (*US*) *n* comissário(-a) *m* de bordo; **flight deck** *n* (*AVIAT*) cabine *f* do piloto; (*NAUT*) pista de aterrissagem (*BR*) or aterragem (*PT*)

flimsy ['flɪmzɪ] *adj* (*thin*) delgado, franzino; (*shoes*) ordinário; (*clothes*) de tecido fino; (*building*) barato; (*weak*) débil; (*excuse*) fraco

flinch [flɪntʃ] *vi* encolher-se; **to ~ from sth/from doing sth** vacilar diante de algo/em fazer algo

fling [flɪŋ] (*pt, pp* **flung**) *vt* lançar

flint [flɪnt] *n* pederneira; (*in lighter*) pedra

flippant ['flɪpənt] *adj* petulante, irreverente

flipper ['flɪpə*] *n* (*of animal*) nadadeira; (*for swimmer*) pé-de-pato, nadadeira

flirt [fləːt] *vi* flertar ♦ *n* namorador(a) *m/f*, paquerador(a) *m/f*

float [fləut] *n* bóia; (*in procession*) carro alegórico; (*sum of money*) caixa ♦ *vi* flutuar; (*swimmer*) boiar

flock [flɔk] *n* rebanho; (*of birds*) bando ♦ *vi*: **to ~** afluir-se

flog [flɔg] *vt* açoitar

flood [flʌd] *n* enchente *f*, inundação *f*; (*of letters, imports etc*) enxurrada ♦ *vt* inundar, alagar ♦ *vi* (*place*) alagar; (*people, goods*): **to ~ into** inun-

dar; **flooding** *n* inundação *f*; **floodlight** *n* refletor *m*, holofote *m*

floor [flɔː*] *n* chão *m*; (*storey*) andar *m*; (*of sea*) fundo ♦ *vt* (*fig: confuse*) confundir, pasmar; (*subj: blow*) derrubar; (: *question, remark*) aturdir; **ground ~** (*BRIT*) or **first ~** (*US*) andar térreo (*BR*), rés-do-chão (*PT*); **first ~** (*BRIT*) or **second ~** (*US*) primeiro andar; **floorboard** *n* tábua de assoalho; **floor show** *n* show *m*

flop [flɔp] *n* fracasso ♦ *vi* fracassar; (*into chair*) cair pesadamente

floppy ['flɔpɪ] *adj* frouxo, mole; **floppy (disk)** *n* disquete *m*

florist ['flɔrɪst] *n* florista *m/f*; **florist's (shop)** *n* floricultura

flounder ['flaundə*] (*pl ~* or *~s*) *n* (*ZOOL*) linguado ♦ *vi* (*swimmer*) debater-se; (*fig: speaker*) atrapalhar-se; (: *economy*) flutuar

flour ['flauə*] *n* farinha

flourish ['flʌrɪʃ] *vi* florescer ♦ *vt* brandir, menear ♦ *n* gesto floreado

flow [fləu] *n* fluxo; (*of river, ELEC*) corrente *f*; (*of blood*) circulação *f* ♦ *vi* correr; (*traffic*) fluir; (*blood, ELEC*) circular; (*clothes, hair*) ondular; **flow chart** *n* fluxograma *m*

flower ['flauə*] *n* flor *f* ♦ *vi* florescer, florir; **flower bed** *n* canteiro; **flowerpot** *n* vaso; **flowery** *adj* (*perfume*) à base de flor; (*pattern*) florido; (*speech*) floreado

flown [fləun] *pp of* **fly**

flu [fluː] *n* gripe *f*

fluctuate ['flʌktjueɪt] *vi* flutuar; (*temperature*) variar

fluent ['fluːənt] *adj* fluente; **he speaks ~ French, he's ~ in French** ele fala francês fluentemente

fluff [flʌf] *n* felpa, penugem *f*; **fluffy** *adj* macio, fofo; (*toy*) de pelúcia

fluid ['fluːɪd] *adj* fluido ♦ *n* fluido

fluke [fluːk] (inf) n sorte f

flung [flʌŋ] pt, pp of fling

fluoride ['fluəraɪd] n fluoreto m

flurry ['flʌrɪ] n (of snow) lufada; ~ of activity muita atividade

flush [flʌʃ] n (on face) rubor m; (fig) resplendor m ♦ vt lavar com água ♦ vi ruborizar-se ♦ adj: ~ with rente com; to ~ the toilet dar descarga; **flush out** vt levantar; **flushed** adj ruborizado, corado

flustered ['flʌstəd] adj atrapalhado

flute [fluːt] n flauta

flutter ['flʌtə*] n agitação f; (of wings) bater m ♦ vi esvoaçar

flux [flʌks] n: in a state of ~ mudando continuamente

fly [flaɪ] (pt flew, pp flown) n mosca; (on trousers: also: **flies**) braguilha ♦ vt (plane) pilotar; (passengers, cargo) transportar (de avião); (distances) percorrer ♦ vi voar; (passengers) ir de avião; (escape) fugir; (flag) hastear-se; **fly away** or **off** vi voar; **flying** n aviação f ♦ adj: **flying visit** visita de médico; **with flying colours** brilhantemente; **flying saucer** n disco voador; **flyover** (BRIT) n viaduto m; **flysheet** n duplo teto

foal [foul] n potro

foam [fəum] n espuma f; (also: ~ rubber) espuma de borracha ♦ vi espumar

focal point ['fəukl] n foco

focus ['fəukəs] (pl ~es) n foco ♦ vt enfocar ♦ vi: to ~ on enfocar, focalizar; **in/out of** ~ em foco/fora de foco

foe [fəu] n inimigo

fog [fɔg] n nevoeiro; **foggy** adj: **it's foggy** está nevoento

foil [fɔɪl] vt frustrar ♦ n folha metálica; (also: **kitchen** ~) folha or papel m de alumínio; (complement) contraste

m, complemento; (FENCING) florete m

fold [fould] n (of animal) dobra, vinco, prega; (of skin) ruga; (AGR) redil m, curral m ♦ vt dobrar; (arms) cruzar; **fold up** vi dobrar; (business) abrir falência ♦ vt dobrar; **folder** n pasta; **folding** adj dobrável

folk [fəuk] npl gente f ♦ cpd popular, folclórico; ~s npl (family) família, parentes mpl; (parents) pais mpl; **folklore** ['fəuklɔː*] n folclore m

follow ['fɔləu] vt seguir; (event, story) acompanhar ♦ vi seguir; (person, period of time) acompanhar; (result) resultar; to ~ **suit** fazer o mesmo; **follow up** vt (letter) responder a; (offer) levar adiante; (case) acompanhar; **follower** n seguidor(a) m/t; **following** adj seguinte ♦ n adeptos mpl

folly ['fɔlɪ] n loucura

fond [fɔnd] adj carinhoso; (hopes) absurdo, descabido; to be ~ of gostar de

fondle ['fɔndl] vt acariciar

font [fɔnt] n (REL) pia batismal; (TYP) fonte f, família

food [fuːd] n comida; **food mixer** n batedeira; **food poisoning** n intoxicação f alimentar; **food processor** n multiprocessador m de cozinha; **foodstuffs** npl gêneros mpl alimentícios

fool [fuːl] n tolo(-a); (CULIN) purê m de frutas com creme ♦ vt enganar ♦ vi (gen: ~ around) brincar; **foolhardy** adj temerário; **foolish** adj burro; (careless) imprudente; **foolproof** adj infalível

foot [fut] (pl **feet**) n pé m; (of animal) pata; (measure) pé (304 mm; 12 inches) ♦ vt (bill) pagar; **on** ~ a pé; **footage** n (CINEMA: length) ≈ metragem f (: material) sequências fpl; **football** n bola; (game: BRIT) futebol *m*; (: *us*) futebol norte-americano; **football player** *n* (*BRIT: also:* **footballer**) jogador *m* de futebol; **footbrake** *n* freio (*BR*) *or* travão *m* (*PT*) de pé; **footbridge** *n* passarela; **foothills** *npl* contraforte *m*; **foothold** *n* apoio para o pé; **footing** *n* (*fig*) posição *f*; **to lose one's footing** escorregar; **footnote** *n* nota ao pé da página, nota de rodapé; **footpath** *n* caminho, atalho; **footprint** *n* pegada; **footstep** *n* passo; **footwear** *n* calçados *mpl*

KEYWORD

---

for [fɔːˀ] *prep* **1** (*indicating destination, direction*) para; **he went ~ the paper** foi pegar *or* jornal; **is this ~ me?** é para mim?; **it's time ~ lunch** é hora de almoçar

2 (*indicating purpose*) para; **what's it ~?** para quê serve?; **to pray ~ peace** orar pela paz

3 (*on behalf of, representing*) por; **he works ~ the government/a local firm** ele trabalha para o governo/uma firma local; **G ~ George** G de George

4 (*because of*) por; **~ this reason** por esta razão; **~ fear of being criticised** com medo de ser criticado

5 (*with regard to*) para; **it's cold ~ July** está frio para julho

6 (*in exchange for*) por; **it was sold ~ £5** foi vendido por £5

7 (*in favour of*) a favor de; **are you ~ or against us?** você está a favor de ou contra nós?; **I'm all ~ it** concordo plenamente, tem todo o meu apoio; **vote ~ X** vote em X

8 (*referring to distance*): **there are roadworks ~ 5 km** há obras na estrada por 5 quilômetros; **we walked ~ miles** andamos quilômetros

9 (*referring to time*) **she will be**

away **~ a month** ela ficará fora um mês; **I have known her ~ years** eu a conheço há anos; **can you do it ~ tomorrow?** você pode fazer isso para amanhã?

10 (*with infinite clause*): **it is not ~ me to decide** não cabe a mim decidir; **it would be best ~ you to leave** seria melhor que você fosse embora; **there is still time ~ you to do it** ainda há tempo para você fazer isso; **~ this to be possible ...** para que isso seja possível ...

11 (*in spite of*) apesar de

♦ *conj* (*since, as: rather formal*) pois, porque

forbid [fəˈbɪd] (*pt* **forbad(e)**, *pp* **forbidden**) *vt* proibir; **to ~ sb to do sth** proibir alguém de fazer algo; **forbidding** *adj* (*prospect*) sombrio; (*look*) severo

force [fɔːs] *n* força ♦ *vt* forçar; **the F~s** *npl* (*BRIT*) as Forças Armadas; **in ~** em vigor; **forceful** *adj* enérgico, vigoroso

forcibly [ˈfɔːsəblɪ] *adv* à força

ford [fɔːd] *n* vau *m*

fore [fɔːˀ] *n*: **to come to the ~** salientar-se

forearm [ˈfɔːrɑːm] *n* antebraço

foreboding [fɔːˈbəʊdɪŋ] *n* mau presságio

forecast [ˈfɔːkɑːst] (*irreg: like* **cast**) *n* previsão *f*; (*also:* **weather ~**) previsão do tempo ♦ *vt* prognosticar, prever

forefinger [ˈfɔːfɪŋgəˀ] *n* (dedo) indicador *m*

foregone [ˈfɔːgɒn] *pp* of **forego** ♦ *adj*: **it's a ~ conclusion** é uma conclusão inevitável

foreground [ˈfɔːgraʊnd] *n* primeiro plano

forehead [ˈfɒrɪd] *n* testa

foreign ['fɔrɪn] adj estrangeiro; (trade) exterior; (object, matter) estranho; **foreigner** n estrangeiro(-a); **foreign exchange** n câmbio; **Foreign Office** (BRIT) n Ministério das Relações Exteriores

foreman ['fɔːmən] (irreg) n capataz m; (in construction) contramestre m

foremost ['fɔːməust] adj principal ♦ adv: **first and ~** antes de mais nada

forensic [fə'rɛnsɪk] adj forense; **~ medicine** medicina legal

forerunner ['fɔːrʌnə*] n precursor(a) m/f

foresee [fɔː'siː] (irreg: like see) vt prever; **foreseeable** adj previsível

foresight ['fɔːsaɪt] n previdência f

forest ['fɔrɪst] n floresta

forestry ['fɔrɪstrɪ] n silvicultura

foretaste ['fɔːteɪst] n amostra

foretell [fɔː'tɛl] (irreg: like tell) vt predizer, profetizar

forever [fə'rɛvə*] adv para sempre

foreword ['fɔːwəːd] n prefácio

forfeit ['fɔːfɪt] vt perder (direito a)

forgave [fə'geɪv] pt of **forgive**

forge [fɔːdʒ] n ferraria ♦ vt falsificar; (metal) forjar; **forge ahead** vi avançar constantemente; **forger** n falsificador(a) m/f; **forgery** n falsificação f

forget [fə'gɛt] (pt forgot, pp forgotten) vt, vi esquecer; **forgetful** adj esquecido; **forget-me-not** n miosótis m

forgive [fə'gɪv] (pt forgave, pp ~n) vt perdoar; **to ~ sb for sth** perdoar algo a alguém, perdoar alguém de algo; **forgiveness** n perdão m

fork [fɔːk] n (for eating) garfo; (for gardening) forquilha; (of roads etc) bifurcação f ♦ vi bifurcar-se; **fork out** (inf) vt (pay) desembolsar,

morrer em

forlorn [fə'lɔːn] adj desolado; (attempt) desesperado; (hope) último

form [fɔːm] n forma; (type) tipo; (SCH) série f, (questionnaire) formulário ♦ vt formar; (organization) criar; **to ~ a queue** (BRIT) fazer fila; **in top ~** em plena forma

formal ['fɔːməl] adj (offer) oficial; (person) cerimonioso; (occasion, education) formal; (dress) a rigor (BR), de cerimônia (PT); (garden) simétrico; **formally** adv formalmente

format ['fɔːmæt] n formato ♦ vt (COMPUT) formatar

former ['fɔːmə*] adj anterior; (earlier) antigo; **the ~ ... the latter ...** aquele ... este ...; **formerly** adv anteriormente

formidable ['fɔːmɪdəbl] adj terrível, temível

formula ['fɔːmjulə] (pl ~s or ~e) n fórmula

forsake [fə'seɪk] (pt forsook, pp forsaken) vt abandonar

fort [fɔːt] n forte m

forth [fɔːθ] adv para adiante; **back and ~** de cá para lá; **and so ~** e assim por diante; **forthcoming** adj próximo, que está para aparecer; (help) disponível; (person) comunicativo; **forthright** adj franco

fortify ['fɔːtɪfaɪ] vt (city) fortificar; (person) fortalecer

fortnight ['fɔːtnaɪt] (BRIT) n quinzena, quinze dias mpl; **fortnightly** adj quinzenal ♦ adv quinzenalmente

fortunate ['fɔːtʃənɪt] adj (event) feliz; (person): **to be ~** ter sorte; **it is ~ that ...** é uma sorte que ...; **fortunately** adv felizmente

fortune ['fɔːtʃən] n sorte f; (wealth)

fortuna; **fortune-teller** n adivinho(-a)

forty ['fɔːtɪ] num quarenta

forward ['fɔːwəd] adj (movement) para a frente; (position) avançado; (in time) futuro; (not shy) imodesto, presunçoso ♦ n (SPORT) atacante m ♦ vt (letter) remeter; (goods, parcel) expedir; (career) promover; (also: **forwards**) adv para a frente; **to move ~** avançar; **forward(s)** adv para a frente

fossil ['fɔsl] n fóssil m

foster ['fɔstə*] vt adotar (por um tempo limitado); (activity) promover; **foster child** (irreg) n filho adotivo (por um tempo limitado)

fought [fɔːt] pt, pp of **fight**

foul [faul] adj horrível; (language) obsceno ♦ n (SPORT) falta ♦ vt sujar; **foul play** n (LAW) crime m

found [faund] pt, pp of **find** ♦ vt (establish) fundar; **foundation** [faun'deɪʃən] n (act, organization) fundação f; (base) base f; (also: **foundation cream**) creme m base; **foundations** npl (of building) alicerces mpl

founder ['faundə*] n fundador(a) m/f ♦ vi naufragar

fountain ['fauntɪn] n chafariz m; **fountain pen** n caneta-tinteiro f

four [fɔː*] num quatro; **on all ~s** de quatro; **fourteen** num catorze; **fourth** num quarto

fowl [faul] n ave f (doméstica)

fox [fɔks] n raposa ♦ vt deixar perplexo

foyer ['fɔɪeɪ] n saguão m

fraction ['frækʃən] n fração f

fracture ['fræktʃə*] n fratura ♦ vt fraturar

fragile ['frædʒaɪl] adj frágil

fragment ['frægmənt] n fragmento

fragrant ['freɪɡrənt] adj fragrante, perfumado

frail [freɪl] adj (person) fraco; (structure) frágil

frame [freɪm] n (of building) estrutura; (body) corpo; (of picture, door) moldura; (of spectacles: also: **~s**) armação f, aro ♦ vt (picture) emoldurar; **frame of mind** n estado de espírito; **framework** n armação f

France [frɑːns] n França

frank [fræŋk] adj franco ♦ vt (letter) franquear; **frankly** adv francamente; (candidly) abertamente

frantic ['fræntɪk] adj frenético; (person) fora de si

fraternity [frə'tɜːnɪtɪ] n (feeling) fraternidade f; (club) confraria

fraud [frɔːd] n fraude f; (person) impostor(a) m/f

fraught [frɔːt] adj tenso; **~ with** repleto de

fray [freɪ] n guerra ♦ vi esfiapar-se; **tempers were ~ed** estavam com os nervos em frangalhos

freak [friːk] n (person) anormal m/f; (event) anomalia

freckle ['frɛkl] n sarda

free [friː] adj livre; (seat) desocupado; (costing nothing) gratis, gratuito ♦ vt pôr em liberdade; (jammed object) soltar; **~ (of charge)** grátis, de graça; **freedom** n liberdade f; **Freefone** ® n número de discagem gratuita; **free gift** n brinde m; **freelance** adj autônomo; **freely** adv livremente; **free-range** (egg) caseiro; **freeway** (US) n autoestrada; **free will** n livre arbítrio; **of one's own free will** por sua própria vontade

freeze [friːz] (pt **froze**, pp **frozen**) vi gelar-se, congelar-se ♦ vt congelar ♦ n geada; (on arms, wages) congelamento; **freezer** n congelador m, freezer m (BR); **freezing** adj: **freezing (cold)** (weather) glacial; (water) gelado; **3 degrees below freezing** 3

graus abaixo de zero; **freezing point** *n* ponto de congelamento
freight [freɪt] *n* (*goods*) carga; (*money charged*) frete *m*; **freight train** (*US*) *n* trem *m* de carga
French [frentʃ] *adj* francês(-esa) ♦ *n* (*LING*) francês *m*; **the ~** *npl* (*people*) os franceses; **French bean** (*BRIT*) *n* feijão *m* comum; **French fried potatoes** (*US* French fries) *npl* batatas *fpl* fritas; **Frenchman** (*irreg*) *n* francês; **Frenchwoman** (*irreg*) *n* francesa
frenzy ['frenzɪ] *n* frenesi *m*
frequent [*adj* 'friːkwənt, *vt* frɪ'kwent] *adj* freqüente ♦ *vt* freqüentar; **frequently** *adv* freqüentemente, a miúdo
fresh [freʃ] *adj* fresco; (*new*) novo; (*cheeky*) atrevido; **freshen** *vi* (*wind, air*) tornar-se mais forte; **freshen up** (*person*) lavar-se, refrescar-se; **freshly** *adv* recentemente, há pouco; **freshness** *n* frescor *m*; **freshwater** *adj* de água doce
fret [fret] *vi* afligir-se
friar ['fraɪə*] *n* frade *m*
friction ['frɪkʃən] *n* fricção *f*; (*between people*) atrito
Friday ['fraɪdɪ] *n* sexta-feira *f*
fridge [frɪdʒ] (*BRIT*) *n* geladeira (*BR*), frigorífico (*PT*)
fried [fraɪd] *adj* frito; **~ egg** ovo estrelado *or* frito
friend [frend] *n* amigo(-a); **friendly** *adj* simpático; (*match*) amistoso; **friendship** *n* amizade *f*
fright [fraɪt] *n* terror *m*; (*scare*) pavor *m*; **to take ~** assustar-se; **frighten** *vt* assustar; **frightened** *adj*: **to be frightened of** ter medo de; **frightening** *adj* assustador(a); **frightful** *adj* terrível, horrível
frigid ['frɪdʒɪd] *adj* frígido, frio
frill [frɪl] *n* babado

fringe [frɪndʒ] *n* franja; (*on shawl etc*) franja, orla; (*edge: of forest etc*) margem *f*
Frisbee ® ['frɪzbɪ] *n* Frisbee ® *m*
frisk [frɪsk] *vt* revistar
fritter ['frɪtə*] *n* bolinho frito; **fritter away** *vt* desperdiçar
frivolous ['frɪvələs] *adj* frívolo; (*activity*) fútil
frizzy ['frɪzɪ] *adj* frisado
fro [frəʊ] *adj* see **to**
frock [frɒk] *n* vestido
frog [frɒg] *n* rã *f*; **frogman** (*irreg*) *n* homem-rã *m*

KEYWORD

---

from [frɒm] *prep* **1** (*indicating starting place*) de; **where do you come ~?** de onde você é?; **~ London to Glasgow** de Londres para Glasgow; **to escape ~ sth/sb** escapar de algo/alguém
2 (*indicating origin etc*) de; **a letter/telephone call ~ my sister** uma carta/um telefonema da minha irmã; **tell him ~ me that ...** diga a ele que da minha parte ...; **to drink ~ the bottle** beber na garrafa
3 (*indicating time*) de; **one o'clock to** *or* **until** *or* **till two** da uma hora até às duas; **~ May (on)** a partir de maio
4 (*indicating distance*) de; **we're still a long way ~ home** ainda estamos muito longe de casa
5 (*indicating price, number etc*) de; **prices range ~ £10 to £50** os preços vão de £10 a £50
6 (*indicating difference*) de; **he can't tell red ~ green** ele não pode diferenciar vermelho do verde
7 (*because of/on the basis of*): **~ what he says** pelo que ele diz; **to act ~ conviction** agir por convicção; **weak ~ hunger** fraco de fome

front [frʌnt] *n* frente *f*; (*of vehicle*) parte *f* dianteira; (*of house, fig*) fachada; (*also:* **sea ~**) orla marítima ♦ *adj* da frente; **in ~ (of)** em frente (de); **front door** *n* porta principal; **frontier** ['frʌntɪə*] *n* fronteira; **front page** *n* primeira página; **front room** (BRIT) *n* salão *m*, sala de estar; **front-wheel drive** *n* tração *f* dianteira

frost [frɔst] *n* geada; (*also:* **hoar~**) gelo; **frostbite** *n* ulceração *f* produzida pelo frio; **frosty** *adj* (*window*) coberto de geada; (*welcome*) glacial

froth [frɔθ] *n* espuma

frown [fraun] *vi* franzir as sobrancelhas, amarrar a cara

froze [frauz] *pt of* **freeze**

frozen ['frauzn] *pp of* **freeze**

fruit [fru:t] *n inv* fruta; (*fig: pl* **~s**) fruto; **fruitful** *adj* proveitoso; **fruit juice** *n* suco (BR) or sumo (PT) de frutas; **fruit machine** (BRIT) *n* caçaníqueis *m inv* (BR), máquina de jogo (PT); **fruit salad** *n* salada de frutas

frustrate [frʌs'treɪt] *vt* frustrar

fry [fraɪ] (*pt, pp* **fried**) *vt* fritar; **frying pan** *n* frigideira

ft. *abbr* = **foot; feet**

fudge [fʌdʒ] *n* (CULIN) ≈ doce *m* de leite

fuel [fjuəl] *n* (*for heating*) combustível *m*; (*for propelling*) carburante *m*; **fuel oil** *n* óleo combustível; **fuel tank** *n* depósito de combustível

fugitive ['fju:dʒɪtɪv] *n* fugitivo(-a)

fulfil [ful'fɪl] (*US* **fulfill**) *vt* (*function*) cumprir; (*condition*) satisfazer; (*wish, desire*) realizar

full [ful] *adj* cheio; (*use, volume*) máximo; (*complete*) completo; (*information*) detalhado; (*price*) integral; (*skirt*) folgado ♦ *adv*: **~ well** perfeitamente; **I'm ~ (up)** estou

satisfeito; **~ employment** pleno emprego; **a ~ two hours** duas horas completas; **at ~ speed** a toda a velocidade; **in ~** integralmente; **full stop** *n* ponto (final); **full-time** *adj, adv* (*work*) de tempo completo or integral; **fully** *adv* completamente; (*at least*) pelo menos; **fully-fledged** *adj* (*teacher etc*) diplomado

fumble ['fʌmbl] *vi*: **to ~ with** ♦ *vt fus* atrapalhar-se com

fume [fju:m] *vi* fumegar; (*be angry*) estar com raiva; **fumes** *npl* gases *mpl*

fun [fʌn] *n* divertimento; **to have ~** divertir-se; **for ~** de brincadeira; **to make ~ of** fazer troça de, zombar de

function ['fʌŋkʃən] *n* função *f*; (*reception, dinner*) recepção *f* ♦ *vi* funcionar; **functional** *adj* funcional; (*practical*) prático

fund [fʌnd] *n* fundo; (*source, store*) fonte *f*; **~s** *npl* (*money*) fundos *mpl*

fundamental [fʌndə'mentl] *adj* fundamental

funeral ['fju:nərəl] *n* (*burial*) enterro

funfair ['fʌnfeə*] (BRIT) *n* parque *m* de diversões

fungus ['fʌŋgəs] (*pl* **fungi**) *n* fungo; (*mould*) bolor *m*, mofo

funnel ['fʌnl] *n* funil *m*; (*of ship*) chaminé *f*

funny ['fʌnɪ] *adj* engraçado, divertido; (*strange*) esquisito, estranho

fur [fə:*] *n* pele *f*; (BRIT: *in kettle etc*) depósito, crosta

furious ['fjuərɪəs] *adj* furioso; (*effort*) incrível

furnace ['fə:nɪs] *n* forno

furnish ['fə:nɪʃ] *vt* mobiliar (BR), mobilar (PT); (*supply*): **to ~ sb with sth** fornecer algo a alguém; **furnishings** *npl* mobília

furniture ['fə:nɪtʃə*] *n* mobília, móveis *mpl*; **piece of ~** móvel *m*

furry ['fəːrɪ] *adj* peludo

further ['fəːðə*] *adj* novo, adicional ♦ *adv* mais longe; (*more*) mais; (*moreover*) além disso ♦ *vt* promover; **further education** (*BRIT*) *n* educação *f* superior; **furthermore** *adv* além disso

furthest ['fəːðɪst] *superl* of **far**

fury ['fjuərɪ] *n* fúria

fuse [fjuːz] *n* fusível *m*; (*for bomb etc*) espoleta, mecha ♦ *vt* fundir; (*fig*) unir ♦ *vi* (*metal*) fundir-se; unir-se; **to ~ the lights** (*BRIT: ELEC*) queimar as luzes; **fuse box** *n* caixa de fusíveis

fuss [fʌs] *n* estardalhaço; (*complaining*) escândalo; **to make a ~** criar caso; **to make a ~ of sb** paparicar alguém; **fussy** *adj* (*person*) exigente; (*dress, style*) espalhafatoso

future ['fjuːtʃə*] *adj* futuro ♦ *n* futuro; **in ~** no futuro

fuze [fjuːz] (*us*) = **fuse**

fuzzy ['fʌzɪ] *adj* (*PHOT*) indistinto; (*hair*) frisado, encrespado

G

G [dʒiː] *n* (*MUS*) sol *m*

G7 *n abbr* (= Group of 7) G7

gable ['ɡeɪbl] *n* cumeeira

gadget ['ɡædʒɪt] *n* aparelho, engenhoca

Gaelic ['ɡeɪlɪk] *adj* gaélico(a) ♦ *n* (*LING*) gaélico

gag [ɡæɡ] *n* (*on mouth*) mordaça; (*joke*) piada ♦ *vt* amordaçar

gain [ɡeɪn] *n* ganho; (*profit*) lucro ♦ *vt* ganhar ♦ *vi* (*watch*) adiantar-se; (*benefit*): **to ~ from sth** tirar proveito de algo; **to ~ on sb** aproximar-se de alguém; **to ~ 3lbs (in weight)** engordar 3 libras

gal. *abbr* = **gallon**

Galapagos (Islands) [ɡə'læpəɡəs-]

npl: **the ~** as ilhas Galápagos

gale [ɡeɪl] *n* ventania; **~ force 10** vento de força 10

gallant ['ɡælənt] *adj* valente; (*polite*) galante

gallery ['ɡælərɪ] *n* (*in theatre etc*) galeria; (*also*: **art ~**: *public*) museu *m*; (: *private*) galeria (de arte)

gallon ['ɡælən] *n* galão *m* (= 8 pints; BRIT = 4.5l; US = 3.8l)

gallop ['ɡæləp] *n* galope *m* ♦ *vi* galopar

gallows ['ɡæləuz] *n* forca

gallstone ['ɡɔːlstəun] *n* cálculo biliar

galore [ɡə'lɔː*] *adv* à beça

gamble ['ɡæmbl] *n* risco ♦ *vt* apostar ♦ *vi* jogar, arriscar; **gambler** *n* jogador(a) *m/f*; **gambling** *n* jogo

game [ɡeɪm] *n* jogo; (*match*) partida; (*esp TENNIS*) jogada; (*strategy*) plano, esquema *m*; (*HUNTING*) caça ♦ *adj* (*willing*): **to be ~ for anything** topar qualquer parada; **big ~** caça grossa; **gamekeeper** *n* guarda-caça *m*

gammon ['ɡæmən] *n* (*bacon*) toucinho (defumado); (*ham*) presunto

gang [ɡæŋ] *n* bando, grupo; (*of criminals*) gangue *f*; (*of workmen*) turma ♦ *vi*: **to ~ up on sb** conspirar contra alguém

gangster ['ɡæŋstə*] *n* gângster *m*, bandido

gaol [dʒeɪl] (*BRIT*) *n*, *vt* = **jail**

gap [ɡæp] *n* brecha, fenda; (*in trees, traffic*) abertura; (*in time*) intervalo; (*difference*) diferença

gape [ɡeɪp] *n* (*person*) estar *or* ficar boquiaberto; (*hole*) abrir-se; **gaping** *adj* (*hole*) muito aberto

garage ['ɡærɑːʒ] *n* garagem *f*; (*for car repairs*) oficina (mecânica)

garbage ['ɡɑːbɪdʒ] (*us*) *n* lixo; (*inf: nonsense*) disparates *mpl*; **garbage can** (*us*) *n* lata de lixo

garbled ['ɡɑːbld] *adj* deturpado,

destorcido

garden ['gɑ:dn] n jardim m; **~s** npl (public park) jardim público, parque m; **gardener** n jardineiro(-a); **gardening** n jardinagem f

gargle ['gɑ:gl] vi gargarejar

garish ['gɛərɪʃ] adj (colour) berrante; (light) brilhante

garland ['gɑ:lənd] n guirlanda

garlic ['gɑ:lɪk] n alho

garment ['gɑ:mənt] n peça de roupa

garrison ['gærɪsn] n guarnição f

garter ['gɑ:tə*] n liga

gas [gæs] n gás m; (US: gasoline) gasolina ♦ vt asfixiar com gás; **gas cooker** (BRIT) n fogão m a gás; **gas cylinder** n bujão m de gás; **gas fire** (BRIT) n aquecedor m a gás

gash [gæʃ] n talho; (tear) corte m ♦ vt talhar; cortar

gasket ['gæskɪt] n (AUT) junta, gaxeta

gasoline ['gæsəli:n] (US) n gasolina

gasp [gɑ:sp] n arfada ♦ vi arfar; **gasp out** vt dizer com voz entrecortada

gas station (US) n posto de gasolina

gate [geɪt] n portão m; **gatecrash** (BRIT) vt entrar de penetra em; **gateway** n portão m, passagem f

gather ['gæðə*] vt colher; (assemble) reunir; (SEWING) franzir; (understand) compreender ♦ vi reunir-se; **to ~ speed** acelerar-se; **gathering** n reunião f, assembléia

gauge [geɪdʒ] n (instrument) medidor m ♦ vt (fig: character) avaliar

gaunt [gɔ:nt] adj descarnado; (bare, stark) desolado

gauze [gɔ:z] n gaze f

gave [geɪv] pt of **give**

gay [geɪ] adj (homosexual) gay; (old-fashioned: cheerful) alegre; (colour) vistoso; (music) vivo

gaze [geɪz] n olhar m fixo ♦ vi: **to ~ at sth** fitar algo

GB abbr = **Great Britain**

GCE (BRIT) n abbr = **General Certificate of Education**

GCSE (BRIT) n abbr = **General Certificate of Secondary Education**

gear [gɪə*] n equipamento; (TECH) engrenagem f; (AUT) velocidade f, marcha (BR), mudança (PT) ♦ vt (fig: adapt): **to ~ sth to** preparar algo para; **top** (BRIT) or **high** (US)/**low ~** quarta/primeira (marcha); **in ~** engrenado; **gearbox** n caixa de mudanças (BR) or de velocidades (PT)

geese [gi:s] npl of **goose**

gel [dʒel] n gel m

gem [dʒem] n jóia, gema

Gemini ['dʒemɪnaɪ] n Gêminis m, Gêmeos mpl

gender ['dʒendə*] n gênero

general ['dʒenərl] n general m ♦ adj geral; **in ~** em geral; **general anaesthetic** n anestesia geral; **generally** adv geralmente; **general practitioner** n clínico(-a) geral

generate ['dʒenəreɪt] vt gerar; **generator** n gerador m

generous ['dʒenərəs] adj generoso; (measure etc) abundante

genetic engineering [dʒɪ'netɪk-] n engenharia genética

Geneva [dʒɪ'ni:və] n Genebra

genial ['dʒi:nɪəl] adj cordial, simpático

genitals ['dʒenɪtlz] npl órgãos mpl genitais

genius ['dʒi:nɪəs] n gênio

gentle ['dʒentl] adj (touch) leve, suave; (landscape) suave; (animal) manso

gentleman ['dʒentlmən] (irreg) n senhor m; (social position) fidalgo; (well-bred man) cavalheiro

gently ['dʒentlɪ] adv suavemente

gentry ['dʒentrɪ] n pequena nobreza

gents [dʒents] n banheiro de

homens (*BR*), casa de banho dos homens (*PT*)

genuine ['dʒɛnjuɪn] *adj* autêntico; (*person*) sincero

geography [dʒɪ'ɒgrəfɪ] *n* geografia

geology [dʒɪ'ɒlədʒɪ] *n* geologia

geometry [dʒɪ'ɒmɪtrɪ] *n* geometria

geranium [dʒɪ'reɪnjəm] *n* gerânio

geriatric [dʒɛrɪ'ætrɪk] *adj* geriátrico

germ [dʒə:m] *n* micróbio, bacilo

German ['dʒə:mən] *adj* alemão(-mã) ♦ *n* alemão(-mã) *m/f*; (*LING*) alemão *m*; **German measles** *n* rubéola

Germany ['dʒə:mənɪ] *n* Alemanha

gesture ['dʒɛstjə*] *n* gesto

KEYWORD

---

get [gɛt] (*pt, pp* **got**) (*US: pp* **gotten**) *vi* **1** (*become, be*) ficar, tornar-se; **to ~ old/tired/cold** envelhecer/cansar-se/resfriar-se; **to ~ annoyed/bored** aborrecer-se/amuar-se; **to ~ drunk** embebedar-se; **to ~ dirty** sujar-se; **to ~ killed/married** ser morto/casar-se; **when do I ~ paid?** quando eu recebo?, quando eu vou ser pago?; **it's ~ting late** está ficando tarde

2 (*go*): **to ~ to/from** ir para/de; **to ~ home** chegar em casa

3 (*begin*) começar a; **to ~ to know sb** começar a conhecer alguém; **let's ~ going** *or* **started** vamos lá!

♦ *modal aux vb*: **you've got to do it** você tem que fazê-lo

♦ *vt* **1**: **to ~ sth done** (*do*) fazer algo; (*have done*) mandar fazer algo; **to ~ one's hair cut** cortar o cabelo; **to ~ the car going** *or* **to go** fazer o carro andar; **to ~ sb to do sth** convencer alguém a fazer algo; **to ~ sth/sb ready** preparar algo/arrumar alguém

2 (*obtain*) ter; (*find*) achar; (*fetch*)

buscar; **to ~ sth for sb** arranjar algo para alguém; (*fetch*) ir buscar algo para alguém; **~ me Mr Jones, please** (*TEL*) pode chamar o Sr Jones por favor; **can I ~ you a drink?** você está servido?

3 (*receive: present, letter*) receber; (*acquire: reputation, prize*) ganhar

4 (*catch*) agarrar; (*hit: target etc*) pegar; **to ~ sb by the arm/throat** agarrar alguém pelo braço/pela garganta; **~ him!** pega ele!

5 (*take, move*) levar; **to ~ sth to sb** levar algo para alguém; **I can't ~ it in/out/through** não consigo enfiá-lo/tirá-lo/passá-lo; **do you think we'll ~ it through the door?** você acha que conseguiremos passar isto na porta?

6 (*plane, bus etc*) pegar, tomar

7 (*understand*) entender; (*hear*) ouvir; **I've got it** entendi; **I don't ~ your meaning** não entendo o que você quer dizer

8 (*have, possess*): **to have got** ter

get down *vi* (*news*) espalhar-se

get along *vi* (*agree*) entender-se; (*depart*) ir embora; (*manage*) = **get by**

get around = **get round**

get at *vt fus* (*attack, criticize*) atacar; (*reach*) alcançar; **what are you ~ting at?** o que você está querendo dizer?

get away *vi* (*leave*) partir; (*escape*) escapar

get away with *vt fus* conseguir fazer impunemente

get back *vi* (*return*) regressar, voltar ♦ *vt* receber de volta, recobrar

get by *vi* (*pass*) passar; (*manage*) virar-se

get down *vi* descer ♦ *vt fus* abaixar ♦ *vt* (*object*) abaixar, descer; (*depress: person*) deprimir

get down to vt fus (work) pôr-se a (fazer)

get in vi entrar; (train) chegar; (arrive home) voltar para casa

get into vt fus entrar em; (vehicle) subir em; (clothes) pôr, vestir, enfiar; **to ~ into bed/a rage** meter-se na cama/ficar com raiva

get off vi (from train etc) saltar (BR), descer (PT); (depart) sair; (escape) escapar ♦ vt (remove: clothes, stain) tirar; (send off) mandar ♦ vt fus (train, bus) saltar de (BR), sair de (PT)

get on vi (at exam etc): **how are you ~ting on?** como vai?; (agree): **to ~ on** (with) entender-se (com) ♦ vt fus (train etc) subir em (BR), subir para (PT); (horse) montar em

get out vi (of place, vehicle) sair ♦ vt (take out) tirar

get out of vt fus (duty etc) escapar de

get over vt fus (illness) restabelecer-se de

get round vt fus rodear; (fig: person) convencer

get through vi (TEL) completar a ligação

get through to vt fus (TEL) comunicar-se com

get together vi (people) reunir-se ♦ vt reunir

get up vi levantar-se ♦ vt fus levantar

get up to vt fus (reach) chegar a; (BRIT: prank etc) fazer

getaway ['gɛtəweɪ] n fuga, escape m

ghastly ['gɑːstlɪ] adj horrível; (building) medonho; (appearance) horripilante; (pale) pálido

gherkin ['gəːkɪn] n pepino em vinagre

ghost [gəust] n fantasma m

giant ['dʒaɪənt] n gigante m ♦ adj gigantesco, gigante

gibberish ['dʒɪbərɪʃ] n algaravia

giblets ['dʒɪblɪts] npl miúdos mpl

Gibraltar [dʒɪ'brɔːltə*] n Gibraltar m (no article)

giddy ['gɪdɪ] adj (dizzy): **to be** or **feel ~** estar com vertigem

gift [gɪft] n presente m, dádiva; (ability) dom m, talento; **gifted** adj bem-dotado

gigantic [dʒaɪ'gæntɪk] adj gigantesco

giggle ['gɪgl] vi dar risadinha boba

gill [dʒɪl] n (measure) = 0.25 pints (BRIT = 0.148l, US = 0.118l)

gills [gɪlz] npl (of fish) guelras fpl, brânquias fpl

gilt [gɪlt] adj dourado ♦ n dourado

gimmick ['gɪmɪk] n truque m or macete m (publicitário)

gin [dʒɪn] n gim m, genebra

ginger ['dʒɪndʒə*] n gengibre m; **gingerbread** n (cake) pão m de gengibre; (biscuit) biscoito de gengibre

gipsy ['dʒɪpsɪ] n cigano

giraffe [dʒɪ'rɑːf] n girafa

girl [gəːl] n (small) menina (BR), rapariga (PT); (young woman) jovem f, moça; (daughter) filha; **girlfriend** n (of girl) amiga; (of boy) namorada

gist [dʒɪst] n essencial m

KEYWORD

---

give [gɪv] (pt **gave**, pp **given**) vt
1 (hand over) dar; **to ~ sb sth, ~ sth to sb** dar algo a alguém
2 (used with n to replace a vb): **to ~ a cry/sigh/push** etc dar um grito/suspiro/empurrão etc; **to ~ a speech/a lecture** fazer um discurso/uma palestra
3 (tell, deliver: news, advice, message etc) dar; **to ~ the right/wrong ans-**

wer dar a resposta certa/errada
4 (*supply, provide*: *opportunity, job etc*) dar; (*bestow*: *title, right*) conceder; **the sun ~s warmth and light** o sol fornece calor e luz
5 (*dedicate*: *time, one's life*) dedicar; **she gave it all her attention** ela dedicou toda sua atenção a isto
6 (*organize*): **to ~ a party/dinner** *etc* dar uma festa/jantar *etc*
♦ *vi* **1** (*also*: **~ way**: *break, collapse*) dar folga; **his legs gave beneath him** suas pernas bambearam; **the roof/floor gave as I stepped on it** o telhado/chão desabou quando eu pisei nele
2 (*stretch*: *fabric*) dar de si
give away *vt* (*money, opportunity*) dar; (*secret, information*) revelar
give back *vt* devolver
give in *vi* (*yield*) ceder ♦ *vt* (*essay etc*) entregar
give off *vt* (*heat, smoke*) soltar
give out *vt* (*distribute*) distribuir; (*make known*) divulgar
give up *vi* (*surrender*) desistir, dar-se por vencido ♦ *vt* (*job, boyfriend, habit*) renunciar a; (*idea, hope*) abandonar; **to ~ smoking** deixar de fumar; **to ~ o.s. up** entregar-se
give way *vi* (*yield*) ceder; (*break, collapse*: *rope*) arrebentar; (: *ladder*) quebrar; (*BRIT*: *AUT*) dar a preferência (*BR*), dar prioridade (*PT*)

glacier ['glæsɪə*] *n* glaciar *m*, geleira
glad [glæd] *adj* contente
gladly ['glædlɪ] *adv* com muito prazer
glamorous ['glæmərəs] *adj* encantador(a), glamuroso
glamour ['glæmə*] *n* encanto, glamour *m*
glance [glɑːns] *n* relance *m*, vista de

olhos ♦ *vi*: **to ~ at** olhar (de relance);
glance off *vt fus* (*bullet*) ricochetear de; **glancing** *adj* (*blow*) oblíquo
gland [glænd] *n* glândula
glare [gleə*] *n* (*of anger*) olhar *m* furioso; (*of light*) luminosidade *f*; (*of publicity*) foco ♦ *vi* brilhar; **to ~ at** olhar furiosamente para; **glaring** *adj* (*mistake*) notório
glass [glɑːs] *n* vidro, cristal *m*; (*for drinking*) copo; **~es** *npl* (*spectacles*) óculos *mpl*; **glassware** *n* objetos *mpl* de cristal
glaze [gleɪz] *vt* (*door*) envidraçar; (*pottery*) vitrificar ♦ *n* verniz *m*
gleam [gliːm] *vi* brilhar
glean [gliːn] *vt* (*information*) colher
glib [glɪb] *adj* (*answer*) pronto; (*person*) labioso
glide [glaɪd] *vi* deslizar; (*AVIAT, birds*) planar; **glider** *n* (*AVIAT*) planador *m*; **gliding** *n* (*AVIAT*) vôo sem motor
glimmer ['glɪmə*] *n* luz *f* trêmula; (*of interest, hope*) lampejo
glimpse [glɪmps] *n* vista rápida, vislumbre *m* ♦ *vt* vislumbrar, ver de relance
glint [glɪnt] *vi* cintilar
glisten ['glɪsn] *vi* brilhar
glitter ['glɪtə*] *vi* reluzir, brilhar
gloat [gləʊt] *vi*: **to ~ (over)** exultar (com)
global ['gləʊbl] *adj* mundial
globe [gləʊb] *n* globo, esfera
gloom [gluːm] *n* escuridão *f*; (*sadness*) tristeza; **gloomy** *adj* escuro; triste
glorious ['glɔːrɪəs] *adj* (*weather*) magnífico; (*future*) glorioso
glory ['glɔːrɪ] *n* glória
gloss [glɒs] *n* (*shine*) brilho; (*also*: **~ paint**) pintura brilhante, esmalte *m*; **gloss over** *vt fus* encobrir
glossary ['glɒsərɪ] *n* glossário

glossy ['glɔsɪ] *adj* lustroso

glove [glʌv] *n* luva

glow [gləu] *vi* (*shine*) brilhar; (*fire*) arder

glower ['glauə*] *vi*: **to ~ at** (**sb**) olhar (alguém) de modo ameaçador

glucose ['glu:kəus] *n* glicose *f*

glue [glu:] *n* cola ♦ *vt* colar

glum [glʌm] *adj* (*mood*) abatido; (*person, tone*) triste

glut [glʌt] *n* abundância, fartura

glutton ['glʌtn] *n* glutão(-ona) *m/f*; **a ~ for work** um(a) trabalhador(a) incansável

GM *adj abbr* (= *genetically modified*) geneticamente modificado

gnat [næt] *n* mosquito

gnaw [nɔ:] *vt* roer

KEYWORD

go [gəu] (*pt* **went**, *pp* **gone**, *pl* **~es**) *vi* **1** (*try*) ir; (*travel, move*) viajar; **a car went by** um carro passou; **he has gone to Aberdeen** ele foi para Aberdeen

2 (*depart*) partir, ir-se

3 (*attend*) ir; **she went to university in Rio** ela foi à universidade no Rio; **he ~es to the local church** ele freqüenta a igreja local

4 (*take part in an activity*) ir; **to ~ for a walk** ir passear

5 (*work*) funcionar; **the bell went just then** a campainha acabou de tocar

6 (*become*): **to ~ pale/mouldy** ficar pálido/mofado

7 (*be sold*): **to ~ for £10** ser vendido por £10

8 (*fit, suit*): **to ~ with** acompanhar, combinar com

9 (*be about to, intend to*): **he's ~ing to do it** ele vai fazê-lo; **are you ~ing to come?** você vem?

10 (*time*) passar

11 (*event, activity*) ser; **how did it ~?** como foi?

12 (*be given*): **the job is to ~ to someone else** o emprego vai ser dado para outra pessoa

13 (*break*) romper-se; **the fuse went** o fusível queimou; **the leg of the chair went** a perna da cadeira quebrou

14 (*be placed*): **where does this cup ~?** onde é que põe esta xícara?; **the milk ~es in the fridge** pode guardar o leite na geladeira

♦ *n* **1** (*try*): **to have a ~ (at)** tentar a sorte (com)

2 (*turn*) vez *f*

3 (*move*): **to be on the ~** ter muito para fazer; **go about** *vi* (*also*: **~ around**: *rumour*) espalhar-se

♦ *vt fus*: **how do I ~ about this?** como é que eu faço isto?

go ahead *vi* (*make progress*) progredir; (*get going*) ir em frente

go along *vi ir* ♦ *vt fus* ladear; **to ~ along with** concordar com

go away *vi* (*leave*) ir-se, ir embora

go back *vi* (*return*) voltar; (*go again*) ir de novo

go back on *vt fus* (*promise*) faltar com

go by *vi* (*years, time*) passar ♦ *vt fus* (*book, rule*) guiar-se por

go down *vi* (*descend*) descer, baixar; (*ship*) afundar; (*sun*) pôr-se ♦ *vt fus* (*stairs, ladder*) descer

go for *vt fus* (*fetch*) ir buscar; (*like*) gostar de; (*attack*) atacar

go in *vi* (*enter*) entrar

go in for *vt fus* (*competition*) inscrever-se em; (*like*) gostar de

go into *vt fus* (*enter*) entrar em; (*investigate*) investigar; (*embark on*) embarcar em

go off *vi* (*leave*) ir-se; (*food*) estragar, apodrecer; (*bomb, gun*) explo-

dir; (event) realizar-se ♦ vt fus (person, food etc) deixar de gostar de
go on vi (continue) seguir, continuar; (happen) acontecer, ocorrer
go out vi sair; (for entertainment): **are you ~ing out tonight?** você vai sair hoje à noite?; (couple): **they went out for 3 years** eles namoraram 3 anos; (fire, light) apagar-se
go over vi (ship) soçobrar ♦ vt fus (check) revisar
go round vi (news, rumour) circular
go through vt fus (town etc) atravessar; (search through) vasculhar; (examine) percorrer de cabo a rabo
go up vi subir; (price) aumentar
go without vt fus passar sem

goad [gəud] vt aguilhoar
go-ahead adj empreendedor(a) ♦ n luz f verde
goal [gəul] n meta, alvo; (SPORT) gol m (BR), golo (PT); **goalkeeper** n goleiro(-a) (BR), guarda-redes m/f inv (PT)
goat [gəut] n cabra
gobble ['gɔbl] vt (also: ~ down, ~ up) engolir rapidamente, devorar
god [gɔd] n deus m; G~ Deus; **godchild** n afilhado(-a); **goddess** n deusa; **godfather** n padrinho; **godmother** n madrinha; **godsend** n dádiva do céu
goggles ['gɔglz] npl óculos mpl de proteção
going ['gəuŋ] n (conditions) estado do terreno ♦ adj: **the ~ rate** tarifa corrente or em vigor
gold [gəuld] n ouro ♦ adj de ouro; **golden** adj (made of gold) de ouro; (gold in colour) dourado; **goldfish** n inv peixe-dourado m; **gold-plated** adj plaquê inv; **goldsmith** n ourives m/f inv
golf [gɔlf] n golfe m; **golf ball** n

bola de golfe; (on typewriter) esfera; **golf club** n clube m de golfe; (stick) taco; **golf course** n campo de golfe; **golfer** n jogador(a) m/f, golfista m/f
gone [gɔn] pp of **go**
gong [gɔŋ] n gongo
good [gud] adj bom (boa); (kind) bom, bondoso; (well-behaved) educado ♦ n bem m; **~s** npl (COMM) mercadorias fpl; **~! bom!; to be ~ at** ser bom em; **to be ~ for** servir para; **it's ~ for you** faz-lhe bem; **a ~ deal (of)** muito; **a ~ many** muitos; **to make ~** reparar; **it's no ~ complaining** não adianta se queixar; **for ~** para sempre, definitivamente; **~ morning/afternoon/evening!** bom dia/boa tarde/boa noite!; **~ night!** boa noite!; **goodbye** excl até logo (BR), adeus (PT); **to say goodbye** despedir-se; **Good Friday** n Sexta-Feira Santa; **good-looking** adj bonito; **good-natured** adj (person) de bom gênio; (pet) de boa índole; **goodwill** n boa vontade f
goose [gu:s] n (pl **geese**) n ganso
gooseberry ['guzbəri] n groselha; **to play ~** (BRIT) ficar de vela
gooseflesh ['gu:sfleʃ] n, **goose pimples** npl pele f arrepiada
gore [gɔ:*] vt escornar ♦ n sangue m
gorge [gɔ:dʒ] n desfiladeiro ♦ vt: **to ~ o.s. (on)** empanturrar-se (de)
gorgeous ['gɔ:dʒəs] adj magnífico, maravilhoso; (person) lindo
gorilla [gə'rɪlə] n gorila m
gorse [gɔ:s] n tojo
gory ['gɔ:rɪ] adj sangrento
gospel ['gɔspl] n evangelho
gossip ['gɔsɪp] n (scandal) fofocas fpl (BR), mexericos mpl (PT); (chat) conversa; (scandalmonger) fofoqueiro(-a) (BR), mexeriqueiro(-a) (PT) ♦ vi (chat) bater (um) papo (BR), cava-

quear (PT)

got [gɒt] pt, pp of **get**

gotten ['gɒtn] (US) pp of **get**

gout [gaut] n gota

govern ['gʌvən] vt governar; (event) controlar

governess ['gʌvənɪs] n governanta

government ['gʌvnmənt] n governo

governor ['gʌvənə*] n governador(a) m/f; (of school, hospital, jail) diretor(a) m/f

gown [gaun] n vestido; (of teacher, judge) toga

GP n abbr (MED) = **general practitioner**

grab [græb] vt agarrar ♦ vi: **to ~ at** tentar agarrar

grace [greɪs] n (REL) graça; (gracefulness) elegância, fineza ♦ vt (honour) honrar; (adorn) adornar; **5 days' ~** um prazo de 5 dias; **graceful** adj elegante, gracioso; **gracious** ['greɪʃəs] adj gracioso; afável

grade [greɪd] n (quality) classe f, qualidade f; (degree) grau m; (US: SCH) série f, classe ♦ vt classificar; **grade crossing** (US) n passagem f de nível; **grade school** (US) n escola primária

gradient ['greɪdɪənt] n declive m

gradual ['grædjuəl] adj gradual, gradativo; **gradually** adv gradualmente, pouco a pouco

graduate [n 'grædjut, vb 'grædjueɪt] n graduado, licenciado; (US) diplomado do colégio ♦ vi formar-se, licenciar-se; **graduation** [grædju-'eɪʃən] n formatura

graffiti [grə'fi:tɪ] n, npl pichações fpl

graft [grɑ:ft] n (AGR, MED) enxerto; (BRIT: inf) trabalho pesado; (bribery) suborno ♦ vt enxertar

grain [greɪn] n grão m; (no pl: cereals) cereais mpl; (in wood) veio, fibra

gram [græm] n grama m

grammar ['græmə*] n gramática; **grammar school** n (BRIT) ≈ liceu; **grammatical** [grə'mætɪkl] adj gramatical

gramme [græm] n = **gram**

grand [grænd] adj esplêndido; (inf: wonderful) ótimo, formidável; **granddad** n vovô m; **granddaughter** n neta; **grandfather** n avô m; **grandma** n avó f, vovó f; **grandmother** n avó f; **grandpa** n = grandad; **grandparents** npl avós mpl; **grand piano** n piano de cauda; **grandson** n neto

granite ['grænɪt] n granito

granny ['grænɪ] n (inf) avó f, vovó f

grant [grɑ:nt] vt (concede) conceder; (a request etc) anuir a; (admit) admitir ♦ n (SCH) bolsa; (ADMIN) subvenção f, subsídio; **to take sth for ~ed** dar algo por certo

grape [greɪp] n uva

grapefruit ['greɪpfru:t] (pl inv or ~s) n toranja, grapefruit m (BR)

graph [grɑ:f] n gráfico; **graphic** ['græfɪk] adj gráfico; **graphics** (art) artes fpl gráficas ♦ npl (drawings) desenhos mpl

grasp [grɑ:sp] vt agarrar, segurar; (understand) compreender, entender ♦ n aperto de mão; (understanding) compreensão f; **grasping** adj avaro

grass [grɑ:s] n grama (BR), relva (PT); **grasshopper** n gafanhoto

grate [greɪt] n (fireplace) lareira ♦ vt ranger ♦ vt (CULIN) ralar

grateful ['greɪtful] adj agradecido, grato

grater ['greɪtə*] n ralador m

gratitude ['grætɪtju:d] n agradecimento

gratuity [grə'tju:ɪtɪ] *n* gratificação f, gorjeta

grave [greɪv] *n* cova, sepultura ♦ *adj* sério; (*mistake*) grave

gravel ['grævl] *n* cascalho

gravestone ['greɪvstəʊn] *n* lápide f

graveyard ['greɪvjɑ:d] *n* cemitério

gravity ['grævɪtɪ] *n* (PHYS) gravidade f; (*seriousness*) seriedade f, gravidade

gravy ['greɪvɪ] *n* molho (de carne)

gray [greɪ] (US) *adj* = **grey**

graze [greɪz] *vi* pastar ♦ *vt* (*touch lightly*) roçar; (*scrape*) raspar ♦ *n* (MED) esfoladura, arranhadura

grease [gri:s] *n* (*fat*) gordura; (*lubricant*) graxa, lubrificante *m* ♦ *vt* untar, lubrificar, engraxar; **greasy** *adj* gordurento, gorduroso; (*skin, hair*) oleoso

great [greɪt] *adj* grande; (*inf*) genial; (*pain, heat*) forte; (*important*) importante; **Great Britain** *n* Grã-Bretanha; *ver quadro*

GREAT BRITAIN

A Grã-Bretanha, **Great Britain** ou **Britain** em inglês, designa a maior das ilhas britânicas e, portanto, engloba a Escócia e o País de Gales. Junto com a Irlanda, a ilha de Man e as ilhas Anglonormandas, a Grã-Bretanha forma as ilhas Britânicas, ou *British Isles* Reino Unido, ou *United Kingdom* ou *UK*, é o nome oficial da entidade política que compreende a Grã-Bretanha e a Irlanda do Norte.

---

great: **great-grandfather** *n* bisavô *m*; **great-grandmother** *n* bisavó f; **greatly** *adv* imensamente, muito

Greece [gri:s] *n* Grécia

greed [gri:d] *n* (*also*: **~iness**) avidez f, cobiça, ganância; **greedy** *adj* avarento; (*for food*) guloso

Greek [gri:k] *adj* grego ♦ *n* grego(-a); (LING) grego

green [gri:n] *adj* verde; (*inexperienced*) inexperiente, ingênuo ♦ *n* verde *m*; (*stretch of grass*) (BR), relvado (PT); (*on golf course*) green *m*; **~s** *npl* (*vegetables*) verduras fpl; **greenery** *n* verdura, **greengrocer** (BRIT) *n* verdureiro(-a); **greenhouse** *n* estufa; **greenhouse effect** *n* efeito estufa; **greenhouse gas** *n* gás provocado pelo efeito estufa

Greenland ['gri:nlənd] *n* Groenlândia

greet [gri:t] *vt* acolher; (*news*) receber; **greeting** *n* acolhimento, **greeting(s) card** *n* cartão *m* comemorativo

grenade [grə'neɪd] *n* granada

grew [gru:] *pt of* **grow**

grey [greɪ] (US **gray**) *adj* cinzento; (*dismal*) sombrio; **grey-haired** *adj* grisalho; **greyhound** *n* galgo

grid [grɪd] *n* grade f; (ELEC) rede f

grief [gri:f] *n* dor f, pesar *m*

grievance ['gri:vəns] *n* motivo de queixa, agravo

grieve [gri:v] *vi* sofrer ♦ *vt* dar pena a, afligir; **to ~ for** chorar por

grill [grɪl] *n* (*on cooker*) grelha; (*also*: **mixed ~**) prato de grelhados ♦ *vt* (BRIT) grelhar; (*inf*: *question*) interrogar cerradamente

grille [grɪl] *n* grade f; (AUT) grelha

grim [grɪm] *adj* desagradável; (*unattractive*) feio; (*stern*) severo

grimace [grɪ'meɪs] *n* careta ♦ *vi* fazer caretas

grime [graɪm] *n* sujeira (BR),

sujidade f (PT)

grin [grɪn] n sorriso largo ♦ vi: **to ~ (at)** dar um sorriso largo (para)

grind [graɪnd] (pt, pp **ground**) vt triturar; (coffee etc) moer; (make sharp) afiar; (US: meat) picar ♦ n (work) trabalho (repetitivo e maçante)

grip [grɪp] n (of person) aperto de mão; (of animal) força; (handle) punho; (of tyre, shoe) aderência; (holdall) valise f ♦ vt agarrar; (attention) prender; **to come to ~s with** arcar com

gripping ['grɪpɪŋ] adj absorvente, emocionante

grisly ['grɪzlɪ] adj horrendo, medonho

gristle ['grɪsl] n (on meat) nervo

grit [grɪt] n areia, grão m de areia; (courage) coragem f ♦ vt (road) pôr areia em; **to ~ one's teeth** cerrar os dentes

groan [grəun] n gemido ♦ vi gemer

grocer ['grəusə*] n dono(-a) de mercearia; **groceries** npl comestíveis mpl; **grocer's (shop)** n mercearia

groin [grɔɪn] n virilha

groom [gru:m] n cavalariço; (also: **bride~**) noivo ♦ vt (horse) tratar; (fig): **to ~ sb for sth** preparar alguém para algo; **well-~ed** bem posto

groove [gru:v] n ranhura, entalhe m

grope [grəup] vi: **to ~ for** procurar às cegas

gross [grəus] adj (flagrant) grave; (vulgar) vulgar; (: building) de mau gosto; (COMM) bruto

grotto ['grɔtəu] n gruta

grotty ['grɔtɪ] (BRIT: inf) adj vagabundo

ground [graund] pt, pp of **grind** ♦ n terra, chão m; (SPORT) campo; (land) terreno; (reason: gen pl) motivo, razão f; (US: also: **~wire**) (ligação f à) terra, fio-terra m ♦ vt (plane) manter em terra; (US: ELEC) ligar à terra; **~s** npl (of coffee etc) borra; (gardens etc) jardins mpl, parque m; **on the ~** no chão; **to the ~** por terra; **ground cloth** (US) n = **groundsheet**; **groundless** adj infundado; **groundsheet** (BRIT) n capa impermeável; **groundwork** n base f, preparação f

group [gru:p] n grupo; (also: **pop ~**) conjunto ♦ vt (also: **~ together**) agrupar ♦ vi (also: **~ together**) agrupar-se

grouse [graus] n inv (bird) tetraz m, galo-silvestre m ♦ vi (complain) queixar-se, resmungar

grove [grəuv] n arvoredo

grovel ['grɔvl] vi (fig): **to ~ (before)** abaixar-se (diante de)

grow [grəu] (pt **grew**, pp **grown**) vi crescer; (increase) aumentar; (develop): **to ~ (out of/from)** originar-se; (become): **to ~ rich/weak** enriquecer(-se)/enfraquecer-se ♦ vt plantar, cultivar; (beard) deixar crescer; **grow up** vi crescer, fazer-se homem/mulher; **grower** n cultivador(a) m/f, produtor(a) m/f; **growing** adj crescente

growl [graul] vi rosnar

grown [grəun] pp of **grow**

grown-up n adulto(-a), pessoa mais velha

growth [grəuθ] n crescimento; (increase) aumento; (MED) abcesso, tumor m

grub [grʌb] n larva, lagarta; (inf: food) comida, rango (BR)

grubby ['grʌbɪ] adj encardido

grudge [grʌdʒ] n motivo de rancor

♦ vt: **to ~ sb sth** dar algo a alguém de má vontade, invejar algo a alguém; **to bear sb a ~ for sth** guardar rancor de alguém por algo

gruelling ['gruəlɪŋ] (US **grueling**) adj duro, árduo

gruesome ['gru:səm] adj horrível

gruff [grʌf] adj (voice) rouco; (manner) brusco

grumble ['grʌmbl] vi resmungar, bufar

grumpy ['grʌmpɪ] adj rabugento

grunt [grʌnt] vi grunhir

G-string n tapa-sexo m

guarantee [gærən'ti:] n garantia ♦ vt garantir

guard [gɑ:d] n guarda; (one person) guarda m; (BRIT: RAIL) guarda-freio; (on machine) dispositivo de segurança; (also: **fire~**) guarda-fogo ♦ vt (protect): **to ~ (against)** proteger (contra); (prisoner) vigiar; **to be on one's ~** estar prevenido; **guard against** vt fus prevenir-se contra; **guarded** (statement) cauteloso; **guardian** n protetor(a) m/f; (of minor) tutor(a) m/f

Guatemala [gwɔtə'mɑ:lə] n Guatemala

guerrilla [gə'rɪlə] n guerrilheiro(-a)

guess [gɛs] vt, vi (estimate) avaliar, conjeturar; (answer) adivinhar; (US) achar, supor ♦ n suposição f, conjetura; **to take** or **have a ~** adivinhar, chutar (inf)

guest [gɛst] n convidado(-a); (in hotel) hóspede m/f; **guest-house** n pensão f; **guest room** n quarto de hóspedes

guffaw [gʌ'fɔ:] vi dar gargalhadas

guidance ['gaɪdəns] n conselhos mpl

guide [gaɪd] n (person) guia m/f;

(book, fig) guia m; (BRIT: also: **girl ~**) escoteira ♦ vt guiar; **guidebook** n guia m; **guide dog** n cão m de guia; **guidelines** npl (advice) orientação f

guillotine ['gɪləti:n] n guilhotina

guilt [gɪlt] n culpa; **guilty** adj culpado

guinea pig ['gɪnɪ-] n porquinho-da-índia m, cobaia; (fig) cobaia

guitar [gɪ'tɑ:*] n violão m

gulf [gʌlf] n golfo; (abyss: also fig) abismo

gull [gʌl] n gaivota

gullible ['gʌlɪbl] adj crédulo

gully ['gʌlɪ] n barranco

gulp [gʌlp] vi engolir em seco ♦ vt (also: **~ down**) engolir

gum [gʌm] n (ANAT) gengiva; (glue) goma; (also: **~ drop**) bala de goma; (also: **chewing-~**) chiclete m (BR), pastilha elástica (PT) ♦ vt colar; **gumboots** (BRIT) npl botas fpl de borracha, galochas fpl

gun [gʌn] n (gen) arma (de fogo); (revolver) revólver m; (small) pistola; (rifle) espingarda; (cannon) canhão m; **gunfire** n tiroteio; **gunman** (irreg) n pistoleiro; **gunpoint** n: **at gunpoint** sob a ameaça de uma arma; **gunpowder** n pólvora; **gunshot** n tiro (de arma de fogo)

gurgle ['gə:gl] vi (baby) balbuciar; (water) gorgolejar

gust [gʌst] n (of wind) rajada

gusto ['gʌstəu] n: **with ~** com garra

gut [gʌt] n intestino, tripa; **~s** npl (ANAT) entranhas fpl; (inf: courage) coragem f, raça (inf)

gutter ['gʌtə*] n (of roof) calha; (in street) sarjeta

guy [gaɪ] n (also: **~rope**) corda; (inf: man) cara m (BR), tipo (PT); **Guy Fawkes' Night** n ver quadro

GUY FAWKES' NIGHT

A **Guy Fawkes' Night**, também chamada de *bonfire night*, é a ocasião em que se comemora o fracasso da conspiração (a *Gunpowder Plot*) contra James I e o Parlamento, em 5 de novembro de 1605. Um dos conspiradores, Guy Fawkes, foi surpreendido no porão do Parlamento quando estava prestes a atear fogo a explosivos. Todo ano, no dia 5 de novembro, as crianças preparam antecipadamente um boneco de Guy Fawkes e pedem às pessoas que passam na rua *a penny for the Guy* (uma moedinha para o Guy), com o qual compram fogos de artifício.

gym [dʒɪm] *n* (*also:* **gymnasium**) ginásio; (*also:* **gymnastics**) ginástica

gymnast ['dʒɪmnæst] *n* ginasta *m/f*

gymnastics [dʒɪm'næstɪks] *n* ginástica

gynaecologist [gaɪnɪ'kɔlədʒɪst] (*US* **gynecologist**) *n* ginecologista *m/f*

gypsy ['dʒɪpsɪ] *n* = **gipsy**

H

haberdashery ['hæbə'dæʃərɪ] (*BRIT*) *n* armarinho

habit ['hæbɪt] *n* hábito, costume *m*; (*addiction*) vício; (*REL*) hábito

habitual [hə'bɪtjuəl] *adj* habitual, costumeiro; (*drinker*, *liar*) inveterado

hack [hæk] *vt* (*cut*) cortar; (*chop*) talhar ♦ *n* (*pej: writer*) escrevinhador(a) *m/f*; **hacker** *n* (*COMPUT*) pirata *m* (de dados de computador)

had [hæd] *pt, pp of* **have**

haddock ['hædək] (*pl inv or* **~s**) *n* hadoque *m* (*BR*), eglefim *m* (*PT*)

hadn't ['hædnt] = **had not**

haemorrhage ['hemərɪdʒ] (*US* **hemorrhage**) *n* hemorragia

haemorrhoids ['hemərɔɪdz] (*US* **hemorrhoids**) *npl* hemorróidas *fpl*

haggle ['hægl] *vi* pechinchar, regatear

Hague [heɪg] *n*: **The ~** Haia

hail [heɪl] *n* granizo; (*of objects*) chuva; (*of criticism*) torrente *f* ♦ *vt* (*greet*) cumprimentar; (*taxi*) chamar; (*person*, *event*) saudar ♦ *vi* chover granizo; **hailstone** *n* pedra de granizo

hair [hɛə*] *n* (*of human*) cabelo; (*of animal*) pêlo; **to do one's ~** pentear-se; **hairbrush** *n* escova de cabelo; **haircut** *n* corte *m* de cabelo; **hairdo** *n* penteado; **hairdresser** *n* cabeleireiro(-a); **hairdresser's** *n* cabeleireiro; **hair dryer** *n* secador *m* de cabelo; **hair gel** *n* gel *m* para o cabelo; **hairgrip** *n* grampo (*BR*), gancho (*PT*); **hairnet** *n* rede *f* de cabelo; **hairpin** *n* grampo (*BR*), gancho (*PT*), pinça; **hair-raising** *adj* horripilante, de arrepiar os cabelos; **hair remover** *n* (*creme m*) depilatório; **hair spray** *n* laquê *m* (*BR*), laca (*PT*); **hairstyle** *n* penteado; **hairy** *adj* cabeludo, peludo; (*inf: situation*) perigoso

hake [heɪk] (*pl inv or* **~s**) *n* abrótea

half [hɑːf] (*pl* **halves**) *n* metade *f*; (*RAIL*, *bus*, *of beer etc*) meia ♦ *adj* meio ♦ *adv* meio, pela metade; **~ a pound** meia libra; **two and a ~** dois e meio; **~ a dozen** meia-dúzia; **to cut sth in ~** cortar algo ao meio; **~ asleep/empty/closed** meio adormecido/vazio/fechado; **half-caste** ['hɑːfkɑːst] *n* mestiço(-a); **half-**

hearted adj irresoluto, indiferente; **half-hour** n meia hora; **half-price** adj, adv pela metade do preço; **half term** (BRIT) n (SCH) dias de folga no meio do semestre; **half-time** n meio tempo; **halfway** adv a meio caminho; (in time) no meio

hall [hɔ:l] n (for concerts) sala; (entrance way) hall m, entrada

hallmark ['hɔ:lmɑ:k] n (also fig) marca

hallo [hə'ləu] excl = **hello**

hall of residence (BRIT) (pl **halls of residence**) n residência universitária

Hallowe'en ['hæləu'i:n] n Dia m das Bruxas (31 de outubro); ver quadro

---

HALLOWE'EN

Segundo a tradição, Hallowe'en é a noite dos fantasmas e dos bruxos. Na Escócia e nos Estados Unidos, sobretudo (bem menos na Inglaterra), as crianças, para festejar o Hallowe'en, se fantasiam e batem de porta em porta pedindo prendas (chocolates, maçãs etc).

---

hallway ['hɔ:lwei] n hall m, entrada

halo ['heiləu] n (of saint etc) auréola

halt [hɔ:lt] n parada f, paragem f (PT) ♦ vt parar ♦ vt deter; (process) interromper

halve [hɑ:v] vt (divide) dividir ao meio; (reduce by half) reduzir à metade

halves [hɑ:vz] npl of **half**

ham [hæm] n presunto, fiambre m (PT)

hamburger ['hæmbə:gə*] n hambúrguer m

hammer ['hæmə*] n martelo ♦ vt martelar ♦ vi (on door) bater insistentemente

hammock ['hæmək] n rede f

hamper ['hæmpə*] vt dificultar, atrapalhar ♦ n cesto

hamster ['hæmstə*] n hamster m

hand [hænd] n mão f; (of clock) ponteiro; (writing) letra; (of cards) cartas fpl; (worker) trabalhador m ♦ vt dar, passar; to give or lend sb a ~ dar uma mãozinha a alguém, dar uma ajuda a alguém; at ~ à mão, disponível; in ~ livre; (situation) sob controle; to be on ~ (person) estar disponível; (emergency services) estar num estado de prontidão; on the one ~ ..., on the other ~ ... por um lado ..., por outro (lado) ...; hand in vt entregar; hand out vt distribuir, entregar; hand over vt entregar; (responsibility) transferir; handbag n bolsa; handbook n manual m; handbrake n freio (BR) or travão m (PT) de mão; handcuffs npl algemas fpl; handful n punhado; (of people) grupo

handicap ['hændikæp] n (MED) incapacidade f; (disadvantage) desvantagem f; (SPORT) handicap m ♦ vt prejudicar; mentally/physically ~ped deficiente menta/físico

handicraft ['hændikrɑ:ft] n artesanato, trabalho manual

handiwork ['hændiwɔ:k] n obra

handkerchief ['hæŋkətʃif] n lenço

handle ['hændl] n (of door etc) maçaneta; (of cup etc) asa; (of knife etc) cabo; (for winding) manivela ♦ vt manusear; (deal with) tratar de; (treat: people) lidar com; "~ with care" "cuidado – frágil"; to fly off the ~ perder as estribeiras; handlebar(s) n(pl) guidom m (BR), guidão m (PT)

hand: hand-luggage n bagagem f de mão; **handmade** adj feito à mão; **handout** n (money, food) doação f; (leaflet) folheto; (at lec-

ture) apostila; **handrail** *n* corrimão *m*; **handshake** *n* aperto de mão

handsome ['hænsəm] *adj* bonito, elegante; (*profit*) considerável

handwriting ['hændraɪtɪŋ] *n* letra, caligrafia

handy ['hændɪ] *adj* (*close at hand*) à mão; (*useful*) útil; (*skilful*) habilidoso, hábil

hang [hæŋ] (*pt, pp* **hung**) *vt* pendurar; (*criminal: pt, pp* ~ed) enforcar ♦ *vi* estar pendurado; (*hair, drapery*) cair ♦ *n* (*inf*): **to get the ~ of sth** pegar o jeito de algo; **hang about** or **around** *vi* vadiar, vagabundear; **hang on** *vi* (*wait*) esperar; **hang up** *vt* (*coat*) pendurar ♦ *vi* (*TEL*) desligar; **to ~ up on sb** bater o telefone na cara de alguém

hanger ['hæŋə*] *n* cabide *m*

hang-gliding *n* vôo livre

hangover ['hæŋəuvə*] *n* ressaca

hanker ['hæŋkə*] *vi*: **to ~ after** (*long for*) ansiar por

hankie ['hæŋkɪ] *n abbr* = **handkerchief**

hanky ['hæŋkɪ] *n abbr* = **handkerchief**

haphazard [hæp'hæzəd] *adj* desorganizado

happen ['hæpən] *vi* acontecer; **to ~ to do sth** fazer algo por acaso; **as it ~s ...** acontece que ...; **happening** *n* acontecimento, ocorrência

happily ['hæpɪlɪ] *adv* (*luckily*) felizmente; (*cheerfully*) alegremente

happiness ['hæpɪnɪs] *n* felicidade *f*

happy ['hæpɪ] *adj* feliz; (*cheerful*) contente, feliz ♦ **to be ~ (with)** estar contente (com); **to be ~ to do** (*willing*) estar disposto a fazer; **~ birthday!** feliz aniversário; **happy-go-lucky** *adj* despreocupado

harass ['hærəs] *vt* importunar;

harassment *n* perseguição *f*

harbour ['hɑːbə*] (*US* **harbor**) *n* porto ♦ *vt* (*hope etc*) abrigar; (*hide*) esconder

hard [hɑːd] *adj* duro; (*difficult*) difícil; (*work*) árduo; (*person*) severo, cruel; (*facts*) verdadeiro ♦ *adv* (*work*) muito, diligentemente; (*think, try*) seriamente; **to look ~ at** olhar firme or fixamente para; **no ~ feelings!** sem ressentimentos!; **to be ~ of hearing** ser surdo; **to be ~ done by** ser tratado injustamente; **hardback** *n* livro de capa dura; **hard disk** *n* (*COMPUT*) disco rígido; **harden** *vt* endurecer; (*steel*) temperar; (*fig*) tornar insensível ♦ *vi* endurecer-se

hardly ['hɑːdlɪ] *adv* (*scarcely*) apenas; (*no sooner*) mal; **~ ever/anywhere** quase nunca/em lugar nenhum

hardship ['hɑːdʃɪp] *n* privação *f*

hard shoulder *n* acostamento *m*

hard up (*inf*) *adj* duro (*BR*), liso (*PT*)

hardware ['hɑːdwɛə*] *n* ferragens *fpl*; (*COMPUT*) hardware *m*

hard-working *adj* trabalhador(a); (*student*) aplicado

hardy ['hɑːdɪ] *adj* forte; (*plant*) resistente

hare [hɛə*] *n* lebre *f*

harm [hɑːm] *n* mal *m*; (*damage*) dano ♦ *vt* (*person*) fazer mal a, prejudicar; (*thing*) danificar; **out of ~'s way** a salvo; **harmful** *adj* prejudicial, nocivo; **harmless** *adj* inofensivo

harmony ['hɑːmənɪ] *n* harmonia

harness ['hɑːnɪs] *n* (*for horse*) arreios *mpl*; (*for child*) correia; (*safety ~*) correia de segurança ♦ *vt* (*horse*) arrear, pôr arreios em; (*resources*) aproveitar

harp [hɑːp] *n* harpa ♦ *vi*: **to ~ on**

about bater sempre na mesma tecla sobre

harrowing ['hærəʊɪŋ] *adj* doloroso, pungente

harsh [hɑːʃ] *adj* (*life*) duro; (*sound*) desarmonioso; (*light*) forte

harvest ['hɑːvɪst] *n* colheita ♦ *vt* colher

has [hæz] *vb see* **have**

hash [hæʃ] *n* (CULIN) picadinho; (*fig: mess*) confusão *f*

hasn't ['hæznt] = **has not**

hassle ['hæsl] (*inf*) *n* complicação *f*

haste [heɪst] *n* pressa; **hasten** ['heɪsn] *vt* acelerar ♦ *vi*: **to hasten to do sth** apressar-se em fazer algo; **hastily** *adv* depressa; **hasty** *adj* apressado; (*rash*) precipitado

hat [hæt] *n* chapéu *m*

hatch [hætʃ] *n* (NAUT: *also:* **~way**) escotilha; (*also:* **service ~**) comunicação *f* entre a cozinha e a sala de jantar ♦ *vi* sair do ovo, chocar

hatchet ['hætʃɪt] *n* machadinha

hate [heɪt] *vt* odiar, detestar ♦ *n* ódio; **hateful** *adj* odioso; **hatred** ['heɪtrɪd] *n* ódio

haughty ['hɔːtɪ] *adj* soberbo, arrogante

haul [hɔːl] *vt* puxar ♦ *n* (*of fish*) redada; (*of stolen goods etc*) pilhagem *f*, presa; **haulage** *n* transporte *m* (rodoviário); (*costs*) gasto com transporte; **haulier** ['hɔːlɪə*] (BRIT) *n* (*firm*) transportadora; (*person*) transportador(a) *m/f*

haunt [hɔːnt] *vt* (*subj: ghost*) assombrar; (*: problem, memory*) perseguir ♦ *n* reduto; (**~ed house**) casa mal-assombrada

[KEYWORD]

have [hæv] (*pt, pp* **had**) *aux vb*
1 (*gen*) ter; **to ~ gone/eaten** ter ido/comido; **he has been kind/pro-**

moted ele foi bondoso/promovido; **having finished** *or* **when he had finished, he left** quando ele terminou, foi embora

2 (*in tag questions*): **you've done it, ~n't you?** você fez isto, né?; **he hasn't done it, has he?** ele não fez isto, fez?

3 (*in short questions and answers*): **you've made a mistake – no I ~n't so I** – você fez um erro – não, eu não fiz/sim, eu fiz; **I've been there before, ~ you?** eu já estive lá, e você?

♦ *modal aux vb* (*be obliged*): **to ~ (got) to do sth** ter que fazer algo; **I ~n't got** *or* **I don't ~ to wear glasses** eu não preciso usar óculos

♦ *vt* **1** (*possess*): **he** *lit*. **has (got) blue eyes/dark hair** ele tem olhos azuis/cabelo escuro

2 (*referring to meals etc*): **to ~ breakfast** tomar café (BR), tomar o pequeno almoço (PT); **to ~ lunch/dinner** almoçar/jantar; **to ~ a drink/a cigarette** tomar um drinque/fumar um cigarro

3 (*receive, obtain etc*): **may I ~ your address?** pode me dar seu endereço?; **you can ~ it for 5 pounds** você pode levá-lo por 5 libras; **to ~ a baby** dar à luz (BR), ter um nenê *or* bebê (PT)

4 (*maintain, allow*): **he will ~ it that he is right** ele vai insistir que ele está certo; **I won't ~ it/this nonsense!** não vou agüentar isso/este absurdo!; **we can't ~ that** não podemos permitir isto

5: **to ~ sth done** mandar fazer algo; **to ~ one's hair cut** ir cortar o cabelo; **to ~ sb do sth** mandar alguém fazer algo

6 (*experience, suffer*): **to ~ a cold** estar resfriado (BR) *or* constipado

(PT); **to ~ flu** estar com gripe; **she had her bag stolen** ela teve sua bolsa roubada; **to ~ an operation** fazer uma operação

7 (+ n: take, hold etc): **to ~ a swim/ walk/bath/rest** ir nadar/passear/ tomar um banho/descansar; **let's ~ a look** vamos dar uma olhada; **to ~ a party** fazer uma festa

8 (inf: dupe): **he's been had** ele comprou gato por lebre

have out vt: **to ~ it out with sb** (settle a problem) explicar-se com alguém

haven ['heɪvn] n porto; (fig) abrigo, refúgio

haven't ['hævnt] = have not

havoc ['hævək] n destruição f; **to play ~ with** (fig) estragar

hawk [hɔːk] n falcão m

hay [heɪ] n feno; **hay fever** n febre f do feno; **haystack** n palheiro

haywire ['heɪwaɪə*] (inf) adj: **to go ~** desorganizar-se, degringolar

hazard ['hæzəd] n perigo, risco ♦ vt aventurar, arriscar; **hazard warning lights** npl (AUT) pisca-alerta m

haze [heɪz] n névoa

hazelnut ['heɪzlnʌt] n avelã f

hazy ['heɪzɪ] adj nublado; (idea) confuso

he [hiː] pron ele; **~ who ...** quem ..., aquele que ...

head [hɛd] n cabeça; (of table) cabeceira; (of queue) frente f; (of organization) chefe m/f; (of school) diretor(a) m/f ♦ vt (list) encabeçar; (group) liderar; (ball) cabecear; **~s or tails** cara ou coroa; **~ first** de cabeça; **~ over heels** de pernas para o ar; **~ over heels in love** apaixonadíssimo; **head for** vt fus dirigir-se a; (disaster) estar procurando; **headache** n dor f de cabeça; **heading** n

título, cabeçalho; **headlamp** (BRIT) n = **headlight**; **headland** n promontório; **headlight** n farol m; **headline** n manchete f; **headlong** adv (fall) de cabeça; (rush) precipitadamente; **headmaster** n diretor m (de escola); **headmistress** n diretora f (de escola); **head office** n matriz f; **head-on** adj (collision) de frente; (confrontation) direto; **headphones** npl fones mpl de ouvido; **headquarters** npl sede f; (MIL) quartel m general; **headrest** n apoio para a cabeça; **headroom** n (in car) espaço (para a cabeça); (under bridge) vão m livre; **headscarf** (irreg) n lenço de cabeça; **headstrong** adj voluntarioso, teimoso; **headway** n: **to make headway** avançar; **headwind** n vento contrário; **heady** adj emocionante; (intoxicating) estonteante

heal [hiːl] vt curar ♦ vi cicatrizar

health [hɛlθ] n saúde f; **good ~!** saúde!; **health food(s)** n(pl) alimentos mpl naturais; **healthy** adj (person) saudável; (air, walk) sadio; (economy) próspero, forte

heap [hiːp] n pilha, montão m ♦ vt: **to ~ sth with** encher algo de; **~s (of)** (inf) um monte (de); **to ~ sth on** empilhar algo em

hear [hɪə*] (pt, pp **~d** [hɜːd]) vt ouvir; (listen to) escutar; (news) saber; **to ~ about** ouvir falar de; **to ~ from sb** ter notícias de alguém; **hearing** n (sense) audição f; (LAW) audiência; **hearing aid** n aparelho para a surdez

hearse [hɜːs] n carro fúnebre

heart [hɑːt] n coração m; (of problem, city) centro; **~s** npl (CARDS) copas fpl; **to lose/take ~** perder o ânimo/criar coragem; **at ~** no fundo; **by ~** (learn, know) de cor;

heart attack n ataque m de coração; **heartbeat** n batida do coração; **heartbreaking** adj desolador(a); **heartbroken** adj: **to be heartbroken** estar inconsolável; **heartburn** n azia; **heart failure** n parada cardíaca; **heartfelt** adj sincero

hearth [hɑ:θ] n lareira

hearty ['hɑ:tɪ] adj (person) energético; (laugh) animado; (appetite) bom (boa); (welcome) sincero, (dislike) absoluto

heat [hi:t] n calor m; (excitement) ardor m; (SPORT: also: **qualifying ~**) (prova) eliminatória ♦ vt esquentar; (room, house) aquecer; **heat up** vi aquecer-se, esquentar ♦ vt esquentar; **heated** adj aquecido; (fig) acalorado; **heater** n aquecedor m

heath [hi:θ] (BRIT) n charneca

heather ['hɛðə*] n urze f

heating ['hi:tɪŋ] n aquecimento, calefação f

heatstroke ['hi:tstrəuk] n insolação f

heave [hi:v] vt (pull) puxar; (push) empurrar (com esforço); (lift) levantar (com esforço) ♦ vi (chest) palpitar; (retch) ter ânsias de vômito ♦ n puxão m; empurrão m; **to ~ a sigh** soltar um suspiro

heaven ['hɛvn] n céu m, paraíso m; **heavenly** adj celestial; (REL) divino

heavily ['hɛvɪlɪ] adv pesadamente; (drink, smoke) excessivamente; (sleep, depend) profundamente

heavy ['hɛvɪ] adj pesado; (work) duro; (responsibility) grande; (rain, meal) forte; (drinker, smoker) inveterado; (weather) carregado; **heavy goods vehicle** (BRIT) n caminhão m de carga pesada; **heavyweight** n (SPORT) peso-pesado

Hebrew ['hi:bru:] adj hebreu

(hebréia) ♦ n (LING) hebraico

Hebrides ['hɛbrɪdi:z] npl: **the ~ as** (ilhas) Hébridas

hectic ['hɛktɪk] adj agitado

he'd [hi:d] = he would; he had

hedge [hɛdʒ] n cerca viva, sebe f ♦ vi dar evasivas ♦ vt: **to ~ one's bets** (fig) resguardar-se

hedgehog ['hɛdʒhɔg] n ouriço

heed [hi:d] vt (also: **take ~ of**) prestar atenção a

heel [hi:l] n (of shoe) salto; (of foot) calcanhar m ♦ vt (shoe) pôr salto em

hefty ['hɛftɪ] adj (person) robusto; (parcel) pesado; (profit) alto

height [haɪt] n (of person) estatura; (of building, tree) altura; (altitude) altitude f; (high ground) monte m; (fig: of power) auge m; (: of luxury) máximo; (: of stupidity) cúmulo; **heighten** vt elevar; (fig) aumentar

heir [ɛə*] n herdeiro; **heiress** n herdeira; **heirloom** n relíquia de família

held [hɛld] pt, pp of **hold**

helicopter ['hɛlɪkɔptə*] n helicóptero

hell [hɛl] n inferno; **~!** (inf) droga!

he'll [hi:l] = he will; he shall

hello [hə'ləu] excl oi! (BR), olá! (PT); (surprise) ora essa!

helm [hɛlm] n (NAUT) timão m, leme m

helmet ['hɛlmɪt] n capacete m

help [hɛlp] n ajuda; (charwoman) faxineira ♦ vt ajudar; **~!** socorro!; **~ yourself** sirva-se; **he can't ~ it** não tem culpa; **helper** n ajudante m/f; **helpful** adj prestativo; (advice) útil; **helping** n porção f; **helpless** adj (incapable) incapaz; (defenceless) indefeso

hem [hɛm] n bainha ♦ vt embainhar; **hem in** vt cercar, encurralar

hemorrhage ['hɛmərɪdʒ] (US) n = **haemorrhage**

hemorrhoids ['hɛmərɔɪdz] (US) npl

= haemorrhoids

hen [hɛn] n galinha; (female bird) fêmea

hence [hɛns] adv daí, portanto; **2 years ~** daqui a 2 anos; **henceforth** adv de agora em diante, doravante

her [hə:*] pron (direct) a; (indirect) lhe; (stressed, after prep) ela ♦ adj seu (sua), dela; see also **me; my**

heraldry ['hɛrəldrɪ] n heráldica

herb [hə:b] n erva

herd [hə:d] n rebanho

here [hɪə*] adv aqui; (at this point) nesse ponto; **~!** (present) presente!; **~ is/are** aqui está/estão; **~ she is!** aqui está ela!; **hereafter** adv daqui por diante

heresy ['hɛrəsɪ] n heresia

heritage ['hɛrɪtɪdʒ] n patrimônio

hermit ['hə:mɪt] n eremita m/f

hernia ['hə:nɪə] n hérnia

hero ['hɪərəu] (pl **~es**) n herói m; (of book, film) protagonista m

heroin ['hɛrəuɪn] n heroína

heroine ['hɛrəuɪn] n heroína; (of book, film) protagonista

heron ['hɛrən] n garça

herring ['hɛrɪŋ] (pl inv or **~s**) n arenque m

hers [hə:z] pron o seu (a sua), o(a) dela; see also **mine[1]**

herself [hə:'sɛlf] pron (reflexive) se; (emphatic) ela mesma; (after prep) si (mesma); see also **oneself**

he's [hi:z] = he is; he has

hesitant ['hɛzɪtənt] adj hesitante, indeciso

hesitate ['hɛzɪteɪt] vi hesitar; **hesitation** [hɛzɪ'teɪʃən] n hesitação f, indecisão f

heterosexual ['hɛtərəu'sɛksjuəl] adj heterossexual

heyday ['heɪdeɪ] n: **the ~ of** o auge or apogeu de

HGV (BRIT) n abbr = **heavy goods vehicle**

hi [haɪ] excl oi!

hibernate ['haɪbəneɪt] vi hibernar

hiccough ['hɪkʌp] vi soluçar ♦ npl: **~s: to have (the) ~s** estar com soluço

hiccup ['hɪkʌp] = **hiccough**

hide [haɪd] (pt **hid**, pp **hidden**) n (skin) pele f ♦ vt esconder, ocultar; (view) obscurecer ♦ vi: **to ~ (from sb)** esconder-se or ocultar-se (de alguém)

hideous ['hɪdɪəs] adj horrível

hiding ['haɪdɪŋ] n (beating) surra; **to be in ~** (concealed) estar escondido

hierarchy ['haɪərɑ:kɪ] n hierarquia

hi-fi ['haɪfaɪ] n alta-fidelidade f; (system) som m ♦ adj de alta-fidelidade

high [haɪ] adj alto; (number) grande; (price) alto, elevado; (wind) forte; (voice) agudo; (opinion) ótimo; (principles) nobre ♦ adv alto, a grande altura; **it is 20 m ~** tem 20 m de altura; **~ in the air** nas alturas; **highbrow** adj intelectual, erudito; **highchair** n cadeira alta (para criança); **higher education** n ensino superior; **high-handed** adj despótico; **high-heeled** adj de salto alto; **high jump** n (SPORT) salto em altura; **the Highlands** npl a Alta Escócia; **highlight** n (fig) ponto alto; (in hair) mecha ♦ vt realçar, ressaltar; **highly** adv: highly paid muito bem pago; (a lot): **to speak/think highly of** falar elogiosamente de/pensar muito bem de; **high-pitched** adj agudo; **high-rise** adj alto; **high school** n (BRIT) escola secundária; (US) científico; ver quadro

HIGH SCHOOL

Uma **high school** é um estabelecimento de ensino secundário. Nos Estados Unidos, existem a *Junior High School*, que equivale aproximadamente aos dois últimos anos do primeiro grau, e a *Senior High School*, que corresponde ao segundo grau. Na Grã-Bretanha, esse termo às vezes é utilizado para as escolas secundárias.

high street (BRIT) n rua principal
highway ['haɪweɪ] (US) n estrada; (main road) rodovia
hijack ['haɪdʒæk] vt sequestrar; **hijacker** n sequestrador(a) m/t (de avião)
hike [haɪk] vi caminhar ♦ n caminhada, excursão f a pé; **hiker** n caminhante m/f, andarilho(-a)
hilarious [hɪ'lɛərɪəs] adj hilariante
hill [hɪl] n colina; (high) montanha; (slope) ladeira, rampa; **hillside** n vertente f; **hill-walking** n caminhada em montanha; **to go hill-walking** fazer trilha; **hilly** adj montanhoso
him [hɪm] pron (direct) o; (indirect) lhe; (stressed, after prep) ele; see also me; **himself** pron (reflexive) se; (emphatic) ele mesmo; (after prep) si (mesmo); see also oneself
hinder ['hɪndə*] vt retardar
hindsight ['haɪndsaɪt] n: **with ~** em retrospecto
Hindu ['hɪnduː] adj hindu
hinge [hɪndʒ] n dobradiça ♦ vi (fig): **to ~ on** depender de
hint [hɪnt] n (suggestion) insinuação f; (advice) palpite m, dica; (sign) sinal m ♦ vt: **to ~ that** insinuar que ♦ vi: **to ~ at** fazer alusão a

hip [hɪp] n quadril m
hippopotamus [hɪpə'pɔtəməs] (pl ~es or **hippopotami**) n hipopótamo
hire ['haɪə*] vt (BRIT: car, equipment) alugar; (worker) contratar ♦ n aluguel m (BR), aluguer m (PT); **for ~** aluga-se; (taxi) livre; **hire purchase** (BRIT) n compra a prazo
his [hɪz] pron o seu (a sua), o(a) dele ♦ adj seu (sua), dele; see also my; **mine**[1]
hiss [hɪs] vi (snake, fat) assoviar; (gas) silvar; (boo) vaiar
historic(al) [hɪ'stɔrɪk(l)] adj histórico
history ['hɪstərɪ] n história
hit [hɪt] (pt, pp hit) vt bater em; (target) acertar, alcançar; (car) bater em, colidir com; (fig: affect) atingir ♦ n golpe m; (success) sucesso; **to ~ it off with sb** dar-se bem com alguém; **hit-and-run driver** n motorista que atropela alguém e foge da cena do acidente
hitch [hɪtʃ] vt (fasten) atar, amarrar; (also: ~ up) levantar ♦ n (difficulty) dificuldade f; **to ~ a lift** pegar carona (BR), arranjar uma boleia (PT)
hitch-hike vi pegar carona (BR), andar à boleia (PT); **hitch-hiker** n pessoa que pega carona (BR) or anda à boleia (PT)
hi-tech adj tecnologicamente avançado ♦ n alta tecnologia
HIV abbr: **~-negative/-positive** ♦ adj HIV negativo/positivo
hive [haɪv] n colméia; **hive off** (inf) vt transferir
HMS (BRIT) abbr = **His (or Her) Majesty's Ship**
hoard [hɔːd] n provisão f; (of money) tesouro ♦ vt acumular; **hoarding** (BRIT) n tapume m, outdoor m
hoarse [hɔːs] adj rouco
hoax [həuks] n trote m
hob [hɔb] n parte de cima do fogão

hobble ['hɔbl] vi mancar

hobby ['hɔbɪ] n hobby m, passatempo predileto

hobo ['həubəu] (US) n vagabundo

hockey ['hɔkɪ] n hóquei m

hog [hɔg] n porco ♦ vt (fig) monopolizar; **to go the whole ~** ir até o fim

hoist [hɔɪst] vt içar

hold [həuld] (pt, pp **held**) vt segurar; (contain) conter; (have) ter; (record etc: meeting) realizar; (detain) deter; (consider): **to ~ sb responsible (for sth)** responsabilizar alguém (por algo); (keep in certain position): **to ~ one's head up** manter a cabeça erigida ♦ vi (withstand pressure) resistir; (be valid) ser válido ♦ n (grasp) pressão f; (: fig) influência, domínio; (of ship) porão m; (of plane) compartimento para cargo; (control) controle m; **~ the line!** (TEL) não desligue!; **to ~ one's own** (fig) virar-se, sair-se bem; **to catch or get (a) ~ of** agarrar, pegar; **hold back** vt reter; (secret) manter, guardar; **hold down** vt (person) segurar; (job) manter; **hold off** vt (enemy) afastar, repelir; **hold on** vi agarrar-se; (wait) esperar; **~ on!** espera aí!; (TEL) não desligue!; **hold on to** vt fus agarrar-se a; (keep) guardar, ficar com; **hold out** vt (hand) estender; (hope) ter ♦ vi (resist) resistir; **hold up** vt (raise) levantar; (support) apoiar; (delay) atrasar; (rob) assaltar; **holdall** (BRIT) n bolsa de viagem; **holder** n (container) recipiente m; (of ticket) portador(a) m/f; (of record) detentor(a) m/f; (of office, title) titular m/f; **hold-up** n (robbery) assalto; (delay) demora; (BRIT: in traffic) engarrafamento

hole [həul] n buraco; (small: in sock etc) furo ♦ vt esburacar

holiday ['hɔlədɪ] n (BRIT: vacation) férias fpl; (day off) dia m de folga; (public ~) feriado; **on ~** de férias; **holiday camp** (BRIT) n colônia de férias; **holiday-maker** (BRIT) n pessoa (que está) de férias; **holiday resort** n local m de férias

Holland ['hɔlənd] n Holanda

hollow ['hɔləu] adj oco, vazio; (cheeks) côncavo; (eyes) fundo; (sound) surdo; (laugh, claim) falso ♦ n (in ground) cavidade f, depressão f ♦ vt: **to ~ out** escavar

holly ['hɔlɪ] n azevinho

holster ['həulstə*] n coldre m

holy ['həulɪ] adj sagrado; (person) santo, bento

homage ['hɔmɪdʒ] n homenagem f; **to pay ~ to** prestar homenagem a, homenagear

home [həum] n casa, lar m; (country) pátria; (institution) asilo ♦ cpd caseiro, doméstico; (ECON, POL) nacional, interno; (SPORT: team) de casa; (: game) no próprio campo ♦ adv (direction) para casa; (right in: nail etc) até o fundo; **at ~** em casa; **make yourself at ~** fique à vontade; **home address** n endereço residencial; **homeland** n terra (natal); **homeless** adj sem casa, desabrigado; **homely** adj (simple) simples inv; **home-made** adj caseiro; **Home Office** (BRIT) n Ministério do Interior; **home page** n (COMPUT) home page f, página inicial; **Home Secretary** n (BRIT) Ministro(-a) do Interior; **homesick** adj: **to be homesick** estar com saudades (do lar); **home town** n cidade f natal; **homework** n dever m de casa

homoeopathic [həumiəu'pæθɪk] (US **homeopathic**) adj homeopático

homosexual [hɔməu'seksjuəl] adj, n homossexual m/f

Honduras [hɔnˈdjuərəs] n Honduras f (no article)

honest [ˈɔnɪst] adj (truthful) franco; (trustworthy) honesto; (sincere) sincero; **honestly** adv honestamente; **honesty** n honestidade f, sinceridade f

honey [ˈhʌnɪ] n mel m; **honeycomb** n favo de mel; **honeymoon** n lua-de-mel f; (trip) viagem f de lua-de-mel

honk [hɔŋk] vi buzinar

honorary [ˈɔnərərɪ] adj (unpaid) não remunerado; (duty, title) honorário

honour [ˈɔnə*] (US **honor**) vt honrar ♦ n honra; **honourable** adj honrado

hood [hud] n capuz m; (of cooker) tampa; (BRIT: AUT) capota, (US: AUT) capô m

hoof [huːf] (pl **hooves**) n casco, pata

hook [huk] n gancho m; (on dress) gancho, colchete m; (for fishing) anzol m ♦ vt prender com gancho (or colchete); (fish) fisgar

hooligan [ˈhuːlɪgən] n desordeiro(-a), bagunceiro(-a)

hoop [huːp] n arco

hooray [huːˈreɪ] excl = **hurrah**

hoot [huːt] vi (AUT) buzinar; (siren) tocar; (owl) piar

hoover [ˈhuːvə*] ® (BRIT) n aspirador m (de pó) ♦ vt passar o aspirador em

hooves [huːvz] npl of **hoof**

hop [hɔp] vi saltar, pular; (on one foot) pular num pé só

hope [həup] vt, vi esperar ♦ n esperança; **I ~ so/not** espero que sim/não; **hopeful** adj (person) otimista, esperançoso; (situation) promissor(a); **hopefully** adv esperançosamente; **hopefully, they'll come back** é de esperar or esperamos que

voltem; **hopeless** adj desesperado, irremediável; (useless) inútil

hops [hɔps] npl lúpulo

horizon [həˈraɪzn] n horizonte m; **horizontal** [hɔrɪˈzɔntl] adj horizontal

horn [hɔːn] n corno, chifre m; (material) chifre; (MUS) trompa; (AUT) buzina

hornet [ˈhɔːnɪt] n vespão m

horoscope [ˈhɔrəskəup] n horóscopo

horrendous [həˈrendəs] adj horrendo

horrible [ˈhɔrɪbl] adj horrível; (terrifying) terrível

horrid [ˈhɔrɪd] adj horrível

horrify [ˈhɔrɪfaɪ] vt horrorizar

horror [ˈhɔrə*] n horror m; **horror film** n filme m de terror

horse [hɔːs] n cavalo; **horseback: on horseback** adj, adv a cavalo; **horse chestnut** n castanha-da-índia; **horsepower** n cavalo-vapor m; **horse-racing** n corridas fpl de cavalo, turfe m; **horseshoe** n ferradura

hose [həuz] n (also: **~pipe**) mangueira

hospitable [ˈhɔspɪtəbl] adj hospitaleiro

hospital [ˈhɔspɪtl] n hospital m

hospitality [hɔspɪˈtælɪtɪ] n hospitalidade f

host [həust] n anfitrião m; (TV, RADIO) apresentador(a) m/f; (REL) hóstia; (large number): **a ~ of** uma multidão de

hostage [ˈhɔstɪdʒ] n refém m/f

hostel [ˈhɔstl] n albergue m, abrigo; (also: **youth ~**) albergue da juventude

hostess [ˈhəustɪs] n anfitriã f; (BRIT: air ~) aeromoça (BR), hospedeira de bordo (PT); (TV, RADIO) apresentadora

hostile ['hɔstaɪl] adj hostil

hostility [hɔ'stɪlɪtɪ] n hostilidade f

hot [hɔt] adj quente; (as opposed to only warm) muito quente; (spicy) picante; (fierce) ardente; **to be ~** (person) estar com calor; (thing, weather) estar quente; **hot dog** n cachorro-quente m

hotel [hə'tɛl] n hotel m

hot: hothouse n estufa; **hotplate** n (on cooker) chapa elétrica; **hotwater bottle** n bolsa de água quente

hound [haund] vt acossar, perseguir ♦ n cão m de caça, sabujo

hour ['auə*] n hora; **hourly** adj de hora em hora; (rate) por hora

house [n haus, vb hauz] n (gen, firm) casa; (POL) câmara; (THEATRE) assistência, lotação f ♦ vt (person) alojar; (collection) abrigar; **on the ~** (fig) por conta da casa; **houseboat** n casa flutuante; **household** n família; (house) casa; **housekeeper** n governanta; **housekeeping** n (work) trabalhos mpl domésticos; (money) economia doméstica; **house-warming (party)** n festa de inauguração de uma casa; **housewife** (irreg) n dona de casa; **housework** n trabalhos mpl domésticos; **housing** n (provision) alojamento; (houses) residências fpl; **housing development** (BRIT **housing estate**) n conjunto residencial

hovel ['hɔvl] n casebre m

hover ['hɔvə*] vi pairar; **hovercraft** n aerobarco

how [hau] adv **1** (in what way) como; **~ was the film?** que tal o filme?; **~ are you?** como vai?
2 (to what degree) quanto; **~ much milk/many people?** quanto de leite/quantas pessoas?; **~ long have you been here?** quanto tempo você está aqui?; **~ old are you?** quantos anos você tem?; **~ tall is he?** qual é a altura dele?; **~ lovely/awful!** que ótimo/terrível!

however [hau'ɛvə*] adv de qualquer modo; (+ adj) por mais ... que; (in questions) como ♦ conj no entanto, contudo

howl [haul] vi uivar

H.P. (BRIT) n abbr = hire purchase

h.p. abbr (AUT: = horsepower) CV

HQ n abbr (= headquarters) QG m

HTML n abbr (= Hypertext Markup Language) HTML f

hub [hʌb] n cubo; (fig) centro

huddle ['hʌdl] vi: **to ~ together** aconchegar-se

hue [hju:] n cor f, matiz m

huff [hʌf] n: **in a ~** com raiva

hug [hʌg] vt abraçar; (thing) agarrar, prender

huge [hju:dʒ] adj enorme, imenso

hulk [hʌlk] n (wreck) navio velho, carcaça; (person) brutamontes m inv; (building) trambolho

hull [hʌl] n (of ship) casco

hullo [hə'ləu] excl = hello

hum [hʌm] vt cantarolar ♦ vi cantarolar; (insect, machine etc) zumbir

human ['hju:mən] adj humano ♦ n (also: **~ being**) ser m humano

humane [hju:'meɪn] adj humano

humanitarian [hju:mænɪ'tɛərɪən] adj humanitário

humanity [hju:'mænɪtɪ] n humanidade f

humble ['hʌmbl] adj humilde ♦ vt humilhar

humid ['hju:mɪd] adj úmido

humiliate [hju:'mɪlɪeɪt] vt humilhar

humorous ['hju:mərəs] adj humorístico; (person) engraçado

humour ['hju:mə*] (*US* humor) *n* humorismo, senso de humor; (*mood*) humor *m* ♦ *vt* fazer a vontade de

hump [hʌmp] *n* (*in ground*) elevação *f*; (*camel's*) corcova, giba; (*deformity*) corcunda

hunch [hʌntʃ] *n* (*premonition*) pressentimento, palpite *m*; **hunchback** *n* corcunda *m/f*; **hunched** *adj* corcunda

hundred ['hʌndrəd] *num* cem; (*before lower numbers*) cento; **~s of people** centenas de pessoas; **hundredweight** *n* (*BRIT*) = 50.8 kg; 112 lb; (*US*) = 45.3 kg; 100 lb

hung [hʌŋ] *pt, pp of* hang

Hungary ['hʌŋgəri] *n* Hungria

hunger ['hʌŋgə*] *n* fome *f* ♦ *vi*: **to ~ for** (*desire*) desejar ardentemente

hungry ['hʌŋgri] *adj* faminto, esfomeado; (*keen*): **~ for** (*fig*) ávido de, ansioso por; **to be ~** estar com fome

hunt [hʌnt] *vt* buscar; (*criminal, fugitive*) perseguir; (*SPORT, for food*) caçar ♦ *vi* caçar, caçada; (*search*) **to ~ (for)** procurar (por) ♦ *n* caça, caçada; **hunter** *n* caçador(a) *m/f*; **hunting** *n* caça

hurdle ['hə:dl] *n* (*SPORT*) barreira; (*fig*) obstáculo

hurl [hə:l] *vt* arremessar, lançar; (*abuse*) gritar

hurrah [hu'rɑ:] *excl* oba!, viva!

hurray [hu'rei] *excl* = hurrah

hurricane ['hʌrikən] *n* furacão *m*

hurried ['hʌrid] *adj* apressado; (*rushed*) feito às pressas; **hurriedly** *adv* depressa, apressadamente

hurry ['hʌri] *n* pressa ♦ *vi* (*also:* **~ up**) apressar-se ♦ *vt* (*also:* **~ up: person**) apressar; (*: work*) acelerar; **to be in a ~** estar com pressa

hurt [hə:t] (*pt, pp* hurt) *vt* machucar; (*injure*) ferir; (*fig*) magoar ♦ *vi* doer; **hurtful** *adj* prejudicial, que magoa, ofensivo

husband ['hʌzbənd] *n* marido, esposo

hush [hʌʃ] *n* silêncio, quietude *f* ♦ *vt* silenciar, fazer calar; **~!** silêncio!, psiu!; **hush up** *vt* abafar, encobrir

husk [hʌsk] *n* (*of wheat*) casca; (*of maize*) palha

husky ['hʌski] *adj* rouco ♦ *n* cão *m* esquimó

hut [hʌt] *n* cabana, choupana; (*shed*) alpendre *m*

hutch [hʌtʃ] *n* coelheira

hyacinth ['haiəsinθ] *n* jacinto

hydrant ['haidrənt] *n* (*also:* **fire ~**) hidrante *m*

hydroelectric [haidrəu'lektrik] *adj* hidroelétrico

hydrofoil ['haidrəfɔil] *n* hidrofoil *m*, aliscafo

hydrogen ['haidrədʒən] *n* hidrogênio

hyena [hai'i:nə] *n* hiena

hygiene ['haidʒi:n] *n* higiene *f*

hymn [him] *n* hino

hype [haip] (*inf*) *n* tititi *m*, falatório

hypermarket ['haipəmɑːkit] (*BRIT*) *n* hipermercado

hyphen ['haifn] *n* hífen *m*

hypnotize ['hipnətaiz] *vt* hipnotizar

hypocrite ['hipəkrit] *n* hipócrita *m/f*; **hypocritical** *adj* hipócrita

hysterical [hi'sterikl] *adj* histérico; (*funny*) hilariante; **hysterics** *npl*: **to be in** *or* **have hysterics** (*anger, panic*) ter uma crise histérica; (*laughter*) ter um ataque de riso

I

I [ai] *pron* eu

ice [ais] *n* gelo; (*~ cream*) sorvete *m* ♦ *vt* (*cake*) cobrir com glacê ♦ *vi* (*also:* **~ over, ~ up**) gelar; **iceberg** *n* iceberg *m*; **icebox** *n* (*US*) geladeira;

(BRIT: in fridge) congelador m; (insulated box) geladeira portátil; **ice cream** n sorvete m (BR), gelado (PT); **ice cube** n pedra de gelo; **iced** adj (drink) gelado; (cake) glaçado; **ice hockey** n hóquei m sobre o gelo

Iceland ['aɪslənd] n Islândia

ice: **ice lolly** (BRIT) n picolé m; **ice rink** n pista de gelo, rinque m; **ice-skating** n patinação f no gelo

icicle ['aɪsɪkl] n pingente m de gelo

icing ['aɪsɪŋ] n (CULIN) glacê m; **icing sugar** (BRIT) n açúcar m glacê

icon ['aɪkɔn] n (gen, COMPUT) ícone m

icy ['aɪsɪ] adj gelado

I'd [aɪd] = I would; I had

idea [aɪ'dɪə] n idéia

ideal [aɪ'dɪəl] n ideal m ♦ adj ideal

identical [aɪ'dɛntɪkl] adj idêntico

identification [aɪdɛntɪfɪ'keɪʃən] n identificação f; **means of** ~ documentos pessoais

identify [aɪ'dɛntɪfaɪ] vt identificar

identity [aɪ'dɛntɪtɪ] n identidade f; **identity card** n carteira de identidade

idiom ['ɪdɪəm] n expressão f idiomática; (style) idioma m, linguagem f

idiosyncrasy [ɪdɪəʊ'sɪŋkrəsɪ] n idiossincrasia

idiot ['ɪdɪət] n idiota m/f; **idiotic** [ɪdɪ'ɔtɪk] adj idiota

idle ['aɪdl] adj (lazy) ocioso; (lazy) preguiçoso; (unemployed) desempregado; (question, conversation) fútil; (pleasure) descontraído ♦ vi (machine) funcionar com a transmissão desligada; **idle away** vt: **to ~ away the time** perder or desperdiçar tempo

idol ['aɪdl] n ídolo; **idolize** vt idolatrar

i.e. abbr (= id est: that is) i.e., isto é

┌─────────────────┐
│ KEYWORD   │
└─────────────────┘

if [ɪf] conj **1** (conditional use) se; ~ **necessary** se necessário; ~ **I were you** se eu fôsse você
2 (whenever) quando
3 (although): (even) ~ mesmo que
4 (whether) se
5: ~ **so/not** sendo assim/do contrário; ~ **only** se pelo menos; see also **as**

ignition [ɪg'nɪʃən] n (AUT) ignição f; **to switch on/off the** ~ ligar/desligar o motor; **ignition key** n (AUT) chave f de ignição

ignorant ['ɪgnərənt] adj ignorante; **to be** ~ **of** ignorar

ignore [ɪg'nɔ:*] vt (person) não fazer caso de; (fact) não levar em consideração, ignorar

I'll [aɪl] = I will; I shall

ill [ɪl] adj doente; (harmful: effects) nocivo ♦ n mal m ♦ adv: **to speak/ think ~ of sb** falar/pensar mal de alguém; **to be taken** ~ ficar doente; **ill-at-ease** adj constrangido, pouco à vontade

illegal [ɪ'li:gl] adj ilegal

illegible [ɪ'lɛdʒɪbl] adj ilegível

illegitimate [ɪlɪ'dʒɪtɪmət] adj ilegítimo

ill-fated adj malfadado

ill feeling n má vontade f, rancor m

illiterate [ɪ'lɪtərət] adj analfabeto

ill-mannered [-'mænəd] adj mal educado, grosseiro

illness ['ɪlnɪs] n doença

ill-treat vt maltratar

illuminate [ɪ'lu:mɪneɪt] vt iluminar, clarear; **illumination** [ɪlu:mɪ'neɪʃən] n iluminação f; **illuminations** npl (decorative lights) luminárias fpl

illusion [ɪ'lu:ʒən] n ilusão f

illustrate ['ɪləstreɪt] vt ilustrar; (point) exemplificar; **illustration** [ɪlə'streɪʃən] n ilustração f; (example) exemplo; (explanation) esclarecimento

ill will n animosidade f

I'm [aɪm] = **I am**

image ['ɪmɪdʒ] n imagem f; **imagery** n imagens fpl

imaginary [ɪ'mædʒɪnərɪ] adj imaginário

imagination [ɪmædʒɪ'neɪʃən] n imaginação f; (inventiveness) inventividade f

imagine [ɪ'mædʒɪn] vt imaginar

imbalance [ɪm'bæləns] n desigualdade f

imitate ['ɪmɪteɪt] vt imitar; **imitation** [ɪmɪ'teɪʃən] n imitação f; (copy) cópia; (mimicry) mimica

immaculate [ɪ'mækjulət] adj impecável; (REL) imaculado

immaterial [ɪmə'tɪərɪəl] adj irrelevante

immature [ɪmə'tjuə*] adj imaturo; (fruit) verde; (cheese) fresco

immediate [ɪ'mi:dɪət] adj imediato; (pressing) urgente, premente; (neighbourhood, family) próximo; **immediately** adv imediatamente; (directly) diretamente; **immediately next to** bem junto a

immense [ɪ'mɛns] adj imenso; (importance) enorme

immerse [ɪ'mə:s] vt submergir; **to be ~d in** (fig) estar absorto em

immersion heater [ɪ'mə:ʃn-] (BRIT) n aquecedor m de imersão

immigrant ['ɪmɪgrənt] n imigrante m/f

immigration [ɪmɪ'greɪʃən] n imigração f

imminent ['ɪmɪnənt] adj iminente

immoral [ɪ'mɔrl] adj imoral

immortal [ɪ'mɔ:tl] adj imortal

immune [ɪ'mju:n] adj: **~ to** imune a, imunizado contra

impact ['ɪmpækt] n impacto (BR), impacte m (PT)

impair [ɪm'pɛə*] vt prejudicar

impartial [ɪm'pɑ:ʃl] adj imparcial

impassable [ɪm'pɑ:səbl] adj (river) intransponível; (road) intransitável

impatience [ɪm'peɪʃəns] n impaciência

impatient [ɪm'peɪʃənt] adj impaciente; **to get** or **grow ~** impacientar-se

impeccable [ɪm'pɛkəbl] adj impecável

impediment [ɪm'pɛdɪmənt] n obstáculo; (also: **speech ~**) defeito (de fala)

impending [ɪm'pɛndɪŋ] adj iminente, próximo

imperative [ɪm'pɛrətɪv] adj (tone) imperioso, obrigatório; (need) vital; (necessary) indispensável ♦ n (LING) imperativo

imperfect [ɪm'pə:fɪkt] adj imperfeito; (goods etc) defeituoso ♦ n (LING: also: **~ tense**) imperfeito

imperial [ɪm'pɪərɪəl] adj imperial

impersonal [ɪm'pə:sənl] adj impessoal

impersonate [ɪm'pə:səneɪt] vt fazer-se passar por, personificar; (THEATRE) imitar

impertinent [ɪm'pə:tɪnənt] adj impertinente, insolente

impervious [ɪm'pə:vɪəs] adj (fig): **~ to** insensível a

impetuous [ɪm'petjuəs] adj impetuoso, precipitado

implement [n 'ɪmplɪmənt, vb 'ɪmplɪment] n instrumento, ferramenta; (for cooking) utensílio ♦ vt efetivar

implicit [ɪm'plɪsɪt] adj implícito;

(*complete*) absoluto

imply [ɪm'plaɪ] vt (*mean*) significar; (*hint*) dar a entender que

impolite [ɪmpə'laɪt] adj indelicado, mal-educado

import [vb ɪm'pɔːt, n 'ɪmpɔːt] vt importar ♦ n importação f; (*article*) mercadoria importada

importance [ɪm'pɔːtəns] n importância

important [ɪm'pɔːtənt] adj importante; **it's not** ~ não tem importância, não importa

impose [ɪm'pəuz] vt impor ♦ vi: **to** ~ **on sb** abusar de alguém; **imposing** adj imponente; **imposition** [ɪmpə-'zɪʃən] n (*of tax etc*) imposição f; **to be an imposition on sb** (*person*) abusar de alguém

impossible [ɪm'pɔsɪbl] adj impossível; (*situation*) inviável; (*person*) insuportável

impotent ['ɪmpətənt] adj impotente

impound [ɪm'paund] vt confiscar

impoverished [ɪm'pɔvərɪʃt] adj empobrecido; (*land*) esgotado

impractical [ɪm'præktɪkl] adj pouco prático

impress [ɪm'prɛs] vt impressionar; (*mark*) imprimir; **to** ~ **sth on sb** inculcar algo em alguém

impression [ɪm'prɛʃən] n impressão f; (*imitation*) caricatura; **to be under the** ~ **that** estar com a impressão de que; **impressionist** n (ART) impressionista m/f; (*entertainer*) caricaturista m/f

impressive [ɪm'prɛsɪv] adj impressionante

imprint ['ɪmprɪnt] n impressão f, marca; (*PUBLISHING*) nome m (da coleção)

imprison [ɪm'prɪzn] vt encarcerar

improbable [ɪm'prɔbəbl] adj im-

provável; (*story*) inverossímil (BR), inverosímil (PT)

improper [ɪm'prɔpə*] adj (*unsuitable*) impróprio; (*dishonest*) desonesto

improve [ɪm'pruːv] vt melhorar ♦ vi melhorar; (*pupils*) progredir; **improvement** n melhora; progresso

improvise ['ɪmprəvaɪz] vt, vi improvisar

impudent ['ɪmpjudnt] adj insolente, impudente

impulse ['ɪmpʌls] n impulso; **on** ~ sem pensar, num impulso

KEYWORD

in [ɪn] prep **1** (*indicating place, position*) em; ~ **the house/garden** na casa/no jardim; **I have it** ~ **my hand** eu estou assegurando isto; ~ **here/there** aqui dentro/lá dentro

2 (*with place names: of town, country, region*) em; ~ **London/Rio** em Londres/no Rio; ~ **England/Japan/the United States** na Inglaterra/no Japão/nos Estados Unidos

3 (*indicating time: during*) em; ~ **spring/autumn** na primavera/no outono; ~ **1988** em 1988; ~ **May** em maio; **I'll see you** ~ **July** até julho; ~ **the morning** de manhã; **at 4 o'clock** ~ **the afternoon** às 4 da tarde

4 (*indicating time: in the space of*) em; **I did it** ~ **3 hours/days** fiz isto em 3 horas/dias; ~ **2 weeks** or ~ **2 weeks' time** daqui a 2 semanas

5 (*indicating manner etc*): ~ **a loud/soft voice** em voz alta/numa voz suave; **written** ~ **pencil/ink** escrito a lápis/à caneta; ~ **English/Portuguese** em inglês/português; **the boy** ~ **the blue shirt** o menino de camisa azul

6 (*indicating circumstances*): ~ the sun ao or sob o sol; ~ the rain na chuva; **a rise** ~ **prices** um aumento nos preços
7 (*indicating mood, state*): ~ **tears** aos prantos; ~ **anger/despair** com raiva/desesperado; ~ **good condition** em boas condições
8 (*with ratios, numbers*): **1 ~ 10** 1 em 10, 1 em cada 10; **20 pence** ~ **the pound** vinte pênis numa libra; **they lined up** ~ **twos** eles se alinharam dois a dois
9 (*referring to people, works*) em
10 (*indicating profession etc*): **to be** ~ **teaching/publishing** ser professor/ trabalhar numa editora
11 (*after superl*): **the best pupil** ~ **the class** o melhor aluno da classe; **the biggest/smallest** ~ **Europe** o maior/menor na Europa
12 (*with present participle*): ~ **saying this** ao dizer isto
♦ *adv*: **to be** ~ (*person: at home*) estar em casa; (: *at work*) estar no trabalho; (*fashion*) estar na moda; (*ship, plane, train*): **it's** ~ chegou; **is he** ~? ele está?; **to ask sb** ~ convidar alguém para entrar; **to run/limp** *etc* ~ entrar correndo/mancando *etc*
♦ *n*: **the** ~**s and outs** (*of proposal, situation etc*) os cantos e recantos, os pormenores

in. *abbr* = **inch**(es)

inability [ɪnəˈbɪlɪtɪ] *n*: ~ (**to do**) incapacidade *f* (de fazer)
inaccurate [ɪnˈækjurət] *adj* inexato, impreciso
inadequate [ɪnˈædɪkwət] *adj* insuficiente; (*person*) impróprio
inadvertently [ɪnədˈvɜːtntlɪ] *adv* inadvertidamente, sem querer
inadvisable [ɪnədˈvaɪzəbl] *adj* desaconselhável, inoportuno

inane [ɪˈneɪn] *adj* tolo
inanimate [ɪnˈænɪmət] *adj* inanimado
inappropriate [ɪnəˈprəʊprɪət] *adj* inadequado; (*word, expression*) impróprio
inarticulate [ɪnɑːˈtɪkjulət] *adj* (*person*) incapaz de expressar-se (bem); (*speech*) inarticulado
inasmuch as [ɪnəzˈmʌtʃ-] *adv* na medida em que
inauguration [ɪˈnɔːgjʊreɪʃən] *n* inauguração *f*; (*of president, official*) posse *f*
inborn [ɪnˈbɔːn] *adj* inato
inbred [ɪnˈbrɛd] *adj* inato; (*family*) de procriação consangüínea
Inc. (*US*) *abbr* = **incorporated**
incapable [ɪnˈkeɪpəbl] *adj* incapaz
incapacitate [ɪnkəˈpæsɪteɪt] *vt* incapacitar
incense [*n* ˈɪnsɛns, *vb* ɪnˈsɛns] *n* incenso ♦ *vt* (*anger*) exasperar, enraivecer
incentive [ɪnˈsɛntɪv] *n* incentivo
incessant [ɪnˈsɛsnt] *adj* incessante, contínuo; **incessantly** *adv* constantemente
inch [ɪntʃ] *n* polegada (= 25 mm; 12 in a foot); **to be within an** ~ **of** estar a um passo de; **he didn't give an** ~ ele não cedeu nem um milímetro; **inch forward** *vi* avançar palmo a palmo
incident [ˈɪnsɪdnt] *n* incidente *m*, evento
incidental [ɪnsɪˈdɛntl] *adj* adicional; ~ **to** relacionado com; **incidentally** *adv* (*by the way*) a propósito
inclination [ɪnklɪˈneɪʃən] *n* (*tendency*) tendência; (*disposition*) inclinação *f*
incline [*n* ˈɪnklaɪn, *vb* ɪnˈklaɪn] *n* inclinação *f*, ladeira ♦ *vt* curvar, inclinar ♦ *vi* inclinar-se; **to be ~d to** ten-

der a, ser propenso a

include [ɪnˈkluːd] vt incluir

including [ɪnˈkluːdɪŋ] prep inclusive

inclusive [ɪnˈkluːsɪv] adj incluído, incluso; ~ **of** incluindo

income [ˈɪŋkʌm] n (earnings) renda, rendimentos mpl; (unearned) renda; **income tax** n imposto de renda (BR), imposto complementar (PT)

incoming [ˈɪnkʌmɪŋ] adj (flight) de chegada; (mail) de entrada; (government) novo; (tide) enchente

incompetent [ɪnˈkɔmpɪtənt] adj incompetente

incomplete [ɪnkəmˈpliːt] adj incompleto; (unfinished) por terminar

inconsiderate [ɪnkənˈsɪdərət] adj sem consideração

inconsistent [ɪnkənˈsɪstnt] adj inconsistente; ~ **with** incompatível com

inconspicuous [ɪnkənˈspɪkjuəs] adj modesto, discreto

inconvenience [ɪnkənˈviːnjəns] n (quality) inconveniência; (problem) inconveniente m ♦ vt incomodar

inconvenient [ɪnkənˈviːnjənt] adj inconveniente, incômodo; (time, place) inoportuno

incorporate [ɪnˈkɔːpəreɪt] vt incorporar; (contain) compreender

incorrect [ɪnkəˈrekt] adj incorreto

increase [n ˈɪnkriːs, vb ɪnˈkriːs] n aumento ♦ vi, vt aumentar; **increasing** adj crescente, em aumento; **increasingly** adv (more intensely) progressivamente; (more often) cada vez mais

incredible [ɪnˈkredɪbl] adj inacreditável; (enormous) incrível

incubator [ˈɪnkjubeɪtə*] n incubadora

incur [ɪnˈkəː*] vt incorrer em; (expenses) contrair

indebted [ɪnˈdetɪd] adj: **to be ~ to**

sb estar em dívida com alguém, dever obrigação a alguém

indecent [ɪnˈdiːsnt] adj indecente

indecisive [ɪndɪˈsaɪsɪv] adj indeciso

indeed [ɪnˈdiːd] adv de fato; (certainly) certamente; (furthermore) aliás; **yes** ~! claro que sim!

indefinitely [ɪnˈdefɪnɪtlɪ] adv indefinidamente

independence [ɪndɪˈpendns] n independência; **Independence Day** n Dia m da Independência; ver quadro

---

INDEPENDENCE DAY

Independence Day é a festa nacional dos Estados Unidos. Todo dia 4 de julho os americanos comemoram a adoção, em 1776, da declaração de Independência escrita por Thomas Jefferson que proclamava a separação das 13 colônias americanas da Grã-Bretanha.

---

independent [ɪndɪˈpendnt] adj independente; (inquiry) imparcial

index [ˈɪndeks] (pl ~**es**) n (in book) índice m; (in library etc) catálogo; (pl: indices: ratio, sign) índice m, expoente m; **index finger** n dedo indicador; **index-linked** (us **indexed**) adj vinculado ao índice (do custo de vida)

India [ˈɪndɪə] n Índia; **Indian** adj, n (from India) indiano(-a); (American, Brazilian) índio(-a); **Red Indian** índio (-a) pele vermelha; **Indian Ocean** n: **the Indian Ocean** o oceano Índico

indicate [ˈɪndɪkeɪt] vt (show) sugerir; (point to, mention) indicar; **indication** [ɪndɪˈkeɪʃən] n indício, sinal m; **indicative** [ɪnˈdɪkətɪv] adj: **indicative of** sintomático de ♦ n (LING) indicativo; **indicator** n indicador m; (AUT) pisca-pisca m

indices ['ɪndɪsi:z] npl of **index**

indifferent [ɪn'dɪfrənt] adj indiferente; (quality) mediócre

indigenous [ɪn'dɪdʒɪnəs] adj indígena, nativo

indigestion [ɪndɪ'dʒestʃən] n indigestão f

indignant [ɪn'dɪgnənt] adj: **to be ~ about sth/with sb** estar indignado com algo/alguém, indignar-se de algo/alguém

indignity [ɪn'dɪgnɪtɪ] n indignidade f

indirect [ɪndɪ'rekt] adj indireto

indiscreet [ɪndɪ'skri:t] adj indiscreto

indiscriminate [ɪndɪ'skrɪmɪnət] adj indiscriminado

indisputable [ɪndɪ'spju:təbl] adj incontestável

individual [ɪndɪ'vɪdjuəl] n indivíduo ♦ adj individual; (personal) pessoal; (characteristic) particular

Indonesia [ɪndə'ni:zɪə] n Indonésia

indoor ['ɪndɔ:*] adj (inner) interno, interior; (inside) dentro de casa; (plant) para dentro de casa; (swimming pool) coberto; (games, sport) de salão; **indoors** adv em lugar fechado

induce [ɪn'dju:s] vt (MED) induzir; (bring about) causar, produzir

indulge [ɪn'dʌldʒ] vt (desire) satisfazer; (whim) condescender com; (person) comprazer; (child) fazer a vontade de ♦ vi: **to ~ in** entregar-se a, satisfazer-se com; **indulgence** n (of desire) satisfação f; (leniency) indulgência, tolerância; **indulgent** adj indulgente

industrial [ɪn'dʌstrɪəl] adj industrial; **industrial action** n greve f

industrious [ɪn'dʌstrɪəs] adj trabalhador(a); (student) aplicado

industry ['ɪndəstrɪ] n indústria; (diligence) aplicação f, diligência

inebriated [ɪ'ni:brɪeɪtɪd] adj embriagado, bêbado

inedible [ɪn'edɪbl] adj não-comestível

ineffective [ɪnɪ'fektɪv] adj ineficaz

ineffectual [ɪnɪ'fektʃuəl] adj = ineffective

inefficient [ɪnɪ'fɪʃənt] adj ineficiente

inequality [ɪnɪ'kwɔlɪtɪ] n desigualdade f

inescapable [ɪnɪ'skeɪpəbl] adj inevitável

inevitable [ɪn'evɪtəbl] adj inevitável; **inevitably** adv inevitavelmente

inexpensive [ɪnɪk'spensɪv] adj barato, econômico

inexperienced [ɪnɪk'spɪərɪənst] adj inexperiente

infallible [ɪn'fælɪbl] adj infalível

infamous ['ɪnfəməs] adj infame, abominável

infancy ['ɪnfənsɪ] n infância

infant ['ɪnfənt] n (baby) bebê m; (young child) criança

infant school (BRIT) n pré-escola

infatuated [ɪn'fætjueɪtɪd] adj: **~ with** apaixonado por

infatuation [ɪnfætjʊ'eɪʃən] n gamação f, paixão f louca

infect [ɪn'fekt] vt (person) contagiar; (food) contaminar; **infection** n infecção f; **infectious** adj contagioso; (fig) infeccioso

infer [ɪn'fə:*] vt deduzir, inferir

inferior [ɪn'fɪərɪə*] adj interior; (goods) de qualidade inferior ♦ n inferior m/f; (in rank) subalterno(-a); **inferiority** [ɪnfɪərɪ'ɔrɪtɪ] n inferioridade f

infertile [ɪn'fə:taɪl] adj infértil; (person, animal) estéril

infinite ['ɪnfɪnɪt] adj infinito

infinitive [ɪn'fɪnɪtɪv] n infinitivo

infinity [ɪn'fɪnɪtɪ] n (also MATH) infinito; (an ~) infinidade f

infirmary [ɪn'fə:mərɪ] n enfermaria, hospital m

inflamed [ɪn'fleɪmd] adj inflamado

inflammable [ɪn'flæməbl] adj inflamável

inflammation [ɪnflə'meɪʃən] n inflamação f

inflatable [ɪn'fleɪtəbl] adj inflável

inflate [ɪn'fleɪt] vt (tyre, balloon) inflar, encher; (price) inflar; **inflation** n (ECON) inflação f

inflict [ɪn'flɪkt] vt: to ~ on infligir em

influence ['ɪnfluəns] n influência ♦ vt influir em, influenciar; **under the ~ of alcohol** sob o efeito do álcool; **influential** [ɪnflu'ɛnʃl] adj influente

influenza [ɪnflu'ɛnzə] n gripe f

infomercial ['ɪnfəuməːʃl] (US) n (for product) infomercial m

inform [ɪn'fɔːml] vt informar ♦ vi: to ~ on sb delatar alguém

informal [ɪn'fɔːml] adj informal; (visit, discussion) extra-oficial; **informality** [ɪnfɔː'mælɪtɪ] n informalidade f

information [ɪnfə'meɪʃən] n informação f, informações fpl; (knowledge) conhecimento; **a piece of ~** uma informação; **information desk** n balcão m de informações

informative [ɪn'fɔːmətɪv] adj informativo

informer [ɪn'fɔːmə*] n informante m/f

infringe [ɪn'frɪndʒ] vt infringir, transgredir ♦ vi: to ~ on violar

infuriating [ɪn'fjuərɪeɪtɪŋ] adj de dar raiva, enfurecedor(a)

ingenious [ɪn'dʒiːnjəs] adj engenhoso; **ingenuity** [ɪndʒɪ'njuːɪtɪ] n engenho, habilidade f

ingot ['ɪŋgət] n lingote m

ingratiate [ɪn'greɪʃɪeɪt] vt: to ~ o.s. with cair nas (boas) graças de

ingredient [ɪn'griːdɪənt] n ingrediente m; (of situation) fator m

inhabit [ɪn'hæbɪt] vt habitar; **inhabitant** n habitante m/f

inhale [ɪn'heɪl] vt inalar ♦ vi (in smoking) tragar

inherent [ɪn'hɪərənt] adj: ~ in or to inerente a

inherit [ɪn'herɪt] vt herdar; **inheritance** n herança

inhibit [ɪn'hɪbɪt] vt inibir; **inhibition** [ɪnhɪ'bɪʃən] n inibição f

inhuman [ɪn'hjuːmən] adj inumano, desumano

initial [ɪ'nɪʃl] adj inicial ♦ n inicial ♦ vt marcar com iniciais; **~s** npl (of name) iniciais fpl; **initially** adv inicialmente, no início

initiate [ɪ'nɪʃɪeɪt] vt (start) iniciar, começar; (person) iniciar; **to ~ sb into a secret** revelar um segredo a alguém

initiative [ɪ'nɪʃətɪv] n iniciativa

inject [ɪn'dʒɛkt] vt (liquid, fig money) injetar; (person) dar uma injeção em; **injection** n injeção f

injure ['ɪndʒə*] vt ferir; (reputation etc) prejudicar; (feelings) ofender; **injured** adj ferido; (feelings) ofendido, magoado; **injury** n ferida

injustice [ɪn'dʒʌstɪs] n injustiça

ink [ɪŋk] n tinta

inkling ['ɪŋklɪŋ] n vaga idéia

inlaid ['ɪnleɪd] adj (with gems, incrustado; (table etc) marchetado

inland [adj 'ɪnlənd, adv ɪn'lænd] adj interior, interno ♦ adv para o interior; **Inland Revenue** (BRIT) n = fisco, receita federal (BR)

inmate ['ɪnmeɪt] n (in prison) presidiário(-a); (in asylum) internado(-a) m

inn [ɪn] n hospedaria, taberna

innate [ɪ'neɪt] adj inato

inner ['ɪnə*] adj (place) interno; (feeling) interior; **inner city** n aglomeração f urbana, metrópole f

innings ['ɪnɪŋz] n (SPORT) turno

innocent ['ɪnəsnt] adj inocente

innocuous [ɪ'nɔkjuəs] adj inócuo

innuendo [ɪnju'ɛndəu] (pl **~es**) n insinuação f, indireta

innumerable [ɪ'nju:mrəbl] adj incontável

in-patient n paciente m/f interno(-a)

input ['ɪnput] n entrada; (resources) investimento

inquest ['ɪnkwɛst] n inquérito judicial

inquire [ɪn'kwaɪə*] vi pedir informação ♦ vt perguntar; **inquire about** vt fus pedir informações sobre; **inquire into** vt fus investigar, indagar; **inquiry** n pergunta; (LAW) investigação f, inquérito

inquisitive [ɪn'kwɪzɪtɪv] adj curioso, perguntador(a)

ins. abbr = **inches**

insane [ɪn'seɪn] adj louco, doido; (MED) demente, insano; **insanity** [ɪn'sænɪtɪ] n loucura; insanidade f, demência

inscription [ɪn'skrɪpʃən] n inscrição f; (in book) dedicatória

inscrutable [ɪn'skru:təbl] adj inescrutável, impenetrável

insect ['ɪnsɛkt] n inseto; **insecticide** [ɪn'sɛktɪsaɪd] n inseticida m

insecure [ɪnsɪ'kjuə*] adj inseguro

insensitive [ɪn'sɛnsɪtɪv] adj insensível

insert [ɪn'sə:t] vt (between things) intercalar; (into sth) introduzir, inserir

inshore [ɪn'ʃɔ:*] adj perto da costa, costeiro ♦ adv (be) perto da costa; (move) em direção à costa

inside ['ɪn'saɪd] n interior m ♦ adj interior, interno ♦ adv (be) dentro; (go) para dentro ♦ prep dentro de; (of time): **~ 10 minutes** em menos de 10 minutos; **~s** npl (inf) entranhas fpl; **inside out** adv às avessas; (know) muito bem; **to turn sth inside out** virar algo pelo avesso

insight ['ɪnsaɪt] n insight m

insignificant [ɪnsɪg'nɪfɪknt] adj insignificante

insincere [ɪnsɪn'sɪə*] adj insincero

insinuate [ɪn'sɪnjueɪt] vt insinuar

insist [ɪn'sɪst] vi insistir; **to ~ on doing** insistir em fazer; **to ~ that** insistir que; (claim) cismar que; **insistent** adj insistente, pertinaz; (continual) persistente

insomnia [ɪn'sɔmnɪə] n insônia

inspect [ɪn'spɛkt] vt inspecionar; (building) vistoriar; (BRIT: tickets) fiscalizar; (troops) passar revista em; **inspection** n inspeção f; vistoria; fiscalização f; **inspector** n inspetor(a) m/f; (BRIT: on buses, trains) fiscal m

inspire [ɪn'spaɪə*] vt inspirar

install [ɪn'stɔ:l] vt instalar; (official) nomear; **installation** [ɪnstə'leɪʃən] n instalação f

instalment [ɪn'stɔ:lmənt] (US **installment**) n (of money) prestação f; (of story) fascículo; (of TV serial etc) capítulo; **in ~s** (pay) a prestações; (receive) em várias vezes

instance ['ɪnstəns] n exemplo; **for ~** por exemplo; **in the first ~** em primeiro lugar

instant ['ɪnstənt] n instante m, momento ♦ adj imediato; (coffee) instantâneo; **instantly** adv imediatamente

instead [ɪn'stɛd] adv em vez disso; **~ of** em vez de, em lugar de

instigate ['ɪnstɪgeɪt] vt fomentar

instil [ɪn'stɪl] vt: **to ~ sth (into)** infundir or incutir algo (em)

instinct ['ɪnstɪŋkt] n instinto

institute ['ɪnstɪtjuːt] n instituto; (professional body) associação f ♦ vt (inquiry) começar, iniciar; (proceedings) instituir, estabelecer

institution [ɪnstɪ'tjuːʃən] n instituição f; (organization) instituto; (MED: home) asilo; (asylum) manicômio; (custom) costume m

instruct [ɪn'strʌkt] vt: **to ~ sb in sth** instruir alguém em or sobre algo; **to ~ sb to do sth** dar instruções a alguém para fazer algo; **instruction** n (teaching) instrução f; **instructions** npl (orders) ordens fpl; **instructions (for use)** modo de usar; **instructor** n instrutor(a) m/f

instrument ['ɪnstrumənt] n instrumento

insufficient [ɪnsə'fɪʃənt] adj insuficiente

insular ['ɪnsjulə*] adj (outlook) estreito; (person) de mente limitada

insulate ['ɪnsjuleɪt] vt isolar; (protect) segregar; **insulation** [ɪnsju'leɪʃən] n isolamento

insulin ['ɪnsjulɪn] n insulina

insult [n 'ɪnsʌlt, vb ɪn'sʌlt] n ofensa ♦ vt insultar, ofender

insurance [ɪn'ʃuərəns] n seguro; **fire/life ~** seguro contra incêndio/de vida

insure [ɪn'ʃuə*] vt segurar

intact [ɪn'tækt] adj intacto, íntegro; (unharmed) ileso, são e salvo

intake ['ɪnteɪk] n (of food) quantidade f ingerida; (BRIT: SCH): **an ~ of 200 a year** 200 matriculados por ano

integral ['ɪntɪgrəl] adj (part) integrante, essencial

integrate ['ɪntɪgreɪt] vt integrar ♦ vi integrar-se

intellect ['ɪntəlekt] n intelecto;

intellectual [ɪntə'lektjuəl] adj, n intelectual m/f

intelligence [ɪn'telɪdʒəns] n inteligência; (MIL etc) informações fpl

intelligent [ɪn'telɪdʒənt] adj inteligente

intend [ɪn'tend] vt (gift etc): **to ~ sth for** destinar algo a; **to ~ to do sth** tencionar or pretender fazer algo; (plan) planejar fazer algo

intense [ɪn'tens] adj intenso; (person) muito emotivo

intensive [ɪn'tensɪv] adj intensivo; **intensive care unit** n unidade f de tratamento intensivo

intent [ɪn'tent] n intenção f ♦ adj: **to be ~ on doing sth** estar resolvido a fazer algo; **to all ~s and purposes** para todos os efeitos

intention [ɪn'tenʃən] n intenção f, propósito; **intentional** adj intencional, propositado; **intentionally** adv de propósito

intently [ɪn'tentlɪ] adv atentamente

interact [ɪntər'ækt] vi interagir; **interactive** adj interactivo

interchange ['ɪntətʃeɪndʒ] n intercâmbio; (exchange) troca, permuta; (on motorway) trevo; **interchangeable** adj permutável

intercom ['ɪntəkɔm] n interfone m

intercourse ['ɪntəkɔːs] n: **sexual ~** relações fpl sexuais

interest ['ɪntrɪst] n interesse m; (COMM: sum) juros mpl; (: in company) participação f ♦ vt interessar; **to be ~ed in** interessar-se por, estar interessado em; **interesting** adj interessante

interface ['ɪntəfeɪs] n (COMPUT) interface f

interfere [ɪntə'fɪə*] vi: **to ~ in** interferir or intrometer-se em; **to ~ with** (objects) mexer em; (hinder) impedir; (plans) interferir em

interference [intə'fiərəns] n intromissão f; (RADIO, TV) interferência

interior [in'tiəriə*] n interior m ♦ adj interno; (ministry) do interior

interjection [intə'dʒekʃən] n interrupção f; (LING) interjeição f, exclamação f

interlude ['intəlu:d] n interlúdin; (rest) descanso; (THEATRE) intervalo

intermediate [intə'mi:diət] adj intermediário

intermission [intə'miʃən] n intervalo

intern [vb in'tə:n, n 'intə:n] vt internar ♦ n (US) médico-interno (médica-interna)

internal [in'tə:nl] adj interno; **internally** adv: "not to be taken internally" "uso externo"; **Internal Revenue Service** (US) n Receita Federal (BR), Direcção f Geral das Contribuições e Impostos (PT)

international [intə'næʃnl] adj internacional ♦ n (BRIT: SPORT: game) jogo internacional

Internet ['intənet] n: **the ~** a Internet; **Internet café** n cibercafé m; **Internet Service Provider** n provedor m de acesso à Internet

interpret [in'tə:prit] vt interpretar; (translate) traduzir ♦ vi interpretar; **interpreter** n intérprete m/f

interrelated [intəri'leitid] adj inter-relacionado

interrogate [in'terəugeit] vt interrogar; **interrogation** [interəu-'geiʃən] n interrogatório

interrupt [intə'rʌpt] vt, vi interromper; **interruption** n interrupção f

intersect [intə'sekt] vi (roads) cruzar-se; **intersection** n cruzamento

interval ['intəvl] n intervalo

intervene [intə'vi:n] vi intervir; (event) ocorrer; (time) decorrer;

intervention n intervenção f

interview ['intəvju:] n entrevista ♦ vt entrevistar; **interviewer** n entrevistador(a) m/f

intestine [in'testin] n intestino

intimacy ['intiməsi] n intimidade f

intimate [adj 'intimət, vb 'intimeit] adj íntimo; (knowledge) profundo ♦ vt insinuar, sugerir

into ['intu] prep em; **she burst ~ tears** ela desatou a chorar; **come ~ the house** venha para dentro; **research ~ cancer** pesquisa sobre o câncer; **he worked late ~ the night** ele trabalhou até altas horas; **he was shocked ~ silence** ele ficou mudo de choque; **~ 3 pieces/French** em 3 pedaços/para o francês

intolerant [in'tɔlərnt] adj: **~ (of)** intolerante (com or para com)

intoxicated [in'tɔksikeitid] adj embriagado

intranet ['intrənet] n intranet f

intricate ['intrikət] adj complexo, complicado

intrigue [in'tri:g] n intriga ♦ vt intrigar; (fascinate) fascinar; **intriguing** adj curioso

introduce [intrə'dju:s] vt introduzir; **to ~ sb (to sb)** apresentar alguém a (alguém); **to ~ sb to** (pastime, technique) iniciar alguém em; **introduction** n introdução f; (of person) apresentação f; **introductory** adj introdutório

intrude [in'tru:d] vi: **to ~ (on)** intrometer-se (em); **intruder** n intruso(-a)

inundate ['inʌndeit] vt: **to ~ with** inundar de

invade [in'veid] vt invadir

invalid [n 'invəlid, adj in'vælid] n inválido(-a) ♦ adj inválido, nulo

invaluable [in'væljuəbl] adj valioso, inestimável

invariably [ɪn'vɛərɪəblɪ] *adv* invariavelmente

invent [ɪn'vɛnt] *vt* inventar; **invention** *n* invenção *f*; (*inventiveness*) engenho; (*lie*) ficção *f*, mentira; **inventor** *n* inventor(a) *m/f*

inventory ['ɪnvəntrɪ] *n* inventário, relação *f*

invert [ɪn'vəːt] *vt* inverter; **inverted commas** (BRIT) *npl* aspas *fpl*

invest [ɪn'vɛst] *vt* investir ♦ *vi*: **to ~ in** investir em; (*acquire*) comprar

investigate [ɪn'vɛstɪgeɪt] *vt* investigar; **investigation** [ɪnvɛstɪ'geɪʃən] *n* investigação *f*

investment [ɪn'vɛstmənt] *n* investimento

invigorating [ɪn'vɪgəreɪtɪŋ] *adj* revigorante

invisible [ɪn'vɪzɪbl] *adj* invisível

invitation [ɪnvɪ'teɪʃən] *n* convite *m*

invite [ɪn'vaɪt] *vt* convidar; (*opinions etc*) incitar; **inviting** *adj* convidativo

invoice ['ɪnvɔɪs] *n* fatura ♦ *vt* faturar

involuntary [ɪn'vɔləntrɪ] *adj* involuntário

involve [ɪn'vɔlv] *vt* (*entail*) implicar; (*require*) exigir; (*concern*) envolver; **to ~ sb (in)** envolver alguém (em); **involved** *adj* (*complex*) complexo; **to be involved in** estar envolvido em; **involvement** *n* envolvimento

inward ['ɪnwəd] *adj* (*movement*) interior, interno; (*thought, feeling*) íntimo; **inward(s)** *adv* para dentro

iodine ['aɪəudiːn] *n* iodo

iota [aɪ'əutə] *n* (*fig*) pouquinho, tiquinho

IOU *n abbr* (= *I owe you*) vale *m*

IQ *n abbr* (= *intelligence quotient*) QI

IRA *n abbr* (= *Irish Republican Army*) IRA *m*

Iran [ɪ'rɑːn] *n* Irã *m* (BR), Irão *m* (PT)

Iraq [ɪ'rɑːk] *n* Iraque *m*

irate [aɪ'reɪt] *adj* irado, enfurecido

Ireland ['aɪələnd] *n* Irlanda

iris ['aɪrɪs] (*pl* **~es**) *n* íris *f*

Irish ['aɪrɪʃ] *adj* irlandês(-esa) ♦ *npl*: **the ~** os irlandeses; **Irishman** (*irreg*) *n* irlandês *m*; **Irish Sea** *n*: **the Irish Sea** o mar da Irlanda; **Irishwoman** (*irreg*) *n* irlandesa

iron ['aɪən] *n* ferro; (*for clothes*) ferro de passar roupa ♦ *adj* de ferro ♦ *vt* (*clothes*) passar; **iron out** *vt* (*problem*) resolver

ironic(al) [aɪ'rɔnɪk(l)] *adj* irônico

ironing ['aɪənɪŋ] *n* (*activity*) passar *m* roupa; (*clothes*) roupa passada; **ironing board** *n* tábua de passar roupa

irony ['aɪrənɪ] *n* ironia

irrational [ɪ'ræʃənl] *adj* irracional

irregular [ɪ'rɛgjulə*] *adj* irregular; (*surface*) desigual

irrelevant [ɪ'rɛləvənt] *adj* irrelevante

irresistible [ɪrɪ'zɪstɪbl] *adj* irresistível

irrespective [ɪrɪ'spɛktɪv]: **~ of** *prep* independente de, sem considerar

irresponsible [ɪrɪ'spɔnsɪbl] *adj* irresponsável

irrigation [ɪrɪ'geɪʃən] *n* irrigação *f*

irritate ['ɪrɪteɪt] *vt* irritar; **irritating** *adj* irritante; **irritation** [ɪrɪ'teɪʃən] *n* irritação *f*

IRS (US) *n abbr* = **Internal Revenue Service**

is [ɪz] *vb see* **be**

ISDN *n abbr* (= *Integrated Services Digital Network*) RDSI *f*, ISDN *f*

Islam ['ɪzlɑːm] *n* islamismo

island ['aɪlənd] *n* ilha; **islander** *n* ilhéu (ilhoa) *m/f*

isle [aɪl] *n* ilha

isn't ['ɪznt] = **is not**

isolate ['aɪsəleɪt] *vt* isolar; **isolated**

adj isolado; **isolation** [aɪsəˈleɪʃən] *n* isolamento

ISP *n abbr* = **Internet Service Provider**

Israel [ˈɪzreɪl] *n* Israel *m (no article)*; **Israeli** [ɪzˈreɪlɪ] *adj*, *n* israelense *m/f*

issue [ˈɪsjuː] *n* questão *f*, tema *m*; *(of book)* edição *f*; *(of stamps)* emissão *f* ♦ *vt (statement)* fazer; *(rations, equipment)* distribuir; *(orders)* dar; **at ~** em debate; **to take ~ with sb (over sth)** discordar de alguém (sobre algo); **to make an ~ of sth** criar caso com algo

---

KEYWORD

it [ɪt] *pron* **1** *(specific: subject)* ele (ela); *(: direct object)* o (a); *(: indirect object)* lhe; **~'s on the table** está em cima da mesa; **I can't find ~** não consigo achá-lo; **give ~ to me** dê-mio; **about/from ~** sobre/de isto; **did you go to ~?** *(party, concert etc)* você foi?

2 *(impers)* isto, isso; *(after prep)* ele, ela; **~'s raining** está chovendo *(BR)* or a chover *(PT)*; **~'s six o'clock/the 10th of August** são seis horas/hoje é *(dia)* 10 de agosto; **who is ~? – ~'s me** quem é? – sou eu

---

Italian [ɪˈtæljən] *adj* italiano ♦ *n* italiano(-a); *(LING)* italiano

italics [ɪˈtælɪks] *npl* itálico

Italy [ˈɪtəlɪ] *n* Itália

itch [ɪtʃ] *n* comichão *f*, coceira *f* ♦ *vi (person)* estar com or sentir comichão or coceira; *(part of body)* comichar, coçar; **I'm itching to do sth** estou louco para fazer algo; **itchy** *adj* que coça; **to be itchy = to itch**

it'd [ˈɪtd] = **it would; it had**

item [ˈaɪtəm] *n* item *m*; *(on agenda)* assunto; *(in programme)* número;

(also: **news ~**) notícia; **itemize** *vt* detalhar, especificar

itinerary [aɪˈtɪnərərɪ] *n* itinerário

it'll [ˈɪtl] = **it will; it shall**

its [ɪts] *adj* seu (sua), dele (dela) ♦ *pron* o seu (a sua), o dele (a dela)

it's [ɪts] = **it is; it has**

itself [ɪtˈself] *pron (reflexive)* si mesmo(-a); *(emphatic)* ele mesmo (ela mesma)

ITV *(BRIT)* *n abbr* (= **Independent Television**) canal de televisão comercial

IUD *n abbr* (= **intra-uterine device**) DIU *m*

I've [aɪv] = **I have**

ivory [ˈaɪvərɪ] *n* marfim *m*

ivy [ˈaɪvɪ] *n* hera

J

jab [dʒæb] *vt* cutucar ♦ *n* cotovelada, murro; *(MED: inf)* injeção *f*; **to ~ sth into sth** cravar algo em algo

jack [dʒæk] *n (AUT)* macaco; *(CARDS)* valete *m*; **jack up** *vt (AUT)* levantar com macaco

jackal [ˈdʒækl] *n* chacal *m*

jacket [ˈdʒækɪt] *n* jaqueta, casaco curto, forro; *(of book)* sobrecapa; **jacket potato** *n* batata assada com a casca

jack-knife *vi*: **the lorry ~d** o reboque do caminhão deu uma guinada

jackpot [ˈdʒækpɔt] *n* bolada, sorte *f* grande

jaded [ˈdʒeɪdɪd] *adj (tired)* cansado; *(fed-up)* aborrecido, enfastiado

jagged [ˈdʒæɡɪd] *adj* dentado, denteado

jail [dʒeɪl] *n* prisão *f*, cadeia ♦ *vt* encarcerar

jam [dʒæm] *n* geléia; *(also:* **traffic ~**) engarrafamento; *(inf)* apuro ♦ *vt* obstruir, atravancar; *(mechanism)*

emperrar; (_RADIO_) bloquear, interferir ♦ _vi_ (mechanism, drawer _etc_) emperrar; **to ~ sth into sth** forçar algo dentro de algo

Jamaica [dʒə'meɪkə] _n_ Jamaica

janitor ['dʒænɪtə*] _n_ zelador _m_

January ['dʒænjuərɪ] _n_ janeiro

Japan [dʒə'pæn] _n_ Japão _m_; **Japanese** [dʒæpə'niːz] _adj_ japonês(-esa) ♦ _n inv_ japonês(-esa) _m/f_; (_LING_) japonês _m_

jar [dʒɑː*] _n_ jarro ♦ _vi_ (sound) ranger, chiar; (colours) destoar

jargon ['dʒɑːgən] _n_ jargão _m_

jaundice ['dʒɔːndɪs] _n_ icterícia

javelin ['dʒævlɪn] _n_ dardo de arremesso

jaw [dʒɔː] _n_ mandíbula, maxilar _m_

jaywalker ['dʒeɪwɔːkə*] _n_ pedestre _m/f_ imprudente (_BR_), peão _m_ imprudente (_PT_)

jazz [dʒæz] _n_ jazz _m_; **jazz up** _vt_ animar, avivar

jealous ['dʒeləs] _adj_ ciumento; **jealousy** _n_ ciúmes _mpl_

jeans [dʒiːnz] _npl_ jeans _m_ (_pl PT_)

jeer [dʒɪə*] _vi_: **to ~ (at)** zombar (de)

jelly ['dʒelɪ] _n_ gelatina; (jam) geléia; **jellyfish** ['dʒelɪfɪʃ] _n inv_ água-viva

jeopardy ['dʒepədɪ] _n_: **to be in ~** estar em perigo, estar correndo risco

jerk [dʒəːk] _n_ solavanco, sacudida; (wrench) puxão _m_; (inf: idiot) babaca _m_ ♦ _vt_ sacudir ♦ _vi_ dar um solavanco

jersey ['dʒəːzɪ] _n_ suéter _m_ or _f_ (_BR_), camisola (_PT_); (fabric) jérsei _m_, malha

Jesus ['dʒiːzəs] _n_ Jesus _m_

jet [dʒet] _n_ (of gas, liquid) jato; (_AVIAT_) avião _m_ a jato; (stone) azeviche _m_; **jet engine** _n_ motor _m_ a jato; **jet lag** _n_ cansaço devido à diferença de fuso horário

jettison ['dʒetɪsn] _vt_ alijar

jetty ['dʒetɪ] _n_ quebra-mar _m_, cais _m_

Jew [dʒuː] _n_ judeu(-dia) _m/f_

jewel ['dʒuːəl] _n_ jóia; **jeweller** (_US_ **jeweler**) _n_ joalheiro(-a); **jeweller's (shop)** _n_ joalheria; **jewellery** (_US_ **jewelry**) _n_ jóias _fpl_

Jewess ['dʒuːɪs] _n_ (offensive) judia

Jewish ['dʒuːɪʃ] _adj_ judeu (judia)

jiffy ['dʒɪfɪ] (_inf_) _n_: **in a ~** num instante

jigsaw ['dʒɪgsɔː] _n_ (also: ~ **puzzle**) quebra-cabeça _m_

jilt [dʒɪlt] _vt_ dar o fora em

jingle ['dʒɪŋgl] _n_ (for advert) música de propaganda ♦ _vi_ tilintar, retinir

jinx [dʒɪŋks] (_inf_) _n_ caipora, pé frio

job [dʒɔb] _n_ trabalho; (task) tarefa; (duty) dever _m_; (post) emprego; **it's not my ~** não faz parte das minhas funções; **it's a good ~ that** ... ainda bem que ...; **just the ~!** justo o que queria!; **jobless** _adj_ desempregado

jockey ['dʒɔkɪ] _n_ jóquei _m_ ♦ _vi_: **to ~ for position** manobrar para conseguir uma posição

jog [dʒɔg] _vt_ empurrar, sacudir ♦ _vi_ fazer jogging ou cooper; **jog along** _vi_ ir levando; **jogging** _n_ jogging _m_

join [dʒɔɪn] _vt_ (things) juntar, unir; (queue) entrar em; (become member of) associar-se a; (meet) encontrar-se com; (accompany) juntar-se a ♦ _vi_ (roads, rivers) confluir ♦ _n_ junção _f_; **join in** _vi_ participar ♦ _vt fus_ participar em; **join up** _vi_ unir-se; (_MIL_) alistar-se

joint [dʒɔɪnt] _n_ (_TECH_) junta, união _f_; (wood) encaixe _m_; (_ANAT_) articulação _f_; (_BRIT_: _CULIN_) quarto; (inf: place) espelunca; (: of marijuana) baseado ♦ _adj_ comum; (combined) conjunto; (committee) misto

joke [dʒəuk] n piada; (also: **practical ~**) brincadeira, peça ♦ vi brincar; **to play a ~ on** pregar uma peça em; **joker** n (CARDS) curingão m

jolly ['dʒɒlɪ] adj (merry) alegre; (enjoyable) divertido ♦ adv (BRIT: inf) muito, extremamente

jolt [dʒəult] n (shake) sacudida, solavanco; (shock) susto ♦ vt sacudir; (emotionally) abalar

Jordan ['dʒɔːdən] n Jordânia; (river) Jordão m

jostle ['dʒɒsl] vt acotovelar, empurrar

jot [dʒɒt] n: **not one ~** nem um pouquinho; **jot down** vt anotar; **jotter** (BRIT) n bloco de anotações

journal ['dʒɜːnl] n jornal m; (magazine) revista; (diary) diário; **journalism** n jornalismo; **journalist** n jornalista m/f

journey ['dʒɜːnɪ] n viagem f; (distance covered) trajeto

joy [dʒɔɪ] n alegria; **joyful** adj alegre; **joystick** n (AVIAT) manche m, alavanca de controle; (COMPUT) joystick m

Jr abbr = **junior**

judge [dʒʌdʒ] n juiz (juíza m/f); (in competition) árbitro; (fig: expert) especialista m/f, conhecedor(a) m/f ♦ vt julgar; (competition) arbitrar; (estimate) avaliar; (consider) considerar; **judg(e)ment** n juízo; (opinion) opinião f; (discernment) discernimento

judo ['dʒuːdəu] n judô m

jug [dʒʌg] n jarro

juggernaut ['dʒʌgənɔːt] (BRIT) n (huge truck) jamanta

juggle ['dʒʌgl] vi fazer malabarismos; **juggler** n malabarista m/f

juice [dʒuːs] n suco (BR), sumo (PT); **juicy** adj suculento

jukebox ['dʒuːkbɒks] n juke-box m

July [dʒuːˈlaɪ] n julho

jumble ['dʒʌmbl] n confusão f, mixórdia ♦ vt (also: **~ up**: mix up) misturar; **jumble sale** n (BRIT) bazar m; ver quadro

---

JUMBLE SALE

As **jumble sales** têm lugar dentro de igrejas, salões de festa e escolas, onde são vendidos diversos tipos de mercadorias, em geral baratas e sobretudo de segunda mão, a fim de coletar dinheiro para uma obra de caridade, uma escola ou uma igreja.

---

jumbo (jet) ['dʒʌmbəu-] n avião m jumbo

jump [dʒʌmp] vi saltar, pular; (start) sobressaltar-se; (increase) disparar ♦ vt pular, saltar ♦ n pulo, salto; (increase) alta; (fence) obstáculo; **to ~ the queue** (BRIT) furar a fila (BR), pôr-se à frente (PT)

jumper ['dʒʌmpə*] n (BRIT: pullover) suéter m (BR), camisola (PT); (US: pinafore dress) avental m; **jumper cables** (US) npl = **jump leads**

jump leads (BRIT) npl cabos mpl para ligar a bateria

jumpy ['dʒʌmpɪ] adj nervoso

Jun. abbr = **junior**

junction ['dʒʌŋkʃən] (BRIT) n (of roads) cruzamento; (RAIL) entroncamento

June [dʒuːn] n junho

jungle ['dʒʌŋgl] n selva, mato

junior ['dʒuːnɪə*] adj (in age) mais novo e moço; (position) subalterno ♦ n jovem m/f

junk [dʒʌŋk] n (cheap goods) tranqueira, velharias fpl; (rubbish) lixo; **junk food** n comida pronta de baixo valor nutritivo; **junk mail** n correspondência não-solicitada; **junk shop** n loja de objetos usados

Junr abbr = **junior**

jury ['dʒʊərɪ] n júri m

just [dʒʌst] adj justo ♦ adv (exactly) justamente, exatamente; (only) apenas, somente; **he's ~ done it/left** ele acabou (BR) ou acaba (PT) de fazê-lo/ir; **~ right** perfeito; **~ two o'clock** duas (horas) em ponto; **she's ~ as clever as you** ela é tão inteligente como você; **it's ~ as well that ...** ainda bem que ...; **~ as he was leaving** no momento em que ele saía; **~ before/enough** justo antes/o suficiente; **~ here** bem aqui; **he ~ missed** falhou por pouco; **~ listen** escute aqui!

justice ['dʒʌstɪs] n justiça; (US: judge) juiz (juíza) m/f; **to do ~ to** (fig) apreciar devidamente

justify ['dʒʌstɪfaɪ] vt justificar

jut [dʒʌt] vi (also: ~ out) sobressair

juvenile ['dʒuːvənaɪl] adj juvenil; (court) de menores; (books) para adolescentes; (humour, mentality) infantil ♦ n menor m/f de idade

K

K abbr (= kilobyte) K ♦ n abbr (= one thousand) mil

kangaroo [kæŋgə'ruː] n canguru m

karate [kə'rɑːtɪ] n karatê m

kebab [kə'bæb] n churrasquinho, espetinho

keen [kiːn] adj (interest, desire) grande, vivo; (eye, intelligence) penetrante; (competition) acirrado, intenso; (edge) afiado; (eager) entusiasmado; **to be ~ to do** or **on doing sth** sentir muita vontade de fazer algo; **to be ~ on sth/sb** gostar de algo/alguém

keep [kiːp] (pt, pp **kept**) vt guardar, ficar com; (house etc) manter; (detain) deter; (shop etc) tomar conta de; (preserve) conservar; (accounts, family) manter; (promise) cumprir; (chickens, bees etc) criar; (prevent): **to ~ sb from doing sth** impedir alguém de fazer algo ♦ vi (food) conservar-se; (remain) ficar ♦ n (of castle) torre f de menagem; (food etc): **to earn one's ~** ganhar a vida; (inf): **for ~s** para sempre; **to ~ doing sth** continuar fazendo algo; **to ~ sb happy** manter alguém satisfeito; **to ~ a place tidy** manter um lugar limpo; **keep on** vi: **to ~ on doing** continuar fazendo; **keep out** vt impedir de entrar; **"~ out"** "entrada proibida"; **keep up** vt manter ♦ vi não atrasar-se, acompanhar; **to ~ up with** (pace) acompanhar; (level) manter-se ao nível de; **keeper** n guarda m, guardião(-diã) m/f; **keep fit** n ginástica

kennel ['kɛnl] n casa de cachorro; **~s** n (establishment) canil m

kerb [kəːb] (BRIT) n meio-fio (BR), borda do passeio (PT)

kernel ['kəːnl] n amêndoa; (fig) cerne m

kettle ['kɛtl] n chaleira

key [kiː] n chave f; (MUS) clave f; (of piano, typewriter) tecla ♦ cpd (issue etc) chave ♦ vt (also: ~ in) colocar; **keyboard** n teclado; **keyhole** n buraco da fechadura; **keyring** n chaveiro

khaki ['kɑːkɪ] adj cáqui

kick [kɪk] vt dar um pontapé em; (ball) chutar; (inf: habit) conseguir superar ♦ vi (horse) dar coices ♦ n (from person) pontapé m; (from animal) coice m, patada; (to ball) chute m; (inf: thrill): **he does it for ~s** faz isso para curtir; **kick off** vi (SPORT) dar o chute inicial

kid [kɪd] n (inf: child) criança; (ani-

mal) cabrito; (*leather*) pelica ♦ *vi* (*inf*) brincar

kidnap ['kɪdnæp] *vt* seqüestrar; **kidnapper** *n* seqüestrador(a) *m/f*; **kidnapping** *n* seqüestro

kidney ['kɪdnɪ] *n* rim *m*

kill [kɪl] *vt* matar; (*murder*) assassinar ♦ *n* ato de matar; **killer** *n* assassino(-a); **killing** *n* assassinato; **to make a killing** (*inf*) faturar uma boa nota; **killjoy** *n* desmancha-prazeres *m inv*

kiln [kɪln] *n* forno

kilo ['kiːləʊ] *n* quilo; **kilobyte** *n* quilobyte *m*; **kilogram(me)** *n* quilograma *m*; **kilometre** (*US* **kilometer**) *n* quilômetro; **kilowatt** *n* quilowatt *m*

kilt [kɪlt] *n* saiote *m* escocês

kin [kɪn] *n see* **next**

kind [kaɪnd] *adj* (*friendly*) gentil; (*generous*) generoso; (*good*) bom (boa) bondoso, amável; (*voice*) suave ♦ *n* espécie *f*, classe *f*; (*species*) gênero; **in ~** (*COMM*) em espécie

kindergarten ['kɪndəgɑːtn] *n* jardim *m* de infância

kind-hearted *adj* de bom coração, bondoso

kindly ['kaɪndlɪ] *adj* bom (boa) bondoso; (*gentle*) gentil, carinhoso ♦ *adv* bondosamente, amavelmente; **will you ~ ...** você pode fazer o favor de ...

kindness ['kaɪndnɪs] *n* bondade *f*, gentileza

king [kɪŋ] *n* rei *m*; **kingdom** *n* reino; **kingfisher** *n* martim-pescador *m*; **king-size(d)** *adj* tamanho grande

kiosk ['kiːɔsk] *n* banca (*BR*), quiosque *m* (*PT*); (*BRIT: TEL*) cabine *f*

kipper ['kɪpə*] *n* arenque defumado

kiss [kɪs] *n* beijo ♦ *vt* beijar; **to ~ (each other)** beijar-se; **kiss of life**

(*BRIT*) *n* respiração *f* artificial

kit [kɪt] *n* (*for sport etc*) kit *m*; (*equipment*) equipamento *m*; (*tools*) caixa de ferramentas; (*for assembly*) kit *m* para montar

kitchen ['kɪtʃɪn] *n* cozinha; **kitchen sink** *n* pia (de cozinha)

kite [kaɪt] *n* (*toy*) papagaio, pipa

kitten ['kɪtn] *n* gatinho

kitty ['kɪtɪ] *n* fundo comum, vaquinha

km *abbr* (= *kilometre*) km

knack [næk] *n* jeito

knapsack ['næpsæk] *n* mochila

knead [niːd] *vt* amassar

knee [niː] *n* joelho; **kneecap** *n* rótula

kneel [niːl] (*pt, pp* **knelt**) *vi* (*also: ~ down*) ajoelhar-se

knew [njuː] *pt of* **know**

knickers ['nɪkəz] (*BRIT*) *npl* calcinha (*BR*), cuecas *fpl* (*PT*)

knife [naɪf] (*pl* **knives**) *n* faca ♦ *vt* esfaquear

knight [naɪt] *n* cavaleiro; (*CHESS*) cavalo; **knighthood** (*BRIT*) *n* (*title*): **to get a knighthood** receber o título de Sir

knit [nɪt] *vt* tricotar; (*brows*) franzir ♦ *vi* tricotar (*BR*), fazer malha (*PT*); (*bones*) consolidar-se; **knitting** *n* tricô *m*; **knitting needle** *n* agulha de tricô (*BR*) or de malha (*PT*); **knitwear** *n* roupa de malha

knives [naɪvz] *npl of* **knife**

knob [nɔb] *n* (*of door*) maçaneta; (*of stick*) castão *m*; (*on TV etc*) botão *m*

knock [nɔk] *vt* bater em; (*bump into*) colidir com; (*inf*) criticar, malhar ♦ *n* pancada, golpe *m*; (*on door*) batida ♦ *vi*: **to ~ at** *or* **on the door** bater à porta; **knock down** *vt* derrubar; (*pedestrian*) atropelar; **knock off** *vi* (*inf: finish*) terminar ♦ *vt* (*inf: steal*) abafar; (*from price*):

to ~ **off £10** fazer um desconto de
£10; **knock out** vt pôr nocaute,
nocautear; (defeat) eliminar; **knock
over** vt derrubar; (pedestrian) atropelar; **knocker** n aldrava

knot [nɔt] n nó m ♦ vt dar nó em

know [nəu] (pt **knew**, pp **known**) vt
saber; (person, author, place) conhecer; **to ~ how to swim** saber nadar;
to ~ about or **of sth** saber de algo;
know-how n know-how m, experiência; **knowingly** adv de propósito; (spitefully) maliciosamente

knowledge ['nɔlidʒ] n conhecimento; (learning) saber m, conhecimentos mpl; **knowledgeable** adj
entendido, versado

knuckle ['nʌkl] n nó m

Koran [kɔ'rɑːn] n: **the ~** o Alcorão

Korea [kə'riə] n Coréia

kosher ['kəuʃə*] adj kosher inv

Kosovo ['kɔsəvəu] n Kosovo m

L

L (BRIT) abbr (AUT) of **learner**

lab [læb] n abbr = **laboratory**

label ['leibl] n etiqueta, rótulo ♦ vt
etiquetar, rotular

labor etc ['leibə*] (US) = **labour** etc

laboratory [lə'bɔrətəri] n laboratório

labour ['leibə*] (US **labor**) n trabalho; (workforce) mão-de-obra f;
(MED): **to be in ~** estar em trabalho
de parto ♦ vi trabalhar ♦ vt insistir
em; **the Labour Party** o
Partido Trabalhista; **labourer** n
operário; **farm labourer** trabalhador
m rural, peão m

lace [leis] n renda; (of shoe etc)
cadarço ♦ vt (shoe) amarrar

lack [læk] n falta ♦ vt (money, confidence) faltar; (intelligence) carecer

de; **through** or **for ~ of** por falta de;
to be ~ing faltar; **to be ~ing in** carecer de

lacquer ['lækə*] n laca; (hair ~) fixa-
dor m

lad [læd] n menino, rapaz m, moço

ladder ['lædə*] n escada f de mão;
(BRIT: in tights) defeito (em forma de
escada)

laden ['leidn] adj: **~ (with)** carregado (de)

ladle ['leidl] n concha (de sopa)

lady ['leidi] n senhora; (distinguished, noble) dama; (in address):
ladies and gentlemen ... senhoras e
senhores ...; **young ~** senhorita;
"ladies' (toilets)" "senhoras"; **ladybird** (US **ladybug**) n joaninha; **lady-
like** adj elegante, refinado

lag [læg] n atraso, retardamento ♦ vi
(also: **~ behind**) ficar para trás ♦ vt
(pipes) revestir com isolante térmico

lager ['lɑːgə*] n cerveja leve e clara

lagoon [lə'guːn] n lagoa

laid [leid] pt, pp of **lay**; **laid-back**
(inf) adj descontraído; **laid up** adj:
to be laid up with flu ficar de cama
com gripe

lain [lein] pp of **lie**

lake [leik] n lago

lamb [læm] n cordeiro

lame [leim] adj coxo, manco; (excuse, argument) pouco convincente,
fraco

lament [lə'mɛnt] n lamento, queixa
♦ vt lamentar-se de

laminated ['læmineitid] adj lami-
nado

lamp [læmp] n lâmpada; **lamppost**
(BRIT) n poste m; **lampshade** n abajur m, quebra-luz m

lance [lɑːns] n lança ♦ vt (MED) lan-
cetar

land [lænd] n terra; (country) país m;
(piece of ~) terreno; (estate) terras

fpl, propriedades *fpl* ♦ *vi* (*from ship*)
desembarcar; (*AVIAT*) pousar, aterrissar (*BR*), aterrar (*PT*); (*fig: arrive*) cair,
terminar ♦ *vt* desembarcar; **to ~ sb
with sth** (*inf*) sobrecarregar alguém
com algo; **land up** *vi* ir parar; **landing** *n* (*AVIAT*) pouso, aterrissagem *f*
(*BR*), aterragem *f* (*PT*); (*of staircase*)
patamar *m*; **landing strip** *n* pista de
aterrissagem (*BR*) or de aterragem
(*PT*); **landlady** *n* senhoria; (*of pub*)
dona, proprietária; **landlord** *n* senhorio, locador *m*; (*of pub*) dono,
proprietário; **landmark** *n* lugar *m*
conhecido; (*fig*) marco; **landowner** *n* latifundiário(-a)

landscape ['lændskeɪp] *n* paisagem
f

landslide ['lændslaɪd] *n* (*GEO*) desmoronamento, desabamento; (*fig:
POL*) vitória esmagadora

lane [leɪn] *n* caminho, estrada estreita; (*AUT*) pista; (*in race*) raia

language ['læŋgwɪdʒ] *n* língua;
(*way one speaks*) linguagem *f*; **bad ~**
palavrões *mpl*; **language laboratory** *n* laboratório de línguas

lank [læŋk] *adj* (*hair*) liso

lanky ['læŋkɪ] *adj* magricela

lantern ['læntn] *n* lanterna

lap [læp] *n* (*of track*) volta; (*of person*)
colo ♦ *vt* (*also: ~ up*) lamber ♦ *vi* (*of
waves*) marulhar; **lap up** *vt* (*fig*)
receber com sofreguidão

lapel [lə'pɛl] *n* lapela

Lapland ['læplænd] *n* Lapônia

lapse [læps] *n* lapso; (*bad behaviour*)
deslize *m* ♦ *vi* (*LAW*) prescrever; **to ~
into bad habits** adquirir maus hábitos

laptop (computer) ['læptɒp-] *n*
laptop *m*

lard [lɑːd] *n* banha de porco

larder ['lɑːdə*] *n* despensa

large [lɑːdʒ] *adj* grande; **at ~** (*free*)

em liberdade; (*generally*) em geral;
largely *adv* em grande parte;
(*introducing reason*) principalmente;
large-scale *adj* (*map*) em grande
escala; (*fig*) importante, de grande
alcance

lark [lɑːk] *n* (*bird*) cotovia; (*joke*)
brincadeira, peça; **lark about** *vi*
divertir-se, brincar

laryngitis [lærɪn'dʒaɪtɪs] *n* laringite
f

laser ['leɪzə*] *n* laser *m*; **laser printer** *n* impressora a laser

lash [læʃ] *n* (*blow*) chicotada; (*also:
eye~*) pestana, cílio ♦ *vt* chicotear,
açoitar; (*subj: rain, wind*) castigar;
(*tie*) atar, **lash out** *vi*: **to ~ out at sb**
atacar alguém violentamente; (*criticize*) atacar alguém verbalmente

lass [læs] (*BRIT*) *n* moça

lasso [læ'suː] *n* laço

last [lɑːst] *adj* último; (*final*) derradeiro ♦ *adv* em último lugar ♦ *vi*
durar; (*continue*) continuar; **~ night/
week** ontem à noite/na semana
passada; **at ~** finalmente; **~ but one**
penúltimo; **lasting** *adj* duradouro;
lastly *adv* por fim, por último;
(*finally*) finalmente; **last-minute**
adj de última hora

latch [lætʃ] *n* trinco, fecho, tranca

late [leɪt] *adj* (*not on time*) atrasado;
(*far on in day etc*) tardio; (*former*)
antigo, ex-, anterior; (*dead*) falecido
♦ *adv* tarde; (*behind time, schedule*)
atrasado; **of ~** recentemente; **in ~
May** no final de maio; **latecomer** *n*
retardatário(-a); **lately** *adv* ultimamente

later ['leɪtə*] *adj* (*date etc*) posterior;
(*version etc*) mais recente ♦ *adv* mais
tarde, depois; **~ on** mais tarde

latest ['leɪtɪst] *adj* último; **at the ~**
no mais tardar

lathe [leɪð] *n* torno

lather ['lɑːðə*] n espuma (de sabão)
♦ vt ensaboar

Latin ['lætɪn] n (LING) latim m ♦ adj
latino; **Latin America** n América
Latina; **Latin American** adj, n
latino-americano(-a)

latitude ['lætɪtjuːd] n latitude f

latter ['lætə*] adj último; (of two)
segundo ♦ n: the ~ o último, este

laugh [lɑːf] n riso, risada ♦ vi rir, dar
risada (or gargalhada); **(to do sth)
for a ~** (fazer algo) só de curtição;
laugh at vt fus rir de; **laugh off** vt
disfarçar sorrindo; **laughable** adj
ridículo, absurdo; **laughter** n riso,
risada

launch [lɔːntʃ] n (boat) lancha,
(COMM, of rocket etc) lançamento ♦ vt
lançar; **launch into** vt fus lançar-se a

launderette [lɔːndə'ret] (BRIT) n
lavanderia automática

Laundromat ['lɔːndrəmæt] ® (US)
n = **launderette**

laundry ['lɔːndrɪ] n lavanderia;
(clothes) roupa para lavar

laurel ['lɒrl] n loureiro

lava ['lɑːvə] n lava

lavatory ['lævətərɪ] n privada (BR),
casa de banho (PT)

lavender ['lævəndə*] n lavanda

lavish ['lævɪʃ] adj (amount) generoso; (person): ~ **with** pródigo em,
generoso com ♦ vt: to ~ **sth on sb**
encher ou cobrir alguém de algo

law [lɔː] n lei f; (rule) regra; (SCH)
direito; **law-abiding** adj obediente
à lei; **law and order** n a ordem
pública; **law court** n tribunal m de
justiça; **lawful** adj legal, lícito

lawn [lɔːn] n gramado (BR), relvado
(PT); **lawnmower** n cortador m de
grama (BR) or de relva (PT); **lawn
tennis** n tênis m de gramado (BR) or
de relvado (PT)

law school (US) n faculdade f de

direito

lawsuit ['lɔːsuːt] n ação f judicial,
processo

lawyer ['lɔːjə*] n advogado(-a); (for
sales, wills etc) notário(-a), tabe-
lião(-liã) m/f

lax [læks] adj (discipline) relaxado;
(person) negligente

laxative ['læksətɪv] n laxante m

lay [leɪ] (pt, pp **laid**) pt of **lie** ♦ adj
leigo ♦ vt colocar; (eggs, table) pôr;
lay aside or **by** vt pôr de lado; **lay
down** vt depositar; (rules etc)
impor, estabelecer; **to ~ down the
law** (pej) impor regras; **to ~ down
one's life** sacrificar voluntariamente
a vida; **lay off** vt (workers) demitir;
lay on vt (meal etc) prover; **lay out**
vt (spread out) dispor em ordem;
layabout (inf) n vadio(-a), pre-
guiçoso(-a); **lay-by** (BRIT) n acostamento

layer ['leɪə*] n camada

layman ['leɪmən] (irreg) n leigo

layout ['leɪaʊt] n (of garden, building) desenho; (of writing) leiaute m

laze [leɪz] vi (also: ~ **about**) vadiar

lazy ['leɪzɪ] adj preguiçoso; (movement) lento

lb. abbr = **pound** (weight)

lead¹ [liːd] (pt, pp **led**) n (front position) dianteira; (SPORT) liderança; (fig)
vantagem f; (clue) pista; (ELEC) fio;
(for dog) correia; (in play, film) papel
m principal ♦ vt levar; (be leader of)
chefiar; (start, guide: activity) encabeçar ♦ vi encabeçar; **to be in the ~**
(SPORT: in race) estar na frente; (: in
match) estar ganhando; **to ~ the
way** assumir a direção; **lead away**
vt levar; **lead back** vt levar de
volta; **lead on** vt (tease) provocar;
lead to vt fus levar a, conduzir a;
lead up to vt fus conduzir a

lead² [led] n chumbo; (in pencil)

grafite f

leader ['liːdə*] n líder m/f; **leader-ship** n liderança; (quality) poder m de liderança

lead-free [lɛd-] adj sem chumbo

leading ['liːdɪŋ] adj principal; (role) de destaque; (first, front) primeiro, dianteiro

lead singer [liːd-] n cantor(a) m/f

leaf [liːf] (pl **leaves**) n folha ♦ vi: **to ~ through** (book) folhear; **to turn over a new ~** mudar de vida, partir para outra (inf)

leaflet ['liːflɪt] n folheto

league [liːg] n liga; **to be in ~ with** estar de comum acordo com

leak [liːk] n (of liquid, gas) escape m, vazamento; (hole) buraco, rombo; (in roof) goteira, (flg: of information) vazamento ♦ vi (ship) fazer água; (shoe) deixar entrar água; (roof) gotejar; (pipe, container, liquid) vazar; (gas) escapar ♦ vt (news) vazar

lean [liːn] (pt, pp ~ed or ~t) adj magro ♦ vt: **to ~ sth on** encostar or apoiar algo em ♦ vi inclinar-se; **to ~ against** encostar-se or apoiar-se contra; **to ~ on** encostar-se or apoiar-se em; **lean forward/back** vi inclinar-se para frente/para trás; **lean out** vi inclinar-se; **lean over** vi debruçar-se ♦ vt fus debruçar-se sobre

leap [liːp] (pt, pp ~ed or ~t) n salto, pulo ♦ vi saltar; **leap year** n ano bissexto

learn [ləːn] (pt, pp ~ed or ~t) vt aprender; (by heart) decorar ♦ vi aprender; **to ~ about sth** (SCH: hear, read) saber de algo; **learned** ['ləːnɪd] adj erudito, **learner** n principiante m/f; (BRIT: also: **learner driver**) aprendiz m/f de motorista

lease [liːs] n arrendamento ♦ vt arrendar

leash [liːʃ] n correia

least [liːst] adj: **the ~ +** n o(a) menor; (smallest amount of) a menor quantidade de ♦ adv: **the ~ +** adj o(a) menos; **at ~** pelo menos; **not in the ~** de maneira nenhuma

leather ['lɛðə*] n couro

leave [liːv] (pt, pp **left**) vt deixar; (go away from) abandonar ♦ vi ir-se, sair; (train) sair ♦ n licença; **to ~ sth to sb** deixar algo para alguém; **to be left** sobrar; **leave behind** vt deixar para trás; (forget) esquecer; **leave out** vt omitir

leaves [liːvz] npl of **leaf**

Lebanon ['lɛbənən] n Líbano

lecherous ['lɛtʃərəs] (pej) adj lascivo

lecture ['lɛktʃə*] n conferência, palestra; (SCH) aula ♦ vi dar aulas, lecionar ♦ vt (scold) passar um sermão em; **lecturer** (BRIT) n (at university) professor(a) m/f

led [lɛd] pt, pp of **lead**[1]

ledge [lɛdʒ] n (of window) peitoril m; (of mountain) saliência, proeminência

ledger ['lɛdʒə*] n livro-razão m, razão m

leech [liːtʃ] n sanguessuga

leek [liːk] n alho-poró m

leeway ['liːweɪ] n (fig): **to have some ~** ter certa liberdade de ação

left [lɛft] pt, pp of **leave** ♦ adj esquerdo ♦ n esquerda ♦ adv à esquerda; **on the ~** à esquerda; **to the ~** para a esquerda; **the Left** (POL) a Esquerda; **left-handed** adj canhoto; **left-hand side** n lado esquerdo; **left-luggage (office)** (BRIT) n depósito de bagagem; **leftovers** npl sobras fpl; **left-wing** adj (POL) de esquerda, esquerdista

leg [lɛg] n perna; (of animal) pata; (CULIN: of meat) perna; (of journey) etapa; **lst/2nd ~** (*SPORT*) primeiro/segundo turno

legacy ['legəsɪ] *n* legado; (*fig*) herança

legal ['li:gl] *adj* legal

legend ['lɛdʒənd] *n* lenda; (*person*) mito

leggings ['legɪŋz] *npl* legging f

legislation [lɛdʒɪs'leɪʃən] *n* legislação f

legislature ['lɛdʒɪslətʃə*] *n* legislatura

legitimate [lɪ'dʒɪtɪmət] *adj* legítimo

leg-room *n* espaço para as pernas

leisure ['lɛʒə*] *n* lazer *m*; **at ~** desocupado, livre

lemon ['lɛmən] *n* limão(-galego) *m*; **lemonade** [lɛmə'neɪd] *n* limonada; **lemon tea** *n* chá *m* de limão

lend [lɛnd] (*pt, pp* **lent**) *vt* emprestar

length [lɛŋθ] *n* comprimento, extensão f; (*amount of time*) duração f; **at ~** (*at lust*) finalmente, afinal; (*lengthily*) por extenso; **lengthen** *vt* encompridar, alongar ♦ *vi* encompridar-se; **lengthways** *adv* longitudinalmente, ao comprido; **lengthy** *adj* comprido, longo; (*meeting*) prolongado

lenient ['li:nɪənt] *adj* indulgente

lens [lɛnz] *n* (*of spectacles*) lente f; (*of camera*) objetiva

Lent [lɛnt] *n* Quaresma

lent [lɛnt] *pt, pp* de **lend**

lentil ['lɛntl] *n* lentilha

Leo ['li:əu] *n* Leão *m*

leotard ['li:ətɑ:d] *n* collant *m*

leprosy ['lɛprəsɪ] *n* lepra

lesbian ['lɛzbɪən] *n* lésbica

less [lɛs] *adj, pron, adv* menos ♦ *prep*: **~ tax/10% discount** menos imposto/10% de desconto; **~ than ever** menos do que nunca; **~ and ~** cada vez menos; **the ~ he works ...** quanto menos trabalha ...

lessen ['lɛsn] *vi* diminuir, minguar ♦ *vt* diminuir, reduzir

lesser ['lɛsə*] *adj* menor; **to a ~ extent** nem tanto

lesson ['lɛsn] *n* aula; (*example, warning*) lição f; **to teach sb a ~** (*fig*) dar uma lição em alguém

let [lɛt] (*pt, pp* **let**) *vt* (*allow*) deixar; (*BRIT: lease*) alugar; **to ~ sb know sth** avisar alguém de algo; **~'s go!** vamos!; **"to ~"** "aluga-se"; **let down** *vt* (*tyre*) esvaziar; (*disappoint*) desapontar; **let go** *vt, vi* soltar; **let in** *vt* deixar entrar; (*visitor etc*) fazer entrar; **let off** *vt* (*culprit*) perdoar; (*firework etc*) soltar; **let on** *vi* revelar; **let out** *vt* deixar sair; (*scream*) soltar; **let up** *vi* cessar, afrouxar

lethal ['li:θl] *adj* letal

letter ['lɛtə*] *n* (*of alphabet*) letra; (*correspondence*) carta; **letter bomb** *n* carta-bomba; **letterbox** (*BRIT*) *n* caixa do correio; **lettering** *n* letras *fpl*

lettuce ['lɛtɪs] *n* alface f

leukaemia [lu:'ki:mɪə] (*US* **leukemia**) *n* leucemia

level ['lɛvl] *adj* (*flat*) plano ♦ *adv*: **to draw ~ with** alcançar ♦ *n* nível *m*; (*height*) altura ♦ *vt* aplanar; **to be ~ with** estar no mesmo nível que; **on the ~** em nível; (*fig: honest*) sincero; **"A" levels** (*BRIT*) *npl* = vestibular *m*; **"O" levels** *npl* exames optativos feitos após o término do 10 Grau; **level off** *or* **out** *vi* (*prices etc*) estabilizar-se; **level crossing** (*BRIT*) *n* passagem f de nível; **level-headed** *adj* sensato

lever ['li:və*] *n* alavanca; (*fig*) estratagema *m*; **leverage** *n* força de uma alavanca; (*fig: influence*) influência

lewd [lu:d] *adj* obsceno, lascivo

liability [laɪə'bɪlətɪ] *n* responsabili-

dade f; (handicap) desvantagem f;
liabilities npl (COMM) exigibilidades
fpl, obrigações fpl
liable ['laɪəbl] adj (subject): ~ to
sujeito a; (responsible): ~ for responsável por; (likely): ~ to do capaz de
fazer
liaise [liː'eɪz] vi: to ~ (with) cooperar
(com)
liaison [liː'eɪzɔn] n (coordination)
ligação f; (affair) relação f amorosa
liar ['laɪə*] n mentiroso(-a)
libel ['laɪbl] n difamação f ♦ vt calu-
niar, difamar
liberal ['lɪbərl] adj liberal; (generous)
generoso
liberation [lɪbə'reɪʃən] n liberação f,
libertação f
liberty ['lɪbətɪ] n liberdade f; (criminal): to be at ~ estar livre; to be at
~ to do ser livre de fazer
Libra ['liːbrə] n Libra, Balança
librarian [laɪ'brɛərɪən] n bibliotecá-
rio(-a)
library ['laɪbrərɪ] n biblioteca
Libya ['lɪbɪə] n Líbia
lice [laɪs] npl of **louse**
licence ['laɪsns] (US **license**) n
(gen, COMM) licença; (AUT) carta de
motorista (BR), carta de condução
(PT)
license ['laɪsns] n (US) = **licence** ♦ vt
autorizar, dar licença a; **licensed**
adj (car) autorizado oficialmente;
(for alcohol) autorizado para vender
bebidas alcoólicas; **license plate**
(US) n (AUT) placa (de identificação)
(do carro)
lick [lɪk] vt lamber; (inf: defeat) arrasar, surrar; to ~ one's lips (also fig)
lamber os beiços
lid [lɪd] n tampa; (eye~) pálpebra
lie [laɪ] (pt **lay**, pp **lain**) vi (act) deitar-
se; (state) estar deitado; (object: be
situated) estar, encontrar-se; (fig:

problem, cause) residir; (in race,
league) ocupar; (tell ~s: pt, pp ~d)
mentir ♦ n mentira; to ~ low (fig)
esconder-se; **lie about** or **around**
vi (things) estar espalhado; (people)
vadiar; **lie-in** (BRIT) n: to have a lie-
in dormir até tarde
lieutenant [lɛf'tɛnənt, (US) luː-
'tɛnənt] n (MIL) tenente m
life [laɪf] (pl **lives**) n vida; to come to
~ animar-se; **lifebelt** (BRIT) n cinto
salva-vidas; **lifeboat** n barco salva-
vidas; **lifeguard** n (guarda m/f)
salva-vidas m/f inv; **life jacket** n
colete m salva-vidas; **lifeless** adj
sem vida; **lifelike** adj natural; (realistic) realista; **lifelong** adj que dura
toda a vida; **life preserver** (US) n ~
lifebelt; **life jacket, life sentence**
n pena de prisão perpétua; **life-
size(d)** adj de tamanho natural; **life-
span** n vida, duração f; **life style** n
estilo de vida; **lifetime** n vida
lift [lɪft] vt levantar ♦ vi (fog)
dispersar-se, dissipar-se ♦ n (BRIT: elevator) elevador m; to give sb a ~
(BRIT) dar uma carona para alguém
(BR), dar uma boleia a alguém (PT);
lift-off n decolagem f
light [laɪt] (pt, pp **lit**) n luz f; (AUT:
headlight) farol m; (: rear ~) luz traseira; (for cigarette etc): **have you
got a ~?** tem fogo? ♦ vt acender;
(room) iluminar ♦ adj (colour, room)
claro; (not heavy, fig) leve; (rain, traffic) fraco; (movement) delicado; ~s
npl (AUT) sinal m de trânsito; to
come to ~ vir à tona; **in the** ~ of à
luz de; **light up** vi iluminar-se ♦ vt
iluminar; **light bulb** n lâmpada;
lighten vt tornar mais leve; **lighter**
n (also: **cigarette lighter**) isqueiro,
acendedor m; **light-hearted** adj
alegre, despreocupado; **lighthouse** n farol m; **lighting** n ilumi-

nação f; **lightly** adv ligeiramente; **to get off lightly** conseguir se safar, livrar a cara (inf)

lightning ['laɪtnɪŋ] n relâmpago, raio

light pen n caneta leitora

lightweight ['laɪtweɪt] adj (suit) leve; (BOXING) peso-leve

like [laɪk] vt gostar de ♦ prep como; (such as) tal qual ♦ adj parecido, semelhante ♦ n: **the ~ coisas** fpl parecidas; **his ~s and dislikes** seus gostos e aversões; **I would ~, I'd ~** (eu) gostaria de; **to be** or **look ~ sb/ sth** parecer-se com alguém/algo, parecer alguém/algo; **do it ~ this** faça isso assim; **it is nothing ~ ...** não se parece nada com ...; **likeable** adj simpático, agradável

likelihood ['laɪklɪhud] n probabilidade f

likely ['laɪklɪ] adj provável; **he's ~ to leave** é provável que ele se vá; **not ~!** (inf) nem morto!

likeness ['laɪknɪs] n semelhança; **that's a good ~** tem uma grande semelhança

likewise ['laɪkwaɪz] adv igualmente; **to do ~** fazer o mesmo

liking ['laɪkɪŋ] n afeição f, simpatia; **to be to sb's ~** ser ao gosto de alguém

lilac ['laɪlək] n lilás m

lily ['lɪlɪ] n lírio, açucena

limb [lɪm] n membro

limbo ['lɪmbəu] n: **to be in ~** (fig) viver na expectativa

lime [laɪm] n (tree) limeira; (fruit) limão m; (also: **~ juice**) suco (BR) or sumo (PT) de limão; (GEO) cal f

limelight ['laɪmlaɪt] n: **to be in the ~** ser o centro das atenções

limerick ['lɪmərɪk] n quintilha humorística

limestone ['laɪmstəun] n pedra calcária

limit ['lɪmɪt] n limite m ♦ vt limitar; **limited** adj limitado; **to be limited to** limitar-se a

limp [lɪmp] n: **to have a ~** mancar, ser coxo ♦ vi mancar ♦ adj frouxo

limpet ['lɪmpɪt] n lapa

line [laɪn] n linha; (rope) corda; (wire) fio; (row) fila, fileira; (on face) ruga ♦ vt (road, room) encarreirar; (container, clothing) forrar; **to ~ the streets** ladear as ruas; **in ~ with** de acordo com; **line up** vi enfileirar-se ♦ vt (set up, have ready) preparar, arranjar

lined [laɪnd] adj (face) enrugado; (paper) pautado

linen ['lɪnɪn] n artigos de cama e mesa; (cloth) linho

liner ['laɪnə*] n navio de linha regular; (also: **bin ~**) saco para lata de lixo

linesman ['laɪnzmən] (irreg) n (SPORT) juiz m de linha

linger ['lɪŋgə*] vi demorar-se, retardar-se; (smell, tradition) persistir

linguistics ['lɪŋgwɪstɪks] n lingüística

lining ['laɪnɪŋ] n forro; (ANAT) parede f

link [lɪŋk] n (of a chain) elo; (connection) conexão f ♦ vt vincular, unir; (associate): **to ~ with** or **to** unir a; **~s** npl (GOLF) campo de golfe; **link up** vt acoplar ♦ vi unir-se

lion ['laɪən] n leão m; **lioness** n leoa

lip [lɪp] n lábio; **lipread** (irreg) vi ler os lábios; **lip salve** n pomada para os lábios; **lipstick** n batom m

liqueur [lɪ'kjuə*] n licor m

liquid ['lɪkwɪd] adj líquido ♦ n líquido

liquidize ['lɪkwɪdaɪz] (BRIT) vt (CULIN) liqüidificar, passar no liqüidificador; **liquidizer** (BRIT) n liqüidificador m

liquor ['lɪkə*] n licor m, bebida alcoólica

liquor store (US) n loja que vende bebidas alcoólicas

Lisbon ['lɪzbən] n Lisboa

lisp [lɪsp] n ceceio ♦ vi cecear, falar com a língua presa

list [lɪst] n lista ♦ vt (write down) fazer uma lista or relação de; (enumerate) enumerar

listen ['lɪsn] vi escutar, ouvir; **to ~ to** escutar; **listener** n ouvinte m/f

lit [lɪt] pt, pp of **light**

liter ['liːtə*] (US) n = **litre**

literacy ['lɪtərəsɪ] n capacidade f de ler e escrever, alfabetização f

literal ['lɪtərl] adj literal

literary ['lɪtərərɪ] adj literário

literate ['lɪtərət] adj alfabetizado, instruído; (educated) culto, letrado

literature ['lɪtrɪtʃə*] n literatura; (brochures etc) folhetos mpl

litre ['liːtə*] (US **liter**) n litro

litter ['lɪtə*] n (rubbish) lixo; (young animals) ninhada; **litter bin** (BRIT) n lata de lixo

little ['lɪtl] adj (small) pequeno; (not much) pouco ♦ (often translated by suffix: eg: **~ house** casinha ♦ adv pouco; **a ~** um pouco (de); **for a while** por um instante; **as ~ as possible** o menos possível; **~ by ~** pouco a pouco

live [vb lɪv, adj laɪv] vi viver; (reside) morar; (wire) eletrizado; (broadcast) ao vivo; (shell) carregado; **~ ammunition** munição de guerra; **live down** vt redimir; **live on** vt fus viver de, alimentar-se de; **to ~ on £50 a week** viver com £50 por semana; **live together** vi viver juntos; **live up to** vt fus (fulfil) cumprir

livelihood ['laɪvlɪhud] n meio de vida, subsistência

lively ['laɪvlɪ] adj vivo

liven up ['laɪvn-] vt animar ♦ vi animar-se

liver ['lɪvə*] n fígado

lives [laɪvz] npl of **life**

livestock ['laɪvstɔk] n gado

livid ['lɪvɪd] adj lívido; (inf: furious) furioso

living ['lɪvɪŋ] adj vivo ♦ n: **to earn** or **make a ~** ganhar a vida; **living room** n sala de estar

lizard ['lɪzəd] n lagarto

load [ləud] n carga; (weight) peso ♦ vt (gen, COMPUT) carregar; **a ~ of**, **~s of** (fig) um monte de, uma porção de; **loaded** adj (vehicle): **to be loaded with** estar carregado de; (question) intencionado; (inf: rich) cheio de nota

loaf [ləuf] (pl **loaves**) n pão-de-forma m

loan [ləun] n empréstimo ♦ vt emprestar; **on ~** emprestado

loath [ləuθ] adj: **to be ~ to do sth** estar pouco inclinado a fazer algo, relutar em fazer algo

loathe [ləuð] vt detestar, odiar

loaves [ləuvz] npl of **loaf**

lobby ['lɔbɪ] n vestíbulo, saguão m; (POL: pressure group) grupo de pressão, lobby m ♦ vt pressionar

lobster ['lɔbstə*] n lagostim m; (large) lagosta

local ['ləukl] adj local ♦ n (pub) bar m (local); **the ~s** npl (~ inhabitants) os moradores locais; **local anaesthetic** n anestesia local

locate [ləu'keɪt] vt (find) localizar, situar; (situate): **to be ~d in** estar localizado em

location [ləu'keɪʃən] n local m, posição f; on ~ (CINEMA) em externas

loch [lɔx] n lago

lock [lɔk] n (of door, box) fechadura; (of canal) eclusa; (of hair) anel m, mecha ♦ vt (with key) trancar ♦ vi (door etc) fechar-se à chave; (wheels) travar-se; **lock in** *vt* trancar dentro; **lock out** *vt* trancar do lado de fora; **lock up** *vt* (*criminal, mental patient*) prender; (*house*) trancar ♦ *vi* fechar tudo

locker ['lɔkə*] *n* compartimento com chave

locket ['lɔkɪt] *n* medalhão *m*

locksmith ['lɔksmɪθ] *n* serralheiro(-a)

lodge [lɔdʒ] *n* casa do guarda, guarita; (*hunting ~*) pavilhão *m* de caça ♦ *vi* (*person*): **to ~ (with)** alojar-se (na casa de) ♦ *vt* (*complaint*) apresentar; **lodger** *n* inquilino(-a), hóspede *m/f*

lodgings ['lɔdʒɪŋz] *npl* quarto *m* (mobiliado)

loft [lɔft] *n* sótão *m*

lofty ['lɔftɪ] *adj* (*haughty*) altivo, arrogante; (*sentiments, aims*) nobre

log [lɔg] *n* (*of wood*) tora; (*book*) = **logbook** ♦ *vt* registrar

logbook ['lɔgbuk] *n* (*NAUT*) diário de bordo; (*AVIAT*) diário de vôo; (*of car*) documentação *f* (do carro)

logic ['lɔdʒɪk] *n* lógica; **logical** *adj* lógico

loin [lɔɪn] *n* (*CULIN*) (carne *f* de) lombo

loiter ['lɔɪtə*] *vi* perder tempo

lollipop ['lɔlɪpɔp] *n* pirulito (*BR*), chupa-chupa *m* (*PT*); **lollipop lady/man** *n* (*BRIT*) ver quadro

---

LOLLIPOP LADY/MAN

Lollipop ladies/men são as pessoas que ajudam as crianças a atravessar a rua nas proximidades das escolas na hora da entrada e da saída. São facilmente localizadas graças a suas longas capas brancas e à placa redonda com a qual pedem aos motoristas que parem. São chamados assim por causa da forma circular da placa, que lembra um pirulito (*lollipop*).

London ['lʌndən] *n* Londres; **Londoner** *n* londrino(-a)

lone [ləun] *adj* (*person*) solitário; (*thing*) único

loneliness ['ləunlɪnɪs] *n* solidão *f*, isolamento

lonely ['ləunlɪ] *adj* (*person*) só; (*place*) solitário, isolado

long [lɔŋ] *adj* longo; (*road, hair, table*) comprido ♦ *adv* muito tempo ♦ *vi*: **to ~ for sth** ansiar or suspirar por algo; **how ~ is the street?** qual é a extensão da rua?; **how ~ is the lesson?** quanto dura a lição?; **all night ~** a noite inteira; **he no ~er comes** ele não vem mais; **~ before/after** muito antes/depois; **before ~** (+ *future*) dentro de pouco; (+ *past*) pouco tempo depois; **at ~ last** por fim, no final; **so** or **as ~ as** contanto que; **long-distance** (*travel*) de longa distância; (*call*) interurbano; **longhand** *n* escrita usual; **longing** *n* desejo, anseio

longitude ['lɔŋgɪtjuːd] *n* longitude *f*

long: **long jump** *n* salto em distância; **long-range** *adj* de longo alcance; (*forecast*) a longo prazo; **long-sighted** *adj* presbita; **long-standing** *adj* de muito tempo; **long-suffering** *adj* paciente, resignado; **long-term** *adj* a longo prazo; **long wave** *n* (*RADIO*) onda longa; **long-winded** *adj* prolixo, cansativo

loo [luː] *n* (*BRIT*: *inf*) *n* banheiro (*BR*), casa de banho (*PT*)

look [luk] *vi* olhar; (*seem*) parecer; (*building etc*): **to ~ south/(out) onto the sea** dar para o sul/o mar ♦ *n* olhar *m*; (*glance*) olhada, vista de olhos; (*appearance*) aparência, aspecto; **~s** *npl* (*good ~s*) físico, aparência; **~ (here)!** (*annoyance*) escuta aqui!; **~!** (*surprise*) olha!;

look after vt fus cuidar de; (deal with) lidar com; **look at** vt fus olhar (para); (read quickly) ler rapidamente; (consider) considerar; **look back** vi: to ~ on (remember) recordar, rever; **look down on** vt fus (fig) desdenhar, desprezar; **look for** vt fus procurar; **look forward to** vi fus aguardar com prazer, ansiar por; (in letter): **we ~ forward to hearing from you** no aguardo de suas notícias; **look into** vt fus investigar; **look on** vi assistir; **look out** vi (beware): **to ~ out (for)** tomar cuidado (com); **look out for** vt fus (await) esperar; **look round** vi virar a cabeça, voltar-se; **look through** vt fus (papers, book) examinar; **look up** vi (rely on) contar com; **look up** vi levantar os olhos; (improve) melhorar ♦ vt (word) procurar

loop [lu:p] n laço ♦ vt: **to ~ sth round sth** prender algo em torno de algo

loose [lu:s] adj solto; (not tight) frouxo ♦ n: **to be on the ~** estar solto; **loose change** n trocado; **loosely** adv frouxamente, folgadamente; **loosen** vt (free) soltar; (slacken) afrouxar

loot [lu:t] n saque m, despojo ♦ vt saquear, pilhar

lopsided [lɔp'saɪdɪd] adj torto

lord [lɔ:d] n senhor m; **L~ Smith** Lord Smith; **the L~** (REL) o Senhor; **good L~!** Deus meu!; **the (House of) L~s** (BRIT) a Câmara dos Lordes

lorry ['lɔrɪ] (BRIT) n caminhão m (BR), camião m (PT); **lorry driver** (BRIT) n caminhoneiro (BR), camionista m/f (PT)

lose [lu:z] (pt, pp lost) vt, vi perder; **to ~ (time)** (clock) atrasar-se; **loser** n perdedor(a) m/f; (inf: failure) derrotado(-a), fracassado(-a)

loss [lɔs] n perda; (COMM): **to make**

a ~ sair com prejuízo; **heavy ~es** (MIL) grandes perdas; **to be at a ~** estar perplexo

lost [lɔst] pt, pp of **lose** ♦ adj perdido; **~ and found** (US) (seção f de) perdidos e achados mpl; **lost property** (BRIT) n (objetos mpl) perdidos e achados mpl

lot [lɔt] n (set of things) porção f; (at auctions) lote m; **the ~** tudo, todos(-as); **a ~** muito, bastante; **a ~ of, ~s of** muito(s); **I read a ~** leio bastante; **to draw ~s** tirar à sorte

lotion ['ləuʃən] n loção f

lottery ['lɔtərɪ] n loteria

loud [laud] adj (voice) alto; (shout) forte; (noise) barulhento; (support, condemnation) veemente; (gaudy) berrante ♦ adv alto; **out ~** em voz alta; **loudly** adv ruidosamente; (aloud) em voz alta; **loudspeaker** n alto-falante m

lounge [laundʒ] n sala f de estar; (of airport) salão m; (BRIT: also: **~ bar**) bar m social ♦ vi recostar-se, espreguiçar-se; **lounge about** vi ficar à-toa; **lounge around** vi = **lounge about**; **lounge suit** (BRIT) n terno (BR), fato (PT)

louse [laus] (pl **lice**) n piolho

lousy ['lauzɪ] (inf) adj ruim, péssimo; (ill): **to feel ~** sentir-se mal

lout [laut] n rústico, grosseiro

lovable ['lʌvəbl] adj adorável, simpático

love [lʌv] n amor m ♦ vt amar; (care for) gostar; (activity): **to ~ to do** gostar (muito); **~ (from) Anne** (on letter) um abraço or um beijo, Anne; **I ~ coffee** adoro o café; **"15 ~"** (TENNIS) "15 a zero"; **to be in ~** with estar apaixonado por; **to fall in ~** with apaixonar-se por; **to make ~** fazer amor; **love affair** n aventura (amorosa), caso (de amor); **love**

life *n* vida sentimental

lovely ['lʌvlɪ] *adj* encantador(a), delicioso; (*beautiful*) lindo, belo; (*holiday*) muito agradável, maravilhoso

lover ['lʌvə*] *n* amante *m/f*

loving ['lʌvɪŋ] *adj* carinhoso, afetuoso; (*actions*) dedicado

low [ləʊ] *adj* baixo; (*depressed*) deprimido; (*ill*) doente ♦ *adv* baixo ♦ *n* (METEOROLOGY) área de baixa pressão; **to be ~ on** (*supplies*) ter pouco; **to reach a new** *or* **an all-time ~** cair ao/a o seu nível mais baixo; **low-alcohol** *adj* de baixo teor alcoólico; **low-calorie** *adj* de baixas calorias; **low-cut** *adj* (*dress*) decotado; **lower** *adj* mais baixo; (*less important*) inferior ♦ *vt* abaixar; (*reduce*) reduzir, diminuir; **low-fat** *adj* magro; **lowlands** *npl* planície *f*; **lowly** *adj* humilde

loyal ['lɔɪəl] *adj* leal; **loyalty** *n* lealdade *f*; **loyalty card** *n* (BRIT) cartão *m* de fidelidade

lozenge ['lɔzɪndʒ] *n* (MED) pastilha

LP *n* *abbr* (= *long-playing record*) elepê *m* (BR), LP *m* (PT)

L-plates ['ɛlpleɪts] (BRIT) *npl* placas *fpl* de aprendiz de motorista; *ver quadro*

L-PLATES

As L-plates são placas quadradas com um "L" vermelho que são colocadas na parte de trás do carro para mostrar que a pessoa ao volante ainda não tem carteira de motorista. Até a obtenção da carteira, o motorista aprendiz possui uma permissão provisória e não tem direito de dirigir sem um motorista qualificado ao lado. Os motoristas aprendizes não podem dirigir em rodovias mesmo que estejam acompanhados.

Ltd (BRIT) *abbr* (= *limited (liability) company*) SA

lubricate ['luːbrɪkeɪt] *vt* lubrificar

luck [lʌk] *n* sorte *f*; **bad ~** azar *m*; **good ~!** boa sorte!; **bad** *or* **hard** *or* **tough ~!** que azar!; **luckily** *adv* por sorte, felizmente; **lucky** *adj* (*person*) sortudo; (*situation*) afortunado; (*object*) de sorte

ludicrous ['luːdɪkrəs] *adj* ridículo

lug [lʌg] (*inf*) *vt* arrastar

luggage ['lʌgɪdʒ] *n* bagagem *f*; **luggage rack** *n* porta-bagagem *m*, bagageiro

lukewarm ['luːkwɔːm] *adj* morno, tépido; (*fig*) indiferente

lull [lʌl] *n* pausa, interrupção *f* ♦ *vt*: **to ~ sb to sleep** acalentar alguém; **to be ~ed into a false sense of security** ser acalmado com uma falsa sensação de segurança

lullaby ['lʌləbaɪ] *n* canção *f* de ninar

lumber ['lʌmbə*] *n* (*junk*) trastes *mpl* velhos; (*wood*) madeira serrada, tábua ♦ *vt*: **to ~ sb with sth/sb** empurrar algo/alguém para cima de alguém; **lumberjack** *n* madeireiro, lenhador *m*

luminous ['luːmɪnəs] *adj* luminoso

lump [lʌmp] *n* torrão *m*; (*fragment*) pedaço; (*on body*) galo, caroço; (*also*: **sugar ~**) cubo de açúcar ♦ *vt*: **to ~ together** amontoar; **a ~ sum** uma quantia global; **lumpy** *adj* encaroçado

lunatic ['luːnətɪk] *adj* louco(-a)

lunch [lʌntʃ] *n* almoço

luncheon ['lʌntʃən] *n* almoço formal; **luncheon meat** *n* bolo de carne

lung [lʌŋ] *n* pulmão *m*

lunge [lʌndʒ] *vi* (*also*: **~ forward**) dar estocada *or* bote; **to ~ at** arremeter-se contra

lurch [ləːtʃ] *vi* balançar ♦ *n* solavanco; **to leave sb in the ~** deixar alguém em apuros, deixar alguém na mão (inf)

lure [luə*] n isca ♦ vt atrair, seduzir

lurid ['luərɪd] adj horrível

lurk [lə:k] vi (hide) esconder-se; (wait) estar à espreita

luscious ['lʌʃəs] adj (person, thing) atraente; (food) delicioso

lush [lʌʃ] adj exuberante

lust [lʌst] n luxúria; (greed) cobiça; **lust after** or **for** vt fus cobiçar

Luxembourg ['lʌksəmbə:g] n Luxemburgo

luxurious [lʌg'zjuərɪəs] adj luxuoso

luxury ['lʌkʃərɪ] n luxo ♦ cpd de luxo

lying ['laɪɪŋ] n mentira(s) f(pl) ♦ adj mentiroso, falso

lyrical ['lɪrɪkəl] adj lírico

lyrics ['lɪrɪks] npl (of song) letra

M

m abbr (= metre) m; (= mile) mil.; = **million**

M.A. abbr (SCH) = **Master of Arts**

mac [mæk] (BRIT) n capa impermeável

Macao [mə'kau] n Macau

macaroni [mækə'rəunɪ] n macarrão m

machine [mə'ʃi:n] n máquina ♦ vt (dress etc) costurar à máquina; (TECH) usinar; **machine gun** n metralhadora; **machinery** n maquinaria; (fig) máquina

mackerel ['mækrl] n inv cavala

mackintosh ['mækɪntɔʃ] (BRIT) n capa impermeável

mad [mæd] adj louco; (foolish) tolo; (angry) furioso, brabo; (keen): **to be ~ about** ser louco por

madam ['mædəm] n senhora, madame f

madden ['mædn] vt exasperar

made [meɪd] pt, pp of **make**

Madeira [mə'dɪərə] n (GEO) Madeira; (wine) (vinho) Madeira m

made-to-measure (BRIT) adj feito sob medida

madly ['mædlɪ] adv loucamente; **~ in love** louco de amor

madman ['mædmən] (irreg) n louco

madness ['mædnɪs] n loucura; (foolishness) tolice f

magazine [mægə'zi:n] n (PRESS) revista; (RADIO, TV) programa m de atualidades

maggot ['mægət] n larva de inseto

magic ['mædʒɪk] n magia, mágica ♦ adj mágico; **magical** adj mágico; **magician** [mə'dʒɪʃən] n mago(-a); (entertainer) mágico(-a)

magistrate ['mædʒɪstreɪt] n magistrado(-a), juiz (juíza) m/f

magnet ['mægnɪt] n ímã m; **magnetic** [mæg'netɪk] adj magnético

magnificent [mæg'nɪfɪsnt] adj magnífico

magnify ['mægnɪfaɪ] vt aumentar; **magnifying glass** n lupa, lente f de aumento

magnitude ['mægnɪtju:d] n magnitude f

magpie ['mægpaɪ] n pega

mahogany [mə'hɔgənɪ] n mogno, acaju m

maid [meɪd] n empregada; **old ~** (pej) solteirona

maiden name n nome m de solteira

mail [meɪl] n correio; (letters) cartas fpl ♦ vt pôr no correio; **mailbox** (US) n caixa do correio; **mailing list** n lista de clientes, mailing list m; **mail order** n pedido por reembolso postal

maim [meɪm] vt mutilar, aleijar

main [meɪn] adj principal ♦ n (pipe)

cano *or* esgoto principal; **the ~s** *npl* (*ELEC, GAS, WATER*) a rede; **in the ~** na maior parte; **mainframe** *n* (*COMPUT*) mainframe *m*; **mainland** *n*: **the mainland** o continente; **mainly** *adv* principalmente; **main road** *n* estrada principal; **mainstay** *n* (*fig*) esteio; **mainstream** *n* corrente *f* principal

maintain [meɪnˈteɪn] *vt* manter; (*keep up*) conservar (em bom estado); (*affirm*) sustentar, afirmar; **maintenance** [ˈmeɪntənəns] *n* manutenção *f*; (*alimony*) alimentos *mpl*, pensão *f* alimentícia

maize [meɪz] *n* milho

majestic [məˈdʒestɪk] *adj* majestoso

majesty [ˈmædʒɪstɪ] *n* majestade *f*

major [ˈmeɪdʒə*] *n* (*MIL*) major *m* ♦ *adj* (*main*) principal; (*considerable*) importante; (*MUS*) maior

Majorca [məˈjɔːkə] *n* Maiorca

majority [məˈdʒɔrɪtɪ] *n* maioria

make [meɪk] (*pt, pp* **made**) *vt* fazer; (*manufacture*) fabricar, produzir; (*cause to be*): **to ~ sb sad** entristecer alguém, fazer alguém ficar triste; (*force*): **to ~ sb do sth** fazer com que alguém faça algo; (*equal*): **2 and 2 ~ 4** dois e dois são quatro ♦ *n* marca; **to ~ a profit/loss** ter um lucro/uma perda; **to ~ it** (*arrive*) chegar; (*succeed*) ter sucesso; **what time do you ~ it?** que horas você tem?; **to ~ do with** contentar-se com; **make for** *vt fus* (*place*) dirigir-se a; **make out** *vt* (*decipher*) decifrar; (*understand*) compreender; (*see*) divisar, avistar; (*cheque*) preencher; **make up** *vt* (*constitute*) constituir; (*invent*) inventar; (*parcel*) embrulhar ♦ *vi* reconciliar-se; (*with cosmetics*) maquiar-se (*BR*), maquilhar-se (*PT*); **make up for** *vt fus* compensar; **make-believe** *n*: **a world of make-**

believe um mundo de faz-de-conta; **maker** *n* (*of film etc*) criador *m*; (*manufacturer*) fabricante *m/f*; **makeshift** *adj* provisório; **make-up** *n* maquilagem *f* (*BR*), maquilhagem *f* (*PT*)

malaria [məˈlɛərɪə] *n* malária

Malaysia [məˈleɪzɪə] *n* Malaísia (*BR*), Malásia (*PT*)

male [meɪl] *n* macho ♦ *adj* masculino; (*child etc*) do sexo masculino

malevolent [məˈlɛvələnt] *adj* malévolo

malfunction [mælˈfʌŋkʃən] *n* funcionamento defeituoso

malice [ˈmælɪs] *n* (*ill will*) malícia; (*rancour*) rancor *m*; **malicious** [məˈlɪʃəs] *adj* malevolente

malignant [məˈlɪgnənt] *adj* (*MED*) maligno

mall [mɔːl] *n* (*also*: **shopping ~**) shopping *m*

mallet [ˈmælɪt] *n* maço, marreta

malt [mɔːlt] *n* malte *m*

Malta [ˈmɔːltə] *n* Malta

mammal [ˈmæml] *n* mamífero

mammoth [ˈmæməθ] *n* mamute *m* ♦ *adj* gigantesco, imenso

man [mæn] (*pl* **men**) *n* homem *m* ♦ *vt* (*NAUT*) tripular; (*MIL*) guarnecer; (*machine*) operar; **an old ~** um velho; **~ and wife** marido e mulher

manage [ˈmænɪdʒ] *vi* arranjar-se, virar-se ♦ *vt* (*be in charge of*) dirigir, administrar; (*business*) gerenciar; (*ship, person*) controlar; **manageable** *adj* manejável; (*task etc*) viável; **management** *n* administração *f*, direção *f*, gerência; **manager** *n* gerente *m/f*; (*SPORT*) técnico(-a); **manageress** [mænɪdʒəˈrɛs] *n* gerente *f*; **managerial** [mænɪˈdʒɪərɪəl] *adj* administrativo, gerencial; **managing director** *n* diretor(a) *m/f* geral, diretor-gerente (diretora-gerente) m/f

mandarin ['mændərɪn] n (fruit) tangerina; (person) mandarim m

mandatory ['mændətərɪ] adj obrigatório

mane [meɪn] n (of horse) crina; (of lion) juba

maneuver [mə'nu:və*] (US) = **manoeuvre**

mangle ['mæŋgl] vt mutilar, estropiar

mango ['mæŋgəu] (pl ~es) n manga

mangy ['meɪndʒɪ] adj sarnento, esfarrapado

manhandle ['mænhændl] vt maltratar

manhole ['mænhəul] n poço de inspeção

manhood ['mænhud] n (age) idade f adulta; (masculinity) virilidade f

man-hour n hora-homem f

manhunt ['mænhʌnt] n caça ao homem

mania ['meɪnɪə] n mania; **maniac** ['meɪnɪæk] n maníaco(-a); (fig) louco(-a)

manic ['mænɪk] adj maníaco

manicure ['mænɪkjuə*] n manicure f (BR), manicura (PT)

manifest ['mænɪfest] vt manifestar, mostrar ♦ adj manifesto, evidente

manipulate [mə'nɪpjuleɪt] vt manipular

mankind [mæn'kaɪnd] n humanidade f, raça humana

man-made adj sintético, artificial

manner ['mænə*] n modo, maneira; (behaviour) conduta, comportamento; (type): **all ~ of things** todos os tipos de coisa; **~s** npl (conduct) boas maneiras fpl, educação f; **bad ~s** falta de educação; **all ~ of** todo tipo de; **mannerism** n maneirismo, hábito

manoeuvre [mə'nu:və*] (US **maneuver**) vt manobrar; (manipulate) manipular ♦ vi manobrar ♦ n manobra

manor ['mænə*] n (also: ~ **house**) casa senhorial, solar m

manpower ['mænpauə*] n potencial m humano, mão-de-obra f

mansion ['mænʃən] n mansão f, palacete m

manslaughter ['mænslɔ:tə*] n homicídio involuntário

mantelpiece ['mæntlpi:s] n consolo da lareira

manual ['mænjuəl] adj manual ♦ n manual m

manufacture [mænju'fæktʃə*] vt manufaturar, fabricar ♦ n fabricação f; **manufacturer** n fabricante m/f

manure [mə'njuə*] n estrume m, adubo

manuscript ['mænjuskrɪpt] n manuscrito

many ['menɪ] adj, pron muitos(-as); **a great ~** muitíssimos; **~ a time** muitas vezes

map [mæp] n mapa m; **map out** vt traçar

maple ['meɪpl] n bordo

mar [mɑ:*] vt estragar

marathon ['mærəθən] n maratona

marble ['mɑ:bl] n mármore m; (toy) bola de gude

March [mɑ:tʃ] n março

march [mɑ:tʃ] vi marchar; (demonstrators) desfilar ♦ n marcha; passeata

mare [meə*] n égua

margarine [mɑ:dʒə'ri:n] n margarina

margin ['mɑ:dʒɪn] n margem f; **marginal** adj marginal; **marginal seat** (POL) cadeira ganha por pequena maioria

marigold ['mærɪgəuld] n malmequer m

marijuana [mærɪ'wɑ:nə] n maconha

marine [mə'ri:n] adj marinho; (engineer) naval ♦ n fuzileiro naval

marital [mærɪtl] adj matrimonial, marital; ~ **status** estado civil

marjoram ['mɑ:dʒərəm] n manjerona

mark [mɑ:k] n marca, sinal m; (imprint) impressão f; (stain) mancha; (BRIT: SCH) nota; (currency) marco ♦ vt marcar; (stain) manchar; (indicate) indicar; (commemorate) comemorar; (: correct) corrigir; **to ~ time** marcar passo; **marker** n (sign) marcador m, marca; (bookmark) marcador

market ['mɑ:kɪt] n mercado ♦ vt (COMM) comercializar; **market garden** (BRIT) n horta; **marketing** n marketing m; **marketplace** n mercado; **market research** n pesquisa de mercado

marksman ['mɑ:ksmən] (irreg) n bom atirador m

marmalade ['mɑ:məleɪd] n geléia de laranja

maroon [mə'ru:n] vt: **to be ~ed** ficar abandonado (numa ilha) ♦ adj de cor castanho-avermelhado, vinho inv

marquee [mɑ:'ki:] n toldo, tenda

marriage ['mærɪdʒ] n casamento

married ['mærɪd] adj casado; (life, love) conjugal

marrow ['mærəu] n medula; (vegetable) abóbora

marry ['mærɪ] vt casar(-se) com; (subj: father, priest etc) casar, unir ♦ vi (also: **get married**) casar(-se)

Mars [mɑ:z] n Marte m

marsh [mɑ:ʃ] n pântano; (salt ~) marisma

marshal ['mɑ:ʃl] n (MIL: also: **field ~**) marechal m; (at sports meeting etc)

oficial m ♦ vt (thoughts, support) organizar; (soldiers) formar

martyr ['mɑ:tə*] n mártir m/f

marvel ['mɑ:vl] n maravilha ♦ vi: **to ~ (at)** maravilhar-se (de ou com); **marvellous** (US **marvelous**) adj maravilhoso

Marxist ['mɑ:ksɪst] adj, n marxista m/f

marzipan ['mɑ:zɪpæn] n maçapão m

mascara [mæs'kɑ:rə] n rímel ® m

masculine ['mæskjulɪn] adj masculino

mash [mæʃ] vt (CULIN) fazer um purê de; (crush) amassar; **mashed potatoes** n purê m de batatas

mask [mɑ:sk] n máscara ♦ vt (face) encobrir; (feelings) esconder, ocultar

mason ['meɪsn] n (also: **stone ~**) pedreiro(-a); (also: **free~**) maçom m; **masonry** n alvenaria

mass [mæs] n quantidade f; (people) multidão f; (PHYS) massa; (REL) missa; (great quantity) montão m ♦ cpd de massa ♦ vi reunir-se, concentrar-se; **the ~es** npl (ordinary people) as massas; **~es of** (inf) montes de

massacre ['mæsəkə*] n massacre m, carnificina

massage ['mæsɑ:ʒ] n massagem f

massive ['mæsɪv] adj (large) enorme; (support) massivo

mass media npl meios mpl de comunicação de massa, mídia

mass production n produção f em massa, fabricação f em série

mast [mɑ:st] n (NAUT) mastro; (RADIO etc) antena

master ['mɑ:stə*] n mestre m; (fig: of situation) dono; (in secondary school) professor m; (title for boys): **M~ X** o menino X ♦ vt controlar; (learn) conhecer a fundo; **masterly**

adj magistral; **mastermind** *n* (*fig*) cabeça ♦ *vt* dirigir, planejar; **Master of Arts/Science** *n* (*degree*) mestrado; **masterpiece** *n* obra-prima

mat [mæt] *n* esteira; (*also:* door~) capacho; (*also:* table~) descanso

match [mætʃ] *n* fósforo; (*game*) jogo, partida; (*equal*) igual *m/f* ♦ *vt* (*also:* ~ **up**) casar, emparelhar; (*go well with*) combinar com; (*equal*) igualar; (*correspond to*) corresponder a ♦ *vi* combinar; (*couple*) formar um bom casal; **matchbox** *n* caixa de fósforos; **matching** *adj* que combina (com)

mate [meit] *n* (*inf*) colega *m/f*; (*assistant*) ajudante *m/f*; (*animal*) macho/fêmea; (*in merchant navy*) imediato ♦ *vi* acasalar-se

material [məˈtiəriəl] *n* (*substance*) matéria; (*equipment*) material *m*; (*cloth*) pano, tecido; (*data*) dados *mpl* ♦ *adj* material; **~s** *npl* (*equipment*) material

maternal [məˈtəːnl] *adj* maternal

maternity [məˈtəːniti] *n* maternidade *f*

mathematical [mæθəˈmætikl] *adj* matemático

mathematics [mæθəˈmætiks] *n* matemática

maths [mæθs] (*us* **math**) *n* matemática

matrimony [ˈmætriməni] *n* matrimônio, casamento

matron [ˈmeitrən] *n* (*in hospital*) enfermeira-chefe *f*; (*in school*) inspetora

matted [ˈmætid] *adj* embaraçado

matter [ˈmætə*] *n* questão *f*, assunto; (*PHYS*) matéria; (*substance*) substância; (*reading ~ etc*) material *m*; (*MED: pus*) pus *m* ♦ *vi* importar; **~s** *npl* (*affairs*) questões *fpl*; **it doesn't ~**

não importa; (*I don't mind*) tanto faz; **what's the ~?** o que (é que) há?, qual é o problema?; **no ~ what** aconteça o que acontecer; **as a ~ of course** por rotina; **as a ~ of fact** na realidade, de fato; **matter-of-fact** *adj* prosaico, prático

mattress [ˈmætris] *n* colchão *m*

mature [məˈtjuə*] *adj* maduro; (*cheese, wine*) amadurecido ♦ *vi* amadurecer

maul [mɔːl] *vt* machucar, maltratar

mauve [məuv] *adj* cor de malva *inv*

maximum [ˈmæksiməm] (*pl* **maxima** *or* **~s**) *adj* máximo ♦ *n* máximo

May [mei] *n* maio

may [mei] (*pt, conditional* **might**) *aux vb* (*indicating possibility*): **he ~ come** pode ser que ele venha, é capaz de vir; (*be allowed to*): **~ I smoke?** posso fumar?; (*wishes*): **~ God bless you!** que Deus lhe abençoe

maybe [ˈmeibiː] *adv* talvez; **~ not** talvez não

mayhem [ˈmeihem] *n* caos *m*

mayonnaise [meiəˈneiz] *n* maionese *f*

mayor [mɛə*] *n* prefeito (*BR*), presidente *m* do município (*PT*); **mayoress** *n* prefeita (*BR*), presidenta do município (*PT*)

maze [meiz] *n* labirinto

me [miː] *pron* me; (*stressed, after prep*) mim; **he heard ~** ele me ouviu; **it's ~** sou eu; **he gave ~ the money** ele deu o dinheiro para mim; **give it to ~** dê-mo; **with ~** comigo; **without ~** sem mim

meadow [ˈmedəu] *n* prado, campina

meagre [ˈmiːgə*] (*us* **meager**) *adj* escasso

meal [miːl] *n* refeição *f*; (*flour*) farinha; **mealtime** *n* hora da refeição

mean [miːn] (*pt, pp* **~t**) *adj* (*with*

money) sovina, avarento, pão-duro *inv* (*BR*); (*unkind*) mesquinho; (*shabby*) malcuidado, dilapidado; (*average*) médio ♦ *vt* (*signify*) significar, querer dizer; (*refer to*): **I thought you ~t her** eu pensei que você estivesse se referindo a ela; (*intend*): **to ~ to do sth** pretender ou tencionar fazer algo ♦ *n* meio, meio termo; **~s** *npl* (*way, money*) meio; **by ~s of** por meio de, mediante; **by all ~s!** claro que sim!, pois não; **do you ~ it?** você está falando sério?

meaning ['mi:nɪŋ] *n* sentido, significado; **meaningful** *adj* significativo; (*relationship*) sério; **meaningless** *adj* sem sentido

meant [mɛnt] *pt, pp of* **mean**

meantime ['mi:ntaɪm] *adv* (*also:* **in the ~**) entretanto, enquanto isso

meanwhile ['mi:nwaɪl] *adv* = **meantime**

measles ['mi:zlz] *n* sarampo

measure ['mɛʒə*] *vt, vi* medir ♦ *n* medida; (*ruler: also:* **tape ~**) fita métrica; **measurements** *npl* (*size*) medidas *fpl*

meat [mi:t] *n* carne *f*; **cold ~s** (*BRIT*) frios; **meatball** *n* almôndega

Mecca ['mɛkə] *n* Meca; (*fig*): **a ~ (for)** a meca (de)

mechanic [mɪ'kænɪk] *n* mecânico; **mechanical** *adj* mecânico

mechanism ['mɛkənɪzəm] *n* mecanismo

medal ['mɛdl] *n* medalha; **medallion** [mɪ'dælɪən] *n* medalhão *m*; **medallist** (*US* **medalist**) *n* (*SPORT*) ganhador(a) *m/f*

meddle ['mɛdl] *vi*: **to ~ in** meter-se em, intrometer-se em; **to ~ with sth** mexer em algo

media ['mi:dɪə] *npl* meios *mpl* de comunicação, mídia

mediaeval [mɛdɪ'i:vl] *adj* = **medieval**

mediate ['mi:dɪeɪt] *vi* mediar

Medicaid ['mɛdɪkeɪd] (*US*) *n* programa de ajuda médica

medical ['mɛdɪkl] *adj* médico ♦ *n* (*examination*) exame *m* médico

Medicare ['mɛdɪkɛə*] (*US*) *n* sistema federal de seguro saúde

medication [mɛdɪ'keɪʃən] *n* medicação *f*

medicine ['mɛdsɪn] *n* medicina; (*drug*) remédio, medicamento

medieval [mɛdɪ'i:vl] *adj* medieval

mediocre [mi:dɪ'əukə*] *adj* mediocre

meditate ['mɛdɪteɪt] *vi* meditar

Mediterranean [mɛdɪtə'reɪnɪən] *adj* mediterrâneo; **the ~ (Sea)** o (mar) Mediterrâneo

medium ['mi:dɪəm] (*pl* **media** or **~s**) *adj* médio ♦ *n* (*means*) meio; (*pl* **~s:** *person*) médium *m/f*

medley ['mɛdlɪ] *n* mistura; (*MUS*) pot-pourri *m*

meek [mi:k] *adj* manso, dócil

meet [mi:t] (*pt, pp* **met**) *vt* encontrar; (*accidentally*) topar com, dar de cara com; (*by arrangement*) encontrar-se com, ir ao encontro de; (*for the first time*) conhecer; (*go and fetch*) ir buscar; (*opponent, problem*) enfrentar; (*obligations*) cumprir; (*need*) satisfazer ♦ *vi* encontrar-se; (*for talks*) reunir-se; (*join*) unir-se; (*get to know*) conhecer-se; **meet with** *vt fus* reunir-se com; (*difficulty*) encontrar; **meeting** *n* encontro; (*session: of club etc*) reunião *f*; (*assembly*) assembléia; (*SPORT*) corrida

megabyte ['mɛgəbaɪt] *n* (*COMPUT*) megabyte *m*

megaphone ['mɛgəfəun] *n* megafone *m*

melancholy ['mɛlənkəlɪ] *n* melancolia ♦ *adj* melancólico

melody ['melǝdɪ] n melodia

melon ['melǝn] n melão m

melt [melt] vi (metal) fundir-se; (snow) derreter ♦ vt derreter; **melt down** vt fundir; **meltdown** n fusão f

member ['membǝ*] n membro(-a); (of club) sócio(-a); (ANAT) membro; **M~ of Parliament** (BRIT) deputado(-a); **membership** n (state) adesão f; (members) número de sócios; **membership card** n carteira de sócio

memento [mǝ'mentǝu] n lembrança

memo ['memǝu] n memorando, nota

memoirs ['memwɑ:z] npl memórias fpl

memorandum [memǝ'rændǝm] (pl **memoranda**) n memorando

memorial [mɪ'mɔ:rɪǝl] n monumento comemorativo ♦ adj comemorativo; **Memorial Day** (US) n ver quadro

---

MEMORIAL DAY

Memorial Day é um feriado nos Estados Unidos, a última segunda-feira de maio na maior parte dos estados, em memória dos soldados americanos mortos em combate.

---

memorize ['memǝraɪz] vt decorar, aprender de cor

memory ['memǝrɪ] n memória; (recollection) lembrança

men [men] npl of **man**

menace ['menǝs] n ameaça; (nuisance) droga ♦ vt ameaçar

mend [mend] vt consertar, reparar; (darn) remendar ♦ n: **to be on the ~** estar melhorando

menial ['mi:nɪǝl] adj (often pej) humilde, subalterno

meningitis [menɪn'dʒaɪtɪs] n meningite f

menopause ['menǝupɔ:z] n menopausa

menstruation [menstru'eɪʃǝn] n menstruação f

mental ['mentl] adj mental; **mentality** [men'tælɪtɪ] n mentalidade f

mention ['menʃǝn] n menção f ♦ vt (speak of) falar de; **don't ~ it!** não tem de quê!, de nada!

menu ['menju:] n (set ~, COMPUT) menu m; (printed) cardápio (BR), ementa (PT)

MEP n abbr = **Member of the European Parliament**

mercenary ['mǝ:sɪnǝrɪ] adj mercenário ♦ n mercenário

merchandise ['mǝ:tʃǝndaɪz] n mercadorias fpl

merchant ['mǝ:tʃǝnt] n comerciante m/f

merciful ['mǝ:sɪful] adj (person) misericordioso, humano; (release) afortunado

merciless ['mǝ:sɪlɪs] adj desumano, inclemente

mercury ['mǝ:kjurɪ] n mercúrio

mercy ['mǝ:sɪ] n piedade f; (REL) misericórdia; **at the ~ of** à mercê de

mere [mɪǝ*] adj mero, simples inv; **merely** adv simplesmente, somente, apenas

merge [mǝ:dʒ] vt unir ♦ vi unir-se; (COMM) fundir-se; **merger** n fusão f

meringue [mǝ'ræŋ] n suspiro, merengue m

merit ['merɪt] n mérito; (advantage) vantagem f ♦ vt merecer

mermaid ['mǝ:meɪd] n sereia

merry ['merɪ] adj alegre; **M~ Christmas!** Feliz Natal!; **merry-go-round** n carrossel m

mesh [meʃ] n malha

mesmerize ['mɛzməraɪz] vt hipnotizar

mess [mɛs] n confusão f; (in room) bagunça; (MIL) rancho; **to be in a ~** ser uma bagunça, estar numa bagunça; **mess about** (inf) vi perder tempo; (pass the time) vadiar; **mess about with** (inf) vt fus mexer com; **mess around** (inf) vi = mess about; **mess around with** (inf) vt fus = mess about with; **mess up** vt (spoil) estragar; (dirty) sujar

message ['mɛsɪdʒ] n recado, mensagem f

messenger ['mɛsɪndʒə*] n mensageiro(-a)

Messrs ['mɛsəz] abbr (on letters: = messieurs) Srs

messy ['mɛsɪ] adj (dirty) sujo; (untidy) desarrumado

met [mɛt] pt, pp of **meet**

metal ['mɛtl] n metal m

meteorology [miːtɪə'rɔlədʒɪ] n meteorologia

meter ['miːtə*] n (instrument) medidor m; (also: **parking ~**) parcômetro; (US: unit) = **metre**

method ['mɛθəd] n método; **methodical** [mɪ'θɔdɪkl] adj metódico

metre ['miːtə*] (US **meter**) n metro

metric ['mɛtrɪk] adj métrico

metropolitan [mɛtrə'pɔlɪtən] adj metropolitano

Mexico ['mɛksɪkəu] n México

miaow [miː'au] vi miar

mice [maɪs] npl of **mouse**

micro... ['maɪkrəu] prefix micro...; **microchip** n microchip m; **microphone** n microfone m; **microscope** n microscópio; **microwave** n (also: **microwave oven**) forno microondas

mid [mɪd] adj: **~ May/afternoon** meados de maio (meio da tarde);

in ~ air em pleno ar; **midday** n meio-dia m

middle ['mɪdl] n meio; (waist) cintura ♦ adj meio; (quantity, size) médio, mediano; **middle-aged** adj de meia-idade; **Middle Ages** npl: **the Middle Ages** a Idade Média; **middle class** n: **the middle class(es)** a classe média ♦ adj (also: **middle-class**) de classe média; **Middle East** n: **the Middle East** o Oriente Médio; **middleman** n intermediário; **middle name** n segundo nome m

midge [mɪdʒ] n mosquito

midget ['mɪdʒɪt] n anão (anã) m/f

Midlands ['mɪdləndz] npl região central da Inglaterra

midnight ['mɪdnaɪt] n meia-noite f

midriff ['mɪdrɪf] n barriga

midst [mɪdst] n: **in the ~ of** no meio de, entre

midsummer [mɪd'sʌmə*] n: **a ~ day** um dia em pleno verão

midway [mɪd'weɪ] adj, adv: **~** (**between**) no meio do caminho (entre)

midweek [mɪd'wiːk] adv no meio da semana

midwife ['mɪdwaɪf] (pl **midwives**) n parteira

might [maɪt] see **may** ♦ n poder m, força; **mighty** adj poderoso, forte

migraine ['miːgreɪn] n enxaqueca

migrant ['maɪgrənt] adj migratório; (worker) emigrante

migrate [maɪ'greɪt] vi emigrar; (birds) arribar

mike [maɪk] n abbr = **microphone**

mild [maɪld] adj (character) pacífico; (climate) temperado; (taste) suave; (illness) leve, benigno; (interest) pequeno

mile [maɪl] n milha (1609 m); **mileage** n número de milhas; (AUT) ≈ quilometragem f

milestone ['maɪlstəun] n marco

miliário

militant ['mɪlɪtnt] *adj, n* militante *m/f*

military ['mɪlɪtəri] *adj* militar

milk [mɪlk] *n* leite *m* ♦ *vt* (cow) ordenhar; (fig) explorar, chupar; **milk chocolate** *n* chocolate *m* de leite; **milkman** (irreg) *n* leiteiro; **milk shake** *n* milk-shake *m*, leite *m* batido com sorvete; **milky** *adj* leitoso; **Milky Way** *n* Via Láctea

mill [mɪl] *n* (wind– etc) moinho; (coffee ~) moedor *m* de café; (factory) moinho, engenho ♦ *vt* moer ♦ *vi* (also: ~ **about**) aglomerar-se, remoinhar

millimetre (us **millimeter**) *n* milímetro

million ['mɪljən] *n* milhão *m*; **a ~ times** um milhão de vezes; **millionaire** *n* milionário(-a)

mime [maɪm] *n* mímo; (actor) mímico(-a), comediante *m/f* ♦ *vt* imitar ♦ *vi* fazer mímica

mimic ['mɪmɪk] *n* mímico(-a), imitador(a) *m/f* ♦ *vt* imitar, parodiar

min. *abbr* (= **minute, minimum**) min.

mince [mɪns] *vt* moer ♦ *vi* (in walking) andar com afetação ♦ *n* (BRIT: CULIN) carne *f* moída; **mincemeat** *n* recheio de sebo e frutas picadas; (us: meat) carne *f* moída; **mince pie** *n* pastel com recheio de sebo e frutas picadas

mind [maɪnd] *n* mente *f*; (intellect) intelecto; (opinion) opinião; **to my ~** a meu ver; (sanity): **to be out of one's ~** estar fora de si ♦ *vt* (attend to, look after) tomar conta de, cuidar de; (be careful of) ter cuidado com; (object to): **I don't ~ the noise** o barulho não me incomoda; **it is on my ~** não me sai da cabeça; **to keep or bear sth in ~** levar algo em consideração, não esquecer-se de algo; **to make up one's ~** decidir-se; **I don't ~** (it doesn't worry me) eu nem ligo; (it's all the same to me) para mim tanto faz; **~ you, ... se bem que ...**; **never ~!** não faz mal!, não importa!; (don't worry) não se preocupe!; **"~ the step"** "cuidado com o degrau"; **mindless** *adj* (violence) insensato; (job) monótono

mine¹ [maɪn] *pron* (o) meu *m*, (a) minha *f*; **a friend of ~** um amigo meu

mine² [maɪn] *n* mina ♦ *vt* (coal) extrair, explorar; (ship, beach) minar

miner ['maɪnə*] *n* mineiro

mineral ['mɪnərəl] *adj* mineral ♦ *n* mineral *m*; **~s** *npl* (BRIT: soft drinks) refrigerantes *mpl*; **mineral water** *n* água mineral

mingle ['mɪŋgl] *vi*: **to ~ with** misturar-se com

miniature ['mɪnətʃə*] *adj* em miniatura ♦ *n* miniatura

minibus ['mɪnɪbʌs] *n* microônibus *m*

MiniDisc ['mɪnɪdɪsk] ® *n* MiniDisc ® *m*

minimal ['mɪnɪml] *adj* mínimo

minimum ['mɪnɪməm] (pl **minima**) *adj* mínimo ♦ *n* mínimo

mining ['maɪnɪŋ] *n* exploração *f* de minas

miniskirt ['mɪnɪskə:t] *n* minissaia

minister ['mɪnɪstə*] *n* (BRIT: POL) ministro(-a); (REL) pastor *m* ♦ *vi*: **to ~ to sb** prestar assistência a alguém; **to ~ to sb's needs** atender às necessidades de alguém

ministry ['mɪnɪstrɪ] *n* (BRIT: POL) ministério; (REL): **to go into the ~** ingressar no sacerdócio

mink [mɪŋk] *n* marta

minor ['maɪnə*] *adj* menor; (unimportant) de pouca importância; (MUS) menor ♦ *n* (LAW) menor *m/f* de idade

minority [mar'nɔrɪtɪ] n minoria

mint [mɪnt] n (plant) hortelã f; (sweet) bala de hortelã ♦ vt (coins) cunhar; **the (Royal) M~** (BRIT) or **the (US) M~** (US) = a Casa da Moeda; **in ~ condition** em perfeito estado

minus ['maɪnəs] n (also: **~ sign**) sinal m de subtração ♦ prep menos

minute¹ [mar'nju:t] adj miúdo, diminuto; (search) minucioso

minute² ['mɪnɪt] n minuto; **~s** npl (of meeting) atas fpl; **at the last ~** no último momento

miracle ['mɪrəkl] n milagre m

mirage ['mɪrɑ:ʒ] n miragem f

mirror ['mɪrə*] n espelho; (in car) retrovisor m

mirth [mə:θ] n risada

misadventure [mɪsəd'ventʃə*] n desgraça, infortúnio

misappropriate [mɪsə'prəuprɪeɪt] vt desviar

misbehave [mɪsbɪ'heɪv] vi comportar-se mal

miscarriage ['mɪskærɪdʒ] n (MED) aborto (espontâneo); (failure): **~ of justice** erro judicial

miscellaneous [mɪsɪ'leɪnɪəs] adj (items, expenses) diverso; (selection) variado

mischief ['mɪstʃɪf] n (naughtiness) travessura; (fun) diabrura; (maliciousness) malícia; **mischievous** ['mɪstʃɪvəs] adj (naughty) travesso; (playful) traquino

misconception [mɪskən'sepʃən] n concepção f errada, conceito errado

misconduct [mɪs'kɔndʌkt] n comportamento impróprio; **professional ~** má conduta profissional

misdemeanour [mɪsdɪ'mi:nə*] (US **misdemeanor**) n má ação f, contravenção f

miser ['maɪzə*] n avaro(-a), sovina m/f

miserable ['mɪzərəbl] adj triste; (wretched) miserável; (weather, person) deprimente; (contemptible: offer) desprezível; (: failure) humilhante

miserly ['maɪzəlɪ] adj avarento, mesquinho

misery ['mɪzərɪ] n (unhappiness) tristeza; (wretchedness) miséria

misfire [mɪs'faɪə*] vi falhar

misfit ['mɪsfɪt] n inadaptado(-a), deslocado(-a)

misfortune [mɪs'fɔːtʃən] n desgraça, infortúnio

misgiving(s) [mɪs'gɪvɪŋ(z)] n(pl) mau pressentimento; **to have ~s about sth** ter desconfianças em relação a algo

misguided [mɪs'gaɪdɪd] adj enganado

mishandle [mɪs'hændl] vt manejar mal

mishap ['mɪshæp] n desgraça, contratempo

misinform [mɪsɪn'fɔːm] vt informar mal

misinterpret [mɪsɪn'tə:prɪt] vt interpretar mal

misjudge [mɪs'dʒʌdʒ] vt fazer um juízo errado de, julgar mal

mislay [mɪs'leɪ] (irreg) vt extraviar, perder

mislead [mɪs'li:d] (irreg) vt induzir em erro, enganar; **misleading** adj enganoso, errôneo

mismanage [mɪs'mænɪdʒ] vt administrar mal; (situation) tratar de modo ineficiente

misplace [mɪs'pleɪs] vt extraviar, perder

misprint ['mɪsprɪnt] n erro tipográfico

Miss [mɪs] n Senhorita (BR), a

menina (PT)

miss [mis] vt (train, class, opportunity) perder; (fail to hit) errar, não acertar em; (fail to see): **you can't ~ it** é impossível não ver; (regret the absence of): **I ~ him** sinto a falta dele ♦ vi falhar ♦ n (shot) tiro perdido or errado; **miss out** (BRIT) vt omitir

misshapen [mis'ʃeipən] adj disforme

missile ['misail] n míssil m; (object thrown) projétil m

missing ['misiŋ] adj (pupil) ausente; (thing) perdido; (removed) que está faltando; (MIL) desaparecido; **to be ~** estar desaparecido; **to go ~** desaparecer

mission ['miʃən] n missão f; (official representatives) delegação f

mist [mist] n (light) neblina, (heavy) névoa; (at sea) bruma ♦ vi (eyes: also: ~ over) enevoar-se; (BRIT: also: ~ over, ~ up: windows) embaçar

mistake [mis'teik] (irreg) n erro, engano ♦ vt entender or interpretar mal; by ~ por engano; **to make a ~** fazer um erro; **to ~ A for B** confundir A com B; **mistaken** pp of **mistake** ♦ adj errado; **to be mistaken** enganar-se, equivocar-se

mister ['mistə*] (inf) n senhor m; see **Mr**

mistletoe ['misltəu] n visco

mistook [mis'tuk] pt of **mistake**

mistress ['mistris] n (lover) amante f; (of house) dona (da casa); (BRIT: in school) professora, mestra; (of situation) dona; see **Mrs**

mistrust [mis'trʌst] vt desconfiar de

misty ['misti] adj (day) nublado; (glasses etc) embaçado

misunderstand [misʌndə'stænd] (irreg) vt entender or interpretar mal; **misunderstanding** n mal-entendido; (disagreement) desen-

tendimento

misuse [n mis'juːs, vb mis'juːz] n uso impróprio; (of power) abuso; (of funds) desvio ♦ vt abusar de; desviar

mitigate ['mitigeit] vt mitigar, atenuar

mix [miks] vt misturar; (combine) combinar ♦ vi (people) entrosar-se ♦ n mistura; (combination) combinação f; **mix up** (confuse: things) misturar; (: people) confundir; **mixed** adj misto; **mixed-up** adj confuso; **mixer** n (for food) batedeira; (person) pessoa sociável; **mixture** n mistura; (MED) preparado; **mix-up** n trapalhada, confusão f

mm abbr (= millimetre) mm

moan [məun] n gemido ♦ vi gemer; (inf: complain): **to ~ (about)** queixar-se (de), bufar (sobre) (inf)

moat [məut] n fosso

mob [mɔb] n multidão f ♦ vt cercar

mobile ['məubail] adj móvel ♦ n móvel m; **mobile phone** n telefone m celular

mock [mɔk] vt ridicularizar; (laugh at) zombar de, gozar de ♦ adj falso, fingido; (exam etc) simulado; **mockery** n zombaria; **to make a mockery of** ridicularizar

mode [məud] n modo; (of transport) meio

model ['mɔdl] n modelo; (ARCH) maqueta; (person: for fashion, ART) modelo m/f ♦ adj exemplar ♦ vt modelar ♦ vi servir de modelo; (in fashion) trabalhar como modelo; **to ~ o.s. on** mirar-se em

modem ['məudem] n modem m

moderate [adj 'mɔdərət, vb 'mɔdəreit] adj moderado ♦ vi moderar-se, acalmar-se ♦ vt moderar

modern ['mɔdən] adj moderno; **modernize** vt modernizar, atualizar

modest ['mɔdɪst] *adj* modesto; **modesty** *n* modéstia

modify ['mɔdɪfaɪ] *vt* modificar

moist [mɔɪst] *adj* úmido (*BR*), húmido (*PT*), molhado (*PT*); **moisten** *vt* umedecer (*BR*), humedecer (*PT*); **moisture** *n* umidade *f* (*BR*), humidade *f* (*PT*); **moisturizer** *n* creme *m* hidratante

molar ['məulə*] *n* molar *m*

mold [məuld] (*US*) *n*, *vt* = **mould**

mole [məul] *n* (*animal*) toupeira; (*spot*) sinal *m*, lunar *m*; (*spy*) espião(-piã) *m/f*

molest [məu'lest] *vt* molestar; (*attack sexually*) atacar sexualmente

mollycoddle ['mɔlɪkɔdl] *vt* mimar

molt [məult] (*US*) *vi* = **moult**

molten ['məultən] *adj* fundido; (*lava*) liquefeito

mom [mɔm] (*US*) *n* = **mum**

moment ['məumənt] *n* momento; **at the ~** neste momento; **momentary** *adj* momentâneo; **momentous** [məu'mentəs] *adj* importantíssimo

momentum [məu'mentəm] *n* momento; (*fig*) ímpeto; **to gather ~** ganhar ímpeto

mommy ['mɔmɪ] (*US*) *n* = **mummy**

Monaco ['mɔnəkəu] *n* Mônaco (*no article*)

monarch ['mɔnək] *n* monarca *m/f*; **monarchy** *n* monarquia

monastery ['mɔnəstərɪ] *n* mosteiro, convento

Monday ['mʌndɪ] *n* segunda-feira

monetary ['mʌnɪtərɪ] *adj* monetário

money ['mʌnɪ] *n* dinheiro; (*currency*) moeda; **to make ~** ganhar dinheiro; **money order** *n* vale *m* (*postal*)

mongrel ['mʌngrəl] *n* (*dog*) viralata *m*

monitor ['mɔnɪtə*] *n* (*TV*, *COMPUT*) terminal *m* (de vídeo) ♦ *vt* (*heartbeat*, *pulse*) controlar; (*broadcasts*, *progress*) monitorar

monk [mʌŋk] *n* monge *m*

monkey ['mʌŋkɪ] *n* macaco

monopoly [mə'nɔpəlɪ] *n* monopólio

monotonous [mə'nɔtənəs] *adj* monótono

monsoon [mɔn'su:n] *n* monção *f*

monster ['mɔnstə*] *n* monstro

monstrous ['mɔnstrəs] *adj* (*huge*) descomunal; (*atrocious*) monstruoso

month [mʌnθ] *n* mês *m*; **monthly** *adj* mensal ♦ *adv* mensalmente

monument ['mɔnjumənt] *n* monumento

mood [mu:d] *n* humor *m*; (*of crowd*) atmosfera; **to be in a good/bad ~** estar de bom/mau humor; **moody** *adj* (*variable*) caprichoso, de veneta; (*sullen*) rabugento

moon [mu:n] *n* lua; **moonlight** *n* luar *m* ♦ *vi* ter dois empregos, ter um bico; **moonlit** *adj*: **a moonlit night** uma noite de lua

moor [muə*] *n* charneca *f* ♦ *vt* (*ship*) amarrar ♦ *vi* fundear, atracar

moorland ['muələnd] *n* charneca

moose [mu:s] *n* *inv* alce *m*

mop [mɔp] *n* esfregão *m*; (*for dishes*) esponja com cabeça; (*of hair*) grenha ♦ *vt* esfregar; **mop up** *vt* limpar

mope [məup] *vi* estar or andar deprimido or desanimado

moped ['məuped] *n* moto *f* pequena (*BR*), motorizada (*PT*)

moral ['mɔrl] *adj* moral ♦ *n* moral *f*; **~s** *npl* (*principles*) moralidade *f*, costumes *mpl*

morale [mɔ'rɑ:l] *n* moral *f*, estado de espírito

morality [mə'rælɪtɪ] *n* moralidade *f*;

(*correctness*) retidão f, probidade f

KEYWORD
---

more [mɔ:*] *adj* **1** (*greater in number etc*) mais; **~ people/work/letters than we expected** mais pessoas/trabalho/cartas do que esperávamos **2** (*additional*) mais; **do you want (some) ~ tea?** você quer mais chá?; **I have no** or **I don't have any ~ money** não tenho mais dinheiro ♦ *pron* **1** (*greater amount*) mais; **~ than 10** mais de 10; **it cost ~ than we expected** custou mais do que esperávamos **2** (*further or additional amount*) mais; **is there any ~?** tem ainda mais?; **there's no ~** não tem mais ♦ *adv* mais; **~ dangerous/difficult etc than** mais perigoso/difícil etc do que; **~ easily (than)** mais fácil (do que); **~ and ~** cada vez mais; **~ or less** mais ou menos; **~ than ever** mais do que nunca

---

moreover [mɔ:'rəuvə*] *adv* além do mais, além disso

morning ['mɔ:nɪŋ] *n* manhã f; (*early ~*) madrugada ♦ *cpd* da manhã; **in the ~** de manhã; **7 o'clock in the ~** as (as) 7 da manhã; **morning sickness** *n* náusea matinal

Morocco [mə'rɔkəu] *n* Marrocos m

moron ['mɔ:rɔn] (*inf*) *n* débil mental *m/f*, idiota *m/f*

Morse [mɔ:s] *n* (*also:* ~ **code**) código Morse

morsel ['mɔ:sl] *n* (*of food*) bocado

mortar ['mɔ:tə*] *n* (*cannon*) morteiro; (*CONSTR*) argamassa; (*dish*) pilão m, almofariz m

mortgage ['mɔ:gɪdʒ] *n* hipoteca ♦ *vt* hipotecar

mortuary ['mɔ:tjuəri] *n* necrotério

(*correctness*) retidão f, probidade f

mosaic [məu'zeɪɪk] *n* mosaico

Moscow ['mɔskəu] *n* Moscou (*BR*), Moscovo (*PT*)

Moslem ['mɔzləm] *adj*, *n* = **Muslim**

mosque [mɔsk] *n* mesquita

mosquito [mɔs'ki:təu] (*pl* **~es**) *n* mosquito

moss [mɔs] *n* musgo

KEYWORD
---

most [məust] *adj* **1** (*almost all: people, things etc*) a maior parte de, a maioria de; **~ people** a maioria das pessoas **2** (*largest, greatest: interest*) máximo; (*money*): **who has (the) ~ money?** quem é que tem mais dinheiro?; **he derived the ~ pleasure from her visit** ele teve o maior prazer em recebê-la ♦ *pron* (*greatest quantity, number*) a maior parte, a maioria; **~ of it/them** a maioria dele/deles; **~ of the money** a maior parte do dinheiro; **do the ~ you can** faça o máximo que você puder; **I saw the ~** vi mais; **to make the ~ of sth** aproveitar algo ao máximo; **at the (very) ~** quando muito, no máximo ♦ *adv* (+ *vb*) o mais; (+ *adj*): **the ~ intelligent/expensive** *etc* o mais inteligente/caro *etc*; (*adv: carefully, easily etc*) o mais; (*very: polite, interesting etc*) muito; **a ~ interesting book** um livro interessantíssimo

mostly ['məustli] *adv* principalmente, na maior parte

MOT (*BRIT*) *n abbr* (= *Ministry of Transport*): **the ~ (test)** vistoria anual dos veículos automotores

motel [məu'tel] *n* motel m

moth [mɔθ] *n* mariposa; (*clothes ~*) traça

mother ['mʌðə*] *n* mãe f ♦ *adj*

materno ♦ vt (care for) cuidar de (como uma mãe); **motherhood** n maternidade f; **mother-in-law** n sogra; **motherly** adj maternal; **mother-of-pearl** n madrepérola; **mother-to-be** n futura mamãe f; **mother tongue** n língua materna

motion ['məuʃən] n movimento; (gesture) gesto, sinal m; (at meeting) moção f ♦ vt, vi: **to ~ (to) sb to do sth** fazer sinal a alguém para que faça algo; **motionless** adj imóvel; **motion picture** n filme m (cinematográfico)

motivated ['məutıveıtıd] adj: ~ (by) motivado (por)

motive ['məutıv] n motivo

motor ['məutə*] n motor m; (BRIT: inf: vehicle) carro, automóvel m ♦ cpd (industry) de automóvel; **motorbike** n moto(cicleta) f, motoca (inf); **motorboat** n barco a motor; **motorcar** (BRIT) n carro, automóvel m; **motorcycle** n motocicleta; **motorist** n motorista m/f; **motor racing** (BRIT) n corrida de carros, automobilismo m; **motorway** (BRIT) n rodovia (BR), autoestrada (PT)

mottled ['mɔtld] adj mosqueado, em furta-cores

motto ['mɔtəu] (pl **~es**) n lema m

mould [məuld] (US **mold**) n molde m; (mildew) mofo, bolor m ♦ vt moldar; (fig) moldar; **mouldy** adj mofado

moult [məult] (US **molt**) vi mudar (de penas etc)

mound [maund] n (of earth) monte m; (of blankets, leaves etc) pilha, montanha

mount [maunt] n monte m ♦ vt (horse etc) montar em, subir a; (stairs) subir; (exhibition) montar; (picture) emoldurar ♦ vi (increase) aumentar; **mount up** vi aumentar

mountain ['mauntın] n montanha ♦ cpd de montanha; **mountain bike** n mountain bike f; **mountaineer** [mauntı'nıə*] n alpinista m/f, montanhista m/f; **mountaineering** n alpinismo; **mountainous** adj montanhoso; **mountainside** n lado da montanha

mourn [mɔ:n] vt chorar, lamentar ♦ vi: **to ~ for** chorar or lamentar a morte de; **mourning** n luto; **in mourning** de luto

mouse [maus] (pl **mice**) n camundongo (BR), rato (PT); (COMPUT) mouse m; **mouse mat** or **pad** n (COMPUT) mouse pad m; **mousetrap** n ratoeira

mousse [mu:s] n musse f; (for hair) mousse f

moustache [məs'ta:ʃ] (US **mustache**) n bigode m

mousy ['mausı] adj pardacento

mouth [mauθ] n boca; (of cave, hole) entrada; (of river) desembocadura; **mouthful** n bocado; **mouth organ** n gaita; **mouthwash** n colutório; **mouth-watering** adj de dar água na boca

movable ['mu:vəbl] adj móvel

move [mu:v] n movimento; (in game) lance m, jogada; (: turn to play) turno, vez f; (of house, job) mudança ♦ vt (change position of) mudar; (: in game) jogar; (emotionally) comover; (POL: resolution etc) propor ♦ vi mexer-se, mover-se; (traffic) circular; (also: ~ house) mudar-se; (develop: situation) desenvolver; **to ~ sb to do sth** convencer alguém a fazer algo; **to get a ~ on** apressar-se; **move about** or **around** vi (fidget) mexer-se; (travel) deslocar-se; **move along** vi avançar; **move away** vi afastar-se;

move back vi voltar; **move forward** vi avançar; **move in** vi (to a house) instalar-se (numa casa); **move on** vi ir andando; **move out** vi sair (de uma casa); **move over** vi afastar-se; **move up** vi ser promovido

movement ['muːvmənt] n movimento; (gesture) gesto; (of goods) transporte m; (in attitude) mudança

movie ['muːvɪ] n filme m; **to go to the ~s** ir ao cinema

moving ['muːvɪŋ] adj (emotional) comovente; (that moves) móvel

mow [məʊ] (pt ~ed, pp ~ed or ~n) vt (grass) cortar; (corn) ceifar; **mow down** vt (massacre) chacinar; **mower** n ceifeira; (also: lawnmower) cortador m de grama (BR) or de relva (PT)

Mozambique [məʊzəm'biːk] n Moçambique m (no article)

MP n abbr = Member of Parliament

mph abbr = miles per hour (60 mph = 96 km/h)

Mr ['mɪstə*] n: ~ Smith (o) Sr. Smith

Mrs ['mɪsɪz] n: ~ Smith (a) Sra. Smith

Ms [mɪz] n (= Miss or Mrs) ver quadro

Ms

Ms é um título utilizado em lugar de Mrs (senhora) ou de Miss (senhorita) para evitar a distinção tradicional entre mulheres casadas e solteiras. É aceito, portanto, como o equivalente de Mr (senhor) para os homens. Muitas vezes reprovado por ter surgido como manifestação de um feminismo exacerbado, é uma forma de tratamento muito comum hoje em dia.

MSc n abbr = Master of Science

KEYWORD

much [mʌtʃ] adj muito; **how ~ money/time do you need?** quanto dinheiro/tempo você precisa?; **he's done so ~ work for the charity** ele trabalhou muito para a obra de caridade; **as ~ as** tanto como
♦ pron muito; **~ has been gained from our discussions** nossas discussões foram muito proveitosas; **how ~ does it cost? – too ~** quanto custa isso? – caro demais
♦ adv 1 (greatly) muito; **thank you very ~** muito obrigado(-a); **we are very ~ looking forward to your visit** estamos aguardando a sua visita com muito ansiedade; **he is very ~ the gentleman/politician** ele é muito cavalheiro/político; **as ~ as** tanto como; **as ~ as you** tanto quanto você
2 (by far) de longe; **I'm ~ better now** estou bem melhor agora
3 (almost) quase; **how are you feeling? – ~ the same** como você está (se sentindo)? – do mesmo jeito

muck [mʌk] n (dirt) sujeira (BR), sujidade f (PT); **muck about** or **around** (inf) vi fazer besteiras; **muck up** (inf) vt estragar

mud [mʌd] n lama

muddle ['mʌdl] n confusão f, bagunça; (mix-up) trapalhada ♦ vt (also: ~ up: person, story) confundir; (: things) misturar; **muddle through** vi virar-se

muddy ['mʌdɪ] adj (road) lamacento

mudguard ['mʌdgaːd] n pára-lama m

muesli ['mjuːzlɪ] n muesli m

muffin ['mʌfɪn] n bolinho redondo e

chato

muffle ['mʌfl] *vt* (*sound*) abafar; (*against cold*) agasalhar; **muffled** *adj* abafado, surdo; **muffler** (*US*) *n* (*AUT*) silencioso (*BR*), panela de escape (*PT*)

mug [mʌg] *n* (*cup*) caneca; (: *for beer*) caneco, canecão; (*inf*: *face*) careta; (: *fool*) bobo(-a) ♦ *vt* (*assault*) assaltar; **mugging** *n* assalto

muggy ['mʌgɪ] *adj* abafado

mule [mjuːl] *n* mula

multimedia [mʌltɪ'miːdɪə] *adj* multimídia

multiple ['mʌltɪpl] *adj* múltiplo ♦ *n* múltiplo; **multiple sclerosis** [-sklɪ'rəusɪs] *n* esclerose f múltipla

multiply ['mʌltɪplaɪ] *vt* multiplicar ♦ *vi* multiplicar-se

multistorey ['mʌltɪ'stɔːrɪ] (*BRIT*) *adj* de vários andares

mum [mʌm] *n* (*BRIT*: *inf*) mamãe f ♦ *adj*: **to keep ~** ficar calado

mumble ['mʌmbl] *vt, vi* resmungar, murmurar

mummy ['mʌmɪ] *n* (*BRIT*: *mother*) mamãe f; (*embalmed*) múmia

mumps [mʌmps] *n* caxumba

mundane [mʌn'deɪn] *adj* banal, mundano

municipal [mjuː'nɪsɪpl] *adj* municipal

murder ['məːdə*] *n* assassinato ♦ *vt* assassinar; **murderer** *n* assassino

murky ['məːkɪ] *adj* escuro; (*water*) turvo

murmur ['məːmə*] *n* murmúrio ♦ *vt, vi* murmurar

muscle ['mʌsl] *n* músculo; (*fig*: *strength*) força (muscular); **muscle in** *vi* imiscuir-se, impor-se; **muscular** *adj* muscular; (*person*) musculoso

museum [mjuː'zɪəm] *n* museu m

mushroom ['mʌʃrum] *n* cogumelo

♦ *vi* crescer da noite para o dia, pipocar

music ['mjuːzɪk] *n* música; **musical** *adj* musical; (*harmonious*) melodioso ♦ *n* musical *m*; **musician** [mjuː'zɪʃən] *n* músico(-a)

Muslim ['mʌzlɪm] *adj, n* muçulmano(-a)

mussel ['mʌsl] *n* mexilhão *m*

must [mʌst] *aux vb* (*obligation*): **I ~ do it** tenho que or devo fazer isso; (*probability*): **he ~ be there by now** ele já deve estar lá; (*suggestion, invitation*): **you ~ come and see me soon** você tem que vir me ver em breve; (*indicating sth unwelcome*): **why ~ he behave so badly?** por que ele tem que se comportar tão mal? ♦ *n* necessidade f; **it's a ~** é imprescindível

mustache ['mʌstæʃ] (*US*) *n* = **moustache**

mustard ['mʌstəd] *n* mostarda

muster ['mʌstə*] *vt* (*support*) reunir; (*energy*) juntar; (*MIL*) formar

mustn't ['mʌsnt] = **must not**

mute [mjuːt] *adj* mudo

mutiny ['mjuːtɪnɪ] *n* motim *m*, rebelião f

mutter ['mʌtə*] *vt, vi* resmungar, murmurar

mutton ['mʌtn] *n* carne f de carneiro

mutual ['mjuːtʃuəl] *adj* mútuo; (*shared*) comum

muzzle ['mʌzl] *n* (*of animal*) focinho; (*guard*: *for dog*) focinheira; (*of gun*) boca ♦ *vt* pôr focinheira em

my [maɪ] *adj meu* (minha); **this is ~ house/car/brother** esta é a minha casa/meu carro/meu irmão; **I've washed ~ hair/cut ~ finger** lavei meu cabelo/cortei meu dedo

myself [maɪ'sɛlf] *pron* (*reflexive*) me;

(*emphatic*) eu mesmo; (*after prep*) mim mesmo; *see also* **oneself**

mysterious [mɪsˈtɪərɪəs] *adj* misterioso

mystery [ˈmɪstərɪ] *n* mistério

mystify [ˈmɪstɪfaɪ] *vt* mistificar

myth [mɪθ] *n* mito; **mythology** [mɪˈθɔlədʒɪ] *n* mitologia

N

n/a *abbr* = **not applicable**

nag [næg] *vt* ralhar, apoquentar; **nagging** *adj* (*doubt*) persistente; (*pain*) contínuo

nail [neɪl] *n* (*human*) unha; (*metal*) prego ♦ *vt* pregar; **to ~ sb down to a date/price** conseguir que alguém se defina sobre a data/o preço; **nailbrush** *n* escova de unhas; **nailfile** *n* lixa de unhas; **nail polish** *n* esmalte *m* (*BR*) or verniz *m* (*PT*) de unhas; **nail polish remover** *n* removedor *m* de esmalte (*BR*) or verniz (*PT*); **nail scissors** *npl* tesourinha de unhas; **nail varnish** *n* = **nail polish**

naïve [naɪˈiːv] *adj* ingênuo

naked [ˈneɪkɪd] *adj* nu (nua)

name [neɪm] *n* nome *m*; (*surname*) sobrenome *m*; (*reputation*) reputação *f*, fama ♦ *vt* (*child*) pôr nome em; (*criminal*) apontar; (*price*) fixar; (*date*) marcar; **what's your ~?** qual é o seu nome?, como (você) se chama?; **by ~** de nome; **in the ~ of** em nome de; **namely** *adv* a saber, isto é; **namesake** *n* xará *m/f* (*BR*), homónimo(-a) (*PT*)

nanny [ˈnænɪ] *n* babá *f*

nap [næp] *n* (*sleep*) soneca ♦ *vi*: **to be caught ~ping** ser pego de surpresa

nape [neɪp] *n*: **~ of the neck** nuca

napkin [ˈnæpkɪn] *n* (*also*: **table ~**) guardanapo

nappy [ˈnæpɪ] (*BRIT*) *n* fralda; **nappy rash** *n* assadura

narcotic [nɑːˈkɔtɪk] *adj* narcótico ♦ *n* narcótico

narrative [ˈnærətɪv] *n* narrativa

narrow [ˈnærəu] *adj* estreito; (*fig: majority*) pequeno; (: *ideas*) tacanho ♦ *vi* (*road*) estreitar-se; (*difference*) diminuir; **to have a ~ escape** escapar por um triz; **to ~ sth down to** restringir or reduzir algo a; **narrowly** *adv* (*miss*) por pouco; **narrowminded** *adj* de visão limitada

nasty [ˈnɑːstɪ] *adj* (*remark*) desagradável; (: *person*) mau, ruim; (*malicious*) maldoso; (*rude*) grosseiro, obsceno; (*taste, smell*) repugnante, asqueroso; (*wound etc*) grave, sério

nation [ˈneɪʃən] *n* nação *f*

national [ˈnæʃənl] *adj*, *n* nacional *m/f*; **national anthem** *n* hino nacional; **National Health Service** (*BRIT*) *n* ≈ Instituto Nacional de Assistência Médica e Previdência Social, ≈ INAMPS *m*; **nationality** [næʃəˈnælɪtɪ] *n* nacionalidade *f*; **nationalize** *vt* nacionalizar; **nationally** *adv* (*nationwide*) de âmbito nacional; (*as a nation*) nacionalmente, como nação; **national park** *n* parque *m* nacional; **National Trust** (*BRIT*) *n* ver quadro

nationwide [ˈneɪʃənwaɪd] *adj* de âmbito or a nível nacional ♦ *adv* em todo o país

native ['neɪtɪv] n natural m/f, nativo(-a); (in colonies) indígena m/f, nativo(-a) ♦ adj (indigenous) indígena; (of one's birth) natal; (language) materno; (innate) inato, natural; **a ~ speaker of Portuguese** uma pessoa de língua (materna) portuguesa

NATO ['neɪtəu] n abbr (= North Atlantic Treaty Organization) OTAN f

natural ['nætʃrəl] adj natural; **naturally** adv naturalmente, (of course) claro, evidentemente

nature ['neɪtʃə*] n natureza; (character) caráter m, índole f

naught [nɔːt] n = **nought**

naughty ['nɔːtɪ] adj travesso, levado

nausea ['nɔːsɪə] n náusea

naval ['neɪvl] adj naval

nave [neɪv] n nave f

navel ['neɪvl] n umbigo

navigate ['nævɪgeɪt] vi navegar; (AUT) ler o mapa; **navigation** [nævɪ'geɪʃən] n (action) navegação f; (science) náutica

navvy ['nævɪ] (BRIT) n trabalhador m braçal, cavouqueira

navy ['neɪvɪ] n marinha (de guerra); **navy(-blue)** adj azul-marinho inv

Nazi ['nɑːtsɪ] n nazista m/f (BR), nazi m/f (PT)

NB abbr (= nota bene) NB

near [nɪə*] adj (place) vizinho; (time) próximo; (relation) íntimo ♦ adv perto ♦ prep (also: ~ **to**: space) perto de; (: time) perto de, quase ♦ vt aproximar-se de; **nearby** [nɪə'baɪ] adj próximo, vizinho ♦ adv à mão, perto; **nearly** adv quase; **I nearly fell** quase que caí; **nearside** n (AUT: right-hand drive) lado esquerdo; (: left-hand drive) lado direito ♦ adj esquerdo, direito; **near-sighted** adj míope

neat [niːt] adj (place) arrumado, em

ordem; (person) asseado, arrumado; (work) organizado; (plan) engenhoso, bem bolado; (spirits) puro; **neatly** adv caprichosamente, com capricho; (skilfully) habilmente

necessarily ['nesɪsrɪlɪ] adv necessariamente

necessary ['nesɪsrɪ] adj necessário

necessity [nɪ'sesɪtɪ] n (thing needed) necessidade f, requisito; (compelling circumstances) necessidade; **necessities** npl (essentials) artigos mpl de primeira necessidade

neck [nek] n (ANAT) pescoço; (of garment) gola; (of bottle) gargalo ♦ vi (inf) ficar de agarramento; **~ and ~** emparelhados

necklace ['neklɪs] n colar m

neckline ['neklaɪn] n decote m

necktie ['nektaɪ] (esp US) n gravata

need [niːd] n (lack) falta, carência; (necessity) necessidade f; (thing) requisito, necessidade ♦ vt precisar de; **I ~ to do it** preciso fazê-lo

needle ['niːdl] n agulha ♦ vt (inf) provocar, alfinetar

needless ['niːdlɪs] adj inútil, desnecessário; **to say** ... desnecessário dizer que ...

needlework ['niːdlwəːk] n (item(s)) trabalho de agulha; (activity) costura

needn't ['niːdnt] = **need not**

needy ['niːdɪ] adj necessitado, carente

negative ['negətɪv] adj negativo ♦ n (PHOT) negativo; (LING) negativa

neglect [nɪ'glekt] vt (one's duty) negligenciar, não cumprir com; (child) descuidar, esquecer-se de ♦ n (of child) descuido, desatenção f; (of house etc) abandono; (of duty) negligência

negotiate [nɪ'gəuʃɪeɪt] vi: **to ~ (with)** negociar (com) ♦ vt (treaty, transaction) negociar; (obstacle)

contornar; (bend in road) fazer;
negotiation [nɪgəʊʃɪˈeɪʃən] n negociação f
neigh [neɪ] vi relinchar
neighbour [ˈneɪbə*] (US **neighbor**)
n vizinho(-a); **neighbourhood** n
(place) vizinhança, bairro; (people)
vizinhos mpl; **neighbouring** adj
vizinho; **neighbourly** adj amistoso,
prestativo
neither [ˈnaɪðə*] conj: **I didn't move
and ~ did he** não me movi nem ele
♦ adj, pron nenhum (dos dois), nem
um nem outro ♦ adv: **~ good nor
bad** nem bom nem mau; **~ story is
true** nenhuma das estórias é verdade
neon [ˈniːɒn] n neônio, néon m;
neon light n luz f de neônio
nephew [ˈnevjuː] n sobrinho
nerve [nɜːv] n (ANAT) nervo; (courage) coragem f; (impudence) descaramento, atrevimento; **to have a fit
of ~s** ter uma crise nervosa; **nerve-
racking** adj angustiante
nervous [ˈnɜːvəs] adj (ANAT) nervoso; (anxious) apreensivo; (timid) tímido, acanhado; **nervous
breakdown** n crise f nervosa
nest [nest] vi aninhar-se ♦ n (of bird)
ninho; (of wasp) vespeiro
net [net] n rede f; (fabric) filó m; (fig)
sistema m ♦ adj (COMM) líquido ♦ vt
pegar na rede; (money: subj: person)
faturar; (: deal, sale) render; **the N~**
(the Internet) a Rede; **netball** n espécie de basquetebol
Netherlands [ˈneðələndz] npl: **the
~ os** Países Baixos
nett [net] adj = **net**
nettle [ˈnetl] n urtiga
network [ˈnetwɜːk] n rede f
neurotic [njʊəˈrɒtɪk] adj, n neuróti-
co(-a)
neuter [ˈnjuːtə*] adj neutro ♦ vt (cat
etc) castrar, capar

neutral [ˈnjuːtrəl] adj neutro ♦ n
(AUT) ponto morto
never [ˈnevə*] adv nunca; see also
mind; **never-ending** adj sem fim,
interminável; **nevertheless** adv
todavia, contudo
new [njuː] adj novo; **newborn**
adj recém-nascido; **newcomer**
n recém-chegado(-a), novato(-a);
new-found adj (friend) novo; (enthusiasm) recente; **newly** adv recém, novamente; **newly-weds** npl
recém-casados mpl
news [njuːz] n notícias fpl; (RADIO, TV)
noticiário; **a piece of ~** uma notícia;
newsagent (BRIT) n jornaleiro(-a);
newscaster n locutor(a) m/f;
news flash n notícia de última
hora; **newsletter** n boletim m
informativo; **newspaper** n jornal
m; **newsreader** n = **newscaster**;
newsreel n jornal m cinematográfico, atualidades fpl
newt [njuːt] n tritão m
New Year n ano novo; **New
Year's Day** n dia m de ano novo;
New Year's Eve n véspera de ano
novo
New Zealand [-ˈziːlənd] n Nova
Zelândia; **New Zealander** n neo-
zelandês(-esa) m/f
next [nekst] adj (in space) próximo,
vizinho; (in time) seguinte, próximo
♦ adv depois; depois, logo; **~ time**
na próxima vez; **~ year** o ano que
vem; **~ to** ao lado de; **~ to nothing**
quase nada; **next door** adv na casa
do lado ♦ adj vizinho; **next-of-kin**
n parentes mpl mais próximos
NHS n abbr = **National Health
Service**
nib [nɪb] n ponta or bico da pena
nibble [ˈnɪbl] vt mordiscar, beliscar
Nicaragua [nɪkəˈrægjuə] n Nicarágua

nice [naɪs] *adj* (*likeable*) simpático; (*kind*) amável, atencioso; (*pleasant*) agradável; (*attractive*) bonito; **nice-ly** *adv* agradavelmente, bem

nick [nɪk] *n* (*wound*) corte *m*; (*cut, indentation*) entalhe *m*, incisão *f* ♦ *vt* (*inf: steal*) furtar, arrochar; **in the ~ of time** na hora H, no momento exato

nickel ['nɪkl] *n* níquel *m*; (*US*) moeda de 5 centavos

nickname ['nɪkneɪm] *n* apelido (*BR*), alcunha (*PT*) ♦ *vt* apelidar de (*BR*), alcunhar de (*PT*)

niece [niːs] *n* sobrinha

Nigeria [naɪ'dʒɪərɪə] *n* Nigéria

niggling ['nɪglɪŋ] *adj* (*trifling*) insignificante, mesquinho; (*annoying*) irritante

night [naɪt] *n* noite *f*; **at** *or* **by ~** à *or* de noite; **the ~ before last** anteontem à noite; **nightcap** *n* bebida *tomada antes de dormir*; **nightclub** *n* boate *f*; **nightdress** (*BR*), camisa de noite (*PT*); **nightfall** *n* anoitecer *m*; **nightgown** *n* = **nightdress**; **nightie** ['naɪtɪ] *n* = **nightdress**

nightingale ['naɪtɪŋgeɪl] *n* rouxinol *m*

nightlife ['naɪtlaɪf] *n* vida noturna

nightly ['naɪtlɪ] *adj* noturno, de noite ♦ *adv* todas as noites, cada noite

nightmare ['naɪtmɛə*] *n* pesadelo

night-time *n* noite *f*

nil [nɪl] *n* nada; (*BRIT: SPORT*) zero

Nile [naɪl] *n*: **the ~** o Nilo

nimble ['nɪmbl] *adj* (*agile*) ágil, ligeiro; (*skilful*) hábil, esperto

nine [naɪn] *num* nove; **nineteen** ['naɪn'tiːn] *num* dezenove (*BR*), dezanove (*PT*); **ninety** ['naɪntɪ] *num* noventa; **ninth** [naɪnθ] *num* nono

nip [nɪp] *vt* (*pinch*) beliscar; (*bite*) morder

nipple ['nɪpl] *n* (*ANAT*) bico do seio, mamilo

nitrogen ['naɪtrədʒən] *n* nitrogênio

┌─────────────────┐
│ **KEYWORD**   │
└─────────────────┘

no [nəu] (*pl* **~es**) *adv* (*opposite of "yes"*) não; **are you coming? – ~ (I'm not)** você vem? – não (eu não) ♦ *adj* (*not any*) nenhum(a), não … algum(a); **I have ~ more money/time/books** não tenho mais dinheiro/tempo/livros; **"~ entry"** "entrada proibida"; **"~ smoking"** "é proibido fumar"

♦ *n* não *m*, negativa

nobility [nəu'bɪlɪtɪ] *n* nobreza

noble ['nəubl] *adj* (*person*) nobre; (*title*) de nobreza

nobody ['nəubədɪ] *pron* ninguém

nod [nɔd] *vi* (*greeting*) cumprimentar com a cabeça; (*in agreement*) acenar (que sim) com a cabeça; (*doze*) cochilar, dormitar ♦ *vt*: **to ~ one's head** inclinar a cabeça ♦ *n* inclinação *f* da cabeça; **nod off** *vi* cochilar

noise [nɔɪz] *n* barulho; **noisy** *adj* barulhento

nominate ['nɔmɪneɪt] *vt* (*propose*) propor; (*appoint*) nomear; **nominee** [nɔmɪ'niː] *n* pessoa nomeada, candidato(-a)

non-alcoholic [nɔn-] *adj* sem álcool

nondescript ['nɔndɪskrɪpt] *adj* qualquer; (*pej*) medíocre

none [nʌn] *pron* (*person*) ninguém; (*thing*) nenhum(a), nada; **~ of you** nenhum de vocês; **I've ~ left** não tenho mais

nonentity [nɔ'nɛntɪtɪ] *n* nulidade *f*, zero à esquerda *m*

nonetheless [nʌnðə'lɛs] *adv* no entanto, apesar disso, contudo

non-existent [nɔnɪg'zɪstənt] *adj*

inexistente

non-fiction [nɒn-] n literatura de não-ficção

nonplussed [nɒn'plʌst] adj perplexo, pasmado

nonsense ['nɒnsəns] n disparate m, besteira, absurdo; ~! bobagem!, que nada!

non [nɒn-]: **non-smoker** n não-fumante m/f; **non-stick** adj tefal ®, não-aderente; **non-stop** adj ininterrupto; (RAIL) direto; (AVIAT) sem escala ♦ adv sem parar

noodles ['nu:dlz] npl talharim m

noon [nu:n] n meio-dia m

no-one pron = nobody

noose [nu:s] n laço corrediço; (hangman's) corda da forca

nor [nɔ:*] conj = neither ♦ adv see neither

norm [nɔ:m] n (convention) norma; (requirement) regra

normal ['nɔ:ml] adj normal

north [nɔ:θ] n norte m ♦ adj do norte, setentrional ♦ adv ao or para o norte; **North America** n América do Norte; **north-east** n nordeste m; **northerly** ['nɔ:ðəlɪ] adj norte; **northern** ['nɔ:ðən] adj do norte, setentrional; **Northern Ireland** n Irlanda do Norte; **North Pole** n: the North Pole o Pólo Norte; **North Sea** n: the North Sea o Mar do Norte; **northward(s)** adv em direção norte; **north-west** n noroeste m

Norway ['nɔ:weɪ] n Noruega; **Norwegian** [nɔ:'wi:dʒən] adj norueguês(-esa) ♦ n norueguês(-esa) m/f; (LING) norueguês m

nose [nəuz] n (ANAT) nariz m; (ZOOL) focinho; (sense of smell: of person) olfato; (: of animal) faro; **nose about** vi bisbilhotar; **nose around** vi = nose about; **nosebleed** n

hemorragia nasal; **nose-dive** n (deliberate) vôo picado; (involuntary) parafuso; **nosey** (inf) adj = nosy

nostalgia [nɒs'tældʒɪə] n nostalgia

nostril ['nɒstrɪl] n narina

nosy ['nəuzɪ] (inf) adj intrometido, abelhudo

not [nɒt] adv não; **he is ~ or isn't here** ele não está aqui; **it's too late, isn't it?** é muito tarde, não?; **he asked me ~ to do it** ele me pediu para não fazer isto; **~ yet/now** ainda/agora não; see also **all**; **only**

notably ['nəutəblɪ] adv (particularly) particularmente; (markedly) notavelmente

notch [nɒtʃ] n (in wood) entalhe m; (in blade) corte m

note [nəut] n (MUS, bank~) nota; (letter) nota, bilhete m; (record) nota, anotação f; (tone) tom m ♦ vt (observe) observar, reparar em; (also: ~ down) anotar, tomar nota de; **notebook** n caderno; **notepad** n bloco de anotações; **notepaper** n papel m de carta

nothing ['nʌθɪŋ] n nada; (zero) zero; **he does** ~ ele não faz nada; **~ new/much** de novo/quase nada; **for** ~ de graça, grátis; (in vain) em vão, por nada

notice ['nəutɪs] n (sign) aviso, anúncio; (warning) aviso; (dismissal) demissão f; (of leaving) aviso prévio; (period of time) prazo ♦ vt reparar em, notar; **at short** ~ de repente, em cima da hora; **until further** ~ até nova ordem; **to hand in one's** ~ demitir, pedir a demissão; **to take** ~ **of** prestar atenção a, fazer caso de; **to bring sth to sb's** ~ levar algo ao conhecimento de alguém; **noticeable** adj evidente, visível; **notice board** (BRIT) n quadro de avisos

notify ['nəutɪfaɪ] vt: **to ~ sb of sth**

avisar alguém de algo
notion ['nəuʃən] n noção f, idéia
nought [nɔːt] n zero
noun [naun] n substantivo
nourish ['nʌrɪʃ] vt nutrir, alimentar; (fig) fomentar, alentar; **nourishing** adj nutritivo, alimentício; **nourishment** n alimento, nutrimento
novel ['nɔvl] n romance m ♦ adj novo, recente; **novelist** n romancista m/f; **novelty** n novidade f
November [nəu'vɛmbə*] n novembro
now [nau] adv agora; (these days) atualmente, hoje em dia ♦ conj: ~ (that) agora que; right ~ agora mesmo; by ~ já; just ~ atualmente; ~ and then, ~ and again de vez em quando; from ~ on de agora em diante; **nowadays** adv hoje em dia
nowhere ['nəuwɛə*] adv (go) a lugar nenhum; (be) em nenhum lugar
nozzle ['nɔzl] n bocal m
nuclear ['njuːklɪə*] adj nuclear
nucleus ['njuːklɪəs] (pl **nuclei**) n núcleo
nude [njuːd] adj nu (nua) ♦ n (ART) nu m; **in the ~** nu, pelado
nudge [nʌdʒ] vt acotovelar, cutucar (BR)
nudist ['njuːdɪst] n nudista m/f
nuisance ['njuːsns] n amolação f, aborrecimento; (person) chato; **what a ~!** que saco! (BR), que chatice! (PT)
numb [nʌm] adj: ~ **with cold** duro de frio; ~ **with fear** paralisado de medo
number ['nʌmbə*] n número; (numeral) algarismo ♦ vt (pages etc) numerar; (amount to) montar a; **a ~ of** vários, muitos; **to be ~ed among** figurar entre; **they were ten in ~** eram em número de dez; **number**

plate (BRIT) n placa (do carro)
numeral ['njuːmərəl] n algarismo
numerical [njuː'mɛrɪkl] adj numérico
numerous ['njuːmərəs] adj numeroso
nun [nʌn] n freira
nurse [nəːs] n enfermeiro(-a) (also: ~maid) ama-seca, babá f ♦ vt (patient) cuidar de, tratar de
nursery ['nəːsəri] n (institution) creche f; (room) quarto das crianças; (for plants) viveiro; **nursery rhyme** n poesia infantil; **nursery school** n escola maternal
nursing ['nəːsɪŋ] n (profession) enfermagem f; (care) cuidado, assistência; **nursing home** n sanatório, clínica de repouso
nut [nʌt] n (TECH) porca; (BOT) noz f; **nutcrackers** npl quebra-nozes m inv
nutmeg ['nʌtmeg] n noz-moscada
nutritious [njuː'trɪʃəs] adj nutritivo
nuts [nʌts] (inf) adj: **he's ~** ele é doido
nutshell ['nʌtʃel] n casca de noz; **in a ~** (fig) em poucas palavras
nylon ['naɪlɔn] n náilon m (BR), nylon m (PT) ♦ adj de náilon

O

oak [əuk] n carvalho ♦ adj de carvalho
OAP (BRIT) n abbr = **old-age pensioner**
oar [ɔː*] n remo
oasis [əu'eɪsɪs] (pl **oases**) n oásis m inv
oath [əuθ] n juramento; (swear word) palavrão m
oatmeal ['əutmiːl] n farinha or mingau m de aveia

oats [əuts] n aveia

obedient [ə'bi:diənt] adj obediente

obey [ə'bei] vt obedecer a; (instructions, regulations) cumprir

obituary [ə'bitjuəri] n necrológio

object [n 'ɔbdʒikt, vb əb'dʒekt] n objeto; (purpose) objetivo ♦ vi: **to ~ to** (attitude) desaprovar, objetar a; (proposal) opor-se a; **I ~!** protesto!; **he ~ed that ...** ele objetou que ...; **expense is no ~** o preço não é problema; **objection** [əb'dʒekʃən] n objeção f; **I have no objection to ...** não tenho nada contra ...; **objectionable** adj desagradável; (conduct) censurável; **objective** n objetivo

obligation [ɔbli'geiʃən] n obrigação f; **without ~** sem compromisso

obligatory [ə'bligətəri] adj obrigatório

oblige [ə'blaidʒ] vt (do a favour for) obsequiar, fazer um favor a; (force) obrigar, forçar, **to be ~d to sb for doing sth** ficar agradecido por alguém fazer algo; **obliging** adj prestativo

oblique [ə'bli:k] adj oblíquo; (allusion) indireto

oblivion [ə'bliviən] n esquecimento; **oblivious** adj: **oblivious of** inconsciente de, esquecido de

oblong [ɔblɔŋ] adj oblongo, retangular ♦ n retângulo

obnoxious [əb'nɔkʃəs] adj odioso, detestável; (smell) enjoativo

oboe ['əubau] n oboé m

obscene [əb'si:n] adj obsceno

obscure [əb'skjuə*] adj obscuro, desconhecido; (difficult to understand) pouco claro ♦ vt ocultar, escurecer; (hide: sun etc) esconder

observant [əb'zə:vnt] adj observador(a)

observation [ɔbzə'veiʃən] n observação f; (MED) exame m

observatory [əb'zə:vətri] n observatório

observe [əb'zə:v] vt observar; (rule) cumprir; **observer** n observador(a) m/f

obsess [əb'ses] vt obsedar, obcecar

obsolete ['ɔbsəli:t] adj obsoleto

obstacle ['ɔbstəkl] n obstáculo; (hindrance) estorvo, impedimento

obstinate ['ɔbstinit] adj obstinado

obstruct [əb'strʌkt] vt obstruir; (block: hinder) estorvar

obtain [əb'tein] vt obter; (achieve) conseguir

obvious ['ɔbviəs] adj óbvio; **obviously** adv evidentemente, obviously not! (é) claro que não!

occasion [ə'keiʒən] n ocasião f; (event) acontecimento; **occasionally** adv de vez em quando; **occasionally** adv de vez em quando

occupation [ɔkju'peiʃən] n ocupação f; (job) profissão f

occupier ['ɔkjupaiə*] n inquilino(-a)

occupy ['ɔkjupai] vt ocupar; (house) morar em; **to ~ o.s. in doing** ocupar-se de fazer

occur [ə'kə:*] vi ocorrer; (phenomenon) acontecer; **to ~ to sb** ocorrer a alguém; **occurrence** n ocorrência, acontecimento; (existence) existência

ocean ['əuʃən] n oceano

o'clock [ə'klɔk] adv: **it is 5 ~** são cinco horas

OCR n abbr = optical character reader; optical character recognition

October [ɔk'təubə*] n outubro

octopus ['ɔktəpəs] n polvo

odd [ɔd] adj (strange) estranho, esquisito; (number) ímpar; (sock etc) desemparelhado; **60-~** 60 e tantos; **at ~ times** às vezes, de vez em quando; **to be the ~ one out** ficar sobrando, ser a exceção; **odd jobs** npl biscates mpl, bicos mpl; **oddly** adv curiosamente; see also **enough**; **odds** npl (in betting) pontos mpl de vantagem; **it makes no odds** dá no mesmo; **at odds** brigados(-as), de mal

odour ['əʊdə*] (US **odor**) n odor m, cheiro; (unpleasant) fedor m

---

KEYWORD

of [ɔv, əv] prep **1** (gen) de; **a friend ~ ours** um amigo nosso; **a boy ~ 10** um menino de 10 anos; **that was very kind ~ you** foi muito gentil da sua parte

2 (expressing quantity, amount, dates etc) de; **how much ~ this do you need?** de quanto você precisa?; **3 ~ them** 3 deles; **3 ~ us went** 3 de nós foram; **the 5th ~ July** dia 5 de julho **3** (from, out of) de; **made ~ wood** feito de madeira

---

KEYWORD

off [ɔf] adv **1** (distance, time): **it's a long way ~** fica bem longe; **the game is 3 days ~** o jogo é daqui a 3 dias

2 (departure): **I'm ~** estou de partida; **to go ~ to Paris/Italy** ir para Paris/a Itália; **I must be ~** devo ir-me **3** (removal): **to take ~** one's hat/ coat/clothes tirar o chapéu/o casaco/a roupa; **the button came ~** o botão caiu; **10% ~** (COMM) 10% de abatimento or desconto **4** (not at work): **to have a day ~** tirar um dia de folga; (: sick): **to be ~ sick** estar ausente por motivo de saúde
♦ adj **1** (not turned on: machine, water, gas) desligado; (: light) apagado; (: tap) fechado
2 (cancelled) cancelado

3 (BRIT: not fresh: food) passado; (: milk) talhado, anulado
4: **on the ~ chance** (just in case) ao acaso; **today I had an ~ day** (not as good as usual) hoje não foi o meu dia
♦ prep **1** (indicating motion, removal etc) de; **the button came ~ my coat** o botão do meu casaco caiu
2 (distant from) de; **5 km ~ (the road)** a 5 km (da estrada); **~ the coast** em frente à costa
3: **to be ~ meat** (no longer eat it) não comer mais carne; (no longer like it) enjoar de carne

offal ['ɔfl] n (CULIN) sobras fpl, restos mpl

off-colour (BRIT) adj (ill) indisposto

offence [ə'fɛns] (US **offense**) n (crime) delito; **to take ~ at** ofender-se com, melindrar-se com

offend [ə'fɛnd] vt ofender; **offender** n delinquente m/f

offensive [ə'fɛnsɪv] adj (weapon, remark) ofensivo; (smell etc) repugnante ♦ n (MIL) ofensiva

offer ['ɔfə*] n (also: proposal) proposta ♦ vt oferecer; (opportunity) proporcionar; **"on ~"** (COMM) "em oferta"

off-hand [ɔf'hænd] adj informal ♦ adv de improviso

office ['ɔfɪs] n (place) escritório; (room) gabinete m; (position) cargo, função f; **to take ~** tomar posse; **doctor's ~** (US) consultório; **office block** (US **office building**) n conjunto de escritórios

officer ['ɔfɪsə*] n (MIL etc) oficial m/f; (of organization) diretor(a) m/f; (also: **police ~**) agente m/f policial or de polícia

office worker n empregado(-a) or funcionário(-a) de escritório

official [əˈfɪʃl] adj oficial ♦ n oficial m/f; (civil servant) funcionário público (funcionária pública)

officious [əˈfɪʃəs] adj intrometido

off-licence (BRIT) n ver quadro

OFF-LICENCE

Uma loja **off-licence** vende bebidas alcoólicas (para viagem) nos horários em que os pubs estão fechados. Nesses estabelecimentos também se pode comprar bebidas não-alcoólicas, cigarros, batatas fritas, balas, chocolates etc.

---

off: **off line** adj, adv (COMPUT) fora de linha; **off-peak** adj (heating etc) de período de pouco consumo; (ticket, train) de período de pouco movimento; **off-putting** (BRIT) adj desconcertante; **off-season** adj, adv fora de estação or temporada

offset [ˈɔfsɛt] (irreg) vt compensar, contrabalançar

offshore [ɔfˈʃɔ:*] adj (breeze) de terra; (fishing) costeiro; ~ **oilfield** campo petrolífero ao largo

offside [ˈɔfˈsaɪd] adj (SPORT) impedido; (AUT) do lado do motorista

offspring [ˈɔfsprɪŋ] n descendência, prole f

offstage [ɔfˈsteɪdʒ] adv nos bastidores

often [ˈɔfn] adv muitas vezes, freqüentemente; **how ~ do you go?** quantas vezes você vai?

oil [ɔɪl] n (CULIN) azeite m; (petroleum) petróleo; (for heating) óleo ♦ vt (machine) lubrificar; **oil painting** n pintura a óleo; **oil rig** n torre f de perfuração; **oil slick** n mancha negra; **oil tanker** n (ship) petroleiro; (truck) carro-tanque m de petróleo; **oil well** n poço petrolífero; **oily** adj oleoso; (food) gorduroso

ointment [ˈɔɪntmənt] n pomada

O.K. [ˈəʊˈkeɪ] excl está bem, está bom, tá (bem or bom) (inf) ♦ adj bom; (correct) certo ♦ vt aprovar

okay [ˈəʊˈkeɪ] = O.K.

old [əʊld] adj velho; (former) antigo, anterior; **how ~ are you?** quantos anos você tem?; **he's 10 years ~** ele tem 10 anos; **~er brother** irmão mais velho; **old age** n velhice f; **old-age pensioner** (BRIT) n aposentado(-a) (BR), reformado(-a) (PT); **old-fashioned** adj fora de moda; (person) antiquado; (values) absoleto, retrógrado

olive [ˈɔlɪv] n (fruit) azeitona; (tree) oliveira ♦ adj (also: ~-green) verde-oliva inv; **olive oil** n azeite m de oliva

Olympic [əʊˈlɪmpɪk] adj olímpico

omelet(te) [ˈɔmlɪt] n omelete f (BR), omeleta (PT)

omen [ˈəʊmən] n presságio, agouro

ominous [ˈɔmɪnəs] adj preocupante

omit [əʊˈmɪt] vt omitir

KEYWORD

on [ɔn] prep **1** (indicating position) sobre, em (cima de); ~ **the wall** na parede; ~ **the left** à esquerda
2 (indicating means, method, condition etc): ~ **foot** a pé; ~ **the train/plane** no trem/avião; ~ **the telephone/radio** no telefone/rádio; ~ **television** na televisão; **to be ~ drugs** (addicted) ser viciado em drogas; (MED) estar sob medicação; **to be ~ holiday** estar de férias
3 (referring to time): ~ **Friday** na sexta-feira; **a week** ~ **Friday** sem ser esta sexta-feira, a outra; ~ **arrival** ao chegar; ~ **seeing this** ao ver isto
4 (about, concerning) sobre
♦ adv **1** (referring to dress, covering): **to have one's coat** ~ estar de casa-

co; **what's she got ~?** o que ela está usando?; **she put her boots ~** ela calçou as botas; **he put his gloves/ hat ~** ele colocou as luvas/o chapéu; **screw the lid ~ tightly** atarraxar bem a tampa

2 (*further, continuously*): **to walk/ drive ~** continuar andando/dirigindo; **to go ~** continuar (em frente); **to read ~** continuar a ler

♦ *adj* **1** (*functioning, in operation: machine*) em funcionamento; (*light*) aceso; (*radio*) ligado; (*tap*) aberto; (*brakes: of car etc*): **to be ~** estar freado; (*meeting*): **is the meeting still ~?** (*in progress*) a reunião ainda está sendo realizada?; (*not cancelled*) ainda vai haver reunião?; **there's a good film ~ at the cinema** tem um bom filme passando no cinema

2: **that's not ~!** (*inf: of behaviour*) isso não se faz!

once [wʌns] *adv* uma vez; (*formerly*) outrora ♦ *conj* depois que; **~ he had left/it was done** depois que ele saiu/foi feito; **at ~** imediatamente; (*simultaneously*) de uma vez, ao mesmo tempo; **~ more** mais uma vez; **~ and for all** uma vez por todas; **~ upon a time** era uma vez

oncoming [ˈɔnkʌmɪŋ] *adj* (*traffic*) que vem de frente

KEYWORD

one [wʌn] *num* um(a); **~ hundred and fifty** cento e cinqüenta; **~ by ~** um por um

♦ *adj* **1** (*sole*) único; **the ~ book which ...** o único livro que ...

2 (*same*) mesmo; **they came in the ~ car** eles vieram no mesmo carro

♦ *pron* **1** um(a); **this ~** este (esta); **that ~** esse (essa), aquele (aquela); **I've already got ~/a red ~** eu já

---

tenho um/um vermelho

2: **~ another** um ao outro; **do you two ever see ~ another?** vocês dois se vêem de vez em quando?

3 (*impers*): **~ never knows** nunca se sabe; **to cut ~'s finger** cortar o dedo; **~ needs to eat** é preciso comer

---

oneself [wʌnˈsɛlf] *pron* (*reflexive*) se; (*after prep, emphatic*) si (mesmo(-a)); **by ~** sozinho(-a); **to hurt ~** ferir-se; **to keep sth for ~** guardar algo para si mesmo; **to talk to ~** falar consigo mesmo

one: **one-sided** *adj* (*argument*) parcial; **one-way** *adj* (*street, traffic*) de mão única (*BR*), de sentido único (*PT*)

ongoing [ˈɔngəʊɪŋ] *adj* (*project*) em andamento; (*situation*) existente

onion [ˈʌnjən] *n* cebola

on line *adj* (*COMPUT*) on-line, em linha ♦ *adv* em linha

onlooker [ˈɔnlʊkə*] *n* espectador(a) m/f

only [ˈəʊnlɪ] *adv* somente, apenas ♦ *adj* único, só ♦ *conj* só que, porém; **an ~ child** um filho único; **not ~ ... but also ...** não só ... mas também ...

onset [ˈɔnsɛt] *n* começo

onshore [ˈɔnʃɔː*] *adj* (*wind*) do mar

onslaught [ˈɔnslɔːt] *n* investida, arremetida

onto [ˈɔntʊ] *prep* = **on to**

onward(s) [ˈɔnwəd(z)] *adv* (*move*) para diante, para a frente; **from this time ~** de (ag)ora em diante

ooze [uːz] *vi* ressumar, filtrar-se

opaque [əʊˈpeɪk] *adj* opaco, fosco

OPEC [ˈəʊpɛk] *n abbr* (= *Organization of Petroleum-Exporting Countries*) OPEP f

open [ˈəʊpn] *adj* aberto; (*car*) descoberto; (*road*) livre; (*fig: frank*) aber-

to, franco; *(meeting)* aberto, sem
restrições ♦ *vt* abrir ♦ *vi* abrir(-se);
(book etc) começar; **in the ~ (air)** ao
ar livre; **open on to** *vt fus (subj:
room, door)* dar para; **open up** *vt*
abrir; *(blocked road)* desobstruir
♦ *vi* (COMM) abrir; **opening** *adj* de
abertura ♦ *n* abertura, *(start)* início; *(opportunity)* oportunidade *f*;
openly *adv* abertamente; **open-
minded** *adj* aberto, imparcial;
open-necked *adj* aberto no colo;
open-plan *adj* sem paredes divisó-
rias; **Open University** (BRIT) *n* ver
quadro

OPEN UNIVERSITY

Fundada em 1969, a **Open
University** oferece um tipo de
ensino que compreende cursos
(alguns blocos da programação da
TV e do rádio são reservados para
esse fim), devem, que são envia-
dos pelo aluno ao diretor ou diretora de estudos e uma estada
obrigatória em uma universidade
de verão. É preciso cumprir um
certo número de unidades ao
longo de um período determinado
e obter a média em um certo
número delas para receber o
diploma almejado.

---

opera ['ɔpərə] *n* ópera
operate ['ɔpəreit] *vt* fazer funcionar,
pôr em funcionamento ♦ *vi* funcionar; (MED). **to ~ on sb** operar alguém
operation [ɔpə'reiʃən] *n* operação
f; *(of machine)* funcionamento, **to
be in ~** *(system)* estar em vigor
operator ['ɔpəreitə*] *n (of machine)*
operador(a) *m/f*, manipulador(a)
m/f; (TEL) telefonista *m/f*
opinion [ə'pinjən] *n* opinião *f*; **in
my ~** na minha opinião, a meu ver;

opinionated *adj* opinioso
opponent [ə'pəunənt] *n* oponente
m/f; (MIL, SPORT) adversário(-a)
opportunity [ɔpə'tju:niti] *n* oportunidade *f*; **to take the ~ of doing**
aproveitar a oportunidade para
fazer
oppose [ə'pəuz] *vt* opor-se a; **to be
~d to sth** opor-se a algo, estar contra algo; **as ~d to** em oposição a
opposing [ə'pəuziŋ] *adj* oposto,
contrário
opposite ['ɔpəzit] *adj* oposto;
(house etc) em frente ♦ *adv* (lá) em
frente ♦ *prep* em frente de, defronte
de ♦ *n* oposto, contrário
opposition [ɔpə'ziʃən] *n* oposição *f*
opt [ɔpt] *vi*: **to ~ for** optar por; **to ~
to do** optar por fazer; **opt out**. **to ~
out of doing sth** optar por não fazer
algo
optician [ɔp'tiʃən] *n* oculista *m/f*
optimist ['ɔptimist] *n* otimista *m/f*;
optimistic [ɔpti'mistik] *adj* otimista
option ['ɔpʃən] *n* opção *f*; **optional**
adj opcional, facultativo
or [ɔ:*] *conj* ou; *(with negative)*: **he
hasn't seen ~ heard anything** ele
não viu nem ouviu nada; **~ else**
senão
oral ['ɔ:rəl] *adj* oral ♦ *n* (exame *m*)
oral *f*
orange ['ɔrindʒ] *n (fruit)* laranja
♦ *adj* cor de laranja *inv*, alaranjado
orbit ['ɔ:bit] *n* órbita ♦ *vt* orbitar
orchard ['ɔ:tʃəd] *n* pomar *m*
orchestra ['ɔ:kistrə] *n* orquestra, *(us:
seating)* platéia
orchid ['ɔ:kid] *n* orquídea
ordeal [ɔ:'di:l] *n* experiência penosa, provação *f*
order ['ɔ:də*] *n* ordem *f*; (COMM)
encomenda; *(good ~)* bom estado
♦ *vt (also: put in ~)* pôr em ordem,

arrumar; (in restaurant) pedir; (COMM) encomendar; (command) mandar, ordenar; **in (working)** ~ em bom estado; **in** ~ **to do/that** para fazer/que (+ sub); **on** ~ (COMM) encomendado; **out of** ~ com defeito, enguiçado; **order form** n impresso para encomendas; **orderly** n (MIL) ordenança m; (MED) servente m/f ♦ adj (room) arrumado, ordenado; (person) metódico

ordinary ['ɔːdɪnrɪ] adj comum, usual; (pej) ordinário, medíocre; **out of the** ~ fora do comum, extraordinário

ore [ɔː*] n minério

organ ['ɔːgən] n órgão m; **organic** [ɔː'gænɪk] adj orgânico

organization [ɔːgənaɪ'zeɪʃən] n organização f

organize ['ɔːgənaɪz] vt organizar

orgasm ['ɔːgæzəm] n orgasmo

Orient ['ɔːrɪənt] n: **the** ~ o Oriente; **oriental** [ɔːrɪ'entl] adj, n oriental m/f

origin ['ɔrɪdʒɪn] n origem f

original [ə'rɪdʒɪnl] adj original ♦ n original m

originate [ə'rɪdʒɪneɪt] vi: **to** ~ **from** originar-se de, surgir de; **to** ~ **in** ter origem em

Orkneys ['ɔːknɪz] npl: **the** ~ (also: **the Orkney Islands**) as ilhas Órcadas

ornament ['ɔːnəmənt] n ornamento; (on dress) enfeite m; **ornamental** [ɔːnə'mentl] adj decorativo, ornamental

ornate [ɔː'neɪt] adj enfeitado, requintado

orphan ['ɔːfn] n órfão (órfã) m/f

orthopaedic [ɔːθə'piːdɪk] (US **orthopedic**) adj ortopédico

ostentatious [ɔsten'teɪʃəs] adj pomposo, espalhafatoso; (person) ostentoso

ostrich ['ɔstrɪtʃ] n avestruz m/f

other ['ʌðə*] adj outro ♦ pron: **the** ~ **(one)** o outro (a outra) ♦ adv (usually in negatives): ~ **than** (apart from) a não ser; (anything but) exceto; ~**s** (~ people) outros; **otherwise** adv (in a different way) de outra maneira; (apart from that) do contrário, caso contrário ♦ conj (if not) senão

otter ['ɔtə*] n lontra

ouch [autʃ] excl ai!

ought [ɔːt] (pt ought) aux vb: **I** ~ **to do it** eu deveria fazê-lo; **he** ~ **to win** ele deve ganhar

ounce [auns] n onça (= 28.35g; 16 in a pound)

our ['auə*] adj nosso; see also **my**; **ours** pron (o) nosso ((a) nossa) etc; see also **mine¹**; **ourselves** [auə'selvz] pron pl (reflexive, after prep) nós; (emphatic) nós mesmos(-as); see also **oneself**

oust [aust] vt expulsar

┌─── KEYWORD ───┐

out [aut] adv **1** (not in) fora; **(to stand)** ~ **in the rain/snow** (estar em pé) na chuva/neve; ~ **loud** em voz alta

2 (not at home, absent) fora (de casa); **Mr Green is** ~ **at the moment** Sr. Green não está no momento; **to have a day/night** ~ passar o dia fora/sair à noite

3 (indicating distance): **the boat was 10 km** ~ o barco estava a 10 km da costa

4 (SPORT): **the ball is/has gone** ~ a bola caiu fora; ~! (TENNIS etc) fora!

♦ adj **1**: **to be** ~ (unconscious) estar inconsciente; (~ of game) estar fora; (~ of fashion) estar fora de moda

2 (have appeared: news, secret) do conhecimento público; (: flowers): **the flowers are** ~ as flores desabrocham

3 (*extinguished: light, fire*) apagado; **before the week was ~** (*finished*) antes da semana acabar

4: to be ~ to do sth (*intend*) pretender fazer algo; **to be ~ in one's calculations** (*wrong*) enganar-se nos cálculos

♦ *prep*: **~ of 1** (*outside, beyond*): **~ of** fora de; **to go ~ of the house** sair da casa; **to look ~ of the window** olhar pela janela

2 (*cause, motive*) por

3 (*origin*): **to drink sth ~ of a cup** beber algo na xícara

4 (*from among*): **1 ~ of every 3 1** entre 3

5 (*without*) sem; **to be ~ of milk/ sugar/petrol** *etc* não ter leite/açúcar/gasolina *etc*

out-and-out *adj* (*liar etc*) completo, rematado

outback ['autbæk] *n* (*in Australia*): **the ~** o interior

outbreak ['autbreɪk] *n* (*of war*) deflagração *f*; (*of disease*) surto; (*of violence etc*) explosão *f*

outburst ['autbɜːst] *n* explosão *f*

outcast ['autkɑːst] *n* pária *m/f*

outcome ['autkʌm] *n* resultado

outcry ['autkraɪ] *n* clamor *m* (de protesto)

outdated [aut'deɪtɪd] *adj* antiquado, fora de moda

outdo [aut'duː] (*irreg*) *vt* ultrapassar, exceder

outdoor [aut'dɔː*] *adj* ao ar livre; (*clothes*) de sair; **outdoors** *adv* ao ar livre

outer ['autə*] *adj* exterior, externo; **outer space** *n* espaço (exterior)

outfit ['autfɪt] *n* roupa, traje *m*

outgoing ['autgəuɪŋ] *adj* de saída; (*character*) extrovertido, sociável; **outgoings** (*BRIT*) *npl* despesas *fpl*

outgrow [aut'grəu] (*irreg*) *vt*: **he has ~n his clothes** a roupa ficou pequena para ele

outing ['autɪŋ] *n* excursão *f*

outlaw ['autlɔː] *n* fora-da-lei *m/f* ♦ *vt* (*person*) declarar fora da lei; (*practice*) declarar ilegal

outlay ['autleɪ] *n* despesas *fpl*

outlet ['autlet] *n* saída, escape *m*; (*of pipe*) desagüe *m*, escoadouro; (*US: ELEC*) tomada; (*also*: **retail ~**) posto de venda

outline ['autlaɪn] *n* (*shape*) contorno, perfil *m*; (*of plan*) traçado; (*sketch*) esboço, linhas *fpl* gerais ♦ *vt* (*theory, plan*) traçar, delinear

outlive [aut'lɪv] *vt* sobreviver a

outlook ['autluk] *n* (*attitude*) ponto de vista; (*fig: prospects*) perspectiva; (: *for weather*) previsão *f*

outnumber [aut'nʌmbə*] *vt* exceder em número

out-of-date *adj* (*passport, ticket*) sem validade; (*clothes*) fora de moda

out-of-the-way *adj* remoto, afastado

outpatient ['autpeɪʃənt] *n* paciente *m/f* externo(-a) *or* de ambulatório

outpost ['autpəust] *n* posto avançado

output ['autput] *n* (*volume m de*) produção *f*; (*COMPUT*) saída ♦ *vt* (*COMPUT*) liberar

outrage ['autreɪdʒ] *n* escândalo; (*atrocity*) atrocidade *f* ♦ *vt* ultrajar; **outrageous** [aut'reɪdʒəs] *adj* ultrajante, escandaloso

outright [*adv* aut'raɪt, *adj* 'autraɪt] *adv* (*kill, win*) completamente; (*ask, refuse*) abertamente ♦ *adj* completo; franco

outset ['autset] *n* início, princípio

outside [aut'saɪd] *n* exterior *m* ♦ *adj* exterior, externo ♦ *adv* (lá) fora

outsize ['autsaɪz] *adj (clothes)* de tamanho extra-grande *or* especial

outskirts ['autskɜːts] *npl* arredores *mpl*, subúrbios *mpl*

outspoken [aut'spəukən] *adj* franco, sem rodeios

outstanding [aut'stændɪŋ] *adj* excepcional; *(work, debt)* pendente

outstay [aut'steɪ] *vt*: to ~ one's welcome abusar da hospitalidade (demorando mais tempo)

outstretched [aut'stretʃt] *adj (hand)* estendido

outstrip ['autstrɪp] *vt* ultrapassar

outward ['autwəd] *adj* externo; *(journey)* de ida

outweigh [aut'weɪ] *vt* ter mais valor do que

outwit [aut'wɪt] *vt* passar a perna em

oval ['əuvl] *adj* ovalado ♦ *n* oval *m*; **Oval Office** *n* ver quadro

---

OVAL OFFICE

O Salão Oval (**Oval Office**) é o escritório particular do presidente dos Estados Unidos na Casa Branca, assim chamado devido a sua forma oval. Por extensão, o termo se refere à presidência em si.

---

ovary ['əuvərɪ] *n* ovário

oven ['ʌvn] *n* forno

KEYWORD

over ['əuvə*] *adv* **1** *(across:* walk, jump, fly *etc)* por cima; **to cross** ~ **to the other side of the road** atravessar para o outro lado da rua; ~ **here** por aqui, cá; ~ **there** por ali, lá; **to ask sb** ~ *(to one's home)* convidar alguém

2: **to fall** ~ cair; **to knock** ~ derrubar; **to turn** ~ virar; **to bend** ~ curvar-se, debruçar-se

3 *(finished):* **to be** ~ estar acabado

4 *(excessively:* clever, rich, fat *etc)* muito, demais; **she's not** ~ **intelligent** ela não é superdotada

5 *(remaining:* money, food *etc):* **there are 3** ~ tem 3 sobrando/sobraram 3

6: **all** ~ *(everywhere)* por todos os lados; ~ **and** ~ *(again)* repetidamente

♦ *prep* **1** *(on top of)* sobre; *(above)* acima de

2 *(on the other side of)* no outro lado de; **he jumped** ~ **the wall** ele pulou o muro

3 *(more than)* mais de; ~ **and above** além de

4 *(during)* durante

overall [*adj, n* 'əuvərɔːl, *adv* əuvər'ɔːl] *adj (length)* total; *(study)* global ♦ *adv (view)* globalmente; *(measure, paint)* totalmente ♦ *n (also:* ~**s**) macacão *m (BR)*, *(fato)* macaco *(PT)*

overawe [əuvər'ɔː] *vt* intimidar

overboard ['əuvəbɔːd] *adv (NAUT)* ao mar

overcast ['əuvəkɑːst] *adj* nublado, fechado

overcharge [əuvə'tʃɑːdʒ] *vt*: **to** ~ **sb** cobrar em excesso a alguém

overcoat ['əuvəkəut] *n* sobretudo

overcome [əuvə'kʌm] *(irreg) vt* vencer, dominar; *(difficulty)* superar

overcrowded [əuvə'kraudɪd] *adj* superlotado

overdo [əuvə'duː] *(irreg) vt* exagerar; *(overcook)* cozinhar demais; **to** ~ **it** *(work too hard)* exceder-se

overdose ['əuvədəus] *n* overdose *f*, dose *f* excessiva

overdraft ['əuvədrɑːft] n saldo negativo

overdrawn [əuvə'drɔːn] adj (account) sem fundos, a descoberto

overdue [əuvə'djuː] adj atrasado; (change) tardio

overestimate [əuvər'estɪmeɪt] vt sobrestimar

overflow [vb əuvə'fləu, n 'əuvəfləu] vi transbordar ♦ n (also: ~ **pipe**) tubo de descarga, ladrão m

overgrown [əuvə'grəun] adj (garden) coberto de vegetação

overhaul [vb əuvə'hɔːl, n 'əuvəhɔːl] vt revisar ♦ n revisão f

overhead [adv əuvə'hed, adj, n 'əuvəhed] adv por cima, em cima; (in the sky) no céu ♦ adj (lighting) superior; (railway) suspenso ♦ n (US) = ~s; ~s npl (expenses) despesas fpl gerais

overhear [əuvə'hɪə*] (irreg) vt ouvir por acaso

overheat [əuvə'hiːt] vi (engine) aquecer demais

overjoyed [əuvə'dʒɔɪd] adj: **to be ~ (at)** estar muito alegre (com)

overland ['əuvəlænd] adj, adv por terra

overlap [əuvə'læp] vi (edges) sobrepor-se em parte; (fig) coincidir

overleaf [əuvə'liːf] adv no verso

overload [əuvə'ləud] vt sobrecarregar

overlook [əuvə'luk] vt (have view on) dar para; (miss) omitir; (forgive) fazer vista grossa a

overnight [adv əuvə'naɪt, adj 'əuvənaɪt] adv durante a noite; (fig) da noite para o dia ♦ adj de uma (or de) noite; **to stay ~** passar a noite, pernoitar

overpass ['əuvəpɑːs] (esp US) n viaduto

overpower [əuvə'pauə*] vt domi-

nar, subjugar; (fig) assolar

overrate [əuvə'reɪt] vt sobrestimar, supervalorizar

override [əuvə'raɪd] (irreg) vt (order, objection) não fazer caso de, ignorar

overrule [əuvə'ruːl] vt (decision) anular; (claim) indeferir

overrun [əuvə'rʌn] (irreg) vt (country etc) invadir; (time limit) ultrapassar, exceder

overseas [əuvə'siːz] adv (abroad) no estrangeiro, no exterior ♦ adj (trade) exterior; (visitor) estrangeiro

overshadow [əuvə'ʃædəu] vt ofuscar

oversight ['əuvəsaɪt] n descuido

oversleep [əuvə'sliːp] (irreg) vi dormir além da hora

overt [əu'vɜːt] adj aberto, indissimulado

overtake [əuvə'teɪk] (irreg) vt ultrapassar

overthrow [əuvə'θrəu] (irreg) vt (government) derrubar

overtime ['əuvətaɪm] n horas fpl extras

overtone ['əuvətəun] n (fig: also: ~s) implicação f, tom m

overture ['əuvətʃuə*] n (MUS) abertura; (fig) proposta, oferta

overturn [əuvə'tɜːn] vt virar; (system) derrubar; (decision) anular ♦ vi (car etc) capotar

overweight [əuvə'weɪt] adj gordo demais, com excesso de peso

overwhelm [əuvə'welm] vt esmagar, assolar; **overwhelming** adj (victory, defeat) esmagador(a); (heat) sufocante; (desire) irresistível

overwrought [əuvə'rɔːt] adj extenuado, superexcitado

owe [əu] vt: **to ~ sb sth, to ~ sth to sb** dever algo a alguém; **owing to** prep devido a, por causa de

owl [aul] n coruja

own [əun] *adj* próprio ♦ *vt* possuir,
ter; **a room of my ~** meu próprio
quarto; **to get one's ~ back** ir à
forra; **on one's ~** sozinho; **own up**
vi: **to ~ up to sth** confessar algo;
owner *n* dono(-a), proprietário(-a);
ownership *n* posse f

ox [ɔks] (*pl* **~en**) *n* boi *m*

oxtail ['ɔksteıl] *n*: **~ soup** sopa de
rabada

oxygen ['ɔksıdʒən] *n* oxigênio

oyster ['ɔıstə*] *n* ostra

oz. *abbr* = **ounce(s)**

ozone ['əuzəun] *n* ozônio; **ozone-
friendly** *adj* (*products*) que não
destrói a camada de ozônio; **ozone
layer** *n* camada de ozônio

P

p [pi:] *abbr* (= *page*) p; (*BRIT*) = **penny;
pence**

PA *n abbr* = **personal assistant;
public address system**

p.a. *abbr* (= *per annum*) p.a.

pace [peıs] *n* passo; (*speed*) velocidade f ♦ *vi*: **to ~ up and down** andar
de um lado para o outro; **to keep
~ with** acompanhar o passo de;
pacemaker *n* (*MED*) marcapasso *m*

Pacific [pə'sıfık] *n*: **the ~ (Ocean)** o
(Oceano) Pacífico

pack [pæk] *n* pacote *m*, embrulho *m*;
(*US: of cigarettes*) maço; (*of hounds*)
matilha; (*of thieves*) bando, quadri-
lha; (*of cards*) baralho; (*back~*)
mochila ♦ *vt* encher; (*in suitcase*)
arrumar (na mala); (*cram*): **to ~ into**
entupir de, entulhar com; **to ~
(one's bags)** fazer as malas; **to ~ sb
off** despedir alguém; **~ it in!** pára
com isso!

package ['pækıdʒ] *n* pacote *m*;
(*bulky*) embrulho, fardo; (*also: ~*

deal) acordo global, pacote; **package tour** (*BRIT*) *n* excursão f organizada

packed lunch [pækt-] (*BRIT*) *n*
merenda

packet ['pækıt] *n* pacote *m*; (*of cigarettes*) maço; (*of washing powder
etc*) caixa

packing ['pækıŋ] *n* embalagem f;
(*act*) empacotamento

pad [pæd] *n* (*of paper*) bloco; (*to prevent friction*) acolchoado; (*inf: home*)
casa ♦ *vt* acolchoar, enchumaçar

paddle ['pædl] *n* remo curto; (*US: for
table tennis*) raquete f ♦ *vt* remar ♦ *vi*
patinhar; **paddling pool** (*BRIT*) *n*
lago de recreação

paddock ['pædək] *n* cercado; (*at
race course*) paddock *m*

padlock ['pædlɔk] *n* cadeado

pagan ['peıgən] *adj*, *n* pagão (pagã)
m/f

page [peıdʒ] *n* página; (*also: ~ boy*)
mensageiro ♦ *vt* mandar chamar

pager ['peıdʒə*], **paging device**
['peıdʒıŋ-] *n* bip *m*

paid [peıd] *pt*, *pp* of **pay** ♦ *adj* (*work*)
remunerado; (*holiday*) pago; (*offi-
cial*) assalariado; **to put ~ to** (*BRIT*)
acabar com

pail [peıl] *n* balde *m*

pain [peın] *n* dor f; **to be in ~** sofrer
or sentir dor; **to take ~s to do sth**
dar-se ao trabalho de fazer algo;
painful *adj* doloroso; (*laborious*)
penoso; (*unpleasant*) desagradável;
painfully *adv* (*fig*) terrivelmente;
painkiller *n* analgésico; **painless**
adj sem dor, indolor; **painstaking**
['peınzteıkıŋ] *adj* (*work*) esmerado;
(*person*) meticuloso

paint [peınt] *n* pintura ♦ *vt* pintar; **paintbrush** *n* (*artist's*) pincel
m; (*decorator's*) broxa; **painter** *n*
(*artist*) pintor(a) *m/f*; (*decorator*)

pintor(a) de paredes; **painting** n pintura; (picture) tela, quadro; **paintwork** n pintura

pair [pɛə*] n par m; a ~ of scissors uma tesoura; a ~ of trousers uma calça (BR), umas calças (PT)

pajamas [pɪ'dʒɑːməz] (US) npl pijama m

Pakistan [pɑːkɪ'stɑːn] n Paquistão m; **Pakistani** adj, n paquistanês(-esa) m/f

pal [pæl] (inf) n camarada m/f, colega m/f

palace ['pæləs] n palácio

pale [peɪl] adj pálido; (colour) claro; (light) fraco ♦ vi empalidecer ♦ n: **to be beyond the ~** passar dos limites

Palestine ['pælɪstaɪn] n Palestina; **Palestinian** [pælɪs'tɪnɪən] adj, n palestino(-a)

palm [pɑːm] n (of hand) palma; (also: ~ **tree**) palmeira ♦ vt: **to ~ sth off on sb** (inf) impingir algo a alguém

pamper ['pæmpə*] vt paparicar, mimar

pamphlet ['pæmflət] n panfleto

pan [pæn] n (also: **sauce~**) panela (BR), caçarola (PT); (also: **frying ~**) frigideira

Panama ['pænəmɑː] n Panamá m

pancake ['pænkeɪk] n panqueca

panda ['pændə] n panda m/f

pane [peɪn] n vidraça, vidro

panel ['pænl] n (of wood, RADIO, TV) painel m; **panelling** (US **paneling**) n painéis mpl

pang [pæŋ] n: a ~ of regret uma sensação de pesar; ~s of hunger fome aguda

panic ['pænɪk] n pânico ♦ vi entrar em pânico; **panicky** adj (person) assustadiço, apavorado; **panic-**

stricken adj tomado de pânico

pansy ['pænzɪ] n (BOT) amor-perfeito; (inf: pej) bicha (BR), maricas m (PT)

pant [pænt] vi arquejar, ofegar

panther ['pænθə*] n pantera

panties ['pæntɪz] npl calcinha (BR), cuecas fpl (PT)

pantihose ['pæntɪhəʊz] (US) n meia-calça (BR), collants mpl (PT)

pantomime ['pæntəmaɪm] (BRIT) n pantomima; ver quadro

PANTOMIME

Uma **pantomime**, também chamada simplesmente de panto, é um gênero de comédia em que o personagem principal em geral é um rapaz e na qual há sempre uma dame, isto é, uma mulher Idosa representada por um homem, e um vilão. Na maior parte das vezes, a história é baseada em um conto de fadas, como "A gata borralheira" ou "O gato de botas", e a platéia é encorajada a participar prevenindo os heróis dos perigos que estão por vir. Esse tipo de espetáculo, voltado sobretudo para as crianças, visa também ao público adulto por meio de diversas brincadeiras que fazem alusão aos fatos atuais.

---

pantry ['pæntrɪ] n despensa

pants [pænts] npl (BRIT: underwear: woman's) calcinha (BR), cuecas fpl (PT); (: man's) cueca (BR), cuecas (PT); (US: trousers) calça (BR), calças fpl (PT)

paper ['peɪpə*] n papel m; (also: **news~**) jornal m; (also: **wall~**) papel de parede; (study, article) artigo, dissertação f; (exam) exame m, prova ♦ adj de papel ♦ vt (room) revestir (com papel de parede); ~s npl (also:

identity ~s) documentos *mpl*;
paperback *n* livro de capa mole;
paper bag *n* saco de papel; **paper
clip** *n* clipe *m*; **paper hankie** *n*
lenço de papel; **paperweight** *n*
pesa-papéis *m inv*; **paperwork** *n*
trabalho burocrático; (*pej*) papelada

par [pa:*] *n* paridade *f*, igualdade *f*;
(*GOLF*) média *f*; **on a ~ with** em pé
de igualdade com

parachute ['pærəʃuːt] *n* pára-
quedas *m inv*

parade [pə'reɪd] *n* desfile *m* ♦ *vt*
(*show off*) exibir ♦ *vi* (*MIL*) passar
revista

paradise ['pærədaɪs] *n* paraíso

paraffin ['pærəfɪn] (*BRIT*) *n*: ~ (**oil**)
querosene *m*

paragraph ['pærəgrɑːf] *n* parágrafo

Paraguay ['pærəgwaɪ] *n* Paraguai *m*

parallel ['pærəlɛl] *adj* (*lines etc*)
paralelo; (*fig*) correspondente ♦ *n*
paralela; correspondência

paralyse ['pærəlaɪz] (*BRIT*) *vt* paralisar

paralysis [pə'rælɪsɪs] (*pl* **paralyses**)
n paralisia

paralyze ['pærəlaɪz] (*US*) *vt* = paralyse

paranoid ['pærənɔɪd] *adj* paranóico

parasol ['pærəsɔl] *n* guarda-sol *m*,
sombrinha

paratrooper ['pærətruːpə*] *n* pára-
quedista *m/f*

parcel ['pɑːsl] *n* pacote *m* ♦ *vt* (*also:
~ up*) embrulhar, empacotar

pardon ['pɑːdn] *n* (*LAW*) indulto ♦ *vt*
perdoar; **~ me!**, **I beg your ~**
(*apologizing*) desculpe(-me); (**I beg
your**) **~?** (*BRIT*), **~ me?** (*US*) (*not hearing*) como?, como disse?

parent ['pɛərənt] *n* (*father*) pai *m*;
(*mother*) mãe *f*; **~s** *npl* (*mother and
father*) pais *mpl*

Paris ['pærɪs] *n* Paris

parish ['pærɪʃ] *n* paróquia, freguesia

park [pɑːk] *n* parque *m* ♦ *vt*, *vi* estacionar

parking ['pɑːkɪŋ] *n* estacionamento; **"no ~"** "estacionamento proibido"; **parking lot** (*US*) *n* (*parque
m de*) estacionamento; **parking
meter** *n* parquímetro; **parking
ticket** *n* multa por estacionamento
proibido

parliament ['pɑːləmənt] (*BRIT*) *n*
parlamento

parlour ['pɑːlə*] (*US* **parlor**) *n* sala
de visitas, salão *m*, saleta

parochial [pə'rəʊkɪəl] (*pej*) *adj* provinciano

parole [pə'rəʊl] *n*: **on ~** em liberdade condicional, sob promessa

parrot ['pærət] *n* papagaio

parsley ['pɑːslɪ] *n* salsa

parsnip ['pɑːsnɪp] *n* cherivia, pasti-
naga

parson ['pɑːsn] *n* padre *m*, clérigo;
(*in Church of England*) pastor *m*

part [pɑːt] *n* parte *f*; (*of machine*)
peça; (*THEATRE etc*) papel *m*; (*of serial*)
capítulo; (*US*: *in hair*) risca, repartido
♦ *adv* = **partly** ♦ *vt* dividir; (*hair*)
repartir ♦ *vi* (*people*) separar-se;
(*crowd*) dispersar-se; **to take ~ in**
participar de, tomar parte em; **to
take sb's ~** defender alguém; **for
my ~** pela minha parte; **for the
most ~** na maior parte; **to take sth
in good ~** não se ofender com algo;
part with *vt fus* ceder, entregar;
(*money*) pagar; **part exchange**
(*BRIT*) *n*: **in part exchange** como
parte do pagamento

partial ['pɑːʃl] *adj* parcial; **to be ~
to** gostar de, ser apreciador(a) de

participate [pɑː'tɪsɪpeɪt] *vi*: **to
~ in** participar de; **participation**
[pɑːtɪsɪ'peɪʃən] *n* participação *f*

particle ['pɑːtɪkl] *n* partícula; (*of*

dust) grão *m*

particular [pə'tɪkjulə*] *adj (special)* especial; *(specific)* específico; *(fussy)* exigente, minucioso; **in ~** em particular; **particularly** *adv* em particular, especialmente; **particulars** *npl* detalhes *mpl; (personal details)* dados *mpl* pessoais

parting ['pɑːtɪŋ] *n (act)* separação *f; (farewell)* despedida; *(BRIT: in hair)* risca, repartido ♦ *cpd* de despedida

partition [pɑː'tɪʃən] *n (POL)* divisão *f; (wall)* tabique *m*, divisória

partly ['pɑːtlɪ] *adv* em parte

partner ['pɑːtnə*] *n (COMM)* sócio(-a); *(SPORT)* parceiro(-a); *(at dance)* par *m; (spouse)* cônjuge *m/f;* **partnership** *n* associação *f*, parceria; *(COMM)* sociedade *f*

partridge ['pɑːtrɪdʒ] *n* perdiz *f*

part-time *adj, adv* de meio expediente

party ['pɑːtɪ] *n (POL)* partido; *(celebration)* festa; *(group)* grupo; *(LAW)* parte *f* interessada, litigante *m/f* ♦ *cpd (POL)* do partido, partidário

pass [pɑːs] *vt* passar; *(exam)* passar em; *(place)* passar por; *(overtake)* ultrapassar; *(approve)* aprovar ♦ *vi* passar; *(SCH)* ser aprovado, passar ♦ *n (permit)* passe *m; (membership card)* carteira; *(in mountains)* desfiladeiro; *(SPORT)* passe *m; (SCH):* **to get a ~ in** ser aprovado em; **to make a ~ at sb** tomar liberdade com alguém; **pass away** *vi* falecer; **pass by** *vi* passar ♦ *vt* passar por cima de; **pass for** *vt fus* passar por; **pass on** *vt (news, illness)* transmitir; *(object)* passar para; **pass out** *vi* desmaiar; **pass up** *vt* deixar passar; **passable** *adj (road)* transitável; *(work)* aceitável

passage ['pæsɪdʒ] *n (also: ~way: indoors)* corredor *m; (: outdoors)* passagem *f; (ANAT)* via; *(act of passing)* trânsito; *(in book)* passagem, trecho; *(by boat)* travessia

passenger ['pæsɪndʒə*] *n* passageiro(-a)

passer-by ['pɑːsə*-] *(pl* **passers-by)** *n* transeunte *m/f*

passing ['pɑːsɪŋ] *adj (fleeting)* passageiro, fugaz; **in ~** de passagem

passion ['pæʃən] *n* paixão *f;* **passionate** *adj* apaixonado

passive ['pæsɪv] *adj* passivo

passport ['pɑːspɔːt] *n* passaporte *m*

password ['pɑːswɔːd] *n* senha, contra-senha

past [pɑːst] *prep (in front of)* por; *(beyond)* mais além de; *(later than)* depois de ♦ *adj* passado; *(president etc)* ex-, anterior ♦ *n* passado; **he's forty** ele tem mais de quarenta anos; **ten/quarter ~ four** quatro e dez/quinze; **for the ~ few/3 days** nos últimos/3 dias

pasta ['pæstə] *n* massa

paste [peɪst] *n* pasta; *(glue)* grude *m*, cola ♦ *vt* grudar; **tomato ~** massa de tomate

pasteurized ['pæstəraɪzd] *adj* pasteurizado

pastille ['pæstl] *n* pastilha

pastime ['pɑːstaɪm] *n* passatempo

pastry ['peɪstrɪ] *n* massa; *(cake)* bolo

pasture ['pɑːstʃə*] *n* pasto

pasty [*n* 'pæstɪ, *adj* 'peɪstɪ] *n* empadão *m* de carne ♦ *adj (complexion)* pálido

pat [pæt] *vt* dar palmadinhas em; *(dog etc)* fazer festa em

patch [pætʃ] *n* retalho; *(eye ~)* tapa-olho *m*, tampão *m; (area* aréa pequena; *(mend)* remendo ♦ *vt* remendar; **(to go through) a bad ~** (passar por) um mau pedaço; **patch up** *vt* consertar provisoriamente; *(quarrel)* resolver; **patchy**

adj (colour) desigual; (information) incompleto

pâté ['pætei] *n* patê *m*

patent ['peitnt] *n* patente *f* ♦ *vt* patentear ♦ *adj* patente, evidente; **patent leather** *n* verniz *m*

paternal [pə'tə:nl] *adj* paternal; (relation) paterno

path [pɑːθ] *n* caminho; (trail, track) trilha, senda; (trajectory) trajetória

pathetic [pə'θetik] *adj* (pitiful) patético, digno de pena; (very bad) péssimo

pathway ['pɑːθwei] *n* caminho, trilha

patience ['peiʃns] *n* paciência

patient ['peiʃnt] *adj*, *n* paciente *m/f*

patio ['pætiəu] *n* pátio

patrol [pə'trəul] *n* patrulha ♦ *vt* patrulhar; **patrol car** *n* carro de patrulha; **patrolman** (US: irreg) *n* guarda *m*, policial *m* (BR), polícia *m* (PT)

patron ['peitrən] *n* (customer) cliente *m/f*, freguês(-esa) *m/f*; (of charity) benfeitor(a) *m/f*; **~ of the arts** mecenas *m*; **patronize** ['pætrənaiz] *vt* (pej) tratar com ar de superioridade; (shop) ser cliente de (business, artist) patrocinar

patter ['pætə*] *n* (of rain) tamborilada; (of feet) passos miúdos *mpl*; (sales talk) jargão *m* profissional ♦ *vi* correr dando passinhos; (rain) tamborilar

pattern ['pætən] *n* (SEWING) molde *m*; (design) desenho

pauper ['pɔːpə*] *n* pobre *m/f*

pause [pɔːz] *n* pausa ♦ *vi* fazer uma pausa

pave [peiv] *vt* pavimentar; **to ~ the way for** preparar o terreno para

pavement ['peivmənt] (BRIT) *n* calçada (BR), passeio (PT)

pavilion [pə'viliən] *n* (SPORT) barraca

paving ['peiviŋ] *n* pavimento, calçamento; **paving stone** *n* laje *f*, paralelepípedo

paw [pɔː] *n* pata; (of cat) garra

pawn [pɔːn] *n* (CHESS) peão *m*; (fig) títere *m* ♦ *vt* empenhar; **pawnbroker** *n* agiota *m/f*

pay [pei] (pt, pp **paid**) *n* salário; (of manual worker) paga ♦ *vt* pagar; (debt) liquidar, saldar; (visit) fazer ♦ *vi* valer a pena, render; **to ~ attention (to)** prestar atenção (a); **to ~ one's respects to sb** fazer uma visita de cortesia a alguém; **pay back** *vt* (money) devolver; (person) pagar; **pay for** *vt fus* pagar a; (fig) recompensar; **pay in** *vt* depositar; **pay off** *vt* (debts) saldar, liquidar; (creditor) pagar, reembolsar ♦ *vi* (plan) valer a pena; **pay up** *vt* pagar; **payable** *adj* pagável; (cheque): **payable to** nominal em favor de; **payee** [pei'i:] *n* beneficiário(-a); **payment** *n* pagamento; **monthly payment** pagamento mensal; **pay packet** (BRIT) *n* envelope *m* de pagamento; **pay phone** *n* telefone *m* público; **pay roll** *n* folha de pagamento; **pay television** *n* televisão *f* por assinatura

PC *n abbr* (= personal computer) PC *m*

pc *abbr* = **per cent**

pea [piː] *n* ervilha

peace [piːs] *n* paz *f*; (calm) tranqüilidade *f*, quietude *f*; **peaceful** *adj* (person) tranqüilo, pacífico; (place, time) tranqüilo, sossegado

peach [piːtʃ] *n* pêssego

peacock ['piːkɔk] *n* pavão *m*

peak [piːk] *n* (of mountain: top) cume *m*; (of cap) pala, viseira; (fig) apogeu *m*

peanut ['piːnʌt] *n* amendoim *m*; **peanut butter** *n* manteiga de amendoim

pear [pɛə*] n pêra

pearl [pə:l] n pérola

peasant ['pɛznt] n camponês(-esa) m/f

peat [pi:t] n turfa

pebble ['pɛbl] n seixo, calhau m

peck [pɛk] vt (also: ~ at) bicar, dar bicadas em ♦ n bicada; (kiss) beijoca; **peckish** (BRIT: inf) adj: **I feel peckish** estou a fim de comer alguma coisa

peculiar [pɪ'kju:lɪə*] adj (strange) estranho, esquisito; (belonging to): ~ **to** próprio de

pedal ['pɛdl] n pedal m ♦ vi pedalar

pedestrian [pɪ'dɛstrɪən] n pedestre m/f (BR), peão m (PT) ♦ adj (fig) prosaico; **pedestrian crossing** (BRIT) n passagem f para pedestres (BR), passadeira (PT)

pedigree ['pɛdɪgri:] n raça; (fig) genealogia ♦ cpd (animal) de raça

pee [pi:] (inf) vi fazer xixi, mijar

peek [pi:k] vi: to ~ at espiar, espreitar

peel [pi:l] n casca ♦ vt descascar ♦ vi (paint, skin) descascar; (wallpaper) desprender-se

peep [pi:p] n (BRIT: look) espiadela; (sound) pio ♦ vi espreitar; **peep out** (BRIT) vi mostrar-se, surgir; **peephole** n vigia, olho mágico

peer [pɪə*] vi: to ~ at perscrutar, fitar ♦ n (noble) par m/f; (equal) igual m/f; (contemporary) contemporâneo(-a)

peg [pɛg] n (for coat etc) cabide m; (BRIT: also: **clothes** ~) pregador m

pelican ['pɛlɪkən] n pelicano

pellet ['pɛlɪt] n bolinha; (for shotgun) pelota de chumbo

pelt [pɛlt] vt: to ~ **sb with sth** atirar algo em alguém ♦ vi (rain: also: ~ **down**) chover a cântaros; (inf: run)

correr ♦ n pele f (não curtida)

pelvis ['pɛlvɪs] n pelvis f, bacia

pen [pɛn] n caneta; (for sheep etc) redil m, cercado

penal ['pi:nl] adj penal, **penalize** ['pi:nəlaɪz] vt impor penalidade a; (SPORT) penalizar

penalty ['pɛnltɪ] n pena, penalidade f; (fine) multa; (SPORT) punição f

pence [pɛns] (BRIT) npl of penny

pencil ['pɛnsl] n lápis m; **pencil case** n lapiseira, porta-lápis m inv; **pencil sharpener** n apontador m (de lápis) (BR), apara-lápis m inv (PT)

pendant ['pɛndnt] n pingente m

pending ['pɛndɪŋ] prep, adj pendente

penetrate ['pɛnɪtreɪt] vt penetrar

penfriend ['pɛnfrɛnd] (BRIT) n amigo(-a) por correspondência, correspondente m/f

penguin ['pɛŋgwɪn] n pingüim m

peninsula [pə'nɪnsjulə] n península

penis ['pi:nɪs] n pênis m

penitentiary [pɛnɪ'tɛnʃərɪ] (US) n penitenciária, presídio

penknife ['pɛnnaɪf] (irreg) n canivete m

penniless ['pɛnɪlɪs] adj sem dinheiro, sem um tostão

penny ['pɛnɪ] (pl **pennies** or (BRIT) pence) n pêni m; (US) cêntimo

penpal ['pɛnpæl] n amigo(-a) por correspondência, correspondente m/f

pension ['pɛnʃən] n pensão f; (old-age ~) aposentadoria, pensão do governo; **pensioner** (BRIT) n aposentado(-a) (BR), reformado(-a) (PT)

Pentagon ['pɛntəgən] n: **the ~** o Pentágono; ver quadro

PENTAGON

O Pentágono **Pentagon** é o nome dado aos escritórios do Ministério da Defesa americano, localizados em Arlington, no estado da Virgínia, por causa da forma pentagonal do edifício onde se encontram. Por extensão, o termo é utilizado também para se referir ao ministério.

---

penthouse ['penthaus] n cobertura

pent-up [pent-] adj reprimido

people ['pi:pl] npl gente f, pessoas fpl; (inhabitants) habitantes m/fpl; (citizens) povo; (POL): **the** ~ o povo ♦ n povo; **several** ~ **came** vieram várias pessoas; ~ **say that** ... dizem que ...

pepper ['pepə*] n pimenta; (vegetable) pimentão m ♦ vt apimentar; (fig): **to** ~ **with** salpicar de; **peppermint** n (sweet) bala de hortelã

peptalk ['peptɔ:k] (inf) n conversa para levantar o espírito

per [pə:*] prep por

perceive [pə'si:v] vt perceber; (notice) notar; (realize) compreender

per cent n por cento

percentage [pə'sentidʒ] n porcentagem f, percentagem f

perceptive [pə'septiv] adj perceptivo

perch [pə:tʃ] (pl **~es**) n (for bird) poleiro; (pl: inv or **~es**: fish) perca ♦ vi: **to** ~ **(on)** (bird) empoleirar-se (em); (person) encarapitar-se (em)

percolator ['pə:kəleitə*] n (also: **coffee** ~) cafeteira de filtro

perfect [adj, n 'pə:fikt, vb pə'fekt] adj perfeito; (utter) completo ♦ n (also: ~ **tense**) perfeito ♦ vt aperfeiçoar; **perfectly** adv perfeitamente

perform [pə'fɔ:m] vt (carry out) realizar, fazer; (piece of music) interpretar ♦ vi (well, badly) interpretar; **performance** n desempenho; (of play, by artist) atuação f; (of car) performance f; **performer** n (actor) artista m/f, ator (atriz) m/f; (MUS) intérprete m/f

perfume ['pə:fju:m] n perfume m

perhaps [pə'hæps] adv talvez

peril ['peril] n perigo, risco

perimeter [pə'rimitə*] n perímetro

period ['piəriəd] n período; (SCH) aula; (full stop) ponto final; (MED) menstruação f, regra ♦ adj (costume, furniture) da época; **periodic(al)** [piəri'ɔdik(l)] adj periódico; **periodical** [piəri'ɔdikl] n periódico

peripheral [pə'rifərəl] adj periférico ♦ n (COMPUT) periférico

perish ['periʃ] vi perecer; (decay) deteriorar-se

perjury ['pə:dʒəri] n (LAW) perjúrio, falso testemunho

perk [pə:k] (inf) n mordomia, regalia; **perk up** vi (cheer up) animar-se

perm [pə:m] n permanente f

permanent ['pə:mənənt] adj permanente

permission [pə'miʃən] n permissão f; (authorization) autorização f

permit [n 'pə:mit, vb pə'mit] n licença; (to enter) passe m ♦ vt permitir; (authorize) autorizar

perplex [pə'pleks] vt deixar perplexo

persecute ['pə:sikju:t] vt importunar

persevere [pə:si'viə*] vi perseverar

Persian ['pə:ʃən] adj persa ♦ n (LING) persa m; **the (~) Gulf** o golfo Pérsico

persist [pə'sist] vi: **to** ~ **(in)** persistir (em); **persistent** [pə'sistənt] adj persistente; (determined) teimoso

person ['pə:sn] n pessoa; **in** ~ em

pessoa; **personal** *adj* pessoal; (*private*) particular; (*visit*) em pessoa, pessoal; **personal assistant** *n* secretário(-a) particular; **personal computer** *n* computador *m* pessoal; **personality** [pəːsəˈnælɪtɪ] *n* personalidade *f*; **personal organizer** *n* agenda; **personal stereo** *n* Walkman ® *m*

personnel [pəːsəˈnel] *n* pessoal *m*

perspective [pəˈspɛktɪv] *n* perspectiva

Perspex [ˈpəːspɛks] ® (*BRIT*) *n* Blindex ® *m*

perspiration [pəːspɪˈreɪʃən] *n* transpiração *f*

persuade [pəˈsweɪd] *vt:* **to ~ sb to do sth** persuadir alguém a fazer algo

Peru [pəˈruː] *n* Peru *m*

pervert [*n* ˈpəːvəːt, *vb* pəˈvəːt] *n* pervertido(-a) ♦ *vt* perverter, corromper; (*truth*) distorcer

pessimist [ˈpɛsɪmɪst] *n* pessimista *m/f*; **pessimistic** [pɛsɪˈmɪstɪk] *adj* pessimista

pest [pɛst] *n* (*insect*) inseto nocivo; (*fig*) peste *f*

pester [ˈpɛstə*] *vt* incomodar

pet [pɛt] *n* animal *m* de estimação ♦ *cpd* predileto ♦ *vt* acariciar ♦ *vi* (*inf*) acariciar-se; **teacher's ~** (*favourite*) preferido(-a) do professor

petal [ˈpɛtl] *n* pétala

peter out [ˈpiːtə*-] *vi* (*conversation*) esgotar-se; (*road etc*) acabar-se

petite [pəˈtiːt] *adj* delicado, mignon

petition [pəˈtɪʃən] *n* petição *f*; (*list of signatures*) abaixo-assinado

petrified [ˈpɛtrɪfaɪd] *adj* (*fig*) petrificado, paralisado

petrol [ˈpɛtrəl] (*BRIT*) *n* gasolina; **two/four-star ~** gasolina de duas/ quatro estrelas

petroleum [pəˈtrəulɪəm] *n* petróleo

petrol: **petrol pump** (*BRIT*) *n* bomba de gasolina; **petrol station** (*BRIT*) *n* posto (*BR*) or bomba (*PT*) de gasolina; **petrol tank** (*BRIT*) *n* tanque *m* de gasolina

petticoat [ˈpɛtɪkəut] *n* anágua

petty [ˈpɛtɪ] *adj* (*mean*) mesquinho; (*unimportant*) insignificante; **petty cash** *n* fundo para despesas miúdas, caixa pequena, fundo de caixa

pew [pjuː] *n* banco (de igreja)

pewter [ˈpjuːtə*] *n* peltre *m*

phantom [ˈfæntəm] *n* fantasma *m*

pharmacy [ˈfaːməsɪ] *n* farmácia

phase [feɪz] *n* fase *f* ♦ *vt:* **to ~ in/out** introduzir/retirar por etapas

PhD *n abbr* = Doctor of Philosophy

pheasant [ˈfɛznt] *n* faisão *m*

phenomenon [fəˈnɔmɪnən] (*pl* **phenomena**) *n* fenômeno

philosophical [fɪləˈsɔfɪkl] *adj* filosófico; (*fig*) calmo, sereno

philosophy [fɪˈlɔsəfɪ] *n* filosofia

phobia [ˈfəubjə] *n* fobia

phone [fəun] *n* telefone *m* ♦ *vt* telefonar para, ligar para; **to be on the ~** ter telefone; (*be calling*) estar no telefone; **phone back** *vt, vi* ligar de volta; **phone up** *vt* telefonar para ♦ *vi* telefonar; **phone book** *n* lista telefônica; **phone box** (*BRIT*) *n* cabine *f* telefônica; **phone call** *n* telefonema *m*, ligada; **phone card** *n* cartão para uso em telefone público; **phone in** (*BRIT*) *n* (*RADIO*) programa *com participação dos ouvintes*; (*TV*) *programa com participação dos espectadores*; **phone number** *n* (número de) telefone

phonetics [fəˈnɛtɪks] *n* fonética

phoney [ˈfəunɪ] *adj* falso; (*person*) fingido

photo [ˈfəutəu] *n* foto *f*

photo... [ˈfəutəu] *prefix* foto...;
photocopier *n* fotocopiadora *f*;

photocopy n fotocópia, xerox ® m ♦ vt fotocopiar, xerocar

photograph ['fəʊtəgrɑ:f] n fotografia ♦ vt fotografar; **photographer** [fə'tɔgrəfə*] n fotógrafo(-a); **photography** [fə'tɔgrəfi] n fotografia

phrase [freɪz] n frase f ♦ vt expressar; **phrase book** n livro de expressões idiomáticas (para turistas)

physical ['fɪzɪkl] adj físico

physician [fɪ'zɪʃən] n médico(-a)

physics ['fɪzɪks] n física

physiotherapy [fɪzɪəʊ'θerəpi] n fisioterapia

physique [fɪ'zi:k] n físico

pianist ['pi:ənɪst] n pianista m/f

piano [pi'ænəʊ] n piano

pick [pɪk] n (tool: also: ~axe) picareta ♦ vt (select) escolher, selecionar; (gather) colher; (remove) tirar; (lock) forçar; **take your ~** escolha o que quiser; **the ~ of** o melhor de; **to ~ one's nose** colocar o dedo no nariz; **to ~ one's teeth** palitar os dentes; **to ~ a quarrel with sb** comprar uma briga com alguém; **pick at** vt fus (food) beliscar; **pick on** vt fus (person: criticize) criticar; (: treat badly) azucrinar, aporrinhar; **pick out** vt escolher; (distinguish) distinguir; **pick up** vi (improve) melhorar ♦ vt (from floor, AUT) apanhar; (POLICE) prender; (collect) buscar; (for sexual encounter) paquerar; (learn) aprender; (RADIO) pegar; **to ~ up speed** acelerar; **to ~ o.s. up** levantar-se

picket ['pɪkɪt] n (in strike) piquete m ♦ vt formar piquete em frente de

pickle ['pɪkl] n (also: ~s: condiment) picles mpl; (fig: mess) apuro ♦ vt (in vinegar) conservar em vinagre; (in salt) conservar em sal e água

pickpocket ['pɪkpɔkɪt] n batedor(a) m/f de carteira (BR),

carteirista m/f (PT)

picnic ['pɪknɪk] n piquenique m

picture ['pɪktʃə*] n quadro; (painting) pintura; (drawing) desenho; (etching) água-forte f; (photograph) foto(grafia) f; (TV) imagem f; (film) filme m; (fig: description) descrição f; (: situation) conjuntura ♦ vt imaginar-se; **the ~s** npl (BRIT: inf) o cinema; **picture book** n livro de figuras

pie [paɪ] n (vegetable) pastelão m; (fruit) torta; (meat) empadão m

piece [pi:s] n pedaço; (portion) fatia; (item): **a ~ of clothing/furniture/advice** uma roupa/um móvel/um conselho ♦ vt: **to ~ together** juntar; **to take to ~s** desmontar; **piecemeal** adv pouco a pouco; **piecework** n trabalho por empreitada or peça

pie chart n gráfico de setores

pier [pɪə*] n cais m; (jetty) embarcadouro, molhe m

pierce [pɪəs] vt furar, perfurar

pig [pɪg] n porco; (fig) porcalhão(-lhona) m/f; (pej: unkind person) grosseiro(-a); (: greedy person) ganancioso(-a)

pigeon ['pɪdʒən] n pombo; **pigeonhole** n escaninho

piggy bank ['pɪgɪ-] n cofre em forma de porquinho

pigskin ['pɪgskɪn] n couro de porco

pigsty ['pɪgstaɪ] n chiqueiro

pigtail ['pɪgteɪl] n rabo-de-cavalo, trança

pike [paɪk] n (pl inv or ~s) (fish) lúcio

pilchard ['pɪltʃəd] n sardinha

pile [paɪl] n (heap) monte m; (of carpet) pêlo; (of cloth) lado felpudo ♦ vt (also: ~ up) empilhar ♦ vi (also: ~ up) empilhar-se; (: problems, work) acumular-se; **pile into** vt fus (car) apinhar-se

piles [paɪlz] *npl* hemorróidas *fpl*

pile-up *n* (AUT) engavetamento

pilgrim ['pɪlgrɪm] *n* peregrino(-a)

pill [pɪl] *n* pílula, **the ~** a pílula

pillar ['pɪlə*] *n* pilar *m*; **pillar box** (BRIT) *n* caixa coletora (do correio) (BR), marco do correio (PT)

pillion ['pɪljən] *n*: **to ride ~** andar na garupa

pillow ['pɪləʊ] *n* travesseiro (BR), almofada (PT); **pillowcase** *n* fronha

pilot ['paɪlət] *n* piloto(-a) ♦ *cpd* (*scheme etc*) piloto *inv* ♦ *vt* pilotar; **pilot light** *n* piloto

pimp [pɪmp] *n* cafetão *m* (BR), cáften *m* (PT)

pimple ['pɪmpl] *n* espinha

PIN [pɪn] *n abbr* (= *personal identification number*) número de identificação pessoal, senha

pin [pɪn] *n* alfinete *m* ♦ *vt* alfinetar; **~s and needles** comichão *f*, sensação *f* de formigamento; **to ~ sth on sb** (*fig*) culpar alguém de algo; **pin down** *vt* (*fig*): **to ~ sb down** conseguir que alguém se defina or tome atitude

pinafore ['pɪnəfɔː*] *n* (*also*: ~ *dress*) avental *m*

pincers ['pɪnsəz] *npl* pinça, tenaz *f*

pinch [pɪntʃ] *n* (*of salt etc*) pitada ♦ *vt* beliscar; (*inf*: *steal*) afanar; **at a ~** em último caso

pincushion ['pɪnkuʃən] *n* alfineteira

pine [paɪn] *n* pinho ♦ *vi*: **to ~ for** ansiar por; **pine away** *vi* consumir-se, definhar

pineapple ['paɪnæpl] *n* abacaxi *m* (BR), ananás *m* (PT)

ping-pong ['pɪŋpɔŋ] ® *n* pingue-pongue *m*

pink [pɪŋk] *adj* cor de rosa *inv* ♦ *n* (*colour*) cor *f* de rosa; (BOT) cravo, cravina

PIN number ['pɪn-] *n* = PIN

pinpoint ['pɪnpɔɪnt] *vt* (*discover*) descobrir; (*explain*) identificar; (*locate*) localizar com precisão

pint [paɪnt] *n* quartilho (BRIT: = 568CC; US: = 473CC)

pioneer [paɪə'nɪə*] *n* pioneiro(-a)

pious ['paɪəs] *adj* pio, devoto

pip [pɪp] *n* (*seed*) caroço, semente *f*; **the ~s** *npl* (BRIT: *time signal on radio*) ≈ o toque de seis segundos

pipe [paɪp] *n* cano; (*for smoking*) cachimbo ♦ *vt* canalizar, encanar; **~s** *npl* (*also*: **bag~**) gaita de foles; **pipe down** (*inf*) *vi* calar o bico, meter a viola no saco; **pipeline** *n* (*for oil*) oleoduto; (*for gas*) gaseoduto

piping ['paɪpɪŋ] *adv*: **~ hot** chiando de quente

pirate ['paɪərət] *n* pirata *m* ♦ *vt* piratear

Pisces ['paɪsiːz] *n* Pisces *m*, Peixes *mpl*

piss [pɪs] (*inf!*) *vi* mijar; **pissed** (*inf!*) *adj* (*drunk*) bêbado, de porre

pistol ['pɪstl] *n* pistola

piston ['pɪstən] *n* pistão *m*, êmbolo

pit [pɪt] *n* cova, fossa; (*quarry, hole in surface of sth*) buraco; (*also*: **coal ~**) mina de carvão ♦ *vt*: **to ~ one's wits against sb** competir em conhecimento or inteligência contra alguém; **~s** *npl* (AUT) box *m*

pitch [pɪtʃ] *n* (MUS) tom *m*; (*fig*: *degree*) intensidade *f*; (BRIT: *SPORT*) campo; (*tar*) piche *m*, breu *m* ♦ *vt* (*throw*) arremessar, lançar; (*tent*) armar ♦ *vi* (*fall forwards*) cair (para frente); **pitch-black** *adj* escuro como o breu

pitfall ['pɪtfɔːl] *n* perigo (imprevisto), armadilha

pitiful ['pɪtɪful] *adj* comovente, tocante

pittance ['pɪtns] n ninharia, miséria

pity ['pɪtɪ] n compaixão f, piedade f
♦ vt ter pena de, compadecer-se de

pizza ['piːtsə] n pizza

placard ['plækɑːd] n placar m; (in march etc) cartaz m

placate [plə'keɪt] vt apaziguar, aplacar

place [pleɪs] n lugar m; (position) posição f; (post) posto; (role) papel m; (home): **at/to his ~** na/para a casa dele ♦ vt pôr, colocar; (identify) identificar, situar; **to take ~** realizar-se; (occur) ocorrer; **out of ~** (not suitable) fora de lugar, deslocado; **in the first ~** em primeiro lugar; **to change ~s with sb** trocar de lugar com alguém; **to be ~d** (in race, exam) classificar-se

plague [pleɪg] n (MED) peste f; (fig) praga ♦ vt atormentar, importunar

plaice [pleɪs] n inv solha

plain [pleɪn] adj (unpatterned) liso; (clear) claro, evidente; (simple) simples inv, despretensioso; (not handsome) sem atrativos ♦ adv claramente, com franqueza ♦ n planície f, campina; **plain chocolate** n chocolate m amargo; **plain-clothes** adj (police officer) à paisana; **plainly** adv claramente, obviamente; (hear, see) facilmente; (state) francamente

plaintiff ['pleɪntɪf] n querelante m/f, queixoso(-a)

plait [plæt] n trança, dobra

plan [plæn] n plano; (scheme) projeto; (schedule) programa m ♦ vt planejar (BR), planear (PT) ♦ vi fazer planos; **to ~ to do** pretender fazer

plane [pleɪn] n (AVIAT) avião m; (also: ~ **tree**) plátano; (fig: level) nível m; (tool) plaina; (MATH) plano

planet ['plænɪt] n planeta m

plank [plæŋk] n tábua

planning ['plænɪŋ] n planejamento

(BR), planeamento (PT); **family ~** planejamento or planeamento familiar

plant [plɑːnt] n planta; (machinery) maquinaria; (factory) usina, fábrica ♦ vt plantar; (field) semear; (bomb) colocar, pôr

plaster ['plɑːstə*] n (for walls) reboco; (also: **~ of Paris**) gesso; (BRIT: also: **sticking ~**) esparadrapo, band-aid m ♦ vt rebocar; (cover): **to ~ with** encher or cobrir de; **plastered** (inf) adj bêbado, de porre

plastic ['plæstɪk] n plástico ♦ adj de plástico; **plastic bag** n sacola de plástico

plastic surgery n cirurgia plástica

plate [pleɪt] n prato, chapa; (dental) chapa; (in book) gravura; **gold-/silver ~** placa de ouro-/prata

plateau ['plætəu] (pl ~**s** or ~**x**) n planalto

platform ['plætfɔːm] n (RAIL) plataforma (BR), cais m (PT); (at meeting) tribuna; (raised structure: for landing etc) plataforma; (BRIT: of bus) plataforma; (POL) programa m partidário

platinum ['plætɪnəm] n platina

plausible ['plɔːzɪbl] adj plausível; (person) convincente

play [pleɪ] n (THEATRE) obra, peça f ♦ vt jogar; (team) jogar contra; (music) tocar; (role) fazer o papel de ♦ vi (music) tocar; (frolic) brincar; **to ~ safe** não se arriscar, não correr riscos; **play down** vt minimizar; **play up** vi (person) dar trabalho; (TV, car) estar com defeito; **playboy** n playboy m; **player** n jogador(a) m/f; (THEATRE) ator (atriz) m/f; (MUS) músico(-a); **playful** adj brincalhão(-lhona); **playground** n (in park) playground m; (in school) pátio de recreio; **playgroup** n espécie de jardim de infância; **playing card** n carta de baralho; **playing**

field n campo de esportes (BR) or jogos (PT); **playmate** n colega m/f, camarada m/f; **playpen** n cercado para crianças; **plaything** n brinquedo; (fig) joguete m; **playtime** n (SCH) recreio; **playwright** n dramaturgo(-a)

plc abbr = **public limited company**

plea [pli:] n (request) apelo, petição f; (LAW) defesa

plead [pli:d] vt (LAW) defender, advogar; (give as excuse) alegar ♦ vi (LAW) declarar-se; (beg): **to ~ with sb** suplicar or rogar a alguém

pleasant ['plɛznt] adj agradável; (person) simpático

please [pli:z] excl por favor ♦ vt agradar a, dar prazer a ♦ vi agradar, dar prazer; (think fit): **do as you ~** faça o que or como quiser; **~ yourself!** (inf) como você quiser!, você que sabe!; **pleased** adj (happy): **pleased (with)** satisfeito (com); **pleased to meet you** prazer (em conhecê-lo); **pleasing** adj agradável

pleasure ['plɛʒə*] n prazer m; **"it's a ~"** "não tem de quê"

pleat [pli:t] n prega

pledge [plɛdʒ] n (promise) promessa ♦ vt prometer; **to ~ support for sb** empenhar-se a apoiar alguém

plentiful ['plɛntiful] adj abundante

plenty ['plɛntɪ] n: **~ of** (food, money) bastante; (jobs, people) muitos(-as)

pliable ['plaɪəbl] adj flexível; (fig: person) adaptável, moldável

pliers ['plaɪəz] npl alicate m

plimsolls ['plɪmsəlz] (BRIT) npl tênis mpl

plod [plɔd] vi caminhar pesadamente; (fig) trabalhar laboriosamente

plonk [plɔŋk] (inf) n (BRIT: wine) zurrapa ♦ vt: **to ~ sth down** deixar cair algo (pesadamente)

plot [plɔt] n (scheme) conspiração f,

complô m; (of story, play) enredo, trama; (of land) lote m ♦ vt (conspire) tramar, planejar (BR), planear (PT); (AVIAT, NAUT, MATH) plotar ♦ vi conspirar; **a vegetable ~** (BRIT) uma horta

plough [plau] (US plow) n arado ♦ vt arar; **to ~ money into** investir dinheiro em; **plough through** vt fus abrir caminho por; **ploughman's lunch** (BRIT) n lanche de pão, queijo e picles

ploy [plɔɪ] n estratagema m

pluck [plʌk] vt (fruit) colher; (musical instrument) dedilhar; (bird) depenar ♦ n coragem f, puxão m; **to ~ one's eyebrows** fazer as sobrancelhas; **to ~ up courage** criar coragem

plug [plʌg] n (ELEC) tomada (BR), ficha (PT); (in sink) tampa; (AUT: also: spark(ing) ~) vela (de ignição) ♦ vt (hole) tapar; (inf: advertise) fazer propaganda de; **plug in** vt (ELEC) ligar

plum [plʌm] n (fruit) ameixa ♦ cpd (inf): **a ~ job** um emprego jóia

plumber ['plʌmə*] n bombeiro(-a) (BR), encanador(a) m/f (BR), canalizador(a) m/f (PT)

plumbing ['plʌmɪŋ] n (trade) ofício de encanador; (piping) encanamento

plummet ['plʌmɪt] vi: **to ~ (down)** (bird, aircraft) cair rapidamente; (price) baixar rapidamente

plump [plʌmp] adj roliço, rechonchudo ♦ vi: **to ~ for** (inf: choose) escolher, optar por; **plump up** vt (cushion) afofar

plunder ['plʌndə*] n pilhagem f; (loot) despojo ♦ vt pilhar, espoliar

plunge [plʌndʒ] n (dive) salto; (fig) queda ♦ vt (hand, knife) enfiar, meter ♦ vi (fall, fig) cair; (dive) mergulhar; **to take the ~** topar a parada

plural ['pluərl] adj plural ♦ n plural m

plus [plʌs] n (also: **~ sign**) sinal m de adição ♦ prep mais; **ten/twenty ~** dez/vinte e tantos

plush [plʌʃ] adj suntuoso

ply [plaɪ] n (of wool) fio ♦ vt (a trade) exercer ♦ vi (ship) ir e vir; **to ~ sb with drink/questions** bombardear alguém com bebidas/perguntas

plywood n madeira compensada

PM (BRIT) n abbr = **Prime Minister**

p.m. adv abbr (= post meridiem) da tarde, da noite

PMT n abbr (= premenstrual tension) TPM f, tensão f pré-menstrual

pneumatic drill [njuː'mætɪk-] n perfuratriz f

poach [pəutʃ] vt (COOK: fish) escaldar; (: eggs) fazer pochê (BR), escalfar (PT); (steal) furtar ♦ vi caçar (or pescar) em propriedade alheia

PO Box n abbr (= Post Office Box) caixa postal

pocket ['pɔkɪt] n bolso; (fig: small area) pedaço ♦ vt meter no bolso; (steal) embolsar; **to be out of ~** (BRIT) perder, ter prejuízo; **pocketbook** (US) n carteira f; **pocket knife** (irreg) n canivete m; **pocket money** n dinheiro para despesas miúdas; (for child) mesada

pod [pɔd] n vagem f

podgy ['pɔdʒɪ] (inf) adj gorducho, rechonchudo

podiatrist [pɔ'diːətrɪst] (US) n pedicuro(-a)

poem ['pəuɪm] n poema m

poet ['pəuɪt] n poeta (poetisa) m/f; **poetic** [pəu'ɛtɪk] adj poético; **poetry** ['pəuɪtrɪ] n poesia

momento; (stage) estágio; (ELEC; also: **power ~**) tomada; (also: **decimal ~**): **2 ~ 3 (2.3)** dois vírgula três ♦ vt mostrar; (gun etc): **to ~ sth at sb** apontar algo para alguém ♦ vi: **to ~ at** apontar para; **~s** npl (AUT) platinado, contato; (RAIL) agulhas fpl; **to be on the ~ of doing sth** estar prestes a or a ponto de fazer algo; **to make a ~ of** fazer questão de, insistir em; **to get the ~** perceber; **to miss the ~** compreender mal; **to come to the ~** ir ao assunto; **there's no ~ (in doing)** não há razão (para fazer); **point out** vt (in debate etc) ressaltar; **point to** vt fus (fig) indicar; **point-blank** adv categoricamente; (also: **at point-blank range**) à queima-roupa; **pointed** adj (stick etc) pontudo; (remark) mordaz; **pointer** n (on chart) indicador m; (on machine) ponteiro; (fig) dica; **pointless** adj (useless) inútil; (senseless) sem sentido; **point of view** n ponto de vista

poise [pɔɪz] n (composure) elegância; (calmness) serenidade f

poison ['pɔɪzn] n veneno ♦ vt envenenar; **poisonous** adj venenoso; (fumes etc) tóxico

poke [pəuk] vt cutucar; (put): **to ~ sth in(to)** enfiar or meter algo em; **poke about** vi escarafunchar

poker ['pəukə*] n atiçador m (de brasas); (CARDS) pôquer m

Poland ['pəulənd] n Polônia

polar ['pəulə*] adj polar; **polar bear** n urso polar

Pole [pəul] n polonês(-esa) m/f

pole [pəul] n vara; (GEO) pólo; (telegraph ~) poste m; (flag~) mastro; **pole bean** (US) n feijão-trepador m; **pole vault** n salto com vara

police [pə'liːs] n polícia ♦ vt policiar; **police car** n rádio-patrulha f;

policeman (*irreg*) *n* policial *m* (*BR*), polícia *m* (*PT*); **police station** *n* delegacia (de polícia) (*BR*), esquadra (*PT*); **policewoman** (*irreg*) *n* policial *f* (feminina) (*BR*), mulher *f* polícia (*PT*)

policy ['pɔlɪsɪ] *n* política; (*also*: **insurance ~**) apólice *f*

polio ['pəulɪəu] *n* pólio(mielite) *f*

Polish ['pəulɪʃ] *adj* polonês(-esa) ♦ *n* (*LING*) polonês *m*

polish ['pɔlɪʃ] *n* (*for shoes*) graxa; (*for floor*) cera (para encerar); (*shine*) brilho; (*fig*) refinamento, requinte *m* ♦ *vt* (*shoes*) engraxar; (*make shiny*) lustrar, dar brilho a; **polish off** *vt* (*work*) dar os arremates a; (*food*) raspar

polite [pə'laɪt] *adj* educado; **politeness** *n* gentileza, cortesia

political [pə'lɪtɪkl] *adj* político

politician [pɔlɪ'tɪʃən] *n* político(-a)

politics ['pɔlɪtɪks] *n, npl* política

poll [pəul] *n* (*votes*) votação *f*; (*also*: **opinion ~**) pesquisa, sondagem *f* ♦ *vt* (*votes*) receber, obter

pollen ['pɔlən] *n* pólen *m*

polling day ['pəulɪŋ-] (*BRIT*) *n* dia *m* de eleição

pollute [pə'luːt] *vt* poluir; **pollution** *n* poluição *f*

polo-necked ['pəuləunɛkt] *adj* de gola rulê

polyester [pɔlɪ'ɛstə*] *n* poliéster *m*

polystyrene [pɔlɪ'staɪriːn] *n* isopor ® *m*

polythene ['pɔlɪθiːn] *n* politeno

pomegranate ['pɔmɪɡrænɪt] *n* romã *f*

pond [pɔnd] *n* (*natural*) lago pequeno; (*artificial*) tanque *m*

ponder ['pɔndə*] *vt, vi* ponderar, meditar (sobre)

pony ['pəunɪ] *n* pônei *m*; **ponytail** *n* rabo-de-cavalo; **pony trekking**

(*BRIT*) *n* excursão *f* em pônei

poodle ['puːdl] *n* cão-d'água *m*

pool [puːl] *n* (*puddle*) poça, charco; (*pond*) lago; (*also*: **swimming ~**) piscina; (*fig: of light*) feixe *m*; (: *of liquid*) poça; (*SPORT*) sinuca ♦ *vt* juntar; **~s** *npl* (*football ~s*) loteria esportiva (*BR*), totobola (*PT*); **typing** (*BRIT*) *or* **secretary** (*US*) **~** seção *f* de datilografia

poor [puə*] *adj* pobre; (*bad*) inferior, mau ♦ *npl*: **the ~** os pobres; **~ in** (*resources etc*) deficiente em; **poorly** *adj* adoentado, indisposto ♦ *adv* mal

pop [pɔp] *n* (*sound*) estalo, estouro; (*MUS*) pop *m*; (*US: inf: father*) papai *m*; (*inf: fizzy drink*) bebida gasosa ♦ *vt*: **to ~ sth into/onto etc** (*put*) pôr em/sobre *etc* ♦ *vi* estourar; (*cork*) saltar; **pop in** *vi* dar um pulo; **pop out** *vi* dar uma saída; **pop up** *vi* surgir, aparecer inesperadamente; **popcorn** *n* pipoca

pope [pəup] *n* papa *m*

poplar ['pɔplə*] *n* álamo, choupo

poppy ['pɔpɪ] *n* papoula

popsicle ['pɔpsɪkl] ® (*US*) *n* picolé *m*

popular ['pɔpjulə*] *adj* popular; (*person*) querido

population [pɔpju'leɪʃən] *n* população *f*

porcelain ['pɔːslɪn] *n* porcelana

porch [pɔːtʃ] *n* pórtico; (*US: verandah*) varanda

porcupine ['pɔːkjupaɪn] *n* porco-espinho

pore [pɔː*] *n* poro ♦ *vi*: **to ~ over** examinar minuciosamente

pork [pɔːk] *n* carne *f* de porco

pornography [pɔː'nɔɡrəfɪ] *n* pornografia

porpoise ['pɔːpəs] *n* golfinho, boto

porridge ['pɔrɪdʒ] *n* mingau *m* (de aveia)

port [pɔ:t] *n* (*harbour*) porto; (NAUT: *left side*) bombordo; (*wine*) vinho do Porto; **~ of call** porto de escala

portable ['pɔ:təbl] *adj* portátil

porter ['pɔ:tə*] *n* (*for luggage*) carregador *m*; (*doorkeeper*) porteiro

portfolio [pɔ:t'fəuliəu] *n* (*case*) pasta; (POL) pasta ministerial; (FINANCE) carteira de ações ou títulos; (*of artist*) pasta, portfólio

porthole ['pɔ:thəul] *n* vigia

portion ['pɔ:ʃən] *n* porção *f*, quinhão *m*; (*of food*) ração *f*

portrait ['pɔ:treit] *n* retrato

portray [pɔ:'trei] *vt* retratar; (*act*) interpretar

Portugal ['pɔ:tjugl] *n* Portugal *m* (*no article*)

Portuguese [pɔ:tju'gi:z] *adj* português(-esa) ♦ *n inv* português(-esa) *m/f*; (LING) português *m*

pose [pəuz] *n* postura, pose *f* ♦ *vi* (*pretend*): **to ~ as** fazer-se passar por ♦ *vt* (*question*) fazer; (*problem*) causar; **to ~ for** (*painting*) posar para

posh [pɔʃ] (*inf*) *adj* fino, chique; (*upper-class*) de classe alta

position [pə'ziʃən] *n* posição *f*; (*job*) cargo; (*situation*) situação *f* ♦ *vt* colocar, situar

positive ['pɔzitiv] *adj* positivo; (*certain*) certo; (*definite*) definitivo

possess [pə'zes] *vt* possuir; **possession** *n* posse *f*, possessão *f*; **possessions** *npl* (*belongings*) pertences *mpl*; **to take possession of sth** tomar posse de algo

possibility [pɔsi'biliti] *n* possibilidade *f*; (*of sth happening*) probabilidade *f*

possible ['pɔsibl] *adj* possível; **possibly** *adv* pode ser, talvez; (*surprise*): **what could they possibly want with me?** o que eles podem querer comigo?; (*emphasizing*

effort): **they did everything they possibly could** eles fizeram tudo o que podiam; **I cannot possibly come** estou impossibilitado de vir

post [pəust] *n* (BRIT: *mail*) correio; (*job*) cargo, posto; (*pole*) poste *m*; (MIL) nomeação *f* ♦ *vt* (BRIT: *send by* ~) pôr no correio; (: *appoint*): **to ~ to** destinar a; **postage** *n* porte *m*, franquia; **postal order** *n* vale *m* postal; **postbox** (BRIT) *n* caixa de correio; **postcard** *n* cartão *m* postal; **postcode** (BRIT) *n* código postal, ≈ CEP *m* (BR)

poster ['pəustə*] *n* cartaz *m*; (*as decoration*) pôster *m*

postman ['pəustmən] (*irreg*) *n* carteiro

postmark ['pəustma:k] *n* carimbo do correio

postmortem [pəust'mɔ:təm] *n* autópsia

post office *n* (*building*) agência do correio, correio; (*organization*) ≈ Empresa Nacional dos Correios e Telégrafos (BR), ≈ Correios, Telégrafos e Telefones (PT)

postpone [pəs'pəun] *vt* adiar

posture ['pɔstʃə*] *n* postura; (*fig*) atitude *f*

postwar [pəust'wɔ:*] *adj* de após-guerra

pot [pɔt] *n* (*for cooking*) panela; (*for flowers*) vaso; (*container*, *tea*~, *coffee*~) pote *m*; (*inf*: *marijuana*) maconha ♦ *vt* (*plant*) plantar em vaso; **to go to ~** (*inf*) arruinar-se, degringolar

potato [pə'teitəu] (*pl* **~es**) *n* batata; **potato peeler** *n* descascador *m* de batatas

potent ['pəutnt] *adj* poderoso; (*drink*) forte; (*man*) potente

potential [pə'tenʃl] *adj* potencial ♦ *n* potencial *m*

pothole ['pɔthəul] n (in road) buraco; (BRIT: underground) caldeirão m, cova; **potholing** (BRIT) n: **to go potholing** dedicar-se à espeleologia

potluck [pɔt'lʌk] n: **to take ~** contentar-se com o que houver

potter ['pɔtə*] n (artistic) ceramista m/f; (artisan) oleiro(-a) ♦ vi (BRIT): **to ~ around, ~ about** ocupar-se com pequenos trabalhos; **pottery** n cerâmica; (factory) olaria

potty ['pɔtɪ] adj (inf: mad) maluco, doido ♦ n penico

pouch [pautʃ] n (ZOOL) bolsa; (for tobacco) tabaqueira

poultry ['pəultrɪ] n aves fpl domésticas; (meat) carne f de aves domésticas

pounce [pauns] vi: **to ~ on** lançar-se sobre; (person) agarrar em; (fig: mistake etc) apontar

pound [paund] n libra (weight = 453g, 16 ounces; money = 100 pence) ♦ vt (beat) socar, esmurrar; (crush) triturar ♦ vi (heart) bater

pour [pɔ:*] vt despejar; (drink) servir ♦ vi correr, jorrar; **pour away** vt esvaziar, decantar; **pour in** vi (people) entrar numa enxurrada; (information) chegar numa enxurrada; **pour off** vt esvaziar, decantar; **pour out** vi (people) sair aos borbotões ♦ vt (drink) servir; (fig) extravasar; **pouring** adj: **pouring rain** chuva torrencial

pout [paut] vi fazer beicinho or biquinho

poverty ['pɔvətɪ] n pobreza, miséria

powder ['paudə*] n pó m; (face ~) pó-de-arroz m ♦ vt (face) empoar, passar pó em; **powdered milk** n leite m em pó; **powder room** n toucador m, banheiro de senhoras

power ['pauə*] n poder m; (of explosion, engine) força, potência; (abil-ity) poder, poderio; (electricity) força; **to be in ~** estar no poder; **power cut** (BRIT) n corte m de energia, blecaute m (BR); **powerful** adj poderoso; (engine) potente; (body) vigoroso; (blow) violento; (argument) convincente; (emotion) intenso; **powerless** adj impotente; **power point** (BRIT) n tomada; **power station** n central f elétrica

pp abbr (= per procurationem) p.p.; = pages

PR n abbr = **public relations**

practical ['præktɪkl] adj prático; **practical joke** n brincadeira, peça

practice ['præktɪs] n (custom) costume m, hábito; (exercise) prática; (of profession) exercício; (training) treinamento; (MED) consultório; (LAW) escritório ♦ vt, vi (US) = **practise**; **in ~** na prática; **out of ~** destreinado

practise ['præktɪs] (US **practice**) vt praticar; (profession) exercer; (sport) treinar ♦ vi (doctor) ter consultório; (lawyer) ter escritório; (train) treinar, praticar

practitioner [præk'tɪʃənə*] n (MED) médico(-a)

prairie ['prɛərɪ] n campina, pradaria

praise [preɪz] n louvor m; (admira-tion) elogio ♦ vt elogiar, louvar; **praiseworthy** adj louvável, digno de elogio

pram [præm] (BRIT) n carrinho de bebê

prance [prɑːns] vi: **to ~ about/up and down** etc (horse) curvetear, fazer cabriolas; (person) andar espalhafatosamente

prank [præŋk] n travessura, peça

prawn [prɔːn] n pitu m; (small) camarão m

pray [preɪ] vi: **to ~ for/that** rezar por/para que; **prayer** [prɛə*] n (activity) reza; (words) oração f, prece f

preach [pri:tʃ] vt apregar ♦ vi pregar; (pej) catequizar

precede [prɪ'si:d] vt preceder

precedent ['presɪdənt] n precedente m

preceding [prɪ'si:dɪŋ] adj anterior

precinct [pri:sɪŋkt] n (US: district) distrito policial; ~s npl (of large building) arredores mpl; **pedestrian ~** (BRIT) zona para pedestres (BR) or peões (PT); **shopping ~** (BRIT) zona comercial

precious ['preʃəs] adj precioso

precipitate [prɪ'sɪpɪteɪt] vt precipitar, acelerar

precise [prɪ'saɪs] adj exato, preciso; (plans) detalhado

precocious [prɪ'kəuʃəs] adj precoce

predecessor ['pri:dɪsesə*] n predecessor(a) m/f, antepassado(-a)

predicament [prɪ'dɪkəmənt] n situação f difícil, apuro

predict [prɪ'dɪkt] vt prever, predizer, prognosticar; **predictable** adj previsível

predominantly [prɪ'dɔmɪnəntlɪ] adv predominantemente, na maioria

preen [pri:n] vt: **to ~ itself** (bird) limpar e alisar as penas (com o bico); **to ~ o.s.** enfeitar-se, envaidecer-se

prefab ['pri:fæb] n casa pré-fabricada

preface ['prefəs] n prefácio

prefect ['pri:fekt] n (BRIT: SCH) monitor(a) m/f, tutor(a) m/f; (in Brazil) prefeito(-a)

prefer [prɪ'fə:*] vt preferir; **preferably** ['prefrəblɪ] adv de preferência; **preferential** [prefə'renʃəl] adj: **preferential treatment** preferência

prefix ['pri:fɪks] n prefixo

pregnancy ['pregnənsɪ] n gravidez

f; (animal) prenhez f

pregnant ['pregnənt] adj grávida; (animal) prenha

prehistoric [pri:hɪs'tɔrɪk] adj pré-histórico

prejudice ['predʒudɪs] n preconceito; **prejudiced** adj cheio de preconceitos; **to be prejudiced against sb/sth** estar com prevenção contra alguém/algo

premarital [pri:'mærɪtl] adj pré-nupcial

premature ['premətʃuə*] adj prematuro

première ['premɪeə*] n estréia

premise ['premɪs] n premissa; **~s** npl (of business, institution) local m

premium ['pri:mɪəm] n prêmio; **to be at a ~** ser caro

premonition [premə'nɪʃən] n presságio, pressentimento

preoccupied [pri:'ɔkjupaɪd] adj preocupado

prepaid [pri:'peɪd] adj com porte pago

preparation [prepə'reɪʃən] n preparação f; **~s** npl (arrangements) preparativos mpl

preparatory [prɪ'pærətərɪ] adj preparatório

prepare [prɪ'peə*] vt preparar ♦ vi: **to ~ for** preparar-se or aprontar-se para; **~d to** disposto a; **~d for** pronto para

preposition [prepə'zɪʃən] n preposição f

preposterous [prɪ'pɔstərəs] adj absurdo, disparatado

prerequisite [pri:'rekwɪzɪt] n pré-requisito, condição f prévia

prescribe [prɪ'skraɪb] vt prescrever; (MED) receitar

prescription [prɪ'skrɪpʃən] n receita

presence ['prezns] n presença; (spirit) espectro

present [adj, n 'preznt, vb pri'zent]
adj presente; (current) actual ♦ n presente m; (actuality): **the ~** o presente ♦ vt (give): **to ~ sth to sb, to ~ sb with sth** entregar algo a alguém; (information, programme, threat) apresentar; (describe) descrever; at ~ no momento, agora; **to give sb a ~** presentear alguém; **presentation** [prezn'teɪʃən] n apresentação f; (ceremony) entrega; (of plan etc) exposição f; **present-day** adj atual, de hoje; **presenter** n apresentador(a) m/f; **presently** adv (after) logo após; (soon) logo, em breve; (now) atualmente

preservative [pri'zə:vətiv] n conservante m

preserve [pri'zə:v] vt (situation) conservar, manter; (building, manuscript) preservar; (food) pôr em conserva ♦ n (often pl: jam) geléia; (: fruit) compota, conserva

president ['prezidant] n presidente(-a) m/f; **presidential** [prezi'denʃl] adj presidencial

press [pres] n (printer's) imprensa, prelo; (newspapers) imprensa; (of switch) pressão f ♦ vt apertar; (clothes: iron) passar; (put pressure on: person) assediar; (insist): **to ~ sth on sb** insistir para que alguém aceite algo ♦ vi (squeeze) apertar; (pressurize): **to ~ for** pressionar por; **we are ~ed for time/money** estamos com pouco tempo/dinheiro; **press on** vi continuar; **pressing** adj urgente; **press stud** (BRIT) n botão m de pressão; **press-up** (BRIT) n flexão f

pressure ['preʃə*] n pressão f; **to put ~ on sb (to do sth)** pressionar alguém (a fazer algo); **pressure cooker** n panela de pressão

prestige [pres'ti:ʒ] n prestígio

presume [pri'zju:m] vt supor

pretence [pri'tens] (US pretense) n pretensão f; **under false ~s** por meios fraudulentos

pretend [pri'tend] vt, vi fingir

pretense [pri'tens] (US) n = **pretence**

pretty ['priti] adj bonito ♦ adv (quite) bastante

prevail [pri'veil] vi triunfar; (be current) imperar

prevalent ['prevələnt] adj (common) predominante

prevent [pri'vent] vt impedir

preview ['pri:vju:] n pré-estréia

previous ['pri:viəs] adj (earlier) anterior; **previously** adv (before) previamente; (in the past) anteriormente

prewar [pri:'wɔ:*] adj anterior à guerra

prey [prei] n presa ♦ vi: **to ~** (feed on) alimentar-se de; **it was ~ing on his mind** preocupava-o, atormentava-o

price [prais] n preço ♦ vt fixar o preço de; **priceless** adj inestimável; (inf: amusing) impagável

prick [prik] n picada ♦ vt picar; (make hole in) furar; **to ~ up one's ears** aguçar os ouvidos

prickle ['prikl] n (sensation) comichão f, ardência; (BOT) espinho; **prickly** adj espinhoso; **prickly heat** n brotoeja

pride [praid] n orgulho; (pej) soberba ♦ vt: **to ~ o.s. on** orgulhar-se de

priest [pri:st] n (Christian) padre m; (non-Christian) sacerdote m

prim [prim] (pej) adj (formal) empertigado; (affected) afetado; (easily shocked) pudico

primarily ['praimərili] adv principalmente

primary ['praiməri] adj primário;

(first in importance) principal ♦ n (US: election) eleição f primária; **primary school** (BRIT) n escola primária; ver quadro

---

PRIMARY SCHOOL

As **primary schools** da Grã-Bretanha acolhem crianças de 5 a 11 anos. Assinalam o início do ciclo escolar obrigatório e são compostas de duas partes: a pré-escola (infant school) e o primário (junior school).

---

prime [praɪm] adj primeiro, principal; (excellent) de primeira ♦ vt (wood) imprimar; (fig) aprontar, preparar ♦ n: in the ~ of life na primavera da vida; ~ **example** exemplo típico; **prime minister** n primeiro-ministro (primeira-ministra)
primeval [praɪˈmiːvl] adj primitivo
primitive [ˈprɪmɪtɪv] adj primitivo; (crude) rudimentar
primrose [ˈprɪmrəuz] n prímula, primavera
prince [prɪns] n príncipe m
princess [prɪnˈses] n princesa
principal [ˈprɪnsɪpl] adj principal ♦ n (of school, college) diretor(a) m/f
principle [ˈprɪnsɪpl] n princípio; in ~ em princípio; on ~ por princípio
print [prɪnt] n (letters) letra de forma; (fabric) estampado, (ART) estampa, gravura; (PHOT) cópia; (foot~) pegada; (finger~) impressão f digital ♦ vt imprimir; (write in capitals) escrever em letra de imprensa; out of ~ esgotado; **printed matter** n impressos mpl; **printer** n (person) impressor(a) m/f; (firm) gráfica; (machine) impressora; **printing** n (art) impressa; (act) impressão f; **printout** n (COMPUT) cópia impressa
prior [ˈpraɪə*] adj anterior, prévio;

(more important) prioritário; ~ **to** doing antes de fazer
priority [praɪˈɔrɪtɪ] n prioridade f
prise [praɪz] vt: to ~ **open** arrombar
prison [ˈprɪzn] n prisão f ♦ cpd carcerário; **prisoner** n (in prison) preso(-a); (under arrest) detido(-a)
privacy [ˈprɪvəsɪ] n isolamento, solidão f, privacidade f
private [ˈpraɪvɪt] adj privado; (personal) particular; (confidential) confidencial, reservado; (personal: belongings) pessoal; (: thoughts, plans) secreto, íntimo; (place) isolado; (quiet: person) reservado; (intimate) íntimo ♦ n soldado raso; "~" (on envelope) "confidencial"; (on door) "privativo"; in ~ em particular; **privatize** vt privatizar
privet [ˈprɪvɪt] n alfena
privilege [ˈprɪvɪlɪdʒ] n privilégio
privy [ˈprɪvɪ] adj: to be ~ to estar inteirado de
prize [praɪz] n prêmio ♦ adj de primeira classe ♦ vt valorizar; **prize-winner** n premiado(-a)
pro [prəu] n (SPORT) profissional m/f ♦ prep a favor de; **the ~s and cons** os prós e os contras
probability [prɔbəˈbɪlɪtɪ] n probabilidade f
probable [ˈprɔbəbl] adj provável; (plausible) verossímil
probation [prəˈbeɪʃən] n: on ~ (employee) em estágio probatório; (LAW) em liberdade condicional
probe [prəub] n (MED, SPACE) sonda; (enquiry) pesquisa ♦ vt investigar, esquadrinhar
problem [ˈprɔbləm] n problema m
procedure [prəˈsiːdʒə*] n procedimento; (method) método, processo
proceed [prəˈsiːd] vi (do afterwards): to ~ **to do sth** passar a fazer algo; (continue): **to ~ (with)** continuar or

prosseguir (com); (activity) continuar; (go) ir em direção a, dirigir-se a; **proceedings** npl evento, acontecimento; (LAW) processo; **proceeds** ['prəusiːdz] npl produto, proventos mpl

process ['prəuses] n processo ♦ vt processar; **procession** [prə'sɛʃən] n desfile m, procissão f; **funeral procession** cortejo fúnebre

proclaim [prə'kleim] vt anunciar

procure [prə'kjuə*] vt obter

prod [prɔd] vt empurrar; (with finger, stick) cutucar ♦ n empurrão m; (cotovelada; espetada

prodigal ['prɔdigl] adj pródigo

prodigy ['prɔdidʒi] n prodígio

produce [n 'prɔdjuːs, vb prə'djuːs] n (AGR) produtos mpl agrícolas ♦ vt produzir; (cause) provocar; (evidence, argument) apresentar, mostrar; (show) apresentar, exibir; (THEATRE) pôr em cena or em cartaz; **producer** n (THEATRE) diretor(a) m/f; (AGR, CINEMA, of record) produtor(a) m/f; (country) produtor m

product ['prɔdʌkt] n produto

production [prə'dʌkʃən] n produção f; (of electricity) geração f; (THEATRE) encenação f; **production line** n linha de produção or de montagem

profession [prə'fɛʃən] n profissão f; (people) classe f; **professional** n profissional m/f ♦ adj profissional; (work) de profissional

professor [prə'fɛsə*] n (BRIT) catedrático(-a); (US, CANADA) professor(a) m/f

profile ['prəufail] n perfil m

profit ['prɔfit] n (COMM) lucro ♦ vi: to ~ by or from (benefit) aproveitar-se de, tirar proveito de; **profitable** adj (ECON) lucrativo, rendoso

profound [prə'faund] adj profundo

programme ['prəugræm] (US pro-gram) n programa m ♦ vt programar; **programming** (US programing) n (COMPUT) programação f

progress [n 'prəugres, vb prə'gres] n progresso ♦ vi progredir, avançar; **in ~** em andamento; **progressive** [prə'gresiv] adj progressivo; (person) progressista

prohibit [prə'hibit] vt proibir

project [n 'prɔdʒekt, vb prə'dʒekt] n projeto; (SCH: research) pesquisa f ♦ vt projetar; (figure) estimar ♦ vi (stick out) ressaltar, sobressair

projection [prə'dʒekʃən] n projeção f; (overhang) saliência

projector [prə'dʒektə*] n projetor m

prolong [prə'lɔŋ] vt prolongar

prom [prɔm] n abbr = promenade; promenade concert

promenade [prɔmə'nɑːd] n (by sea) passeio (à orla marítima); (US: ball) baile m de estudantes; **promenade concert** (BRIT) n concerto (de música clássica); ver quadro

---

PROMENADE CONCERT

Na Grã-Bretanha, um **promenade concert** (ou **prom**) é um concerto de música clássica, assim chamado porque originalmente o público não ficava sentado, mas de pé ou caminhando. Hoje em dia, uma parte do público permanece de pé, mas há também lugares sentados (mais caros). Os **Proms** mais conhecidos são os londrinos. A última sessão (the Last Night of the Proms) é um acontecimento carregado de emoção, quando são executadas árias tradicionais e patrióticas. Nos Estados Unidos e no Canadá, o **prom**, ou **promenade**, é um baile organizado pelas escolas secundárias.

prominent ['prɔmɪnənt] adj (standing out) proeminente; (important) eminente, notório

promise ['prɔmɪs] n promessa; (hope) esperança ♦ vt, vi prometer; **promising** adj promissor(a), prometedor(a)

promote [prə'məut] vt promover; (product) promover, fazer propaganda de; **promoter** n (of sporting event) patrocinador(a) m/f; (of cause etc) partidário(-a); **promotion** n promoção f

prompt [prɔmpt] adj pronto, rápido ♦ adv (exactly) em ponto, pontualmente ♦ n (COMPUT) sinal m de orientação, prompt m ♦ vt (urge) incitar, impelir; (cause) provocar, ocasionar; **to ~ sb to do sth** induzir alguém a fazer algo; **promptly** adv imediatamente; (exactly) pontualmente

prone [prəun] adj (lying) de bruços; **~ to** propenso a, predisposto a

pronoun ['prəunaun] n pronome m

pronounce [prə'nauns] vt pronunciar; (verdict, opinion) declarar

pronunciation [prənʌnsɪ'eɪʃən] n pronúncia

proof [pru:f] n prova ♦ adj: **~ against** à prova de

prop [prɔp] n suporte m, escora; (fig) amparo, apoio ♦ vt (also: **~ up**) apoiar, escorar; (lean): **to ~ sth against** apoiar algo contra

propaganda [prɔpə'gændə] n propaganda

propel [prə'pel] vt propelir, propulsionar; (fig) impelir; **propeller** n hélice f

proper ['prɔpə*] adj (correct) correto; (socially acceptable) respeitável, digno; (authentic) genuíno, autêntico; (referring to place): **the village ~** a cidadezinha propriamente dita; **properly** adv (eat, study) bem;

(behave) decentemente

property ['prɔpətɪ] n propriedade f; (goods) posses fpl, bens mpl; (buildings) imóveis mpl

prophesy ['prɔfɪsaɪ] vt profetizar

prophet ['prɔfɪt] n profeta m/f

proportion [prə'pɔ:ʃən] n porção f; **proportional** adj proporcional; **proportionate** adj proporcionado

proposal [prə'pəuzl] n proposta; (of marriage) pedido

propose [prə'pəuz] vt propor; (toast) erguer ♦ vi propor casamento; **to ~ to do** propor-se fazer

proposition [prɔpə'zɪʃən] n proposta, proposição f; (offer) oferta

proprietor [prə'praɪətə*] n proprietário(-a), dono(-a)

prose [prəuz] n prosa

prosecute ['prɔsɪkju:t] vt processar; **prosecution** [prɔsɪ'kju:ʃən] n acusação f; (accusing side) autor m da demanda

prospect [n 'prɔspekt, vb prə'spekt] n (chance) probabilidade f; (outlook) perspectiva ♦ vi: **to ~ (for)** prospectar (por); **~s** npl (for work etc) perspectivas fpl

prospectus [prə'spektəs] n prospecto, programa m

prostitute ['prɔstɪtju:t] n prostituta; **male ~** prostituto

protect [prə'tekt] vt proteger; **protection** n proteção f; **protective** adj protetor(a)

protein ['prəuti:n] n proteína

protest [n 'prəutest, vb prə'test] n protesto ♦ vi protestar ♦ vt insistir

Protestant ['prɔtɪstənt] adj, n protestante m/f

protester [prə'testə*] n manifestante m/f

protrude [prə'tru:d] vi projetar-se

proud [praud] adj orgulhoso; (pej)

vaidoso, soberbo

prove [pruːv] vt comprovar ♦ vi: **to ~ (to be) correct** etc vir a ser correto etc; **to ~ o.s.** pôr-se à prova

proverb [ˈprɔvəːb] n provérbio

provide [prəˈvaid] vt fornecer, proporcionar; **to ~ sb with sth** fornecer alguém de algo, fornecer algo a alguém, **provide for** vt fus (person) prover à subsistência de; **provided (that)** conj contando que (+ sub), sob condição de (que) (+ sub)

providing [prəˈvaidɪŋ] conj: ~ **(that)** contando que (+ sub)

province [ˈprɔvɪns] n província; (fig) esfera; **provincial** [prəˈvɪnʃəl] adj provincial; (pej) provinciano

provision [prəˈvɪʒən] n (supplying) abastecimento; (in contract) cláusula, condição f; **~s** npl (food) mantimentos mpl; **provisional** adj provisório, interino; (agreement, licence) provisório

proviso [prəˈvaizəu] n condição f

provocative [prəˈvɔkətiv] adj provocante; (sexually) excitante

provoke [prəˈvəuk] vt provocar; (cause) causar

prowl [praul] vi (also: ~ **about, ~ around**) rondar, andar à espreita ♦ n: **on the ~** de ronda, rondando; **prowler** n tarado(-a)

proxy [ˈprɔksi] n: **by ~** por procuração

prudent [ˈpruːdənt] adj prudente

prune [pruːn] n ameixa seca ♦ vt podar

pry [prai] vi: **to ~ (into)** intrometer-se (em)

PS n abbr (= postscript) PS m

pseudonym [ˈsjuːdənim] n pseudônimo

psychiatrist [saiˈkaiətrist] n psiquiatra m/f

psychic [ˈsaikik] adj psíquico; (also:

~al: person) sensível a forças psíquicas

psychoanalyst [saikəuˈænəlist] n psicanalista m/f

psychologist [saiˈkɔlədʒist] n psicólogo(-a)

psychology [saiˈkɔlədʒi] n psicologia

PTO abbr (= please turn over) v.v., vire

pub [pʌb] n abbr (= public house) pub m, bar m, botequim m; ver quadro

---

PUB

Um **pub** geralmente consiste em duas salas: uma (the lounge) é bastante confortável, com poltronas e bancos estofados, enquanto a outra (the public bar) é simplesmente um bar onde a consumação é em geral mais barata. O public bar é muitas vezes também um salão de jogos, dos quais os mais comuns são os dardos, dominó e bilhar. Atualmente muitos pubs servem refeições, sobretudo na hora do almoço, e essa é a única hora em que a entrada de crianças é permitida, desde que estejam acompanhadas por adultos. Em geral os pubs funcionam das 11 às 23 horas, mas isso pode variar de acordo com sua permissão de funcionamento; alguns pubs fecham à tarde.

---

public [ˈpʌblik] adj público ♦ n público; **in ~** em público; **to make ~** tornar público; **public address system** n sistema m (de reforço) de som

publican [ˈpʌblikən] n dono(-a) de pub

public: public convenience (BRIT) n banheiro público; **public holiday** n feriado; **public house** (BRIT) n pub m, bar m, taberna

publicity [pʌb'lɪsɪtɪ] n publicidade f
publicize ['pʌblɪsaɪz] vt divulgar
public: **public relations** relações fpl públicas; **public school** n (BRIT) escola particular; (US) escola pública; **public transport** (US **public transportation**) n transporte m coletivo
publish ['pʌblɪʃ] vt publicar; **publisher** n editor(a) m/f; (company) editora; **publishing** n a indústria editorial
pudding ['pudɪŋ] n (BRIT: dessert) sobremesa; (cake) pudim m, doce m; **black** (BRIT) or **blood** (US) ~ morcela
puddle ['pʌdl] n poça
puff [pʌf] n sopro; (of cigarette) baforada; (of air, smoke) lufada ♦ vt: **to ~ one's pipe** tirar baforadas do cachimbo ♦ vi (pant) arquejar; **puff out** (cheeks) encher; **puff pastry** (US **puff paste**) n massa folhada; **puffy** adj inchado
pull [pul] n (tug): **to give sth a ~** dar um puxão em algo ♦ vt puxar; (trigger) apertar; (curtain, blind) fechar ♦ vi puxar, dar um puxão; **to ~ to pieces** picar em pedacinhos; **to ~ one's punches** não usar toda a força; **to ~ one's weight** fazer a sua parte; **to ~ o.s. together** recompor-se; **to ~ sb's leg** (fig) brincar com alguém, sacanear alguém (inf); **pull apart** vt (break) romper; **pull down** vt (building) demolir, derrubar; **pull in** vi (AUT: at the kerb) encostar; (RAIL) chegar (na plataforma); **pull off** vt tirar; (fig) acertar; **pull out** vi (AUT: from kerb) sair; (RAIL) partir ♦ vt tirar, arrancar; **pull over** vi (AUT) encostar; **pull through** vi (MED) sobreviver; **pull up** vi (stop) deter-se, parar ♦ vt levantar; (uproot) desarraigar, arrancar
pulley ['pulɪ] n roldana

pullover ['puləuvə*] n pulôver m
pulp [pʌlp] n (of fruit) polpa
pulsate [pʌl'seɪt] vi pulsar, palpitar
pulse [pʌls] n (ANAT) pulso; (of music, engine) cadência; (BOT) legume m
pump [pʌmp] n bomba; (shoe) sapatilha (de dança) ♦ vt bombear; **pump up** vt encher
pumpkin ['pʌmpkɪn] n abóbora
pun [pʌn] n jogo de palavras, trocadilho
punch [pʌntʃ] n (blow) soco, murro; (tool) punção m; (drink) ponche m ♦ vt (hit): **to ~ sb/sth** esmurrar or socar alguém/algo; **punchline** n remate m
punctual ['pʌŋktjuəl] adj pontual
puncture ['pʌŋktʃə*] n furo ♦ vt furar
pungent ['pʌndʒənt] adj acre
punish ['pʌnɪʃ] vt punir, castigar; **punishment** n castigo, punição f
punk [pʌŋk] n (also: ~ **rocker**) punk m/f; (also: ~ **rock**) punk m; (US: inf: hoodlum) pinta-brava m
punt [pʌnt] n (boat) chalana
puny ['pju:nɪ] adj débil, fraco
pupil ['pju:pl] n (SCOL) aluno(-a); (of eye) pupila
puppet ['pʌpɪt] n marionete f, títere m; (fig) fantoche m
puppy ['pʌpɪ] n cachorro, cachorrinho (BR)
purchase ['pə:tʃɪs] n compra ♦ vt comprar
pure [pjuə*] adj puro
purge [pə:dʒ] n (POL) expurgo
purple ['pə:pl] adj roxo, purpúreo
purpose ['pə:pəs] n propósito, objetivo; **on ~** de propósito; **purposeful** adj decidido, resoluto
purr [pə:*] vi ronronar
purse [pə:s] n (BRIT) carteira; (US) bolsa ♦ vt enrugar, franzir
purser ['pə:sə*] n (NAUT) comissário

de bordo

pursue [pə'sjuː] vt perseguir; (fig: activity) exercer; (: interest, plan) dedicar-se a; (: result) lutar por

pursuit [pə'sjuːt] n caça; (fig) busca; (pastime) passatempo

push [puʃ] n empurrão m; (of button) aperto ♦ vt empurrar; (button) apertar; (promote) promover ♦ vi empurrar; (press) apertar; (fig): **to ~ for** reivindicar; **push aside** vt afastar com a mão; **push off** (inf) vi dar o fora; **push on** vi prosseguir; **push through** vi abrir caminho ♦ vt (measure) forçar a aceitação de; **push up** vt forçar a alta de; **push-chair** (BRIT) n carrinho; **pusher** n (also: **drug pusher**) traficante m/f or passador(a) m/f de drogas; **push-up** (US) n flexão f; **pushy** (pej) adj intrometido, agressivo

pussy(cat) ['pusɪ(kæt)] (inf) n gatinho

put [put] (pt, pp put) vt pôr, colocar; (~ into) meter; (: person: in institution etc) internar; (say) dizer, expressar; (case) expor; (question) fazer; (estimate) avaliar, calcular; (write, type etc) colocar; **put about** vt (rumour) espalhar; **put across** vt (ideas) comunicar; **put away** vt guardar; **put back** vt (replace) repor; (postpone) adiar; (delay) atrasar; **put by** vt (money etc) poupar, pôr de lado; **put down** vt pôr em; (animal) sacrificar; (in writing) anotar, inscrever; (revolt etc) sufocar; (attribute: case, view): **to ~ sth down to** atribuir algo a; **put forward** vt apresentar, propor; **put in** vt (application, complaint) apresentar; (time, effort) investir, gastar; **put off** vt adiar, protelar; (discourage) desencorajar; **put on** vt (clothes, make-up, dinner) pôr; (light) acender; (play)

encenar; (weight) ganhar; (brake) aplicar; (record, video, kettle) ligar; (accent, manner) assumir; **put out** vt (take out) colocar fora; (fire, cigarette, light) apagar; (one's hand) estender; (inf: person): **to be ~ out** estar aborrecido; **put through** vt (call) transferir; (plan) ser aprovado; **put up** vt (raise) levantar, erguer; (hang) prender; (build) construir, edificar; (tent) armar; (increase) aumentar; (accommodate) hospedar; **put up with** vt fus suportar, agüentar

putty ['pʌtɪ] n massa de vidraceiro, betume m

puzzle ['pʌzl] n charada; (jigsaw) quebra-cabeça m; (also: **crossword ~**) palavras cruzadas fpl; (mystery) mistério ♦ vt desconcertar, confundir ♦ vi: **to ~ over** sth tentar entender algo; **puzzling** adj intrigante, confuso

pyjamas [pɪ'dʒɑːməz] (US **pajamas**) npl pijama m or f

pylon ['paɪlən] n pilono, poste m

pyramid ['pɪrəmɪd] n pirâmide f

Pyrenees [pɪrə'niːz] npl: **the ~** os Pirineus

Q

quack [kwæk] n grasnido; (pej: doctor) curandeiro(-a), charlatão(-tã) m/f

quadrangle ['kwɔdræŋgl] n pátio quadrangular

quaint [kweɪnt] adj (ideas) curioso, esquisito; (village etc) pitoresco

quake [kweɪk] vi (with fear) tremer ♦ n abbr = **earthquake**

qualification [kwɔlɪfɪ'keɪʃən] n (skill, quality) qualificação f; (reservation) restrição f, ressalva; (modification) modificação f; (often pl: degree, training) título, qualificação f

qualified ['kwɔlɪfaɪd] adj (trained) habilitado, qualificado; (professionally) diplomado; (fit): ~ **to** apto para, capaz de; (limited) limitado

qualify ['kwɔlɪfaɪ] vt (modify) modificar ♦ vi: **to ~ (as)** (pass examination(s)) formar-se or diplomar-se (em); **to ~ (for)** reunir os requisitos (para)

quality ['kwɔlɪtɪ] n qualidade f; **quality (news)papers** npl ver quadro

---

QUALITY (NEWS)PAPERS

Os **quality (news)papers** (ou quality press) englobam os jornais "sérios", diários ou semanais, em oposição aos jornais populares (tabloid press). Esses jornais visam a um público que procura informações detalhadas sobre uma grande variedade de assuntos e que está disposto a dedicar um bom tempo à leitura. Geralmente os **quality newspapers** são publicados em formato grande.

---

quantity ['kwɔntɪtɪ] n quantidade f
quarantine ['kwɔrəntiːn] n quarentena
quarrel ['kwɔrl] n (argument) discussão f ♦ vi: **to ~ (with)** brigar (com)
quarry ['kwɔrɪ] n (for stone) pedreira; (animal) presa, caça
quart [kwɔːt] n quarto de galão (1.136 l)
quarter ['kwɔːtə*] n quarto, quarta parte f; (of year) trimestre m; (district) bairro; (us: 25 cents) (moeda de) 25 centavos mpl de dólar ♦ vt dividir em quatro; (MIL: lodge) aquartelar; **~s** npl (MIL) quartel m; (living ~s) alojamento; **a ~ of an hour** um quarto de hora; **quarter final** n quarta de final; **quarterly** adj trimestral ♦ adv trimestralmente
quaver ['kweɪvə*] n (BRIT: MUS) col-

cheia ♦ vi tremer
quay [kiː] n (also: ~side) cais m
queasy ['kwiːzɪ] adj (sickly) enjoado
queen [kwiːn] n rainha; (also: ~ bee) abelha-mestra, rainha; (CARDS etc) dama; **queen mother** n rainha-mãe f
queer [kwɪə*] adj (odd) esquisito, estranho ♦ n (inf: homosexual) bicha m (BR), maricas m inv (PT)
quench [kwentʃ] vt: **to ~ one's thirst** matar a sede
query ['kwɪərɪ] n pergunta ♦ vt questionar
quest [kwest] n busca
question ['kwestʃən] n pergunta; (doubt) dúvida; (issue) questão f; (in text) problema m ♦ vt (doubt) duvidar; (interrogate) interrogar, inquirir; **beyond ~** sem dúvida; **out of the ~** fora de cogitação, impossível; **questionable** adj discutível; (doubtful) duvidoso; **question mark** n ponto de interrogação; **questionnaire** [kwestʃə'nɛə*] n questionário
queue [kjuː] (BRIT) n fila (BR), bicha (PT) ♦ vi (also: ~ up) fazer fila (BR) or bicha (PT)
quibble ['kwɪbl] vi: **to ~ about** or over/with tergiversar sobre/com
quick [kwɪk] adj rápido; (agile) ágil; (mind) sagaz, despachado ♦ n: **to cut sb to the ~** ferir alguém; **be ~!** ande depressa!, vai rápido!; **quicken** vt apressar ♦ vi apressar-se; **quickly** adv rapidamente, depressa; **quicksand** n areia movediça; **quick-witted** adj perspicaz, vivo
quid [kwɪd] (BRIT: inf) n inv libra
quiet ['kwaɪət] adj (voice, music) baixo; (peaceful: place) tranqüilo; (person: calm) calmo; (not noisy: place) silencioso; (: person) calado; (silent) silencioso; (ceremony) discreto ♦ n (peacefulness) sossego; (si-

lence) quietude *f* ♦ *vt, vi* (*US*) = ~**en**;

quieten (*also*: **quieten down**) *vi* (*grow calm*) acalmar-se; (*grow silent*) calar-se ♦ *vt* tranqüilizar; fazer calar; **quietly** *adv* silenciosamente; (*talk*) baixo

quilt [kwɪlt] *n* acolchoado, colcha; (**continental**) ~ (*BRIT*) edredom *m* (*BR*), edredão *m* (*PT*)

quip [kwɪp] *n* escárnio, dito espirituoso

quirk [kwə:k] *n* peculiaridade *f*

quit [kwɪt] (*pt, pp* **quit** *or* ~**ted**) *vt* (*smoking etc*) parar; (*job*) deixar; (*premises*) desocupar ♦ *vi* desistir; (*resign*) demitir-se, deixar o emprego

quite [kwaɪt] *adv* (*rather*) bastante; (*entirely*) completamente, totalmente; **that's not** ~ **big enough** não é suficientemente grande; ~ **a few of them** um bom número deles; ~ (**so**)! exatamente!, isso mesmo!

quiver [ˈkwɪvə*] *vi* estremecer

quiz [kwɪz] *n* concurso (de cultura geral) ♦ *vt* interrogar; **quizzical** *adj* zombeteiro

quota [ˈkwəutə] *n* cota, quota

quotation [kwəuˈteɪʃən] *n* citação *f*; (*estimate*) orçamento; **quotation marks** *npl* aspas *fpl*

quote [kwəut] *n* citação *f*; (*estimate*) orçamento ♦ *vt* citar; (*price*) propor; ~**s** *npl* aspas *fpl*

R

rabbi [ˈræbaɪ] *n* rabino

rabbit [ˈræbɪt] *n* coelho

rabble [ˈræbl] (*pej*) *n* povinho, ralé *f*

rabies [ˈreɪbi:z] *n* raiva

RAC (*BRIT*) *n abbr* (= *Royal Automobile Club*) ≈ TCB *m* (*BR*), ≈ ACP *m* (*PT*)

raccoon [rəˈku:n] *n* mão-pelada *m*, guaxinim *m*

race [reɪs] *n* corrida; (*species*) raça ♦ *vt* (*horse*) fazer correr ♦ *vi* (*compete*) competir; (*run*) correr; (*pulse*) bater rapidamente; **race car** (*US*) *n* = **racing car**; **racecourse** *n* hipódromo; **racehorse** *n* cavalo de corridas; **racetrack** *n* pista de corridas; (*for cars*) autódromo

racing [ˈreɪsɪŋ] *n* corrida; **racing car** (*BRIT*) *n* carro de corrida; **racing driver** (*BRIT*) *n* piloto(-a) de corrida

racism [ˈreɪsɪzəm] *n* racismo; **racist** (*pej*) *adj, n* racista *m/f*

rack [ræk] *n* (*also*: **luggage** ~) bagageiro; (*shelf*) estante *f*; (*also*: **roof** ~) xalmas *fpl*, porta bagagem *m*; (*dish*) secador *m* de prato ♦ *vt*: ~**ed by** (*pain, anxiety*) tomado por; **to** ~ **one's brains** quebrar a cabeça

racket [ˈrækɪt] *n* (*for tennis*) raquete *f* (*BR*), raqueta (*PT*); (*noise*) barulheira, zoeira; (*swindle*) negócio ilegal, fraude *f*

racquet [ˈrækɪt] *n* raquete *f* (*BR*), raqueta (*PT*)

racy [ˈreɪsɪ] *adj* ousado, picante

radiant [ˈreɪdɪənt] *adj* radiante, brilhante

radiate [ˈreɪdɪeɪt] *vt* irradiar ♦ *vi* difundir-se, estender-se

radiation [reɪdɪˈeɪʃən] *n* radiação *f*

radiator [ˈreɪdɪeɪtə*] *n* radiador *m*

radical [ˈrædɪkl] *adj* radical

radii [ˈreɪdɪaɪ] *npl of* **radius**

radio [ˈreɪdɪəu] *n* rádio ♦ *vt*: **to** ~ **sb** comunicar-se por rádio com alguém

radio... [reɪdɪəu] *prefix* radio...;

radioactive [ˈreɪdɪəuˈæktɪv] *adj* radioativo; **radio station** *n* emissora, estação *f* de rádio

radish [ˈrædɪʃ] *n* rabanete *m*

radius ['reɪdɪəs] (*pl* **radii**) *n* raio

RAF (*BRIT*) *n abbr* = **Royal Air Force**

raffle ['ræfl] *n* rifa

raft [rɑːft] *n* balsa

rafter ['rɑːftə*] *n* viga, caibro

rag [ræg] *n* trapo; (*torn cloth*) farrapo; (*pej: newspaper*) jornaleco; (*UNIVERSITY*) atividades estudantis beneficentes; **~s** *npl* (*torn clothes*) trapos *mpl*, farrapos *mpl*; **rag doll** *n* boneca de trapo

rage [reɪdʒ] *n* (*fury*) raiva, furor *m* ♦ *vi* (*person*) estar furioso; (*storm*) assolar; (*debate*) continuar calorosamente; **it's all the ~** é a última moda

ragged ['rægɪd] *adj* (*edge*) irregular, desigual; (*clothes*) puído, gasto; (*appearance*) esfarrapado, andrajoso

raid [reɪd] *n* (*MIL*) incursão *f*; (*criminal*) assalto; (*attack*) ataque *m*; (*by police*) batida ♦ *vt* invadir, atacar; assaltar; atacar; fazer uma batida em

rail [reɪl] *n* (*on stair*) corrimão *m*; (*on bridge*) parapeito, antepara; (*of ship*) amurada; **~s** *npl* (*for train*) trilhos *mpl*; **by ~** de trem (*BR*), por caminho de ferro (*PT*); **railing(s)** *n(pl)* grade *f*; **railroad** (*US*) *n* = **railway**; **railway** *n* estrada *or* caminho *m* (*PT*) de ferro; **railway line** (*BRIT*) *n* linha de trem (*BR*) *or* de comboio (*PT*); **railway station** (*BRIT*) *n* estação *f* ferroviária (*BR*) *or* de caminho de ferro (*PT*)

rain [reɪn] *n* chuva ♦ *vi* chover; **it's ~ing** está chovendo (*BR*), está a chover (*PT*); **rainbow** *n* arco-íris *m inv*; **raincoat** *n* impermeável *m*, capa de chuva; **raindrop** *n* gota de chuva; **rainfall** *n* chuva; (*measurement*) pluviosidade *f*; **rainforest** *n* floresta tropical; **rainy** *adj* chuvoso; **a rainy day** um dia de chuva

raise [reɪz] *n* aumento ♦ *vt* (*lift*) levantar; (*salary, production*) aumentar; (*morale, standards*) melhorar; (*doubts*) suscitar, despertar; (*cattle, family*) criar; (*crop*) cultivar, plantar; (*army*) recrutar, alistar; (*funds*) angariar; (*loan*) levantar, obter; **to ~ one's voice** levantar a voz

raisin ['reɪzn] *n* passa, uva seca

rake [reɪk] *n* ancinho ♦ *vt* (*garden*) revolver *or* limpar com o ancinho; (*with machine gun*) varrer

rally ['rælɪ] *n* (*POL etc*) comício; (*AUT*) rally *m*, rali *m*; (*TENNIS*) rebatida ♦ *vt* reunir ♦ *vi* reorganizar-se; (*sick person, Stock Exchange*) recuperar-se; **rally round** *vt fus* dar apoio a

RAM [ræm] *n abbr* (*COMPUT*) (= *random access memory*) RAM *f*

ram [ræm] *n* carneiro ♦ *vt* (*push*) cravar; (*crash into*) colidir com

ramble ['ræmbl] *n* caminhada, excursão *f* a pé ♦ *vi* caminhar; (*talk: also:* **~ on**) divagar; **rambler** *n* caminhante *m/f*; (*BOT*) roseira trepadeira; **rambling** *adj* (*speech*) desconexo, incoerente; (*house*) cheio de recantos; (*plant*) rastejante

ramp [ræmp] *n* (*incline*) rampa; **on/off ~** (*US: AUT*) entrada (*para a rodovia*)/saída da rodovia

rampage [ræm'peɪdʒ] *n*: **to be on the ~** alvoroçar-se

ramshackle ['ræmʃækl] *adj* caindo aos pedaços

ran [ræn] *pt of* **run**

ranch [rɑːntʃ] *n* rancho, fazenda, estância; **rancher** *n* rancheiro(-a), fazendeiro(-a)

rancid ['rænsɪd] *adj* rançoso, râncio

rancour ['ræŋkə*] (*US* **rancor**) *n* rancor *m*

random ['rændəm] *adj* ao acaso, casual, fortuito; (*COMPUT, MATH*) aleatório ♦ *n*: **at ~** a esmo, aleatoriamente

randy ['rændɪ] (BRIT: inf) adj de fogo

rang [ræŋ] pt of **ring**

range [reɪndʒ] n (of mountains) cadeia, cordilheira; (of missile) alcance m; (of voice) extensão f; (series) série f; (of products) gama, sortimento; (MIL: also: **shooting ~**) estande m; (also: **kitchen ~**) fogão m ♦ vt (place) colocar; (arrange) arrumar, ordenar ♦ vi: **to ~ over** (extend) estender-se por; **to ~ from ... to ...** variar de ... a ..., oscilar entre ... e ...

rank [ræŋk] n (row) fila, fileira; (MIL) posto; (status) categoria, posição f; (BRIT: also: **taxi ~**) ponto de táxi ♦ vi: **to ~ among** figurar entre ♦ adj fétido, malcheiroso; **the ~ and file** (fig) a gente comum

ransack ['rænsæk] vt (search) revistar; (plunder) saquear, pilhar

ransom ['rænsəm] n resgate m; **to hold sb to ~** (fig) encostar alguém contra a parede

rant [rænt] vi arengar

rap [ræp] vt bater de leve ♦ n: **~ (music)** rap m

rape [reɪp] n estupro; (BOT) colza ♦ vt violentar, estuprar

rapid ['ræpɪd] adj rápido; **rapids** npl (GEO) cachoeira

rapist ['reɪpɪst] n estuprador m

rapport [ræ'pɔ:*] n harmonia, afinidade f

rare [reə*] adj raro; (CULIN: steak) mal passado

rascal ['rɑ:skl] n maroto, malandro

rash [ræʃ] adj impetuoso, precipitado ♦ n (MED) exantema m, erupção f cutânea; (of events) série f, torrente f

rasher ['ræʃə*] n fatia fina

raspberry ['rɑ:zbərɪ] n framboesa

rat [ræt] n rato (BR), ratazana (PT)

rate [reɪt] n (ratio) razão f; (price) preço, taxa; (: of hotel) diária; (of

interest, change) taxa; (speed) velocidade f ♦ vt (value) taxar; (estimate) avaliar; **~s** npl (BRIT) imposto predial e territorial; (fees) pagamento; **to ~ sb/sth as** considerar alguém/algo como

rather ['rɑ:ðə*] adv (somewhat) um tanto, meio; (to some extent) até certo ponto; (more accurately) ou melhor; **it's ~ expensive** (quite) é meio caro; (too) é caro demais; **there's ~ a lot** há bastante or muito; **I would ~ go** preferiria or preferia ir

ratio ['reɪʃɪəʊ] n razão f, proporção f

ration ['ræʃən] n ração f ♦ vt racionar; **~s** npl (MIL) mantimentos mpl, víveres mpl

rational ['ræʃənl] adj lógico; (person) sensato, razoável; **rationale** [ræʃə'nɑ:l] n razão f fundamental

rat race n: **the ~** a competição acirrada na vida moderna

rattle ['rætl] n (of door) batida; (of train etc) chocalhada; (of coins) chocalhar m; (object: for baby) chocalho ♦ vi (small objects) tamborilar; (vehicle): **to ~ along** mover-se ruidosamente ♦ vt sacudir, fazer bater; (unnerve) perturbar; **rattlesnake** n cascavel f

raucous ['rɔːkəs] adj espalhafatoso, banelhento

rave [reɪv] vi (in anger) encolerizar-se; (MED) delirar; (with enthusiasm): **to ~ about** vibrar com

raven ['reɪvən] n corvo

ravenous ['rævənəs] adj morto de forne, esfomeado

ravine [rə'vi:n] n ravina, barranco

raving ['reɪvɪŋ] adj: **~ lunatic** doido(-a) varrido(-a)

ravishing ['rævɪʃɪŋ] adj encantador(a)

raw [rɔ:] adj (uncooked) cru(a); (not processed) bruto; (sore) vivo; (inex-

perienced) inexperiente, novato; (*weather*) muito frio; **raw material** *n* matéria-prima

ray [reɪ] *n* raio; **~ of hope** fio de esperança

razor ['reɪzə*] *n* (*open*) navalha; (*safety ~*) aparelho de barbear; (*electric*) aparelho de barbear elétrico; **razor blade** *n* gilete *m* (*BR*), lâmina de barbear (*PT*)

Rd *abbr* = **road**

re [riː] *prep* referente a

reach [riːtʃ] *n* alcance *m*; (*of river etc*) extensão *f* ♦ *vt* alcançar; (*arrive at: place*) chegar em; (: *agreement*) chegar a; (*by telephone*) conseguir falar com ♦ *vi* (*stretch out*) esticar-se; **within ~** ao alcance (da mão); **out of ~** fora do alcance; **reach out** *vt* (*hand*) esticar ♦ *vi*: **to ~ out for sth** estender or esticar ã mão para pegar (em) algo

react [riːˈækt] *vi* reagir; **reaction** *n* reação *f*; **~ions** *npl* (*reflexes*) reflexos *mpl*

reactor [riːˈæktə*] *n* (*also:* **nuclear ~**) reator *m* nuclear

read [riːd, *pt, pp* **red**] (*pt, pp* **read**) *vi* ler ♦ *vt* ler; (*understand*) compreender; (*study*) estudar; **read out** *vt* ler em voz alta; **reader** *n* leitor(a) *m/f*; (*book*) livro de leituras (*BRIT*: *at university*) professor(a) *m/f*(-a)

readily ['rɛdɪlɪ] *adv* (*willingly*) de boa vontade; (*easily*) facilmente; (*quickly*) sem demora, prontamente

reading ['riːdɪŋ] *n* leitura *f*; (*on instrument*) indicação *f*, registro (*BR*), registo (*PT*)

ready ['rɛdɪ] *adj* pronto, preparado; (*willing*) disposto; (*available*) disponível ♦ *n*: **at the ~** (*MIL*) pronto para atirar; **to get ~** *vi* preparar-se ♦ *vt* preparar; **ready-made** *adj* (já) feito; (*clothes*) pronto; **ready-to-**

wear *adj* pronto, prêt à porter *inv*

real [rɪəl] *adj* real; (*genuine*) verdadeiro, autêntico; **in ~ terms** em termos reais; **real estate** *n* bens *mpl* imobiliários *or* de raiz; **realistic** [rɪəˈlɪstɪk] *adj* realista

reality [riːˈælɪt] *n* realidade *f*

realization [rɪəlaɪˈzeɪʃən] *n* (*fulfilment*) realização *f*; (*understanding*) compreensão *f*; (*COMM*) conversão *f* em dinheiro, realização

realize ['rɪəlaɪz] *vt* (*understand*) perceber; (*fulfil, COMM*) realizar

really ['rɪəlɪ] *adv* (*for emphasis*) realmente; (*actually*): **what ~ happened?** o que aconteceu na verdade?; **~?** (*interest*) é mesmo?; (*surprise*) verdade!; **~!** (*annoyance*) realmente!

realm [rɛlm] *n* reino; (*fig*) esfera, domínio

realtor ['rɪəltə*] (*US*) *n* corretor(a) *m/f* de imóveis (*BR*), agente *m/f* imobiliário(-a) (*PT*)

reap [riːp] *vt* segar, ceifar; (*fig*) colher

reappear [riːəˈpɪə*] *vi* reaparecer

rear [rɪə*] *adj* traseiro, de trás ♦ *n* traseira ♦ *vt* criar ♦ *vi* (*also:* **~ up**) empinar-se

reason ['riːzn] *n* (*cause*) razão *f*; (*ability*) raciocínio; (*sense*) bom-senso ♦ *vi*: **to ~ with sb** argumentar com alguém, persuadir alguém; **it stands to ~ that** é razoável *or* lógico que; **reasonable** *adj* (*fair*) razoável; (*sensible*) sensato; **reasonably** *adv* razoavelmente; sensatamente; **reasoning** *n* raciocínio

reassurance [riːəˈʃʊərəns] *n* garantia

reassure [riːəˈʃʊə*] *vt* tranqüilizar; **to ~ sb** reafirmar a confiança de alguém acerca de

rebate ['riːbeɪt] *n* devolução *f*

rebel [n 'rɛbl, vb rɪ'bɛl] n rebelde m/f ♦ vi rebelar-se; **rebellious** [rɪ'bɛljəs] adj insurreto; (behaviour) rebelde

rebound [vb rɪ'baund, n 'riːbaund] vi (ball) ressaltar ♦ n: on the ~ res-salto; (person): **she married him on the ~** ela casou com ele logo após o rompimento do casamento (or relacionamento) anterior

rebuff [rɪ'bʌf] n repulsa, recusa

rebuke [rɪ'bjuːk] vt repreender

recall [vb rɪ'kɔːl, n 'riːkɔl] vt recordar, lembrar; (parliament) reunir de volta; (ambassador) chamar de volta ♦ n (memory) recordação f, lembrança; (of ambassador) chamada (de volta)

recap ['riːkæp] vt sintetizar ♦ vi recapitular

recd. abbr = received

receding [rɪ'siːdɪŋ] adj (chin) metido or puxado para dentro; (hair) que está escasseando nas têmporas

receipt [rɪ'siːt] n recibo; (act) recebimento (BR), recepção f (PT); **~s** npl (COMM) receitas fpl

receive [rɪ'siːv] vt receber; (guest) acolher; (wound, criticism) sofrer; **receiver** n (TEL) fone m (BR), auscultador m (PT); (RADIO, TV) receptor m; (of stolen goods) receptador(a) m/f; (COMM) curador(a) m/f síndico(-a) de massa falida

recent ['riːsnt] adj recente; **recently** adv recentemente; (in recent times) ultimamente

reception [rɪ'sɛpʃən] n recepção f; (welcome) acolhida; **reception desk** n (mesa de) recepção f; **receptionist** n recepcionista m/f

recess [rɪ'sɛs] n (in room) recesso, vão m; (secret place) esconderijo; (POL etc: holiday) férias fpl

recession [rɪ'sɛʃən] n recessão f

recipe ['rɛsɪpɪ] n receita

recipient [rɪ'sɪpɪənt] n recipiente m/f, recebedor(a) m/f; (of letter) destinatário(-a)

recite [rɪ'saɪt] vt recitar

reckless ['rɛkləs] adj (driver) imprudente; (speed) imprudente, excessivo; (spending) irresponsável

reckon ['rɛkən] vt (calculate) calcular, contar; (think): **I ~ that ...** acho que ...; **reckon on** vt fus contar com

reclaim [rɪ'kleɪm] vt (demand back) reivindicar; (land: from sea) aterrar; (waste materials) reaproveitar

recline [rɪ'klaɪn] vi reclinar-se; **reclining** adj (seat) reclinável

recognition [rɛkəg'nɪʃən] n reconhecimento

recognize ['rɛkəgnaɪz] vt reconhecer

recoil [vb rɪ'kɔɪl, n 'riːkɔɪl] vi (person): **to ~ from doing sth** recusar-se a fazer algo ♦ n (of gun) coice m

recollect [rɛkə'lɛkt] vt lembrar, recordar; **recollection** n (memory) recordação f; (remembering) lembrança

recommend [rɛkə'mɛnd] vt recomendar

reconcile ['rɛkənsaɪl] vt reconciliar; (facts) conciliar, harmonizar; **to ~ o.s. to sth** resignar-se a or conformar-se com algo

reconsider [riːkən'sɪdə*] vt reconsiderar

reconstruct [riːkən'strʌkt] vt reconstruir; (event) reconstituir

record [n, adj 'rɛkɔːd, vb rɪ'kɔːd] n (MUS) disco; (of meeting etc) ata, minuta; (COMPUT, of attendance) registro (BR), registo (PT); (written) história; (also: **criminal ~**) antecedentes mpl; (SPORT) recorde m ♦ vt (write down) anotar; (temperature, *speed*) registrar (*BR*), registar (*PT*); (*MUS*: *song etc*) gravar ♦ *adj*: **in ~ time** num tempo recorde; **off the ~** ♦ *adj* confidencial ♦ *adv* confidencialmente; **recorder** *n* (*MUS*) flauta; **recording** *n* (*MUS*) gravação *f*; **record player** *n* toca-discos *m inv* (*BR*), gira-discos *m inv* (*PT*)

re-count ['ri:kaunt] *n* (*POL*: *of votes*) nova contagem *f*, recontagem *f*

recoup [rɪ'ku:p] *vt*: **to ~ one's losses** recuperar-se dos prejuízos

recover [rɪ'kʌvə*] *vt* recuperar ♦ *vi* (*from illness*) recuperar-se; (*from shock*) refazer-se; **recovery** *n* recuperação *f*; (*MED*) recuperação, melhora

recreation [rɛkrɪ'eɪʃən] *n* recreio; **recreational** *adj* recreativo

recruit [rɪ'kru:t] *n* recruta *m/f*; (*in company*) novato(-a) ♦ *vt* recrutar

rectangle ['rɛktæŋgl] *n* retângulo

rector ['rɛktə*] *n* (*REL*) pároco

recuperate [rɪ'ku:pəreɪt] *vi* recuperar-se

recur [rɪ'kə:*] *vi* repetir-se, ocorrer outra vez; (*symptoms*) reaparecer; **recurrent** *adj* repetido, periódico

recycle [ri:'saɪkl] *vt* reciclar; **recycling** *n* reciclagem *f*

red [rɛd] *n* vermelho; (*POL*: *pej*) vermelho(-a) ♦ *adj* vermelho; (*hair*) ruivo; (*wine*) tinto; **to be in the ~** não ter fundos; **Red Cross** *n* Cruz *f* Vermelha; **redden** *vt* avermelhar ♦ *vi* corar, ruborizar-se

redeem [rɪ'di:m] *vt* (*REL*) redimir; (*sth in pawn*) tirar do prego; (*loan, fig*: *situation*) salvar; **redeeming** *adj*: **redeeming feature** lado bom or que salva

red: **red-haired** *adj* ruivo; **red-handed** *adj*: **to be caught red-handed** ser apanhado em flagrante, ser flagrado; **redhead** *n* ruivo(-a);

red herring *n* (*fig*) pista falsa; **red-hot** *adj* incandescente

redirect [ri:daɪ'rɛkt] *vt* (*mail*) endereçar de novo

red-light district *n* zona (de meretrício)

redo [ri:'du:] (*irreg*) *vt* refazer

redress [rɪ'drɛs] *n* compensação *f* ♦ *vt* retificar

Red Sea *n*: **the ~** o mar Vermelho

redskin ['rɛdskɪn] *n* pele-vermelha *m/f*

red tape *n* (*fig*) papelada, burocracia

reduce [rɪ'dju:s] *vt* reduzir; (*lower*) rebaixar; **"~ speed now"** (*AUT*) "diminua a velocidade"; **to ~ sb to** (*silence, begging*) levar alguém a; (*tears*) reduzir alguém a; **reduction** [rɪ'dʌkʃən] *n* redução *f*; (*of price*) abatimento

redundancy [rɪ'dʌndənsɪ] (*BRIT*) *n* (*dismissal*) demissão *f*; (*unemployment*) desemprego

redundant [rɪ'dʌndnt] *adj* (*BRIT*: *worker*) desempregado; (*detail, object*) redundante, supérfluo; **to be made ~** ficar desempregado or sem trabalho

reed [ri:d] *n* (*BOT*) junco; (*MUS*: *of clarinet etc*) palheta

reef [ri:f] *n* (*at sea*) recife *m*

reek [ri:k] *vi*: **to ~ (of)** cheirar (a), feder (a)

reel [ri:l] *n* carretel *m*, bobina; (*of film*) rolo, filme *m*; (*on fishing-rod*) carretilha; (*dance*) dança típica da Escócia ♦ *vi* (*sway*) cambalear, oscilar; **reel in** *vt* puxar enrolando a linha

ref [rɛf] (*inf*) *n abbr* = **referee**

refectory [rɪ'fɛktərɪ] *n* refeitório

refer [rɪ'fə:*] *vt* (*matter, problem*): **to ~ sth to** submeter algo à apreciação de; (*person, patient*): **to ~ sb to** encaminhar alguém a ♦ *vi*: **to ~ to**

referir-se or aludir a; (*consult*) recorrer a

referee [rɛfə'ri:] n árbitro(-a); (*BRIT: for job application*) referência ♦ vt apitar

reference ['rɛfrəns] n referência; (*mention*) menção f; **with ~ to** com relação a; (*COMM: in letter*) com referência a; **reference book** n livro de consulta

refill [vb ri:'fɪl, n ri:'fɪl] vt reencher; (*lighter etc*) reabastecer ♦ n (*for pen*) carga nova

refine [rɪ'faɪn] vt refinar; **refined** adj refinado, culto

reflect [rɪ'flɛkt] vt refletir ♦ vi (*think*) refletir, meditar; **it ~s badly/well on him** isso repercute mal/bem para ele; **reflection** n reflexo; (*thought, act*) reflexão f; (*criticism*): **reflection on** crítica de; **on reflection** pensando bem

reflex [ri:'flɛks] adj reflexo ♦ n reflexo; **reflexive** [rɪ'flɛksɪv] adj (*LING*) reflexivo

reform [rɪ'fɔ:m] n reforma ♦ vt reformar; **reformatory** [rɪ'fɔ:mətərɪ] (*US*) n reformatório

refrain [rɪ'freɪn] vi: **to ~ from doing** abster-se de fazer ♦ n estribilho, refrão m

refresh [rɪ'frɛʃ] vt refrescar; **refresher course** (*BRIT*) n curso de reciclagem; **refreshing** adj refrescante; (*sleep*) repousante; **refreshments** npl bebidas fpl (não alcoólicas) e guloseimas

refrigerator [rɪ'frɪdʒəreɪtə*] n refrigerador m, geladeira (*BR*), frigorífico (*PT*)

refuel [ri:'fjuəl] vi reabastecer

refuge ['rɛfju:dʒ] n refúgio; **to take ~ in** refugiar-se em

refugee [rɛfju'dʒi:] n refugiado(-a)

refund [n 'ri:fʌnd, vb rɪ'fʌnd] n

reembolso ♦ vt devolver, reembolsar

refurbish [ri:'fə:bɪʃ] vt renovar

refusal [rɪ'fju:zəl] n recusa, negativa; **first ~** primeira opção

refuse¹ [rɪ'fju:z] vt recusar; (*order*) recusar-se a ♦ vi recusar-se, negar-se; (*horse*) recusar-se a pular a cerca

refuse² ['rɛfju:s] n refugo, lixo

regain [rɪ'geɪn] vt recuperar, recobrar

regal ['ri:gl] adj real, régio

regard [rɪ'gɑ:d] n (*gaze*) olhar m firme; (*attention*) atenção f; (*esteem*) estima, consideração f ♦ vt (*consider*) considerar; **to give one's ~s to** dar lembranças a; **"with kindest ~s"** "cordialmente"; **as ~s, with ~ to** com relação a, com respeito a, quanto a; **regarding** prep com relação a; **regardless** adv apesar de tudo; **regardless of** apesar de

régime [reɪ'ʒi:m] n regime m

regiment ['rɛdʒɪmənt] n regimento

region ['ri:dʒən] n região f; **in the ~ of** (*fig*) por volta de, ao redor de; **regional** adj regional

register ['rɛdʒɪstə*] n registro (*BR*), registo (*PT*); (*SCH*) chamada ♦ vt registrar (*BR*), registar (*PT*); (*subj: instrument*) marcar, indicar ♦ vi (*at hotel*) registrar-se (*BR*), registar-se (*PT*); (*for work*) candidatar-se; (*as student*) inscrever-se; (*make impression*) causar impressão; **registered** adj (*letter, parcel*) registrado (*BR*), registado (*PT*)

registrar ['rɛdʒɪstrɑ:*] n oficial m/f de registro (*BR*) or registo (*PT*), escrivão(-vã) m/f; (*in college*) funcionário(-a) administrativo(-a) sênior; (*in hospital*) médico(-a) sênior

registration [rɛdʒɪs'treɪʃən] n (*act*) registro (*BR*), registo (*PT*); (*AUT: also: ~ number*) número da placa

registry ['rɛdʒɪstrɪ] n registro (*BR*),

registo (PT), cartório; **registry office** (BRIT) n registro (BR) or registo (PT) civil, cartório; **to get married in a ~ office** casar-se no civil

regret [rɪ'grɛt] n desgosto, pesar ♦ vt lamentar; (repent of) arrepender-se de; **regretfully** adv com pesar, pesarosamente

regular ['rɛgjulə*] adj regular; (frequent) freqüente; (usual) habitual; (soldier) de linha ♦ n habitual m/f; **regularly** adv regularmente; (shaped) simetricamente; (often) freqüentemente

regulate ['rɛgjuleɪt] vt (speed) regular; (spending) controlar; (TECH) regular, ajustar; **regulation** [rɛgju-'leɪʃən] n (rule) regra, regulamento; (adjustment) ajuste m

rehearsal [rɪ'hɜːsəl] n ensaio

rehearse [rɪ'hɜːs] vt ensaiar

reign [reɪn] n reinado; (fig) domínio ♦ vi reinar; imperar

reimburse [riːɪm'bɜːs] vt reembolsar

rein [reɪn] n (for horse) rédea

reindeer ['reɪndɪə*] n inv rena

reinforce [riːɪn'fɔːs] vt reforçar; **reinforcements** npl (MIL) reforços mpl

reinstate [riːɪn'steɪt] vt (worker) readmitir; (tax, law) reintroduzir

reject [n 'riːdʒɛkt, vb rɪ'dʒɛkt] n (COMM) artigo defeituoso ♦ vt rejeitar; (offer of help) recusar; (goods) refugar; **rejection** n rejeição f; recusa

rejoice [rɪ'dʒɔɪs] vi: **to ~ at** or **over** regozijar-se or alegrar-se de

relapse [rɪ'læps] n (MED) recaída

relate [rɪ'leɪt] vt (tell) contar, relatar; (connect): **to ~ sth to** relacionar algo com ♦ vi: **to ~ to** relacionar-se com; **~d to** ligado a, relacionado a; **relating: relating to** prep relativo a, acerca de

relation [rɪ'leɪʃən] n (person) parente m/f; (link) relação f; **~s** npl (dealings) relações fpl; (relatives) parentes mpl; **relationship** n relacionamento; (between two things) relação f; (also: **family relationship**) parentesco

relative ['rɛlətɪv] n parente m/f ♦ adj relativo; **relatively** adv relativamente

relax [rɪ'læks] vi (unwind) descontrair-se; (muscle) relaxar-se ♦ vt (grip) afrouxar; (control) relaxar; (mind, person) descansar; **relaxation** [riːlæk'seɪʃən] n (rest) descanso; (of muscle, control) relaxamento; (of grip) afrouxamento; (recreation) lazer m; **relaxed** adj relaxado; (tranquil) descontraído

relay [n 'riːleɪ, vb rɪ'leɪ] n (race) (corrida de) revezamento ♦ vt (message) retransmitir

release [rɪ'liːs] n (from prison) libertação f; (from obligation) liberação f; (of gas) escape m; (of water) despejo; (of film, book etc) lançamento ♦ vt (prisoner) pôr em liberdade; (book, film) lançar; (report, news) publicar; (gas etc) soltar; (free: from wreckage etc) soltar; (TECH: catch, spring etc) desengatar, desapertar

relegate ['rɛləgeɪt] vt relegar; (SPORT): **to be ~d** ser rebaixado

relent [rɪ'lɛnt] vi (yield) ceder; **relentless** adj (unceasing) contínuo; (determined) implacável

relevant ['rɛləvənt] adj pertinente; **~ to** relacionado com

reliable [rɪ'laɪəbl] adj (person, firm: digno) de confiança, confiável, sério; (method, machine) seguro; (news) fidedigno; **reliably** adv: **to be reliably informed that ...** saber através de fonte segura que ...

relic ['rɛlɪk] n (REL) relíquia; (of the

past) vestígio

relief [rɪˈliːf] n alívio; (*help, supplies*) ajuda, socorro; (ART, GEO) relevo

relieve [rɪˈliːv] vt (*pain, fear*) aliviar; (*bring help to*) ajudar, socorrer; (*take over from: gen*) substituir, revezar; (: *guard*) render; **to ~ sb of sth** (*luad*) tirar algo de alguém; (*duties*) destituir alguém de algo; **to ~ o.s.** fazer as necessidades

religion [rɪˈlɪdʒən] n religião f; **religious** adj religioso

relinquish [rɪˈlɪŋkwɪʃ] vt abandonar; (*plan, habit*) renunciar a

relish [ˈrelɪʃ] n (CULIN) condimento, tempero; (*enjoyment*) entusiasmo ♦ vt (*food etc*) saborear; (*thought*) ver com satisfação

reluctant [rɪˈlʌktənt] adj relutante; **reluctantly** adv relutantemente, de má vontade

rely on [rɪˈlaɪ-] vt fus confiar em, contar com; (*be dependent on*) depender de

remain [rɪˈmeɪn] vi (*survive*) sobreviver; (*stay*) ficar, permanecer; (*be left*) sobrar; (*continue*) continuar; **remainder** n resto, restante m; **remaining** adj restante; **remains** npl (*of body*) restos mpl; (*of meal*) sobras fpl; (*of building*) ruínas fpl

remand [rɪˈmɑːnd] n: **on ~** sob prisão preventiva ♦ vt: **to be ~ed in custody** continuar sob prisão preventiva, manter sob custódia

remark [rɪˈmɑːk] n observação f, comentário ♦ vt comentar; **remarkable** adj (*outstanding*) notável

remarry [riːˈmærɪ] vi casar-se de novo

remedial [rɪˈmiːdɪəl] adj de reforço; (*exercise*) terapêutico

remedy [ˈremədɪ] n: **~ (for)** remédio (contra or a) ♦ vt remediar

remember [rɪˈmembə*] vt lembrar-se de, lembrar; (*bear in mind*) ter

em mente; (*send greetings*): **~ me to her** dê lembranças a ela

remembrance [rɪˈmembrəns] n (*memory*) memória; (*souvenir*) lembrança, recordação f; **Remembrance Day** or **Sunday** n Dia m do Armistício; ver quadro

---

REMEMBRANCE DAY

Remembrance Day ou Remembrance Sunday é o domingo mais próximo do dia 11 de novembro, dia em que a Primeira Guerra Mundial terminou oficialmente e no qual se homenageia as vítimas das duas guerras mundiais. Nessa ocasião são observados dois minutos de silêncio às 11 horas, horário da assinatura do armistício com a Alemanha em 1918. Nos dias anteriores, papoulas de papel são vendidas por associações de caridade e a renda é revertida aos ex-combatentes e suas famílias.

---

remind [rɪˈmaɪnd] vt: **to ~ sb to do sth** lembrar a alguém que tem de fazer algo; **to ~ sb of sth** lembrar algo a alguém, lembrar alguém de algo; **reminder** n lembrança; (*letter*) carta de advertência

reminisce [remɪˈnɪs] vi relembrar velhas histórias; **reminiscent** adj: **tu be reminiscent of sth** lembrar algo

remit [rɪˈmɪt] vt remeter, enviar, mandar; **remittance** n remessa

remnant [ˈremnənt] n resto; (*of cloth*) retalho; **~s** npl (COMM) retalhos mpl

remorse [rɪˈmɔːs] n remorso; **remorseful** adj arrependido

remote [rɪˈməut] adj remoto; (*person*) reservado, afastado; **remote**

control n controle m remoto;
remotely adv remotamente; (slightly) levemente

removal [rɪ'muːvəl] n (taking away)
remoção f; (BRIT: from house)
mudança; (from office: sacking) afastamento, demissão f; (MED)
extração f; **removal van** (BRIT) n
caminhão m (BR) or camião m (PT)
de mudanças

remove [rɪ'muːv] vt tirar, retirar;
(clothing) tirar; (stain) remover;
(employee) afastar, demitir; (name
from list, obstacle) eliminar, remover;
(doubt, abuse) afastar; (MED) extrair

render ['rendə*] vt (thanks) trazer;
(service) prestar; (make) fazer, tornar

rendezvous ['rɔndɪvuː] n encontro; (place) ponto de encontro

renew [rɪ'njuː] vt retomar, recomeçar;
(loan etc) prorrogar; (negotiations)
reatar; **renewal** n (of contract)
renovação f; (resumption) retomada

renounce [rɪ'nauns] vt renunciar a

renovate ['renəveɪt] vt renovar;
(house) reformar

renown [rɪ'naun] n renome m;
renowned adj renomado, famoso

rent [rent] n aluguel m (BR), aluguer
m (PT) ♦ vt (also: ~ out) alugar;
rental n (for television, car) aluguel
m (BR), aluguer m (PT)

rep [rep] n abbr (COMM) = **representative**

repair [rɪ'pɛə*] n reparação f, conserto ♦ vt consertar; **in good/bad ~**
em bom/mau estado; **repair kit** n
caixa de ferramentas

repay [riː'peɪ] (irreg) vt (money)
reembolsar, restituir; (person) pagar
de volta; (debt) saldar, liquidar; (sb's
efforts) corresponder, retribuir; (favour) retribuir; **repayment** n reembolso; (of debt) pagamento

repeal [rɪ'piːl] n (of law) revogação f

♦ vt revogar

repeat [rɪ'piːt] n (RADIO, TV) repetição
f ♦ vt repetir; (COMM: order) renovar
♦ vi repetir-se

repel [rɪ'pel] vt repelir; (disgust)
repugnar; **repellent** adj repugnante ♦ n: **insect repellent** repelente m
de insetos

repent [rɪ'pent] vi arrepender-se;
repentance n arrependimento

repetitive [rɪ'petɪtɪv] adj repetitivo

replace [rɪ'pleɪs] vt (put back)
repor, devolver; (take the place of)
substituir; **replacement** n (substitution) substituição f; (substitute)
substituto(-a)

replay ['riːpleɪ] n (of match) partida
decisiva; (TV: also: **action ~**) replay m

replenish [rɪ'plenɪʃ] vt (glass) reencher; (stock etc) completar, prover

replica ['replɪkə] n réplica, cópia,
reprodução f

reply [rɪ'plaɪ] n resposta ♦ vi responder

report [rɪ'pɔːt] n relatório; (PRESS etc)
reportagem f; (BRIT: also: **school ~**)
boletim m escolar; (of gun) estampido, detonação f ♦ vt informar sobre;
(PRESS etc) fazer uma reportagem
sobre; (bring to notice) comunicar,
anunciar ♦ vi (make a report): **to
~ (on)** apresentar um relatório
(sobre); (present o.s.): **to ~ (to sb)**
apresentar-se (a alguém); (be responsible to): **to ~ to sb** obedecer
as ordens de alguém; **report card**
(US, SCOTTISH) n boletim m escolar;
reportedly adv: **she is reportedly
living in Spain** dizem que ela mora
na Espanha; **reporter** n repórter m/f

represent [reprɪ'zent] vt representar; (constitute) constituir; (COMM)
ser representante de; **representation** [reprɪzen'teɪʃən] n represen-

tação f; (picture, statue) representação, retrato; (petition) petição f; ~ations npl (protest) reclamação f, protesto; **representative** [reprı-'zentətıv] n representante m/f; (US: POL) deputado(-a) ♦ adj: **representative (of)** representativo (de)

repress [rı'prɛs] vt reprimir; **repression** n repressão f

reprisal [rı'praızl] n represália

reproach [rı'prəutʃ] n reprovação f, censura ♦ vt: to ~ **sb for sth** reprender alguém por algo; **reproachful** adj repreensivo, acusatório

reproduce [ri:prə'dju:s] vt reproduzir ♦ vi reproduzir-se

reproof [rı'pru:f] n reprovação f, repreensão f

reptile ['rɛptaıl] n réptil m

republic [rı'pʌblık] n república; **republican** adj, n republicano(-a); (US: POL): **Republican** membro(-a) do Partido Republicano

reputable ['rɛpjutəbl] adj (make etc) bem conceituado, de confiança; (person) honrado, respeitável

reputation [rɛpju'teıʃən] n reputação f

reputedly [rı'pju:tıdlı] adv segundo se diz, supostamente

request [rı'kwɛst] n pedido; (formal) petição f ♦ vt: to ~ **sth of** or **from sb** pedir algo a alguém; (formally) solicitar algo a alguém; **request stop** (BRIT) n (for bus) parada não obrigatória

require [rı'kwaıə*] vt (need: subj: person) precisar de, necessitar; (: thing, situation) requerer, exigir; (want) pedir; (order): to ~ **sb to do sth/sth of sb** exigir que alguém faça algo/algo de alguém; **requirement** n (need) necessidade f; (want) pedido

rescue ['rɛskju:] n salvamento, resgate m ♦ vt: to ~ **(from)** resgatar (de); (save, fig) salvar (de); **rescue party** n grupo or expedição f de resgate

research [rı'sə:tʃ] n pesquisa ♦ vt pesquisar

resemblance [rı'zɛmbləns] n semelhança

resemble [rı'zɛmbl] vt parecer-se com

resent [rı'zɛnt] vt (attitude) ressentir-se de; (person) estar ressentido com; **resentful** adj ressentido

reservation [rɛzə'veıʃən] n reserva

reserve [rı'zə:v] n reserva; (SPORT) suplente m/f, reserva m/f (BR) ♦ vt reservar; ~s npl (MIL) (tropas fpl da) reserva; (COMM) reserva; **in** ~ de reserva; **reserved** adj reservado

residence ['rɛzıdəns] n residência; (formal: home) domicílio; **residence permit** (BRIT) n autorização f de residência

resident ['rɛzıdənt] n (of country, town) habitante m/f; (in hotel) hóspede m/f ♦ adj (population) permanente; (doctor) interno, residente; **residential** [rɛzı'dɛnʃəl] adj residencial

residue ['rɛzıdju:] n resto

resign [rı'zaın] vt renunciar a, demitir-se de ♦ vi: to ~ **(from)** demitir-se (de); to ~ **o.s. to** resignar-se a; **resignation** n demissão f; (state of mind) resignação f; **resigned** adj resignado

resilient [rı'zılıənt] adj (person) forte; (material) resistente

resist [rı'zıst] vt resistir a

resolution [rɛzə'lu:ʃən] n resolução f; (of problem) solução f

resolve [rı'zɔlv] n resolução f ♦ vt resolver ♦ vi: to ~ **to do** resolver-se a fazer

resort [rɪ'zɔ:t] n local m turístico, estação f de veraneio; (recourse) recurso ♦ vi: **to ~ to** recorrer a; **in the last ~** em último caso, em última instância

resounding [rɪ'zaundɪŋ] adj retumbante

resource [rɪ'sɔ:s] n (raw material) recurso natural; **~s** npl (coal, money, energy) recursos mpl; **resourceful** adj engenhoso, habilidoso

respect [rɪs'pɛkt] n o respeito ♦ vt respeitar; **~s** npl (greetings) cumprimentos mpl; **respectable** adj respeitável; (large) considerável; (result, player) razoável; **respectful** adj respeitoso

respond [rɪs'pɔnd] vi (answer) responder; (react) reagir; **response** n resposta; reação f

responsibility [rɪspɔnsɪ'bɪlɪtɪ] n responsabilidade f; (duty) dever m

responsible [rɪs'pɔnsɪbl] adj sério, responsável; (job) de responsabilidade; (liable): **~ (for)** responsável (por)

responsive [rɪs'pɔnsɪv] adj receptivo

rest [rɛst] n descanso, repouso; (pause) pausa, intervalo; (support) apoio; (remainder) resto; (MUS) pausa ♦ vi descansar; (stop) parar; (be supported): **to ~ on** apoiar-se em ♦ vt descansar; (lean): **to ~ sth on/against** apoiar algo em or sobre/contra; **the ~ of them** os outros, it **~s with him to do it** cabe a ele fazê-lo

restaurant ['rɛstərɒŋ] n restaurante m; **restaurant car** (BRIT) n vagão-restaurante m

restful ['rɛstful] adj tranqüilo, repousante

restive ['rɛstɪv] adj inquieto, impaciente; (horse) rebelão(-ona), teimoso

restless ['rɛstlɪs] adj desassossegado, irrequieto

restore [rɪ'stɔ:*] vt (building, order) restaurar; (sth stolen) restituir; (health) restabelecer

restrain [rɪs'treɪn] vt (feeling) reprimir; (growth, inflation) refrear; (person): **to ~ (from doing)** impedir (de fazer); **restrained** adj (style) moderado, comedido; (person) comedido; **restraint** n (restriction) restrição f; (moderation) moderação f, comedimento; (of style) sobriedade f

restrict [rɪs'trɪkt] vt restringir, limitar; (people, animals) confinar; (activities) limitar; **restriction** n restrição f, limitação f

rest room (US) n banheiro (BR), lavabo (PT)

result [rɪ'zʌlt] n resultado ♦ vi: **to ~** in resultar em; **as a ~ of** como resultado or conseqüência de

resume [rɪ'zju:m] vt (work, journey) retomar, recomeçar ♦ vi recomeçar

résumé ['reɪzju:meɪ] n (summary) resumo; (US: curriculum vitae) curriculum vitae m, currículo

resurrection [rɛzə'rɛkʃən] n ressurreição f

resuscitate [rɪ'sʌsɪteɪt] vt (MED) ressuscitar, reanimar

retail ['ri:teɪl] adj a varejo (BR), a retalho (PT) ♦ adv a varejo (BR), a retalho (PT); **retailer** n varejista m/f (BR), retalhista m/f (PT)

retain [rɪ'teɪn] vt (keep) reter, conservar; **retainer** n (fee) adiantamento

retaliate [rɪ'tælieɪt] vi: **to ~ (against)** revidar (contra); **retaliation** [rɪtæli'eɪʃən] n represálias fpl, vingança

retch [rɛtʃ] vi fazer esforço para vomitar

retire [rɪ'taɪə*] vi aposentar-se; (withdraw) retirar-se; (go to bed) deitar-se; **retired** adj aposentado (BR), reformado (PT); **retirement** n aposentadoria (BR), reforma (PT); **retiring** adj de saída; (shy) acanhado, retraído

retort [rɪ'tɔ:t] vi replicar, retrucar

retrace [ri:'treɪs] vt: to ~ one's steps voltar sobre (os) seus passos, refazer o mesmo caminho

retract [rɪ'trækt] vt (statement) retirar, retratar; (claws) encolher; (undercarriage, aerial) recolher

retrain [ri:'treɪn] vt reciclar

retreat [rɪ'tri:t] n (place) retiro; (act) retirada ♦ vi retirar-se

retrieval [rɪ'tri:vəl] n recuperação f

retrieve [rɪ'tri:v] vt (sth lost) reaver, recuperar; (situation, honour) salvar; (error, loss) reparar

retrospect ['retrəspekt] n: in ~ retrospectivamente, em retrospecto; **retrospective** [retrə'spektɪv] adj retrospectivo; (law) retroativo

return [rɪ'tɜ:n] n regresso, volta, (of sth stolen etc) devolução f; (FINANCE: from land, shares) rendimento ♦ cpd (journey) de volta; (BRIT: ticket) de ida e volta; (match) de revanche ♦ vi voltar, regressar; (symptoms) voltar; (regain): to ~ to (consciousness) recobrar; (power) retornar a ♦ vt devolver; (favour etc) retribuir; (verdict) proferir, anunciar; (POL: candidate) eleger; ~s npl (COMM) receita; in ~ (for) em troca (de); many happy ~s (of the day)! parabéns!; by ~ (of post) por volta do correio

reunion [ri:'ju:nɪən] n (family) reunião f; (two people, class) reencontro

reunite [ri:ju:'naɪt] vt reunir; (reconcile) reconciliar

rev [rev] n abbr (AUT: = revolution) revolução f ♦ vt (also: ~ up) aumen-

tar a velocidade de

revamp [ri:'væmp] vt dar um jeito em

reveal [rɪ'vi:l] vt revelar; (make visible) mostrar; **revealing** adj revelador(a)

revel ['revl] vi: to ~ in sth/in doing sth deleitar-se com algo/em fazer algo

revenge [rɪ'vendʒ] n vingança, desforra; to take ~ on vingar-se de

revenue ['revənju:] n receita, renda

reverberate [rɪ'vɜ:bəreɪt] vi (sound) ressoar, repercutir, ecoar; (fig) repercutir

reversal [rɪ'vɜ:sl] n (of order) reversão f, (of direction) mudança em sentido contrário; (of decision) revogação f; (of roles) inversão f

reverse [rɪ'vɜ:s] n (opposite) contrário; (of cloth) avesso; (of coin) reverso; (of paper) dorso; (AUT: also: ~ gear) marcha à ré (BR), marcha atrás (PT); (setback) revés m, derrota ♦ adj (order) inverso, oposto; (direction) contrário; (process) inverso ♦ vt inverter; (position) mudar; (process, decision) revogar; (car) dar marcha a ré em ♦ vi (BRIT: AUT) dar (marcha à) ré (BR), fazer marcha atrás (PT); **reverse-charge call** (BRIT) n (TEL) ligação f a cobrar

revert [rɪ'vɜ:t] vi: to ~ to voltar a; (LAW) reverter a

review [rɪ'vju:] n (magazine, MIL) revista; (of book, film) crítica, resenha; (examination) recapitulação f, exame m ♦ vt rever, examinar; (MIL) passar em revista; (book, film) fazer a crítica or resenha de

revise [rɪ'vaɪz] vt (manuscript) corrigir; (opinion, procedure) alterar; (price) revisar; **revision** [rɪ'vɪʒn] n correção f; (for exam) revisão f

revival [rɪ'vaɪvl] n (recovery) restabelecimento; (of interest) renascença, renascimento; (THEATRE) reestréia; (of faith) despertar m

revive [rɪ'vaɪv] vt (person) reanimar, ressuscitar; (economy) recuperar; (custom) restabelecer, restaurar; (hope, courage) despertar ♦ (play) reapresentar ♦ vi (person: from faint) voltar a si, recuperar os sentidos; (: from ill-health) recuperar-se; (activity, economy) reativar; (hope, interest) renascer

revolt [rɪ'vəult] n revolta, rebelião f, insurreição f ♦ vi revoltar-se ♦ vt causar aversão a, repugnar; **revolting** adj revoltante, repulsivo

revolution [revə'lu:ʃən] n revolução f; (of wheel, earth) rotação f

revolve [rɪ'vɔlv] vi girar

revolver [rɪ'vɔlvə*] n revólver m

revolving [rɪ'vɔlvɪŋ] adj giratório

revulsion [rɪ'vʌlʃən] n aversão f, repugnância

reward [rɪ'wɔ:d] n recompensa ♦ vt: **to ~ (for)** recompensar or premiar (por); **rewarding** adj (fig) gratificante, compensador(a)

rewind [ri:'waɪnd] (irreg) vt (tape) voltar para trás

rewire [ri:'waɪə*] vt (house) renovar a instalação elétrica de

rheumatism ['ru:mətɪzəm] n reumatismo

rhinoceros [raɪ'nɔsərəs] n rinoceronte m

rhubarb ['ru:bɑ:b] n ruibarbo

rhyme [raɪm] n rima f; (verse) verso(s) m(pl) rimado(s), poesia

rhythm ['rɪðm] n ritmo

rib [rɪb] n (ANAT) costela ♦ vt (mock) zombar de, encarnar em

ribbon ['rɪbən] n fita; **in ~s** (torn) em tirinhas, esfarrapado

rice [raɪs] n arroz m; **rice pudding** n arroz m doce

rich [rɪtʃ] adj rico; (clothes) valioso; (soil) fértil; (food) suculento, forte; (colour) intenso; (voice) suave, cheio ♦ npl: **the ~** os ricos; **~es** npl (wealth) riquezas fpl

rickets ['rɪkɪts] n raquitismo

rid [rɪd] (pt, pp rid) vt: **to ~ sb of sth** livrar alguém de algo; **to get ~ of** livrar-se de; (sth no longer required) desfazer-se de

riddle ['rɪdl] n (conundrum) adivinhação f; (mystery) enigma m, charada ♦ vt: **to be ~d with** estar cheio de

ride [raɪd] (pt rode, pp ridden) n (gen) passeio; (on horse) passeio a cavalo; (distance covered) percurso, trajeto ♦ vi (as sport) montar; (go somewhere: on horse, bicycle) ir (a cavalo, de bicicleta); (journey: on bicycle, motorcycle, bus) viajar ♦ vt (a horse) montar a; (bicycle, motorcycle) andar de; (distance) percorrer; **to ~ at anchor** (NAUT) estar ancorado; **to take sb for a ~** (fig) enganar alguém; **rider** n (on horse: male) cavaleiro; (: female) amazona; (on bicycle) ciclista m/f; (on motorcycle) motociclista m/f

ridge [rɪdʒ] n (of hill) cume m, topo; (of roof) cumeeira; (wrinkle) ruga

ridicule ['rɪdɪkju:l] n escárnio, zombaria, mofa ♦ vt ridicularizar, zombar de; **ridiculous** adj ridículo

riding ['raɪdɪŋ] n equitação f

rife [raɪf] adj: **to be ~** ser comum; **to be ~ with** estar repleto de, abundar em

rifle ['raɪfl] n rifle m, fuzil m ♦ vt saquear; **rifle through** vt fus vasculhar

rift [rɪft] n fenda, fratura; (in clouds) brecha; (fig: between friends) desentendimento; (: in party) rompimento, divergência

rig [rɪg] n (also: **oil ~**) torre f de perfuração ♦ *vt* adulterar *or* falsificar os resultados de; **rig out** (*BRIT*) *vt*: to ~ **out as/in** ataviar *or* vestir como/com; **rig up** *vt* instalar, montar, improvisar

right [raɪt] *adj* certo, correto; (*suitable*) adequado, conveniente; (*: decision*) certo; (*just*) justo; (*morally good*) bom; (*not left*) direito ♦ *n* direito; (*not left*) direita ♦ *adv* bem, corretamente; (*fairly*) adequadamente, justamente; (*not on the left*) à direita; (*exactly*): ~ **now** agora mesmo ♦ *vt* colocar em pé; (*correct*) corrigir, indireitar ♦ *excl* bom!; **to be** ~ (*person*) ter razão; (*answer, clock*) estar certo; **by** ~**s** por direito; **on the** ~ à direita; **to be in the** ~ ter razão; ~ **away** imediatamente, logo, já; ~ **in the middle** bem no meio; **righteous** ['raɪtʃəs] *adj* justo, honrado; (*anger*) justificado; **rightful** *adj* (*heir*) legítimo; (*place*) justo, legítimo; **right-handed** *adj* destro; **right-hand man** *n* braço direito; **right-hand side** *n* lado direito; **rightly** *adv* (*with reason*) com razão; **right of way** *n* prioridade *f* de passagem; (*AUT*) preferência; **right-wing** *adj* de direita

rigid ['rɪdʒɪd] *adj* rígido; (*principle*) inflexível

rim [rɪm] *n* borda, beira; (*of spectacles, wheel*) aro

rind [raɪnd] *n* (*of bacon*) pele *f*, (*of lemon etc*) casca; (*of cheese*) crosta, casca

ring [rɪŋ] (*pt* **rang**, *pp* **rung**) *n* (*of metal*) aro; (*on finger*) anel *m*; (*of people, objects*) círculo, grupo; (*for boxing*) ringue *m*; (*of circus*) pista, picadeiro; (*bull~*) picadeiro, arena; (*of light, smoke*) círculo; (*of small bell*) toque *m*; (*of large bell*) badalada, repique *m* ♦ *vi* (*on telephone*)

telefonar; (*bell*) tocar; (*also*: ~ **out**) soar; (*ears*) zumbir ♦ *vt* (*BRIT*: *TEL*) telefonar a, ligar para; (*bell etc*) badalar; (*doorbell*) tocar; **to give sb a** ~ (*BRIT*: *TEL*) dar uma ligada *or* ligar para alguém; **ring back** (*BRIT*) *vi* (*TEL*) telefonar *or* ligar de volta ♦ *vt* (*TEL*) telefonar *or* ligar de volta para; **ring off** (*BRIT*) *vt* (*TEL*) desligar; **ring up** (*BRIT*) *vt* (*TEL*) telefonar a, ligar para; **ringing** ['rɪŋɪŋ] *n* (*of telephone*) toque *m*; (*of bell*) repicar *m*; (*in ears*) zumbido; **ringing tone** (*BRIT*) *n* (*TEL*) sinal *m* de chamada; **ring-leader** *n* cabeça *m/f*, cérebro

ringlets ['rɪŋlɪts] *npl* caracóis *mpl*, anéis *mpl*

ring road (*BRIT*) *n* estrada periférica *or* perimetral

rink [rɪŋk] *n* (*also*: **ice** ~) pista de patinação, rinque *m*

rinse [rɪns] *n* enxaguada ♦ *vt* enxaguar; (*also*: ~ **out**: *mouth*) bochechar

riot ['raɪət] *n* distúrbio, motim *m*, desordem *f*; (*of colour*) festival *m*, profusão *f* ♦ *vi* provocar distúrbios, amotinar-se; **to run** ~ desenfrear-se; **riotous** *adj* (*crowd*) desordeiro; (*behaviour*) turbulento; (*party*) tumultuado, barulhento

rip [rɪp] *n* rasgão *m* ♦ *vt* rasgar ♦ *vi* rasgar-se

ripe [raɪp] *adj* maduro; **ripen** *vt*, *vi* amadurecer

ripple ['rɪpl] *n* ondulação *f*, encrespação *f*; (*of laughter etc*) onda ♦ *vi* encrespar-se

rise [raɪz] (*pt* **rose**, *pp* **risen**) *n* elevação *f*, ladeira; (*hill*) colina, rampa; (*in wages*: *BRIT*) aumento; (*in prices, temperature*) subida; (*to power etc*) ascensão *f* ♦ *vi* levantar-se, erguer-se; (*prices, waters*) subir; (*sun*) nascer; (*from bed etc*) levantar(-se);

(sound) aumentar, erguer-se; (also: ~ up: building) erguer-se; (: rebel) sublevar-se; (in rank) ascender, subir; **to give ~** to ocasionar, dar origem a; **to ~ to the occasion** mostrar-se à altura da situação; **rising** adj (prices) em alta; (number) crescente, cada vez maior; (tide) montante; (sun, moon) nascente

risk [rɪsk] n risco, perigo; (INSURANCE) risco ♦ vt pôr em risco; (chance) arriscar, aventurar; **to take** or **run the ~ of doing** correr o risco de fazer; **at ~** em perigo; **at one's own ~** por sua própria conta e risco; **risky** adj perigoso

rite [raɪt] n rito; **last ~s** últimos sacramentos

ritual ['rɪtjuəl] adj ritual ♦ n ritual m; (of initiation) rito

rival ['raɪvl] adj, n rival m/f; (in business) concorrente m/f ♦ vt competir com; **rivalry** ['raɪvlrɪ] n rivalidade f

river ['rɪvə*] n rio ♦ cpd (port, traffic) fluvial; **up/down ~** rio acima/abaixo; **riverbank** n margem f (do rio); **riverbed** n leito do rio

rivet ['rɪvɪt] n rebite m, cravo ♦ vt (fig) fixar

road [rəud] n via; (motorway etc) estrada (de rodagem); (in town) rua ♦ cpd rodoviário; **roadblock** n barricada; **roadhog** n dono da estrada; **road map** n mapa m rodoviário; **road rage** n conduta agressiva dos motoristas no trânsito; **roadside** n beira da estrada; **road sign** n placa de sinalização; **roadway** n pista, estrada; **road works** npl obras fpl (na estrada); **road worthy** adj em bom estado de conservação e segurança

roam [rəum] vi vagar, perambular, errar

roar [rɔː*] n (of animal) rugido, urro; (of crowd) bramido; (of vehicle, storm) estrondo; (of laughter) barulho ♦ vi (animal, engine) rugir; (person, crowd) bradar; **to ~ with laughter** dar gargalhadas

roast [rəust] n carne f assada, assado ♦ vt assar; (coffee) torrar; **roast beef** n rosbife m

rob [rɔb] vt roubar; (bank) assaltar; **to ~ sb of sth** roubar algo de alguém; (fig: deprive) despojar alguém de algo; **robber** n ladrão (ladra) m/f; **robbery** n roubo

robe [rəub] n toga, beca; (also: bath ~) roupão m (de banho)

robin ['rɔbɪn] n pisco-de-peito-ruivo (BR), pintarroxo (PT)

robot ['rəubɔt] n robô m

robust [rəu'bʌst] adj robusto, forte; (appetite) sadio; (economy) forte

rock [rɔk] n rocha; (boulder) penhasco, rochedo; (US: small stone) cascalho; (BRIT: sweet) pirulito ♦ vt (swing gently: cradle) balançar, oscilar; (: child) embalar, acalentar; (shake) sacudir ♦ vi (object) balançar-se; (person) embalar-se; **on the ~s** (drink) com gelo; (marriage etc) arruinado, em dificuldades; **rock and roll** n rock-and-roll m; **rock-bottom** adj (fig) mínimo, ínfimo; **rockery** n jardim de plantas rasteiras entre pedras

rocket ['rɔkɪt] n foguete m

rocky ['rɔkɪ] adj rochoso, bambo, instável; (marriage) instável

rod [rɔd] n vara, varinha; (also: fishing ~) vara de pescar

rode [rəud] pt of ride

rodent ['rəudnt] n roedor m

rodeo ['rəudɪəu] (US) n rodeio m

roe [rəu] n (also: ~ deer) corça, cerva; (of fish): **hard/soft ~** ova/esperma m de peixe

rogue [rəug] n velhaco, maroto

role [rəul] n papel m

roll [rəul] n rolo; (of banknotes) maço; (also: **bread ~**) pãozinho; (register) rol m, lista; (of drums etc) rufar m ♦ vt rolar; (also: **~ up**: string) enrolar; (: sleeves) arregaçar; (cigarette) enrolar; (eyes) virar; (also. **~ out**: pastry) esticar; (lawn, road etc) aplanar ♦ vi rolar; (drum) rufar; (vehicle: also: **~ along**) rodar; (ship) balançar, jogar; **roll about** or **around** vi ficar rolando; **roll by** vi (time) passar; **roll in** vi (mail, cash) chegar em grande quantidade; **roll over** vi dar uma volta; **roll up** vi (inf) pintar, chegar, aparecer ♦ vt enrolar; **roll call** n chamada, toque m de chamada; **roller** n (in machine) rolo, cilindro; (wheel) roda, roldana; (tor lawn, road) rolo compressor; (for hair) rolo; **Rollerblades** ® [ˈrəuləbleɪdz] n patins mpl em linha; **roller coaster** n montanha-russa; **roller skates** npl patins mpl de roda

rolling pin [ˈrəulɪŋ-] n rolo de pastel

ROM [rɔm] n abbr (COMPUT: = read-only memory) ROM m

Roman [ˈrəumən] adj, n romano(-a); **Roman Catholic** adj, n católico(-a) (romano(-a))

romance [rəˈmæns] n aventura amorosa, romance m; (book) história de amor; (charm) romantismo

Romania [ru:ˈmeɪnɪə] n Romênia;
Romanian adj romeno ♦ n romeno(-a); (LING) romeno

romantic [rəˈmæntɪk] adj romântico

Rome [rəum] n Roma

romp [rɔmp] n brincadeira, travessura ♦ vi (also: **~ about**) brincar ruidosamente

rompers [ˈrɔmpəz] npl macacão m de bebê

roof [ru:f] n (of house) telhado; (of car) capota, teto ♦ vt telhar, cobrir com telhas; the **~ of the mouth** o céu da boca; **roof rack** n (AUT) bagageiro

rook [ruk] n (bird) gralha; (CHESS) torre f

room [ru:m] n (in house) quarto, aposento; (also: **bed~**) quarto, dormitório; (in school etc) sala; (space) espaço, lugar m; (scope: for improvement etc) espaço; **~s** npl (lodging) alojamento; "**~s to let**" (BRIT), "**~s for rent**" (US) "alugam-se quartos or apartamentos"; **roommate** n companheiro(-a) de quarto; **room service** n serviço de quarto; **roomy** adj espaçoso; (garment) folgado

rooster [ˈru:stə*] n galo

root [ru:t] n raiz f; (fig) origem f ♦ vi enraizar, arraigar; **~s** npl (family origins) raízes fpl; **root about** vi (fig): **to ~ about in** (drawer) vasculhar; (house) esquadrinhar; **root for** vt fus torcer por; **root out** vt extirpar

rope [rəup] n corda; (NAUT) cabo m ♦ vt (tie) amarrar; (climbers: also: **~ together**) amarrar or atar com uma corda; (area: also: **~ off**) isolar; **to know the ~s** (fig) estar por dentro (do assunto); **rope in** vt (fig): **to ~ sb in** persuadir alguém a tomar parte

rosary [ˈrəuzərɪ] n rosário

rose [rəuz] pt of **rise** ♦ n rosa; (also: **~bush**) roseira; (on watering can) crivo

rosé [ˈrəuzeɪ] n rosado, rosé m

rosemary [ˈrəuzmərɪ] n alecrim m

rosy [ˈrəuzɪ] adj rosado, rosáceo; (cheeks) rosado; (situation) cor-de-rosa inv; **a ~ future** um futuro promissor

rot [rɒt] *n* (*decay*) putrefação *f*, podridão *f*; (*fig: pej*) besteira ♦ *vt, vi* apodrecer

rota ['rəʊtə] *n* lista de tarefas, escala de serviço

rotate [rəʊ'teɪt] *vt* fazer girar, dar voltas em; (*jobs*) alternar, revezar ♦ *vi* girar, dar voltas; **rotating** *adj* rotativo

rotten ['rɒtn] *adj* podre; (*wood*) carcomido; (*fig*) corrupto; (*inf: bad*) péssimo; **to feel ~** (*ill*) sentir-se podre

rough [rʌf] *adj* (*skin, surface*) áspero; (*terrain*) acidentado; (*road*) desigual; (*voice*) áspero, rouco; (*person, manner: violent*) violento; (: *brusque*) ríspido; (*weather*) tempestuoso; (*treatment*) brutal, mau (má); (*sea*) agitado; (*district*) violento; (*plan*) preliminar; (*work*) grosseiro; (*guess*) aproximado ♦ *n* (*GOLF*): **in the ~** na grama crescida; **to sleep ~** (*BRIT*) dormir na rua; **roughage** *n* fibras *fpl*; **rough copy** *n* rascunho; **rough draft** *n* rascunho; **roughly** *adv* bruscamente; (*make*) toscamente; (*approximately*) aproximadamente

roulette [ruː'let] *n* roleta

Roumania *etc* [ruː'meɪnɪə] *n* = **Romania** *etc*

round [raʊnd] *adj* redondo ♦ *n* (*BRIT: of toast*) rodela; (*of policeman*) ronda; (*of milkman*) trajeto; (*of doctor*) visitas *fpl*; (*game: of cards etc*) partida; (*of ammunition*) cartucho; (*BOXING*) rounde *m*, assalto; (*of talks*) ciclo ♦ *vt* virar, dobrar ♦ *prep* (*surrounding*): ~ **his neck/the table** em volta da sua pescoço/da redor da mesa; (*in a circular movement*): **to move ~ the room/~ the world** mover-se pelo quarto/dar a volta

ao mundo; (*in various directions*) por; (*approximately*): ~ **about** aproximadamente ♦ *adv*: **all** ~ por todos os lados; **the long way** ~ o caminho mais comprido; **all the year** ~ durante todo o ano; **it's just** ~ **the corner** (*fig*) está pertinho; ~ **the clock** ininterrupto; **to go** ~ **the back** passar por detrás; **to go** ~ **a house** visitar uma casa; **enough to go** ~ suficiente para todos; **a** ~ **of applause** uma salva de palmas; **a** ~ **of drinks** uma rodada de bebidas; ~ **of sandwiches** sanduíche *m* (*BR*), sandes *f inv* (*PT*); **round off** *vt* terminar, completar; **round up** *vt* (*cattle*) encurralar; (*people*) reunir; (*price, figure*) arredondar; **round-about** *n* (*BRIT: AUT*) rotatória; (: *at fair*) carrossel *m* ♦ *adj* indireto; **round trip** *n* viagem *f* de ida e volta

rouse [raʊz] *vt* (*wake up*) despertar, acordar; (*stir up*) suscitar; **rousing** *adj* emocionante, vibrante

route [ruːt] *n* caminho, rota; (*of bus*) trajeto; (*of shipping*) rumo, rota; (*of procession*) rota

routine [ruː'tiːn] *adj* (*work*) rotineiro; (*procedure*) de rotina ♦ *n* rotina; (*THEATRE*) número

row¹ [rəʊ] *n* (*line*) fila, fileira; (*in theatre, boat*) fileira; (*KNITTING*) carreira, fileira ♦ *vi, vt* remar; **in a** ~ (*fig*) a fio, seguido

row² [raʊ] *n* barulho, balbúrdia; (*dispute*) discussão *f*, briga; (*scolding*) repreensão *f* ♦ *vi* brigar

rowboat ['rəʊbəʊt] (*US*) *n* barco a remo

rowdy ['raʊdɪ] *adj* (*person: noisy*) barulhento; (*occasion*) tumultuado

rowing ['rəʊɪŋ] *n* remo; **rowing boat** (*BRIT*) *n* barco a remo

royal ['rɔɪəl] adj real
Royal Academy (of Arts) (BRIT) n ver quadro

ROYAL ACADEMY

A Royal Academy, ou Royal Academy of Arts, fundada em 1768 por George III para desenvolver a pintura, a escultura e a arquitetura, situa-se em Burlington House, Piccadilly, em Londres. A cada verão há uma exposição de obras de artistas contemporâneos. A Royal Academy também oferece cursos de pintura, escultura e arquitetura.

Royal Air Force (BRIT) n força aérea britânica
royalty n família real, realeza; (payment: to author) direitos mpl autorais
rpm abbr (= revolutions per minute) rpm
RSVP abbr (= répondez s'il vous plaît) ER
Rt Hon. (BRIT) abbr (= Right Honourable) título honorífico de conselheiro do estado ou juiz
rub [rʌb] vt friccionar; (part of body) esfregar ♦ n: **to give sth a ~** dar uma esfregada em algo; **to ~ sb up** (BRIT) or **~ sb** (US) **the wrong way** irritar alguém; **rub off** vi tus esfregando; **rub off on** vt fus transmitir-se para, influir sobre; **rub out** vt apagar
rubber ['rʌbə*] n borracha; (BRIT: eraser) borracha; **rubber band** n elástico, tira elástica
rubbish ['rʌbɪʃ] n (waste) refugo; (from household, in street) lixo; (junk) coisas fpl sem valor; (fig: pej: nonsense) disparates mpl, asneiras fpl; **rubbish bin** (BRIT) n lata de lixo; **rubbish dump** n (in town) depósito (de lixo)

rubble ['rʌbl] n (debris) entulho; (CONSTR) escombros mpl
ruby ['ru:bɪ] n rubi m
rucksack ['rʌksæk] n mochila
rudder ['rʌdə*] n leme m; (of plane) leme de direção
rude [ru:d] adj (person) grosso, mal-educado; (word, manners) grosseiro; (shocking) obsceno, chocante
rug [rʌg] n tapete m; (BRIT: for knees) manta (de viagem)
rugby ['rʌgbɪ] n (also: ~ football) rúgbi m (BR), râguebi m (PT)
rugged ['rʌgɪd] adj (landscape) acidentado, irregular; (features) marcado; (character) severo, austero
ruin ['ru:ɪn] n ruína; (of plans) destruição f; (downfall) queda; (bankruptcy) bancarrota ♦ vt destruir; (future, person) arruinar; (spoil) estragar; **~s** npl (of building) ruínas fpl
rule [ru:l] n (norm) regra; (regulation) regulamento; (government) governo, domínio; (ruler) régua ♦ vt governar ♦ vi governar; (monarch) reger; (LAW): **to ~ in favour of/against** decidir oficialmente a favor de/contra; **as a ~** por via de regra, geralmente; **rule out** vt excluir; **ruler** n (sovereign) soberano(-a); (for measuring) régua; **ruling** adj (party) dominante; (class) dirigente ♦ n (LAW) parecer m, decisão f
rum [rʌm] n rum m
Rumania etc [ru:'meɪnɪə] n = **Romania** etc
rumble ['rʌmbl] n ruído surdo, barulho; (of thunder) estrondo, ribombo ♦ vi ribombar, ressoar; (stomach) roncar; (pipe) fazer barulho; (thunder) ribombar
rummage ['rʌmɪdʒ] vi vasculhar
rumour ['ru:mə*] (US **rumor**) n rumor m, boato ♦ vt: **it is ~ed that** ... corre o boato de que ...

rump steak [rʌmp-] n alcatra

rumpus ['rʌmpəs] n barulho, confusão f, zorra

run [rʌn] (pt **ran**, pp **run**) n corrida; (in car) passeio (de carro); (distance travelled) trajeto, percurso; (journey) viagem f; (series) série f; (THEATRE) temporada (SKI) pista; (in stockings) fio puxado ♦ vt (race) correr; (operate: business) dirigir; (: competition, course) organizar; (: hotel, house) administrar; (water) deixar correr; (bath) encher; (PRESS: feature) publicar; (COMPUT) rodar; (hand, finger) passar ♦ vi correr; (work: machine) funcionar; (bus, train: operate) circular; (: travel) ir; (continue: play) continuar em cartaz; (: contract) ser válido; (river, bath) fluir, correr; (colours) desbotar; (in election) candidatar-se; (nose) escorrer; **there was a ~** on houve muita procura em; **in the long ~** no final das contas, mais cedo ou mais tarde; **on the ~** em fuga, foragido; **run about** or **around** vi correr por todos os lados; **run across** vt fus encontrar por acaso, topar com, dar com; **run away** vi fugir; **run down** vt (AUT) atropelar; (production) reduzir; (criticize) criticar; **to be ~ down** estar enfraquecido or exausto; **run in** (BRIT) vt (car) rodar; **run into** vt fus (meet: person) dar com, topar com; (: trouble) esbarrar em; (collide with) bater em; **run off** vi fugir; **run out** vi (person) sair correndo; (liquid) escorrer, esgotar-se; (lease, passport) caducar, vencer; (money) acabar; **run out of** vt fus ficar sem; **run over** vt (AUT) atropelar ♦ vt fus (revise) recapitular; **run through** vt fus (instructions, play) recapitular; **run up** vt (debt) acumular ♦ vi: **to ~ up against** esbarrar em; **runaway** adj (horse)

desembestado; (truck) desgovernado; (person) fugitivo

rung [rʌŋ] pp of **ring** ♦ n (of ladder) degrau m

runner ['rʌnə*] n (in race) corredor(a) m/f; (horse) corredor m; (on sledge) patim m, lâmina; (for drawer) corrediça; **runner bean** (BRIT) n (BOT) vagem f (BR), feijão m verde (PT); **runner-up** n segundo(-a) colocado(-a)

running ['rʌnɪŋ] n (sport) corrida; (of business) direção f ♦ adj (water) corrente; (commentary) contínuo, seguido; **6 days** ~ 6 dias seguidos or consecutivos; **to be in/out of the ~ for sth** disputar algo/estar fora da disputa por algo

runny ['rʌnɪ] adj aguado; (egg) mole; **to have a ~ nose** estar com coriza, estar com o nariz escorrendo

runt [rʌnt] n (animal) nanico; (pej: person) anão (anã) m/f

run-up n: ~ **to sth** (election etc) período que antecede algo

runway ['rʌnweɪ] n (AVIAT) pista (de decolagem or de pouso)

rupture ['rʌptʃə*] n (MED) hérnia

rural ['ruərl] adj rural

rush [rʌʃ] n (hurry) pressa; (COMM) grande procura or demanda; (BOT) junco; (current) torrente f; (of emotion) ímpeto ♦ vt apressar ♦ vi apressar-se, precipitar-se; **rush hour** n rush m (BR), hora de ponta (PT)

rusk [rʌsk] n rosca

Russia ['rʌʃə] n Rússia; **Russian** adj russo ♦ n russo(-a); (LING) russo

rust [rʌst] n ferrugem f ♦ vi enferrujar

rustle ['rʌsl] vi sussurrar ♦ vt (paper) farfalhar; (US: cattle) roubar, afanar

rustproof ['rʌstpruːf] adj inoxidável, à prova de ferrugem

rusty ['rʌstɪ] adj enferrujado

rut [rʌt] n sulco; (ZOOL) cio; **to be in a ~** ser escravo da rotina

ruthless ['ruːθlɪs] adj implacável, sem piedade

rye [raɪ] n centeio

S

Sabbath ['sæbəθ] n (Christian) domingo; (Jewish) sábado

sabotage ['sæbətɑːʒ] n sabotagem f ♦ vt sabotar

saccharin(e) ['sækərɪn] n sacarina

sachet ['sæʃeɪ] n sachê m

sack [sæk] n (bag) saco, saca ♦ vt (dismiss) despedir; (plunder) saquear; **to get the ~** ser demitido; **sacking** n (dismissal) demissão f; (material) aniagem f

sacred ['seɪkrɪd] adj sagrado

sacrifice ['sækrɪfaɪs] n sacrifício ♦ vt sacrificar

sad [sæd] adj triste; (deplorable) deplorável, triste

saddle ['sædl] n sela; (of cycle) selim m ♦ vt selar; **to ~ sb with sth** (inf: task, bill) pôr algo nas costas de alguém; (: responsibility) sobrecarregar alguém com algo; **saddlebag** n alforje m

sadistic [sə'dɪstɪk] adj sádico

sadly ['sædlɪ] adv tristemente; (regrettably) infelizmente; (mistaken, neglected) gravemente; **~ lacking (in)** muito carente (de)

sadness ['sædnɪs] n tristeza

sae abbr = **stamped addressed envelope**

safe [seɪf] adj seguro; (out of danger) fora de perigo; (unharmed) ileso, incólume ♦ n cofre m, caixa-forte f;

~ from protegido de; **~ and sound** são e salvo; **(just) to be on the ~ side** por via das dúvidas; **safeguard** n salvaguarda, proteção f ♦ vt proteger, defender; **safekeeping** n custódia, proteção f; **safely** adv com segurança, a salvo; (without mishap) sem perigo

safety ['seɪftɪ] n segurança; **safety belt** n cinto de segurança; **safety pin** n alfinete m de segurança

sag [sæg] vi (breasts) cair; (roof) afundar; (hem) desmanchar

sage [seɪdʒ] n salva; (man) sábio

Sagittarius [sædʒɪ'tɛərɪəs] n Sagitário

Sahara [sə'hɑːrə] n: **the ~ (Desert)** o Saara

sail [seɪl] n (on boat) vela; (trip): **to go for a ~** dar um passeio de barco a vela ♦ vt (boat) governar ♦ vi (travel: ship) navegar, velejar; (: passenger) ir de barco; (SPORT) velejar; (set off) zarpar; **they ~ed into Rio de Janeiro** entraram no porto do Rio de Janeiro; **sail through** vt fus (fig) fazer com facilidade; **sailboat** (US) n barco a vela; **sailing** n (SPORT) navegação f a vela, vela; **to go sailing** ir velejar; **sailing boat** n barco a vela; **sailing ship** n veleiro

sailor ['seɪlə*] n marinheiro, marujo

saint [seɪnt] n santo(-a)

sake [seɪk] n: **for the ~ of** por (causa de), em consideração a; **for sb's/sth's ~** pelo bem de alguém/algo

salad ['sæləd] n salada; **salad cream** (BRIT) n maionese f; **salad dressing** n tempero or molho da salada

salami [sə'lɑːmɪ] n salame m

salary ['sælərɪ] n salário

sale [seɪl] n venda; (at reduced prices) liquidação f, saldo; (auction) leilão m; ~s npl (total amount sold) vendas fpl; "for ~" "vende-se"; on ~ à venda; on ~ or return em consignação; **sales assistant** (US **sales clerk**) n vendedor(a) m/f; **salesman/woman** (irreg) n vendedor(a) m/f; (representative) vendedor(a) m/f viajante

salmon ['sæmən] n inv salmão m
salon ['sælən] n (hairdressing ~) salão m (de cabeleireiro); (beauty ~) salão (de beleza)
saloon [sə'luːn] n (US) bar m, botequim m; (BRIT: AUT) sedã m; (ship's lounge) salão m
salt [sɔːlt] n sal m ♦ vt salgar; **salt cellar** n saleiro m; **saltwater** adj de água salgada; **salty** adj salgado
salute [sə'luːt] n (greeting) saudação f; (of guns) salva; (MIL) continência ♦ vt saudar; (MIL) fazer continência a
salvage ['sælvɪdʒ] n (saving) salvamento, recuperação f; (things saved) salvados mpl ♦ vt salvar
salvation [sæl'veɪʃən] n salvação f
same [seɪm] adj mesmo ♦ pron: the ~ o mesmo (a mesma); the ~ book as o mesmo livro que; all or just the ~ apesar de tudo, mesmo assim; the ~ to you! igualmente!
sample ['sɑːmpl] n amostra ♦ vt (food, wine) provar, experimentar
sanction ['sæŋkʃən] n sanção f ♦ vt sancionar
sanctity ['sæŋktɪtɪ] n santidade f
sanctuary ['sæŋktjuərɪ] n (holy place) santuário; (refuge) refúgio, asilo; (for animals) reserva
sand [sænd] n areia; (beach: also: ~s) praia ♦ vt (also: ~ down) lixar
sandal ['sændl] n sandália
sand: sandbox (US) n caixa de areia; **sandcastle** n castelo de areia; **sandpaper** n lixa; **sandpit** n (for children) caixa de areia; **sand-**

stone n arenito, grés m
sandwich ['sændwɪtʃ] n sanduíche m (BR), sandes f inv (PT) ♦ vt: ~ed between encaixado entre
sandy ['sændɪ] adj arenoso; (colour) vermelho amarelado
sane [seɪn] adj são (sã) do juízo; (sensible) ajuizado, sensato
sang [sæŋ] pt of sing
sanitary ['sænɪtərɪ] adj (system, arrangements) sanitário; (clean) higiênico; **sanitary towel** (US **sanitary napkin**) n toalha higiênica or absorvente
sanitation [sænɪ'teɪʃən] n (in house) instalações fpl sanitárias; (in town) saneamento; **sanitation department** (US) n comissão f de limpeza urbana
sanity ['sænɪtɪ] n sanidade f, equilíbrio mental; (common sense) juízo, sensatez f
sank [sæŋk] pt of sink
Santa Claus [sæntə'klɔːz] n Papai Noel m
sap [sæp] n (of plants) seiva ♦ vt (strength) esgotar, minar
sapling ['sæplɪŋ] n árvore f nova
sapphire ['sæfaɪə*] n safira
sarcasm ['sɑːkæzm] n sarcasmo
sardine [sɑː'diːn] n sardinha
Sardinia [sɑː'dɪnɪə] n Sardenha
sash [sæʃ] n faixa, banda
sat [sæt] pt, pp of sit
satchel ['sætʃl] n sacola
satellite ['sætəlaɪt] n satélite m; **satellite dish** n antena parabólica; **satellite television** n televisão f via satélite
satin ['sætɪn] n cetim m ♦ adj acetinado
satire ['sætaɪə*] n sátira
satisfaction [sætɪs'fækʃən] n satisfação f; (refund, apology etc) compensação f; **satisfactory** adj

satisfatório

satisfy ['sætɪsfaɪ] vt satisfazer; (convince) convencer, persuadir; **satisfying** adj satisfatório

Saturday ['sætədɪ] n sábado

sauce [sɔ:s] n molho; (sweet) calda; **saucepan** (BR), caçarola (PT)

saucer ['sɔ:sə*] n pires m inv

Saudi ['saudɪ]: ~ **Arabia** n Arábia Saudita; **Saudi (Arabian)** adj saudita

sauna ['sɔ:nə] n sauna

saunter ['sɔ:ntə*] vi: **to ~ over/ along** andar devagar para/por; **to ~ into** entrar devagar em

sausage ['sɔsɪdʒ] n salsicha, lingüiça; (cold meat) frios mpl; **sausage roll** n folheado de salsicha

savage ['sævɪdʒ] adj (cruel, fierce) cruel, feroz; (primitive) selvagem ♦ n selvagem m/f

save [seɪv] vt (rescue, COMPUT) salvar; (money) poupar, economizar; (time) ganhar; (SPORT) impedir; (avoid: trouble) evitar; (keep: seat) guardar ♦ vi (also: ~ up) poupar ♦ n (SPORT) salvamento ♦ prep salvo, exceto

saving ['seɪvɪŋ] n (on price etc) economia ♦ adj: **the ~ grace** of o único mérito de; **~s** npl (money) economias fpl; **savings account** n (caderneta de) poupança

saviour ['seɪvjə*] (US **savior**) n salvador(a) m/f

savour ['seɪvə*] (US **savor**) vt saborear; (experience) apreciar; **savoury** adj (dish: not sweet) salgado

saw [sɔ:] (pt **~ed**, pp **~ed** or **~n**) pt of **see** ♦ n (tool) serra ♦ vt serrar; **sawdust** n serragem f, pó m de serra; **sawn-off shotgun** (BRIT) n espingarda de cano serrado

saxophone ['sæksəfəun] n saxofone m

say [seɪ] (pt, pp **said**) n: **to have one's ~** exprimir sua opinião, ven-

der seu peixe (inf) ♦ vt dizer, falar; **to have a ~ or some ~ in** sth opinar sobre algo, ter que ver com algo; **could you ~ that again?** poderia repetir?; **that is to ~** ou seja; **saying** n ditado, provérbio

scab [skæb] n casca, crosta (de ferida); (pej) fura-greve m/f inv

scaffold ['skæfəuld] n (for execution) cadafalso, patíbulo; **scaffolding** n andaime m

scald [skɔ:ld] n escaldadura ♦ vt escaldar, queimar

scale [skeɪl] n escala; (of fish) escama; (of salaries, fees etc) tabela ♦ vt (mountain) escalar; **~s** npl (for weighing) balança; **~ of charges** tarifa, lista de preços; **scale down** vt reduzir

scallop ['skɔləp] n (ZOOL) vieira, venera; (SEWING) barra, arremate m

scalp [skælp] n couro cabeludo ♦ vt escalpar

scampi ['skæmpɪ] npl camarões mpl fritos

scan [skæn] vt (examine) esquadrinhar, perscrutar; (glance at quickly) passar uma vista de olhos por; (TV, RADAR) explorar ♦ n (MED) exame m

scandal ['skændl] n escândalo; (gossip) fofocas fpl; (fig: disgrace) vergonha

Scandinavian [skændɪ'neɪvɪən] adj escandinavo

scanner ['skænə*] n (MED, COMPUT) scanner m

scant [skænt] adj escasso, insuficiente; **scanty** ['skæntɪ] adj (meal) insuficiente, pobre; (underwear) sumário

scapegoat ['skeɪpgəut] n bode m expiatório

scar [skɑ:*] n cicatriz f ♦ vt marcar (com uma cicatriz)

scarce [skɛəs] adj escasso, raro; **to make o.s. ~** (inf) dar o fora, cair fora; **scarcely** adv mal, quase não; (barely) apenas

scare [skeə*] n susto; (panic) pânico ♦ vt assustar; **to ~ sb stiff** deixar alguém morrendo de medo; **bomb ~** alarme de bomba; **scare away** vt espantar; **scare off** vt = scare away; **scarecrow** n espantalho; **scared** adj: **to be scared** estar assustado or com medo

scarf [skɑ:f] (pl ~s or scarves) n cachecol m, (square) lenço (de cabeça)

scarlet ['skɑ:lɪt] adj escarlate; **scarlet fever** n escarlatina

scary ['skeərɪ] (inf) adj assustador(a)

scathing ['skeɪðɪŋ] adj mordaz

scatter ['skætə*] vt espalhar; (put to flight) dispersar ♦ vi espalhar-se; **scatterbrained** (inf) adj esquecido

scene [si:n] n (THEATRE, fig) cena; (of crime, accident) cenário; (sight) vista, panorama m; (fuss) escândalo; **scenery** ['si:nərɪ] n (THEATRE) cenário; (landscape) paisagem f; **scenic** adj pitoresco

scent [sɛnt] n perfume m; (smell) aroma; (track, fig) pista, rastro

schedule ['ʃɛdju:l, (us) 'skɛdju:l] n (of trains) horário; (of events) programa m; (list) lista ♦ vt (timetable) planejar; (visit) marcar (a hora de); **on ~** na hora, sem atraso; **to be ahead of/behind ~** estar adiantado/atrasado

scheme [ski:m] n (plan) maquinação f; (pension ~) projeto; (arrangement) arranjo ♦ vi conspirar

scholar ['skɔlə*] n aluno(-a), estudante m/f; (learned person) sábio(-a), erudito(-a); **scholarship** n erudição f; (grant) bolsa de estudos

school [sku:l] n escola; (secondary ~) colégio; (us: university) universidade f ♦ cpd escolar; **schoolboy** n aluno;

schoolchildren npl alunos mpl; **schoolgirl** n aluna; **schooling** n educação f, ensino; **schoolmaster** n professor m; **schoolmistress** n professora; **schoolteacher** n professor(a) m/f

science ['saɪəns] n ciência; **science fiction** n ficção f científica; **scientific** [saɪən'tɪfɪk] adj científico; **scientist** n cientista m/f

scissors ['sɪzəz] npl tesoura; **a pair of ~** uma tesoura

scoff [skɔf] vt (BRIT: inf: eat) engolir ♦ vi: **to ~ (at)** (mock) zombar (de)

scold [skəuld] vt ralhar

scone [skɔn] n bolinho de trigo

scoop [sku:p] n colherona; (for flour etc) pá f; (PRESS) furo (jornalístico); **scoop out** vt escavar; **scoop up** vt recolher

scooter ['sku:tə*] n (also: motor ~) lambreta; (toy) patinete m

scope [skəup] n liberdade f de ação; (of undertaking) âmbito; (of person) competência; (opportunity) oportunidade f

scorch [skɔ:tʃ] vt (clothes) chamuscar; (earth, grass) secar, queimar

score [skɔ:*] n (points etc) escore m, contagem f; (MUS) partitura; (twenty) vintena ♦ vt (goal, point) fazer; (mark) marcar, entalhar; (success) alcançar ♦ vi (in game) marcar; (FOOTBALL) marcar or fazer um gol; (keep score) marcar o escore; **on that ~** a esse respeito, por esse motivo; **~s of** (fig) um monte de; **to ~ 6 out of 10** conseguir um escore de 6 num total de 10; **score out** vt riscar; **scoreboard** n marcador m, placar m

scorn [skɔ:n] n desprezo ♦ vt desprezar, rejeitar

Scorpio ['skɔ:pɪəu] n Escorpião m

Scot [skɔt] n escocês(-esa) m/f

Scotch [skɔtʃ] *n* uísque *m* (*BR*) or whisky *m* (*PT*) escocês

Scotland ['skɔtlənd] *n* Escócia; **Scots** *adj* escocês(-esa); **Scotsman** (*irreg*) *n* escocês *m*; **Scotswoman** (*irreg*) *n* escocesa; **Scottish** *adj* escocês(-esa)

scoundrel ['skaundrəl] *n* canalha *m/f*, patife *m*

scour ['skauə*] *vt* (*search*) esquadrinhar, procurar em

scout [skaut] *n* (*MIL*) explorador *m*, batedor *m*; (*also:* **boy ~**) escoteiro; **girl ~** (*US*) escoteira; **scout around** *vi* explorar

scowl [skaul] *vi* franzir a testa; **to ~ at sb** olhar de cara feia para alguém

scrabble ['skræbl] *vi* (*claw*): **to ~ at** arranhar ♦ *vt*: **S~** ® mexe-mexe *m*; **to ~ (around) for sth** (*search*) tatear procurando algo

scram [skræm] (*inf*) *vi* dar o fora, safar-se

scramble ['skræmbl] *n* (*climb*) escalada (difícil); (*struggle*) luta ♦ *vi*: **to ~ out/through** conseguir sair com dificuldade; **to ~ for** lutar por; **scrambled eggs** *npl* ovos *mpl* mexidos

scrap [skræp] *n* (*of paper*) pedacinho; (*of material*) fragmento; (*fig: of truth*) mínimo; (*fight*) rixa, luta; (*also:* **~ iron**) ferro velho, sucata ♦ *vt* sucatar, jogar no ferro velho; (*fig*) descartar, abolir ♦ *vi* brigar; **~s** *npl* (*leftovers*) sobras *fpl*, restos *mpl*; **scrapbook** *n* álbum *m* de recortes

scrape [skreɪp] *n* (*fig*): **to be in a ~** meter-se numa enrascada ♦ *vt* raspar; (**~ against**: *hand, car*) arranhar, roçar ♦ *vi*: **to ~ through** (*in exam*) passar raspando; **scrape together** *vt* (*money*) juntar com dificuldade

scrap: scrapheap *n* (*fig*): **on the scrapheap** rejeitado, jogado fora;

scrap paper *n* papel *m* de rascunho

scratch [skrætʃ] *n* arranhão *m*; (*from claw*) arranhadura ♦ *cpd*: **~ team** time *m* improvisado, escrete *m* ♦ *vt* (*rub*) coçar; (*with claw, nail*) arranhar, unhar; (*damage*) arranhar ♦ *vi* coçar(-se); **to start from ~** partir do zero; **to be up to ~** estar à altura (das circunstâncias)

scrawl [skrɔ:l] *n* garrancho, garatujas *fpl* ♦ *vi* garatujar, rabiscar

scream [skri:m] *n* grito ♦ *vi* gritar

screech [skri:tʃ] *vi* guinchar

screen [skri:n] *n* (*CINEMA, TV, COMPUT*) tela (*BR*), écran *m* (*PT*); (*movable*) biombo; (*fig*) cortina ♦ *vt* (*conceal*) esconder, tapar; (*from the wind etc*) proteger; (*film*) projetar; (*candidates etc*) examinar; **screenplay** *n* roteiro; **screensaver** *n* protetor *m* de tela

screw [skru:] *n* parafuso ♦ *vt* apara-fusar; (*also:* **~ in**) aparar, atarraxar; **to ~ up one's eyes** franzir os olhos; **screw up** *vt* (*paper etc*) amassar; **screwdriver** *n* chave *f* de fenda or de parafuso

scribble ['skrɪbl] *n* garrancho ♦ *vt* escrevinhar ♦ *vi* rabiscar

script [skrɪpt] *n* (*CINEMA etc*) roteiro, script *m*; (*writing*) escrita, caligrafia

Scripture(s) ['skrɪptʃə(z)] *n(pl)* Sagrada Escritura

scroll [skrəul] *n* rolo de pergaminho

scrounge [skraundʒ] (*inf*) *vt* filar ♦ *n*: **to be on the ~** viver às custas de alguém (*or* dos outros *etc*)

scrub [skrʌb] *n* mato, cerrado ♦ *vt* esfregar; (*inf*) cancelar, eliminar

scruff [skrʌf] *n*: **by the ~ of the neck** pelo cangote

scruffy ['skrʌfɪ] *adj* desmazelado

scruple ['skru:pl] *n* escrúpulo

scrutiny ['skru:tɪnɪ] *n* escrutínio, exame *m* cuidadoso

scuff [skʌf] vt desgastar

scuffle ['skʌfl] n tumulto

sculptor ['skʌlptə*] n escultor(a) m/f

sculpture ['skʌlptʃə*] n escultura

scum [skʌm] n (on liquid) espuma; (pej: people) ralé f, gentinha

scurry ['skʌrɪ] vi sair correndo; **scurry off** vi sair correndo, dar no pé

scythe [saɪð] n segadeira, foice f grande

SDP (BRIT) n abbr = **Social Democratic Party**

sea [si:] n mar m ♦ cpd do mar, marino; **on the ~** (boat) no mar; (town) junto ao mar; (to go) **to ~** viajar por mar; **out to** or **at ~** em alto mar; **to be all at ~** (fig) estar confuso or desorientado; **seafood** n mariscos mpl; **seafront** n orla marítima; **seagoing** adj (ship) de longo curso; **seagull** n gaivota

seal [si:l] n (animal) foca; (stamp) selo ♦ vt fechar; **seal off** vt fechar

sea level n nível m do mar

sea lion n leão-marinho m

seam [si:m] n costura; (where edges meet) junta; (of coal) veio, filão m

seaman ['si:mən] (irreg) n marinheiro

search [sə:tʃ] n busca, procura; (COMPUT) procura; (inspection) exame m, investigação f ♦ vt (look in) procurar em; (examine) examinar; (person) revistar ♦ vi: **to ~ for** procurar; **in ~ of** à procura de; **search through** vt fus dar busca em; **search engine** n (on Internet) ferramenta f de busca; **searching** adj penetrante, perscrutador(a); **searchlight** n holofote m; **search party** n equipe f de salvamento

sea: **seashore** n praia, beira-mar f, litoral m; **seasick** adj: **to be seasick** enjoar; **seaside** n praia; **seaside resort** n balneário

season ['si:zn] n (of year) estação f; (sporting etc) temporada; (of films etc) série f ♦ vt (food) temperar; **to be in/out of ~** (fruit) estar na época/ fora de época; **seasoned** adj (fig: traveller) experiente; **season ticket** n bilhete m de temporada

seat [si:t] n (in bus, train: place) assento; (chair) cadeira; (POL) lugar m, cadeira; (buttocks) traseiro, nádegas fpl; (of trousers) fundilhos mpl ♦ vt sentar; (have room for) ter capacidade para; **to be ~ed** estar sentado; **seat belt** n cinto de segurança

sea: **sea water** n água do mar; **seaweed** n alga marinha; **seaworthy** adj em condições de navegar, resistente

sec. abbr (= second) seg

secluded [sɪ'klu:dɪd] adj (place) afastado; (life) solitário

second¹ [sɪ'kɔnd] (BRIT) vt (employee) transferir temporariamente

second² ['sɛkənd] adj segundo ♦ adv (in race etc) em segundo lugar ♦ n segundo; (AUT: also: ~ gear) segunda; (COMM) artigo defeituoso; (BRIT: SCH: degree) qualificação boa mas sem distinção ♦ vt (motion) apoiar, secundar; **secondary** adj secundário; **secondary school** n escola secundária, colégio; ver quadro

---

SECONDARY SCHOOL

Uma **secondary school** é um estabelecimento de ensino para alunos de 11 a 18 anos, alguns dos quais interrompem os estudos aos 16 anos. A maior parte dessas escolas é formada por comprehensive schools, mas algumas secondary schools ainda têm sistemas rigorosos de seleção.

second ['sɛkənd]: **second-class** adv em segunda classe; **secondhand** adj de (BR) or em (PT) segunda mão, usado; **second hand** n (on clock) ponteiro de segundos; **secondly** adv em segundo lugar; **second-rate** adj de segunda categoria; **second thoughts** (US **second thought**) npl: **to have second thoughts** (about doing sth) pensar duas vezes (antes de fazer algo); **on second thoughts** pensando bem

secrecy ['siːkrəsɪ] n sigilo

secret ['siːkrɪt] adj secreto ♦ n segredo

secretary ['sɛkrətərɪ] n secretário(-a); (BRIT: POL): **S~ of State** Ministro(-a) de Estado

secretive ['siːkrətɪv] adj sigiloso, reservado

section ['sɛkʃən] n seção f; (part) parte f, porção f; (of document) parágrafo, artigo; (of opinion) setor m; **cross-~** corte m transversal

sector ['sɛktə*] n setor m

secular ['sɛkjulə*] adj (priest) secular; (music, society) leigo

secure [sɪ'kjuə*] adj (safe) seguro; (firmly fixed) firme, rígido ♦ vt (fix) prender; (get) conseguir, obter; **security** n segurança; (for loan) fiança, garantia; **security guard** n guarda m

sedate [sɪ'deɪt] adj calmo ♦ vt sedar, tratar com calmantes; **sedative** n calmante m, sedativo

seduce [sɪ'djuːs] vt seduzir; **seductive** adj sedutor(a)

see [siː] (pt **saw**, pp **~n**) vt ver; (understand) entender; (accompany): **to ~ sb to the door** acompanhar or levar alguém até a porta ♦ vi ver; (find out) achar ♦ n sé f; **to ~ that** (ensure) assegurar que; **~ you soon!** até logo!; **see about**

vt fus tratar de; **see off** vt despedir-se de; **see through** vt fus enxergar através de ♦ vt levar a cabo; **see to** vt fus providenciar

seed [siːd] n semente f; (sperm) esperma m; (fig: gen pl) germe m; (TENNIS) pré-selecionado(-a); **to go to ~** produzir sementes; (fig) deteriorar-se; **seedling** n planta brotada da semente, muda; **seedy** adj (shabby: place) mal-cuidado; (: person) maltrapilho

seeing ['siːɪŋ] conj: **~ (that)** visto (que), considerando (que)

seek [siːk] (pt, pp **sought**) vt procurar; (post) solicitar

seem [siːm] vi parecer; **there ~s to be ...** parece que há ...

seen [siːn] pp of **see**

seep [siːp] vi filtrar-se, penetrar

seesaw ['siːsɔː] n gangorra, balanço

seethe [siːð] vi ferver; **to ~ with anger** estar danado (da vida)

see-through adj transparente

segment ['sɛgmənt] n segmento; (of orange) gomo

seize [siːz] vt agarrar, pegar; (power, hostage) apoderar-se de, confiscar; (territory) tomar posse de; (opportunity) aproveitar; **seize up** vi (TECH) gripar; **seize (up)on** vt fus valer-se de; **seizure** n (MED) ataque m, acesso; (LAW, of power) confisco, embargo

seldom ['sɛldəm] adv raramente

select [sɪ'lɛkt] adj seleto, fino ♦ vt escolher, selecionar; (SPORT) selecionar, escalar; **selection** n seleção f, escolha; (COMM) sortimento

self [sɛlf] (pl **selves**) pron see **herself**; **himself**; **itself**; **myself**; **oneself**; **ourselves**; **themselves**; **yourself** ♦ n: **the ~** o eu

self... [sɛlf] prefix: **self-assured** adj seguro de si; **self-catering**

(BRIT) adj (flat) com cozinha; (holiday) em casa alugada; **self-centred** (US self-centered) adj egocêntrico; **self-confidence** n autoconfiança, confiança em si; **self-conscious** adj inibido, constrangido; **self-control** n autocontrole m, autodomínio; **self-defence** (US self-defense) n legítima defesa, autodefesa; **in self-defence** em legítima defesa; **self-discipline** n autodisciplina; **self-employed** adj autônomo; **self-evident** adj patente; **self-interest** n egoísmo; **selfish** adj egoísta; **selfless** adj desinteressado; **self-pity** n pena de si mesmo; **self-respect** n amor m próprio; **self-righteous** adj farisaico, santarrão(-rona); **self-sacrifice** n abnegação f, altruísmo; **self-satisfied** adj satisfeito consigo mesmo; **self-service** adj de auto-serviço; **self-sufficient** adj auto-suficiente; **self-tanning** adj autobronzeador; **self-taught** adj autodidata

sell [sɛl] (pt, pp sold) vt vender; (fig): **to ~ sb an idea** convencer alguém de uma idéia ♦ vi vender-se; **to ~ at** or **for £10** vender a or por £10; **sell off** vt liquidar; **sell out** vi vender todo o estoque ♦ vt: **the tickets are all sold out** todos os ingressos já foram vendidos; **sell-by date** n vencimento; **seller** n vendedor(a) m/f; **selling price** n preço de venda

sellotape ['sɛləuteɪp] ® (BRIT) n fita adesiva, durex ® m (BR)

selves [sɛlvz] pl of **self**

semi... prefix semi..., meio...; **semicircle** n semicírculo; **semicolon** n ponto e vírgula; **semi-detached (house)** (BRIT) n (casa) geminada; **semifinal** n semifinal f

seminar ['sɛmɪnɑ:*] n seminário

semiskilled [sɛmɪ'skɪld] adj (work, worker) semi-especializado

semi-skimmed milk [sɛmɪ-'skɪmd-] n leite m semidesnatado

senate ['sɛnɪt] n senado; **senator** n senador(a) m/f

send [sɛnd] (pt, pp sent) vt mandar, enviar; (dispatch) expedir, remeter; (transmit) transmitir; **send away** vt (letter, goods) expedir, mandar; (unwelcome visitor) mandar embora; **send away for** vt fus encomendar, pedir pelo correio; **send back** vt devolver, mandar de volta; **send for** vt fus mandar buscar; (by post) encomendar, pedir pelo correio; **send off** vt (goods) despachar, expedir; (BRIT: SPORT: player) expulsar; **send out** vt (invitation) distribuir; (signal) emitir; **send up** vt (person, price) fazer subir; (BRIT: parody) parodiar; **sender** n remetente m/f; **send-off** n: **a good send-off** uma boa despedida

senior ['si:nɪə*] adj (older) mais velho or idoso; (on staff) mais antigo; (of higher rank) superior; **senior citizen** n idoso(-a); **seniority** [si:nɪ'ɔrɪtɪ] n (in service) status m

sensation [sɛn'seɪʃən] n sensação f; **sensational** adj sensacional; (headlines, result) sensacionalista

sense [sɛns] n sentido; (feeling) sensação f; (good ~) bom senso ♦ vt sentir, perceber; **it makes ~** faz sentido; **senseless** adj insensato, estúpido; (unconscious) sem sentidos, inconsciente; **sensible** adj sensato, de bom senso; (reasonable: price) razoável; (: advice, decision) sensato

sensitive ['sɛnsɪtɪv] adj sensível; (fig: touchy) suscetível

sensual ['sɛnsjuəl] adj sensual

sensuous ['sɛnsjuəs] *adj* sensual

sent [sɛnt] *pt, pp of* **send**

sentence ['sɛntəns] *n* (*LING*) frase *f*, oração *f*; (*LAW*) sentença ♦ *vt*: **to ~ sb to death/to 5 years** condenar alguém à morte/a 5 anos de prisão

sentiment ['sɛntɪmənt] *n* sentimento; (*opinion: also pl*) opinião *f*; **sentimental** [sɛntɪ'mɛntl] *adj* sentimental

separate [*adj* 'sɛprɪt, *vb* 'sɛpəreɪt] *adj* separado; (*distinct*) diferente ♦ *vt* separar; (*part*) dividir ♦ *vi* separar-se; **separately** *adv* separadamente

September [sɛp'tɛmbə*] *n* setembro

septic ['sɛptɪk] *adj* sético; (*wound*) infeccionado

sequel ['si:kwl] *n* conseqüência, resultado; (*of film, story*) continuação *f*

sequence ['si:kwəns] *n* série *f*, seqüência; (*CINEMA*) série *f*

sequin ['si:kwɪn] *n* lantejoula, paetê *m*

serene [sɪ'ri:n] *adj* sereno, tranqüilo

sergeant ['sɑ:dʒənt] *n* sargento

serial ['sɪərɪəl] *n* seriado; **serial number** *n* número de série

series ['sɪəri:z] *n inv* série *f*

serious ['sɪərɪəs] *adj* sério; (*matter*) importante; (*illness*) grave; **seriously** *adv* a sério, com seriedade; (*hurt*) gravemente

sermon ['sə:mən] *n* sermão *m*

serrated [sɪ'reɪtɪd] *adj* serrado, dentado

servant ['sə:vənt] *n* empregado(-a); (*fig*) servidor(a) *m/f*

serve [sə:v] *vt* servir; (*customer*) atender; (*subj: train*) passar por; (*apprenticeship*) fazer; (*prison term*) cumprir ♦ *vi* (*at table*) servir; (*TENNIS*) sacar; (*be useful*): **to ~ as/for/to do** servir como/para/para fazer ♦ *n*

(*TENNIS*) saque *m*; **it ~s him right** é bem feito para ele; **serve out** *vt* (*food*) servir; **serve up** *vt* = **serve out**

service ['sə:vɪs] *n* serviço; (*REL*) culto; (*AUT*) revisão *f*; (*TENNIS*) saque *m*; (*also:* **dinner ~**) aparelho de jantar ♦ *vt* (*car, washing machine*) fazer a revisão de, revisar; **the S~s** *npl* (*army, navy etc*) as Forças Armadas; **to be of ~ to sb** ser útil a alguém; **service area** *n* (*on motorway*) posto de gasolina com bar, restaurante *etc*; **service charge** (*BRIT*) *n* serviço; **serviceman** (*irreg*) *n* militar *m*; **service station** *n* posto de gasolina (*BR*), estação *f* de serviço (*PT*)

serviette [sə:vɪ'ɛt] (*BRIT*) *n* guardanapo

session ['sɛʃən] *n* sessão *f*; **to be in ~** estar reunido em sessão

set [sɛt] (*pt, pp* **set**) *n* (*of things*) jogo; (*radio ~, TV ~*) aparelho; (*of utensils*) bateria de cozinha; (*of cutlery*) talher *m*; (*of books*) coleção *f*; (*of people*) grupo; (*TENNIS*) set *m*; (*THEATRE, CINEMA*) cenário; (*HAIRDRESSING*) penteado ♦ *adj* fixo; (*ready*) pronto ♦ *vt* pôr, colocar; (*table*) pôr; (*price*) fixar; (*rules etc*) estabelecer, decidir; (*record*) estabelecer; (*time*) marcar; (*adjust*) ajustar; (*task, exam*) passar ♦ *vi* (*sun*) pôr-se; (*jam, jelly, concrete*) endurecer, solidificar-se; **to be ~ on doing sth** estar decidido a fazer algo; **to ~ to music** pôr música em; **to ~ on fire** botar fogo em, incendiar; **to ~ free** libertar; **to ~ sth going** pôr algo em movimento; **set about** *vt fus* começar com; **set aside** *vt* deixar de lado; **set back** *vt* (*cost*): **it ~ me back £5** me deu um prejuízo de £5; (*in time*): **to**

~ **sb back (by)** atrasar alguém (em);
set off vi partir, ir indo ♦ vt (bomb)
fazer explodir; (alarm) disparar;
(chain of events) iniciar; (show up
well) ressaltar; **set out** vi partir ♦ vt
(arrange) colocar, dispor; (state)
expor, explicar; **to ~ out to do sth**
pretender fazer algo; **set up** vt fundar, estabelecer; **setback** n revés
m, contratempo; **set menu** n
refeição f a preço fixo
settee [sɛ'ti:] n sofá m
setting ['sɛtɪŋ] n (background)
cenário; (position) posição f; (of
sun) pôr(-do-sol) m; (of jewel)
engaste m
settle ['sɛtl] vt (argument, matter)
resolver, esclarecer; (accounts) ajustar, liquidar; (MED: calm) acalmar,
tranquilizar ♦ vi (dust etc) assentar; (calm down: children) acalmar-se; (also: ~ **down**) instalar-se,
estabilizar-se; **to ~ for sth** concordar em aceitar algo; **to ~ on sth**
optar por algo; **settle in** vi instalar-se; **settle up** vi: **to ~ up with sb**
ajustar as contas com alguém; **settlement** n (payment) liquidação f;
(agreement) acordo, convênio; (of
village etc) povoado, povoação
f; **settler** n colono(-a), colonizador(a) m/f
setup ['sɛtʌp] n (organization) organização f; (situation) situação f
seven ['sɛvn] num sete; **seventeen**
num dezessete; **seventh** num sétimo; **seventy** num setenta
sever ['sɛvə*] vt cortar; (relations)
romper
several ['sɛvərl] adj, pron vários(-as); ~ **of us** vários de nós
severe [sɪ'vɪə*] adj severo; (serious)
grave; (hard) duro; (pain) intenso;
(dress) austero
sew [səu] vt (pt ~**ed**, pp **sewn**) vt

coser, costurar; **sew up** vt coser,
costurar
sewage ['su:ɪdʒ] n detritos mpl
sewer ['su:ə*] n (cano do) esgoto,
bueiro
sewing ['səuɪŋ] n costura; **sewing
machine** n máquina de costura
sewn [səun] pp of **sew**
sex [sɛks] n sexo; **sexist** adj sexista
sexual ['sɛksjuəl] adj sexual
sexy ['sɛksɪ] adj sexy
shabby ['ʃæbɪ] adj (person) esfarrapado, maltrapilho; (clothes) usado,
surrado; (behaviour) indigno
shack [ʃæk] n choupana, barraca
shade [ʃeɪd] n sombra; (for lamp)
quebra-luz m; (of colour) tom m,
tonalidade f; (small quantity): **a ~
(more/too large)** um pouquinho
(mais/grande) ♦ vt dar sombra a;
(eyes) sombrear; **in the ~** à sombra
shadow ['ʃædəu] n sombra ♦ vt
(follow) seguir de perto (sem ser
visto)
shady ['ʃeɪdɪ] adj à sombra; (fig: dishonest: person) suspeito, duvidoso;
(: deal) desonesto
shaft [ʃɑːft] n (of arrow, spear) haste
f; (AUT, TECH) eixo, manivela; (of
mine, of lift) poço; (of light) raio
shaggy ['ʃægɪ] adj desgrenhado
shake [ʃeɪk] (pt **shook**, pp **shaken**)
vt sacudir; (building, confidence)
abalar; (surprise) surpreender ♦ vi
tremer; **to ~ hands with sb** apertar
a mão de alguém; **to ~ one's head**
(in refusal etc) dizer não com a
cabeça; (in dismay) sacudir a
cabeça; **shake off** vt sacudir; (fig)
livrar-se de; **shake up** vt sacudir;
(fig) reorganizar; **shaky** adj (hand,
voice) trêmulo; (table) instável;
(building) abalado
shall [ʃæl] aux vb: **I ~ go** irei; **~ I
open the door?** posso abrir a

porta?; **I'll get some, ~ I?** eu vou pegar algum, está bem?

shallow ['ʃæləʊ] adj raso; (breathing) fraco; (fig) superficial

sham [ʃæm] n fraude f, fingimento ♦ vt fingir, simular

shambles ['ʃæmblz] n confusão f

shame [ʃeɪm] n vergonha ♦ vt envergonhar; **it is a ~ (that/to do)** é (uma) pena (que/fazer); **what a ~!** que pena!; **shameful** adj vergonhoso; **shameless** adj sem vergonha, descarado

shampoo [ʃæm'puː] n xampu m (BR), champô m (PT) ♦ vt lavar o cabelo (com xampu ou champô)

shandy ['ʃændɪ] n mistura de cerveja com refresco gaseificado

shan't [ʃɑːnt] = **shall not**

shanty town ['ʃæntɪ-] n favela

shape [ʃeɪp] n forma ♦ vt (form) moldar; (sb's ideas) formar; (sb's life) definir, determinar; **to take ~** tomar forma; **shape up** vi (events) desenrolar-se; (person) tomar jeito; **shapeless** adj informe, sem forma definida; **shapely** adj escultural

share [ʃeə*] n parte f; (contribution) cota; (COMM) ação f ♦ vt dividir; (have in common) compartilhar; **share out** vi distribuir; **shareholder** n acionista m/f

shark [ʃɑːk] n tubarão m

sharp [ʃɑːp] adj (razor, knife) afiado; (point, features) pontiagudo; (outline) definido, bem marcado; (pain, voice) agudo; (taste) acre; (MUS) desafinado; (contrast) marcado; (quick-witted) perspicaz; (dishonest) desonesto ♦ n (MUS) sustenido ♦ adv: **at 2 o'clock ~** às 2 (horas) em ponto; **sharpen** vt afiar; (pencil) apontar, fazer a ponta de; (fig) aguçar; **sharpener** n (also: **pencil sharpener**) apontador m (BR),

apara-lápis m inv (PT); **sharply** adv (abruptly) bruscamente; (clearly) claramente; (harshly) severamente

shatter ['ʃætə*] vt despedaçar, estilhaçar; (fig: ruin) destruir, acabar com; (: upset) arrasar ♦ vi despedaçar-se, estilhaçar-se

shave [ʃeɪv] vt barbear, fazer a barba de ♦ vi fazer a barba, barbear-se ♦ n: **to have a ~** fazer a barba; **shaver** n (also: **electric shaver**) barbeador m elétrico; **shaving** n (action) barbeação f; **shavings** npl (of wood) aparas fpl; **shaving brush** n pincel m de barba; **shaving cream** n creme m de barbear; **shaving foam** n espuma de barbear

shawl [ʃɔːl] n xale m

she [ʃiː] pron ela ♦ prefix: **~-elephant** etc elefante etc fêmea

sheaf [ʃiːf] (pl **sheaves**) n (of corn) gavela; (of papers) maço

shear [ʃɪə*] (pt ~ed, pp **shorn**) vt (sheep) tosquiar, tosar; **shear off** vi cisalhar; **shears** npl (for hedge) tesoura de jardim

sheath [ʃiːθ] n bainha; (contraceptive) camisa-de-vênus f, camisinha

shed [ʃed] (pt, pp **shed**) n alpendre m, galpão m ♦ vt (skin) mudar; (load) perder; (tears, blood) derramar; (workers) despedir

she'd [ʃiːd] = **she had; she would**

sheen [ʃiːn] n brilho

sheep [ʃiːp] n inv ovelha; **sheepdog** n pastor; **sheepskin** n pele f de carneiro, pelego

sheer [ʃɪə*] adj (utter) puro, completo; (steep) íngreme, empinado; (almost transparent) fino, translúcido ♦ adv a pique

sheet [ʃiːt] n (on bed) lençol m; (of paper) folha; (of glass, metal) lâmina, chapa; (of ice) camada

sheik(h) [ʃeɪk] n xeque m

shelf [ʃelf] (pl **shelves**) n prateleira

shell [ʃel] n (on beach) concha; (of egg, nut etc) casca; (explosive) obus m; (of building) armação f, esqueleto ♦ vt (peas) descascar; (MIL) bombardear

she'll [ʃiːl] = she will; she shall

shellfish [ʃelfɪʃ] n inv crustáceo; (pl: as food) frutos mpl do mar, mariscos mpl

shell suit n conjunto de náilon para jogging

shelter [ʃeltə*] n (building) abrigo; (protection) refúgio ♦ vt (protect) proteger; (give lodging to) abrigar ♦ vi abrigar-se, refugiar-se

shelve [ʃelv] vt (fig) pôr de lado, engavetar; **shelves** npl of **shell**

shepherd [ʃepəd] n pastor m ♦ vt guiar, conduzir; **shepherd's pie** (BRIT) n empadão m de carne e batata

sheriff [ʃerɪf] (US) n xerife m

sherry [ʃerɪ] n (vinho de) Xerez m

she's [ʃiːz] = she is; she has

Shetland [ʃetlənd] n (also: **the ~s**, **the ~ Isles**) as ilhas Shetland

shield [ʃiːld] n escudo; (SPORT) escudo, brasão m; (protection) proteção f ♦ vt: **to ~ (from)** proteger (contra)

shift [ʃɪft] n mudança; (of work) turno; (of workers) turma ♦ vt transferir; (remove) tirar ♦ vi mudar; **shifty** adj esperto, trapaceiro; (eyes) velhaco, maroto

shimmer [ʃɪmə*] vi cintilar, tremeluzir

shin [ʃɪn] n canela (da perna)

shine [ʃaɪn] n brilho, lustre m ♦ vi brilhar ♦ vt (glasses) polir; (shoes: pt, pp ~d) lustrar; **to ~ a torch on sth** apontar uma lanterna para algo

shingles [ʃɪŋɡlz] n (MED) herpeszoster m

shiny [ʃaɪnɪ] adj brilhante, lustroso

ship [ʃɪp] n (goods) embarcar; (send) transportar or mandar (por via marítima); **shipment** n carregamento; **shipping** n (ships) navios mpl; (cargo) transporte m de mercadorias (por via marítima); (traffic) navegação f; **shipwreck** n (event) malogro; (ship) naufrágio ♦ vt: **to be shipwrecked** naufragar; **shipyard** n estaleiro

shirt [ʃəːt] n (man's) camisa; (woman's) blusa; **in ~ sleeves** em manga de camisa

shit [ʃɪt] (inf!) excl merda (!)

shiver [ʃɪvə*] n tremor m, arrepio ♦ vi tremer, estremecer, tiritar

shoal [ʃəul] n (of fish) cardume m; (fig: also: **~s**) bando, multidão f

shock [ʃɔk] n (impact) choque m; (ELEC) descarga; (emotional) comoção f, abalo; (start) susto, sobressalto; (MED) trauma m ♦ vt dar um susto em, chocar; (offend) escandalizar; **shock absorber** n amortecedor m; **shocking** adj chocante, lamentável; (outrageous) revoltante, chocante

shoddy [ʃɔdɪ] adj de má qualidade

shoe [ʃuː] n (pt, pp **shod**) n sapato; (for horse) ferradura ♦ vt (horse) ferrar; **shoelace** n cadarço, cordão m (de sapato); **shoe polish** n graxa de sapato; **shoeshop** n sapataria

shone [ʃɔn] pt, pp of **shine**

shook [ʃuk] pt of **shake**

shoot [ʃuːt] n (pt, pp **shot**) n (on branch, seedling) broto ♦ vt disparar; (kill) matar à bala, balear; (wound) ferir à bala, balear; (execute) fuzilar; (film) filmar, rodar ♦ vi: **to ~ (at)** atirar (em); (FOOTBALL) chutar; **shoot down** vt (plane) derrubar, abater; **shoot in/out** vi entrar/sair correndo; **shoot up** vi (fig) subir vertiginosamente; **shooting star** n estrela cadente

shop [ʃɔp] n loja; (workshop) oficina ♦ vi (also: **go ~ping**) ir fazer compras; **shop assistant** (BRIT) n vendedor(a) m/f; **shopkeeper** n lojista m/f; **shoplifting** n furto (em lojas); **shopper** n comprador(a) m/f; **shopping** n (goods) compras fpl; **shopping bag** n bolsa de compras; **shopping centre** (US **shopping center**) n shopping (center) m; **shop window** n vitrine f (BR), montra f (PT)

shore [ʃɔː*] n (of sea) costa, praia; (of lake) margem f ♦ vt: **to ~ (up)** reforçar, escorar; **on ~** em terra

shorn [ʃɔːn] pp of **shear**

short [ʃɔːt] adj curto; (in time) breve, de curta duração; (person) baixo; (curt) seco, brusco; (insufficient) insuficiente, em falta; **to be ~ of sth** estar em falta de algo; **in ~** em resumo; **~ of doing ...** a não ser fazer ...; **everything ~ of ...** tudo a não ser ...; **it is ~ for** é a abreviatura de; **to cut ~** (speech, visit) encurtar; **to fall ~ of** não ser à altura de; **to run ~ of sth** ficar sem algo; **to stop ~** parar de repente; **to stop ~ of** chegar quase a; **shortage** n escassez f, falta; **shortbread** n biscoito amanteigado; **short circuit** n curto-circuito ♦ vt provocar um curto-circuito ♦ vi entrar em curto-circuito; **shortcoming** n defeito, imperfeição f, falha; **short(crust) pastry** (BRIT) n massa amanteigada; **shortcut** n atalho; **shorten** vt encurtar; (visit) abreviar; **shorthand** (BRIT) n estenografia; **short list** (BRIT) n lista dos candidatos escolhidos; **shortly** adv em breve, dentro em pouco; **shorts** npl: **(a pair of) shorts** um

calção (BR), um short (BR), uns calções (PT); **short-sighted** (BRIT) adj míope; (fig) imprevidente; **short-staffed** adj com falta de pessoal; **short story** n conto; **short-tempered** adj irritadiço; **short-term** adj a curto prazo; **short wave** n (RADIO) onda curta

shot [ʃɔt] pt, pp of **shoot** ♦ n (of gun) tiro; (pellets) chumbo; (try, FOOTBALL) tentativa; (injection) injeção f; (PHOT) fotografia; **to be a good/bad ~** (person) ter boa/má pontaria; **like a ~** com um relâmpago, de repente; **shotgun** n espingarda

should [ʃud] aux vb: **I ~ go now** devo ir embora agora; **he ~ be there now** ele já deve ter chegado; **I ~ go if I were you** se eu fosse você eu iria; **I ~ like to** eu gostaria de

shoulder [ˈʃəuldə*] n ombro ♦ vt (fig) arcar com; **shoulder blade** n omoplata m

shouldn't [ˈʃudnt] = **should not**

shout [ʃaut] n grito ♦ vt gritar ♦ vi (also: **~ out**) gritar, berrar; **shout down** vt fazer calar com gritos; **shouting** n gritaria, berreiro

shove [ʃʌv] vt empurrar; (inf: put): **to ~ sth in** botar algo em; **shove off** (inf) vi dar o fora

shovel [ˈʃʌvl] n pá f; (mechanical) escavadeira vt cavar com pá

show [ʃəu] (pt **-ed**, pp **~n**) n (of emotion) demonstração f; (semblance) aparência; (exhibition) exibição f; (THEATRE) espetáculo, representação f; (CINEMA) sessão f ♦ vt mostrar; (courage etc) demonstrar, dar prova de; (exhibit) mostrar, expor; (depict) ilustrar; (film) exibir ♦ vi mostrar-se; (appear) aparecer; **to be on ~** estar em exposição; **show in** vt mandar entrar; **show off** vi (pej) mostrar-se, exibir-se ♦ vt (*display*) exibir, mostrar; **show out** *vt* levar até a porta; **show up** *vi* (*stand out*) destacar-se; (*inf: turn up*) aparecer, pintar ♦ *vt* descobrir; **show business** *n* o mundo do espetáculo; **showdown** *n* confrontação *f*

shower ['ʃauə*] *n* (*rain*) pancada de chuva; (*of stones etc*) chuva, enxurrada; (*also: ~ bath*) chuveiro ♦ *vi* tomar banho (de chuveiro) ♦ *vt*: to **~ sb with** (*gifts etc*) cumular alguém de; **to have** *or* **take a ~** tomar banho (de chuveiro)

showing ['ʃəuɪŋ] *n* (*of film*) projeção *f*, exibição *f*

show jumping [-'dʒʌmpɪŋ] *n* hipismo

shown [ʃəun] *pp* of **show**

show: **show-off** (*inf*) *n* (*person*) exibicionista *m/f*, faroleiro(-a); **showpiece** *n* (*of exhibition etc*) obra mais importante; **showroom** *n* sala de exposição

shrank [ʃræŋk] *pt* of **shrink**

shred [ʃred] *n* (*gen pl*) tira, pedaço ♦ *vt* rasgar em tiras, retalhar; (*CULIN*) desfiar, picar

shrewd [ʃru:d] *adj* perspicaz

shriek [ʃri:k] *n* grito ♦ *vi* gritar, berrar

shrill [ʃrɪl] *adj* agudo, estridente

shrimp [ʃrɪmp] *n* camarão *m*

shrine [ʃraɪn] *n* santuário

shrink [ʃrɪŋk] (*pt* **shrank**, *pp* **shrunk**) *vi* encolher; (*be reduced*) reduzir-se; (*also: ~ away*) encolher-se ♦ *vt* (*cloth*) fazer encolher ♦ *vi* (*inf: pej*) psicanalista *m/f*; **to ~ from doing sth** não se atrever a fazer algo

shrivel ['ʃrɪvl] *vt* (*also: ~ up: dry*) secar; (: *crease*) enrugar ♦ *vi* secar-se, enrugar-se, murchar

Shrove Tuesday [ʃrəuv-] *n* terça-

feira gorda

shrub [ʃrʌb] *n* arbusto; **shrubbery** *n* arbustos *mpl*

shrug [ʃrʌg] *n* encolhimento dos ombros ♦ *vt*, *vi*: **to ~ (one's shoulders)** encolher os ombros, dar de ombros (*BR*); **shrug off** *vt* negar a importância de

shrunk [ʃrʌŋk] *pp* of **shrink**

shudder ['ʃʌdə*] *n* estremecimento, tremor *m* ♦ *vi* estremecer, tremer de medo

shuffle ['ʃʌfl] *vt* (*cards*) embaralhar ♦ *vi*: **to ~ (one's feet)** arrastar os pés

shun [ʃʌn] *vt* evitar, afastar-se de

shut [ʃʌt] (*pt*, *pp* **shut**) *vt* fechar ♦ *vi* fechar(-se); **shut down** *vt*, *vi* fechar; **shut off** *vt* cortar, interromper; **shut up** *vi* (*inf: keep quiet*) calar-se, calar a boca ♦ *vt* (*close*) fechar; (*silence*) calar; **shutter** *n* veneziana; (*PHOT*) obturador *m*

shuttle ['ʃʌtl] *n* (*plane: also: ~ service*) ponte *f* aérea; (*space ~*) ônibus *m* espacial

shuttlecock ['ʃʌtlkɔk] *n* peteca

shy [ʃaɪ] *adj* tímido; (*reserved*) reservado

sick [sɪk] *adj* (*ill*) doente; (*nauseated*) enjoado; (*humour*) negro; (*vomiting*): **to be ~** vomitar; **to feel ~** estar enjoado; **to be ~ of** (*fig*) estar cheio *or* farto de; **sickbay** *n* enfermaria; **sicken** *vt* (*disgust*) enojar, repugnar; **sickening** *adj* (*fig*) repugnante

sickle ['sɪkl] *n* foice *f*

sick: **sick leave** *n* licença por doença; **sickly** *adj* doentio; (*causing nausea*) nauseante; **sickness** *n* doença, indisposição *f*; (*vomiting*) náusea, enjôo

side [saɪd] *n* lado; (*of body*) flanco *m*; (*of lake*) margem *f*; (*aspect*) aspecto *m*; (*team*) time *m* (*BR*), equipa (*PT*);

(of hill) declive m ♦ cpd (door, entrance) lateral ♦ vi: **to ~ with sb** tomar o partido de alguém; **by the ~ of** ao lado de; **~ by ~** lado a lado, juntos; **from ~ to ~** para lá e para cá; **to take ~s with** pôr-se ao lado de; **sideboard** n aparador m; **sideboards** npl (BRIT) = sideburns; **sideburns** npl suíças fpl, costeletas fpl; **side effect** n efeito colateral; **sidelight** n (AUT) luz f lateral; **sideshow** n (stall) barraca; **sidestep** vt evitar; **sidetrack** vt (fig) desviar (do seu propósito); **sidewalk** (US) n calçada; **sideways** adv de lado

siege [siːdʒ] n sítio, assédio

sieve [sɪv] n peneira ♦ vt peneirar

sift [sɪft] vt peneirar; (fig) esquadrinhar, analisar minuciosamente

sigh [saɪ] n suspiro ♦ vi suspirar

sight [saɪt] n (faculty) vista, visão f; (spectacle) espetáculo ♦ vt avistar; **in ~** à vista; **on ~** (shoot) no local; **out of ~** longe dos olhos, **sightseeing** n turismo; **to go sightseeing** fazer turismo, passear

sign [saɪn] n (with hand) sinal m, aceno; (indication) indício; (notice) letreiro, tabuleta; (written) signo ♦ vt assinar; **to ~ sth over to sb** assinar a transferência de algo para alguém; **sign on** vi (MIL) alistar-se; (BRIT: as unemployed) cadastrar-se para receber auxílio-desemprego; (for course) inscrever-se ♦ vt (MIL) alistar; (employee) efetivar; **sign up** vi (MIL) alistar-se; (for course) inscrever-se ♦ vt recrutar

signal [ˈsɪɡnl] n sinal m, aviso ♦ vt (also: AUT) sinalizar, dar sinal ♦ vt (person) fazer sinais para; (message) transmitir

signature [ˈsɪɡnətʃə*] n assinatura; **signature tune** n tema m (de abertura)

significance [sɪɡˈnɪfɪkəns] n importância; **significant** adj significativo; (important) importante

sign language n mímica, linguagem f através de sinais

silence [ˈsaɪləns] n silêncio ♦ vt silenciar, impor silêncio a; **silencer** n (on gun) silenciador m; (BRIT: AUT) silencioso

silent [ˈsaɪlənt] adj silencioso; (not speaking) calado; (film) mudo; **to remain ~** manter-se em silêncio

silhouette [sɪluːˈet] n silhueta

silicon chip [ˈsɪlɪkən-] n placa or chip m de silício

silk [sɪlk] n seda ♦ adj de seda; **silky** adj sedoso

silly [ˈsɪlɪ] adj (person) bobo, idiota, imbecil; (idea) absurdo, ridículo

silt [sɪlt] n sedimento, aluvião m

silver [ˈsɪlvə*] n prata; (money) moedas fpl; (also: ~ware) prataria ♦ adj de prata; **silver-plated** adj prateado, banhado a prata; **silvery** adj prateado

similar [ˈsɪmɪlə*] adj: **~ to** parecido com, semelhante a

simmer [ˈsɪmə*] vi cozer em fogo lento, ferver lentamente

simple [ˈsɪmpl] adj simples inv; (foolish) ingênuo; **simply** adv de maneira simples; (merely) simplesmente

simultaneous [sɪməlˈteɪnɪəs] adj simultâneo

sin [sɪn] n pecado ♦ vi pecar

since [sɪns] adv desde então, depois ♦ prep desde ♦ conj (time) desde que; (because) porque, visto que, já que; **~ then** desde então; **(ever) ~** desde que

sincere [sɪnˈsɪə*] adj sincero; **sincerely** adv: **yours sincerely** (at end of letter) atenciosamente; **sincerity**

[sɪn'serɪtɪ] n sinceridade f
sing [sɪŋ] (pt **sang**, pp **sung**) vt, vi
cantar
Singapore [sɪŋgə'pɔ:*] n Cingapura (no article)
singe [sɪndʒ] vt chamuscar
singer ['sɪŋə*] n cantor(a) m/f
singing ['sɪŋɪŋ] n canto; (songs) canções fpl
single ['sɪŋgl] adj único, só; (unmarried) solteiro; (not double) simples inv ♦ n (BRIT: also: ~ ticket) passagem f de ida; (record) compacto; **single out** vt (choose) escolher; (distinguish) distinguir; **single file** n: in single file em fila indiana; **single-handed** adv sem ajuda, sozinho; **single-minded** adj determinado; **single room** n quarto individual; **singly** adv separadamente
singular ['sɪŋgjulə*] adj (odd) esquisito; (outstanding) extraordinário, excepcional; (LING) singular ♦ n (LING) singular m
sinister ['sɪnɪstə*] adj sinistro
sink [sɪŋk] (pt **sank**, pp **sunk**) n pia ♦ vt (ship) afundar; (foundations) escavar ♦ vi afundar-se; (heart) partir; (spirits) ficar deprimido; (also: ~ back, ~ down) cair or mergulhar gradativamente; **to ~ sth into** enterrar algo em; **sink in** vi (fig) penetrar
sinner ['sɪnə*] n pecador(a) m/f
sinus ['saɪnəs] n (ANAT) seio paranasal
sip [sɪp] n gole m ♦ vt sorver, bebericar
siphon ['saɪfən] n sifão m; **siphon off** vt extrair com sifão; (funds) desviar
sir [sə*] n senhor m; S~ John Smith Sir John Smith; **yes, ~** sim, senhor
siren ['saɪərn] n sirena
sirloin ['sə:lɔɪn] n lombo de vaca

sissy ['sɪsɪ] (inf) n fresco
sister ['sɪstə*] n irmã f; (BRIT: nurse) enfermeira-chefe f; (nun) freira; **sister-in-law** n cunhada
sit [sɪt] (pt, pp **sat**) vi sentar-se; (be sitting) estar sentado; (assembly) reunir-se; (for painter) posar ♦ vt (exam) prestar; **sit down** vi sentar-se; **sit in on** vt fus assistir a; **sit up** vi (after lying) levantar-se; (straight) endireitar-se; (not go to bed) aguardar acordado, velar
sitcom ['sɪtkɔm] n abbr (= situation comedy) comédia de costumes
site [saɪt] n local m, sítio; (also: building ~) lote m (de terreno) ♦ vt situar, localizar
sit-in n (demonstration) ocupação de um local como forma de protesto, manifestação f pacífica
sitting ['sɪtɪŋ] n (in canteen) turno; **sitting room** n sala de estar
situation [sɪtjuˈeɪʃən] n situação f; (job) posição f; (location) local m; "~s vacant" (BRIT) "empregos oferecem-se"
six [sɪks] num seis; **sixteen** num dezesseis; **sixth** num sexto; **sixty** num sessenta
size [saɪz] n tamanho; (extent) extensão f; (of clothing) tamanho, medida; (of shoes) número; **size up** vt avaliar, formar uma opinião sobre; **sizeable** adj considerável, importante
sizzle ['sɪzl] vi chiar
skate [skeɪt] n patim m; (fish: pl inv) arraia ♦ vi patinar; **skateboard** n skate m, patim-tábua m; **skating** n patinação f; **skating rink** n rinque m de patinação
skeleton ['skelɪtn] n esqueleto; (TECH) armação f; (outline) esquema m, esboço
sketch [sketʃ] n (drawing) desenho;

(*outline*) esboço, croqui *m*; (*THEATRE*) quadro, esquete *m* ♦ *vt* desenhar, esboçar; (*ideas: also:* ~ **out**) esbuçar; **sketchbook** *n* caderno de rascunho; **sketchy** *adj* incompleto, superficial

skewer ['skju:ə*] *n* o espetinho

ski [ski:] *n* esqui *m* ♦ *vi* esquiar; **ski boot** *n* bota de esquiar

skid [skɪd] *n* derrapagem *f* ♦ *vi* deslizar; (*AUT*) derrapar

ski: skier *n* esquiador(a) *m/f*; **skiing** *n* esqui *m*

skilful ['skɪlful] (*US* **skillful**) *adj* habilidoso, jeitoso

ski lift *n* ski lift *m*

skill [skɪl] *n* habilidade *f*, perícia; (*for work*) técnica; **skilled** *adj* hábil, perito; (*worker*) especializado, qualificado; **skillful** (*US*) *adj* = **skilful**

skim [skɪm] *vt* (*milk*) desnatar; (*glide over*) roçar ♦ *vi*: **to** ~ **through** (*book*) folhear; **skimmed milk** *n* leite *m* desnatado

skimpy ['skɪmpɪ] *adj* (*meagre*) escasso, insuficiente; (*skirt*) apertado

skin [skɪn] *n* pele *f*; *of fruit, vegetable*) casca *f* ♦ *vt* (*fruit etc*) descascar; (*animal*) tirar a pele de; **skin-deep** *adj* superficial; **skin diving** *n* caça-submarina; **skinny** *adj* magro, descarnado; **skintight** *adj* justo, grudado (no corpo)

skip [skɪp] *n* salto, pulo; (*BRIT: container*) balde *m* ♦ *vi* saltar; (*with rope*) pular corda ♦ *vt* (*pass over*) omitir, saltar; (*miss*) deixar de

skipper ['skɪpə*] *n* capitão *m*

skipping rope ['skɪpɪŋ-] (*BRIT*) *n* corda (de pular)

skirt [skɜ:t] *n* saia ♦ *vt* orlar, circundar; **skirting board** (*BRIT*) *n* rodapé *m*

ski suit *n* traje *m* de esqui

skittle ['skɪtl] *n* pau *m*; ~**s** *n* (*game*)

(*jogo de*) boliche *m* (*BR*), jogo da bola (*PT*)

skive [skaɪv] (*BRIT: inf*) *vi* evitar trabalhar

skull [skʌl] *n* caveira *f*; (*ANAT*) crânio

skunk [skʌŋk] *n* gambá *m*

sky [skaɪ] *n* céu *m*; **skylight** *n* claraboia, escotilha; **skyscraper** *n* arranha-céu *m*

slab [slæb] *n* (*stone*) bloco; (*flat*) laje *f*; (*of cake*) fatia grossa

slack [slæk] *adj* (*loose*) frouxo; (*slow*) lerdo; (*careless*) descuidoso, desmazelado; **slacks** *npl* (*trousers*) calça (*BR*), calças *fpl* (*PT*)

slam [slæm] *vt* (*door*) bater or fechar (com violência); (*throw*) atirar violentamente; (*criticize*) malhar, criticar ♦ *vi* fechar-se (com violência)

slander ['slɑ:ndə*] *n* calúnia, difamação *f*

slang [slæŋ] *n* gíria; (*jargon*) jargão *m*

slant [slɑ:nt] *n* declive *m*, inclinação *f*; (*fig*) ponto de vista; **slanted**, **slanting** *adj* inclinado; (*eyes*) puxado

slap [slæp] *n* tapa *m* or *f* ♦ *vt* dar um(a) tapa em; (*paint etc*): **to** ~ **sth on sth** passar algo em algo descuidadamente ♦ *adv* diretamente, exatamente; **slapstick** *n* (*comédia-*)pastelão *m*

slash [slæʃ] *vt* cortar, talhar; (*fig: prices*) cortar

slate [sleɪt] *n* ardósia ♦ *vt* (*fig: criticize*) criticar duramente, arrasar

slaughter ['slɔ:tə*] *n* (*of animals*) matança; (*of people*) carnificina ♦ *vt* abater; matar, massacrar; **slaughterhouse** *n* matadouro

slave [sleɪv] *n* escravo(-a) ♦ *vi* (*also:* ~ **away**) trabalhar como escravo; **slavery** *n* escravidão *f*

slay [sleɪ] (*pt* **slew**, *pp* **slain**) *vt* (*literary*) matar

sleazy ['sli:zɪ] *adj* sórdido

sledge [slɛdʒ] *n* trenó *m*; **sledge-hammer** *n* marreta, malho

sleek [sli:k] *adj* (*hair, fur*) macio, lustroso; (*car, boat*) aerodinâmico

sleep [sli:p] (*pt, pp* **slept**) *n* sono ♦ *vi* dormir; **to go to ~** dormir, adormecer; **sleep around** *vi* ser promíscuo sexualmente; **sleep in** *vi* (*oversleep*) dormir demais; **sleeper** *n* (*RAIL: train*) vagão-leitos *m* (*BR*), carruagem-camas *f* (*PT*); **sleeping bag** *n* saco de dormir; **sleeping car** *n* vagão-leitos *m* (*BR*), carruagem-camas *f* (*PT*); **sleeping partner** (*BRIT*) *n* (*COMM*) sócio comanditário; **sleeping pill** *n* pílula para dormir; **sleepless** *adj*: **a sleepless night** uma noite em claro; **sleepy** *adj* sonolento; (*fig*) morto

sleet [sli:t] *n* chuva com neve *or* granizo

sleeve [sli:v] *n* manga; (*of record*) capa

sleigh [sleɪ] *n* trenó *m*

slender ['slɛndə*] *adj* esbelto, delgado; (*means*) escasso, insuficiente

slept [slɛpt] *pt, pp of* **sleep**

slice [slaɪs] *n* (*of meat, bread*) fatia; (*of lemon*) rodela; (*utensil*) pá *f or* espátula de bolo ♦ *vt* cortar em fatias

slick [slɪk] *adj* (*skilful*) jeitoso, ágil, engenhoso; (*clever*) esperto, astuto ♦ *n* (*also:* **oil ~**) mancha de óleo

slide [slaɪd] (*pt, pp* **slid**) *n* deslizamento, escorregão *m*; (*in playground*) escorregador *m*; (*PHOT*) slide *m*; (*BRIT: also:* **hair ~**) passador *m* ♦ *vt* deslizar ♦ *vi* escorregar; **sliding** *adj* (*door*) corrediço

slight [slaɪt] *adj* (*slim*) fraco, franzino; (*frail*) delicado; (*small*) pequeno; (*trivial*) insignificante ♦ *n*

desfeita, desconsideração *f*; **not in the ~est** em absoluto, de maneira alguma; **slightly** *adv* ligeiramente, um pouco

slim [slɪm] *adj* esbelto, delgado; (*chance*) pequeno ♦ *vi* emagrecer

slime [slaɪm] *n* lodo, lima, lama

slimming ['slɪmɪŋ] *n* emagrecimento

sling [slɪŋ] (*pt, pp* **slung**) *n* (*MED*) tipóia; (*for baby*) bebêbag *m*; (*weapon*) estilingue *m*, funda ♦ *vt* atirar, arremessar, lançar

slip [slɪp] *n* (*fall*) escorregão *m*; (*mistake*) erro, lapso; (*underskirt*) combinação *f*; (*of paper*) tira ♦ *vt* deslizar ♦ *vi* (*slide*) deslizar; (*lose balance*) escorregar; (*decline*) decair; (*move smoothly*): **to ~ into/out of** entrar furtivamente em/sair furtivamente de; **to ~ sth on/off** enfiar/tirar algo; **to give sb the ~** esgueirar-se de alguém; **a ~ of the tongue** um lapso da língua; **slip away** *vi* escapulir; **slip in** *vt* meter ♦ *vi* (*errors*) surgir; **slip out** *vi* (*go out*) sair (um momento); **slip up** *vi* cometer um erro

slipper ['slɪpə*] *n* chinelo

slippery ['slɪpərɪ] *adj* escorregadio

slip-up *n* equívoco, mancada

slit [slɪt] (*pt, pp* **slit**) *n* fenda; (*cut*) corte *m* ♦ *vt* (*cut*) rachar, cortar; (*open*) abrir

slither ['slɪðə*] *vi* escorregar, deslizar

sliver ['slɪvə*] *n* (*of glass, wood*) lasca; (*of cheese etc*) fatia fina

slob [slɔb] (*inf*) *n* (*in manners*) porco(-a); (*in appearance*) maltrapilho(-a)

slog [slɔg] (*BRIT*) *vi* mourejar ♦ *n*: **it was a ~** deu um trabalho louco

slogan ['sləugən] *n* lema *m*, slogan *m*

slope [sləup] *n* ladeira; (*side of*

mountain) encosta, vertente *f*; *(ski ~)* pista; *(slant)* inclinação *f*, declive *m* ♦ *vi*: **to ~ down** estar em declive; **to ~ up** inclinar-se; **sloping** *adj* inclinado, em declive; *(handwriting)* torto

sloppy ['slɔpɪ] *adj (work)* descuidado; *(appearance)* relaxado

slot [slɔt] *n (in machine)* fenda ♦ *vt*: **to ~ into** encaixar em

slouch [slaʊtʃ] *vi* ter má postura

slovenly ['slʌvənlɪ] *adj (dirty)* desalinhado, sujo; *(careless)* desmazelado

slow [sləʊ] *adj* lento; *(not clever)* bronco, de raciocínio lento; *(watch)*: **to be ~** atrasar ♦ *adv* lentamente, devagar ♦ *vt*, *vi* ir *(mais)* devagar; **"~"** *(road sign)* "devagar"; **slowly** *adv* lentamente, devagar; **slow motion** *n*: **in slow motion** em câmara lenta

sludge [slʌdʒ] *n* lama, lodo

slug [slʌg] *n* lesma; **sluggish** *adj* vagaroso; *(business)* lento

sluice [sluːs] *n (gate)* comporta, eclusa; *(channel)* canal *m*

slum [slʌm] *n (area)* favela; *(house)* cortiço, barraco

slump [slʌmp] *n (economic)* depressão *f*; *(COMM)* baixa, queda ♦ *vi (person)* cair; *(prices)* baixar repentinamente

slung [slʌŋ] *pt*, *pp* de **sling**

slur [sləː] *n* calúnia ♦ *vt* pronunciar indistintamente

slush [slʌʃ] *n* neve *f* meio derretida

slut [slʌt] *n (pej)* mulher *f* desmazelada

sly [slaɪ] *adj (person)* astuto; *(smile, remark)* malicioso, velhaco

smack [smæk] *n* palmada ♦ *vt* bater; *(child)* dar uma palmada em; *(on face)* dar um tabefe em ♦ *vi*: **to ~ of** cheirar a, saber a

small [smɔːl] *adj* pequeno; **small change** *n* trocado; **small hours** *npl*: **in the small hours** na madrugada, lá pelas tantas *(inf)*; **smallpox** *n* varíola; **small talk** *n* conversa fiada

smart [smaːt] *adj* elegante; *(clever)* inteligente, astuto; *(quick)* vivo, esperto ♦ *vi* sofrer; **smart card** *n* smart card *m*, cartão *m* inteligente; **smarten up** *vi* arrumar-se ♦ *vt* arrumar

smash [smæʃ] *n (also: ~-up)* colisão *f*, choque *m*; *(~ hit)* sucesso de bilheteira ♦ *vt (break)* escangalhar, despedaçar; *(car etc)* bater com; *(SPORT: record)* quebrar ♦ *vi* despedaçar-se; *(against wall etc)* espatifar-se; **smashing** *(inf) adj* excelente

smattering ['smætərɪŋ] *n*: **a ~ of** um conhecimento superficial de

smear [smɪə] *n* mancha, nódoa; *(MED)* esfregaço ♦ *vt* untar; *(to make dirty)* lambuzar

smell [smɛl] *(pt, pp* **smelt** or **~ed)** *n* cheiro; *(sense)* olfato ♦ *vt* cheirar ♦ *vi (food etc)* cheirar; *(pej)* cheirar mal; **to ~ of** cheirar a; **smelly** *(pej) adj* fedorento, malcheiroso

smile [smaɪl] *n* sorriso ♦ *vi* sorrir

smirk [sməːk] *(pej) n* sorriso falso or afetado

smock [smɔk] *n* guarda-pó *m*; *(children's)* avental *m*

smog [smɔg] *n* nevoeiro com fumaça *(BR)* or fumo *(PT)*

smoke [sməʊk] *n* fumaça *(BR)*, fumo *(PT)* ♦ *vi* fumar; *(chimney)* fumegar ♦ *vt (cigarettes)* fumar; **smoked** *adj (bacon)* defumado; *(glass)* fumée; **smoker** *n (person)* fumante *m/f*; *(RAIL)* vagão *m* para fumantes; **smokescreen** *n* cortina de fumaça; **smoking** *n*: **"no smok-**

ing" (sign) "proibido fumar";
smoky adj enfumaçado; (taste) defumado

smolder ['sməuldə*] (US) vi = **smoulder**

smooth [smu:ð] adj liso, macio; (sauce) cremoso; (sea) tranqüilo, calmo; (flavour, movement) suave; (person: pej) meloso ♦ vt (also: ~ out) alisar; (: difficulties) aplainar

smother ['smʌðə*] vt (fire) abafar; (person) sufocar; (emotions) reprimir

smoulder ['sməuldə*] (US **smolder**) vi arder sem chamas; (fig) estar latente

smudge [smʌdʒ] n mancha ♦ vt manchar, sujar

smug [smʌg] (pej) adj convencido

smuggle ['smʌgl] vt contrabandear; **smuggler** n contrabandista m/f; **smuggling** n contrabando

smutty ['smʌtɪ] adj (fig) obsceno, indecente

snack [snæk] n lanche m (BR), merenda (PT); **snack bar** n lanchonete f (BR), snackbar m (PT)

snag [snæg] n dificuldade f, obstáculo

snail [sneɪl] n caracol m

snake [sneɪk] n cobra

snap [snæp] n (sound) estalo; (photograph) foto f ♦ adj repentino ♦ vt quebrar; (fingers) estalar ♦ vi quebrar; (fig: person) retrucar asperamente; **to ~ shut** fechar com um estalo; **snap at** vt fus (subj: dog) tentar morder; **snap off** vt (break) partir; **snap up** vt arrebatar, comprar rapidamente; **snappy** (inf) adj rápido; (slogan) vigoroso; **make it snappy!** faça rápido!; **snapshot** n foto f (instantânea)

snare [snɛə*] n armadilha, laço

snarl [snɑ:l] vi grunhir

snatch [snætʃ] n (small piece) tre-

cho ♦ vt agarrar; (fig: look) roubar

sneak [sni:k] (pt ~ed or (US) snuck) vi: **to ~ in/out** entrar/sair furtivamente ♦ n (inf) dedo-duro; **to ~ up on sb** chegar de mausinho perto de alguém; **sneakers** npl tênis m (BR), sapatos mpl de treino (PT)

sneer [snɪə*] vi rir-se com desdém; (mock): **to ~** zombar de, desprezar

sneeze [sni:z] n espirro ♦ vi espirrar

sniff [snɪf] n fungada; (of dog) farejada; (of person) fungadela ♦ vi fungar ♦ vt fungar, farejar; (glue, drug) cheirar

snigger ['snɪgə*] vi rir-se com dissimulação

snip [snɪp] n tesourada; (BRIT: inf) pechincha ♦ vt cortar com tesoura

sniper ['snaɪpə*] n franco-atirador(a) m/f

snob [snɔb] n esnobe m/f; **snobbish** adj esnobe

snooker ['snu:kə*] n sinuca

snoop [snu:p] vi: **to ~ about** bisbilhotar

snooze [snu:z] n soneca ♦ vi tirar uma soneca, dormitar

snore [snɔ:*] vi roncar ♦ n ronco

snorkel ['snɔ:kl] n tubo snorkel

snort [snɔ:t] n bufo, bufido ♦ vi bufar

snout [snaut] n focinho

snow [snəu] n neve f ♦ vi nevar; **snowball** n bola de neve ♦ vi (fig) aumentar (como bola de neve); **snowbound** adj bloqueado pela neve; **snowdrift** n monte m de neve (formado pelo vento); **snowdrop** n campainha branca; **snowfall** n nevada; **snowflake** n floco de neve; **snowman** (irreg) n boneco de neve; **snowplough** (US **snowplow**) n máquina limpa-neve, removedor m de neve; **snow-**

storm n nevasca, tempestade f de neve

snub [snʌb] vt desdenhar, menosprezar ♦ n repulsa

snug [snʌg] adj (sheltered) abrigado, protegido; (fitted) justo, cômodo

snuggle ['snʌgl] vi: to ~ up to sb aconchegar-se or aninhar-se a alguém

---
KEYWORD
---

so [səu] adv 1 (thus, likewise) assim, deste modo; ~ saying he walked away falou isto e foi embora; if ~ se for assim, se assim é; I didn't do it - you did ~ não fiz isso – você fez!; ~ do I, ~ am I etc eu também; ~ it is! é verdade!; I hope/think ~ espero/ acho que sim; ~ far até aqui

2 (in comparisons etc: to such a degree) tão; ~ big/quickly (that) tão grande/rápido (que)

3: ~ much ♦ adj, adv tanto; I've got ~ much work tenho tanto trabalho; ~ many tantos(-as); there are ~ many people to see tem tanta gente para ver

4 (phrases): 10 or ~ 10 mais ou menos; ~ long! (inf: goodbye) tchau!

♦ conj 1 (expressing purpose): ~ as to do para fazer; we hurried ~ as not to be late nós apressamos para não chegarmos atrasados; ~ (that) para que, a fim de que

2 (result) de modo que; he didn't arrive, ~ I left como ele não chegou, eu fui embora; ~ I was right after all então eu estava certo no final das contas

soak [səuk] vt embeber, ensopar; (put in water) pôr de molho ♦ vi estar de molho, impregnar-se;

soak in vi infiltrar; **soak up** vt absorver

soap [səup] n sabão m; **soap opera** n novela; **soap powder** n sabão m em pó; **soapy** adj ensaboado

soar [sɔ:ʳ] vi (on wings) elevar-se em vôo; (rocket, temperature) subir; (building etc) levantar-se; (price, production) disparar

sob [sɔb] n soluço ♦ vi soluçar

sober ['səubəʳ] adj (serious) sério; (not drunk) sóbrio; (colour, style) discreto; **sober up** vi ficar sóbrio

so-called [-kɔːld] adj chamado

soccer ['sɔkəʳ] n futebol m

social ['səuʃl] adj social ♦ n reunião f social; **socialism** n socialismo; **socialist** adj, n socialista m/f; **socialize** vi: to socialize (with) socializar (com); **social security** (BRIT) n previdência social; **social work** n assistência social, serviço social; **social worker** n assistente m/f social

society [sə'saɪətɪ] n sociedade f; (club) associação f; (also: high ~) alta sociedade

sociology [səusɪ'ɔlədʒɪ] n sociologia

sock [sɔk] n meia (BR), peúga (PT)

socket ['sɔkɪt] n bocal m, encaixe m; (BRIT: ELEC) tomada

soda ['səudə] n (CHEM) soda; (also: ~ water) água com gás; (US: also: ~ pop) soda

sofa ['səufə] n sofá m

soft [sɔft] adj mole; (voice, music, light) suave; (kind) meigo, bondoso; **soft drink** n refrigerante m; **soften** vt amolecer, amaciar; (effect) abrandar; (expression) suavizar ♦ vi amolecer-se; (voice, expression) suavizar-se; **softly** adv suavemente; (gently) delicadamente; **softness** n maciez f; (gentleness) suavidade f; **software** n (COMPUT) software m

soggy ['sɔgɪ] adj ensopado, encharcado

soil [sɔɪl] n terra, solo; (territory) território ♦ vt sujar, manchar

solar ['səulə*] adj solar

sold [səuld] pt, pp of **sell** ♦ adj: ~ **out** (COMM) esgotado

solder ['səuldə*] vt soldar ♦ n solda

soldier ['səuldʒə*] n soldado; (army man) militar m

sole [səul] n (of foot, shoe) sola; (fish: pl inv) solha, linguado ♦ adj único

solemn ['sɔləm] adj solene

solicitor [sə'lɪsɪtə*] n (BRIT) n (for wills etc) tabelião(-lioa) m/f; (in court) = advogado(-a)

solid ['sɔlɪd] adj sólido; (gold etc) maciço; (person) sério ♦ n sólido; ~s npl (food) comida sólida

solitary ['sɔlɪtərɪ] adj solitário, só; (walk) só; (isolated) isolado, retirado; (single) único

solo ['səuləu] n, adv solo; **soloist** n solista m/f

solution [sə'lu:ʃən] n solução f

solve [sɔlv] vt resolver, solucionar

solvent ['sɔlvənt] adj (COMM) solvente ♦ n (CHEM) solvente m

KEYWORD

---

some [sʌm] adj 1 (a certain number or amount): ~ **tea/water/biscuits** um pouco de chá/água/uns biscoitos; ~ **children came** algumas crianças vieram

2 (certain: in contrasts) algum(a); ~ **people say that ...** algumas pessoas dizem que ...

3 (unspecified) um pouco de; ~ **woman was asking for you** uma mulher estava perguntando por você; ~ **day** um dia

♦ pron 1 (a certain number) alguns

(algumas); **I've got** ~ (books etc) tenho alguns; ~ **went for a taxi and** ~ **walked** alguns foram pegar um táxi e outros foram andando

2 (a certain amount) um pouco; **I've got** ~ (milk etc) tenho um pouco

♦ adv: ~ **10 people** umas 10 pessoas

some: somebody ['sʌmbədɪ] pron = someone; **somehow** ['sʌmhau] adv de alguma maneira; (for some reason) por uma razão ou outra; **someone** ['sʌmwʌn] pron alguém; **someplace** ['sʌmpleɪs] (US) adv = somewhere

somersault ['sʌməsɔ:lt] n (deliberate) salto-mortal; (accidental) cambalhota ♦ vi dar um salto-mortal (or uma cambalhota)

something ['sʌmθɪŋ] pron alguma coisa, algo (BR)

sometime ['sʌmtaɪm] adv (in future) algum dia, em outra oportunidade; (in past): ~ **last month** durante o mês passado

sometimes ['sʌmtaɪmz] adv às vezes, de vez em quando

somewhat ['sʌmwɔt] adv um tanto

somewhere ['sʌmwɛə*] adv (be) em algum lugar; (go) para algum lugar; ~ **else** em outro lugar; para outro lugar

son [sʌn] n filho

song [sɔŋ] n canção f; (of bird) canto

son-in-law ['sʌnɪnlɔ:] n genro

soon [su:n] adv logo, brevemente; (a short time after) logo após; (early) cedo; ~ **afterwards** pouco depois; see also **as**; **sooner** adv antes, mais cedo; (preference): **I would sooner do that** preferia fazer isso; **sooner or later** mais cedo ou mais tarde

soot [sut] n fuligem f

soothe [suːð] vt acalmar, sossegar; (pain) aliviar, suavizar

sophomore ['sɔfəmɔː*] (US) n segundanista m/f

sopping ['sɔpiŋ] adj: ~ (wet) encharcado

soppy ['sɔpi] (pej) adj piegas inv

soprano [sə'prɑːnəu] n soprano m/f

sorcerer ['sɔːsərə*] n feiticeiro

sore [sɔː*] adj dolorido ♦ n chaga, ferida; **sorely** ['sɔːli] adv: **I am sorely tempted (to)** estou muito tentado (a)

sorrow ['sɔrəu] n tristeza, mágoa, dor f; **~s** npl (causes of grief) tristezas fpl

sorry ['sɔri] adj (regretful) arrependido; (condition, excuse) lamentável; **~!** desculpe!, perdão!, sinto muito!; **to feel ~ for sb** sentir pena de alguém

sort [sɔːt] n tipo ♦ vt (also: ~ out: papers) classificar; (: problems) solucionar, resolver

SOS n abbr (= save our souls) S.O.S. m

so-so adv mais ou menos, regular

sought [sɔːt] pt, pp of **seek**

soul [səul] n alma; (person) criatura; **soulful** ['səulful] adj emocional, sentimental

sound [saund] adj (healthy) saudável, sadio; (safe, not damaged) sólido, completo; (secure) seguro; (reliable) confiável; (sensible) sensato ♦ adv: **~ asleep** dormindo profundamente ♦ n (noise) som m, ruído, barulho; (volume: on TV etc) volume m; (GEO) estreito, braço (de mar) ♦ vt (alarm) soar ♦ vi soar, tocar; (fig: seem) parecer; **to ~ like** parecer; **sound out** vi sondar; **sound barrier** n barreira do som; **sound effects** npl efeitos mpl

sonoros; **soundly** adv (sleep) profundamente; (beat) completamente; **soundproof** adj à prova de som; **soundtrack** n trilha sonora

soup [suːp] n sopa; **in the ~** (fig) numa encrenca; **soupspoon** n colher f de sopa

sour ['sauə*] adj azedo, ácido; (milk) talhado; (fig) mal-humorado, rabugento; **it's ~ grapes!** (fig) é despeito!

source [sɔːs] n fonte f

south [sauθ] n sul m ♦ adj do sul, meridional ♦ adv ao or para o sul; **South Africa** n África do Sul; **South African** adj, n sul-african(-a); **South America** n América do Sul; **South American** adj, n sul-americano(-a); **southeast** n sudeste m; **southerly** ['sʌðəli] adj para o sul; (from the south) do sul; **southern** ['sʌðən] adj (to the south) para o sul, em direção do sul; (from the south) do sul, sulista; **the southern hemisphere** o Hemisfério Sul; **South Pole** n Pólo Sul; **southward(s)** adv para o sul; **south-west** n sudoeste m

souvenir [suːvə'niə*] n lembrança

sovereign ['sɔvrin] n soberano(-a)

soviet ['səuviət] adj soviético; **the S~ Union** a União Soviética

sow[1] [sau] n porca

sow[2] [səu] (pt ~**ed**, pp ~**n**) vt semear; (fig: spread) disseminar, espalhar

soya ['sɔiə] (US **soy**) n: ~ **bean** semente f de soja; ~ **sauce** molho de soja

spa [spɑː] n (town) estância hidromineral; (US: also: **health ~**) estância balnear

space [speis] n (gen) espaço; (room) lugar m; (cpd) espacial ♦ vt (also: ~ out) espaçar; **spacecraft** n nave f espacial; **spaceman** (irreg) n astro-

nauta *m*, cosmonauta *m*; **spaceship** *n* = **spacecraft**; **spacious**
['speɪʃəs] *adj* espaçoso

spade [speɪd] *n* pá *f*; **~s** *npl* (CARDS)
espadas *fpl*

Spain [speɪn] *n* Espanha

span [spæn] *n* (*also:* **wing~**) enver-
gadura; (*of arch*) vão *m*; (*in time*)
lapso, espaço ♦ *vt* estender-se sobre,
atravessar; (*fig*) abarcar

Spaniard ['spænjəd] *n* espanhol(a)
m/f

Spanish ['spænɪʃ] *adj* espanhol(a)
♦ *n* (LING) espanhol *m*, castelhano; **the ~** *npl* os espanhóis

spank [spæŋk] *vt* bater, dar palma-
das em

spanner ['spænə*] (BRIT) *n* chave *f*
inglesa

spare [spɛə*] *adj* vago, desocupado;
(*surplus*) de sobra, a mais ♦ *n* = **~
part** ♦ *vt* dispensar, passar sem;
(*make available*) dispor de; (*refrain
from hurting*) perdoar, poupar; **to ~**
de sobra; **spare part** *n* peça
sobressalente; **spare time** *n* tempo
livre; **spare wheel** *n* estepe *m*;
sparingly *adv* frugalmente, com
moderação

spark [spaːk] *n* chispa, faísca; (*fig*)
centelha

sparkle ['spaːkl] *n* cintilação *f*, brilho ♦ *vi* (*shine*) brilhar, faiscar; **sparkling** *adj* (*mineral water*) gasoso;
(*wine*) espumante; (*conversation*)
animado; (*performance*) brilhante

sparrow ['spærəu] *n* pardal *m*

sparse [spaːs] *adj* escasso; (*hair*)
ralo

spasm ['spæzəm] *n* (MED) espasmo

spastic ['spæstɪk] *n* espástico(-a)

spat [spæt] *pt, pp of* **spit**

speak [spiːk] (*pt* **spoke**, *pp* **spoken**)
vt (*language*) falar; (*truth*) dizer ♦ *vi*
falar; (*make a speech*) discursar; **~**

up! fale alto!; **speaker** *n* (*in public*)
orador(a) *m/f*; (*also:* **loudspeaker**)
alto-falante *m*; (POL:) **the Speaker** o
Presidente da Câmara

spear [spɪə*] *n* lança ♦ *vt* lancear,
arpoar

spec [spɛk] (*inf*) *n:* **on ~** por acaso

special ['spɛʃl] *adj* especial; (*edition
etc*) extra; (*delivery*) rápido; **specialist** *n* especialista *m/f*; **speciality**
[spɛʃɪˈælɪtɪ] *n* especialidade *f*; **specialize** *vi:* **to specialize (in)** especializar-se (em); **specially** *adv*
especialmente; **specialty** ['spɛʃltɪ]
(*esp US*) *n* = **speciality**

species ['spiːʃiːz] *n inv* espécie *f*

specific [spəˈsɪfɪk] *adj* específico;
specification [spɛsɪfɪˈkeɪʃən] *n*
especificação *f*; (*requirement*) re-
quinto; **~ations** *npl* (TECH) ficha técnica

specimen ['spɛsɪmən] *n* espécime
m, amostra; (*for testing*, MED) espécime

speck [spɛk] *n* mancha, pinta

speckled ['spɛkld] *adj* pintado

specs [spɛks] (*inf*) *npl* óculos *mpl*

spectacle ['spɛktəkl] *n* espetáculo;
~s *npl* (*glasses*) óculos *mpl*; **spectacular** [spɛkˈtækjulə*] *adj* espetacular ♦ *n* (CINEMA *etc*) superprodução
f

spectator [spɛkˈteɪtə*] *n* especta-
dor(a) *m/f*

spectrum ['spɛktrəm] (*pl* **spectra**)
n espectro

speech [spiːtʃ] *n* (*faculty*, THEATRE)
fala; (*formal talk*) discurso; **speechless** *adj* estupefato, emudecido

speed [spiːd] *n* velocidade *f*; (*rate*)
rapidez *f*; (*haste*) pressa; (*prompt-
ness*) prontidão *f*; **at full** *ou* **top ~** a
toda a velocidade; **speed up** (*pt,
pp* **speeded up**) *vt, vi* acelerar;
speedboat *n* lancha; **speedily**

adv depressa, rapidamente; **speeding** *n* (AUT) excesso de velocidade; **speed limit** *n* limite *m* de velocidade, velocidade *f* máxima; **speedometer** [spɪ'dɔmɪtə*] *n* velocímetro; **speedway** *n* (SPORT: also: **speedway racing**) corrida de motocicleta; **speedy** *adj* veloz, rápido; (*prompt*) pronto, imediato

spell [spel] (*pt, pp* ~**ed**, (BRIT) **spelt**) *n* (*also:* **magic ~**) encanto, feitiço; (*period of time*) período, temporada ♦ *vt* (*also:* ~ **out**) soletrar; (*fig*) pressagiar, ser sinal de; **to cast a ~ on sb** enfeitiçar alguém; **he can't ~** não sabe escrever bem, comete erros de ortografia; **spellbound** *adj* enfeitiçado, fascinado; **spelling** *n* ortografia

spend [spend] (*pt, pp* **spent**) *vt* (*money*) gastar; (*time*) passar

sperm [spɜ:m] *n* esperma

sphere [sfɪə*] *n* esfera

spice [spaɪs] *n* especiaria ♦ *vt* condimentar

spicy ['spaɪsɪ] *adj* condimentado

spider ['spaɪdə*] *n* aranha

spike [spaɪk] *n* (*point*) ponta, espigão *m*; (BOT) espiga

spill [spɪl] (*pt, pp* **spilt** or ~**ed**) *vt* entornar, derramar ♦ *vi* derramar-se; **spill over** *vi* transbordar

spin [spɪn] (*pt* **spun** or **span**, *pp* **spun**) *n* (AVIAT) parafuso; (*trip in car*) volta or passeio de carro; (*ball*): **to put ~ on** fazer rolar ♦ *vt* (*wool etc*) fiar, tecer ♦ *vi* girar, rodar; (*make thread*) tecer; **spin out** *vt* prolongar; (*money*) fazer render

spinach ['spɪnɪtʃ] *n* espinafre *m*

spinal cord ['spaɪnl-] *n* espinha dorsal

spin-dryer (BRIT) *n* secadora

spine [spaɪn] *n* espinha dorsal; (*thorn*) espinho; **spineless** *adj* (*fig*)

fraco, covarde

spinster ['spɪnstə*] *n* solteira

spiral ['spaɪərl] *n* espiral *f* ♦ *vi* (*prices*) disparar; **spiral staircase** *n* escada em caracol

spire ['spaɪə*] *n* flecha, agulha

spirit ['spɪrɪt] *n* (*soul*) alma; (*ghost*) fantasma *m*; (*courage*) coragem f, ânimo; (*frame of mind*) estado de espírito; (*sense*) sentido; **~s** *npl* (*drink*) álcool *m*; **in good ~s** alegre, de bom humor; **spirited** *adj* animado, espirituoso; **spiritual** *adj* espiritual ♦ *n* (*also:* **Negro spiritual**) *canto religioso dos negros*

spit [spɪt] (*pt, pp* **spat**) *n* (*for roasting*) espeto; (*saliva*) saliva ♦ *vi* cuspir; (*sound*) escarrar; (*rain*) chuviscar

spite [spaɪt] *n* rancor *m*, ressentimento ♦ *vt* contrariar; **in ~ of** apesar de, a despeito de; **spiteful** *adj* maldoso, malévolo

splash [splæʃ] *n* (*sound*) borrifo, respingo; (*of colour*) mancha ♦ *vt*: **to ~ (with)** salpicar (de) ♦ *vi* (*also:* ~ **about**) borrifar, respingar

spleen [spli:n] *n* (ANAT) baço

splendid ['splendɪd] *adj* esplêndido; (*impressive*) impressionante

splint [splɪnt] *n* tala

splinter ['splɪntə*] *n* (*of wood, glass*) lasca; (*in finger*) farpa ♦ *vi* lascar-se, estilhaçar-se, despedaçar-se

split [splɪt] (*pt, pp* **split**) *n* fenda, brecha; (*fig: division*) rompimento; (: *difference*) diferença; (POL) divisão ♦ *vt* partir, fender; (*party, work*) dividir; (*profits*) repartir ♦ *vi* (*divide*) dividir-se, repartir-se; **split up** *vi* (*couple*) separar-se, acabar; (*meeting*) terminar

spoil [spɔɪl] (*pt, pp* ~**t** or ~**ed**) *vt* (*damage*) danificar; (*mar*) estragar,

arruinar; (child) mimar; **spoils** npl
desejo, saque m; **spoilsport** (pej)
n desmancha-prazeres m/f inv

spoke [spəuk] pt of **speak** ♦ n raio

spoken ['spəukn] pp of **speak**

spokesman ['spəuksmən] (irreg) n
porta-voz m

spokeswoman ['spəukswumən]
(irreg) n porta-voz f

sponge [spʌndʒ] n esponja; (cake)
pão-de-ló m ♦ vt lavar com esponja
♦ vi: **to ~ on sb** viver às custas de
alguém; **sponge bag** (BRIT) n bolsa
de toalete

sponsor ['spɔnsə*] n patrocina-
dor(a) m/f ♦ vt patrocinar; apadri-
nhar; fiar; (applicant, proposal)
apoiar, defender; **sponsorship** n
patrocínio

spontaneous [spɔn'teɪnɪəs] adj
espontâneo

spooky ['spu:kɪ] (inf) adj arrepiante

spoon [spu:n] n colher f; **spoon-
feed** (irreg) vt dar de comer com
colher; (fig) dar tudo mastigado a;
spoonful n colherada

sport [spɔ:t] n esporte m (BR), desporto m (PT); (person) bom perdedor
(boa perdedora) m/f ♦ vt (wear) exibir; **sporting** adj esportivo (BR),
desportivo (PT); (generous) nobre;
to give sb a sporting chance dar
uma grande chance a alguém;
sport jacket (US) n = **sports jacket**; **sports car** n carro esporte
(BR), carro de sport (PT); **sports
jacket** (BRIT) n casaco esportivo (BR)
or desportivo (PT); **sportsman**
(irreg) n esportista m (BR), desportista m (PT); **sportsmanship** n espírito esportivo (BR) or desportivo (PT);
sportswear n roupa esportiva (BR)
or esporte (PT) or esporte;
sportswoman (irreg) n esportista
(BR), desportista (PT); **sporty** adj

esportivo (BR), desportivo (PT)

spot [spɔt] n (mark) marca; (place)
lugar m, local m; (dot: on pattern)
mancha, ponto; (on skin) espinha;
(RADIO, TV) hora; (small amount): **a ~
of** um pouquinho de ♦ vt notar; on
the **~** na hora; (there) ali mesmo; (in
difficulty) em apuros; **spot check** n
fiscalização f de surpresa; **spotless**
adj sem mancha, imaculado; **spot-
light** n holofote m, refletor m;
spotted adj com bolinhas; **spotty**
adj cheio de espinhas

spouse [spauz] n cônjuge m/f

spout [spaut] n (of jug) bico; (of
pipe) cano ♦ vi jorrar

sprain [spreɪn] n distensão f, torce-
dura ♦ vt torcer

sprang [spræŋ] pt of **spring**

sprawl [sprɔ:l] vi esparramar-se

spray [spreɪ] n borrifo; (container)
spray m, atomizador m; (garden ~)
vaporizador m; (of flowers) ramalhe-
te m ♦ vt pulverizar; (crops) borrifar,
regar

spread [spred] (pt, pp **spread**) n
extensão f; (distribution) expansão f,
difusão f; (CULIN) pasta; (inf: food)
banquete m ♦ vt espalhar; (butter)
untar, passar; (wings, sails) abrir,
desdobrar; (workload, wealth) distribuir; (scatter) disseminar ♦ vi (news,
stain) espalhar-se; (disease) alastrar-
se; **spread out** vi dispersar-se;
spread-eagled adj estirado;
spreadsheet n (COMPUT) planilha

spree [spri:] n: **to go on a ~** cair na
farra

sprightly ['spraitli] adj ativo, ágil

spring [sprɪŋ] (pt **sprang**, pp
sprung) n salto, pulo; (coiled metal)
mola; (season) primavera; (of water)
fonte f, **spring up** vi aparecer de
repente; **springboard** n trampolim m; **spring-cleaning** n limpeza

total, faxina (geral); **springtime** n primavera

sprinkle ['sprɪŋkl] vt (liquid) salpicar; (salt, sugar) borrifar; **to ~ water on, ~ with water** salpicar de água

sprint [sprɪnt] n corrida de pequena distância ♦ vi correr a toda velocidade; **sprinter** n corredor(a) m/f

sprout [spraʊt] vi brotar, germinar; **sprouts** npl (also: **Brussels ~s**) couves-de-Bruxelas fpl

sprung [sprʌŋ] pp of **spring**

spun [spʌn] pt, pp of **spin**

spur [spəː*] n espora; (fig) estímulo ♦ vt (also: **~ on**) incitar, estimular; **on the ~ of the moment** de improviso, de repente

spurn [spəːn] vt desdenhar, desprezar

spurt [spəːt] n (of energy) acesso; (of blood etc) jorro ♦ vi jorrar

spy [spaɪ] n espião (espiã) m/f ♦ vi: **to ~ on** espiar, espionar ♦ vt enxergar, avistar; **spying** n espionagem f

sq. abbr (MATH etc) = **square**

squabble ['skwɔbl] vi brigar, discutir

squad [skwɔd] n (MIL, POLICE) pelotão m, esquadra; (FOOTBALL) seleção f

squadron ['skwɔdrən] n (MIL) esquadrão m; (AVIAT) esquadrilha f; (NAUT) esquadra

squalid ['skwɔlɪd] adj (conditions) esquálido; (story etc) sórdido

squall [skwɔːl] n (storm) tempestade f; (wind) pé m (de vento), rajada f

squalor ['skwɔlə*] n sordidez f

squander ['skwɔndə*] vt esbanjar, dissipar; (chances) desperdiçar

square [skwɛə*] n quadrado; (in town) praça; (inf: person) quadrado(-a), careta m/f ♦ adj quadrado; (inf: ideas, tastes) careta, antiquado ♦ vt (arrange) ajustar, acertar; (MATH) elevar ao quadrado; (reconcile) con-

ciliar; **all ~** igual, quite; **a ~ meal** uma refeição substancial; **2 metres ~** um quadrado de 2 metros de lado; **2 ~ metres** 2 metros quadrados; **squarely** adv diretamente; (fully) em cheio

squash [skwɔʃ] n (BRIT: drink): **lemon/orange ~** limonada/laranjada concentrada; (SPORT) squash m; (US: vegetable) abóbora ♦ vt esmagar

squat [skwɔt] adj atarracado ♦ vi (also: **~ down**) agachar-se, acocorar-se; **squatter** n posseiro(-a)

squeak [skwiːk] vi (door) ranger; (mouse) guinchar

squeal [skwiːl] vi guinchar, gritar agudamente

squeamish ['skwiːmɪʃ] adj melindroso, delicado

squeeze [skwiːz] n (gen, of hand) aperto; (ECON) arrocho ♦ vt comprimir, socar; (hand, arm) apertar; **squeeze out** vt espremer; (fig) extorquir

squelch [skwɛltʃ] vi fazer ruído de passos na lama

squid [skwɪd] n (pl inv or **~s**) lula

squiggle ['skwɪgl] n garatuja

squint [skwɪnt] vi olhar or ser vesgo ♦ n (MED) estrabismo

squirm [skwəːm] vi retorcer-se

squirrel ['skwɪrəl] n esquilo

squirt [skwəːt] vi, vt jorrar, esguichar

Sr abbr = **senior**

St abbr (= saint) S.; = **street**

stab [stæb] n (with knife etc) punhalada; (of pain) pontada; (inf: try): **to have a ~ at (doing) sth** tentar (fazer) algo ♦ vt apunhalar

stable ['steɪbl] adj estável ♦ n estábulo, cavalariça

stack [stæk] n montão m, pilha ♦ vt amontoar, empilhar

stadium ['steɪdɪəm] (pl **stadia** or

~s) n estádio

staff [stɑ:f] n (work force) pessoal m, quadro; (BRIT: SCH: also: teaching ~) corpo docente ♦ vt prover de pessoal

stag [stæg] n veado, cervo

stage [steɪdʒ] n palco, cena; (point) etapa, fase f; (platform) plataforma, estrado; (profession): **the** ~ o palco, o teatro ♦ vt pôr em cena, representar; (demonstration) montar, organizar; **in** ~**s** por etapas; **stagecoach** n diligência

stagger ['stægə*] vi cambalear ♦ vt (amaze) surpreender, chocar; (hours, holidays) escalonar; **staggering** adj (amazing) surpreendente, chocante

stag party n despedida de solteiro

staid [steɪd] adj sério, sóbrio

stain [steɪn] n mancha; (colouring) tinta, tintura ♦ vt manchar; (wood) tingir; **stained glass window** n janela com vitral; **stain remover** n tira-manchas m

stair [steə*] n (step) degrau m; ~**s** npl (flight of steps) escada; **staircase** n escadaria, escada; **stairway** n = staircase

stake [steɪk] n estaca, poste m; (COMM: interest) interesse m, participação f; (BETTING: gen pl) aposta ♦ vt apostar; (claim) reivindicar; **to be at** ~ estar em jogo

stale [steɪl] adj (bread) dormido; (food) estragado; (air) viciado; (smell) mofado; (beer) velho

stalk [stɔ:k] n talo, haste f ♦ vt caçar de tocaia; **to** ~ **in/out** entrar/sair silenciosamente; **to** ~ **off** andar com arrogância

stall [stɔ:l] n (BRIT: in market) barraca; (in stable) baia ♦ vt (AUT) fazer morrer; (fig: delay) impedir, atrasar ♦ vi morrer; esquivar-se, ganhar

tempo; ~**s** npl (BRIT: in cinema, theatre) platéia

stallion ['stælɪən] n garanhão m

stamina ['stæmɪnə] n resistência

stammer ['stæmə*] n gagueira ♦ vi gaguejar, balbuciar

stamp [stæmp] n selo; (rubber ~) carimbo, timbre m; (mark, also fig) marca, impressão f ♦ vi (also: ~'s foot) bater com o pé ♦ vt (letter) selar; (mark) marcar; (with rubber ~) carimbar; **stamp collecting** n filatelia

stampede [stæm'pi:d] n debandada, estouro (da boiada)

stance [stæns] n postura, posição f

stand [stænd] (pt, pp **stood**) n posição f, postura; (for taxis) ponto; (also: **hall** ~) pedestal m; (also: **music** ~) estante f; (SPORT) tribuna, palanque m; (stall) barraca ♦ vi (be) estar, encontrar-se; (be on foot) estar em pé; (rise) levantar-se; (remain: decision, offer) estar de pé; (in election) candidatar-se ♦ vt (place) pôr, colocar; (tolerate) agüentar, suportar; (cost) pagar; **to make a** ~ resistir; (fig) ater-se a um princípio; **to** ~ **for parliament** (BRIT) apresentar-se como candidato ao parlamento; **stand by** vi estar a postos ♦ vt fus (opinion) aferrar-se a; (person) ficar ao lado de; **stand down** vi retirar-se; **stand for** vt fus (signify) significar; (represent) representar; (tolerate) tolerar, permitir; **stand in for** vt fus substituir; **stand out** vi (be prominent) destacar-se; **stand up** vi levantar-se; **stand up for** vt fus defender; **stand up to** vt fus enfrentar

standard ['stændəd] n padrão m, critério; (flag) estandarte m; (level) nível m ♦ adj padronizado, regular, normal; **~s** *npl* (*morals*) valores *mpl* morais; **standard lamp** (*BRIT*) *n* abajur *m* de pé; **standard of living** *n* padrão *m* de vida (*BR*), nível *m* de vida (*PT*)

stand-by *adj* de reserva ♦ *n*: **to be on ~** estar de sobreaviso or de prontidão; **stand-by ticket** *n* bilhete *m* de stand-by

stand-in *n* suplente *m/f*

standing ['stændiŋ] *adj* (*on foot*) em pé; (*permanent*) permanente ♦ *n* posição *f*, reputação *f*; **of many years' ~** de muitos anos; **standing joke** *n* piada conhecida; **standing order** (*BRIT*) *n* instrução *f* permanente

standpoint ['stændpɔint] *n* ponto de vista

standstill ['stændstil] *n*: **at a ~** paralisado, parado; **to come to a ~** (*car*) parar; (*factory, traffic*) ficar paralisado

stank [stæŋk] *pt of* **stink**

staple ['steipl] *n* (*for papers*) grampo ♦ *adj* (*food etc*) básico ♦ *vt* grampear; **stapler** *n* grampeador *m*

star [staː*] *n* estrela; (*celebrity*) astro/estrela ♦ *vi*: **to ~ in** ser a estrela em, estrelar ♦ *vt* (*CINEMA*) ser estrelado por; **the ~s** *npl* (*horoscope*) o horóscopo

starboard ['staːbəd] *n* estibordo

starch [staːtʃ] *n* (*in food*) amido, fécula; (*for clothes*) goma

stardom ['staːdəm] *n* estrelato

stare [stɛə*] *n* olhar *m* fixo ♦ *vi*: **to ~ at** olhar fixamente, fitar

starfish ['staːfiʃ] *n inv* estrela-do-mar *f*

stark [staːk] *adj* severo, áspero ♦ *adv*: **~ naked** completamente nu, em pêlo

starling ['staːliŋ] *n* estorninho

starry ['staːri] *adj* estrelado; **starry-**

eyed *adj* (*innocent*) deslumbrado

start [staːt] *n* princípio, começo; (*departure*) partida; (*sudden movement*) sobressalto, susto; (*advantage*) vantagem *f* ♦ *vt* começar, iniciar; (*cause*) causar; (*found*) fundar; (*engine*) ligar ♦ *vi* começar, iniciar; (*with fright*) sobressaltar-se, assustar-se; (*train etc*) sair; **start off** *vi* começar, principiar; (*leave*) sair, pôr-se a caminho; **start up** *vi* começar; (*car*) pegar, pôr-se em marcha ♦ *vt* começar; (*car*) ligar; **starter** *n* (*AUT*) arranque *m*; (*SPORT: official*) juiz (juíza) *m/f* da partida; (*BRIT: CULIN*) entrada; **starting point** *n* ponto de partida

startle ['staːtl] *vt* assustar, aterrar; **startling** *adj* surpreendente

starvation [staː'veiʃən] *n* fome *f*

starve ['staːv] *vi* passar fome; (*to death*) morrer de fome ♦ *vt* fazer passar fome; (*fig*) privar

state [steit] *n* estado ♦ *vt* afirmar, declarar; **the S~s** *npl* (*GEO*) os Estados Unidos; **to be in a ~** estar agitado; **stately** *adj* majestoso, imponente; **statement** *n* declaração *f*; **statesman** (*irreg*) *n* estadista *m*

static ['stætik] *n* (*RADIO, TV*) interferência ♦ *adj* estático

station ['steiʃən] *n* estação *f*; (*POLICE*) delegacia; (*RADIO*) emissora ♦ *vt* colocar

stationary ['steiʃnəri] *adj* estacionário

stationer ['steiʃənə*] *n* dono de papelaria; **stationer's (shop)** *n* papelaria; **stationery** *n* artigos *mpl* de papelaria

station wagon (*US*) *n* perua (*BR*), canadiana (*PT*)

statistic [stə'tistik] *n* estatística; **statistics** [stə'tistiks] *n* (*science*) estatística

statue ['stætju:] n estátua

status ['steɪtəs] n posição f; (classification) categoria; (importance) status m

statute ['stætju:t] n estatuto, lei f

staunch [stɔ:ntʃ] adj fiel

stay [steɪ] n estadia, estada ♦ vi ficar; (as guest) hospedar-se; (spend some time) demorar-se; **to ~ put** não se mexer; **to ~ the night** pernoitar; **stay behind** vi ficar atrás; **stay in** vi ficar em casa; **stay on** vi ficar; **stay out** vi ficar fora de casa; **stay up** vi (at night) velar, ficar acordado

steadfast ['stedfɑ:st] adj firme, estável, resoluto

steadily ['stedɪlɪ] adv (firmly) firmemente; (unceasingly) sem parar, constantemente; (walk) regularmente

steady ['stedɪ] adj (job, boyfriend) constante; (speed) fixo; (regular) regular; (person, character) sensato; (calm) calmo, sereno ♦ vt (stabilize) estabilizar; (nerves) acalmar

steak [steɪk] n filé m; (beef) bife m

steal [sti:l] (pt **stole**, pp **stolen**) vt roubar ♦ vi mover-se furtivamente

steam [sti:m] n vapor m ♦ vt (CULIN) cozinhar no vapor ♦ vi fumegar; **steam engine** n máquina a vapor; **steamer** n vapor m, navio (a vapor); **steamy** adj vaporoso; (room) cheio de vapor, úmido (BR), húmido (PT); (heat, atmosphere) vaporoso

steel [sti:l] n aço ♦ adj de aço

steep [sti:p] adj íngreme; (increase) acentuado; (price) exorbitante ♦ vt (food) colocar de molho; (cloth) ensopar, encharcar

steeple ['sti:pl] n campanário, torre f

steer [stɪə*] vt (person) guiar; (vehicle) dirigir ♦ vi conduzir; **steering** n

(AUT) direção f; **steering wheel** n volante m

stem [stem] n (of plant) caule m, haste f; (of glass) pé m ♦ vt deter, reter; (blood) estancar; **stem from** vt fus originar-se de

stench [stentʃ] (pej) n fedor m

stencil ['stensl] n (pattern, design) estêncil m; (lettering) gabarito de letra ♦ vt imprimir com estêncil

stenographer [ste'nɔgrəfə*] (us) n estenógrafo(-a)

step [step] n passo m; (stair) degrau m ♦ vi: **to ~ forward** dar um passo a frente/atrás; **~s** npl (BRIT) = **~ladder**; **to be in ~ (with)** (fig) manter a paridade (com); **to be out of ~ (with)** (fig) estar em disparidade (com); **step down** vi (fig) renunciar; **step on** vt fus pisar; **step up** vt aumentar; **stepbrother** n meio-irmão m; **stepdaughter** n enteada; **stepfather** n padrasto; **stepladder** (BRIT) n escada portátil or de abrir; **stepmother** n madrasta; **stepsister** n meia-irmã f; **stepson** n enteado

stereo ['stɪərɪəʊ] n estéreo; (record player) (aparelho de) som m ♦ adj (also: **~phonic**) estereofônico

sterile ['steraɪl] adj esterelizado; (barren) estéril; **sterilize** ['sterɪlaɪz] vt esterilizar

sterling ['stɜ:lɪŋ] adj esterlino; (silver) de lei ♦ n (currency) libra esterlina; **one pound** = uma libra esterlina

stern [stɜ:n] adj severo, austero ♦ n (NAUT) popa, ré f

stew [stju:] n guisado, ensopado ♦ vt guisar, ensopar; (fruit) cozinhar

steward ['stju:əd] n (AVIAT) comissário de bordo; **stewardess** n aeromoça (BR), hospedeira de bordo (PT)

stick [stɪk] (pt, pp **stuck**) n pau m; (as weapon) cacete m; (walking ~)

bengala, cajado ♦ vt (glue) colar; (thrust): **to ~ sth into** cravar or enfiar algo em; (inf: put) meter; (: tolerate) agüentar, suportar ♦ vi (become attached) colar-se; (be unmoveable) emperrar; (in mind etc) gravar-se; **stick out** vi estar saliente, projetar-se; **stick up** vi estar saliente, projetar-se; **stick up for** vt fus defender; **sticker** n adesivo; **sticking plaster** n esparadrapo

sticky ['stɪkɪ] adj pegajoso; (label) adesivo; (fig) delicado

stiff [stɪf] adj (strong) forte; (hard) duro; (difficult) difícil; (moving with difficulty: person) teso; (: door, zip) empenado; (formal) formal ♦ adv (bored, worried) extremamente; **stiffen** vi enrijecer-se; (grow stronger) fortalecer-se

stifle ['staɪfl] vt sufocar, abafar; (opposition) sufocar

stigma ['stɪgmə] n estigma m

stiletto [stɪ'letəʊ] (BRIT) n (also: ~ heel) salto alto e fino

still [stɪl] adj parado ♦ adv (up to this time) ainda; (even, yet) ainda; (nonetheless) entretanto, contudo; **stillborn** adj nascido morto, natimorto; **still life** n natureza morta

stilted ['stɪltɪd] adj afetado

stimulate ['stɪmjʊleɪt] vt estimular

stimulus ['stɪmjʊləs] (pl stimuli) n estímulo, incentivo

sting [stɪŋ] (pt, pp stung) n (wound) picada; (pain) ardência; (of insect) ferrão m ♦ vt arguilhar ♦ vi (insect, animal) picar; (eyes, ointment) queimar

stingy ['stɪndʒɪ] (pej) adj pão-duro, sovina

stink [stɪŋk] (pt stank, pp stunk) n fedor m, catinga ♦ vi feder, cheirar mal; **stinking** (inf) adj (fig) maldito

stint [stɪnt] n tarefa, parte f ♦ vi: **to ~ on** ser parco com

stir [stɜ:*] n (fig) comoção f, rebuliço ♦ vt mexer; (fig) comover ♦ vi mover-se, remexer-se; **stir up** vt excitar; (trouble) provocar

stirrup ['stɪrəp] n estribo

stitch [stɪtʃ] n (SEWING, KNITTING, MED) ponto; (pain) pontada ♦ vt costurar; (MED) dar pontos em, suturar

stoat [stəʊt] n arminho

stock [stɔk] n suprimento; (COMM: reserves) estoque m, provisão f; (: selection) sortimento; (AGR) gado; (CULIN) caldo; (lineage) estirpe f, linhagem f; (FINANCE) valores mpl, títulos mpl ♦ adj (reply etc) de sempre, costumeiro ♦ vt ter em estoque, estocar; **in/out of ~** em estoque/ esgotado; **to take ~ of** (fig) fazer um balanço de; **~s and shares** valores e títulos mobiliários; **stock up** vi: **to ~ up (with)** abastecer-se (de); **stockbroker** n corretor/a m/f de valores or da Bolsa; **stock cube** (BRIT) n cubo de caldo; **stock exchange** n Bolsa de Valores

stocking ['stɔkɪŋ] n meia

stock: **stock market** (BRIT) n Bolsa, mercado de valores; **stockpile** n reservas fpl, estocagem f ♦ vt acumular reservas de, estocar; **stock-taking** (BRIT) n (COMM) inventário

stocky ['stɔkɪ] adj (strong) robusto; (short) atarracado

stodgy ['stɔdʒɪ] adj pesado

stoke [stəʊk] vt atiçar, alimentar

stole [stəʊl] pt of steal ♦ n estola

stolen ['stəʊln] pp of steal

stomach ['stʌmək] n (ANAT) estômago; (belly) barriga, ventre m ♦ vt suportar, tolerar; **stomach ache** n dor f de estômago

stone [stəʊn] n pedra; (pebble)

pedrinha; (in fruit) caroço; (MED) pedra, cálculo; (BRIT: weight) = 6.348kg; 14 pounds ♦ adj de pedra ♦ vt apedrejar; (fruit) tirar o(s) caroço(s) de; **stone-cold** adj gelado; **stone-deaf** adj surdo como uma porta; **stonework** n cantaria

stood [stud] pt, pp of **stand**

stool [stu:l] n tamborete m, banco

stoop [stu:p] vi (also: **have a ~**) ser corcunda; (also: **~ down**) debruçar-se, curvar-se

stop [stɔp] n parada, interrupção f; (for bus etc) parada (BR), ponto (BR), paragem f (PT) (also: **full ~**) ponto ♦ vt parar, deter; (break off) interromper; (cheque) sustar, suspender; (also: **put a ~ to**) impedir ♦ vi parar, deter-se; (watch, noise) parar; (end) acabar; **to ~ doing sth** deixar de fazer algo; **stop dead** vi parar de repente; **stop off** vi dar uma parada; **stop up** vt tapar; **stopover** n parada rápida; (AVIAT) escala; **stopper** n tampa, rolha; **stopwatch** n cronômetro

storage ['stɔ:rɪdʒ] n armazenagem f

store [stɔ:*] n (stock) suprimento; (depot) armazém m; (reserve) estoque m; (BRIT: large shop) loja de departamentos; (US: shop) loja ♦ vt armazenar; **~s** npl (provisions) víveres mpl, provisões fpl; **who knows what is in ~ for us?** quem sabe o que nos espera?; **store up** vt acumular; **storeroom** n depósito, almoxarifado

storey ['stɔ:rɪ] (US **story**) n andar m

stork [stɔ:k] n cegonha

storm [stɔ:m] n tempestade f; (fig) tumulto ♦ vi (fig) enfurecer-se ♦ vt tomar de assalto, assaltar; **stormy** adj tempestuoso

story ['stɔ:rɪ] n história, estória; (lie) mentira; (US) = **storey**; **storybook** n livro de contos

stout [staut] adj sólido, forte; (fat) gordo, corpulento; (resolute) decidido, resoluto ♦ n cerveja preta

stove [stauv] n (for cooking) fogão m; (for heating) estufa, fogareiro

stow [stau] vt guardar; **stowaway** n passageiro(-a) clandestino(-a)

straddle ['strædl] vt cavalgar

straggle ['strægl] vi (houses) espalhar-se desordenadamente; (people) vagar, perambular

straight [streɪt] adj reto; (back) esticado; (hair) liso; (honest) honesto; (simple) simples inv ♦ adv reto; (drink) puro; **to put** or **get sth ~** esclarecer algo; **~ away**, **~ off** imediatamente; **straighten** vt arrumar; **straighten out** vt endireitar; (fig) esclarecer; **to straighten things out** arrumar as coisas; **straightforward** adj (simple) simples inv, direto; (honest) honesto, franco

strain [streɪn] n tensão f; (TECH) esforço; (MED: back ~) distensão f; (: tension) luxação f; (breed) raça, estirpe f ♦ vt forçar, torcer, distender; (stretch) puxar, estirar; (CULIN) coar; **~s** npl (MUS) acordes mpl; **strained** adj distendido; (laugh) forçado; (relations) tenso; **strainer** n coador m; (sieve) peneira

strait [streɪt] n estreito; **~s** npl (fig): **to be in dire ~s** estar em apuros; **straitjacket** n camisa-de-força

strand [strænd] n (of thread, hair) fio; (of rope) tira; **stranded** adj preso

strange [streɪndʒ] adj (not known) desconhecido; (odd) estranho, esquisito; **strangely** adv estranhamente; **stranger** n desconhecido(-a); (from another area) forasteiro(-a)

strangle ['stræŋgl] vt estrangular;

(fig) sufocar

strap [stræp] *n* correia; *(of slip, dress)* alça

strategic [strəˈtiːdʒɪk] *adj* estratégico

strategy [ˈstrætɪdʒɪ] *n* estratégia

straw [strɔː] *n* palha; *(drinking ~)* canudo; **that's the last ~!** essa foi a última gota!

strawberry [ˈstrɔːbərɪ] *n* morango

stray [streɪ] *adj (animal)* extraviado; *(bullet)* perdido; *(scattered)* espalhado ♦ *vi* perder-se

streak [striːk] *n* listra, traço; *(in hair)* mecha ♦ *vt* listrar ♦ *vi:* **to ~ past** passar como um raio

stream [striːm] *n* riacho, córrego; *(of people, vehicles)* fluxo; *(of smoke)* rastro; *(of questions etc)* torrente *f* ♦ *vt (SCH)* classificar ♦ *vi* correr, fluir; **to ~ in/out** entrar/sair em massa

streamer [ˈstriːmə*] *n* serpentina; *(pennant)* flâmula

streamlined [ˈstriːmlaɪnd] *adj* aerodinâmico

street [striːt] *n* rua; **streetcar** *(US)* *n* bonde *m* *(BR)*, eléctrico *(PT)*; **street lamp** *n* poste *m* de iluminação; **street plan** *n* mapa *m*; **streetwise** *(inf)* *adj* malandro

strength [streŋθ] *n* força; *(of girder etc)* firmeza, resistência; *(fig)* poder *m*; **strengthen** *vt* fortificar; *(fig)* fortalecer

strenuous [ˈstrenjuəs] *adj* enérgico; *(determined)* tenaz

stress [stres] *n* pressão *f*; *(mental strain)* tensão *f*, stress *m*; *(emphasis)* ênfase *f*; *(TECH)* tensão ♦ *vt* realçar, dar ênfase a; *(syllable)* acentuar

stretch [stretʃ] *n* *(of sand etc)* trecho, extensão *f* ♦ *vi* espreguiçar-se; *(extend)* **to ~ to** or **as far as** estender-se até ♦ *vt* estirar, esticar; *(fig: subj: job, task)* exigir o máximo

de; **stretch out** *vi* esticar-se ♦ *vt (arm etc)* esticar; *(spread)* estirar

stretcher [ˈstretʃə*] *n* maca, padiola

strewn [struːn] *adj:* **~ with** coberto *or* cheio de

stricken [ˈstrɪkən] *adj (wounded)* ferido; *(devastated)* arrasado; *(ill)* acometido; **~ with** tomado por

strict [strɪkt] *adj (person)* severo, rigoroso; *(meaning)* exato, estrito

stride [straɪd] *(pt* **strode***, pp* **stridden** [ˈstrɪdən]*) n* passo largo ♦ *vi* andar a passos largos

strife [straɪf] *n* conflito

strike [straɪk] *(pt, pp* **struck***) n* greve *f*; *(of oil etc)* descoberta; *(attack)* ataque *m* ♦ *vt* bater em; *(fig):* **me ocorre que …;** *(oil etc)* descobrir; *(deal)* fechar, acertar ♦ *vi* estar em greve; *(attack: soldiers, illness)* atacar; *(: disaster)* assolar; *(clock)* bater; **on ~** em greve; **to ~ a match** acender um fósforo; **strike down** *vt* derrubar; **strike up** *vt (MUS)* começar a tocar; *(conversation, friendship)* travar; **striker** *n* grevista *m/f*; *(SPORT)* atacante *m/f*; **striking** *adj* impressionante

string [strɪŋ] *(pt, pp* **strung***) n* *(cord)* barbante *m* *(BR)*, cordel *m* *(PT)*; *(of beads)* cordão *m*; *(of onions)* réstia; *(MUS)* corda ♦ *vt:* **to ~ out** esticar; **the ~s** *npl (MUS)* os instrumentos de corda; **to ~ together** *(words)* unir; *(ideas)* concatenar; **to get a job by pulling ~s** *(fig)* usar pistolão; **string(ed) instrument** *n* *(MUS)* instrumento de corda

stringent [ˈstrɪndʒənt] *adj* rigoroso

strip [strɪp] *n* tira; *(of land)* faixa; *(of metal)* lâmina, tira ♦ *vt* despir; *(also:* **~ down***: machine)* desmontar ♦ *vi* despir-se; **strip cartoon** *n* história em quadrinhos (BR), banda desenhada (PT)

stripe [straɪp] n listra; (MIL) galão m; **striped** adj listrado, com listras

strive [straɪv] (pt strove, pp ~n [strɪvən]) vi: **to ~ for sth/to do sth** esforçar-se por or batalhar para algo/para fazer algo

strode [strəud] pt of **stride**

stroke [strəuk] n (blow) golpe m; (MED) derrame m cerebral; (of paintbrush) pincelada; (SWIMMING: style) nado ♦ vt acariciar, afagar; **at a ~ de** repente, de golpe

stroll [strəul] n volta, passeio ♦ vi passear, dar uma volta; **stroller** (US) n carrinho (de criança)

strong [strɔŋ] adj forte; (imagination) fértil; (personality) forte, dominante; (nerves) de aço; **they are 50 ~** são 50; **stronghold** n fortaleza; (fig) baluarte m; **strongly** adv firmemente; (defend) vigorosamente; (believe) profundamente

strove [strəuv] pt of **strive**

struck [strʌk] pt, pp of **strike**

structure ['strʌktʃə*] n estrutura; (building) construção f

struggle ['strʌgl] n luta, contenda ♦ vi (fight) lutar; (try hard) batalhar

strum [strʌm] vt (guitar) dedilhar

strung [strʌŋ] pt, pp of **string**

strut [strʌt] n escora, suporte m ♦ vi pavonear-se, empertigar-se

stub [stʌb] n (of ticket etc) canhoto; (of cigarette) toco, ponta; **to ~ one's toe** dar uma topada; **stub out** vt apagar

stubble ['stʌbl] n restolho; (on chin) barba por fazer

stubborn ['stʌbən] adj teimoso, cabeçudo, obstinado

stuck [stʌk] pt, pp of **stick** ♦ adj (jammed) emperrado; **stuck-up** adj convencido, metido, esnobe

stud [stʌd] n (shirt ~) botão m; (earring) tarraxa, rosca; (of boot) cravo; (also: ~ **farm**) fazenda de cavalos; (also: ~ **horse**) garanhão m ♦ vt (fig): **~ded with** salpicado de

student ['stju:dənt] n estudante m/f ♦ adj estudantil; **student driver** (US) n aprendiz m/f

studio ['stju:dɪəu] n estúdio; (sculptor's) ateliê m

studious ['stju:dɪəs] adj estudioso, aplicado; (careful) cuidadoso; **studiously** adv (carefully) com esmero

study ['stʌdɪ] n estudo; (room) sala de leitura or estudo ♦ vt estudar; (examine) examinar, investigar ♦ vi estudar; **studies** npl (subjects) estudos mpl, matérias fpl

stuff [stʌf] n (substance) troço; (things) troços mpl, coisas fpl ♦ vt (CULIN) rechear; (animals) empalhar; (inf: push) enfiar; **~ed toy** brinquedo de pelúcia; **stuffing** n recheio; **stuffy** adj (room) abafado, mal ventilado; (person) rabujento, melindroso

stumble ['stʌmbl] vi tropeçar; **to ~ across** or on (fig) topar com; **stumbling block** n pedra no caminho

stump [stʌmp] n (of tree) toco; (of limb) coto ♦ vt: **to be ~ed** ficar perplexo

stun [stʌn] vt (subj: blow) aturdir; (: news) pasmar

stung [stʌŋ] pt, pp of **sting**

stunk [stʌŋk] pp of **stink**

stunning ['stʌnɪŋ] adj (news) atordoante; (appearance) maravilhoso

stunt [stʌnt] n façanha sensacional; (publicity ~) truque m publicitário; **stuntman** ['stʌntmæn] (irreg) n dublê m

stupendous [stju:'pɛndəs] adj monumental

stupid ['stju:pɪd] adj estúpido, idiota

sturdy ['stə:dɪ] adj (person) robusto, firme; (thing) sólido

stutter ['stʌtə*] n gagueira, gaguez f ♦ vi gaguejar

sty [staɪ] n (for pigs) chiqueiro

stye [staɪ] n (MED) terçol m

style [staɪl] n estilo; (elegance) elegância; **stylish** adj elegante, chique

suave [swɑ:v] adj suave, melífluo

subconscious [sʌb'kɔnʃəs] adj do subconsciente

subdue [səb'dju:] vt subjugar; (passions) dominar; **subdued** adj (light) tênue; (person) desanimado

subject [n 'sʌbdʒɪkt, vb səb'dʒɛkt] n (of king) súdito(-a); (theme) assunto; (SCH) matéria; (LING) sujeito ♦ vt: **to ~ sb to sth** submeter alguém a algo; **to be ~ to** estar sujeito a; **subjective** [səb'dʒɛktɪv] adj subjetivo; **subject matter** n assunto; (content) conteúdo

sublet [sʌb'lɛt] vt sublocar, subalugar

submarine ['sʌbməri:n] n submarino

submerge [səb'mə:dʒ] vt submergir ♦ vi submergir-se

submission [səb'mɪʃən] n submissão f; (to committee) petição f; (of plan) apresentação f, exposição f

submit [səb'mɪt] vt submeter ♦ vi submeter-se

subnormal [sʌb'nɔ:məl] adj (temperature) abaixo do normal

subordinate [sə'bɔ:dɪnət] adj, n subordinado(-a)

subscribe [səb'skraɪb] vi subscrever; **to ~ to** (opinion) concordar com; (fund) contribuir para; (newspaper) assinar; **subscription** [səb'skrɪpʃən] n assinatura

subsequent ['sʌbsɪkwənt] adj

subseqüente, posterior; **subsequently** adv posteriormente, depois

subside [səb'saɪd] vi (feeling, wind) acalmar-se; (flood) baixar; **subsidence** [səb'saɪdns] n (in road etc) afundamento da superfície

subsidiary [səb'sɪdɪərɪ] adj secundário ♦ n (also: ~ **company**) subsidiária

subsidize ['sʌbsɪdaɪz] vt subsidiar

subsidy ['sʌbsɪdɪ] n subsídio

substance ['sʌbstəns] n substância

substantial [səb'stænʃl] adj (solid) sólido; (reward, meal) substancial; **substantially** adv consideravelmente; (in essence) substancialmente

substitute ['sʌbstɪtju:t] n substituto(-a); (person) suplente m/f ♦ vt: **to ~ A for B** substituir B por A

subterranean [sʌbtə'reɪnɪən] adj subterrâneo

subtitle ['sʌbtaɪtl] n (CINEMA) legenda

subtle ['sʌtl] adj sutil

subtotal [sʌb'təutl] n total m parcial, subtotal m

subtract [səb'trækt] vt subtrair, deduzir

suburb ['sʌbə:b] n subúrbio; **suburban** [sə'bə:bən] adj suburbano; (train etc) de subúrbio; **suburbia** [sə'bə:bɪə] n os subúrbios

subway ['sʌbweɪ] n (BRIT) passagem f subterrânea; (US) metrô m (BR), metro(-politano) (PT)

succeed [sək'si:d] vi (person) ser bem sucedido, ter êxito; (plan) sair bem ♦ vt suceder a; **to ~ in doing** conseguir fazer; **succeeding** adj sucessivo, posterior

success [sək'sɛs] n êxito; (hit, person) sucesso; **successful** adj (venture) bem sucedido; (writer) de sucesso, bem sucedido; **to be successful (in doing)** conseguir (fazer); **successfully** adv com sucesso, com êxito

succession [sək'sɛʃən] n sucessão f, série f; **(to throne)** sucessão

such [sʌtʃ] adj tal, semelhante; (of that kind: sg): **~ a book** um livro parecido, tal livro; (: pl): **~ books** tais livros; (so much): **~ courage** tanta coragem ♦ adv tão; **~ a long trip** uma viagem tão longa; **~ a lot of** tanto; **~ as** tal como; **as ~** como tal; **such-and-such** adj tal e qual

suck [sʌk] vt chupar; (breast) mamar; **sucker** n (ZOOL) ventosa; (inf) trouxa m/f, otário(-a)

sudden ['sʌdn] adj (rapid) repentino, súbito; (unexpected) imprevisto; **all of a ~** inesperadamente; **suddenly** adv inesperadamente

sue [su:] vt processar

suede [sweid] n camurça

suet ['suit] n sebo

suffer ['sʌfə*] vt sofrer; (bear) agüentar, suportar ♦ vi sofrer, padecer; **to ~ from** sofrer de, estar com; **sufferer** n: **a ~er from** (MED) uma pessoa que sofre de; **suffering** n sofrimento

sufficient [sə'fɪʃənt] adj suficiente, bastante; **sufficiently** adv suficientemente

suffocate ['sʌfəkeɪt] vi sufocar(-se), asfixiar(-se)

sugar ['ʃugə*] n açúcar m ♦ vt pôr açúcar em, açucarar; **sugar cane** n cana-de-açúcar f

suggest [sə'dʒɛst] vt sugerir; (indicate) indicar; **suggestion** n sugestão f; indicação f

suicide ['suɪsaɪd] n suicídio; (person) suicida m/f; see also **commit**

suit [su:t] n (man's) terno (BR), fato (PT); (woman's) conjunto; (LAW) pro-

cesso; (CARDS) naipe m ♦ vt convir a; (clothes) ficar bem a; (adapt): **to ~ sth to** adaptar or acomodar algo a; **they are well ~ed** fazem um bom par; **suitable** adj conveniente; (appropriate) apropriado; **suitably** adv (dressed) apropriadamente; (impressed) bem

suitcase ['su:tkeɪs] n mala

suite [swi:t] n (of rooms) conjunto de salas; (MUS) suíte f; (furniture) conjunto

suitor ['su:tə*] n pretendente m

sulfur ['sʌlfə*] (US) n = **sulphur**

sulk [sʌlk] vi ficar emburrado, fazer beicinho or biquinho (inf); **sulky** adj emburrado

sullen ['sʌlən] adj rabugento; (silence) pesado

sulphur ['sʌlfə*] (US **sulfur**) n enxofre m

sultana [sʌl'tɑ:nə] n passa branca

sultry ['sʌltrɪ] adj abafado

sum [sʌm] n soma, (calculation) cálculo; **sum up** vt, vi resumir

summarize ['sʌməraɪz] vt resumir

summary ['sʌmərɪ] n resumo

summer ['sʌmə*] n verão m ♦ adj de verão; **in ~** no verão; **summertime** n (season) verão m

summit ['sʌmɪt] n topo, cume m; (also: **~ conference**) (conferência de) cúpula

summon ['sʌmən] vt (person) mandar chamar; (meeting) convocar; (LAW: witness) convocar; **summon up** vt concentrar

sun [sʌn] n sol m; **sunbathe** vi tomar sol; **sunblock** n bloqueador m solar; **sunburn** n queimadura do sol; **sunburned** adj = **sunburnt**; **sunburnt** adj bronzeado; (painfully) queimado

Sunday ['sʌndɪ] n domingo; **Sunday school** n escola dominical

sundial ['sʌndaɪəl] n relógio de sol

sundown ['sʌndaun] n pôr m do sol

sundries ['sʌndrɪz] npl gêneros mpl diversos

sundry ['sʌndrɪ] adj vários, diversos; **all and ~** todos

sunflower ['sʌnflauə*] n girassol m

sung [sʌŋ] pp of **sing**

sunglasses ['sʌŋglɑ:sɪz] npl óculos mpl de sol

sunk [sʌŋk] pp of **sink**

sun: sunlight n (luz f do) sol m; **sunlit** adj ensolarado, iluminado pelo sol; **sunny** adj cheio de sol; (day) ensolarado, de sol; **sunrise** n nascer m do sol; **sun roof** n (AUT) teto solar; **sunscreen** n protetor m solar; **sunset** n pôr m do sol; **sunshade** n para-sol m; **sunshine** n (luz f do) sol m; **sunstroke** n insolação f; **suntan** n bronzeado; **suntan lotion** n loção f de bronzear

super ['su:pə*] (inf) adj bacana (RR), muito giro (PT)

superannuation [su:pərænju-'eɪʃən] n pensão f de aposentadoria

superb [su:'pɜ:b] adj excelente

supercilious [su:pə'sɪlɪəs] adj arrogante, desdenhoso; (haughty) altivo

superintendent [su:pərɪn'tend-ənt] n superintendente m/f; (POLICE) chefe m/f de polícia

superior [su'pɪərɪə*] adj superior; (smug) desdenhoso ♦ n superior m

supermarket ['su:pəmɑ:kɪt] n supermercado

supernatural [su:pə'nætʃərəl] adj sobrenatural ♦ n: **the ~ o** sobrenatural

superpower ['su:pəpauə*] n (POL) superpotência

superstitious [su:pə'stɪʃəs] adj supersticioso

supervise ['su:pəvaɪz] vt supervisar,

supervisionar; **supervision** [su:pə-'vɪʒən] n supervisão f; **supervisor** n supervisor(a) m/f; (academic) orientador(a) m/f

supper ['sʌpə*] n jantar m; (late evening) ceia

supple ['sʌpl] adj flexível

supplement [n 'sʌplɪmənt, vb sʌplɪ'mɛnt] n suplemento ♦ vt suprir, completar; **supplementary** [sʌplɪ'mɛntərɪ] adj suplementar

supplier [sə'plaɪə*] n abastecedor(a) m/f, fornecedor(a) m/f

supply [sə'plaɪ] vt (provide): **to ~** sth (to sb) fornecer algo (para alguém); (equip): **to ~ (with)** suprir (de) ♦ n fornecimento, provisão f; (stock) estoque m; (supplying) abastecimento; **supplies** npl (food) víveres mpl, (MIL) apetrechos mpl

support [sə'pɔ:t] n (moral, financial etc) apoio; (TECH) suporte m ♦ vt apoiar; (financially) manter; (TECH: hold up) sustentar; (theory etc) defender; **supporter** n (POL etc) partidário(-a); (SPORT) torcedor(a) m/f

suppose [sə'pəuz] vt supor; (imagine) imaginar; (duty): **to be ~d to** do sth dever fazer algo; **supposedly** [sə'pəuzɪdlɪ] adv supostamente, pretensamente; **supposing** conj caso, supondo-se que

suppress [sə'prɛs] vt (information) suprimir; (feelings, revolt) reprimir; (yawn) conter

supreme [su'pri:m] adj supremo

surcharge ['sɜ:tʃɑ:dʒ] n sobretaxa

sure [ʃuə*] adj seguro; (definite) certo; (aim) certeiro; **to make ~ of** sth/that assegurar-se de algo/que; **~!** claro que sim!; **~ enough** efetivamente; **surely** adv (certainly; US: also: **sure**) certamente

surf [sə:f] n (waves) ondas fpl, arrebentação f
surface ['sə:fɪs] n superfície f ♦ vt (road) revestir ♦ vi vir à superfície or à tona; (fig: news, feeling) vir à tona; **surface mail** n correio comum
surfboard ['sə:bɔ:d] n prancha de surfe
surfing ['sə:fɪŋ] n surfe m
surge [sə:dʒ] n onda ♦ vi (sea) encapelar-se; (people, vehicles) precipitar-se; (feeling) aumentar repentinamente
surgeon ['sə:dʒən] n cirurgião(-giã) m/f
surgery ['sə:dʒərɪ] n cirurgia; (BRIT: room) consultório; (: also: ~ hours) horas fpl de consulta
surgical ['sə:dʒɪkl] adj cirúrgico; **surgical spirit** (BRIT) n álcool m
surname ['sə:neɪm] n sobrenome m (BR), apelido (PT)
surplus ['sə:pləs] n excedente m; (COMM) superávit m ♦ adj excedente, de sobra
surprise [sə'praɪz] n surpresa ♦ vt surpreender; **surprising** adj surpreendente
surrender [sə'rɛndə*] n rendição f, entrega f ♦ vi render-se, entregar-se
surrogate ['sʌrəgɪt] n (BRIT) substituto(-a)
surround [sə'raund] vt circundar, rodear; (MIL etc) cercar; **surrounding** adj circundante, adjacente; **surroundings** npl arredores mpl, cercanias fpl
surveillance [sə:'veɪləns] n vigilância
survey [n 'sə:veɪ, vb sə:'veɪ] n inspeção f; (of habits etc) pesquisa; (of land) levantamento; (of house) inspeção f ♦ vt observar, contemplar; (land) fazer um levantamento de;

surveyor n (of land) agrimensor(a) m/f; (of building) inspetor(a) m/f
survival [sə'vaɪvl] n sobrevivência; (relic) remanescente m
survive [sə'vaɪv] vi sobreviver; (custom etc) perdurar ♦ vt sobreviver a; **survivor** n sobrevivente m/f
susceptible [sə'sɛptəbl] adj: ~ (to) (injury) suscetível or sensível (a); (flattery, pressure) vulnerável (a)
suspect [adj, n 'sʌspɛkt, vb səs-'pɛkt] adj, n suspeito(-a) ♦ vt suspeitar, desconfiar
suspend [səs'pɛnd] vt suspender; **suspenders** npl (BRIT) ligas fpl; (US) suspensórios mpl
suspense [səs'pɛns] n incerteza, ansiedade f; (in film etc) suspense m; **to keep sb in ~** manter alguém em suspense or na expectativa
suspension [səs'pɛnʃən] n suspensão f; (of driving licence) cassação f
suspicion [səs'pɪʃən] n suspeita; **suspicious** adj (suspecting) suspeitoso; (causing suspicion) suspeito
sustain [səs'teɪn] vt sustentar; (suffer) sofrer; **sustained** adj (effort) contínuo; **sustenance** ['sʌstɪnəns] n sustento
swab [swɔb] n (MED) mecha de algodão
swagger ['swægə*] vi andar com ar de superioridade
swallow ['swɔləu] n (bird) andorinha ♦ vt engolir, tragar; (fig: story) engolir; (pride) pôr de lado; (one's words) retirar; **swallow up** vt (savings etc) consumir
swam [swæm] pt de **swim**
swamp [swɔmp] n pântano, brejo ♦ vt atolar, inundar; (fig) assoberbar
swan [swɔn] n cisne m
swap [swɔp] n troca, permuta ♦ vt:

to ~ (for) trocar (por); *(replace (with))* substituir (por)

swarm [swɔːm] *n (of bees)* enxame *m*; *(of people)* multidão *f* ♦ *vi* enxamear; aglomerar-se; *(place)*: **to be ~ing with** estar apinhado de

swastika ['swɔstɪkə] *n* suástica

swat [swɔt] *vt* esmagar

sway [sweɪ] *vi* balançar-se, oscilar ♦ *vt (influence)* influenciar

swear [swɛə*] *(pt* **swore**, *pp* **sworn)** *vi (curse)* xingar ♦ *vt (promise)* jurar; **swearword** *n* palavrão *m*

sweat [swɛt] *n* suor *m* ♦ *vi* suar; **sweater** *n* suéter *m* or *f (BR)*, camisola *(PT)*; **sweaty** *adj* suado

Swede [swiːd] *n* sueco(-a)

swede [swiːd] *n* tipo de nabo

Sweden ['swiːdən] *n* Suécia; **Swedish** *adj* sueco ♦ *n (LING)* sueco

sweep [swiːp] *(pt, pp* **swept)** *n (act)* varredura; *(also:* **chimney ~)** limpador *m* de chaminés ♦ *vt* varrer; *(with arm)* empurrar; *(subj: current)* arrastar; *(: fashion, craze)* espalhar-se por ♦ *vi* varrer; **sweep away** *vt* varrer; **sweep past** *vi* passar rapidamente; **sweep up** *vi* varrer; **sweeping** *adj (gesture)* dramático; *(statement)* generalizado

sweet [swiːt] *n (candy)* bala *(BR)*, rebuçado *(PT)*; *(BRIT: pudding)* sobremesa ♦ *adj* doce; *(fig: air)* fresco; *(: water, smell)* doce; *(: sound)* suave; *(: kind)* meigo; *(baby, kitten)* bonitinho; **sweetcorn** ['swiːtkɔːn] *n* milho; **sweeten** *vt* pôr açúcar em; *(temper)* abrandar; **sweetheart** *n* namorado(-a); **sweet pea** *n* ervilha-de-cheiro *f*

swell [swɛl] *(pt ~ed, pp* **swollen** or ~**ed**) *n (of sea)* vaga, onda ♦ *adj (US: inf: excellent)* bacana ♦ *vi (increase)* aumentar; *(get stronger)* intensificar-se; *(also:* ~ **up)** inchar-

se; **swelling** *n (MED)* inchação *f*

sweltering ['swɛltərɪŋ] *adj (heat)* sufocante; *(day)* mormacento

swept [swɛpt] *pt, pp of* **sweep**

swerve [swəːv] *vi* desviar-se

swift [swɪft] *n (bird)* andorinhão *m* ♦ *adj* rápido

swim [swɪm] *(pt* **swam**, *pp* **swum)** *n*: **to go for a ~** ir nadar ♦ *vi* nadar; *(head, room)* rodar ♦ *vt* atravessar a nado; *(distance)* percorrer (a nado); **swimmer** *n* nadador(a) *m/f*; **swimming** *n* natação *f*; **swimming cap** *n* touca de natação; **swimming costume** *(BRIT)* *n (woman's)* maiô *m (BR)*, fato de banho *(PT)*; *(man's)* calção *m* de banho *(BR)*, calções *mpl* de banho *(PT)*; **swimming pool** *n* piscina; **swimming trunks** *npl* sunga *(BR)*, calções *mpl* de banho *(PT)*; **swimsuit** *n* maiô *m (BR)*, fato de banho *(PT)*

swindle ['swɪndl] *n* fraude *f* ♦ *vt* defraudar

swine [swaɪn] *(inf!)* *n* canalha *m*, calhorda *m*

swing [swɪŋ] *(pt, pp* **swung)** *n (in playground)* balanço; *(movement)* balanceio, oscilação *f*; *(in opinion)* mudança, virada; *(rhythm)* ritmo ♦ *vt* balançar; *(also:* ~ **round)** girar, rodar ♦ *vi* oscilar; *(on swing)* balançar; *(also:* ~ **round)** voltar-se bruscamente; **to be in full ~** estar a todo vapor; **swing door** *n (US* **swinging door)** *n* porta de vaivém

swipe [swaɪp] *(inf)* *vt (steal)* afanar, roubar

swirl [swəːl] *vi* redemoinhar

Swiss [swɪs] *adj, n inv* suíço(-a)

switch [swɪtʃ] *n (for light, radio etc)* interruptor *m*; *(change)* mudança ♦ *vt (change)* trocar; **switch off** *vt* apagar; *(engine)* desligar; **switch**

on *vt* acender; ligar; **switchboard**
n (TEL) mesa telefônica
Switzerland ['swɪtsələnd] *n* Suíça
swivel ['swɪvl] *vi* (*also*: ~ **round**)
girar (sobre um eixo), fazer pião
swollen ['swəulən] *pp of* **swell**
swoop [swu:p] *n* (*by police etc*) batida ♦ *vi* (*also*: ~ **down**) precipitar-se,
cair
swop [swɔp] *n*, *vt* = **swap**
sword [sɔ:d] *n* espada
swore [swɔ:*] *pt of* **swear**
sworn [swɔ:n] *pp of* **swear** ♦ *adj*
(*statement*) sob juramento; (*enemy*)
declarado
swum [swʌm] *pp of* **swim**
swung [swʌŋ] *pt*, *pp of* **swing**
syllable ['sɪləbl] *n* sílaba
syllabus ['sɪləbəs] *n* programa *m*
de estudos
symbol ['sɪmbl] *n* símbolo
symmetry ['sɪmɪtrɪ] *n* simetria
sympathetic [sɪmpə'θetɪk] *adj*
(*understanding*) compreensivo; (*likeable*) agradável; (*supportive*): ~ **to**
(*wards*) solidário com
sympathize ['sɪmpəθaɪz] *vi*: **to** ~
with (*person*) compadecer-se de;
(*sb's feelings*) compreender; (*cause*)
simpatizar com; **sympathizer** *n*
(POL) simpatizante *m/f*
sympathy ['sɪmpəθɪ] *n* compaixão
f; **sympathies** *npl* (*tendencies*) simpatia; **in** ~ em acordo; (*strike*) em
solidariedade; **with our deepest** ~
com nossos mais profundos pêsames
symphony ['sɪmfənɪ] *n* sinfonia
symptom ['sɪmptəm] *n* sintoma *m*;
(*sign*) indício
syndicate ['sɪndɪkɪt] *n* sindicato;
(*of newspapers*) cadeia
synthetic [sɪn'θetɪk] *adj* sintético
syphon ['saɪfən] = **siphon**
Syria ['sɪrɪə] *n* Síria
syringe [sɪ'rɪndʒ] *n* seringa

syrup ['sɪrəp] *n* xarope *m*; (*also*:
golden ~) melaço
system ['sɪstəm] *n* sistema *m*;
(*method*) método; (ANAT) organismo; **systematic** [sɪstə'mætɪk] *adj*
sistemático; **system disk** *n* (COM-
PUT) disco do sistema; **systems
analyst** *n* analista *m/f* de sistemas

T

tab [tæb] *n* lingüeta, aba; (*label*) etiqueta; **to keep ~s on** (*fig*) vigiar
tabby ['tæbɪ] *n* (*also*: ~ **cat**) gato
malhado or listrado
table ['teɪbl] *n* mesa ♦ *vt* (*motion etc*)
apresentar; **to lay** or **set the ~** pôr a
mesa; ~ **of contents** índice *m*,
sumário; **tablecloth** *n* toalha de
mesa; **tablemat** *n* descanso;
tablespoon *n* colher *f* de sopa;
(*also*: **tablespoonful**: *as measurement*) colherada
tablet ['tæblɪt] *n* (MED) comprimido;
(*of stone*) lápide *f*
table tennis *n* pingue-pongue *m*,
tênis *m* de mesa
table wine *n* vinho de mesa
tabloid ['tæblɔɪd] *n* tablóide *m*;
tabloid press *n ver quadro*

TABLOID PRESS

O termo **tabloid press** refere-se
aos jornais populares de formato
meio jornal que apresentam muitas fotografias e adotam um estilo
bastante conciso. O público-alvo
desses jornais é composto por lei-
tores que se interessam pelos
fatos do dia que contenham um
certo toque de escândalo; veja
quality (news)papers.

---

tack [tæk] *n* (*nail*) tachinha, percevejo ♦ *vt* prender com tachinha; (*stitch*) alinhavar ♦ *vi* virar de bordo

tackle ['tækl] *n* (*gear*) equipamento; (*also: fishing ~*) apetrechos *mpl*; (*for lifting*) guincho; (*FOOTBALL*) ato de tirar a bola de adversário ♦ *vt* (*difficulty*) atacar; (*challenge: person*) desafiar; (*grapple with*) atracar-se com; (*FOOTBALL*) tirar a bola de

tacky ['tækɪ] *adj* pegajoso, grudento; (*inf: tasteless*) cafona

tact [tækt] *n* tato, diplomacia; **tactful** *adj* diplomático

tactics ['tæktɪks] *n, npl* tática

tactless ['tæktlɪs] *adj* sem diplomacia

tadpole ['tædpəul] *n* girino

tag [tæg] *n* (*label*) etiqueta; **tag along** *vi* seguir

tail [teɪl] *n* rabo; (*of comet, plane*) cauda; (*of shirt, coat*) aba ♦ *vt* (*follow*) seguir bem de perto; **tail away** *or* **off** *vi* diminuir gradualmente

tailor ['teɪlə*] *n* alfaiate *m*; **tailormade** *adj* feito sob medida; (*fig*) especial

tailwind ['teɪlwɪnd] *n* vento de popa or de cauda

tainted ['teɪntɪd] *adj* (*food*) estragado, passado; (*water, air*) poluído; (*fig*) manchado

take [teɪk] (*pt* **took**, *pp* **taken**) *vt* tomar; (*photo, holiday*) tirar; (*grab*) pegar (em); (*prize*) ganhar; (*effort, courage*) requerer, exigir; (*tolerate*) agüentar; (*accompany, bring: person*) acompanhar, trazer; (: *thing*) trazer, carregar; (*exam*) fazer; (*passengers etc*): **it ~s 50 people** cabem 50 pessoas; **to ~ sth from** (*drawer etc*) tirar algo de; (*person*) pegar algo de; **I ~ it that ...** suponho que ...; **take after** *vt fus* parecer-se com; **take apart** *vt* desmontar;

take away *vt* (*extract*) tirar; (*carry off*) levar; (*subtract*) subtrair; **take back** *vt* (*return*) devolver; (*one's words*) retirar; **take down** *vt* (*building*) demolir; (*dismantle*) desmontar; (*letter etc*) tomar por escrito; **take in** *vt* (*deceive*) enganar; (*understand*) compreender; (*include*) abranger; (*lodger*) receber; **take off** *vt* (*AVIAT*) decolar; (*go away*) ir-se ♦ *vt* (*remove*) tirar; **take on** *vt* (*work*) empreender; (*employee*) empregar; (*opponent*) desafiar; **take out** *vt* (*extract*) extrair; (*invite*) acompanhar; **take over** *vt* (*business*) assumir; (*country*) tomar posse de ♦ *vi*: **to ~ over from sb** suceder a alguém; **take to** *vt fus* (*person*) simpatizar com; (*activity*) afeiçoar-se a; **to ~ to doing sth** criar o hábito de fazer algo; **take up** *vt* (*dress*) encurtar; (*time, space*) ocupar; (*hobby etc*) dedicar-se a; (*offer*) aceitar; **to ~ sb up on a suggestion/offer** aceitar a oferta/sugestão de alguém sobre algo; **takeaway** (*BRIT*) *adj* (*food*) para levar; **takeoff** *n* (*AVIAT*) decolagem *f*; **takeover** *n* (*COMM*) aquisição *f* de controle; **takings** *npl* (*COMM*) receita, renda

talc [tælk] *n* (*also: ~um powder*) talco

tale [teɪl] *n* (*story*) conto; (*account*) narrativa; **to tell ~s** (*fig: lie*) dizer mentiras

talent ['tælənt] *n* talento; **talented** *adj* talentoso

talk [tɔːk] *n* conversa, fala; (*gossip*) mexerico, fofocas *fpl*; (*conversation*) conversa, conversação *f* ♦ *vi* falar; **~s** *npl* (*POL etc*) negociações *fpl*; **to ~ about** falar sobre; **to ~ sb into/out of doing sth** convencer alguém a fazer algo/dissuadir alguém de fazer algo; **to ~ shop** falar sobre negócios/questões profissionais; **talk over** vt discutir; **talkative** adj loquaz, tagarela; **talk show** n programa m de entrevistas

tall [tɔ:l] adj alto; **to be 6 feet ~** = medir 1,80 m

tally ['tælɪ] n conta ♦ vi: **to ~ (with)** conferir (com)

talon ['tælən] n garra

tame [teɪm] adj domesticado; (fig: story, style) sem graça, insípido

tamper ['tæmpə*] vi: **to ~ with** mexer em

tampon ['tæmpɔn] n tampão m

tan [tæn] n (also: **sun~**) bronzeado ♦ vi bronzear-se ♦ adj (colour) bronzeado, marrom claro

tangent ['tændʒənt] n (MATH) tangente f; **to go off at a ~** (fig) sair pela tangente

tangerine [tændʒə'ri:n] n tangerina, mexerica

tangle ['tæŋgl] n emaranhado; **to get in(to) a ~** meter-se num rolo

tank [tæŋk] n depósito, tanque m; (for fish) aquário; (MIL) tanque

tanker ['tæŋkə*] n (ship) navio-tanque m; (truck) caminhão-tanque m

tantalizing ['tæntəlaɪzɪŋ] adj tentador(a)

tantamount ['tæntəmaunt] adj: **~ to** equivalente a

tantrum ['tæntrəm] n chilique m, acesso (de raiva)

tap [tæp] n (on sink etc) torneira; (gentle blow) palmadinha; (gas ~) chave f ♦ vt dar palmadinha em, bater de leve; (resources) utilizar, explorar; (telephone) grampear; **on ~** disponível; **tap-dancing** n sapateado

tape [teɪp] n fita; (also: **magnetic ~**) fita magnética; (sticky ~) fita adesiva ♦ vt (record) gravar (em fita); (stick

with tape) colar; **tape deck** n gravador m, toca-fitas m inv; **tape measure** n fita métrica, trena

taper ['teɪpə*] n círio ♦ vi afilar-se, estreitar-se

tape recorder n gravador m

tapestry ['tæpɪstrɪ] n (object) tapete m de parede; (art) tapeçaria

tar [tɑ:*] n alcatrão m

target ['tɑ:gɪt] n alvo

tariff ['tærɪf] n tarifa

tarmac ['tɑ:mæk] n (BRIT: on road) macadame m; (AVIAT) pista

tarnish ['tɑ:nɪʃ] vt empanar o brilho de

tarpaulin [tɑ:'pɔ:lɪn] n lona alcatroada

tart [tɑ:t] n (CULIN) torta; (BRIT: inf: pej: woman) piranha ♦ adj (flavour) ácido, azedo; **tart up** (inf) vt arrumar, dar um jeito em; **to ~ o.s. up** arrumar-se; (pej) empetecar-se

tartan ['tɑ:tn] n tartan m (pano escocês axadrezado) ♦ adj axadrezado

tartar ['tɑ:tə*] n (on teeth) tártaro; **tartar(e) sauce** n molho tártaro

task [tɑ:sk] n tarefa; **to take to ~** repreender

tassel ['tæsl] n borla, pendão m

taste [teɪst] n gosto; (also: **after~**) gosto residual; (sample, fig) amostra, idéia ♦ vt provar; (test) experimentar ♦ vi: **to ~ of** or like ter gosto or sabor de; **you can ~ the garlic (in it)** sente-se o gosto de alho; **good/bad ~** de bom/mau gosto; **tasteful** adj de bom gosto; **tasteless** adj insípido, insosso; (remark) de mau gosto; **tasty** adj saboroso, delicioso

tatters ['tætəz] npl: **in ~** (clothes) em farrapos; (papers etc) em pedaços

tattoo [tə'tu:] n tatuagem f; (spec-

tacle) espetáculo militar ♦ *vt* tatuar

tatty ['tætɪ] (*BRIT: inf*) *adj* (*clothes*) surrado; (*shop, area*) mal-cuidado

taught [tɔːt] *pt, pp* of **teach**

taunt [tɔːnt] *n* zombaria, escárnio ♦ *vt* zombar de, mofar de

Taurus ['tɔːrəs] *n* Touro

taut [tɔːt] *adj* esticado

tax [tæks] *n* imposto ♦ *vt* tributar; (*fig: test*) sobrecarregar; (*: patience*) esgotar; **taxation** [tæk'seɪʃən] *n* (*system*) tributação f; (*money paid*) imposto; **tax-free** *adj* isento de impostos

taxi ['tæksɪ] *n* táxi *m* ♦ *vi* (*AVIAT*) taxiar; **taxi driver** *n* motorista *m/f* de táxi; **taxi rank** (*BRIT*) *n* ponto de táxi; **taxi stand** *n* = **taxi rank**

tax payer *n* contribuinte *m/f*

tax return *n* declaração f de rendimentos

TB *abbr* of **tuberculosis**

tea [tiː] *n* chá *m*; (*BRIT: meal*) refeição f à noite; **high ~** (*BRIT*) *n* jantar(ado; **tea bag** *n* saquinho (*BR*) *or* carteira (*PT*) de chá; **tea break** (*BRIT*) *n* pausa (para o chá)

teach [tiːtʃ] (*pt, pp* **taught**) *vt*: **to ~ sb sth, ~ sth to sb** ensinar algo a alguém; (*in school*) lecionar ♦ *vi* ensinar; (*be a teacher*) lecionar; **teacher** *n* professor(a) *m/f*; **teaching** *n* ensino; (*as profession*) magistério

tea cosy *n* coberta do bule, abafador *m*

teacup ['tiːkʌp] *n* xícara (*BR*) *or* chávena (*PT*) de chá

teak [tiːk] *n* madeira de teca

tea leaves *npl* folhas *fpl* de chá

team [tiːm] *n* (*SPORT*) time *m* (*BR*), equipa (*PT*); (*group*) equipe f (*BR*), equipa (*PT*); (*of animals*) parelha; **teamwork** *n* trabalho de equipe

teapot ['tiːpɔt] *n* bule *m* de chá

tear¹ [tɛəʳ] (*pt* **tore**, *pp* **torn**) *n*

rasgão *m* ♦ *vt* rasgar ♦ *vi* rasgar-se;

tear along *vi* (*rush*) precipitar-se;

tear up *vt* rasgar

tear² [tɪəʳ] *n* lágrima; **in ~s** chorando, em lágrimas; **tearful** *adj* choroso; **tear gas** *n* gás *m* lacrimogênio

tearoom ['tiːruːm] *n* salão *m* de chá

tease [tiːz] *vt* implicar com

tea set *n* aparelho de chá

teaspoon ['tiːspuːn] *n* colher f de chá; (*also: ~ful: as measurement*) (conteúdo de) colher de chá

teat [tiːt] *n* bico (de mamadeira)

teatime ['tiːtaɪm] *n* hora do chá

tea towel (*BRIT*) *n* pano de prato

technical ['tɛknɪkl] *adj* técnico; **technicality** [tɛknɪ'kælɪtɪ] *n* detalhe *m* técnico; (*point of law*) particularidade f

technician [tɛk'nɪʃn] *n* técnico(-a)

technique [tɛk'niːk] *n* técnica

technology [tɛk'nɔlədʒɪ] *n* tecnologia

teddy (bear) ['tɛdɪ-] *n* ursinho de pelúcia

tedious ['tiːdɪəs] *adj* maçante, chato

teem [tiːm] *vi* abundar, pulular; **to ~ with** abundar em; **it is ~ing (with rain)** está chovendo a cântaros

teenage ['tiːneɪdʒ] *adj* (*fashions etc*) de ou para adolescentes; **teenager** *n* adolescente *m/f*, jovem *m/f*

teens [tiːnz] *npl*: **to be in one's ~** estar entre os 13 e 19 anos, estar na adolescência

tee-shirt *n* = **T-shirt**

teeth [tiːθ] *npl* of **tooth**; **teethe** *vi* começar a ter dentes; **teething troubles** *npl* (*fig*) dificuldades *fpl* iniciais

teetotal ['tiː'təutl] *adj* abstêmio

teleconferencing [tɛlɪ'kɒnfərənsɪŋ] *n* teleconferência f

telegram ['tɛlɪgræm] n telegrama m

telegraph ['tɛlɪgrɑːf] n telégrafo

telephone ['tɛlɪfəun] n telefone m ♦ vt (person) telefonar para; (message) telefonar; **to be on the ~** (BRIT), **to have a ~** (subscriber) ter telefone; **to be on the ~** (be speaking) estar falando no telefone; **telephone booth** (BRIT **telephone box**) n cabine f telefônica; **telephone call** n telefonema m; **telephone directory** n lista telefônica, catálogo (BR); **telephone number** n (número de) telefone m; **telephonist** [tə'lɛfənɪst] (BRIT) n telefonista m/f

telesales ['tɛlɪseɪlz] npl televendas fpl

telescope ['tɛlɪskəup] n telescópio

television ['tɛlɪvɪʒən] n televisão f; **on ~** na televisão; **television set** n (aparelho de) televisão f, televisor m

teleworking ['tɛlɪwəːkɪŋ] n teletrabalho m

telex ['tɛlɛks] n telex m ♦ vt (message) enviar por telex, telexar; (person) mandar um telex para

tell [tɛl] (pt, pp **told**) vt dizer; (relate: story) contar; (distinguish): **to ~ sth from** distinguir algo de ♦ vi (have effect) ter efeito; (talk): **to ~ (of)** falar (de or em); **to ~ sb to do sth** dizer para alguém fazer algo; **tell off** vt repreender; **telltale** adj (sign) revelador(a)

telly ['tɛlɪ] (BRIT: inf) n abbr = **television**

temp [tɛmp] (BRIT: inf) abbr (= temporary) ♦ n temporário(-a) ♦ vi trabalhar como temporário(-a)

temper ['tɛmpə*] n (nature) temperamento; (mood) humor m; (fit of anger) cólera ♦ vt (moderate) moderar; **to be in a ~** estar de mau

humor; **to lose one's ~** perder a paciência or a calma, ficar zangado

temperament ['tɛmprəmənt] n temperamento; **temperamental** [tɛmprə'mɛntl] adj temperamental

temperate ['tɛmprət] adj moderado; (climate) temperado

temperature ['tɛmprətʃə*] n temperatura; **to have** or **run a ~** ter febre

temple ['tɛmpl] n (building) templo; (ANAT) têmpora

temporary ['tɛmpərərɪ] adj temporário; (passing) transitório

tempt [tɛmpt] vt tentar; **tempting** adj tentador(a)

ten [tɛn] num dez

tenancy ['tɛnənsɪ] n aluguel m

tenant ['tɛnənt] n inquilino(-a), locatário(-a)

tend [tɛnd] vt (sick etc) cuidar de ♦ vi: **to ~ to do sth** tender a fazer algo

tendency ['tɛndənsɪ] n tendência

tender ['tɛndə*] adj terno; (age) tenro; (sore) sensível, dolorido; (meat) macio ♦ n (COMM: offer) oferta, proposta; (money): **legal ~** moeda corrente or legal ♦ vt oferecer; **to ~ one's resignation** pedir demissão

tenement ['tɛnəmənt] n conjunto habitacional

tennis ['tɛnɪs] n tênis m; **tennis ball** n bola de tênis; **tennis court** n quadra de tênis; **tennis player** n jogador(a) m/f de tênis; **tennis racket** n raquete f de tênis

tenor ['tɛnə*] n (MUS) tenor m

tenpin bowling ['tɛnpɪn-] (BRIT) n boliche m com 10 paus

tense [tɛns] adj tenso; (muscle) rígido, teso ♦ n (LING) tempo

tension ['tɛnʃən] n tensão f

tent [tɛnt] n tenda, barraca

tentative ['tɛntətɪv] adj provisório, tentativo; (person) hesitante, indeciso

tenth [tɛnθ] num décimo

tent peg n estaca

tent pole n pau m

tenure ['tɛnjuə*] n (of property) posse f; (of job) estabilidade f

tepid ['tɛpɪd] adj tépido, morno

term [tə:m] n (expression) termo, expressão f; (period) período; (SCH) trimestre m ♦ vt denominar; **~s** npl (conditions) condições fpl; (COMM) cláusulas fpl, termos mpl; **in the short/long ~** a curto/longo prazo; **to be on good ~s with sb** dar-se bem com alguém; **to come to ~s with** aceitar

terminal ['tə:mɪnl] adj incurável ♦ n (ELEC) borne m; (BRIT: also: **air ~**) terminal m; (also COMPUT) terminal m; (BRIT: also: **coach ~**) estação f rodoviária

terminate ['tə:mɪneɪt] vt terminar; **to ~ a pregnancy** fazer um aborto

terminus ['tə:mɪnəs] (pl **termini**) n terminal m

terrace ['tɛrəs] n terraço; (BRIT: houses) lance m de casas; **the ~s** npl (BRIT: SPORT) a arquibancada (BR), a geral (PT); **terraced** adj (house) ladeado por outras casas; (garden) em dois níveis

terrain [tɛ'reɪn] n terreno

terrible ['tɛrɪbl] adj terrível, horroroso; (conditions) precário; (inf: awful) terrível; **terribly** adv terrivelmente; (very badly) pessimamente

terrific [tə'rɪfɪk] adj terrível, magnífico; (wonderful) maravilhoso, sensacional

terrify ['tɛrɪfaɪ] vt apavorar

territory ['tɛrɪtərɪ] n território

terror ['tɛrə*] n terror m; **terrorist** n terrorista m/f

test [tɛst] n (trial, check) prova, ensaio; (of courage etc, CHEM) prova; (MED) exame m; (exam) teste m, prova; (also: **driving ~**) exame de motorista ♦ vt testar, pôr à prova

testament ['tɛstəmənt] n testamento; **the Old/New T~** o Velho/Novo Testamento

testicle ['tɛstɪkl] n testículo

testify ['tɛstɪfaɪ] vi (LAW) depor, testemunhar; **to ~ to sth** atestar algo, testemunhar algo

testimony ['tɛstɪmənɪ] n (LAW) testemunho, depoimento; **to be (a) ~** to ser uma prova de

test: test match n (CRICKET, RUGBY) jogo internacional; **test tube** n proveta, tubo de ensaio

tetanus ['tɛtənəs] n tétano

text [tɛkst] n texto; **textbook** n livro didático; (SCH) livro escolar

texture ['tɛkstʃə*] n textura

Thailand ['taɪlænd] n Tailândia

Thames [tɛmz] n: **the ~** o Tâmisa (BR), o Tamisa (PT)

than [ðæn, ðən] conj (in comparisons) do que; **more ~ 10** mais de 10; **I have more/less ~ you** tenho mais/menos do que você; **she has more apples ~ pears** ela tem mais maçãs do que peras; **she is older ~ you think** ela é mais velha do que você pensa

thank [θæŋk] vt agradecer; **~ you (very much)** muito obrigado(-a); **thankful** adj: **thankful (for)** agradecido (por); **thankful that** aliviado que; **thankless** adj ingrato; **thanks** npl agradecimentos mpl ♦ excl obrigado(-a); **Thanksgiving (Day)** n Dia m de Ação de Graças; ver quadro

THANKSGIVING DAY

O feriado de Ação de graças **Thanksgiving Day** nos Estados Unidos, quarta quinta-feira do mês de novembro, é o dia em que se comemora a boa colheita feita pelos peregrinos originários da Grã-Bretanha em 1621; tradicionalmente, é um dia em que se agradece a Deus e se organiza um grande banquete. Uma festa semelhante é celebrada no Canadá na segunda segunda-feira de outubro.

KEYWORD

that [ðæt, ðət] (*pl* those) *adj* (*demonstrative*) esse (essa); (*more remote*) aquele (aquela); **~ man/ woman/book** aquele homem/ aquela mulher/aquele livro; **~ one** esse (essa)
♦ *pron* **1** (*demonstrative*) esse (essa), aquele (aquela); (*neuter*) isso, aquilo; **who's/what's ~?** quem é?/o que é isso?; **is ~ you?** é você?; **I prefer this to ~** eu prefiro isto a aquilo; **~'s what he said** foi isso o que ele disse; **~ is (to say)** isto é, quer dizer
2 (*relative: direct: thing, person*) que; (: *person*) quem; (*relative: indirect: thing, person*) o qual (a qual) *sg*, os quais (as quais) *pl*; (: *person*) quem; **the book (~)** I read o livro que eu li; **the box (~)** I put it in a caixa na qual eu botei-o; **the man (~)** I spoke to o homem com quem or o qual falei
3 (*relative: of time*): **on the day ~ he came** no dia em que ele veio
♦ *conj* que; **she suggested ~ I phone you** ela sugeriu que eu telefonasse para você

♦ *adv* (*demonstrative*): **I can't work ~ much** não posso trabalhar tanto; **I didn't realize it was ~ bad** não pensei que fôsse tão ruim; **~ high** dessa altura, até essa altura

thatched [θætʃt] *adj* (*roof*) de sapê; **~ cottage** chalé *m* com telhado de sapê or de colmo

thaw [θɔ:] *n* degelo ♦ *vi* (*ice*) derreter-se; (*food*) descongelar-se ♦ *vt* (*food*) descongelar

KEYWORD

the [ði:, ðə] *def art* **1** (*gen: sg*) o (a); (: *pl*) os (as); **~ books/children** os livros/as crianças; **she put it on ~ table** ela colocou-o na mesa; **he took it from ~ drawer** ele tirou isto da gaveta; **to play ~ piano/violin** tocar piano/violino; **I'm going to ~ cinema** vou ao cinema
2 (+ *adj to form n*): **~ rich and ~ poor** os ricos e os pobres; **to attempt ~ impossible** tentar o impossível
3 (*in titles*): **Richard ~ Second** Ricardo II; **Peter ~ Great** Pedro o Grande
4 (*in comparisons*: + *adv*): **~ more he works, ~ more he earns** quanto mais ele trabalha, mais ele ganha

theatre ['θɪətə*] (*us* theater) *n* teatro; (*MED: also: operating ~*) sala de operação; **theatrical** [θɪˈætrɪkl] *adj* teatral

theft [θɛft] *n* roubo

their [ðɛə*] *adj* seu (sua), deles (delas); **theirs** *pron* (o) seu ((a) sua); *see also* mine²

them [ðɛm, ðəm] *pron* (*direct*) os (as); (*indirect*) lhes; (*stressed, after prep*) a eles (a elas)

theme [θi:m] *n* tema *m*; **theme**

park n parque de diversões em torno de um único tema

themselves [ðəm'selvz] pron eles mesmos (elas mesmas), se; (after prep) si (mesmos(-as))

then [ðen] adv (at that time) então; (next) em seguida; (later) logo, depois; (and also) além disso ♦ conj (therefore) então, nesse caso, portanto ♦ adj: **the ~ president** o então presidente; **by ~** (past) até então; (future) até lá; **from ~ on** a partir de então

theology [θɪ'ɔlədʒɪ] n teologia

theoretical [θɪə'retɪkl] adj teórico

theory [θɪərɪ] n teoria; **in ~** em teoria, teoricamente

therapy ['θerəpɪ] n terapia

KEYWORD

there [ðeə*] adv **1 ~ is, ~ are** há, tem; **~ are 3 of them** há 3 deles; **~ is no-one here/no bread left** não tem ninguém aqui/não tem mais pão; **~ has been an accident** houve um acidente
2 (referring to place) aí, ali, lá; **put it in/on/up/down ~** põe isto lá dentro/cima/em cima/embaixo; **I want that book ~** quero aquele livro lá; **~ he is!** lá está ele!
3: ~, ~! (esp to child) calma!

---

thereabouts ['ðeərəbauts] adv por aí; (amount) aproximadamente

thereafter [ðeər'ɑːftə*] adv depois disso

thereby ['ðeəbaɪ] adv assim, deste modo

therefore ['ðeəfɔː] adv portanto

there's [ðeəz] = there is; there has

thermal ['θəːml] adj térmico

thermometer [θə'mɔmɪtə*] n termômetro

Thermos ['θəːməs] ® n (also: ~

flask) garrafa térmica (BR), termo (PT)

thermostat ['θəːməustæt] n termostato

thesaurus [θɪ'sɔːrəs] n tesouro, dicionário de sinônimos

these [ðiːz] pl adj, pron estes (estas)

thesis ['θiːsɪs] (pl theses) n tese f

they [ðeɪ] pl pron eles (elas); ~ **say that ...** (it is said that) diz-se que ..., dizem que ...; **they'd** = they had; **they would; they'll** = they shall; they will; **they've** = they have

thick [θɪk] adj espesso; (mud, fog, forest) denso; (sauce) grosso; (stupid) burro ♦ n: **in the ~ of the battle** em plena batalha; **it's 20 cm ~** tem 20 cm de espessura; **thick en** vi (fog) adensar-se; (plot etc) complicar-se ♦ vt engrossar; **thickness** n espessura, grossura; **thickset** adj troncudo

thief [θiːf] (pl thieves) n ladrão (ladra) m/f

thigh [θaɪ] n coxa

thimble ['θɪmbl] n dedal m

thin [θɪn] adj magro; (slice) fino; (light) leve; (hair) ralo; (crowd) pequeno; (soup, sauce) aguado ♦ vt (also: ~ **down**) diluir

thing [θɪŋ] n coisa; (object) negócio; (matter) assunto, negócio; (mania) mania; **~s** npl (belongings) pertences mpl; **to have a ~ about sb/sth** ser vidrado em alguém/algo; **the best ~ would be to ...** o melhor seria ...; **how are ~s?** como vai?, tudo bem?; **she's got a ~ about ...** ela detesta ...; **poor ~!** coitadinho(-a)!

think [θɪŋk] (pt, pp thought) vi pensar; (believe) achar ♦ vt pensar, achar; (imagine) imaginar; **what did you ~ of them?** o que você achou deles?; **to ~ about sb/sth** pensar em alguém/algo; **I'll ~ about it** vou pensar sobre isso; **to ~ of doing sth** pensar em fazer algo; **I ~ so/not** acho que sim/não; **to ~ well of sb** fazer bom juízo de alguém; **think over** vt refletir sobre, meditar sobre; **think up** vt inventar, bolar

thinly ['θɪnlɪ] adv (cut) em fatias finas; (spread) numa camada fina

third [θəːd] adj terceiro ♦ n terceiro(-a); (fraction) terço; (AUT) terceira; (SCH: degree) terceira categoria; **thirdly** adv em terceiro lugar; **third party insurance** n seguro contra terceiros; **third-rate** adj medíocre; **Third World** n: the Third World o Terceiro Mundo

thirst [θəːst] n sede f; **thirsty** adj (person) sedento, com sede; (work) que dá sede; **to be thirsty** estar com sede

thirteen ['θəː'tiːn] num treze

thirty ['θəːtɪ] num trinta

KEYWORD

this [ðɪs] (pl these) adj (demonstrative) este (esta); **~ man/woman/book** este homem/esta mulher/este livro; **these people/children/records** estas pessoas/crianças/estes discos; **~ one** este aqui
♦ pron (demonstrative) este (esta); (neuter) isto; **who/what is ~?** quem é esse?/o que é isso?; **~ is where I live** é aqui que eu moro; **~ is Mr Brown** este é o Sr Brown; (on phone) aqui é o Sr Brown
♦ adv (demonstrative): **~ high/long** desta altura/deste comprimento; **we can't stop now we've gone ~ far** não podemos parar agora que fomos tão longe

thistle ['θɪsl] n cardo

thorn [θɔːn] n espinho

thorough ['θʌrə] adj (search) minucioso; (knowledge, research, person) metódico, profundo; **thoroughbred** adj (horse) de puro sangue; **thoroughfare** n via, passagem f; **"no thoroughfare"** "passagem proibida"; **thoroughly** adv minuciosamente; (search) profundamente; (wash) completamente; (very) muito

those [ðəuz] pl pron, adj esses (essas)

though [ðəu] conj embora, se bem que ♦ adv no entanto

thought [θɔːt] pt, pp of **think** ♦ n pensamento; (idea) idéia; (opinion) opinião f; (reflection) reflexão f; **thoughtful** adj pensativo; (serious) sério; (considerate) atencioso; **thoughtless** adj desatencioso; (words) inconseqüente

thousand ['θauzənd] num mil; **two ~** dois mil; **~s (of)** milhares mpl (de); **thousandth** num milésimo

thrash [θræʃ] vt surrar, malhar; (defeat) derrotar; **thrash about** vi debater-se; **thrash out** vt discutir exaustivamente

thread [θrɛd] n fio, linha; (of screw) rosca ♦ vt (needle) enfiar

threat [θrɛt] n ameaça; **threaten** vi ameaçar ♦ vt: **to threaten sb with sth/to do** ameaçar alguém com algo/de fazer

three [θriː] num três; **three-dimensional** adj tridimensional, em três dimensões; **three-piece suit** n terno (3 peças), fato de 3 peças (PT); **three-piece suite** n conjunto de sofá e duas poltronas

threshold ['θrɛʃhəuld] n limiar m

threw [θruː] pt of **throw**

thrifty ['θrɪftɪ] adj econômico, frugal

thrill [θrɪl] n emoção f; (shudder) estremecimento ♦ vt emocionar, vibrar; **to be ~ed** (with gift etc) estar emocionado; **thriller** n romance m (or filme m) de suspense; **thrilling** adj emocionante

thrive [θraɪv] (pt ~d or throve, pp ~d or thriven) vi (grow) vicejar; (do well) to ~ on sth realizar-se ao fazer algo; **thriving** adj próspero

throat [θrəut] n garganta; **to have a sore ~** estar com dor de garganta

throb [θrɔb] n (of heart) batida; (of engine) vibração f; (of pain) latejo ♦ vi (heart) bater, palpitar; (pain) dar pontadas; (engine) vibrar

throne [θrəun] n trono

throng [θrɔŋ] n multidão f ♦ vt apinhar, apinhar-se em

throttle ['θrɔtl] n (AUT) acelerador m ♦ vt estrangular

through [θru:] prep por, através de; (time) durante; (by means of) por meio de, por intermédio de; (owing to) devido a ♦ adj (ticket, train) direto ♦ adv através; **to put sb ~ to sb** (TEL) ligar alguém com alguém; **to be ~** (TEL) estar na linha; (have finished) acabar; **"no – road"** "rua sem saída"; **I'm halfway ~ the book** estou na metade do livro; **throughout** prep (place) por todo(-a) o (a); (time) durante todo(-a) o (a) ♦ adv por or em todas as partes

throw [θrəu] (pt threw, pp thrown) n arremesso, tiro; (SPORT) lançamento ♦ vt jogar, atirar; lançar; (rider) derrubar; (fig) desconcertar; **to ~ a party** dar uma festa; **throw away** vt (dispose of) jogar fora; (waste) desperdiçar; **throw off** vt desfazer-se de; (habit, cold) livrar-se de; **throw out** vt expulsar; (rubbish) jogar fora; (idea) rejeitar; **throw up** vi vomitar, botar para fora; **throwaway** adj descartável; (remark) gratuito

throw-in n (SPORT) lance m

thru [θru:] (US) prep, adj, adv = **through**

thrush [θrʌʃ] n (ZOOL) tordo

thrust [θrʌst] (pt, pp thrust) n impulso; (TECH) empuxo ♦ vt empurrar

thud [θʌd] n baque m, som m surdo

thug [θʌg] n facínora m/f

thumb [θʌm] n (ANAT) polegar m; **to ~ a lift** pegar carona (BR), arranjar uma boléia (PT); **thumb through** vt fus folhear; **thumbtack** (US) n percevejo, tachinha

thump [θʌmp] n murro, pancada; (sound) baque m ♦ vt dar um murro em ♦ vi bater

thunder ['θʌndə*] n trovão m ♦ vi trovejar; (train etc): **to ~ past** passar como um raio; **thunderbolt** n raio; **thunderclap** n estampido do trovão; **thunderstorm** n tempestade f com trovoada, temporal m

Thursday ['θəːzdɪ] n quinta-feira

thus [ðʌs] adv assim, desta maneira; (consequently) conseqüentemente

thwart [θwɔːt] vt frustrar

thyme [taɪm] n tomilho

tiara [tɪ'ɑːrə] n tiara, diadema m

tick [tɪk] n (of clock) tique-taque m; (mark) toque m, marca; (ZOOL) carrapato; (BRIT: inf): **in a ~** num instante ♦ vi fazer tique-taque ♦ vt marcar, ticar; **tick off** vt assinalar, ticar; (person) dar uma bronca em; **tick over** (BRIT) vi (engine) funcionar em marcha lenta; (fig) ir indo

ticket [ˈtɪkɪt] n (for bus, plane) passagem f; (for theatre, raffle) bilhete m; (for cinema) entrada; (in shop: on goods) etiqueta; (parking ~: fine) multa; (for library) cartão m; **to get a (parking) ~** (AUT) ganhar uma multa (por estacionamento ilegal); **ticket collector** n revisor(a) m/f;

ticket office n bilheteria (BR), bilheteira (PT)

tickle ['tɪkl] vt fazer cócegas em ♦ vi fazer cócegas; **ticklish** adj coceguento; (problem) delicado

tidal ['taɪdl] adj de maré; **tidal wave** n macaréu m, onda gigantesca

tidbit ['tɪdbɪt] (esp US) n = **titbit**

tide [taɪd] n maré f; (fig) curso; **high/low** ~ maré alta/baixa; **the ~ of public opinion** a corrente da opinião pública; **tide over** vt ajudar num período difícil

tidy ['taɪdɪ] adj (room) arrumado; (dress, work) limpo; (person) bem arrumado ♦ vt (also: ~ **up**) pôr em ordem, arrumar

tie [taɪ] n (string etc) fita, corda; (BRIT: also: **neck**~) gravata; (fig: link) vínculo, laço; (SPORT: draw) empate m ♦ vt amarrar ♦ vi (SPORT) empatar; **to ~ in a bow** dar um laço em; **to ~ a knot in sth** dar um nó em algo; **tie down** vt amarrar; (fig: restrict) limitar, restringir; (to date, price etc) obrigar; **tie up** vt embrulhar; (dog) prender; (boat, prisoner) amarrar; (arrangements) concluir; **to be ~d up** estar ocupado

tier [tɪə*] n fileira; (of cake) camada

tiger ['taɪgə*] n tigre m

tight [taɪt] adj (rope) esticado, firme; (money) escasso; (clothes, shoes) justo; (bend) fechado; (budget, programme) rigoroso; (inf: drunk) bêbado ♦ adv (squeeze) bem forte; (shut) hermeticamente; **tighten** vt (rope) esticar; (screw, grip) apertar; (security) aumentar ♦ vi esticar-se; apertar-se; **tight-fisted** adj pãoduro; **tightly** adv firmemente; **tight-rope** n corda (bamba)

tights [taɪts] (BRIT) npl collant m

tile [taɪl] n (on roof) telha; (on floor) ladrilho; (on wall) azulejo, ladrilho; **tiled** adj ladrilhado; (roof) de telhas

till [tɪl] n caixa (registradora) ♦ vt (land) cultivar ♦ prep, conj = **until**

tiller ['tɪlə*] n (NAUT) cana do leme

tilt [tɪlt] vt inclinar ♦ vi inclinar-se

timber ['tɪmbə*] n (material) madeira; (trees) mata, floresta

time [taɪm] n tempo; (epoch: often pl) época; (by clock) hora; (moment) momento; (occasion) vez f; (MUS) compasso ♦ vt calcular or medir o tempo de; (visit etc) escolher o momento para; **a long** ~ muito tempo; **4 at a** ~ quatro de uma vez; **for the** ~ **being** por enquanto; **from ~ to** ~ de vez em quando; **at** ~**s** às vezes; **in** ~ (soon enough) a tempo; (after some time) com o tempo; (MUS) no compasso; **in a week's** ~ dentro de uma semana; **in no** ~ num abrir e fechar de olhos; **any** ~ a qualquer hora; **on** ~ na hora; **5 ~s 5** is 25 5 vezes 5 são 25; **what** ~ **is it?** que horas são?; **to have a good** ~ divertir-se; **time bomb** n bomba-relógio f; **timeless** adj eterno; **timely** adj oportuno; **time switch** (BRIT) n interruptor m horário; **timetable** n horário; **time zone** n fuso horário

timid ['tɪmɪd] adj tímido

timing ['taɪmɪŋ] n escolha do momento; (SPORT) cronometragem f; **the ~ of his resignation** o momento que escolheu para se demitir

tin [tɪn] n estanho; (also: ~ **plate**) folha-de-flandres f; (BRIT: can) lata; **tin foil** n papel m de estanho

tingle ['tɪŋgl] n formigar

tinned [tɪnd] (BRIT) adj (food) em lata, em conserva

tin opener (BRIT) n abridor m de latas (BR), abre-latas m inv (PT)

tinsel ['tɪnsl] n ouropel m

tint [tɪnt] n matiz m; (for hair) tintura, tinta; **tinted** adj (hair) pintado; (spectacles, glass) fumê inv

tiny ['taɪnɪ] adj pequenininho, minúsculo

tip [tɪp] n ponta; (gratuity) gorjeta; (BRIT: for rubbish) depósito; (advice) dica ♦ vt dar uma gorjeta a; (tilt) inclinar; (overturn: also: ~ over) virar, emborcar; (empty: also: ~ out) esvaziar, entornar; **tipped** (BRIT) adj (cigarette) com filtro

tipsy ['tɪpsɪ] adj embriagado, tocado

tiptoe ['tɪptəʊ] n: **on ~** na ponta dos pés

tire ['taɪə*] n (US) = **tyre** ♦ vt cansar ♦ vi cansar-se; (become bored) chatear-se; **tired** adj cansado; **to be tired of sth** estar farto or cheio de algo; **tireless** adj incansável; **tiresome** adj enfadonho, chato; **tiring** adj cansativo

tissue ['tɪʃuː] n tecido; (paper handkerchief) lenço de papel; **tissue paper** n papel m de seda

tit [tɪt] n (bird) passarinho; **to give ~ for tat** pagar na mesma moeda

titbit ['tɪtbɪt] n (food) guloseima; (news) boato, rumor m

title ['taɪtl] n título

TM n abbr = **trademark**

to [tuː, tə] prep **1** (direction) a, para; (towards) para; **to go ~ France/ London/school/the station** ir à França/a Londres/ao colégio/à estação; **to go ~ Lígia's/the doctor's** ir à casa de Lígia/ao médico; **the road ~ Edinburgh** a estrada para Edinburgo; **the left/right** à esquerda/direita

2 (as far as) até; **to count ~ 10** con-

tar até 10; **from 40 ~ 50 people** de 40 a 50 pessoas

3 (with expressions of time): **a quarter ~ 5** quinze para as 5 (BR), 5 menos um quarto (PT)

4 (for, or) de, para; **the key ~ the front door** a chave da porta da frente; **a letter ~ his wife** uma carta para a sua mulher

5 (expressing indirect object): **to give sth ~ sb** dar algo a alguém; **to talk ~ sb** falar com alguém; **I sold it ~ a friend** vendi isto para um amigo; **to cause damage ~ sth** causar danos em algo

6 (in relation to) para; **3 goals ~ 2** 3 a 2; **8 apples ~ the kilo** 8 maçãs por quilo

7 (purpose, result) para; **to come ~ sb's aid** prestar ajuda a alguém; **to sentence sb ~ death** condenar alguém à morte; **my surprise ~** para minha surpresa

♦ with vb **1** (simple infin): **~ go/eat** ir/comer

2 (following another vb): **~ want/try ~ do** querer/tentar fazer; **~ start ~ do** começar a fazer

3 (with vb omitted): **I don't want ~** eu não quero; **you ought ~** você deve

4 (purpose, result) para

5 (equivalent to relative clause) para, a; **I have things ~ do** eu tenho coisas para fazer; **the main thing is ~ try** o principal é tentar

6 (after adj etc) para; **ready ~ go** pronto para ir; **too old/young ~ ...** muito velho/jovem para ...

♦ adv: **pull/push the door ~** puxar/empurrar a porta

toad [təud] n sapo

toadstool ['təudstuːl] n chapéu-de-cobra m, cogumelo venenoso

toast [təust] n (CULIN) torradas fpl;

(drink, speech) brinde m ♦ vt torrar; brindar; **toaster** n torradeira

tobacco [tə'bækəu] n tabaco, fumo (BR); **tobacconist** n vendedor(a) m/f de tabaco

toboggan [tə'bɔgən] n tobogã m

today [tə'deɪ] adv, n hoje m

toddler [ˈtɔdlə*] n criança que começa a andar

toe [təu] n dedo do pé; *(of shoe)* bico ♦ vt: **to ~ the line** *(fig)* conformar-se, cumprir as obrigações

toffee ['tɔfɪ] n puxa-puxa m (BR), caramelo (PT); **toffee apple** (BRIT) n maçã f do amor

together [tə'gɛðə*] adv juntos; *(at same time)* ao mesmo tempo; **~ with** junto com

toil [tɔɪl] n faina, labuta ♦ vi labutar, trabalhar arduamente

toilet ['tɔɪlət] n privada, vaso sanitário; *(BRIT: lavatory)* banheiro (BR), casa de banho (PT) ♦ cpd de toalete; **toilet paper** n papel m higiênico; **toiletries** npl artigos mpl de toalete; **toilet roll** n rolo de papel higiênico

token ['təukən] n *(sign)* sinal m, símbolo, prova; *(souvenir)* lembrança; *(substitute coin)* ficha ♦ adj simbólico; **book/record ~** (BRIT) vale para comprar livros/discos

told [təuld] pt, pp de **tell**

tolerable ['tɔlərəbl] adj *(bearable)* suportável; *(fairly good)* passável

tolerant ['tɔlərnt] adj: **~ of** tolerante com

tolerate ['tɔləreɪt] vt suportar; *(MED, TECH)* tolerar

toll [təul] n *(of casualties)* número de baixas; *(charge)* pedágio m (BR), portagem f (PT) ♦ vi dobrar, tanger

tomato [tə'mɑːtəu] *(pl ~es)* n

tomate m

tomb [tuːm] n tumba

tomboy ['tɔmbɔɪ] n menina moleque

tombstone ['tuːmstəun] n lápide f

tomcat ['tɔmkæt] n gato

tomorrow [tə'mɔrəu] adv, n amanhã m; **the day after ~** depois de amanhã; **~ morning** amanhã de manhã

ton [tʌn] n tonelada (BRIT = 1016kg; US = 907kg); **~s of** *(inf)* um monte de

tone [təun] n tom m ♦ vi harmonizar; **tone down** vt *(colour, criticism)* suavizar; *(sound)* baixar; *(MUS)* entoar; **tone up** vt *(muscles)* tonificar; **tone-deaf** adj que não tem ouvido

tongs [tɔŋz] npl *(for coal)* tenaz f; *(for hair)* ferros mpl de frisar cabelo

tongue [tʌŋ] n língua; **~ in cheek** ironicamente; **tongue-tied** adj *(fig)* calado; **tongue-twister** n trava-língua m

tonic ['tɔnɪk] n *(MED)* tônico; *(also: ~ water)* (água) tônica

tonight [tə'naɪt] adv, n esta noite, hoje à noite

tonsil ['tɔnsl] n amígdala; **tonsillitis** [tɔnsɪ'laɪtɪs] n amigdalite f

too [tuː] adv *(excessively)* demais, muito; *(also)* também; **~ much** *(adv)* demais; *(adj)* demasiado; **~ many** demasiados(-as)

took [tuk] pt de **take**

tool [tuːl] n ferramenta

toot [tuːt] n *(of horn)* buzinada; *(of whistle)* apito ♦ vi buzinar

tooth [tuːθ] *(pl teeth)* n *(ANAT, TECH)* dente m; *(molar)* molar m; **toothache** n dor f de dente; **to have toothache** estar com dor de dente; **toothbrush** n escova de dentes; **toothpaste** n pasta de dentes, creme *m* dental; **toothpick** *n* palito

top [tɔp] *n* (of mountain) cume *m*, cimo; (of tree) topo; (of head) cocuruto; (of cupboard, table) superfície *f*, topo; (of box, jar, bottle) tampa; (of ladder, page) topo *m*; (toy) pião *m*; (blouse etc) top *m*, blusa *f* ♦ adj (shelf, step) mais alto; (marks) máximo; (in rank) principal, superior ♦ vt exceder; (be first in) estar à cabeça de; **on ~ of** sobre, em cima de; (in addition to) além de; **from ~ to toe** (BRIT) da cabeça aos pés; **from ~ to bottom** de cima abaixo; **top up** (US **top off**) vt completar; **top floor** *n* último andar *m*; **top hat** *n* cartola; **top-heavy** adj desequilibrado

topic ['tɔpɪk] *n* tópico, assunto; **topical** adj atual

topless adj (bather etc) topless inv, sem a parte superior do biquíni

topmost adj o mais alto

topple ['tɔpl] vt derrubar ♦ vi cair para frente

top-secret adj ultra-secreto, supersecreto

topsy-turvy ['tɔpsɪ'təːvɪ] adj, adv de pernas para o ar, confuso, às avessas

torch [tɔːtʃ] *n* (BRIT: electric) lanterna

tore [tɔː*] pt of **tear**

torment [*n* 'tɔːmɛnt, vb tɔː'mɛnt] *n* tormento, suplício ♦ vt atormentar; (fig: annoy) chatear, aborrecer

torn [tɔːn] pp of **tear**

tornado [tɔː'neɪdəu] (pl **~es**) *n* tornado

torrent ['tɔrənt] *n* torrente *f*

tortoise ['tɔːtəs] *n* tartaruga

torture ['tɔːtʃə*] *n* tortura ♦ vt torturar; (fig) atormentar

Tory ['tɔːrɪ] (BRIT) adj, *n* (POL) conservador(a) *m/f*

toss [tɔs] vt atirar, arremessar; (head) lançar para trás ♦ vi: **to ~ and**

turn in bed virar de um lado para o outro na cama; **to ~ a coin** tirar cara ou coroa; **to ~ up for sth** (BRIT) jogar cara ou coroa por algo

tot [tɔt] *n* (BRIT: drink) copinho, golinho; (child) criancinha

total ['təutl] adj total ♦ *n* total *m*, soma ♦ vt (add up) somar; (amount to) montar a

totter ['tɔtə*] vi cambalear

touch [tʌtʃ] *n* (sense) toque *m*; (contact) contato ♦ vt tocar (em); (tamper with) mexer com; (make contact with) fazer contato com; (emotionally) comover; **a ~ of** (fig) um traço de; **to get in ~ with sb** entrar em contato com alguém; **to lose ~** perder o contato; **touch on** vt fus (topic) tocar em, fazer menção de; **touch up** vt (paint) retocar; **touchdown** *n* aterrissagem *f* (BR), aterragem *f* (PT); (on sea) amerissagem *f* (BR), amaragem *f* (PT); (US: FOOTBALL) touchdown *m*; **touching** adj comovedor(a); **touchy** adj suscetível, sensível

tough [tʌf] adj duro; (difficult) difícil; (resistant) resistente; (person: physically) forte; (: mentally) tenaz; (firm) firme, inflexível

tour ['tuə*] *n* viagem *f*, excursão *f*; (also: package ~) excursão organizada; (of town, museum) visita; (by artist) turnê *f* ♦ vt (country, city) excursionar por; (factory) visitar

tourism ['tuərɪzm] *n* turismo

tourist ['tuərɪst] *n* turista *m/f* ♦ cpd turístico; **tourist office** *n* (in country) escritório de turismo; (in embassy etc) departamento de turismo

tournament ['tuənəmənt] *n* torneio

tow [təu] vt rebocar; **"on ~"** (BRIT), **"in ~"** (US) (AUT) "rebocado"

toward(s) [tə'wɔːd(z)] *prep* em direção a; (*of attitude*) para com; (*of purpose*) para; ~ **noon/the end of the year** perto do meio-dia/do fim do ano

towel ['tauəl] *n* toalha; **towelling** *n* (*fabric*) tecido para toalhas

tower ['tauə*] *n* torre *f*; **tower block** (*BRIT*) *n* prédio alto, espigão *m*, cortiço (*BR*); **towering** *adj* elevado; (*figure*) eminente

town [taun] *n* cidade *f*; **to go to** ~ **in** à cidade; (*fig*) fazer com entusiasmo, mandar brasa (*BR*); **town centre** *n* centro (da cidade); **town hall** *n* prefeitura (*BR*), concelho (*PT*)

towrope ['təurəup] *n* cabo de reboque

tow truck (*US*) *n* reboque *m* (*BR*), pronto socorro (*PT*)

toy [tɔɪ] *n* brinquedo; **toy with** *vt fus* brincar com; (*idea*) contemplar

trace [treɪs] *n* (*sign*) sinal *m*; (*small amount*) traço ♦ *vt* (*draw*) traçar, esboçar; (*follow*) seguir a pista de; (*locate*) encontrar

track [træk] *n* (*mark*) pegada, vestígio; (*path: gen*) caminho, vereda; (: *of bullet etc*) trajetória; (: *of suspect, animal*) pista, rasto; (*RAIL*) trilhos (*BR*), carris *mpl* (*PT*); (*on tape*) trilha; (*SPORT*) pista; (*on record*) faixa ♦ *vt* seguir a pista de; **to keep** ~ **of** não perder de vista; (*fig*) manter-se informado sobre; **track down** *vt* (*prey*) seguir a pista de; (*sth lost*) procurar e encontrar; **track suit** *n* roupa de jogging

tractor ['træktə*] *n* trator *m*

trade [treɪd] *n* comércio; (*skill, job*) ofício ♦ *vi* negociar, comerciar ♦ *vt*: **to** ~ **sth** (**for sth**) trocar algo (por algo); **trade in** *vt* dar como parte do pagamento; **trademark** *n* marca registrada; **trade name** *n*

marca *or* nome comercial de um produto; (*of company*) razão *f* social; **trader** *n* comerciante *m/f*; **tradesman** (*irreg*) *n* lojista *m*; **trade union** *n* sindicato

tradition [trə'dɪʃən] *n* tradição *f*; **traditional** *adj* tradicional

traffic ['træfɪk] *n* trânsito; (*air ~ etc*) tráfego; (*illegal*) tráfico ♦ *vi*: **to** ~ **in** (*pej: liquor, drugs*) traficar com, fazer tráfico com; **traffic circle** (*US*) *n* rotatória; **traffic jam** *n* engarrafamento, congestionamento; **traffic lights** *npl* sinal *m* luminoso; **traffic warden** *n* guarda *m/f* de trânsito

tragedy ['trædʒədɪ] *n* tragédia

tragic ['trædʒɪk] *adj* trágico

trail [treɪl] *n* (*tracks*) rasto, pista; (*path*) caminho, trilha; (*of smoke, dust*) rasto ♦ *vt* (*drag*) arrastar; (*follow*) seguir a pista de ♦ *vi* arrastar-se; (*hang loosely*) pender; (*in game, contest*) ficar para trás; **trail behind** *vi* atrasar-se; **trailer** *n* (*AUT*) reboque *m*; (*US: caravan*) trailer *m* (*BR*), rulote *f* (*PT*); (*CINEMA*) trailer; **trailer truck** (*US*) *n* caminhão-reboque *m*

train [treɪn] *n* trem *m* (*BR*), comboio (*PT*); (*of dress*) cauda ♦ *vt* formar; (*teach skills to*) instruir; (*SPORT*) treinar; (*dog*) adestrar, amestrar; (*point: gun etc*): **to** ~ **on** apontar para ♦ *vi* (*learn a skill*) instruir; (*SPORT*) treinar; (*be educated*) ser treinado; **to lose one's** ~ **of thought** perder o fio; **trained** *adj* especializado; (*teacher*) formado; (*animal*) adestrado; **trainee** [treɪ'niː] *n* estagiário(-a); **trainer** *n* (*SPORT*) treinador(a) *m/f*; (*of animals*) adestrador(a) *m/f*; **trainers** *npl* (*shoes*) tênis *m*; **training** *n* instrução *f*, formação *f*; (*SPORT*) treinamento; (*professional*) formação f; **training college** n (for teachers) ≈ escola normal

trait [treɪt] n traço

traitor ['treɪtə*] n traidor(a) m/f

tram [træm] (BRIT) n (also: ~car) bonde m (BR), eléctrico (PT)

tramp [træmp] n (person) vagabundo(-a); (inf: pej: woman) piranha ♦ vi caminhar pesadamente

trample ['træmpl] vt: **to ~ (underfoot)** calcar aos pés

trampoline ['træmpəli:n] n trampolim m

tranquil ['træŋkwɪl] adj tranqüilo; **tranquillizer** n (MED) tranqüilizante m

transact [træn'zækt] vt (business) negociar; **transaction** n transação f, negócio

transfer [n 'trænsfə:*, vb træns'fə:*] n transferência; (picture, design) decalcomania ♦ vt transferir; **to ~ the charges** (BRIT: TEL) ligar a cobrar

transform [træns'fɔ:m] vt transformar

transfusion [træns'fju:ʒən] n (also: blood ~) transfusão f (de sangue)

transistor [træn'zɪstə*] n (ELEC: also: ~ radio) transistor m

transit ['trænzɪt] n: **in ~** em trânsito, de passagem

translate [trænz'leɪt] vt traduzir; **translation** n tradução f; **translator** n tradutor(a) m/f

transmission [trænz'mɪʃən] n transmissão f

transmit [trænz'mɪt] vt transmitir

transparency [træns'pɛərnsɪ] n transparência; (BRIT: PHOT) diapositivo

transparent [træns'pærnt] adj transparente

transplant [vb træns'plɑ:nt, n 'trænsplɑ:nt] vt transplantar ♦ n (MED) transplante m

transport [n 'trænspɔ:t, vb træns'pɔ:t] n transporte m ♦ vt transportar; (carry) acarretar; **transportation** ['trænspɔ:'teɪʃən] n transporte m

trap [træp] n (snare) armadilha, cilada; (trick) cilada; (carriage) aranha, charrete f ♦ vt pegar em armadilha; (person: trick) armar; (: in bad marriage) prender; (: in fire): **to be ~ped** ficar preso; (immobilize) bloquear; **trap door** n alçapão m

trapeze [trə'pi:z] n trapézio

trappings ['træpɪŋz] npl adornos mpl, enfeites mpl

trash [træʃ] n (pej: nonsense) besteiras fpl, (US: rubbish) lixo; **trash can** (US) n lata de lixo

trauma ['trɔ:mə] n trauma m

travel ['trævl] n viagem f ♦ vi viajar; (sound) propagar-se; (news) levar; (wine): **this wine ~s well** este vinho não sofre alteração ao ser transportado ♦ vt percorrer; **~s** npl (journeys) viagens fpl; **travel agent** n agente m/f de viagens; **traveller** (US traveler) n viajante m/f; (COMM) caixeiro (-a) viajante; **traveller's cheque** (US traveler's check) n cheque m de viagem; **travelling** (US traveling) n as viagens, viajar m ♦ adj (circus, exhibition) itinerante; (salesman) viajante ♦ cpd de viagem; **travel sickness** n enjôo

trawler ['trɔ:lə*] n traineira

tray [treɪ] n bandeja; (on desk) cesta

treacherous ['tretʃərəs] adj traiçoeiro; (ground, tide) perigoso

treacle ['tri:kl] n melado

tread [tred] (pt trod, pp trodden) n (step) passo, pisada; (sound) passada; (of stair) piso; (of tyre) banda de rodagem ♦ vi pisar; **tread on** vt fus pisar (em)

treason ['triːzn] n traição f

treasure ['treʒə*] n tesouro; (person) jóia ♦ vt (value) apreciar, estimar; ~s npl (art ~s etc) preciosidades fpl

treasurer ['treʒərə*] n tesoureiro(-a)

treasury ['treʒəri] n tesouraria

treat [triːt] n regalo, deleite m ♦ vt tratar; **to ~ sb to sth** convidar alguém para algo

treatment ['triːtmənt] n tratamento

treaty ['triːti] n tratado, acordo

treble ['trebl] adj tríplice ♦ vt triplicar ♦ vi triplicar(-se)

tree [triː] n árvore f

trek [trek] n (long journey) jornada; (walk) caminhada

tremble ['trembl] vi tremer

tremendous [trɪ'mendəs] adj tremendo; (enormous) enorme; (excellent) sensacional, fantástico

tremor ['tremə*] n tremor m; (also: **earth ~**) tremor de terra

trench [trentʃ] n trincheira

trend [trend] n (tendency) tendência; (of events) curso; (fashion) modismo, tendência; **trendy** adj (idea) de acordo com a tendência atual; (clothes) da última moda

trespass ['trespəs] vi: **to ~ on** invadir; **"no ~ing"** "entrada proibida"

trial ['traɪəl] n (LAW) processo; (test: of machine etc) prova, teste m; **~s** npl (unpleasant experiences) dissabores mpl; **by ~ and error** por tentativas; **to be on ~** ser julgado; **trial period** n período de experiência

triangle ['traɪæŋgl] n (MATH, MUS) triângulo

tribe [traɪb] n tribo f

tribunal [traɪ'bjuːnl] n tribunal m

tributary ['trɪbjutəri] n afluente m

tribute ['trɪbjuːt] n homenagem f;

to pay ~ to prestar homenagem a, homenagear

trick [trɪk] n truque m; (joke) peça, brincadeira; (skill, knack) habilidade f; (CARDS) vaza ♦ vt enganar; **to play a ~ on sb** pregar uma peça em alguém; **that should do the ~** (inf) isso deveria dar resultado; **trickery** n trapaça, astúcia

trickle ['trɪkl] n (of water etc) fio (de água) ♦ vi gotejar, pingar

tricky ['trɪki] adj difícil, complicado

tricycle ['traɪsɪkl] n triciclo

trifle ['traɪfl] n bobagem f, besteira; (CULIN) tipo de bolo com fruta e creme ♦ adv: **a ~ long** um pouquinho longo; **trifling** adj insignificante

trigger ['trɪgə*] n (of gun) gatilho; **trigger off** vt desencadear

trim [trɪm] adj (figure) elegante; (house) arrumado; (garden) bem cuidado ♦ n (haircut) aparada; (on car) estofamento ♦ vt aparar, cortar; (decorate): **to ~ (with)** enfeitar (com); (NAUT: sail) ajustar; **trimmings** npl decoração f; (CULIN) acompanhamentos mpl

trinket ['trɪŋkɪt] n bugiganga; (piece of jewellery) berloque m, bijuteria

trip [trɪp] n viagem f; (outing) excursão f; (stumble) tropeção m ♦ vi tropeçar; (go lightly) andar com passos ligeiros; **on a ~** de viagem; **trip up** vi tropeçar ♦ vt passar uma rasteira em

tripe [traɪp] n (CULIN) bucho, tripa; (pej: rubbish) bobagem f

triple ['trɪpl] adj triplo, tríplice; **triplets** npl trigêmeos(-as) m/fpl

tripod ['traɪpɔd] n tripé m

trite [traɪt] adj gasto, banal

triumph ['traɪʌmf] n (satisfaction) satisfação f; (great achievement) triunfo ♦ vi: **to ~ (over)** triunfar

(sobre)

trivia ['trɪvɪə] *npl* trivialidades *fpl*

trivial ['trɪvɪəl] *adj* insignificante; (*commonplace*) trivial

trod [trɒd] *pt of* **tread**; **trodden** *pp of* **tread**

trolley ['trɒlɪ] *n* carrinho; (*table on wheels*) mesa volante

trombone [trɒm'bəun] *n* trombone *m*

troop [truːp] *n* bando, grupo ♦ *vi*: to ~ in/out entrar/sair em bando; ~s *npl* (MIL) tropas *fpl*; ~ing the colour (BRIT) saudação da bandeira

trophy ['trəufɪ] *n* troféu *m*

tropic ['trɒpɪk] *n* trópico *m*; **tropical** *adj* tropical

trot [trɒt] *n* trote *m*; (*fast pace*) passo rápido ♦ *vi* trotar; (*person*) andar rapidamente; **on the ~** (*fig*: *inf*) a fio

trouble ['trʌbl] *n* problema(s) *m(pl)*, dificuldade(s) *f(pl)*; (*worry*) preocupação *f*; (*effort*) incômodo, trabalho; (*POL*) distúrbios *mpl*; (MED): **stomach** *etc* ~ problemas *mpl* gástricos *etc* ♦ *vt* perturbar; (*worry*) preocupar, incomodar ♦ *vi*: to ~ to do sth incomodar-se or preocupar-se fazer algo; ~s *npl* (*POL etc*) distúrbios *mpl*; to be in ~ estar num aperto; (*ship, climber etc*) estar em dificuldade; what's the ~? qual é o problema?; **troubled** *adj* preocupado; (*epoch, life*) agitado; **troublemaker** *n* criador(a)-de-casos *m/f*; (*child*) encrenqueiro(-a); **troublesome** *adj* importuno; (*child, cough*) incômodo

trough [trɒf] *n* (*also*: **drinking** ~) bebedouro, cocho; (*also*: **feeding** ~) gamela; (*depression*) depressão *f*

trousers ['trauzəz] *npl* calça (BR), calças *fpl* (PT)

trout [traut] *n inv* truta

truant ['truənt] (BRIT) *n*: to play ~

matar aula (BR), fazer gazeta (PT)

truce [truːs] *n* trégua, armistício

truck [trʌk] *n* caminhão *m* (BR), camião *m* (PT); (RAIL) vagão *m*; **truck driver** *n* caminhoneiro(-a) (BR), camionista *m/f* (PT); **truck farm** (US) *n* horta

true [truː] *adj* verdadeiro; (*accurate*) exato; (*genuine*) autêntico; (*faithful*) fiel, leal; to come ~ realizar-se, tornar-se realidade

truffle ['trʌfl] *n* trufa; (*sweet*) docinho de chocolate *or* rum

truly ['truːlɪ] *adv* realmente; (*truthfully*) verdadeiramente; (*faithfully*) fielmente; **yours ~** (*in letter*) atenciosamente

trump [trʌmp] *n* trunfo

trumpet ['trʌmpɪt] *n* trombeta

truncheon ['trʌntʃən] *n* cassetete *m*

trunk [trʌŋk] *n* tronco; (*of elephant*) tromba; (*case*) baú *m*; (US: AUT) mala (BR), porta-bagagens *m* (PT); ~s *npl* (*also*: **swimming** ~s) sunga (BR), calções *mpl* de banho (PT)

trust [trʌst] *n* confiança; (*responsibility*) responsibilidade *f*; (LAW) fideicomisso ♦ *vt* (*rely on*) confiar em; (*entrust*): to ~ sth to sb confiar algo a alguém; (*hope*): to ~ (that) esperar que; to take sth on ~ aceitar algo sem verificação prévia; **trusted** *adj* de confiança; **trustful** *adj* confiante; **trustworthy** *adj* digno de confiança

truth [truːθ] *n* verdade *f*; **truthful** *adj* (*person*) sincero, honesto

try [traɪ] *n* tentativa; (RUGBY) ensaio ♦ *vt* (LAW) julgar; (*test*: *sth new*) provar, pôr à prova; (*strain*) cansar ♦ *vi* tentar; to have a ~ fazer uma tentativa; to ~ to do sth tentar fazer algo; **try on** *vt* (*clothes*) experimentar, provar; **trying** *adj* exasperante

T-shirt n camiseta (*BR*), T-shirt f (*PT*)

tub [tʌb] n tina; (*bath*) banheira

tubby ['tʌbɪ] adj gorducho

tube [tjuːb] n tubo; (*pipe*) cano; (*BRIT: underground*) metrô m (*BR*), metro(-politano) (*PT*); (*for tyre*) câmara-de-ar f

tuberculosis [tjubəːkju'ləusɪs] n tuberculose f

TUC n abbr (= *Trades Union Congress*) ≈ CUT f

tuck [tʌk] vt (*put*) enfiar, meter; **tuck away** vt esconder; **to be ~ed away** estar escondido; **tuck in** vi enfiar para dentro; (*child*) aconchegar ♦ vi (*eat*) comer com apetite; **tuck up** vt (*child*) aconchegar

Tuesday ['tjuːzdɪ] n terça-feira

tuft [tʌft] n penacho; (*of grass etc*) tufo

tug [tʌg] n (*ship*) rebocador m ♦ vt puxar; **tug-of-war** n cabo-de-guerra m; (*fig*) disputa

tuition [tjuː'ɪʃən] n ensino; (*private ~*) aulas fpl particulares; (*US: fees*) taxas fpl escolares

tulip ['tjuːlɪp] n tulipa

tumble ['tʌmbl] n (*fall*) queda ♦ vi cair, tombar; **to ~ to sth** (*inf*) sacar algo; **tumbledown** adj em ruínas; **tumble dryer** (*BRIT*) n máquina de secar roupa

tumbler ['tʌmblə*] n copo

tummy ['tʌmɪ] (*inf*) n (*belly*) barriga; (*stomach*) estômago

tumour ['tjuːmə*] (*US* **tumor**) n tumor m

tuna ['tjuːnə] n inv (*also:* ~ **fish**) atum m

tune [tjuːn] n melodia ♦ vt (*MUS*) afinar; (*RADIO, TV*) sintonizar; (*AUT*) regular; **to be in/out of ~** (*instrument*) estar afinado/desafinado; (*singer*) cantar afinado/desafinar; **to be in/out of ~ with** (*fig*) harmonizar-se com/destoar de; **tune in** vi (*RADIO, TV*): **to ~ in** (**to**) sintonizar (com); **tune up** vi (*musician*) afinar (seu instrumento); **tuneful** adj melodioso; **tuner** n: **piano tuner** afinador(a) m/f de pianos

tunic ['tjuːnɪk] n túnica

Tunisia [tjuː'nɪzɪə] n Tunísia

tunnel ['tʌnl] n túnel m; (*in mine*) galeria ♦ vi abrir um túnel (*or* uma galeria)

turbulence ['təːbjuləns] n (*AVIAT*) turbulência

tureen [tə'riːn] n terrina

turf [təːf] n torrão m ♦ vt relvar, gramar; **turf out** (*inf*) vt (*person*) pôr no olho da rua

Turk [təːk] n turco(-a)

Turkey ['təːkɪ] n Turquia

turkey ['təːkɪ] n peru(a) m/f

Turkish ['təːkɪʃ] adj turco(-a) ♦ n (*LING*) turco

turmoil ['təːmɔɪl] n tumulto, distúrbio, agitação f; **in ~** agitado, tumultuado

turn [təːn] n volta, turno; (*in road*) curva; (*of mind, events*) propensão f, tendência; (*THEATRE*) número; (*MED*) choque m ♦ vt dar volta a, fazer girar; (*collar*) virar; (*change*): **to ~ sth into** converter algo em ♦ vi virar; (*person: look back*) voltar-se; (*reverse direction*) mudar de direção; (*milk*) azedar; (*become*) tornar-se, virar; **to ~ nasty** engrossar; **to ~ forty** fazer quarenta anos; **a good ~** um favor; **it gave me quite a ~** me deu um susto enorme; **"no left ~"** (*AUT*) "proibido virar à esquerda"; **it's your ~** é a sua vez; **in ~** por sua vez; **to take ~s (at)** revezar (em); **turn away** vi virar a cabeça ♦ vt recusar; **turn back** vi voltar atrás ♦ vt voltar para trás; (*clock*) atrasar; **turn down** vt (*refuse*) recusar;

(*reduce*) baixar; (*fold*) dobrar, virar para baixo; **turn in** vi (*inf: go to bed*) ir dormir ♦ vt (*fold*) dobrar para dentro; **turn off** vi (*from road*) virar, sair do caminho ♦ vt (*light, radio etc*) apagar; (*engine*) desligar; **turn on** vt (*light*) acender; (*engine, radio*) ligar; (*tap*) abrir; **turn out** vt (*light, gas*) apagar; (*produce*) produzir ♦ vi (*troops*) ser mobilizado; **to ~ out to be ...** revelar-se (ser) ..., resultar (ser) ..., vir a ser ...; **turn over** vi (*person*) virar-se ♦ vt (*object*) virar; **turn round** vi voltar-se, virar-se; **turn up** vi (*person*) aparecer, pintar; (*lost object*) aparecer ♦ vt (*collar*) subir; (*radio etc*) aumentar; **turning** n (*in road*) via lateral

turnip ['tə:nɪp] n nabo

turnout ['tə:naut] n assistência; (*in election*) comparecimento às urnas

turnover ['tə:nəuvə*] n (*COMM: amount of money*) volume m de negócios; (*: of goods*) movimento; (*of staff*) rotatividade f

turnpike ['tə:npaɪk] (*US*) n estrada ou rodovia com pedágio (*BR*) or portagem (*PT*)

turnstile ['tə:nstaɪl] n borboleta (*BR*), torniquete m (*PT*)

turntable ['tə:nteɪbl] n (*on record player*) prato

turn-up (*BRIT*) n (*on trousers*) volta, dobra

turpentine ['tə:pəntaɪn] n (*also: turps*) aguarrás f

turquoise ['tə:kwɔɪz] n (*stone*) turquesa ♦ adj azul-turquesa inv

turret ['tʌrɪt] n torrinha

turtle ['tə:tl] n tartaruga, cágado

tusk [tʌsk] n defesa (de elefante)

tutor ['tju:tə*] n professor(a) m/f; (*private ~*) professor(a) m/f particular; **tutorial** [tju:'tɔ:rɪəl] n (*SCH*)

seminário

tuxedo [tʌk'si:dəu] (*US*) n smoking m

TV n abbr (= *television*) TV f

twang [twæŋ] n (*of instrument*) dedilhado; (*of voice*) timbre m nasal

tweed [twi:d] n tweed m, pano grosso de lã

tweezers ['twi:zəz] npl pinça (pequena)

twelfth [twelfθ] num décimo segundo

twelve [twelv] num doze; **at ~ (o'clock)** (*midday*) ao meio-dia; (*midnight*) à meia-noite

twentieth ['twentɪθ] num vigésimo

twenty ['twentɪ] num vinte

twice [twaɪs] adv duas vezes; **~ as much** duas vezes mais

twig [twɪg] n graveto, varinha ♦ vi (*inf*) sacar

twilight ['twaɪlaɪt] n crepúsculo, meia-luz f

twin [twɪn] adj gêmeo; (*beds*) separado ♦ n gêmeo ♦ vt irmanar; **twin (-bedded) room** n quarto com duas camas

twine [twaɪn] n barbante m (*BR*), cordel m (*PT*) ♦ vi enroscar-se, enrolar-se

twinge [twɪndʒ] n (*of pain*) pontada; (*of conscience*) remorso

twinkle ['twɪŋkl] vi cintilar; (*eyes*) pestanejar

twirl [twə:l] vt fazer girar ♦ vi girar rapidamente

twist [twɪst] n torção f; (*in road, coil*) curva; (*in flex*) virada; (*in story*) mudança imprevista ♦ vt torcer, retorcer; (*ankle*) torcer; (*weave*) entrelaçar; (*roll around*) enrolar; (*fig*) deturpar ♦ vi serpentear

twit [twɪt] (*inf*) n idiota m/f, bobo(-a)

twitch [twɪtʃ] n puxão m; (nervous) tique m nervoso ♦ vi contrair-se

two [tu:] num dois; **to put ~ and ~ together** (fig) tirar conclusões; **two-faced** (pej) adj (person) falso; **two-way** adj: **two-way traffic** trânsito em mão dupla

tycoon [taɪˈku:n] n: (business) ~ magnata m

type [taɪp] n (category) tipo, espécie f; (model) modelo; (TYP) tipo, letra ♦ vt (letter etc) datilografar, bater (à máquina); **typescript** n texto datilografado; **typewriter** n máquina de escrever

typhoid [ˈtaɪfɔɪd] n febre f tifóide

typical [ˈtɪpɪkl] adj típico

typing [ˈtaɪpɪŋ] n datilografia

typist [ˈtaɪpɪst] n datilógrafo(-a) m/f

tyrant [ˈtaɪərənt] n tirano(-a)

tyre [ˈtaɪə*] n (US tire) n pneu m

U

ubiquitous [juːˈbɪkwɪtəs] adj ubíquo, onipresente

udder [ˈʌdə*] n ubre f

UFO [ˈjuːfəʊ] n abbr (= unidentified flying object) óvni m

Uganda [juːˈgændə] n Uganda (no article)

ugly [ˈʌglɪ] adj feio; (dangerous) perigoso

UK n abbr = **United Kingdom**

ulcer [ˈʌlsə*] n úlcera; **mouth** ~ afta

Ulster [ˈʌlstə*] n Ulster m

ulterior [ʌlˈtɪərɪə*] adj: ~ **motive** segundas intenções fpl

ultimate [ˈʌltɪmət] adj último, final; (authority) máximo; **ultimately** adv (in the end) no final, por último; (fundamentally) no fundo

ultrasound [ˈʌltrəsaʊnd] n (MED) ultra-som m

umbilical cord [ʌmbɪˈlaɪkl-] n cordão m umbilical

umbrella [ʌmˈbrɛlə] n guarda-chuva m; (for sun) guarda-sol m, barraca (da praia)

umpire [ˈʌmpaɪə*] n árbitro ♦ vt arbitrar

umpteen [ʌmpˈtiːn] adj inúmeros(-as)

UN n abbr (= United Nations) ONU f

unable [ʌnˈeɪbl] adj: **to be ~ to do sth** não poder fazer algo

unaccompanied [ʌnəˈkʌmpənɪd] adj desacompanhado; (singing, song) sem acompanhamento

unanimous [juːˈnænɪməs] adj unânime

unarmed [ʌnˈɑːmd] adj (without a weapon) desarmado; (defenceless) indefeso

unattached [ʌnəˈtætʃt] adj (person) livre; (part etc) solto, separado

unattended [ʌnəˈtɛndɪd] adj (car, luggage) abandonado

unattractive [ʌnəˈtræktɪv] adj sem atrativos; (building, appearance, idea) pouco atraente

unauthorized [ʌnˈɔːθəraɪzd] adj não autorizado, sem autorização

unavoidable [ʌnəˈvɔɪdəbl] adj inevitável

unaware [ʌnəˈwɛə*] adj: **to be ~ of** ignorar, não perceber

unawares [ʌnəˈwɛəz] adv improvisadamente, de surpresa

unbalanced [ʌnˈbælənst] adj desequilibrado

unbearable [ʌnˈbɛərəbl] adj insuportável

unbeatable [ʌnˈbiːtəbl] adj (team) invencível; (price) sem igual

unbelievable [ʌnbɪˈliːvəbl] adj inacreditável; (amazing) incrível

unborn [ʌnˈbɔːn] adj por nascer

unbroken [ʌnˈbrəʊkən] adj (seal)

intacto; (line) contínuo; (silence, series) ininterrupto; (record) mantido; (spirit) indômito

unbutton [ʌn'bʌtn] vt desabotoar

uncalled-for [ʌn'kɔ:ld-] adj desnecessário, gratuito

uncanny [ʌn'kænɪ] adj estranho; (knack) excepcional

uncertain [ʌn'sɜ:tn] adj incerto; (character) indeciso; (unsure): **about** inseguro sobre; **in no ~ terms** em termos precisos; **uncertainty** n incerteza; (also: doubts) dúvidas fpl

uncivilized [ʌn'sɪvɪlaɪzd] adj (country, people) primitivo; (fig: behaviour) incivilizado; (: hour) de manhã bem cedo

uncle ['ʌŋkl] n tio

uncomfortable [ʌn'kʌmfətəbl] adj incômodo; (uneasy) pouco à vontade; (situation) desagradável

uncommon [ʌn'kɔmən] adj raro, incomum, excepcional

uncompromising [ʌn'kɔmprəmaɪzɪŋ] adj intransigente, inflexível

unconcerned [ʌnkən'sɜ:nd] adj indiferente, despreocupado

unconditional [ʌnkən'dɪʃənl] adj incondicional

unconscious [ʌn'kɔnʃəs] adj sem sentidos, desacordado; (unaware): **~ of** inconsciente de ♦ n: **the ~ o** inconsciente

uncontrollable [ʌnkən'trəuləbl] adj (temper) ingovernável; (child, animal, laughter) incontrolável

unconventional [ʌnkən'venʃənl] adj inconvencional

uncouth [ʌn'ku:θ] adj rude, grosseiro

uncover [ʌn'kʌvə*] vt descobrir; (take lid off) destapar, destampar

undecided [ʌndɪ'saɪdɪd] adj indeci-

so; (question) não respondido, pendente

under ['ʌndə*] prep embaixo de (BR), debaixo de (PT); (fig) sob; (less than) menos de; (according to) segundo, de acordo com ♦ adv embaixo; (movement) por baixo; **there** ali embaixo; **~ repair** em conserto

under... [ʌndə*] prefix: **under-age** adj menor de idade; **undercarriage** (BRIT) n (AVIAT) trem de aterrissagem; **undercharge** vt não cobrar o suficiente; **underclothes** npl roupa de baixo, roupa íntima; **undercover** adj secreto, clandestino; **undercurrent** n (fig) tendência; **undercut** (irreg) vt (person) prejudicar; (prices) vender por menos que; **underdog** n o mais fraco; **underdone** adj (CULIN) mal passado; **underestimate** vt subestimar; **underexposed** adj (PHOT) sem exposição suficiente; **underfed** adj subnutrido; **underfoot** adv sob os pés; **undergo** (irreg) vt sofrer; (test) passar por; (operation, treatment) ser submetido a; **undergraduate** n universitário(-a); **underground** n (BRIT) metrô m (BR), metro(-politano) (PT); (POL) organização f clandestina ♦ adj subterrâneo; (fig) clandestino ♦ adv (work) embaixo da terra; (fig) na clandestinidade; **undergrowth** n vegetação f rasteira; **underhand(ed)** adj (fig) secreto e desonesto; **underlie** (irreg) vt ser a base de; **underline** vt sublinhar; **undermine** vt minar, solapar; **underneath** adv embaixo, debaixo, por baixo ♦ prep embaixo de (BR), debaixo de (PT); **underpaid** adj mal pago; **underpants** (BRIT) npl cueca(s) f (pl) (BR), cuecas fpl (PT);

underpass (BRIT) n passagem f inferior; **underprivileged** adj menos favorecido; **underrate** vt depreciar, subestimar; **undershirt** (US) n camiseta; **undershorts** (US) npl cueca (BR), cuecas fpl (PT); **underside** n parte f inferior; **underskirt** (BRIT) n anágua

understand [ʌndə'stænd] (irreg) vt entender, compreender ♦ vi: **to ~ that** acreditar que; **understandable** adj compreensível; **understanding** adj compreensivo ♦ n compreensão f; (knowledge) entendimento; (agreement) acordo

understatement [ʌndə'steɪtmənt] n (quality) subestimação f; (euphemism) eufemismo; **it's an ~ to say that** ... é uma subestimação dizer que ...

understood [ʌndə'stud] pt, pp of **understand** ♦ adj entendido; (implied) subentendido, implícito

understudy ['ʌndəstʌdɪ] n ator m substituto (atriz f substituta)

undertake [ʌndə'teɪk] (irreg: like **take**) vt incumbir-se de, encarregar-se de; **to ~ to do sth** comprometer-se a fazer algo

undertaker ['ʌndəteɪkə*] n agente m/f funerário(-a)

undertaking ['ʌndəteɪkɪŋ] n empreendimento; (promise) promessa

underwater [ʌndə'wɔːtə*] adv sob a água ♦ adj subaquático

underwear ['ʌndəwεə*] n roupa de baixo, roupa íntima

underworld ['ʌndəwəːld] n (of crime) submundo

undies ['ʌndɪz] (inf) npl roupa de baixo, roupa íntima

undo [ʌn'duː] (irreg: like **do**) vt (unfasten) desatar; (spoil) desmanchar

undoing [ʌn'duːɪŋ] n ruína, desgraça

undoubted [ʌn'dautɪd] adj indubitável

undress [ʌn'drεs] vi despir-se, tirar a roupa

undue [ʌn'djuː] adj excessivo

unduly [ʌn'djuːlɪ] adv excessivamente

unearth [ʌn'əːθ] vt desenterrar; (fig) revelar

uneasy [ʌn'iːzɪ] adj (person) preocupado; (feeling) incômodo; (peace, truce) desconfortável

uneconomic(al) [ʌniːkə'nɔmɪk(l)] adj antieconômico

uneducated [ʌn'εdjukeɪtɪd] adj inculto, sem instrução, não escolarizado

unemployed [ʌnɪm'plɔɪd] adj desempregado ♦ npl: **the ~** os desempregados

unemployment [ʌnɪm'plɔɪmənt] n desemprego

unending [ʌn'εndɪŋ] adj interminável

unerring [ʌn'əːrɪŋ] adj infalível

uneven [ʌn'iːvn] adj desigual; (road etc) irregular, acidentado

unexpected [ʌnɪk'spεktɪd] adj inesperado; **unexpectedly** [ʌnɪks'pεktɪdlɪ] adv inesperadamente

unfair [ʌn'fεə*] adj: **~ (to)** injusto (com)

unfaithful [ʌn'feɪθful] adj infiel

unfamiliar [ʌnfə'mɪlɪə*] adj pouco familiar, desconhecido; **to be ~ with sth** não estar familiarizado com algo

unfashionable [ʌn'fæʃnəbl] adj fora da moda

unfasten [ʌn'fɑːsn] vt desatar; (open) abrir

unfavourable [ʌn'feɪvərəbl] (US **unfavorable**) adj desfavorável

unfeeling [ʌn'fiːlɪŋ] *adj* insensível

unfinished [ʌn'fɪnɪʃt] *adj* incompleto, inacabado

unfit [ʌn'fɪt] *adj* sem preparo físico; (*incompetent*): ~ **(for)** incompetente (para), incapaz (de); ~ **for work** inapto para trabalhar

unfold [ʌn'fəuld] *vt* desdobrar ♦ *vi* (*situation*) desdobrar-se

unforeseen [ʌnfɔː'siːn] *adj* imprevisto

unfortunate [ʌn'fɔːtʃənət] *adj* infeliz; (*event, remark*) inoportuno

unfounded [ʌn'faundɪd] *adj* infundado

unfriendly [ʌn'frendlɪ] *adj* antipático

ungainly [ʌn'geɪnlɪ] *adj* desalinhado

ungrateful [ʌn'greɪtful] *adj* mal agradecido, ingrato

unhappiness [ʌn'hæpɪnɪs] *n* infelicidade *f*

unhappy [ʌn'hæpɪ] *adj* triste; (*unfortunate*) desventurado; (*childhood*) infeliz; (*dissatisfied*): ~ **with** descontente com, insatisfeito com

unharmed [ʌn'hɑːmd] *adj* ileso

unhealthy [ʌn'helθɪ] *adj* insalubre; (*person*) doentio; (*fig*) anormal

unheard-of [ʌn'hɜːd-] *adj* insólito

unhurt [ʌn'hɜːt] *adj* ileso

uniform ['juːnɪfɔːm] *n* uniforme *m* ♦ *adj* uniforme

uninhabited [ʌnɪn'hæbɪtɪd] *adj* inabitado

unintentional [ʌnɪn'tenʃənəl] *adj* involuntário, não intencional

union ['juːnjən] *n* união *f*; (*also:* **trade ~**) sindicato (de trabalhadores) ♦ *cpd* sindical; **Union Jack** *n* bandeira britânica

unique [juː'niːk] *adj* único, sem igual

unison ['juːnɪsn] *n*: **in ~** em harmonia, em uníssono

unit ['juːnɪt] *n* unidade *f*; (*of furniture etc*) seção *f*; (*team, squad*) equipe *f*; **kitchen ~** armário de cozinha

unite [juː'naɪt] *vt* unir ♦ *vi* unir-se; **united** *adj* unido; (*effort*) conjunto; **United Kingdom** *n* Reino Unido; **United Nations (Organization)** *n* (Organização *f* das) Nações *fpl* Unidas; **United States (of America)** *n* Estados Unidos *mpl* (da América)

universal [juːnɪ'vɜːsl] *adj* universal

universe ['juːnɪvɜːs] *n* universo

university [juːnɪ'vɜːsɪtɪ] *n* universidade *f*

unjust [ʌn'dʒʌst] *adj* injusto

unkempt [ʌn'kempt] *adj* desleixado, descuidado; (*hair*) despenteado; (*beard*) mal tratado

unkind [ʌn'kaɪnd] *adj* maldoso; (*comment etc*) cruel

unknown [ʌn'nəun] *adj* desconhecido

unlawful [ʌn'lɔːful] *adj* ilegal

unleaded [ʌn'ledɪd] *adj* (*petrol, fuel*) sem chumbo

unleash [ʌn'liːʃ] *vt* (*fig*) desencadear

unless [ʌn'les] *conj* a menos que, a não ser que; ~ **he comes** a menos que ele venha

unlike [ʌn'laɪk] *adj* diferente ♦ *prep* diferentemente de, ao contrário de

unlikely [ʌn'laɪklɪ] *adj* (*not likely*) improvável; (*unexpected*) inesperado

unlisted [ʌn'lɪstɪd] (*US*) *adj* (*TEL*) que não consta na lista telefônica

unload [ʌn'ləud] *vt* descarregar

unlock [ʌn'lɔk] *vt* destrancar

unlucky [ʌn'lʌkɪ] *adj* infeliz; (*object, number*) de mau agouro; **to be ~** ser azarado, ter azar

unmarried [ʌn'mærɪd] *adj* solteiro

unmistak(e)able [ʌnmɪs'teɪkəbl] *adj* inconfundível

unnatural [ʌn'nætʃrəl] *adj* antinatural, artificial; (*manner*) afetado; (*habit*) depravado

unnecessary [ʌn'nesəsərɪ] *adj* desnecessário, inútil

unnoticed [ʌn'nəʊtɪst] *adj:* (**to go** *or* **pass**) ~ (passar) despercebido

UNO ['juːnəʊ] *n abbr* (= *United Nations Organization*) ONU f

unobtainable [ʌnəb'teɪnəbl] *adj* inacessível; (*TEL*) ocupado

unofficial [ʌnə'fɪʃl] *adj* não-oficial, informal; (*strike*) desautorizado

unpack [ʌn'pæk] *vi* desembrulhar ♦ *vt* desfazer

unpalatable [ʌn'pælətəbl] *adj* desagradável

unparalleled [ʌn'pærəleld] *adj* sem paralelo

unpleasant [ʌn'pleznt] *adj* desagradável; (*person, manner*) antipático

unplug [ʌn'plʌg] *vt* desligar

unpopular [ʌn'pɔpjulə*] *adj* impopular

unprecedented [ʌn'presɪdəntɪd] *adj* sem precedentes

unpredictable [ʌnprɪ'dɪktəbl] *adj* imprevisível

unprofessional [ʌnprə'feʃənl] *adj* (*conduct*) pouco profissional

unravel [ʌn'rævl] *vt* desemaranhar; (*mystery*) desvendar

unreal [ʌn'rɪəl] *adj* irreal, ilusório; (*extraordinary*) extraordinário

unrealistic [ʌnrɪə'lɪstɪk] *adj* pouco realista

unreasonable [ʌn'riːznəbl] *adj* insensato; (*demand*) absurdo

unrelated [ʌnrɪ'leɪtɪd] *adj* sem relação; (*family*) sem parentesco

unreliable [ʌnrɪ'laɪəbl] *adj* (*person*)

indigno de confiança; (*machine*) incerto, perigoso

unrest [ʌn'rest] *n* inquietação f, desassossego; (*POL*) distúrbios *mpl*

unroll [ʌn'rəʊl] *vt* desenrolar

unruly [ʌn'ruːlɪ] *adj* indisciplinado; (*hair*) desalinhado

unsafe [ʌn'seɪf] *adj* perigoso

unsatisfactory [ʌnsætɪs'fæktərɪ] *adj* insatisfatório

unsavoury [ʌn'seɪvərɪ] (*US* **unsavory**) *adj* (*fig*) repugnante, vil

unscrew [ʌn'skruː] *vt* desparafusar

unscrupulous [ʌn'skruːpjuləs] *adj* inescrupuloso, imoral

unsettled [ʌn'setld] *adj* (*weather*) instável; (*person*) inquieto

unshaven [ʌn'ʃeɪvn] *adj* com a barba por fazer

unsightly [ʌn'saɪtlɪ] *adj* feio, disforme

unskilled [ʌn'skɪld] *adj* não-especializado

unspeakable [ʌn'spiːkəbl] *adj* indescritível; (*awful*) inqualificável

unstable [ʌn'steɪbl] *adj* em falso; (*mentally*) instável

unsteady [ʌn'stedɪ] *adj* trêmulo; (*ladder*) em falso

unstuck [ʌn'stʌk] *adj:* **to come** ~ despregar-se; (*fig*) fracassar

unsuccessful [ʌnsək'sesful] *adj* (*attempt*) frustrado, vão (vã); (*writer, proposal*) sem êxito; **to be** ~ (*in attempting sth*) ser mal sucedido, não conseguir; (*application*) ser recusado

unsuitable [ʌn'suːtəbl] *adj* inadequado; (*time*) inconveniente

unsure [ʌn'ʃuə*] *adj* inseguro, incerto; **to be** ~ **of o.s.** não ser seguro de si

unsympathetic [ʌnsɪmpə'θetɪk] *adj* insensível; (*unlikeable*) antipático

unthinkable [ʌn'θɪŋkəbl] *adj* impensável, inconcebível, incalculável

untidy [ʌn'taɪdɪ] *adj* (*room*) desarrumado, desleixado; (*appearance*) desmazelado, desalinhado.

untie [ʌnˈtaɪ] *vt* desatar, desfazer; (*dog, prisoner*) soltar

until [ənˈtɪl] *prep* até ♦ *conj* até que; ~ **he comes** até que ele venha; ~ **now** até agora; ~ **then** até então

unused [ʌnˈjuːzd] *adj* novo, sem uso

unusual [ʌnˈjuːʒuəl] *adj* (*strange*) estranho; (*rare*) incomum; (*exceptional*) extraordinário

unveil [ʌnˈveɪl] *vt* desvelar, descobrir

unwanted [ʌnˈwɒntɪd] *adj* não desejado, indesejável

unwelcome [ʌnˈwɛlkəm] *adj* (*guest*) inoportuno; (*news*) desagradável

unwell [ʌnˈwɛl] *adj*: **to be ~** estar doente; **to feel ~** estar indisposto

unwilling [ʌnˈwɪlɪŋ] *adj*: **to be ~ to do sth** relutar em fazer algo, não querer fazer algo; **unwillingly** *adv* de má vontade

unwind [ʌnˈwaɪnd] (*irreg*) *vt* desenrolar ♦ *vi* (*relax*) relaxar-se

unwise [ʌnˈwaɪz] *adj* imprudente

unworthy [ʌnˈwəːðɪ] *adj* indigno

unwrap [ʌnˈræp] *vt* desembrulhar

unwritten [ʌnˈrɪtən] *adj* (*agreement*) tácito

KEYWORD

---

up [ʌp] *prep*: **to go/be ~ sth** subir algo/estar em cima de algo; **we climbed/walked ~ the hill** nós subimos/andamos até em cima da colina; **they live further ~ the street** eles moram mais adiante nesta rua ♦ *adv* **1** (*upwards, higher*) em cima, para cima; ~ **in the sky/the mountains** lá no céu/nas montanhas; ~ **there** lá em cima; ~ **above** em cima

2: **to be ~** (*out of bed*) estar de pé; (*prices, level*) estar elevado; (*building, tent*) estar erguido

3: ~ **to** (*as far as*) até; ~ **to now** até agora

4: **to be ~ to** (*depending on*): **it is ~ to you** você é quem sabe, você decide

5: **to be ~ to** (*equal to*) estar à altura de; **he's not ~ to it** (*job, task etc*) ele não é capaz de fazê-lo; **his work is not ~ to the required standard** seu trabalho não atende aos padrões exigidos

6: **to be ~ to** (*inf: be doing*) estar fazendo (*BR*) or a fazer (*PT*); **what is he ~ to?** o que ele está querendo?, o que ele está tramando?

♦ *n*: ~**s and downs** altos *mpl* e baixos *mpl*

---

upbringing [ˈʌpbrɪŋɪŋ] *n* educação *f*, criação *f*

update [ʌpˈdeɪt] *vt* atualizar, pôr em dia

upgrade [ʌpˈgreɪd] *vt* (*person*) promover; (*job*) melhorar; (*house*) reformar

upheaval [ʌpˈhiːvl] *n* transtorno; (*unrest*) convulsão *f*

uphill [ʌpˈhɪl] *adj* ladeira acima; (*fig: task*) trabalhoso, árduo ♦ *adv*: **to go ~** ir morro acima; (*face, look*) para cima

uphold [ʌpˈhəʊld] (*irreg: like hold*) *vt* defender, preservar

upholstery [ʌpˈhəʊlstərɪ] *n* estofamento

upkeep [ˈʌpkiːp] *n* manutenção *f*

upon [əˈpɒn] *prep* sobre

upper [ˈʌpə*] *adj* superior, de cima ♦ *n* (*of shoe*) gáspea, parte *f* superior; **upper-class** *adj* de classe alta; **upper hand** *n*: **to have the upper hand** ter controle *or* domínio; **uppermost** *adj* mais elevado; **what was uppermost in my mind** o que me preocupava mais

upright ['ʌpraɪt] *adj* vertical; (*straight*) reto; (*fig*) honesto

uprising ['ʌpraɪzɪŋ] *n* revolta, rebelião *f*, sublevação *f*

uproar ['ʌprɔ:*] *n* tumulto, algazarra *f*

uproot [ʌp'ru:t] *vt* (*tree*) arrancar; (*fig*) desarraigar

upset [*n* 'ʌpsɛt, *vb*, *adj* ʌp'sɛt (*irreg: like* set)] *n* (*to plan etc*) revés *m*, reviravolta; (*stomach* ~) indisposição *f* ♦ *vt* (*glass etc*) virar; (*plan*) perturbar; (*person: annoy*) aborrecer ♦ *adj* aflito; (*stomach*) indisposto

upshot ['ʌpʃɔt] *n* resultado, conclusão *f*

upside down ['ʌpsaɪd-] *adv* de cabeça para baixo; **to turn a place ~** (*fig*) deixar um lugar de cabeça para baixo

upstairs [ʌp'stɛəz] *adv* (*be*) em cima; (*go*) lá em cima ♦ *adj* (*room*) de cima ♦ *n* andar *m* de cima

upstart ['ʌpstɑ:t] (*pej*) *n* novo-rico, pessoa sem classe

upstream [ʌp'stri:m] *adv* rio acima

uptight [ʌp'taɪt] (*inf*) *adj* nervoso

up-to-date *adj* (*person*) moderno, atualizado; (*information*) atualizado

upward ['ʌpwəd] *adj* ascendente, para cima; **upward(s)** *adv* para cima; (*more than*): **upward(s) of** para cima de

urban ['ə:bən] *adj* urbano, da cidade

urge [ə:dʒ] *n* desejo ♦ *vt*: **to ~ sb to do sth** incitar alguém a fazer algo

urgent ['ə:dʒənt] *adj* urgente; (*tone, plea*) insistente

urinal ['juərɪnl] (*BRIT*) *n* (*vessel*) urinol *m*; (*building*) mictório

urine ['juərɪn] *n* urina

urn [ə:n] *n* urna; (*also*: **tea** ~) samovar *m*

Uruguay ['juərəgwaɪ] *n* Uruguai *m*

us [ʌs] *pron* nos; (*after prep*) nós; *see also* **me**

US(A) *n abbr* (= *United States (of America)*) EUA *mpl*

use [*n* ju:s, *vb* ju:z] *n* uso, emprego; (*usefulness*) utilidade *f* ♦ *vt* usar, utilizar; (*phrase*) empregar; **in ~** em uso; **out of ~** fora de uso; **to be of ~** ser útil; **it's no ~** (*pointless*) é inútil; (*not useful*) não serve; **to be ~d to** estar acostumado a; **she ~d to do it** ela costumava fazê-lo; **use up** *vt* esgotar, consumir; (*money*) gastar; **used** [ju:zd] *adj* usado; **useful** ['ju:sful] *adj* útil; **usefulness** *n* utilidade *f*; **useless** ['ju:slɪs] *adj* inútil; (*person*) incapaz; **user** ['ju:zə*] *n* usuário(-a) (*BR*), utente *m/f* (*PT*); **user-friendly** *adj* de fácil utilização

usher ['ʌʃə*] *n* (*at wedding*) oficial *m* de justiça; **usherette** [ʌʃə'rɛt] *n* (*in cinema*) lanterninha (*BR*), arrumadora (*PT*)

usual ['ju:ʒuəl] *adj* usual, habitual; **as ~** como de hábito, como sempre; **usually** ['ju:ʒuəlɪ] *adv* normalmente

utensil [ju:'tɛnsl] *n* utensílio

utmost ['ʌtməust] *adj* maior ♦ *n*: **to do one's ~** fazer todo o possível

utter ['ʌtə*] *adj* total ♦ *vt* (*sounds*) emitir; (*words*) proferir, pronunciar; **utterly** *adv* completamente, totalmente

U-turn *n* retorno

V

v *abbr* = **verse**; (= *vide: see*) vide; (= *versus*) x; (= *volt*) v

vacancy ['veɪkənsɪ] *n* (*BRIT: job*) vaga; (*room*) quarto livre

vacant ['veɪkənt] *adj* desocupado, livre; (*expression*) distraído

vacate [və'keɪt] *vt* (*house*) desocupar; (*job*) deixar

vacation [vəˈkeɪʃən] (*esp US*) *n* férias *fpl*

vaccinate [ˈvæksɪneɪt] *vt* vacinar

vacuum [ˈvækjum] *n* vácuo *m*; **vacuum cleaner** *n* aspirador *m* de pó

vagina [vəˈdʒaɪnə] *n* vagina

vagrant [ˈveɪɡrənt] *n* vagabundo(-a), vadio(-a)

vague [veɪɡ] *adj* vago; (*blurred: memory*) fraco; **vaguely** *adv* vagamente

vain [veɪn] *adj* vaidoso; (*useless*) vão (vã) inútil; **in ~** em vão

valentine [ˈvæləntaɪn] *n* (*also: ~ card*) cartão *m* do Dia dos Namorados; (*person*) namorado

valiant [ˈvæliənt] *adj* corajoso

valid [ˈvælɪd] *adj* válido

valley [ˈvælɪ] *n* vale *m*

valuable [ˈvæljuəbl] *adj* (*jewel*) de valor; (*time*) valioso; (*help*) precioso; **valuables** *npl* objetos *mpl* de valor

valuation [væljuˈeɪʃən] *n* avaliação *f*; (*of quality*) apreciação *f*

value [ˈvæljuː] *n* valor *m*; (*importance*) importância ♦ *vt* (*fix price of*) avaliar; (*appreciate*) valorizar, estimar; **~s** *npl* (*principles*) valores *mpl*; **valued** *adj* (*appreciated*) valorizado

valve [vælv] *n* válvula

van [væn] *n* (*AUT*) camionete *f* (*BR*), camioneta (*PT*)

vandal [ˈvændl] *n* vândalo(-a); **vandalize** *vt* destruir, depredar

vanilla [vəˈnɪlə] *n* baunilha

vanish [ˈvænɪʃ] *vi* desaparecer, sumir

vanity [ˈvænɪtɪ] *n* vaidade *f*

vapour [ˈveɪpə*] (*US* **vapor**) *n* vapor *m*

variety [vəˈraɪətɪ] *n* variedade *f*, diversidade *f*; (*type, quantity*) variedade

various [ˈvɛərɪəs] *adj* vários(-as), diversos(-as); (*several*) vários(-as)

varnish [ˈvɑːnɪʃ] *n* verniz *m*; (*nail ~*) esmalte *m* ♦ *vt* envernizar, pintar (com esmalte)

vary [ˈvɛərɪ] *vt* mudar ♦ *vi* variar; (*become different*): **to ~ with** variar de acordo com

vase [vɑːz] *n* vaso

vaseline [ˈvæsɪliːn] ® *n* vaselina ®

vast [vɑːst] *adj* enorme

VAT [væt] (*BRIT*) *n abbr* (= *value added tax*) ≈ ICM *m* (*BR*), IVA *m* (*PT*)

vat [væt] *n* tina, cuba

vault [vɔːlt] *n* (*of roof*) abóbada; (*tomb*) sepulcro; (*in bank*) caixa-forte *f* ♦ *vt* (*also: ~ over*) saltar (por cima de)

VCR *n abbr* = **video cassette recorder**

VDU *n abbr* = **visual display unit**

veal [viːl] *n* carne *f* de vitela

veer [vɪə*] *vi* virar

vegan [ˈviːɡən] *n* vegetalista *m/f*

vegetable [ˈvɛdʒtəbl] *n* (*BOT*) vegetal *m*; (*edible plant*) legume *m*, hortaliça ♦ *adj* vegetal

vegetarian [vɛdʒɪˈtɛərɪən] *adj*, *n* vegetariano(-a)

vehement [ˈviːmənt] *adj* veemente; (*attack*) violento

vehicle [ˈviːɪkl] *n* veículo

veil [veɪl] *n* véu *m* ♦ *vt* velar

vein [veɪn] *n* veia; (*of ore etc*) filão *m*; (*on leaf*) nervura

velvet [ˈvɛlvɪt] *n* veludo ♦ *adj* aveludado

vending machine [ˈvɛndɪŋ-] *n* vendedor *m* automático

veneer [vəˈnɪə*] *n* (*wood*) compensado; (*fig*) aparência

venereal [vɪˈnɪərɪəl] *adj*: **~ disease** doença venérea

Venetian blind [vɪˈniːʃən-] *n* persiana

Venezuela [vɛnɛ'zweɪlə] n Venezuela

vengeance ['vɛndʒəns] n vingança; **with a ~** (fig) para valer

venison ['vɛnɪsn] n carne f de veado

venom ['vɛnəm] n veneno; (bitterness) malevolência

vent [vɛnt] n (in jacket) abertura; (also: **air ~**) respiradouro ♦ vt (fig: feelings) desabafar, descarregar

ventriloquist [vɛn'trɪləkwɪst] n ventríloquo

venture ['vɛntʃə*] n empreendimento ♦ vt (opinion) arriscar ♦ vi arriscar-se; **business ~** empreendimento comercial

venue ['vɛnju:] n local m

verb [vɜːb] n verbo

verbatim [vɜː'beɪtɪm] adj, adv palavra por palavra

verdict ['vɜːdɪkt] n veredicto, decisão f; (fig) opinião f, parecer m

verge [vɜːdʒ] n beira, margem f; (on road) acostamento (BR), berma (PT); **"soft ~s"** (BRIT: AUT) "acostamento mole"; **to be on the ~ of doing sth** estar a ponto or à beira de fazer algo; **verge on** vt fus beirar em

vermin ['vɜːmɪn] npl (animals) bichos mpl; (insects) insetos mpl nocivos

vermouth ['vɜːməθ] n vermute m

versatile ['vɜːsətaɪl] adj (person) versátil; (machine, tool etc) polivalente

verse [vɜːs] n verso, poesia; (stanza) estrofe f; (in bible) versículo

version ['vɜːʃn] n versão f

versus ['vɜːsəs] prep contra, versus

vertical ['vɜːtɪkl] adj vertical

vertigo ['vɜːtɪgəu] n vertigem f

verve [vɜːv] n garra, pique m

very ['vɛrɪ] adv muito ♦ adj: **the ~ book which** o mesmo livro que; **the ~ last** o último (de todos), bem o último; **at the ~ least** no mínimo; **~ much** muitíssimo

vessel ['vɛsl] n (NAUT) navio, barco; (container) vaso, vasilha

vest [vɛst] n (BRIT) camiseta (BR), camisola interior (PT); (US: waistcoat) colete m

vet [vɛt] n abbr (= veterinary surgeon) veterinário(-a) ♦ vt examinar

veteran ['vɛtərn] n (also: **war ~**) veterano de guerra

veto ['viːtəu] (pl **~es**) n veto ♦ vt vetar

vex [vɛks] vt irritar, apoquentar; **vexed** adj (question) controvertido, discutido

via [vaɪə] prep por, via

vibrate [vaɪ'breɪt] vi vibrar

vicar ['vɪkə*] n vigário; **vicarage** n vicariato

vice [vaɪs] n (evil) vício; (TECH) torno mecânico

vice- [vaɪs] prefix vice-

vice versa ['vaɪsɪ'vɜːsə] adv vice-versa

vicinity [vɪ'sɪnɪtɪ] n: **in the ~ of** nas proximidades de

vicious ['vɪʃəs] adj violento; (cruel) cruel; **vicious circle** n círculo vicioso

victim ['vɪktɪm] n vítima f

victor ['vɪktə*] n vencedor(a) m/f

Victorian [vɪk'tɔ:rɪən] adj vitoriano

victory ['vɪktərɪ] n vitória f

video ['vɪdɪəu] (~ film) vídeo; (also: **~ cassette**) videocassete m; (also: **~ cassette recorder**) videocassete m

Vienna [vɪ'ɛnə] n Viena

Vietnam ['vjet'næm] n Vietnã m;
Vietnamese [vjetnə'mi:z] adj vietnamita ♦ n inv vietnamita m/f; (LING)
vietnamita m

view [vju:] n vista; (outlook) perspectiva; (opinion) opinião f, parecer
m ♦ vt olhar; in full ~ (of) à plena
vista (de); in my ~ na minha opinião; in ~ of the weather/the fact
that em vista do tempo/do fato de
que; **viewer** n telespectador(a)
m/f; **viewfinder** n visor m; **viewpoint** n ponto de vista; (place)
lugar m

vigorous ['vɪgərəs] adj vigoroso;
(plant) viçoso

vile [vaɪl] adj vil, infame; (smell)
repugnante, repulsivo; (temper) violento

villa ['vɪlə] n (country house) casa de
campo; (suburban house) vila, quinta

village ['vɪlɪdʒ] n aldeia, povoado;
villager n aldeão (aldeã) m/f

villain ['vɪlən] n (scoundrel) patife
m; (in novel etc) vilão m; (BRIT: criminal) marginal m/f

vindicate ['vɪndɪkeɪt] vt vingar;
(justify) justificar

vindictive [vɪn'dɪktɪv] adj vingativo

vine [vaɪn] n planta trepadeira

vinegar ['vɪnɪgə*] n vinagre m

vineyard ['vɪnjɑ:d] n vinha, vinhedo

vintage ['vɪntɪdʒ] n vindima; (year)
safra, colheita ♦ cpd (comedy) de
época; (performance) clássico; the
1970 ~ a safra de 1970; **vintage
car** n carro antigo; **vintage wine**
n vinho velho

viola [vɪ'əulə] n viola

violate ['vaɪəleɪt] vt violar

violence ['vaɪələns] n violência;
(strength) força

violent ['vaɪələnt] adj violento;
(intense) intenso

violet ['vaɪələt] adj violeta ♦ n violeta

violin [vaɪə'lɪn] n violino; **violinist**
[vaɪə'lɪnɪst] n violinista m/f

VIP n abbr (= very important person)
VIP m/f

virgin ['və:dʒɪn] n virgem m/f ♦ adj
virgem

Virgo ['və:gəu] n Virgem f

virtually ['və:tjuəlɪ] adv praticamente

virtue ['və:tju:] n virtude f; (advantage) vantagem f; **by ~ of** em virtude de

virtuous ['və:tjuəs] adj virtuoso

virus ['vaɪərəs] n vírus m

visa ['vi:zə] n visto

visible ['vɪzəbl] adj visível

vision ['vɪʒən] n (sight) vista, visão
f; (foresight, in dream) visão f

visit ['vɪzɪt] n visita ♦ vt (person: us:
also: ~ with) visitar, fazer uma visita
a; (place) ir a, ir conhecer; **visiting
hours** npl horário de visita; **visitor**
n visitante m/f; (to one's house) visita; (tourist) turista m/f

visor ['vaɪzə*] n viseira

visual ['vɪzjuəl] adj visual; **visual
display unit** n terminal m de
vídeo; **visualize** vt visualizar

vital ['vaɪtl] adj essencial, indispensável; (important) de importância
vital; (crucial) crucial; (person) vivo;
(of life) vital; **vitally** adv: **~ly
important** de importância vital

vitamin ['vɪtəmɪn] n vitamina

vivacious [vɪ'veɪʃəs] adj vivaz, animado

vivid ['vɪvɪd] adj (account) vívido;
(light) claro, brilhante; (imagination,
colour) vivo; **vividly** adv vivamente; (remember) distintamente

V-neck n: ~ **jumper, ~ pullover** svéter f com decote em V

vocabulary [vəˈkæbjulərɪ] n vocabulário

vocal [ˈvəukl] adj vocal; (noisy) clamoroso; (articulate) claro, eloqüente; **vocal cords** npl cordas fpl vocais

vocation [vəuˈkeɪʃən] n vocação f

vociferous [vəˈsɪfərəs] adj vociferante

vodka [ˈvɔdkə] n vodca

vogue [vəug] n voga, moda; **to be in ~** estar na moda

voice [vɔɪs] n voz f ♦ vt expressar; **voice mail** n (TEL) correio m de voz

void [vɔɪd] n vazio; (hole) oco ♦ adj nulo; (empty): **~ of** destituído de

volatile [ˈvɔlətaɪl] adj volátil; (situation, person) imprevisível

volcano [vɔlˈkeɪnəu] (pl **~es**) n vulcão m

volley [ˈvɔlɪ] n (of gunfire) descarga, salva; (of stones etc) chuva; (of questions etc) enxurrada, chuva; (TENNIS etc) voleio; **volleyball** n voleibol m, vôlei m (BR)

volt [vəult] n volt m

volume [ˈvɔljuːm] n volume m; (of tank) capacidade f

voluntarily [ˈvɔləntrɪlɪ] adv livremente, voluntariamente

voluntary [ˈvɔləntərɪ] adj voluntário; (unpaid) (a título) gratuito

volunteer [vɔlənˈtɪə*] n voluntário(-a) ♦ vt oferecer voluntariamente ♦ vi (MIL) alistar-se voluntariamente; **to ~ to do** oferecer-se voluntariamente para fazer

vomit [ˈvɔmɪt] n vômito ♦ vt, vi vomitar

vote [vəut] n voto; (votes cast) votação f; (right to ~) direito de votar ♦ vt: **to be ~d chairman** etc ser eleito presidente etc; (propose): **to ~ that** propor que; (in election) votar

♦ vi votar; **voter** n votante m/f, eleitor(a) m/f

voucher [ˈvautʃə*] n (also: lunch-eon ~) vale-refeição m; (with petrol etc) vale m; (gift ~) vale m para presente

vouch for [vautʃ-] vt fus garantir, responder por

vow [vau] n voto ♦ vt: **to ~ to do/ that** prometer solenemente fazer/ que

vowel [ˈvauəl] n vogal f

voyage [ˈvɔɪdʒ] n viagem f

vulgar [ˈvʌlgə*] adj grosseiro, ordinário; (in bad taste) vulgar, baixo

vulture [ˈvʌltʃə*] n abutre m, urubu m

W

wad [wɔd] n (of cotton wool) chumaço; (of paper) bola; (of banknotes etc) maço

wade [weɪd] vi: **to ~ through** andar em; (fig: a book) ler com dificuldade

wafer [ˈweɪfə*] n (biscuit) bolacha

waffle [ˈwɔfl] n (CULIN) waffle m; (empty talk) lengalenga ♦ vi encher lingüiça

waft [wɔft] vt levar ♦ vi flutuar

wag [wæg] vt (tail) sacudir; (finger) menear ♦ vi abanar

wage [weɪdʒ] n (also: **~s**) salário, ordenado ♦ vt: **to ~ war** empreender or fazer guerra; **wage earner** n assalariado(-a)

wager [ˈweɪdʒə*] n aposta, parada

wag(g)on [ˈwægən] n (horse-drawn) carroça; (BRIT: RAIL) vagão m

wail [weɪl] n lamento, gemido ♦ vi lamentar-se, gemer; (siren) tocar

waist [weɪst] n cintura; **waistcoat** n colete m; **waistline** n cintura

wait [weɪt] n espera ♦ vi esperar; I

can't ~ to (*fig*) estou morrendo de vontade de; **to ~ for sb/sth** esperar por alguém/algo; **wait behind** vi ficar para trás; **wait on** vt fus servir; **waiter** n garçom m (*BR*), empregado (*PT*); **waiting list** n lista de espera; **waiting room** n sala de espera; **waitress** n garçonete f (*BR*), empregada (*PT*)

waive [weɪv] vt abrir mão de

wake [weɪk] (*pt* **woke** or **~d**, *pp* **woken** or **~d**) vt (*also:* **~ up**) acordar ♦ vi acordar ♦ n (*for dead person*) velório; (*NAUT*) esteira

Wales [weɪlz] n País m de Gales

walk [wɔːk] n passeio; (*hike*) excursão f a pé, caminhada; (*gait*) passo, modo de andar; (*in park etc*) alameda, passeio ♦ vi andar; (*for pleasure, exercise*) passear ♦ vt (*distance*) percorrer a pé, andar; (*dog*) levar para passear; **it's 10 minutes' ~ from here** daqui são 10 minutos a pé; **people from all ~s of life** pessoas de todos os níveis; **walk out** vi sair; (*audience*) retirar-se (em protesto); (*strike*) entrar em greve; **walk out on** vt fus abandonar; **walkie-talkie** n transmissor-receptor m portátil, walkie-talkie m; **walking** n o andar; **walking shoes** npl sapatos mpl para caminhar; **walking stick** n bengala; **Walkman** ® n Walkman ® m; **walkover** (*inf*) n barbada; **walkway** n passeio, passadiço

wall [wɔːl] n parede f; (*exterior*) muro; (*city ~ etc*) muralha; **walled** adj (*city*) cercado por muralhas; (*garden*) murado, cercado

wallet [ˈwɔlɪt] n carteira

wallow [ˈwɔləʊ] vi (*in mud*) chafurdar; (*in water*) rolar; (*person: in guilt*) regalar-se

wallpaper [ˈwɔːlpeɪpə*] n papel m de parede ♦ vt colocar papel de parede em

walnut [ˈwɔːlnʌt] n noz f; (*tree, wood*) nogueira

walrus [ˈwɔːlrəs] (*pl inv or* **~es**) n morsa, vaca marinha

waltz [wɔːlts] n valsa ♦ vi valsar

wand [wɔnd] n (*also:* **magic ~**) varinha de condão

wander [ˈwɔndə*] vi (*person*) vagar, perambular; (*thoughts*) divagar ♦ vt perambular

wane [weɪn] vi diminuir; (*moon*) minguar

want [wɔnt] vt querer; (*demand*) exigir; (*need*) precisar de, necessitar, **to ~ sb to do sth** querer que alguém faça algo; **wanted** adj (*criminal etc*) procurado (pela polícia); **"cook wanted"** (*in advertisement*) "precisa-se cozinheiro"

war [wɔː*] n guerra; **to make ~ (on)** fazer guerra (contra)

ward [wɔːd] n (*in hospital*) ala; (*POL*) distrito eleitoral; (*LAW: child*) tutelado(-a), pupilo(-a); **ward off** vt desviar, aparar; (*attack*) repelir

warden [ˈwɔːdn] n (*BRIT: of institution*) diretor(a) m/f; (*of park, youth hostel*) administrador(a) m/f; (*BRIT: also:* **traffic ~**) guarda m/f

warder [ˈwɔːdə*] (*BRIT*) n carcereiro(-a)

wardrobe [ˈwɔːdrəʊb] n guarda-roupa m; (*CINEMA, THEATRE*) figurinos mpl

warehouse [ˈwɛəhaʊs] n armazém m, depósito

warfare [ˈwɔːfɛə*] n guerra, combate m

warhead [ˈwɔːhɛd] n ogiva

warm [wɔːm] adj quente; (*thanks, welcome*) caloroso; **it's ~** está quente; **I'm ~** estou com calor; **warm up** vt, vi esquentar; **warm-**

hearted adj afetuoso; **warmly** adv (applaud, dress) calorosamente; (dress): **to dress warmly** vestir-se com roupas de inverno; **warmth** n calor m; (friendliness) calor humano

warn [wɔ:n] vt prevenir, avisar; **to ~ sb that/of/(not) to do** prevenir alguém de que/de/para (não) fazer

warning [wɔ:nɪŋ] n advertência; (in writing) aviso; (signal) sinal m

warp [wɔ:p] vt deformar ♦ vi empenar, deformar-se

warrant [wɔrnt] n (voucher) comprovante m; (LAW: to arrest) mandado de prisão; (: to search) mandado de busca; **warranty** n garantia

warrior [wɔrɪə*] n guerreiro(-a)

Warsaw [wɔ:sɔ:] n Varsóvia

warship [wɔ:ʃɪp] n navio de guerra

wart [wɔ:t] n verruga

wartime [wɔ:taɪm] n: **in ~** em tempo de guerra

wary [wɛərɪ] adj cauteloso, precavido

was [wɔz] pt of **be**

wash [wɔʃ] vt lavar ♦ vi lavar-se; (subj: ~ing machine) lavar; (sea etc): **to ~ over/against sth** bater contra/chocar-se contra algo; (clothes): **this shirt ~es well** esta camisa resiste bem à lavagem ♦ n (clothes etc) lavagem f; (~ing programme) programa m de lavagem; (of ship) esteira; **to have a ~** lavar-se; **wash away** vt (stain) tirar ao lavar; (subj: river etc) levar, arrastar; **wash off** vt tirar lavando ♦ vi sair ao lavar; **wash up** vi (BRIT) lavar a louça; (US) lavar-se; **washbasin** n pia (BR), lavatório (PT); **washcloth** (US) n toalhinha para lavar o rosto; **washing** n (dirty) roupa suja; (clean) roupa lavada; **washing machine** n máquina de lavar roupa, lavadora; **washing powder** (BRIT) n sabão m

em pó; **washing-up** n: **to do the washing-up** lavar a louça; **washing-up liquid** n detergente m; **wash-out** (inf) n fracasso, fiasco; **washroom** (US) n banheiro (BR), casa de banho (PT)

wasn't [wɔznt] = **was not**

wasp [wɔsp] n vespa

wastage [weɪstɪdʒ] n desgaste m, desperdício; (loss) perda

waste [weɪst] n desperdício, esbanjamento; (of time) perda; (also: **household ~**) detritos mpl domésticos; (rubbish) lixo ♦ adj (material) de refugo; (left over) de sobra; (land) baldio ♦ vt (squander) esbanjar, desperdiçar; (time, opportunity) perder; **~s** npl (land) ermos mpl; **to lay ~** devastar; **waste away** vi definhar; **wasteful** adj esbanjador(a); (process) anti-econômico; **wastepaper basket** n cesta de papéis

watch [wɔtʃ] n (clock) relógio; (also: **wrist~**) relógio de pulso; (act of ~ing) vigia; (guard: MIL) sentinela; (NAUT: spell of duty) quarto ♦ vt (look at) observar, olhar; (programme, match) assistir a; (television) ver; (spy on, guard) vigiar; (be careful of) tomar cuidado com ♦ vi ver, olhar; (keep guard) montar guarda; **watch out** vi ter cuidado; **watchdog** n cão m de guarda; (fig) vigia m/f; **watchful** adj vigilante, atento; **watchmaker** n relojoeiro(-a); **watchman** (irreg) n see **night**; **watchstrap** n pulseira de relógio

water [wɔ:tə*] n água ♦ vt (plant) regar ♦ vi (eyes) lacrimejar; (mouth) salivar; **in British ~s** nas águas territoriais britânicas; **water down** vt (milk) aguar; (fig) diluir; **watercolour** (US **watercolor**) n aquarela; **waterfall** n cascata, cachoeira;

watering can n regador m; **water lily** n nenúfar m; **waterline** n (NAUT) linha d'água; **waterlogged** adj alagado; **watermelon** n melancia; **waterproof** adj impermeável; **watershed** n (GEO) linha divisória das águas; (fig) momento crítico; **water-skiing** n esqui m aquático; **watertight** adj hermético, à prova d'água; **waterworks** npl usina hidráulica; **watery** adj (eyes) húmido

watt [wɔt] n watt m

wave [weɪv] n onda; (of hand) aceno, sinal m; (in hair) onda, ondulação ♦ vi acenar com a mão; (flag, grass) tremular ♦ vt (hand) acenar; (handkerchief) acenar com; (weapon) brandir; **wavelength** n comprimento de onda; **to be on the same wavelength** as ter os mesmos gostos e atitudes que

waver ['weɪvə*] vi vacilar; (voice, eyes, love) hesitar

wavy ['weɪvɪ] adj (hair) ondulado; (line) ondulante

wax [wæks] n cera ♦ vt encerar; (car) polir ♦ vi (moon) crescer; **waxworks** n museu m de cera ♦ npl (models) figuras fpl de cera

way [weɪ] n caminho; (distance) percurso; (direction) direção f, sentido; (manner) maneira, modo; (habit) costume m; **which ~? - this ~** por onde? – por aqui; **on the ~** (to) a caminho (de); **to be on one's ~** estar a caminho; **to be in the ~** atrapalhar; **to go out of one's ~ to do sth** dar-se ao trabalho de fazer algo; **to lose one's ~** perder-se; **to be under ~** estar em andamento; **in a ~** de certo modo, até certo ponto; **in some ~s** a certos respeitos; **by the ~** a propósito; **"~ in"** (BRIT) "entrada"; **"~ out"** (BRIT) "saída";

the ~ back o caminho de volta; **"give ~"** (BRIT: AUT) "dê a preferência"; **no ~!** (inf) de jeito nenhum!; **waylay** vt armar uma cilada para; **wayward** adj caprichoso, voluntarioso

WC ['dʌblju:'si:] n abbr (= water closet) privada

we [wi:] pl pron nós

weak [wi:k] adj fraco, débil; (morally, currency) fraco; (excuse) pouco convincente; (tea) aguado, ralo; **weaken** vi enfraquecer(-se); (give way) ceder; (influence, power) diminuir ♦ vt enfraquecer; **weakling** n pessoa fraca or delicada; (morally) pessoa de personalidade fraca, **weakness** n fraqueza; (fault) ponto fraco; **to have a weakness for** ter uma queda por

wealth [wɛlθ] n riqueza; (of details) abundância; **wealthy** adj rico, abastado; (country) rico

wean [wi:n] vt desmamar

weapon ['wɛpən] n arma

wear [wɛə*] (pt wore, pp worn) n (use) uso; (deterioration) desgaste m; (clothing): **baby/sports ~** roupa infantil/de esporte ♦ vt (clothes) usar; (shoes) usar, calçar; (put on) vestir; (damage: through use) desgastar ♦ vi (last) durar; (rub through etc) gastar-se; **town/evening ~** traje m de passeio/de noite; **wear away** vt gastar ♦ vi desgastar-se; **wear down** vt gastar; (strength) esgotar; **wear off** vi (pain etc) passar; **wear out** vt desgastar; (person, strength) esgotar; **wear and tear** n desgaste m

weary ['wɪərɪ] adj cansado; (dispirited) deprimido ♦ vi: **to ~ of** cansar-se de

weasel ['wi:zl] n (ZOOL) doninha

weather ['wɛðə*] n tempo ♦ vt

(*storm, crisis*) resistir a; **under the ~** (*fig: ill*) doente; **weather-beaten** *adj* curtido; (*building, stone*) castigado, erodido; **weather forecast** *n* previsão *f* do tempo; **weatherman** (*irreg: inf*) *n* meteorologista *m*

weave [wiːv] (*pt* **wove**, *pp* **woven**) *vt* tecer

web [wɛb] *n* (*of spider*) teia; (*on foot*) membrana; (*network*) rede *f*; **the (World Wide) W~** a (World Wide) Web; **website** ['wɛbsaɪt] *n* site *m*, website *m*

wed [wɛd] (*pt, pp* **~ded**) *vt* casar ♦ *vi* casar-se

we'd [wiːd] = **we had; we would**

wedding ['wɛdɪŋ] *n* casamento, núpcias *fpl*; **silver/golden ~** (*anniversary*) bodas *fpl* de prata/de ouro; **wedding dress** *n* vestido de noiva; **wedding ring** *n* anel *m* or aliança de casamento

wedge [wɛdʒ] *n* (*of wood etc*) cunha, calço; (*of cake*) fatia ♦ *vt* (*pack tightly*) apinhar; (*door*) pôr calço em

Wednesday ['wɛnzdɪ] *n* quarta-feira

wee [wiː] (*SCOTTISH*) *adj* pequeno, pequenino

weed [wiːd] *n* erva daninha ♦ *vt* capinar; **weedkiller** *n* herbicida *m*; **weedy** *adj* (*man*) fraquinho

week [wiːk] *n* semana; **a ~ today** daqui a uma semana; **a ~ on Tuesday** sem ser essa terça-feira, a próxima; **weekday** *n* dia *m* de semana; (*COMM*) dia útil; **weekend** *n* fim *m* de semana; **weekly** *adv* semanalmente ♦ *adj* semanal ♦ *n* semanário

weep [wiːp] (*pt, pp* **wept**) *vi* (*person*) chorar; **weeping willow** *n* salgueiro chorão

weigh [weɪ] *vt, vi* pesar; **to ~ anchor**

levantar ferro; **weigh down** *vt* sobrecarregar; (*fig: with worry*) deprimir, acabrunhar; **weigh up** *vt* ponderar, avaliar

weight [weɪt] *n* peso; **to lose/put on ~** emagrecer/engordar; **weight-lifter** *n* levantador *m* de pesos; **weighty** *adj* pesado; (*matters*) importante

weir [wɪə*] *n* represa, açude *m*

weird [wɪəd] *adj* esquisito, estranho

welcome ['wɛlkəm] *adj* bem-vindo ♦ *n* acolhimento, recepção *f* ♦ *vt* dar as boas-vindas a; (*be glad of*) saudar; **you're ~** (*after thanks*) de nada

weld [wɛld] *n* solda ♦ *vt* soldar, unir

welfare ['wɛlfɛə*] *n* bem-estar *m*; (*social aid*) assistência social; **welfare state** *n* país auto-financiador da sua assistência social

well [wɛl] *n* poço ♦ *adv* bem ♦ *adj*: **to be ~** estar bem (de saúde) ♦ *excl* bem!, então!; **as ~** também; **as ~ as** assim como; ~ **done!** muito bem!; **get ~ soon!** melhoras!; **to do ~** ir or sair-se bem; (*business*) ir bem; **well up** *vi* brotar

we'll [wiːl] = **we will; we shall**

well: **well-behaved** *adj* bem comportado; **well-being** *n* bem-estar *m*; **well-built** *adj* robusto; **well-deserved** *adj* bem merecido; **well-dressed** *adj* bem vestido

wellingtons ['wɛlɪŋtənz] *n* (*also:* **wellington boots**) botas *fpl* de borracha até os joelhos

well: **well-known** *adj* conhecido; **well-meaning** *adj* bem intencionado; **well-off** *adj* próspero, rico; **well-read** *adj* lido, versado; **well-to-do** *adj* abastado

Welsh [wɛlʃ] *adj* galês (galesa) ♦ *n* (*LING*) galês *m*; **the ~** *npl* (*people*) os galeses; **Welshman** (*irreg*) *n* galês *m*; **Welshwoman** (*irreg*) *n* galesa

went [wɛnt] *pt of* **go**

wept [wɛpt] *pt, pp of* **weep**

were [wəː*] *pt of* **be**

we're [wɪə*] = **we are**

weren't [wəːnt] = **were not**

west [wɛst] *n* oeste *m* ♦ *adj* ocidental, do oeste ♦ *adv* para o oeste or ao oeste; **the W~** (*POL*) o Oeste, o Ocidente; **West Country** (*BRIT*) *n*: **the West Country** o sudoeste da Inglaterra; **westerly** *adj* (*situation*) ocidental; (*wind*) oeste; **western** *adj* ocidental ♦ *n* (*CINEMA*) western *m*, bangue-bangue (*BR: INF*); **West Indian** *adj, n* antilhano(-a); **West Indies** *npl* Antilhas *fpl*; **westward(s)** *adv* para o oeste

wet [wɛt] *adj* molhado; (*damp*) úmido; (~ *through*) encharcado; (*rainy*) chuvoso ♦ *n* (*BRIT: POL*) político de tendência moderada, **to get ~** molhar-se; **"~ paint"** "tinta fresca"; **wetsuit** *n* roupa de mergulho

we've [wiːv] = **we have**

whale [weɪl] *n* (*ZOOL*) baleia

wharf [wɔːf] (*pl* **wharves**) *n* cais *m inv*

---

fez/estava na mesa; **he asked me ~ she had said** ele me perguntou o que ela tinha dito
♦ *excl* (*disbelieving*): ~, **no coffee!** o que, não tem café!

---

whatever [wɔtˈɛvə*] *adj*: ~ **book** qualquer livro ♦ *pron*: **do ~ is necessary/you want** faça tudo o que for preciso/o que você quiser; ~ **happens** aconteça o que acontecer; **no reason** ~ or **whatsoever** nenhuma razão seja qual for or em absoluto; **nothing** ~ nada em absoluto

whatsoever [wɔtsəuˈɛvə*] *adj* = **whatever**

wheat [wiːt] *n* trigo

wheel [wiːl] *n* roda; (*also:* **steering** ~) volante *m*; (*NAUT*) roda do leme ♦ *vt* (*pram etc*) empurrar ♦ *vi* (*birds*) dar voltas; (*also:* ~ **round**) girar, dar voltas, virar-se; **wheelbarrow** *n* carrinho de mão; **wheelchair** *n* cadeira de rodas; **wheel clamp** *n* (*AUT*) grampo com que se imobiliza carros estacionados ilegalmente

wheeze [wiːz] *vi* respirar ruidosamente

KEYWORD

what [wɔt] *adj* **1** (*in direct/indirect questions*) que, qual; ~ **size is it?** que tamanho é este? ~ **colour/shape is it?** qual é a cor/o formato?; **he asked me ~ books I needed** ele me perguntou de quais de livros eu precisava
2 (*in exclamations*) quê!, como!; ~ **a mess!** que bagunça!
♦ *pron* **1** (*interrogative*) que, o que; ~ **are you doing?** o que é que você está fazendo?; ~ **is it called?** como se chama?; ~ **about me?** e eu?; ~ **about doing ...?** que tal fazer ...?
2 (*relative*) o que; **I saw ~ you did/was on the table** eu vi o que você

KEYWORD

when [wɛn] *adv* quando
♦ *conj* **1** (*at, during, after the time that*) quando; ~ **you've read it, tell me what you think** depois que você tiver lido isto, diga-me o que acha; **that was ~ I needed you** foi quando eu precisei de você
2 (*on, at which*) quando, em que; **on the day ~ I met him** no dia em que o conheci; **one day ~ it was raining** um dia quando estava chovendo
3 (*whereas*) ao passo que; **you said I was wrong ~ in fact I was right**

você disse que eu estava errado quando, na verdade, eu estava certo

whenever [wɛnˈevə*] *conj* quando, quando quer que; *(every time that)* sempre que ♦ *adv* quando você quiser

where [wɛə*] *adv* onde ♦ *conj* onde, aonde; **this is ~** ... aqui é onde ...; **whereabouts** ['wɛərəbauts] *adv* (por) onde ♦ *n*: **nobody knows his whereabouts** ninguém sabe o seu paradeiro; **whereas** [wɛərˈæz] *conj* uma vez que, ao passo que; **whereby** *adv* (formal) pelo qual (or pela qual etc); **wherever** [wɛərˈevə*] *conj* onde quer que ♦ *adv* (interrogative) onde?

whether ['wɛðə*] *conj* se; **I don't know ~ to accept or not** não sei se aceito ou não; **~ you go or not** quer você vá quer não; **it's doubtful ~** ... não é certo que ...

☐ KEYWORD

which [wɪtʃ] *adj* **1** *(interrogative: direct, indirect)* que, qual; **~ picture do you want?** que quadro você quer?; **~ books are yours?** quais são os seus livros?; **~ one?** qual? que? qual?

2: **in ~ case** em cujo caso; **by ~ time** momento em que

♦ *pron* **1** *(interrogative)* qual; **~ (of these) are yours?** quais (destes) são seus?

2 *(relative)* que, o que, o qual *etc*; **the apple ~ you ate** a maçã que você comeu; **the chair on ~ you are sitting** a cadeira na qual você está sentado; **he said he knew, ~ is true** ele disse que sabia, o que é verdade; **after ~** depois do que

whichever [wɪtʃˈevə*] *adj*: **take ~**

book you prefer pegue o livro que preferir; **~ book you take** qualquer livro que você pegue

while [waɪl] *n* tempo, momento ♦ *conj* enquanto, ao mesmo tempo que; *(as long as)* contanto que; *(although)* embora; **for a ~** durante algum tempo; **while away** *vt (time)* encher

whim [wɪm] *n* capricho, veneta

whimper ['wɪmpə*] *n* *(moan)* lamúria ♦ *vi* choramingar, soluçar

whimsical ['wɪmzɪkl] *adj* *(person)* caprichoso, de veneta; *(look)* excêntrico

whine [waɪn] *n* *(of pain)* gemido; *(of engine, siren)* zunido ♦ *vi* gemer; zunir; *(fig)* lamuriar-se

whip [wɪp] *n* açoite *m*; *(for riding)* chicote *m*; *(POL)* líder *m/f* da bancada ♦ *vt* chicotear; *(snatch)* apanhar de repente; *(cream, eggs)* bater; *(move quickly)*: **to ~ sth out/off/away** *etc* arrancar algo; **whipped cream** *n* (creme *m*) chantilly *m*; **whip-round** *(BRIT)* *n* coleta, vaquinha

whirl [wəːl] *vt* fazer girar ♦ *vi* *(dancers)* rodopiar; *(leaves, water etc)* redemoinhar; **whirlpool** *n* remoinho; **whirlwind** *n* furacão *m*, remoinho

whirr [wəː*] *vi* zumbir

whisk [wɪsk] *n* *(CULIN)* batedeira ♦ *vt* bater; **to ~ sb away** *or* **off** levar alguém rapidamente

whiskers ['wɪskəz] *npl* *(of animal)* bigodes *mpl*; *(of man)* suíças *fpl*

whisky ['wɪskɪ] *(US, IRELAND* **whiskey)** *n* uísque *m* *(BR)*, whisky *m* *(PT)*

whisper ['wɪspə*] *n* sussurro, murmúrio ♦ *vt*, *vi* sussurrar

whistle ['wɪsl] *n* *(sound)* assobio; *(object)* apito ♦ *vt*, *vi* assobiar

white [waɪt] *adj* branco; *(pale)* pálido ♦ n branco; (of egg) clara; **white coffee** n café m com leite; **White House** n: **the W~ House** a Casa Branca; ver quadro

---

WHITE HOUSE

A White House é um grande edifício branco situado em Washington D.C. onde reside o presidente dos Estados Unidos. Por extensão, o termo se refere também ao poder executivo americano.

---

white lie n mentira inofensiva or social

whitewash n (paint) cal f ♦ vt caiar; (fig) encobrir

whiting ['waɪtɪŋ] n inv pescada

Whitsun ['wɪtsn] n Pentecostes m

whizz [wɪz] vi: **to ~ past** or by passar a toda velocidade; **whizz kid** (inf) n prodígio

KEYWORD

who [huː] pron **1** (interrogative) quem?; **~ is it?** quem é?
2 (relative) que, o qual etc, quem; **my cousin, ~ lives in New York** meu primo que mora em Nova Iorque; **the man ~ spoke to me** o homem que falou comigo

KEYWORD

whole [həʊl] adj (complete) todo, inteiro; (not broken) intacto ♦ n (all): **the ~ of the time** o tempo todo; (entire unit) conjunto; **on the ~, as a ~** como um todo, no conjunto; **wholefoods** n comida integral; **wholehearted** adj total; **wholemeal** (BRIT) adj integral; **wholesale** n venda por atacado ♦ adj por atacado; (destruction) em grande escala ♦ adv por atacado; **wholesaler** n atacadista m/f; **wholesome** adj

saudável, sadio; **wholewheat** adj = **wholemeal**; **wholly** ['həʊlɪ] adv totalmente, completamente

KEYWORD

whom [huːm] pron **1** (interrogative) quem?; **to ~ did you give it?** para quem você deu isto?
2 (relative) quem, quem; **the man ~ I saw/to ~ I spoke** o homem que eu vi/com quem eu falei

whooping cough ['huːpɪŋ-] n coqueluche f

whore [hɔː*] (inf: pej) n puta

KEYWORD

whose [huːz] adj **1** (possessive: interrogative): **~ book is this?, ~ is this book?** de quem é este livro?
2 (possessive: relative): **the man ~ son you rescued** o homem cujo filho você salvou; **the woman ~ car was stolen** a mulher de quem o carro foi roubado
♦ pron de quem; **I don't know ~ it is** eu não sei de quem é isto

KEYWORD

why [waɪ] adv por que (RR), porque (PT); (at end of sentence) por quê (BR), porquê (PT)
♦ conj por que; **that's not ~ I'm here** não e por isso que estou aqui; **the reason ~** a razão por que
♦ excl (expressing surprise, shock, annoyance) ora essa!; (explaining) bem!; **~, it's you!** ora, é você!

---

wicked ['wɪkɪd] adj perverso; (smile) malicioso

wicket ['wɪkɪt] n (CRICKET) arco

wide [waɪd] adj largo; (area, publicity, knowledge) amplo ♦ adv: **to**

open ~ abrir totalmente; **to shoot** ~ atirar longe do alvo; **wide-awake** adj bem acordado; **widely** adv extremamente; (travelled) muito; (believed, known) amplamente; **widen** vt alargar; (one's experience) aumentar ♦ vi alargar-se; **wide open** adj (eyes) arregalado; (door) escancarado; **widespread** adj (belief etc) difundido, comum

widow ['wɪdəu] n viúva; **widowed** adj viúvo; **widower** n viúvo

width [wɪdθ] n largura

wield [wi:ld] vt (sword) brandir, empunhar; (power) exercer

wife [waɪf] (pl **wives**) n mulher f, esposa

wig [wɪg] n peruca

wiggle ['wɪgl] vt menear, agitar

wild [waɪld] adj (animal) selvagem; (plant) silvestre; (rough) violento, furioso; (idea) disparatado, extravagante; (person) insensato; **wilderness** ['wɪldənɪs] n ermo; **wildlife** n animais mpl selvagens; **wildly** adv (behave) freneticamente; (hit, guess) irrefletidamente; (happy) extremamente

wilful ['wɪlful] (us **willful**) adj (person) teimoso, voluntarioso; (action) deliberado, intencional

will [wɪl] (vt) (pt, pp ~**ed**) aux vb
1 (forming future tense): **I** ~ **finish it tomorrow** vou acabar isto amanhã; **I** ~ **have finished it by tomorrow** até amanhã eu terei terminado isto; ~ **you do it?** – **yes I** ~/**no I won't** você vai fazer isto? – sim, vou/não eu não vou
2 (in conjectures, predictions): **he** ~ **come** ele virá; **he** ~ **or he'll be there by now** nesta altura ele está lá; **that** ~ **be the postman** deve ser o cartei-

ro; **this medicine** ~/**won't help you** este remédio vai/não vai fazer efeito em você
3 (in commands, requests, offers): ~ **you be quiet!** fique quieto, por favor!; ~ **you come?** você vem?; ~ **you help me?** você pode me ajudar?; ~ **you have a cup of tea?** você vai querer uma xícara de chá or um chá?; **I won't put up with it** eu não vou tolerar isto
♦ vt: **to** ~ **sb to do sth** desejar que alguém faça algo; **he** ~**ed himself to go on** reuniu grande força de vontade para continuar
♦ n (volition) vontade f; (testament) testamento

willful ['wɪlful] (us) adj = **wilful**

willing ['wɪlɪŋ] adj disposto, pronto; (enthusiastic) entusiasmado; **willingly** adv de bom grado, de boa vontade; **willingness** n boa vontade f, disposição f

willow ['wɪləu] n salgueiro

willpower ['wɪlpauə*] n força de vontade

wilt [wɪlt] vi (flower) murchar; (plant) morrer

win [wɪn] (pt, pp **won**) n vitória ♦ vt ganhar, vencer; (obtain) conseguir, obter; (support) alcançar ♦ vi ganhar; **win over** vt conquistar; **win round** (BRIT) vt = **win over**

wince [wɪns] vi encolher-se, estremecer

winch [wɪntʃ] n guincho

wind¹ [wɪnd] n vento; (MED) gases mpl, flatulência; (breath) fôlego ♦ vt (take breath away from) deixar sem fôlego

wind² [waɪnd] (pt, pp **wound**) vt enrolar, bobinar; (wrap) envolver; (clock, toy) dar corda a ♦ vi (road, river) serpentear; **wind up** vt (clock) dar corda em; (*debate*) rematar, concluir

windfall ['wɪndfɔ:l] *n* golpe *m* de sorte

winding ['waɪndɪŋ] *adj* (*road*) sinuoso, tortuoso; (*staircase*) de caracol, em espiral

wind instrument *n* (*MUS*) instrumento de sopro

windmill ['wɪndmɪl] *n* moinho de vento

window ['wɪndəu] *n* janela; (*in shop etc*) vitrine *f* (*BR*), montra (*PT*); **window box** *n* jardineira (no peitoril da janela); **window cleaner** *n* limpador(a) *m/f* de janelas; **window ledge** *n* peitoril *m* da janela; **window pane** *n* vidraça, vidro; **window-shopping** *n*: **to go window-shopping** ir ver vitrines; **windowsill** ['wɪndəusɪl] *n* (*inside*) peitoril *m*; (*outside*) soleira

windpipe ['wɪndpaɪp] *n* traquéia

wind power *n* energia eólica

windscreen ['wɪndskri:n] (*BRIT*) *n* pára-brisa *m*; **windscreen wiper** (*BRIT*) *n* limpador *m* de pára-brisa

windshield *etc* ['wɪndʃi:ld] (*US*) *n* = **windscreen** *etc*

windswept ['wɪndswɛpt] *adj* varrido pelo vento

windy ['wɪndɪ] *adj* com muito vento, batido pelo vento; **it's ~** está ventando (*BR*), faz vento (*PT*)

wine [waɪn] *n* vinho; **wine bar** *n* bar *m* (para degustação de vinhos); **wine cellar** *n* adega, **wine glass** *n* cálice *m* (de vinho); **wine list** *n* lista de vinhos; **wine waiter** *n* garção *m* dos vinhos

wing [wɪŋ] *n* asa; *cf* (*of building*) ala; (*AUT*) aleta, pára-lamas *m inv*; **~s** *npl* (*THEATRE*) bastidores *mpl*

wink [wɪŋk] *n* piscadela ♦ *vi* piscar o olho; (*light etc*) piscar

winner ['wɪnə*] *n* vencedor(a) *m/f*

winning ['wɪnɪŋ] *adj* (*team*) vencedor(a); (*goal*) decisivo; (*smile*) sedutor(a); **winnings** *npl* ganhos *mpl*

winter ['wɪntə*] *n* inverno; **winter sports** *npl* esportes *mpl* (*BR*) or desportos *mpl* (*PT*) de inverno

wipe [waɪp] *n*: **to give sth a ~** limpar algo com um pano ♦ *vt* limpar; (*rub*) esfregar; (*erase: tape*) apagar; **wipe off** *vt* remover esfregando; **wipe out** *vt* (*debt*) liquidar; (*memory*) apagar; (*destroy*) exterminar; **wipe up** *vt* limpar

wire ['waɪə*] *n* arame *m*; (*ELEC*) fio (elétrico); (*telegram*) telegrama *m* ♦ *vt* (*house*) instalar a rede elétrica em; (*also*: **~ up**) conectar; (*telegram*) telegrafar para

wiring ['waɪərɪŋ] *n* instalação *f* elétrica

wiry ['waɪərɪ] *adj* nervoso; (*hair*) grosso

wisdom ['wɪzdəm] *n* prudência; (*of action, remark*) bom-senso, sabedoria; **wisdom tooth** (*irreg*) *n* dente *m* do siso

wise [waɪz] *adj* prudente; (*action, remark*) sensato

wish [wɪʃ] *n* desejo ♦ *vt* (*want*) querer; **best ~es** (*on birthday etc*) parabéns *mpl*, felicidades *fpl*; **with best ~es** (*in letter*) cumprimentos; **to ~ sb goodbye** despedir-se de alguém; **he ~ed me well** me desejou boa sorte; **to ~ to do/sb to do sth** querer fazer/que alguém faça algo; **to ~ for** desejar; **wishful** *adj*: **it's wishful thinking** é doce ilusão

wistful ['wɪstful] *adj* melancólico

wit [wɪt] *n* (*wittiness*) presença de espírito, engenho; (*intelligence: also*: **~s**) entendimento; (*person*) espirituoso(-a)

witch [wɪtʃ] *n* bruxa

with [wɪð, wɪθ] *prep* **1** *(accompanying, in the company of)* com; **I was ~ him** eu estava com ele; **to stay overnight ~ friends** dormir na casa de amigos; **we'll take the children ~ us** vamos levar as crianças conosco; **I'll be ~ you in a minute** vou vê-lo num minuto; **I'm ~ you** *(I understand)* compreendo; **to be ~ it** *(inf)* estar por dentro; *(aware)* estar a par da situação; (: *up-to-date)* estar atualizado com
2 *(descriptive)* com, de; **a room ~ a view** um quarto com vista; **the man ~ the grey hat/blue eyes** o homem do chapéu cinza/de olhos azuis
3 *(indicating manner, means, cause)* com, de; **~ tears in her eyes** com os olhos cheios de lágrimas; **to fill sth ~ water** encher algo de água

withdraw [wɪð'drɔ:] *(irreg)* vt tirar, remover; *(offer)* retirar ♦ *vi* retirar-se; **to ~ money (from the bank)** retirar dinheiro (do banco); **withdrawal** *n* retirada; **withdrawal symptoms** *npl* síndrome *f* de abstinência; **withdrawn** *adj* *(person)* reservado, introvertido
wither ['wɪðə*] *vi* murchar
withhold [wɪð'həuld] *(irreg: like* **hold**) vt *(money)* reter; *(permission)* negar; *(information)* ocultar
within [wɪð'ɪn] *prep* dentro de ♦ *adv* dentro; **~ reach (of)** ao alcance (de); **~ sight (of)** à vista (de); **~ the week** antes do fim da semana; **~ a mile of** a uma milha de
without [wɪð'aut] *prep* sem; **~ anybody knowing** sem ninguém saber; **to go ~ sth** passar sem algo
withstand [wɪð'stænd] *(irreg: like* **stand**) vt resistir a

witness ['wɪtnɪs] *n* testemunha ♦ *vt* testemunhar, presenciar; *(document)* legalizar; **to bear ~ to sth** *(fig)* testemunhar algo; **witness box** *(US* ~ **stand**) *n* banco das testemunhas
witty ['wɪtɪ] *adj* espirituoso
wives [waɪvz] *npl of* **wife**
wizard ['wɪzəd] *n* feiticeiro, mago
wk *abbr* = **week**
wobble ['wɔbl] *vi* oscilar; *(chair)* balançar
woe [wəu] *n* dor f, mágoa
woke [wəuk] *pt of* **wake**; **woken** *pp* **of wake**
wolf [wulf] *(pl* **wolves**) *n* lobo
woman ['wumən] *(pl* **women**) *n* mulher f; **~ doctor** médica
womb [wu:m] *n* *(ANAT)* matriz f, útero
women ['wɪmɪn] *npl of* **woman**
won [wʌn] *pt, pp of* **win**
wonder ['wʌndə*] *n* maravilha, prodígio; *(feeling)* espanto ♦ *vi* perguntar-se a si mesmo; **to ~ at** admirar-se de; **to ~ about** pensar sobre or em; **it's no ~ that** não é de admirar que; **wonderful** *adj* maravilhoso; *(miraculous)* impressionante
won't [wəunt] = **will not**
wood [wud] *n* *(timber)* madeira f; *(forest)* floresta, bosque *m*; **wood carving** *n* *(act)* escultura em madeira; *(object)* entalhe em; **wooded** *adj* arborizado; **wooden** *adj* de madeira; *(fig)* inexpressivo; **woodpecker** *n* pica-pau *m*; **woodwind** *n* *(MUS)* instrumentos *mpl* de sopro de madeira; **woodwork** *n* carpintaria; **woodworm** *n* carcoma, caruncho
wool [wul] *n* lã f; **to pull the ~ over sb's eyes** *(fig)* enganar alguém, vender a alguém gato por lebre; **woollen** *adj* de lã; **woolly** *(US*

wooly adj de lã; (fig) confuso

word [wɜːd] n palavra; (news) notícia ♦ vt redigir; **in other ~s** em outras palavras, ou seja; **to break/ keep one's ~** faltar à palavra/cumprir a promessa; **to have ~s with sb** discutir com alguém; **wording** n fraseado; **word processing** n processamento de textos; **word processor** n processador m de textos

wore [wɔː*] pt of **wear**

work [wɜːk] n trabalho; (job) emprego, trabalho; (ART, LITERATURE) obra ♦ vi trabalhar; (mechanism) funcionar; (medicine etc) surtir efeito, ser eficaz ♦ vt (clay) moldar; (wood) talhar; (mine etc) explorar; (machine) fazer trabalhar, manejar; (effect, miracle) causar; to ~ **loose** (part) soltar-se; (knot) afrouxar-se; **work on** vt fus trabalhar em, dedicar-se a; (person: influence) tentar convencer; (principle) basear-se em; **work out** vi dar certo, sair efeito ♦ vt (problem) resolver; (plan) elaborar, formular; **it ~s out at £100** monta or soma a £100; **workaholic** [wɜːkə'hɒlɪk] n burro de carga; **worker** n trabalhador(a) m/f, operário(-a); **working class** n proletariado, classe f operária ♦ adj; **working-class** do proletariado, da classe operária; **working order** n: **in working order** em perfeito estado; **workman** (irreg) n operário, trabalhador m; **workmanship** n (skill) habilidade f; **workshop** n oficina; (practical session) aula prática; **work station** n estação f de trabalho

world [wɜːld] n mundo ♦ cpd mundial; **to think the ~ of sb** (fig) ter alguém em alto conceito; **worldly** adj mundano; (knowledgeable) experiente; **worldwide** adj mundial, universal

worm [wɜːm] n (also: **earth~**) minhoca, lombriga

worn [wɔːn] pp of **wear** ♦ adj gasto; **worn-out** adj (object) gasto; (person) esgotado, exausto

worry ['wʌrɪ] n preocupação ♦ vt preocupar, inquietar ♦ vi preocupar-se, afligir-se

worse [wɜːs] adj, adv pior ♦ n o pior; **a change for the ~** uma mudança para pior, uma piora; **worsen** vt, vi piorar; **worse off** adj com menos dinheiro; (fig): **you'll be worse off this way** assim você ficará pior que nunca

worship ['wɜːʃɪp] n adoração ♦ vt adorar, venerar; (person, thing) adorar; **Your W~** (BRIT: to mayor) vossa Excelência; (: to judge) senhor Juiz

worst [wɜːst] adj (o a) pior ♦ adv pior ♦ n o pior; **at ~** na pior das hipóteses

worth [wɜːθ] n valor m, mérito ♦ adj: **to be ~** valer; **it's ~ it** vale a pena; **to be ~ one's while (to do)** valer a pena (fazer); **worthless** adj (person) imprestável; (thing) inútil; **worthwhile** adj (activity) que vale a pena; (cause) de mérito, louvável

worthy ['wɜːðɪ] adj (person) merecedor(a), respeitável; (motive) justo, ~ **of** digno de

╔══════════════════════╗
║ KEYWORD ║
╚══════════════════════╝

would [wud] aux vb **1** (conditional tense): **if you asked him, he ~ do it** se você pedisse, ele faria isto; **if you had asked him, he ~ have done it** se você tivesse pedido, ele teria feito o que

2 (in offers, invitations, requests): ~ **you like a biscuit?** você quer um biscoito?; ~ **you ask him to come in?** pode pedir a ele para entrar?;

you close the door, please? quer fechar a porta, por favor?
3 (in indirect speech): **I said I ~ do it** eu disse que eu faria isto
4 (emphatic) **you WOULD say that, ~n't you?** é lógico que você vai dizer isso
5 (insistence): **she ~n't behave** não houve feito dela se comportar
6 (conjecture): **it ~ have been midnight** devia ser meia-noite; **it ~ seem so** parece que sim
7 (indicating habit): **he ~ go on Mondays** costumava ir às segundas-feiras

wouldn't ['wudnt] = **would not**
wound¹ [waund] pt, pp of **wind²**
wound² [wu:nd] n ferida ♦ vt ferir
wove [wəuv] pt of **weave**; **woven** pp of **weave**
wrap [ræp] n (stole) xale m; (cape) capa ♦ vt (cover) envolver; (also: ~ up) embrulhar; (wind: tape etc) amarrar; **wrapper** n invólucro; (BRIT: of book) capa; **wrapping paper** n papel m de embrulho; (fancy) papel de presente
wreak [ri:k] vt: **to ~ havoc (on)** causar estragos (em); **to ~ vengeance on** vingar-se em, tirar vingança de
wreath [ri:θ] n coroa
wreck [rɛk] n (vehicle) destroços mpl; (ship) restos mpl do naufrágio; (pej: person) ruína, caco ♦ vt destruir, danificar; (fig) arruinar, arrasar; **wreckage** n (of car, plane) destroços mpl; (of ship) restos mpl (of building) escombros mpl
wren [rɛn] n (ZOOL) carriça
wrench [rɛntʃ] n (TECH) chave f inglesa; (tug) puxão m; (fig) separação f penosa ♦ vt torcer com força; **to ~ sth from sb** arrancar algo de alguém

wrestle ['rɛsl] vi: **to ~ (with sb)** lutar (com or contra alguém); **wrestler** n lutador m; **wrestling** n luta (livre)
wretched ['rɛtʃid] adj desventurado, infeliz; (inf) maldito
wriggle ['rigl] vi (also: ~ about) retorcer-se, contorcer-se
wring [rin] (pt, pp **wrung**) vt (clothes, neck) torcer; (hands) apertar; (fig): **to ~ sth out of sb** arrancar algo de alguém
wrinkle ['riŋkl] n (on skin) ruga; (on paper) prega ♦ vt franzir ♦ vi enrugar-se
wrist [rist] n pulso; **wristwatch** n relógio m de pulso
write [rait] (pt **wrote**, pp **written**) vt escrever; (cheque, prescription) passar ♦ vi escrever; **to ~ to sb** escrever para alguém; **write down** vt (note) anotar; (put on paper) pôr no papel; **write off** vt cancelar; **write out** vt escrever por extenso; (cheque etc) passar; **write up** vt redigir; **write-off** n perda total; **writer** n escritor(a) m/f
writing ['raitiŋ] n escrita; (hand~) caligrafia, letra; (of author) obra; **in ~** por escrito
wrong [rɔŋ] adj (bad) errado, mau; (unfair) injusto; (incorrect) errado, equivocado; (inappropriate) impróprio ♦ adv mal, errado ♦ n injustiça ♦ vt ser injusto com; **you are ~ to do it** você se engana ao fazê-lo; **you are ~ about that, you've got it ~** você está enganado sobre isso; **to be in the ~** não ter razão; **what's ~?** o que é que há?; **to go ~** (person) desencaminhar-se; (plan) dar errado; (machine) sofrer uma avaria; **wrongful** ['rɔŋful] adj injusto; **wrongly** ['rɔŋli] adv errado

wrote [rəut] *pt of* write
wrung [rʌŋ] *pt, pp of* wring
wt. *abbr* = weight
WWW *n abbr* (= World Wide Web):
the ~ a WWW

X

Xmas ['ɛksməs] *n abbr* = Christmas
X-ray [eks'reɪ] *n* radiografia ♦ *vt*
radiografar, tirar uma chapa de

Y

yacht [jɔt] *n* iate *m*; **yachting** *n*
iatismo
Yank [jæŋk] (*pej*) *n* ianque *m/f*
yap [jæp] *vi* (*dog*) ganir
yard [jɑːd] *n* pátio, quintal *m*;
(*measure*) jarda (*914 mm; 3 feet*)
yarn [jɑːn] *n* fio; (*tale*) história inverossímil
yawn [jɔːn] *n* bocejo ♦ *vi* bocejar
yd *abbr* = yard(s)
yeah [jɛə] (*inf*) *adv* é
year [jɪə*] *n* ano; **to be 8 ~s old** ter
8 anos; **an eight-~-old child** uma
criança de oito anos (de idade);
yearly *adj* anual ♦ *adv* anualmente
yearn [jɔːn] *vi*: **to ~ to do/for sth**
ansiar fazer/por algo
yeast [jiːst] *n* levedura, fermento
yell [jɛl] *n* grito, berro ♦ *vi* gritar,
berrar
yellow ['jɛləu] *adj* amarelo
yes [jɛs] *adv, n* sim *m*
yesterday ['jɛstədɪ] *adv, n* ontem *m*
yet [jɛt] *adv* ainda ♦ *conj* porém, no
entanto; **the best ~** o melhor até
agora; **as ~** até agora, ainda
yew [juː] *n* teixo
yield [jiːld] *n* (*AGR*) colheita; (*COMM*)
rendimento ♦ *vt* produzir; (*profit*)

render; (*surrender*) ceder ♦ *vi*
render-se, ceder; (*US: AUT*) ceder
YMCA *n abbr* (= Young Men's
Christian Association) ≈ ACM *f*
yog(h)ourt ['jəugət] *n* iogurte *m*
yoke [jəuk] *n* (*of oxen*) junta; (*fig*)
jugo
yolk [jəuk] *n* gema (do ovo)

KEYWORD

you [juː] *pron* **1** (*subj: sg*) tu, você;
(: *pl*) vós, vocês; **~ French enjoy
your food** vocês franceses gostam
de comer; **~ and I will go** nós iremos
2 (*direct object: sg*) te, o (a); (: *pl*)
vos, os (as); (*indirect object: sg*) te,
lhe; (: *pl*) vos, lhes; **I know ~** eu te
conheço; **I gave it to ~** dei isto para
você
3 (*stressed*) você; **I told YOU to do
it** eu disse para você fazer isto
4 (*after prep, in comparisons: sg*) ti,
você; (: *pl*) vós, vocês; (*polite form:
sg*) o senhor (a senhora); (: *pl*) os
senhores (as senhoras); **it's for ~**
para você; **with ~** contigo, com
você; convosco, com vocês; com o
senhor *etc*
5 (*impers: one*): **~ never know**
nunca se sabe; **apples do ~ good** as
maçãs fazem bem à saúde

you'd [juːd] = **you had**; **you would**
you'll [juːl] = **you will**; **you shall**
young [jʌŋ] *adj* jovem ♦ *npl* (*of animal*) filhotes *mpl*, crias *fpl*; (*people*): **the ~** a juventude, os jovens;
younger [jʌŋgə*] *adj* mais novo;
youngster *n* jovem *m/f*, moço(-a)
your [jɔː*] *adj* teu (tua), seu (sua);
(*pl*) vosso, seu (sua); (*formal*) do
senhor (da senhora); *see also* **my**
you're [juə*] = **you are**
yours [jɔːz] *pron* teu (tua), seu (sua);
(*pl*) vosso, seu (sua); (*formal*) do

senhor (da senhora); **~ sincerely** or **faithfully** atenciosamente; *see also* **mine¹**

yourself [jɔːˈsɛlf] *pron (emphatic)* tu mesmo, você mesmo; *(object, reflexive)* te, se; *(after prep)* ti mesmo, si mesmo; *(formal)* o senhor mesmo (a senhora mesma); *see also* **oneself**

yourselves *pl, pron* vós mesmos, vocês mesmos; vos, se; vós mesmos, vocês mesmos; os senhores mesmos (as senhoras mesmas); *see also* **oneself**

youth [juːθ] *n* mocidade f, juventude f; *(young man)* jovem *m*; **youth club** *n* associação f de juventude; **youthful** *adj* juvenil; **youth hostel** *n* albergue *m* da juventude

you've [juːv] = **you have**

YTS *(BRIT) n abbr (= Youth Training Scheme) programa de ensino profissionalizante*

Yugoslav [ˈjuːgəuslɑːv] *adj, n* iugoslavo(-a)

Yugoslavia [juːgəuˈslɑːvɪə] *n* Iugoslávia

yuppie [ˈjʌpɪ] *(inf) adj, n* yuppie *m/f*

YWCA *n abbr (= Young Women's Christian Association)* ≈ ACM f

Z

zany [ˈzeɪnɪ] *adj* tolo, bobo

zap [zæp] *vt (COMPUT)* apagar

zebra [ˈziːbrə] *n* zebra; **zebra crossing** *(BRIT) n* faixa (para pedestres) *(BR)*, passadeira *(PT)*

zero [ˈzɪərəu] *n* zero

zest [zɛst] *n* vivacidade f, entusiasmo; *(of lemon etc)* zesto

zigzag [ˈzɪgzæg] *n* ziguezague *m* ♦ *vi* ziguezaguear

Zimbabwe [zɪmˈbɑːbwɪ] *n* Zimbábue *m*

zinc [zɪŋk] *n* zinco

zip [zɪp] *n (also: ~ fastener)* fecho ecler *(BR)* or éclair *(PT)* ♦ *vt (also: ~ up)* fechar o fecho ecler de, subir o fecho ecler de; **zip code** *(US) n* código postal; **zipper** *(US)* = **zip**

zodiac [ˈzəudɪæk] *n* zodíaco

zone [zəun] *n* zona

zoo [zuː] *n* (jardim *m*) zoológico

zoom [zuːm] *vi*: **to ~** *past* passar zunindo; **zoom lens** *n* zoom *m*, zum *m*

zucchini [zuːˈkiːnɪ] *(US) n(pl)* abobrinha

PORTUGUÊS-INGLÊS
PORTUGUESE-ENGLISH

A

PALAVRA CHAVE

a [a] (*a* + *o(s)* = ao(s); *a* + *a(s)* =
à(s); *a* + *aquele/a(s)* = àquele/a(s))
art def the; *V tb* **o**
♦ *pron* (*ela*) her; (*você*) you; (*coisa*)
it; *V tb* **o**
♦ *prep* **1** (*direção*) to; **à direita/
esquerda** to ou on the right/left
2 (*distância*): **está ~ 15 km daqui** it's
15 km from here
3 (*posição*): **ao lado de** beside, at
the side of
4 (*tempo*) at; **~ que horas?** at what
time?; **às 5 horas** at 5 o'clock; **à
noite** at night; **aos 15 anos** at 15
years of age
5 (*maneira*): **à francesa** in the
French way; **~ cavalo/pé** on horse-
back/foot
6 (*meio, instrumento*): **à força** by
force; **~ mão** by hand; **~ lápis** in
pencil; **fogão ~ gás** gas stove
7 (*razão*): **~ R$1 o quilo** at R$1 a
kilo; **~ mais de 100 km/h** at over
100 km/h
8 (*depois de certos verbos*): **começou
~ nevar** it started snowing ou to
snow; **passar ~ fazer** to become
9 (+ *infin*): **ao vê-lo, o reconheci
imediatamente** when I saw him, I
recognized him immediately; **ele
ficou muito nervoso ao falar com o
professor** he became very nervous
while he was talking to the teacher
10 (*PT*: + *infin*: *gerúndio*): **~ correr**
running; **estou ~ trabalhar** I'm
working

à [a] = **a** + **a**

(a) *abr* (= *assinado*) signed
aba ['aba] *f* (*de chapéu*) brim; (*de
casaco*) tail; (*de montanha*) foot
abacate [aba'katʃi] *m* avocado
(pear)
abacaxi [abaka'ʃi] (*BR*) *m* pineapple
abade, ssa [a'badʒi, aba'desa] *m/f*
abbot/abbess; **abadia** [aba'dʒia] *f*
abbey
abafado, -a [aba'fadu, a] *adj* (*ar*)
stuffy; (*tempo*) humid, close; (*ocupado*) (extremely) busy; (*angustia-
do*) anxious
abafar [aba'fa*] *vt* to suffocate,
(*ocultar*) to suppress; (*col*) to pinch
abagunçar [abagũ'sa*] *vt* to mess
up
abaixar [abaj'ʃa*] *vt* to lower; (*luz,
som*) to turn down; **abaixar-se** *vr*
to stoop
abaixo [a'bajʃu] *adv* down ♦ *prep*: **~
de** below; **~ o governo!** down with
the government!; **morro ~** downhill; **rio ~** downstream; **mais ~** further down; **~ e acima** up and
down; **~ assinado** undersigned;
abaixo-assinado [-asi'nadu] (*pl*
abaixo-assinados) *m* petition
abalado, -a [aba'ladu, a] *adj* (*objeto*) unstable, unsteady; (*fig: pessoa*)
shaken
abalar [aba'la*] *vt* to shake; (*fig:
comover*) to affect ♦ *vi* to shake;
abalar-se *vr* to be moved
abalo [a'balu] *m* (*comoção*) shock;
(*ação*) shaking; **~ sísmico** earth
tremor
abanar [aba'na*] *vt* to shake; (*rabo*)
to wag; (*com leque*) to fan
abandonar [abãdo'na*] *vt* to leave;

(idéia) to reject; (esperança) to give up; (descuidar) to neglect; **abandonar-se** vr: **~-se a** to abandon o.s. to; **abandono** [abã'donu] m (ato) desertion; (estado) neglect

abarcar [abax'ka*] vt (abranger: assunto, país) to cover; (: suj: vista) to take in

abarrotado, -a [abaxo'tadu, a] adj (gaveta) crammed full; (lugar) packed

abastado, -a [abaʃ'tadu, a] adj wealthy

abastecer [abaʃte'se*] vt to supply; (motor) to fuel; (AUTO) to fill up; (AER) to refuel; **abastecer-se** vr: **~-se de** to stock up with

abastecimento [abaʃtesi'mẽtu] m supply; (comestíveis) provisions pl; (ato) supplying; **~s** mpl (suprimentos) supplies

abater [aba'te*] vt (gado) to slaughter; (preço) to reduce; (desalentar) to upset; **abatido, -a** [aba'tʃidu, a] adj depressed, downcast; **abatimento** [abatʃi'mẽtu] m (fraqueza) weakness; (de preço) reduction; (prostração) depression; **fazer um abatimento em** to give a discount on

abdicar [abdʒi'ka*] vt, vi to abdicate

abdômen [ab'domẽ] m abdomen

á-bê-cê [abe'se] m alphabet

abecedário [abese'darju] m alphabet, ABC

abelha [a'beʎa] f bee

abelhudo, -a [abe'ʎudu, a] adj nosy

abençoar [abẽ'swa*] vt to bless

aberto, -a [a'bɛxtu, a] pp de **abrir** ♦ adj open; (céu) clear; (sinal) green; (torneira) running; **a torneira estava aberta** the tap was on

abertura [abex'tura] f opening; (FOTO) aperture; (ranhura) gap, crevice; (POL) liberalization

abestalhado, -a [abeʃta'ʎadu, a] adj stupid

abismado, -a [abiʒ'madu, a] adj astonished

abismo [a'biʒmu] m abyss, chasm; (fig) depths pl

abjeção [abʒe'sãw] (PT **-cç-**) f baseness

abjeto, -a [ab'ʒetu, a] (PT **-ct-**) adj abject, contemptible

ABL abr f = **Academia Brasileira de Letras**

abnegação [abnega'sãw] f self-denial

abnegado, -a [abne'gadu, a] adj self-sacrificing

abnegar [abne'ga*] vt to renounce

abóbada [a'bɔbada] f vault; (telhado) arched roof

abobalhado, -a [aboba'ʎadu, a] adj (criança) simple

abóbora [a'bɔbora] f pumpkin

abobrinha [abo'briɲa] f courgette (BRIT), zucchini (US)

abolir [abo'li*] vt to abolish

abonar [abo'na*] vt to guarantee

abono [a'bɔnu] m guarantee; (JUR) bail; (louvor) praise; **~ de família** child benefit

abordar [abox'da*] vt (NÁUT) to board; (pessoa) to approach; (assunto) to broach, tackle

aborrecer [aboxe'se*] vt (chatear) to annoy; (maçar) to bore; **aborrecer-se** vr to get upset; to get bored; **aborrecido, -a** [aboxe'sidu, a] adj annoyed; boring; **aborrecimento** [aboxesi'mẽtu] m annoyance; boredom

abortar [abox'ta*] vi (MED) to have a miscarriage; (: de propósito) to have an abortion; **aborto** [a'boxtu] m miscarriage; abortion; **fazer/ter um aborto** to have an abortion/a miscarriage

abotoadura [abotwa'dura] f cufflink

abotoar [abo'twa*] vt to button up ♦ vi (BOT) to bud

abraçar [abra'sa*] vt to hug; (causa) to embrace; **abraçar-se** vr to embrace; **ele abraçou-se a mim** he embraced me; **abraço** [a'brasu] m embrace, hug; **com um abraço** (em carta) with best wishes

abrandar [abrã'da*] vt to reduce; (suavizar) to soften ♦ vi to diminish; (acalmar) to calm down

abranger [abrã'ʒe*] vt (assunto) to cover; (alcançar) to reach

abre-garrafas ['abri-] (PT) m inv bottle opener

abre-latas ['abri-] (PT) m inv tin (BRIT) ou can opener

abreviar [abre'vja*] vt to abbreviate; (texto) to abridge; **abreviatura** [abrevja'tura] f abbreviation

abridor [abri'do*] (BR) m: ~ de (lata) tin (BRIT) ou can opener, ~ de garrafa bottle opener

abrigar [abri'ga*] vt to shelter; (proteger) to protect; **abrigar-se** vr to take shelter

abrigo [a'brigu] m shelter, cover; ~ **anti-aéreo** air-raid shelter; ~ **anti-nuclear** fall-out shelter

abril [a'briw] (PT A~) m April; **25 de Abril** (PT) see boxed note

25 DE ABRIL

On 25 April 1974 in Portugal, the MAF (Armed Forces Movement) instigated the bloodless revolution that was to topple the 48-year-old dictatorship presided over until 1968 by António de Oliveira Salazar. The red carnation has come to symbolize the coup, as it is said that the Armed Forces took to the streets with carnations in the barrels of their rifles. 25 April is now a public holiday in Portugal.

abrir [a'bri*] vt to open; (fechadura) to unlock; (vestuário) to unfasten; (torneira) to turn on; (exceção) to make ♦ vi to open; (sinal) to turn green; **abrir-se** vr: ~**se com alguém** to confide in sb

abrupto, -a [a'bruptu, a] adj abrupt; (repentino) sudden

absolutamente [absoluta'mẽtʃi] adv absolutely; (em resposta) absolutely not, not at all

absoluto, -a [abso'lutu, a] adj absolute; **em ~** absolutely not, not at all

absolver [absow've*] vt to absolve; (JUR) to acquit; **absolvição** [absowvi'sãw] (pl -ões) f absolution; acquittal

absorto, -a [ab'soxtu, a] pp de absorver ♦ adj absorbed, engrossed

absorvente [absox'vẽtʃi] adj (papel etc) absorbent; (livro etc) absorbing

absorver [absox've*] vt to absorb; **absorver-se** vr: ~**se em** to concentrate on

abstêmio, -a [abʃ'temju, a] adj abstemious; (álcool) teetotal ♦ m/f abstainer; teetotaller (BRIT), teetotaler (US)

abster-se [abʃ'texsi] (irreg: como ter) vr: ~ **de** to abstain ou refrain from

abstinência [abʃtʃi'nẽsja] f abstinence; (jejum) fasting

abstracto, -a [abʃ'tratu, a] (PT) adj = abstrato

abstrair [abʃtra'i*] vt to abstract; (omitir) to omit; (separar) to separate

abstrato, -a [abʃ'tratu, a] adj abstract

absurdo, -a [abi'suxdu, a] adj absurd ♦ m nonsense

abundante [abũ'dãtʃi] adj abundant; **abundar** [abũ'da*] *vi* to abound

abusar [abu'za*] *vi* to go too far; ~ **de** to abuse

abuso [a'buzu] *m* abuse; (*JUR*) indecent assault

a.C. *abr* (= *antes de Cristo*) B.C.

a/c *abr* (= *aos cuidados de*) c/o

acabado, -a [aka'badu, a] *adj* finished; (*esgotado*) worn out

acabamento [akaba'mẽtu] *m* finish

acabar [aka'ba*] *vt* to finish, complete; (*consumir*) to use up; (*rematar*) to finish off ♦ *vi* to finish, end; **acabar-se** *vr* to be over; (*prazo*) to expire; (*esgotar-se*) to run out; ~ **com** to put an end to; ~ **de chegar** to have just arrived; ~ **por fazer** to end up (by) doing; **acabou-se!** it's all over!; (*basta!*) that's enough!

academia [akade'mia] *f* academy; **A~ Brasileira de Letras** *see boxed note*

ACADEMIA BRASILEIRA DE LETRAS

Founded in 1896 in Rio de Janeiro, on the initiative of the author Machado de Assis, the **Academia Brasileira de Letras**, or ABL, aims to preserve and develop the Portuguese language and Brazilian literature. Machado de Assis was its president until 1908. It is made up of forty life members known as the *imortais*. The Academia's activities include publication of reference books, promotion of literary prizes, and running a library, museum and archive.

---

acadêmico, -a [aka'demiku, a] *adj, m/f* academic

açafrão [asa'frãw] *m* saffron

acalmar [akaw'ma*] *vt* to calm ♦ *vi* (*vento etc*) to abate; **acalmar-se** *vr* to calm down

acamado, -a [aka'madu, a] *adj* bedridden

acampamento [akãpa'mẽtu] *m* camping; (*MIL*) camp, encampment

acampar [akã'pa*] *vi* to camp

acanhado, -a [aka'ɲadu, a] *adj* shy

acanhamento [akaɲa'mẽtu] *m* shyness

acanhar-se [aka'ɲaxsi] *vr* to be shy

ação [a'sãw] (*pl* **-ões**) *f* action; (*ato*) act, deed; (*MIL*) battle; (*enredo*) plot; (*JUR*) lawsuit; (*COM*) share; ~ **ordinária/preferencial** (*COM*) ordinary/preference share

acarajé [akara'ʒɛ] *m* (*CULIN*) beans fried in palm oil

acariciar [akari'sja*] *vt* to caress; (*fig*) to cherish

acarretar [akaxe'ta*] *vt* to result in, bring about

acaso [a'kazu] *m* chance; **ao** ~ at random; **por** ~ by chance

acatar [aka'ta*] *vt* to respect; (*lei*) to obey

acção [a'sãw] (*PT*) *f* = **ação**

accionar *etc* [asjo'na*] (*PT*) = **acionar** *etc*

aceitação [asejta'sãw] *f* acceptance; (*aprovação*) approval

aceitar [asej'ta*] *vt* to accept; (*aprovar*) to approve; **aceitável** [asej'tavew] (*pl* **-eis**) *adj* acceptable; **aceito, -a** [a'sejtu, a] *pp de* **aceitar**

acelerado, -a [asele'radu, a] *adj* (*rápido*) quick; (*apressado*) hasty

acelerador [aselera'do*] *m* accelerator

acelerar [asele'ra*] *vt* (*AUTO*): ~ **o carro** to accelerate; (*ritmo, negociações*) to speed up ♦ *vi* to accelerate; ~ **o passo** to go faster

acenar [ase'na*] *vi* (*com a mão*) to

wave; (*com a cabeça: afirmativo*) to nod; (: *negativo*) to shake one's head

acender [asē'de*] *vt* (*cigarro, fogo*) to light; (*luz*) to switch on; (*fig*) to excite, inflame

aceno [a'sɛnu] *m* sign, gesture; (*com a mão*) wave; (*com a cabeça: afirmativo*) nod; (: *negativo*) shake

acento [a'sētu] *m* accent; (*de intensidade*) stress; **acentuar** [asē'twa*] *vt* to accent; (*salientar*) to stress, emphasize

acepção [asep'sāw] (*pl* -ões) *f* (*de uma palavra*) sense

acerca [a'sexka]: ~ **de** *prep* about, concerning

acertado, -a [asex'tadu, a] *adj* right, correct; (*sensato*) sensible

acertar [asex'ta*] *vt* (*ajustar*) to put right; (*relógio*) to set; (*alvo*) to hit; (*acordo*) to reach; (*pergunta*) to get right ♦ *vi* to get it right, be right; ~ **o caminho** to find the right way; ~ **com** to hit upon

aceso, -a [a'sezu, a] *pp de* **acender** ♦ *adj*: **a luz estava acesa/o fogo estava** ~ the light was on/the fire was alight; (*excitado*) excited; (*furioso*) furious

acessar [ase'sa*] *vt* (*COMPUT*) to access

acessível [ase'sivew] (*pl* -eis) *adj* accessible; (*pessoa*) approachable

acesso [a'sɛsu] *m* access; (*MED*) fit, attack

acessório, -a [ase'sɔrju, a] *adj* (*máquina, equipamento*) backup; (*EDUC*): **matéria acessória** subsidiary subject ♦ *m* accessory

achado, -a [a'ʃadu, a] *m* find, discovery; (*pechincha*) bargain; (*sorte*) godsend

achar [a'ʃa*] *vt* (*descobrir*) to find; (*pensar*) to think; **achar-se** *vr* to

think (that) one is; (*encontrar-se*) to be; ~ **de fazer** (*resolver*) to decide to do; **o que é que você acha disso?** what do you think of that?; **acho que sim** I think so

achatar [aʃa'ta*] *vt* to squash, flatten

acidentado, -a [asidē'tadu, a] *adj* (*terreno*) rough; (*estrada*) bumpy; (*viagem*) eventful; (*vida*) difficult ♦ *m/f* injured person

acidental [asidē'taw] (*pl* -ais) *adj* accidental

acidente [asi'dētʃi] *m* accident; **por** ~ by accident

acidez [asi'deʒ] *f* acidlty

ácido, -a [a'sidu, a] *adj* acid; (*azedo*) sour ♦ *m* acid

acima [a'sima] *adv* above; (*para cima*) up ♦ *prep*: ~ **de** above; (*além de*) beyond; **mais** ~ higher up; **rio** ~ up river; **passar rua** ~ to go up the street; ~ **de 1000** more than 1000

aclonado, -a [asjo'nadu, a] *m/f* (*JUR*) defendant

acionar [asjo'na*] *vt* to set in motion; (*máquina*) to operate; (*JUR*) to sue

acionista [asjo'niʃta] *m/f* shareholder

acirrado, -a [asi'xadu, a] *adj* (*luta, competição*) tough

acirrar [asi'xa*] *vt* to incite, stir up

aclamação [aklama'sāw] *f* acclamation; (*ovação*) applause

aclamar [akla'ma*] *vt* to acclaim; (*aplaudir*) to applaud

aço [a'su] *m* steel

acocorar-se [akoko'raxsi] *vr* to squat, crouch

acode *etc* [a'kɔdʒi] *vb V* **acudir**

ações [a'sōjʃ] *fpl de* **ação**

açoitar [asoj'ta*] *vt* to whip, lash; **açoite** [a'sojtʃi] *m* whip, lash

acolá [ako'la] *adv* over there

acolchoado [akow'ʃwadu] *m* quilt
acolhedor, a [akoʎe'do*, a] *adj* welcoming; (*hospitaleiro*) hospitable
acolher [ako'ʎe*] *vt* to welcome; (*abrigar*) to shelter; (*aceitar*) to accept; **acolher-se** *vr* to shelter;
acolhida [ako'ʎida] *f* (*recepção*) reception, welcome; (*refúgio*) refuge; **acolhimento** [akoʎi'mẽtu] *m* = **acolhida**
acomodação [akomoda'sãw] (*pl* -ões) *f* accommodation; (*arranjo*) arrangement; (*adaptação*) adaptation
acomodar [akomo'da*] *vt* to accommodate; (*arrumar*) to arrange; (*adaptar*) to adapt
acompanhamento [akõpaɲa'mẽtu] *m* attendance; (*cortejo*) procession; (*MÚS*) accompaniment; (*CULIN*) side dish
acompanhante [akõpa'ɲãtʃi] *m/f* companion; (*MÚS*) accompanist
acompanhar [akõpa'ɲa*] *vt* to accompany
aconchegante [akõʃe'gãtʃi] *adj* cosy (*BRIT*), cozy (*US*)
aconchego [akõ'ʃegu] *m* cuddle
aconselhar [akõse'ʎa*] *vt* to advise; **aconselhar-se** *vr*: **~-se com** to consult
acontecer [akõte'se*] *vi* to happen; **acontecimento** [akõtesi'mẽtu] *m* event
acordar [akox'da*] *vt* to wake (up); (*concordar*) to agree (on) ♦ *vi* to wake up
acorde [a'kɔrdʒi] *m* chord
acordeão [akox'dʒjãw] (*pl* -ões) *m* accordion
acordo [a'koxdu] *m* agreement; **"de ~!"** "agreed!"; **de ~ com** (*pessoa*) in agreement with; (*conforme*) in accordance with; **estar de ~** to agree

Açores [a'sorif] *mpl*: **os ~** the Azores; **açoriano, -a** [aso'rjanu, a] *adj, m/f* Azorean
acossar [ako'sa*] *vt* (*perseguir*) to pursue; (*atormentar*) to harass
acostamento [akoʃta'mẽtu] *m* hard shoulder (*BRIT*), berm (*US*)
acostumado, -a [akoʃtu'madu, a] *adj* usual, customary; **estar ~ a algo** to be used to sth
acostumar [akoʃtu'ma*] *vt* to accustom; **acostumar-se** *vr*: **~-se a** to get used to
açougue [a'sogi] *m* butcher's (shop); **açougueiro** [aso'gejru] *m* butcher
acovardar-se [akovax'daxsi] *vr* (*desanimar*) to lose courage; (*amedrontar-se*) to flinch, cower
acre ['akri] *adj* (*gosto*) bitter; (*cheiro*) acrid; (*fig*) harsh
acreditado, -a [akredʒi'tadu, a] *adj* accredited
acreditar [akredʒi'ta*] *vt* to believe; (*COM*) to credit; (*afiançar*) to guarantee ♦ *vi*: **~ em** to believe in
acre-doce *adj* (*CULIN*) sweet and sour
acrescentar [akresẽ'ta*] *vt* to add
acrescer [akre'se*] *vt* to increase; (*juntar*) to add ♦ *vi* to increase;
acréscimo [a'kresimu] *m* increase; addition; (*elevação*) rise
activo, -a *etc* [a'tivu, a] (*PT*) = **ativo** *etc*
acto [a'tu] (*PT*) *m* = **ato**
actor [a'to*] (*PT*) *m* = **ator**
actriz [a'triʒ] (*PT*) *f* = **atriz**
actual *etc* [a'twaw] (*PT*) = **atual** *etc*
actuar *etc* [a'twa*] (*PT*) = **atuar** *etc*
açúcar [a'suka*] *m* sugar; **açucareiro** [asuka'rejru] *m* sugar bowl
açude [a'sudʒi] *m* dam
acudir [aku'dʒi*] *vt* (*ir em socorro*) to help, assist ♦ *vi* (*responder*) to

reply, respond; ~ **a** to come to the aid of

acumular [akunu'la*] vt to accumulate; (reunir) to collect; (funções) to combine

acusação [akuza'sãw] (pl -ões) f accusation, charge; (JUR) prosecution

acusar [aku'za*] vt to accuse; (revelar) to reveal; (culpar) to blame; ~ **o recebimento de** to acknowledge receipt of

acústica [a'kuʃtʃika] f (ciência) acoustics sg; (de uma sala) acoustics pl

acústico, -a [a'kuʃtʃiku, a] adj acoustic

adaptar [adap'ta*] vt to adapt; (acomodar) to fit; **adaptar-se** vr: ~-**se a** to adapt to

adega [a'dɛga] f cellar

ademais [adʒi'majʃ] adv besides, moreover

adentro [a'dẽtru] adv inside, in; **mata** ~ into the woods

adepto, -a [a'dɛptu, a] m/f follower; (de time) supporter

adequado, -a [ade'kwadu, a] adj appropriate

adereço [ade'resu] m adornment; **adereços** mpl (TEATRO) stage props

aderente [ade'rẽtʃi] adj adhesive, sticky ♦ m/f supporter

aderir [ade'ri*] vi to adhere

adesão [ade'zãw] f adhesion; (patrocínio) support

adesivo, -a [ade'zivu, a] adj adhesive, sticky ♦ m adhesive tape; (MED) sticking plaster

adestrar [adeʃ'tra*] vt to train; (cavalo) to break in

adeus [a'dewʃ] excl goodbye!

adiamento [adʒja'mẽtu] m postponement; (de uma sessão) adjournment

adiantado, -a [adʒjã'tadu, a] adj advanced; (relógio) fast; **chegar** ~ to arrive ahead of time; **pagar** ~ to pay in advance

adiantamento [adʒjãta'mẽtu] m progress; (dinheiro) advance (payment)

adiantar [adʒjã'ta*] vt (dinheiro, trabalho) to advance; (relógio) to put forward; **não adianta reclamar** there's no point ou it's no use complaining

adiante [a'dʒjãtʃi] adv (na frente) in front; (para a frente) forward; **mais** ~ further on; (no futuro) later on

adiar [a'dʒja*] vt to postpone, put off; (sessão) to adjourn

adição [adʒi'sãw] (pl -ões) f addition; (MAT) sum; **adicionar** [adʒi-sju'na*] vt to add

adido, -a [a'dʒidu, a] m/f attaché

adiro etc [a'diru] vb V **aderir**

adivinhação [adʒivina'sãw] f (destino) fortune-telling; (conjectura) guessing, guesswork

adivinhar [adʒivi'na*] vt to guess; (ler a sorte) to foretell ♦ vi to guess; ~ **o pensamento de alguém** to read sb's mind; **adivinho, -a** [adʒi'vinu, a] m/f fortune-teller

adjetivo [adʒe'tʃivu] m adjective

adjudicar [adʒudʒi'ka*] vt to award, grant

administração [adʒiminiʃtra'sãw] (pl -ões) f administration; (direção) management; (comissão) board

administrador, a [adʒiminiʃtra'do*, a] m/f administrator; (diretor) director; (gerente) manager

administrar [adʒiminiʃ'tra*] vt to administer, manage; (governar) to govern

admiração [adʒimira'sãw] f wonder; (estima) admiration; **ponto de** ~ (PT) exclamation mark

admirado, -a [adʒimiˈradu, a] *adj* astonished, surprised

admirar [adʒimiˈra*] *vt* to admire; **admirar-se** *vr*: ~-**se** **de** to be surprised at; **admirável** [adʒimiˈravew] (*pl* -**eis**) *adj* amazing

admissão [adʒimiˈsãw] (*pl* -**ões**) *f* admission; (*consentimento para entrar*) admittance; (*de escola*) intake

admitir [adʒimiˈtʃi*] *vt* to admit; (*permitir*) to allow; (*funcionário*) to take on

adoção [adoˈsãw] *f* adoption

adoçar [adoˈsa*] *vt* to sweeten

adoecer [adoeˈse*] *vi*: ~ (**de** *ou* **com**) to fall ill (with) ♦ *vt* to make ill

adoidado, -a [adojˈdadu, a] *adj* crazy

adolescente [adoleˈsẽtʃi] *adj*, *m/f* adolescent

adoptar *etc* [adoˈta*] (*PT*) = **adotar** *etc*

adorar [adoˈra*] *vt* to adore; (*venerar*) to worship

adormecer [adoxmeˈse*] *vi* to fall asleep; (*entorpecer-se*) to go numb; **adormecido, -a** [adoxmeˈsidu, a] *adj* sleeping ♦ *m/f* sleeper

adorno [aˈdoxnu] *m* adornment

adotar [adoˈta*] *vt* to adopt; **adotivo, -a** [adoˈtʃivu, a] *adj* (*filho*) adopted

adquirir [adʒikiˈri*] *vt* to acquire

Adriático, -a [aˈdrjatʃiku, a] *adj*: **o** (**mar**) ~ the Adriatic

adro [ˈadru] *m* (church) forecourt; (*em volta da igreja*) churchyard

adulação [adulaˈsãw] *f* flattery

adulterar [aduwteˈra*] *vt* to adulterate; (*contas*) to falsify ♦ *vi* to commit adultery

adultério [aduwˈtɛrju] *m* adultery

adulto, -a [aˈduwtu, a] *adj*, *m/f* adult

advento [adˈvẽtu] *m* advent; **o A~** Advent

advérbio [adˈvexbju] *m* adverb

adverso, -a [adʒiˈvexsu, a] *adj* adverse; (*oposto*): ~ **a** opposed to

advertência [adʒivexˈtẽsja] *f* warning

advertir [adʒivexˈtʃi*] *vt* to warn; (*repreender*) to reprimand; (*chamar a atenção a*) to draw attention to

advogado, -a [adʒivoˈgadu, a] *m/f* lawyer

advogar [adʒivoˈga*] *vt* to advocate; (*JUR*) to plead ♦ *vi* to practise (*BRIT*) *ou* practice (*US*) law

aéreo, -a [aˈɛrju, a] *adj* air *atr*

aerobarco [aeroˈbaxku] *m* hovercraft

aeromoço, -a [aeroˈmosu, a] (*BR*) *m/f* steward/air hostess

aeronáutica [aeroˈnawtʃika] *f* air force; (*ciência*) aeronautics *sg*

aeronave [aeroˈnavi] *f* aircraft

aeroporto [aeroˈpoxtu] *m* airport

aerossol [aeroˈsɔw] (*pl* -**óis**) *m* aerosol

afã [aˈfã] *m* (*entusiasmo*) enthusiasm; (*diligência*) diligence; (*ânsia*) eagerness; (*esforço*) effort

afagar [afaˈga*] *vt* to caress; (*cabelo*) to stroke

afanar [afaˈna*] (*col*) *vt* to nick, pinch

afastado, -a [afaʃˈtadu, a] *adj* (*distante*) remote; (*isolado*) secluded; **manter-se** ~ to keep to o.s.

afastamento [afaʃtaˈmẽtu] *m* removal; (*distância*) distance; (*de pessoal*) lay-off

afastar [afaʃˈta*] *vt* to remove; (*separar*) to separate; (*idéia*) to put out of one's mind; (*pessoal*) to lay off; **afastar-se** *vr* to move away

afável [aˈfavew] (*pl* -**eis**) *adj* friendly

afazeres [afa'zerif] mpl business sg; (dever) duties, tasks; ~ domésticos household chores

afectar etc [afek'ta*] (PT) = **afetar** etc

afeição [afej'sãw] f affection, fondness; (dedicação) devotion; **afeiçoado, -a** [afej'swadu, a] adj: **afeiçoado a** (amoroso) fond of; (devotado) devoted to; **afeiçoar-se** [afej'swaxsi] vr: **afeiçoar-se a** to take a liking to

afeito, -a [a'fejtu, a] adj: ~ a accustomed to, used to

aferrado, -a [afe'xadu, a] adj obstinate, stubborn

afetado, -a [afe'tadu, a] adj affected

afetar [afe'ta*] vt to affect; (fingir) to feign

afetivo, -a [afe'tʃivu, a] adj affectionate; (problema) emotional

afeto [a'fetu] m affection; **afetuoso, -a** [afe'twozu, ɔza] adj affectionate

afiado, -a [a'fjadu, a] adj sharp; (pessoa) well-trained

afiar [a'fja*] vt to sharpen

aficionado, -a [afisjo'nadu, a] m/f enthusiast

afilhado, -a [afi'ʎadu, a] m/f godson/goddaughter

afim [a'fĩ] (pl -ns) adj (semelhante) similar; (consanguíneo) related ♦ m/f relative, relation

afinado, -a [afi'nadu, a] adj in tune

afinal [afi'naw] adv at last, finally; ~ (de contas) after all

afinar [afi'na*] vt (MÚS) to tune

afinco [a'fĩku] m tenacity, persistence

afins [a'fĩʃ] pl de **afim**

afirmação [afixma'sãw] (pl -ões) f affirmation; (declaração) statement

afirmar [afix'ma*] vt, vi to affirm,

assert; (declarar) to declare

afirmativo, -a [afixma'tʃivu, a] adj affirmative

afixar [afik'sa*] vt (cartazes) to stick, post

aflição [afli'sãw] f affliction; (ansiedade) anxiety; (angústia) anguish

afligir [afli'ʒi*] vt to distress; (atormentar) to torment; (inquietar) to worry; **afligir-se** vr: ~-se com to worry about; **aflito, -a** [a'flitu, a] pp de **afligir** ♦ adj distressed, anxious

afluência [a'flwẽsja] f affluence; (corrente copiosa) flow; (de pessoas) stream; **afluente** [a'flwẽtʃi] adj copious; (rico) affluent ♦ m tributary

afobação [afoba'sãw] f fluster; (ansiedade) panic

afobado, -a [a'fo'badu, a] adj flustered; (ansioso) panicky, nervous

afobar [afo'ba*] vt to fluster; (deixar ansioso) to make nervous ou panicky ♦ vi to get flustered, to panic, get nervous; **afobar-se** vr to get flustered

afogar [afo'ga*] vt to drown ♦ vi (AUTO) to flood; **afogar-se** vr to drown

afoito, -a [a'fojtu, a] adj bold, daring

afortunado, -a [afoxtu'nadu, a] adj fortunate, lucky

África ['afrika] f: a ~ Africa; a ~ do Sul South Africa; **africano, -a** [afri'kanu, a] adj, m/f African

afro-brasileiro, -a [a'fru-] (pl ~s) adj Afro-Brazilian

afronta [a'frõta] f insult, affront; **afrontar** [afrõ'ta*] vt to insult; (ofender) to offend

afrouxar [afro'ʃa*] vt (desapertar) to slacken; (soltar) to loosen ♦ vi to come loose

afta ['afta] f (mouth) ulcer

afugentar [afuʒẽ'ta*] vt to drive away, put to flight

afundar [afũ'da*] vt to sink; (cavidade) to deepen; **afundar-se** vr to sink

agachar-se [aga'ʃaxsi] vr (acaçaparse) to crouch, squat; (curvar-se) to stoop

agarrar [aga'xa*] vt to seize, grasp; **agarrar-se** vr: ~-se a to cling to, hold on to

agasalhar [agaza'ʎa*] vt to dress warmly, wrap up; **agasalhar-se** vr to wrap o.s. up

agasalho [aga'zaʎu] m (casaco) coat; (suéter) sweater

ágeis ['aʒejʃ] pl de **ágil**

agência [a'ʒẽsja] f agency; (escritório) office; ~ **de correio** (BR) post office; ~ **de viagens** travel agency

agenda [a'ʒẽda] f diary

agente [a'ʒẽtʃi] m/f agent; (de polícia) policeman/woman

ágil ['aʒiw] (pl -eis) adj agile

agir [a'ʒi*] vi to act

agitação [aʒita'sãw] (pl -ões) f agitation; (perturbação) disturbance; (inquietação) restlessness

agitado, -a [aʒi'tadu, a] adj agitated, disturbed; (inquieto) restless

agitar [aʒi'ta*] vt to agitate, disturb; (sacudir) to shake; (cauda) to wag; (mexer) to stir; **agitar-se** vr to get upset; (mar) to get rough

aglomeração [aglomera'sãw] (pl -ões) f gathering; (multidão) crowd

aglomerado [aglome'radu] m: ~ **urbano** city

aglomerar [aglome'ra*] vt to heap up, pile up; **aglomerar-se** vr (multidão) to crowd together

agonia [ago'nia] f agony, anguish; (ânsia da morte) death throes pl;

agonizante [agoni'zãtʃi] adj dying

♦ m/f dying person; **agonizar** [agoni'za*] vi to be dying; (afligir-se) to agonize

agora [a'gɔra] adv now; ~ **mesmo** right now; (há pouco) a moment ago; **até** ~ so far, up to now; **por** ~ for now

agosto [a'goʃtu] (PT A~) m August

agouro [a'goru] m omen

agraciar [agra'sja*] vt to decorate

agradar [agra'da*] vt to please; (fazer agrados a) to be nice to ♦ vi to be pleasing; (satisfazer) to go down well

agradável [agra'davew] (pl -eis) adj pleasant

agradecer [agrade'se*] vt: ~ **algo a alguém** (afagar) to thank sb for sth; ~ **a alguém por algo** to thank sb for sth; **agradecido, -a** [agrade'sidu, a] adj grateful; **mal agradecido** ungrateful; **agradecimento** [agradesi'mẽtu] m gratitude; **agradecimentos** mpl (gratidão) thanks

agrado [a'gradu] m: **fazer um** ~ **a alguém** to be affectionate with sb; (ser agradável) to be nice to sb

agrário, -a [a'grarju, a] adj agrarian; **reforma agrária** land reform

agravante [agra'vãtʃi] adj aggravating ♦ f aggravating circumstance

agravar [agra'va*] vt to aggravate, make worse; **agravar-se** vr (piorar) to get worse

agravo [a'gravu] m (JUR) appeal

agredir [agre'dʒi*] vt to attack; (insultar) to insult

agregar [agre'ga*] vt (juntar) to collect; (acrescentar) to add

agressão [agre'sãw] (pl -ões) f aggression; (ataque) attack; (assalto) assault

agressivo, -a [agre'sivu, a] adj aggressive

agressões [agre'sõjʃ] *fpl de* agressão

agreste [a'grɛʃtʃi] *adj* rural, rustic; (*terreno*) wild

agrião [a'grjãw] *m* watercress

agrícola [a'grikola] *adj* agricultural

agricultor [agrikuw'to*] *m* farmer

agricultura [agrikuw'tura] *f* agriculture, farming

agrido *etc* [a'grɪdu] *vb* V **agredir**

agridoce [agri'dosi] *adj* bittersweet

agronomia [agrono'mia] *f* agronomy

agropecuária [agrope'kwarja] *f* farming, agriculture

agrupar [agru'pa*] *vt* to group; **agrupar-se** *vr* to group together

agrura [a'grura] *f* bitterness

água ['agwa] *f* water; ~s *fpl* (*mar*) waters; (*chuvas*) rain *sg*; (*maré*) tides; ~ **abaixo/acima** downstream/upstream; **dar** ~ **na boca** (*comida*) to be mouthwatering; **estar na** ~ (*bêbado*) to be drunk; **fazer** ~ (*NÁUT*) to leak; ~ **benta/corrente/doce** holy/running/fresh water; ~ **dura/leve** hard/soft water; ~ **mineral** mineral water; ~ **oxigenada** peroxide; ~ **salgada** salt water; ~ **sanitária** household bleach

aguaceiro [agwa'sejru] *m* (*chuva*) (heavy) shower, downpour

água-de-coco *f* coconut milk

água-de-colônia (*pl* **águas-de-colônia**) *f* eau-de-cologne

aguado, -a [a'gwadu, a] *adj* watery

aguardar [agwax'da*] *vt* to wait for; (*contar com*) to expect ♦ *vi* to wait

aguardente [agwax'dẽtʃi] *m* kind of brandy

aguarrás [agwa'xajʃ] *f* turpentine

aguçados, -a [agu'sadu, a] *adj* pointed; (*espírito, sentidos*) acute

agudo, -a [a'gudu, a] *adj* sharp, shrill; (*intenso*) acute

agüentar [agwẽ'ta*] *vt* (*muro etc*) to hold up; (*dor, injustiças*) to stand, put up with; (*peso*) to withstand ♦ *vi* to last; **agüentar-se** *vr* to remain, hold on; ~ **fazer algo** to manage to do sth; **não ~ de** not to be able to stand

águia ['agja] *f* eagle; (*fig*) genius

agulha [a'guʎa] *f* (*de coser, tricô*) needle; (*NÁUT*) compass; (*FERRO*) points *pl* (*BRIT*), switch (*US*); **trabalho de ~** needlework

ai [aj] *excl* (*suspiro*) oh!; (*de dor*) ouch! ♦ *m* (*suspiro*) sigh; (*gemido*) groan; ~ **de mim** poor me!

aí [a'i] *adv* there; (*então*) then; **por ~** (*em lugar indeterminado*) somewhere over there, thereabouts; **espera ~**! wait!, hang on a minute!; **está ~**! (*col*) right!; **e ~?** and then what?

AIDS ['ajdʒs] *abr f* AIDS

ainda [a'ĩda] *adv* still; (*mesmo*) even; ~ **agora** just now; ~ **assim** even so, nevertheless; ~ **bem** just as well; ~ **por cima** on top of all that, in addition; ~ **não** not yet; ~ **que** even if; **maior** ~ even bigger

aipo ['ajpu] *m* celery

ajeitar [aʒej'ta*] *vt* (*roupa, cabelo*) to adjust; (*emprego*) to arrange; **ajeitar-se** *vr* to adapt

ajo *etc* [a'ʒu] *vb* V **agir**

ajoelhar [aʒwe'ʎa*] *vi* to kneel (down); **ajoelhar-se** *vr* to kneel down

ajuda [a'ʒuda] *f* help; (*subsídio*) grant, subsidy; **dar** ~ **a alguém** to lend ou give sb a hand; ~ **de custo** allowance; **ajudante** [aʒu'dãtʃi] *m/f* assistant, helper; (*MIL*) adjutant

ajudar [aʒu'da*] *vt* to help

ajuizado, -a [aʒwi'zadu, a] *adj* (*sensato*) sensible; (*sábio*) wise; (*prudente*) discreet

ajuntamento [aʒũta'mẽtu] *m* gathering

ajuntar [aʒũ'ta*] *vt* (*unir*) to join; (*documentos*) to attach; (*reunir*) to gather

ajustagem [aʒuʃ'taʒẽ] (BR) (*pl* **-ns**) *f* (TEC) adjustment

ajustamento [aʒuʃta'mẽtu] *m* adjustment; (*de contas*) settlement

ajustar [aʒuʃ'ta*] *vt* to adjust; (*conta*, *disputa*) to settle; (*acomodar*) to fit; (*roupa*) to take in; (*preço*) to agree on; **ajustar-se** *vr*: **~-se a** to conform to; (*adaptar-se*) to adapt to

ajuste [a'ʒuʃtʃi] *m* (*acordo*) agreement; (*de contas*) settlement; (*adaptação*) adjustment

ala ['ala] *f* wing; (*fileira*) row; (*passagem*) aisle

alagar [ala'ga*] *vt*, *vi* to flood

alameda [ala'meda] *f* (*avenida*) avenue; (*arvoredo*) grove

alarde [a'laxdʒi] *m* ostentation; (*jactância*) boasting; **fazer ~ de** to boast about; **alardear** [alax'dʒia*] *vt* to show off; (*gabar-se de*) to boast of ♦ *vi* to show off; to boast; **alardear-se** *vr* to boast

alargar [alax'ga*] *vt* to extend; (*fazer mais largo*) to widen, broaden; (*afrouxar*) to loosen, slacken

alarma [a'laxma] *f* alarm; (*susto*) panic; (*tumulto*) tumult; (*vozearia*) outcry; **dar o sinal de ~** to raise the alarm; **~ de roubo** burglar alarm; **alarmante** [alax'mãtʃi] *adj* alarming; **alarmar** [alax'ma*] *vt* to alarm; **alarmar-se** *vr* to be alarmed

alarme [a'laxmi] *m* = **alarma**

alastrar [alaʃ'tra*] *vt* to scatter; (*disseminar*) to spread; **alastrar-se** *vr* (*epidemia*, *rumor*) to spread

alavanca [ala'vãka] *f* lever; (*pé-de-*

cabra) crowbar; **~ de mudanças** gear lever

albergue [aw'bɛxgi] *m* (*estalagem*) inn; (*refúgio*) hospice, shelter; **~ noturno** hotel; **~ para jovens** youth hostel

albufeira [awbu'fejra] *f* lagoon

álbum ['awbũ] (*pl* **-ns**) *m* album; **~ de recortes** scrapbook

alça ['awsa] *f* strap; (*asa*) handle; (*de fusil*) sight

alcachofra [awka'ʃofra] *f* artichoke

alcançar [awkã'sa*] *vt* to reach; (*estender*) to hand, pass; (*obter*) to obtain, get; (*atingir*) to attain; (*compreender*) to understand; (*desfalcar*): **~ uma firma em $1 milhão** to embezzle $1 million from a firm

alcance [aw'kãsi] *m* reach; (*competência*) power; (*compreensão*) understanding; (*de tiro*, *visão*) range; **ao ~ de** within reach *ou* range of; **ao ~ da voz** within earshot; **de grande ~** far-reaching; **fora do ~ da mão** out of reach; **fora do ~ de alguém** beyond sb's grasp

alcaparra [awka'paxa] *f* caper

alçar [aw'sa*] *vt* to lift (up); (*voz*) to raise

alcatrão [awka'trãw] *m* tar

álcool ['awkow] *m* alcohol; **alcoólatra** [aw'kɔlatra] *m/f* alcoholic; **alcoólico, -a** [aw'kɔliku, a] *adj*, *m/f* alcoholic

Alcorão [awko'rãw] *m* Koran

alcova [aw'kova] *f* bedroom

alcunha [aw'kuɲa] *f* nickname

aldeão, -eã [aw'dʒjãw, jã] (*pl* **-ões**, **~s**) *m/f* villager

aldeia [aw'deja] *f* village

aldeões [aw'dʒjõjʃ] *mpl de* **aldeão**

alecrim [ale'krĩ] *m* rosemary

alegar [ale'ga*] *vt* to allege; (JUR) to plead

alegoria [alego'ria] f allegory

alegórico, -a [ale'gɔriku, a] adj allegorical; **carro alegórico** float

alegrar [ale'gra*] vt to cheer (up), gladden; (ambiente) to brighten up; (animar) to liven up); **alegrar-se** vr to cheer up

alegre [a'legri] adj cheerful; (contente) happy, glad; (cores) bright; (embriagado) merry, tight; **alegria** [ale'gria] f joy, happiness

aleijado, -a [alej'ʒadu, a] adj crippled ♦ m/f cripple

aleijar [alej'ʒa*] vt to maim

além [a'lẽj] adv (lá ao longe) over there; (mais adiante) further on ♦ m: **o ~** the hereafter ♦ prep: ~ **de** beyond; (no outro lado de) on the other side of; (para mais de) over; (ademais de) apart from, besides; ~ **disso** moreover; **mais ~** further

alemã [ale'mã] f de **alemão**

alemães [ale'mãjʃ] mpl de **alemão**

Alemanha [ale'maɲa] f: **a ~** Germany

alemão, -mã [ale'mãw, 'mã] (pl -ães, ~s) adj, m/f German ♦ m (LING) German

alentador, a [alẽta'do*, a] adj encouraging

alento [a'lẽtu] m (fôlego) breath; (ânimo) courage; **dar ~** to encourage; **tomar ~** to draw breath

alergia [alex'ʒia] f: ~ (a) allergy (to); (fig) aversion (to); **alérgico, -a** [a'lexʒiku, a] adj: **alérgico (a)** allergic (to); **ele é alérgico a João/à política** he can't stand João/politics

alerta [a'lɛxta] adj alert ♦ adv on the alert ♦ m alert

alfabetizar [awfabetʃi'za*] vt to teach to read and write; **alfabetizar-se** vr to learn to read and write

alfabeto [awfa'bɛtu] m alphabet

alface [aw'fasi] f lettuce

alfaiate [awfa'jatʃi] m tailor

alfândega [aw'fãdʒiga] f customs pl, customs house; **alfandegário, -a** [awfãde'garju, a] m/f customs officer

alfazema [awfa'zema] f lavender

alfinete [awfi'netʃi] m pin; ~ **de segurança** safety pin

alga ['awga] f seaweed

algarismo [awga'riʒmu] m numeral, digit

Algarve [aw'gaxvi] m: **o ~** the Algarve

algazarra [awga'zaxa] f uproar, racket

álgebra ['awʒebra] f algebra

algemas [aw'ʒemaʃ] fpl handcuffs

algo ['awgu] adv somewhat, rather ♦ pron something; (qualquer coisa) anything

algodão [awgo'dãw] m cotton; ~ **(hidrófilo)** cotton wool (BRIT), absorbent cotton (US)

alguém [aw'gẽj] pron someone, somebody; (em frases interrogativas ou negativas) anyone, anybody

algum, a [aw'gũ, 'guma] (pl -ns, ~s) adj some; (em frases interrogativas ou negativas) any ♦ pron one; (no plural) some; (negativa): **de modo ~** in no way; **coisa ~a** nothing; ~ **dia** one day; ~ **tempo** for a while; ~**a coisa** something; ~**a vez** sometime

algures [aw'guriʃ] adv somewhere

alheio, -a [a'ʎeju, a] adj (de outrem) someone else's; (estranho) alien; (estrangeiro) foreign; (impróprio) irrelevant

alho ['aʎu] m garlic

ali [a'li] adv there; **até ~** up to there; **por ~** around there; (direção) that way; ~ **por** (tempo) round about; **de ~ por diante** from then on;

~ **dentro** in there

aliado, -a [a'ljadu, a] *adj* allied
♦ *m/f* ally

aliança [a'ljãsa] *f* alliance; (*anel*) wedding ring

aliar [a'lja*] *vt* to ally; **aliar-se** *vr* to form an alliance

aliás [a'ljajʃ] *adv* (*a propósito*) as a matter of fact; (*ou seja*) rather, that is; (*contudo*) nevertheless; (*diga-se de passagem*) incidentally

álibi ['alibi] *m* alibi

alicate [ali'katʃi] *m* pliers *pl*; ~ **de unhas** nail clippers *pl*

alienação [aljena'sãw] *f* alienation; (*de bens*) transfer (of property); ~ **mental** insanity

alienado, -a [alje'nadu, a] *adj* alienated; (*demente*) insane; (*bens*) transferred ♦ *m/f* lunatic

alienar [alje'na*] *vt* (*afastar*) to alienate; (*bens*) to transfer

alimentação [alimẽta'sãw] *f* (*alimentos*) food; (*ação*) feeding; (*nutrição*) nourishment; (*ELET*) supply

alimentar [alimẽ'ta*] *vt* to feed; (*fig*) to nurture ♦ *adj* (*produto*) food *atr*; (*hábitos*) eating *atr* **alimentar-se** *vr*: ~**-se de** to feed on

alimento [ali'mẽtu] *m* food; (*nutrição*) nourishment

alinhado, -a [ali'ɲadu, a] *adj* (*elegante*) elegant; (*texto*): ~ **à esquerda/direita** ranged left/right

alinhar [ali'ɲa*] *vt* to align; **alinhar-se** *vr* to form a line

alinho [a'liɲu] *m* (*alinhamento*) alignment; (*elegância*) neatness

alisar [ali'za*] *vt* to smooth; (*cabelo*) to straighten; (*acariciar*) to stroke

aliviar [ali'vja*] *vt* to relieve

alívio [a'livju] *m* relief

alma ['awma] *f* soul; (*entusiasmo*) enthusiasm; (*caráter*) character

almejar [awme'ʒa*] *vt* to long for,

yearn for

almirante [awmi'rãtʃi] *m* admiral

almoçar [awmo'sa*] *vi* to have lunch ♦ *vt*: ~ **peixe** to have fish for lunch

almoço [aw'mosu] *m* lunch; **pequeno** ~ (*PT*) breakfast

almofada [awmo'fada] *f* cushion; (*PT*: *travesseiro*) pillow

almoxarifado [awmoʃari'fadu] *m* storeroom

alô [a'lo] (*BR*) *excl* (*TEL*) hullo

alocar [alo'ka*] *vt* to allocate

alojamento [aloʒa'mẽtu] *m* accommodation (*BRIT*), accommodations *pl* (*US*); (*habitação*) housing

alojar [alo'ʒa*] *vt* (*hóspede*: *numa pensão*) to accommodate; (: *numa casa*) to put up; (*sem teto, refugiado*) to house; (*MIL*) to billet; **alojar-se** *vr* to stay

alongar [alõ'ga*] *vt* to lengthen; (*braço*) to stretch out; (*prazo, contrato*) to extend; (*reunião, sofrimento*) to prolong; **alongar-se** *vr* (*sobre um assunto*) to dwell

aloprado, -a [alo'pradu, a] (*col*) *adj* nutty

alpendre [aw'pẽdri] *m* (*telheiro*) shed; (*pórtico*) porch

Alpes ['awpiʃ] *mpl*: **os** ~ the Alps

alpinismo [awpi'niʒmu] *m* mountaineering, climbing; **alpinista** [awpi'niʃta] *m/f* mountaineer, climber

alta ['awta] *f* (*de preços*) rise; (*de hospital*) discharge

altar [aw'ta*] *m* altar

alteração [awtera'sãw] (*pl* -ões) *f* alteration; (*desordem*) disturbance; (*falsificação*) falsification

alterado, -a [awte'radu, a] *adj* bad-tempered, irritated

alterar [awte'ra*] *vt* to alter; (*falsificar*) to falsify; **alterar-se** *vr* to change; (*enfurecer-se*) to get angry, lose one's temper

alternar [awtex'na*] vt, vi to alternate; **alternar-se** vr to alternate; (*por turnos*) to take turns

alternativa [awtexna'tʃiva] f alternative

alternativo, -a [awtexna'tʃivu, a] adj alternative; (ELET) alternating

alteza [aw'teza] f highness

altitude [awtʃi'tudʒi] f altitude

altivez [awtʃi'veʒ] f (*arrogância*) haughtiness; (*nobreza*) loftiness;

altivo, -a [aw'tʃivu, a] adj haughty; lofty

alto, -a ['awtu, a] adj high; (*pessoa*) tall; (*som*) high, sharp; (*voz*) loud; (GEO) upper ♦ adv (*falar*) loudly, loud; (*voar*) high ♦ excl halt! ♦ m top, summit; **do ~** from above; **por ~** superficially; **alta fidelidade** high fidelity, hi-fi; **na alta noite** at dead of night

alto-falante (pl ~s) m loudspeaker

altura [aw'tura] f height; (*momento*) point, juncture; (*altitude*) altitude; (*de um som*) pitch; **em que ~ do Rio Branco fica a livraria?** whereabouts in Rio Branco is the bookshop?; **nesta ~** at this juncture; **estar à ~ de** (*ser capaz de*) to be up to; **ter 1.80 metros de ~** to be 1.80 metres (BRIT) ou meters (US) tall

alucinado, -a [alusi'nadu, a] adj crazy

alucinante [alusi'nãtʃi] adj crazy

alugar [alu'ga*] vt (*tomar de aluguel*) to rent, hire; (*dar de aluguel*) to let, rent out; **alugar-se** vr to let; **aluguel** [alu'gεw] (pl -éis) (BR) m rent; (*ação*) renting; **aluguel de carro** car hire (BRIT) ou rental (US); **aluguer** [alu'gε*] (PT) m = **aluguel**

alumiar [alu'mja*] vt to light (up) ♦ vi to give light

alumínio [alu'minju] m aluminium (BRIT), aluminum (US)

aluno, -a [a'lunu, a] m/f pupil, student

alvejar [awve'ʒa*] vt (*tomar como alvo*) to aim at; (*branquear*) to bleach

alvenaria [awvena'ria] f masonry; **de ~** brick atr, brick-built

alvéolo [aw'vεolu] m cavity

alvo, -a ['awvu, a] adj white ♦ m target

alvorada [awvo'rada] f dawn

alvorecer [awvore'se*] vi to dawn

alvoroço [awvo'rosu] m commotion; (*entusiasmo*) enthusiasm

amabilidade [amabili'dadʒi] f kindness; (*simpatia*) friendliness

amaciante [ama'sjatʃi] m: **~ (de roupa)** fabric conditioner

amaciar [ama'sja*] vt (*tornar macio*) to soften; (*carro*) to run in

amado, -a [a'madu, a] m/f beloved, sweetheart

amador, a [ama'do*, a] adj, m/f amateur

amadurecer [amadure'se*] vt, vi (*frutos*) to ripen; (*fig*) to mature

âmago ['amagu] m (*centro*) heart, core; (*medula*) pith; (*essência*) essence

amaldiçoar [amawdʒi'swa*] vt to curse, swear at

amalgamar [amawga'ma*] vt to amalgamate; (*combinar*) to fuse (BRIT), fuze (US), blend

amalucado, -a [amalu'kadu, a] adj crazy, whacky

amamentar [amamē'ta*] vt, vi to breast-feed

amanhã [ama'ɲã] adv, m tomorrow

amanhecer [amaɲe'se*] vi (*alvorecer*) to dawn; (*encontrar-se pela manhã*): **amanhecemos em Paris** we were in Paris at daybreak ♦ m dawn; **ao ~** at daybreak

amansar [amã'sa*] vt (animais) to tame; (cavalos) to break in; (aplacar) to placate

amante [a'mãtʃi] m/f lover

amar [a'ma*] vt to love

amarelo, -a [ama'rɛlu, a] adj yellow ♦ m yellow

amargar [amax'ga*] vt to make bitter; (fig) to embitter

amargo, -a [a'maxgu, a] adj bitter; **amargura** [amax'gura] f bitterness

amarrar [ama'xa*] vt to tie (up); (NÁUT) to moor; **~ a cara** to frown, scowl

amarrotar [amaxo'ta*] vt to crease

amassar [ama'sa*] vt (pão) to knead; (misturar) to mix; (papel) to screw up; (roupa) to crease; (carro) to dent

amável [a'mavew] (pl **-eis**) adj kind

Amazonas [ama'zɔnaʃ] m: **o ~** the Amazon

Amazônia [ama'zonja] f: **~** the Amazon region; see boxed note

---

AMAZÔNIA

Amazônia is the region formed by the basin of the river Amazon (the river with the largest volume of water in the world) and its tributaries. With a total area of almost 7 million square kilometres, it stretches from the Atlantic to the Andes. Most of Amazônia is in Brazilian territory, although it also extends into Peru, Colombia, Venezuela and Bolivia. It contains the richest biodiversity and largest area of tropical rainforest in the world.

---

ambição [ambi'sãw] (pl **-ões**) f ambition; **ambicionar** [ãbisjo'na*] vt to aspire to; **ambicioso, -a**

[ãbi'sjozu, ɔza] adj ambitious

ambidestro, -a [ãbi'dɛʃtru, a] adj ambidextrous

ambientar [ãbjẽ'ta*] vt (filme etc) to set; (adaptar): **~ alguém a algo** to get sb used to sth; **ambientar-se** vr to fit in

ambiente [ã'bjẽtʃi] m atmosphere; (meio, COMPUT) environment; **meio ~** environment; **temperatura ~** room temperature

ambíguo, -a [ã'bigwu, a] adj ambiguous

âmbito ['ãbitu] m extent; (campo de ação) scope, range

ambos, -as ['ãbuʃ, aʃ] adj pl both

ambulância [ãbu'lãsja] f ambulance

ambulante [ãbu'lãtʃi] adj walking; (errante) wandering; (biblioteca) mobile

ambulatório [ãbula'tɔrju] m outpatient department

ameaça [ame'asa] f threat; **ameaçar** [amea'sa*] vt to threaten

amedrontar [amedrõ'ta*] vt to scare, intimidate; **amedrontar-se** vr to be frightened

ameixa [a'mejʃa] f plum; (passa) prune

amém [a'mẽj] excl amen

amêndoa [a'mẽdwa] f almond; **amendoeira** [amẽ'dwejra] f almond tree

amendoim [amẽdo'ĩ] (pl **-ns**) m peanut

amenidade [ameni'dadʒi] f wellbeing; **~s** fpl (assuntos superficiais) small talk sg

amenizar [ameni'za*] vt (abrandar) to soften; (tornar agradável) to make pleasant; (facilitar) to ease

ameno, -a [a'mɛnu, a] adj pleasant; (clima) mild

América [a'mɛrika] f: **a ~** America;

a ~ do Norte/do Sul North/South America; **a ~ Central/Latina** Central/Latin America; **americano, -a** [ameri'kanu, a] *adj, m/f* American

amestrar [ames'tra*] *vt* to train

amianto [a'mjãtu] *m* asbestos

amido [a'midu] *m* starch

amigável [ami'gavew] (*pl* **-eis**) *adj* amicable, friendly

amígdala [a'migdala] *f* tonsil; **amigdalite** [amigda'litʃi] *f* tonsillitis

amigo, -a [a'migu, a] *adj* friendly ♦ *m/f* friend; **ser ~ de** to be friends with

amistoso, -a [amiʃ'tozu, ɔza] *adj* friendly, cordial ♦ *m* (*jogo*) friendly

amiúde [a'mjudʒi] *adv* often, frequently

amizade [ami'zadʒi] *f* (*relação*) friendship; (*simpatia*) friendliness

amnistia [amniʃ'tia] (*PT*) *f* = **anistia**

amolação [amola'sãw] (*pl* **-ões**) *f* bother, annoyance

amolar [amo'la*] *vt* to sharpen; (*aborrecer*) to annoy, bother ♦ *vi* to be annoying

amolecer [amole'se*] *vt* to soften ♦ *vi* to soften; (*abrandar-se*) to relent

amônia [a'mɔnja] *f* ammonia

amoníaco [amo'niaku] *m* ammonia

amontoar [amõ'twa*] *vt* to pile up, accumulate; **~ riquezas** to amass a fortune

amor [a'mo*] *m* love; **por ~ de** for the sake of; **fazer ~** to make love

amora [a'mɔra] *f*: **~ silvestre** blackberry

amordaçar [amoxda'sa*] *vt* to gag

amoroso, -a [amo'rozu, ɔza] *adj* loving, affectionate

amor-perfeito (*pl* **amores-perfeitos**) *m* pansy

amortecedor [amoxtese'do*] *m* shock absorber

amortização [amoxtʃiza'sãw] *f* payment in instalments (*BRIT*) *ou* installments (*US*)

amortizar [amoxtʃi'za*] *vt* to pay in instalments (*BRIT*) *ou* installments (*US*)

amostra [a'mɔʃtra] *f* sample

amparar [ãpa'ra*] *vt* to support; (*ajudar*) to help, assist; **amparar-se vr: ~-se em** to lean on

amparo [ã'paru] *m* support; help, assistance

ampliação [amplja'sãw] (*pl* **-ões**) *f* enlargement; (*extensão*) extension

ampliar [ã'plja*] *vt* to enlarge; (*conhecimento*) to broaden

amplificador [ãplifika'do*] *m* amplifier

amplificar [ãplifi'ka*] *vt* to amplify

amplitude [ãpli'tudʒi] *f* (*espaço*) spaciousness; (*fig*: *extensão*) extent

amplo, -a [a'plu, a] *adj* (*sala*) spacious; (*conhecimento, sentido*) broad; (*possibilidade*) ample

amputar [ãpu'ta*] *vt* to amputate

Amsterdã [amiʃtex'dã] (*BR*) *n* Amsterdam

Amsterdão [amiʃtex'dãw] (*PT*) *n* = **Amsterdã**

amuado, -a [a'mwadu, a] *adj* sulky

anã [a'nã] *f de* **anão**

anais [a'najʃ] *mpl* annals

analfabeto, -a [anawfa'betu, a] *adj, m/f* illiterate

analgésico [anaw'ʒeziku] *m* painkiller, analgesic

analisar [anali'za*] *vt* to analyse; **análise** [a'nalizi] *f* analysis; **analista** [ana'liʃta] *m/f* analyst

ananás [ana'najʃ] (*pl* **ananases**) *m* (*BR*) variety of pineapple (*PT*) pineapple

anão, -anã [a'nãw, a'nã] (*pl* **-ões**,

~s) m/f dwarf

anarquia [anax'kia] f anarchy;
anarquista [anax'kiʃta] m/f anarchist

anatomia [anato'mia] f anatomy

anca ['ɐ̃ka] f (de pessoa) hip; (de animal) rump

ancião, -anciã [ɐ̃'sjɐ̃w, ɐ̃'sjɐ̃] (pl
-ões, ~s) adj old ♦ m/f old man/
woman; (de uma tribo) elder

anciões [ɐ̃'sjõjʃ] mpl de ancião

âncora ['ɐ̃kora] f anchor; **ancorar**
[ɐ̃ko'ra*] vt, vi to anchor

andaime [ɐ̃'dajmi] m (ARQ) scaffolding

andamento [ɐ̃da'mẽtu] m (progresso) progress; (rumo) course; (MÚS)
tempo; **em ~** in progress

andar [ɐ̃'da*] vi vi to walk; (máquina)
to work; (progredir) to progress; (estar): **ela anda triste** she's been
sad lately ♦ m gait; (pavimento)
floor, storey (BRIT), story (US); **anda!**
hurry up!; **~ a cavalo** to ride; **~ de
trem/avião/bicicleta** to travel by
train/fly/ride a bike

Andes ['ɐ̃dʒiʃ] mpl: **os ~** the Andes

andorinha [ɐ̃do'riɲa] f (pássaro)
swallow

anedota [ane'dɔta] f anecdote

anel [a'nɛw] (pl -éis) m ring; (elo)
link; (de cabelo) curl; **~ de casamento** wedding ring

anemia [ane'mia] f anaemia (BRIT),
anemia (US)

anestesia [aneʃte'zia] f anaesthesia
(BRIT), anesthesia (US); (anestésico)
anaesthetic (BRIT), anesthetic (US)

anexar [anek'sa*] vt to annex; (juntar) to attach; (documento) to
enclose; **anexo, -a** [a'nɛksu, a] adj
attached ♦ m annexe; (em carta)
enclosure; **segue em anexo** please
find enclosed

anfitrião, -triã [ɐ̃fi'trjɐ̃w, 'trjɐ̃] (pl

-ões, ~s) m/f host/hostess

angina [ɐ̃'ʒina] f: **~ do peito** angina
(pectoris)

Angola [ɐ̃'gɔla] f Angola

angu [ɐ̃'gu] m corn-meal purée

ângulo ['ɐ̃gulu] m angle; (canto)
corner

angústia [ɐ̃'guʃtʃia] f anguish, distress; **angustiante** [ɐ̃guʃ'tʃiɐ̃tʃi]
adj distressing; (momentos) anxious,
nerve-racking

animação [anima'sɐ̃w] f (vivacidade) liveliness; (movimento) bustle;
(entusiasmo) enthusiasm

animado, -a [ani'madu, a] adj lively; (alegre) cheerful; **~ com** enthusiastic about

animador, a [anima'do*, a] adj
encouraging ♦ m/f (BR: TV) presente-

animal [ani'maw] (pl -ais) adj, m
animal; **~ de estimação** pet (animal)

animar [ani'ma*] vt to liven up;
(encorajar) to encourage; **animar-
se** vr to cheer up; (festa etc) to liven
up; **~-se a** to bring o.s. to

ânimo ['animu] m (coragem)
courage; **~!** cheer up!; **perder o ~**
to lose heart; **recobrar o ~** to pluck
up courage; (alegrar-se) to cheer up

aninhar [ani'ɲa*] vt to nestle,
aninhar-se vr to nestle

anis [a'niʃ] m aniseed

anistia [aniʃ'tʃia] f amnesty

aniversário [anivex'sarju] m
anniversary; (de nascimento) birthday; (: festa) birthday party

anjo ['ɐ̃ʒu] m angel; **~ da guarda**
guardian angel

ano ['anu] m year; **Feliz A~ Novo!**
Happy New Year!; **o ~ que vem**
next year; **por** per annum; **fazer ~s**
to have a birthday; **ter dez ~s** to be
ten (years old); **dia de ~s** (PT) birthday; **~ letivo** academic year; (do

escola) school year

anões [a'nõjʃ] *mpl de* **anão**

anoitecer [anojte'se*] *vi* to grow dark ♦ *m* nightfall

anomalia [anoma'lia] *f* anomaly

anônimo, -a [a'nonimu, a] *adj* anonymous

anoraque [ano'raki] *m* anorak

anormal [anox'maw] (*pl* **-ais**) *adj* abnormal; (*excepcional*) handicapped; **anormalidade** [anoxmali'dadʒi] *f* abnormality

anotação [anota'sãw] (*pl* **-ões**) *f* annotation; (*nota*) note

anotar [ano'ta*] *vt* to annotate; (*tomar nota*) to note down

anseio *etc* [ã'seju] *vb V* **ansiar**

ânsia ['ãsja] *f* anxiety; (*desejo*): ~ (**de**) longing (for); **ter** ~**s** (**de vômito**) to feel sick

ansiar [ã'sja*] *vi*: ~ **por** (*desejar*) to yearn for; ~ **por fazer** to long to do

ansiedade [ãsje'dadʒi] *f* anxiety; (*desejo*) eagerness

ansioso, -a [ã'sjozu, ɔza] *adj* anxious; (*desejoso*) eager

Antártico [ã'taxtʃiku] *m*: **o** ~ **the** Antarctic

ante ['ãtʃi] *prep* (*na presença de*) before; (*em vista de*) in view of, faced with

antecedência [ãtese'dẽsja] *f*: **com** ~ in advance; **3 dias de** ~ three days' notice

antecedente [ãtese'dẽtʃi] *adj* preceding ♦ *m* antecedent; ~**s** *mpl* (*registro*) record *sg*; (*passado*) background *sg*

anteceder [ãtese'de*] *vt* to precede

antecipação [ãtesipa'sãw] *f* anticipation; **com um mês de** ~ a month in advance; ~ **de pagamento** advance (payment)

antecipadamente [ãtesipada'mẽtʃi] *adv* in advance, beforehand

antecipado, -a [ãtesi'padu, a] *adj* (*pagamento*) in advance

antecipar [ãtesi'pa*] *vt* to anticipate, forestall; (*adiantar*) to bring forward

antemão [ante'mãw]: **de** ~ *adv* beforehand

antena [ã'tena] *f* (*BIO*) antenna, feeler; (*RÁDIO*, *TV*) aerial

anteontem [ãtʃi'õtẽ] *adv* the day before yesterday

antepassado [ãtʃipa'sadu] *m* ancestor

anterior [ãte'rjo*] *adj* previous; (*antigo*) former; (*de posição*) front

antes ['ãtʃiʃ] *adv* before; (*antigamente*) formerly; (*ao contrário*) rather ♦ *prep*: ~ **de** before; **o quanto** ~ as soon as possible; ~ **de partir** before leaving; ~ **de tudo** above all; ~ **que** before

anti- [ãtʃi] *prefixo* anti-

antiácido, -a [ã'tʃjasidu, a] *adj* antacid ♦ *m* antacid

antibiótico, -a [ãtʃi'bjɔtʃiku, a] *adj* antibiotic ♦ *m* antibiotic

anticaspa [ãtʃi'kaʃpa] *adj inv*: **xampu** ~ dandruff shampoo

anticlímax [ãtʃi'klimakʃ] *m* anticlimax

anticoncepcional [ãtʃikõsepsjo'naw] (*pl* **-ais**) *adj*, *m* contraceptive

anticongelante [ãtʃikõʒe'lãtʃi] *m* antifreeze

antidepressivo [ãtʃidepre'sivu] *m* antidepressant

antigamente [ãtʃiga'mẽtʃi] *adv* formerly; (*no passado*) in the past

antigo, -a [ã'tʃigu, a] *adj* old; (*histórico*) ancient; (*de estilo*) antique; (*chefe etc*) former

antiguidade [ãtʃigi'dadʒi] *f* antiquity, ancient times *pl*; (*de emprego*) seniority; ~**s** *fpl* (*monumentos*) ancient monuments; (*artigos*) antiques

anti-horário, -a adj anticlockwise

antilhano, -a [ãtʃi'ʎanu, a] adj, m/f West Indian

Antilhas [ã'tʃiʎaʃ] fpl: **as ~** the West Indies

antipatia [ãtʃipa'tʃia] f dislike; **antipático, -a** [ãtʃi'patʃiku, a] adj unpleasant, unfriendly

antipatizar [ãtʃipatʃi'za*] vi: **~ com alguém** to dislike sb

antiquado, -a [ãtʃi'kwadu, a] adj antiquated; (fora de moda) out of date, old-fashioned

antiquário, -a [ãtʃi'kwarju, a] m/f antique dealer ♦ m (loja) antique shop

anti-semita adj anti-Semitic

anti-séptico, -a adj antiseptic ♦ m antiseptic

anti-social (pl -ais) adj antisocial

antologia [ãtolo'ʒia] f anthology

anual [a'nwaw] (pl -ais) adj annual, yearly

anulação [anula'sãw] (pl -ões) f cancellation; (de contrato, casamento) annulment

anular [anu'la*] vt to cancel; (contrato, casamento) to annul; (efeito) to cancel out ♦ m ring finger

anunciante [anũ'sjãtʃi] m (COM) advertiser

anunciar [anũ'sja*] vt to announce; (COM) to advertise

anúncio [a'nũsju] m announcement; (COM) advertisement; (cartaz) notice; **~s classificados** small ou classified ads

ânus ['anuʃ] m inv anus

anzol [ã'zɔw] (pl -óis) m fish-hook

ao [aw] = **a + o**

aonde [a'õdʒi] adv where; **~ quer que** wherever

aos [awʃ] = **a + os**

Ap. abr = **apartamento**

apagado, -a [apa'gadu, a] adj: **o fogo estava ~/a luz estava apagada** the fire was out/the light was off

apagar [apa'ga*] vt to put out; (luz elétrica) to switch off; (vela) to blow out; (com borracha) to rub out, erase; **apagar-se** vr to go out

apaixonado, -a [apajʃo'nadu, a] adj (discurso) impassioned; (pessoa): **ele está ~ por ela** he is in love with her; **ele é ~ por tênis** he's mad about tennis

apaixonar-se [apajʃo'naxsi] vr: **~ por** to fall in love with

apalpar [apaw'pa*] vt to touch, feel; (MED) to examine

apanhado [apa'ɲadu] m (de flores) bunch; (resumo) summary

apanhar [apa'ɲa*] vt to catch; (algo à mão, do chão) to pick up; (surra, táxi) to get; (flores, frutas) to pick; (agarrar) to grab ♦ vi to get a beating; **~ sol/chuva** to sunbathe/get soaked

aparador [apara'do*] m sideboard

apara-lápis [apara'lapiʃ] (PT) m inv pencil sharpener

aparar [apa'ra*] vt (cabelo) to trim; (lápis) to sharpen; (algo arremessado) to catch

aparato [apa'ratu] m pomp; (coleção) array

aparecer [apare'se*] vi to appear; (apresentar-se) to turn up; (ser publicado) to be published; **~ em casa de alguém** to call on sb; **aparecimento** [aparesi'mẽtu] m appearance; (publicação) publication

aparelhado, -a [apare'ʎadu, a] adj ready, prepared

aparelho [apa'reʎu] m apparatus; (equipamento) equipment; (PESCA) tackle; (máquina) machine; (PT: fone) telephone; **~ de barbear** electric shaver; **~ de chá** tea set; **~ de rádio/TV** radio/TV set; **~ doméstico** domestic appliance

aparência [apaˈrẽsja] f appearance; **na ~** apparently; **sob a ~ de** under the guise of; **ter ~ de** to look like, seem

aparentar [aparẽˈta*] vt (fingir) to feign; (parecer) to look; **não aparenta a sua idade** he doesn't look his age

aparente [apaˈrẽtʃi] adj apparent

aparição [apariˈsãw] (pl -ões) f (visão) apparition; (fantasma) ghost

apartamento [apaxtaˈmẽtu] m apartment, flat (BRIT)

apartar [apax'ta*] vt to separate; **apartar-se** vr to separate

apartheid [apaxˈtajdʒi] m apart heid

apatia [apaˈtʃia] f apathy

apático, -a [aˈpatʃiku, a] adj apathetic

apavorado, -a [apavoˈradu, a] adj terrified

apavorante [apavoˈrãtʃi] adj terrifying

apavorar [apavoˈra*] vt to terrify ♦ vi to be terrifying; **apavorar-se** vr to be terrified

apear-se [aˈpjaxsi] vr: **~ de** (cavalo) to dismount from

apegado, -a [apeˈgadu, a] adj. **ser ~ a** (gostar de) to be attached to

apegar-se [apeˈgaxsi] vr: **~ a** (afeiçoar-se) to become attached to

apego [aˈpegu] m (afeição) attachment

apelação [apelaˈsãw] (pl -ões) f appeal

apelar [apeˈla*] vi to appeal; **~ da sentença** (JUR) to appeal against the sentence; **~ para** to appeal to; **~ para a ignorância/violência** to resort to abuse/violence

apelido [apeˈlidu] m (BR: alcunha) nickname; (PT: nome de família) surname

apelo [aˈpelu] m appeal

apenas [aˈpenaʃ] adv only

apendicite [apẽdʒiˈsitʃi] f appendicitis

aperfeiçoamento [apexfejswaˈmẽtu] m (perfeição) perfection; (melhoramento) improvement

aperfeiçoar [apexfejˈswa*] vt to perfect; (melhorar) to improve; **aperfeiçoar-se** vr to improve o.s.

apertado, -a [apexˈtadu, a] adj tight; (estreito) narrow; (sem dinheiro) hard-up; (vida) hard

apertar [apex'ta*] vt (agarrar) to hold tight; (roupa) to take in; (esponja) to squeeze; (botão) to press; (despesas) to limit; (vigilância) to step up; (coração) to break; (fig: pessoa) to put pressure on ♦ vi (sapatos) to pinch; (chuva, frio) to get worse; (estrada) to narrow; **~ em** (insistir) to insist on; **~ a mão de alguém** to shake hands with sb

aperto [aˈpextu] m pressure; (situação difícil) spot of bother, jam; **um ~ de mãos** a handshake

apesar [apeˈza*]: **~ de** prep in spite of, despite; **~ disso** nevertheless; **~ de que** even though

apetecer [apeteˈse*] vi (comida) to be appetizing

apetite [apeˈtʃitʃi] m appetite; **bom ~!** enjoy your meal!

apetrechos [apeˈtreʃuʃ] mpl gear sg; (PESCA) tackle sg

ápice [ˈapisi] m (cume) summit, top; (vértice) apex

apiedar-se [apjeˈdaxsi] vr: **~ de** to pity; (compadecer-se) to take pity on

apinhado, -a [apiˈɲadu, a] adj crowded

apinhar [api'ɲa*] vt to crowd, pack; **apinhar-se** vr to crowd together; **~-se de** (gente) to be filled ou packed with

apitar [api'ta*] vi to whistle; **apito** [a'pitu] m whistle

aplacar [apla'ka*] vt to placate ♦ vi to calm down; **aplacar-se** vr to calm down

aplaudir [aplaw'dʒi*] vt to applaud

aplauso [a'plawzu] m applause; (apoio) support; (elogio) praise; (aprovação) approval; **~s** applause sg

aplicação [aplika'sãw] (pl -ões) f application; (esforço) effort; (da lei) enforcement; (de dinheiro) investment

aplicado, -a [apli'kadu, a] adj hard-working

aplicar [apli'ka*] vt to apply; (lei) to enforce; (dinheiro) to invest; **aplicar-se** vr: **~-se a** to devote o.s. to

apoderar-se [apode'raxsi] vr: **~** de to seize, take possession of

apodrecer [apodre'se*] vt to rot; (dente) to decay ♦ vi to rot; to decay

apogeu [apo'ʒew] m (fig) height, peak

apoiar [apo'ja*] vt to support; (basear) to base; (moção) to second; **apoiar-se** vr: **~-se em** to rest on

apoio [a'poju] m support; (financeiro) backing

apólice [a'polisi] f (certificado) policy, certificate; (ação) share, bond; **~ de seguro** insurance policy

apontamento [apõta'mẽtu] m (nota) note

apontar [apõ'ta*] vt (fusil) to aim; (erro) to point out; (com o dedo) to point at ou to; (razão) to put forward ♦ vi to begin to appear; (brotar) to sprout; (com o dedo) to

point; **~ para** to point to; (com arma) to aim at

após [a'pɔjʃ] prep after

aposentado, -a [apoze'tadu, a] adj retired ♦ m/f retired person, pensioner; **ser ~** to be retired; **aposentadoria** [apozetado'ria] f retirement; (dinheiro) pension

aposentar [apoze'ta*] vt to retire; **aposentar-se** vr to retire

aposento [apo'zẽtu] m room

apossar-se [apo'saxsi] vr: **~ de** to take possession of, seize

aposta [a'poʃta] f bet

apostar [apoʃ'ta*] vt to bet ♦ vi: **~ em** to bet on

apóstolo [a'poʃtolu] m apostle

apóstrofo [a'poʃtrofu] m apostrophe

aprazível [apra'zivew] (pl -eis) adj pleasant

apreciação [apresja'sãw] f appreciation

apreciar [apre'sja*] vt to appreciate; (gostar de) to enjoy

apreço [a'presu] m esteem, regard; (consideração) consideration; **em ~** in question

apreender [aprjẽ'de*] vt to apprehend; (tomar) to seize; (entender) to grasp

apreensão [aprjẽ'sãw] (pl -ões) f (percepção) perception; (tomada) seizure; (receio) apprehension

apreensivo, -a [aprjẽ'sivu, a] adj apprehensive

apreensões [aprjẽ'sõjʃ] fpl de **apreensão**

apregoar [apre'gwa*] vt to proclaim, announce; (mercadorias) to cry

aprender [aprẽ'de*] vt, vi to learn; **a ler** to learn to read; **~ de cor** to learn by heart

aprendizagem [aprẽdʒi'zaʒẽ] f

(num ofício) apprenticeship; *(numa profissão)* training; *(escolar)* learning

apresentação [aprezẽta'sãw] *(pl -ões)* f presentation; *(de peça, filme)* performance; *(de pessoas)* introduction; *(porte pessoal)* appearance

apresentador, a [aprezẽta'do*, a] *m/f* presenter

apresentar [aprezẽ'ta*] *vt* to present; *(pessoas)* to introduce; **apresentar-se** *vr* to introduce o.s.; *(problema)* to present itself; *(à polícia etc)* to report; **quero apresentar-lhe** may I introduce you to

apressado, -a [apre'sadu, a] *adj* hurried, hasty; **estar ~ to** be in a hurry

apressar [apre'sa*] *vt* to hurry; **apressar-se** *vr* to hurry up

aprisionar [aprizjo'na*] *vt* *(cativar)* to capture; *(encarcerar)* to imprison

aprontar [aprõ'ta*] *vt* to get ready, prepare; **aprontar-se** *vr* to get ready

apropriação [aproprja'sãw] *(pl -ões)* f appropriation; *(tomada)* seizure

apropriado, -a [apro'prjadu, a] *adj* appropriate, suitable

apropriar [apro'prja*] *vt* to appropriate; **apropriar-se** *vr*: **~-se de** to seize, take possession of

aprovação [aprova'sãw] f approval; *(louvor)* praise; *(num exame)* pass

aprovado, -a [apro'vadu, a] *adj* approved; **ser ~ num exame** to pass an exam

aprovar [apro'va*] *vt* to approve of; *(exame)* to pass ♦ *vi* to make the grade

aproveitador, a [aprovejta'do*, a] *m/f* opportunist

aproveitamento [aprovejta'mẽtu] *m* use, utilization; *(nos estudos)* progress

aproveitar [aprovej'ta*] *vt* to take advantage of; *(utilizar)* to use; *(oportunidade)* to take ♦ *vi* to make the most of it; *(PT)* to be of use; **aproveite!** enjoy yourself!

aproximação [aprosima'sãw] *(pl -ões)* f approximation; *(chegada)* approach; *(proximidade)* nearness

aproximar [aprosi'ma*] *vt* to bring near; *(aliar)* to bring together; **aproximar-se** *vr*: **~-se de** to approach

aptidão [aptʃi'dãw] f aptitude; *(jeito)* knack; **~ física** physical fitness

apto, -a [ˈaptu, a] *adj* apt; *(capaz)* capable

apto. *abr* = **apartamento**

apunhalar [apuɲa'la*] *vt* to stab

apurado, -a [apu'radu, a] *adj* refined

apurar [apu'ra*] *vt* to perfect; *(averiguar)* to investigate; *(dinheiro)* to raise, get; *(votos)* to count; **apurar-se** *vr* to dress up

aquarela [akwa'rɛla] f watercolour *(BRIT)*, watercolor *(US)*

aquário [a'kwarju] *m* aquarium; **A~** *(ASTROLOGIA)* Aquarius

aquático, -a [a'kwatʃiku, a] *adj* aquatic, water *atr*

aquecer [ake'se*] *vt* to heat ♦ *vi* to heat up; **aquecer-se** *vr* to heat up; **aquecido, -a** [ake'sidu, a] *adj* heated; **aquecimento** [akesi-'mẽtu] *m* heating; **aquecimento central** central heating

aquele, -ela [a'keli, ɛla] *adj (sg)* that; *(pl)* those ♦ *pron (sg)* that one; *(pl)* those

àquele, -ela [a'keli, ɛla] = **a + aquele/ela**

aquém [a'kẽj] *adv* on this side; **~ de** on this side of

aqui [a'ki] *adv* here; **eis ~** here is/ are; **~ mesmo** right here; **até ~** up to here; **por ~** hereabouts; *(nesta direção)* this way

aquilo [aˈkilu] *pron* that; **~ que** what

àquilo [aˈkilu] = **a** + **aquilo**

aquisição [akiziˈsãw] *(pl* -ões) *f* acquisition

ar [aˈ*] *m* air; *(aspecto)* look; *(brisa)* breeze; *(PT: AUTO)* choke; **~es** *mpl (atitude)* airs; *(clima)* climate *sg;* **ao ~ livre** in the open air; **no ~** *(TV, RÁDIO)* on air; *(fig: planos)* up in the air; **dar-se ~es** to put on airs; **~ condicionado** *(aparelho)* air conditioner; *(sistema)* air conditioning

árabe [ˈarabi] *adj, m/f* Arab ♦ *m (LING)* Arabic

Arábia [aˈrabja] *f:* **a ~ Saudita** Saudi Arabia

arame [aˈrami] *m* wire

aranha [aˈraɲa] *f* spider

arara [aˈrara] *f* macaw

arbitragem [axbiˈtraʒẽ] *f* arbitration

arbitrar [axbiˈtra*] *vt* to arbitrate; *(ESPORTE)* to referee

arbitrário, -a [axbiˈtrarju, a] *adj* arbitrary

arbítrio [axˈbitrju] *m* decision; **ao ~ de** at the discretion of

árbitro [ˈaxbitru] *m (juiz)* arbiter; *(JUR)* arbitrator; *(FUTEBOL)* referee; *(TÊNIS etc)* umpire

arbusto [axˈbuʃtu] *m* shrub, bush

arca [ˈaxka] *f* chest, trunk; **~ de Noé** Noah's Ark

arcar [axˈka*] *vt:* **~ com** *(responsabilidades)* to shoulder; *(despesas)* to handle; *(consequências)* to take

arcebispo [arseˈbiʃpu] *m* archbishop

arco [ˈaxku] *m (ARQ)* arch; *(MIL, MÚS)* bow; *(ELET, MAT)* arc

arco-íris *m inv* rainbow

ardente [axˈdẽtʃi] *adj* burning;

(intenso) fervent; *(apaixonado)* ardent

arder [axˈde*] *vi* to burn; *(pele, olhos)* to sting; **~ de raiva** to seethe (with rage)

ardiloso, -a [axdʒiˈlozu, ɔza] *adj* cunning

ardor [axˈdo*] *m* ardour *(BRIT)*, ardor *(US)*; **ardoroso, -a** [axdoˈrozu, ɔza] *adj* ardent

árduo, -a [ˈaxdwu, a] *adj* arduous; *(difícil)* hard, difficult

área [ˈarja] *f* area; *(ESPORTE)* penalty area; *(fig)* field; **~ (de serviço)** balcony *(for hanging washing etc)*

areia [aˈreja] *f* sand; **~ movediça** quicksand

arejar [areˈʒa*] *vt* to air ♦ *vi* to get some air; *(descansar)* to have a breather; **arejar-se** *vr* to get some air; to have a break

arena [aˈrena] *f* arena; *(de circo)* ring

Argélia [axˈʒɛlja] *f:* **a ~** Algeria

Argentina [axʒẽˈtʃina] *f:* **a ~** Argentina

argila [axˈʒila] *f* clay

argola [axˈɡɔla] *f* ring; **~s** *fpl (brincos)* hooped earrings; **~ (de porta)** door-knocker

argumentação [axɡumẽtaˈsãw] *f* line of argument

argumentar [axɡumẽˈta*] *vt, vi* to argue

argumento [axɡuˈmẽtu] *m* argument; *(de obra)* theme

aridez [ariˈdeʒ] *f* dryness; *(esterilidade)* barrenness; *(falta de interesse)* dullness

árido, -a [ˈaridu, a] *adj* arid, dry; *(estéril)* barren; *(maçante)* dull

Áries [ˈariʃ] *f* Aries

aristocrata [ariʃtoˈkrata] *m/f* aristocrat

aritmética [aritʃˈmɛtʃika] *f* arithmetic

arma ['axma] f weapon; **~s** fpl (nucleares etc) arms; (brasão) coat sg of arms; **passar pelas ~s** to shoot, execute; **~ convencional/ nuclear** conventional/nuclear weapon; **~ de fogo** firearm

armação [axma'sãw] (pl -ões) f (armadura) frame; (PESCA) tackle; (NÁUT) rigging; (de óculos) frames pl

armadilha [axma'dʒiʎa] f trap

armado, -a [ax'madu, a] adj armed

armamento [axma'mẽtu] m (armas) armaments pl, weapons pl; (NÁUT) equipment; (ato) arming

armar [ax'ma*] vt to arm; (montar) to assemble; (barraca) to pitch; (um aparelho) to set up; (armadilha) to set; (NÁUT) to fit out; **armar-se** vr to arm o.s.; **~ uma briga com** to pick a quarrel with

armarinho [axma'riɲu] m haberdashery (BRIT), notions pl (US)

armário [ax'marju] m cupboard; (de roupa) wardrobe

armazém [axma'zẽj] (pl -ns) m (depósito) warehouse; (loja) grocery store; **armazenar** [axmaze'na*] vt to store; (provisões) to stock

aro ['aru] m (argola) ring; (de óculos, roda) rim; (de porta) frame

aroma [a'roma] m aroma; **aromático, -a** [aro'matʃiku, a] adj (comida) aromatic; (perfume) fragrant

arpão [ax'pãw] (pl -ões) m harpoon

arqueiro, -a [ax'kejru, a] m/f archer; (goleiro) goalkeeper

arqueologia [axkjolu'ʒia] f archaeology (BRIT), archeology (US); **arqueólogo, -a** [ax'kjɔlogu, a] m/f archaeologist (BRIT), archeologist (US)

arquiteto, -a [axki'tetu, a] (PT -ect-) m/f architect; **arquitetônico, -a** [axkite'toniku, a] (PT -ectó-) adj architectural; **arquitetura**

[axkite'tura] (PT -ect-) f architecture

arquivar [axki'va*] vt to file; (projeto) to shelve

arquivo [ax'kivu] m (ger, COMPUT) file; (lugar) archive; (de empresa) files pl; (móvel) filing cabinet

arraial [axa'jaw] (pl -ais) (PT) m (festa) fair

arraigado, -a [axaj'gadu, a] adj deep-rooted; (fig) ingrained

arraigar [axaj'ga*] vi to root; **arraigar-se** vr to take root; (estabelecer-se) to settle

arrancada [axã'kada] f (movimento, puxão) jerk; **dar uma ~ em** (puxar) to jerk; **dar uma ~ (em carro)** to pull away (suddenly)

arrancar [axã'ka*] vt to pull out; (botão etc) to pull off; (arrebatar) to snatch (away); (fig: confissão) to extract ♦ vi to start (off); **arrancar-se** vr to leave; (fugir) to run off

arranha-céu [a'xaɲa-] (pl ~s) m skyscraper

arranhão [axa'ɲãw] (pl -ões) m scratch

arranhar [axa'ɲa*] vt to scratch

arranjar [axã'ʒa*] vt to arrange; (emprego, namorado) to get, find; (doença) to get, catch; (questão) to settle; **arranjar-se** vr to manage; (conseguir emprego) to get a job; **~- se sem** to do without

arranjo [a'xãʒu] m arrangement

arranque [a'xãki] m: **motor de ~** starter (motor)

arrasar [axa'za*] vt to devastate; (demolir) to demolish; (estragar) to ruin; **arrasar-se** vr to be devastated; (destruir-se) to destroy o.s.; (arruinar-se) to lose everything

arrastão [axaʃ'tãw] (pl -ões) m tug; (rede) dragnet

arrastar [axaʃ'ta*] vt to drag; (atrair) to draw ♦ vi to trail; **arrastar-se** vr to crawl; (*tempo, processo*) to drag (on)

arrebatado, -a [axeba'tadu] *adj* rash, impetuous

arrebatar [axeba'ta*] *vt* to snatch (away); (*levar*) to carry off; (*enlevar*) to entrance; (*enfurecer*) to enrage; **arrebatar-se** *vr* to be entranced

arrebentado, -a [axebē'tadu, a] *adj* broken; (*estafado*) worn out

arrebentar [axebē'ta*] *vi* to break; (*porta*) to break down; (*corda*) to snap ♦ *vi* to break; (*corda*) to snap; (*guerra*) to break out

arrebitado, -a [axebi'tadu, a] *adj* turned-up; (*nariz*) snub

arrecadar [axeka'da*] *vt* (*impostos etc*) to collect

arredondado, -a [axedő'dadu, a] *adj* round, rounded

arredondar [axedő'da*] *vt* to round (off); (*conta*) to round up

arredores [axe'dɔrlʃ] *mpl* suburbs; (*cercanias*) outskirts

arrefecer [axefe'se*] *vt* to cool; (*febre*) to lower; (*desanimar*) to discourage ♦ *vi* to cool (off); to get discouraged

ar-refrigerado [-xefriʒe'radu] *m* air conditioning

arregaçar [axega'sa*] *vt* to roll up

arregalado, -a [axega'ladu, a] *adj* (*olhos*) wide

arregalar [axega'la*] *vt*: **~ os olhos** to stare in amazement

arrematar [axema'ta*] *vt* (*dizer concluindo*) to conclude; (*comprar*) to buy by auction; (*vender*) to sell by auction; (*COSTURA*) to finish off

arremessar [axeme'sa*] *vt* to throw, hurl; **arremesso** [axe'mesu] *m* throw

arremeter [axeme'te*] *vi* to lunge; **~ contra** (*acometer*) to attack, assail

arrendamento [axẽda'mẽtu] *m* (*ação*) leasing; (*contrato*) lease

arrendar [axẽ'da*] *vt* to lease

arrendatário, -a [axẽda'tarju, a] *m/f* tenant

arrepender-se [axepẽ'dexsi] *vr* to repent; (*mudar de opinião*) to change one's mind; **~ de** to regret, be sorry for; **arrependido, -a** [axepẽ'dʒidu, a] *adj* (*pessoa*) sorry; **arrependimento** [axepẽdʒi'mẽtu] *m* regret; (*REL, de crime*) repentance

arrepiar [axe'pja*] *vt* (*amedrontar*) to horrify; (*cabelo*) to cause to stand on end; **arrepiar-se** *vr* to shiver; (*cabelo*) to stand on end; (**ser) de ~ os cabelos** (to be) hair-raising

arrepio [axe'piu] *m* shiver; (*de frio*) chill; **isso me dá ~s** it gives me the creeps

arriar [a'xja*] *vt* to lower; (*depor*) to lay down ♦ *vi* to drop; (*vergar*) to sag; (*desistir*) to give up; (*fig*) to collapse

arriscado, -a [axiʃ'kadu, a] *adj* risky; (*audacioso*) daring

arriscar [axiʃ'ka*] *vt* to risk; (*pôr em perigo*) to endanger, jeopardize; **arriscar-se** *vr* to take a risk; **~-se a fazer** to risk doing

arroba [a'xoba] *f* (*símbolo*) @, 'at' sign

arrogante [axo'gãtʃi] *adj* arrogant

arroio [a'xɔju] *m* stream

arrojado, -a [axo'ʒadu, a] *adj* (*design*) bold; (*temerário*) rash; (*ousado*) daring

arrolar [axo'la*] *vt* to list

arrombar [axő'ba*] *vt* (*porta*) to break down; (*cofre*) to crack

arrotar [axo'ta*] *vi* to belch ♦ *vt* (*alardear*) to boast of

arroz [a'xoʒ] *m* rice; **~ doce** rice pudding

arruinar [axwi'na*] *vt* to ruin; (*destruir*) to destroy; **arruinar-se** *vr* to be ruined; (*perder a saúde*) to ruin one's health

arrumação [axuma'sāw] *f* arrangement; (*de um quarto etc*) tidying up; (*de malas*) packing

arrumadeira [axuma'dejra] *f* cleaning lady; (*num hotel*) chambermaid

arrumar [axu'ma*] *vt* to put in order, arrange; (*quarto etc*) to tidy up; (*malas*) to pack; (*emprego*) to get; (*vestir*) to dress up; (*desculpa*) to make up, find; (*vida*) to sort out; **arrumar-se** *vr* (*aprontar-se*) to get dressed, get ready; (*na vida*) to sort o.s. out; (*virar-se*) to manage

arte ['axtʃi] *f* art; (*habilidade*) skill; (*ofício*) trade, craft

artefato [axtʃi'fatu] (*PT* **-act-**) *m* (*manufactured*) article

artéria [ax'tɛrja] *f* (*ANAT*) artery

artesão, -sã [axte'zãw, zã] (*pl* ~s, ~ãs) *m/f* artisan, craftsman/woman

ártico, -a ['axtʃiku, a] *adj* Arctic ♦ *m*: **o A~** the Arctic

artificial [axtʃifi'sjaw] (*pl* -ais) *adj* artificial

artifício [axtʃi'fisju] *m* stratagem, trick

artigo [ax'tʃigu] *m* article; (*COM*) item; ~s *mpl* (*produtos*) goods

artilharia [axtʃiʎa'ria] *f* artillery

artista [ax'tʃista] *m/f* artist; **artístico, -a** [ax'tʃiftʃiku, a] *adj* artistic

artrite [ax'tritʃi] *f* (*MED*) arthritis

árvore ['axvori] *f* tree; (*TEC*) shaft; ~ **de Natal** Christmas tree

as [aʃ] *art def* V **a**

às [ajʃ] *m* ace

às [ajʃ] = **a** + **as**

asa ['aza] *f* wing; (*de xícara etc*) handle

ascendência [asē'dēsja] *f* (*antepassados*) ancestry; (*domínio*) ascendancy, sway; **ascendente** [asē'dētʃi] *adj* rising, upward

ascender [asē'de*] *vi* to rise, ascend

ascensão [asē'sãw] (*pl* -ões) *f* ascent; (*REL*): **dia da A~** Ascension Day

asco ['aʃku] *m* loathing, revulsion; **dar** ~ **a** to revolt, disgust

asfalto [aʃ'fawtu] *m* asphalt

asfixia [aʃfik'sia] *f* asphyxia, suffocation

Ásia ['azja] *f*: **a** ~ Asia

asiático, -a [a'zjatʃiku, a] *adj, m/f* Asian

asilo [a'zilu] *m* (*refúgio*) refuge; (*estabelecimento*) home; ~ **político** political asylum

asma ['aʒma] *f* asthma

asneira [aʒ'nejra] *f* (*tolice*) stupidity; (*ato, dito*) stupid thing

asno ['aʒnu] *m* donkey; (*fig*) ass

aspas ['aʃpaʃ] *fpl* inverted commas

aspecto [aʃ'pɛktu] *m* aspect; (*aparência*) look, appearance; (*característica*) feature; (*ponto de vista*) point of view

aspereza [aʃpe'reza] *f* roughness; (*severidade*) harshness; (*rudeza*) rudeness

áspero, -a ['aʃperu, a] *adj* rough; (*severo*) harsh; (*rude*) rude

aspiração [aʃpira'sãw] (*pl* -ões) *f* aspiration; (*inalação*) inhalation

aspirador [aʃpira'do*] *m*: ~ **(de pó)** vacuum cleaner; **passar o** ~ **(em)** to vacuum

aspirante [aʃpi'rātʃi] *adj* aspiring ♦ *m/f* candidate

aspirar [aʃpi'ra*] *vt* to breathe in; (*bombear*) to suck up ♦ *vi* to breathe; (*soprar*) to blow; (*desejar*): ~ **a algo** to aspire to sth

aspirina [aʃpi'rina] *f* aspirin

asqueroso, -a [aʃke'rozu, ɔza] *adj* disgusting, revolting

assado, -a [a'sadu, a] *adj* roasted; (*CULIN*) roast ♦ *m* roast; **carne assada**

roast beef

assaltante [asaw'tãtʃi] *m/f* assailant; (*de banco*) robber; (*de casa*) burglar; (*na rua*) mugger

assaltar [asaw'ta*] *vt* to attack; (*casa*) to break into; (*banco*) to rob; (*pessoa na rua*) to mug; **assalto** [a'sawtu] *m* attack; raid, robbery; burglary, break-in; mugging; (BOXE) round

assar [a'sa*] *vt* to roast; (*na grelha*) to grill

assassinar [asasi'na*] *vt* to murder, kill; (POL) to assassinate; **assassinato** [asasi'natu] *m* murder, killing; assassination; **assassino, -a** [asa'sinu, a] *m/f* murderer; assassin

assaz [a'saʒ] *adv* (*suficientemente*) sufficiently; (*muito*) rather

assediar [ase'dʒja*] *vt* (*sitiar*) to besiege; (*importunar*) to pester; **assédio** [a'sedʒu] *m* siege; (*insistência*) insistence

assegurar [asegu'ra*] *vt* to secure; (*garantir*) to ensure; (*afirmar*) to assure; **assegurar-se** *vr*: **~-se de** to make sure of

asseio [a'seju] *m* cleanliness

assembléia [asẽ'bleja] *f* assembly; (*reunião*) meeting; **~ geral** (*ordinária*) annual general meeting

assentar [asẽ'ta*] *vt* (*fazer sentar*) to seat; (*colocar*) to place; (*estabelecer*) to establish; (*decidir*) to decide upon ♦ *vi* (*pó etc*) to settle; **assentar-se** *vr* to sit down; **~ em** *ou* **a** (*roupa*) to suit

assentir [asẽ'tʃi*] *vi*: **~ (em)** to agree (to)

assento [a'sẽtu] *m* seat; (*base*) base

assíduo, -a [a'sidwu, a] *adj* (*aluno*) who attends regularly; (*diligente*) assiduous; (*constante*) constant; **ser ~ num lugar** to be a regular visitor to a place

assim [a'sĩ] *adv* (*deste modo*) like this, in this way, thus; (*portanto*) therefore; (*igualmente*) likewise; **~ ~** so-so; **~ mesmo** in any case; **e ~ por diante** and so on; **~ como** as well as; **como ~?** how do you mean?; **~ que** (*logo que*) as soon as

assimilar [asimi'la*] *vt* to assimilate; (*apreender*) to take in; (*assemelhar*) to compare

assinante [asi'nãtʃi] *m/f* (*de jornal etc*) subscriber

assinar [asi'na*] *vt* to sign

assinatura [asina'tura] *f* (*nome*) signature; (*de jornal etc*) subscription; (TEATRO) season ticket

assinto *etc* [a'sĩtu] *vb* V **assentir**

assistência [asiʃ'tẽsja] *f* (*presença*) presence; (*público*) audience; (*auxílio*) aid; **~ social** social work

assistente [asiʃ'tẽtʃi] *adj* assistant ♦ *m/f* spectator, onlooker; (*ajudante*) assistant; **~ social** social worker

assistir [asiʃ'tʃi*] *vt*, *vi*: **~ (a)** (MED) to attend (to); **~ a** to assist; (TV, filme, jogo) to watch; (*reunião*) to attend

assoar [aso'a*] *vt*: **~ o nariz** to blow one's nose; **assoar-se** *vr* (PT) to blow one's nose

assobiar [aso'bja*] *vi* to whistle

assobio [aso'biu] *m* whistle

associação [asosja'sãw] (*pl -ões*) *f* association; (*organização*) society; (*parceria*) partnership

associado, -a [aso'sjadu, a] *adj* associate ♦ *m/f* associate, member; (COM) associate; (*sócio*) partner

associar [aso'sja*] *vt* to associate; **associar-se** *vr*: **~-se a** to associate with

assombração [asõbra'sãw] (*pl -ões*) *f* ghost

assombro [a'sõbru] *m* amazement,

astonishment; (*maravilha*) marvel;
assombroso, -a [asõˈbrozu, ˌɔza]
adj astonishing, amazing
assoviar [asoˈvja*] vt = **assobiar**
assovio [asoˈviu] m = **assobio**
assumir [asuˈmi*] vt to assume,
take on; (*reconhecer*) to accept
assunto [aˈsũtu] m subject, matter;
(*enredo*) plot
assustador, a [asuʃtaˈdo*, a] adj
(*alarmante*) startling; (*amedronta-
dor*) frightening
assustar [asuʃˈta*] vt to frighten;
(*alarmar*) to startle; **assustar-se**
vr to be frightened
asteca [aʃˈtɛka] adj, m/f Aztec
astrologia [aʃtroloˈʒia] f astrology
astronauta [aʃtroˈnawta] m/f astronaut
astronave [aʃtroˈnavi] f spaceship
astronomia [aʃtronoˈmia] f astronomy
astucia [aʃˈtusja] f cunning
ata [ˈata] f (*de reunião*) minutes pl
atacado [ataˈkadu] m: **por ~** wholesale
atacante [ataˈkãtʃi] adj attacking
♦ m/f attacker, assailant ♦ m
(FUTEBOL) forward
atacar [ataˈka*] vt to attack; (*problema etc*) to tackle
atado, -a [aˈtadu, a] adj (*desajeitado*) clumsy, awkward; (*perplexo*)
puzzled
atalho [aˈtaʎu] m (*caminho*) short
cut
ataque [aˈtaki] m attack; **~ aéreo** air
raid
atar [aˈta*] vt to tie (up), fasten; **não
~ nem desatar** (*pessoa*) to waver;
(*negócio*) to be in the air
atarefado, -a [atareˈfadu, a] adj
busy
atarracado, -a [ataxaˈkadu, a] adj
stocky

até [aˈtɛ] prep (PT: + a: *lugar*) up to,
as far as; (*tempo etc*) until, till ♦ adv
(tb: **~ mesmo**) even; **~ certo ponto**
to a certain extent; **~ em cima** to
the top; **~ já** see you soon; **~ logo**
bye!; **~ onde** as far as; **~ que** until;
~ que enfim! at last!
atear [ateˈa*] vt (*fogo*) to kindle; (*fig*)
to incite, inflame; **atear-se** vr to
blaze; (*paixões*) to flare up
atéia [aˈtɛja] f de **ateu**
atemorizar [atemoriˈza*] vt to
frighten; (*intimidar*) to intimidate
Atenas [aˈtenaʃ] n Athens
atenção [atẽˈsãw] (pl **-ões**) f attention; (*cortesia*) courtesy; (*bondade*)
kindness; **~!** be careful; **chamar
a ~** to attract attention, **atencioso, -a** [atẽˈsjozu, ˌɔza] adj considerate
atender [atẽˈde*] vt: **~ (a)** to attend
to; (*receber*) to receive; (*deferir*) to
grant; (*telefone etc*) to answer;
(*paciente*) to see ♦ vi to answer; (*dar
atenção*) to pay attention; **atendimento** [atẽdʒiˈmẽtu] m service;
(*recepção*) reception; **horário de
atendimento** opening hours; (*em
consultório*) surgery (BRIT) ou office
(us) hours
atentado [atẽˈtadu] m attack;
(*crime*) crime; (*contra a vida de
alguém*) attempt on sb's life
atento, -a [aˈtẽtu, a] adj attentive;
estar ~ a to be aware ou mindful
of
atenuante [ateˈnwãtʃi] adj extenuating ♦ m extenuating circumstance
atenuar [ateˈnwa*] vt to reduce,
lessen
aterragem [ateˈxaʒẽj] (PT) (pl **-ns**) f
(AER) landing
aterrar [ateˈxa*] (PT) vi (AER) to land
aterrissagem [atexiˈsaʒẽ] (BR) (pl
-ns) f (AER) landing

aterrissar [atexi'sa*] (BR) vi (AER) to land

aterrorizante [atexori'zãtʃi] adj terrifying

aterrorizar [atexori'za*] vt to terrorize

atestado [ateʃ'tadu] m certificate; (prova) proof; (JUR) testimony

ateu, atéia [a'tew, a'tɛja] adj, m/f atheist

atiçar [atʃi'sa*] vt (fogo) to poke; (incitar) to incite; (provocar) to provoke; (sentimento) to induce

atinar [atʃi'na*] vt (acertar) to guess correctly ♦ vi: ~ com (solução) to find; ~ em to notice; ~ a fazer algo to succeed in doing sth

atingir [atʃĩ'ʒi*] vt to reach; (acertar) to hit; (afetar) to affect; (objetivo) to achieve; (compreender) to grasp

atirador, a [atʃira'do*, a] m/f marksman/woman; ~ de tocaia sniper

atirar [atʃi'ra*] vt to throw, fling ♦ vi (arma) to shoot; **atirar-se** vr: ~-se a to hurl o.s. at

atitude [atʃi'tudʒi] f attitude; (postura) posture

atividade [atʃivi'dadʒi] f activity

ativo, -a [a'tʃivu, a] adj active ♦ m (COM) assets pl

atlântico, -a [at'lãtʃiku, a] adj Atlantic ♦ m: o (Oceano) A~ the Atlantic (Ocean)

atlas ['atlaʃ] m inv atlas

atleta [at'leta] m/f athlete; **atlético, -a** [at'lɛtʃiku, a] adj athletic; **atletismo** [atle'tʃiʒmu] m athletics sg

atmosfera [atmoʃ'fɛra] f atmosphere

ato ['atu] m act, action; (cerimônia) ceremony; (TEATRO) act; **em ~ contínuo** straight after; **no ~** on the

spot; **no mesmo ~** at the same time

à-toa adj (insignificante) insignificant; (simples) simple, easy ♦ adv V toa

atômico, -a [a'tomiku, a] adj atomic

atomizador [atomiza'do*] m atomizer

átomo ['atomu] m atom

atônito, -a [a'tonitu, a] adj astonished, amazed

ator [a'to*] m actor

atordoado, -a [atox'dwadu, a] adj dazed

atordoar [atox'dwa*] vt to daze, stun

atormentar [atoxmẽ'ta*] vt to torment

atração [atra'sãw] (pl -ões) f attraction

atracar [atra'ka*] vt, vi (NÁUT) to moor; **atracar-se** vr to grapple

atrações [atra'sõjʃ] fpl de **atração**

atractivo, -a [atra'tivu, a] (PT) adj = **atrativo**

atraente [atra'ẽtʃi] adj attractive

atraiçoar [atraj'swa*] vt to betray

atrair [atra'i*] vt to attract; (fascinar) to fascinate

atrapalhar [atrapa'ʎa*] vt to confuse; (perturbar) to disturb; (dificultar) to hinder ♦ vi to be a nuisance

atrás [a'trajʃ] adv behind; (no fundo) at the back ♦ prep: ~ de behind; (no tempo) after; **dois meses ~** two months ago

atrasado, -a [atra'zadu, a] adj late; (país etc) backward; (relógio etc) slow; (pagamento) overdue; **atrasados** [atra'zaduʃ] mpl (COM) arrears

atrasar [atra'za*] vt to delay; (progresso, desenvolvimento: progresso) to hold back; (relógio) to put back; (pagamento) to be late with ♦ vi

atraso 351 **ausentar-se**

(*relógio etc*) to be slow; (*avião, pessoa*) to be late; **atrasar-se** *vr* to be late; (*num trabalho*) to fall behind; (*num pagamento*) to get into arrears

atraso [a'trazu] *m* delay; (*de país etc*) backwardness; **~s** *mpl* (*com*) arrears; **com 20 minutos de ~ 20** minutes late

atrativo, -a [atra'tʃivu, a] *adj* attractive ♦ *m* attraction; (*incentivo*) incentive; **~s** *mpl* (*encantos*) charms

através [atra'vɛʃ] *adv* across; **~ de** across; (*pelo centro de*) through

atravessar [atrave'sa*] *vt* to cross; (*pôr ao través*) to put ou lay across; (*traspassar*) to pass through

atrever-se [atre'vexsi] *vr*: **~ a** to dare to; **atrevido, -a** [atre'vidu, a] *adj* cheeky; (*corajoso*) bold; **atrevimento** [atrevi'mẽtu] *m* cheek; boldness

atribuir [atri'bwi*] *vt*: **~ algo a** to attribute sth to; (*prêmios, regalias*) to confer sth on

atributo [atri'butu] *m* attribute

átrio ['atrju] *m* hall; (*pátio*) courtyard

atrito [a'tritu] *m* (*fricção*) friction; (*desentendimento*) disagreement

atriz [a'triz] *f* actress

atropelamento [atropela'mẽtu] *m* (*de pedestre*) road accident

atropelar [atrope'la*] *vt* to knock down, run over; (*empurrar*) to jostle

atuação [atwa'sãw] (*pl* **-ões**) *f* acting; (*de ator etc*) performance

atual [a'twaw] (*pl* **-ais**) *adj* current; (*pessoa, carro*) modern; **atualidade** [atwali'dadʒi] *f* present (time); **atualidades** *fpl* (*notícias*) news *sg*; **atualizar** [atwali'za*] *vt* to update; **atualmente** [atwaw'mẽtʃi] *adv* at present, currently; (*hoje em dia*) nowadays

atuante [a'twãtʃi] *adj* active

atuar [a'twa*] *vi* to act; **~ para** to contribute to; **~ sobre** to influence

atum [a'tũ] (*pl* **-ns**) *m* tuna (fish)

aturdido, -a [atux'dʒidu, a] *adj* stunned; (*com barulho*) deafened; (*com confusão, movimento*) bewildered

aturdir [atux'dʒi*] *vt* to stun; (*suj: barulho*) to deafen; (: *confusão, movimento*) to bewilder

audácia [aw'dasja] *f* boldness; (*insolência*) insolence; **audacioso, -a** [awda'sjozu, ɔza] *adj* daring; insolent

audição [awdʒi'sãw] (*pl* **-ões**) *f* audition

audiência [aw'dʒjẽsja] *f* audience; (*de tribunal*) session, hearing

audiovisual [awdʒjovi'zwaw] (*pl* **-ais**) *adj* audiovisual

auditar [awdʒi'ta*] *vt* to audit

auditor, a [awdʒi'to*, a] *m/f* auditor; (*juiz*) judge; (*ouvinte*) listener

auditoria [awdʒito'ria] *f*: **fazer a ~** de to audit

auditório [awdʒi'tɔrju] *m* audience; (*recinto*) auditorium

auge ['awʒi] *m* height, peak

aula ['awla] *f* (*PT: sala*) classroom; (*lição*) lesson, class; **dar ~** to teach

aumentar [awmẽ'ta*] *vt* to increase; (*salários, preços: salários*) to raise; (*sala, casa*) to expand, extend; (*suj: lente*) to magnify; (*acrescentar*) to add ♦ *vi* to increase; (*preço, salário: preço*) to rise, go up

aumento [aw'mẽtu] *m* increase; rise; (*ampliação*) enlargement; (*crescimento*) growth

aurora [aw'rɔra] *f* dawn

ausência [aw'zẽsja] *f* absence

ausentar-se [awzẽ'taxsi] *vr* (*ir-se*) to go away; (*afastar-se*) to stay away

ausente [aw'zẽtʃi] *adj* absent

austeridade [awʃteri'dadʒi] *f* austerity

austral [awʃ'traw] (*pl* -ais) *adj* southern

Austrália [awʃ'tralja] *f*: **a ~** Australia; **australiano, -a** [awʃtra-'ljanu, a] *adj, m/f* Australian

Áustria ['awʃtrja] *f*: **a ~** Austria; **austríaco, -a** [awʃ'triaku, a] *adj, m/f* Austrian

autêntico, -a [aw'tẽtʃiku, a] *adj* authentic; (*pessoa*) genuine; (*verdadeiro*) true, real

auto ['awtu] *m* car; **~s** *mpl* (*JUR*: *processo*) legal proceedings; (*documentos*) legal papers

autobiografia [awtobjogra'fia] *f* autobiography

autobronzeador [awtobrõza'do*] *adj* self-tanning

autocarro [awto'kaxu] (*PT*) *m* bus

autodefesa [awtode'feza] *f* self-defence (*BRIT*), self-defense (*US*)

autodidata [awtodʒi'data] *adj* self-taught

autodisciplina [awtodʒisi'plina] *f* self-discipline

autódromo [aw'tɔdromu] *m* race track

auto-escola *f* driving school

auto-estrada *f* motorway (*BRIT*), expressway (*US*)

autografar [awtogra'fa*] *vt* to autograph

autógrafo [aw'tɔgrafu] *m* autograph

automático, -a [awto'matʃiku, a] *adj* automatic

automobilismo [awtomobi'liʒmu] *m* motoring; (*ESPORTE*) motor car racing

automóvel [awto'mɔvew] (*pl* -eis) *m* motor car (*BRIT*), automobile (*US*)

autonomia [awtono'mia] *f* autonomy

autópsia [aw'tɔpsja] *f* postmortem, autopsy

autor, a [aw'to*, a] *m/f* author; (*de um crime*) perpetrator; (*JUR*) plaintiff

autoral [awto'raw] (*pl* -ais) *adj*: **direitos autorais** copyright *sg*

autoridade [awtori'dadʒi] *f* authority

autorização [awtoriza'sãw] (*pl* -ões) *f* permission, authorization; **dar ~ a alguém para** to authorize sb to

autorizar [awtori'za*] *vt* to authorize

auto-serviço *m* self-service

auto-suficiente *adj* self-sufficient

auxiliar [awsi'lja*] *adj* auxiliary ♦ *m/f* assistant ♦ *vt* to help; **auxílio** [aw'silju] *m* help, assistance

Av *abr* (= *avenida*) Ave

aval [a'vaw] (*pl* -ais) *m* guarantee

avalancha [ava'lãʃa] *f* avalanche

avaliação [avalja'sãw] (*pl* -ões) *f* valuation; (*apreciação*) assessment

avaliar [ava'lja*] *vt* to value; (*apreciar*) to assess

avançado, -a [avã'sadu, a] *adj* advanced; (*idéias, pessoa*) progressive

avançar [avã'sa*] *vt* to move forward ♦ *vi* to advance; **avanço** [a'vãsu] *m* advancement; (*progresso*) progress

avarento, -a [ava'rẽtu, a] *adj* mean ♦ *m/f* miser

avaria [ava'ria] *f* (*TEC*) breakdown; **avariado, -a** [ava'rjadu, a] *adj* (*máquina*) out of order; (*carro*) broken down; **avariar** [ava'rja*] *vt* to damage ♦ *vi* to suffer damage; (*TEC*) to break down

ave ['avi] *f* bird

aveia [a'veja] *f* oats *pl*

avelã [ave'lã] *f* hazelnut

avenida [ave'nida] f avenue

avental [avē'taw] (pl -**ais**) m apron; (vestido) pinafore dress (BRIT); jumper (US)

aventura [avē'tura] f adventure; **aventurar** [avētu'ra*] vt to risk, venture

averiguação [averigwa'sãw] (pl -**ões**) f investigation, inquiry; (verificação) verification

averiguar [averi'gwa*] vt to investigate; (verificar) to verify

avermelhado, -a [avexme'ʎadu, a] adj reddish

avesso, -a [a'vesu, a] adj (lado) opposite, reverse ♦ m wrong side, reverse; **ao ~** inside out; **às avessas** (inverso) upside down; (oposto) the wrong way round

avestruz [avej'truʒ] m ostrich

aviação [avja'sãw] f aviation, flying

aviador, a [avja'do*, a] m/f aviator, airman/woman

avião [a'vjãw] (pl -**ões**) m aeroplane; **~ a jato** jet

avidez [avi'deʒ] f greed; (desejo) eagerness; **ávido, -a** ['avidu, a] adj greedy; eager

aviões [a'vjõjʃ] mpl de **avião**

avisar [avi'za*] vt to warn; (informar) to tell, let know; **aviso** [a'vizu] m (comunicação) notice

avistar [avij'ta*] vt to catch sight of

avô, -ó [a'vo, a'vɔ] m/f grandfather/mother; **avós** mpl grandparents

avulso, -a [a'vuwsu, a] adj separate, detached

axila [ak'sila] f armpit

azar [a'za*] m bad luck; **~!** too bad, bad luck!; **estar com ~, ter ~** to be unlucky; **azarento, -a** [aza'rētu, a] adj unlucky

azedar [aze'da*] vt to turn sour ♦ vi to turn sour; (leite) to go off;

azedo, -a [a'zedu, a] adj sour; off; (fig) grumpy

azeite [a'zejtʃi] m oil; (de oliva) olive oil

azeitona [azej'tɔna] f olive

azia [a'zia] f heartburn

azougue [a'zogi] m (QUÍM) mercury

azul [a'zuw] (pl -**uis**) adj blue

azulejo [azu'leʒu] m (glazed) tile

azul-marinho adj inv navy blue

azul-turquesa adj inv turquoise

B

baba ['baba] f dribble

babá [ba'ba] f nanny

babaca [ba'baka] (col) adj stupid ♦ m/f idiot

babado [ba'badu] m frill; (col) piece of gossip

babador [baba'do*] m bib

babar [ba'ba*] vi to dribble; **babar-se** vr to dribble

baby-sitter ['bejbisite*] (pl -**s**) m/f baby-sitter

bacalhau [baka'ʎaw] m (dried) cod

bacana [ba'kana] (col) adj great

bacharel [baʃa'rew] (pl -**éis**) m graduate

bacia [ba'sia] f basin; (ANAT) pelvis

backup [ba'kapi] (pl -**s**) m (COMPUT) back up; **tirar um ~ de** to back up

baço, -a ['basu, a] adj dull; (metal) tarnished ♦ m (ANAT) spleen

bactéria [bak'tɛrja] f germ, bacterium; **~s** bacteria pl

badalar [bada'la*] vt, vi to ring

baderna [ba'dexna] f commotion

bafo ['bafu] m (bad) breath

bagaço [ba'gasu] m (de frutos) pulp; (PT: cachaça) brandy; **estar/ficar um ~** (fig: pessoa) to be/get run down

bagageiro [baga'ʒejru] m (AUTO)

roofrack; (*PT*) porter

bagagem [ba'gaʒẽ] *f* luggage; (*fig*) baggage; **recebimento de ~** (*AER*) baggage reclaim

bagatela [baga'tɛla] *f* trinket; (*fig*) trifle

bago ['bagu] *m* (*fruto*) berry; (*uva*) grape; (*de chumbo*) pellet

bagulho [ba'guʎu] *m* (*objeto*) piece of junk

bagunça [ba'gũsa] *f* mess, shambles *sg*; **bagunçado, -a** [bagũ'sadu, a] *adj* in a mess; **bagunçar** [bagũ'sa*] *vt* to mess up; **bagunceiro, -a** [bagũ'sejru, a] *adj* messy

baía [ba'ia] *f* bay

bailado [baj'ladu] *m* dance; (*balé*) ballet

bailarino, -a [bajla'rinu, a] *m/f* ballet dancer

baile ['bajli] *m* dance; (*formal*) ball; **~ à fantasia** fancy-dress ball

bainha [ba'iɲa] *f* (*de arma*) sheath; (*de costura*) hem

bairro ['bajxu] *m* district

baixa ['bajʃa] *f* decrease; (*de preço*: *redução*) reduction; (: *queda*) fall; (*em vendas*) drop; (*em combate*) casualty; (*de serviço*) discharge

baixar [baj'ʃa*] *vt* to lower; (*ordem*) to issue; (*lei*) to pass; (*COMPUT*) to download ♦ *vi* to go (*ou* come) down; (*temperatura, preço*) to drop, fall

baixinho [baj'ʃiɲu] *adv* (*falar*) softly, quietly; (*em segredo*) secretly

baixo, -a ['bajʃu, a] *adj* low; (*pessoa*) short, small; (*rio*) shallow; (*linguagem*) common; (*olhos, cabeça*) lowered; (*atitude*) mean; (*metal*) base ♦ *adv* low; (*em posição baixa*) low down; (*falar*) softly ♦ *m* (*MÚS*) bass; **em ~** below; (*em casa*) downstairs; **em voz baixa** in a quiet voice; **para ~** down, downwards;

(*em casa*) downstairs; **por ~ de** under, underneath; **baixo-astral** (*col*) *m*: **estar num baixo-astral** to be on a downer

bala ['bala] *f* bullet; (*BR*: *doce*) sweet

balança [ba'lãsa] *f* scales *pl*; **B~** (*ASTROLOGIA*) Libra; **~ comercial** balance of trade; **~ de pagamentos** balance of payments

balançar [balã'sa*] *vt* to swing; (*pesar*) to weigh (up) ♦ *vi* to swing; (*carro, avião*) to shake; (*em cadeira*) to rock; **balançar-se** *vr* to swing; **balanço** [ba'lãsu] *m* (*movimento*) swaying; (*brinquedo*) swing; (*de carro, avião*) shaking; (*COM*: *registro*) balance (sheet); (: *verificação*) audit; **fazer um balanço de** (*fig*) to take stock of

balão [ba'lãw] (*pl* -**ões**) *m* balloon

balbuciar [bawbu'sja*] *vt*, *vi* to babble

balbúrdia [baw'buxdʒja] *f* uproar, bedlam

balcão [baw'kãw] (*pl* -**ões**) *m* balcony; (*de loja*) counter; (*TEATRO*) circle; **~ de informações** information desk; **balconista** [bawko'niʃta] *m/f* shop assistant

balde ['bawdʒi] *m* bucket, pail

balé [ba'lɛ] *m* ballet

baleia [ba'leja] *f* whale

baliza [ba'liza] *f* (*estaca*) post; (*bóia*) buoy; (*luminosa*) beacon; (*ESPORTE*) goal

balneário [baw'njarju] *m* bathing resort

balões [ba'lõjʃ] *mpl de* **balão**

baloiço [ba'lojsu] (*PT*) *m* (*de criança*) swing; (*ação*) swinging

balsa ['bawsa] *f* raft; (*barca*) ferry

bamba ['bãba] *adj*, *m/f* expert

bambo, -a ['bãbu, a] *adj* slack, loose

banana [ba'nana] *f* banana; **bananeira** [bana'nejra] *f* banana tree

banca ['bãka] f bench; (escritório) office; (em jogo) bank; ~ (de jornais) newsstand; **bancada** [bã'kada] f (banco, POL) bench; (de cozinha) worktop

bancar [bã'ka*] vt to finance ♦ vi (fingir): ~ **que** to pretend that; **bancário, -a** [bã'karju, a] adj bank atr ♦ m/f bank employee

bancarrota [bãka'xota] f bankruptcy; **ir a ~** to go bankrupt

banco ['bãku] m (assento) bench; (COM) bank; ~ **de areia** sandbank; ~ **de dados** (COMPUT) database

banda ['bãda] f band; (lado) side; (cinto) sash; **de ~** sideways; **pôr de ~** to put aside; ~ **desenhada** (PT) cartoon

bandeira [bã'dejra] f flag; (estandarte) banner; **bandeirinha** [bãdej'riɲa] m (ESPORTE) linesman

bandeja [bã'deʒa] f tray

bandido [bã'dʒidu, a] m bandit

bando ['bãdu] m band; (grupo) group; (de malfeitores) gang; (de ovelhas) flock; (de gado) herd; (de livros etc) pile

banha ['baɲa] f fat; (de porco) lard

banhar [ba'ɲa*] vt to wet; (mergulhar) to dip; (lavar) to wash; **banhar-se** vr to bathe

banheira [ba'ɲejra] f bath

banheiro [ba'ɲejru] m bathroom

banho ['baɲu] m bath; (mergulho) dip; **tomar ~** to have a bath; (de chuveiro) to have a shower; ~ **de chuveiro** shower; ~ **de sol** sunbathing

banir [ba'ni*] vt to banish

banqueiro, -a [bã'kejru, a] m/f banker

banquete [bã'ketʃi] m banquet

baptismo etc [ba'tiʒmu] (PT) = **batismo** etc

bar [ba*] m bar

baralho [ba'raʎu] m pack of cards

barata [ba'rata] f cockroach

barateiro, -a [bara'tejru, a] adj cheap

barato, -a [ba'ratu, a] adj cheap ♦ adv cheaply

barba ['baxba] f beard; **fazer a ~** to shave

bárbaro, -a ['baxbaru, a] adj barbaric; (dor, calor) terrible; (maravilhoso) great

barbeador [baxbja'do*] m razor; (tb: ~ **elétrico**) shaver

barbear [bax'bja*] vt to shave; **barbear-se** vr to shave; **barbearia** [baxbja'ria] f barber's (shop)

barbeiro [bax'bejru] m barber; (loja) barber's

barca ['baxka] f barge; (de travessia) ferry

barco ['baxku] m boat; ~ **a motor** motorboat; ~ **a remo** rowing boat; ~ **a vela** sailing boat

barganha [bax'gaɲa] f bargain; **barganhar** [baxga'ɲa*] vt, vi to negotiate

barman [bax'mã] (pl -**men**) m barman

barra ['baxa] f bar; (faixa) strip; (traço) stroke; (alavanca) lever

barraca [ba'xaka] f (tenda) tent; (de feira) stall; (de madeira) hut; (de praia) sunshade; **barracão** [baxa'kãw] (pl -**ões**) m shed; **barraco** [ba'xaku] m shack, shanty

barragem [ba'xaʒẽ] (pl -**ns**) f dam; (impedimento) barrier

barranco [ba'xãku] m ravine, gully; (de rio) bank

barrar [ba'xa*] vt to bar

barreira [ba'xejra] f barrier; (cerca) fence; (ESPORTE) hurdle

barricada [baxi'kada] f barricade

barriga [ba'xiga] f belly; **estar de ~** to be pregnant; ~ **da perna** calf;

barrigudo, -a [baxi'gudu, a] *adj*
paunchy, pot-bellied

barril [ba'xiw] (*pl* **-is**) *m* barrel, cask

barro ['baxu] *m* clay; (*lama*) mud

barulhento, -a [baru'ʎẽtu, a] *adj*
noisy

barulho [ba'ruʎu] *m* (*ruído*) noise;
(*tumulto*) din

base ['bazi] *f* base; (*fig*) basis; **sem ~**
groundless; **com ~ em** based on; **na
~ de** by means of

basear [ba'zja*] *vt* to base; **basear-
se** *vr*: **~-se em** to be based on

básico, -a ['baziku, a] *adj* basic

basquete [baʃ'ketʃi] *m* = **basquetebol**

basquetebol [baʃkete'bɔw] *m*
basketball

basta ['baʃta] *m*: **dar um ~ em** to
call a halt to

bastante [baʃ'tãtʃi] *adj* (*suficiente*)
enough; (*muito*) quite a lot (of) ♦ *adv* enough; a lot

bastão [baʃ'tãw] (*pl* **-ões**) *m* stick

bastar [baʃ'ta*] *vi* to be enough, be
sufficient; **bastar-se** *vr* to be self-
sufficient; **basta!** (that's) enough!; **~
para** to be enough to

bastardo, -a [baʃ'taxdu, a] *adj,
m/f* bastard

bastões [baʃ'tõjʃ] *mpl de* **bastão**

bata ['bata] *f* (*de mulher*) smock; (*de
médico*) overall

batalha [ba'taʎa] *f* battle; **bata-
lhador, a** [bataʎa'do*, a] *adj* strug-
gling ♦ *m/f* fighter; **batalhão**
[bata'ʎãw] (*pl* **-ões**) *m* battalion;
batalhar [bata'ʎa*] *vi* to battle,
fight; (*esforçar-se*) to make an effort,
try hard ♦ *vt* (*emprego*) to go after

batata [ba'tata] *f* potato; **~ doce**
sweet potato; **~s fritas** chips *pl*
(*BRIT*), French fries *pl* (*US*); (*de pacote*)
crisps *pl* (*BRIT*), (potato) chips *pl* (*US*)

bate-boca ['batʃi-] (*pl* **~s**) *m* row,

quarrel

batedeira [bate'dejra] *f* beater; (*de
manteiga*) churn; **~ elétrica** mixer

batente [ba'tẽtʃi] *m* doorpost

bate-papo ['batʃi-] (*pl* **~s**) (*BR*) *m*
chat

bater [ba'te*] *vt* to beat, strike; (*pé*)
to stamp; (*foto*) to take; (*porta*) to
slam; (*asas*) to flap; (*recorde*) to
break; (*roupa*) to wear all the time
♦ *vi* to slam; (*sino*) to ring; (*janela*)
to bang; (*coração*) to beat; (*sol*) to
beat down; **bater-se** *vr*: **~-se para**
fazer/por to fight to do/for; **~ (à
porta**) to knock (at the door); **~ à
maquina** to type; **~ em** to hit; **~
com o carro** to crash one's car; **~
com a cabeça** to bang one's head;
~ com o pé (em) to kick

bateria [bate'ria] *f* battery; (*MÚS*)
drums *pl*; **~ de cozinha** kitchen
utensils *pl*; **baterista** [bate'riʃta]
m/f drummer

batida [ba'tʃida] *f* beat; (*da porta*)
slam; (*à porta*) knock; (*da polícia*)
raid; (*AUTO*) crash; (*bebida*) cocktail
of cachaça, fruit and sugar

batido, -a [ba'tʃidu, a] *adj* beaten;
(*roupa*) worn ♦ *m*: **~ de leite** (*PT*)
milkshake

batina [ba'tʃina] *f* (*REL*) cassock

batismo [ba'tʃiʒmu] *m* baptism,
christening

batizar [batʃi'za*] *vt* to baptize,
christen

batom [ba'tõ] (*pl* **-ns**) *m* lipstick

batucada [batu'kada] *f* dance percussion group

batucar [batu'ka*] *vt, vi* to drum

baú [ba'u] *m* trunk

baunilha [baw'niʎa] *f* vanilla

bazar [ba'za*] *m* bazaar; (*loja*) shop

BCE *m* (= *Banco Central Europeu*)
ECB

bêbado, -a ['bebadu, a] *adj, m/f*

drunk

bebê [be'be] m baby

bebedeira [bebe'dejra] f drunkenness; **tomar uma ~** to get drunk

bêbedo, -a ['bebedu, a] adj, m/f = **bêbado**

bebedouro [bebe'douru] m drinking fountain

beber [be'be*] vt to drink; (absorver) to soak up ♦ vi to drink; **beber** [be'bida] f drink

beça ['besa] (col) f: **à ~** (com vb): **ele comeu à ~** he ate a lot; (com n): **ela tinha livros à ~** she had a lot of books

beco ['beku] m alley, lane; **~ sem saída** cul-de-sac

bege ['beʒi] adj inv beige

beija-flor [bejʒa-'flɔ*] (pl **~es**) m hummingbird

beijar [hej'ʒa*] vt to kiss; **beijar-se** vr to kiss (one another); **beijo** ['bejʒu] m kiss; **dar beijos em alguém** to kiss sb

beira ['bejra] f edge; (de rio) bank; (orla) border; **à ~ de** on the edge of; (ao lado de) beside, by; (fig) on the verge of; **~ do telhado** eaves pl; **beira-mar** f seaside

belas-artes fpl fine arts

beldade [bew'dadʒi] f beauty

beleza [be'leza] f beauty; **que ~!** how lovely!

belga ['bewga] adj, m/f Belgian

Bélgica ['bɛwʒika] f: **a ~** Belgium

beliche [be'liʒi] m bunk

beliscão [beliʃ'kãw] (pl **-ões**) m pinch; **beliscar** [beliʃ'ka*] vt to pinch, nip; (comida) to nibble

Belize [be'lizi] m Belize

belo, -a ['bɛlu, a] adj beautiful

bem [bẽj] adv **1** (de maneira satisfatória, correta etc) well; **trabalha/**come ~ she works/eats well; **respondeu ~** he answered correctly; **me sinto/não me sinto ~** I feel fine/I don't feel very well; **tudo ~?** – **tudo ~** how's it going? – fine **2** (valor intensivo) very; **um quarto ~ quente** a nice warm room; **~ se vê que ...** it's clear that ... **3** (bastante) quite, fairly; **a casa é ~ grande** the house is quite big **4** (exatamente): **~ ali** right there; **não é ~ assim** it's not quite like that **5** (estar ~): **estou muito ~ aqui** I feel very happy here; **está ~!** vou **fazê-lo** oh all right, I'll do it! **6** (de bom grado): **eu ~ que iria mas ...** I'd gladly go but ... **7** (cheirar) good, nice

♦ m **1** (bem-estar) good; **estou dizendo isso para o seu ~** I'm telling you for your own good; **o ~ e o mal** good and evil **2** (posses): **bens** goods, property sg; **bens de consumo** consumer goods; **bens de família** family possessions; **bens móveis/imóveis** moveable property sg/real estate sg

♦ excl **1** (aprovação): **~!** OK!; **muito ~!** well done! **2** (desaprovação): **~ feito!** it serves you right!

♦ adj inv (tom depreciativo): **gente ~** posh people

♦ conj **1**: **nem ~** as soon as, no sooner than; **nem ~ ela chegou começou a dar ordens** as soon as she arrived she started to give orders, no sooner had she arrived than she started to give orders **2**: **se ~ que** though; **gostaria de ir se ~ que não tenho dinheiro** I'd like to go even though I've got no money **3**: **~ como** as well as; **o livro ~ como a peça foram escritos por ele** the book as well as the play was written by him

bem-conceituado, -a [bējkõsej'twadu, a] *adj* highly regarded

bem-disposto, -a [bējdʒiʃ'poʃtu, 'poʃta] *adj* well, in good form

bem-estar *m* well-being

bem-me-quer (*pl* ~**es**) *m* daisy

bem-vindo, -a *adj* welcome

bênção ['bēsãw] (*pl* ~**s**) *f* blessing

beneficência [benefi'sēsja] *f* kindness; (*caridade*) charity

beneficiar [benefi'sja*] *vt* to benefit; (*melhorar*) to improve; **beneficiar-se** *vr* to benefit

benefício [bene'fisju] *m* benefit; (*vantagem*) profit; (*favor*) favour (*BRIT*), favor (*US*); **em ~ de** in aid of; (*TEATRO*) in benefit of

benéfico, -a [be'nefiku, a] *adj* beneficial; (*generoso*) generous

benévolo, -a [be'nɛvolu, a] *adj* benevolent, kind

benfeitor, a [bēfej'to*, a] *m/f* benefactor/benefactress

bengala [bē'gala] *f* walking stick

benigno, -a [be'nignu, a] *adj* kind; (*agradável*) pleasant; (*MED*) benign

bens [bējʃ] *mpl de* **bem**

bento, -a ['bētu, a] *pp de* **benzer** ♦ *adj* blessed; (*água*) holy

benzer [bē'ze*] *vt* to bless; **benzer-se** *vr* to cross o.s.

berço ['bexsu] *m* cradle; (*cama*) cot; (*origem*) birthplace

Berlim [bex'lĩ] *n* Berlin

berma ['bɛxma] (*PT*) *f* hard shoulder (*BRIT*), berm (*US*)

berrar [be'xa*] *vi* to bellow; (*criança*) to bawl; **berreiro** [be'xejru] *m*: **abrir o berreiro** to burst out crying; **berro** ['bɛxu] *m* yell

besta ['beʃta] *adj* stupid; (*convencido*) full of oneself; **~ de carga** beast of burden; **besteira** [beʃ'tejra] *f*

foolishness; **dizer besteiras** to talk nonsense; **fazer uma besteira** to do something silly; **bestial** [beʃ'tʃjaw] (*pl* -**ais**) *adj* bestial; (*repugnante*) repulsive

best-seller ['bɛst'sɛlɛ*] (*pl* ~**s**) *m* best seller

betão [be'tãw] (*PT*) *m* concrete

beterraba [bete'xaba] *f* beetroot

bexiga [be'ʃiga] *f* bladder

bezerro, -a [be'zexu, a] *m/f* calf

BI *abr m* (*PT*: *bilhete de identidade*) identity card; *see boxed note*

BI

All Portuguese citizens are required to carry an identity card, known as the BI or *bilhete de identidade*. The photocard, which gives the holder's name, date of birth, marital status, height and a fingerprint, can be used instead of a passport for travel within the European Union. Failure to produce a valid identity card when stopped by the police can result in a fine.

Bíblia ['biblja] *f* Bible

bibliografia [bibljogra'fia] *f* bibliography

biblioteca [bibljo'tɛka] *f* library; (*estante*) bookcase; **bibliotecário, -a** [bibljote'karju, a] *m/f* librarian

bica ['bika] *f* tap; (*PT*) black coffee, expresso

bicha ['biʃa] *f* (*lombriga*) worm; (*BR*: *col, pej*: *homossexual*) queer; (*PT*: *fila*) queue

bicho ['biʃu] *m* animal; (*inseto*) insect, bug

bicicleta [bisi'kleta] *f* bicycle; (*col*) bike; **andar de ~** to cycle; **~ do exército** exercise bike

bico ['biku] *m* (*de ave*) beak; (*ponta*)

point; (de chaleira) spout; (boca) mouth; (de pena) nib; (de peito) nipple; (de gás) jet; (col: emprego) casual job; (chupeta) dummy; **calar o ~** to shut up

bidê [bi'de] m bidet

bife ['bifi] m (beef) steak; **~ a cavalo** steak with fried eggs; **~ à milanesa** beef escalope; **~ de panela** beef stew

bifurcação [bifuxka'sãw] (pl -ões) f fork

bifurcar-se [bifux'kaxsi] vr to fork, divide

bigode [bi'gɔdʒi] m moustache

bijuteria [biʒute'ria] f (costume) jewellery (BRIT) ou jewelry (US)

bilhão [bi'ʎãw] (pl -ões) m billion

bilhar [bi'ʎa*] m (jogo) billiards sg

bilhete [bi'ʎetʃi] m ticket; (cartinha) note; **~ de ida** single (BRIT) ou one-way ticket; **~ de ida e volta** return (BRIT) ou round-trip (US) ticket; **bilheteira** [biʎe'tejra] (PT) f = **~ria**; **bilheteiro, -a** [biʎe'tejru, a] m/f ticket seller; **bilheteria** [biʎete'ria] f ticket office

bilhões [bi'ʎõjʃ] mpl de **bilhão**

bilíngüe [bi'lĩgwi] adj bilingual

binóculo [bi'nɔkulu] m binoculars pl; (para teatro) opera glasses pl

biografia [bjogra'fia] f biography

biologia [bjolo'ʒia] f biology

biombo ['bjõbu] m screen

bip [bip] n pager, paging device

biquíni [bi'kini] m bikini

birita [bi'rita] (col) f drink

Birmânia [bix'manja] f: **a ~** Burma

biruta [bi'ruta] adj crazy ♦ f windsock

bis [biʃ] excl encore!

bisavô, -ó [biza'vo, ɔ] m/f great-grandfather/great-grandmother; **bisavós** [biza'vɔʃ] mpl great-grandparents

biscate [biʃ'katʃi] m odd job

biscoito [biʃ'kojtu] m biscuit (BRIT), cookie (US)

bispo ['biʃpu] m bishop

bissexto, -a [bi'seʃtu, a] adj: **ano ~** leap year

bit ['bitʃi] m (COMPUT) bit

bizarro, -a [bi'zaxu, a] adj bizarre

blasfemar [blaʃfe'ma*] vt to curse ♦ vi to blaspheme; **blasfêmia** [blaʃ'femja] f blasphemy; (ultraje) curse

blazer ['blejze*] (pl ~s) m blazer

blecaute [ble'kawtʃi] m power cut

blindado, -a [blĩ'dadu, a] adj armoured (BRIT), armored (US)

blitz [blits] f police raid; (na estrada) police road block

bloco ['blɔku] m block; (POL) bloc; (de escrever) writing pad; **~ de carnaval** carnival troupe

bloqueador [blokja'do*] m: **~ solar** sunblock

bloquear [blo'kja*] vt to blockade; (obstruir) to block; **bloqueio** [blo'keju] m blockade; blockage

blusa ['bluza] f (de mulher) blouse; (de homem) shirt; **~ de lã** jumper; **blusão** [blu'zãw] (pl -ões) m jacket

boa ['boa] adj f de **bom** ♦ f boa constrictor

boate ['bwatʃi] f nightclub

boato ['bwatu] m rumour (BRIT), rumor (US)

bobagem [bo'baʒẽ] (pl -ns) f silliness, nonsense; (dito, ato) silly thing

bobo, -a ['bobu, a] adj silly, daft ♦ m/f fool ♦ m (de corte) jester; **fazer-se de ~** to act the fool

bobó [bo'bɔ] m beans, palm oil and manioc

boca ['boka] f mouth; (entrada) entrance; (de fogão) ring; **de ~ aberta** amazed; **bater ~** to argue

bocadinho [boka'dʒiɲu] m: **um ~** (pouco tempo) a little while; (pouquinho) a little bit

bocado [bo'kadu] *m* mouthful, bite; (*pedaço*) piece, bit; **um ~ de tempo** quite some time

boçal [bo'saw] (*pl* **-ais**) *adj* ignorant; (*grosseiro*) uncouth

bocejar [bose'ʒa*] *vi* to yawn; **bocejo** [bo'seʒu] *m* yawn

bochecha [bo'ʃeʃa] *f* cheek; **bochecho** [bo'ʃeʃu] *m* mouthwash

boda ['boda] *f* wedding; **~s** *fpl* (*aniversário de casamento*) wedding anniversary *sg*

bode ['bɔdʒi] *m* goat; **~ expiatório** scapegoat

bofetada [bofe'tada] *f* slap

bofetão [bofe'tãw] (*pl* **-ões**) *m* punch

boi [boj] *m* ox

bóia ['bɔja] *f* buoy; (*col*) grub; (*de braço*) armband, water wing

boiar [bo'ja*] *vt*, *vi* to float

boi-bumbá [-bũ'ba] *n* (*BR*) *see boxed note*

BOI-BUMBÁ

The **boi-bumbá**, or **bumba-meu-boi**, is a traditional folk dance from north-eastern Brazil, which brings together human, animal and mythological characters in a theatrical performance. The ox, which the dance is named after, is played by a dancer wearing an iron frame covered in pieces of colourful fabric. Eventually the beast is "killed" and its meat is symbolically shared out before it comes back to life in the finale.

---

boicotar [bojko'ta*] *vt* to boycott; **boicote** [boj'kɔtʃi] *m* boycott

bola ['bɔla] *f* ball; **dar ~ para** (*flertar*) to flirt with; **ela não dá a menor ~ (para isso)** she couldn't care less (about it); **não ser certo da ~** (*col*)

not to be right in the head

bolacha [bo'laʃa] *f* biscuit (*BRIT*), cookie (*US*); (*col: bofetada*) wallop; (*para chope*) beermat

boleia [bo'leja] *f* driver's seat; **dar uma ~ a alguém** (*PT*) to give sb a lift

boletim [bole'tʃĩ] (*pl* **-ns**) *m* report; (*publicação*) newsletter; **~ meteorológico** weather forecast

bolha ['boʎa] *f* (*na pele*) blister; (*de ar, sabão*) bubble

boliche [bo'liʃi] *m* bowling, skittles *sg*

bolinho [bo'liɲu] *m*: **~ de carne** meat ball; **~ de arroz/bacalhau** rice/dry cod cake

Bolívia [bo'livja] *f*: **a ~** Bolivia

bolo ['bolu] *m* cake; (*monte: de gente*) bunch; (: *de papéis*) bundle; **dar o ~ em alguém** to stand sb up; **vai dar ~** (*col*) there's going to be trouble

bolor [bo'lo*] *m* mould (*BRIT*), mold (*US*); (*nas plantas*) mildew

bolota [bo'lɔta] *f* acorn

bolsa ['bowsa] *f* bag; (*COM: tb:* **~ de valores**) stock exchange; **~ (de estudos)** scholarship

bolso ['bowsu] *m* pocket; **de ~** pocket *atr*

PALAVRA CHAVE

---

bom, boa [bõ, 'boa] (*pl* **bons, boas**) *adj* **1** (*ótimo*) good; **é um livro ~ ou um ~ livro** it's a good book; **a comida está boa** the food is delicious; **o tempo está ~** the weather's fine; **ele foi muito ~ comigo** he was very nice ou kind to me

2 (*apropriado*): **ser ~ para** to be good for; **acho ~ você não ir** I think it's better if you don't go

3 (*irônico*): **um ~ quarto de hora** a good quarter of an hour; **que ~ motorista você é!** a fine ou some driver you are!; **seria ~ que ...!** a fine thing it would be if ...!; **essa é boa!** what a cheek!

4 (*saudação*): **~ dia!** good morning!; **boa tarde!** good afternoon!; **boa noite!** good evening!; (*ao deitar-se*) good night!; **tudo ~?** how's it going?

5 (*outras fraises*): **está ~?** OK?

♦ *excl*: **~!** all right!; **~, ... right, ...**

bomba ['bɔba] f bomb; (*TEC*) pump; (*fig*) bombshell; **~ atômica/relógio/de fumaça** atomic/time/smoke bomb; **~ de gasolina** petrol (*BRIT*) ou gas (*US*) pump; **~ de incêndio** fire extinguisher

bombardear [bõbax'dʒja*] *vt* to bomb; (*fig*) to bombard; **bombardeio** [bõbax'deju] *m* bombing, bombardment

bombeiro [bõ'bejru] *m* fireman; (*BR: encanador*) plumber; **o corpo de ~s** fire brigade

bombom [bõ'bõ] (*pl* **-ns**) *m* chocolate

bondade [bõ'dadʒi] f goodness, kindness; **tenha a ~ de vir** would you please come

bonde ['bõdʒi] (*BR*) *m* tram

bondoso, -a [bõ'dozu, ɔza] *adj* kind, good

boné [bo'nɛ] *m* cap

boneca [bo'nɛka] f doll

boneco [bo'nɛku] *m* dummy

bonito, -a [bo'nitu, a] *adj* pretty; (*gesto, dia*) nice ♦ *m* (*peixe*) tuna (fish), tunny

bônus ['bonuʃ] *m inv* bonus

boquiaberto, -a [bokja'bɛxtu, a] *adj* dumbfounded, astonished

borboleta [boxbo'leta] f butterfly; (*BR: roleta*) turnstile

borbotão [boxbo'tãw] (*pl* **-ões**) *m* gush, spurt; **sair aos borbotões** to gush out

borbulhar [boxbu'ʎa*] *vi* to bubble

borda ['bɔxda] f edge; (*do rio*) bank; **à ~ de** on the edge of

bordado [box'dadu] *m* embroidery

bordar [box'da*] *vt* to embroider

bordo ['bɔxdu] *m* (*de navio*) side; **a ~ on board**

borra ['bɔxa] f dregs *pl*

borracha [bo'xaʃa] f rubber; **borracheiro** [boxa'ʃejru] *m* tyre (*BRIT*) ou tire (*US*) specialist

borrão [bo'xãw] (*pl* **-ões**) *m* (*rascunho*) rough draft; (*mancha*) blot

borrar [bo'xa*] *vt* to blot; (*riscar*) to cross out

borrifar [boxi'fa*] *vt* to sprinkle; **borrifo** [bo'xifu] *m* spray

borrões [bo'xõjʃ] *mpl de* **borrão**

bosque ['bɔʃki] *m* wood, forest

bossa ['bɔsa] f charm; (*inchaço*) swelling; **~ nova** (*Mús*) *see boxed note*

BOSSA NOVA

Bossa nova is a type of music invented by young, middle-class inhabitants of Rio de Janeiro at the end of the 1950s. It has an obvious jazz influence, an unusual, rhythmic beat and lyrics praising beauty and love. Bossa nova became known around the world through the work of the conductor and composer Antônio Carlos Jobim whose compositions, working with the poet Vinícius de Morais, include the famous song "The Girl from Ipanema".

---

bota ['bɔta] f boot; **~s de borracha** wellingtons

botânica [bo'tanika] f botany

botão [bo'tãw] (*pl* **-ões**) *m* button; (*flor*) bud

botar [bo'ta*] *vt* to put; (*roupa, sa-*

patos) to put on; (*mesa*) to set; (*defeito*) to find; (*ovos*) to lay

bote [ˈbɔtʃi] *m* boat; (*com arma*) thrust; (*salto*) spring

botequim [botʃiˈkĩ] *m* bar

botija [boˈtʃiʒa] *f* (earthenware) jug

botões [boˈtõjʃ] *mpl de* **botão**

boxe [ˈbɔksi] *m* boxing

brabo, -a [ˈbrabu, a] *adj* fierce; (*zangado*) angry; (*ruim*) bad; (*calor*) unbearable

braçada [braˈsada] *f* armful; (NATAÇÃO) stroke

bracelete [braseˈletʃi] *m* bracelet

braço [ˈbrasu] *m* arm; **de ~s cruzados** with arms folded; (*fig*) without lifting a finger; **de ~ dado** arm-in-arm

bradar [braˈdaˈ] *vt, vi* to shout, yell; **brado** [ˈbradu] *m* shout, yell

braguilha [braˈgiʎa] *f* flies *pl*

branco, -a [ˈbrãku, a] *adj* white ♦ *m/f* white man/woman ♦ *m* (*espaço*) blank; **em ~** blank; **noite em ~** sleepless night; **brancura** [brãˈkura] *f* whiteness

brando, -a [ˈbrãdu, a] *adj* gentle; (*mole*) soft

brasa [ˈbraza] *f* hot coal; **em ~** red-hot; **pisar em ~** to be on tenter-hooks

brasão [braˈzãw] (*pl* -**ões**) *m* coat of arms

braseiro [braˈzejru] *m* brazier

Brasil [braˈziw] *m*: **o ~** Brazil; **brasileiro, -a** [braziˈlejru, a] *adj, m/f* Brazilian

Brasília [braˈzilja] *n* Brasília

brasões [braˈzõjʃ] *mpl de* **brasão**

bravata [braˈvata] *f* bravado, boasting

bravio, -a [braˈviu, a] *adj* (*selvagem*) wild; (*feroz*) ferocious

bravo, -a [ˈbravu, a] *adj* brave; (*furioso*) angry; (*mar*) rough ♦ *m*

brave man; **~!** bravo!; **bravura** [braˈvura] *f* courage, bravery

brecar [breˈkaˈ] *vt* (*carro*) to stop; (*reprimir*) to curb ♦ *vi* to brake

brecha [ˈbreʃa] *f* breach; (*abertura*) opening; (*dano*) damage; (*col*) chance

breu [brew] *m* tar, pitch

breve [ˈbrɛvi] *adj* short; (*conciso, rápido*) brief ♦ *adv* soon; **em ~** soon, shortly; **até ~** see you soon

bridge [ˈbridʒi] *m* bridge

briga [ˈbriga] *f* fight; (*verbal*) quarrel

brigada [briˈgada] *f* brigade

brigão, -ona [briˈgãw, ɔna] (*pl* -**ões**, ~**s**) *adj* quarrelsome ♦ *m/f* troublemaker

brigar [briˈgaˈ] *vi* to fight; (*altercar*) to quarrel

brigões [briˈgõjʃ] *mpl de* **brigão**

brigona [briˈgɔna] *f de* **brigão**

brilhante [briˈʎãtʃi] *adj* brilliant ♦ *m* diamond

brilhar [briˈʎaˈ] *vi* to shine

brilho [ˈbriʎu] *m* (*luz viva*) brilliance; (*esplendor*) splendour (BRIT), splendor (US); (*nos sapatos*) shine; (*de metais, olhos*) gleam

brincadeira [brĩkaˈdejra] *f* fun; (*graceja*) joke; (*de criança*) game; **deixe de ~s!** stop fooling!; **de ~** for fun

brincalhão, -ona [brĩkaˈʎãw, ɔna] (*pl* -**ões**, ~**s**) *adj* playful ♦ *m/f* joker, teaser

brincar [brĩˈkaˈ] *vi* to play; (*gracejar*) to joke; **estou brincando** I'm only kidding; **~ de soldados** to play (at) soldiers; **~ com alguém** to tease sb

brinco [ˈbrĩku] *m* (*jóia*) earring

brindar [brĩˈdaˈ] *vt* to drink to; (*presentear*) to give a present to; **brinde** [ˈbrĩdʒi] *m* toast; free gift

brinquedo [brĩˈkedu] *m* toy

brio [ˈbriu] *m* self-respect, dignity

brisa ['briza] f breeze

britânico, -a [bri'taniku, a] adj British ♦ m/f Briton

broche ['brɔʃi] m brooch

brochura [bro'ʃura] f (livro) paperback; (folheto) brochure, pamphlet

brócolis ['brɔkoliʃ] mpl broccoli sg

bronca ['brõka] (col) f telling off; **dar uma ~ en** to tell off; **levar uma ~ to** get told off

bronco, -a ['brõku, a] adj (rude) coarse; (burro) thick

bronquite [brõ'kitʃi] f bronchitis

bronze ['brõzi] m bronze; **bronzeado, -a** [brõ'zjadu, a] adj (cor) bronze; (pelo sol) suntanned ♦ m suntan; **bronzear** [brõ'zja*] vt to tan; **bronzear-se** vr to get a tan

brotar [bro'ta*] vt to produce ♦ vi (manar) to flow; (ʀoᴛ) to sprout; (nascer) to spring up

broto ['brotu] m bud; (fig) youngster

broxa ['brɔʃa] f (large) paint brush

bruços ['brusuʃ]: **de ~** adv face down

bruma ['bruma] f mist, haze

brusco, -a ['bruʃku, a] adj brusque; (súbito) sudden

brutal [bru'taw] (pl -ais) adj brutal

bruto, -a ['brutu, a] adj brutish; (grosseiro) coarse; (móvel) heavy; (petróleo) crude; (peso, coм) gross ♦ m brute; **em ~** raw, unworked

bruxa ['bruʃa] f witch; **bruxaria** [bruʃa'ria] f witchcraft

Bruxelas [bru'ʃelaʃ] n Brussels

bruxo ['bruʃu] m wizard

budismo [bu'dʒizmu] m Buddhism

bufar [bu'fa*] vi to puff, pant; (com raiva) to snort; (reclamar) to moan, grumble

bufê [bu'fe] m sideboard; (comida) buffet

buffer ['bafe*] (pl ~s) m (coмᴘuᴛ) buffer

bugiganga [buʒi'gãga] f trinket; **~s** fpl (coisas sem valor) knicknacks

bula ['bula] f (мᴇᴅ) directions pl for use

bule ['buli] m (de chá) teapot; (de café) coffeepot

Bulgária [buw'garja] f: **a ~** Bulgaria; **búlgaro, -a** ['buwgaru, a] adj, m/f Bulgarian ♦ m (ᴌɪɴɢ) Bulgarian

bunda ['bũda] (col) f bottom, backside

buquê [bu'ke] m bouquet

buraco [bu'raku] m hole; (de agulha) eye; **ser um ~** to be tough; **~ da fechadura** keyhole

burguês, -guesa [bux'geʃ, 'geza] adj middle-class, bourgeois; **burguosia** [buxge'zia] f middle class, bourgeoisie

burocracia [burokra'sia] f bureaucracy

burro, -a ['buxu, a] adj stupid ♦ m/f (zooᴌ) donkey; (pessoa) fool, idiot; **pra ~** (col) a lot; (com adj) really; **~ de carga** (fig) hard worker

busca ['buʃka] f search; **em ~ de** in search of; **dar ~ a** to search for

buscar [buʃ'ka*] vt to fetch; (procurar) to look ou search for; **ir ~** to fetch, go for; **mandar ~** to send for

bússola ['busola] f compass

busto ['buʃtu] m bust

buzina [bu'zina] f horn; **buzinar** [buzi'na*] vi to sound one's horn, toot the horn ♦ vt to hoot

búzio ['buzju] m conch

C

c/ abr = **com**

Ca abr (= companhia) Co

cá [ka] adv here; **de ~** on this side; **para ~** here, over here; **para lá e para ~** back and forth; **de lá para ~** since then

caatinga [kaˈtʃĩga] (*BR*) f scrub(-land)

cabana [kaˈbana] f hut

cabeça [kaˈbesa] f head; (*inteligência*) brains *pl*; (*de uma lista*) top ♦ *m/f* leader; **de ~** off the top of one's head; (*calcular*) in one's head; **de ~ para baixo** upside down; **por ~** per person, per head; **cabeçada** [kabeˈsada] f (*pancada com cabeça*) butt; (*FUTEBOL*) header; (*asneira*) blunder; **cabeçalho** [kabeˈsaʎu] *m* (*de livro*) title page; (*de página, capítulo*) heading

cabeceira [kabeˈsejra] f (*de cama*) head

cabeçudo, -a [kabeˈsudu, a] *adj* big-headed; (*teimoso*) pigheaded

cabeleira [kabeˈlejra] f head of hair; (*postiça*) wig; **cabeleireiro, -a** [kabelejˈrejru, a] *m/f* hairdresser

cabelo [kaˈbelu] *m* hair; **cortar/fazer o ~** to have one's hair cut/done; **cabeludo, -a** [kabeˈludu, a] *adj* hairy

caber [kaˈbe*] *vi:* **~ (em)** to fit; (*ser compatível*) to be appropriate (in); **~ a** (*em partilha*) to fall to; **cabe a alguém fazer** it is up to sb to do; **não cabe aqui fazer comentários** this is not the time or place to comment

cabide [kaˈbidʒi] *m* (*coat*) hanger; (*móvel*) hat stand; (*fixo à parede*) coat rack

cabine [kaˈbini] f cabin; (*em loja*) fitting room; **~ do piloto** (*AER*) cockpit; **~ telefônica** telephone box (*BRIT*) *ou* booth

cabo [ˈkabu] *m* (*extremidade*) end; (*de faca, vassoura etc*) handle; (*corda*) rope; (*elétrico etc*) cable; (*GEO*) cape; (*MIL*) corporal; **ao ~ de** at the end of; **de ~ a rabo** from

beginning to end; **levar a ~** to carry out; **dar ~ de** to do away with

caboclo, -a [kaˈboklu, a] (*BR*) *m/f* mestizo

cabra [ˈkabra] f goat

cabreiro, -a [kaˈbrejru, a] (*col*) *adj* suspicious

cabrito [kaˈbritu] *m* kid

caça [ˈkasa] f hunting; (*busca*) hunt; (*animal*) quarry, game ♦ *m* (*AER*) fighter (plane); **caçador, a** [kasaˈdo*, a] *m/f* hunter

cação [kaˈsãw] (*pl* -ões) *m* shark

caçar [kaˈsa*] *vt* to hunt; (*com espingarda*) to shoot; (*procurar*) to seek ♦ *vi* to hunt, go hunting

caçarola [kasaˈrɔla] f (*sauce*)pan

cacau [kaˈkaw] *m* cocoa; (*BOT*) cacao

cacetada [kaseˈtada] f blow (with a stick)

cachaça [kaˈʃasa] f (white) rum

cachaceiro, -a [kaʃaˈsejru, a] *adj* drunk ♦ *m/f* drunkard

cachê [kaˈʃe] *m* fee

cachecol [kaʃeˈkɔw] (*pl* -óis) *m* scarf

cachimbo [kaˈʃĩbu] *m* pipe

cacho [ˈkaʃu] *m* bunch; (*de cabelo*) curl; (: *longo*) ringlet

cachoeira [kaʃˈwejra] f waterfall

cachorra [kaˈʃoxa] f bitch; (*cadela*) (female) puppy

cachorrinho, -a [kaʃoˈxiɲu, a] *m/f* puppy

cachorro [kaˈʃoxu] *m* dog; (*cãozinho*) puppy; **cachorro-quente** (*pl* **cachorros-quentes**) *m* hot dog

cacique [kaˈsiki] *m* (*Indian*) chief; (*mandachuva*) local boss

caco [ˈkaku] *m* bit, fragment; (*pessoa velha*) old relic

caçoar [kaˈswa*] *vt, vi* to mock

cacoete [kaˈkwetʃi] *m* twitch, tic

cacto [ˈkaktu] *m* cactus

cada ['kada] *adj inv* each; *(todo)* every; ~ **um** each one; ~ **semana** each week; **a** ~ **3 horas** every 3 hours; ~ **vez mais** more and more

cadastro [ka'daʃtru] *m* register; *(ato)* registration; *(de criminosos)* criminal record

cadáver [ka'dave*] *m* corpse, (dead) body

cadê [ka'de] *(col) adv*: ~ ...? where's/where are ...?, what's happened to ...?

cadeado [ka'dʒjadu] *m* padlock

cadeia [ka'deja] *f* chain; *(prisão)* prison; *(rede)* network

cadeira [ka'dejra] *f* chair; *(disciplina)* subject; *(TEATRO)* stall; *(função)* post; ~**s** *fpl (ANAT)* hips; ~ **de balanço/rodas** rocking chair/wheelchair

cadela [ka'dɛla] *f (cão)* bitch

caderneta [kadex'neta] *f* notebook, ~ **de poupança** savings account

caderno [ka'dexnu] *m* exercise book; *(de notas)* notebook; *(de jornal)* section

caducar [kadu'ka*] *vi* to lapse, expire; **caduco, -a** [ka'duku, a] *adj* invalid, expired; *(senil)* senile; *(BOT)* deciduous

cães [kãjʃ] *mpl de* **cão**

cafajeste [kafa'ʒeʃtʃi] *(col) adj* roguish; *(vulgar)* vulgar, coarse ♦ *m/f* rogue; rough customer

café [ka'fɛ] *m* coffee; *(estabelecimento)* café; ~ **com leite** white coffee *(BRIT)*, coffee with cream *(US)*; ~ **preto** black coffee; ~ **da manhã** *(BR)* breakfast

cafeteira [kafe'tejra] *f* coffee pot; *(máquina)* percolator; **cafezal** [kafe'zaw] *(pl* -**ais**) *m* coffee plantation; **cafezinho** [kafe'ziɲu] *m* small

black coffee

cagada [ka'gada] *(col!) f* shit *(!)*

cágado ['kagadu] *m* turtle

cagar [ka'ga*] *(col!) vi* to (have a) shit *(!)*

cagüetar [kagwe'ta*] *vt* to inform on; **cagüete** [ka'gwetʃi] *m* informer

caiba *etc* ['kajba] *vb V* **caber**

cãibra ['kãjbra] *f (MED)* cramp

caída [ka'ida] *f* = **queda**

caído, -a [ka'idu, a] *adj* dejected; *(derrubado)* fallen; *(pendente)* droopy; ~ **por** *(apaixonado)* in love with

câimbra ['kãjbra] *f* = **cãibra**

caipirinha [kajpi'riɲa] *f cocktail of cachaça, lemon and sugar*

cair [ka'i*] *vi* to fall; ~ **bem/mal** *(roupa)* to fit well/badly; *(col: pessoa)* to look good/bad; ~ **em si** to come to one's senses; **ao** ~ **da noite** at nightfall; **essa comida me caiu mal** that food did not agree with me

Cairo ['kajru] *m*: **o** ~ Cairo

cais [kajʃ] *m (NÁUT)* quay; *(PT: FERRO)* platform

caixa ['kajʃa] *f* box; *(cofre)* safe; *(de uma loja)* cashdesk ♦ *m/f (pessoa)* cashier ♦ *m*: ~ **automático** cash machine; **pequena** ~ petty cash; ~ **de correio** letter box; ~ **econômica** savings bank; ~ **de mudanças** *(BR)* ou **de velocidades** *(PT)* gearbox; ~ **postal** P.O. box; ~ **registradora** cash register; **caixa-forte** *(pl* **caixas-fortes**) *f* vault

caixão [kaj'ʃãw] *(pl* -**ões**) *m (ataúde)* coffin; *(caixa grande)* large box

caixeiro-viajante, caixeira-viajante *(pl* **caixeiros-viajantes, caixeiras-viajantes**) *m/f* commercial traveller *(BRIT)* ou traveler *(US)*

caixilho [kaj'ʃiʎu] *m* (*moldura*) frame

caixões [kaj'ʃõjʃ] *mpl de* **caixão**

caixote [kaj'ʃɔtʃi] *m* packing case; ~ **do lixo** (*PT*) dustbin (*BRIT*), garbage can (*US*)

caju [ka'ʒu] *m* cashew fruit

cal [kaw] *f* lime; (*na água*) chalk; (*para caiar*) whitewash

calabouço [kala'bosu] *m* dungeon

calado, -a [ka'ladu, a] *adj* quiet

calafrio [kala'friu] *m* shiver; **ter ~s** to shiver

calamidade [kalami'dadʒi] *f* calamity, disaster

calão [ka'lãw] (*PT*) *m*: (*baixo*) ~ slang

calar [ka'la*] *vt* to keep quiet about; (*impor silêncio a*) to silence ♦ *vi* to go quiet; (*manter-se calado*) to keep quiet; **calar-se** *vr* to go quiet; to keep quiet; **cala a boca!** shut up!

calça ['kawsa] *f* (*tb*: ~**s**) trousers *pl* (*BRIT*), pants *pl* (*US*)

calçada [kaw'sada] *f* (*BR*: *passeio*) pavement (*BRIT*), sidewalk (*US*); (*PT*: *rua*) roadway

calçadão [kawsa'dãw] (*pl* -**ões**) *m* pedestrian precinct (*BRIT*)

calçado, -a [kaw'sadu, a] *adj* (*rua*) paved ♦ *m* shoe; ~**s** *mpl* (*para os pés*) footwear *sg*

calçadões [kawsa'dõjʃ] *mpl de* **calçadão**

calçamento [kawsa'mẽtu] *m* paving

calcanhar [kawka'ɲa*] *m* (*ANAT*) heel

calção [kaw'sãw] (*pl* -**ões**) *m* shorts *pl*; ~ **de banho** swimming trunks *pl*

calcar [kaw'ka*] *vt* to tread on; (*espezinhar*) to trample on

calçar [kaw'sa*] *vt* (*sapatos, luvas*) to put on; (*pavimentar*) to pave;

calçar-se *vr* to put on one's shoes; **ela calça (número) 28** she takes size 28 (in shoes)

calcário [kaw'karju] *m* limestone

calcinha [kaw'siɲa] *f* panties *pl*

calço ['kawsu] *m* wedge

calções [kaw'sõjʃ] *mpl de* **calção**

calculador [kawkula'do*] *m* = **calculadora**

calculadora [kawkula'dora] *f* calculator

calcular [kawku'la*] *vt* to calculate; (*imaginar*) to imagine; ~ **que** to reckon that

cálculo ['kawkulu] *m* calculation; (*MAT*) calculus; (*MED*) stone

calda ['kawda] *f* (*de doce*) syrup; ~**s** *fpl* (*águas termais*) hot springs

caldeirada [kawdej'rada] (*PT*) *f* (*guisado*) fish stew

caldo ['kawdu] *m* broth; (*de fruta*) juice; ~ **de carne/galinha** beef/chicken stock; ~ **verde** potato and cabbage broth

calendário [kalẽ'darju] *m* calendar

calhar [ka'ʎa*] *vi*: **calhou viajarmos no mesmo avião** we happened to travel on the same plane; **calhou que** it so happened that; ~ **a** (*cair bem*) to suit; **se** ~ (*PT*) perhaps, maybe

calibre [ka'libri] *m* calibre (*BRIT*), caliber (*US*)

cálice ['kalisi] *m* wine glass; (*REL*) chalice

calista [ka'liʃta] *m/f* chiropodist (*BRIT*), podiatrist (*US*)

calma ['kawma] *f* calm

calmante [kaw'mãtʃi] *adj* soothing ♦ *m* (*MED*) tranquillizer

calmo, -a ['kawmu, a] *adj* calm

calo ['kalu] *m* callus; (*no pé*) corn

calor [ka'lo*] *m* heat; (*agradável, fig*) warmth; **está** ou **faz** ~ it is hot; **estar com** ~ to be hot

calorento, -a [kalo'rētu, a] *adj* (*pessoa*) sensitive to heat; (*lugar*) hot

caloria [calo'ria] *f* calorie

caloroso, -a [kalo'rozu, ɔza] *adj* warm; (*entusiástico*) enthusiastic

calouro, -a [ka'loru, a] *m/f* (*EDUC*) fresher (*BRIT*), freshman (*US*)

calúnia [ka'lunja] *f* slander

calvo, -a [ˈkavvu, a] *adj* bald

cama [ˈkama] *f* bed; ~ **de casal** double bed; ~ **de solteiro** single bed; **de** ~ (*doente*) ill (in bed)

camada [ka'mada] *f* layer; (*de tinta*) coat

câmara [ˈkamara] *f* chamber; (*FOTO*) camera; ~ **municipal** (*BR*) town council; (*PT*) town hall; ~ **digital** digital camera; **em** ~ **lenta** in slow motion

camarada [kama'rada] *adj* friendly, nice; (*preço*) good ♦ *m/f* comrade; (*sujeito*) guy/woman

câmara-de-ar (*pl* **câmaras-de-ar**) *f* inner tube

camarão [kama'rāw] (*pl* -**ões**) *m* shrimp; (*graúdo*) prawn

camarões [kama'rõjʃ] *mpl de* **camarão**

camarote [kama'rɔtʃi] *m* (*NÁUT*) cabin; (*TEATRO*) box

cambaleante [kãba'ljātʃi] *adj* unsteady (on one's feet)

cambalear [kãba'lja*] *vi* to stagger, reel

cambalhota [kãba'ʎɔta] *f* somersault

câmbio [ˈkãbju] *m* (*dinheiro etc*) exchange; (*preço de câmbio*) rate of exchange; ~ **livre** free trade; ~ **paralelo** black market

cambista [kã'biʃta] *m* money changer

Camboja [kã'bɔja] *m*: **o** ~ Cambodia

camelo [ka'melu] *m* camel

camião [ka'mjãw] (*pl* -**ões**) (*PT*) *m* lorry (*BRIT*), truck (*US*)

caminhada [kami'nada] *f* walk

caminhão [kami'nãw] (*pl* -**ões**) (*BR*) *m* lorry (*BRIT*), truck (*US*)

caminhar [kami'na*] *vi* to walk; (*processo*) to get under way; (*negócios*) to progress

caminho [ka'minu] *m* way; (*vereda*) road, path; ~ **de ferro** (*PT*) railway (*BRIT*), railroad (*US*); **a** ~ on the way, en route; **cortar** ~ to take a short cut; **pôr-se a** ~ to set off

caminhões [kami'nõjʃ] *npl de* **caminhão**

caminhoneiro, -a [kamino'nejru, a] *m/f* lorry driver (*BRIT*), truck driver (*US*)

camiões [ka'mjõjʃ] *mpl de* **camião**

camioneta [kamjo'neta] (*PT*) *f* (*para passageiros*) coach; (*comercial*) van

camionista [kamjo'niʃta] (*PT*) *m/f* lorry driver (*BRIT*), truck driver (*US*)

camisa [ka'miza] *f* shirt; ~ **de dormir** nightshirt; ~ **esporte/pólo/social** sports/polo/dress shirt; **mudar de** ~ (*ESPORTE*) to change sides; **camisa-de-força** (*pl* **camisas-de-força**) *f* straitjacket

camiseta [kami'zeta] (*BR*) *f* T-shirt; (*interior*) vest

camisinha [kami'zina] (*col*) *f* condom

camisola [kami'zɔla] *f* (*BR*) nightdress; (*PT*: *pulôver*) sweater; ~ **interior** (*PT*) vest

campainha [kampa'ina] *f* bell

campanário [kãpa'narju] *m* church tower, steeple

campanha [kã'pana] *f* (*MIL etc*) campaign; (*planície*) plain

campeão, -peã [kã'pjãw, 'pjã] (*pl* -**ões**, ~**s**) *m/f* champion; **campeo-**

nato [kãpjo'natu] *m* championship

campestre [kã'peſtri] *adj* rural, rustic

camping ['kãpĩŋ] (BR) (*pl* **~s**) *m* camping; (*lugar*) campsite

campismo [kã'piʒmu] *m* camping; **parque de ~** campsite

campista [kã'piſta] *m/f* camper

campo [kãpu] *m* field; (*fora da cidade*) countryside; (ESPORTE) ground; (*acampamento*) camp; (TÉNIS) court

camponês, -esa [kãpo'neʃ, eza] *m/f* countryman/woman; (*agricultor*) farmer

campus ['kãpuʃ] *m inv* campus

camuflagem [kamu'flaʒẽ] *f* camouflage

camundongo [kamũ'dõgu] (BR) *m* mouse

camurça [ka'muxsa] *f* suede

cana ['kana] *f* cane; (*col: cadeia*) nick; (*de açúcar*) sugar cane

Canadá [kana'da] *m*: **o ~** Canada; **canadense** [kana'dẽsi] *adj, m/f* Canadian

canal [ka'naw] (*pl* **-ais**) *m* channel; (*de navegação*) canal; (ANAT) duct

canalha [ka'naʎa] *f* rabble, mob ♦ *m/f* wretch, scoundrel

canalização [kanaliza'sãw] *f* plumbing

canalizador, a [kanaliza'do*, (PT) *m/f* plumber

canário [ka'narju] *m* canary

canastra [ka'naſtra] *f* (big) basket

canção [kã'sãw] (*pl* **-ões**) *f* song; **~ de ninar** lullaby

cancela [kã'sɛla] *f* gate

cancelamento [kãsela'mẽtu] *m* cancellation

cancelar [kãse'la*] *vt* to cancel; (*riscar*) to cross out

câncer ['kãse*] *m* cancer; **C~** (ASTROLOGIA) Cancer

canções [kã'sõjʃ] *fpl de* canção

cancro ['kãkru] (PT) *m* cancer

candelabro [kãde'labru] *m* candlestick; (*lustre*) chandelier

candidato, -a [kãdʒi'datu, a] *m/f* candidate; (*a cargo*) applicant

cândido, -a ['kãdʒidu, a] *adj* naive; (*inocente*) innocent

candomblé [kãdõ'ble] *m see boxed note*

CANDOMBLÉ

Candomblé is Brazil's most influential Afro-Brazilian religion. Practised mainly in Bahia, it mixes catholicism and Yoruba traditions. According to **candomblé**, believers become possessed by spirits and thus become an instrument of communication between divine and mortal forces. **Candomblé** ceremonies are great spectacles of African rhythm and dance, and are held in *terreiros*.

---

caneca [ka'nɛka] *f* mug

canela [ka'nɛla] *f* cinnamon; (ANAT) shin

caneta [ka'neta] *f* pen; **~ esferográfica/pilot** ballpoint/felt-tip pen; **~ seletora** (COMPUT) light pen

cangaceiro [kãga'sejru] (BR) *m* bandit

canguru [kãgu'ru] *m* kangaroo

canhão [ka'ɲãw] (*pl* **-ões**) *m* cannon; (GEO) canyon

canhoto, -a [ka'ɲotu, a] *adj* left-handed ♦ *m/f* left-handed person ♦ *m* (*de cheque*) stub

canibal [kani'baw] (*pl* **-ais**) *m/f* cannibal

canil [ka'niw] (*pl* **-is**) *m* kennel

canivete [kani'vetʃi] *m* penknife

canja ['kãʒa] *f* chicken broth; (*col*)

cinch, pushover

canjica [kã'ʒika] f maize porridge

cano ['kanu] m pipe; (tubo) tube; (de arma de fogo) barrel; (de bota) top; ~ **de esgoto** sewer

canoa [ka'noa] f canoe

cansaço [kã'sasu] m tiredness

cansado, -a [kã'sadu, a] adj tired

cansar [kã'sa*] vt to tire; (entediar) to bore ♦ vi to get tired; **cansar-se** vr to get tired; **cansativo, -a** [kãsa'tʃivu, a] adj tiring; (tedioso) tedious

cantar [kã'ta*] vt, vi to sing ♦ m song

cantarolar [kãtaro'la*] vt to hum

canteiro [kã'tejru] m stonemason; (de flores) flower bed

cantiga [kã'tʃiga] f ballad; ~ **de ninar** lullaby

cantil [kã'tʃiw] (pl -**is**) m canteen

cantina [kã'tʃina] f canteen

cantis [kã'tʃiʃ] mpl de **cantil**

canto ['kãtu] m corner; (lugar) place; (canção) song

cantor, a [kã'to*, a] m/f singer

cão [kãw] (pl **cães**) m dog

caolho, -a [ka'oʎu, a] adj cross-eyed

caos ['kaoʃ] m chaos

capa ['kapa] f cape; (cobertura) cover; **livro de ~ dura/mole** hardback/paperback (book)

capacete [kapa'setʃi] m helmet

capacidade [kapasi'dadʒi] f capacity; (aptidão) ability, competence

capaz [ka'paʒ] adj able, capable; **ser ~ de** to be able to (ou capable of); **sou ~ de ...** (talvez) I might ...; **é ~ de chover hoje** it might rain today

capela [ka'pɛla] f chapel

capim [ka'pĩ] m grass

capitães [kapi'tãjʃ] mpl de **capitão**

capital [kapi'taw] (pl -**ais**) adj, m

capital ♦ f (cidade) capital; ~ **(em) ações** (COM) share capital

capitalismo [kapita'liʒmu] m capitalism; **capitalista** [kapita'liʃta] m/f capitalist

capitalizar [kapitali'za*] vt to capitalize on; (COM) to capitalize

capitão [kapi'tãw] (pl -**ães**) m captain

capítulo [ka'pitulu] m chapter

capô [ka'po] m (AUTO) bonnet (BRIT), hood (US)

capoeira [ka'pwejra] f (PT) hencoop; (dança) see boxed note

CAPOEIRA

Capoeira is a fusion of martial arts and dance which originated among African slaves in colonial Brazil. It is danced in a circle to the sound of the **berimbau**, a percussion instrument of African origin. Opposed by the Brazilian authorities until the beginning of the twentieth century, today **capoeira** is regarded as a national sport.

---

capota [ka'pɔta] f (AUTO) hood, top

capotar [kapo'ta*] vi to overturn

capricho [ka'priʃu] m whim, caprice; (teimosia) obstinacy; (apuro) care; **caprichoso, -a** [kapri'ʒozu, ɔza] adj capricious; (com apuro) meticulous

Capricórnio [kapri'kɔxnju] m Capricorn

cápsula ['kapsula] f capsule

captar [kap'ta*] vt (atrair) to win; (RÁDIO) to pick up

captura [kap'tura] f capture; **capturar** [kaptu'ra*] vt to capture

capuz [ka'puʒ] m hood

cáqui ['kaki] adj khaki

cara ['kara] f face; (aspecto) appearance ♦ m (col) guy; ~ **ou coroa?**

heads or tails?; **de ~** straightaway;
dar de ~ com to bump into; **ser a ~
de** (col) to be the spitting image of;
ter ~ de to look (like)

caracol [kara'kɔw] (pl **-óis**) m snail;
(de cabelo) curl; **escada em ~** spiral
staircase

caracteres [karak'tεriʃ] mpl de
caráter

característica [karakte'riʃtʃika] f
characteristic, feature

característico, -a [karakte-
'riʃtʃika, a] adj characteristic

cara-de-pau (pl **caras-de-pau**) adj
brazen; **ele é ~** he's very forward

caramelo [kara'mεlu] m caramel;
(bala) toffee

caranguejo [karã'geʒu] m crab

caras-pintadas fpl see boxed note

CARAS-PINTADAS

In 1992, during popular demon-
strations calling for the impeach-
ment of the then president
Fernando Collor de Mello, students known as **caras-pintadas**,
because they had the Brazilian
flag painted on their faces, went
through the streets shouting
"Collor, out!" and similar slogans.

---

caratê [kara'te] m karate

caráter [ka'rate*] (pl **caracteres**) m
character

caravana [kara'vana] f caravan

carbonizar [kaxboni'za*] vt to car-
bonize; (queimar) to char

carbono [kax'bɔnu] m carbon

carburador [kaxbura'do*] m carburettor (BRIT), carburetor (US)

cárcere ['kaxseri] m prison;
carcereiro, -a [kaxse'rejru, a] m/f
jailer, warder

cardápio [kax'dapju] (BR) m menu

cardeal [kax'dʒjaw] (pl **-ais**) adj, m
cardinal

cardíaco, -a [kax'dʒiaku, a] adj
cardiac; **ataque/parada ~** heart
attack/cardiac arrest

cardigã [kaxdʒi'gã] m cardigan

careca [ka'rεka] adj bald

carecer [kare'se*] vi: **~ de** to lack;
(precisar) to need

carência [ka'rẽsja] f lack; (necessidade) need; (privação) deprivation;
carente [ka'rẽtʃi] adj wanting;
(pessoa) needy, deprived

careta [ka'reta] adj (col) straight,
square ♦ f grimace; **fazer uma ~** to
pull a face

carga ['kaxga] f load; (de navio,
avião) cargo; (ato de carregar) loading; (ELET) charge; (fig: peso) burden;
(MIL) attack, charge; **dar ~ em** (COM-
PUT) to boot (up)

cargo ['kaxgu] m responsibility;
(função) post; **a ~ de** in charge of;
ter a ~ to be in charge of; **tomar a
~** to take charge of

Caribe [ka'ribi] m: **o ~** the Caribbean (Sea)

carícia [ka'risja] f caress

caridade [kari'dadʒi] f charity; **obra
de ~** charity

cárie ['kari] f tooth decay

carimbar [karĩ'ba*] vt to stamp; (no
correio) to postmark

carimbo [ka'rĩbu] m stamp; (postal) postmark

carinho [ka'riɲu] m affection, fondness; (carícia) caress; **fazer ~** to
caress; **com ~** affectionately; (com
cuidado) with care; **carinhoso, -a**
[kari'ɲozu, ɔza] adj affectionate

carioca [ka'rjɔka] adj of Rio de
Janeiro ♦ m/f native of Rio de Janeiro
♦ m (PT: café) type of weak coffee

carnal [kax'naw] (pl **-ais**) adj carnal;
primo ~ first cousin

carnaval [kaxna'vaw] (pl **-ais**) m

carnival; (*fig*) mess; *see boxed note*

CARNAVAL

In Brazil, **Carnaval** is the popular festival held each year in the four days before Lent. It is celebrated in very different ways in different parts of the country. In Rio de Janeiro, for example, the big attraction is the parades of the *escolas de samba*, in Salvador the *trios elétricos*, in Recife the *frevo* and, in Olinda, the giant figures, such as the *Homem da meia-noite* and *Mulher do meio-dia*. In Portugal, **Carnaval** is celebrated on Shrove Tuesday, with street parties and processions taking place throughout the country.

---

carne ['kaxni] *f* flesh; (*CULIN*) meat; **em ~ e osso** in the flesh

carnê [kax'ne] *m* (*para compras*) payment book

carneiro [kax'nejru] *m* sheep; (*macho*) ram; **perna/costeleta de ~** leg of lamb/lamb chop

carnificina [kaxnifi'sina] *f* slaughter

caro, -a ['karu, a] *adj* dear; **cobrar/ pagar ~** to charge a lot/pay dearly

carochinha [karo'ʃiɲa] *f*: **conto ou história da ~** fairy tale ou story

caroço [ka'rosu] *m* (*de frutos*) stone; (*endurecimento*) lump

carona [ka'rɔna] *f* lift, viajar de ~ to hitchhike; **pegar uma ~** to get a lift

carpete [kax'petʃi] *m* (fitted) carpet

carpinteiro [kaxpĩ'tejru] *m* carpenter

carrapato [kaxa'patu] *m* (*inseto*) tick

carrasco [ka'xaʃku] *m* executioner; (*fig*) tyrant

carregado, -a [kaxe'gadu, a] *adj*

loaded; (*semblante*) sullen; (*céu*) dark; (*ambiente*) tense

carregador [kaxega'do*] *m* porter

carregamento [kaxega'mẽtu] *m* (*ação*) loading; (*carga*) load, cargo

carregar [kaxe'ga*] *vt* to load; (*levar*) to carry; (*bateria*) to charge; (*PT*: *apertar*) to press; (*levar para longe*) to take away ♦ *vi*: **~ em** to overdo; (*pôr enfase*) to bring out

carreira [ka'xejra] *f* run, running; (*profissão*) career; (*TURFE*) race; (*NÁUT*) slipway; (*fileira*) row; **às ~s** in a hurry

carretel [kaxe'tɛw] (*pl* -**éis**) *m* spool, reel

carrinho [ka'xiɲu] *m* trolley; (*brinquedo*) toy car; **~ (de criança)** pram; **~ de mão** wheelbarrow

carro ['kaxu] *m* car; (*de bois*) cart; (*de mão*) barrow; (*de máquina de escrever*) carriage; **~ de corrida/passeio/esporte** racing/saloon/sports car; **~ de praça** cab; **~ de bombeiro** fire engine

carroça [ka'xɔsa] *f* cart, waggon

carroceria [kaxose'ria] *f* (*AUTO*) bodywork

carro-chefe (*pl* **carros-chefes**) *m* (*de desfile*) main float; (*fig*) flagship, centrepiece (*BRIT*), centerpiece (*US*)

carrossel [kaxo'sɛw] (*pl* -**éis**) *m* merry-go-round

carruagem [ka'xwaʒẽ] (*pl* -**ns**) *f* carriage, coach

carta ['kaxta] *f* letter; (*de jogar*) card; (*mapa*) chart; **~ aérea/registrada** airmail/registered letter; **~ de condução** (*PT*) driving licence (*BRIT*), driver's license (*US*); **dar as ~s** to deal; **carta-bomba** (*pl* **cartas-bomba**) *f* letter bomb

cartão [kax'tãw] (*pl* -**ões**) *m* card; (*PT*: *material*) cardboard; **~ de crédito** credit card; **cartão-postal**

(*pl* **cartões-postais**) *m* postcard

cartaz [kax'taʒ] *m* poster, bill (US); **(estar) em ~** (*TEATRO*, *CINEMA*) (to be) showing

carteira [kax'tejra] *f* desk; (*para dinheiro*) wallet; (*de ações*) portfolio; **~ de identidade** identity card; **~ de motorista** driving licence (*BRIT*), driver's license (*US*)

carteiro [kax'tejru] *m* postman (*BRIT*), mailman (*US*)

cartões [kax'tõjʃ] *mpl de* **cartão**

cartola [kax'tɔla] *f* top hat

cartolina [kaxto'lina] *f* card

cartório [kax'tɔrju] *m* registry office

cartucho [kax'tuʃu] *m* cartridge; (*saco de papel*) packet

cartum [kax'tũ] (*pl* **-ns**) *m* cartoon

carvalho [kax'vaʎu] *m* oak

carvão [kax'vãw] (*pl* **-ões**) *m* coal; (*de madeira*) charcoal

casa ['kaza] *f* house; (*lar*) home; (*COM*) firm; (*MAT*: *decimal*) place; **em/para ~** (at) home/home; **~ de saúde** hospital; **~ da moeda** mint; **~ de banho** (*PT*) bathroom; **~ e comida** board and lodging; **~ de cômodos** tenement; **~ popular** = council house

casacão [kaza'kãw] (*pl* **-ões**) *m* overcoat

casaco [ka'zaku] *m* coat; (*paletó*) jacket

casacões [kaza'kõjʃ] *mpl de* casacão

casal [ka'zaw] (*pl* **-ais**) *m* couple

casamento [kaza'mẽtu] *m* marriage; (*boda*) wedding

casar [ka'za*] *vt* to marry; (*combinar*) to match (up); **casar-se** *vr* to get married; to combine well

casarão [kaza'rãw] (*pl* **-ões**) *m* mansion

casca ['kaʃka] *f* (*de árvore*) bark; (*de banana*) skin; (*de ferida*) scab; (*de laranja*) peel; (*de nozes*, *ovos*) shell; (*de milho etc*) husk; (*de pão*) crust

cascata [kaʃ'kata] *f* waterfall

casco ['kaʃku] *m* skull; (*de animal*) hoof; (*de navio*) hull; (*para bebidas*) empty bottle; (*de tartaruga*) shell

casebre [ka'zɛbri] *m* hovel, shack

caseiro, -a [ka'zejru, a] *adj* homemade; (*pessoa*, *vida*) domestic ♦ *m/f* housekeeper

caso ['kazu] *m* case; (*tb*: **~ amoroso**) affair; (*estória*) story ♦ *conj* in case, if; **no ~ de** in case (of); **em todo ~** in any case; **neste ~** in that case; **~ necessário** if necessary; **criar ~** to cause trouble; **não fazer ~ de** to ignore; **~ de emergência** emergency

caspa ['kaʃpa] *f* dandruff

casquinha [kaʃ'kiɲa] *f* (*de sorvete*) cone; (*pele*) skin

cassar [ka'sa*] *vt* (*direitos*, *licença*) to cancel, withhold; (*políticos*) to ban

cassete [ka'setʃi] *m* cassette

cassetete [kase'tetʃi] *m* truncheon (*BRIT*), nightstick (*US*)

cassino [ka'sinu] *m* casino

castanha [kaʃ'taɲa] *f* chestnut; **~ de caju** cashew nut; **castanha-do-pará** [-pa'ra] (*pl* **castanhas-do-pará**) *f* Brazil nut

castanheiro [kaʃta'ɲejru] *m* chestnut tree

castanho, -a [kaʃ'taɲu, a] *adj* brown

castelo [kaʃ'tɛlu] *m* castle

castiçal [kaʃtʃi'saw] (*pl* **-ais**) *m* candlestick

castiço, -a [kaʃ'tʃisu, a] *adj* pure

castidade [kaʃtʃi'dadʒi] *f* chastity

castigar [kaʃtʃi'ga*] *vt* to punish; **castigo** [kaʃ'tʃigu] *m* punishment; (*fig*: *mortificação*) pain

casto, -a ['kaʃtu, a] *adj* chaste

casual [ka'zwaw] (pl -ais) adj chance atr, accidental; (fortuito) fortuitous; **casualidade** [kazwali'dadʒi] f chance; (acidente) accident

cata ['kata] f: **à ~ de** in search of

catalizador [kataliza'do*] m catalyst

catalogar [katalo'ga*] vt to catalogue (BRIT), catalog (US)

catálogo [ka'talogu] m catalogue (BRIT), catalog (US); **~ (telefônico)** telephone directory

catapora [kata'pɔra] (BR) f chickenpox

catar [ka'ta*] vt to pick (up); (procurar) to look for, search for; (recolher) to collect, gather

catarata [kata'rata] f waterfall; (MED) cataract

catarro [ka'taxu] m catarrh

catástrofe [ka'taʃtrofi] f catastrophe

cata-vento m weathercock

catedral [kate'draw] (pl -ais) f cathedral

categoria [katego'ria] f category; (social) rank; (qualidade) quality; **de alta ~** first-rate

cativar [katʃi'va*] vt to enslave; (fascinar) to captivate; (atrair) to charm

cativeiro [katʃi'vejru] m captivity; (escravidão) slavery; (cadeia) prison

cativo, -a [ka'tʃivu, a] m/f slave; (prisioneiro) prisoner

católico, -a [ka'tɔliku, a] adj, m/f catholic

catorze [ka'toxzi] num fourteen

caução [kaw'sãw] (pl -ões) f security, guarantee; (JUR) bail; **sob ~** on bail

caule ['kauli] m stalk, stem

causa ['kawza] f cause; (motivo) motive, reason; (JUR) lawsuit; **por ~ de** because of; **causador, a** [kawza'do*, a] adj which caused ♦ m

cause; **causar** [kaw'za*] vt to cause, bring about

cautela [kaw'tɛla] f caution; (senha) ticket; **~ (de penhor)** pawn ticket; **cauteloso, -a** [kawte'lozu, ɔza] adj cautious, wary

cavado, -a [ka'vadu, a] adj (olhos) sunken; (roupa) low-cut

cavala [ka'vala] f mackerel

cavalaria [kavala'ria] f cavalry

cavaleiro [kava'lejru] m rider, horseman; (medieval) knight

cavalete [kava'letʃi] m stand; (FOTO) tripod; (de pintor) easel; (de mesa) trestle

cavalgar [kavaw'ga*] vt to ride ♦ vi: **~ em** to ride on; **~ (sobre)** to jump over

cavalheiro, -a [kava'ʎejru, a] adj courteous, gallant ♦ m gentleman

cavalo [ka'valu] m horse; (XADREZ) knight; **a ~** on horseback; **50 ~s (-vapor)** ou **(de força)** 50 horsepower; **~ de corrida** racehorse

cavaquinho [kava'kiɲu] m small guitar

cavar [ka'va*] vt to dig; (esforçar-se para obter) to try to get ♦ vi to dig; (fig) to delve; (animal) to burrow

cave ['kavi] (PT) f wine-cellar

caveira [ka'vejra] f skull

cavidade [kavi'dadʒi] f cavity

caxumba [ka'ʃũba] f mumps sg

CD abr m CD

cê [se] (col) pron = **você**

cear [sja*] vt to have for supper ♦ vi to dine

cebola [se'bola] f onion; **cebolinha** [sebo'liɲa] f spring onion

ceder [se'de*] vt to give up; (dar) to hand over; (emprestar) to lend ♦ vi to give in, yield

cedilha [se'dʒiʎa] f cedilla

cedo ['sedu] adv early; (em breve) soon

cedro ['sɛdru] m cedar

cédula ['sedula] f banknote; (eleitoral) ballot paper

CEE abr f (= Comunidade Econômica Européia) EEC

cegar [se'ga*] vt to blind; (ofuscar) to dazzle ♦ vi to be dazzling

cego, -a ['sɛgu, a] adj blind; (total) complete, total; (tesoura) blunt ♦ m/f blind man/woman; **às cegas** blindly

cegonha [se'gɔɲa] f stork

cegueira [se'gejra] f blindness

CEI abr f (= Comunidade de Estados Independentes) CIS

ceia ['seja] f supper

cela ['sɛla] f cell

celebração [selebra'sãw] (pl -ões) f celebration

celebrar [sele'bra*] vt to celebrate; (exaltar) to praise; (acordo) to seal

célebre ['sɛlebri] adj famous, well-known

celeiro [se'lejru] m granary; (depósito) barn

celeste [se'lɛʃtʃi] adj celestial, heavenly

celibatário, -a [seliba'tarju, a] adj unmarried, single ♦ m/f bachelor/spinster

celofane [selo'fani] m cellophane; **papel ~** cling film

célula ['sɛlula] f (BIO, ELET) cell; **celular** [selu'la*] adj cellular ♦ n: (telefone) **celular** mobile (phone)

cem [sẽ] num hundred

cemitério [semi'tɛrju] m cemetery, graveyard

cena ['sena] f scene; (palco) stage

cenário [se'narju] m scenery; (CINEMA) scenario; (de um acontecimento) setting

cenoura [se'nora] f carrot

censo ['sɛsu] m census

censor, a [sẽ'so*, a] m/f censor

censura [sẽ'sura] f censorship; (reprovação) censure, criticism; **censurar** [sẽsu'ra*] vt to censure; (filme, livro etc) to censor

centavo [sẽ'tavu] m cent; **estar sem um ~** to be penniless

centeio [sẽ'teju] m rye

centelha [sẽ'teʎa] f spark

centena [sẽ'tena] f hundred; **às ~s** in hundreds

centenário, -a [sẽte'narju, a] m centenary

centígrado [sẽ'tʃigradu] m centigrade

centímetro [sẽ'tʃimetru] m centimetre (BRIT), centimeter (US)

cento ['sẽtu] m: **~ e um** one hundred and one; **por ~** per cent

centopeia [sẽto'peja] f centipede

central [sẽ'traw] (pl -ais) adj central ♦ f (de polícia etc) head office; **~ elétrica** (electric) power station; **~ telefônica** telephone exchange; **centralizar** [sẽtrali'za*] vt to centralize

centrar [sẽ'tra*] vt to centre (BRIT), center (US)

centro ['sẽtru] m centre (BRIT), center (US); (de uma cidade) town centre; **centroavante** [sẽtroa'vãtʃi] m (FUTEBOL) centre forward

CEP ['sɛpi] (BR) abr m (= Código de Endereçamento Postal) postcode (BRIT), zip code (US)

céptico, -a etc ['septiku, a] (PT) = **cético** etc

cera ['sera] f wax

cerâmica [se'ramika] f pottery

cerca ['sexka] f fence ♦ prep: **~ de** (aproximadamente) around, about; **~ viva** hedge

cercado [sex'kadu] m enclosure; (para animais) pen; (para crianças) playpen

cercanias [sexka'niaʃ] fpl outskirts;

(*vizinhança*) neighbourhood *sg* (*BRIT*), neighborhood *sg* (*US*)

cercar [sex'ka*] *vt* to enclose; (*rodear*) to surround; (*assediar*) to besiege

cerco ['sexku] *m* siege; **pôr ~ a** to besiege

cereal [se'rjaw] (*pl* -**ais**) *m* cereal

cérebro ['serebru] *m* brain; (*fig*) brains *pl*

cereja [se'reʒa] *f* cherry

cerimônia [seri'monja] *f* ceremony

cerração [sexa'sãw] *f* fog

cerrado, -a [se'xadu, a] *adj* shut, closed; (*denso*) thick ♦ *m* scrub (land)

certeza [sex'teza] *f* certainty; **com ~** certainly, surely; (*provavelmente*) probably; **ter ~ de/de que** to be certain ou sure of/to be sure that

certidão [sextʃi'dãw] (*pl* -**ões**) *f* certificate

certificado [sextʃifi'kadu] *m* certificate

certificar [sextʃifi'ka*] *vt* to certify; (*assegurar*) to assure; **certificar-se** *vr*: **~-se de** to make sure of

certo, -a ['sextu, a] *adj* certain, sure; (*exato, direito*) right; (*um, algum*) a certain ♦ *adv* correctly; **na certa** certainly; **ao ~** for certain; **está ~** okay, all right

cerveja [sex'veʒa] *f* beer; **cervejaria** [sexveʒa'ria] *f* (*fábrica*) brewery; (*bar*) bar, public house

cervical [sexvi'kaw] (*pl* -**ais**) *adj* cervical

cessação [sesa'sãw] *f* halting, ceasing

cessão [se'sãw] (*pl* -**ões**) *f* surrender

cessar [se'sa*] *vi* to cease, stop; **sem ~** continually; **cessar-fogo** *m inv* cease-fire

cessões [se'sõjʃ] *fpl* de **cessão**

cesta ['seʃta] *f* basket

cesto ['seʃtu] *m* basket; (*com tampa*) hamper

cético, -a ['setʃiku, a] *m/f* sceptic (*BRIT*), skeptic (*US*)

cetim [se'tʃĩ] *m* satin

céu [sɛw] *m* sky; (*REL*) heaven; (*da boca*) roof

cevada [se'vada] *f* barley

CFC *abr m* (= *clorofluorocarbono*) CFC

chá [ʃa] *m* tea

chácara ['ʃakara] *f* farm; (*casa de campo*) country house

chacina [ʃa'sina] *f* slaughter; **chacinar** [ʃasi'na*] *vt* (*matar*) to slaughter

chacota [ʃa'kɔta] *f* mockery

chafariz [ʃafa'riʒ] *m* fountain

chalé [ʃa'lɛ] *m* chalet

chaleira [ʃa'lejra] *f* kettle; (*bajulador*) crawler, toady

chama ['ʃama] *f* flame

chamada [ʃa'mada] *f* call; (*MIL*) roll call; (*EDUC*) register; (*no jornal*) headline; **dar uma ~ em alguém** to tell sb off

chamar [ʃa'ma*] *vt* to call; (*convidar*) to invite; (*atenção*) to attract ♦ *vi* to call; (*telefone*) to ring; **chamar-se** *vr* to be called; **chamo-me João** my name is John; **~ alguém de idiota/Dudu** to call sb an idiot/Dudu; **mandar ~** to summon, send for

chamariz [ʃama'riʒ] *m* decoy

chamativo, -a [ʃama'tʃivu, a] *adj* showy, flashy

chaminé [ʃami'nɛ] *f* chimney; (*de navio*) funnel

champanha [ʃã'paɲa] *m ou f* champagne

champanhe [ʃã'paɲi] *m ou f* = **champanha**

champu [ʃã'pu] (*PT*) *m* shampoo

chance ['ʃãsi] *f* chance

chantagear [ʃãtaˈʒjaʳ] vt to black-mail

chantagem [ʃãˈtaʒẽ] f blackmail

chão [ʃãw] (pl ~s) m ground; (terra) soil; (piso) floor

chapa [ˈʃapa] f (placa) plate; (eleitoral) list; ~ de matrícula (PT: AUTO) number (BRIT) ou license (US) plate; oi, meu ~! hi, mate!

chapéu [ʃaˈpew] m hat

charco [ˈʃaxku] m marsh, bog

charme [ˈʃaxmi] m charm; fazer ~ to be nice, use one's charm; **charmoso, -a** [ʃaxˈmozu, ɔza] adj charming

charrete [ʃaˈxetʃi] f cart

charuto [ʃaˈrutu] m cigar

chassi [ʃaˈsi] m (AUTO, ELET) chassis

chata [ˈʃata] f barge; V tb **chato**

chateação [ʃatʃiaˈsãw] (pl -ões) f bother, upset; (maçada) bore

chatear [ʃaˈtʃjaʳ] vt to bother, upset; (importunar) to pester; (entediar) to bore; (irritar) to annoy ♦ vi to be upsetting; to be boring; to be annoying; **chatear-se** vr to get upset; to get bored; to get annoyed

chatice [ʃaˈtʃisi] f nuisance

chato, -a [ˈʃatu, a] adj flat; (tedioso) boring; (irritante) annoying; (que fica mal) rude ♦ m/f bore; (quem irrita) pain

chauvinista [ʃawviˈniʃta] adj chauvinistic ♦ m/f chauvinist

chavão [ʃaˈvãw] (pl -ões) m cliché

chave [ˈʃavi] f key; (ELET) switch; ~ de porcas spanner; ~ inglesa (monkey) wrench; ~ de fenda screwdriver

chávena [ˈʃavena] (PT) f cup

checar [ʃeˈkaʳ] vt to check

check-up [tʃeˈkapi] (pl ~s) m check-up

chefe [ˈʃefi] m/f head, chief; (patrão) boss; ~ de estação station-master; **chefia** [ʃeˈfia] f leadership; (direção) management; (repartição) headquarters sg; **chefiar** [ʃeˈfjaʳ] vt to lead

chegada [ʃeˈgada] f arrival

chegado, -a [ʃeˈgadu, a] adj near; (íntimo) close

chegar [ʃeˈgaʳ] vt to bring near ♦ vi to arrive; (ser suficiente) to be enough; **chegar-se** vr: ~-se a to approach; **chega!** that's enough!; ~ a (atingir) to reach; (conseguir) to manage to

cheio, -a [ˈʃeju, a] adj full; (repleto) full up; (col: farto) fed up

cheirar [ʃejˈraʳ] vt, vi to smell; ~ a to smell of; (pressagiar) to smack of; **cheiro** [ˈʃejru] m smell; **ter cheiro de** to smell of; **cheiroso, -a** [ʃejˈrozu, ɔza] adj: **ser** ou **estar cheiroso** to smell nice

cheque [ˈʃɛki] m cheque (BRIT), check (US); ~ de viagem traveller's cheque (BRIT), traveler's check (US)

chiar [ʃjaʳ] vt to squeak; (porta) to creak; (vapor) to hiss; (col: reclamar) to grumble

chiclete [ʃiˈkletʃi] m chewing gum

chicória [ʃiˈkɔrja] f chicory

chicote [ʃiˈkotʃi] m whip

chifre [ˈʃifri] m horn

Chile [ˈʃili] m: o ~ Chile

chimarrão [ʃimaˈxãw] (pl -ões) m mate tea without sugar taken from a pipe-like cup

chimpanzé [ʃĩpãˈze] m chimpanzee

China [ˈʃina] f: a ~ China

chinelo [ʃiˈnelu] m slipper

chinês, -esa [ʃiˈneʃ, eza] adj, m/f Chinese ♦ m (LING) Chinese

chip [ˈʃipi] m (COMPUT) chip

Chipre [ˈʃipri] f Cyprus

chique [ˈʃiki] adj stylish, chic

chocalho [ʃoˈkaʎu] m (MÚS, brinquedo) rattle; (para animais) bell

chocante [ʃoˈkɑ̃tʃi] *adj* shocking; (*col*) amazing

chocar [ʃoˈka*] *vt* to hatch, incubate; (*ofender*) to shock, offend ♦ *vi* to shock; **chocar-se** *vr* to crash, collide; to be shocked

chocho, -a [ˈʃoʃu, a] *adj* hollow, empty; (*fraco*) weak; (*sem graça*) dull

chocolate [ʃokoˈlatʃi] *m* chocolate

chofer [ʃoˈfe*] *m* driver

chope [ˈʃopi] *m* draught beer

choque¹ [ˈʃɔki] *m* shock; (*colisão*) collision; (*impacto*) impact; (*conflito*) clash

choque² *etc vb V* **chocar**

choramingar [ʃoramĩˈga*] *vi* to whine, whimper

chorão, -rona [ʃoˈrãw, rɔna] (*pl* -ões, ~s) *adj* tearful ♦ *m/f* crybaby ♦ *m* (*BOT*) weeping willow

chorar [ʃoˈra*] *vt, vi* to weep, cry

chorinho [ʃoˈriɲu] *m* type of Brazilian music

choro [ˈʃoru] *m* crying; (*MÚS*) type of Brazilian music

choupana [ʃoˈpana] *f* shack, hut

chouriço [ʃoˈrisu] *m* (*BR*) black pudding; (*PT*) spicy sausage

chover [ʃoˈve*] *vi* to rain; **~ a cântaros** to rain cats and dogs

chulé [ʃuˈle] *m* foot odour (*BRIT*) ou odor (*US*)

chulo, -a [ˈʃulu, a] *adj* vulgar

chumaço [ʃuˈmasu] *m* (*de papel, notas*) wad

chumbo [ˈʃũbu] *m* lead; (*de caça*) gunshot; (*PT: de dente*) filling; **sem ~** (*gasolina*) unleaded

chupar [ʃuˈpa*] *vt* to suck

chupeta [ʃuˈpeta] *f* dummy (*BRIT*), pacifier (*US*)

churrasco [ʃuˈxaʃku] *m*, **churrasqueira** [ʃuxaʃˈkejra] ♦ *f* barbecue

churrasquinho [ʃuxaʃˈkiɲu] *m* kebab

chutar [ʃuˈta*] *vt* to kick; (*col: adivinhar*) to guess at; (: *dar o fora em*) to dump ♦ *vi* to kick, to guess; (: *mentir*) to lie

chute [ˈʃutʃi] *m* kick; (*col: mentira*) fib; **dar o ~ em alguém** (*col*) to give sb the boot

chuteira [ʃuˈtejra] *f* football boot

chuva [ˈʃuva] *f* rain; **chuveiro** [ʃuˈvejru] *m* shower

chuviscar [ʃuviʃˈka*] *vi* to drizzle; **chuvisco** [ʃuˈviʃku] *m* drizzle

chuvoso, -a [ʃuˈvozu, ɔza] *adj* rainy

Cia. *abr* = **companhia**) Co.

cibercafé [sibexkaˈfɛ] *m* cybercafé

ciberespaço [sibexʃˈpasu] *m* cyberspace

cicatriz [sikaˈtriʒ] *f* scar; **cicatrizar** [sikatriˈza*] *vi* to heal; (*rosto*) to scar

cicerone [siseˈrɔni] *m* tourist guide

ciclismo [siˈkliʒmu] *m* cycling

ciclista [siˈkliʃta] *m/f* cyclist

ciclo [ˈsiklu] *m* cycle

ciclovia [sikloˈvia] *f* cycle lane ou path

cidadã [sidaˈdã] *f de* **cidadão**

cidadania [sidadaˈnia] *f* citizenship

cidadão, -cidadã [sidaˈdãw, sidaˈdã] (*pl* ~s, ~s) *m/f* citizen

cidade [siˈdadʒi] *f* town; (*grande*) city

ciência [ˈsjesja] *f* science

ciente [ˈsjẽtʃi] *adj* aware

científico, -a [sjẽˈtʃifiku, a] *adj* scientific

cientista [sjẽˈtʃiʃta] *m/f* scientist

cifra [ˈsifra] *f* cipher; (*algarismo*) number, figure; (*total*) sum

cigano, -a [siˈganu, a] *adj, m/f* gypsy

cigarra [siˈgaxa] *f* cicada; (*ELET*) buzzer

cigarrilha [siga'xiʎa] f cheroot

cigarro [si'gaxu] m cigarette

cilada [si'lada] f ambush; (armadilha) trap; (embuste) trick

cilindro [si'lĩdru] m cylinder; (rolo) roller

cima ['sima] f: **de ~ para baixo** from top to bottom; **para ~** up; **em ~ de** on, on top of; **por ~ de** over; **de ~** from above; **lá em ~** up there; (em casa) upstairs; **ainda por ~** on top of that

cimento [si'mẽtu] m cement; (fig) foundation

cimo ['simu] m top, summit

cinco ['sĩku] num five

cineasta [sine'aʃta] m/f film maker

cinema [si'nɛma] f cinema

Cingapura [sĩga'pura] f Singapore

cínico, -a ['siniku, a] adj cynical ♦ m/f cynic; **cinismo** [si'niʒmu] m cynicism

cinqüenta [sĩ'kwẽta] num fifty

cinta ['sĩta] f sash; (de mulher) girdle

cintilar [sĩtʃi'la*] vi to sparkle, glitter

cinto ['sĩtu] m belt; **~ de segurança** safety belt; (AUTO) seatbelt

cintura [sĩ'tura] f waist; (linha) waistline

cinza ['sĩza] adj inv grey (BRIT), gray (US) ♦ f ash, ashes pl

cinzeiro [sĩ'zejru] m ashtray

cinzento, -a [sĩ'zẽtu, a] adj grey (BRIT), gray (US)

cio [siu] m: **no ~** on heat, in season

cipreste [si'prɛʃtʃi] m cypress (tree)

cipriota [si'prjɔta] adj, m/f Cypriot

circo ['sixku] m circus

circuito [six'kwitu] m circuit

circulação [sixkula'sãw] f circulation

circular [sixku'la*] adj circular ♦ f (carta) circular ♦ vi to circulate; (girar, andar) to go round ♦ vt to cir-

culate; (estar em volta de) to surround; (percorrer em roda) to go round

círculo ['sixkulu] m circle

circundar [sixkũ'da*] vt to surround

circunferência [sixkũfe'rẽsja] f circumference

circunflexo [sixkũ'fleksu] m circumflex (accent)

circunstância [sixkũ'ʃtãsja] f circumstance; **~s atenuantes** mitigating circumstances

cirurgia [sirux'ʒia] f surgery; **~ plástica/estética** plastic/cosmetic surgery

cirurgião, -giã [sirux'ʒjãw, 'ʒjã] (pl -ões, ~s) m/f surgeon

cirúrgico, -a [si'ruxʒiku, a] adj surgical

cirurgiões [sirux'ʒjõjʃ] mpl de **cirurgião**

cisco ['siʃku] m speck

cismado, -a [siʒ'madu, a] adj with fixed ideas

cismar [siʒ'ma*] vi (pensar): **~ em** to brood over; (antipatizar): **~ com** to take a dislike to ♦ vt: **~ que** to be convinced that; **~ de** ou **em fazer** (meter na cabeça) to get into one's head to do; (insistir) to insist on doing

cisne ['siʒni] m swan

cisterna [siʃ'tɛxna] f cistern, tank

citação [sita'sãw] (pl -ões) f quotation; (JUR) summons sg

citar [si'ta*] vt to quote; (JUR) to summon

ciúme ['sjumi] m jealousy; **ter ~s de** to be jealous of; **ciumento, -a** [sju'mẽtu, a] adj jealous

cívico, -a ['siviku, a] adj civic

civil [si'viw] (pl -is) adj civil ♦ m/f civilian; **civilidade** [sivili'dadʒi] f politeness

civilização [siviliza'sãw] (pl -ões) f civilization

civis [si'viʃ] pl de **civil**

clamar [kla'ma*] vt to clamour (BRIT) ou clamor (US) for ♦ vi to cry out, clamo(u)r

clamor [kla'mo*] m outcry, uproar

clandestino, -a [klãdeʃ'tʃinu, a] adj clandestine; (ilegal) underground

clara ['klara] f egg white

clarabóia [klara'bɔja] f skylight

clarão [kla'rãw] (pl -ões) m (cintilação) flash; (claridade) gleam

clarear [kla'rja*] vi (dia) to dawn; (tempo) to clear up, brighten up ♦ vt to clarify

claridade [klari'dadʒi] f brightness

clarim [kla'rĩ] (pl -ns) m bugle

clarinete [klari'netʃi] m clarinet

clarins [kla'rĩʃ] mpl de **clarim**

claro, -a ['klaru, a] adj clear; (luminoso) bright; (cor) light; (evidente) clear, evident ♦ m (na escrita) space; (clareira) clearing ♦ adv clearly; ~! of course!; ~ que sim!/não! of course!/of course not!; às claras openly

classe ['klasi] f class

clássico, -a ['klasiku, a] adj classical; (fig) classic; (habitual) usual ♦ m classic

classificação [klasifika'sãw] (pl -ões) f classification; (ESPORTE) place, placing

classificado, -a [klasifi'kadu, a] adj (em exame) successful; (anúncio) classified; (ESPORTE) placed ♦ m classified ad

classificar [klasifi'ka*] vt to classify; **classificar-se** vr: ~-se de algo to call o.s. sth, describe o.s. as sth

claustro ['klawʃtru] m cloister

cláusula ['klawzula] f clause

clausura [klaw'zura] f enclosure

clavícula [kla'vikula] f collarbone

clemência [kle'mẽsja] f mercy

clero ['kleru] m clergy

clicar [kli'ka*] vi (COMPUT) to click

clichê [kli'ʃe] m (FOTO) plate; (chavão) cliché

cliente ['kljẽtʃi] m client, customer; (de médico) patient; **clientela** [kljẽ'tela] f clientele; (de loja) customers pl

clima ['klima] m climate

clímax ['klimaks] m inv climax

clínica ['klinika] f clinic; V tb **clínico**

clínico, -a ['kliniku, a] adj clinical ♦ m/f doctor; ~ geral general practitioner, GP

clipe ['klipi] m clip; (para papéis) paper clip

clique ['kliki] m (COMPUT) click; **dar um ~ duplo em** to double-click on

cloro ['klɔru] m chlorine

close ['klɔzi] m close-up

clube ['klubi] m club

coadjuvante [koadʒu'vãtʃi] adj supporting ♦ m/f (num crime) accomplice; (TEATRO, CINEMA) co-star

coador [koa'do*] m strainer; (de café) filter bag; (para legumes) colander

coalhada [koa'ʎada] f curd

coalizão [koali'zãw] (pl -ões) f coalition

coar [ko'a*] vt (líquido) to strain

coberta [ko'bexta] f cover, covering; (NÁUT) deck

cobertor [kobex'to*] m blanket

cobertura [kobex'tura] f covering; (telhado) roof; (apartamento) penthouse; (TV, RÁDIO, JORNALISMO) coverage; (SEGUROS) cover

cobiça [ko'bisa] f greed

cobiçar [kobi'sa*] vt to covet

cobra ['kɔbra] f snake

cobrador, a [kobra'do*, a] m/f collector; (em transporte) conductor

cobrança [ko'brãsa] *f* collection; *(ato de cobrar)* charging

cobrar [ko'bra*] *vt* to collect; *(preço)* to charge

cobre ['kɔbri] *m* copper; **~s** *mpl* *(dinheiro)* money *sg*

cobrir [ko'bri*] *vt* to cover

cocada [ko'kada] *f* coconut sweet

cocaína [koka'ina] *f* cocaine

coçar [ko'sa*] *vt* to scratch ♦ *vi* to itch; **coçar-se** *vr* to scratch o.s.

cócegas ['kɔsegaʃ] *fpl*: **fazer ~ em** to tickle; **tenho ~ nos pés** my feet tickle; **sentir ~** to be ticklish

coceira [ko'sejra] *f* itch; *(qualidade)* itchiness

cochichar [koʃi'ʃa*] *vi* to whisper; **cochicho** [ko'ʃiʃu] *m* whispering

cochilar [koʃi'la*] *vi* to snooze, doze; **cochilo** [ko'ʃilu] *m* nap

coco ['koku] *m* coconut

cócoras ['kɔkoraʃ] *fpl*: **de ~** squatting; **ficar de ~** to squat (down)

código ['kɔdʒigu] *m* code; **~ de barras** bar code

coelho [ko'eʎu] *m* rabbit

coerente [koe'rẽtʃi] *adj* coherent; *(conseqüente)* consistent

cofre ['kɔfri] *m* safe; *(caixa)* strongbox; **os ~s públicos** public funds

cogitar [koʒi'ta*] *vt*, *vi* to contemplate

cogumelo [kogu'mɛlu] *m* mushroom; **~ venenoso** toadstool

coice ['kojsi] *m* kick; *(de arma)* recoil; **dar ~s em** to kick

coincidência [koĩsi'dẽsja] *f* coincidence

coincidir [koĩsi'dʒi*] *vi* to coincide; *(concordar)* to agree

coisa ['kojza] *f* thing; *(assunto)* matter; **~ de about**

coitado, -a [koj'tadu, a] *adj* poor, wretched

cola ['kɔla] *f* glue

colaborador, a [kolabora'do*, a] *m/f* collaborator; *(em jornal)* contributor

colaborar [kolabo'ra*] *vi* to collaborate; *(ajudar)* to help; *(escrever artigos etc)* to contribute

colante [ko'lãtʃi] *adj* *(roupa)* skintight

colapso [ko'lapsu] *m* collapse; **~ cardíaco** heart failure

colar [ko'la*] *vt* to stick, glue; *(BR: copiar)* to crib ♦ *vi* to stick; to cheat ♦ *m* necklace

colarinho [kola'riɲu] *m* collar

colarinho-branco *(pl* **colarinhos-brancos)** *m* white-collar worker

colcha ['ko|ʃa] *f* bedspread

colchão [kow'ʃãw] *(pl* **-ões)** *m* mattress

colchete [kow'ʃetʃi] *m* clasp, fastening; *(parêntese)* square bracket; **~ de gancho** hook and eye; **~ de pressão** press stud, popper

colchões [kow'ʃõjʃ] *mpl de* **colchão**

coleção [kole'sãw] *(PT* **-cç-)** *(pl* **-ões)** *f* collection; **colecionador, a** [kolesjona'do*, a] *(PT* **-cc-)** *m/f* collector; **colecionar** [kolesjo'na*] *(PT* **-cc-)** *vt* to collect

colectar *etc* [kolek'ta*] *(PT)* = **coletar** *etc*

colega [ko'lɛga] *m/f* colleague; *(de escola)* classmate

colegial [kole'ʒjaw] *(pl* **-ais)** *m/f* schoolboy/girl

colégio [ko'lɛʒu] *m* school

coleira [ko'lejra] *f* collar

cólera ['kɔlera] *f* anger ♦ *m ou f* *(MED)* cholera

colesterol [koleʃte'rɔw] *m* cholesterol

coleta [ko'lɛta] *f* collection; **coletar** [kole'ta*] *vt* to tax; *(arrecadar)* to collect

colete [ko'letʃi] *m* waistcoat *(BRIT)*,

vest (US); ~ **salva-vidas** life jacket (BRIT), life preserver (US)

coletivo, -a [kole'tʃivu, a] adj collective; (transportes) public ♦ m bus

colheita [ko'ʎejta] f harvest

colher [ko'ʎe*] vt to gather, pick; (dados) to gather ♦ f spoon; ~ **de chá/sopa** teaspoon/tablespoon

colidir [koli'dʒi*] vi: ~ **com** to collide with, crash into

coligação [koliga'sãw] (pl -ões) f coalition

colina [ko'lina] f hill

colisão [koli'zãw] (pl -ões) f collision

collant [ko'lã] (pl ~s) m tights of (BRIT), pantihose (US); (blusa) leotard

colmeia [kow'meja] f beehive

colo [ˈkɔlu] m neck; (regaço) lap

colocar [kolo'ka*] vt to put, place; (empregar) to find a job for, place; (COM) to market; (pneus, tapetes) to fit; (questão, idéia) to put forward; (COMPUT: dados) to key (in)

Colômbia [ko'lõbja] f: **a ~** Colombia

colônia [ko'lonja] f colony; (perfume) cologne; **colonial** [kolo'njaw] (pl -ais) adj colonial

colonizador, a [koloniza'do*, a] m/f colonist, settler

colono [ko'lɔnu] m/f settler; (cultivador) tenant farmer

coloquial [kolo'kjaw] (pl -ais) adj colloquial

colóquio [ko'lɔkju] m conversation; (congresso) conference

colorido, -a [kolo'ridu, a] adj colourful (BRIT), colorful (US) ♦ m colouring (BRIT), coloring (US)

colorir [kolo'ri*] vt to colour (BRIT), color (US)

coluna [ko'luna] f column; (pilar) pillar; ~ **dorsal** ou **vertebral** spine; **colunável** [kolu'navew] (pl -eis)

adj famous ♦ m/f celebrity; **colunista** [kolu'niʃta] m/f columnist

com [kõ] prep with; ~ **cuidado** carefully; **estar** ~ **câncer** to have cancer; **estar** ~ **dinheiro** to have some money on one; **estar** ~ **fome** to be hungry

coma [ˈkɔma] f coma

comandante [komã'dãtʃi] m commander; (MIL) commandant; (NÁUT) captain

comandar [komã'da*] vt to command

comando [ko'mãdu] m command

combate [kõ'batʃi] m combat; **combater** [kõba'te*] vt to fight; (opor-se a) to oppose ♦ vi to fight; **combater-se** vr to fight

combinação [kõbina'sãw] (pl -ões) f combination; (QUÍM) compound; (acordo) arrangement; (plano) scheme; (roupa) slip

combinar [kõbi'na*] vt to combine; (jantar etc) to arrange; (fuga etc) to plan ♦ vi (roupas etc) to go together; **combinar-se** vr to combine; (pessoas) to get on well together; ~ **com** (harmonizar-se) to go with; ~ **de fazer** to arrange to do; **combinado!** agreed!

comboio [kõ'boju] m (PT) train; (de navios, carros) convoy

combustível [kõbuʃ'tʃivew] m fuel

começar [kome'sa*] vt, vi to begin, start; ~ **a fazer** to begin ou start to do

começo [ko'mesu] m beginning, start

comédia [ko'medʒja] f comedy

comemorar [komemo'ra*] vt to commemorate

comentar [komẽ'ta*] vt to comment on; (maliciosamente) to make comments about

comentário [komẽ'tarju] m comment, remark; (análise) commentary

comer [ko'me*] vt to eat; (DAMAS, XADREZ) to take, capture ♦ vi to eat; **dar de ~ a** to feed

comercial [komex'sjaw] (pl -ais) adj commercial; (relativo ao negócio) business atr ♦ m commercial

comercializar [komexsjali'za*] vt to market

comerciante [komex'sjãtʃi] m/f trader

comércio [ko'mεxsju] m commerce; (tráfico) trade; (negócio) business; (lojas) shops pl; ~ **eletrônico** e-commerce

comes ['kɔmiʃ] mpl: ~ **e bebes** food and drink

comestíveis [komeʃ'tʃiveis] mpl foodstuffs, food sg

comestível [komeʃ'tʃivew] (pl -eis) adj edible

cometer [kome'te*] vt to commit

comichão [komi'ʃãw] f itch, itching

comício [ko'misju] m (POL) rally, meeting; (assembléia) assembly

cômico, -a ['komiku, a] adj comic(al) ♦ m comedian; (de teatro) actor

comida [ko'mida] f (alimento) food; (refeição) meal

comigo [ko'migu] pron with me

comilão, -lona [komi'lãw, lɔna] (pl -ões, ~s) adj greedy ♦ m/f glutton

comiserar-se [komize'raxsi] vr: ~-**se (de)** to sympathize (with)

comissão [komi'sãw] (pl -ões) f commission; (comitê) committee

comissário [komi'sarju] m commissioner; (COM) agent; ~ **de bordo** (AER) steward; (NÁUT) purser

comissões [komi'sõjʃ] fpl de **comissão**

comitê [komi'te] m committee

PALAVRA CHAVE

como ['komu] adv 1 (modo) as; **ela fez ~ eu pedi** she did as I asked; ~ **se** as if; ~ **quiser** as you wish; **seja ~ for** be that as it may

2 (assim ~) like; **ela tem olhos azuis ~ o pai** she has blue eyes like her father's; **ela trabalha numa loja, ~ a mãe** she works in a shop, as does her mother

3 (de que maneira) how; ~? pardon?; ~! what!; ~ **assim?** what do you mean?; ~ **não!** of course!

♦ conj (porque) as, since; **como estava tarde ele dormiu aqui** since it was late he slept here

comoção [komo'sãw] (pl -ões) f distress; (revolta) commotion

cômoda ['komoda] f chest of drawers (BRIT), bureau (US)

comodidade [komodʒi'dadʒi] f comfort; (conveniência) convenience

comodismo [komo'dʒiʒmu] m complacency

cômodo, -a ['komodu, a] adj comfortable; (conveniente) convenient ♦ m room

comovente [komo'vẽtʃi] adj moving, touching

comover [komo've*] vt to move ♦ vi to be moving; **comover-se** to be moved

compacto, -a [kõ'paktu, a] adj compact; (espesso) thick; (sólido) solid ♦ m (disco) single

compadecer-se [kõpade'sexsi] vr: ~-**se de** to be sorry for, pity

compadre [kõ'padri] m (col: companheiro) buddy, pal

compaixão [kõpaj'ʃãw] m compassion; (misericórdia) mercy

companheirismo [kõpaɲej-'riʒmu] *m* companionship

companheiro, -a [kõpa'ɲejru, a] *m/f* companion; (*colega*) friend; (*col*) buddy, mate

companhia [kõpa'ɲia] *f* company

comparação [kõpara'sãw] (*pl -ões*) *f* comparison

comparar [kõpa'ɾaʁ] *vt* to compare; ~ **a** to liken to; ~ **com** to compare with

comparecer [kõpare'se*] *vi* to appear, make an appearance; ~ **a uma reunião** to attend a meeting

comparsa [kõ'paxsa] *m/f* (*TEATRO*) extra; (*cúmplice*) accomplice

compartilhar [kõpaxtʃi'ʎa*] *vt* to share ♦ *vi*: ~ **de** to share in, participate in

compartimento [kõpaxtʃi'mẽtu] *m* compartment; (*aposento*) room

compasso [kõ'pasu] *m* (*instrumento*) pair of compasses; (*MÚS*) time; (*ritmo*) beat

compatível [kõpa'tʃivew] (*pl -eis*) *adj* compatible

compatriota [kõpa'trjɔta] *m/f* fellow countryman/woman

compensação [kõpẽsa'sãw] (*pl -ões*) *f* compensation; **em** ~ on the other hand

compensar [kõpẽ'sa*] *vt* to make up for, compensate for; (*equilibrar*) to offset; (*cheque*) to clear

competência [kõpe'tẽsja] *f* competence, ability; (*responsabilidade*) responsibility; (*competente* [kõpe'tẽtʃi] *adj* competent; (*apropriado*) appropriate; (*responsável*) responsible

competição [kõpetʃi'sãw] (*pl -ões*) *f* competition

competidor, a [kõpetʃi'do*, a] *m/f* competitor

competir [kõpe'tʃi*] *vi* to compete;

~ **a alguém** to be sb's responsibility; (*caber*) to be up to sb

competitivo, -a [kõpetʃi'tʃivu, a] *adj* competitive

compito *etc* [kõ'pitu] *vb V* **competir**

complementar [kõplemẽ'ta*] *adj* complementary ♦ *vt* to supplement

complemento [kõple'mẽtu] *m* complement

completamente [kõpleta'mẽtʃi] *adv* completely, quite

completar [kõple'ta*] *vt* to complete; (*tanque, carro*) to fill up; ~ **dez anos** to be ten

completo, -a [kõ'plɛtu, a] *adj* complete; (*cheio*) full (up); **por** ~ completely

complexo, -a [kõ'plɛksu, a] *adj* complex ♦ *m* complex

complicação [kõplika'sãw] (*pl -ões*) *f* complication

complicado, -a [kõpli'kadu, a] *adj* complicated

complicar [kõpli'ka*] *vt* to complicate

complô [kõ'plo] *m* plot, conspiracy

componente [kõpo'nẽtʃi] *adj, m* component

compor [kõ'po*] (*irreg: como* **pôr**) *vt* to compose; (*discurso, livro*) to write; (*arranjar*) to arrange ♦ *vi* to compose; **compor-se** *vt* (*controlarse*) to compose o.s.; ~ **-se de** to consist of

comporta [kõ'pɔxta] *f* (*de canal*) lock

comportamento [kõpoxta'mẽtu] *m* behaviour (*BRIT*), behavior (*US*)

comportar-se [kõpox'taxsi] *vt, vr* to behave; ~ **mal** to misbehave, behave badly

composição [kõpozi'sãw] (*pl -ões*) *f* composition; (*TIP*) typesetting

compositor, a [kõpozi'to*, a] *m/f*

composer; (*TIP*) typesetter

compota [kõ'pɔta] f fruit in syrup

compra ['kõpra] f purchase; **fazer ~s** to go shopping; **comprador, a** [kõpra'do*, a] m/f buyer, purchaser

comprar [kõ'pra*] vt to buy

compreender [kõprjẽn'de*] vt to understand; (*constar de*) to be comprised of, consist of; (*abranger*) to cover

compreensão [kõprjẽ'sãw] f understanding, comprehension; **compreensivo, -a** [kõprjẽ'sivu, a] adj understanding

compressa [kõ'prɛsa] f compress

comprido, -a [kõ'pridu, a] adj long; (*alto*) tall; **ao ~** lengthways

comprimento [kõpri'mẽtu] m length

comprimido [kõpri'midu] m pill, tablet

comprimir [kõpri'mi*] vt to compress

comprometer [kõprome'te*] vt to compromise; (*envolver*) to involve; (*arriscar*) to jeopardize; (*empenhar*) to pledge; **comprometer-se** vr: **~-se a** to undertake to, promise to

compromisso [kõpro'misu] m promise; (*obrigação*) commitment; (*hora marcada*) appointment; (*acordo*) agreement

comprovante [kõpro'vãtʃi] m receipt

comprovar [kõpro'va*] vt to prove; (*confirmar*) to confirm

compulsão [kõpuw'sãw] (*pl -ões*) f compulsion; **compulsivo, -a** [kõpuw'sivu, a] adj compulsive; **compulsório, -a** [kõpuw'sɔrju, a] adj compulsory

computação [kõputa'sãw] f computer science, computing

computador [kõputa'do*] m computer

computar [kõpu'ta*] vt (*calcular*) to calculate; (*contar*) to count

comum [ko'mũ] (*pl -ns*) adj ordinary, common; (*habitual*) usual; **em ~** in common

comungar [komũ'ga*] vi to take communion

comunhão [komu'ɲãw] (*pl -ões*) f (*ger, REL*) communion

comunicação [komunika'sãw] (*pl -ões*) f communication; (*mensagem*) message; (*acesso*) access

comunicado [komuni'kadu] m notice

comunicar [komuni'ka*] vt, vi to communicate; **comunicar-se** vr to communicate; **~-se com** (*entrar em contato*) to get in touch with

comunidade [komuni'dadʒi] f community; **C~ dos Estados Independentes** Commonwealth of Independent States

comunismo [komu'niʒmu] m communism; **comunista** [komu'niʃta] adj, m/f communist

comuns [ko'mũʃ] pl de **comum**

conceber [kõse'be*] vt, vi to conceive

conceder [kõse'de*] vt to allow; (*outorgar*) to grant; (*dar*) to give ♦ vi: **~ em** to agree to

conceito [kõ'sejtu] m concept, idea; (*fama*) reputation; (*opinião*) opinion; **conceituado, -a** [kõsej'twadu, a] adj well thought of, highly regarded

concentração [kõsẽtra'sãw] (*pl -ões*) f concentration

concepção [kõsep'sãw] (*pl -ões*) f (*geração*) conception; (*noção*) idea, concept; (*opinião*) opinion

concerto [kõ'sextu] m concert

concessão [kõse'sãw] (*pl -ões*) f concession; (*permissão*) permissão

concha ['koʃa] f shell; (*para líquidos*) ladle

conchavo [ko'ʃavu] m conspiracy

conciliar [kosi'lja*] vt to reconcile

concluir [ko'klwi*] vt, vi to conclude

conclusão [koklu'zãw] (*pl* -ões) f end; (*dedução*) conclusion

conclusões [koklu'zõjʃ] fpl de **conclusão**

concordância [kokox'dãsja] f agreement

concordar [kokox'da*] vi, vt to agree

concorrência [koko'xẽsja] f competition; (*a um cargo*) application

concorrente [koko'xẽtʃi] m/f competitor; (*candidato*) candidate

concorrer [koko'xe*] vi to compete; ~ **a** to apply for

concretizar [kokretʃi'za*] vt to make real, **concretizar-se** vr (*sonho*) to come true; (*ambições*) to be realized

concreto, -a [ko'kretu, a] adj concrete ♦ m concrete

concurso [ko'kuxsu] m contest; (*exame*) competition

conde ['kodʒi] m count

condenação [kodena'sãw] (*pl* -ões) f (*JUR*) conviction

condenar [kode'na*] vt to condemn; (*JUR: sentenciar*) to sentence; (*: declarar culpado*) to convict

condensar [kodẽ'sa*] vt to condense; **condensar-se** vr to condense

condescendência [kodesẽ'dẽsja] f acquiescence

condescender [kodesẽ'de*] vi to acquiesce; ~ **a** ou **em** to condescend to, deign to

condessa [ko'desa] f countess

condição [kodʒi'sãw] (*pl* -ões) f condition; (*social*) status; (*quali-dade*) capacity; **com a ~ de que** on condition that, provided that; **em condições de fazer** (*pessoa*) able to do; (*carro etc*) in condition to do

condimento [kodʒi'mẽtu] m seasoning

condomínio [kodo'minju] m condominium

condução [kodu'sãw] f driving; (*transporte*) transport; (*ônibus*) bus

conduta [ko'duta] f conduct, behaviour (*BRIT*), behavior (*US*)

condutor, a [kodu'to*, a] m/f (*de veículo*) driver ♦ m (*ELET*) conductor

conduzir [kodu'zi*] vt (*levar*) to lead; (*rís*) to conduct; **conduzir-se** vr to behave; **conduzir a** to lead to

cone ['koni] m cone

conectar [konek'ta*] vt to connect

conexão [konek'sãw] (*pl* -ões) f connection

confecção [kofek'sãw] (*pl* -ões) f making; (*de um boletim*) production; (*roupa*) ready-to-wear clothes pl; (*negócio*) business selling ready-to-wear clothes

confeccionar [kofeksjo'na*] vt to make; (*fabricar*) to manufacture

confecções [kofek'sõjʃ] fpl de **confecção**

confeitaria [kofejta'ria] f patisserie

conferência [kofe'rẽsja] f conference; (*discurso*) lecture

conferir [kofe'ri*] vt to check; (*comparar*) to compare; (*outorgar*) to grant ♦ vi to tally

confessar [kofe'sa*] vt, vi to confess; **confessar-se** vr to confess

confete [ko'fetʃi] m confetti

confiança [ko'fjãsa] f confidence; (*fé*) trust; **de ~** reliable; **ter ~ em alguém** to trust sb

confiante [ko'fjãtʃi] adj: ~ **(em)** confident (of)

confiar [ko'fja*] vt to entrust; (*se-*

gredo) to confide ♦ *vi:* ~ **em** to trust; (*ter fé*) to have faith in

confiável [kõ'fjavew] (*pl* **-eis**) *adj* reliable

confidência [kõfi'dẽsja] *f* secret; **em** ~ in confidence; **confidencial** [kõfidẽ'sjaw] (*pl* **-ais**) *adj* confidential

confins [kõ'fĩʃ] *mpl* limits, boundaries

confirmação [kõfixma'sãw] (*pl* **-ões**) *f* confirmation

confirmar [kõfix'ma*] *vt* to confirm

confiro *etc* [kõ'firu] *vb V* **conferir**

confiscar [kõfiʃ'ka*] *vt* to confiscate

confissão [kõfi'sãw] (*pl* **-ões**) *f* confession

conflito [kõ'flitu] *m* conflict

conformar [kõfox'ma*] *vt* to form ♦ *vi:* ~ **com** to conform to; **conformar-se** *vr:* ~**-se com** to resign o.s. to; (*acomodar-se*) to conform to

conforme [kõ'fɔxmi] *prep* according to; (*dependendo de*) depending on ♦ *conj* (*logo que*) as soon as; (*como*) as, according to what; (*à medida que*) as; **você vai?** – ~ are you going? – it depends

conformidade [kõfoxmi'dadʒi] *f* agreement; **em** ~ **com** in accordance with

confortar [kõfox'ta*] *vt* to comfort, console

confortável [kõfox'tavew] (*pl* **-eis**) *adj* comfortable

conforto [kõ'foxtu] *m* comfort

confrontar [kõfrõ'ta*] *vt* to confront; (*comparar*) to compare

confronto [kõ'frõtu] *m* confrontation; (*comparação*) comparison

confundir [kõfũ'dʒi*] *vt* to confuse; **confundir-se** *vr* to get mixed up

confusão [kõfu'zãw] (*pl* **-ões**) *f* confusion; (*tumulto*) uproar; (*problemas*) trouble

confuso, -a [kõ'fuzu, a] *adj* confused; (*problema*) confusing

confusões [kõfu'zõjʃ] *fpl de* **confusão**

congelador [kõʒela'do*] *m* freezer, deep freeze

congelamento [kõʒela'mẽtu] *m* freezing; (*ECON*) freeze

congelar [kõʒe'la*] *vt* to freeze; **congelar-se** *vr* to freeze

congestão [kõʒeʃ'tãw] *f* congestion; **congestionado, -a** [kõʒeʃtʃjo'nadu, a] *adj* congested; (*olhos*) bloodshot; (*rosto*) flushed; **congestionamento** [kõʒeʃtʃjona-'mẽtu] *m* congestion; **um congestionamento (de tráfego)** a traffic jam

congestionar [kõʒeʃtʃjo'na*] *vt* to congest; **congestionar-se** *vr* (*rosto*) to go red

congressista [kõgre'siʃta] *m/f* congressman/woman

congresso [kõ'gresu] *m* congress, conference

conhaque [ko'ɲaki] *m* cognac, brandy

conhecedor, a [koɲese'do*, a] *adj* knowing ♦ *m/f* connoisseur, expert

conhecer [koɲe'se*] *vt* to know; (*travar conhecimento com*) to meet; (*descobrir*) to discover; **conhecer-se** *vr* to meet; (*ter conhecimento*) to know each other

conhecido, -a [koɲe'sidu, a] *adj* known; (*célebre*) well-known ♦ *m/f* acquaintance

conhecimento [koɲesi'mẽtu] *m* (*tb:* ~**s**) knowledge; (*idéia*) idea; (*conhecido*) acquaintance; (*com*) bill of lading; **levar ao** ~ **de alguém** to bring to sb's notice

conjugado [kõʒu'gadu] *m* studio

cônjuge ['kõʒuʒi] *m* spouse

conjunção [kõʒũ'sãw] (*pl* -ões) *f* union; (*LING*) conjunction

conjuntivite [kõʒũtʃi'vitʃi] *f* conjunctivitis

conjuntivo [kõʒũ'tʃivu] (*PT*) *m* (*LING*) subjunctive

conjunto, -a [kõ'ʒũtu, a] *adj* joint ♦ *m* whole; (*coleção*) collection; (*músicos*) group; (*roupa*) outfit

conosco [ko'noʃku] *pron* with us

conquista [kõ'kiʃta] *f* conquest; **conquistador, a** [kõkiʃta'do*, a] *adj* conquering ♦ *m* conqueror

conquistar [kõkiʃ'ta*] *vt* to conquer; (*alcançar*) to achieve; (*ganhar*) to win

consagrado, -a [kõsa'gradu, a] *adj* established

consciência [kõ'sjẽsja] *f* conscience; (*percepção*) awareness; (*senso de responsabilidade*) conscientiousness

consciente [kõ'sjẽtʃi] *adj* conscious

conseguinte [kõse'gĩtʃi] *adj*: **por ~** consequently

conseguir [kõse'gi*] *vt* to get, obtain; **~ fazer** to manage to do, succeed in doing

conselho [kõ'seʎu] *m* piece of advice; (*corporação*) council; **~s** *mpl* (*advertência*) advice *sg*; **~ de guerra** court martial; **C~ de ministros** (*POL*) Cabinet

consentimento [kõsẽtʃi'mẽtu] *m* consent

consentir [kõsẽ'tʃi*] *vt* to allow, permit; (*aprovar*) to agree to ♦ *vi*: **~ em** to agree to

consequência [kõse'kwẽsja] *f* consequence; **por ~** consequently

consertar [kõsex'ta*] *vt* to mend, repair; (*remediar*) to put right; **conserto** [kõ'sextu] *m* repair

conserva [kõ'sexva] *f* pickle; **em ~** pickled

conservação [kõsexva'sãw] *f* conservation; (*de vida, alimentos*) preservation

conservador, a [kõsexva'do*, a] *adj* conservative ♦ *m/f* (*POL*) conservative

conservante [kõsex'vãtʃi] *m* preservative

conservar [kõsex'va*] *vt* to preserve, maintain; (*reter, manter*) to keep, retain; **conservar-se** *vr* to keep

conservatório [kõsexva'tɔrju] *m* conservatory

consideração [kõsĩdera'sãw] (*pl* -ões) *f* consideration; (*estima*) respect, esteem; **levar em ~** to take into account

considerar [kõside'ra*] *vt* to consider; (*prezar*) to respect ♦ *vi* to consider

considerável [kõside'ravew] (*pl* -eis) *adj* considerable

consigo[1] [kõ'sigu] *pron* (*m*) with him; (*f*) with her; (*pl*) with them; (*com você*) with you

consigo[2] *etc vb V* **conseguir**

consinto *etc* [kõ'sĩtu] *vb V* **consentir**

consistente [kõsiʃ'tẽtʃi] *adj* solid; (*espesso*) thick

consistir [kõsiʃ'tʃi*] *vi*: **~ em** to be made up of, consist of

consoante [kõso'ãtʃi] *f* consonant ♦ *prep* according to ♦ *conj*: **~ prometera** as he had promised

consolação [kõsola'sãw] (*pl* -ões) *f* consolation

consolar [kõso'la*] *vt* to console

consolidar [kõsoli'da*] *vt* to consolidate; (*fratura*) to knit ♦ *vi* to become solid; to knit together

consolo [kõ'solu] *m* consolation

consome *etc* [kõ'somi] *vb V* **consumir**

consórcio [kõ'sɔxsju] *m* (*união*) partnership; (COM) consortium

conspiração [kõʃpira'sãw] (*pl* -ões) *f* plot, conspiracy

conspirar [kõʃpi'ra*] *vt, vi* to plot

constante [kõʃ'tãtʃi] *adj* constant

constar [kõʃ'ta*] *vi* to be in; **ao que me consta** as far as I know

constatar [kõʃta'ta*] *vt* to establish; (*notar*) to notice; (*evidenciar*) to show up

consternado, -a [kõʃtex'nadu, a] *adj* depressed; (*desolado*) distressed

constipação [kõʃtʃipa'sãw] (*pl* -ões) *f* constipation; (PT) cold; **apanhar uma ~** (PT) to catch a cold

constipado, -a [kõʃtʃi'padu, a] *adj*: **estar ~** to be constipated; (PT) to have a cold

constituição [kõʃtʃitwi'sãw] (*pl* -ões) *f* constitution

constituinte [kõʃtʃi'twĩtʃi] *m/f* (*deputado*) member ♦ *f* (BR): **a C~** the Constituent Assembly, ≈ Parliament

constituir [kõʃtʃi'twi*] *vt* to constitute; (*formar*) to form; (*estabelecer*) to establish; (*nomear*) to appoint

constrangimento [kõʃtrãʒi'mẽtu] *m* constraint; embarrassment

construção [kõʃtru'sãw] (*pl* -ões) *f* building, construction

construir [kõʃ'trwi*] *vt* to build, construct

construtivo, -a [kõʃtru'tʃivu, a] *adj* constructive

construtor, a [kõʃtru'to*, a] *m/f* builder

cônsul ['kõsuw] (*pl* ~es) *m* consul; **consulado** [kõsu'ladu] *m* consulate

consulta [kõ'suwta] *f* consultation;

livro de ~ reference book; **horário de ~** surgery hours *pl* (BRIT), office hours *pl* (US); **consultar** [kõsuw-'ta*] *vt* to consult; **consultor, a** [kõsuw'to*, a] *m/f* consultant

consultório [kõsuw'tɔrju] *m* surgery

consumidor, a [kõsumi'do*, a] *adj* consumer *atr* ♦ *m/f* consumer

consumir [kõsu'mi*] *vt* to consume; (*gastar*) to use up; **consumir-se** *vr* to waste away

consumo [kõ'sumu] *m* consumption; **artigos de ~** consumer goods

conta ['kõta] *f* count; (*em restaurante*) bill; (*fatura*) invoice; (*bancária*) account; (*de colar*) bead; **~s** *fpl* (COM) accounts; **levar** *ou* **ter em ~** to take into account; **tomar ~ de** to take care of; (*dominar*) to take hold of; **afinal de ~s** after all; **dar-se ~ de** to realize; (*notar*) to notice; **~ corrente** current account

contabilidade [kõtabili'dadʒi] *f* book-keeping, accountancy

contabilista [kõtabi'liʃta] (PT) *m/f* accountant

contabilizar [kõtabili'za*] *vt* to write up, book

contacto *etc* [kõ'tatu] (PT) = **contato** *etc*

contador, a [kõta'do*, a] *m/f* (COM) accountant ♦ *m* (TEC: *medidor*) meter

contagiante [kõta'ʒjãtʃi] *adj* (*alegria*) contagious

contagiar [kõta'ʒja*] *vt* to infect

contágio [kõ'taʒju] *m* infection

contagioso, -a [kõta'ʒjozu, ɔza] *adj* (*doença*) contagious

contaminar [kõtami'na*] *vt* to contaminate

contanto que [kõ'tãtu ki] *conj* provided that

conta-quilómetros (PT) *m inv* speedometer

contar [kõ'ta*] vt to count; (narrar) to tell; (pretender) to intend ♦ vi to count; ~ **com** to count on; (esperar) to expect; ~ **em fazer** to count on doing, expect to do

contatar [kõta'ta*] vt to contact; **contato** [kõ'tatu] m contact; **entrar em contato com** to get in touch with, contact

contemplar [kõtẽ'pla*] vt to contemplate; (olhar) to gaze at

contemplativo, -a [kõtẽpla'tʃivu, a] adj (pessoa) thoughtful

contemporâneo, -a [kõtẽpo-'ranju, a] adj, m/f contemporary

contentamento [kõtẽta'mẽtu] m (felicidade) happiness; (satisfação) contentment

contente [kõ'tẽtʃi] adj happy; (satisfeito) pleased, satisfied

contento [kõ'tẽtu] m: **a ~** satisfactorily

conter [kõ'te*] (irreg: como **ter**) vt to contain, hold; (refrear) to restrain, hold back; (gastos) to curb

contestação [kõtʃeʃta'sãw] (pl -ões) f challenge; (negação) denial

contestar [kõtʃeʃ'ta*] vt to dispute, contest; (impugnar) to challenge

conteúdo [kõte'udu] m contents pl; (de um texto) content

contexto [kõ'teʃtu] m context

contigo [kõ'tʃigu] pron with you

contíguo, -a [kõ'tʃigwu, a] adj: ~ **a** next to

continental [kõtʃinẽ'taw] (pl -ais) adj continental

continente [kõtʃi'nẽtʃi] m continent

contingência [kõtʃi'ʒẽsja] f contingency

continuação [kõtʃinwa'sãw] f continuation

continuar [kõtʃi'nwa*] vt, vi to continue; ~ **falando** ou **a falar** to go

on talking; **ela continua doente** she is still sick

continuidade [kõtʃinwi'dadʒi] f continuity

contínuo, -a [kõ'tʃinwu, a] adj (persistente) continual; (sem interrupção) continuous ♦ m office boy

conto ['kõtu] m story, tale; (PT: dinheiro) 1000 escudos

contorcer [kõtox'se*] vt to twist; **contorcer-se** vr to writhe

contornar [kõtox'na*] vt (rodear) to go round; (ladear) to skirt; (fig: problema) to get round

contorno [kõ'toxnu] m outline; (da terra) contour; (do rosto) profile

contra ['kõtra] prep against ♦ m: **os prós e os ~os ~s** the pros and cons; **dar o ~** (a) to be opposed (to)

contra-ataque m counterattack

contrabandear [kõtrabã'dʒja*] vt to smuggle; **contrabandista** [kõtrabã'dʒiʃta] m/f smuggler; **contrabando** [kõtra'bãdu] m smuggling; (artigos) contraband

contraceptivo, -a [kõtrasep'tʃivu, a] adj contraceptive ♦ m contraceptive

contracheque [kõtra'ʃeki] m pay slip (BRIT), check stub (US)

contradição [kõtradʒi'sãw] (pl -ões) f contradiction

contraditório, -a [kõtradʒi'tɔrju, a] adj contradictory

contradizer [kõtradʒi'ze*] (irreg: como **dizer**) vt to contradict

contragosto [kõtra'goʃtu] m: **a ~** against one's will, unwillingly

contrair [kõtra'i*] vt to contract; (hábito) to form

contramão [kõtra'mãw] adj one-way ♦ f: **na ~** the wrong way down a one-way street

contraproducente [kõtraprodu-'sẽtʃi] adj counterproductive

contrariar [kõtra'rja*] *vt* to contradict; (*aborrecer*) to annoy

contrário, -a [kõ'trarju, a] *adj* (*oposto*) opposite; (*pessoa*) opposed; (*desfavorável*) unfavourable (*BRIT*), unfavorable (*US*), adverse ♦ *m* opposite; **do ~** otherwise; **pelo** ou **ao ~** on the contrary; **ao ~** the other way round

contra-senso *m* nonsense

contrastar [kõtraʃ'ta*] *vt* to contrast; **contraste** [kõ'traʃtʃi] *m* contrast

contratação [kõtrata'sãw] *f* (*de pessoal*) employment

contratar [kõtra'ta*] *vt* (*serviços*) to contract; (*pessoa*) to employ, take on

contratempo [kõtra'tẽpu] *m* setback; (*aborrecimento*) upset; (*dificuldade*) difficulty

contrato [kõ'tratu] *m* contract; (*acordo*) agreement

contribuição [kõtribwi'sãw] (*pl -ões*) *f* contribution; (*imposto*) tax

contribuinte [kõtri'bwĩtʃi] *m/f* contributor; (*que paga impostos*) taxpayer

contribuir [kõtri'bwi*] *vt* to contribute ♦ *vi* to contribute; (*pagar impostos*) to pay taxes

controlar [kõtro'la*] *vt* to control

controle [kõ'troli] *m* control; **~ remoto** remote control; **~ de crédito** (*COM*) credit control; **~ de qualidade** (*COM*) quality control

controvérsia [kõtro'vɛxsja] *f* controversy; (*discussão*) debate; **controverso, -a** [kõtro'vɛxsu, a] *adj* controversial

contudo [kõ'tudu] *conj* nevertheless, however

contumaz [kõtu'majʒ] *adj* obstinate, stubborn

contusão [kõtu'zãw] (*pl -ões*) *f* bruise

convalescer [kõvale'se*] *vi* to convalesce

convenção [kõvẽ'sãw] (*pl -ões*) *f* convention; (*acordo*) agreement

convencer [kõvẽ'se*] *vt* to convince; (*persuadir*) to persuade; **convencer-se** *vr*: **~-se de** to be convinced about; **convencido, -a** [kõvẽ'sidu, a] *adj* convinced; (*col: imodesto*) conceited, smug

convencional [kõvẽsjo'naw] (*pl -ais*) *adj* conventional

convenções [kõvẽ'sõjʃ] *fpl de* **convenção**

conveniência [kõve'njẽsja] *f* convenience

conveniente [kõve'njẽtʃi] *adj* convenient, suitable; (*vantajoso*) advantageous

convênio [kõ'venju] *m* (*reunião*) convention; (*acordo*) agreement

convento [kõ'vẽtu] *m* convent

conversa [kõ'vɛxsa] *f* conversation; **~-fiada** idle chat; (*promessa falsa*) hot air

conversão [kõvex'sãw] (*pl -ões*) *f* conversion

conversar [kõvex'sa*] *vi* to talk

conversões [kõvex'sõjʃ] *fpl de* **conversão**

converter [kõvex'te*] *vt* to convert

convés [kõ'vɛʃ] (*pl -eses*) *m* (*NÁUT*) deck

convexo, -a [kõ'vɛksu, a] *adj* convex

convicção [kõvik'sãw] (*pl -ões*) *f* conviction

convidado, -a [kõvi'dadu, a] *m/f* guest

convidar [kõvi'da*] *vt* to invite

convincente [kõvĩ'sẽtʃi] *adj* convincing

convir [kõ'vi*] (*irreg: como* **vir**) *vi* to

suit, be convenient; (*ficar bem*) to be appropriate; (*concordar*) to agree; **convém fazer isso o mais rápido possível** we must do this as soon as possible

convite [kõ'vitʃi] *m* invitation

convivência [kõvi'vẽsjɐ] *f* living together; (*familiaridade*) familiarity, intimacy

conviver [kõvi've*] *vi*: **~ com** (*viver em comum*) to live with; (*ter familiaridade*) to get on with; **convívio** [kõ'vivju] *m* living together; (*familiaridade*) familiarity

convocar [kõvo'ka*] *vt* to summon, call upon; (*reunião, eleições*) to call; (*para o serviço militar*) to call up

convosco [kõ'voʃku] *adv* with you

convulsão [kõvuw'sɐ̃w] (*pl* -**ões**) *f* convulsion

cooper [ˈkupe*] *m* jogging; **fazer ~** to go jogging

cooperação [koopera'sɐ̃w] *f* co-operation

cooperar [koope'ra*] *vi* to cooperate

cooperativa [koopera'tʃiva] *f* (*COM*) cooperative

cooperativo, -a [koopera'tʃivu, a] *adj* cooperative

coordenada [kooxde'nada] *f* coordinate

coordenar [kooxde'na*] *vt* to coordinate

copa [ˈkɔpa] *f* (*de árvore*) top; (*torneio*) cup, **~s** *fpl* (*CARTAS*) hearts

cópia [ˈkɔpja] *f* copy; **tirar ~ de** to copy; **copiadora** [kopja'dora] *f* duplicating machine

copiar [ko'pja*] *vt* to copy

copo [ˈkɔpu] *m* glass

coque [ˈkɔki] *m* (*penteado*) bun

coqueiro [ko'kejru] *m* (*BOT*) coconut palm

coquetel [koke'tɛw] (*pl* -**éis**) *m*

cocktail; (*festa*) cocktail party

cor¹ [kɔ*] *m*: **de ~** by heart

cor² [kO*] *f* colour (*BRIT*), color (*US*); **de ~** colo(u)red

coração [kora'sɐ̃w] (*pl* -**ões**) *m* heart; **de bom ~** kind-hearted; **de todo o ~** wholeheartedly

corado, -a [ko'radu, a] *adj* ruddy

coragem [ko'raʒẽj] *f* courage; (*atrevimento*) nerve

corais [ko'rajʃ] *mpl de* **coral**

corajoso, -a [kora'ʒozu, ɔza] *adj* courageous

coral [ko'raw] (*pl* -**ais**) *m* (*MÚS*) choir; (*ZOOL*) coral

corante [ko'rãtʃi] *adj, m* colouring (*BRIT*), coloring (*US*)

corar [ko'ra*] *vt* (*roupa*) to bleach (in the sun) ♦ *vi* to blush; (*tornar-se branco*) to bleach

corcunda [kox'kũda] *adj* hunchbacked ♦ *f* hump ♦ *m/f* (*pessoa*) hunchback

corda [ˈkɔxda] *f* rope, line; (*MÚS*) string; (*varal*) clothes line; (*de relógio*) spring; **dar ~ em** to wind up; **~s vocais** vocal chords

cordão [kox'dɐ̃w] (*pl* -**ões**) *m* string, twine; (*jóia*) chain; (*no carnaval*) group; (*ELET*) lead; (*fileira*) row

cordeiro [kox'dejru] *m* lamb

cordel [kox'dɛw] (*pl* -**éis**) *m* (*PT*) string; **literatura de ~** pamphlet literature

cor-de-rosa *adj inv* pink

cordial [kox'dʒjaw] (*pl* -**ais**) *adj* cordial ♦ *m* (*bebida*) cordial

cordões [kox'dõjʃ] *mpl de* **cordão**

coreano, -a [ko'rjanu, a] *adj* Korean ♦ *m/f* Korean ♦ (*LING*) Korean

Coréia [ko'rɛja] *f*: **a ~** Korea

coreto [ko'retu] *m* bandstand

córner [ˈkɔxne*] *m* (*FUTEBOL*) corner

coro ['koɾu] *m* chorus; (*conjunto de cantores*) choir

coroa [ko'ɾoa] *f* crown; (*de flores*) garland ♦ *m/f* (*BR*: *col*) old timer

coroar [koɾo'a*] *vt* to crown; (*premiar*) to reward

coronel [koɾo'nɛw] (*pl* **-éis**) *m* colonel; (*político*) local political boss

corpo ['koɾpu] *m* body; (*aparência física*) figure; (: *de homem*) build; (*de vestido*) bodice; (*MIL*) corps *sg*; **de ~ e alma** (*fig*) wholeheartedly; **~ diplomático** diplomatic corps *sg*

corporal [koɾpo'ɾaw] (*pl* **-ais**) *adj* physical

corpulento, -a [koɾpu'lẽtu, a] *adj* stout

correção [koɾe'sãw] (*PT* **-cç-**) (*pl* **-ões**) *f* correction; (*exatidão*) correctness; **casa de ~** reformatory

corre-corre [kɔɾi'kɔɾi] (*pl* **~s**) *m* rush

correcto, -a *etc* [ko'ɾɛktu, a] (*PT*) = **correto** *etc*

corredor, -a [koɾe'do*, a] *m/f* runner ♦ *m* corridor; (*em avião etc*) aisle; (*cavalo*) racehorse

correia [ko'ɾeja] *f* strap; (*de máquina*) belt; (*para cachorro*) leash

correio [ko'ɾeju] *m* mail, post; (*local*) post office; (*carteiro*) postman (*BRIT*), mailman (*US*); **~ aéreo** air mail; **~ eletrônico** e-mail, electronic mail; **~ de voz** voice mail; **pôr no ~** to post

corrente [ko'ɾẽtʃi] *adj* (*atual*) current; (*águas*) running; (*comum*) usual, common ♦ *f* current; (*cadeia, jóia*) chain; **~ de ar** draught (*BRIT*), draft (*US*); **correnteza** [koɾẽ'teza] *f* (*de ar*) draught (*BRIT*), draft (*US*); (*de rio*) current

correr [ko'ɾe*] *vt* to run; (*viajar por*) to travel across ♦ *vi* to run; (*em carro*) to drive fast, speed; (*o tempo*)

to elapse; (*boato*) to go round; (*atuar com rapidez*) to rush; **correria** [koxe'ɾia] *f* rush

correspondência [koxeʃpõ'dẽsja] *f* correspondence; **correspondente** [koxeʃpõ'dẽtʃi] *adj* corresponding ♦ *m* correspondent

corresponder [koxeʃpõ'de*] *vi*: **~ a** to correspond to; (*ser igual*) to match (up to); **corresponder-se** *vr*: **~-se com** to correspond with

correto, -a [ko'ɾɛtu, a] *adj* correct; (*conduta*) right; (*pessoa*) straight, honest

corretor, a [koɾe'to*, a] *m/f* broker; **~ de fundos** *ou* **de bolsa** stockbroker; **~ de imóveis** estate agent (*BRIT*), realtor (*US*)

corrida [ko'ɾida] *f* running; (*certame*) race; (*de taxi*) fare; **~ de cavalos** horse race

corrido, -a [ko'ɾidu, a] *adj* quick; (*expulso*) driven out ♦ *adv* quickly

corrigir [koxi'ʒi*] *vt* to correct

corrimão [koxi'mãw] (*pl* **~s**) *m* handrail

corriqueiro, -a [koxi'kejɾu, a] *adj* common; (*problema*) trivial

corromper [koxõ'pe*] *vt* to corrupt; (*subornar*) to bribe; **corromper-se** *vr* to be corrupted

corrosão [koxo'zãw] *f* corrosion; (*fig*) erosion

corrosivo, -a [koxo'zivu, a] *adj* corrosive

corrupção [koxup'sãw] *f* corruption

corrupto, -a [ko'ɾuptu, a] *adj* corrupt

Córsega ['kɔɾsega] *f*: **a ~** Corsica

cortada [koɾ'tada] *f*: **dar uma ~ em alguém** (*fig*) to cut sb short

cortante [koɾ'tãtʃi] *adj* cutting

cortar [koɾ'ta*] *vt* to cut; (*eliminar*) to cut out; (*água, telefone etc*) to cut off; (*efeito*) to stop ♦ *vi* to cut; (*encurtar caminho*) to take a short cut; ~ **o cabelo** (*no cabeleireiro*) to have one's hair cut; ~ **a palavra de alguém** to interrupt sb

corte[1] ['kɔxtʃi] *m* cut; (*de luz*) power cut; **sem** ~ (*tesoura etc*) blunt; ~ **de cabelo** haircut

corte[2] ['kɔxtʃi] *f* court; ~**s** *fpl* (*PT*) parliament *sg*

cortejo [kox'teʒu] *m* procession

cortês [kox'teʃ] (*pl* -**eses**) *adj* polite

cortesia [koxte'zia] *f* politeness; (*de empresa*) free offer

cortiça [kox'tʃisa] *f* cork

cortiço [kox'tʃisu] *m* slum tenement

cortina [kox'tʃina] *f* curtain

coruja [ko'ruʒa] *f* owl

corvo ['koxvu] *m* crow

coser [ku'ze*] *vt, vi* to sew

cosmético, -a [koʒ'mɛtʃiku, a] *adj* cosmetic ♦ *m* cosmetic

cospe *etc* ['kɔʃpi] *vb V* **cuspir**

costa ['kɔʃta] *f* coast; ~**s** *fpl* (*dorso*) back *sg*; **dar as** ~**s a** to turn one's back on

Costa Rica *f*: **a** ~ Costa Rica

costela [koʃ'tɛla] *f* rib

costeleta [koʃte'leta] *f* chop, cutlet; ~**s** *fpl* (*suíças*) side-whiskers

costumar [koʃtu'ma*] *vt* (*habituar*) to accustom ♦ *vi*: **ele costuma chegar às 6.00** he usually arrives at 6.00; **costumava dizer ...** he used to say ...

costume [koʃ'tumi] *m* custom, habit; (*traje*) costume; ~**s** *mpl* (*comportamento*) behaviour *sg* (*BRIT*), behavior *sg* (*US*); (*conduta*) conduct *sg*; (*de um povo*) customs; **de** ~ usual; **como de** ~ as usual

costumeiro, -a [koʃtu'mejru, a] *adj* usual, habitual

costura [koʃ'tura] *f* sewing; (*sutura*)

seam; **costurar** [koʃtu'ra*] *vt, vi* to sew; **costureira** [koʃtu'rejra] *f* dressmaker

cota ['kɔta] *f* quota, share

cotação [kota'sãw] (*pl* -**ões**) *f* (*de preços*) list, quotation; (*BOLSA*) price; (*consideração*) esteem; ~ **bancária** bank rate

cotado, -a [ko'tadu, a] *adj* (*COM: ação*) quoted; (*bem-conceituado*) well thought of; (*num concurso*) fancied

cotar [ko'ta*] *vt* (*ações*) to quote; ~ **algo em** to value sth at

cotejar [kote'ʒa*] *vt* to compare

cotidiano, -a [kotʃi'dʒjanu, a] *adj* daily, everyday ♦ *m*: **o** ~ daily life

cotonete [koto'nɛtʃi] *m* cotton bud

cotovelada [kotove'lada] *f* shove; (*cutucada*) nudge

cotovelo [koto'velu] *m* (*ANAT*) elbow; (*curva*) bend; **falar pelos** ~**s** to talk non-stop

coube *etc* ['kobi] *vb V* **caber**

couro ['koru] *m* leather; (*de um animal*) hide

couve ['kovi] *f* spring greens *pl*; **couve-flor** (*pl* **couves-flores**) *f* cauliflower

couvert [ku'vex] *m* cover charge

cova ['kɔva] *f* pit; (*caverna*) cavern; (*sepultura*) grave

covarde [ko'vaxdʒi] *adj* cowardly ♦ *m/f* coward; **covardia** [kovax-'dʒia] *f* cowardice

covil [ko'viw] (*pl* -**is**) *m* den, lair

covinha [ko'viɲa] *f* dimple

covis [ko'viʃ] *mpl de* **covil**

coxa ['kɔʃa] *f* thigh

coxear [koʃ'ʃa*] *vi* to limp

coxia [ko'ʃia] *f* aisle, gangway

coxo, -a ['koʃu, a] *adj* lame

cozer [ko'ze*] *vt, vi* to cook

cozido [ko'zidu] *m* stew

cozinha [ko'ziɲa] f kitchen; (arte) cookery

cozinhar [kozi'ɲa*] vt, vi to cook

cozinheiro, -a [kozi'ɲejru, a] m/f cook

CP abr = **Caminhos de Ferro Portugueses**

CPF (BR) abr m (= Cadastro de Pessoa Física) identification number

CPLP abr f (= Comunidade de Países de Língua Portuguesa) see boxed note

---

CPLP

The **CPLP** or Comunidade de Países de Língua Portuguesa was set up in 1996 to establish economic and diplomatic links between all countries where the official language is Portuguese. The members are Brazil, Portugal, Angola, Mozambique, Guinea-Bissau, Cape Verde and São Tomé e Príncipe. Portuguese is spoken by around 170 million people around the world today.

---

crachá [kra'ʃa] m badge

crânio ['kranju] m skull

craque ['kraki] m/f ace, expert

crasso, -a ['krasu, a] adj crass

cratera [kra'tera] f crater

cravar [kra'va*] vt (prego etc) to drive (in); (com os olhos) to stare at; **cravar-se** vr to penetrate

cravo ['kravu] m carnation; (MÚS) harpsichord; (especiaria) clove; (na pele) blackhead; (prego) nail

creche ['krɛʃi] f crèche

credenciais [kredē'sjajʃ] fpl credentials

creditar [kredʒi'ta*] vt to guarantee; (COM) to credit; ~ **algo a alguém** to credit sb with sth; (garantir) to assure sb of sth

crédito ['krɛdʒitu] m credit; digno

de ~ reliable

credo ['krɛdu] m creed; ~! heavens!

credor, a [kre'do*, a] adj worthy, deserving; (COM: saldo) credit atr ♦ m/f creditor

creme ['krɛmi] adj inv cream ♦ m cream; (CULIN: doce) custard; ~ **dental** toothpaste; **cremoso, -a** [kre'mozu, ɔza] adj creamy

crença ['krẽsa] f belief

crente ['krẽtʃi] m/f believer

crepúsculo [kre'puʃkulu] m dusk, twilight

crer [kre*] vt, vi to believe; **crer-se** vr to believe o.s. to be; ~ **em** to believe in; **creio que sim** I think so

crescente [kre'sẽtʃi] adj growing ♦ m crescent

crescer [kre'se*] vi to grow; **crescimento** [kresi'mētu] m growth

crespo, -a ['kreʃpu, a] adj (cabelo) curly

cretinice [kretʃi'nisi] f stupidity; (ato, dito) stupid thing

cretino [kre'tʃinu] m cretin, imbecile

cria ['kria] f (animal: sg) baby animal; (: pl) young pl

criação [kria'sãw] (pl -ões) f creation; (de animais) raising, breeding; (educação) upbringing; (animais domésticos) livestock pl; **filho de ~** adopted child

criado, -a ['kriadu, a] m/f servant

criador, a [krja'do*, a] m/f creator; ~ **de gado** cattle breeder

criança ['krjãsa] adj childish ♦ f child; **criançada** [krjã'sada] f: **a criançada** the kids

criar [krja*] vt to create; (crianças) to bring up; (animais) to raise; (amamentar) to suckle, nurse; (planta) to grow; **criar-se** vr: **~-se (com)** to grow up (with); **criar caso** to make trouble

criatura [kria'tura] f creature; (indi-

vídu) individual

crime ['krimi] *m* crime; **criminal** [krimi'naw] (*pl* **-ais**) *adj* criminal; **criminalidade** [kriminali'dadʒi] *f* crime; **criminoso, -a** [krimi'nozu, ɔza] *adj, m/f* criminal

crina ['krina] *f* mane

crioulo, -a ['krjolu, a] *adj* creole ♦ *m/f* creole; (*BR*: *negro*) Black (person)

crise ['krizi] *f* crisis; (*escassez*) shortage; (*MED*) attack, fit

crista ['kriʃta] *f* (*de serra, onda*) crest; (*de galo*) cock's comb

cristal [kriʃ'taw] (*pl* **-ais**) *m* crystal; (*vidro*) glass; **cristais** *mpl* (*copos*) glassware *sg*; **cristalino, -a** [kriʃta'linu, a] *adj* crystal-clear

cristão, -tã [kriʃ'tãw, 'tã] (*pl* **-s**, **~s**) *adj, m/f* Christian

cristianismo [kriʃtʃja'niʒinu] *m* Christianity

Cristo ['kriʃtu] *m* Christ

critério [kri'tɛrju] *m* criterion; (*juízo*) discretion, judgement; **criterioso, -a** [krite'rjozu, ɔza] *adj* thoughtful, careful

crítica ['kritʃika] *f* criticism; *V tb* crítico

criticar [kritʃi'ka*] *vt* to criticize; (*um livro*) to review

crítico, -a ['kritʃiku, a] *adj* critical ♦ *m/f* critic

crivar [kri'va*] *vt* (*com balas etc*) to riddle

crivo ['krivu] *m* sieve

crocante [kro'katʃi] *adj* crunchy

crônica ['kronika] *f* chronicle; (*coluna de jornal*) newspaper column; (*texto jornalístico*) feature; (*conto*) short story

crônico, -a ['kroniku, a] *adj* chronic

cronológico, -a [krono'lɔʒiku, a] *adj* chronological

cronômetro [kro'nometru] *m*

stopwatch

croquete [kro'ketʃi] *m* croquette

cru, a [kru, 'krua] *adj* raw; (*não refinado*) crude

crucial [kru'sjaw] (*pl* **-ais**) *adj* crucial

crucificação [krusifika'sãw] (*pl* **-ões**) *f* crucifixion

crucificar [krusifi'ka*] *vt* to crucify

crucifixo [krusi'fiksu] *m* crucifix

cruel [kru'ew] (*pl* **-éis**) *adj* cruel; **crueldade** [kruew'dadʒi] *f* cruelty

cruz [kruʒ] *f* cross; **C~ Vermelha** Red Cross

cruzado, -a [kru'zadu, a] *adj* crossed ♦ *m* (*moeda*) cruzado

cruzamento [kruza'mẽtu] *m* crossroads

cruzar [kru'za*] *vt* to cross ♦ *vi* (*NÁUT*) to cruise; (*pessoas*) to pass each other by; **~ com** to meet

cruzeiro [kru'zejru] *m* (*cruz*) (*monumental*) cross; (*moeda*) cruzeiro; (*viagem de navio*) cruise

cu [ku] (*col!*) *m* arse (!); **vai tomar no ~** fuck off (!)

Cuba ['kuba] *f* Cuba

cubo ['kubu] *m* cube; (*de roda*) hub

cubro *etc* ['kubru] *vb V* **cobrir**

cuca ['kuka] (*col*) *f* head; **fundir a ~** (*quebrar a cabeça*) to rack one's brain; (*baratinar*) to boggle the mind; (*perturbar*) to drive crazy

cuco ['kuku] *m* cuckoo

cueca ['kweka] *f* (*BR*: *tb*: **~s**: *para homens*) underpants *pl*; **~s** *fpl* (*PT*) underpants *pl*; (: *para mulheres*) panties *pl*

cuíca ['kwika] *f* kind of musical instrument

cuidado [kwi'dadu] *m* care; **aos ~s de** in the care of; **ter ~** to be careful; **~!** watch out!, be careful!; **tomar ~ (de)** to be careful (of); **cuidadoso, -a** [kwida'dozu, ɔza] *adj* careful

cuidar [kwi'da*] *vi*: ~ **de** to take care of, look after; **cuidar-se** *vr* to look after o.s.

cujo, -a [ˈkuʒu, a] *pron* (*de quem*) whose; (*de que*) of which

culinária [kuliˈnarja] *f* cookery

culpa [ˈkuwpa] *f* fault; (*JUR*) guilt; **ter ~ de** to be to blame for; **por ~ de** because of; **culpado, -a** [kuwˈpadu, a] *adj* guilty ♦ *m/f* culprit; **culpar** [kuwˈpa*] *vt* to blame; (*acusar*) to accuse; **culpar-se** *vr* to take the blame; **culpável** [kuwˈpavew] (*pl* -**eis**) *adj* guilty

cultivar [kuwtʃiˈva*] *vt* to cultivate; (*plantas*) to grow; **cultivo** [kuwˈtʃivu] *m* cultivation

culto, -a [ˈkuwtu, a] *adj* cultured ♦ *m* (*homenagem*) worship; (*religião*) cult

cultura [kuwˈtura] *f* culture; (*da terra*) cultivation; **cultural** [kuwtuˈraw] (*pl* **culturais**) *adj* cultural

cume [ˈkumi] *m* top, summit; (*fig*) climax

cúmplice [ˈkũplisi] *m/f* accomplice

cumprimentar [kũprimẽˈta*] *vt* to greet; (*dar parabéns*) to congratulate

cumprimento [kũpriˈmẽtu] *m* fulfilment; (*saudação*) greeting; (*elogio*) compliment; ~s *mpl* (*saudações*) best wishes; ~ **de uma lei/ordem** compliance with a law/an order

cumprir [kũˈpri*] *vt* (*desempenhar*) to carry out; (*promessa*) to keep; (*lei*) to obey; (*pena*) to serve ♦ *vi* to be necessary; ~ **a palavra** to keep one's word; **fazer** ~ to enforce

cúmulo [ˈkumulu] *m* height; **é o ~!** that's the limit!

cunha [ˈkuɲa] *f* wedge

cunhado, -a [kuˈɲadu, a] *m/f*

brother-in-law/sister-in-law

cunho [ˈkuɲu] *m* (*marca*) hallmark; (*caráter*) nature

cupim [kuˈpĩ] (*pl* -**ns**) *m* termite

cupins [kuˈpĩʃ] *mpl* **de cupim**

cúpula [ˈkupula] *f* dome; (*de abajur*) shade; (*de partido etc*) leadership; (**reunião de**) ~ summit (meeting)

cura [ˈkura] *f* cure; (*tratamento*) treatment; (*de carnes etc*) curing, preservation ♦ *m* priest

curar [kuˈra*] *vt* (*doença, carne*) to cure; (*ferida*) to treat; **curar-se** *vr* to get well

curativo [kuraˈtʃivu] *m* dressing

curiosidade [kurjoziˈdadʒi] *f* curiosity; (*objeto raro*) curio

curioso, -a [kuˈrjozu, ɔza] *adj* curious ♦ *m/f* snooper, inquisitive person; ~**s** *mpl* (*espectadores*) onlookers

curral [kuˈxaw] (*pl* -**ais**) *m* pen, enclosure

currículo [kuˈxikulu] *m* (*curriculum*) curriculum vitae

cursar [kux'sa*] *vt* (*aulas, escola*) to attend; (*cursos*) to follow; **ele está cursando História** he's studying *ou* doing history

curso [ˈkuxsu] *m* course; (*direção*) direction; **em** ~ (*ano etc*) current; (*processo*) in progress

cursor [kux'so*] *m* (*COMPUT*) cursor

curtição [kuxtʃiˈsãw] (*col*) *f* fun

curtir [kux'tʃi*] *vt* (*couro*) to tan; (*tornar rijo*) to toughen up; (*padecer*) to suffer, endure; (*col*) to enjoy

curto, -a [ˈkuxtu, a] *adj* short ♦ *m* (*ELET*) short (circuit); **curto-circuito** (*pl* **curtos-circuitos**) *m* short circuit

curva [ˈkuxva] *f* curve; (*de estrada, rio*) bend; ~ **fechada** hairpin bend

curvo, -a ['kuxvu, a] *adj* curved; (*estrada*) winding

cuscuz [kuʃ'kuʒ] *m* couscous

cuspe ['kuʃpi] *m* spit, spittle

cuspir [kuʃ'pi*] *vt, vi* to spit

custa ['kuʃta] *f*: **à ~ de** at the expense of; **~s** *fpl* (*JUR*) costs

custar [kuʃ'ta*] *vi* to cost; (*ser difícil*): **~ a fazer** to have trouble doing; (*demorar*): **~ a fazer** to take a long time to do; **~ caro** to be expensive

custo ['kuʃtu] *m* cost; **a ~** with difficulty; **a todo ~** at all costs

cutelo [ku'telu] *m* cleaver

cutícula [ku'ʃikula] *f* cuticle

cutucar [kutu'ka*] *vt* (*com o dedo*) to prod, poke; (*com o cotovelo*) to nudge

D

D *abr* = **Dom; Dona;** (= *direito*) r; (= *deve*) d

d/ *abr* = **dia**

da [da] = **de + a**

dá [da] *vb V* **dar**

dactilografar *etc* [datilogra'fa*] (*PT*) = **datilografar** *etc*

dádiva ['dadʒiva] *f* donation; (*oferta*) gift

dado, -a ['dadu, a] *adj* given; (*sociável*) sociable ♦ *m* (*em jogo*) die; (*fato*) fact; **~s** *mpl* dice; (*fatos, COMPUT*) data *sg*; **~ que** supposing that; (*uma vez que*) given that

daí [da'ji] *adv* = **de + aí** (*desse lugar*) from there; (*desse momento*) from then; **~ a um mês** a month later

dali [da'li] *adv* = **de + ali** (*desse lugar*) from there

daltônico, -a [daw'toniku, a] *adj* colour-blind (*BRIT*), color-blind (*US*)

dama ['dama] *f* lady; (*XADREZ, CARTAS*)

queen; **~s** *fpl* (*jogo*) draughts (*BRIT*), checkers (*US*); **~ de honra** bridesmaid

damasco [da'maʃku] *m* apricot

danado, -a [da'nadu, a] *adj* damned; (*zangado*) furious; (*menino*) mischievous

dança ['dãsa] *f* dance; **dançar** [dã'sa*] *vi* to dance

danificar [danifi'ka*] *vt* to damage

dano ['danu] *m* (*tb*: **~s**) damage, harm; (*a uma pessoa*) injury

dantes ['dãtʃiʃ] *adv* before, formerly

daquele, -a [da'keli, a] = **de + aquele/a**

daqui [da'ki] *adv* = **de + aqui** (*deste lugar*) from here; **~ a pouco** soon, in a little while; **~ a uma semana** a week from now; **~ em diante** from now on

daquilo [da'kilu] = **de + aquilo**

┌─── *PALAVRA CHAVE* ───

dar [da*] *vt* **1** (*ger*) to give; (*festa*) to hold; (*problemas*) to cause; **~ algo a alguém** to give sb sth, give sth to sb; **~ de beber a alguém** to give sb a drink; **~ aula de francês** to teach French

2 (*produzir: fruta etc*) to produce

3 (*notícias no jornal*) to publish

4 (*cartas*) to deal

5 (+ *n: perífrase de vb*): **me dá medo/pena** it frightens/upsets me

♦ *vi* **1**: **~ com** (*coisa*) to find; (*pessoa*) to meet

2: **~ em** (*bater*) to hit; (*resultar*) to lead to; (*lugar*) to come to

3: **dá no mesmo** it's all the same

4: **~ de si** (*sapatos etc*) to stretch, give

5: **~ para** (*impess: ser possível*): **dá para trocar dinheiro aqui?** can I change money here?; **vai ~ para eu**

ir amanhã I'll be able to go tomorrow; **dá para você vir amanhã – não, amanhã não vai** ~ can you come tomorrow? – no, I can't

6: ~ **para** (*ser suficiente*): ~ **para/ para fazer** to be enough for/to do; **dá para todo mundo?** is there enough for everyone?; **dar-se** *vr* **1** (*sair-se*): ~**-se bem/mal** to do well/badly

2: ~**-se (com alguém)** to be acquainted (with sb); ~**-se bem (com alguém)** to get on well (with sb)

3: ~**-se por vencido** to give up

das [daʃ] = **de** + **as**

data ['data] *f* date; (*época*) time; ~ **de validade** best before date; **datar** [da'ta*] *vt* to date ♦ *vi*: **datar de** to date from

datilografar [datʃilogra'fa*] *vt* to type; **datilografia** [datʃilogra'fia] *f* typing; **datilógrafo, -a** [datʃi'lɔgrafu, a] *m/f* typist (*BRIT*), stenographer (*US*)

d.C. *abr* (= *depois de Cristo*) A.D.

DDD *abr* (= *discagem direta à distância*) STD (*BRIT*), direct dialling

DDI *abr* (= *discagem direta internacional*) IDD, international direct call

---PALAVRA CHAVE---

de [dʒi] (*de* + *o(s)/a(s)* = *do(s)/da(s)*; + *ele(s)/a(s)* = *dele(s)/da(s)*; + *esse(s)/ a(s)* = *desse(s)/a(s)*; + *isso* = *disso*; + *este(s)/a(s)* = *deste(s)/a(s)*; + *isto* = *disto*; + *aquele(s)/a(s)* = *daquele(s)/ a(s)*; + *aquilo* = *daquilo*) *prep* **1** (*posse*) of; **a casa ~ João/da irmã João's/my sister's house; é dele** it's his; **um romance ~** a novel by

2 (*origem, distância, com números*) from; **sou ~ São Paulo** I'm from São Paulo; ~ **8 a 20** from 8 to 20; **sair do**

cinema to leave the cinema; ~ **dois em dois** two by two, two at a time

3 (*valor descritivo*): **um copo ~ vinho** a glass of wine; **um homem ~ cabelo comprido** a man with long hair; **o infeliz do homem** (*col*) the poor man; **um bilhete ~ avião** an air ticket; **uma criança ~ três anos** a three-year-old (child); **uma máquina ~ costurar** a sewing machine; **aulas ~ inglês** English lessons; **feito ~ madeira** made of wood; **vestido ~ branco** dressed in white

4 (*modo*): ~ **trem/avião** by train/ plane; ~ **lado** sideways

5 (*hora, tempo*): **às 8 da manhã** at 8 o'clock in the morning; ~ **dia/noite** by day/night; ~ **hoje a oito dias** a week from now; ~ **dois em dois dias** every other day

6 (*comparações*): **mais/menos ~ cem pessoas** more/less than a hundred people; **é o mais caro da loja** it's the most expensive in the shop; **ela é mais bonita do que sua irmã** she's prettier than her sister; **gastei mais do que pretendia** I spent more than I intended

7 (*causa*): **estou morto ~ calor** I'm boiling hot; **ela morreu ~ câncer** she died of cancer

8 (*adj* + ~ + *infin*): **fácil ~ entender** easy to understand

dê *etc* [de] *vb* V **dar**

debaixo [de'bajʃu] *adv* below, underneath ♦ *prep*: ~ **de** under, beneath

debate [de'batʃi] *m* discussion, debate; (*disputa*) argument; **debater** [deba'te*] *vt* to debate; (*discutir*) to discuss; **debater-se** *vr* to struggle

débeis ['dɛbejʃ] *pl de* **débil**

débil ['debiw] (*pl* -eis) *adj* weak, feeble ♦ *m*: ~ mental mentally handicapped person; **debilidade** [debili'dadʒi] *f* weakness; **debilidade mental** mental handicap; **debilitar** [debili'ta*] *vt* to weaken; **debilitar-se** *vr* to become weak, weaken; **debilóide** [debi'lɔjdʒi]; (*col*) *adj* idiotic ♦ *m/f* idiot

debitar [debi'ta*] *vt*: ~ $40 à *ou* na conta de alguém to debit $40 to sb's account; **débito** ['dɛbitu] *m* debit

debochado, -a [debo'ʃadu, a] *adj* (*pessoa*) sardonic; (*jeito*, *tom*) mocking

década ['dɛkada] *f* decade

decadência [deka'dēsja] *f* decadence

decair [deka'i*] *vi* to decline

decapitar [dekapi'ta*] *vt* to behead, decapitate

decente [de'sētʃi] *adj* decent; (*apropriado*) proper; (*honrado*) honourable (*BRIT*), honorable (*US*); (*trabalho*) neat; **decentemente** [desētʃi'mētʃi] *adv* decently; properly; hono(u)rably

decepção [desep'sãw] (*pl* -ões) *f* disappointment; **decepcionar** [desepsjo'na*] *vt* to disappoint; (*desiludir*) to disillusion; **decepcionar-se** *vr* to be disappointed; to be disillusioned

decidido, -a [desi'dʒidu, a] *adj* (*pessoa*) determined; (*questão*) resolved

decidir [desi'dʒi*] *vt* to decide; (*solucionar*) to resolve; **decidir-se** *vr*: ~**-se a** to make up one's mind to; ~**-se por** to decide on, go for

decifrar [desi'fra*] *vt* to decipher; (*futuro*) to foretell; (*compreender*) to understand

decimal [desi'maw] (*pl* -ais) *adj*, *m* decimal

décimo, -a ['dɛsimu, a] *adj* tenth ♦ *m* tenth

decisão [desi'zãw] (*pl* -ões) *f* decision; **decisivo, -a** [desi'zivu, a] *adj* (*fator*) decisive; (*jogo*) deciding

declaração [deklara'sãw] (*pl* -ões) *f* declaration; (*depoimento*) statement

declarado, -a [dekla'radu, a] *adj* (*intenção*) declared; (*opinião*) professed; (*inimigo*) sworn; (*alcoólatra*) self-confessed; (*cristão etc*) avowed

declarar [dekla'ra*] *vt* to declare; (*confessar*) to confess

declinar [dekli'na*] *vt* (*qer*) to decline ♦ *vi* (*sol*) to go down; (*terreno*) to slope down; **declínio** [de'klinju] *m* decline

declive [de'klivi] *m* slope, incline

decolagem [deko'laʒē] (*pl* -ns) *f* (*AER*) take-off

decolar [deko'la*] *vi* (*AER*) to take off

decompor [dekõ'po*] (*irreg*: *como* **pôr**) *vt* to analyse; (*apodrecer*) to rot; **decompor-se** *vr* to rot, decompose

decomposição [dekõposi'sãw] (*pl* -ões) *f* decomposition; (*análise*) dissection

decoração [dekora'sãw] *f* decoration; (*TEATRO*) scenery

decorar [deko'ra*] *vt* to decorate; (*aprender*) to learn by heart; **decorativo, -a** [dekora'tʃivu, a] *adj* decorative

decoro [de'koru] *m* decency; (*dignidade*) decorum

decorrente [deko'xētʃi] *adj*: ~ **de** resulting from

decorrer [deko'xe*] *vi* (*tempo*) to pass; (*acontecer*) to take place, happen ♦ *m*: **no** ~ **de** in the course of; ~ **de** to result from

decrescer [dekre'se*] *vi* to decrease, diminish

decretar [dekre'ta*] vt to decree, order; **decreto** [de'krɛtu] m decree, order; **decreto-lei** (pl **decretos-leis**) m act, law

dedal [de'daw] (pl **-ais**) m thimble

dedetizar [dedetʃi'za*] vt to spray with insecticide

dedicação [dedʒika'sãw] f dedication; (devotamento) devotion

dedicar [dedʒi'ka*] vt to dedicate; (tempo, atenção) to devote; **dedicar-se** vr: **~-se a** to devote o.s. to; **dedicatória** [dedʒika'tɔrja] f (de obra) dedication

dedo ['dedu] m finger; (do pé) toe; **~ anular/indicador/mínimo** ou **mindinho** ring/index/little finger; **~ polegar** thumb

dedução [dedu'sãw] (pl **-ões**) f deduction

deduzir [dedu'zi*] vt to deduct; (concluir) to deduce, infer

defasagem [defa'zaʒẽ] (pl **-ns**) f discrepancy

defeito [de'fejtu] m defect, flaw; **pôr ~s em** to find fault with; **com ~** broken, out of order; **para ninguém botar ~** (col) perfect; **defeituoso, -a** [defej'twozu, ɔza] adj defective, faulty

defender [defẽ'de*] vt to defend; **defender-se** vr to stand up for o.s.; (numa língua) to get by

defensiva [defẽ'siva] f: **estar** ou **ficar na ~** to be on the defensive

defensor, a [defẽ'so*, a] m/f defender; (JUR) defending counsel

defesa [de'feza] f defence (BRIT), defense (US); (JUR) counsel for the defence ♦ m (FUTEBOL) back

deficiente [defi'sjẽtʃi] adj (imperfeito) defective; (carente): **~ (em)** deficient (in)

déficit ['dɛfisitʃi] (pl **-s**) m deficit

definição [defini'sãw] (pl **-ões**) f definition

definir [defi'ni*] vt to define; **definir-se** vr to make a decision; (explicar-se) to make one's position clear; **~-se a favor de/contra algo** to come out in favo(u)r of/against sth

definitivamente [definitʃiva'mẽtʃi] adv definitively; (permanentemente) for good; (sem dúvida) definitely

definitivo, -a [defini'tʃivu, a] adj final, definitive; (permanente) permanent; (resposta, data) definite

deformação [defoxma'sãw] (pl **-ões**) f loss of shape; (de corpo) deformation; (de imagem, pensamento) distortion

deformar [defox'ma*] vt to put out of shape; (corpo) to deform; (imagem, pensamento) to distort; **deformar-se** vr to lose shape; to become distorted

defronte [de'frõtʃi] adv opposite ♦ prep: **~ de** opposite

defumar [defu'ma*] vt (presunto) to smoke; (perfumar) to perfume

defunto, -a [de'fũtu, a] adj dead ♦ m/f dead person

degelar [deʒe'la*] vt to thaw; (geladeira) to defrost ♦ vi to thaw out; to defrost

degenerar [deʒene'ra*] vi: **~ (em)** to degenerate (into)

degolar [dego'la*] vt to decapitate

degradar [degra'da*] vt to degrade, debase; **degradar-se** vr to demean o.s.

degrau [de'graw] m step; (de escada de mão) rung

degustação [deguʃta'sãw] (pl **-ões**) f tasting, sampling; (saborear) savouring (BRIT), savoring (US)

degustar [deguʃ'ta*] vt (provar) to

taste; (saborear) to savour (BRIT),
savor (US)

dei etc [dej] vb V **dar**

deitada [dej'tada] (col) f: **dar uma
~** to have a lie-down

deitado, -a [dej'tadu, a] adj (estendido) lying down; (na cama) in bed

deitar [dej'ta*] vt to lay down; (na
cama) to put to bed; (colocar) to
put, place; (lançar) to cast; (PT: líquido) to pour; **deitar-se** vr to lie
down; to go to bed; **~ sangue** (PT)
to bleed; **~ abaixo** to knock down,
flatten; **~ a fazer algo** to start doing
sth; **~ uma carta** (PT) to post a letter; **~ fora** (PT) to throw away ou
out; **~ e rolar** (col) to do as one likes

deixa [dejʃa] f clue, hint; (TEATRO)
cue; (chance) chance

deixar [dej'ʃa*] vt to leave; (abandonar) to abandon; (permitir) to let,
allow ♦ vi: **~ de** (parar) to stop; (não
fazer) to fail to; **não posso ~ de** ir I
must go; **~ cair** to drop; **~ alguém
louco** to drive sb crazy ou mad; **~
alguém cansado/nervoso** etc to
make sb tired/nervous etc; **deixa
disso!** come off it!; **deixa para
lá!** (col) forget it!

dela ['dɛla] = de + ela

delatar [dela'ta*] vt (pessoa) to
inform on; (abusos) to reveal; (à
polícia) to report; **delator, a**
[dela'to*, a] m/f informer

dele ['deli] = de + ele

delegacia [delega'sia] f office; **~ de
polícia** police station

delegado, -a [dele'gadu, a] m/f
delegate, representative; **~ de polícia** police chief

delegar [dele'ga*] vt to delegate

deleitar [delej'ta*] vt to delight;
deleitar-se vr: **~-se com** to delight
in

delgado, -a [dew'gadu, a] adj thin;

(esbelto) slim; (fino) fine

deliberação [delibera'sãw] (pl
-ões) f deliberation; (decisão) decision

deliberar [delibe'ra*] vt to decide,
resolve ♦ vi to deliberate

delicadeza [delika'dɛza] f delicacy;
(cortesia) kindness

delicado, -a [deli'kadu, a] adj delicate; (frágil) fragile; (cortês) polite;
(sensível) sensitive

delícia [de'lisja] f delight; (prazer)
pleasure; **que ~!** how lovely!; **deliciar** [deli'sja*] vt to delight;
deliciar-se vr: **deliciar-se com
algo** to take delight in sth

delicioso, -a [deli'sjozu, ɔza] adj
lovely; (comida, bebida) delicious

delinear [deli'nja*] vt to outline

delinqüente [deliˈkwẽtʃi] adj, m/f
delinquent, criminal

delirante [deli'rãtʃi] adj delirious;
(show, atuação) thrilling

delirar [deli'ra*] vi (com febre) to be
delirious; (de ódio, prazer) to go
mad, go wild

delírio [de'lirju] m (MED) delirium;
(êxtase) ecstasy; (excitação) excitement

delito [de'litu] m (crime) crime;
(falta) offence (BRIT), offense (US)

demais [dʒiˈmajʃ] adv (em demasia)
too much; (muitíssimo) a lot, very
much ♦ pron: **os/as ~** the rest (of
them); **já é ~!** this is too much!; **é
bom ~** it's really good; **foi ~** (col:
bacana) it was great

demanda [de'mãda] f lawsuit; (disputa) claim; (requisição) request;
(ECON) demand; **em ~ de** in search
of; **demandar** [demã'da*] vt (JUR)
to sue; (exigir, reclamar) to demand

demasia [dema'zia] f excess, surplus; (imoderação) lack of moderation; **em ~** (dinheiro, comida etc) too

much; (cartas, problemas etc) too many

demasiadamente [demazjada-'metʃi] adv too much; (com adj) too

demasiado, -a [dema'zjadu, a] adj too much; (pl) too many ♦ adv too much; (com adj) too

demente [de'mētʃi] adj insane, demented

demissão [demi'sãw] (pl -ões) f dismissal; **pedir ~** to resign

demitir [demi'tʃi*] vt to dismiss; (col) to sack, fire; **demitir-se** vr to resign

democracia [demokra'sia] f democracy

democrático, -a [demo'kratʃiku, a] adj democratic

demolir [demo'li*] vt to demolish, knock down; (fig) to destroy

demônio [de'monju] m devil, demon; (col: criança) brat

demonstração [demõʃtra'sãw] (pl -ões) f demonstration; (de amizade) show, display; (prova) proof

demonstrar [demõʃ'tra*] vt to demonstrate; (provar) to prove; (amizade etc) to show

demora [de'mɔra] f delay; (parada) stop; **sem ~** at once, without delay; **qual é a ~ disso?** how long will this take?; **demorado, -a** [demo'radu, a] adj slow; **demorar** [demo'ra*] vt to delay, slow down ♦ vi (permanecer) to stay; (tardar a vir) to be late; (conserto) to take (a long) time; **demorar-se** vr to stay for a long time, linger; **demora a chegar** to be a long time coming; **vai demorar muito?** will it take long?; **não vou demorar** I won't be long

dendê [dē'de] m (CULIN: óleo) palm oil; (BOT) oil palm

dengoso, -a [dē'gozu, ɔza] adj coy; (criança: choramingento): **ser ~** to

be a crybaby

dengue ['dēgi] m (MED) dengue

denominar [denomi'na*] vt: ~ **algo/alguém ...** to call sth/sb ...; **denominar-se** vr to be called; (a si mesmo) to call o.s.

denotar [deno'ta*] vt (indicar) to show, indicate; (significar) to signify

densidade [dēsi'dadʒi] f density; **disco de ~ simples/dupla** (COMPUT) single-/double-density disk

denso, -a ['dēsu, a] adj dense; (espesso) thick; (compacto) compact

dentada [dē'tada] f bite

dentadura [dēta'dura] f teeth pl, set of teeth; (artificial) dentures pl

dente ['dētʃi] m tooth; (de animal) fang; (de elefante) tusk; (de alho) clove; **falar entre os ~s** to mutter, mumble; **~ de leite/do siso** milk/ wisdom tooth; **~s postiços** false teeth

dentista [dē'tʃista] m/f dentist

dentre ['dētri] prep (from) among

dentro ['dētru] adv inside ♦ prep: ~ **de** inside; (tempo) (with)in; ~ **em pouco** ou **em breve** soon, before long; **de ~ para fora** inside out; **dar uma ~** (col) to get it right; **aí ~** in there; **por ~** on the inside; **estar por ~** (col: fig) to be in the know

denúncia [de'nũsja] f denunciation; (acusação) accusation; (de roubo) report; **denunciar** [denũ'sja*] vt (acusar) to denounce; (delatar) to inform on; (revelar) to reveal

deparar [depa'ra*] vt to reveal; (fazer aparecer) to present ♦ vi: ~ **com** to come across, meet; **deparar-se** vr: **~-se com** to come across, meet

departamento [depaxta'mētu] m department

dependência [depē'dēsja] f dependence; (edificação) annexe

(BRIT), annex (US); (colonial) dependency; (cômodo) room

dependente [depẽ'dẽtʃi] m/f dependant

depender [depẽ'de*] vi: ~ de to depend on

depilar [depi'la*] vt (pernas) to wax; **depilatório** [depila'tɔrju] m hair-remover

deplorável [deplo'ravew] (pl -eis) adj deplorable; (lamentável) regrettable

depoimento [depoj'mẽtu] m testimony, evidence; (na polícia) statement

depois [de'pojʃ] adv afterwards ♦ prep: ~ de after; ~ de comer after eating; ~ que after

depor [de'po*] (irreg: como pôr) vt (pôr) to place; (indicar) to indicate; (rei) to depose; (governo) to overthrow ♦ vi (JUR) to testify, give evidence; (na polícia) to give a statement

depositar [depozi'ta*] vt to deposit; (voto) to cast; (colocar) to place

depósito [de'pɔzitu] m deposit; (armazém) warehouse, depot; (de lixo) dump; (reservatório) tank; ~ de bagagens left-luggage office (BRIT), checkroom (US)

depreciação [depresja'sãw] f depreciation

depreciar [depre'sja*] vt (desvalorizar) to devalue; (COM) to write down; (menosprezar) to belittle; **depreciar-se** vr to depreciate, lose value

depredar [depre'da*] vt to wreck

depressa [dʒi'prɛsa] adv fast, quickly; **vamos ~** let's get a move on!

depressão [depre'sãw] (pl -ões) f depression

deprimente [depri'mẽtʃi] adj depressing

deprimido, -a [depri'midu, a] adj depressed

deprimir [depri'mi*] vt to depress; **deprimir-se** vr to get depressed

deputado, -a [depu'tadu, a] m/f deputy; (agente) agent (POL) ≈ Member of Parliament (BRIT), ≈ Representative (US)

der etc [de*] vb V **dar**

deriva [de'riva] f drift; **ir à ~** to drift; **ficar à ~** to be adrift

derivar [deri'va*] vt to divert; (LING) to derive ♦ vi to drift; **derivar-se** vr to be derived; (ir à deriva) to drift; (provir): ~(-se) (de) to derive ou be derived (from)

derradeiro, -a [dexa'dejru, a] adj last, final

derramamento [dexama'mẽtu] m spilling; (de sangue, lágrimas) shedding

derramar [dexa'ma*] vt to spill; (entornar) to pour; (sangue, lágrimas) to shed; **derramar-se** vr to pour out

derrame [de'xami] m haemorrhage (BRIT), hemorrhage (US)

derrapar [dexa'pa*] vi to skid

derreter [dexe'te*] vt to melt; **derreter-se** vr to melt; (coisa congelada) to thaw; (enternecer-se) to be touched

derrota [de'xɔta] f defeat, rout; (NÁUT) route; **derrotar** [dexo'ta*] vt (vencer) to defeat; (em jogo) to beat

derrubar [dexu'ba*] vt to knock down; (governo) to bring down; (suj: doença) to lay low; (col: prejudicar) to put down

desabafar [dʒizaba'fa*] vt (sentimentos) to give vent to ♦ vi: ~ (com) to unburden o.s. (to); **desabafar-se** vr: ~-se (com) to unburden o.s.

(to); **desabafo** [dʒiza'bafu] *m* confession

desabamento [dʒizaba'mẽtu] *m* collapse

desabar [dʒiza'ba*] *vi* (*edifício*, *ponte*) to collapse; (*chuva*) to pour down; (*tempestade*) to break

desabitado, -a [dʒizabi'tadu, a] *adj* uninhabited

desabotoar [dʒizabo'twa*] *vt* to unbutton

desabrigado, -a [dʒizabri'gadu, a] *adj* (*sem casa*) homeless; (*exposto*) exposed

desabrochar [dʒizabro'ʃa*] *vi* (*flores*, *fig*) to blossom

desacatar [dʒizaka'ta*] *vt* (*desrespeitar*) to have ou show no respect for; (*afrontar*) to defy; (*desprezar*) to scorn; **desacato** [dʒiza'katu] *m* disrespect; (*desprezo*) disregard

desacompanhado, -a [dʒizakõpa'ɲadu, a] *adj* on one's own, alone

desaconselhar [dʒizakõse'ʎa*] *vt*: ~ **algo** (**a alguém**) to advise (sb) against sth

desacordado, -a [dʒizakox'dadu, a] *adj* unconscious

desacordo [dʒiza'koxdu] *m* disagreement; (*desarmonia*) discord

desacostumado, -a [dʒizakoʃtu'madu, a] *adj*: ~ (**a**) unaccustomed (to)

desacreditar [dʒizakredʒi'ta*] *vt* to discredit; **desacreditar-se** *vr* to lose one's reputation

desafiador, a [dʒizafja'do*, a] *adj* challenging; (*pessoa*) defiant ♦ *m/f* challenger

desafiar [dʒiza'fja*] *vt* to challenge; (*afrontar*) to defy

desafinado, -a [dʒizafi'nadu, a] *adj* out of tune

desafio [dʒiza'fiu] *m* challenge; (*PT*: *ESPORTE*) match, game

desaforado, -a [dʒizafo'radu, a] *adj* rude, insolent

desaforo [dʒiza'foru] *m* insolence, abuse

desafortunado, -a [dʒizafoxtu-'nadu, a] *adj* unfortunate, unlucky

desagradar [dʒizagra'da*] *vt* to displease ♦ *vi*: ~ **a alguém** to displease sb; **desagradável** [dʒizagra'davew] (*pl* -**eis**) *adj* unpleasant; **desagrado** [dʒiza'gradu] *m* displeasure

desaguar [dʒiza'gwa*] *vt* to drain ♦ *vi*: ~ (**em**) to flow ou empty (into)

desajeitado, -a [dʒizaʒej'tadu, a] *adj* clumsy, awkward

desalentado, -a [dʒizalẽ'tadu, a] *adj* disheartened

desalentar [dʒizalẽ'ta*] *vt* to discourage; (*deprimir*) to depress; **desalento** [dʒiza'lẽtu] *m* discouragement

desalinhado, -a [dʒizali'ɲadu, a] *adj* untidy

desalinho [dʒiza'liɲu] *m* untidiness

desalmado, -a [dʒizaw'madu, a] *adj* cruel, inhuman

desalojar [dʒizalo'ʒa*] *vt* (*expulsar*) to oust; **desalojar-se** *vr* to move out

desamarrar [dʒizama'xa*] *vt* to untie ♦ *vi* (*NÁUT*) to cast off

desamor [dʒiza'mo*] *m* dislike

desamparado, -a [dʒizãpa'radu, a] *adj* abandoned; (*sem apoio*) helpless

desanimação [dʒizanima'sãw] *f* dejection

desanimado, -a [dʒizani'madu, a] *adj* (*pessoa*) fed up, dispirited; (*festa*) dull; **ser ~** (*pessoa*) to be apathetic

desanimar [dʒizani'ma*] *vt* to discourage; (*desencorajar*): ~ (**de fazer**) to discourage (from doing) ♦ *vi* to lose heart; to be discouraging; ~ **de**

fazer algo to lose the will to do sth; (*desistir*) to give up doing sth

desanuviar [dʒɪzanu'vjaˈ] *vt* (*céu*) to clear; **desanuviar-se** *vr* to clear; (*fig*) to stop; **desanuviar alguém** to put sb's mind at rest

desaparafusar [dʒɪzaparafu'zaˈ] *vt* to unscrew

desaparecer [dʒɪzapare'seˈ] *vi* to disappear, vanish; **desaparecido, -a** [dʒɪzapare'sidu, a] *adj* lost, missing ♦ *m/f* missing person; **desaparecimento** [dʒɪzaparesi'mětu] *m* disappearance; (*falecimento*) death

desapego [dʒɪza'pegu] *m* indifference, detachment

desapercebido, -a [dʒɪzapexse'bidu, a] *adj* unnoticed

desapertar [dʒɪzapex'taˈ] *vt* to loosen; (*livrar*) to free

desapontamento [dʒɪzapõta'mětu] *m* disappointment

desapontar [dʒɪzapõ'taˈ] *vt* to disappoint

desapropriar [dʒɪzapro'prjaˈ] *vt* (*bens*) to expropriate; (*pessoa*) to dispossess

desaprovar [dʒɪzapro'vaˈ] *vt* to disapprove of; (*censurar*) to object to

desarmamento [dʒɪzaxma'mětu] *m* disarmament

desarmar [dʒɪzax'maˈ] *vt* to disarm; (*desmontar*) to dismantle; (*bomba*) to defuse

desarmonia [dʒɪzaxmo'nia] *f* discord

desarranjo [dʒɪza'xãʒu] *m* disorder; (*enguiço*) breakdown; (*diarréia*) diarrhoea (*BRIT*), diarrhea (*US*)

desarrumado, -a [dʒɪzaxu'madu, a] *adj* untidy, messy

desarrumar [dʒɪzaxu'maˈ] *vt* to mess up; (*mala*) to unpack

desassossego [dʒɪzaso'segu] *m*

(*inquietação*) disquiet; (*perturbação*) restlessness

desastrado, -a [dʒɪzaʃ'tradu, a] *adj* clumsy

desastre [dʒɪ'zaʃtri] *m* disaster; (*acidente*) accident; (*de avião*) crash

desatar [dʒɪza'taˈ] *vt* (*nó*) to undo, untie ♦ *vi*: ~ **a fazer** to begin to do; ~ **a chorar** to burst into tears; ~ **a rir** to burst out laughing

desatento, -a [dʒɪza'tětu, a] *adj* inattentive

desatinado, -a [dʒɪzatʃi'nadu, a] *adj* crazy, wild ♦ *m/f* lunatic

desatino [dʒɪza'tʃinu] *m* madness; (*ato*) folly

desativar [dʒɪzatʃi'vaˈ] *vt* (*firma*, *usina*) to shut down; (*veículos*) to withdraw from service; (*bomba*) to deactivate, defuse

desatualizado, -a [dʒɪzatwali'zadu, a] *adj* out of date; (*pessoa*) out of touch

desavença [dʒɪza'věsa] *f* (*briga*) quarrel; (*discórdia*) disagreement; **em ~** at loggerheads

desavergonhado, -a [dʒɪza-vexgo'nadu, a] *adj* shameless

desavisado, -a [dʒɪzavi'zadu, a] *adj* careless

desbastar [dʒɪʒbaʃ'taˈ] *vt* (*cabelo*, *plantas*) to thin (out); (*vegetação*) to trim

desbocado, -a [dʒɪʒbo'kadu, a] *adj* foul-mouthed

desbotar [dʒɪʒbo'taˈ] *vt* to discolour (*BRIT*), discolor (*US*) ♦ *vi* to fade

desbragadamente [dʒɪʒbragada-'mětʃi] *adv* (*beber*) to excess; (*mentir*) blatantly

desbravar [dʒɪʒbra'vaˈ] *vt* (*terras desconhecidas*) to explore

descabelar [dʒiʃkabe'laˈ] *vt*: ~ **alguém** to mess up sb's hair; **descabelar-se** *vr* to get one's hair messed up

descabido, -a [dʒiʃka'bidu, a] *adj*
improper; (*inoportuno*) inappropriate

descafeinado [dʒiʃkafej'nadu] *adj*
decaffeinated ♦ *n* decaff

descalçar [dʒiʃkaw'sa*] *vt* (*sapatos*)
to take off; **descalçar-se** *vr* to take
off one's shoes

descalço, -a [dʒiʃ'kawsu, a] *adj*
barefoot

descansado, -a [dʒiʃkã'sadu, a]
adj calm, quiet; (*vagaroso*) slow;
fique ~ don't worry; **pode ficar ~
que** ... you can rest assured that ...

descansar [dʒiʃkã'sa*] *vt* to rest;
(*apoiar*) to lean ♦ *vi* to rest; to lean;
descanso [dʒiʃ'kãsu] *m* rest;
(*folga*) break; (*para prato*) mat

descarado, -a [dʒiʃka'radu, a] *adj*
cheeky, impudent

descaramento [dʒiʃkara'mẽtu] *m*
cheek, impudence

descarga [dʒiʃ'kaxga] *f* unloading;
(MIL) volley; (ELET) discharge; (*de vaso
sanitário*): **dar a ~** to flush the toilet

descarregamento [dʒiʃkaxega-
'mẽtu] *m* (*de carga*) unloading;
(ELET) discharge

descarregar [dʒiʃkaxe'ga*] *vt*
(*carga*) to unload; (ELET) to discharge; (*aliviar*) to relieve; (*raiva*) to
vent, give vent to; (*arma*) to fire ♦ *vi*
to unload; (*bateria*) to run out; **~ a
raiva em alguém** to take it out on sb

descartar [dʒiʃkax'ta*] *vt* to discard; **descartar-se** *vr*: **~-se de** to
get rid of; **descartável** [dʒiʃkax-
'tavew] (*pl* **-eis**) disposable

descascar [dʒiʃkaʃ'ka*] *vt* (*fruta*) to
peel; (*ervilhas*) to shell ♦ *vi* (*depois do
sol*) to peel; (*cobra*) to shed its skin

descaso [dʒiʃ'kazu] *m* disregard

descendência [desẽ'dẽsja] *f*
descendants *pl*, offspring *pl*

descendente [desẽ'dẽtʃi] *adj*
descending, going down ♦ *m/f*

descendant

descer [de'se*] *vt* (*escada*) to go (*ou*
come) down; (*bagagem*) to take
down ♦ *vi* (*saltar*) to get off; (*baixar*)
to go (*ou* come) down; **descida**
[de'sida] *f* descent; (*declive*) slope;
(*abaixamento*) fall, drop

desclassificar [dʒiʃklasifi'ka*] *vt* to
disqualify; (*desacreditar*) to discredit

descoberta [dʒiʃko'bexta] *f* discovery; (*invenção*) invention

descoberto, -a [dʒiʃko'bextu, a] *pp
de* **descobrir** ♦ *adj* bare, naked; (*exposto*) exposed ♦ *m* overdraft; **a ~** openly;
conta a ~ overdrawn account; **pôr** *ou*
sacar a ~ (*conta*) to overdraw

descobridor, a [dʒiʃkobri'do*, a]
m/f discoverer; (*explorador*) explorer

descobrimento [dʒiʃkobri'mẽtu]
m discovery; **D~s** *mpl*: **os D~s** the
Discoveries; *see boxed note*

DESCOBRIMENTOS

Portugal enjoyed a period of unri-
valled overseas expansion during
the 15th century, mainly due to
the seafaring expertise of Henry
the Navigator. He organized and
financed several voyages to Africa,
which eventually led to the
rounding of the Cape of Good
Hope in 1488 by Bartolomeu
Dias. In 1497, Vasco da Gama
became the first European to travel by sea to India, where he established a lucrative spice trade, and
a few years later, in 1500, Pedro
Álvares Cabral reached Brazil,
which he claimed for Portugal.
Brazil remained under Portuguese
rule until 1822.

---

descobrir [dʒiʃko'bri*] *vt* to discover; (*tirar a cobertura de*) to uncover;
(*panela*) to take the lid off;

(*averiguar*) to find out; (*enigma*) to solve

escolar [dʒiʃko'la*] vt to unstick ♦ vi: **a criança não descola da mãe** the child won't leave his (ou her) mother's side

escolorante [dʒiʃkolo'rãtʃi] m bleach

escolorir [dʒiʃkolo'ri*] vt to discolour (*BRIT*), discolor (*US*); (*cabelo*) to bleach ♦ vi to fade

escompostura [dʒiʃkõpoʃ'tura] f (*repreensão*) dressing-down; (*insulto*) abuse; **passar uma ~ em alguém** to give sb a dressing-down; to hurl abuse at sb

escomunal [dʒiʃkomu'naw] (*pl* -ais) *adj* extraordinary; (*colossal*) huge, enormous

esconcentrar [dʒiʃkõse'tra*] vt to distract; **desconcentrar-se** vr to lose one's concentration

esconexo, -a [dʒiʃko'neksu, a] *adj* (*desunido*) disconnected, unrelated; (*incoerente*) incoherent

esconfiado, -a [dʒiʃkõ'fjadu, a] *adj* suspicious, distrustful ♦ m/f suspicious person

esconfiança [dʒiʃkõ'fjãsa] f suspicion, distrust

esconfiar [dʒiʃkõ'fja*] vi to be suspicious; **~ de alguém** (*não ter confiança em*) to distrust sb; (*suspeitar*) to suspect sb; **~ que ...** to have the feeling that ...

esconfortável [dʒiʃkõfox'tavew] (*pl* -eis) *adj* uncomfortable

esconforto [dʒiʃkõ'foxtu] m discomfort

escongelar [dʒiʃkõʒe'la*] vt to thaw out; **descongelar-se** vr to melt

esconhecer [dʒiʃkoɲe'se*] vt (*ignorar*) not to know; (*não reconhecer*) not to recognize; (*um benefício*)

not to acknowledge; (*não admitir*) not to accept; **desconhecido, -a** [dʒiʃkoɲe'sidu, a] *adj* unknown ♦ m/f stranger; **desconhecimento** [dʒiʃkoɲesi'mẽtu] m ignorance

desconsolado, -a [dʒiʃkõso'ladu, a] *adj* miserable, disconsolate

descontar [dʒiʃkõ'ta*] vt to deduct; (*não levar em conta*) to discount; (*não fazer caso de*) to make light of

descontentamento [dʒiʃkõtẽta-'mẽtu] m discontent; (*desprazer*) displeasure

descontente [dʒiʃkõ'tẽtʃi] *adj* discontented, dissatisfied

desconto [dʒiʃ'kõtu] m discount; **com ~** at a discount; **dar um ~ (para)** (*fig*) to make allowances (for)

descontraído, -a [dʒiʃkõtra'idu, a] *adj* casual, relaxed

descontrair [dʒiʃkõtra'i*] vt to relax; **descontrair-se** vr to relax

descontrolar-se [dʒiʃkõtro'laxsi] vr (*situação*) to get out of control; (*pessoa*) to lose one's self-control

desconversar [dʒiʃkõvex'sa*] vi to change the subject

descortesia [dʒiʃkoxte'zia] f rudeness, impoliteness

descoser [dʒiʃko'ze*] vt (*descostular*) to unstitch, (*rasgar*) to rip apart; **descoser-se** vr to come apart at the seams

descrença [dʒiʃ'krẽsa] f disbelief, incredulity

descrente [dʒiʃ'krẽtʃi] *adj* sceptical (*BRIT*), skeptical (*US*) ♦ m/f sceptic (*BRIT*), skeptic (*US*)

descrever [dʒiʃkre've*] vt to describe

descrição [dʒiʃkri'sãw] (*pl* -ões) f description; **descritivo, -a** [dʒiʃkri'tʃivu, a] *adj* descriptive

descrito, -a [dʒiʃˈkritu, a] pp de
descrever

descubro etc [dʒiʃˈkubru] vb V
descobrir

descuidado, -a [dʒiʃkwiˈdadu, a]
adj careless

descuidar [dʒiʃkwiˈda*] vt to
neglect ♦ vi: ~ **de** to neglect, disregard; **descuido** [dʒiʃˈkwidu] m
carelessness; (negligência) neglect;
(erro) oversight, slip; **por descuido**
inadvertently

desculpa [dʒiʃˈkuwpa] f excuse;
(perdão) pardon; **pedir ~s a
alguém por** ou **algo** to apologise
to sb for sth; **desculpar** [dʒiʃ-
kuwˈpa*] vt to excuse; (perdoar) to
pardon, forgive; **desculpar-se** vr
to apologize; **desculpar algo a
alguém** to forgive sb for sth; **desculpe!** (I'm) sorry, I beg your pardon; **desculpável** [dʒiʃkuw-
ˈpavew] (pl -eis) adj forgivable

PALAVRA CHAVE

desde [ˈdeʒdʒi] prep **1** (lugar): ~ ...
até ... from ... to ...; **andamos ~ a
praia até o restaurante** we walked
from the beach to the restaurant
2 (tempo: + adv, n): ~ **então** from
then on, ever since; ~ **já** (de agora)
from now on; (imediatamente) at
once, right now; ~ **o casamento**
since the wedding
3 (tempo: + vb) since; for;
conhecemo-nos ~ 1978/há 20 anos
we've known each other since
1978/for 20 years; **não o vejo
~ 1983** I haven't seen him since
1983
4 (variedade): ~ **os mais baratos
até os mais luxuosos** from the
cheapest to the most luxurious
♦ conj: ~ **que** since; ~ **que comecei
a trabalhar não o vi mais** I haven't

seen him since I started work; **nã̃o
saiu de casa ~ que chegou** he
hasn't been out since he arrived

desdém [deʒˈdẽ] m scorn, disdain
desdenhar [deʒdeˈɲa*] vt to scorn,
disdain
desdizer [dʒiʒdʒiˈze*] (irreg: com:
dizer) vt to contradict; **desdizer-
se** vr to go back on one's word
desdobrar [dʒiʒdoˈbra*] vt (abrir)
to unfold; (esforços) to increase,
redouble; (tropas) to deploy; (bandeira) to unfurl; (dividir em grupos)
to split up; **desdobrar-se** vr to
unfold; (empenhar-se) to work hard,
make a big effort
desejar [deseˈʒa*] vt to want, desire
desejo [deˈzeʒu] m wish, desire;
desejoso, -a [dezeˈʒozu, ɔza] adj:
desejoso de algo wishing for sth;
desejoso de fazer keen to do
desembaraçar [dʒizẽbaraˈsa*] vt
(livrar) to free; (cabelo) to untangle;
desembaraçar-se vr (desinibir-se)
to lose one's inhibitions; **~-se de** to
get rid of
desembaraço [dʒizẽbaˈrasu] m
liveliness; (facilidade) ease; (confiança) self-assurance
desembarcar [dʒizẽbaxˈka*] vt
(carga) to unload; (passageiros) to
let off ♦ vi to disembark; **desembarque** [dʒizẽˈbaxki] m landing,
disembarkation; **"desembarque"**
(no aeroporto) "arrivals"
desembolsar [dʒizẽbowˈsa*] vt to
spend
desembrulhar [dʒizẽbruˈʎa*] vt to
unwrap
desempacotar [dʒizẽpakoˈta*] vt
to unpack
desempatar [dʒizẽpaˈta*] vt to
decide ♦ vi to decide the match (ou
race etc); **desempate** [dʒizẽˈpatʃi]

desempenhar 409 **desenvolver**

m: **partida de desempate** (*jogo*) play-off, decider

desempenhar [dʒizēpe'naʃ] *vt* (*cumprir*) to carry out, fulfil (*BRIT*), fulfill (*US*); (*papel*) to play; **desempenho** [dʒizē'peɲu] *m* performance; (*de obrigações etc*) fulfilment (*BRIT*), fulfillment (*US*)

desempregado, -a [dʒizēpre-'gadu, a] *adj* unemployed ♦ *m/f* unemployed person

desempregar-se [dʒizēpre'gaxsi] *vr* to lose one's job

desemprego [dʒizē'pregu] *m* unemployment

desencadear [dʒizēka'dʒja*] *vt* to unleash; (*despertar*) to provoke, trigger off ♦ *vi* (*chuva*) to start; **desencadear-se** *vr* to break loose; (*tempestade*) to break

desencaixar [dʒizēkaj'ʃa*] *vt* to put out of joint; (*deslocar*) to dislodge; **desencaixar-se** *vr* to become dislodged

desencaixotar [dʒizēkajʃo'ta*] *vt* to unpack

desencarregar-se [dʒizēkaxe-'gaxsi] *vr* (*de obrigação*) to discharge o.s.

desencontrar-se [dʒizēkõ'traxsi] *vr* (*não se encontrar*) to miss each other; (*perder-se um do outro*: *perder-se*) to lose each other; **~ de** to miss; to get separated from

desencorajar [dʒizēkora'ʒa*] *vt* to discourage

desencostar [dʒizēkoʃ'ta*] *vt* to move away; **desencostar-se** *vr*: **desencostar-se de** to move away from

desenfreado, -a [dʒizē'frjadu, a] *adj* wild

desenganado, -a [dʒizēga'nadu, a] *adj* incurable; (*desiludido*) disillusioned

desenganar [dʒizēga'na*] *vt*: **~ alguém** to disillusion sb; (*de falsas crenças*) to open sb's eyes; (*doente*) to give up hope of curing; **desenganar-se** *vr* to become disillusioned; (*sair de erro*) to realize the truth; **desengano** [dʒizē'ganu] *m* disillusionment; (*desapontamento*) disappointment

desengonçado, -a [dʒizēgõ'sadu, a] *adj* (*mal-seguro*) rickety; (*pessoa*) ungainly

desenhar [deze'ɲa*] *vt* to draw; (*TEC*) to design; **desenhar-se** *vr* (*destacar-se*) to stand out; (*figurar-se*) to take shape; **desenhista** [deze'niʃta] *m/f* (*TEC*) designer

desenho [de'zeɲu] *m* drawing; (*modelo*) design; (*esboço*) sketch; (*plano*) plan; **~ animado** cartoon

desenlace [dʒizē'lasi] *m* outcome

desenrolar [dʒizēxo'la*] *vt* to unroll; (*narrativa*) to develop; **desenrolar-se** *vr* to unfold

desentender [dʒizētē'de*] *vt* to misunderstand; **desentender-se** *vr*: **~-se com** to have a disagreement with; **desentendido, -a** [dʒizētē'dʒidu, a] *adj*: **fazer-se de desentendido** to pretend not to understand; **desentendimento** [dʒizētēdʒi'mētu] *m* misunderstanding

desenterrar [dʒizēte'xa*] *vt* (*cadáver*) to exhume; (*tesouro*) to dig up; (*descobrir*) to bring to light

desentupir [dʒizētu'pi*] *vt* to unblock

desenvoltura [dʒizēvow'tura] *f* self-confidence

desenvolver [dʒizēvow've*] *vt* to develop; **desenvolver-se** *vr* to develop; **desenvolvimento** [dʒizēvowvi'mētu] *m* development; (*crescimento*) growth; **país em**

desenvolvimento developing country

desequilibrado, -a [dʒizekili'bradu, a] *adj* unbalanced

deserção [dezex'sãw] *f* desertion

desertar [desex'ta*] *vt* to desert, abandon ♦ *vi* to desert; **deserto, -a** [de'zɛxtu, a] *adj* deserted ♦ *m* desert; **desertor, a** [dezex'to*, a] *m/f* deserter

desesperado, -a [dʒizeʃpe'radu, a] *adj* desperate; *(furioso)* furious

desesperador, a [dʒizeʃpera'do*, a] *adj* desperate; *(enfurecedor)* maddening

desesperança [dʒizeʃpe'rãsa] *f* despair

desesperar [dʒizeʃpe'ra*] *vt* to drive to despair; *(enfurecer)* to infuriate; **desesperar-se** *vr* to despair; *(enfurecer-se)* to become infuriated; **desespero** [dʒizeʃ'peru] *m* despair, desperation; *(raiva)* fury

desestimular [dʒizeʃtʃimu'la*] *vt* to discourage

desfalcar [dʒiʃfaw'ka*] *vt (dinheiro)* to embezzle; *(reduzir)*: ~ **(de)** to reduce (by); **a jogo está desfalcado** the game is incomplete

desfalecer [dʒiʃfale'se*] *vt (enfraquecer)* to weaken ♦ *vi (enfraquecer)* to weaken; *(desmaiar)* to faint

desfalque [dʒiʃ'fawki] *m (de dinheiro)* embezzlement; *(diminuição)* reduction

desfavorável [dʒiʃfavo'ravew] *(pl -eis) adj* unfavourable *(BRIT)*, unfavorable *(US)*

desfazer [dʒiʃfa'ze*] *(irreg: como fazer) vt (costura)* to undo; *(dúvidas)* to dispel; *(agravo)* to redress; *(grupo)* to break up; *(noivado)* to dissolve; *(noivado)* to break off ♦ *vi*: ~ **de alguém** to belittle sb; **desfazer-se** *vr* to vanish; *(tecido)*

to come to pieces; *(grupo)* to break up; *(vaso)* to break; **~-se de** *(livrar-se)* to get rid of; **~-se em lágrimas/ gentilezas** to burst into tears/go out of one's way to please

desfecho [dʒiʃ'feʃu] *m* ending, outcome

desfeito, -a [dʒiʃ'fejtu, a] *adj* undone; *(cama)* unmade; *(contrato)* broken

desfigurar [dʒiʃfigu'ra*] *vt (pessoa, cidade)* to disfigure; *(texto)* to mutilate; **desfigurar-se** *vr* to be disfigured

desfilar [dʒiʃfi'la*] *vi* to parade; **desfile** [dʒiʃ'fili] *m* parade, procession

desforra [dʒiʃ'fɔxa] *f* revenge; *(reparação)* redress; **tirar** ~ to get even

desfrutar [dʒiʃfru'ta*] *vt* to enjoy ♦ *vi*: ~ **de** to enjoy

desgarrado, -a [dʒiʒga'xadu, a] *adj* stray; *(navio)* off course

desgastante [dʒiʒgaʃ'tãtʃi] *adj* stressful

desgastar [dʒiʒgaʃ'ta*] *vt* to wear away, erode; *(pessoa)* to wear out, get down; **desgastar-se** *vr* to be worn away; *(pessoa)* to get worn out; **desgaste** [dʒiʒ'gaʃtʃi] *m* wear and tear; *(mental)* stress

desgosto [dʒiʒ'goʃtu] *m* displeasure; *(pesar)* sorrow, unhappiness

desgraça [dʒiʒ'graza] *f* misfortune; *(miséria)* misery; *(desfavor)* disgrace; **desgraçado, -a** [dʒiʒgra'sadu, a] *adj* poor ♦ *m/f* wretch; **estou com uma gripe desgraçada** *(col)* I've got a hell of a cold

desgrudar [dʒiʒgru'da*] *vt* to unstick ♦ *vi*: ~ **de** to tear o.s. away from; ~ **algo de algo** to take sth off sth

desidratar [dʒizidra'ta*] *vt* to

dehydrate

design [dʒi'zãjn] m design

designar [dezig'na*] vt to designate; (nomear) to name, appoint; (dia, data) to fix

desigual [dezi'gwaw] (pl -ais) adj unequal; (terreno) uneven; **desigualdade** [dʒizigwaw'dadʒi] f inequality

desiludir [dʒizilu'dʒi*] vt to disillusion; (causar decepção a) to disappoint; **desiludir-se** vr to lose one's illusions

desimpedido, -a [dʒizĩpe'dʒidu, a] adj free

desinfetante [dʒizĩfe'tãtʃi] (PT -ct-) adj, m disinfectant

desinfetar [dʒizĩfe'ta*] (PT -ct-) vt to disinfect

desintegração [dʒizĩtegra'sãw] f disintegration, break-up

desintegrar [dʒizĩte'gra*] vt to separate; **desintegrar-se** vr to disintegrate, fall to pieces

desinteressado, -a [dʒizĩtere'sadu, a] adj disinterested

desinteresse [dʒizĩte'resi] m lack of interest

desistir [dezi'tʃi*] vi to give up; ~ **de fumar** to stop smoking; **ele ia, mas no final desistiu** he was going, but in the end he gave up the idea ou he decided not to

desjejum [dʒize'ʒũ] m breakfast

deslavado, -a [dʒizla'vadu, a] adj (pessoa, atitude) shameless; (mentira) blatant

desleal [dʒizle'aw] (pl -ais) adj disloyal

desleixado, -a [dʒizlej'ʃadu, a] adj sloppy

desleixo [dʒiz'lejʃu] m sloppiness

desligado, -a [dʒizli'gadu, a] adj (eletricidade) off; (pessoa) absent-minded; **estar ~** to be miles away

desligar [dʒizli'ga*] vt (TEC) to disconnect; (luz, TV, motor) to switch off; (telefone) to hang up; **desligar-se** vr: ~-se de algo (afastar-se) to leave sth; (problemas etc) to turn one's back on sth; **não desligue** (TEL) hold the line

deslizar [dʒizli'za*] vi to slide; (por acidente) to slip; (passar de leve) to glide; **deslize** [dʒiz'lizi] m lapse; (escorregadela) slip

deslocado, -a [dʒizlo'kadu, a] adj (membro) dislocated; (desambientado) out of place

deslocar [dʒizlo'ka*] vt to move; (articulação) to dislocate; (funcionário) to transfer; **deslocar-se** vr to move; to be dislocated

deslumbramento [dʒizlũbra'mẽtu] m dazzle; (fascinação) fascination

deslumbrante [dʒizlũ'brãtʃi] adj dazzling; (casa, festa) amazing

deslumbrar [dʒizlũ'bra*] vt to dazzle; (maravilhar) to amaze; (fascinar) to fascinate ♦ vi to be dazzling; to be amazing; **deslumbrar-se** vr: ~-se com to be fascinated by

desmaiado, -a [dʒiʒma'jadu, a] adj unconscious; (cor) pale

desmaiar [dʒiʒma'ja*] vi to faint; **desmaio** [dʒiʒ'maju] m faint

desmancha-prazeres [dʒiʒ-'mãnʃa-] m/f inv kill-joy, spoilsport

desmanchar [dʒiʒmãn'ʃa*] vt (costura) to undo; (contrato) to break; (noivado) to break off; (penteado) to mess up; **desmanchar-se** vr (costura) to come undone

desmarcar [dʒiʒmax'ka*] vt (compromisso) to cancel

desmascarar [dʒiʒmaʃka'ra*] vt to unmask

desmazelado, -a [dʒiʒmaze'ladu, a] adj slovenly, untidy

desmedido, -a [dʒiʒme'dʒidu, a] *adj* excessive

desmentido [dʒiʒmẽ'tʃidu] *m* (*negação*) denial; (*contradição*) contradiction

desmentir [dʒiʒmẽ'tʃi*] *vt* (*contradizer*) to contradict; (*negar*) to deny

desmiolado, -a [dʒiʒmjo'ladu, a] *adj* brainless; (*esquecido*) forgetful

desmontar [dʒiʒmõ'ta*] *vt* (*máquina*) to take to pieces ♦ *vi* (*do cavalo*) to dismount, get off

desmoronamento [dʒiʒmorona-'mẽtu] *m* collapse

desmoronar [dʒiʒmoro'na*] *vt* to knock down ♦ *vi* to collapse

desnatado, -a [dʒiʒna'tadu, a] *adj* (*leite*) skimmed

desnaturado, -a [dʒiʒnatu'radu, a] *adj* inhumane ♦ *m/f* monster

desnecessário, -a [dʒiʒnese-'sarju, a] *adj* unnecessary

desnutrição [dʒiʒnutri'sãw] *f* malnutrition

desobedecer [dʒizobede'se*] *vt* to disobey; **desobediência** [dʒizobe-'dʒjẽsja] *f* disobedience; **desobediente** [dʒizobe'dʒjẽtʃi] *adj* disobedient

desobstruir [dʒizobiʃ'trwi*] *vt* to unblock

desocupado, -a [dʒizoku'padu, a] *adj* (*casa*) empty, vacant; (*disponível*) free; (*sem trabalho*) unemployed

desocupar [dʒizoku'pa*] *vt* (*casa*) to vacate; (*liberar*) to free

desodorante [dʒizodo'rãtʃi] (*PT* -dorizante*) *m* deodorant

desolação [dezola'sãw] *f* (*consternação*) grief; (*de um lugar*) desolation; **desolado, -a** [dezo'ladu, a] *adj* distressed; desolate

desonesto, -a [dezo'nɛʃtu, a] *adj* dishonest

desonra [dʒi'zõxa] *f* dishonour (*BRIT*), dishonor (*US*); (*descrédito*) disgrace; **desonrar** [dʒizõ'xa*] *vt* (*infamar*) to disgrace; (*mulher*) to seduce; **desonrar-se** *vr* to disgrace o.s.

desordem [dʒi'zoxdẽ] *f* disorder, confusion; **em ~** (*casa*) untidy

desorganizar [dʒizoxgani'za*] *vt* to disorganize; (*dissolver*) to break up; **desorganizar-se** *vr* to become disorganized; to break up

desorientação [dʒizorjẽta'sãw] *f* bewilderment, confusion

desorientar [dʒizorjẽ'ta*] *vt* (*desnortear*) to throw off course; (*perturbar*) to confuse; (*desvairar*) to unhinge; **desorientar-se** *vr* to lose one's way; to get confused; to go mad

desovar [dʒizo'va*] *vt* to lay; (*peixe*) to spawn

despachado, -a [dʒiʃpa'ʃadu, a] *adj* (*pessoa*) efficient

despachar [dʒiʃpa'ʃa*] *vt* to dispatch, send off; (*atender, resolver*) to deal with; (*despedir*) to sack; **despachar-se** *vr* to hurry (up); **despacho** [dʒiʃ'paʃu] *m* dispatch; (*de negócios*) handling; (*nota em requerimento*) ruling; (*consulta*) consultation; (*macumba*) witchcraft

despeço *etc* [dʒiʃ'pɛsu] *vb* V **despedir**

despedaçar [dʒiʃpeda'sa*] *vt* (*quebrar*) to smash; (*rasgar*) to tear apart; **despedaçar-se** *vr* to smash; to tear

despedida [dʒiʃpe'dʒida] *f* farewell; (*de trabalhador*) dismissal

despedir [dʒiʃpe'dʒi*] *vt* (*de emprego*) to dismiss, sack; **despedir-se** *vr*: ~-se (**de**) to say goodbye (to)

despeitado, -a [dʒiʃpej'tadu, a] *adj* spiteful; (*ressentido*) resentful

despeito [dʒiʃ'pejtu] *m* spite; **a ~ de** in spite of, despite

despejar [dʒiʃpe'ʒa*] *vt* (*água*) to pour; (*esvaziar*) to empty; (*inquilino*) to evict; **despejo** [dʒiʃ'peʒu] *m* eviction; **quarto de despejo** junk room

despencar [dʒiʃpẽ'ka*] *vi* to fall down, tumble down

despensa [dʒiʃ'pẽsa] *f* larder

despentear [dʒiʃpẽ'tʃja*] *vt* (*cabelo: sem querer*) to mess up; (: *de propósito*) to let down; **despentear-se** *vr* to mess one's hair up, to let one's hair down

despercebido, -a [dʒiʃpexse'bidu, a] *adj* unnoticed

desperdiçar [dʒiʃpexdʒi'sa*] *vt* to waste; (*dinheiro*) to squander; **desperdício** [dʒiʃpex'dʒisju] *m* waste

despertador [dʒiʃpexta'do*] *m* (*tb: relógio ~*) alarm clock

despertar [dʒiʃpex'ta*] *vt* to wake; (*suspeitas, interesse*) to arouse; (*reminiscências*) to revive; (*apetite*) to whet ♦ *vi* to wake up ♦ *m* awakening; **desperto, -a** [dʒiʃ'pextu, a] *adj* awake

despesa [dʒiʃ'peza] *f* expense; **~s** *fpl* (*de uma empresa*) expenses, costs; **~s gerais** (COM) overheads

despido, -a [dʒiʃ'pidu, a] *adj* naked, bare; (*livre*) tree

despir [dʒiʃ'pi*] *vt* (*roupa*) to take off; (*pessoa*) to undress; (*despojar*) to strip; **despir-se** *vr* to undress

despojar [dʒiʃpo'ʒa*] *vt* (*casas*) to loot, sack; (*pessoas*) to rob

despontar [dʒiʃpõ'ta*] *vi* to emerge; (*sol*) to come out; (: *ao amanhecer*) to come up; **ao ~ do dia** at daybreak

desporto [dʒiʃ'poxtu] (*esp PT*) *m* sport

desprender [dʒiʃprẽ'de*] *vt* to loosen; (*desatar*) to unfasten; (*emitir*) to emit; **desprender-se** *vr* (*botão*) to come off; (*cheiro*) to be given off

despreocupado, -a [dʒiʃpreoku'pado, a] *adj* carefree, unconcerned

desprezar [dʒiʃpre'za*] *vt* to despise, disdain; (*não dar importância a*) to disregard, ignore; **desprezível** [dʒiʃpre'zivew] (*pl -eis*) *adj* despicable; **desprezo** [dʒiʃ'prezu] *m* scorn, contempt; **dar ao desprezo** to ignore

desproporcional [dʒiʃpropoxsjo-'naw] *adj* disproportionate

despropósito [dʒiʃpro'pɔzitu] *m* nonsense

desprovido, -a [dʒiʃpro'vidu, a] *adj* deprived; **~ de** without

desqualificar [dʒiʃkwalifi'ka*] *vt* (*ESPORTE etc*) to disqualify; (*tornar indigno*) to disgrace, lower

desregrado, -a [dʒiʒxe'gradu, a] *adj* disorderly, unruly; (*devasso*) immoderate

desrespeito [dʒiʒxe'ʃpejtu] *m* disrespect

desse *etc* ['desi] *vb V* **dar**

desse, -a ['desi, a] = **de** + **esse/a**

destacar [dʒiʃta'ka*] *vt* (*MIL*) to detail; (*separar*) to detach; (*enfatizar*) to emphasize ♦ *vi* to stand out; **destacar-se** *vr* to stand out; (*pessoa*) to be outstanding

destampar [dʒiʃtã'pa*] *vt* to take the lid off

destapar [dʒiʃta'pa*] *vt* to uncover

destaque [dʒiʃ'taki] *m* distinction; (*pessoa, coisa*) highlight

deste, -a ['deʃtʃi, a] = **de** + **este, -a**

destemido, -a [deʃte'midu, a] *adj* fearless, intrepid

destilar [deʃtʃi'la*] *vt* to distil (*BRIT*),

destinação 414 **detetive**

distill (us)

destinação [deʃtʃina'sãw] (pl -ões) f destination

destinar [deʃtʃi'na*] vt to destine; (dinheiro): ~ (para) to set aside (for); **destinar-se** vr: ~-se a to be intended for; (carta) to be addressed to

destinatário, -a [deʃtʃina'tarju, a] m/f addressee

destino [deʃ'tʃinu] m destiny, fate; (lugar) destination; **com ~ a** bound for

destituir [deʃtʃi'twi*] vt to dismiss; ~ **de** (privar de) to deprive of

destrancar [dʒiʃtrã'ka*] vt to unlock

destratar [dʒiʃtra'ta*] vt to abuse, insult

destreza [deʃ'treza] f skill; (agilidade) dexterity

destro, -a ['deʃtru, a] adj skilful (BRIT), skillful (US); (ágil) agile; (não canhoto) right-handed

destrocar [dʒiʃtro'ka*] vt to give back, return

destroçar [dʒiʃtro'sa*] vt to destroy; (quebrar) to smash, break; **destroços** [dʒiʃ'trɔsuʃ] mpl wreckage sg

destruição [dʒiʃtrwi'sãw] f destruction

destruir [dʒiʃ'trwi*] vt to destroy

desvairado, -a [dʒiʒvaj'radu, a] adj (louco) crazy, demented; (desorientado) bewildered

desvalorizar [dʒiʒvalori'za*] vt to devalue

desvantagem [dʒiʒvã'taʒẽ] (pl -ns) f disadvantage

desvão [dʒiʒ'vãw] (pl -s) m loft

desventura [dʒiʒvẽ'tura] f misfortune; (infelicidade) unhappiness

desviar [dʒiʒ'vja*] vt to divert;

(golpe) to deflect; (dinheiro) to embezzle; **desviar-se** vr to turn away; ~-**se de** to avoid; ~ **os olhos** to look away

desvio [dʒiʒ'viu] m diversion, detour; (curva) bend; (fig) deviation; (de dinheiro) embezzlement

detalhadamente [detaʎada-'mẽtʃi] adv in detail

detalhado, -a [deta'ʎadu, a] adj detailed

detalhar [deta'ʎa*] vt to (give in) detail

detalhe [de'taʎi] m detail

detectar [detek'ta*] vt to detect

detective [detek'tiva] (PT) m/f = **detetive**

detector [detek'to*] m detector

detenção [detẽ'sãw] (pl -ões) f detention

deter [de'te*] (irreg: como ter) vt to stop; (prender) to arrest; (manter preso) to detain; (reter) to keep; (conter: riso) to contain; **deter-se** vr to stop; (ficar) to stay; (conter-se) to restrain o.s.

detergente [detex'ʒẽtʃi] m detergent

deteriorar [deterjo'ra*] vt to spoil, damage; **deteriorar-se** vr to deteriorate; (relações) to worsen

determinação [detexmina'sãw] f determination; (decisão) decision; (ordem) order

determinado, -a [detexmi'nadu, a] adj determined; (certo) certain, given

determinar [detexmi'na*] vt to determine; (decretar) to order; (resolver) to decide (on); (causar) to cause

detestar [deteʃ'ta*] vt to hate; **detestável** [deteʃ'tavew] (pl -eis) adj horrible, hateful

detetive [dete'tʃivi] m/f detective

detido, -a [de'tʃidu, a] adj (preso) under arrest; (minucioso) thorough ♦ m/f person under arrest, prisoner

detonação [detona'sãw] (pl -ões) f explosion

detonar [deto'na*] vt, vi to detonate

detrás [de'trajʃ] adv behind ♦ prep. ~ de behind

detrimento [detri'mẽtu] m: em ~ de to the detriment of

detrito [de'tritu] m debris sg; (de comida) remains pl; (resíduo) dregs pl

deturpação [detuxpa'sãw] f corruption; (de palavras) distortion

deturpar [detux'pa*] vt to corrupt; (desfigurar) to disfigure; (palavras) to twist

deu [dew] vb V dar

deus, a [dewʃ, dewsa] m/f god/goddess; D~ me livre! God forbid!; graças a D~ thank goodness; meu D~! good Lord!

devagar [dʒiva'ga*] adv slowly

devaneio [deva'neju] m daydream

devassa [de'vasa] f investigation, inquiry

devassidão [devasi'dãw] f debauchery

devasso, -a [de'vasu, a] adj dissolute

devastar [devaʃ'ta*] vt to devastate; (arruinar) to ruin

deve [ˈdɛvi] m debit

devedor, a [deve'do*, a] adj (pessoa) in debt ♦ m/f debtor

dever [de've*] m duty ♦ vt to owe ♦ vi (suposição): deve (de) estar doente he must be ill; (obrigação): devo partir às oito I must go at eight; você devia ir ao médico you should go to the doctor; que devo fazer? what shall I do?

devidamente [devida'mẽtʃi] adv

properly; (preencher formulário etc) duly

devido, -a [de'vidu, a] adj (maneira) proper; (respeito) due; ~ a due to, owing to; no ~ tempo in due course

devoção [dɛvɔ'sãw] f devotion

devolução [devolu'sãw] f devolution; (restituição) return; (reembolso) refund; ~ de impostos tax rebate

devolver [devow've*] vt to give back, return; (COM) to refund

devorar [devo'ra*] vt to devour; (destruir) to destroy

devotar [devo'ta*] vt to devote

dez [dɛʒ] num ten

dezanove [dɛza'nɔvɛ] (PT) num = dezenove

dezasseis [deza'sejʃ] (PT) num = dezesseis

dezassete [deza'setɛ] (PT) num = dezessete

dezembro [de'zẽbru] (PT D~) m December

dezena [de'zena] f: uma ~ de ... ten ...

dezenove [deze'nɔvi] num nineteen

dezesseis [deze'sejʃ] num sixteen

dezessete [dezi'setʃi] num seventeen

dezoito [dʒi'zojtu] num eighteen

dia ['dʒia] m day; (claridade) daylight; ~ a ~ day by day; ~ santo holy day; ~ útil weekday; estar ou andar em ~ (com) to be up to date (with); de ~ in the daytime, by day; mais ~ menos ~ sooner or later; ~ sim, ~ não every other day; no ~ seguinte the next day; bom ~ good morning; dia-a-dia m daily life, everyday life

diabete(s) [dʒia'betʃi(ʃ)] f diabetes sg; **diabético, -a** [dʒia'betʃiku, a] *adj, m* /'f/ diabetic

diabo ['dʒjabu] *m* devil; **que ~!** (*col*) damn it!

diabrura [dʒja'brura] *f* prank; **~s** *fpl* (*travessura*) mischief *sg*

diafragma [dʒja'fragma] *m* diaphragm

diagnóstico [dʒjag'nɔʃtʃiku] *m* diagnosis

diagonal [dʒjago'naw] (*pl* -ais) *adj*, *f* diagonal

diagrama [dʒja'grama] *m* diagram

dialeto [dʒja'letu] (*PT* -ect-) *m* dialect

dialogar [dʒjalo'ga*] *vi*: ~ (**com alguém**) to talk (to sb); (*POL*) to have *ou* hold talks (with sb)

diálogo ['dʒjalogu] *m* dialogue; (*conversa*) talk, conversation

diamante [dʒja'mãtʃi] *m* diamond

diâmetro ['dʒjametru] *m* diameter

diante ['dʒjãtʃi] *prep*: ~ **de** before; (*na frente de*) in front of; (*problemas etc*) in the face of; **e assim por** ~ and so on; **para** ~ forward

dianteira [dʒjã'tejra] *f* front, vanguard; **tomar a** ~ to get ahead

dianteiro, -a [dʒjã'tejru, a] *adj* front

diapositivo [dʒjapozi'tʃivu] *m* (*FOTO*) slide

diária ['dʒjarja] *f* (*de hotel*) daily rate

diário, -a ['dʒjarju, a] *adj* daily ♦ *m* diary; (*jornal*) (daily) newspaper; ~ **de bordo** (*AER*) logbook

diarréia [dʒja'xeja] *f* diarrhoea (*BRIT*), diarrhea (*US*)

dica ['dʒika] (*col*) *f* hint

dicionário [dʒisjo'narju] *m* dictionary

dieta ['dʒjeta] *f* diet; **fazer** ~ to be on a diet; (*começar*) to go on a diet

diferença [dʒife'rẽsa] *f* difference; **ela tem uma ~ comigo** she's got

something against me

diferenciar [dʒjiferẽ'sja*] *vt* to differentiate

diferente [dʒife'rẽtʃi] *adj* different; **estar ~ com alguém** to be at odds with sb

difícil [dʒi'fisiw] (*pl* -eis) *adj* difficult; (*improvável*) unlikely; **o ~ é ...** the difficult thing is ...; **acho ~ ela aceitar nossa proposta** I think it's unlikely she will accept our proposal; **dificilmente** [dʒifisiw'mẽtʃi] *adv* with difficulty; (*mal*) hardly; (*raramente*) hardly ever

dificuldade [dʒifikuw'dadʒi] *f* difficulty; (*aperto*): **em ~s** in trouble

dificultar [dʒifikuw'ta*] *vt* to make difficult; (*complicar*) to complicate

difundir [dʒifũ'dʒi*] *vt* to diffuse; (*boato, rumor*) to spread

digerir [dʒize'ri*] *vt, vi* to digest

digestão [dʒize'ʃtãw] *f* digestion

digital [dʒiʒi'taw] (*pl* -ais) *adj*: **impressão ~** fingerprint

digitar [dʒiʒi'ta*] *vt* (*COMPUT: dados*) to key (in)

dígito ['dʒiʒitu] *m* digit

dignidade [dʒigni'dadʒi] *f* dignity

digno, -a ['dʒignu, a] *adj* (*merecedor*) worthy; (*nobre*) dignified

digo *etc* ['dʒigu] *vb* V **dizer**

dilatar [dʒila'ta*] *vt* to dilate, expand; (*prolongar*) to prolong; (*retardar*) to delay

dilema [dʒi'lema] *m* dilemma

diluir [dʒi'lwi*] *vt* to dilute

dilúvio [dʒi'luvju] *m* flood

dimensão [dʒimẽ'sãw] (*pl* -ões) *f* dimension; **dimensões** *fpl* (*medidas*) measurements

diminuição [dʒiminwi'sãw] *f* reduction

diminuir [dʒimi'nwi*] *vt* to reduce; (*som*) to turn down; (*interesse*) to lessen ♦ *vi* to lessen, diminish;

(*preço*) to go down; (*dor*) to wear off; (*barulho*) to die down

diminutivo, -a [dʒiminuˈtʃivu, a] *adj* diminutive ♦ *m* (LING) diminutive

Dinamarca [dʒinaˈmaxka] *f* Denmark; **dinamarquês, -quesa** [dʒinamaxˈkeʃ, ˈkeza] *adj* Danish ♦ *m/f* Dane ♦ *m* (LING) Danish

dinâmico, -a [dʒiˈnamiku, a] *adj* dynamic

dínamo [ˈdʒinamu] *m* dynamo

dinheirão [dʒinejˈrãw] *m*: **um ~** loads *pl* of money

dinheiro [dʒiˈnejru] *m* money; **~ à vista** cash for paying in cash; **~ em caixa** money in the till; **~ em espécie** cash

dinossauro [dʒinoˈsawru] *m* dinosaur

diploma [dʒipˈlɔma] *m* diploma

diplomacia [dʒiplomaˈsia] *f* diplomacy; (*fig*) tact

diplomata [dʒiploˈmata] *m/f* diplomat; **diplomático, -a** [dʒiploˈmatʃiku, a] *adj* diplomatic

dique [ˈdʒiki] *m* dam; (GEO) dyke

direção [dʒireˈsãw] (PT -**cç**-; *pl* -**ões**) *f* direction; (*endereço*) address; (AUTO) steering; (*administração*) management; (*comando*) leadership; (*diretoria*) board of directors; **em ~ a** towards

directo, -a *etc* [diˈrɛktu, a] (PT) = **direto** *etc*

direi *etc* [dʒiˈrej] *vb* V **dizer**

direita [dʒiˈrejta] *f* (*mão*) right hand; (*lado*) right-hand side; (POL) right wing; **à ~ on** the right

direito, -a [dʒiˈrejtu, a] *adj* (*lado*) right-hand; (*mão*) right; (*honesto*) honest; (*devido*) proper; (*justo*) right, just ♦ *m* right; (JUR) law ♦ *adv* straight; (*bem*) right; (*de maneira certa*) properly; **~s** *mpl* (*humanos*) rights; (*alfandegários*)

duty *sg*

direto, -a [dʒiˈrɛtu, a] *adj* direct ♦ *adv* straight; **transmissão direta** (TV) live broadcast

diretor, a [dʒireˈto*, a] *adj* directing, guiding ♦ *m/f* director; (*de jornal*) editor; (*de escola*) head teacher; **diretoria** [dʒiretoˈria] *f* (COM) management

dirigente [dʒiriˈʒẽtʃi] *m/f* (*de país, partido*) leader; (*diretor*) director; (*gerente*) manager

dirigir [dʒiriˈʒi*] *vt* to direct; (COM) to manage; (*veículo*) to drive ♦ *vi* (AUTO) to drive; **dirigir-se** *vr*: **~-se a** (*falar com*) to speak to; (*ir, recorrer*) to go to; (*esforços*) to be directed towards

discagem [dʒiʃˈkaʒẽ] *f* (TEL) dialling

discar [dʒiʃˈka*] *vt* to dial

disciplina [dʒisiˈplina] *f* discipline; **disciplinar** [dʒisipliˈna*] *vt* to discipline

discípulo, -a [dʒiˈsipulu, a] *m/f* disciple; (*aluno*) pupil

disc-jóquei [dʒiʃk-] *m/f* disc jockey, DJ

disco [ˈdʒiʃku] *m* disc; (COMPUT) disk; (MÚS) record; (*de telefone*) dial; **~ laser** (*máquina*) compact disc player, CD player; (*disco*) compact disc, CD; **~ flexível/rígido** (COMPUT) floppy/hard disk; **~ do sistema** system disk; **~ voador** flying saucer

discordar [dʒiʃkoxˈda*] *vi*: **~ de alguém em algo** to disagree with sb on sth

discórdia [dʒiʃˈkoxdʒia] *f* discord, strife

discoteca [dʒiʃkoˈteka] *f* discotheque, disco

discrepância [dʒiʃkreˈpãsja] *f* discrepancy; (*desacordo*) disagreement; **discrepante** [dʒiʃkreˈpãtʃi] *adj* conflicting

discreto, -a [dʒiʃ'kretu, a] *adj* discreet; (*modesto*) modest; (*prudente*) shrewd; (*roupa*) plain; **discrição** [dʒiʃkri'sãw] *f* discretion

discriminação [dʒiʃkrimina'sãw] *f* discrimination

discriminar [dʒiʃkrimi'na*] *vt* to distinguish ♦ *vi*: ~ **entre** to discriminate between

discurso [dʒiʃ'kuxsu] *m* speech

discussão [dʒiʃku'sãw] (*pl* -ões) *f* discussion; (*contenda*) argument

discutir [dʒiʃku'tʃi*] *vt* to discuss ♦ *vi*: ~ (**sobre algo**) to talk (about sth); (*contender*) to argue (about sth)

disenteria [dʒizẽte'ria] *f* dysentery

disfarçar [dʒiʃfax'sa*] *vt* to disguise ♦ *vi* to pretend; **disfarçar-se** ~ **se em** *ou* **de algo** to disguise o.s. as sth; **disfarce** [dʒiʃ'faxsi] *m* disguise; (*máscara*) mask

dislexia [dʒiʃlek'sja] *f* dyslexia

disparar [dʒiʃpa'ra*] *vt* to shoot, fire ♦ *vi* to fire; (*arma*) to go off; (*correr*) to shoot off, bolt

disparatado, -a [dʒiʃpara'tadu, a] *adj* silly, absurd

disparate [dʒiʃpa'ratʃi] *m* nonsense, rubbish

disparidade [dʒiʃpari'dadʒi] *f* disparity

dispensar [dʒiʃpẽ'sa*] *vt* to excuse; (*prescindir de*) to do without; (*conferir*) to grant; **dispensável** [dʒiʃpẽ'savew] (*pl* -eis) *adj* expendable

dispersar [dʒiʃpex'sa*] *vt, vi* to disperse; **disperso, -a** [dʒiʃ'pexsu, a] *adj* scattered

displicência [dʒiʃpli'sẽsja] (*BR*) *f* negligence, carelessness; **displicente** [dʒiʃpli'sẽtʃi] *adj* careless

dispo *etc* ['dʒiʃpu] *vb* V **despir**

disponível [dʒiʃpo'nivew] (*pl* -eis)

adj available

dispor [dʒiʃ'po*] (*irreg: como* **pôr**) *vt* to arrange ♦ *vi*: ~ **de** to have the use of; (*ter*) to have, own; (*pessoas*) to have at one's disposal; **dispor-se** *vr*: ~**se a** (*estar pronto a*) to be prepared to, be willing to; (*decidir*) to decide to; ~ **sobre** to talk about; **disponha!** feel free!

disposição [dʒiʃpozi'sãw] (*pl* -ões) *f* arrangement; (*humor*) disposition; (*inclinação*) inclination; **à sua** ~ at your disposal

dispositivo [dʒiʃpozi'tʃivu] *m* gadget, device; (*determinação de lei*) provision

disposto, -a [dʒiʃ'poʃtu, 'poʃta] *adj*: **estar** ~ **a** to be willing to; **estar bem** ~ to look well

disputa [dʒiʃ'puta] *f* dispute, argument; (*competição*) contest; **disputar** [dʒiʃpu'ta*] *vt* to dispute; (*concorrer a*) to compete for; (*lutar por*) to fight over ♦ *vi* to quarrel, argue; to compete; **disputar uma corrida** to run a race

disquete [dʒiʃ'ketʃi] *m* (*COMPUT*) floppy disk, diskette

disse *etc* ['dʒisi] *vb* V **dizer**

disseminar [dʒisemi'na*] *vt* to disseminate; (*espalhar*) to spread

dissertar [dʒisex'ta*] *vi* to speak

dissidência [dʒisi'dẽsja] *f* (*cisão*) difference of opinion

disso ['dʒisu] = **de** + **isso**

dissolução [dʒisolu'sãw] *f* (*libertinagem*) debauchery; (*de casamento*) dissolution

dissolver [dʒisow've*] *vt* to dissolve; (*dispersar*) to disperse; (*motim*) to break up

dissuadir [dʒiswa'dʒi*] *vt* to dissuade; ~ **alguém de fazer algo** to talk sb out of doing sth, dissuade sb from doing sth

distância [dʒiʃ'tãsja] f distance; **a 3 quilómetros de ~** 3 kilometres (BRIT) ou kilometers (US) away

distanciar [dʒiʃtã'sja*] vt to distance, set apart; (colocar por intervalos) to space out; **distanciar-se** vr to move away; (fig) to distance o.s.

distante [dʒiʃ'tãtʃi] adj distant

distender [dʒiʃtẽ'de*] vt to expand; (estirar) to stretch; (dilatar) to distend; (músculo) to pull; **distender-se** vr to expand; to distend

distinção [dʒiʃtʃĩ'sãw] (pl -ões) f distinction; **fazer a ~** to make a distinction

distinguir [dʒiʃtʃĩ'gi*] vt to distinguish; (avistar, ouvir) to make out; **distinguir-se** vr to stand out

distintivo, -a [dʒiʃtʃĩ'tʃivu, a] adj distinctive ♦ m (insígnia) badge; (emblema) emblem

distinto, -a [dʒiʃ'tʃĩtu, a] adj different; (eminente) distinguished; (claro) distinct; (refinado) refined

disto ['dʒiʃtu] = **de** + **isto**

distorcer [dʒiʃtox'se*] vt to distort

distração [dʒiʃtra'sãw] (PT -cç-; pl -ões) f (alheamento) absent-mindedness; (divertimento) pastime; (descuido) oversight

distraído, -a [dʒiʃtra'idu, a] adj absent-minded; (não atento) inattentive

distrair [dʒiʃtra'i*] vt to distract; (divertir) to amuse

distribuição [dʒiʃtribwi'sãw] f distribution; (de cartas) delivery

distribuidor, a [dʒiʃtribwi'do*, a] m/f distributor ♦ m (AUTO) distributor ♦ f (COM) distribution company, distributor

distribuir [dʒiʃtri'bwi*] vt to distribute; (repartir) to share out; (cartas) to deliver

distrito [dʒiʃ'tritu] m district; (dele-

gacia) police station; **~ eleitoral** constituency; **~ federal** federal area

distúrbio [dʒiʃ'tuxbju] m disturbance

ditado [dʒi'tadu] m dictation; (provérbio) saying

ditador [dʒita'do*] m dictator; **ditadura** [dʒita'dura] f dictatorship

ditar [dʒi'ta*] vt to dictate; (impor) to impose

dito, -a ['dʒitu, a] pp de **dizer**; **~ e feito** no sooner said than done

DIU abr m (= dispositivo intra-uterino) IUD

diurno, -a ['dʒjuxnu, a] adj daytime atr

divã [dʒi'vã] m couch, divan

divergir [dʒivex'ʒi*] vi to diverge; (discordar): **~ (de alguém)** to disagree (with sb)

diversão [dʒivex'sãw] (pl -ões) f amusement; (passatempo) pastime

diverso, -a [dʒi'vexsu, a] adj different; **~s** various, several

diversões [dʒivex'sõjʃ] fpl de **diversão**

diversos [dʒi'vexsuʃ] mpl (COM) sundries

divertido, -a [dʒivex'tʃidu, a] adj amusing, funny

divertimento [dʒivextʃi'mẽtu] m amusement, entertainment

divertir [dʒivex'tʃi*] vt to amuse, entertain; **divertir-se** vr to enjoy o.s., have a good time

dívida ['dʒivida] f debt; **contrair ~s** to run into debt; **~ externa** foreign debt

dividir [dʒivi'dʒi*] vt to divide; (despesas, lucro, comida etc) to share; (separar) to separate ♦ vi (MAT) to divide; **dividir-se** vr to divide, split up

divindade [dʒivĩ'dadʒi] f divinity

divino, -a [dʒi'vinu, a] adj divine

♦ *m* Holy Ghost

divirjo [dʒi'virʒu] *vb V* **divergir**

divisa [dʒi'viza] *f* emblem; (*frase*) slogan; (*fronteira*) border; (MIL) stripe; **~s** *fpl* (*câmbio*) foreign exchange *sg*

divisão [dʒivi'zāw] (*pl* **-ões**) *f* division; (*discórdia*) split; (*partilha*) sharing

divisões [dʒivi'zōjʃ] *fpl* de **divisão**

divisória [dʒivi'zɔrja] *f* partition

divorciado, -a [dʒivox'sjadu, a] *adj* divorced ♦ *m/f* divorciado(e)

divorciar [dʒivox'sja*] *vt* to divorce; **divorciar-se** *vr* to get divorced; **divórcio** [dʒi'vɔxsju] *m* divorce

divulgar [dʒivuw'ga*] *vt* (*notícias*) to spread; (*segredo*) to divulge; (*produto*) to market; (*livro*) to publish; **divulgar-se** *vr* to leak out

dizer [dʒi'ze*] *vt* to say ♦ *m* saying; **dizer-se** *vr* to claim to be; **diz-se** ou **dizem que** ... it is said that ...; **~ algo a alguém** to tell sb sth; (*falar*) to say sth to sb; **~ a alguém que** ... to tell sb that ...; **o que você diz da minha sugestão?** what do you think of my suggestion?; **querer ~** to mean; **quer ~** that is to say; **digo** (*ou seja*) I mean; **não diga!** you don't say!; **por assim ~** so to speak; **até ~ chega** as much as possible

do [du] = **de +o**

doação [doa'sāw] (*pl* **-ões**) *f* donation

doador, a [doa'do*, a] *m/f* donor

doar [do'a*] *vt* to donate, give

dobra ['dɔbra] *f* fold; (*prega*) pleat; (*de calças*) turn-up

dobradiça [dobra'dʒisa] *f* hinge

dobradinha [dobra'dʒiɲa] *f* (CULIN) tripe stew

dobrar [do'bra*] *vt* to double;

(*papel*) to fold; (*joelho*) to bend; (*esquina*) to turn, go round; (*fazer ceder*): **~ alguém** to talk sb round ♦ *vi* to double; (*sino*) to toll; (*vergar*) to bend; **dobrar-se** *vr* to double (up)

dobro ['dobru] *m* double

doce ['dosi] *adj* sweet; (*terno*) gentle ♦ *m* sweet

dóceis ['dɔsejʃ] *adj pl* de **dócil**

dócil ['dɔsiw] (*pl* **-eis**) *adj* docile

documentação [dokumēta'sāw] *f* documentation; (*documentos*) papers *pl*

documentário, -a [dokumē'tarju, a] *adj* documentary ♦ *m* documentary

documento [doku'mētu] *m* document

doçura [do'sura] *f* sweetness; (*brandura*) gentleness

doença [do'ēsa] *f* illness

doente [do'ētʃi] *adj* ill, sick ♦ *m/f* sick person; (*cliente*) patient

doentio, -a [doē'tʃiu, a] *adj* (*pessoa*) sickly; (*clima*) unhealthy; (*curiosidade*) morbid

doer [do'e*] *vi* to hurt, ache; **~ a alguém** (*pesar*) to grieve sb

doido, -a ['dojdu, a] *adj* mad, crazy ♦ *m/f* madman/woman

doído, -a [do'idu, a] *adj* painful; (*moralmente*) hurt; (*que causa dor*) painful

dois, duas [dojʃ, 'duaʃ] *num* two; **conversa a ~** tête-à-tête

dólar ['dɔla*] *m* dollar; **~ oficial/paralelo** dollar at the official/black-market rate; **~-turismo** dollar at the special tourist rate; **doleiro, -a** [do'lejru, a] *m/f* (*black market*) dollar dealer

dolorido, -a [dolo'ridu, a] *adj* painful, sore

doloroso, -a [dolo'rozu, ɔza] *adj*

painful

dom [dõ] *m* gift; (*aptidão*) knack

domar [do'ma*] *vt* to tame

doméstica [do'mɛʃtʃika] *f* maid

domesticado, -a [domeʃtʃi'kadu, a] *adj* domesticated; (*manso*) tame

domesticar [domeʃtʃi'ka*] *vt* to domesticate; (*povo*) to tame

doméstico, -a [do'mɛʃtʃiku, a] *adj* domestic; (*vida*) home *atr*

domicílio [domi'silju] *m* home, residence; **"entregamos a ~"** "we deliver"

dominador, a [domina'do*, a] *adj* (*pessoa*) domineering; (*olhar*) imposing ♦ *m/f* ruler

dominante [domi'nãtʃi] *adj* dominant; (*predominante*) predominant

dominar [domi'na*] *vt* to dominate; (*reprimir*) to overcome ♦ *vi* to dominate; **dominar-se** *vr* to control o.s.

domingo [do'mĩgu] *m* Sunday

domínio [do'minju] *m* power; (*dominação*) control; (*território*) domain; (*esfera*) sphere; **~ próprio** self-control

dona [ˈdɔna] *f* owner; (*col: mulher*) lady; **~ de casa** housewife; **D~** Lígia Lígia; **D~ Luísa Souza** Mrs Luísa Souza

donde [ˈdõdʒi] (*PT*) *adv* from where; (*daí*) thus

dono [ˈdonu] *m* owner

dopar [do'pa*] *vt* to drug

dor [do*] *f* ache; (*aguda*) pain; (*fig*) grief, sorrow; **~ de cabeça/dentes/estômago** headache/toothache/stomachache

dormente [dox'mẽtʃi] *adj* numb ♦ *m* (*FERRO*) sleeper

dormir [dox'mi*] *vi* to sleep; **~ fora** to spend the night away

dormitório [doxmi'tɔrju] *m* bed-room; (*coletivo*) dormitory

dorso [ˈdoxsu] *m* back

dos [duʃ] = **de + os**

dosagem [do'zaʒẽ] *m* dosage

dose [ˈdɔzi] *f* dose

dossiê [do'sje] *m* dossier, file

dotado, -a [do'tadu, a] *adj* gifted; **~ de** endowed with

dotar [do'ta*] *vt* to endow

doze [ˈdozi] *vt* V **dar**

dou [do] *vb* V **dar**

dourado, -a [do'radu, a] *adj* golden; (*com camada de ouro*) gilt ♦ *m* gilt

doutor, a [do'to*, a] *m/f* doctor; **D~** (*forma de tratamento*) Sir; **D~ Eduardo Souza** Mr Eduardo Souza

doutrina [do'trina] *f* doctrine

doze [ˈdozi] *num* twelve

Dr(a). *abr* (= *Doutor(a)*) Dr.

dragão [dra'gãw] (*pl* **-ões**) *m* drag-on

dragões [dra'gõjʃ] *mpl de* **dragão**

drama [ˈdrama] *m* drama; **dramático, -a** [dra'matʃiku, a] *adj* dramatic; **dramatizar** [dramatʃi'za*] *vt, vi* to dramatize

drástico, -a [ˈdraʃtʃiku, a] *adj* drastic

dreno [ˈdrenu] *m* drain

driblar [dri'bla*] *vt, vi* (*FUTEBOL*) to dribble

drinque [ˈdrĩki] *m* drink

droga [ˈdrɔga] *f* drug; (*fig*) rubbish; **drogado, -a** [dro'gadu, a] *m/f* drug addict; **drogar** [dro'ga*] *vt* to drug; **drogar-se** *vr* to take drugs

drogaria [droga'ria] *f* chemist's shop (*BRIT*), drugstore (*US*)

DTP *abr m* (= *desktop publishing*) DTP

duas [ˈduaʃ] *f de* **dois**

dublê [du'ble] *m/f* double

ducha [ˈduʃa] *f* shower

dueto [ˈdwetu] *m* duet

duna [ˈduna] *f* dune

dupla ['dupla] *f* pair; (ESPORTE): ~ **masculina/feminina/mista** men's/women's/mixed doubles

duplicar [dupli'ka*] *vt* to duplicate ♦ *vi* to double; **duplicata** [dupli'kata] *f* duplicate; (título) trade note, bill

duplo, -a ['duplu, a] *adj* double ♦ *m* double

duque ['duki] *m* duke

duração [dura'sãw] *f* duration; **de pouca ~** short-lived

duradouro, -a [dura'doru, a] *adj* lasting

durante [du'rãtʃi] *prep* during; ~ **uma hora** for an hour

durar [du'ra*] *vi* to last

durável [du'ravew] (*pl* **-eis**) *adj* lasting

durex [du'rεks] ® *adj*: **fita ~** adhesive tape, sellotape ® (BRIT), scotchtape ® (US)

durmo *etc* ['duxmu] *vb V* **dormir**

duro, -a ['duru, a] *adj* hard; (severo) harsh; (resistente, fig) tough; **estar ~** (col) to be broke

dúvida ['duvida] *f* doubt; **sem ~** undoubtedly, without a doubt; **duvidar** [duvi'da*] *vt* to doubt ♦ *vi* to have one's doubts; **duvidar de alguém/algo** to doubt sb/sth; **duvidar que** ... to doubt that ...; **duvido!** I doubt it!; **duvidoso, -a** [duvi'dozu, ɔza] *adj* doubtful; (suspeito) dubious

duzentos, -as [du'zẽtuf, aʃ] *num* two hundred

dúzia ['duzja] *f* dozen; **meia ~** half a dozen

DVD *abr m* (= *disco digital versátil*) DVD

dz. *abr* = **dúzia**

E

e [i] *conj* and; **~ a bagagem?** what about the luggage?

é [ε] *vb V* **ser**

ébano ['εbanu] *m* ebony

eclipse [e'klipsi] *m* eclipse

eco ['εku] *m* echo; **ter ~** to catch on; **ecoar** [e'kwa*] *vt* to echo ♦ *vi* (ressoar) to echo

ecologia [ekolo'ʒia] *f* ecology

economia [ekono'mia] *f* economy; (ciência) economics *sg*; **~s** *fpl* (poupanças) savings; **fazer ~ (de)** to economize (with)

econômico, -a [eko'nomiku, a] *adj* economical; (pessoa) thrifty; (COM) economic

economizar [ekonomi'za*] *vt* (gastar com economia) to economize on; (poupar) to save (up) ♦ *vi* to economize; to save up

écran ['εkrã] (PT) *m* screen

ECU *abr m* ECU

edição [edʒi'sãw] (*pl* **-ões**) *f* publication; (conjunto de exemplares) edition; (TV, CINEMA) editing

edifício [edʒi'fisju] *m* building; **~ garagem** multistorey car park (BRIT), multistory parking lot (US)

Edimburgo [edʒi'buxgu] *n* Edinburgh

editar [edʒi'ta*] *vt* to publish; (COMPUT etc) to edit

editor, a [edʒi'to*, a] *adj* publishing *atr* ♦ *m/f* publisher; (redator) editor ♦ *f* publishing company; **casa ~a** publishing house; **editoração** [edʒitora'sãw] *f*: **editoração eletrônica** desktop publishing; **editorial** [edʒitor'jaw] (*pl* **-ais**) *adj* publishing *atr* ♦ *m* editorial

edredão [adrə'dãw] (*pl* **-ões**) (PT) *m* = **edredom**

edredom [edre'dõ] (*pl* **-ns**) *m* eiderdown

educação [eduka'sãw] f education; (criação) upbringing; (de animais) training; (maneiras) good manners pl; **educacional** [edukasjo'naw] (pl -ais) adj education atr

educar [edu'ka*] vt to educate; (criar) to bring up; (animal) to train

efectivo, -a etc [efek'tivu, a] (PT) adj = efetivo etc

efectuar [efek'twa*] (PT) vt = efetuar

efeito [e'fejtu] m effect; **fazer ~** to work; **levar a ~** to put into effect; **com ~** indeed

efeminado [efemi'nadu] adj effeminate

efervescente [efexve'sẽtʃi] adj fizzy

efetivamente [efetʃiva'mẽtʃi] adv effectively; (realmente) really, in fact

efetivo, -a [efe'tʃivu, a] adj effective; (real) actual, real; (cargo, funcionário) permanent

efetuar [efe'twa*] vt to carry out; (soma) to do, perform

eficácia [efi'kasja] f (de pessoa) efficiency; (de tratamento) effectiveness

eficaz [efi'kaʒ] adj (pessoa) efficient; (tratamento) effective

eficiência [efi'sjẽsja] f efficiency; **eficiente** [efi'sjẽtʃi] adj efficient

egípcio, -a [e'ʒipsju, a] adj, m/f Egyptian

Egito [e'ʒitu] (PT -pt-) m: **o ~** Egypt

egoísmo [ego'iʒmu] m selfishness, egoism; **egoísta** [ego'ifta] adj selfish, egoistic ♦ m/f egoist

égua ['ɛgwa] f mare

ei [ej] excl hey!

ei-lo etc = **eis** + **o**

eis [ejʃ] adv (sg) here is; (pl) here are; **~ aí** there is; there are

eixo ['ejʃu] m (de rodas) axle; (MAT)

axis; (de máquina) shaft; **~ de transmissão** drive shaft

ejacular [eʒaku'la*] vt (sêmen) to ejaculate; (líquido) to spurt ♦ vi to ejaculate

ela ['ɛla] pron (pessoa) she; (coisa) it; (com prep) her; it; **~s** fpl they; (com prep) them; **~s por ~s** (col) tit for tat

elaboração [elabora'sãw] (pl -ões) f (de uma teoria) working out; (preparo) preparation

elaborar [elabo'ra*] vt to prepare; (fazer) to make; (teoria) to work out

elástico, -a [e'laʃtʃiku, a] adj elastic; (flexível) flexible; (colchão) springy ♦ m elastic band

ele ['eli] pron he; (coisa) it; (com prep) him; it; **~s** mpl they; (com prep) them

electri... etc [elektri] (PT) = **eletri...** etc

eléctrico, -a [e'lɛktriku, a] (PT) adj = **elétrico** ♦ m tram (BRIT), streetcar (US)

electro... etc [elektru] (PT) = **eletro...** etc

eléctrodo [e'lɛktrodu] (PT) m = **eletrodo**

elefante, -ta [ele'fãtʃi, ta] m/f elephant

elegante [ele'gãtʃi] adj elegant; (da moda) fashionable

eleger [ele'ʒe*] vt to elect; (escolher) to choose

eleição [elej'sãw] (pl -ões) f election; (escolha) choice

eleito, -a [e'lejtu, a] pp de **eleger** ♦ adj elected; chosen

eleitor, a [elej'to*, a] m/f voter

elejo etc [e'leʒu] vb V **eleger**

elementar [elemẽ'ta*] adj elementary; (fundamental) basic, fundamental

elemento [ele'mẽtu] m element;

(*parte*) component; (*recurso*) means; (*informação*) grounds *pl*; **~s** *mpl* (*rudimentos*) rudiments

elenco [e'lẽku] *m* list; (*de atores*) cast

eletricidade [eletrisi'dadʒi] *f* electricity

eletricista [eletri'siʃta] *m/f* electrician

elétrico, -a [e'lɛtriku, a] *adj* electric; (*fig: agitado*) worked up

eletrificar [eletrifi'ka*] *vt* to electrify

eletrizar [eletri'za*] *vt* to electrify; (*fig*) to thrill

eletro... [eletru] *prefixo* electro...; **eletrocutar** [eletroku'ta*] *vt* to electrocute; **eletrodo** [ele'trodu] *m* electrode; **eletrodomésticos** [eletrodo'meʃtʃikuʃ] (*BR*) *mpl* (electrical) household appliances

eletrônica [ele'tronika] *f* electronics *sg*

eletrônico, -a [ele'troniku, a] *adj* electronic

elevação [eleva'sãw] (*pl* **-ões**) *f* (*ARQ*) elevation; (*aumento*) rise; (*ato*) raising; (*altura*) height; (*promoção*) promotion; (*ponto elevado*) bump

elevador [eleva'do*] *m* lift (*BRIT*), elevator (*US*)

elevar [ele'va*] *vt* to lift up; (*voz, preço*) to raise; (*exaltar*) to exalt; (*promover*) to promote; **elevar-se** *vr* to rise

eliminar [elimi'na*] *vt* to remove; (*suprimir*) to delete; (*possibilidade*) to rule out; (*MED, banir*) to expel; (*ESPORTE*) to eliminate; **eliminatória** [elimina'tɔrja] *f* (*ESPORTE*) heat, preliminary round; (*exame*) test

elite [e'litʃi] *f* elite

elogiar [elo'ʒja*] *vt* to praise; **elogio** [elo'ʒiu] *m* praise; (*cumprimento*) compliment

El Salvador [ew-] *n* El Salvador

PALAVRA CHAVE

em [ẽ] (*em* + *o*(*s*)/*a*(*s*) = *no*(*s*)/*na*(*s*); + *ele*(*s*)/*a*(*s*) = *nele*(*s*)/*a*(*s*); + *esse*(*s*)/*a*(*s*) = *nesse*(*s*)/*a*(*s*); + *isso* = *nisso*; + *este*(*s*)/*a*(*s*) = *neste*(*s*)/*a*(*s*); + *isto* = *nisto*; + *aquele*(*s*)/*a*(*s*) = *naquele*(*s*)/*a*(*s*); + *aquilo* = *naquilo*) *prep* **1** (*posição*) in; (: *sobre*) on; **está na gaveta/no bolso** it's in the drawer/pocket; **está na mesa/no chão** it's on the table/floor

2 (*lugar*) in; (: *casa, escritório etc*) at; (: *andar, meio de transporte*) on; **no Brasil/em São Paulo** in Brazil/São Paulo; **~ casa/no dentista** at home/the dentist; **no avião** on the plane; **no quinto andar** on the fifth floor

3 (*ação*) into; **ela entrou na sala de aula** she went into the classroom; **colocar algo no bolso** to put sth into one's bag

4 (*tempo*) in, on; **~ 1962/3 semanas** in 1962/3 weeks; **no inverno** in the winter; **~ janeiro, no mês de janeiro** in January; **nessa ocasião/altura** on that occasion/at that time; **~ breve** soon

5 (*diferença*): **reduzir/aumentar ~ um 20%** to reduce/increase by 20%

6 (*modo*): **escrito ~ inglês** written in English

7 (*após vb que indica gastar etc*) on; **a metade do seu salário vai ~ comida** he spends half his salary on food

8 (*tema, ocupação*): **especialista no assunto** expert on the subject; **ele trabalha na construção civil** he works in the building industry

emagrecer [imagre'se*] *vt* to make thin ♦ *vi* to grow thin; (*mediante regime*) to slim; **emagrecimento**

[imagreʃi'mẽtu] m (mediante regime) slimming

emaranhado, -a [imara'naḍu, a] adj tangled ♦ m tangle

embaixada [ẽbaj'faḍa] f embassy

embaixador, a [ẽbajʃa'do*, a] m/f ambassador

embaixatriz [ẽbajʃa'trɪʒ] f ambassador; (mulher de embaixador) ambassador's wife

embaixo [ẽ'bajʃu] adv below, underneath ♦ prep: ~ **de** under, underneath; (lá) ~ (em andar inferior) downstairs

embalagem [ẽba'laʒẽ] f packing; (de produto: caixa etc) packaging

embalar [ẽba'la*] vt to pack; (balançar) to rock

embaraçar [ẽbara'sa*] vt to hinder; (complicar) to complicate; (encabular) to embarrass; (confundir) to confuse; (obstruir) to block; **embaraçar-se** vr to become embarrassed

embaraço [ẽba'rasu] m hindrance; (cábula) embarrassment; **embaraçoso, -a** [ẽbara'sozu, ɔza] adj embarrassing

embarcação [ẽbaxka'sãw] (pl -ões) f vessel

embarcar [ẽbax'ka*] vt to embark, put on board; (mercadorias) to ship, stow ♦ vi to go on board, embark

embarque [ẽ'baxki] m (de pessoas) boarding, embarkation; (de mercadorias) shipment

embebedar [ẽbebe'da*] vt to make drunk ♦ vi: **o vinho embebeda** wine makes you drunk; **embebedar-se** vr to get drunk

embelezar [ẽbele'za*] vt to make beautiful; (casa) to brighten up; **embelezar-se** vr to make o.s. beautiful

emblema [ẽ'blɛma] m emblem; (na roupa) badge

êmbolo [ẽ'bolu] m piston

embolsar [ẽbow'sa*] vt to pocket; (herança) to come into; (indenizar) to refund

embora [ẽ'bɔra] conj though, although ♦ excl even so; **ir(-se)** ~ to go away

emboscada [ẽboʃ'kaḍa] f ambush

embriagar [ẽbrja'ga*] vt to make drunk, intoxicate; **embriagar-se** vr to get drunk; **embriaguez** [ẽbrja-'geʒ] f drunkenness; (fig) rapture

embrião [e'brjãw] (pl -ões) m embryo

embromar [ẽbro'ma*] vt (udiar) to put off; (enganar) to cheat ♦ vi (prometer e não cumprir) to make empty promises, be all talk (and no action); (protelar) to stall; (falar em rodeios) to beat about the bush

embrulhar [ẽbru'ʎa*] vt (pacote) to wrap; (enrolar) to roll up; (confundir) to muddle up; (enganar) to cheat; (estômago) to upset; **embrulhar-se** vr to get into a muddle

embrulho [ẽ'bruʎu] m package, parcel; (confusão) mix-up

emburrar [ẽbu'xa*] vi to sulk

embutido, -a [ẽbu'tʃiḍu, a] adj (armário) built-in, fitted

emenda [e'mẽḍa] f correction; (de lei) amendment; (de uma pessoa) improvement; (ligação) join; (sambladura) joint; (costura) seam

emendar [emẽ'da*] vt to correct; (reparar) to mend; (injustiças) to make amends for; (lei) to amend; (ajuntar) to put together; **emendar-se** vr to mend one's ways

ementa [e'mẽta] (PT) f menu

emergência [imex'ʒẽsja] f emergence; (crise) emergency

emigrado, -a [emi'gradu, a] *adj* emigrant

emigrante [emi'grãtʃi] *m/f* emigrant

emigrar [emi'gra*] *vi* to emigrate; (*aves*) to migrate

eminência [emi'nẽsja] *f* eminence; (*altura*) height; **eminente** [emi'nẽtʃi] *adj* eminent, distinguished; (*GEO*) high

emissão [emi'sãw] (*pl -ões*) *f* emission; (*RÁDIO*) broadcast; (*de moeda, ações*) issue

emissário, -a [emi'sarju, a] *m/f* emissary ♦ *m* outlet

emissões [emi'sõjʃ] *fpl de* **emissão**

emissor, a [emi'so*, a] *adj* (*de moeda-papel*) issuing ♦ *m* (*RÁDIO*) transmitter ♦ *f* (*estação*) broadcasting station; (*empresa*) broadcasting company

emitir [emi'tʃi*] *vt* (*som*) to give out; (*cheiro*) to give off; (*moeda, ações*) to issue; (*RÁDIO*) to broadcast; (*opinião*) to express ♦ *vi* (*emitir moeda*) to print money

emoção [emo'sãw] (*pl -ões*) *f* emotion; (*excitação*) excitement; **emocional** [imosjo'naw] (*pl -ais*) *adj* emotional; **emocionante** [imosjo-'nãtʃi] *adj* moving; exciting; **emocionar** [imosjo'na*] *vt* to move; (*perturbar*) to upset; (*excitar*) to excite, thrill ♦ *vi* to be exciting; (*comover*) to be moving; **emocionar-se** *vr* to get emotional

emotivo, -a [emo'tʃivu, a] *adj* emotional

empacotar [empako'ta*] *vt* to pack, wrap up

empada [ẽ'pada] *f* pie

empadão [ẽpa'dãw] (*pl -ões*) *m* pie

empalidecer [ẽpalide'se*] *vi* to turn pale

empanturrar [ẽpãtu'xa*] *vt:* ~

alguém de algo to stuff sb full of sth

empatar [ẽpa'ta*] *vt* to hinder; (*dinheiro*) to tie up; (*no jogo*) to draw; (*tempo*) to take up ♦ *vi* (*no jogo*): ~ (**com**) to draw (with); **empate** [ẽ'patʃi] *m* draw; tie; (*XADREZ*) stalemate; (*em negociações*) deadlock

empecilho [ẽpe'siʎu] *m* obstacle; (*col*) snag

empenhar [ẽpe'ɲa*] *vt* (*objeto*) to pawn; (*palavra*) to pledge; (*empregar*) to exert; (*compelir*) to oblige; **empenhar-se** *vr:* ~-**se em fazer** to strive to do, do one's utmost to do; **empenho** [ẽ'peɲu] *m* pawning; pledge; (*insistência*): **empenho (em)** commitment (to)

empilhar [ẽpi'ʎa*] *vt* to pile up

empinado, -a [ẽpi'nadu, a] *adj* upright; (*cavalo*) rearing; (*colina*) steep

empinar [ẽpi'na*] *vt* to raise, uplift

empobrecer [ẽpobre'se*] *vt* to impoverish ♦ *vi* to become poor; **empobrecimento** [ẽpobresi-'mẽtu] *m* impoverishment

empolgação [ẽpowga'sãw] *f* excitement; (*entusiasmo*) enthusiasm

empolgante [ẽpow'gãtʃi] *adj* exciting

empolgar [ẽpow'ga*] *vt* to stimulate, fill with enthusiasm; (*prender a atenção de*): ~ **alguém** to keep sb riveted

empossar [ẽpo'sa*] *vt* to appoint

empreendedor, a [ẽprjede'do*, a] *adj* enterprising ♦ *m/f* entrepreneur

empreender [ẽprje'de*] *vt* to undertake; **empreendimento** [ẽprjedʒi'mẽtu] *m* undertaking

empregada [ẽpre'gada] *f* (*BR:* doméstica) maid; (*PT: de restaurante*) waitress; *V tb* **empregado**

empregado, -a [ẽpre'gadu, a] *m/f*

employee; (*em escritório*) clerk ♦ *m* (*PT: de restaurante*) waiter

empregador, a [ẽprega'do*, a] *m/f* employer

empregar [ẽpre'ga*] *vt* (*pessoa*) to employ; (*coisa*) to use; **empregar-se** *vr* to get a job

emprego [ẽ'pregu] *m* job; (*uso*) use

empreiteiro [ẽprej'tejru] *m* contractor

empresa [ẽ'preza] *f* undertaking; (*COM*) enterprise, firm; **empresário, -a** [ẽpre'zarju, a] *m/f* businessman/woman; (*de cantor, boxeador etc*) manager

emprestado, -a [ẽpreʃ'tadu, a] *adj* on loan; **pedir** ~ to borrow; **tomar algo** ~ to borrow sth

emprestar [ẽpreʃ'ta*] *vt* to lend; **empréstimo** [ẽ'prɛʃtʃĩmu] *m* loan

empunhar [ẽpu'ɲa*] *vt* to grasp, seize

empurrão [ẽpu'xãw] (*pl* -ões) *m* push, shove; **aos empurrões** jostling

empurrar [ẽpu'xa*] *vt* to push

empurrões [ẽpu'xõjʃ] *mpl de* empurrão

emudecer [emude'se*] *vt* to silence ♦ *vi* to fall silent, go quiet

enamorado, -a [enamo'radu, a] *adj* enchanted; (*apaixonado*) in love

encabulado, -a [ẽkabu'ladu, a] *adj* shy

encadernação [ẽkadexna'sãw] (*pl* -ões) *f* (*de livro*) binding

encadernado, -a [ẽkadex'nadu, a] *adj* bound; (*de capa dura*) hardback

encadernar [ẽkadex'na*] *vt* to bind

encaixar [ẽkaj'ʃa*] *vt* (*colocar*) to fit in; (*inserir*) to insert ♦ *vi* to fit; **encaixe** [ẽ'kajʃi] *m* (*ato*) fitting; (*ranhura*) groove; (*buraco*) socket

encalço [ẽ'kawsu] *m* pursuit; **ir no** ~

de to pursue

encalhar [ẽka'ʎa*] *vi* (*embarcação*) to run aground; (*fig: processo*) to grind to a halt; (: *mercadoria*) to be returned, not to sell; (*col: ficar solteiro*) to be left on the shelf

encaminhar [ẽkami'ɲa*] *vt* to direct; (*no bom caminho*) to put on the right path; (*processo*) to set in motion; **encaminhar-se** *vr*: ~-se **para/a** to set out for/to

encanar [ẽka'na*] *vt* to channel

encantado, -a [ẽkã'tadu, a] *adj* delighted; (*castelo etc*) enchanted; (*fascinado*): ~ (**por**) smitten (with)

encantador, a [ẽkãta'do*, a] *adj* delightful, charming

encantamento [ẽkãta'mẽtu] *m* (*magia*) spell; (*fascinação*) charm

encantar [ẽkã'ta*] *vt* to bewitch; to charm; (*deliciar*) to delight

encanto [ẽ'kãtu] *m* delight; charm

encarar [ẽka'ra*] *vt* to face; (*olhar*) to look at; (*considerar*) to consider

encargo [ẽ'kaxgu] *m* responsibility; (*ocupação*) job, assignment; (*fardo*) burden

encarnação [ẽkaxna'sãw] (*pl* -ões) *f* incarnation

encarnado, -a [ẽkax'nadu, a] *adj* red, scarlet

encarnar [ẽkax'na*] *vt* to embody, personify; (*TEATRO*) to play

encarregado, -a [ẽkaxe'gadu, a] *adj*: ~ **de** in charge of ♦ *m/f* person in charge ♦ *m* (*de operários*) foreman

encarregar [ẽkaxe'ga*] *vt*: ~ **alguém de algo** to put sb in charge of sth; **encarregar-se** *vr*: ~-**se de fazer** to undertake to do

encenação [ẽsena'sãw] (*pl* -ões) *f* (*de peça*) staging, putting on; (*produção*) production; (*fingimento*) playacting; (*atitude fingida*) put-on

encerar [ẽse'ra*] vt to wax

encerramento [ẽsexa'mẽtu] m close, end

encerrar [ẽse'xa*] vt to shut in, lock up; (conter) to contain; (concluir) to close

encharcar [ẽʃax'ka*] vt to flood; (ensopar) to soak, drench; **encharcar-se** vr to get soaked ou drenched

enchente [ẽ'ʃẽtʃi] f flood

encher [ẽ'ʃe*] vt to fill (up); (balão) to blow up; (tempo) to fill, take up ♦ vi (col) to be annoying; **encher-se** vr to fill up; **~se (de)** (col) to get fed up (with); **enchimento** [ẽʃi'mẽtu] m filling

enciclopédia [ẽsiklo'pedʒja] f encyclopedia, encyclopaedia (BRIT)

encoberto, -a [ẽko'bextu, a] pp de encobrir ♦ adj concealed; (tempo) overcast

encobrir [ẽko'bri*] vt to conceal, hide

encolher [ẽko'ʎe*] vt (pernas) to draw up; (os ombros) to shrug; (roupa) to shrink ♦ vi to shrink; **encolher-se** vr (de frio) to huddle

encomenda [ẽko'mẽda] f order; **feito de ~** made to order, custom-made; **encomendar** [ẽkomẽ'da*] vt: **encomendar algo a alguém** to order sth from sb

encontrar [ẽkõ'tra*] vt to find; (pessoa) to meet; (inesperadamente) to come across; (dar com) to bump into ♦ vi: **~ com** to bump into; **encontrar-se** vr (achar-se) to be; (ter encontro): **~-se (com alguém)** to meet (sb)

encontro [ẽ'kõtru] m (de pessoas) meeting; (MIL) encounter; **~ marcado** appointment; **ir/vir ao ~ de** to go/come and meet

encorajar [ẽkora'ʒa*] vt to encourage

encosta [ẽ'kɔʃta] f slope

encostar [ẽkoʃ'ta*] vt (cabeça) to put down; (carro) to park; (pôr de lado) to put to one side; (pôr junto) to put side by side; (porta) to leave ajar ♦ vi to pull in; **encostar-se** vr: **~-se em** to lean against; (deitar-se) to lie down on; **~ em** to lean against; **~ a mão em** (bater) to hit

encosto [ẽ'koʃtu] m (arrimo) support; (de cadeira) back

encrencar [ẽkrẽ'ka*] (col) vt (situação) to complicate; (pessoa) to get into trouble ♦ vi to get complicated; (carro) to break down; **encrencar-se** vr to get complicated; to get into trouble

encruzilhada [ẽkruzi'ʎada] f crossroads sg

encurtar [ẽkux'ta*] vt to shorten

endereçar [ẽdere'sa*] vt (carta) to address; (encaminhar) to direct

endereço [ẽde'resu] m address

endiabrado, -a [ẽdʒja'bradu, a] adj devilish; (travesso) mischievous

endinheirado, -a [ẽdʒiɲej'radu, a] adj rich, wealthy

endireitar [ẽdʒirej'ta*] vt (objeto) to straighten; (fig: retificar) to put right; **endireitar-se** vr to straighten up

endividar-se [ẽdʒivi'daxsi] vr to run into debt

endossar [ẽdo'sa*] vt to endorse

endurecer [ẽdure'se*] vt, vi to harden

energia [enex'ʒia] f energy, drive; (TEC) power, energy; **enérgico, -a** [e'nexʒiku, a] adj energetic, vigorous

enervante [enex'vãtʃi] adj annoying

enevoado, -a [ene'vwadu, a] adj misty, hazy

enfado [ẽ'fadu] *m* annoyance;
enfadonho, -a [ẽfa'doɲu, a] *adj*
tiresome; (*aborrecido*) boring

enfarte [ẽ'faxtʃi] *m* (MED) coronary

ênfase [ˈẽfazi] *f* emphasis, stress

enfastiado, -a [ẽfaʃ'tʃjadu, a] *adj*
bored

enfático, -a [ẽ'fatʃiku, a] *adj*
emphatic

enfatizar [ẽfatʃi'za*] *vt* to emphasize

enfeitar [ẽfej'ta*] *vt* to decorate;
enfeitar-se *vr* to dress up; **enfeite**
[ẽ'fejtʃi] *m* decoration

enfeitiçar [ẽfejtʃi'sa*] *vt* to bewitch, cast a spell on

enfermaria [ẽfexma'ria] *f* ward

enfermeiro, -a [ẽfex'mejru, a] *m/f*
nurse

enfermidade [ẽfexmi'dadʒi] *f* illness

enfermo, -a [ẽ'fexmu, a] *adj* ill, sick
♦ *m/f* sick person, patient

enferrujar [ẽfexu'ʒa*] *vt* to rust,
corrode ♦ *vi* to go rusty

enfiar [ẽ'fja*] *vt* (*meter*) to put;
(*agulha*) to thread; (*vestir*) to slip
on; **enfiar-se** *vr*: ~-**se em** to slip
into

enfim [ẽ'fi] *adv* finally, at last; (*em
suma*) in short; **até que ~!** at last!

enfoque [ẽ'fɔki] *m* approach

enforcar [ẽfox'ka*] *vt* to hang; (*trabalho, aulas*) to skip; **enforcar-se**
vr to hang o.s.

enfraquecer [ẽfrake'se*] *vt* to
weaken ♦ *vi* to grow weak

enfrentar [ẽfrẽ'ta*] *vt* to face; (*confrontar*) to confront; (*problemas*) to
face up to

enfurecer [ẽfure'se*] *vt* to infuriate;
enfurecer-se *vr* to get furious

enganado, -a [ẽga'nadu, a] *adj*
mistaken; (*traído*) deceived

enganar [ẽga'na*] *vt* to deceive;

(*desonrar*) to seduce; (*cônjuge*) to
be unfaithful to; (*fome*) to stave off;
enganar-se *vr* to be wrong, be
mistaken; (*iludir-se*) to deceive o.s.

engano [ẽ'gãnu] *m* mistake; (*ilusão*)
deception; (*logro*) trick; **é ~** (TEL)
I've (*ou* you've) got the wrong
number

engarrafamento [ẽgaxafa'mẽtu]
m bottling; (*de trânsito*) traffic jam

engarrafar [ẽgaxa'fa*] *vt* to bottle;
(*trânsito*) to block

engasgar [ẽgaʒ'ga*] *vt* to choke ♦ *vi*
to choke; (*máquina*) to splutter;
engasgar-se *vr* to choke

engatinhar [ẽgatʃi'ɲa*] *vi* to crawl

engenharia [ẽʒeɲa'ria] *f* engineering; **engenheiro, -a** [ẽʒe'ɲejru, a]
m/f engineer

engenhoso, -a [ẽʒe'ɲozu, ɔza] *adj*
clever, ingenious

engessar [ẽʒe'sa*] *vt* (*perna*) to put
in plaster; (*parede*) to plaster

englobar [ẽglo'ba*] *vt* to include

engodo [ẽ'godu] *m* bait

engolir [ẽgo'li*] *vt* to swallow

engordar [ẽgox'da*] *vt* to fatten ♦ *vi*
to put on weight

engraçado, -a [ẽgra'sadu, a] *adj*
funny, amusing

engradado [ẽgra'dadu] *m* crate

engraxador [ẽgraʃa'do*] (*PT*) *m*
shoe shiner

engraxar [ẽgra'ʃa*] *vt* to polish

engrenagem [ẽgre'naʒẽ] (*pl* -**ns**)
f (AUTO) gear

engrenar [ẽgre'na*] *vt* to put into
gear; (*fig: conversa*) to strike up ♦ *vi*:
~ **com alguém** to get on with sb

engrossar [ẽgro'sa*] *vt* (*sopa*) to
thicken; (*aumentar*) to swell; (*voz*)
to raise ♦ *vi* to thicken; to swell; to
rise; (*col: pessoa, conversa*) to turn
nasty

enguia [ẽ'gia] *f* eel

enguiçar [ēgi'sa*] vi (máquina) to break down ♦ vt to cause to break down; **enguiço** [ē'gisu] m snag; (desarranjo) breakdown

enigma [e'nigima] m enigma; (mistério) mystery

enjeitado, -a [ēʒej'tadu, a] m/f foundling, waif

enjoado, -a [ē'ʒwadu, a] adj sick; (enfastiado) bored; (enfadonho) boring; (mal-humorado) in a bad mood

enjoar [ē'ʒwa*] vt to make sick; to bore ♦ vi (pessoa) to be sick; (remédio, comida) to cause nausea; **enjoar-se** vr: **~-se de** to get sick of

enjôo [ē'ʒou] m sickness; (em carro) travel sickness; (em navio) seasickness; boredom

enlatado, -a [ēla'tadu, a] adj tinned (BRIT), canned ♦ m (pej: filme) foreign import; **~s** mpl (comida) tinned (BRIT) ou canned foods

enlouquecer [ēloke'se*] vt to drive mad ♦ vi to go mad

enlutado, -a [ēlu'tadu, a] adj in mourning

enojar [eno'ja*] vt to disgust, sicken

enorme [e'nɔxmi] adj enormous, huge; **enormidade** [enoxmi-'dadʒi] f enormity; **uma enormidade (de)** (col) a hell of a lot (of)

enquanto [ē'kwãtu] conj while; (considerado como) as; **~ isso** meanwhile; **por ~** for the time being; **~ ele não vem** until he comes; **~ que** whereas

enquête [ē'ketʒi] f survey

enraivecer [ēxajve'se*] vt to enrage

enredo [ē'xedu] m (de uma obra) plot; (intriga) intrigue

enriquecer [ēxike'se*] vt to make rich; (fig) to enrich ♦ vi to get rich; **enriquecer-se** vr to get rich

enrolar [ēxo'la*] vt to roll up; (agasalhar) to wrap up; (col: enganar) to con ♦ vi (col) to waffle; **enrolar-se** vr to roll up; to wrap up; (col: confundir-se) to get mixed ou muddled up

enroscar [ēxoʒ'ka*] vt (torcer) to twist, wind (round); **enroscar-se** vr to coil up

enrugar [ēxu'ga*] vt (pele) to wrinkle; (testa) to furrow; (tecido) to crease ♦ vi (pele, mãos) to go wrinkly; (pessoa) to get wrinkles

ensaiar [ēsa'ja*] vt to test, try out; (treinar) to practise (BRIT), practice (US); (TEATRO) to rehearse

ensaio [ē'saju] m test; (tentativa) attempt; (treino) practice; (TEATRO) rehearsal; (literário) essay

ensangüentar [ēsãgwē'ta*] vt to stain with blood

enseada [ē'sjada] f inlet, cove; (baía) bay

ensejo [ē'seʒu] m chance, opportunity

ensinamento [ēsina'mētu] m teaching; (exemplo) lesson

ensinar [ēsi'na*] vt, vi to teach

ensino [ē'sinu] m teaching, tuition; (educação) education

ensolarado, -a [ēsola'radu, a] adj sunny

ensopado, -a [ēso'padu, a] adj soaked ♦ m stew

ensurdecer [ēsuxde'se*] vt to deafen ♦ vi to go deaf

entalar [ēta'la*] vt to wedge, jam; (encher) **ela me entalou de comida** she stuffed me full of food

entalhar [ēta'ʎa*] vt to carve; **entalhe** [ē'taʎi] m groove, notch

entanto [ē'tãtu] **: no ~** adv yet, however

então [ē'tãw] adv then; **até ~** up to that time; **desde ~** ever since; **e ~?**

well then?; **para ~** so that; **pois ~** in
that case; **~, você vai ou não?** so,
are you going or not?

entardecer [ětaxde'se*] vi to get
late ♦ m sunset

ente [ětʃi] m being

enteado, -a [ě'tʃjadu, a] m/f step-
son/stepdaughter

entediar [ěte'dʒja*] vt to bore;
entediar-se vr to get bored

entender [ětě'de*] vt to understand; (pensar) to think; (ouvir) to
hear; **entender-se** vr to understand one another; **dar a ~** to imply;
no meu ~ in my opinion; **~ de
música** to know about music; **~ de
fazer** to decide to do; **~se por** to
be meant by; **~se com alguém** to
get along with sb; (dialogar) to sort
things out with sb

entendido, -a [ětě'dʒidu, a] adj
(col) gay, (conhecedor): **~ em** good
at ♦ m/f expert; (col) homosexual,
gay; **bem ~** that is

entendimento [ětědʒi'mětu] m
understanding; (opinião) opinion;
(combinação) agreement

enterrar [ěte'xa*] vt to bury; (faca)
to plunge; (lever à ruina) to ruin;
(assunto) to close

enterro [ě'texu] m burial; (funeral)
funeral

entidade [ětʃi'dadʒi] f (ser) being;
(corporação) body; (coisa que existe)
entity

entornar [ětox'na*] vt to spill; (fig:
copo) to drink ♦ vi to drink a lot

entorpecente [ětoxpe'sětʃi] m
narcotic

entorpecimento [ětoxpesi'mětu]
m numbness; (torpor) lethargy

entorse [ě'tɔxsi] f sprain

entortar [ětox'ta*] vt (curvar) to
bend; (empenar) to warp; **~ os
olhos** to squint

entrada [ě'trada] f (ato) entry;
(lugar) entrance; (TEC) inlet; (de
casa) doorway; (começo) beginning; (bilhete) ticket; (CULIN) starter,
entrée; (COMPUT) input; (pagamento
inicial) down payment; (corredor de
casa) hall; **~s** fpl (no cabelo) receding hairline sg; **~ gratuita** admission
free; **"~ proibida"** "no entry", "no
admittance"; **meia ~** half-price ticket

entra-e-sai ['ětrai'saj] m comings
and goings pl

entranhado, -a [ětra'ɲadu, a] adj
deep-rooted

entranhas [ě'traɲaʃ] fpl bowels,
entrails; (sentimentos) feelings; (centro) heart sg

entrar [ě'tra*] vi to go (ou come) in,
enter; **~ com** (COMPUT: dados etc) to
enter; **eu entrei com £10** I con-
tributed £10; **~ de férias/licença** to
start one's holiday (BRIT) ou vacation
(US)/leave; **~ em** to go (ou come)
into, enter; (assunto) to get onto;
(comida, bebida) to start in on

entrave [ě'travi] m (fig) impediment

entre ['ětri] prep (dois) between;
(mais de dois) among(st); **~ si**
amongst themselves

entreaberto, -a [ětrja'bɛxtu, a] adj
half-open; (porta) ajar

entrega [ě'trega] f (de mercadorias)
delivery; (a alguém) handing over;
(rendição) surrender; **~ rápida** special delivery

entregar [ětre'ga*] vt to hand over;
(mercadorias) to deliver; (confiar)
to entrust; (devolver) to return;
entregar-se vr (render-se) to give
o.s. up; (dedicar-se) to devote o.s.

entregue [ě'tregi] pp de **entregar**

entrelinha [ětre'liɲa] f line space;
ler nas ~s to read between the lines

entreolhar-se [ětrio'ʎaxsı] vr to exchange glances

entretanto [ětri'tãtu] conj however

entretenimento [ětriteni'mẽtu] m entertainment; (distração) pastime

entreter [ětri'te*] (irreg: como **ter**) vt to entertain, amuse; (ocupar) to occupy; (manter) to keep up; (esperanças) to cherish; **entreter-se** vr to amuse o.s.; to occupy o.s.

entrevista [ětre'vi∫ta] f interview; ~ **coletiva (à imprensa)** press conference; **entrevistar** [ětrevi∫'ta*] vt to interview; **entrevistar-se** vr to have an interview

entristecer [ětri∫te'se*] vt to sadden, grieve ♦ vi to feel sad; **entristecer-se** vr to feel sad

entroncamento [ětrõka'mẽtu] m junction

entrudo [ě'trudu] (PT) m carnival; (REL) Shrovetide

entulhar [ětu'ʎa*] vt to cram full; (suj: multidão) to pack

entupido, -a [ětu'pidu, a] adj blocked; **estar** ~ (col: congestionado) to have a blocked-up nose; (de comida) to be fit to burst, be full up

entupimento [ětupi'mẽtu] m blockage

entupir [ětu'pi*] vt to block, clog; **entupir-se** vr to become blocked; (de comida) to stuff o.s.

entusiasmar [ětuzja∫'ma*] vt to fill with enthusiasm; (animar) to excite; **entusiasmar-se** vr to get excited

entusiasmo [ětu'zja∫mu] m enthusiasm; (júbilo) excitement

entusiasta [ětu'zja∫ta] adj enthusiastic ♦ m/f enthusiast

enumerar [enume'ra*] vt to enumerate; (com números) to number

envelhecer [ěveʎe'se*] vt to age ♦ vi to grow old, age

envelope [ěve'lɔpi] m envelope

envenenamento [ěvenena'mẽtu] m poisoning; ~ **do sangue** blood poisoning

envenenar [ěvene'na*] vt to poison; (fig) to corrupt; (: declaração, palavras) to distort, twist; (tornar amargo) to sour ♦ vi to be poisonous; **envenenar-se** vr to poison o.s.

envergonhado, -a [ěvexgo'ɲadu, a] adj ashamed; (tímido) shy

envergonhar [ěvexgo'ɲa*] vt to shame; (degradar) to disgrace; **envergonhar-se** vr to be ashamed

enviado, -a [ě'vjadu, a] m/f envoy, messenger

enviar [ě'vja*] vt to send

envio [ě'viu] m sending; (expedição) dispatch; (remessa) remittance; (de mercadorias) consignment

enviuvar [ěvju'va*] vi to be widowed

envolto, -a [ě'vowtu, a] pp de **envolver**

envolver [ěvow've*] vt to wrap (up); (cobrir) to cover; (comprometer, acarretar) to involve; (nos braços) to embrace; **envolver-se** vr (intrometer-se) to become involved; (cobrir-se) to wrap o.s. up

envolvimento [ěvowvi'mẽtu] m involvement

enxada [ě'∫ada] f hoe

enxaguar [ě∫a'gwa*] vt to rinse

enxame [ě'∫ami] m swarm

enxaqueca [ě∫a'keka] f migraine

enxergar [ě∫ex'ga*] vt (avistar) to catch sight of; (divisar) to make out; (notar) to observe, see

enxofre [ě'∫ofri] m sulphur (BRIT), sulfur (US)

enxotar [ě∫o'ta*] vt to drive out

enxoval [ě∫o'vaw] (pl **-ais**) m (de noiva) trousseau; (de recém-nascido) layette

enxugar [ẽʃu'ga*] vt to dry; (fig: texto) to tidy up

enxurrada [ẽʃu'xada] f (de água) torrent; (fig) spate

enxuto, -a [ẽ'ʃutu, a] adj dry; (corpo) shapely; (bonito) good-looking

épico, -a ['ɛpiku, a] adj epic ♦ m epic poet

epidemia [epide'mia] f epidemic

epilepsia [epile'psia] f epilepsy

episódio [epi'zɔdʒu] m episode

época ['ɛpoka] f time, period; (da história) age, epoch; **naquela ~** at that time; **fazer ~** to be epoch-making

equação [ekwa'sãw] (pl -ões) f equation

equador [ekwa'do*] m equator; **o E~** Ecuador

equilibrar [ekili'bra*] vt to balance; **equilibrar-se** vr to balance; **equilíbrio** [eki'librju] m balance

equipa [e'kipa] (PT) f team

equipamento [ekipa'mẽtu] m equipment, kit

equipar [eki'pa*] vt: **~ (com)** (navio) to fit out (with); (prover) to equip (with)

equipe [e'kipi] (BR) f team

equitação [ekita'sãw] f (ato) riding; (arte) horsemanship

equivalente [ekiva'lẽtʃi] adj, m equivalent

equivaler [ekiva'le*] vi: **~ a** to be the same as, equal

equivocado, -a [ekivo'kadu, a] adj mistaken, wrong

equivocar-se [ekivo'kaxsi] vr to make a mistake, be wrong

equívoco, -a [e'kivoku, a] adj ambiguous ♦ m (engano) mistake

era¹ ['ɛra] f era, age

era² etc vb V ser

erário [e'rarju] m exchequer

erecto, -a [e'rɛktu, a] (PT) adj = ereto

ereto, -a [e'rɛtu, a] adj upright, erect

erguer [ex'ge*] vt to raise, lift; (edificar) to build, erect; **erguer-se** vr to rise, (pessoa) to stand up

eriçar [eri'sa*] vt: **~ o cabelo de alguém** to make sb's hair stand on end; **eriçar-se** vr to bristle; (cabelos) to stand on end

erigir [eri'ʒi*] vt to erect

erosão [ero'zãw] f erosion

erótico, -a [e'rɔtʃiku, a] adj erotic

errado, -a [e'xadu, a] adj wrong; **dar ~** to go wrong

errar [e'xa*] vt (alvo) to miss; (conta) to get wrong ♦ vi to wander, roam; (enganar-se) to be wrong, make a mistake; **~ o caminho** to lose one's way

erro ['exu] m mistake; **salvo ~** unless I am mistaken; **~ de imprensa** misprint

errôneo, -a [e'xonju, a] adj wrong, mistaken; (falso) false, untrue

erudito, -a [eru'dʒitu, a] adj learned, scholarly ♦ m scholar

erva ['ɛxva] f herb; (col: dinheiro) dosh; (: maconha) dope; **~ daninha** weed

erva-mate (pl **ervas-mates**) f mate

ervilha [ex'viʎa] f pea

esbanjar [iʒbã'ʒa*] vt to squander, waste

esbarrar [iʒba'xa*] vi: **~ em** to bump into; (obstáculo, problema) to come up against

esbelto, -a [iʒ'bɛwtu, a] adj slim, slender

esboçar [iʒbo'sa*] vt to sketch; (delinear) to outline; (traçar) to draw up; **esboço** [iʒ'bosu] m sketch; (primeira versão) draft; (fig: resumo) outline

esbofetear [iʒbofe'tʃja*] vt to slap, hit

esburacar [iʒbura'ka*] vt to make holes (ou a hole) in

esc (PT) abr = **escudo**

escabroso, -a [iʃka'brozu, ɔza] adj (difícil) tough; (indecoroso) indecent

escada [iʃ'kada] f (dentro da casa) staircase, stairs pl; (fora da casa) steps pl; (de mão) ladder; ~ **de incêndio** fire escape; ~ **rolante** escalator; **escadaria** [iʃkada'ria] f staircase

escala [iʃ'kala] f scale; (NÁUT) port of call; (parada) stop; **fazer** ~ **em** to call at; **sem** ~ non-stop

escalada [iʃka'lada] f (de guerra) escalation

escalão [iʃka'lãw] (pl -ões) m step; (MIL) echelon

escalar [iʃka'la*] vt (montanha) to climb; (muro) to scale; (designar) to select

escaldar [iʃkaw'da*] vt to scald; **escaldar-se** vr to scald o.s.

escalões [eʃka'lõjʃ] mpl de **escalão**

escama [iʃ'kama] f (de peixe) scale; (de pele) flake

escancarado, -a [iʃkãka'radu, a] adj wide open

escandalizar [iʃkãdali'za*] vt to shock; **escandalizar-se** vr to be shocked; (ofender-se) to be offended

escândalo [iʃ'kãdalu] m scandal; (indignação) outrage; **fazer** ou **dar um** ~ to make a scene; **escandaloso, -a** [iʃkãda'lozu, ɔza] adj shocking, scandalous

Escandinávia [iʃkãdʒi'navja] f: **a** ~ Scandinavia; **escandinavo, -a** [iʃkãdʒi'navu, a] adj, m/f Scandinavian

escangalhar [iʃkãga'ʎa*] vt to break, smash (up); (a própria saúde)

to ruin; **escangalhar-se** vr: ~**-se de rir** to split one's sides laughing

escapar [iʃka'pa*] vi: ~ **a** ou **de** to escape from; (fugir) to run away from; **escapar-se** vr to run away, flee; **deixar** ~ (uma oportunidade) to miss; (palavras) to blurt out; ~ **de boa** (col) to have a close shave

escapatória [iʃkapa'tɔrja] f way out; (desculpa) excuse

escape [iʃ'kapi] m (de gás) leak; (AUTO) exhaust

escapulir [iʃkapu'li*] vi: ~ (**de**) to get away (from); (suj: coisa) to slip (from)

escárnio [iʃ'kaxnju] m mockery; (desprezo) derision

escarrar [iʃka'xa*] vt to spit, cough up ♦ vi to spit

escarro [iʃ'kaxu] m phlegm, spit

escassear [iʃka'sja*] vt to skimp on ♦ vi to become scarce

escassez [iʃka'seʒ] f (falta) shortage

escasso, -a [iʃ'kasu, a] adj scarce

escavar [iʃka'va*] vt to excavate

esclarecer [iʃklare'se*] vt (situação) to explain; (mistério) to clear up, explain; **esclarecer-se** vr: ~ **se (sobre algo)** to find out (about sth); **esclarecimento** [iʃklaresi'mẽtu] m explanation; (informação) information

escoadouro [iʃkoa'doru] m drain; (cano) drainpipe

escocês, -esa [iʃko'seʃ, seza] adj Scottish, Scots ♦ m/f Scot, Scotsman/woman

Escócia [iʃ'kɔsja] f Scotland

escola [iʃ'kɔla] f school; ~ **naval** naval college; ~ **primária** primary (BRIT) ou elementary (US) school; ~ **secundária** secondary (BRIT) ou high (US) school; ~ **particular/pública** private/state (BRIT) ou public (US)

escolar 435 **escritório**

school; **~ de samba** *see boxed note*;
~ superior college

ESCOLAS DE SAMBA

Escolas de samba are musical
and recreational associations
made up, among others, of
samba dancers, percussionists and
carnival dancers. Although they
exist throughout Brazil, the most
famous schools are in Rio de
Janeiro. The schools in Rio
rehearse all year long for the **carnaval**, where they appear for two
days in the *Sambódromo*, the
samba parade, and compete for
the samba school championship.
Characterised by their extravagance, the biggest schools have
up to 4,000 members and are one
of Brazil's major tourist attrac-
tions.

---

escolar [iʃko'la*] *adj* school *atr*
♦ *m/f* schoolboy/girl
escolha [iʃ'koʎa] *f* choice
escolher [iʃko'ʎe*] *vt* to choose,
select
escolho [iʃ'koʎu] *m* (*recife*) reef;
(*rocha*) rock
escolta [iʃ'kɔwta] *f* escort;
escoltar [iʃkow'ta*] *vt* to escort
escombros [iʃ'kõbruʃ] *mpl* ruins,
debris *sg*
esconde-esconde [iʃkõdʒiʃ-
'kõdʒi] *m* hide-and-seek
esconder [iʃkõ'de*] *vt* to hide, conceal; **esconder-se** *vr* to hide
esconderijo [iʃkõde'riʒu] *m* hiding
place; (*de bandidos*) hideout
escondidas [iʃkõ'dʒidaʃ] *fpl*: **às ~**
secretly
escopo [iʃ'kopu] *m* aim, purpose
escorar [iʃko'ra*] *vt* to prop (up);
(*amparar*) to support; (*esperar de*

espreita) to lie in wait for ♦ *vi* to
lie in wait; **escorar-se** *vr*: **~-se
em** (*fundamentar-se*) to go by;
(*amparar-se*) to live off
escore [iʃ'kɔri] *m* score
escoriação [iʃkorja'sãw] (*pl -ões*) *f*
abrasion, scratch
escorpião [iʃkoxpi'ãw] (*pl -ões*) *m*
scorpion; **E~** (*ASTROLOGIA*) Scorpio
escorrega [iʃko'xega] *f* slide;
escorregadela [iʃkoxega'dɛla] *f*
slip; **escorregadiço, -a** [iʃkoxega-
'dʒi(s)u, a] *adj* slippery; **escorregão** [iʃkoxe'gãw] (*pl -ões*) *m* slip;
(*fig*) slip(-up); **escorregar**
[iʃkoxe'ga*] *vi* to slip; (*errar*) to slip
up
escorrer [iʃko'xe*] *vt* to drain (*oʃʃ*);
(*verter*) to pour out ♦ *vi* (*pingar*) to
drip; (*correr em fio*) to trickle
escoteiro [iʃko'tejru] *m* scout
escova [iʃ'kova] *f* brush; (*penteado*)
blow-dry; **~ de dentes** toothbrush;
escovar [iʃko'va*] *vt* to brush
escravatura [iʃkrava'tura] *f*
(*tráfico*) slave trade; (*escravidão*)
slavery
escravidão [iʃkravi'dãw] *f* slavery
escravizar [iʃkravi'za*] *vt* to
enslave; (*cativar*) to captivate
escravo, -a [iʃ'kravu, a] *adj* captive
♦ *m/f* slave
escrever [iʃkre've*] *vt, vi* to write;
escrever-se *vr* to write to each
other; **~ à máquina** to type
escrita [eʃ'krita] *f* writing; (*letra*)
handwriting
escrito, -a [eʃ'kritu, a] *pp de* es-
crever ♦ *adj* written ♦ *m* piece of
writing; **~ à mão** handwritten; **dar
por ~** to put in writing
escritor, -a [iʃkri'to*, a] *m/f* writer;
(*autor*) author
escritório [iʃkri'tɔrju] *m* office; (*em
casa*) study

escritura [iʃkri'tura] f (JUR) deed; (na compra de imóveis) ≈ exchange of contracts; **as Sagradas E~s** the Scriptures

escrivã [iʃkri'vã] f de **escrivão**

escrivaninha [iʃkriva'niɲa] f writing desk

escrivão, -vã [iʃkri'vãw, vã] (pl -ões, ~s) m/f registrar, recorder

escrúpulo [iʃ'krupulu] m scruple; (cuidado) care; **sem ~** unscrupulous; **escrupuloso, -a** [iʃkrupu'lozu, ɔza] adj scrupulous; careful

escudo [iʃ'kudu] m shield; (moeda) escudo

esculhambado, -a [iʃkuʎã'badu, a] (col!) adj shabby, slovenly; (estragado) knackered

esculhambar [iʃkuʎã'ba*] (col!) vt to mess up, fuck up (!); **~ alguém** (criticar) to give sb stick; (descompor) to give sb a bollocking (!)

esculpir [iʃkuw'pi*] vt to carve, sculpt; (gravar) to engrave

escultor, a [iʃkuw'to*, a] m/f sculptor

escultura [iʃkuw'tura] f sculpture

escuras [iʃ'kuraʃ] fpl: **às ~** in the dark

escurecer [iʃkure'se*] vt to darken ♦ vi to get dark; **ao ~** at dusk

escuridão [iʃkuri'dãw] f (trevas) dark

escuro, -a [iʃ'kuru, a] adj dark; (dia) overcast; (pessoa) swarthy; (negócios) shady ♦ m darkness

escusar [iʃku'za*] vt to excuse, forgive; (justificar) to justify; (dispensar) to exempt; (não precisar de) not to need; **escusar-se** vr to apologize; **~-se de fazer** to refuse to do

escuta [iʃ'kuta] f listening; **à ~** listening out; **ficar na ~** to stand by

escutar [iʃku'ta*] vt to listen to;

(sem prestar atenção) to hear ♦ vi to listen; to hear

esfacelar [iʃfase'la*] vt to destroy

esfaquear [iʃfaki'a*] vt to stab

esfarrapado, -a [iʃfaxa'padu, a] adj ragged, tattered

esfera [iʃ'fɛra] f sphere; (globo) globe; (TIP, COMPUT) golfball

esfolar [iʃfo'la*] vt to skin; (arranhar) to graze; (cobrar demais a) to overcharge, fleece

esfomeado, -a [iʃfo'mjadu, a] adj famished, starving

esforçado, -a [iʃfox'sadu, a] adj committed, dedicated

esforçar-se [iʃfox'saxsi] vr: **~ para** to try hard to, strive to

esforço [iʃ'foxsu] m effort

esfregar [iʃfre'ga*] vt to rub; (com água) to scrub

esfriar [iʃ'frja*] vt to cool, chill ♦ vi to get cold; (fig) to cool off

esganar [iʃga'na*] vt to strangle, choke

esgotado, -a [iʃgo'tadu, a] adj exhausted; (consumido) used up; (livros) out of print; (ingressos) sold out

esgotamento [izgota'mẽtu] m exhaustion

esgotar [izgo'ta*] vt to drain, empty; (recursos) to use up; (pessoa, assunto) to exhaust; **esgotar-se** vr to become exhausted; (mercadorias, edição) to be sold out; (recursos) to run out

esgoto [iʒ'gotu] m drain; (público) sewer

esgrima [iʒ'grima] f (esporte) fencing

esgueirar-se [izgej'raxsi] vr to slip away, sneak off

esguelha [iʒ'geʎa] f slant; **olhar alguém de ~** to look at sb out of the corner of one's eye

esguio, -a [eʒ'giu, a] adj slender

esmaecer [iʒmaje'se*] vi to fade

esmagador, a [iʒmagado*, a] adj crushing; (provas) irrefutable; (maioria) overwhelming

esmagar [iʒma'ga*] vt to crush

esmalte [iʒ'mawtʃi] m enamel; (de unhas) nail polish

esmeralda [iʒme'rawda] f emerald

esmerar-se [iʒme'raxsi] vr: ~ em fazer algo to take great care in doing sth

esmigalhar [iʒmiga'ʎa*] vt to crumble; (despedaçar) to shatter; (esmagar) to crush; **esmigalhar-se** vr to crumble; to smash, shatter

esmo ['eʒmu] m: a ~ at random; falar a ~ to prattle

esmola [iʒ'mɔla] f alms pl; pedir ~s to beg

esmurrar [iʒmu'xa*] vt to punch

esnobe [iʒ'nɔbi] adj snobbish ♦ m/f snob

espacial [iʃpa'sjaw] (pl -ais) adj space atr; nave ~ spaceship

espaço [iʃ'pasu] m space; (tempo) period; ~ para 3 pessoas room for 3 people; a ~ from time to time; **espaçoso, -a** [iʃpa'sozu, ɔza] adj spacious, roomy

espada [iʃ'pada] f sword; ~s fpl (CARTAS) spades

espadarte [iʃpa'daxtʃi] m swordfish

espairecer [iʃpajre'se*] vt to amuse, entertain ♦ vi to relax; **espairecer-se** vr to relax

espaldar [iʃpaw'da*] m (chair) back

espalhafato [iʃpaʎa'fatu] m din, commotion

espalhar [iʃpa'ʎa*] vt to scatter; (boato, medo) to spread; (luz) to shed; **espalhar-se** vr to spread; (refestelar-se) to lounge

espanador [iʃpana'do*] m duster

espancar [iʃpã'ka*] vt to beat up

Espanha [iʃ'paɲa] f: a ~ Spain; **espanhol, a** [iʃpa'ɲow, ɔla] (pl -óis, ~s) adj Spanish ♦ m/f Spaniard ♦ m (LING) Spanish; os espanhóis mpl the Spanish

espantado, -a [iʃpã'tadu, a] adj astonished, amazed; (assustado) frightened

espantalho [iʃpã'taʎu] m scarecrow

espantar [iʃpã'ta*] vt to frighten; (admirar) to amaze, astonish; (afugentar) to frighten away ♦ vi to be amazing; **espantar-se** vr to be astonished ou amazed; to be frightened

espanto [iʃ'pãtu] m fright, fear; (admiração) astonishment, amazement; **espantoso, -a** [iʃpã'tozu, ɔza] adj amazing

esparadrapo [iʃpara'drapu] m (sticking) plaster (BRIT), bandaid ® (US)

esparramar [iʃpaxa'ma*] vt to splash; (espalhar) to scatter

esparso, -a [iʃ'paxsu, a] adj scattered; (solto) loose

espasmo [iʃ'paʒmu] m spasm, convulsion

espatifar [iʃpatʃi'fa*] vt to smash; **espatifar-se** vr to smash; (avião) to crash

especial [iʃpe'sjaw] (pl -ais) adj special; em ~ especially; **especialidade** [iʃpesjali'dadʒi] f speciality (BRIT), specialty (US); (ramo de atividades) specialization; **especialista** [iʃpesja'liʃta] m/f specialist; (perito) expert; **especializar-se** [iʃpesjali'zaxsi] vr: especializar-se (em) to specialize (in)

espécie [iʃ'pɛsi] f (BIO) species; (tipo) sort, kind; causar ~ to be surprising; pagar em ~ to pay in cash

especificar [iʃpesifi'ka*] vt to

specify; **específico, -a** [iʃpɛ'sifiku, a] *adj* specific

espécime [iʃ'pɛsimi] *m* specimen

espécimen [iʃ'pɛsimẽ] (*pl* ~s) *m* = espécime

espectáculo *etc* [iʃpek'takulu] (*PT*) *m* = espetáculo *etc*

espectador, a [iʃpekta'do*, a] *m/f* onlooker; (*TV*) viewer; (*ESPORTE*) spectator; (*TEATRO*) member of the audience; **~es** *mpl* (*TV*, *TEATRO*) audience *sg*

especular [iʃpeku'la*] *vi*: ~ (*sobre*) to speculate (on)

espelho [iʃ'peʎu] *m* mirror; (*fig*) model; ~ **retrovisor** (*AUTO*) rearview mirror

espera [iʃ'pera] *f* (*demora*) wait; (*expectativa*) expectation; **à ~ de** waiting for; **à minha ~** waiting for me

esperança [iʃpe'rãsa] *f* hope; (*expectativa*) expectation; **dar ~s a alguém** to raise sb's hopes; **esperançoso, -a** [iʃperã'sozu, ɔza] *adj* hopeful

esperar [iʃpe'ra*] *vt* to wait for; (*contar com: bebê*) to expect; (*desejar*) to hope for ♦ *vi* to wait; to hope; to expect

esperma [iʃ'pexma] *f* sperm

espertalhão, -lhona [iʃpexta-'ʎãw, ʎɔna] (*pl* -ões, ~s) *adj* crafty, shrewd

esperteza [iʃpex'teza] *f* cleverness; (*astúcia*) cunning

esperto, -a [iʃ'pextu, a] *adj* clever; (*espertalhão*) crafty

espesso, -a [iʃ'pesu, a] *adj* thick; **espessura** [iʃpe'sura] *f* thickness

espetacular [iʃpetaku'la*] *adj* spectacular

espetáculo [iʃpe'takulu] *m* (*TEATRO*) show; (*vista*) sight; (*cena ridícula*) spectacle; **dar ~** to make a spectacle

of o.s.

espetar [iʃpe'ta*] *vt* (*carne*) to put on a spit; (*cravar*) to stick; **espetar-se** *vr* to prick o.s.; ~ **algo em algo** to pin sth to sth

espeto [iʃ'petu] *m* spit; (*pau*) pointed stick; **ser um ~** (*ser difícil*) to be awkward

espevitado, -a [iʃpevi'tadu, a] *adj* (*fig: vivo*) lively

espiã [iʃ'pjã] *f de* espião

espiada [iʃ'pjada] *f*: **dar uma ~** to have a look

espião, -piã [iʃ'pjãw, 'pjã] (*pl* -ões, ~s) *m/f* spy

espiar [iʃ'pja*] *vt* to spy on; (*uma ocasião*) to watch out for; (*olhar*) to watch ♦ *vi* to spy; (*olhar*) to peer

espiga [iʃ'piga] *f* (*de milho*) ear

espinafre [iʃpi'nafri] *m* spinach

espingarda [iʃpĩ'gaxda] *f* shotgun, rifle

espinha [iʃ'piɲa] *f* (*de peixe*) bone; (*na pele*) spot, pimple; (*coluna vertebral*) spine

espinho [iʃ'piɲu] *m* thorn; (*de animal*) spine; (*fig: dificuldade*) snag; **espinhoso, -a** [iʃpi'ɲozu, ɔza] *adj* (*planta*) prickly, thorny; (*fig: difícil*) difficult; (*: problema*) thorny

espiões [iʃ'pjõjʃ] *mpl de* espião

espionagem [iʃpjo'naʒẽ] *f* spying, espionage

espionar [iʃpjo'na*] *vt* to spy on ♦ *vi* to spy, snoop

espírito [iʃ'piritu] *m* spirit; (*pensamento*) mind; ~ **esportivo** sense of humo(u)r; **E~ Santo** Holy Spirit

espiritual [iʃpiri'twaw] (*pl* -ais) *adj* spiritual

espirituoso, -a [iʃpiri'twozu, ɔza] *adj* witty

espirrar [iʃpi'xa*] *vi* to sneeze; (*jorrar*) to spurt out ♦ *vt* (*água*) to spurt; to pin sth to sth **espirro** [iʃ'pixu] *m* sneeze

esplêndido, -a [iʃ'plẽdʒidu, a] adj splendid

esplendor [iʃplẽ'do*] m splendour (BRIT), splendor (US)

esponja [iʃ'põʒa] f sponge

espontâneo, -a [iʃpõ'tanju, a] adj spontaneous; (pessoa) straightforward

esporádico, -a [iʃpo'radʒiku, a] adj sporadic

esporte [iʃ'pɔxtʃi] (BR) m sport; **esportista** [iʃpox'tʃiʃta] adj sporting ♦ m/f sportsman/woman; **esportivo, -a** [iʃpox'tʃivu, a] adj sporting

esposa [iʃ'poza] f wife

esposo [iʃ'pozu] m husband

espreguiçadeira [iʃpregiza'dejra] f deck chair; (com lugar para as pernas) lounger

espreguiçar-se [iʃpregi'saxsi] vr to stretch

espreita [iʃ'prejta] f: **ficar à ~ to keep watch**

espreitar [iʃprej'ta*] vt to spy on; (observar) to observe, watch

espremer [iʃpre'me*] vt (fruta) to squeeze; (roupa molhada) to wring out; (pessoas) to squash; **espremer-se** vr (multidão) to be squashed together; (uma pessoa) to squash up

espuma [iʃ'puma] f foam; (de cerveja) froth, head; (de sabão) lather; (de ondas) surf; **~ de borracha** foam rubber; **espumante** [iʃpu'mãtʃi] adj frothy, foamy; (vinho) sparkling

esq. abr (= esquerdo/a) l

esquadra [iʃ'kwadra] f (NÁUT) fleet; (PT: da polícia) police station

esquadrão [iʃkwa'drãw] (pl -ões) m squadron

esquadrilha [iʃkwa'driʎa] f squadron

esquadrões [iʃkwa'drõjʃ] mpl de

esquadrão

esquálido, -a [iʃ'kwalidu, a] adj squalid, filthy

esquartejar [iʃkwaxte'ʒa*] vt to quarter

esquecer [iʃke'se*] vt, vi to forget; **esquecer-se** vr: **~-se de to forget**; **esquecido, -a** [iʃke'sidu, a] adj forgotten; (pessoa) forgetful

esqueleto [iʃke'letu] m skeleton; (arcabouço) framework

esquema [iʃ'kema] m outline; (plano) scheme; (diagrama) diagram, plan

esquentar [iʃkẽ'ta*] vt to heat (up), warm (up); (fig: irritar) to annoy ♦ vi to warm up; (casaco) to be warm; **esquentar-se** vr to get annoyed

esquerda [iʃ'kexda] f (tb: POL) left; **à ~ on the left**

esquerdista [iʃkex'dʒiʃta] adj left-wing ♦ m/f left-winger

esquerdo, -a [iʃ'kexdu, a] adj left

esqui [iʃ'ki] m (patim) ski; (esporte) skiing; **~ aquático** water skiing; **fazer ~ to go skiing; esquiar** [iʃ'kja*] vi to ski

esquilo [iʃ'kilu] m squirrel

esquina [iʃ'kina] f corner

esquisito, -a [iʃki'zitu, a] adj strange, odd

esquivar-se [iʃki'vaxsi] vr: **~ de to escape from, get away from; (deveres) to get out of**

esquivo, -a [iʃ'kivu, a] adj aloof, standoffish

essa ['esa] pron: **~ é/foi boa that is/was a good one; ~ não, sem ~ come off it; vamos nessa let's go!; ainda mais ~! that's all I need!; corta ~! cut it out!; por ~ e outras for these and other reasons; ~ de fazer ... this business of doing ...**

esse ['esi] adj (sg) that; (pl) those; (BR: este: sg) this; (: pl) these ♦ pron *(sg)* that one; *(pl)* those; *(BR: este: sg)* this one; *(: pl)* these

essência [e'sẽsja] f essence; **essencial** [esẽ'sjaw] *(pl* -ais*)* adj essential; *(principal)* main ♦ m: **o essencial** the main thing

esta ['ɛʃta] f de **este**

estabelecer [iʃtabele'se*] vt to establish; *(fundar)* to set up

estabelecimento [iʃtabelesi-'mẽtu] m establishment; *(casa comercial)* business

estábulo [iʃ'tabulu] m cow-shed

estaca [iʃ'taka] f post, stake; *(de barraca)* peg

estação [iʃta'sãw] *(pl* -ões*)* f station; *(do ano)* season; ~ **de águas** spa; ~ **balneária** seaside resort; ~ **emissora** broadcasting station

estacionamento [iʃtasjona'mẽtu] m *(ato)* parking; *(lugar)* car park *(BRIT)*, parking lot *(US)*

estacionar [iʃtasjo'na*] vt to park ♦ vi to park; *(não mover)* to remain stationary

estacionário, -a [iʃtasjo'narju, a] adj *(veículo)* stationary; *(COM)* slack

estações [iʃta'sõjʃ] fpl de **estação**

estada [iʃ'tada] f stay

estadia [iʃta'dʒia] f = **estada**

estádio [iʃ'tadʒu] m stadium

estadista [iʃta'dʒiʃta] m/f statesman/woman

estado [iʃ'tadu] m state; **E~s Unidos (da América)** United States (of America); ~ **civil** marital status; ~ **de espírito** state of mind; ~ **maior** staff; **estadual** [iʃta'dwaw] *(pl* -ais*)* adj state *atr*

estafa [iʃ'tafa] f fatigue; *(esgotamento)* nervous exhaustion

estagiário, -a [iʃta'ʒjarju, a] m/f probationer, trainee; *(professor)* student teacher; *(médico)* junior doctor

estágio [iʃ'taʒu] m *(aprendizado)* traineeship; *(fase)* stage

estagnado, -a [iʃtag'nadu, a] adj stagnant

estalar [iʃta'la*] vt to break; *(os dedos)* to snap ♦ vi to split, crack; *(crepitar)* to crackle

estalido [iʃta'lidu] m pop

estalo [iʃ'talu] m *(do chicote)* crack; *(dos dedos)* snap; *(dos lábios)* smack; *(de foguete)* bang; ~ **de trovão** thunderclap; **de** ~ suddenly

estampa [iʃ'tãpa] f *(figura impressa)* print; *(ilustração)* picture

estampado, -a [iʃtã'padu, a] adj printed ♦ m *(tecido)* print; *(num tecido)* pattern

estampar [iʃtã'pa*] vt to print; *(marcar)* to stamp

estancar [iʃtã'ka*] vt to staunch; *(fazer cessar)* to stop; **estancar-se** vr to stop

estância [iʃ'tãsja] f ranch, farm

estandarte [iʃtã'daxtʃi] m standard, banner

estanho [iʃ'taɲu] m *(metal)* tin

estante [iʃ'tãtʃi] f bookcase; *(suporte)* stand

PALAVRA CHAVE

---

estar [iʃ'ta*] vi 1 *(lugar)* to be; *(em casa)* to be in; *(no telefone)*: **a Lúcia está?** – não, ela não está **a Lúcia** there? – no, she's not here

2 *(estado)* to be; ~ **doente** to be ill; ~ **bem** *(de saúde)* to be well; *(financeiramente)* to be well off; ~ **calor/frio** to be hot/cold; ~ **com fome/sede/medo** to be hungry/thirsty/afraid

3 *(ação contínua)*: ~ **fazendo** *(BR)* ou **a fazer** *(PT)* to be doing

4 *(+ pp: = adj)*: ~ **sentado/cansado** to be sitting down/tired

5 *(+ pp: uso passivo)*: **está condenado à morte** he's been condemned

to death; **o livro está emprestado** the book's been borrowed

6: ~ de: ~ de férias/licença to be on holiday (BRIT) ou vacation (US)/leave; **ela estava de chapéu** she had a hat on, she was wearing a hat

7: ~ para: ~ para fazer to be about to do; **ele está para chegar a qualquer momento** he'll be here any minute; **não ~ para conversas** not to be in the mood for talking

8: ~ por fazer to be still to be done

9: ~ sem: ~ sem dinheiro to have no money; **~ sem dormir** not to have slept; **estou sem dormir há três dias** I haven't slept for three days; **está sem terminar** it isn't finished yet

10 (frases): **está bem, tá (bem)** (col) OK; **~ bem com** to be on good terms with

estardalhaço [iʃtaxdaˈʎasu] m fuss; (ostentação) ostentation

estas [ˈeʃtaʃ] fpl de **este**

estatal [iʃtaˈtaw] (pl **-ais**) adj nationalized, state-owned ♦ f state-owned company

estático, -a [iʃˈtatʃiku, a] adj static

estatística [iʃtaˈtʃiʃtʃika] f statistic; (ciência) statistics sg

estatizar [iʃtatʃiˈzaʰ] vt to nationalize

estátua [iʃˈtatwa] f statue

estatura [iʃtaˈtura] f stature

estatuto [iʃtaˈtutu] m statute; (de cidade) bye-law; (de associação) rule

estável [iʃˈtavew] (pl **-eis**) adj stable

este [ˈeʃtʃi] m east ♦ adj inv (região) eastern; (vento, direção) easterly

este, -ta [ˈeʃtʃi, ˈeʃta] adj (sg) this; (pl) these ♦ pron this one; (pl) these; (a quem/que se referiu por último) the latter; **esta noite** (noite passada) last night; (noite de hoje)

tonight

esteira [iʃˈtejra] f mat; (de navio) wake; (rumo) path

esteja etc [iʃˈteʒa] vb V **estar**

estelionato [iʃteljoˈnatu] m fraud

estender [iʃteˈdeʰ] vt to extend; (mapa) to spread out; (pernas) to stretch; (massa) to roll out; (conversa) to draw out; (corda) to pull tight; (roupa molhada) to hang out; **estender-se** vr to lie down; (fila, terreno) to stretch, extend; **~ a mão** to hold out one's hand; **~-se sobre algo** to dwell on sth, expand on sth

estéreis [iʃˈterejʃ] adj pl de **estéril**

estereo... [iʃˈterju] prefixo stereo...;
estereofônico, -a [iʃterjoˈfoniku, a] adj stereo(phonic); **estereótipo** [iʃteˈrjɔtʃipu] m stereotype

estéril [iʃˈteriw] (pl **-eis**) adj sterile; (terra) infertile; (fig) futile; **esterilizar** [iʃteriliˈzaʰ] vt to sterilize

estético, -a [iʃˈtetʃiku, a] adj aesthetic (BRIT), esthetic (US)

esteve [iʃˈtevi] vb V **estar**

estibordo [iʃtʃiˈbɔxdu] m starboard

esticar [iʃtʃiˈkaʰ] vt to stretch; **esticar-se** vr to stretch out

estigma [iʃˈtʃigma] m mark, scar; (fig) stigma

estilhaçar [iʃtʃiʎaˈsaʰ] vt to splinter; (despedaçar) to shatter; **estilhaçar-se** vr to shatter; **estilhaço** [iʃtʃiˈʎasu] m fragment, chip; (de pedra) chip; (de madeira, metal) splinter

estilo [iʃˈtʃilu] m style; (TEC) stylus; **~ de vida** way of life

estima [iʃˈtʃima] f esteem; (afeto) affection; **ter ~ a** to have a high regard for

estimação [iʃtʃimaˈsãw] f: ... **de ~** favourite (BRIT) ..., favorite (US) ...

estimado, -a [iʃtʃiˈmadu, a] adj respected; (em cartas): **E~ Senhor**

Dear Sir

estimar [iʃtʃiˈmaˈ] vt to appreciate; (avaliar) to value; (ter estima a) to have a high regard for; (calcular aproximadamente) to estimate

estimativa [iʃtʃimaˈtʃiva] f estimate

estimulante [iʃtʃimuˈlãtʃi] adj stimulating ♦ m stimulant

estimular [iʃtʃimuˈlaˈ] vt to stimulate; (incentivar) to encourage; **estímulo** [iʃˈtʃimulu] m stimulus; (ânimo) encouragement

estipular [iʃtʃipuˈlaˈ] vt to stipulate

estirar [iʃtʃiˈraˈ] vt to stretch (out); **estirar-se** vr to stretch

estive etc [iʃˈtʃivi] vb V **estar**

estocada [iʃtoˈkada] f stab, thrust

estocar [iʃtoˈkaˈ] vt to stock

estofo [iʃˈtofu] m (tecido) material; (para acolchoar) padding, stuffing

estojo [iʃˈtoʒu] m case; ~ **de ferramentas** tool kit; ~ **de unhas** manicure set

estômago [iʃˈtomagu] m stomach; **ter** ~ **para (fazer) algo** to be up to (doing) sth

estontear [iʃtõˈtʃjaˈ] vt to stun, daze

estoque [iʃˈtɔki] m (COM) stock

estorvo [iʃˈtoxvu] m hindrance, obstacle; (amolação) bother, nuisance

estourado, -a [iʃtoˈradu, a] adj (temperamental) explosive; (col: cansado) shattered, worn out

estourar [iʃtoˈraˈ] vi to explode; (pneu) to burst; (escândalo) to blow up; (guerra) to break out; (BR: chegar) to turn up, arrive; ~ (com alguém) (zangar-se) to blow up (at sb)

estouro [iʃˈtoru] m explosion; **dar o** ~ (fig: zangar-se) to blow up, blow one's top

estrábico, -a [iʃˈtrabiku, a] adj cross-eyed

estraçalhar [iʃtrasaˈʎaˈ] vt (livro, objeto) to pull to pieces; (pessoa) to tear to pieces

estrada [iʃˈtrada] f road; ~ **de ferro** (BR) railway (BRIT), railroad (US); ~ **principal** main road (BRIT), state highway (US)

estrado [iʃˈtradu] m (tablado) platform; (de cama) base

estragado, -a [iʃtraˈgadu, a] adj ruined; (fruta) rotten; (muito mimado) spoiled, spoilt (BRIT)

estraga-prazeres [iʃtraga-] m/f inv spoilsport

estragar [iʃtraˈgaˈ] vt to spoil; (arruinar) to ruin, wreck; (desperdiçar) to waste; (saúde) to damage; (mimar) to spoil; **estrago** [iʃˈtragu] m destruction; waste; damage; **os estragos da guerra** the ravages of war

estrangeiro, -a [iʃtrãˈʒejru, a] adj foreign ♦ m/f foreigner; **no** ~ abroad

estrangular [iʃtrãguˈlaˈ] vt to strangle

estranhar [iʃtraˈɲaˈ] vt to be surprised at; (achar estranho): ~ **algo** to find sth strange; **estranhei o clima** the climate did not agree with me; **não é de se** ~ it's not surprising

estranho, -a [iʃˈtraɲu, a] adj strange, odd; (influências) outside ♦ m/f (desconhecido) stranger; (de fora) outsider

estratégia [iʃtraˈtɛʒa] f strategy

estrear [iʃˈtrjaˈ] vt (vestido) to wear for the first time; (peça de teatro) to perform for the first time; (veículo) to use for the first time; (filme) to show for the first time, première; (iniciar): ~ **uma carreira** to embark on ou begin a career ♦ vi (ator, jogador) to make one's first appearance; (filme, peça) to open

estrebaria [iʃtrebaˈria] f stable

estréia [iʃˈtreja] f (de artista) debut; (de uma peça) first night; (de um filme) première, opening

estreitar [iʃtrejˈta*] vt to narrow; (roupa) to take in; (abraçar) to hug; (laços de amizade) to strengthen ♦ vi (estrada) to narrow

estreito, -a [iʃˈtrejtu, a] adj narrow; (saia) straight; (vínculo, relação) close; (medida) strict ♦ m strait

estrela [iʃˈtrela] f star; ~ **cadente** falling star; **estrelado, -a** [iʃtreˈladu, a] adj (céu) starry; (ovo) fried

estremecer [iʃtremeˈse*] vt to shake; (amizade) to strain; (fazer tremer): ~ **alguém** to make sb shudder ♦ vi to shake; (tremer) to tremble; (horrorizar-se) to shudder; (amizade) to be strained

estremecimento [iʃtremesiˈmetu] m shaking, trembling; (tremor) tremor; (numa amizade) tension

estresse [iʃˈtresi] m stress

estribeira [iʃtriˈbejra] f: **perder as ~s** (col) to fly off the handle, lose one's temper

estribo [iʃˈtribu] m (de cavalo) stirrup; (degrau) step; (fig: apoio) support

estridente [iʃtriˈdetʃi] adj shrill, piercing

estrofe [iʃˈtrɔfi] f stanza

estrondo [iʃˈtrodu] m (de trovão) rumble; (de armas) din

estrutura [iʃtruˈtura] f structure; (armação) framework; (de edifício) fabric

estudante [iʃtuˈdatʃi] m/f student; **estudantil** [iʃtudaˈtʃiw] (pl **-is**) adj student atr

estudar [iʃtuˈda*] vt, vi to study

estúdio [iʃˈtudʒu] m studio

estudioso, -a [iʃtuˈdʒozu, ɔza] adj studious ♦ m/f student

estudo [iʃˈtudu] m study

estufa [iʃˈtufa] f (fogão) stove; (de plantas) greenhouse; (de fogão) plate warmer; **efeito ~** greenhouse effect

estufado, -a [iʃtuˈfadu] (PT) m stew

estupefato, -a [iʃtupeˈfatu, a] (PT -ct-) adj dumbfounded

estupendo, -a [iʃtuˈpedu, a] adj wonderful, terrific

estupidez [iʃtupiˈdeʒ] f stupidity; (ato, dito) stupid thing; (grosseria) rudeness

estúpido, -a [iʃˈtupidu, a] adj stupid; (grosseiro) rude, churlish ♦ m/f idiot; oaf

estuprar [iʃtuˈpra*] vt to rape; **estupro** [iʃˈtupru] m rape

esvaziar [iʒvaˈzja*] vt to empty; **esvaziar-se** vr to empty

etapa [eˈtapa] f stage

etc. abr (= et cetera) etc.

eternidade [etexniˈdadʒi] f eternity; **eterno, -a** [eˈtexnu, a] adj eternal

ética [ˈetʃika] f ethics pl

ético, -a [ˈetʃiku, a] adj ethical

Etiópia [eˈtʃjɔpja] f: **a ~** Ethiopia

etiqueta [etʃiˈketa] f etiquette; (rótulo, em roupa) label; (que se amarra) tag

étnico, -a [ˈetʃniku, a] adj ethnic

etos [ˈetuʃ] m inv ethos

eu [ew] pron I ♦ m self; **sou ~** it's me

EUA abr mpl (= Estados Unidos da América) USA

eucaristia [ewkariʃˈtʃia] f Holy Communion

euro [ˈewru] m (moeda) euro

Europa [ewˈrɔpa] f: **a ~** Europe; **europeu, -péia** [ewroˈpeu, ˈpeja] adj, m/f European

evacuar [evaˈkwa*] vt to evacuate;

(*sair de*) to leave; (*MED*) to discharge
♦ *vi* to defecate

evadir [eva'dʒi*] *vt* to evade;
evadir-se *vr* to escape

evangelho [evã'ʒeʎu] *m* gospel

evaporar [evapo'ra*] *vt*, *vi* to
evaporate; **evaporar-se** *vr* to evaporate; (*desaparecer*) to vanish

evasão [eva'zãw] (*pl* -ões) *f* escape,
flight; (*fig*) evasion

evasiva [eva'ziva] *f* excuse

evasivo, -a [eva'zivu, a] *adj* evasive

evasões [eva'zõjʃ] *fpl de* **evasão**

evento [e'vẽtu] *m* event; (*eventuali-
dade*) eventuality

eventual [evẽ'tuaw] (*pl* -ais) *adj*
fortuitous, accidental; **eventuali-
dade** [evẽtuali'dadʒi] *f* eventuality

evidência [evi'dẽsja] *f* evidence,
proof; **evidenciar** [evidẽ'sja*] *vt* to
prove; (*mostrar*) to show;
evidenciar-se *vr* to be evident, be
obvious

evidente [evi'dẽtʃi] *adj* obvious,
evident

evitar [evi'ta*] *vt* to avoid; ~ **de
fazer algo** to avoid doing sth

evocar [evo'ka*] *vt* to evoke; (*espíri-
tos*) to invoke

evolução [evolu'sãw] (*pl* -ões) *f*
development; (*MIL*) manoeuvre
(*BRIT*), maneuver (*US*); (*movimento*)
movement; (*BIO*) evolution

evoluir [evo'lwi*] *vi* to evolve; ~
para to evolve into

ex- [eʃ-, eʒ-] *prefixo* ex-, former

Ex.ª *abr* = **Excelência**

exacto, -a *etc* [e'zatu, a] (*PT*) =
exato *etc*

exagerar [ezaʒe'ra*] *vt* to exaggerate ♦ *vi* to exaggerate; (*agir com
exagero*) to overdo it; **exagero**
[eza'ʒeru] *m* exaggeration

exalar [eza'la*] *vt* (*odor*) to give off

exaltado, -a [ezaw'tadu, a] *adj*

fanatical; (*apaixonado*) overexcited

exaltar [ezaw'ta*] *vt* (*elevar: pessoa,
virtude*) to exalt; (*louvar*) to praise;
(*excitar*) to excite; (*irritar*) to annoy;
exaltar-se *vr* (*irritar-se*) to get
worked up; (*arrebatar-se*) to get
carried away

exame [e'zami] *m* (*EDUC*) examination, exam; (*MED etc*) examination;
fazer um ~ (*EDUC*) to take an exam;
(*MED*) to have an examination

examinar [ezami'na*] *vt* to examine

exasperar [ezaʃpe'ra*] *vt* to exasperate; **exasperar-se** *vr* to get
exasperated

exatidão [ezatʃi'dãw] *f* accuracy;
(*perfeição*) correctness

exato, -a [e'zatu, a] *adj* right, correct; (*preciso*) exact; ~**!** exactly!

exaustão [ezaw'ʃtãw] *f* exhaustion;
exausto, -a [e'zawʃtu, a] *adj*
exhausted

exaustor [ezaw'ʃto*] *m* extractor
fan

exceção [ese'sãw] (*pl* -ões) *f* exception; **com** ~ **de** with the exception
of; **abrir** ~ to make an exception

excedente [ese'dẽtʃi] *adj* excess;
(*COM*) surplus ♦ *m* (*COM*) surplus

exceder [ese'de*] *vt* to exceed;
(*superar*) to surpass; **exceder-se** *vr*
(*cometer excessos*) to go too far;
(*cansar-se*) to overdo things

excelência [ese'lẽsja] *f* excellence;
por ~ par excellence; **Vossa E~**
Your Excellency; **excelente**
[ese'lẽtʃi] *adj* excellent

excêntrico, -a [e'sẽtriku, a] *adj*,
m/f eccentric

exceção [ese'sãw] (*PT*) *f* =
exceção

excepcional [esepsjo'naw] (*pl*
-ais) *adj* exceptional; (*especial*) special; (*MED*) handicapped

excepto etc [e'sɛtu] (PT) = **exceto** etc

excessivo, -a [ese'sivu, a] adj excessive

excesso [e'sɛsu] m excess; (COM) surplus

exceto [e'sɛtu] prep except (for), apart from

excitação [esita'sãw] f excitement

excitado, -a [esi'tadu, a] adj excited; (estimulado) aroused

excitante [esi'tãtʃi] adj exciting

excitar [esi'ta*] vt to excite; (estimular) to arouse; **excitar-se** vr to get excited

exclamação [iʃklama'sãw] (pl -ões) f exclamation

exclamar [iʃkla'ma*] vi to exclaim

excluir [iʃ'klwi*] vt to exclude, leave out; (eliminar) to rule out; (ser incompatível com) to preclude; **exclusão** [iʃklu'zãw] f exclusion; **exclusivo, -a** [iʃklu'zivu, a] adj exclusive

excursão [iʃkux'sãw] (pl -ões) f outing, excursion; ~ **a pé** hike; **excursionista** [iʃkuxsjo'niʃta] m/f tourist; (para o dia) day-tripper; (a pé) hiker

execução [ezeku'sãw] (pl -ões) f execution; (de música) performance

executar [ezeku'ta*] vt to execute; (MÚS) to perform; (plano) to carry out; (papel teatral) to play

executivo, -a [ezeku'tʃivu, a] adj, m/f executive

exemplar [ezẽ'pla*] adj exemplary ♦ m model, example; (BIO) specimen; (livro) copy; (peça) piece

exemplo [e'zẽplu] m example; por ~ for example

exercer [ezex'se*] vt to exercise; (influência, pressão) to exert; (função) to perform; (profissão) to practise (BRIT), practice (US); (obri-

gações) to carry out

exercício [ezex'sisju] m exercise; (de medicina) practice; (MIL) drill; (COM) financial year

exercitar [ezexsi'ta*] vt (profissão) to practise (BRIT), practice (US); (direitos, músculos) to exercise; (adestrar) to train

exército [e'zɛxsitu] m army

exibição [ezibi'sãw] (pl -ões) f show, display; (de filme) showing

exibir [ezi'bi*] vt to show, display; (alardear) to show off; (filme) to show, screen; **exibir-se** vr to show off; (indecentemente) to expose o.s.

exigência [ezi'ʒẽsja] f demand; (o necessário) requirement; **exigente** [ezi'ʒẽtʃi] adj demanding

exigir [ezi'ʒi*] vt to demand

exíguo, -a [e'zigwu, a] adj (diminuto) small; (escasso) scanty

exilado, -a [ezi'ladu, a] m/f exile

exilar [ezi'la*] vt to exile; **exilar-se** vr to go into exile; **exílio** [e'zilju] m exile; (forçado) deportation

existência [eziʃ'tẽsja] f existence; (vida) life

existir [eziʃ'tʃi*] vi to exist; **existe/ existem** ... (há) there is/are ...

êxito ['ezitu] m result; (sucesso) success; (música, filme etc) hit; **ter ~ (em)** to succeed (in), be successful (in)

Exmo(s)/a(s) abr = Excelentíssimo(s)/a(s)) Dear

êxodo ['ezodu] m exodus

exorcista [ezox'siʃta] m/f exorcist

exótico, -a [e'zɔtʃiku, a] adj exotic

expandir [iʃpã'dʒi*] vt to expand; (espalhar) to spread; **expandir-se** vr to expand; ~-**se com alguém** to be frank with sb

expansão [iʃpã'sãw] f expansion, spread; (de alegria) effusiveness

expansivo, -a [iʃpã'sivu, a] adj

(*pessoa*) outgoing

expeça *etc* [iʃˈpesa] *vb V* expedir

expectativa [iʃpektaˈtʃiva] *f* expectation

expedição [iʃpedʒiˈsãw] (*pl* -ões) *f* (*viagem*) expedition; (*de mercadorias*) despatch; (*por navio*) shipment; (*de passaporte etc*) issue

expediente [iʃpeˈdʒjētʃi] *m* means; (*serviço*) working day; (*correspondência*) correspondence ♦ *adj* expedient; ~ **bancário** banking hours *pl*; ~ **do escritório** office hours *pl*

expedir [iʃpeˈdʒi*] *vt* to send, despatch; (*bilhete, passaporte, decreto*) to issue

expelir [iʃpeˈli*] *vt* to expel; (*sangue*) to spit

experiência [iʃpeˈrjẽsja] *f* experience; (*prova*) experiment, test; **em** ~ on trial

experiente [iʃpeˈrjẽtʃi] *adj* experienced

experimentar [iʃperimẽˈta*] *vt* (*comida*) to taste; (*vestido*) to try on; (*pôr à prova*) to try out, test; (*conhecer pela experiência*) to experience; (*sofrer*) to suffer, undergo; **experimento** [iʃperiˈmẽtu] *m* experiment

expilo *etc* [iʃˈpilu] *vb V* expelir

expirar [iʃpiˈra*] *vt* to exhale, breathe out ♦ *vi* to die; (*terminar*) to end

explicação [iʃplikaˈsãw] (*pl* -ões) *f* explanation

explicar [iʃpliˈka*] *vt, vi* to explain; **explicar-se** *vr* to explain o.s.

explícito, -a [iʃˈplisitu, a] *adj* explicit, clear

explodir [iʃploˈdʒi*] *vt, vi* to explode

exploração [iʃploraˈsãw] *f* exploration; (*abuso*) exploitation; (*de uma mina*) working

explorador, a [iʃploraˈdo*, a] *m/f* explorer; (*de outros*) exploiter

explorar [iʃploˈra*] *vt* (*região*) to explore; (*mina*) to work, run; (*ferida*) to probe; (*trabalhadores etc*) to exploit

explosão [iʃploˈzãw] (*pl* -ões) *f* explosion; (*fig*) outburst; **explosivo, -a** [iʃploˈzivu, a] *adj* explosive; (*pessoa*) hot-headed ♦ *m* explosive

expor [iʃˈpo*] (*irreg: como* pôr) *vt* to expose; (*a vida*) to risk; (*teoria*) to explain; (*revelar*) to reveal; (*mercadorias*) to display; (*quadros*) to exhibit; **expor-se** *vr* to expose o.s.

exportação [iʃpoxtaˈsãw] *f* (*ato*) export(ing); (*mercadorias*) exports *pl*

exportador, a [iʃpoxtaˈdo*, a] *adj* exporting ♦ *m/f* exporter

exportar [iʃpoxˈta*] *vt* to export

exposição [iʃposiˈzãw] (*pl* -ões) *f* exhibition; (*explicação*) explanation; (*declaração*) statement; (*narração*) account; (*FOTO*) exposure

exposto, -a [iʃˈpoʃtu, ˈpoʃta] *adj* (*lugar*) exposed; (*quadro, mercadoria*) on show ou display ♦ *m*: **o** **acima** ~ the above

expressão [iʃpreˈsãw] (*pl* -ões) *f* expression

expressar [iʃpreˈsa*] *vt* to express; **expressivo, -a** [iʃpreˈsivu, a] *adj* expressive; (*pessoa*) demonstrative

expresso, -a [iʃˈpresu, a] *pp de* exprimir ♦ *adj* definite, clear; (*trem, ordem, carta*) express ♦ *m* express

expressões [iʃpreˈsõjʃ] *fpl de* expressão

exprimir [iʃpriˈmi*] *vt* to express

expulsão [iʃpulˈsãw] (*pl* -ões) *f* expulsion; (*ESPORTE*) sending off

expulsar [iʃpuwˈsa*] *vt* to expel; (*de uma festa, clube etc*) to throw out; (*inimigo*) to drive out; (*estrangeiro*) to expel, deport, (*jogador*) to send off

expulso, -a [iʃ'puwsu, a] *pp de* **expulsar**

expulsões [iʃpul'sõjʃ] *fpl de* **expulsão**

êxtase ['eʃtazi] *m* ecstasy

extensão [iʃtẽ'sãw] (*pl* **-ões**) *f* (*ger*, *TEL*) extension; (*de uma empresa*) expansion; (*terreno*) expanse; (*tempo*) length, duration; (*de conhecimentos*) extent

extenso, -a [iʃ'tẽsu, a] *adj* extensive; (*comprido*) long; (*artigo*) full, comprehensive; **por ~** in full

extenuante [iʃte'nwãtʃi] *adj* exhausting, (*debilitante*) debilitating

exterior [iʃte'rjo*] *adj* (*de fora*) outside, exterior; (*aparência*) outward; (*comércio*) foreign ♦ *m* (*da casa*) outside; (*aspecto*) outward appearance; **do ~** (*do estrangeiro*) from abroad; **no ~** abroad

exterminar [iʃtexmi'na*] *vt* (*inimigo*) to wipe out, exterminate; (*acabar com*) to do away with

externo, -a [iʃ'texnu, a] *adj* external; (*aparente*) outward; **aluno ~** day pupil

extinguir [iʃtʃĩ'gi*] *vt* (*fogo*) to put out, extinguish; (*um povo*) to wipe out; **extinguir-se** *vr* (*fogo, luz*) to go out; (*BIO*) to become extinct

extinto, -a [iʃ'tʃĩtu, a] *adj* (*fogo*) extinguished; (*língua, pessoa*) dead; (*animal, vulcão*) extinct; (*associação etc*) defunct; **extintor** [iʃtʃĩ'to*] *m* (*fire*) extinguisher

extorquir [iʃtox'ki*] *vt* to extort

extorsão [iʃtox'sãw] *f* extortion

extra ['eʃtra] *adj* extra ♦ *m/f* extra person; (*TEATRO*) extra

extração [iʃtra'sãw] (*PT* **-cç-**) (*pl* **-ões**) *f* extraction; (*de loteria*) draw

extracto [iʃ'tratu] (*PT*) *m* = **extrato**

extrair [iʃtra'ji*] *vt* to extract, take out

extraordinário, -a [iʃtraoxdʒi-'narju, a] *adj* extraordinary; (*despesa*) extra; (*reunião*) special

extrato [iʃ'tratu] *m* extract; (*resumo*) summary; **~ (bancário)** (bank) statement

extravagância [iʃtrava'gãsja] *f* extravagance; **extravagante** [iʃtrava'gãtʃi] *adj* extravagant; (*roupa*) outlandish; (*conduta*) wild

extravasar [iʃtrava'za*] *vi* to overflow

extraviado, -a [iʃtra'vjadu, a] *adj* lost, missing

extraviar [iʃtra'vja*] *vt* to mislay; (*pessoa*) to lead astray; (*dinheiro*) to embezzle; **extraviar-se** *vr* to get lost; **extravio** [iʃtra'viu] *m* loss; embezzlement; (*fig*) deviation

extremado, -a [iʃtre'madu, a] *adj* extreme

extremidade [iʃtremi'dadʒi] *f* extremity; (*do dedo*) tip; (*ponta*) end; (*beira*) edge

extremo, -a [iʃ'tremu, a] *adj* extreme ♦ *m* extreme; **ao ~** extremely

extrovertido, -a [eʃtrovex'tʃidu, a] *adj* extrovert, outgoing ♦ *m/f* extrovert

exultante [ezuw'tãtʃi] *adj* jubilant, exultant

F

fã [fã] (*col*) *m/f* fan

fábrica ['fabrika] *f* factory; **~ de cerveja** brewery; **a preço de ~** wholesale

fabricação [fabrika'sãw] *f* manufacture; **~ em série** mass production

fabricar [fabri'ka*] vt to manufacture, make

fábula ['fabula] f fable; (conto) tale

fabuloso, -a [fabu'lozu, ɔza] adj fabulous

faca ['faka] f knife; **facada** [fa'kada] f stab, cut

façanha [fa'saɲa] f exploit, deed

facção [fak'sãw] (pl -ões) f faction

face ['fasi] f face; (bochecha) cheek; **em ~ de** in view of; **fazer ~ a** to face up to; **disquete de ~ simples/dupla** (COMPUT) single/double-sided disk

fáceis ['fasejʃ] adj pl de **fácil**

faceta [fa'seta] f facet

fachada [fa'ʃada] f façade, front

fácil ['fasiw] (pl -eis) adj easy; (temperamento, pessoa) easy-going ♦ adv easily; **facilidade** [fasili'dadʒi] f ease; (jeito) facility; **facilidades** fpl (recursos) facilities; **ter facilidade para algo** to have a talent for sth

facilitar [fasili'ta*] vt to facilitate, make easy; (fornecer): **~ algo a alguém** to provide sb with sth

faço ['fasu] vb V **fazer**

fac-símile [fak'simili] (pl ~s) m (cópia) facsimile; (carta) fax; (máquina) fax (machine); **enviar por ~** to fax

facto ['faktu] (PT) m = **fato**

factor [fak'to*] (PT) m = **fator**

factual [fak'twaw] (pl -ais) adj factual

factura etc [fak'tura] (PT) = **fatura** etc

faculdade [fakuw'dadʒi] f (ger, EDUC) faculty; (poder) power

facultativo, -a [fakuwta'tʃivu, a] adj optional ♦ m/f doctor

fadado, -a [fa'dadu, a] adj destined

fadiga [fa'dʒiga] f fatigue

fadista [fa'dʒiʃta] m/f fado singer ♦ m (PT) ruffian

fado ['fadu] m fate; (canção) fado;

see boxed note

FADO

The best-known musical form in Portugal is the melancholic **fado**, which is traditionally sung by a soloist (known as a **fadista**) accompanied by the Portuguese *guitarra*. There are two main types of **fado**: Coimbra **fado** is traditionally sung by men, and is considered to be more cerebral than the **fado** from Lisbon, which is sung by both men and women. The theme is nearly always one of deep nostalgia known as *saudade*, and the harsh reality of life.

---

faia ['faja] f beech (tree)

faisão [faj'zãw] (-ies, pl -ães) m pheasant

faísca [fa'iʃka] f spark; (brilho) flash

faisões [faj'zõjʃ] mpl de **faisão**

faixa ['fajʃa] f (cinto, JUDÔ) belt; (tira) strip; (área) zone; (AUTO: pista) lane; (BR: para pedestres) zebra crossing (BRIT), crosswalk (US); (MED) bandage; (num disco) track

fala ['fala] f speech; **chamar às ~s** to call to account; **sem ~** speechless

falante [fa'lãtʃi] adj talkative

falar [fa'la*] vt (língua) to speak; (besteira etc) to talk; (dizer) to say; (verdade, mentira) to tell ♦ vi to speak; **~ algo a alguém** to tell sb sth; **~ de** ou **em algo** to talk about sth; **~ com alguém** to talk to sb; **por ~ em** speaking of; **sem ~ em** not to mention; **falou!, 'tá falado!** (col) OK!

falcão [faw'kãw] (pl -ões) m falcon

falecer [fale'se*] vi to die; **falecimento** [falesi'mẽtu] m death

falência [fa'lẽsja] f bankruptcy; **abrir ~** to declare o.s. bankrupt; **ir à**

~ to go bankrupt; **levar à** ~ to bankrupt

falésia [fa'lɛzja] f cliff

falha ['faʎa] f fault; (*lacuna*) omission; (*de caráter*) flaw

falhar [fa'ʎa*] vi to fail; (*não acertar*) to miss; (*errar*) to be wrong

falho, -a ['faʎu, a] adj faulty; (*deficiente*) wanting

falido, -a [fa'lidu, a] adj, m/f bankrupt

falir [fa'li*] vi to fail; (COM) to go bankrupt

falsário, -a [faw'sarju, a] m/f forger

falsidade [fawsi'dadʒi] f falsehood; (*fingimento*) pretence (BRIT), pretense (US)

falsificar [fawsifi'ka*] vt (*forjar*) to forge; (*falsear*) to falsify; (*adulterar*) to adulterate; (*desvirtuar*) to misrepresent

falso, -a ['fawsu, a] adj false; (*fraudulento*) dishonest; (*errôneo*) wrong; (*jóia, moeda, quadro*) fake; **pisar em ~** to blunder

falta ['fawta] f (*carência*) lack; (*ausência*) absence; (*defeito, culpa*) fault; (FUTEBOL) foul; **por ou na ~ de** for lack of; **sem ~** without fail; **fazer ~** to be lacking, be needed; **sentir ~ de alguém/algo** to miss sb/sth; **ter ~ de** to lack, be in need of

faltar [faw'ta*] vi to be lacking, be wanting; (*pessoa*) to be absent; (*falhar*) to fail; **~ ao trabalho** to be absent from work; **~ à palavra** to break one's word; **falta pouco para ... it won't be long until ...

fama ['fama] f (*renome*) fame; (*reputação*) reputation

família [fa'milja] f family

familiar [fami'lja*] adj (*da família*) family atr; (*conhecido*) familiar ♦ m/f relation, relative; **familiaridade** [familjari'dadʒi] f familiarity; (*sem*

cerimônia) informality

faminto, -a [fa'mĩtu, a] adj hungry; (fig): **~ de** eager for

famoso, -a [fa'mozu, ɔza] adj famous

fanático, -a [fa'natʃiku, a] adj fanatical ♦ m/f fanatic

fantasia [fãta'zia] f fantasy; (*imaginação*) imagination; (*capricho*) fancy; (*traje*) fancy dress

fantasiar [fãta'zja*] vt to imagine ♦ vi to daydream; **fantasiar-se** vr to dress up (in fancy dress)

fantasma [fã'taʒma] m ghost; (*alucinação*) illusion

fantástico, -a [fã'tajtʃiku, a] adj fantastic; (*ilusório*) imaginary; (*incrível*) unbelievable

fantoche [fã'tɔʃi] m puppet

farda ['faxda] f uniform

fardo ['faxdu] m bundle; (*carga*) load; (fig) burden

farei etc [fa'rej] vb V **fazer**

farinha [fa'riɲa] f: **~ (de mesa)** (manioc) flour; **~ de rosca** breadcrumbs pl; **~ de trigo** plain flour

farmacêutico, -a [faxma-'sewtʃiku, a] adj pharmaceutical ♦ m/f pharmacist, chemist (BRIT)

farmácia [fax'masja] f pharmacy, chemist's (shop) (BRIT)

faro ['faru] m sense of smell; (fig) flair

farofa [fa'rɔfa] f (CULIN) side dish based on manioc flour

farol [fa'rɔw] m (pl -óis) m lighthouse; (AUTO) headlight; **com ~ alto** (AUTO) on full (BRIT) ou high (US) beam; **com ~ baixo** dipped headlights pl (BRIT), dimmed beam (US)

farra ['faxa] f binge, spree

farrapo [fa'xapu] m rag

farsa ['faxsa] f farce; **farsante** [fax'sãtʃi] m/f joker

fartar [fax'ta*] vt to satiate; (*encher*)

to fill up; **fartar-se** *vr* to gorge o.s.

farto, -a ['faxtu, a] *adj* full, satiated; (*abundante*) plentiful; (*aborrecido*) fed up

fartura [fax'tura] *f* abundance

fascinante [fasi'nãtʃi] *adj* fascinating

fascinar [fasi'na*] *vt* to fascinate; (*encantar*) to charm; **fascínio** [fa'sinju] *m* fascination

fascismo [fa'siʒmu] *m* fascism

fase ['fazi] *f* phase

fatal [fa'taw] (*pl* **-ais**) *adj* (*mortal*) fatal; (*inevitável*) inevitable; **fatalidade** [fatali'dadʒi] *f* fate; (*desgraça*) disaster

fatia [fa'tʃia] *f* slice

fatigante [fatʃi'gãtʃi] *adj* tiring; (*aborrecido*) tiresome

fatigar [fatʃi'ga*] *vt* to tire; (*aborrecer*) to bore; **fatigar-se** *vr* to get tired

Fátima ['fatima] *f* Fatima; *see boxed note*

FÁTIMA

Fátima, situated in central Portugal, is known worldwide as a site of pilgrimage for Catholics. It is said that, in 1917, the Virgin Mary appeared six times to three shepherd children (*os três pastorinhos*). Millions of pilgrims visit Fátima every year.

---

fato ['fatu] *m* fact; (*acontecimento*) event; (*PT: traje*) suit; **~ de banho** (*PT*) swimming costume (*BRIT*), bathing suit (*US*); **de ~** in fact, really

fator [fa'to*] *m* factor

fatura [fa'tura] *f* bill, invoice; **faturar** [fatu'ra*] *vt* to invoice; (*dinheiro*) to make ♦ *vi* (*col: ganhar dinheiro*) to rake it in

fava ['fava] *f* broad bean; **mandar**

alguém às **~s** to send sb packing

favela [fa'vɛla] *f* slum

favor [fa'vo*] *m* favour (*BRIT*), favor (*US*); **a ~ de** in favo(u)r of; **por ~** please; **faça ou faz o ~ de** ... would you be so good as to ...; **kindly** ...;

favorável [favo'ravew] (*pl* **-eis**) *adj*: **favorável (a)** favo(u)rable (to);

favorecer [favore'se*] *vt* to favo(u)r; (*beneficiar*) to benefit; (*suj: vestido*) to suit; (*: retrato*) to flatter;

favorito [favo'ritu, a] *adj, m/f* favo(u)rite

fax [faks] *m* (*carta*) fax; (*máquina*) fax (machine); **enviar por ~** to fax

faxina [fa'ʃina] *f*: **fazer ~** to clean up; **faxineiro, -a** [faʃi'nejru, a] *m/f* cleaner

fazenda [fa'zẽda] *f* farm; (*de café*) plantation; (*de gado*) ranch; (*pano*) cloth, fabric; (*ECON*) treasury; **fazendeiro** [fazẽ'dejru] *m* farmer; (*de café*) plantation-owner; (*de gado*) rancher, ranch-owner

---

PALAVRA CHAVE

fazer [fa'ze*] *vt* **1** (*fabricar, produzir*) to make; (*construir*) to build; (*pergunta*) to ask; (*poema, música*) to write; **~ um filme/ruído** to make a film/noise

2 (*executar*) to do; **o que você está fazendo?** what are you doing?; **~ a comida** to do the cooking; **~ o papel de** (*TEATRO*) to play

3 (*estudos, alguns esportes*) to do; **~ medicina/direito** to do *ou* study medicine/law; **~ ioga/ginástica** to do yoga/keep-fit

4 (*transformar, tornar*): **sair o fará sentir melhor** going out will make him feel better; **sua partida fará o trabalho mais difícil** his departure will make work more difficult

5 (*como sustituto de vb*): **ele bebeu**

e eu fiz o mesmo he drank and I did likewise

6: ~ **anos**: ele faz anos hoje it's his birthday today; **fiz 30 anos ontem** I was 30 yesterday

♦ vi 1 (*portar-se*) to act, behave; ~ **bem/mal** to do the right/wrong thing; **não fiz por mal** I didn't mean it; **faz como quem não sabe** act as if you don't know anything

2: ~ **com que alguém faça algo** to make sb do sth

♦ vb impess 1: **faz calor/frio** it's hot/cold

2 (*tempo*): **faz um ano** a year ago; **faz dois anos que ele se formou** it's two years since he graduated; **faz três meses que ele está aqui** he's been here for three months

3: **nao faz mal** never mind, **tanto faz** it's all the same; **fazer-se** vr 1: ~-**se de desentendido** to pretend not to understand

2: **faz-se com ovos e leite** it's made with eggs and milk; **isso não se faz** that's not done

fé [fe] f faith; (*crença*) belief; (*confiança*) trust; **de boa/má** ~ in good/bad faith

febre ['fɛbri] f fever; (*fig*) excitement; ~ **do feno** hay fever; **febril** [fe'briw] (*pl* -**is**) *adj* feverish

fechado, -a [fe'ʃadu, a] *adj* shut, closed; (*pessoa*) reserved; (*sinal*) red; (*luz, torneira*) off; (*tempo*) overcast; (*cara*) stern

fechadura [feʃa'dura] f lock

fechar [fe'ʃa*] vt to close, shut; (*concluir*) to finish, conclude; (*luz, torneira*) to turn off; (*rua*) to close off; (*ferida*) to close up; (*bar, loja*) to close down ♦ vi to close (up), shut; to close down; (*tempo*) to cloud over; **fechar-se** vr to close, shut;

(*pessoa*) to withdraw; ~ **à chave** to lock

fecho ['feʃu] m fastening; (*trinco*) latch; (*término*) close; ~ **ecler** zip fastener (*BRIT*), zipper (*US*)

fécula ['fɛkula] f starch

feder [fe'de*] vi to stink

federação [federa'sãw] (*pl* -**ões**) f federation

federal [fede'raw] (*pl* -**ais**) *adj* federal; (*col: grande*) huge

fedor [fe'do*] m stink

feijão [fej'ʒãw] (*pl* -**ões**) m bean(s) (*pl*); (*preto*) black bean(s) (*pl*); **feijoada** [fej'ʒwada] f (*CULIN*) meat, rice and black beans

felo, -a ['fɛju, a] *adj* (*situação*) grim; (*atitude*) bad; (*tempo*) horrible ♦ *adv* (*perder*) badly

feira ['fejra] f fair; (*mercado*) market

feiticeira [fejtʃi'sejra] f witch

feiticeiro, -a [fejtʃi'sejru, a] *adj* bewitching, enchanting ♦ m wizard

feitiço [fej'tʃisu] m charm, spell

feitio [fej'tʃiu] m shape, pattern; (*caráter*) nature, manner; (*TEC*) workmanship

feito, -a ['fejtu, a] *pp de* **fazer** ♦ *adj* finished, ready ♦ m act, deed; (*façanha*) feat ♦ *conj* like; ~ **à mão** hand-made; **homem** ~ grown man

feiúra [fe'jura] f ugliness

felicidade [felisi'dadʒi] f happiness; (*sorte*) good luck; (*êxito*) success; ~**s** *fpl* (*congratulações*) congratulations

felicitações [felisita'sõjʃ] *fpl* congratulations, best wishes

feliz [fe'liʒ] *adj* happy; (*afortunado*) lucky; **felizmente** [feliʒ'mẽtʃi] *adv* fortunately

feltro ['fewtru] m felt

fêmea ['femja] f female

feminino, -a [femi'ninu, a] *adj* feminine; (*sexo*) female; (*equipe*, *roupa*) women's ♦ *m* (*LING*) feminine

feminista [femi'niʃta] *adj, m/f* feminist

fenda ['fẽda] *f* slit, crack; (*GEO*) fissure

feno ['fenu] *m* hay

fenomenal [fenome'naw] (*pl* **-ais**) *adj* phenomenal; (*espantoso*) amazing; (*pessoa*) brilliant

fenômeno [fe'nomenu] *m* phenomenon

fera ['fɛra] *f* wild animal

feriado [fe'rjadu] *m* holiday (*BRIT*), vacation (*US*)

férias ['fɛrjaʃ] *fpl* holidays, vacation *sg*; **de ~** on holiday; **tirar ~** to have *ou* take a holiday

ferida [fe'rida] *f* wound, injury; *V tb* ferido

ferido, -a [fe'ridu, a] *adj* injured; (*em batalha*) wounded; (*magoado*) hurt ♦ *m/f* casualty

ferimento [feri'mẽtu] *m* injury; (*em batalha*) wound

ferir [fe'ri*] *vt* to injure; (*tb fig*) to hurt; (*em batalha*) to wound; (*ofender*) to offend

fermentar [fexmẽ'ta*] *vi* to ferment

fermento [fex'mẽtu] *m* yeast; **~ em pó** baking powder

feroz [fe'rɔʒ] *adj* fierce, ferocious; (*cruel*) cruel

ferradura [fexa'dura] *f* horseshoe

ferragem [fexa'ʒẽ] (*pl* **-ns**) *f* (*peças*) hardware; (*guarnição*) metalwork; **loja de ferragens** ironmonger's (*BRIT*), hardware store

ferramenta [fexa'mẽta] *f* tool; (*caixa de ~s*) tool kit; **~ de busca** (*COMPUT*) search engine

ferrão [fe'xãw] (*pl* **-ões**) *m* goad; (*de inseto*) sting

ferreiro [fe'xejru] *m* blacksmith

ferrenho, -a [fe'xeɲu, a] *adj* (*von-*

tade) iron

ferro ['fexu] *m* iron; **~s** *mpl* (*algemas*) shackles, chains; **~ batido** wrought iron; **~ de passar** iron; **~ fundido** cast iron; **~ ondulado** corrugated iron

ferrões [fe'xõjʃ] *mpl* de **ferrão**

ferrolho [fe'xoʎu] *m* (*trinco*) bolt

ferrovia [fexo'via] *f* railway (*BRIT*), railroad (*US*); **ferroviário, -a** [fexo'vjarju, a] *adj* railway (*BRIT*), railroad *atr* (*US*) ♦ *m/f* railway *ou* railroad worker

ferrugem [fe'xuʒẽ] *f* rust

fértil ['fɛxtʃiw] (*pl* **-eis**) *adj* fertile; **fertilizante** [fextʃili'zãtʃi] *m* fertilizer; **fertilizar** [fextʃili'za*] *vt* to fertilize

ferver [fex've*] *vt, vi* to boil; **~ de raiva/indignação** to seethe with rage/indignation; **~ em fogo baixo** (*CULIN*) to simmer

fervilhar [fexvi'ʎa*] *vi* to simmer; (*com atividade*) to hum; (*pulular*): **~ de** to swarm with

fervor [fex'vo*] *m* fervour (*BRIT*), fervor (*US*)

festa ['fɛʃta] *f* (*reunião*) party; (*conjunto de cerimônias*) festival; **~s** *fpl* (*carícia*) embrace *sg*; **boas ~s** Merry Christmas and a Happy New Year; **dia de ~** public holiday

festejar [feʃte'ʒa*] *vt* to celebrate; (*acolher*) to welcome, greet; **festejo** [feʃ'teʒu] *m* festivity; (*ato*) celebration

festival [feʃtʃi'vaw] (*pl* **-ais**) *m* festival

festividade [feʃtʃivi'dadʒi] *f* festivity

festivo, -a [feʃ'tʃivu, a] *adj* festive

fetiche [fe'tʃiʃi] *m* fetish

feto ['fetu] *m* (*MED*) foetus (*BRIT*), fetus (*US*)

fevereiro [feve'rejru] (*PT* **F-**) *m*

February

fez [feʒ] vb V **fazer**

fezes ['fezif] fpl faeces (BRIT), feces (US)

fiado, -a ['fjadu, a] adv: **comprar/vender ~** to buy/sell on credit

fiador, a [fja'do*, a] m/f (JUR) guarantor; (COM) backer

fiambre ['fjãbri] m cold meat; (presunto) ham

fiança ['fjãsa] f guarantee; (JUR) bail; **prestar ~ por** to stand bail for; **sob ~** on bail

fiar ['fja*] vt (algodão etc) to spin; (confiar) to entrust; (vender a crédito) to sell on credit; **fiar-se** vr: **~-se em** to trust

fibra ['fibra] f fibre (BRIT), fiber (US)

───── *PALAVRA CHAVE* ─────

ficar [fi'ka*] vi 1 (permanecer) to stay; (sobrar) to be left; **~ perguntando/olhando** etc to keep asking/looking etc; **~ por fazer** to have still to be done; **~ para trás** to be left behind

2 (tornar-se) to become; **~ cego/surdo/louco** to go blind/deaf/mad; **fiquei contente ao saber da notícia** I was happy when I heard the news; **~ com raiva/medo** to get angry/frightened; **~ de bem/mal com alguém** (col) to make up/fall out with sb

3 (posição) to be: **a casa fica ao lado da igreja** the house is next to the church; **~ sentado/deitado** to be sitting down/lying down

4 (tempo: durar): **ele ficou duas horas para resolver** he took two hours to decide; (: ser adiado): **a reunião ficou para amanhã** the meeting was postponed until the following day

5: **~ bem** (comportamento): **sua atitude não ficou bem** his (ou her etc) behaviour was inappropriate; (cor): **você fica bem em azul** blue suits you, you look good in blue; (roupa): **~ bem para** to suit

6: **~ bom** (de saúde) to be cured; (trabalho, foto etc) to turn out well

7: **~ de fazer algo** (combinar) to arrange to do sth; (prometer) to promise to do sth

8: **~ de pé** to stand up

─────────────

ficção [fik'sãw] f fiction

ficha ['fiʃa] f (tb: **~ de telefone**) token; (tb: **~ de jogo**) chip; (de fichário) (index) card; (POLÍCIA) record; (PT: ELET) plug; (em loja, lanchonete) ticket

fichário [fi'ʃarju] m filing cabinet; (caixa) card index; (caderno) file

ficheiro [fi'ʃejru] (PT) m = **fichário**

fictício, -a [fik'tʃisju, a] adj fictitious

fidelidade [fideli'dadʒi] f fidelity, loyalty; (exatidão) accuracy

fiel [fjew] (pl -**éis**) adj (leal) faithful, loyal; (acurado) accurate; (que não falha) reliable

figa ['figa] f talisman; **fazer uma ~** to make a figa = cross one's fingers; **de uma ~** (col) damned

fígado ['figadu] m liver

figo ['figu] m fig; **figueira** [fi'gejra] f fig tree

figura [fi'gura] f figure; (forma) form, shape; (LING) figure of speech; (aspecto) appearance

figurino [figu'rinu] m model; (revista) fashion magazine

fila ['fila] f row, line; (BR: fileira de pessoas) queue (BRIT), line (US); (num teatro, cinema) row; **em ~** in a row; **fazer ~** to form a line, queue; **~ indiana** single file

filé [fi'le] m (bife) steak; (peixe) fillet

fileira [fi'lejru] f row, line; **~s** fpl (serviço militar) military service sg

filho, -a ['fiʎu, a] m/f son/daughter; **~s** mpl children; (de animais) young

filhote [fi'ʎɔtʃi] m (de leão, urso etc) cub; (cachorro) pup(py)

filial [fi'ljaw] (pl **-ais**) f (sucursal) branch

Filipinas [fili'pinaʃ] fpl: **as ~** the Philippines

filmadora [fiwma'doru] f camcorder

filmar [fiw'ma*] vt, vi to film

filme ['fiwmi] m film (BRIT), movie (US)

filosofia [filozo'fia] f philosophy; **filósofo, -a** [fi'lɔzofu, a] m/f philosopher

filtrar [fiw'tra*] vt to filter; **filtrar-se** vr to filter; (infiltrar-se) to infiltrate

filtro ['fiwtru] m (TEC) filter

fim [fĩ] (pl **-ns**) m end; (motivo) aim, purpose; (de história, filme) ending; **a ~ de** in order to; **no ~ das contas** after all; **por ~** finally; **sem ~** endless; **levar ao ~** to carry through; **pôr** ou **dar ~ a** to put an end to; **ter ~** to come to an end; **~ de semana** weekend

finado, -a [fi'nadu, a] m/f deceased; **dia dos F~s** day of the dead; see boxed note

---

DIA DOS FINADOS

The **dia dos Finados**, 2 November, a holiday throughout Brazil, is dedicated to remembering the dead. On this day, people usually gather in cemeteries to honour their family dead, and also to worship at the graves of popular figures from Brazilian culture and society, such as singers, actors and other personalities. It is popularly believed that these people can work miracles.

---

final [fi'naw] (pl **-ais**) adj final, last ♦ m end; (MÚS) finale ♦ f (ESPORTE) final; **finalista** [fina'liʃta] m/f finalist; **finalizar** [finali'za*] vt to finish, conclude

finanças [fi'nãsaʃ] fpl finance sg; **financeiro, -a** [finã'sejru, a] adj financial ♦ m/f financier; **financiar** [finã'sja*] vt to finance

fingimento [fiʒi'mẽtu] m pretence (BRIT), pretense (US)

fingir [fi'ʒi*] vt to feign ♦ vi to pretend; **fingir-se** vr: **~-se de** to pretend to be

finito, -a [fi'nitu, a] adj finite

finlandês, -esa [filã'deʃ, eza] adj Finnish ♦ m/f Finn ♦ m (LING) Finnish

Finlândia [fi'lãdʒja] f: **a ~** Finland

fino, -a ['finu, a] adj fine; (delgado) slender; (educado) polite; (som, voz) shrill; (elegante) refined ♦ adv: **falar ~** to talk in a high voice

fins [fĩʃ] mpl de **fim**

fio ['fiu] m thread; (BOT) fibre (BRIT), fiber (US); (ELET) wire; (TEL) line; (de líquido) trickle; (gume) edge; (encadeamento) series; **horas/dias a ~** hours/days on end

firma ['fixma] f signature; (COM) firm, company

firmar [fix'ma*] vt to secure, make firm; (assinar) to sign; (estabelecer) to establish; (basear) to base ♦ vi (tempo) to settle; **firmar-se** vr: **~-se em** (basear-se) to rest on, be based on

firme ['fixmi] adj firm; (estável) stable; (sólido) solid; (tempo) settled ♦ adv firmly; **firmeza** [fix'meza] f firmness; stability; solidity

fiscal [fiʃ'kaw] (pl **-ais**) m/f supervisor; (aduaneiro) customs officer; (de impostos) tax inspector; **fiscalizar** [fiʃkali'za*] vt to supervise; (examinar) to inspect, check

fisco ['fiʃku] m: **o ~** ≈ the Inland Revenue (BRIT), ≈ the Internal Revenue Service (US)

física ['fizika] f physics sg; V tb **físico**

físico, -a ['fiziku, a] adj physical ♦ m/f (cientista) physicist ♦ m (corpo) physique

fisionomia [fizjono'mia] f (rosto) face; (ar) expression, look; (aspecto de algo) appearance

fissura [fi'sura] f crack

fita ['fita] f tape; (tira) strip, band; (filme) film; (para máquina de escrever) ribbon; **~ durex** ® adhesive tape, sellotape ® (BRIT), scotchtape ® (US); **~ métrica** tape measure

fitar [fi'ta*] vt to stare at, gaze at

fivela [fi'vɛla] f buckle

fixar [fik'sa*] vt to fix; (colar, prender) to stick; (data, prazo, regras) to set; (atenção) to concentrate; **fixar-se** vr: **~-se em** (assunto) to concentrate on; (detalhe) to fix on; (apegar-se a) to be attached to; **~ os olhos em** to stare at; **~ residência** to set up house

fixo, -a ['fiksu, a] adj fixed; (firme) firm; (permanente) permanent; (cor) fast

fiz etc [fiʒ] vb V **fazer**

flagelado, -a [flaʒe'ladu, a] m/f: **os ~s** the afflicted, the victims

flagrante [fla'grãtʃi] adj flagrant; **apanhar em ~** (delito) to catch red-handed ou in the act

flagrar [fla'gra*] vt to catch

flanela [fla'nɛla] f flannel

flash [flaʃ] m (FOTO) flash

flauta ['flawta] f flute

flecha ['flɛʃa] f arrow

fleu(g)ma ['flewma] f phlegm

flexível [flek'sivew] (pl -eis) adj flexible

floco ['flɔku] m flake; **~ de milho** cornflake; **~ de neve** snowflake

flor [flo*] f flower; (o melhor): **a ~ de** the cream of, the pick of; **em ~** in bloom; **à ~ de** on the surface of

florescente [flore'sẽtʃi] adj (BOT) in flower; (próspero) flourishing

florescer [flore'se*] vi (BOT) to flower; (prosperar) to flourish

floresta [flo'rɛʃta] f forest; **~ tropical** rainforest; **florestal** [florej'taw*] (pl **florestais**) adj forest atr

florido, -a [flo'ridu, a] adj (jardim) in flower

fluente [flu'ẽtʃi] adj fluent

fluido, -a ['flwidu, a] adj fluid ♦ m fluid

fluir [flwi*] vi to flow

fluminense [flumi'nẽsi] adj from the state of Rio de Janeiro ♦ m/f native ou inhabitant of the state of Rio de Janeiro

flutuar [flu'twa*] vi to float; (bandeira) to flutter; (fig: vacilar) to waver

fluvial [flu'vjaw*] (pl -ais) adj river atr

fluxo ['fluksu] m (corrente) flow; (ELET) flux; **~ de caixa** (COM) cash flow

fobia [fo'bia] f phobia

foca ['fɔka] f seal

focinho [fo'siɲu] m snout; (col: cara) face, mug (col)

foco ['fɔku] m focus; (MED, fig) seat, centre (BRIT), center (US); **fora de ~/em foco** out of focus, in/out of focus

fofo, -a ['fofu, a] adj soft; (col: pessoa) cute

fofoca [fo'fɔka] f piece of gossip; **~s** fpl (mexericos) gossip sg; **fofocar** [fofo'ka*] vi to gossip

fogão [fo'gãw] (pl -ões) m stove, cooker

fogareiro [foga'rejru] m stove

foge etc ['fɔʒi] vb V **fugir**

fogo ['fogu] m fire; (fig) ardour (BRIT), ardor (US); **você tem ~?** have you got a light?; **~s de artifício** fireworks; **pôr ~ a** to set fire to

fogões [fo'gõjʃ] mpl de **fogão**

fogueira [fo'gejra] f bonfire

foguete [fo'getʃi] m rocket

foi [foj] vb V **ir**; **ser**

folclore [fowk'lɔri] m folklore

folclórico, -a [fowk'lɔriku, a] adj (música etc) folk; (comida, roupa) ethnic

fôlego ['folegu] m breath; (folga) breathing space; **perder o ~** to get out of breath

folga ['fowga] f rest, break; (espaço livre) clearance; (ócio) inactivity; (col: atrevimento) cheek; **dia de ~** day off; **folgado, -a** [fow'gadu, a] adj (roupa) loose; (vida) leisurely; (col: atrevido) cheeky; **folgar** [fow'ga*] vt to loosen ♦ vi (descansar) to rest; (divertir-se) to have fun

folha ['foʎa] f leaf; (de papel, de metal) sheet; (página) page; (de faca) blade; (jornal) paper; **novo em ~** brand new; **~ de estanho** tinfoil (BRIT), aluminum foil (US)

folhagem [fo'ʎaʒẽ] f foliage

folheto [fo'ʎetu] m booklet, pamphlet

fome ['fɔmi] f hunger; (escassez) famine; (fig: avidez) longing; **passar ~** to go hungry; **estar com** ou **ter ~** to be hungry

fomentar [fomẽ'ta*] vt to instigate, incite; **fomento** [fo'mẽtu] m (estímulo) incitement

fone ['fɔni] m telephone, phone; (peça de telefone) receiver

fonte ['fõtʃi] f (nascente) spring; (chafariz) fountain; (origem) source; (ANAT) temple

for etc [fo*] vb V **ir**; **ser**

fora¹ ['fɔra] adv out, outside ♦ prep (além de) apart from ♦ m: **dar o ~** (bateria, radio) to give out; (pessoa) to leave, be off; **dar um ~** to slip up; **dar um ~ em/levar um ~** (namorado) to chuck ou dump/be given the boot; (esnobar) to snub sb/get the brush-off; **~ de** outside; **~ de si** beside o.s.; **estar ~** (viajando) to be away; **estar ~ (de casa)** (de casa) to be out; **lá ~** outside; (no exterior) abroad; **jantar ~** to eat out; **com os braços de ~** with bare arms; **ser de ~** to be from out of town; **ficar de ~** not to join in; **lá para ~** outside; **ir para ~** (viajar) to go out of town; **com a cabeça para ~ da janela** with one's head sticking out of the window; **costurar/cozinhar para ~** to do sewing/cooking for other people; **por ~** on the outside; **cobrar por ~** (cobrar) to charge extra, extra; **~ de dúvida** beyond doubt; **~ de propósito** irrelevant

fora² etc vb V **ir**; **ser**

foragido, -a [fora'ʒidu, a] adj, m/f (fugitivo) fugitive

forasteiro, -a [foraʃ'tejru, a] m/f outsider, stranger; (de outro país) foreigner

forca ['foxka] f gallows sg

força ['foxsa] f strength; (TEC, ELET) power; (esforço) effort; (coerção) force; **à ~** by force; **à ~ de** by dint of; **com ~** hard; **por ~** of necessity; **fazer ~** to try (hard); **~ de trabalho** workforce

forçado, -a [fox'sadu, a] adj forced; (afetado) false

forçar [fox'sa*] vt to force; (olhos, voz) to strain

forma ['fɔxma] f form; (de um objeto) shape; (físico) figure; (maneira) way; (MED) fitness; **desta ~** in this way; **de qualquer ~** anyway; **manter a ~** to keep fit

fôrma ['foxma] f (CULIN) cake tin; (*molde*) mould (BRIT), mold (US)

formação [foxma'sãw] (pl -ões) f formation; (*antecedentes*) background; (*caráter*) make-up; (*protissional*) training

formado, -a [fox'madu, a] adj (*modelado*): **ser ~ de** to consist of ♦ m/f graduate

formal [fox'maw] (pl -ais) adj formal; **formalidade** [foxmali'dadʒi] f formality

formar [fox'ma*] vt to form; (*constituir*) to constitute, make up; (*educar*) to train; **formar-se** vr to form; (EDUC) to graduate

formatar [foxma'ta*] vt (COMPUT) to format

formidável [foxmi'davew] (pl -eis) adj tremendous, great

formiga [fox'miga] f ant

formigar [foxmi'ga*] vi to abound; (*sentir comichão*) to itch

formoso, -a [fox'mozu, ɔza] adj beautiful; (*esplêndido*) superb

fórmula ['fɔxmula] f formula

formular [foxmu'la*] vt to formulate; (*queixas*) to voice

formulário [foxmu'larju] m form; **~s** mpl: **~s contínuos** (COMPUT) continuous stationery sg

fornecedor, a [foxnese'do*, a] m/f supplier ♦ f (*empresa*) supplier

fornecer [foxne'se*] vt to supply, provide; **fornecimento** [foxnesi'mẽtu] m supply

forno ['foxnu] m (CULIN) oven; (TEC) furnace; (*para cerâmica*) kiln; **alto ~** blast furnace

foro ['foru] m forum; (JUR) Court of Justice; **~s** mpl (*privilégios*) privileges

forro ['foxu] m covering; lining

fortalecer [foxtale'se*] vt to strengthen

fortaleza [foxta'leza] f fortress; (*força*) strength; (*moral*) fortitude

forte ['fɔxtʃi] adj strong; (*pancada*) hard; (*chuva*) heavy; (*tocar*) loud; (*dor*) sharp ♦ adv strongly; (*tocar*) loud(ly) ♦ m fort; (*talento*) strength; **ser ~ em algo** (*versado*) to be good at sth ou strong in sth

fortuito, -a [fox'twitu, a] adj accidental

fortuna [fox'tuna] f fortune, (good) luck; (*riqueza*) fortune, wealth

fosco, -a ['fɔʃku, a] adj dull; (*opaco*) opaque

fósforo ['fɔʃforu] m match

fossa ['fɔsa] f pit

fosse etc ['fɔsi] vb V ir; ser

fóssil ['fɔsiw] (pl -eis) m fossil

fosso ['fosu] m trench, ditch

foto ['fɔtu] f photo

fotocópia [foto'kɔpja] f photocopy; **fotocopiadora** [fotokoja'dora] f photocopier; **fotocopiar** [fotoko'pja*] vt to photocopy

fotografar [fotogra'fa*] vt to photograph

fotografia [fotogra'fia] f photography; (*uma ~*) photograph

fotógrafo, -a [fo'tɔgrafu, a] m/f photographer

foz [fɔʒ] f mouth of river

fração [fra'sãw] (pl -ões) f fraction

fracassar [fraka'sa*] vi to fail; **fracasso** [fra'kasu] m failure

fracção [fra'sãw] (PT) f = **fração**

fraco, -a ['fraku, a] adj weak; (*sol, som*) faint

fractura etc [fra'tura] (PT) f = **fratura** etc

frade ['fradʒi] m (REL) friar; (: *monge*) monk

frágil ['fraʒiw] (pl -eis) adj (*débil*) fragile; (COM) breakable; (*pessoa*) frail; (saúde) delicate, poor

fragmento [fraɡˈmẽtu] m fragment

fragrância [fraˈɡrãsja] f fragrance, perfume

fralda [ˈfrawda] f (da camisa) shirt tail; (para bebê) nappy (BRIT), diaper (US); (de montanha) foot

framboesa [frãˈbeza] f raspberry

França [ˈfrãsa] f France

francamente [frãkaˈmẽtʃi] adv (abertamente) frankly; (realmente) really

francês, -esa [frãˈseʃ, eza] adj French ♦ m/f Frenchman/woman ♦ m (LING) French

franco, -a [ˈfrãku, a] adj frank; (isento de pagamento) free; (óbvio) clear ♦ m franc; **entrada franca** free admission

frango [ˈfrãɡu] m chicken

franja [ˈfrãʒa] f fringe (BRIT), bangs pl (US)

franqueza [frãˈkeza] f frankness

franquia [frãˈkia] f (COM) franchise; (isenção) exemption

franzino, -a [frãˈzinu, a] adj skinny

fraqueza [fraˈkeza] f weakness

frasco [ˈfraʃku] m bottle

frase [ˈfrazi] f sentence; ~ **feita** set phrase

fratura [fraˈtura] f fracture, break; **fraturar** [fratuˈra*] vt to fracture

fraude [ˈfrawdʒi] f fraud

freada [freˈada] (BR) f: **dar uma ~** to slam on the brakes

frear [freˈa*] (BR) vt to curb, restrain; (veículo) to stop ♦ vi (veículo) to brake

freezer [ˈfrize*] m freezer

freguês, -guesa [freˈɡeʃ, ˈɡeza] m/f customer; (PT) parishioner; **freguesia** [freɡeˈzia] f customers pl; parish

freio [ˈfreju] m (BR: de veículo) brake; (de cavalo) bridle; (bocado do ~) bit;

~ **de mão** handbrake

freira [ˈfrejra] f nun

frenesi [freneˈzi] m frenzy; **frenético, -a** [freˈnɛtʃiku, a] adj frantic, frenzied

frente [ˈfrẽtʃi] f front; (rosto) face; (fachada) façade; ~ **a** ~ face to face; **de** ~ **para** facing; **em** ~ **de** in front of; (de fronte a) opposite; **para a** ~ ahead, forward; **porta da** ~ front door; **seguir em** ~ to go straight on; **na minha** (ou **sua** etc) ~ in front of me (ou you etc); **sair da** ~ to get out of the way; **pra** ~ (col) fashionable, trendy

freqüência [freˈkwẽsja] f frequency; **com** ~ often, frequently

freqüentar [frekwẽˈta*] vt to frequent

freqüente [freˈkwẽtʃi] adj frequent

fresco, -a [ˈfreʃku, a] adj fresh; (vento, tempo) cool; (col: efeminado) camp; (: afetado) pretentious; (: cheio de luxo) fussy ♦ m (ar) fresh air

frescobol [freʃkoˈbɔw] m (kind of) racketball (played mainly on the beach)

frescura [freʃˈkura] f freshness; (frialdade) coolness; (col: luxo) fussiness; (: afetação) pretentiousness

frete [ˈfretʃi] m (carregamento) freight, cargo; (tarifa) freightage

frevo [ˈfrevu] m improvised Carnival dance

fria [ˈfria] f: **dar uma ~ em alguém** to give sb the cold shoulder; **estar/entrar numa ~** (col) to be in/get into a mess

fricção [frikˈsãw] f friction; (ato) rubbing; (MED) massage; **friccionar** [friksjoˈna*] vt to rub

frieza [friˈeza] f coldness; (indiferença) coolness

frigideira [friʒiˈdejra] f frying pan

frigorífico [friɡoˈrifiku] m frigrigerator; (*congelador*) freezer

frio, -a ['friu, a] *adj* cold ♦ *m* cold; **~s** *mpl* (CULIN) cold meats; **estou com ~** I'm cold; **faz** *ou* **está ~** it's cold

frisar [fri'za*] *vt* (*encrespar*) to curl; (*salientar*) to emphasize

fritar [fri'ta*] *vt* to fry

fritas ['fritaʃ] *fpl* chips (BRIT), French fries (US)

frito, -a ['fritu, a] *adj* fried; (*col*): **estar ~** to be done for

frívolo, -a ['frivulu, a] *adj* frivolous

fronha ['fɾoɲa] *f* pillowcase

fronteira [fɾõ'tejra] *f* frontier, border

frota ['fɾɔta] *f* fleet

frouxo, -a ['fɾoʃu, a] *adj* loose; (*corda, fig: pessoa*) slack; (*fraco*) weak; (*col: condescendente*) soft

frustrar [fɾuʃ'tɾa*] *vt* to frustrate

fruta ['fɾuta] *f* fruit; **frutífero, -a** [fɾu'tʃiferu, a] *adj* (*proveitoso*) fruitful; (*árvore*) fruit-bearing

fruto ['fɾutu] *m* (BOT) fruit; (*resultado*) result, product; **dar ~** (*fig*) to bear fruit

fubá [fu'ba] *m* corn meal

fuga ['fuga] *f* flight, escape; (*de gás etc*) leak

fugir [fu'ʒi*] *vi* to flee, escape; (*prisioneiro*) to escape

fugitivo, -a [fuʒi'tʃivu, a] *adj, m/f* fugitive

fui [fuj] *vb* V **ir; ser**

fulano, -a [fu'lanu, a] *m/f* so-and-so

fuligem [fu'liʒẽ] *f* soot

fulminante [fuwmi'nãtʃi] *adj* devastating; (*palavras*) scathing

fulo, -a ['fulu, a] *adj*: **estar** *ou* **ficar ~ de raiva** to be furious

fumaça [fu'masa] (BR) *f* (*de fogo*) smoke; (*de gás*) fumes *pl*

fumador, a [fuma'do*, a] *m/f* (PT) smoker

fumante [fu'mãtʃi] *m/f* smoker

fumar [fu'ma*] *vt, vi* to smoke

fumo ['fumu] *m* (PT: *de fogo*) smoke; (: *de gás*) fumes *pl*; (BR: *tabaco*) tobacco; (*fumar*) smoking

função [fũ'sãw] (*pl* **-ões**) *f* function; (*ofício*) duty; (*papel*) role; (*espetáculo*) performance

funcionalismo [fũsjona'liʒmu] *m*: **~ público** civil service

funcionamento [fũsjona'mẽtu] *m* functioning, working; **pôr em ~** to set going, start

funcionar [fũsjo'na*] *vi* to function; (*máquina*) to work, run; (*dar bom resultado*) to work

funcionário, -a [fũsjo'narju, a] *m/f* official; **~ (público)** civil servant

funções [fũ'sõjʃ] *fpl* de **função**

fundação [fũda'sãw] (*pl* **-ões**) *f* foundation

fundamental [fũdamẽ'taw] (*pl* **-ais**) *adj* fundamental, basic

fundamento [fũda'mẽtu] *m* (*fig*) foundation, basis; (*motivo*) motive

fundar [fũ'da*] *vt* to establish, found; (*basear*) to base; **fundar-se** *vr*: **~-se em** to be based on

fundir [fũ'dʒi*] *vt* to fuse; (*metal*) to smelt, melt down; (COM: *empresas*) to merge; (*em molde*) to cast; **fundir-se** *vr* to melt; (*juntar-se*) to merge

fundo, -a ['fũdu, a] *adj* deep; (*fig*) profound ♦ *m* (*do mar, jardim*) bottom; (*profundidade*) depth; (*base*) basis; (*da loja, casa, do papel*) back; (*de quadro*) background; (*de dinheiro*) fund ♦ *adv* deeply; **~s** *mpl* (COM) funds; (*da casa etc*) back *sg*; **a ~ thoroughly; **no ~** at the bottom; (*da casa etc*) at the back; (*fig*) basically

fúnebre ['funebri] *adj* funeral *atr*, funereal; (*fig*) gloomy

funeral [fune'raw] (*pl* **-ais**) *m* funeral

funil [fu'niw] (*pl* **-is**) *m* funnel

furacão [fura'kãw] (*pl* **-ões**) *m*

hurricane

furado, -a [fu'radu, a] *adj* perforated; (*pneu*) flat; (*orelha*) pierced

furão, -rona [fu'rãw, 'rɔna] (*pl* **-ões, ~s**) *m* ferret ♦ *m/f* (*col*) go-getter ♦ *adj* (*col*) hard-working, dynamic

furar [fu'ra*] *vt* to perforate; (*orelha*) to pierce; (*penetrar*) to penetrate; (*frustrar*) to foil; (*fila*) to jump ♦ *vi* (*col: programa*) to fall through

fúria ['furja] *f* fury, rage; **furioso, -a** [fu'rjozu, ɔza] *adj* furious

furo ['furu] *m* hole; (*num pneu*) puncture

furões [fu'rõjʃ] *mpl de* **furão**

furona [fu'rona] *f de* **furão**

furor [fu'ro*] *m* fury, rage; **fazer ~** to be all the rage

furtar [fux'ta*] *vt, vi* to steal; **furtar-se** *vr*: **~-se a** to avoid

furtivo, -a [fux'tʃivu, a] *adj* furtive, stealthy

furto ['fuxtu] *m* theft

fusão [fu'zãw] (*pl* **-ões**) *f* fusion; (COM) merger; (*derretimento*) melting; (*união*) union

fusível [fu'zivew] (*pl* **-eis**) *m* fuse

fuso ['fuzu] *m* (TEC) spindle; **~ horário** time zone

fusões [fu'zõjʃ] *fpl de* **fusão**

futebol [futʃi'bɔw] *m* football; **~ de salão** five-a-side football

futevôlei [futʃi'volej] *m see boxed note*

FUTEVÔLEI

Futevôlei is a type of volleyball in which the ball is allowed to touch only the feet, legs, trunk and head of the players. It is very popular on the beaches of Rio de Janeiro, where tournaments take place during the summer, in which many famous footballers take part.

---

fútil ['futʃiw] (*pl* **-eis**) *adj* (*pessoa*) shallow; (*insignificante*) trivial

futilidade [futʃili'dadʒi] *f* (*de pessoa*) shallowness; (*insignificância*) triviality; (*coisa*) trivial thing

futuro, -a [fu'turu, a] *adj* future ♦ *m* future; **no ~** in the future

fuzil [fu'ziw] (*pl* **-is**) *m* rifle; **fuzilar** [fuzi'la*] *vt* to shoot

fuzis [fu'ziʃ] *mpl de* **fuzil**

G

g. *abr* (= **grama**) gr.

G7 *abr* (= **Grupo dos Sete**) G7

gabar [ga'ba*] *vt* to praise; **gabar-se** *vr*: **~-se de** to boast about

gabinete [gabi'netʃi] *m* (COM) office; (*escritório*) study; (POL) cabinet

gado ['gadu] *m* livestock; (*bovino*) cattle; **~ leiteiro** dairy cattle; **~ suíno** pigs *pl*

gafanhoto [gafa'ɲotu] *m* grasshopper

gafe ['gafi] *f* gaffe, faux pas

gagueira [ga'gejra] *f* stutter

gaguejar [gage'ʒa*] *vi* to stammer, stutter

gaiato, -a [ga'jatu, a] *adj* funny

gaiola [ga'jɔla] *f* cage; (*cadeia*) jail ♦ *m* (*barco*) riverboat

gaita ['gajta] *f* harmonica; **~ de foles** bagpipes *pl*

gaivota [gaj'vɔta] *f* seagull

gajo [ga'ʒu] (PT: *col*) *m* guy, fellow

gala ['gala] *f*: **traje de ~** evening dress; **festa de ~** gala

galão [ga'lãw] (*pl* **-ões**) *m* (MIL) stripe; (*medida*) gallon; (PT: *café*) white coffee; (*passamanaria*) braid

Galápagos [ga'lapaguʃ]: **(as) Ilhas ~** *fpl* (the) Galapagos Islands

galáxia [ga'laksja] *m* galaxy

galera [ga'lɛra] f (NÁUT) galley; (col: pessoas, público) crowd

galeria [gale'ria] f gallery; (TEATRO) circle

Gales ['galiʃ] m: **País de ~** Wales

galho ['gaʎu] m (de árvore) branch

galinha [ga'liɲa] f hen; (CULIN) chicken; **galinheiro** [gali'ɲejru] m hen-house

galo ['galu] m cock, rooster; (inchação) bump; **missa do ~** midnight mass

galões [ga'lõjʃ] mpl de **galão**

galopar [galo'pa*] vi to gallop; **galope** [ga'lɔpi] m gallop

gama ['gama] f (MÚS) scale; (fig) range; (ZOOL) doe

gambá [gã'ba] m (ZOOL) opossum

Gana ['gana] m Ghana

ganá ['gana] f craving, desire; (ódio) hate; **ter ~s de (fazer) algo** to feel like (doing) sth; **ter ~ de alguém** to hate sb

ganância [ga'nãsja] f greed; **ganancioso, -a** [ganã'sjozu, ɔza] adj greedy

gancho ['gãʃu] m hook; (de calça) crotch

gangue ['gãgi] (col) f gang

ganhador, a [gaɲa'do*, a] adj winning ♦ m/f winner

ganha-pão [gaɲa-] (pl -ões) m living, livelihood

ganhar [ga'ɲa*] vt to win; (salário) to earn; (adquirir) to get; (lugar) to reach; (lucrar) to gain ♦ vi to win; **~ de alguém** (num jogo) to beat sb; **ganho, -a** ['gaɲu, a] pp de **ganhar** ♦ m profit, gain; **ganhos** mpl (ao jogo) winnings

ganso, -a ['gãsu, a] m/f gander/goose

garagem [ga'raʒẽ] (pl -ns) f garage

garanhão [gara'ɲãw] (pl -ões) m stallion

garantia [garã'tʃia] f guarantee; (de dívida) surety

garantir [garã'tʃi*] vt to guarantee; **garantir-se** vr: **~-se contra algo** to defend o.s. against sth; **~ que ...** to maintain that ...

garçom [gax'sõ] (BR) (pl -ns) m waiter

garçonete [gaxso'netʃi] (BR) f waitress

garçons [gax'sõʃ] mpl de **garçom**

garfo ['gaxfu] m fork

gargalhada [gaxga'ʎada] f burst of laughter; **rir às ~s** to roar with laughter; **dar ou soltar uma ~** to burst out laughing

gargalo [gax'galu] m (tb fig) bottleneck

garganta [gax'gãta] f throat; (GEO) gorge, ravine

gargarejo [gaxga'reʒu] m (ato) gargling; (líquido) gargle

gari ['gari] m/f (na rua) roadsweeper (BRIT), streetsweeper (US); (lixeiro) dustman (BRIT), garbage man (US)

garoa [ga'roa] f drizzle; **garoar** [ga'rwa*] vi to drizzle

garotada [garo'tada] f: **a ~** the kids pl

garoto, -a [ga'rotu, a] m/f boy/girl, (namorado) boyfriend/girlfriend ♦ m (PT: café) coffee with milk

garoupa [ga'ropa] f (peixe) grouper

garra ['gaxa] f claw; (de ave) talon; (fig: entusiasmo) enthusiasm, drive; **~s** fpl (fig) clutches

garrafa [ga'xafa] f bottle

garupa [ga'rupa] f (de cavalo) hindquarters pl; (de moto) back seat; **andar na ~** (de moto) to ride pillion

gás [gajʃ] m gas; **gases** mpl (do intestino) wind sg; **~ natural** natural gas

gasóleo [ga'zɔlju] m diesel oil

gasolina [gazo'lina] f petrol (BRIT), gas(oline) (US)

gasosa [ga'zɔza] f fizzy drink

gasoso, -a [ga'zozu, ɔza] adj (água) sparkling; (bebida) fizzy

gastador, -deira [gaʃta'do*, 'dejra] adj, m/f spendthrift

gastar [gaʃ'ta*] vt to spend; (gasolina, eletricidade) to use; (roupa, sapato) to wear out; (salto, piso etc) to wear down; (saúde) to damage; (desperdiçar) to waste ♦ vi to spend; to wear out; to wear down; **gastar-se** vr to wear out; to wear down

gasto, -a ['gaʃtu, a] pp de **gastar** ♦ adj spent; (frase) trite; (sapato etc, fig: pessoa) worn out; (salto, piso) worn down ♦ m (despesa) expense; **~s** mpl (COM) expenses, expenditure sg

gata ['gata] f (she-)cat

gatilho [ga'tʃiʎu] m trigger

gato ['gatu] m cat; **~ montês** wild cat

gatuno, -a [ga'tunu, a] adj thieving ♦ m/f thief

gaveta [ga'veta] f drawer

gaze ['gazi] f gauze

geada ['ʒjada] f frost

geladeira [ʒela'dejra] (BR) f refrigerator, icebox (US)

gelado, -a [ʒe'ladu, a] adj frozen ♦ m (PT: sorvete) ice cream

gelar [ʒe'la*] vt to freeze; (vinho etc) to chill ♦ vi to freeze

gelatina [ʒela'tʃina] f gelatine; (sobremesa) jelly (BRIT), jello (US)

geléia [ʒe'lɛja] f jam

gélido, -a ['ʒɛlidu, a] adj chill, icy

gelo ['ʒelu] adj inv light grey (BRIT) ou gray (US) ♦ m ice; (cor) light grey (BRIT) ou gray (US)

gema ['ʒema] f yolk; (pedra preciosa) gem

gêmeo, -a ['ʒemju, a] adj, m/f twin;

G~s mpl (ASTROLOGIA) Gemini sg

gemer [ʒe'me*] vi (de dor) to groan, moan; (lamentar-se) to wail; (animal) to whine; (vento) to howl; **gemido** [ʒe'midu] m groan, moan; wail; whine

gene ['ʒeni] m gene

Genebra [ʒe'nebra] n Geneva

general [ʒene'raw] (pl **-ais**) m general

generalizar [ʒenerali'za*] vt to propagate ♦ vi to generalize; **generalizar-se** vr to become general, spread

gênero ['ʒeneru] m type, kind; (BIO) genus; (LING) gender; **~s** mpl (produtos) goods; **~s alimentícios** foodstuffs; **~ humano** humankind, human race

generosidade [ʒenerozi'dadʒi] f generosity

generoso, -a [ʒene'rozu, ɔza] adj generous

genética [ʒe'nɛtʃika] f genetics sg

gengibre [ʒẽ'ʒibri] m ginger

gengiva [ʒẽ'ʒiva] f (ANAT) gum

genial [ʒe'njaw] (pl **-ais**) adj inspired, brilliant; (col) terrific, fantastic

gênio ['ʒenju] m (temperamento) nature; (irascibilidade) temper; (talento, pessoa) genius; **de bom/mau ~** good-natured/bad-tempered

genital [ʒeni'taw] (pl **-ais**) adj: **órgãos genitais** genitals pl

genro ['ʒẽxu] m son-in-law

gente ['ʒẽtʃi] f people pl; (col) folks pl, family; (: alguém): **tem ~ batendo à porta** there's somebody knocking at the door; **a ~** (nós: suj) we; (: objeto) us; **a casa da ~** our house; **toda a ~** everybody; **~ grande** grown-ups pl

gentil [ʒẽ'tʃiw] (pl **-is**) adj kind; **gentileza** [ʒẽtʃi'leza] f kindness,

por gentileza if you please; **tenha a gentileza de fazer ...?** would you be so kind as to do ...?

genuíno, -a [ʒe'nwinu, a] *adj* genuine

geografia [ʒeogra'fia] *f* geography

geometria [ʒeome'tria] *f* geometry

geração [ʒera'sãw] (*pl* -**ões**) *f* generation

gerador, a [ʒera'do*, a] *m/f* (*produtor*) creator ♦ *m* (*TEC*) generator

geral [ʒe'raw] (*pl* -**ais**) *adj* general ♦ *f* (*TEATRO*) gallery; **em ~** in general, generally; **de um modo ~** on the whole; **geralmente** [ʒeraw'mẽtʃi] *adv* generally, usually

gerânio [ʒe'ranju] *m* geranium

gerar [ʒe'ra*] *vt* to produce; (*eletricidade*) to generate

gerência [ʒe'rẽsja] *f* management; **gerenciar** [ʒerẽ'sja*] *vt, vi* to manage

gerente [ʒe'rẽtʃi] *adj* managing ♦ *m/f* manager

gerir [ʒe'ri*] *vt* to manage, run

germe ['ʒexmi] *m* (*embrião*) embryo; (*micróbio*) germ

gesso ['ʒesu] *m* plaster (of Paris)

gestante [ʒeʃ'tãtʃi] *f* pregnant woman

gesticular [ʒeʃtʃiku'la*] *vi* to make gestures, gesture

gesto ['ʒeʃtu] *m* gesture

Gibraltar [ʒibraw'ta*] *f* Gibraltar

gigante, -ta [ʒi'gãtʃi, ta] *adj* gigantic, huge ♦ *m* giant; **gigantesco, -a** [ʒigã'teʃku, a] *adj* gigantic

gim [ʒĩ] (*pl* -**ns**) *m* gin

ginásio [ʒi'nazju] *m* gymnasium; (*escola*) secondary (*BRIT*) *ou* high (*US*) school

ginástica [ʒi'naʃtʃika] *f* gymnastics *sg*; (*para fortalecer o corpo*) keep-fit

ginecologia [ʒinekolo'ʒia] *f* gynaecology (*BRIT*), gynecology (*US*)

ginecologista [ʒinekolo'ʒiʃta] *m/f* gynaecologist (*BRIT*), gynecologist (*US*)

ginjinha [ʒĩ'ʒiɲa] (*PT*) *f* cherry brandy

gira-discos ['ʒira-] (*PT*) *m inv* record-player

girafa [ʒi'rafa] *f* giraffe

girar [ʒi'ra*] *vt* to turn, rotate; (*como pião*) to spin ♦ *vi* to go round; to spin; (*vaguear*) to wander

girassol [ʒira'sɔw] (*pl* -**óis**) *m* sunflower

giratório, -a [ʒira'tɔrju, a] *adj* revolving

gíria ['ʒirja] *f* (*calão*) slang; (*jargão*) jargon

giro¹ ['ʒiru] *m* turn; **dar um ~** to go for a wander; (*em veículo*) to go for a spin; **que ~!** (*PT*) terrific!

giro² *etc vb* V **gerir**

giz [ʒiʃ] *m* chalk

glacê [gla'se] *m* icing

glacial [gla'sjaw] (*pl* -**ais**) *adj* icy

glamouroso, -a [glamu'rozu, ɔza] *adj* glamorous

glândula [gla'dula] *f* gland

global [glo'baw] (*pl* -**ais**) *adj* global; (*total*) overall; **quantia ~** lump sum

globo ['globu] *m* globe; ~ **ocular** eyeball

glória ['glɔrja] *f* glory; **glorificar** [glorifi'ka*] *vt* to glorify; **glorioso, -a** [glo'rjozu, ɔza] *adj* glorious

glossário [glo'sarju] *m* glossary

gnomo ['gnomu] *m* gnome

Goa ['goa] *n* Goa

goiaba [go'jaba] *f* guava; **goiabada** [goja'bada] *f* guava jelly

gol [gow] (*pl* -**s**) *m* goal

gola ['gola] *f* collar

gole ['gɔli] *m* gulp, swallow; (*pequeno*) sip; **tomar um ~ de** to sip

goleiro [go'lejru] (*BR*) *m* goalkeeper

golfe ['gowfi] *m* golf; **campo de ~**

golf course

golfinho [gow'fiɲu] *m* (*ZOOL*) dolphin

golfo ['gowfu] *m* gulf

golinho [go'liɲu] *m* sip; **beber algo aos ~s** to sip sth

golo ['golu] (*PT*) *m* = **gol**

golpe ['gɔwpi] *m* (*tb fig*) blow; (*de mão*) smack; (*de punho*) punch; (*manobra*) ploy; (*de vento*) gust; **de um só ~** at a stroke; **dar um ~ em alguém** to hit sb; (*fig: trapacear*) to trick sb; **~ (de estado)** coup (d'état); **~ de mestre** masterstroke;

golpear [gow'pja*] *vt* to hit; (*com navalha*) to stab; (*com o punho*) to punch

goma ['gɔma] *f* gum, glue; (*de roupa*) starch; **~ de mascar** chewing gum

gomo ['gomu] *m* (*de laranja*) slice

gordo, -a ['goxdu, a] *adj* fat; (*gordurento*) greasy; (*carne*) fatty; (*fig: quantia*) considerable, ample ♦ *m/f* fat man/woman

gordura [gox'dura] *f* fat; (*derretida*) grease; (*obesidade*) fatness; **gorduroso, -a** [goxdu'rozu, ɔza] *adj* (*pele*) greasy; (*comida*) fatty

gorila [go'rila] *m* gorilla

gorjeta [gox'ʒeta] *f* tip, gratuity

gorro ['goxu] *m* cap; (*de lã*) hat

gosma ['gɔʒma] *f* spittle; (*fig*) slime

gostar [goʃ'ta*] *vi*: **~ de** to like; (*férias, viagem etc*) to enjoy; **gostar-se** *vr* to like each other; **~ mais de** ... to prefer ..., like ... better

gosto ['goʃtu] *m* taste; (*prazer*) pleasure; **a seu ~** to your liking; **com ~** willingly; (*vestir-se*) tastefully; (*comer*) heartily; **de bom/mau ~** in good/bad taste; **ter ~ de** to taste of;

gostoso, -a [goʃ'tozu, ɔza] *adj* tasty; (*agradável*) pleasant; (*cheiro*

lovely; (*risada*) good; (*col: pessoa*) gorgeous

gota ['gota] *f* drop; (*de suor*) bead; (*MED*) gout; **~ a ~** drop by drop

goteira [go'tejra] *f* (*cano*) gutter; (*buraco*) leak

gourmet [gux'me] (*pl* **~s**) *m/f* gourmet

governador, a [govexnado*, a] *m/f* governor

governamental [govexname'taw] (*pl* **-ais**) *adj* government *atr*

governanta [govex'nãta] *f* (*de casa*) housekeeper; (*de criança*) governess

governante [govex'nãtʃi] *adj* ruling ♦ *m/f* ruler ♦ *f* governess

governar [govex'na*] *vt* to govern, rule; (*barco*) to steer

governo [go'vexnu] *m* government; (*controle*) control

gozação [goza'sãw] (*pl* **-ões**) *f* enjoyment; (*zombaria*) teasing; (*uma* **~**) joke

gozado, -a [go'zadu, a] *adj* funny; (*estranho*) strange, odd

gozar [go'za*] *vt* to enjoy; (*col: rir de*) to make fun of ♦ *vi* to enjoy o.s.; **~ de** to enjoy; to make fun of; **gozo** ['gozu] *m* (*prazer*) pleasure; (*uso*) enjoyment, use; (*orgasmo*) orgasm

Grã-Bretanha [grã-bre'taɲa] *f* Great Britain

graça ['grasa] *f* (*REL*) grace; (*charme*) charm; (*gracejo*) joke; (*JUR*) pardon; **de ~** (*grátis*) for nothing; (*sem motivo*) for no reason; **sem ~** dull, boring; **fazer** *ou* **ter ~** to be funny; **ficar sem ~** to be embarrassed; **~s a** thanks to

gracejar [grase'ʒa*] *vi* to joke; **gracejo** [gra'seʒu] *m* joke

gracioso, -a [gra'sjozu, ɔza] *adj* (*pessoa*) charming; (*gestos*) gracious

grade ['gradʒi] f (no chão) grating; (grelha) grill; (na janela) bars pl; (col: cadeia) nick, clink

gradear [gra'dʒja*] vt (janela) to put bars up at; (jardim) to fence off

graduação [gradwa'sãw] (pl -ões) f (classificação) grading; (EDUC) graduation; (MIL) rank

gradual [gra'dwaw] (pl -ais) adj gradual

graduar [gra'dwa*] vt (classificar) to grade; (luz, fogo) to regulate; **graduar-se** vr to graduate

gráfica [grafika] f graphics sg; V tb gráfico

gráfico, -a ['grafiku, a] adj graphic ♦ m/f printer ♦ m (MAT) graph; (diagrama) diagram, chart; **~s** mpl (COMPUT) graphics; **~ de barras** bar chart

grã-fino, -a [grã'finu, a] (col) adj posh ♦ m/f nob, toff

grama ['grama] m gramme ♦ f (BR: capim) grass

gramado [gra'madu] (BR) m lawn; (FUTEBOL) pitch

gramática [gra'matʃika] f grammar; **gramatical** [gramatʃi'kaw] (pl -ais) adj grammatical

grampeador [grãpja'do*] m stapler

grampear [grã'pja*] vt to staple

grampo ['grãpu] m staple; (no cabelo) hairgrip; (de carpinteiro) clamp; (de chapéu) hatpin

granada [gra'nada] f (MIL) shell; **~ de mão** hand grenade

grande ['grãdʒi] adj big, large; (alto) tall; (notável, intenso) great; (longo) long; (adulto) grown-up; **mulher ~** big woman; **~ mulher** great woman; **grandeza** [grã'deza] f size; (fig) greatness; (ostentação) grandeur

grandioso, -a [grã'dʒjozu, ɔza] adj magnificent, grand

granito [gra'nitu] m granite

granizo [gra'nizu] m hailstone; **chover ~** to hail; **chuva de ~** hailstorm

granulado, -a [granu'ladu, a] adj grainy; (açúcar) granulated

grão ['grãw] (pl **~s**) m grain; (semente) seed; (de café) bean; **grão-de-bico** (pl **grãos-de-bico**) m chickpea

gratidão [gratʃi'dãw] f gratitude

gratificação [gratʃifika'sãw] (pl -ões) f gratuity, tip; (bônus) bonus; (recompensa) reward

gratificar [gratʃifi'ka*] vt to tip; (dar bônus a) to give a bonus to; (recompensar) to reward

grátis ['gratʃiʃ] adj free

grato, -a ['gratu, a] adj grateful; (agradável) pleasant

gratuito, -a [gra'twitu, a] adj (grátis) free; (infundado) gratuitous

grau [graw] m degree; (nível) level; (EDUC) class; **em alto ~** to a high degree; **ensino de primeiro/segundo ~** primary (BRIT) ou elementary (US)/secondary education

gravação [grava'sãw] f (em madeira) carving; (em disco, fita) recording

gravador [grava'do*] m tape recorder

gravar [gra'va*] vt to carve; (metal, pedra) to engrave; (na memória) to fix; (disco, fita) to record

gravata [gra'vata] f tie; **~ borboleta** bow tie

grave ['gravi] adj serious; (tom) deep; **gravemente** [grave'metʃi] adv (doente, ferido) seriously

grávida [gra'vida] adj pregnant

gravidade [gravi'dadʒi] f gravity

gravidez [gravi'deʒ] f pregnancy

gravura [gra'vura] f (em madeira)

engraving; (*estampa*) print

graxa ['graʃa] f (*para sapatos*) polish; (*lubrificante*) grease

Grécia ['gresja] f: a ~ Greece; **grego, -a** ['gregu, a] adj, m/f Greek ♦ m (LING) Greek

grelha ['greʎa] f grill; (*de fornalha*) grate; **bife na ~** grilled steak; **grelhado** [gre'ʎadu] m (*prato*) grill

grêmio ['gremju] m (*associação*) guild; (*clube*) club

grená [gre'na] adj, m dark red

greve ['grevi] f strike; **fazer ~** to go on strike; **~ branca** go-slow; **grevista** [gre'viʃta] m/f striker

grilo ['grilu] m cricket; (AUTO) squeak; (*col: de pessoa*) hang-up; **qual é o ~?** what's the matter?; **não tem ~!** (col) (there's) no problem!

gringo, -a ['grĩgu, a] (*col: pej*) m/f foreigner

gripado, -a [gri'padu, a] adj: **estar/ficar ~** to have/get a cold

gripe ['gripi] f flu, influenza

grisalho, -a [gri'zaʎu, a] adj (*cabelo*) grey (BRIT), gray (US)

gritante [gri'tãtʃi] adj (*hipocrisia*) glaring; (*desigualdade*) gross; (*mentira*) blatant; (*cor*) loud, garish

gritar [gri'ta*] vt to shout, yell ♦ vi to shout; (*de dor, medo*) to scream; **~ com alguém** to shout at sb; **gritaria** [grita'ria] f shouting, din; **grito** ['gritu] m shout; (*de medo*) scream; (*de dor*) cry; (*de animal*) call; **dar um grito** to cry out; **falar aos gritos** to shout

Groenlândia [grwẽ'lãdʒja] f: a ~ Greenland

grosseiro, -a [gro'sejru, a] adj (*piada*) crude; (*modos, tecido*) coarse; **grosseria** [grose'ria] f rudeness; (*ato*): **fazer uma grosseria** to be rude; (*dito*): **dizer uma grosseria** to be rude, say something rude

grosso, -a ['grosu, 'grɔsa] adj thick; (*áspero*) rough; (*voz*) deep; (*col: pessoa, piada*) rude ♦ m: **o ~ de** the bulk of; **grossura** [gro'sura] f thickness

grotesco, -a [gro'teʃku, a] adj grotesque

grudar [gru'da*] vt to glue, stick ♦ vi to stick

grude ['grudʒi] f glue; **grudento, -a** [gru'dẽtu, a] adj sticky

grunhir [gru'ɲi*] vi (*porco*) to grunt; (*tigre*) to growl; (*resmungar*) to grumble

grupo ['grupu] m group

gruta ['gruta] f grotto

guarda ['gwaxda] m/f policeman/woman ♦ f (*vigilância*) guarding; (*de objeto*) safekeeping ♦ m (MIL) guard; **estar de ~** to be on guard; **pôr-se em ~** to be on one's guard; **a G~ Civil** the Civil Guard; **guarda-chuva** (*pl* **guarda-chuvas**) m umbrella; **guarda-costas** m inv (NÁUT) coastguard boat; (*capanga*) bodyguard; **guardados** [gwax-'daduʃ] mpl keepsakes, valuables; **guarda-louça** (*pl* **guarda-louças**) m sideboard; **guardanapo** [gwaxda'napu] m napkin; **guarda-noturno** (*pl* **guardas-noturnos**) m night watchman; **guardar** [gwax'da*] vt to put away; (*zelar por*) to keep; (*lembrança, segredo*) to keep; **guardar-se** vr (*defender-se*) to protect o.s.; **guardar-se de** (*acautelar-se*) to guard against; **guarda-redes** (PT) m inv goalkeeper; **guarda-roupa** (*pl* **guarda-roupas**) m wardrobe; **guarda-sol** (*pl* **guarda-sóis**) m sunshade, parasol

guardião, -diã [gwax'dʒjãw, 'dʒjã] (*pl* -ães *ou* -ões, -s) m/f guardian

guarnição [gwaxni'sãw] (*pl* -ões *-s*) f (MIL) garrison; (NÁUT) crew; (CULIN) garnish

Guatemala [gwateˈmala] f: **a** ~ Guatemala

gude [ˈgudʒi] m: **bola de** ~ marble; (jogo) marbles pl

guerra [ˈgɛxa] f war; **em** ~ at war; **fazer** ~ to wage war; ~ **civil** civil war; ~ **mundial** world war; **guerreiro, -a** [geˈxejru, a] adj (espírito) fighting; (belicoso) warlike ♦ m warrior

guerrilha [geˈxiʎa] f (luta) guerrilla warfare; (tropa) guerrilla band; **guerrilheiro, -a** [gexiˈʎejru, a] m/f guerrilla

guia [ˈgia] f guidance; (COM) permit, bill of lading; (formulário) advice slip ♦ m (livro) guide(book) ♦ m/f (pessoa) guide

Guiana [ˈgjana] f: **a** ~ Guyana

guiar [gjaˈ] vt to guide; (AUTO) to drive ♦ vi to drive; **guiar-se** vr: ~-**se por** to go by

guichê [giˈʃe] m ticket window; (em banco, repartição) window, counter

guinada [giˈnada] f: **dar uma** ~ (com o carro) to swerve

guincho [ˈgĩʃu] m (de animal, rodas) squeal; (de pessoa) shriek

guindaste [gĩˈdaʃtʃi] m hoist, crane

guisado [giˈzadu] m stew

guitarra [giˈtaxa] f (electric) guitar

gula [ˈgula] f gluttony, greed

guloseima [guloˈzejma] f delicacy, titbit

guloso, -a [guˈlozu, ɔza] adj greedy

H

há [a] vb V haver

hábil [ˈabiw] (pl -eis) adj competent, capable; (astucioso, esperto) clever; (sutil) diplomatic; **em tempo** ~ in reasonable time; **habilidade**

[abiliˈdadʒi] f skill, ability; (astúcia, esperteza) shrewdness; (tato) discretion; **habilidoso, -a** [abiliˈdozu, ɔza] adj skilled, clever

habilitação [abilitaˈsãw] (pl -ões) f competence; (ato) qualification; **habilitações** fpl (conhecimentos) qualifications

habilitar [abiliˈtaˈ] vt to enable; (dar direito a) to qualify, entitle; (preparar) to prepare

habitação [abitaˈsãw] (pl -ões) f dwelling, residence; (alojamento) housing

habitante [abiˈtãtʃi] m/f inhabitant

habitar [abiˈtaˈ] vt to live in; (povoar) to inhabit ♦ vi to live

hábito [ˈabitu] m habit; (social) custom; (REL: traje) habit

habituado, -a [abiˈtwadu, a] adj: ~ **a (fazer) algo** used to (doing) sth

habitual [abiˈtwaw] (pl -ais) adj usual

habituar [abiˈtwaˈ] vt: ~ **alguém a** to get sb used to, accustom sb to; **habituar-se** vr: ~-**se a** to get used to

hacker [ˈakeˈ] (pl ~**s**) m (COMPUT) hacker

Haia [ˈaja] n The Hague

haja etc [ˈaʒa] vb V haver

hálito [ˈalitu] m breath

hall [xɔw] (pl ~**s**) m hall; (de teatro, hotel) foyer; ~ **de entrada** entrance hall

hambúrguer [ãˈbuxgeˈ] m hamburger

hão [ãw] vb V haver

hardware [ˈxadweˈ] m (COMPUT) hardware

harmonia [axmoˈnia] f harmony

harmonioso, -a [axmoˈnjozu, ɔza] adj harmonious

harmonizar [axmoni'za*] *vt* (*MÚS*) to harmonize; (*conciliar*): ~ **algo (com algo)** to reconcile sth (with sth); **harmonizar-se** *vi*: ~(**-se**) (*idéias etc*) to coincide; (*pessoas*) to be in agreement

harpa ['axpa] *f* harp

Havaí [avaj'i] *m*: **o ~** Hawaii

PALAVRA CHAVE

---

haver [a've*] *vb aux* **1** (*ter*) to have; **ele havia saído/comido** he had left/eaten

2: ~ **de**: **quem ~ia de dizer que ...?** who would have thought that ...?

♦ *vb impess* **1** (*existência*): **há** (*sg*) there is; (*pl*) there are; **o que é que há?** what's the matter?; **o que é que houve?** what happened?, what was that?; **não há de quê** don't mention it, you're welcome; **haja o que houver** come what may

2 (*tempo*): **há séculos/cinco dias que não o vejo** I haven't seen him for ages/five days; **há um ano que ela chegou** it's a year since she arrived; **há cinco dias (atrás)** five days ago

♦ **haver-se** *vr*: **~-se com alguém** to sort things out with sb

♦ *m* (*COM*) credit; **~es** *mpl* (*pertences*) property *sg*, possessions; (*riqueza*) wealth *sg*

haxixe [a'ʃiʃi] *m* hashish

hebraico, -a [e'brajku, a] *adj* Hebrew ♦ *m* (*LING*) Hebrew

Hébridas ['ɛbridaʃ] *fpl*: **as (ilhas) ~** the Hebrides

hediondo, -a [e'dʒjõdu, a] *adj* vile, revolting; (*crime*) heinous

hei [ej] *vb* V **haver**

hélice ['ɛlisi] *f* propeller

helicóptero [eli'kɔpteru] *m* helicopter

hematoma [ema'tɔma] *m* bruise

hemorragia [emoxa'ʒia] *f* haemorrhage (*BRIT*), hemorrhage (*US*); **~ nasal** nosebleed

hemorróidas [emo'xɔjdaʃ] *fpl* haemorrhoids (*BRIT*), hemorrhoids (*US*), piles

hepatite [epa'tʃitʃi] *f* hepatitis

hera ['ɛra] *f* ivy

herança [e'rãsa] *f* inheritance; (*fig*) heritage

herdar [ex'da*] *vt*: ~ **algo (de)** to inherit sth (from); ~ **a** to bequeath to

herdeiro, -a [ex'dejru, a] *m/f* heir(ess)

herói [e'rɔj] *m* hero

heroína [ero'ina] *f* heroine; (*droga*) heroin

hesitação [ezita'sãw] *f* (*pl* **-ões**) hesitation

hesitante [ezi'tãtʃi] *adj* hesitant

hesitar [ezi'ta*] *vi* to hesitate

heterossexual [eterosek'swaw] (*pl* **-ais**) *adj*, *m/f* heterosexual

híbrido, -a ['ibridu, a] *adj* hybrid

hidratante [idra'tãtʃi] *m* moisturizer

hidráulico, -a [i'drawliku, a] *adj* hydraulic

hidrelétrico, -a [idre'lɛtriku, a] (*PT* **-ct-**) *adj* hydroelectric

hidro... [idru] *prefixo* hydro..., water... *atr*

hidrogênio [idro'ʒenju] *m* hydrogen

hierarquia [jerax'kia] *f* hierarchy

hífen ['ifẽ] (*pl* **~s**) *m* hyphen

higiene [i'ʒjeni] *f* hygiene; **higiênico, -a** [i'ʒjeniku, a] *adj* hygienic; (*pessoa*) clean; **papel higiênico** toilet paper

hindu [ĩ'du] *adj*, *m/f* Hindu

hino ['inu] *m* hymn; ~ **nacional** national anthem

hipermercado [ipexmex'kadu] *m*

hypermarket

hipertensão [ipextẽ'sãw] f high blood pressure

hipismo [i'piʒmu] m (turfe) horse racing; (equitação) (horse) riding

hipnotizar [ipnotʃi'za*] vt to hypnotize

hipocrisia [ipokri'sia] f hypocrisy; **hipócrita** [i'pɔkrita] adj hypocritical ♦ m/f hypocrite

hipódromo [i'pɔdromu] m racecourse

hipopótamo [ipo'pɔtamu] m hippopotamus

hipoteca [ipo'teka] f mortgage; **hipotecar** [ipote'ka*] vt to mortgage

hipótese [i'pɔtezi] f hypothesis; na ~ de in the event of; em ~ alguma under no circumstances; na melhor/pior das ~s at best/worst

hispânico, -a [iʃ'paniku, a] adj Hispanic

histeria [iʃte'ria] f hysteria; **histérico, -a** [iʃ'tɛriku, a] adj hysterical

história [iʃ'tɔrja] f history; (conto) story; ~s fpl (chateação) bother sg, fuss sg; isso é outra ~ that's a different matter; que ~ é essa? what's going on?; **historiador, a** [iʃtorja'do*, a] m/f historian; **histórico, -a** [iʃ'tɔriku, a] adj historical; (fig: notável) historic ♦ m history

hobby ['xɔbi] (pl -bies) m hobby

hoje ['oʒi] adv today; (tb.: ~ em dia) now(adays); ~ à noite tonight

Holanda [o'lãda] f: a ~ Holland; **holandês, -esa** [olã'deʃ, eza] adj Dutch ♦ m/f Dutchman/woman ♦ m (LING) Dutch

holocausto [olo'kawʃtu] m holocaust

holofote [olo'fɔtʃi] m searchlight; (em campo de futebol etc) floodlight

homem ['omẽ] (pl -ns) m man; (a humanidade) mankind; ~ de empresa ou negócios businessman; ~ de estado statesman

homenagear [omena'ʒja*] vt (pessoa) to pay tribute to, honour (BRIT), honor (US)

homenagem [ome'naʒẽ] f tribute; (REL) homage; prestar ~ a alguém to pay tribute to sb

homens ['omẽʃ] mpl de homem

homeopático, -a [omjo'patʃiku] adj homoeopathic

homicida [omi'sida] adj homicidal ♦ m/f murderer; **homicídio** [omi'sidʒju] m murder; homicídio involuntário manslaughter

homologar [omolo'ga*] vt to ratify

homólogo, -a [o'mɔlogu, a] adj homologous; (fig) equivalent ♦ m/f opposite number

homossexual [omosek'swal] (pl -ais) adj, m/f homosexual

Honduras [õ'duraʃ] f Honduras

honestidade [oneʃtʃi'dadʒi] f honesty; (decência) decency; (justeza) fairness

honesto, -a [o'nɛʃtu, a] adj honest; (decente) decent; (justo) fair, just

honorário, -a [ono'rarju, a] adj honorary; **honorários** [ono'rarjuʃ] mpl fees

honra ['õxa] f honour (BRIT), honor (US); em ~ de in hono(u)r of

honrado, -a [õ'xadu, a] adj honest; (respeitado) honourable (BRIT), honorable (US)

honrar [õ'xa*] vt to honour (BRIT), honor (US)

honroso, -a [õ'xozu, ɔza] adj hono(u)rable

hóquei ['ɔkej] m hockey; ~ sobre gelo ice hockey

hora ['ɔra] f (60 minutos) hour; (momento) time; a que ~s? (at) what time?; **que ~s são?** what time is it?; **são duas ~s** it's two o'clock; **você tem as ~s?** have you got the time?; **fazer ~** to kill time; **de ~ em ~** every hour; **na ~** on the spot; **chegar na ~** to be on time; **de última ~** ♦ adj last-minute ♦ adv at the last minute; **meia ~** half an hour; **~s extras** overtime sg; **horário, -a** [o'rarju, a] adj: **100 km horários** 100 km an hour ♦ m timetable; (hora) time; **horário de expediente** working hours pl; (de um escritório) office hours pl

horizontal [orizõ'taw] (pl -ais) adj horizontal

horizonte [ori'zõtʃi] m horizon

horóscopo [o'rɔʃkopu] m horoscope

horrendo, -a [o'xẽdu, a] adj horrendous, frightful

horripilante [oxipi'lãtʃi] adj horrifying, hair-raising

horrível [o'xivew] (pl -eis) adj awful, horrible

horror [o'xo*] m horror; **que ~!** how awful!; **ter ~ a algo** to hate sth; **horrorizar** [oxori'za*] vt to horrify, frighten; **horroroso, -a** [oxo'rozu, ɔza] adj horrible, ghastly

horta ['ɔxta] f vegetable garden

hortaliças [oxta'lisaʃ] fpl vegetables

hortelã [oxte'lã] f mint; **~ pimenta** peppermint

horticultor, a [oxtʃikuw'to*, a] m/f market gardener (BRIT), truck farmer (US)

hortifrutigranjeiros [oxtʃifrutʃigrã'ʒejruʃ] mpl fruit and vegetables

horto ['oxtu] m market garden (BRIT), truck farm (US)

hospedagem [oʃpe'daʒẽ] f guest house

hospedar [oʃpe'da*] vt to put up; **hospedar-se** vr to stay, lodge; **hospedaria** [oʃpeda'ria] f guest house

hóspede ['ɔʃpedʒi] m (amigo) guest; (estranho) lodger

hospedeira [oʃpe'dejra] f landlady; (PT: de bordo) stewardess, air hostess (BRIT)

hospício [oʃ'pisju] m mental hospital

hospital [oʃpi'taw] (pl -ais) m hospital

hospitalidade [oʃpitali'dadʒi] f hospitality

hostil [oʃ'tʃiw] (pl -is) adj hostile; **hostilizar** [oʃtʃili'za*] vt to antagonize; (MIL) to wage war on

hotel [o'tɛw] (pl -éis) m hotel; **hoteleiro, -a** [ote'lejru, a] m/f hotelier

houve etc ['ovi] vb V **haver**

humanidade [umani'dadʒi] f (os homens) man(kind); (compaixão) humanity

humanitário, -a [umani'tarju, a] adj humane

humano, -a [u'manu, a] adj human; (bondoso) humane

húmido, -a (PT) adj = **úmido**

humildade [umiw'dadʒi] f humility; (pobreza) poverty

humilde [u'miwdʒi] adj humble; (pobre) poor

humilhar [umi'ʎa*] vt to humiliate

humor [u'mo*] m mood, temper; (graça) humour (BRIT), humor (US); **de bom/mau ~** in a good/bad mood; **humorista** [umo'riʃta] m/f comedian; **humorístico, -a** [umo'riʃtʃiku, a] adj humorous

húngaro, -a ['ũgaru, a] adj, m/f Hungarian

Hungria [ũ'gria] f: **a ~** Hungary

hurra ['uxa] m cheer ♦ excl hurrah!

I

ia etc ['ia] vb V **ir**

iate ['jatʃi] m yacht; **~ clube** yacht club

ibérico, -a [i'bεriku, a] adj, m/f Iberian

ibero-americano, -a [ibεru-] adj, m/f Ibero-American

ICM (BR) abr m (= Imposto sobre Circulação de Mercadorias) ≈ VAT

ícone [i'kɔni] m (gen, COMPUT) icon

icterícia [ikte'risja] f jaundice

ida ['ida] f going, departure; **~ e volta** round trip, return; **a (viagem de) ~** the outward journey; **na ~ on** the way there

idade [i'dadʒi] f age; **ter cinco anos de ~** to be five (years old); **de meia ~** middle-aged; **qual é a ~ dele?** how old is he?; **na minha ~** in my age; **ser menor/maior de ~** to be under/of age; **pessoa de ~** elderly person; **I~ Média** Middle Ages pl

ideal [ide'jaw] (pl -**ais**) adj, m ideal; **idealista** [idea'liʃta] adj idealistic ♦ m/f idealist

idéia [i'dεja] f idea; (mente) mind; **mudar de ~** to change one's mind; **não ter a mínima ~** to have no idea; **não faço ~** I can't imagine; **estar com ~ de fazer** to plan to do

idem [i'dẽ] pron ditto

idêntico, -a [i'dẽtʃiku, a] adj identical

identidade [idẽtʃi'dadʒi] f identity

identificação [idẽtʃifika'sãw] f identification

identificar [idẽtʃifi'ka*] vt to identify; **identificar-se** vr: **~-se com** to identify with

idioma [i'dʒɔma] m language

idiota [i'dʒɔta] adj idiotic ♦ m/f idiot

ido, -a ['idu, a] adj past

idolatrar [idola'tra*] vt to idolize

ídolo ['idolu] m idol

idoso, -a [i'dozu, ɔza] adj elderly, old

ignição [igni'sãw] (pl -**ões**) f ignition

ignorado, -a [igno'radu, a] adj unknown

ignorância [igno'rãsja] f ignorance; **ignorante** [igno'rãtʃi] adj ignorant, uneducated ♦ m/f ignoramus

ignorar [igno'ra*] vt not to know; (não dar atenção a) to ignore

igreja [i'greʒa] f church

igual [i'gwaw] (pl -**ais**) adj equal; (superfície) even ♦ m/f equal

igualar [igwa'la*] vt to equal; (fazer igual) to make equal; (nivelar) to level ♦ vi: **~ a** ou **com** to be equal to, be the same as; (ficar no mesmo nível) to be level with; **igualar-se** vr: **~-se a alguém** to be sb's equal

igualdade [igwaw'dadʒi] f equality; (uniformidade) uniformity

igualmente [igwaw'mẽtʃi] adv equally; (também) likewise, also; **~!** (saudação) the same to you!

ilegal [ile'gaw] (pl -**ais**) adj illegal

ilegítimo, -a [ile'ʒitʃimu, a] adj illegitimate; (ilegal) unlawful

ilegível [ile'ʒivew] (pl -**eis**) adj illegible

ileso, -a [i'lεzu, a] adj unhurt

iletrado, -a [ile'tradu, a] adj illiterate

ilha ['iʎa] f island; **ilhéu, ilhoa** [i'ʎεw, i'ʎoa] m/f islander

ilícito, -a [i'lisitu, a] adj illicit

ilimitado, -a [ilimi'tadu, a] adj unlimited

iludir [ilu'dʒi*] vt to delude; (enganar) to deceive; (a lei) to evade

iluminação [ilumina'sãw] (pl -**ões**) f lighting; (fig) enlightenment

iluminar 472 impedir

iluminar [ilumi'na*] vt to light up; (estádio etc) to floodlight; (fig) to enlighten

ilusão [ilu'zãw] (pl -ões) f illusion; (quimera) delusion; **ilusório, -a** [ilu'zɔrju, a] adj deceptive

ilustração [iluʃtra'sãw] (pl -ões) f illustration

ilustrado, -a [iluʃ'tradu, a] adj illustrated; (erudito) learned

ilustrar [iluʃ'tra*] vt to illustrate; (instruir) to instruct

ilustre [i'luʃtri] adj illustrious; **um ~ desconhecido** a complete stranger

ímã ['imã] m magnet

imagem [i'maʒẽ] (pl -ns) f image; (semelhança) likeness; (TV) picture; **imagens** fpl (LITERATURA) imagery

imaginação [imaʒina'sãw] (pl -ões) f imagination

imaginar [imaʒi'na*] vt to imagine; (supor) to suppose; **imaginar-se** vr to imagine o.s.; **imagine só!** just imagine!; **imaginário, -a** [imaʒi'narju, a] adj imaginary

imaturo, -a [ima'turu, a] adj immature

imbatível [ĩba'tʃivew] (pl -eis) adj invincible

imbecil [ĩbe'siw] (pl -is) adj stupid ♦ m/f imbecile; **imbecilidade** [ĩbesili'dadʒi] f stupidity

imediações [imedʒa'sõjʃ] fpl vicinity sg, neighbourhood sg (BRIT), neighborhood sg (US)

imediatamente [imedʒata'mẽtʃi] adv immediately, right away

imediato, -a [ime'dʒatu, a] adj immediate; (seguinte) next; **~ a** next to; **de ~** straight away

imenso, -a [i'mẽsu, a] adj immense, huge; (ódio, amor) great

imigração [imigra'sãw] (pl -ões) f immigration

imigrante [imi'grãtʃi] adj, m/f immigrant

iminente [imi'nẽtʃi] adj imminent

imitação [imita'sãw] (pl -ões) f imitation

imitar [imi'ta*] vt to imitate; (assinatura) to copy

imobiliária [imobi'ljarja] f estate agent's (BRIT), real estate broker's (US)

imobiliário, -a [imobi'ljarju, a] adj property atr

imobilizar [imobili'za*] vt to immobilize; (fig) to bring to a standstill

imoral [imo'raw] (pl -ais) adj immoral

imortal [imox'taw] (pl -ais) adj immortal

imóvel [i'mɔvew] (pl -eis) adj motionless, still; (não movediço) immovable ♦ m property; (edifício) building; **imóveis** mpl (propriedade) real estate sg, property sg

impaciência [ĩpa'sjẽsja] f impatience; **impacientar-se** [ĩpasjẽ'taxsi] vr to lose one's patience; **impaciente** [ĩpa'sjẽtʃi] adj impatient

impacto [ĩ'paktu] (PT -cte) m impact

ímpar ['ĩpa*] adj (número) odd; (sem igual) unique, unequalled

imparcial [ĩpax'sjaw] (pl -ais) adj fair, impartial

impecável [ĩpe'kavew] (pl -eis) adj perfect, impeccable

impeço etc [ĩ'pɛsu] vb V **impedir**

impedido, -a [ĩpe'dʒidu, a] adj (FUTEBOL) offside; (PT: TEL) engaged (BRIT), busy (US)

impedimento [ĩpedʒi'mẽtu] m impediment

impedir [ĩpe'dʒi*] vt to obstruct; (estrada, tráfego) to block; (movimento, progresso) to impede; **~ alguém de fazer algo** to prevent sb from doing sth; (*proibir*) to forbid sb to do sth; ~ **(que aconteça)** algo to prevent sth (happening)

impenetrável [ĩpene'travew] (*pl -eis*) *adj* impenetrable

impensado, -a [ĩpẽ'sadu, a] *adj* thoughtless; (*não calculado*) unpremeditated; (*imprevisto*) unforeseen

impensável [ĩpẽ'savew] (*pl -eis*) *adj* unthinkable

imperador [ĩpera'do*] *m* emperor

imperativo, -a [ĩpera'tʃivu, a] *adj* imperative ♦ *m* imperative

imperatriz [ĩpera'triʒ] *f* empress

imperdoável [ĩpex'dwavew] (*pl -eis*) *adj* unforgivable, inexcusable

imperfeito, -a [ĩpex'fejtu, a] *adj* imperfect ♦ *m* (*LING*) imperfect (tense)

imperial [ĩpe'rjaw] (*pl -ais*) *adj* imperial

imperícia [ĩpe'risja] *f* inability; (*inexperiência*) inexperience

império [ĩ'prrju] *m* empire

impermeável [ĩpex'mjavew] (*pl -eis*) *adj* ~ **a** (*tb fig*) impervious to; (*à água*) waterproof ♦ *m* raincoat

impertinente [ĩpextʃi'nẽtʃi] *adj* irrelevant; (*insolente*) impertinent

impessoal [ĩpe'swaw] (*pl -ais*) *adj* impersonal

ímpeto [ĩ'pɛtu] *m* (*TEC*) impetus; (*movimento súbito*) start; (*de cólera*) fit; (*de emoção*) surge; (*de chamas*) fury; **agir com ~** to act on impulse; **levantar-se num ~** to get up with a start

impetuoso, -a [ĩpe'twozu, ɔza] *adj* (*pessoa*) headstrong, impetuous; (*ato*) rash, hasty

impiedoso, -a [ĩpje'dozu, ɔza] *adj* merciless, cruel

implacável [ĩpla'kavew] (*pl -eis*) *adj* relentless; (*pessoa*) unforgiving

implantação [ĩplãta'sãw] (*pl -ões*) *f* introduction; (*MED*) implant

implementar [ĩplemẽ'ta*] *vt* to implement

implicar [ĩpli'ka*] *vt* (*envolver*) to implicate; (*pressupor*) to imply ♦ *vi*: ~ **com alguém** (*chatear*) to tease sb, pick on sb; **implicar-se** *vr* to get involved; ~ **(em) algo** to involve sth

implícito, -a [ĩ'plisitu, a] *adj* implicit

implorar [ĩplo'ra*] *vt*: ~ **(algo a alguém)** to beg *ou* implore (sb for sth)

imponente [ĩpo'nẽtʃi] *adj* impressive, imposing

impopular [ĩpopu'la*] *adj* unpopular; **impopularidade** [ĩpopulari'dadʒi] *f* unpopularity

impor [ĩ'po*] (*irreg: como pôr*) *vt* to impose; (*respeito*) to command; **impor-se** *vr* to assert o.s.; ~ **algo a alguém** to impose sth on sb

importação [impoxta'sãw] (*pl -ões*) *f* (*ato*) importing; (*mercadoria*) import

importador, a [impoxta'do*, a] *adj* import *atr* ♦ *m/f* importer

importância [impox'tãsja] *f* importance; (*de dinheiro*) sum, amount; **não tem ~** it doesn't matter, never mind; **ter ~** to be important; **sem ~** unimportant; **importante** [impox'tãtʃi] *adj* important ♦ *m*: **o (mais) importante** the (most) important thing

importar [ĩpox'ta*] *vt* (*COM*) to import; (*trazer*) to bring in; (*causar: prejuízos etc*) to cause; (*implicar*) to imply, involve ♦ *vi* to matter, be important; **importar-se** *vr*: ~**se com algo** to mind sth; **não me importo** I don't care

importunar [ĩpoxtu'na*] *vt* to

bother, annoy

importuno, -a [ĩpoxˈtunu, a] *adj* annoying; (*inoportuno*) inopportune ♦ *m/f* nuisance

imposição [ĩpoziˈsãw] (*pl* -ões) *f* imposition

impossibilitado, -a [ĩposibiliˈtadu, a] *adj*: ~ **de fazer** unable to do

impossibilitar [ĩposibiliˈta*] *vt*: ~ **algo** to make sth impossible; ~ **alguém de fazer, ~ a alguém fazer** to prevent sb doing; ~ **algo a alguém, ~ alguém para algo** to make sth impossible for sb

impossível [ĩpoˈsivew] (*pl* -eis) *adj* impossible; (*insuportável*: *pessoa*) insufferable; (*incrível*) incredible

imposto [ĩpoˈftu] *m* tax; **antes/depois de ~s** before/after tax; ~ **de renda** (*BR*) income tax; ~ **predial** rates *pl*; **I~ sobre Circulação de Mercadorias (e Serviços)** (*RR*), ~ **sobre valor acrescentado** (*PT*) value added tax (*BRIT*), sales tax (*US*)

impotente [ĩpoˈtẽtʃi] *adj* powerless; (*MED*) impotent

impraticável [ĩpratʃiˈkavew] (*pl* -eis) *adj* impracticable; (*rua, rio etc*) impassable

impreciso, -a [ĩpreˈsizu, a] *adj* vague; (*falta de rigor*) inaccurate

imprensa [ĩˈprẽsa] *f* printing; (*máquina, jornais*) press

imprescindível [ĩpresĩˈdʒivew] (*pl* -eis) *adj* essential, indispensable

impressão [ĩpreˈsãw] (*pl* -ões) *f* impression; (*de livros*) printing; (*marca*) imprint; **causar boa ~** to make a good impression; **ficar com/ter a ~ (de) que** to get/have the impression that

impressionante [ĩpresjoˈnãtʃi] *adj* impressive

impressionar [ĩpresjoˈna*] *vt* to af-

fect ♦ *vi* to be impressive; (*pessoa*) to make an impression; **impressionar-se** *vr*: **~-se (com algo)** to be moved (by sth)

impresso, -a [ĩˈpresu, a] *pp de* **imprimir** ♦ *adj* printed ♦ *m* (*para preencher*) form; (*folheto*) leaflet; **~s** *mpl* (*formulário*) printed matter *sg*

impressões [ĩpreˈsõjʃ] *fpl de* **impressão**

impressora [ĩpreˈsora] *f* printing machine; (*COMPUT*) printer; **~ matricial/a laser** dot-matrix/laser printer

imprestável [ĩpreʃˈtavew] (*pl* -eis) *adj* (*inútil*) useless; (*pessoa*) unhelpful

imprevisível [ĩpreviˈzivew] (*pl* -eis) *adj* unforeseeable

imprevisto, -a [ĩpreˈviʃtu, a] *adj* unexpected, unforeseen ♦ *m*: **um ~** something unexpected

imprimir [ĩpriˈmi*] *vt* to print; (*marca*) to stamp; (*infundir*) to instil (*BRIT*), instill (*US*); (*COMPUT*) to print out

impróprio, -a [ĩˈprɔprju, a] *adj* inappropriate; (*indecente*) improper

improvável [ĩproˈvavew] (*pl* -eis) *adj* unlikely

improvisar [ĩproviˈza*] *vt, vi* to improvise; (*TEATRO*) to ad-lib

improviso [ĩproˈvizu]: **de ~** *adv* (*de repente*) suddenly; (*sem preparação*) without preparation

imprudente [ĩpruˈdẽtʃi] *adj* (*irrefletido*) rash; (*motorista*) careless

impulsivo, -a [ĩpuwˈsivu, a] *adj* impulsive

impulso [ĩˈpuwsu] *m* impulse; (*fig*: *estímulo*) urge

impune [ĩˈpuni] *adj* unpunished; **impunidade** [ĩpuniˈdadʒi] *f* impunity

imundície [imũˈdʒisji] *f* filth; **imundo, -a** [iˈmũdu, a] *adj* filthy;

(*obsceno*) dirty

imune [i'muni] *adj*: ~ **a** immune to;
imunidade [imuni'dadʒi] *f* immunity

inábil [i'nabiw] (*pl* **-eis**) *adj* incapable; (*desajeitado*) clumsy

inabitado, -a [inabi'tadu, a] *adj* uninhabited

inacabado, -a [inaka'badu, a] *adj* unfinished

inacreditável [inakredʒi'tavew] (*pl* **-eis**) *adj* unbelievable, incredible

inactivo, -a *etc* [ina'tivu, a] (*PT*) = **inativo/a** *etc*

inadequado, -a [inade'kwadu, a] *adj* inadequate; (*impróprio*) unsuitable

inadiável [ina'dʒjavew] (*pl* **-eis**) *adj* pressing

inadimplência [inadʒi'plẽsja] *f* (*JUR*) breach of contract, default

inanimado, -a [inani'madu, a] *adj* inanimate

inaptidão [inaptʃi'dãw] (*pl* **-ões**) *f* inability

inatingível [inatʃī'ʒivew] (*pl* **-eis**) *adj* unattainable

inativo, -a [ina'tʃivu, a] *adj* inactive; (*aposentado, reformado*) retired

inato, -a [i'natu, a] *adj* innate, inborn

inauguração [inawgura'sãw] (*pl* **-ões**) *f* inauguration; (*de exposição*) opening; **inaugural** [inawgu'raw] (*pl* **-ais**) *adj* inaugural; **inaugurar** [inawgu'ra*] *vt* to inaugurate; (*exposição*) to open

incansável [ĩkã'savew] (*pl* **-eis**) *adj* tireless, untiring

incapacidade [ĩkapasi'dadʒi] *f* incapacity; (*incompetência*) incompetence

incapacitado, -a [ĩkapasi'tadu, a] *adj* (*inválido*) disabled, handicapped ♦ *m/f* handicapped person; **estar ~**

de fazer to be unable to do

incapaz [ĩka'pajʒ] *adj*, *m/f* incompetent; ~ **de fazer** incapable of doing; ~ **para** unfit for

incendiar [isẽ'dʒja*] *vt* to set fire to; (*fig*) to inflame; **incendiar-se** *vr* to catch fire

incêndio [i'sẽdʒju] *m* fire; ~ **criminoso** *ou* **premeditado** arson

incenso [i'sẽsu] *m* incense

incentivar [isẽtʃi'va*] *vt* to stimulate, encourage

incentivo [isẽ'tʃivu] *m* incentive; ~ **fiscal** tax incentive

incerteza [ĩsex'teza] *f* uncertainty

incerto, -a [ĩ'sextu, a] *adj* uncertain

incessante [ĩse'sãtʃi] *adj* incessant

incesto [ĩ'seʃtu] *m* incest

inchado, -a [ĩ'ʃadu, a] *adj* swollen; (*fig*) conceited

inchar [ĩ'ʃa*] *vt*, *vi* to swell

incidência [ĩsi'dẽsja] *f* incidence, occurrence

incidente [ĩsi'dẽtʃi] *m* incident

incisivo, -a [ĩsi'zivu, a] *adj* cutting, sharp; (*fig*) incisive

incitar [ĩsi'ta*] *vt* to incite; (*pessoa, animal*) to drive on

inclinação [ĩklina'sãw] (*pl* **-ões**) *f* inclination; ~ **da cabeça** nod

inclinado, -a [ĩkli'nadu, a] *adj* (*terreno*) sloping, (*corpo, torre*) leaning

inclinar [ĩkli'na*] *vt* to tilt; (*cabeça*) to nod ♦ *vi* to slope; (*objeto*) to tilt; **inclinar-se** *vr* to tilt; (*dobrar o corpo*) to bow, stoop; **~-se sobre algo** to lean over sth

incluir [i'klwi*] *vt* to include; (*em carta*) to enclose; **incluir-se** *vr* to be included

inclusão [ĩklu'zãw] *f* inclusion; **inclusive** [ĩklu'zivi] *prep* including ♦ *adv* inclusive; (*até mesmo*) even

incoerente [ĩkoe'rẽtʃi] *adj* incoherent; (*contraditório*) inconsistent

incógnita [ĩ'kɔgnita] f (MAT) unknown; (fato incógnito) mystery; **incógnito, -a** [ĩ'kɔgnitu, a] adj unknown ♦ adv incognito

incolor [ĩko'lo*] adj colourless (BRIT), colorless (US)

incomodar [ĩkomo'da*] vt to bother, trouble; (aborrecer) to annoy ♦ vi to be bothersome; **incomodar-se** vr to bother, put o.s. out; **~-se com algo** to be bothered by sth, mind sth; **não se incomode!** don't worry!

incômodo, -a [ĩ'komodu, a] adj uncomfortable; (incomodativo) troublesome; (inoportuno) inconvenient

incompetente [ĩkõpe'tẽtʃi] adj, m/f incompetent

incompleto, -a [ĩkõ'pletu, a] adj incomplete

incompreendido, -a [ĩkõprjẽ-'dʒidu, a] adj misunderstood

incomum [ĩko'mũ] adj uncommon

incomunicável [ĩkomuni'kavew] (pl **-eis**) adj cut off; (privado de comunicação, fig) incommunicado; (preso) in solitary confinement

inconformado, -a [ĩkõfox'madu, a] adj bitter; **~ com** unreconciled to

inconfundível [ĩkõfũ'dʒivew] (pl **-eis**) adj unmistakeable

inconsciência [ĩkõ'sjẽsja] f (MED) unconsciousness; (irreflexão) thoughtlessness

inconsciente [ĩkõ'sjẽtʃi] adj unconscious ♦ m unconscious

inconseqüente [ĩkõse'kwẽtʃi] adj inconsistent; (contraditório) illogical; (irresponsável) irresponsible

inconsistente [ĩkõsiʃ'tẽtʃi] adj inconsistent; (sem solidez) runny

inconstante [ĩkõ'tãtʃi] adj fickle; (tempo) changeable

incontável [ĩkõ'tavew] (pl **-eis**) adj countless

incontestável [ĩkõteʃ'tavew] (pl **-eis**) adj undeniable

incontrolável [ĩkõtro'lavew] (pl **-eis**) adj uncontrollable

inconveniência [ĩkõve'njẽsja] f inconvenience; (impropriedade) inappropriateness

inconveniente [ĩkõve'njẽtʃi] adj inconvenient; (inoportuno) awkward; (grosseiro) rude; (importuno) annoying ♦ m disadvantage; (obstáculo) difficulty, problem

incorporar [ĩkoxpo'ra*] vt to incorporate; (juntar) to add; (COM) to merge; **incorporar-se** vr: **~-se a** ou **em** to join

incorreto, -a [ĩko'xetu, a] (PT **-ect-**) adj incorrect; (desonesto) dishonest

incrédulo, -a [ĩ'krɛdulu, a] adj incredulous; (cético) sceptical (BRIT), skeptical (US) ♦ m/f sceptic (BRIT), skeptic (US)

incrível [ĩ'krivew] (pl **-eis**) adj incredible

incumbência [ĩkũ'bẽsja] f task, duty

incumbir [ĩkũ'bi*] vt: **~ alguém de algo** ou **algo a alguém** to put sb in charge of sth ♦ vi: **~ a alguém** to be sb's duty; **incumbir-se** vr: **~-se de** to undertake, take charge of

indagação [ĩdaga'sãw] (pl **-ões**) f investigation; (pergunta) inquiry, question

indagar [ĩda'ga*] vt to investigate ♦ vi to inquire; **indagar-se** vr: **~-se a si mesmo** to ask o.s.; **~ algo de alguém** to ask sb about sth

indecente [ĩde'sẽtʃi] adj indecent, improper; (obsceno) rude, vulgar

indeciso, -a [ĩde'sizu, a] adj undecided; (indistinto) vague; (hesitante) hesitant, indecisive

indecoroso, -a [ĩdeko'rozu, ɔza] adj indecent, improper

indefeso 477 indispor

indefeso, -a [ĩde'fezu, a] *adj* undefended; (*população*) defenceless (*BRIT*), defenseless (*US*)

indefinido, -a [ĩdefi'nidu, a] *adj* indefinite; (*vago*) vague, undefined; **por tempo ~** indefinitely

indefiro *etc* [ĩde'firu] *vb* V **indeferir**

indelicado, -a [ĩdeli'kadu, a] *adj* impolite, rude

indenização [ĩdeniza'sãw] (*PT* -**mn**-) (*pl* -**ões**) *f* compensation; (*COM*) indemnity

indenizar [ĩdeni'za*] (*PT* -**mn**-) *vt*: **~ alguém por** ou **de algo** (*compensar*) to compensate sb for sth; (*por gastos*) to reimburse sb for sth

independência [ĩdepẽ'dẽsja] *f* independence; **independente** [ĩdepẽ'dẽtʃi] *adj* independent

indesejável [ĩdeze'ʒavew] (*pl* -**eis**) *adj* undesirable

indevido, -a [ĩde'vidu, a] *adj* (*imerecido*) unjust; (*impróprio*) inappropriate

Índia ['ĩdʒa] *f*: **a ~** India; **as ~s Ocidentais** the West Indies; **indiano, -a** [ĩ'dʒjanu, a] *adj*, *m/f* Indian

indicação [ĩdʒika'sãw] (*pl* -**ões**) *f* indication; (*de termômetro*) reading; (*para um cargo, prêmio*) nomination; (*recomendação*) recommendation; (*de um caminho*) directions *pl*

indicado, -a [ĩdʒi'kadu, a] *adj* appropriate

indicador, a [ĩdʒika'do*, a] *adj*: **~ de** indicative of ♦ *m* indicator; (*TEC*) gauge; (*dedo*) index finger; (*ponteiro*) pointer

indicar [ĩdʒi'ka*] *vt* to indicate; (*apontar*) to point to; (*temperatura*) to register; (*recomendar*) to recommend; (*para um cargo*) to nominate; (*determinar*) to determine; **~ o caminho a alguém** to give sb

directions

indicativo, -a [ĩdʒika'tʃivu, a] *adj* (*tb*: *LING*) indicative

índice ['ĩdʒisi] *m* (*de livro*) index; (*taxa*) rate

indício [ĩ'dʒisju] *m* (*sinal*) sign; (*vestígio*) trace; (*JUR*) clue

indiferença [ĩdʒife'rẽsa] *f* indifference; **indiferente** [ĩdʒife'rẽtʃi] *adj* indifferent; **isso me é indiferente** it's all the same to me

indígena [ĩ'dʒiʒena] *adj*, *m/f* native; (*índio: da América*) Indian

indigência [ĩdʒi'ʒẽsja] *f* poverty; (*fig*) lack, need

indigestão [ĩdʒiʒeʃ'tãw] *f* indigestion

indigesto, -a [ĩdʒi'ʒeʃtu, a] *adj* indigestible

indignação [ĩdʒigna'sãw] *f* indignation; **indignado, -a** [ĩdʒig'nadu, a] *adj* indignant

indignar [ĩdʒig'na*] *vt* to anger, incense; **indignar-se** *vr* to get angry

indigno, -a [ĩ'dʒignu, a] *adj* unworthy; (*desprezível*) disgraceful, despicable

índio, -a ['ĩdʒju, a] *adj*, *m/f* (*da América*) Indian; **o Oceano Í~** the Indian Ocean

indireto, -a [ĩdʒi'rɛtu, a] (*PT* -**ct**-) *adj* indirect

indiscreto, -a [ĩdʒiʃ'krɛtu, a] *adj* indiscreet

indiscriminado, -a [ĩdʒiʃkrimi'nadu, a] *adj* indiscriminate

indiscutível [ĩdʒiʃku'tʃivew] (*pl* -**eis**) *adj* indisputable

indispensável [ĩdʒiʃpẽ'savew] (*pl* -**eis**) *adj* essential, vital ♦ *m*: **o ~** the essentials *pl*

indispor [ĩdʒiʃ'po*] (*irreg*: *como* **pôr**) *vt* (*de saúde*) to make ill; (*aborrecer*) to upset; **indisposto, -a**

indistinto [ĩdʒiʃ'poʃtu, 'pɔʃta] adj unwell, poorly; upset

indistinto, -a [ĩdʒiʃ'tʃĩtu, a] adj indistinct

individual [ĩdʒivi'dwaw] (pl -ais) adj individual

indivíduo [ĩdʒi'vidwu] m individual; (col: sujeito) guy

indócil [ĩ'dɔsiw] (pl -eis) adj unruly, wayward; (impaciente) restless

índole ['ĩdoli] f (temperamento) nature; (tipo) sort, type

indolor [ĩdo'lo*] adj painless

indomável [ĩdo'mavew] (pl -eis) adj (animal) untameable; (coragem) indomitable

Indonésia [ĩdo'nɛzja] f: a ~ Indonesia

indulgente [ĩduw'ʒẽtʃi] adj indulgent; (atitude) lenient

indústria [ĩ'duʃtrja] f industry; **industrial** [ĩduʃ'trjaw] (pl -ais) adj industrial ♦ m/f industrialist; **industrializar** [ĩduʃtrjali'za*] vt (país) to industrialize; (aproveitar) to process

induzir [ĩdu'zi*] vt to induce; (persuadir) to persuade

inédito, -a [i'nɛdʒitu, a] adj (livro) unpublished; (incomum) unheard-of, rare

ineficaz [inefi'kaʒ] adj (remédio, medida) ineffective; (empregado, máquina) inefficient

ineficiente [inefi'sjẽtʃi] adj inefficient

inegável [ine'gavew] (pl -eis) adj undeniable

inelutável [inelu'tavew] (pl -eis) adj inescapable

inepto, -a [i'nɛptu, a] adj inept, incompetent

inequívoco, -a [ine'kivoku, a] adj (evidente) clear; (inconfundível) unmistakeable

inércia [i'nɛxsja] f lethargy; (Fís) inertia

inerente [ine'rẽtʃi] adj: ~ a inherent in ou to

inerte [i'nɛxtʃi] adj lethargic; (Fís) inert

inescrupuloso, -a [ineʃkrupu'lozu, ɔza] adj unscrupulous

inesgotável [ineʒgo'tavew] (pl -eis) adj inexhaustible; (superabundante) boundless

inesperado, -a [ineʃpe'radu, a] adj unexpected, unforeseen ♦ m: o ~ the unexpected

inesquecível [ineʃke'sivew] (pl -eis) adj unforgettable

inestimável [ineʃtʃi'mavew] (pl -eis) adj invaluable

inevitável [inevi'tavew] (pl -eis) adj inevitable

inexato, -a [ine'zatu, a] (PT -ct-) adj inaccurate

inexistência [ineziʃ'tẽsja] f lack

inexistente [ineziʃ'tẽtʃi] adj nonexistent

inexperiência [ineʃpe'rjẽsja] f inexperience; **inexperiente** [ineʃpe'rjẽtʃi] adj inexperienced; (ingênuo) naive

inexpressivo, -a [ineʃpre'sivu, a] adj expressionless

infalível [ĩfa'livew] (pl -eis) adj infallible; (sucesso) guaranteed

infância [ĩ'fãsja] f childhood

infantil [ĩfã'tʃiw] (pl -is) adj (ingênuo) childlike; (pueril) childish; (para crianças) children's

infarto [ĩ'faxtu] m heart attack

infecção [ĩfek'sãw] (pl -ões) f infection; **infeccionar** [ĩfeksjo'na*] (ferida) to infect; **infeccioso, -a** [ĩfek'sjozu, ɔza] adj infectious

infectar [ĩfek'ta*] (PT) vt = infetar

infelicidade [ĩfelisi'dadʒi] f unhappiness; (desgraça) misfortune

infeliz [ĩfe'liʒ] *adj* unhappy; (*infausto*) unlucky; (*ação, medida*) unfortunate; (*sugestão, idéia*) inappropriate ♦ *m/f* unhappy person; **infelizmente** [ĩfeliʒ'mẽtʃi] *adv* unfortunately

inferior [ĩfe'rjo*] *adj*: ~ **(a)** (*em valor, qualidade*) inferior (to); (*mais baixo*) lower (than) ♦ *m/f* inferior, subordinate; **inferioridade** [ĩferjori'dadʒi] *f* inferiority

infernal [ĩfex'naw] (*pl* -**ais**) *adj* infernal

inferno [ĩ'fexnu] *m* hell; **vá pro ~!** (*col*) piss off!

infetar [ĩfe'ta*] *vt* to infect

infiel [ĩ'fjɛw] (*pl* -**eis**) *adj* disloyal; (*marido, mulher*) unfaithful; (*texto*) inaccurate ♦ *m/f* (*REL*) non-believer

ínfimo, -a [ĩ'fimu, a] *adj* lowest; (*qualidade*) poorest

infindável [ĩfĩ'davew] (*pl* -**eis**) *adj* unending, constant

infinidade [ĩfini'dadʒi] *f* infinity; **uma ~ de** countless

infinitivo [ĩfini'tʃivu] *m* (*LING*) infinitive

infinito, -a [ĩfi'nitu, a] *adj* infinite ♦ *m* infinity

inflação [ĩfla'sãw] *f* inflation; **inflacionário, -a** [ĩflasjo'narju, a] *adj* inflationary

inflamação [ĩflama'sãw] (*pl* -**ões**) *f* inflammation; **inflamado, -a** [ĩfla'madu, a] (*MED*) inflamed; (*discurso*) heated

inflamar [ĩfla'ma*] *vt* (*madeira, pólvora*) to set fire to; (*MED, fig*) to inflame; **inflamar-se** *vr* to catch fire; (*fig*) to get worked up; **~se de algo** to be consumed with sth

inflamável [ĩfla'mavew] (*pl* -**eis**) *adj* inflammable

inflar [ĩ'fla*] *vt* to inflate, blow up; **inflar-se** *vr* to swell (up)

inflexível [ĩflek'sivew] (*pl* -**eis**) *adj* stiff, rigid; (*fig*) unyielding

influência [ĩ'flwẽsja] *f* influence; **sob a ~ de** under the influence of; **influenciar** [ĩflwẽ'sja*] *vt* to influence ♦ *vi*: **influenciar em algo** to influence sth, have an influence on sth; **influenciar-se** *vr*: **influenciar-se por** to be influenced by; **influente** [ĩ'flwẽtʃi] *adj* influential; **influir** [ĩ'flwi*] *vi* to matter, be important; **influir em** *ou* **sobre** to influence, have an influence on

informação [ĩfoxma'sãw] (*pl* -**ões**) *f* (*piece of*) information; (*notícia*) news *sg*; **informações** *fpl* (*detalhes*) information *sg*; **Informações** (*TEL*) directory enquiries (*BRIT*), information (*US*); **pedir informações sobre** to ask about, inquire about

informal [ĩfox'maw] (*pl* -**ais**) *adj* informal; **informalidade** [ĩfoxmali'dadʒi] *f* informality

informante [ĩfox'mãtʃi] *m* informant; (*JUR*) informer

informar [ĩfox'ma*] *vt*: ~ **alguém (de/sobre algo)** to inform sb (of/about sth) ♦ *vi* to inform, be informative; **informar-se** *vr*: **~-se de** to find out about, inquire about; **~-se de** to report on

informática [ĩfox'matʃika] *f* computer science; (*ramo*) computing, computers *pl*

informativo, -a [ĩfoxma'tʃivu, a] *adj* informative

informatizar [ĩfoxmatʃi'za*] *vt* to computerize

infortúnio [ĩfox'tunju] *m* misfortune

infração [ĩfra'sãw] (*PT* -**cç**-; *pl* -**ões**) *f* breach, infringement; (*ESPORTE*) foul

infrator, a [ĩfra'to*, a] (*PT*) *m/f* = **infrator, a**

infrator, a [ĩfra'to*, a] *m/f* offender

infringir [ĩfrĩ'ʒi*] vt to infringe, contravene

infrutífero, -a [ĩfru'tʃiferu, a] adj fruitless

infundado, -a [ĩfũ'dadu, a] adj groundless, unfounded

ingênuo, -a [ĩ'ʒenwu, a] adj ingenuous, naïve; (comentário) harmless ♦ m/f naïve person

ingerir [ĩʒe'ri*] vt to ingest; (engolir) to swallow

Inglaterra [ĩgla'texa] f: a ~ England; **inglês, -esa** [ĩ'gleʃ, eza] adj English ♦ m/f Englishman/woman ♦ m (LING) English; **os ingleses** mpl the English

ingrato, -a [ĩ'gratu, a] adj ungrateful

ingrediente [ĩgre'dʒjẽtʃi] m ingredient

íngreme ['ĩgremi] adj steep

ingressar [ĩgre'sa*] vi: ~ **em** to enter, go into; (um clube) to join

ingresso [ĩ'gresu] m (entrada) entry; (admissão) admission; (bilhete) ticket

inibição [inibi'sãw] (pl -ões) f inhibition

inibido, -a [ini'bidu, a] adj inhibited

inibir [ini'bi*] vt to inhibit

iniciação [inisja'sãw] (pl -ões) f initiation

inicial [ini'sjaw] (pl -ais) adj, f initial

iniciar [ini'sja*] vt, vi (começar) to begin, start; ~ **alguém em algo** (arte, seita) to initiate sb into sth

iniciativa [inisja'tʃiva] f initiative; **a ~ privada** (ECON) private enterprise

início [i'nisju] m beginning, start; **no ~** at the start

inimigo, -a [ini'migu, a] adj, m/f enemy

inimizade [inimi'zadʒi] f enmity, hatred

ininterrupto, -a [inĩte'xuptu, a] adj continuous; (esforço) unstinting; (vôo) non-stop; (serviço) 24-hour

injeção [ĩʒe'sãw] (PT -cç-; pl -ões) f injection

injetar [ĩʒe'ta*] (PT -ct-) vt to inject

injúria [ĩ'ʒurja] f insult

injustiça [ĩʒuʃ'tʃisa] f injustice

injusto, -a [ĩ'ʒuʃtu, a] adj unfair, unjust

inocência [ino'sẽsja] f innocence

inocentar [inosẽ'ta*] vt: ~ **alguém (de algo)** to clear sb (of sth)

inocente [ino'sẽtʃi] adj innocent ♦ m/f innocent man/woman

inócuo, -a [i'nɔkwu, a] adj harmless

inofensivo, -a [inofẽ'sivu, a] adj harmless, inoffensive

inoportuno, -a [inopox'tunu, a] adj inconvenient, inopportune

inovação [inova'sãw] (pl -ões) f innovation

inoxidável [inoksi'davew] (pl -eis) adj: **aço ~** stainless steel

INPS (BR) abr m (= Instituto Nacional de Previdência Social) ≈ DSS (BRIT), ≈ Welfare Dept (US)

inquérito [ĩ'keritu] m inquiry; (JUR) inquest

inquietação [ĩkjeta'sãw] f anxiety, uneasiness; (agitação) restlessness

inquietante [ĩkje'tãtʃi] adj worrying, disturbing

inquietar [ĩkje'ta*] vt to worry, disturb; **inquietar-se** vr to worry, bother; **inquieto, -a** [ĩ'kjetu, a] adj anxious, worried; (agitado) restless

inquilino, -a [ĩki'linu, a] m/f tenant

insalubre [ĩsa'lubri] adj unhealthy

insanidade [ĩsani'dadʒi] f madness, insanity; **insano, -a** [ĩ'sanu, a] adj insane

insatisfação [ĩsatʃiʃfa'sãw] f dissatisfaction

insatisfatório, -a [ĩsatʃiʃfa'tɔrju, a] adj unsatisfactory

insatisfeito, -a [ĩsatʃiʃ'fejtu, a] adj dissatisfied, unhappy

inscrever [ĩʃkre've*] vt to inscribe; (aluno) to enrol (BRIT), enroll (US); (em registro) to register

inscrição [ĩʃkri'sãw] (pl -ões) f Inscription

inscrito, -a [ĩʃ'kritu, a] pp de inscrever

insecto etc [ĩ'setu] (PT) = **inseto** etc

insegurança [ĩsegu'rãsa] f insecurity; **inseguro, -a** [ĩse'guru, a] adj insecure

insensatez [ĩsēsa'teʒ] f folly, madness; **insensato, -a** [ĩsē'satu, a] adj unreasonable, foolish

insensível [ĩsē'sivew] (pl -eis) adj insensitive; (dormente) numb

inserir [ĩse'ri*] vt to insert, put in; (COMPUT: dados) to enter

inseticida [ĩsetʃi'sida] m insecticide

inseto [ĩ'setu] m insect

insignificante [ĩsignifi'kãtʃi] f insignificant

insinuar [ĩsi'nwa*] vt to insinuate, imply

insípido, -a [ĩ'sipidu, a] adj insipid

insiro etc [ĩ'siru] vb V **inserir**

insistência [ĩsiʃ'tēsja] f: ~ (em) insistence (on); (obstinação) persistence (in); **insistente** [ĩsiʃ'tētʃi] adj (pessoa) insistent; (apelo) urgent

insistir [ĩsiʃ'tʃi*] vi: ~ (em) to insist (on); (perseverar) to persist (in); ~ (em) que to insist that

insolação [ĩsola'sãw] f sunstroke; **pegar uma ~** to get sunstroke

insolente [ĩso'lētʃi] adj insolent

insólito, -a [ĩ'sɔlitu, a] adj unusual

insônia [ĩ'sonja] f insomnia

insosso, -a [ĩ'sosu, a] adj unsalted; (sem sabor) tasteless; (pessoa) uninteresting, dull

inspeção [ĩʃpe'sãw] (PT -cç-; pl -ões) f inspection, check; **inspecionar** [ĩʃpesjo'na*] (PT -cc-) vt to inspect

inspetor, a [ĩʃpe'to*, a] (PT -ct-) m/f inspector

inspiração [ĩʃpira'sãw] (pl -ões) f inspiration

inspirador, a [ĩʃpira'do*, a] adj inspiring

inspirar [ĩʃpi'ra*] vt to inspire; (MED) to inhale; **inspirar-se** vr to be inspired

instalação [ĩʃtala'sãw] (pl -ões) f installation; ~ **elétrica** (de casa) wiring

instalar [ĩʃta'la*] vt to install; (estabelecer) to set up; **instalar-se** vr (numa cadeira) to settle down

instantâneo, -a [ĩʃtã'tanju, a] adj instant, instantaneous ♦ m (FOTO) snap

instante [ĩʃ'tãtʃi] adj urgent ♦ m moment; **num ~** in an instant, quickly; **só um ~!** just a moment!

instável [ĩʃ'tavew] (pl -eis) adj unstable; (tempo) unsettled

instintivo, -a [ĩʃtʃĩ'tʃivu, a] adj instinctive

instinto [ĩʃ'tʃĩtu] m instinct; **por ~** instinctively

instituição [ĩʃtʃitwi'sãw] (pl -ões) f institution

instituto [ĩʃtʃi'tutu] m (escola) institute; (instituição) institution; ~ **de beleza** beauty salon

instrução [ĩʃtru'sãw] (PT -cç-; pl -ões) f education; (erudição) learning; (diretriz) instruction; (MIL) training; **instruções** fpl (para o uso) instructions (for use)

instructor, a [ĩʃtru'tor, a] (PT) m/f

= **instrutor, a**

instruído, -a [ĩʃ'trwidu, a] *adj* educated

instruir [ĩʃ'trwi*] *vt* to instruct; (MIL) to train; **instruir-se** *vr*: ~-**se em algo** to learn sth; ~ **alguém de** *ou* **sobre algo** to inform sb about sth

instrumento [ĩʃtru'mẽtu] *m* instrument; (*ferramenta*) implement; (JUR) deed, document; ~ **de cordas/percussão/sopro** stringed/percussion/ wind instrument; ~ **de trabalho** tool

instrutivo, -a [ĩʃtru'tʃivu, a] *adj* instructive

instrutor, a [ĩʃtru'to*, a] *m/f* instructor; (ESPORTE) coach

insubordinação [ĩsuboxdʒina'sãw] *f* rebellion; (MIL) insubordination

insubstituível [ĩsubiʃtʃi'twivew] (*pl* -**eis**) *adj* irreplaceable

insuficiência [ĩsufi'sjẽsja] *f* inadequacy; (*carência*) shortage; (MED) deficiency; ~ **cardíaca** heart failure; **insuficiente** [ĩsufi'sjẽtʃi] *adj* insufficient; (EDUC: *nota*) = fail; (*pessoa*) incompetent

insulina [ĩsu'lina] *f* insulin

insultar [ĩsuw'ta*] *vt* to insult; **insulto** [ĩ'suwtu] *m* insult

insuperável [ĩsupe'ravew] (*pl* -**eis**) *adj* (*dificuldade*) insuperable; (*qualidade*) unsurpassable

insuportável [ĩsupox'tavew] (*pl* -**eis**) *adj* unbearable

insurgir-se [ĩsux'ʒixsi] *vr* to rebel, revolt

insurreição [ĩsuxej'sãw] (*pl* -**ões**) *f* rebellion, insurrection

intato, -a [ĩ'tatu, a] (PT -**act-**) *adj* intact

íntegra [ĩ'tegra] *f*: **na** ~ in full

integral [ĩte'graw] (*pl* -**eis**) *adj*

whole ♦ *f* (MAT) integral; **pão** ~ wholemeal (BRIT) *ou* wholewheat (US) bread; **integralmente** [ĩtegraw'mẽtʃi] *adv* in full, fully

integrar [ĩte'gra*] *vt* to unite, combine; (*completar*) to form, make up; (MAT, *raças*) to integrate; **integrar-se** *vr* to become complete; ~-**se em** *ou* **a algo** to join sth; (*adaptar-se*) to integrate into sth

integridade [ĩtegri'dadʒi] *f* entirety; (*fig*: *de pessoa*) integrity

íntegro, -a [ĩ'tegru, a] *adj* entire; (*honesto*) upright, honest

inteiramente [ĩtejra'mẽtʃi] *adv* completely

inteirar [ĩtej'ra*] *vt* (*completar*) to complete; **inteirar-se** *vr*: ~-**se de** to find out about; ~ **alguém de** to inform sb of

inteiro, -a [ĩ'tejru, a] *adj* whole, entire; (*ileso*) unharmed; (*não quebrado*) undamaged

intelecto [ĩte'lektu] *m* intellect; **intelectual** [ĩtelek'twaw] (*pl* -**ais**) *adj, m/f* intellectual

inteligência [ĩteli'ʒẽsja] *f* intelligence; **inteligente** [ĩteli'ʒẽtʃi] *adj* intelligent, clever

inteligível [ĩteli'ʒivew] (*pl* -**eis**) *adj* intelligible

intenção [ĩtẽ'sãw] (*pl* -**ões**) *f* intention; **segundas intenções** ulterior motives; **ter a** ~ **de** to intend to; **intencionado, -a** [ĩtẽsjo'nadu, a] *adj*: **bem intencionado** well-meaning; **mal intencionado** spiteful; **intencional** [ĩtẽsjo'naw] (*pl* -**ais**) *adj* intentional, deliberate; **intencionar** [ĩtẽsjo'na*] *vt* to intend

intensificar [ĩtẽsifi'ka*] *vt* to intensify; **intensificar-se** *vr* to intensify

intensivo, -a [ĩtẽ'sivu, a] *adj* intensive

intenso, -a [ĩ'tẽsu, a] *adj* intense; (*emoção*) deep; (*impressão*) vivid; (*vida social*) full

interação [ĩtera'sãw] (*PT* -cç-) *f* interaction

interativo, -a [ĩtera'tʃivu, a] (*PT* -ct-) *adj* (*COMPUT*) interactive

intercâmbio [ĩtex'kãbju] *m* exchange

interdição [ĩtexdʒi'sãw] (*pl* -ões) *f* (*de estrada, porta*) closure; (*JUR*) injunction

interditar [ĩtexdʒi'ta*] *vt* (*importação etc*) to ban; (*estrada, praia*) to close off; (*cinema etc*) to close down

interessado, -a [ĩtere'sadu, a] *adj* interested; (*amizade*) self-seeking

interessante [ĩtere'sãtʃi] *adj* interesting

interessar [ĩtere'sa*] *vt* to interest ♦ *vi* to be interesting; **interessar-se** *vr*: ~ **se em** *ou* **por** to take an interest in, be interested in; **a quem possa** ~ to whom it may concern

interesse [ĩte'resi] *m* interest; (*próprio*) self-interest; (*proveito*) advantage; **no** ~ **de** for the sake of; **por** ~ (*próprio*) for one's own ends; **interesseiro, -a** [ĩtere'sejru, a] *adj* self-seeking

interface [ĩtex'fasi] *f* (*COMPUT*) interface

interferência [ĩtexfe'rẽsja] *f* interference

interferir [ĩtexfe'ri*] *vi*: ~ **em** to interfere in

interfone [ĩtex'fɔni] *m* intercom

interior [ĩte'rjo*] *adj* inner, inside; (*COM*) domestic, internal ♦ *m* inside, interior; (*do país*): **no** ~ inland; **Ministério do I~** = Home Office (*BRIT*), ≈ Department of the Interior (*US*)

interjeição [ĩtexʒej'sãw] (*pl* -ões) *f* interjection

interlocutor, a [ĩtexloku'to*, a]

m/f speaker; **meu** ~ the person I was speaking to

intermediário, -a [ĩtexme-'dʒjarju, a] *adj* intermediary ♦ *m/f* (*COM*) middleman; (*mediador*) intermediary, mediator

intermédio [ĩtex'mɛdʒu] *m*: **por** ~ **de** through

interminável [ĩtexmi'navew] (*pl* -eis) *adj* endless

internação [ĩtexna'sãw] (*pl* -ões) *f* (*de doente*) admission

internacional [ĩtexnasjo'naw] (*pl* -ais) *adj* international

internações [ĩtexna'sõjʃ] *fpl de* internação

internar [ĩtex'na*] *vt* (*aluno*) to put into boarding school; (*doente*) to take into hospital; (*MIL, POL*) to intern

internauta [ĩtex'nawta] *m/f* Internet user

Internet [ĩtex'nɛtʃi] *f*: **a** ~ the Internet

interno, -a [ĩ'texnu, a] *adj* internal; (*POL*) domestic ♦ *m/f* (*tb*: **aluno** ~) boarder; (*MED*: *estudante*) houseman (*BRIT*), intern (*US*); **de uso** ~ (*MED*) for internal use

interpretação [ĩtexpreta'sãw] (*pl* -ões) *f* interpretation; (*TEATRO*) performance

interpretar [ĩtexpre'ta*] *vt* to interpret; (*um papel*) to play; **intérprete** [ĩ'tɛxpretʃi] *m/f* interpreter; (*TEATRO*) performer, artist

interrogação [ĩtexoga'sãw] (*pl* -ões) *f* interrogation; **ponto de** ~ question mark

interrogar [ĩtexo'ga*] *vt* to question, interrogate; (*JUR*) to cross-examine

interromper [ĩtexõ'pe*] *vt* to interrupt; (*parar*) to stop; (*ELET*) to cut off

interrupção [ĩtexup'sãw] (*pl* -ões) *f* interruption; (*intervalo*) break

interruptor [ĩtexup'to*] *m* (*ELET*) switch

interseção [ĩtexse'sãw] (*PT* -cç-; *pl* -ões) *f* intersection

interurbano, -a [ĩterux'banu, a] *adj* (*TEL*) long-distance ♦ *m* long-distance *ou* trunk call

intervalo [ĩtex'valu] *m* interval; (*descanso*) break; **a ~s** every now and then

intervenção [ĩtexvẽ'sãw] (*pl* -ões) *f* intervention; **~ cirúrgica** (*MED*) operation

intervir [ĩtex'vi*] (*irreg: como vir*) *vi* to intervene; (*sobrevir*) to come up

intestino [ĩtej'tʃinu] *m* intestine

intimação [ĩtʃima'sãw] (*pl* -ões) *f* (*ordem*) order; (*JUR*) summons

intimar [ĩtʃi'ma*] *vt* (*JUR*) to summon; **~ alguém a fazer** *ou* **a alguém que faça** to order sb to do

intimidade [ĩtʃimi'dadʒi] *f* intimacy; (*vida privada*) private life; (*familiaridade*) familiarity; **ter ~ com alguém** to be close to sb

íntimo, -a ['ĩtʃimu, a] *adj* intimate; (*sentimentos*) innermost; (*amigo*) close; (*vida*) private ♦ *m/f* close friend; **no ~** at heart

intolerante [ĩtole'rãtʃi] *adj* intolerant

intolerável [ĩtole'ravew] (*pl* -eis) *adj* intolerable, unbearable

intoxicação [ĩtoksika'sãw] *f* poisoning; **~ alimentar** food poisoning

intoxicar [ĩtoksi'ka*] *vt* to poison

intranet [ĩtra'netʃi] *f* intranet

intransigente [ĩtrãsi'ʒẽtʃi] *adj* uncompromising; (*fig: rígido*) strict

intransitável [ĩtrãsi'tavew] (*pl* -eis) *adj* impassable

intransitivo, -a [ĩtrãsi'tʃivu, a] *adj* intransitive

intransponível [ĩtrãʃpo'nivew] (*pl* -eis) *adj* (*rio*) impossible to cross; (*problema*) insurmountable

intratável [ĩtra'tavew] (*pl* -eis) *adj* (*pessoa*) contrary, awkward; (*doença*) untreatable; (*problema*) insurmountable

intriga [ĩ'triga] *f* intrigue; (*enredo*) plot; (*fofoca*) piece of gossip; **~s** (*fofocas*) gossip *sg*; **~ amorosa** (*PT*) love affair; **intrigante** [ĩtri'gãtʃi] *m/f* troublemaker ♦ *adj* intriguing; **intrigar** [ĩtri'ga*] *vt* to intrigue ♦ *vi* to be intriguing

introdução [ĩtrodu'sãw] (*pl* -ões) *f* introduction

introduzir [ĩtrodu'zi*] *vt* to introduce

intrometer-se [ĩtrome'texsi] *vr* to interfere, meddle; **intrometido, -a** [ĩtrome'tʃidu, a] *adj* interfering; (*col*) nosey ♦ *m/f* busybody

introvertido, -a [ĩtrovex'tʃidu, a] *adj* introverted ♦ *m/f* introvert

intruso, -a [ĩ'truzu, a] *m/f* intruder

intuição [ĩtwi'sãw] (*pl* -ões) *f* intuition

intuito [ĩ'tuito] *m* intention, aim

inumano, -a [inu'manu, a] *adj* inhuman

inúmero, -a [i'numeru, a] *adj* countless, innumerable

inundação [inũda'sãw] (*pl* -ões) *f* (*enchente*) flood; (*ato*) flooding

inundar [inũ'da*] *vt* to flood; (*fig*) to inundate ♦ *vi* to flood

inusitado, -a [inuzi'tadu, a] *adj* unusual

inútil [i'nutʃiw] (*pl* -eis) *adj* useless; (*esforço*) futile; (*desnecessário*) pointless; **inutilizar** [inutʃili'za*] *vt* to make useless, render useless; (*incapacitar*) to put out of action; (*danificar*) to ruin; (*esforços*) to thwart; **inutilmente** [inutʃiw-

'mɛtʃi] adv in vain

invadir [ĩva'dʒi*] vt to invade; (suj: água) to overrun; (: sentimento) to overcome

inválido, -a [ĩ'validu, a] adj, m/f invalid

invariável [ĩva'rjavew] (pl -eis) adj invariable

invasão [ĩva'zãw] (pl -ões) f invasion

invasor, a [ĩva'zo*, a] adj invading ♦ m/f invader

inveja [ĩ'veʒa] f envy; **invejar** [ĩve'ʒa*] vt to envy; (cobiçar) to covet ♦ vi to be envious; **invejoso, -a** [ĩve'ʒozu, ɔza] adj envious

invenção [ĩvẽ'sãw] (pl -ões) f invention

inventar [ĩvẽ'ta*] vt to invent

inventivo, -a [ĩvẽ'tʃivu, a] adj inventive

inventor, a [ĩvẽ'to*, a] m/f inventor

inverno [ĩ'vɛxnu] m winter

inverossímil [ĩvero'simiw] (PT -osí-; pl -eis) adj unlikely, improbable; (inacreditável) implausible

inverso, -a [ĩ'vɛxsu, a] adj inverse; (oposto) opposite; (ordem) reverse ♦ m opposite, reverse; **ao ~ de** contrary to

inverter [ĩvex'te*] vt to alter; (ordem) to invert, reverse; (colocar às avessas) to turn upside down, invert

invés [ĩ'vɛʃ] m: **ao ~ de** instead of

investigação [ĩveʃtʃiga'sãw] (pl -ões) f investigation; (pesquisa) research

investigar [ĩveʃtʃi'ga*] vt to investigate; (examinar) to examine

investimento [ĩveʃtʃi'mẽtu] m investment

investir [ĩveʃ'tʃi*] vt (dinheiro) to invest

inviável [ĩ'vjavew] (pl -eis) adj impracticable

invicto, -a [ĩ'viktu, a] adj unconquered

invisível [ĩvi'zivew] (pl -eis) adj invisible

invisto etc [ĩ'viʃtu] vb V **investir**

invocar [ĩvo'ka*] vt to invoke

invólucro [ĩ'volukru] m (cobertura) covering; (envoltório) wrapping; (caixa) box

involuntário, -a [ĩvolũ'tarju, a] adj involuntary; (ofensa) unintentional

iodo ['jodu] m iodine

ioga ['jɔga] f yoga

iogurte [jo'guxtʃi] m yogurt

IR (BR) abr m = **Imposto de Renda**

┌─ PALAVRA CHAVE ──────────┐

ir [i*] vi **1** to go; (a pé) to walk; (a cavalo) to ride; (viajar) to travel; **~ caminhando** to walk; **fui de trem** I went ou travelled by train; **vamos!**, **vamos nessa!** (col), **vamos embora!** let's go!; **já vou!** I'm coming!; **~ atrás de alguém** (seguir) to follow sb; (confiar) to take sb's word for it

2 (progredir: pessoa, coisa) to go; **o trabalho vai muito bem** work is going very well; **como vão as coisas?** how are things going?; **vou muito bem** I'm very well; (na escola etc) I'm getting on very well

♦ vb aux **1** (+ infin): **vou fazer** I will do, I am going to do

2 (+ gerúndio): **~ fazendo** to keep on doing

♦ **ir-se** vr to go away, leave

└──────────────────────────┘

ira ['ira] f anger, rage

Irã [i'rã] m: **o ~** Iran

irado, -a [i'radu, a] adj angry, irate

iraniano, -a [ira'njanu, a] adj, m/f Iranian

Irão [i'rãw] (PT) m = Irã

Iraque [i'raki] m: o ~ Iraq; **ira-quiano, -a** [ira'kjanu, a] adj, m/f Iraqi

ir-e-vir (pl **ires-e-vires**) m comings and goings pl

Irlanda [ix'lãda] f: a ~ Ireland; a ~ do Norte Northern Ireland; **irlandês, -esa** [ixlã'deʃ, eza] adj Irish ♦ m/f Irishman/woman ♦ m (LING) Irish

irmã [ix'mã] f sister; ~ de criação adoptive sister; ~ gêmea twin sister

irmão [ix'mãw] (pl ~s) m brother; (fig: similar) twin; (col: companheiro) mate; ~ de criação adoptive brother; ~ gêmeo twin brother

ironia [iro'nia] f irony

irra! ['ixa] (PT) excl damn!

irracional [ixasjo'naw] (pl -ais) adj irrational

irreal [ixe'aw] (pl -ais) adj unreal

irregular [ixegu'la*] adj irregular; (vida) unconventional; (feições) unusual; (aluno, gênio) erratic

irrelevante [ixele'vãtʃi] adj irrelevant

irremediável [ixeme'dʒjavew] (pl -eis) adj irremediable; (sem remédio) incurable

irrequieto, -a [ixe'kjetu, a] adj restless

irresistível [ixeziʃ'tʃivew] (pl -eis) adj irresistible

irresponsável [ixeʃpõ'savew] (pl -eis) adj irresponsible

irrigar [ixi'ga*] vt to irrigate

irritação [ixita'sãw] (pl -ões) f irritation

irritadiço, -a [ixita'dʒisu, a] adj irritable

irritante [ixi'tãtʃi] adj irritating, annoying

irritar [ixi'ta*] vt to irritate; **irritar-se** vr to get angry, get annoyed

irromper [ixõ'pe*] vi (entrar subitamente): ~ (em) to burst in(to)

isca [iʃka] f (PESCA) bait; (fig) lure, bait

isenção [izẽ'sãw] (pl -ões) f exemption

isentar [izẽ'ta*] vt to exempt; (livrar) to free

Islã [iʒ'lã] m Islam

Islândia [iʒ'lãdʒa] f: a ~ Iceland

isolado, -a [izo'ladu, a] adj isolated; (solitário) lonely

isolamento [izola'mẽtu] m isolation; (ELET) insulation

isolar [izo'la*] vt to isolate; (ELET) to insulate

isqueiro [iʃ'kejru] m (cigarette) lighter

Israel [iʒxa'ɛw] m Israel; **israelense** [iʒxae'lẽsi] adj, m/f Israeli

isso ['isu] pron that; (col: isto) this; ~ mesmo exactly; por ~ therefore, so; por ~ mesmo for that very reason; só ~? is that all?

isto ['iʃtu] pron this; ~ é that is, namely

Itália [i'talja] f: a ~ Italy; **italiano, -a** [ita'ljanu, a] adj, m/f Italian ♦ m (LING) Italian

Itamarati [itamara'tʃi] m: o ~ the Brazilian Foreign Ministry; see boxed note

---

ITAMARATI

The Palace of Itamarati was built in 1855 in Rio de Janeiro. It became the seat of government when Brazil became a republic in 1889, and was later the Foreign Ministry. It ceased to be this when the Brazilian capital was transferred to Brasília, but **Itamarati** is still used to refer to the Foreign Ministry.

---

item ['itẽ] (pl -ns) m item

itinerário [itʃiˈne'rarʒu] *m* itinerary; (*caminho*) route

lugoslávia [jugoʒ'lavja] *f*: **a ~** Yugoslavia; **iugoslavo, -a** [jugoʒ-'lavu, a] *adj, m/f* Yugoslav(ian)

J

já [ʒa] *adv* already; (*em perguntas*) yet; (*agora*) now; (*imediatamente*) right away; (*agora mesmo*) right now ♦ *conj* on the other hand; **até ~** bye; **desde ~** from now on; **~ não** no longer; **~ que** as, since; **~ se vê** of course; **~ vou** I'm coming; **~ até** even; **~, ~** right away

jabuti [ʒabu'tʃi] *m* giant tortoise

jabuticaba [ʒabutʃi'kaba] *f* jaboti-cába (*type of berry*)

jaca [ʒaka] *f* jack fruit

jacaré [ʒaka'rɛ] (*BR*) *m* alligator

jacto [ʒaktu] (*PT*) *m* = **jato**

jaguar [ʒa'gwa*] *m* jaguar

jaguatirica [ʒagwatʃi'rika] *f* leop-ard cat

Jamaica [ʒa'majka] *f*: **a ~** Jamaica

jamais [ʒa'majʃ] *adv* never; (*com palavra negativa*) ever

janeiro [ʒa'nejru] (*PT* J-) *m* January

janela [ʒa'nɛla] *f* window

jangada [ʒãˈgada] *f* raft

jantar [ʒã'ta*] *m* dinner ♦ *vt* to have for dinner ♦ *vi* to have dinner

Japão [ʒa'pãw] *m*: **o ~** Japan; **japonês, -esa** [ʒapo'neʃ, eza] *adj, m/f* Japanese ♦ *m* (*LING*) Japanese

jararaca [ʒara'raka] *f* jararaca (*snake*)

jardim [ʒax'dʒĩ] (*pl* -ns) *m* garden; **~ zoológico** zoo; **jardim-de-infância** (*pl* jardins-de-infância) *m* kindergarten; **jardinagem** [ʒaxdʒi-'naʒẽ] *f* gardening

jardineira [ʒaxdʒi'nejra] *f* (*caixa*) trough; (*calça*) dungarees *pl*; V tb jardineiro

jardineiro, -a [ʒaxdʒi'nejru, a] *m/f* gardener

jardins [ʒax'dʒĩʃ] *mpl de* **jardim**

jargão [ʒax'gãw] *m* jargon

jarra [ˈʒaxa] *f* pot

jarro [ˈʒaxu] *m* jug

jasmim [ʒaʒ'mĩ] *m* jasmine

jato [ˈʒatu] *m* jet; (*de luz*) flash; (*de ar*) blast; **a ~** at top speed

jaula [ˈʒawla] *f* cage

javali [ʒava'li] *m* wild boar

jazigo [ʒa'zigu] *m* grave; (*monu-mento*) tomb

jazz [dʒɛz] *m* jazz

jeito [ˈʒejtu] *m* (*maneira*) way; (*aspecto*) appearance; (*habilidade*) skill, knack; (*modos pessoais*) man-ner; **ter ~ de** to look like; **não ter ~ (pessoa)** to be awkward; (*situação*) to be hopeless; **dar um ~ em (pé)** to twist; (*quarto, casa, papéis*) to tidy up; (*consertar*) to fix; **dar um ~** to find a way; **o ~ é ...** the thing to do is ...; **é o ~** it's the best way; **ao ~ de** in the style of; **com ~** tactfully; **daquele ~** (in) that way; (*col: em desordem, mal*) anyhow; **de qualquer ~** anyway; **de ~ nenhum!** no way!

jejuar [ʒe'ʒwa*] *vi* to fast

jejum [ʒe'ʒũ] (*pl* -ns) *m* fast; **em ~** fasting

Jesus [ʒe'zuʃ] *m* Jesus ♦ *excl* heav-ens!

jibóia [ʒi'bɔja] *f* boa (constrictor)

jiló [ʒi'lɔ] *m* kind of vegetable

jingle [ˈdʒiŋgew] *m* jingle

joalheria [ʒoaʎe'ria] *f* jeweller's (shop) (*BRIT*), jewelry store (*US*)

joaninha [ʒwa'niɲa] *f* ladybird (*BRIT*), ladybug (*US*)

joelho [ʒo'eʎu] *m* knee; **de ~s** kneeling; **ficar de ~s** to kneel down

jogada [ʒo'gada] *f* move; (*lanço*)

throw; (*negócio*) scheme, move

jogador, a [ʒoga'do*, a] *m/f* player; (*de jogo de azar*) gambler

jogar [ʒo'ga*] *vt* to play; (*em jogo de azar*) to gamble; (*atirar*) to throw; (*indiretas*) to drop ♦ *vi* to play; to gamble; (*barco*) to pitch; ~ **fora** to throw away

jogging ['ʒɔɡĩ] *m* jogging; (*roupa*) track suit; **fazer** ~ to go jogging, jog

jogo ['ʒogu] *m* game; (*jogar*) play; (*de azar*) gambling; (*conjunto*) set; (*artimanha*) trick; **J~s Olímpicos** Olympic Games

jóia ['ʒɔja] *f* jewel

Jordânia [ʒox'danja] *f*: **a** ~ Jordan; **Jordão** [ʒox'dãw] *m*: **o (rio) Jordão** the Jordan (River)

jornada [ʒox'nada] *f* journey; ~ **de trabalho** working day

jornal [ʒox'naw] (*pl* **-ais**) *m* newspaper; (*TV*, *RÁDIO*) news *sg*; **jornaleiro, -a** [ʒoxna'lejru, a] *m/f* newsagent (*BRIT*), newsdealer (*US*)

jornalismo [ʒoxna'liʒmu] *m* journalism; **jornalista** [ʃoxna'liʃta] *m/f* journalist

jovem ['ʒovẽ] (*pl* **-ns**) *adj* young ♦ *m/f* young person

jovial [ʒo'vjaw] (*pl* **-ais**) *adj* jovial, cheerful

Jr *abr* = **Júnior**

judaico, -a [ʒu'dajku, a] *adj* Jewish

judeu, judia [ʒu'dew, ʒu'dʒia] *adj* Jewish ♦ *m/f* Jew

judiação [ʒudʒja'sãw] *f* ill-treatment

judiar [ʒu'dʒja*] *vi*: ~ **de** to ill-treat

judicial [ʒudʒi'sjaw] (*pl* **-ais**) *adj* judicial

judiciário, -a [ʒudʒi'sjarju, a] *adj* judicial; **o (poder)** ~ the judiciary

judô [ʒu'do] *m* judo

juiz, -íza [ʒwiʒ, 'iza] *m/f* judge; (*em jogos*) referee; ~ **de paz** justice of

the peace; **juizado** [ʒwi'zado] *m* court

juízo ['ʒwizu] *m* judgement; (*parecer*) opinion; (*siso*) common sense; (*foro*) court; **perder o** ~ to lose one's mind; **não ter** ~ to be foolish; **tomar** *ou* **criar** ~ to come to one's senses; **chamar/levar a** ~ to summon/take to court; ~**!** behave yourself!

julgamento [ʒuwga'mẽtu] *m* judgement; (*audiência*) trial; (*sentença*) sentence

julgar [ʒuw'ga*] *vt* to judge; (*achar*) to think; (*JUR*: *sentenciar*) to sentence; **julgar-se** *vr*: ~**-se algo** to consider o.s. sth, think of o.s. as sth

julho ['ʒuʎu] (*PT* **J-**) *m* July

jumento, -a [ʒu'mẽtu, a] *m/f* donkey

junção [ʒũ'sãw] (*pl* **-ões**) *f* (*ato*) joining; (*junta*) join

junco ['ʒũku] *m* reed, rush

junções [ʒũ'sõjʃ] *fpl de* **junção**

junho ['ʒuɲu] (*PT* **J-**) *m* June

júnior ['ʒunjo*] (*pl* **juniores**) *adj* younger, junior ♦ *m/f* (*ESPORTE*) junior; **Eduardo Autran J~** Eduardo Autran Junior

junta ['ʒũta] *f* board, committee; (*POL*) junta; (*articulação, juntura*) joint

juntar [ʒũ'ta*] *vt* to join; (*reunir*) to bring together; (*aglomerar*) to gather together; (*recolher*) to collect up; (*acrescentar*) to add; (*dinheiro*) to save up ♦ *vi* to gather; **juntar-se** to gather; (*associar-se*) to join up; ~**-se a alguém** to join sb

junto, -a ['ʒũtu, a] *adj* joined; (*chegado*) near; **ir** ~**s** to go together; ~ **a/de** near/next to, by; **segue** ~ (*COM*) please find enclosed

jura ['ʒura] *f* vow

jurado, -a [ʒu'radu, a] *adj* sworn

♦ *m/f* juror

juramento [ʒuraˈmẽtu] *m* oath

jurar [ʒuˈra*] *vt, vi* to swear; **jura?** really?

júri [ˈʒuri] *m* jury

jurídico, -a [ʒuˈridʒiku, a] *adj* legal

juros [ˈʒuruʃ] *mpl* (*ECON*) interest *sg*; **~ simples/compostos** simple/compound interest

justamente [ʒuʃtaˈmẽtʃi] *adv* fairly, justly; (*precisamente*) exactly

justiça [ʒuʃˈtʃisa] *f* justice; (*poder judiciário*) judiciary; (*eqüidade*) fairness; (*tribunal*) court; **com ~** justly, fairly; **ir à ~** to go to court; **justiceiro, -a** [ʒuʃtʃiˈsejru, a] *adj* righteous; (*inflexível*) inflexible

justificação [ʒuʃtʃifikaˈsãw] (*pl -ões*) *f* justification

justificar [ʒuʃtʃifiˈka*] *vt* to justify

justo, -a [ˈʒuʃtu, a] *adj* just, fair; (*legítimo: queixa*) legitimate, justified; (*exato*) exact; (*apertado*) tight ♦ *adv* just

juvenil [ʒuveˈniw] (*pl -is*) *adj* youthful; (*roupa*) young; (*livro*) for young people; (*ESPORTE: equipe, campeonato*) youth *atr*, junior

juventude [ʒuvẽˈtudʒi] *f* youth; (*jovialidade*) youthfulness; (*jovens*) young people *pl*, youth

K

kg *abr* (= *quilograma*) kg

kit [ˈkitʃi] (*pl ~s*) *m* kit

kitchenette [kitʃeˈnetʃi] *f* studio flat

km *abr* (= *quilômetro*) km

km/h *abr* (= *quilômetros por hora*) km/h

L

-la [la] *pron* her; (*você*) you; (*coisa*) it

lá [la] *adv* there ♦ *m* (*MÚS*) A; **~ fora** outside; **~ em baixo** down there; **por ~** (*direção*) that way; (*situação*) over there; **até ~** (*no espaço*) there; (*no tempo*) until then

lã [lã] *f* wool

lábia [ˈlabja] *f* (*astúcia*) cunning; **ter ~** to have the gift of the gab

lábio [ˈlabju] *m* lip

labirinto [labiˈrĩtu] *m* labyrinth, maze

laboratório [laboraˈtɔrju] *m* laboratory

laca [ˈlaka] *f* lacquer

laçar [laˈsa*] *vt* to bind, tie

laço [ˈlasu] *m* bow; (*de gravata*) knot; (*armadilha*) snare; (*fig*) bond; **dar um ~** to tie a bow

lacrar [laˈkra*] *vt* to seal (with wax); **lacre** [ˈlakri] *m* sealing wax

lacuna [laˈkuna] *f* gap; (*omissão*) omission; (*espaço em branco*) blank

ladeira [laˈdejra] *f* slope

lado [ˈladu] *m* side; (*MIL*) flank; (*rumo*) direction; **ao ~** (*perto*) close by; **a casa ao ~** the house next door; **ao ~ de** beside; **deixar de ~** to set aside; (*fig*) to leave out; **de um ~ para outro** back and forth

ladra [ˈladra] *f* thief, robber; (*picareta*) crook

ladrão, -ona [laˈdrãw, ɔna] (*pl -ões, ~s*) *adj* thieving ♦ *m/f* thief, robber; (*picareta*) crook

ladrilho [laˈdriʎu] *m* tile; (*chão*) tiled floor, tiles *pl*

ladrões [laˈdrõjʃ] *mpl de* **ladrão**

lagarta [laˈgaxta] *f* caterpillar

lagartixa [lagaxˈtʃiʃa] *f* gecko

lagarto [laˈgaxtu] *m* lizard

lago [ˈlagu] *m* lake; (*de jardim*) pond

lagoa [la'goa] f pool, pond; (*lago*) lake

lagosta [la'goʃta] f lobster

lagostim [lagoʃ'tʃĩ] (*pl* -ns) m crayfish

lágrima ['lagrima] f tear

laje ['laʒi] f paving stone, flagstone

lama ['lama] f mud

lamaçal [lama'saw] (*pl* -ais) m quagmire; (*pântano*) bog, marsh

lamber [lã'be*] vt to lick; **lambida** [lã'bida] f: **dar uma lambida em algo** to lick sth

lambuzar [lãbu'za*] vt to smear

lamentar [lamẽ'ta*] vt to lament; (*sentir*) to regret; **lamentar-se** vr: **~-se (de algo)** to lament (sth); **~(que)** to be sorry (that); **lamentável** [lamẽ'tavew] (*pl* -eis) adj regrettable; (*deplorável*) deplorable; **lamento** [la'mẽtu] m lament; (*gemido*) moan

lâmina ['lamina] f (*chapa*) sheet; (*placa*) plate; (*de faca*) blade; (*de persiana*) slat

lâmpada ['lãpada] f lamp; (*tb*: **~ elétrica**) light bulb; **~ de mesa** table lamp

lança ['lãsa] f lance, spear

lançamento [lãsa'mẽtu] m throwing; (*de navio, produto, campanha*) launch; (*de disco, filme*) release; (*COM: em livro*) entry

lançar [lã'sa*] vt to throw; (*navio, produto, campanha*) to launch; (*disco, filme*) to release; (*COM: em livro*) to enter; (*em leilão*) to bid

lance ['lãsi] m (*arremesso*) throw; (*incidente*) incident; (*história*) story; (*situação*) position; (*fato*) fact; (*ESPORTE: jogada*) shot; (*em leilão*) bid; (*de escada*) flight; (*de casas*) row; (*episódio*) moment; (*de muro, estrada*) stretch

lancha ['lãʃa] f launch; **~ torpedeira** torpedo boat

lanchar [lã'ʃa*] vi to have a snack ♦ vt to have as a snack; **lanche** ['lãʃi] m snack

lanchonete [lãʃo'netʃi] (*BR*) f snack bar

lânguido, -a ['lãgidu, a] adj languid, listless

lanterna [lã'texna] f lantern; (*portátil*) torch (*BRIT*), flashlight (*US*)

lápide ['lapidʒi] f (*tumular*) tombstone; (*comemorativa*) memorial stone

lápis ['lapiʃ] m inv pencil; **~ de cor** coloured (*BRIT*) ou colored (*US*) pencil, crayon; **~ de olho** eyebrow pencil; **lapiseira** [lapi'zejra] f propelling (*BRIT*) ou mechanical (*US*) pencil; (*caixa*) pencil case

Lapônia [la'ponja] f: a ~ Lapland

lapso ['lapsu] m lapse; (*de tempo*) interval; (*erro*) slip

lar [la*] m home

laranja [la'rãʒa] adj inv orange ♦ f orange ♦ m (*cor*) orange; **laranjada** [larã'ʒada] f orangeade; **laranjeira** [larã'ʒejra] f orange tree

lareira [la'rejra] f hearth, fireside

larga ['laxga] f: **à ~** lavishly; **dar ~s a** to give free rein to; **viver à ~** to lead a lavish life

largada [lax'gada] f start; **dar a ~** to start; (*fig*) to make a start

largar [lax'ga*] vt to let go of, release; (*deixar*) to leave; (*deixar cair*) to drop; (*risada*) to let out; (*velas*) to unfurl; (*piada*) to tell; (*pôr em liberdade*) to let go ♦ vi (*NÁUT*) to set sail; **largar-se** vr (*desprender-se*) to free o.s.; (*ir-se*) to go off; (*pôr-se*) to proceed

largo, -a ['laxgu, a] adj wide, broad; (*amplo*) extensive; (*roupa*) loose, baggy; (*conversa*) long ♦ m (*praça*) square; (*alto-mar*) open sea; **ao ~** at a distance, far off; **passar de ~**

sobre um assunto to gloss over a subject; **passar ao ~ de algo** (fig) to sidestep sth; **largura** [lax'gura] f width, breadth

laringite [larĩ'ʒitʃi] f laryngitis

lasanha [la'zaɲa] f lasagna

lasca ['laʃka] f (de madeira, metal) splinter; (de pedra) chip; (fatia) slice

laser ['lejze*] m laser; **raio ~** laser beam

lástima ['laʃtʃima] f pity, compassion; (infortúnio) misfortune; **é uma ~ (que)** it's a shame (that); **lastimar** [laʃtʃi'ma*] vt to lament; **lastimar-se** vr to complain, be sorry for o.s

lata ['lata] f tin (BRIT), can; (material) tin-plate; **~ de lixo** rubbish bin (BRIT), garbage can (US); **~ velha** (col: carro) old banger (BRIT) ou clunker (US)

latão [la'tãw] m brass

lataria [lata'ria] f (AUTO) bodywork; (enlatados) canned food

latejar [late'ʒa*] vi to throb

latente [la'tẽtʃi] adj latent

lateral [late'raw] (pl **-ais**) adj side, lateral ♦ f (FUTEBOL) sideline ♦ m (FUTEBOL) throw-in

latido [la'tʃidu] m bark(ing), yelp(ing)

latifundiário, -a [latʃifũ'dʒjarju, a] m/f landowner

latifúndio [latʃi'fũdʒju] m large estate

latim [la'tʃĩ] m (LING) Latin; **gastar o seu ~** to waste one's breath

latino, -a [la'tʃinu, a] adj Latin; **latino-americano, -a** adj, m/f Latin-American

latir [la'tʃi*] vi to bark, yelp

latitude [latʃi'tudʒi] f latitude; (largura) breadth; (fig) scope

latrocínio [latro'sinju] m armed robbery

laudo ['lawdu] m (JUR) decision; (resultados) findings pl; (peça escrita) report

lava ['lava] f lava

lavabo [la'vabu] m toilet

lavadeira [lava'dejra] f washerwoman

lavadora [lava'dora] f washing machine

lavagem [la'vaʒẽ] f washing; **~ a seco** dry cleaning; **~ cerebral** brainwashing

lavanda [la'vãda] f (BOT) lavender; (colónia) lavender water; (para lavar os dedos) fingerbowl

lavar [la'va*] vt to wash; (culpa) to wash away; **~ a seco** to dry clean

lavatório [lava'tɔrju] m washbasin; (aposento) toilet

lavoura [la'vora] f tilling; (agricultura) farming; (terreno) plantation

lavrador, a [lavra'do*, a] m/f farmhand

laxativo, -a [laʃa'tʃivu, a] adj laxative ♦ m laxative

lazer [la'ze*] m leisure

leal [le'aw] (pl **-ais**) adj loyal; **lealdade** [leaw'dadʒi] f loyalty

leão [le'ãw] (pl **-ões**) m lion; **L~** (ASTROLOGIA) Leo

lebre ['lɛbri] f hare

lecionar [lesjo'na*] (PT **-cc-**) vt, vi to teach

lectivo, -a [lɛk'tivu, a] (PT) adj = **letivo**

legal [le'gaw] (pl **-ais**) adj legal, lawful; (col) fine; (: pessoa) nice ♦ adv (col) well; (tá) **~!** OK!; **legalidade** [legali'dadʒi] f legality, lawfulness; **legalizar** [legali'za*] vt to legalize; (documento) to authenticate

legendário, -a [leʒẽ'darju, a] adj legendary

legislação [leʒiʒla'sãw] f legislation

legislar [leʒiʒ'la*] vi to legislate ♦ vt

to pass

legislativo, -a [leʒiʒla'tʃivu, a] *adj* legislative ♦ *m* legislature

legitimar [leʒitʃi'ma*] *vt* to legitimize; (*justificar*) to legitimate

legítimo, -a [le'ʒitʃimu, a] *adj* legitimate; (*justo*) rightful; (*autêntico*) genuine; **legítima defesa** self-defence (*BRIT*), self-defense (*US*)

legume [le'gumi] *m* vegetable

lei [lej] *f* law; (*regra*) rule; (*metal*) standard

leigo, -a ['lejgu, a] *adj* (*REL*) lay, secular ♦ *m* layman; **ser ~ em algo** (*fig*) to be no expert at sth, be unversed in sth

leilão [lej'lãw] (*pl -ões*) *m* auction; **vender em ~** to sell by auction, auction off; **leiloar** [lej'lwa*] *vt* to auction

leio *etc* ['leju] *vb* V **ler**

leitão, -toa [lej'tãw, 'toa] (*pl -ões*, **~s**) *m/f* sucking (*BRIT*) ou suckling (*US*) pig

leite ['lejtʃi] *m* milk; **~ em pó** powdered milk; **~ desnatado** ou **magro** skimmed milk; **~ de magnésia** milk of magnesia; **~ semidesnatado** semi-skimmed milk; **leiteira** [lej'tejra] *f* (*para ferver*) milk pan; (*para servir*) milk jug; **leiteiro, -a** [lej'tejru, a] *adj* (*vaca, gado*) dairy ♦ *m/f* milkman/woman

leito ['lejtu] *m* bed

leitões [lej'tõjʃ] *mpl de* **leitão**

leitor, a [lej'to*, a] *m/f* reader; (*professor*) lector

leitura [lej'tura] *f* reading; (*livro etc*) reading matter

lema ['lema] *m* motto; (*POL*) slogan

lembrança [lẽ'brãsa] *f* recollection, memory; (*presente*) souvenir; **~s** (*pl*) (*recomendações*): **~s a sua mãe!** regards to your mother!

lembrar [lẽ'bra*] *vt, vi* to remem-

ber; **lembrar-se** *vr*: **~-(se)** de to remember; **~-(se) (de) que** to remember that; **~ algo a alguém, ~ alguém de algo** to remind sb of sth; **~ alguém de que, ~ a alguém que** to remind sb that; **ele lembra meu irmão** he reminds me of my brother, he is like my brother; **lembrete** [lẽ'bretʃi] *m* reminder

leme ['lemi] *m* rudder; (*NÁUT*) helm; (*fig*) control

lenço ['lẽsu] *m* handkerchief; (*de pescoço*) scarf; (*de cabeça*) headscarf; **~ de papel** tissue

lençol [lẽ'sɔw] (*pl -óis*) *m* sheet; **estar em maus lençóis** to be in a fix

lenda ['lẽda] *f* legend; (*fig: mentira*) lie; **lendário, -a** [lẽ'darju, a] *adj* legendary

lenha ['leɲa] *f* firewood

lente ['lẽtʃi] *f* lens *sg*; **~ de aumento** magnifying glass; **~s de contato** contact lenses

lentidão [lẽtʃi'dãw] *f* slowness

lento, -a ['lẽtu, a] *adj* slow

leoa [le'oa] *f* lioness

leões [le'õjʃ] *mpl de* **leão**

leopardo [ljo'paxdu] *m* leopard

lepra ['lepra] *f* leprosy

leque ['lɛki] *m* fan; (*fig*) array

ler [le*] *vt, vi* to read

lesão [le'zãw] (*pl -ões*) *f* harm, injury; (*JUR*) violation; (*MED*) lesion; **~ corporal** (*JUR*) bodily harm

lesar [le'za*] *vt* to harm, damage; (*direitos*) to violate

lésbica ['lɛʒbika] *f* lesbian

lesma ['leʒma] *f* slug; (*fig: pessoa*) slowcoach

lesões [le'zõjʃ] *fpl de* **lesão**

lesse *etc* ['lesi] *vb* V **ler**

leste ['lɛʃtʃi] *m* east

letal [le'taw] (*pl -ais*) *adj* lethal

letargia [letax'ʒia] *f* lethargy

letivo, -a [le'tʃivu, a] *adj* school *atr*;

ano ~ academic year

letra ['letɾa] f letter; (*caligrafia*) handwriting; (*de canção*) lyrics pl; **L~s** fpl (*curso*) language and literature; **à ~** literally; **ao pé da ~** literally, word for word; **~ de câmbio** (*COM*) bill of exchange; **~ de imprensa** print; **letrado, -a** [le'tɾadu, a] adj learned, erudite ♦ m/f scholar; **letreiro** [le'tɾejɾu] m sign, notice; (*inscrição*) inscription; (*CINEMA*) subtitle

leu etc [lew] vb V **ler**

léu [lɛw] m: **ao ~** (*à toa*) aimlessly; (*à mostra*) uncovered

leucemia [lewse'mia] f leukaemia (*BRIT*), leukemia (*US*)

levado, -a [le'vadu, a] adj mischievous; (*criança*) naughty

levantador, a [levãta'do*, a] adj lifting ♦ m/f: **~ de pesos** weightlifter

levantamento [levãta'mẽtu] m lifting, raising; (*revolta*) uprising, rebellion; (*arrolamento*) survey

levantar [levã'ta*] vt to lift, raise; (*voz, capital*) to raise; (*apanhar*) to pick up; (*suscitar*) to arouse; (*ambiente*) to brighten up ♦ vi to stand up; (*da cama*) to get up; (*da mesa*) to brighten; **levantar-se** vr to stand up; (*da cama*) to get up; (*rebelar-se*) to rebel

levar [le'va*] vt to take; (*portar*) to carry; (*tempo*) to pass, spend; (*roupa*) to wear; (*lidar com*) to handle; (*induzir*) to lead; (*filme*) to show; (*peça teatral*) to put on; (*vida*) to lead ♦ vi to get a beating; **~ a** to lead to; **~ a mal** to take amiss

leve ['lɛvi] adj light; (*insignificante*) slight; **de ~** lightly, softly

leviandade [levjã'dadʒi] f frivolity

leviano, -a [le'vjanu, a] adj frivolous

lha(s) [ʎa(ʃ)] = **lhe + a(s)**

lhe [ʎi] pron (*a ele*) to him; (*a ela*) to her; (*a você*) to you

lhes [ʎiʃ] pron pl (*a eles/elas*) to them; (*a vocês*) to you

lho(s) [ʎu(ʃ)] = **lhe + o(s)**

li etc [li] vb V **ler**

Líbano ['libanu] m: **o ~** (the) Lebanon

libélula [li'bɛlula] f dragonfly

liberação [libeɾa'sãw] f liberation

liberal [libe'ɾaw] (*pl -ais*) adj, m/f liberal

liberar [libe'ɾa*] vt to release; (*libertar*) to free

liberdade [libex'dadʒi] f freedom; **~s** fpl (*direitos*) liberties; **pôr alguém em ~** to set sb free; **~ condicional** probation; **~ de palavra** freedom of speech; **~ sob palavra** parole

libertação [libexta'sãw] f release

libertar [libex'ta*] vt to free, release

libertino, -a [libex'tʃinu, a] adj loose-living ♦ m/f libertine

liberto, -a [li'bɛxtu, a] pp de **libertar**

Líbia ['libja] f: **a ~** Libya

libidinoso, -a [libidʒi'nozu, ɔza] adj lecherous, lustful

líbio, -a [li'libju, a] adj, m/f Libyan

libra ['libɾa] f pound; **L~** (*ASTROLOGIA*) Libra

lição [li'sãw] (*pl -ões*) f lesson

licença [li'sẽsa] f license (*BRIT*), license (*US*); (*permissão*) permission; (*do trabalho, MIL*) leave; **com ~** excuse me; **estar de ~** to be on leave; **dá ~?** may I?

licenciado, -a [lisẽ'sjadu, a] m/f graduate

licenciar [lisẽ'sja*] vt to license; **licenciar-se** vr (*EDUC*) to graduate; (*ficar de licença*) to take leave;

licenciatura [lisẽsja'tuɾa] f (*título*) degree; (*curso*) degree course

liceu [li'sew] (*PT*) m secondary (*BRIT*) ou high (*US*) school

lições [li'sõjʃ] *fpl de* **lição**

licor [li'ko*] *m* liqueur

lidar [li'da*] *vi*: ~ **com** (*ocupar-se*) to deal with; (*combater*) to struggle against; ~ **em algo** to work in sth

líder ['lide*] *m/f* leader; **liderança** [lide'rãsa] *f* leadership; (*ESPORTE*) lead; **liderar** [lide'ra*] *vt* to lead

liga ['liga] *f* league; (*de meias*) suspender (*BRIT*), garter (*US*); (*metal*) alloy

ligação [liga'sãw] (*pl* -ões) *f* connection; (*fig: de amizade*) bond; (*TEL*) call; (*relação amorosa*) liaison; **fazer uma ~ para alguém** to call sb; **não consigo completar a ~** (*TEL*) I can't get through; **caiu a ~** (*TEL*) I (*ou he etc*) was cut off

ligado, -a [li'gadu, a] *adj* (*TEC*) connected; (*luz, rádio etc*) on; (*metal*) alloy

ligadura [liga'dura] *f* bandage

ligamento [liga'mẽtu] *m* ligament

ligar [li'ga*] *vt* to tie, bind; (*unir*) to join, connect; (*luz, TV*) to switch on; (*afetivamente*) to bind together; (*carro*) to start (up) ♦ *vi* (*telefonar*) to ring; **ligar-se** *vr* to join; ~**se com alguém** to join with sb; ~**se a algo** to be connected with sth; ~ **para alguém** to ring sb up; ~ **para** *ou* **a algo** (*dar atenção*) to take notice of sth; (*dar importância*) to care about sth; **eu nem ligo** it doesn't bother me; **não ligo a mínima (para)** I couldn't care less (about)

ligeiro, -a [li'ʒejru, a] *adj* light; (*ferimento*) slight; (*referência*) passing; (*conhecimentos*) scant; (*rápido*) quick, swift; (*ágil*) nimble ♦ *adv* swiftly, nimbly

lilás [li'laʃ] *adj, m* lilac

lima ['lima] *f* (*laranja*) type of (*very sweet*) orange; (*ferramenta*) file; ~ **de unhas** nailfile

limão [li'mãw] (*pl* -ões) *m* lime; **limão(-galego)** (*pl* **limões(-galegos)**) *m* lemon

limiar [li'mja*] *m* threshold

limitação [limita'sãw] (*pl* -ões) *f* limitation, restriction

limitar [limi'ta*] *vt* to limit, restrict; **limitar-se** *vr*: ~**se a** to limit o.s. to; ~**se com** to border on; **limite** [li'mitʃi] *m* limit, boundary; (*fig*) limit; **passar dos limites** to go too far

limo ['limu] *m* (*BOT*) water weed; (*lodo*) slime

limoeiro [li'mwejru] *m* lemon tree

limões [li'mõjʃ] *mpl de* **limão**

limonada [limo'nada] *f* lemonade (*BRIT*), lemon soda (*US*)

limpar [lĩ'pa*] *vt* to clean; (*lágrimas, suor*) to wipe away; (*polir*) to shine, polish; (*fig*) to clean up; (*roubar*) to rob

limpeza [lĩ'peza] *f* cleanliness; (*esmero*) neatness; (*ato*) cleaning; ~ **pública** rubbish (*BRIT*) *ou* garbage (*US*) collection, sanitation

limpo, -a [ˈlĩpu, a] *pp de* **limpar** ♦ *adj* clean; (*céu, consciência*) clear; (*COM*) net; (*fig*) pure; (*col: pronto*) ready; **passar a ~** to make a fair copy; **tirar a ~** to find out the truth about, clear up; **estar ~ com alguém** (*col*) to be in with sb

linchar [lĩ'ʃa*] *vt* to lynch

lindo, -a [ˈlĩdu, a] *adj* lovely

lingerie [lĩʒe'ri] *m* lingerie

língua [ˈlĩgwa] *f* tongue; (*linguagem*) language; **botar a ~ para fora** to stick out one's tongue; **dar com a ~ nos dentes** to let the cat out of the bag; **estar na ponta da ~** to be on the tip of one's tongue

linguado [lĩ'gwadu] *m* (*peixe*) sole

linguagem [lĩ'gwaʒẽ] (*pl* -ns) *f* (*tb: COMPUT*) language; (*falada*) speech;

~ de máquina (*COMPUT*) machine language

linguarudo, -a [lĩgwa'rudu, a] *adj* gossiping ♦ *m/f* gossip

lingüiça [lĩ'gwisa] *f* sausage

linha ['liɲa] *f* line; (*para costura*) thread; (*barbante*) string, cord; **~s** *fpl* (*carta*) letter *sg*; **em ~**, in line, in a row; (*COMPUT*) on line; **fora de ~** (*COMPUT*) off line; **manter/perder a ~** to keep/lose one's cool; **o telefone não deu ~** the line was dead; **~ aérea** airline; **~ de mira** sights *pl*; **~ de montagem** assembly line; **~ férrea** railway (*BRIT*), railroad (*US*)

linho ['liɲu] *m* linen; (*planta*) flax

liquidação [likida'sãw] (*pl -ões*) *f* liquidation; (*em loja*) (clearance) sale; (*de conta*) settlement; **em ~** on sale

liquidar [liki'da*] *vt* to liquidate; (*conta*) to settle; (*mercadoria*) to sell off; (*assunto*) to lay to rest ♦ *vi* (*loja*) to have a sale; **liquidar-se** *vr* (*destruir-se*) to be destroyed; **~ (com)** **alguém** (*fig: arrasar*) to destroy sb; (: *matar*) to do away with sb

liqüidificador [likwidʒifika'do*] *m* liquidizer

líquido, -a ['likidu, a] *adj* liquid, fluid; (*COM*) net ♦ *m* liquid

lira ['lira] *f* lyre; (*moeda*) lira

lírico, -a ['liriku, a] *adj* lyric(al)

lírio ['liriu] *m* lily

Lisboa [liʒ'boa] *n* Lisbon; **lisboeta** [liʒ'bweta] *adj* Lisbon *atr* ♦ *m/f* inhabitant *ou* native of Lisbon

liso, -a ['lizu, a] *adj* smooth; (*tecido*) plain; (*cabelo*) straight; (*col: sem dinheiro*) broke

lisonjear [lizõ'ʒja*] *vt* to flatter

lista ['liʃta] *f* list; (*listra*) stripe; (*PT: menu*) menu; **~ negra** blacklist; **~ telefônica** telephone directory; **listar** [liʃ'ta*] *vt* (*COMPUT*) to list

listra ['liʃtra] *f* stripe; **listrado, -a** [liʃ'tradu, a] *adj* striped

literal [lite'raw] (*pl -ais*) *adj* literal

literário, -a [lite'rarju, a] *adj* literary

literatura [litera'tura] *f* literature; **~ de cordel** see boxed note

---

LITERATURA DE CORDEL

Literatura de cordel is a type of literature typical of the north-east of Brazil, and published in the form of cheaply printed booklets. Their authors hang these booklets from wires attached to walls in the street so that people can look at them. While they do this, the authors sing their stories aloud. Literatura de cordel deals both with local events and people, and with everyday public life, almost always in an irreverent manner.

---

litoral [lito'raw] (*pl -ais*) *adj* coastal ♦ *m* coast, seaboard

litro ['litru] *m* litre (*BRIT*), liter (*US*)

livrar [li'vra*] *vt* to release, liberate; (*salvar*) to save; **livrar-se** *vr* to escape; **~-se de** to get rid of; (*compromisso*) to get out of; **Deus me livre!** Heaven forbid!

livraria [livra'ria] *f* bookshop (*BRIT*), bookstore (*US*)

livre ['livri] *adj* free; (*lugar*) unoccupied; (*desimpedido*) clear, open; **~ de impostos** tax-free; **livre-arbítrio** *m* free will

livro ['livru] *m* book; **~ brochado** paperback; **~ de bolso** pocket-sized book; **~ de cheques** cheque book (*BRIT*), check book (*US*); **~ de consulta** reference book; **~ encadernado** *ou* **de capa dura** hardback

lixa ['liʃa] *f* sandpaper; (*de unhas*) nailfile; (*peixe*) dogfish; **lixar** [li'ʃa*] *vt* to sand

lixeira [li'ʃejra] *f* dustbin (*BRIT*), garbage can (*US*)

lixeiro [li'ʃejru] *m* dustman (*BRIT*), garbage man (*US*)

lixo ['liʃu] *m* rubbish, garbage (*US*); **ser um ~** (*col*) to be rubbish; **~ atômico** nuclear waste

-lo [lu] *pron* him; (*você*) you; (*coisa*) it

lobo ['lobu] *m* wolf

locação [loka'sãw] (*pl* -**ões**) *f* lease; (*de vídeo etc*) rental

locador, a [loka'do*, a] *m/f* (*de casa*) landlord; (*de carro, filme*) rental agent ♦ *f* rental company; **~a de vídeo** video rental shop

local [lo'kaw] (*pl* -**ais**) *adj* local ♦ *m* site, place ♦ *f* (*notícia*) story; **localidade** [lokali'dadʒi] *f* (*lugar*) locality; (*povoação*) town; **localização** [lokaliza'sãw] (*pl* -**ões**) *f* location; **localizar** [lokali'za*] *vt* to locate; (*situar*) to place; **localizar-se** *vr* to be located; (*orientar-se*) to get one's bearings

loção [lo'sãw] (*pl* -**ões**) *f* lotion; **~ após-barba** aftershave (lotion)

locatário, -a [loka'tarju, a] *m/f* (*de casa*) tenant; (*de carro, filme*) hirer

loções [lo'sõjʃ] *fpl* de **loção**

locomotiva [lokomo'tʃiva] *f* railway (*BRIT*) ou railroad (*US*) engine, locomotive

locomover-se [lokomo'vexsi] *vr* to move around

locutor, a [loku'to*, a] *m/f* (*TV, RÁDIO*) announcer

lodo ['lodu] *m* (*lama*) mud; (*limo*) slime

lógica ['lɔʒika] *f* logic; **lógico, -a** ['lɔʒiku, a] *adj* logical; (**é**) **lógico!** of course!

logo ['lɔgu] *adv* (*imediatamente*) right away, at once; (*em breve*) soon; (*justamente*) just, right; (*mais tarde*) later; **~, ~** straightaway, without delay; **~ mais** later; **~ no começo** right at the start; **~ que, tão ~** as soon as; **até ~!** bye!; **~ antes/depois** just before/shortly afterwards; **~ de saída** ou **de cara** straightaway, right away

logotipo [logo'tʃipu] *m* logo

lograr [lo'gra*] *vt* (*alcançar*) to achieve; (*obter*) to get, obtain; (*enganar*) to cheat; **~ fazer** to manage to do

loiro, -a ['lojru, a] *adj* = **louro/a**

loja ['lɔʒa] *f* shop; **lojista** [lo'ʒiʃta] *m/f* shopkeeper

lombo ['lõbu] *m* back; (*carne*) loin

lona ['lona] *f* canvas

Londres ['lõdriʃ] *n* London; **londrino, -a** [lõ'drinu, a] *adj* London atr ♦ *m/f* Londoner

longa-metragem (*pl* **longas-metragens**) *m*: (**filme de**) **~** feature (film)

longe ['lõʒi] *adv* far, far away ♦ *adj* distant; **ao ~** in the distance; **de ~** from far away; (*sem dúvida*) by a long way; **~ de** a long way ou far from; **~ disso** far from it; **ir ~ demais** (*fig*) to go too far

longínquo, -a [lõ'ʒĩkwu, a] *adj* distant, remote

longitude [lõʒi'tudʒi] *f* (*GEO*) longitude

longo, -a ['lõgu, a] *adj* long ♦ *m* (*vestido*) long dress, evening dress; **ao ~ de** along, alongside

lotação [lota'sãw] *f* capacity; (*de funcionários*) complement; (*BR: ônibus*) bus; **~ completa** ou **esgotada** (*TEATRO*) sold out

lotado, -a [lo'tadu, a] *adj* (*TEATRO*) full; (*ônibus*) full up; (*bar, praia*) packed, crowded

lotar [lo'ta*] *vt* to fill, pack; (*funcionário*) to place ♦ *vi* to fill up

lote ['lɔtʃi] *m* portion, share; *(em leilão)* lot; *(terreno)* plot, *(de ações)* parcel, batch

loteria [lote'ria] *f* lottery; ~ **esportiva** football pools *pl (BRIT)*, lottery *(US)*

louça ['losa] *f* china; *(conjunto)* crockery; *(tb:* ~ **sanitária**) bathroom suite; **de** ~ china *atr;* ~ **de barro** earthenware; ~ **de jantar** dinner service; **lavar a** ~ to do the washing up *(BRIT)* ou the dishes

louco, -a ['loku, a] *adj* crazy, mad; *(sucesso)* runaway; *(frio)* freezing ♦ *m/f* lunatic; ~ **varrido** raving mad; ~ **de fome/raiva** ravenous/hopping mad; ~ **por** crazy about; **deixar alguém** ~ to drive sb crazy; **loucura** [lo'kura] *f* madness; *(ato)* crazy thing; **ser loucura (fazer)** to be crazy (to do); **ser uma loucura** to be crazy; *(col: ser muito bom)* to be fantastic

louro, -a ['loru, a] *adj* blond, fair ♦ *m* laurel; *(CULIN)* bay leaf; *(papagaio)* parrot; ~**s** *mpl (fig)* laurels

louva-a-deus ['lova-] *m inv* praying mantis

louvar [lo'va*] *vt* to praise ♦ *vi:* ~ **a** to praise; **louvável** [lo'vavew] *(pl -eis) adj* praiseworthy

louvor [lo'vo*] *m* praise

LP *abr m* LP

Ltda. *abr (= Limitada)* Ltd *(BRIT)*, Inc. *(US)*

lua ['lua] *f* moon; **estar** ou **viver no mundo da** ~ to have one's head in the clouds; **estar de** ~ *(col)* to be in a mood; **ser de** ~ *(col)* to be moody; ~ **cheia/nova** full/new moon; **lua-de-mel** *f* honeymoon

luar ['lwa*] *m* moonlight

lubrificante [lubrifi'kātʃi] *m* lubricant

lubrificar [lubrifi'ka*] *vt* to lubricate

lúcido, -a ['lusidu, a] *adj* lucid

lúcio ['lusju] *m (peixe)* pike

lucrar [lu'kra*] *vt (tirar proveito)* to profit from ou by; *(dinheiro)* to make; *(gozar)* to enjoy ♦ *vi* to make a profit; ~ **com** ou **em** to profit by

lucrativo, -a [lukra'tʃivu, a] *adj* lucrative, profitable

lucro ['lukru] *m* gain; *(COM)* profit; ~**s e perdas** *(COM)* profit and loss

lugar [lu'ga*] *m* place; *(espaço)* space, room; *(para sentar)* seat; *(emprego)* job; *(ocasião)* opportunity; **em** ~ **de** instead of; **dar** ~ **a** *(causar)* to give rise to; ~ **comum** commonplace; **em primeiro** ~ in the first place; **em algum/nenhum/todo** ~ somewhere/nowhere/everywhere; **em outro** ~ somewhere else, elsewhere; **ter** ~ *(acontecer)* to take place; ~ **de nascimento** place of birth; **lugarejo** [luga'reʒu] *m* village

lula ['lula] *f* squid

lume ['lumi] *m* fire; *(luz)* light

luminária [lumi'narja] *f* lamp; ~**s** *fpl (iluminações)* illuminations

luminosidade [luminozi'dadʒi] *f* brightness

luminoso, -a [lumi'nozu, ɔza] *adj* luminous; *(fig: raciocínio)* clear; *(: idéia, talento)* brilliant; *(letreiro)* illuminated

lunar [lu'na*] *adj* lunar ♦ *m (na pele)* mole

lunático, -a [lu'natʃiku, a] *adj* mad

lusitano, -a [luzi'tanu, a] *adj* Portuguese, Lusitanian

luso, -a ['luzu, a] *adj* Portuguese; **luso-brasileiro, -a** *(pl lusos-brasileiros, -as) adj* Luso-Brazilian

lustre ['luʃtri] *m* gloss, sheen; *(fig)* lustre *(BRIT)*, luster *(US)*; *(luminária)* chandelier

luta ['luta] f fight, struggle; ~ **de boxe** boxing; ~ **livre** wrestling; **lutador, a** [luta'do*, a] m/f fighter; (atleta) wrestler; **lutar** [lu'ta*] vi to fight, struggle; (luta livre) to wrestle ♦ vt (caratê, judô) to do; **lutar contra/por algo** to fight against/for sth; **lutar para fazer algo** to fight ou struggle to do sth; **lutar com** (dificuldades) to struggle against; (competir) to fight with

luto ['lutu] m mourning; (tristeza) grief; **de ~** in mourning; **pôr ~** to go into mourning

luva ['luva] f glove; ~**s** fpl (pagamento) payment sg; (ao locador) fee sg

Luxemburgo [luʃẽ'buxgu] m: **o ~** Luxembourg

luxo ['luʃu] m luxury; **de ~** luxury atr; **dar-se ao ~ de** to allow o.s. to; **luxuoso, -a** [lu'ʃwozu, ɔza] adj luxurious

luxúria [lu'ʃurja] f lust

luz [luʒ] f light; (eletricidade) electricity; **à ~ de** by the light of; (fig) in the light of; **a meia ~** with subdued lighting; **dar à ~ (um filho)** to give birth (to a son); **deu-me uma ~** I had an idea

M

ma [ma] pron = **me** + **a**

má [ma] f de **mau**

maca ['maka] f stretcher

maçã [ma'sã] f apple; ~ **do rosto** cheekbone

macabro, -a [ma'kabru, a] adj macabre

macacão [maka'kãw] (pl -ões) m (de trabalhador) overalls pl (BRIT), coveralls pl (US); (da moda) jumpsuit

macaco, -a [ma'kaku, a] m/f monkey ♦ m (MECÂNICA) jack; (fato) ~ (PT) overalls pl (BRIT), coveralls pl (US); ~ **velho** (fig) old hand

macacões [maka'kõjʃ] mpl de **macacão**

maçador, a [masa'do*, a] (PT) adj boring

maçaneta [masa'neta] f knob

maçante [ma'sãtʃi] (BR) adj boring

macarrão [maka'xãw] m pasta; (em forma de canudo) spaghetti; **macarronada** [makaxo'nada] f pasta with cheese and tomato sauce

Macau [ma'kaw] n Macao

macete [ma'setʃi] m mallet

machado [ma'ʃadu] m axe (BRIT), ax (US)

machista [ma'ʃiʃta] adj chauvinistic, macho ♦ m male chauvinist

macho ['maʃu] adj male; (fig) virile, manly; (valentão) tough ♦ m male; (TEC) tap

machucado, -a [maʃu'kadu, a] adj hurt; (pé, braço) bad ♦ m injury; (área machucada) sore patch

machucar [maʃu'ka*] vt to hurt; (produzir contusão) to bruise ♦ vi to hurt; **machucar-se** vr to hurt o.s

maciço, -a [ma'sisu, a] adj solid; (espesso) thick; (quantidade) massive

macieira [ma'sjejra] f apple tree

macio, -a [ma'siu, a] adj soft; (liso) smooth

maço ['masu] m (de folhas, notas) bundle; (de cigarros) packet

maçom [ma'sõ] (pl -ns) m (free)mason

maconha [ma'kɔɲa] f dope; **cigarro de ~** joint

maçons [ma'sõʃ] mpl de **maçom**

má-criação (pl -ões) f rudeness; (ato, dito) rude thing

mácula ['makula] f stain, blemish

macumba [ma'kũba] f ≈ voodoo; (*despacho*) macumba offering; **macumbeiro, -a** [makũ'bejru, a] adj ≈ voodoo atr ♦ m/f follower of macumba

madama [ma'dama] f = **madame**

madame [ma'dami] f (*senhora*) lady; (col: *dona-de-casa*) lady of the house

Madeira [ma'dejra] f: **a ~** Madeira

madeira [ma'dejra] f wood ♦ m Madeira (wine); **de ~** wooden; **bater na ~** (fig) to touch (BRIT) ou knock on (US) wood; **~ compensada** plywood

madeirense [madej'rẽsi] adj, m/f Madeiran

madeixa [ma'dejʃa] f (*de cabelo*) lock

madrasta [ma'dɾaʃta] f stepmother

madrepérola [madɾe'pɛrola] f mother of pearl

Madri [ma'dɾi] n Madrid

Madrid [ma'dɾid] (PT) n Madrid

madrinha [ma'dɾiɲa] f godmother

madrugada [madɾu'gada] f (early) morning; (*alvorada*) dawn, daybreak

madrugar [madɾu'ga*] vi to get up early; (*aparecer cedo*) to be early

maduro, -a [ma'duɾu, a] adj ripe; (fig) mature; (: *prudente*) prudent

mãe [mãj] f mother; **~ adotiva** ou **de criação** adoptive mother

maestro, -trina [ma'ɛʃtɾu, 'tɾina] m/f conductor

má-fé f malicious intent

magia [ma'ʒia] f magic

mágica ['maʒika] f magic; (*truque*) magic trick; V tb **mágico**

mágico, -a ['maʒiku, a] adj magic ♦ m/f magician

magistério [maʒiʃ'tɛrju] m (*ensino*) teaching; (*profissão*) teaching pro-

fession, (*professorado*) teachers pl

magnata [mag'nata] m magnate, tycoon

magnético, -a [mag'nɛtʃiku, a] adj magnetic

magnífico, -a [mag'nifiku, a] adj splendid, magnificent

magnitude [magni'tudʒi] f magnitude

mago ['magu] m magician; **os reis ~s** the Three Wise Men, the Three Kings

mágoa ['magwa] f (*tristeza*) sorrow, grief; (fig: *desagrado*) hurt

magoado, -a [ma'gwadu, a] adj hurt

magoar [ma'gwa*] vt, vi to hurt; **magoar-se** vr: **~-se com algo** to be hurt by sth

magro, -a ['magru, a] adj (*pessoa*) slim; (*carne*) lean; (fig: *parco*) meagre (BRIT), meager (US); (*leite*) skimmed

maio ['maju] (PT **M-**) m May

maiô [ma'jo] (BR) m swimsuit

maionese [majo'nezi] f mayonnaise

maior [ma'jɔ*] adj (*compar: de tamanho*) bigger; (: *de importância*) greater; (*superl: de tamanho*) biggest; (: *de importância*) greatest ♦ m/f adult; **~ de idade** of age, adult; **~ de 21 anos** over 21; **maioria** [majo'ria] f majority; **a maioria de** most of; **maioridade** [majori'dadʒi] f adulthood

---

PALAVRA CHAVE

---

mais [majʃ] adv **1** (*compar*): **~ magro/inteligente (do que)** thinner/more intelligent (than); **ele trabalha ~ (do que eu)** he works more (than me)

2 (*superl*): **o ~ ... the** most ...; **o ~ magro/inteligente** the thinnest/

most intelligent
3 (*negativo*): **ele não trabalha ~ aqui** he doesn't work here any more; **nunca ~** never again
4 (+ *adj: valor intensivo*): **que livro ~ chato!** what a boring book!
5: **por ~ que** however much; **por ~ que se esforce** ... no matter how hard you try ...; **por ~ que eu quisesse** ... much as I should like to ...
6: **a ~: temos um a ~** we've got one extra
7 (*tempo*): **~ cedo ou ~ tarde** sooner or later; **a ~ tempo** sooner; **logo ~** later on; **no ~ tardar** at the latest
8 (*frases*): **~ ou menos** more or less; **~ uma vez** once more; **cada vez ~** more and more; **sem ~ nem menos** out of the blue
♦ *adj* 1 (*compar*): **~ (do que)** more (than); **ele tem ~ dinheiro (do que o irmão)** he's got more money (than his brother)
2 (*superl*): **ele é quem tem ~ dinheiro** he's got most money
3 (+ *números*): **ela tem ~ de dez bolsas** she's got more than ten bags
4 (*negativo*): **não tenho ~ dinheiro** I haven't got any more money
5 (*adicional*) else; **~ alguma coisa?** anything else?; **nada/ninguém ~** nothing/no-one else
♦ *prep*: **2 ~ 2 são 4** 2 and 2 or 2 ou plus 2 are 4
♦ *m*: **o ~ the rest**

maisena [maj'zena] *f* cornflower
maiúscula [ma'juʃkula] *f* capital letter
majestade [maʒeʃ'tadʒi] *f* majesty; **majestoso, -a** [maʒeʃ'tozu, ɔza] *adj* majestic
major [ma'ʒɔ*] *m* (MIL) major

majoritário, -a [maʒori'tarju, a] *adj* majority *atr*
mal [maw] (*pl* **-es**) *m* harm; (MED) illness ♦ *adv* badly; (*quase não*) hardly ♦ *conj* hardly; **~ desliguei o fone, a campainha tocou** I had hardly put the phone down when the doorbell rang; **falar ~ de alguém** to speak ill of sb, run sb down; **não faz ~** never mind; **estar ~ (*doente*) to be ill; passar ~ to be sick; estar de ~ com alguém** not to be speaking to sb
mal- [mal-] *prefixo* badly
mala ['mala] *f* suitcase; (BR: AUTO) boot, trunk (US); **~s** *fpl* (*bagagem*) luggage *sg*; **fazer as ~s** to pack
malabarismo [malaba'riʒmu] *m* juggling; **malabarista** [malab-'riʃta] *m/f* juggler
mal-acabado, -a *adj* badly finished; (*pessoa*) deformed
malagueta [mala'geta] *f* chilli (BRIT)
Malaísia [mala'izja] *f*: **a ~** Malaysia
malandragem [malã'draʒẽ] *f* (*patifaria*) double-dealing; (*preguiça*) idleness; (*esperteza*) cunning
malandro, -a [ma'lãdru, a] *adj* double-dealing; (*preguiçoso*) idle; (*esperto*) wily, cunning ♦ *m/f* crook; idler, layabout; streetwise person
malária [ma'larja] *f* malaria
mal-arrumado, -a [-axu'madu, a] *adj* untidy
malcomportado, -a [mawkõpox-'tadu, a] *adj* badly behaved
malcriado, -a [maw'krjadu, a] *adj* rude ♦ *m/f* slob
maldade [maw'dadʒi] *f* cruelty; (*malícia*) malice
maldição [mawdʒi'sãw] (*pl* **-ões**) *f* curse
maldito, -a [maw'dʒitu, a] *adj*

damned

maldizer [mawdʒi'ze*] (irreg: como dizer) vt to curse

maldoso, -a [maw'dozu, ɔza] adj wicked; (malicioso) malicious

maledicência [maledʒi'sẽsja] f slander

mal-educado, -a adj rude ♦ m/f slob

malefício [male'fisju] m harm;

maléfico, -a [ma'lefiku, a] adj (pessoa) malicious; (prejudicial: efeito) harmful, injurious

mal-entendido, -a adj misunderstood ♦ m misunderstanding

mal-estar m indisposition; (embaraço) uneasiness

malfeito, -a [maw'fejtu, a] adj (roupa) poorly made; (corpo) misshapen

malfeitor, a [mawfej'to*, a] m/f wrong-doer

malha ['maʎa] f (de rede) mesh; (tecido) jersey; (suéter) sweater, (de ginástica) leotard; fazer ~ (PT) to knit; artigos de ~ knitwear

malhar [ma'ʎa*] vt (bater) to beat; (cereais) to thresh; (col: criticar) to knock, run down

mal-humorado, -a [-umo'radu, a] adj grumpy, sullen

malícia [ma'lisja] f malice; (astúcia) slyness; (esperteza) cleverness;

malicioso, -a [mali'sjozu, ɔza] adj malicious; sly; clever; (mente suja) dirty-minded

maligno, -a [ma'lignu, a] adj evil, malicious; (danoso) harmful; (MED) malignant

malograr [malo'gra*] vt (planos) to upset; (frustrar) to thwart, frustrate ♦ vi (planos) to fall through; (fracassar) to fail; **malograr-se** vr to fall through; to fail

mal-passado, -a adj underdone;

(bife) rare

malsucedido, -a [mawsuse'dʒidu, a] adj unsuccessful

Malta ['mawta] f Malta

malta ['mawta] (PT) f gang, mob

maltrapilho, -a [mawtra'piʎu, a] adj in rags, ragged ♦ m/f ragamuffin

maltratar [mawtra'ta*] vt to illtreat; (com palavras) to abuse; (estragar) to ruin, damage

maluco, -a [ma'luku, a] adj crazy, daft ♦ m/f madman/woman

malvadeza [mawva'deza] f wickedness; (ato) wicked thing

malvado, -a [maw'vadu, a] adj wicked

Malvinas [maw'vinaʃ] fpl: **as (ilhas) ~** the Falklands, the Falkland Islands

mama ['mama] f breast

mamadeira [mama'dejra] (BR) f feeding bottle

mamãe [ma'mãj] f mum, mummy

mamão [ma'mãw] (pl -ões) m papaya

mamar [ma'ma*] vt to suck; (dinheiro) to extort ♦ vi to be breastfed; dar de ~ a um bebê to (breast)feed a baby

mamífero [ma'miferu] m mammal

mamilo [ma'milu] m nipple

mamões [ma'mõjʃ] mpl de **mamão**

manada [ma'nada] f herd, drove

mancada [mã'kada] f (erro) mistake; (gafe) blunder; dar uma ~ to blunder

mancar [mã'ka*] vt to cripple ♦ vi to limp; **mancar-se** vr (col) to get the message, take the hint

Mancha ['mãʃa] f: **o canal da ~** the English Channel

mancha ['mãʃa] f stain; (na pele) mark, spot; sem ~s (reputação) spotless; **manchado, -a** [mã'ʃadu, a] adj soiled; (malhado) mottled;

spotted; **manchar** [mã'ʃa*] vt to stain, mark; (reputação) to soil

manchete [mã'ʃetʃi] f headline

manco, -a ['mãku, a] adj crippled, lame ♦ m/f cripple

mandado [mã'dadu] m order; (JUR) writ; (: tb: ~ de segurança) injunction; ~ de prisão/busca warrant for sb's arrest/search warrant; ~ de segurança injunction

mandão, -dona [mã'dãw, 'dɔna] (pl -ões, ~s) adj bossy, domineering

mandar [mã'da*] vt (ordenar) to order; (enviar) to send ♦ vi to be in charge; **mandar-se** vr (col: partir) to make tracks, get going; (fugir) to take off; ~ **buscar** ou **chamar** to send for; ~ **fazer um vestido** to have a dress made; ~ **que alguém faça, ~ alguém fazer** to tell sb to do; **o que é que você manda?** (col) what can I do for you?; ~ **em alguém** to boss sb around

mandato [mã'datu] m mandate; (ordem) order; (POL) term of office

mandioca [mã'dʒɔka] f cassava, manioc

mandões [mã'dõjʃ] mpl de **mandão**

mandona [mã'dɔna] f de **mandão**

maneira [ma'nejra] f (modo) way; (estilo) style, manner; ~s fpl (modas) manners; **à ~ de** like; **de ~ que** so that; **de ~ alguma** ou **nenhuma** not at all; **desta ~** in this way; **de qualquer ~** anyway; **não houve ~ de convencê-lo** it was impossible to convince him

maneiro, -a [ma'nejru, a] adj (ferramenta) easy to use; (roupa) attractive; (trabalho) easy; (pessoa) capable; (col: bacana) great, brilliant

manejar [mane'ʒa*] vt (instrumento) to handle; (máquina) to work; **manejo** [ma'neʒu] m handling

manequim [mane'kĩ] (pl -ns) m (boneco) dummy ♦ m/f model

manga ['mãga] f sleeve; (fruta) mango; **em ~s de camisa** in (one's) shirt sleeves

mangueira [mã'gejra] f hose(pipe); (árvore) mango tree

manha ['maɲa] f guile, craftiness; (destreza) skill; (ardil) trick; (birra) tantrum; **fazer ~** to have a tantrum

manhã [ma'ɲã] f morning; **de** ou **pela ~** in the morning; **amanhã/hoje de ~** tomorrow/this morning

manhoso, -a [ma'ɲozu, ɔza] adj crafty, sly; (criança) whining

mania [ma'nia] f (MED) mania; (obsessão) craze; **estar com ~ de ...** to have a thing about ...; **maníaco, -a** [ma'niaku, a] adj manic ♦ m/f maniac

manicômio [mani'komju] m asylum, mental hospital

manifestação [manifeʃta'sãw] (pl -ões) f show, display; (expressão) expression, declaration; (política) demonstration

manifestar [manifeʃ'ta*] vt to show, display; (declarar) to express, declare

manifesto, -a [mani'feʃtu, a] adj obvious, clear ♦ m manifesto

manipulação [manipula'sãw] f handling; (fig) manipulation

manipular [manipu'la*] vt to manipulate; (manejar) to handle

manivela [mani'vela] f crank

manjericão [mãʒeri'kãw] m basil

manobra [ma'nɔbra] f manoeuvre (BRIT), maneuver (US); (de mecanismo) operation; (de trens) shunting; **manobrar** [mano'bra*] vt to manoeuvre ou maneuver; (mecanismo) to operate, work; (governar) to take charge of; (manipular) to manipulate ♦ vi to manoeuvre ou maneuver

manso, -a ['mãsu, a] adj gentle;

(*mar*) calm; (*animal*) tame

manta ['mãta] f blanket; (*xale*) shawl; (*agasalho*) cloak

manteiga [mã'tejga] f butter; ~ **de cacau** cocoa butter

manter [mã'te*] (*irreg: como* ter) vt to maintain; (*num lugar*) to keep; (*uma família*) to support; (*a palavra*) to keep; (*princípios*) to abide by; **manter-se** vr to support o.s.; (*permanecer*) to remain; **mantimento** [mãtʃi'mẽtu] m maintenance; **mantimentos** mpl (*alimentos*) provisions

manual [ma'nwaw] (*pl* -**ais**) adj manual ♦ m handbook, manual

manufatura [manufa'tura] (*PT* -**ct**-) f manufacture; **manufaturar** [manufatu'ra*] (*PT* -**ct**-) vt to manufacture

manusear [manu'zja*] vt to handle; (*livro*) to leaf through

manutenção [manutẽ'sãw] f maintenance; (*da casa*) upkeep

mão [mãw] (*pl* ~**s**) f hand; (*de animal*) paw; (*de pintura*) coat; (*de direção*) flow of traffic; **à** ~ by hand; (*perto*) at hand; (*feito*) to keep; **de segunda** ~ second-hand; **em** ~ by hand; **dar a** ~ **a alguém** to hold sb's hand; (*cumprimentar*) to shake hands with sb; **dar uma** ~ **a alguém** to give sb a hand, help sb out; ~ **única/dupla** one-way/two-way traffic; **rua de duas** ~**s** two-way street; **mão-de-obra** f (*trabalhadores*) labour (*BRIT*), labor (*US*); (*coisa difícil*) tricky thing

mapa ['mapa] m map; (*gráfico*) chart

maquiagem [ma'kjaʒẽ] f = **maquilagem**

maquiar [ma'kja*] vt to make up; **maquiar-se** vr to make o.s. up, put on one's make-up

maquilagem [maki'laʒẽ] (*PT* -**lha**-)

f make-up; (*ato*) making up

máquina ['makina] f machine; (*de trem*) engine; (*fig*) machinery; ~ **de calcular/costura/escrever** calculator/sewing machine/typewriter; ~ **fotográfica** camera; ~ **de filmar** camera; (*de vídeo*) camcorder; ~ **de lavar** (*roupa*)/**pratos** washing machine/dishwasher; **escrito à** ~ typewritten

maquinar [maki'na*] vt to plot ♦ vi to conspire

maquinista [maki'niʃta] m (*FERRO*) engine driver; (*NÁUT*) engineer

mar [ma*] m sea; **por** ~ by sea; **fazer-se ao** ~ to set sail; **pleno** ~, ~ **alto** high sea; **o** ~ **Morto/Negro/Vermelho** the Dead/Black/Red Sea

maracujá [maraku'ʒa] m passion fruit; **pé de** ~ passion flower

maratona [mara'tona] f marathon

maravilha [mara'viʎa] f marvel, wonder; **maravilhoso, -a** [maravi'ʎozu, ɔza] adj marvellous (*BRIT*), marvelous (*US*)

marca ['maxka] f mark; (*COM*) make, brand; (*carimbo*) stamp; ~ **de fábrica** trademark; ~ **registrada** registered trademark

marcação [maxka'sãw] (*pl* -**ões**) f marking; (*em jogo*) scoring; (*de instrumento*) reading; (*TEATRO*) action; (*PT: TEL*) dialling

marcador [maxka'do*] m marker; (*de livro*) bookmark; (*ESPORTE: quadro*) scoreboard; (: *jogador*) scorer

marcapasso [maxka'pasu] m (*MED*) pacemaker

marcar [max'ka*] vt to mark; (*hora, data*) to fix, set; (*PT: TEL*) to dial; (*gol, ponto*) to score ♦ vi to make one's mark; ~ **uma consulta**, ~ **hora** to make an appointment; ~ **um encontro com alguém** to arrange to meet sb

marcha ['maxʃa] f march; (de acontecimentos) course; (passo) pace; (AUTO) gear; (progresso) progress; ~ à ré (BR), ~ atrás (PT) reverse (gear); pôr-se em ~ to set off

marchar [max'ʃa*] vi to go; (andar a pé) to walk; (MIL) to march

marco ['maxku] m landmark; (de janela) frame; (fig) frontier; (moeda) mark

março ['maxsu] (PT M-) m March

maré [ma're] f tide

marechal [mare'ʃaw] (pl -ais) m marshal

maremoto [mare'mɔtu] m tidal wave

marfim [max'fĩ] m ivory

margarida [maxga'rida] f daisy; (COMPUT) daisy wheel

margarina [maxga'rina] f margarine

margem ['maxʒẽ] (pl -ns) f (borda) edge; (de rio) bank; (litoral) shore; (de impresso) margin; (fig: tempo) time; (: lugar) space; à ~ de alongside

marginal [maxʒi'naw] (pl -ais) adj marginal ♦ m/f delinquent

marido [ma'ridu] m husband

marimbondo [marĩ'bõdu] m hornet

marinha [ma'riɲa] f (tb: ~ de guerra) navy; ~ mercante merchant navy; **marinheiro** [mari'ɲejru] m seaman, sailor

marinho, -a [ma'riɲu, a] adj sea atr, marine

mariposa [mari'poza] f moth

marítimo, -a [ma'ritʃimu, a] adj sea atr

marketing ['maxketʃĩ] m marketing

marmelada [maxme'lada] f quince jam

marmelo [max'mɛlu] m quince

marmita [max'mita] f (vasilha) pot

mármore ['maxmori] m marble

marquês, -quesa [max'keʃ, 'keza] m/f marquis/marchioness

marquise [max'kizi] f awning, canopy

Marrocos [ma'xɔkuʃ] m: o ~ Morocco

marrom [ma'xõ] (pl -ns) adj, m brown

martelar [maxte'la*] vt to hammer; (amolar) to bother ♦ vi to hammer; (insistir): ~ (em algo) to harp on (about sth); **martelo** [max'tɛlu] m hammer

mártir ['maxtʃi*] m/f martyr; **martírio** [max'tʃirju] m martyrdom; (fig) torment

marxista [max'ksiʃta] adj, m/f Marxist

mas [ma(j)ʃ] conj but ♦ pron = me + as

mascar [maʃ'ka*] vt to chew

máscara ['maʃkara] f mask; (para limpeza de pele) face pack; **sob a ~ de** under the guise of; **mascarar** [maʃka'ra*] vt to mask; (disfarçar) to disguise; (encobrir) to cover up

mascote [maʃ'kɔtʃi] f mascot

masculino, -a [maʃku'linu, a] adj masculine; (BIO) male

massa ['masa] f (ris, fig) mass; (de tomate) paste; (CULIN: de pão) dough; (: macarrão etc) pasta

massacrar [masa'kra*] vt to massacre; **massacre** [ma'sakri] f massacre

massagear [masa'ʒja*] vt to massage; **massagem** [ma'saʒẽ] (pl -ns) f massage

mastigar [maʃtʃi'ga*] vt to chew

mastro ['maʃtru] m (NÁUT) mast; (para bandeira) flagpole

masturbar-se [maʃtux'baxsi*] vr to masturbate

mata ['mata] f forest, wood

matadouro [mata'doru] *m* slaughter-house

matança [ma'tãsa] *f* massacre; (*de reses*) slaughter(ing)

matar [ma'ta*] *vt* to kill; (*sede*) to quench; (*fome*) to satisfy; (*aula*) to skip; (*trabalho: não aparecer*) to skive off; (*: fazer rápido*) to dash off; (*adivinhar*) to guess ♦ *vi* to kill; **matar-se** *vr* to kill o.s.; (*esfalfar-se*) to wear o.s. out; **um calor/uma dor de ~** stifling heat/excruciating pain

mate [ˈmatʃi] *adj* matt ♦ *m* (*chá*) maté tea; (*xeque-*) checkmate

matemática [mateˈmatʃika] *f* mathematics *sg*, maths *sg* (BRIT), math (US); **matemático, -a** [mateˈmatʃiku, a] *adj* mathematical ♦ *m/f* mathematician

matéria [maˈterja] *f* matter; (TEC) material; (EDUC: *assunto*) subject; (*tema*) topic; (*jornalística*) story, article; **em ~ de** on the subject of

material [mateˈrjaw] (*pl* **-ais**) *adj* material; (*físico*) physical ♦ *m* material; (TEC) equipment; **materialista** [materjaˈliʃta] *adj* materialistic; **materializar** [materjaliˈza*] *vt* to materialize; **materializar-se** *vr* to materialize

matéria-prima (*pl* **matérias-primas**) *f* raw material

maternal [matexˈnaw] (*pl* **-ais**) *adj* motherly, maternal; **escola ~** nursery (school); **maternidade** [matexniˈdadʒi] *f* motherhood, maternity; (*hospital*) maternity hospital

materno, -a [maˈtexnu, a] *adj* motherly, maternal; (*língua*) native

matinê [matʃiˈne] *f* matinée

matiz [maˈtʃiʒ] *m* (*de cor*) shade

mato [ˈmatu] *m* scrubland, bush; (*plantas agrestes*) scrub; (*o campo*) country

matraca [maˈtraka] *f* rattle

matrícula [maˈtrikula] *f* (*lista*) register; (*inscrição*) registration; (*pagamento*) enrolment (BRIT) *ou* enrollment (US) fee; (PT: AUTO) registration number (BRIT), license number (US); **fazer a ~** to enrol (BRIT), enroll (US)

matrimonial [matrimoˈnjaw] (*pl* **-ais**) *adj* marriage *atr*, matrimonial

matrimônio [matriˈmonju] *m* marriage

matriz [maˈtriʒ] *f* (MED) womb; (*fonte*) source; (*molde*) mould (BRIT), mold (US); (COM) head office

maturidade [maturiˈdadʒi] *f* maturity

mau, má [maw, ma] *adj* bad; (*malvado*) evil, wicked ♦ *m* bad; (REL) evil; **os ~s** *mpl* (*pessoas*) bad people; (*num filme*) the baddies

maus-tratos *mpl* ill-treatment *sg*

maxila [makˈsila] *f* jawbone

maxilar [maksiˈla*] *m* jawbone

máxima [ˈmasima] *f* maxim

máximo, -a [ˈmasimu, a] *adj* (*maior que todos*) greatest; (*o maior possível*) maximum ♦ *m* maximum; (*o cúmulo*) peak; (*temperature*) high; **no ~** at most; **ao ~** to the utmost

MCE *abr m* = Mercado Comum Europeu

me [mi] *pron* (*direto*) me; (*indireto*) (to) me; (*reflexivo*) (to) myself

meado [ˈmjadu] *m* middle; **em ~s ou no(s) ~(s) de** in the middle; **em ~s de julho** in mid-July

Meca [ˈmɛka] *n* Mecca

mecânica [meˈkanika] *f* (*ciência*) mechanics *sg*; (*mecanismo*) mechanism; V *tb* **mecânico**

mecânico, -a [meˈkaniku, a] *adj* mechanical ♦ *m/f* mechanic

mecanismo [mekaˈniʒmu] *m* mechanism

meço *etc* [ˈmesu] *vb* V **medir**

medalha [me'daʎa] f medal; **medalhão** [meda'ʎãw] (pl -ões) m medallion

média ['mɛdʒia] f average; (café) coffee with milk; **em ~** on average

mediano, -a [me'dʒjanu, a] adj medium; (médio) average; (mediócre) mediocre

mediante [me'dʒjãtʃi] prep by (means of), through; (a troco de) in return for

medicação [medʒika'sãw] (pl -ões) f treatment; (medicamentos) medication

medicamento [medʒika'mẽtu] m medicine

medicina [medʒi'sina] f medicine

médico, -a ['mɛdʒiku, a] adj medical ♦ m/f doctor; **receita médica** prescription

medida [me'dʒida] f measure; (providência) step; (medição) measurement; (moderação) prudence; **à ~ que** while, as; **na ~ em que** in so far as; **feito sob ~** made to measure; **ir além da ~** to go too far; **tirar as ~s de alguém** to take sb's measurements; **tomar ~s** to take steps; **tomar as ~s de** to measure

medieval [medʒje'vaw] (pl -ais) adj medieval

médio, -a ['mɛdʒju, a] adj (dedo, classe) middle; (tamanho, estatura) medium; (mediano) average; **ensino ~** secondary education

mediócre [me'dʒiokri] adj mediócre

medir [me'dʒi*] vt to measure; (atos, palavras) to weigh; (avaliar: consequências, distâncias) to weigh up ♦ vi to measure; **quanto você mede? – meço 1,60 m** how tall are you? – I'm 1.60 m (tall)

meditar [medʒi'ta*] vi to meditate; **~ sobre algo** to ponder (on) sth

mediterrâneo, -a [medʒite'xanju, a] adj Mediterranean ♦ m: **o M~** the Mediterranean

medo ['medu] m fear; **com ~** afraid; **meter ~ em alguém** to frighten sb; **ter ~ de** to be afraid of

medonho, -a [me'doɲu, a] adj terrible, awful

medroso, -a [me'drozu, ɔza] adj (com medo) frightened; (tímido) timid

megabyte [mega'bajtʃi] m megabyte

meia ['meja] f stocking; (curta) sock; (meia-entrada) half-price ticket ♦ num six; **meia-idade** f middle age; **pessoa de meia-idade** middle-aged person; **meia-noite** f midnight

meigo, -a ['mejgu, a] adj sweet

meio, -a ['meju, a] adj half ♦ adv a bit, rather ♦ m middle; (social, profissional) milieu; (tb: **~ ambiente**) environment; (maneira) way; (recursos: tb: **~s**) means pl; **~ quilo** half a kilo; **um mês e ~** one and a half months; **cortar ao ~** to cut in half; **dividir algo ao ~** to divide sth in half ou fifty-fifty; **em ~ a** amid; **no ~ (de)** in the middle (of); **~s de comunicação (de massa)** (mass) media pl; **por ~ de** through; **meio-dia** m midday, noon; **meio-fio** m kerb (BRIT), curb (US); **meio-termo** (pl **meios-termos**) m (fig) compromise

mel [mɛw] m honey

melaço [me'lasu] m treacle (BRIT), molasses pl (US)

melancia [melã'sia] f watermelon

melancolia [melãko'lia] f melancholy, sadness; **melancólico, -a** [melã'kɔliku, a] adj melancholy, sad

melão me'lãw] (pl -ões) m melon

melhor [me'ʎɔ*] adj, adv (compar)

better; (*superl*) best; ~ **que nunca** better than ever, **quanto mais** ~ the more the better; **seria** ~ **começarmos** we had better begin; **tanto** ~ so much the better; **ou** ~ ... (*ou antes*) or rather ...; **melhora** [me'ʎɔra] *f* improvement; **melhoras!** get well soon!, **melhorar** [meʎo'ra*] *vt* to improve, make better; (*doente*) to cure ♦ *vi* to improve, get better

melindroso, -a [meli'drozu, ɔza] *adj* sensitive, touchy; (*problema, situação*) tricky; (*operação*) delicate

melodia [melo'dʒia] *f* melody; (*composição*) tune

melodrama [melo'drama] *m* melodrama

melões [me'lõjʃ] *mpl de* **melão**

melro ['mewxu] *m* blackbird

membro ['mẽbru] *m* member; (ANAT: *braço, perna*) limb

memória [me'mɔrja] *f* memory; **~s** *fpl* (*de autor*) memoirs; **de** ~ by heart

memorizar [memori'za*] *vt* to memorize

mencionar [mẽsjo'na*] *vt* to mention

mendigar [mẽdʒi'ga*] *vt* to beg for ♦ *vi* to beg; **mendigo, -a** [mẽ'dʒigu, a] *m/f* beggar

menina [me'nina] *f*: ~ **do olho** pupil; **ser a ~ dos olhos de alguém** (*fig*) to be the apple of sb's eye; *V tb* **menino**

meninada [meni'nada] *f* kids *pl*

menino, -a [me'ninu, a] *m/f* boy/ girl

menopausa [meno'pawza] *f* menopause

menor [me'nɔ*] *adj* (*mais pequeno*: *compar*) smaller; (: *superl*) smallest; (*mais jovem*: *compar*) younger; (: *superl*) youngest; (*o mínimo*) least,

slightest; (*tb*: ~ **de idade**) under age ♦ *m/f* juvenile, young person; (JUR) minor; **não tenho a ~ idéia** I haven't the slightest idea

menos ['menuʃ] *adj* **1** (*compar*): ~ (**do que**) (*quantidade*) less (than); (*número*) fewer (than); **com** ~ **entusiasmo** with less enthusiasm; ~ **gente** fewer people

2 (*superl*) least; **é o que tem** ~ **culpa** he is the least to blame

♦ *adv* **1** (*compar*): ~ (**do que**) less (than); **gostei** ~ **do que do outro** I liked it less than the other one

2 (*superl*): **é o** ~ **inteligente da classe** he is the least bright in his class; **de todas elas è a que** ~ **me agrada** out of all of them she's the one I like least; **pelo** ~ at (the very) least

3 (*frases*): **temos sete a** ~ we are seven short; **não é para** ~ it's no wonder; **isso é o de** ~ that's nothing

♦ *prep* (*exceção*) except; (*números*) minus; **todos** ~ **eu** everyone except (for) me; **5** ~ **2** 5 minus 2

♦ *conj*: **a** ~ **que** unless; **a** ~ **que ele venha amanhã** unless he comes tomorrow

♦ *m*: **o** ~ the least

────────────────────

menosprezar [menuʃpre'za*] *vt* (*subestimar*) to underrate; (*desprezar*) to despise, scorn

mensageiro, -a [mẽsa'ʒejru, a] *m/f* messenger

mensagem [mẽ'saʒẽ] (*pl* -**ns**) *f* message

mensal [mẽ'saw] (*pl* -**ais**) *adj* monthly; **ele ganha £1000 mensais** he earns £1000 a month; **mensalidade** [mẽsali'dadʒi] *f* monthly payment; **mensalmente** [mẽsaw-'mẽt∫i] *adv* monthly

menstruação [mẽt∫rwa'sãw] *f* period; (*MED*) menstruation

menta ['mẽta] *f* mint

mental [mẽ'taw] (*pl* **-ais**) *adj* mental; **mentalidade** [mẽtali'dadʒi] *f* mentality

mente ['mẽt∫i] *f* mind; **de boa** ~ willingly; **ter em** ~ to bear in mind

mentir [mẽ't∫i*] *vi* to lie

mentira [mẽ't∫ira] *f* lie; (*ato*) lying; **parece** ~ **que** it seems incredible that; **de** ~ not for real; **~!** (*acusação*) that's a lie!, you're lying!; (*de surpresa*) you don't say!, no!; **mentiroso, -a** [mẽt∫i'rozu, ɔza] *adj* lying ♦ *m/f* liar

menu [me'nu] *m* (*tb: COMPUT*) menu

mercado [mex'kadu] *m* market; **M~ Comum** Common Market; **negro** *ou* **paralelo** black market

mercadoria [mexkado'ria] *f* commodity; **~s** *fpl* (*produtos*) goods

mercearia [mexsja'ria] *f* grocer's (shop) (*BRIT*), grocery store

mercúrio [mex'kurju] *m* mercury

merda ['mexda] (*col!*) *f* shit (!) ♦ *m/f* (*pessoa*) jerk; **a ~ do carro** the bloody (*BRIT*) *ou* goddamn (*US!*) car

merecer [mere'se*] *vt* to deserve; (*consideração*) to merit; (*valer*) to be worth ♦ *vi* to be worthy; **merecido, -a** [mere'sidu, a] *adj* deserved; (*castigo, prêmio*) just

merenda [me'rẽda] *f* packed lunch

merengue [me'rẽgi] *m* meringue

mergulhador, a [mexguʎa'do*, a] *m/f* diver

mergulhar [mexgu'ʎa*] *vi* to dive; (*penetrar*) to plunge ♦ *vt*: ~ **algo em** (*num líquido*) to dip sth into sth; (*na terra etc*) to plunge sth into sth; **mergulho** [mex'guʎu] *m* dip(ping), immersion; (*em natação*)

dive; **dar um mergulho** (*na praia*) to go for a dip

mérito ['meritu] *m* merit

mero, -a ['meru, a] *adj* mere

mês [mes] *m* month

mesa ['meza] *f* table; (*de trabalho*) desk; (*comitê*) board; (*numa reunião*) panel; **pôr/tirar a** ~ to lay/clear the table; **à** ~ at the table; **~ de toalete** dressing table; **~ telefônica** switchboard

mesada [me'zada] *f* monthly allowance; (*de criança*) pocket money

mesa-de-cabeceira (*pl* **mesas-de-cabeceira**) *f* bedside table

mesmo, -a ['meʒmu, a] *adj* same; (*enfático*) very ♦ *adv* (*exatamente*) right; (*até*) even; (*realmente*) really ♦ *m/f*: **o** ~, **a mesma** the same (one); **o** ~ (*a mesma coisa*) the same (thing); **este** ~ **homem** this very man; **ele** ~ **o fez** he did it himself; **dá no** ~ *ou* **na mesma** it's all the same; **aqui/agora/hoje** ~ right here/right now/this very day; ~ **que** even if; **é** ~ it's true; **é ~?** really?; (é) **isso ~!** exactly!; **por isso** ~ that's why; **nem** ~ not even; **só** ~ only; **por si** ~ by oneself

mesquinho, -a [meʃ'kiɲu, a] *adj* mean

mesquita [meʃ'kita] *f* mosque

mestiço, -a [meʃ't∫isu, a] *adj* half-caste, of mixed race; (*animal*) crossbred ♦ *m/f* half-caste; (*crossbreed*) crossbreed

mestre, -a ['meʃtri, a] *adj* (*chave, viga*) master; (*linha, estrada*) main ♦ *m/f* master/mistress; (*professor*) teacher; **obra mestra** masterpiece

meta ['meta] *f* (*em corrida*) finishing post; (*gol*) goal; (*objetivo*) aim

metade [me'tadʒi] *f* half; (*meio*) middle

metáfora [me'tafora] *f* metaphor

metal [me'taw] (*pl* **-ais**) *m* metal;

metais *mpl* (*MÚS*) brass *sg*; **metálico, -a** [me'taliku, a] *adj* metallic; (*de metal*) metal *atr*

metalúrgico, -a [meta'luxʒiku, a] *m/f* metalworker

meteorologia [meteorolo'ʒia] *f* meteorology; **meteorologista** [meteorolo'ʒiʃta] *m/f* meteorologist; (*TV, RÁDIO*) weather forecaster

meter [me'te*] *vt* (*colocar*) to put; (*envolver*) to involve; (*introduzir*) to introduce; **meter-se** *vr* (*esconder-se*) to hide; **~-se a fazer algo** to decide to have a go at sth; **~-se com** (*provocar*) to pick a quarrel with; (*associar-se*) to get involved with; **~-se em** to get involved in; (*intrometer-se*) to interfere in

meticuloso, -a [metʃiku'lozu, ɔza] *adj* meticulous

metido, -a [mɪ'tʃidu, a] *adj* (*envolvido*) involved; (*intrometido*) meddling; **~ (a besta)** snobbish

metódico, -a [me'tɔdʒiku, a] *adj* methodical

método ['metodu] *m* method

metralhadora [metraʎa'dora] *f* sub-machine gun

métrico, -a ['metriku, a] *adj* metric

metro ['metru] *m* metre (*BRIT*), meter (*US*); (*PT*) = **metrô**

metrô [me'tro] (*BR*) *m* underground (*BRIT*), subway (*US*)

metrópole [me'trɔpɔli] *f* metropolis; (*capital*) capital

meu, minha [mew, 'miɲa] *adj* my ♦ *pron* mine; **os ~s** *mpl* (*minha família*) my family *ou* folks (*col*); **um amigo ~** a friend of mine

mexer [me'ʃe*] *vt* to move; (*cabeça: dizendo sim*) to nod; (: *dizendo não*) to shake; (*misturar*) to stir; (*ovos*) to scramble ♦ *vi* to move; **mexer-se** *vr* to move; (*apressar-se*) to get a move on; **~ em algo** to touch sth;

mexa-se! get going!, move yourself!

mexerico [meʃe'riku] *m* piece of gossip; **~s** *mpl* (*fofocas*) gossip *sg*

México ['meʃiku] *m*: **o ~** Mexico

mexido, -a [me'ʃidu, a] *adj* (*papéis*) mixed up; (*ovos*) scrambled

mexilhão [meʃi'ʎãw] (*pl -ões*) *m* mussel

mi [mi] *m* (*MÚS*) E

miar [mja*] *vi* to miaow; (*vento*) to whistle

miau [mjaw] *m* miaow

micro... [mikru] *prefixo* micro...; **micro(computador)** [mikro(kõputa'do*)] *m* micro(computer); **microfone** [mikro'fɔni] *m* microphone; **microondas** [mikro'õdaʃ] *m inv* (*tb: forno de microondas*) microwave (oven); **microprocessador** [mikroprosesa'do*] *m* microprocessor; **microscópio** [mikro'ʃkɔpju] *m* microscope

mídia ['midʒia] *f* media *pl*

migalha [mi'gaʎa] *f* crumb; **~s** *fpl* (*restos, sobras*) scraps

migrar [mi'gra*] *vi* to migrate

mijar [mi'ʒa*] (*col*) *vi* to pee; **mijar-se** *vr* to wet o.s

mil [miw] *num* thousand; **dois ~** two thousand

milagre [mi'lagri] *m* miracle; **por ~** miraculously; **milagroso, -a** [mila'grozu, ɔza] *adj* miraculous

milhão [mi'ʎãw] (*pl -ões*) *m* million; **um ~ de vezes** hundreds of times

milhar [mi'ʎa*] *m* thousand; **turistas aos ~es** tourists in their thousands

milho ['miʎu] *m* maize (*BRIT*), corn (*US*)

milhões [mi'ʎõjʃ] *mpl de* **milhão**

miligrama [mili'grama] *m* milligram(me)

milionário, -a [milio'narju, a] *m/f* millionaire

militante [mili'tãtʃi] *adj* militant ♦ *m/f* activist; (*extremista*) militant

militar [mili'ta*] *adj* military ♦ *m* soldier ♦ *vi* to fight; ~ **em** (*MIL: regimento*) to serve in; (*POL: partido*) to belong to, be active in; (*profissão*) to work in

mim [mĩ] *pron* me; (*reflexivo*) myself; **de ~ para ~** to myself

mimar [mi'ma*] *vt* to pamper, spoil

mímica ['mimika] *f* mime

mimo ['mimu] *m* gift; (*pessoa, coisa encantadora*) delight; (*carinho*) tenderness; (*gentileza*) kindness; **cheio de ~s** (*criança*) spoiled, spoilt (*BRIT*); **mimoso, -a** [mi'mozu, ɔza] *adj* (*delicado*) delicate; (*carinhoso*) tender, loving; (*encantador*) delightful

mina ['mina] *f* mine

mindinho [mĩ'dʒiɲu] *m* (*tb*: **dedo ~**) little finger

mineiro, -a [mi'nejru, a] *adj* mining *atr* ♦ *m/f* miner

mineral [mine'raw] (*pl* **-ais**) *adj*, *m* mineral

minério [mi'nɛrju] *m* ore

míngua ['mĩgwa] *f* lack; **à ~ de** for want of; **viver à ~** to live in poverty; **minguado, -a** [mĩ'gwadu, a] *adj* scant; (*criança*) stunted; **minguado de algo** short of sth

minguar [mĩ'gwa*] *vi* (*diminuir*) to decrease, dwindle; (*faltar*) to run short

minha ['miɲa] *f de* **meu**

minhoca [mi'ɲɔka] *f* (earth)worm

mini... [mini] *prefixo* mini...

miniatura [minja'tura] *adj*, *f* miniature

MiniDisc [mini'dʒiʃki] ® *m* MiniDisc ®

mínima ['minima] *f* (*temperatura*) low; (*MÚS*) minim

mínimo, -a ['minimu, a] *adj* minimum ♦ *m* minimum; (*tb*: **dedo ~**) little finger; **não dou** ou **ligo a mínima para isso** I couldn't care less about it; **a mínima importância/ idéia** the slightest importance/idea; **no ~** at least

minissaia [mini'saja] *f* miniskirt

ministério [minis'tɛrju] *m* ministry; **~ da Fazenda** ≈ Treasury (*BRIT*), ≈ Treasury Department (*US*); **M~ das Relações Exteriores** ≈ Foreign Office (*BRIT*), ≈ State Department (*US*)

ministro, -a [mi'niʃtru, a] *m/f* minister

minoria [mino'ria] *f* minority

minto *etc* ['mĩtu] *vb V* **mentir**

minucioso, -a [minu'sjozu, ɔza] *adj* (*indivíduo, busca*) thorough; (*explicação*) detailed

minúsculo, -a [mi'nuʃkulu, a] *adj* minute, tiny; **letra minúscula** lower case

minuta [mi'nuta] *f* rough draft

minuto [mi'nutu] *m* minute

miolo ['mjolu] *m* inside; (*polpa*) pulp; (*de maçã*) core; **~s** *mpl* (*cérebro, inteligência*) brains

míope ['mjopi] *adj* short-sighted

mira ['mira] *f* (*de fuzil*) sight; (*pontaria*) aim; (*fig*) aim, purpose; **à ~ de** on the lookout for; **ter em ~** to have one's eye on

miragem [mi'raʒẽ] (*pl* **-ns**) *f* mirage

miscelânea [mise'lanja] *f* miscellany; (*confusão*) muddle

miserável [mize'ravew] (*pl* **-eis**) *adj* (*digno de compaixão*) wretched; (*pobre*) impoverished; (*avaro*) stingy, mean; (*insignificante*) paltry; (*lugar*) squalid; (*infame*) despicable ♦ *m* wretch; (*coitado*) poor thing; (*pessoa infame*) rotter

miséria 511 **modo**

miséria [mi'zɛrja] f misery; (*pobreza*) poverty, (*avareza*) stinginess

misericórdia [mizeri'kɔxdʒja] f (*compaixão*) pity, compassion; (*graça*) mercy

missa ['misa] f (REL) mass

missão [mi'sãw] (*pl* -**ões**) f mission; (*dever*) duty

míssil ['misiw] (*pl* -**eis**) m missile

missionário, -a [misjo'narju, a] m/f missionary

missões [mi'sõjʃ] fpl de **missão**

mistério [miʃ'tɛrju] m mystery; **misterioso, -a** [miʃte'rjozu, ɔza] adj mysterious

mistificar [miʃtʃifi'ka*] vt, vi to fool

misto, -a ['miʃtu, a] adj mixed; (*confuso*) mixed up ♦ m mixture; **misto-quente** (*pl* mistos-quentes) m toasted cheese and ham sandwich

mistura [miʃ'tura] f mixture; (*ato*) mixing; **misturar** [miʃtu'ra*] vt to mix; (*confundir*) to mix up; **misturar-se** vr: **~-se com** to mingle with

mitigar [mitʃi'ga*] vt (*raiva*) to temper; (*dor*) to relieve; (*sede*) to lessen

mito ['mitu] m myth

miudezas [mju'dezaʃ] fpl minutiae; (*bugigangas*) odds and ends; (*objetos pequenos*) trinkets

miúdo, -a ['mjudu, a] adj tiny, minute ♦ m/f (PT: *criança*) youngster, kid; **~s** mpl (*dinheiro*) change sg; (*de aves*) giblets; **dinheiro ~** small change

mm abr (= milímetro) mm

mo [mu] pron = **me** + **o**

moa etc ['moa] vb V **moer**

móbil ['mɔbiw] (*pl* -**eis**) adj = **móvel**

móbile ['mɔbili] m mobile

mobília [mo'bilja] f furniture; **mobiliar** [mobi'lja*] (BR) vt to furnish; **mobiliário** [mobi'ljarju] m

furnishings pl

moça ['mosa] f girl, young woman

Moçambique [mosã'biki] m Mozambique

moção [mo'sãw] (*pl* -**ões**) f motion

mochila [mo'ʃila] f rucksack

mocidade [mosi'dadʒi] f youth; (*os moços*) young people pl

moço, -a ['mosu, a] adj young ♦ m young man, lad

moções [mo'sõjʃ] fpl de **moção**

moda ['mɔda] f fashion; **estar na ~** to be in fashion, be all the rage; **fora da ~** old-fashioned; **sair da** ou **cair de ~** to go out of fashion

modalidade [modali'dadʒi] f kind; (ESPORTE) event

modelo [mo'delu] m model; (*criação de estilista*) design

moderado, -a [mode'radu, a] adj moderate; (*clima*) mild

moderar [mode'ra*] vt to moderate; (*violência*) to control, restrain; (*velocidade*) to reduce; (*voz*) to lower; (*gastos*) to cut down

modernizar [modexni'za*] vt to modernize; **modernizar-se** vr to modernize

moderno, -a [mo'dexnu, a] adj modern; (*atual*) present-day

modéstia [mo'dɛʃtʃja] f modesty

modesto, -a [mo'dɛʃtu, a] adj modest; (*simples*) simple, plain; (*vida*) frugal

módico, -a ['mɔdʒiku, a] adj moderate; (*preço*) reasonable; (*bens*) scant

modificar [modʒifi'ka*] vt to modify, alter

modista [mo'dʒiʃta] f dressmaker

modo ['mɔdu] m (*maneira*) way, manner; (*método*) way; (MÚS) mode; **~s** mpl (*comportamento*) manners; **de (tal) ~ que** so (that); **de ~ nenhum** in no way; **de qualquer**

anyway, anyhow; **~ de emprego** instructions *pl* for use

módulo ['mɔdulu] *m* module

moeda ['mwɛda] *f* (*uma* ~) coin; (*dinheiro*) currency; **uma ~ de 10p** a 10p piece; **~ corrente** currency; **Casa da M~** ≈ the Mint (*BRIT*), ≈ the (*US*) Mint

moedor [moe'do*] *m* (*de café*) grinder; (*de carne*) mincer

moer [mwe*] *vt* (*café*) to grind; (*cana*) to crush

mofado, -a [mo'fadu, a] *adj* mouldy (*BRIT*), moldy (*US*)

mofo ['mofu] *m* (*BOT*) mo(u)ld; **cheiro de ~** musty smell

mogno ['mɔgnu] *m* mahogany

mói *etc* [mɔj] *vb* V **moer**

moía *etc* [mo'ia] *vb* V **moer**

moído, -a [mo'idu, a] *adj* (*café*) ground; (*carne*) minced; (*cansado*) tired out; (*corpo*) aching

moinho ['mwiɲu] *m* mill; (*de café*) grinder; **~ de vento** windmill

mola ['mɔla] *f* (*TEC*) spring; (*fig*) motive, motivation

moldar [mow'da*] *vt* to mould (*BRIT*), mold (*US*); (*metal*) to cast;

molde ['mɔwdʒi] *m* mo(u)ld; (*de papel*) pattern; (*fig*) model; **molde de vestido** dress pattern

moldura [mow'dura] *f* (*de pintura*) frame

mole ['mɔli] *adj* soft; (*sem energia*) listless; (*carnes*) flabby; (*col: fácil*) easy; (*lento*) slow; (*preguiçoso*) sluggish ♦ *adv* (*lentamente*) slowly

moleque [mo'lɛki] *m* (*de rua*) urchin; (*menino*) youngster; (*pessoa sem palavra*) unreliable person; (*canalha*) scoundrel ♦ *adj* (*levado*) mischievous; (*brincalhão*) funny

molestar [moleʃ'ta*] *vt* to upset; (*enfadar*) to annoy; (*importunar*) to bother

moléstia [mo'lɛʃtʃa] *f* illness

moleza [mo'leza] *f* softness; (*falta de energia*) listlessness; (*falta de força*) weakness; **ser (uma) ~** (*col*) to be easy; **na ~** without exerting oneself

molhado, -a [mo'ʎadu, a] *adj* wet, damp

molhar [mo'ʎa*] *vt* to wet; (*de leve*) to moisten, dampen; (*mergulhar*) to dip; **molhar-se** *vr* to get wet

molho¹ ['mɔʎu] *m* (*de chaves*) bunch; (*de trigo*) sheaf

molho² ['moʎu] *m* (*CULIN*) sauce; (*: de salada*) dressing; (*: de carne*) gravy; **pôr de ~** to soak; **estar/deixar de ~** (*roupa etc*) to be/leave to soak

momentâneo, -a [momē'tanju, a] *adj* momentary

momento [mo'mētu] *m* moment; (*TEC*) momentum; **a todo ~** constantly; **de um ~ para outro** suddenly; **no ~ em que** just as

Mônaco ['mɔnaku] *m* Monaco

monarquia [monax'kia] *f* monarchy

monitor [moni'to*] *m* monitor

monopólio [mono'pɔlju] *m* monopoly; **monopolizar** [monopoli-'za*] *vt* to monopolize

monotonia [monoto'nia] *f* monotony; **monótono, -a** [mo'nɔtonu, a] *adj* monotonous

monstro, -a ['mõʃtru, a] *adj inv* giant ♦ *m* (*tb fig*) monster; **monstruoso, -a** [mõʃt'rwozu, ɔza] *adj* monstrous; (*enorme*) gigantic, huge

montagem [mõ'taʒē] (*pl* **-ns**) *f* assembly; (*ARQ*) erection; (*CINEMA*) editing; (*TEATRO*) production

montanha [mõ'taɲa] *f* mountain; **montanha-russa** *f* roller coaster

montante [mõ'tãtʃi] *m* amount, sum; **a ~** (*nadar*) upstream

montar [mõ'ta*] *vt* (*cavalo*) to mount, get on; (*colocar em*) to put on; (*cavalgar*) to ride; (*peças*) to assemble, put together; (*loja, máquina*) to set up; (*casa*) to put up; (*peça teatral*) to put on ♦ *vi* to ride; **~ a ou em** (*animal*) to get on; (*cavalgar*) to ride; (*despesa*) to come to

monte ['mõtʃi] *m* hill; (*pilha*) heap, pile; **um ~ de** (*muitos*) a lot of, lots of; **gente aos ~s** loads of people

montra ['mõtra] (*PT*) *f* shop window

monumental [monumẽ'taw] (*pl* -**ais**) *adj* monumental, (*fig*) magnificent, splendid

monumento [monu'mẽtu] *m* monument

moqueca [mo'keka] *f* fish or seafood simmered in coconut cream and palm oil; **~ de camarão** prawn moqueca

morada [mo'rada] *f* home, residence; (*PT*: *endereço*) address; **moradia** [mora'dʒia] *f* home, dwelling; **morador, a** [mora'do*, a] *m/f* resident; (*de casa alugada*) tenant

moral [mo'raw] (*pl* -**ais**) *adj* moral ♦ *f* (*ética*) ethics *pl*; (*conclusão*) moral ♦ *m* (*de pessoa*) sense of morality; (*ânimo*) morale; **moralidade** [morali'dadʒi] *f* morality

morango [mo'rãgu] *m* strawberry

morar [mo'ra*] *vi* to live, reside

mórbido, -a ['mɔxbidu, a] *adj* morbid

morcego [mox'segu] *m* (*BIO*) bat

mordaça [mox'dasa] *f* (*de animal*) muzzle; (*fig*) gag

mordaz [mox'daʒ] *adj* scathing

morder [mox'de*] *vt* to bite; (*corroer*) to corrode; **mordida** [mox'dʒida] *f* bite

mordomia [moxdo'mia] *f* (*de executivos*) perk; (*col: regalia*) luxury,

comfort

mordomo [mox'dɔmu] *m* butler

moreno, -a [mo'renu, a] *adj* dark(-skinned); (*de cabelos*) dark(-haired); (*de tomar sol*) brown ♦ *m/f* dark person

mormaço [mox'masu] *m* sultry weather

morno, -a ['mɔxnu, 'mɔxna] *adj* lukewarm, tepid

morrer [mo'xe*] *vi* to die; (*luz, cor*) to fade; (*fogo*) to die down; (*AUTO*) to stall

morro ['moxu] *m* hill; (*favela*) slum

mortadela [moxta'dɛla] *f* salami

mortal [mox'taw] (*pl* -**ais**) *adj* mortal; (*letal, insuportável*) deadly ♦ *m* mortal

mortalidade [moxtali'dadʒi] *f* mortality

morte ['mɔxtʃi] *f* death

mortífero, -a [mox'tʃiferu, a] *adj* deadly, lethal

morto, -a ['moxtu, 'mɔxta] *pp* de **matar** ♦ *pp* de **morrer** ♦ *adj* dead; (*cor*) dull; (*exausto*) exhausted; (*inexpressivo*) lifeless ♦ *m/f* dead man/woman; **estar/ser ~** to be dead/killed; **estar ~ de inveja** to be green with envy; **estar ~ de vontade de** to be dying to

mos [muʃ] *pron* = **me + os**

mosca ['moʃka] *f* fly; **estar às ~s** (*bar etc*) to be deserted

Moscou [moʃ'ku] (*BR*) *n* Moscow

Moscovo [moʃ'kovu] (*PT*) *n* Moscow

mosquito [moʃ'kitu] *m* mosquito

mostarda [moʃ'taxda] *f* mustard

mosteiro [moʃ'tejru] *m* monastery; (*de monjas*) convent

mostrador [moʃtra'do*] *m* (*de relógio*) face, dial

mostrar [moʃ'tra*] *vt* to show; (*mercadorias*) to display; (*provar*) to

motel 514 **mula**

demonstrate, prove; **mostrar-se** *vr*
to show o.s. to be; (*exibir-se*) to
show off

motel [mo'tew] (*pl* **-éis**) *m* motel

motivar [motʃi'va*] *vt* (*causar*) to
cause, bring about; (*estimular*) to
motivate; (*de carro, avião*) to
drive; **motivo** (**de** *ou* **para**) cause
(of), reason (for); (*fim*) motive;
(*ARTE, MÚS*) motif; **por motivo de**
because of, owing to

moto ['mɔtu] *f* motorbike ♦ *m* (*lema*)
motto

motocicleta [motosi'kleta] *f*
motorcycle, motorbike

motociclista [motosi'kliʃta] *m/f*
motorcyclist

motociclo [moto'siklu] (*PT*) *m* =
motocicleta

motor, motriz [mo'to*, mo'triʒ]
adj: **força motriz** driving force ♦ *m*
motor; (*de carro, avião*) engine; ~
diesel/de explosão diesel/internal
combustion engine

motorista [moto'riʃta] *m/f* driver

móvel ['mɔvew] (*pl* **-eis**) *adj* moveable ♦ *m* piece of furniture; **móveis**
mpl (*mobília*) furniture *sg*

mover [mo've*] *vt* to move; (*
cabeça*) to shake; (*mecanismo*) to
drive; (*campanha*) to start (up);
mover-se *vr* to move

movimentado, -a [movimē'tadu,
a] *adj* (*rua, lugar*) busy; (*pessoa*)
active; (*show, música*) up-tempo

movimentar [movimē'ta*] *vt* to
move; (*animar*) to liven up

movimento [movi'mētu] *m* movement; (*TEC*) motion; (*na rua*) activity,
bustle; **de muito** ~ busy

muamba [mu'āba] (*col*) *f* (*contrabando*) contraband; (*objetos roubados*) loot

muçulmano, -a [musuw'manu, a]
adj, m/f Moslem

muda ['muda] *f* (*planta*) seedling;
(*vestuário*) outfit; ~ **de roupa**
change of clothes

mudança [mu'dāsa] *f* change; (*de
casa*) move; (*AUTO*) gear

mudar [mu'da*] *vt* to change;
(*deslocar*) to move ♦ *vi* to change;
(*ave*) to moult (*BRIT*), molt (*US*)
mudar-se *vr* (*de casa*) to move
(away); ~ **de roupa/de assunto** to
change clothes/the subject; ~ **de
casa** to move (house); ~ **de idéia** to
change one's mind

mudez [mu'deʒ] *f* muteness; (*silêncio*) silence

mudo, -a ['mudu, a] *adj* dumb; (*cala, CINEMA*) silent; (*telefone*) dead
♦ *m/f* mute

muito, -a ['mwĩtu, a] *adj* (*quantidade*) a lot of; (: *em frase negativa
ou interrogativa*) much; (*número*)
lots of, a lot of; many; ~ **esforço** a
lot of effort; **faz** ~ **calor** it's very hot;
~ **tempo** a long time; **muitas ami-
gas** lots *ou* a lot of friends; **muitas
vezes** often

♦ *pron* a lot; (*em frase negativa ou
interrogativa: sg*) much; (: *pl*) many;
tenho ~ **que fazer** I've got a lot to
do; ~**s dizem que** ... a lot of people
say that ...

♦ *adv* **1** a lot; (+ *adj*) very; (+ *compar*): ~ **melhor** much *ou* far *ou* a lot
better; **gosto** ~ **disto** I like it a lot;
sinto ~ I'm very sorry; ~ **interessante** very interesting

2 (*resposta*) very; **está cansado?** – ~
are you tired? – very

3 (*tempo*): ~ **depois** long after; **há** ~
a long time ago; **não demorou** ~ it
didn't take long

mula ['mula] *f* mule

mulato, -a [mu'latu, a] adj, m/f mulatto

muleta [mu'leta] f crutch; (fig) support

mulher [mu'ʎe*] f woman; (esposa) wife

multa ['muwta] f fine; **levar uma ~** to be fined; **multar** [muw'ta*] vt to fine; **multar alguém em $1000** to fine sb $1000

multi... [muwtʃi] prefixo multi...

multidão [muwtʃi'dãw] (pl -ões) f crowd; **uma ~ de** (muitos) lots of

multimídia [muwtʃi'midʒja] adj multimedia

multinacional [muwtʃinasjo'naw] (pl -ais) adj, f multinational

multiplicar [muwtʃipli'ka*] vt to multiply; (aumentar) to increase

múltiplo, -a ['muwtʃiplu, a] adj multiple ♦ m multiple

múmia ['mumja] f mummy

mundial [mũ'dʒjaw] (pl -ais) adj worldwide; (guerra, recorde) world atr ♦ m world championship

mundo ['mũdu] m world; **todo o ~** everybody; **um ~ de** lots of, a great many

munição [muni'sãw] (pl -ões) f (de armas) ammunition; (chumbo) shot; (MIL) munitions pl, supplies pl

municipal [munisi'paw] (pl -ais) adj municipal

município [muni'sipju] m local authority; (cidade) town; (condado) county

munições [muni'sõjʃ] fpl de munição

munir [mu'ni*] vt: ~ **de** to provide with, supply with; **munir-se** vr: **~-se de** (provisões) to equip o.s. with

muralha [mu'raʎa] f (de fortaleza) rampart; (muro) wall

murchar [mux'ʃa*] vt (BOT) to wither; (sentimentos) to dull; (pessoa) to

sadden ♦ vi to wither, wilt; (fig) to fade

murmurar [muxmu'ra*] vi to murmur, whisper; (queixar-se) to mutter, grumble; (água) to ripple; (folhagem) to rustle ♦ vt to murmur; **murmúrio** [mux'murju] m murmuring, whispering; grumbling; rippling; rustling

muro ['muru] m wall

murro ['muxu] m punch; **dar um ~ em alguém** to punch sb

musa ['muza] f muse

musculação [muʃkula'sãw] f body-building

músculo ['muʃkulu] m muscle; **musculoso, -a** [muʃkʊ'lozu, ɔza] adj muscular

museu [mu'zew] m museum; (de pintura) gallery

musgo ['muʒgu] m moss

música ['muzika] f music; (canção) song; **músico, -a** ['muziku, a] adj musical ♦ m/f musician

mutilar [mutʃi'la*] vt to mutilate; (pessoa) to maim; (texto) to cut

mútuo, -a ['mutwu, a] adj mutual

N

N abr (= norte) N

na [na] = **em** + **a**

-na [na] pron her; (coisa) it

nabo ['nabu] m turnip

nação [na'sãw] (pl -ões) f nation

nacional [nasjo'naw] (pl -ais) adj national; (carro, vinho etc) domestic; home-produced; **nacionalidade** [nasjonali'dadʒi] f nationality; **nacionalismo** [nasjona'liʒmu] m nationalism; **nacionalista** [nasjona'liʃta] adj, m/f nationalist

nações [na'sõjʃ] fpl de nação

nada ['nada] pron nothing ♦ adv at

all; **antes de mais ~** first of all; **não é ~ difícil** it's not at all hard, it's not hard at all; **~ mais** nothing else; **~ de novo** nothing new; **obrigado – de –** thank you – not at all *ou* don't mention it

nadador, a [nada'do*, a] *m/f* swimmer

nadar [na'da*] *vi* to swim

nádegas ['nadegaʃ] *fpl* buttocks

nado ['nadu] *m*: **atravessar a ~** to swim across; **~ borboleta/de costas/de peito** butterfly (stroke)/ backstroke/breaststroke

naipe ['najpi] *m* (*cartas*) suit

namorado, -a [namo'radu, a] *m/f* boyfriend/girlfriend

namorar [namo'ra*] *vt* (*ser namorado de*) to be going out with

namoro [na'moru] *m* relationship

não [nãw] *adv* not; (*resposta*) no ♦ *m* no; **~ sei** I don't know; **~ muito** not much; **~ só ... mas também** not only ... but also; **agora ~** not now; **~ tem de quê** don't mention it; **~ é?** isn't it?, won't you? (*etc*, *segundo o verbo precedente*); **eles são brasileiros, ~ é?** they're Brazilian, aren't they?

não- [nãw-] *prefixo* non-

naquele(s), -a(s) [na'keli(ʃ), na-'kɛla(ʃ)] = **em + aquele(s), a(s)**

naquilo [na'kilu] = **em + aquilo**

narcótico, -a [nax'kɔtʃiku, a] *adj* narcotic ♦ *m* narcotic

narina [na'rina] *f* nostril

nariz [na'riʒ] *m* nose

narração [naxa'sãw] (*pl* **-ões**) *f* narration; (*relato*) account

narrar [na'xa*] *vt* to narrate

narrativa [naxa'tʃiva] *f* narrative; (*história*) story

nas [naʃ] = **em + as**

-nas [naʃ] *pron* them

nascença [na'sẽsa] *f* birth; **de ~** by

birth; **ele é surdo de ~** he was born deaf

nascente [na'sẽtʃi] *m*: **o ~** the East, the Orient ♦ *f* (*fonte*) spring

nascer [na'se*] *vi* to be born; (*plantas*) to sprout; (*o sol*) to rise; (*ave*) to hatch; (*fig: ter origem*) to come into being ♦ *m*: **~ do sol** sunrise; **ele nasceu para médico** *etc* he's a born doctor *etc*; **nascimento** [nasi'mẽtu] *m* birth; (*fig*) origin; (*estirpe*) descent

nata ['nata] *f* cream

natação [nata'sãw] *f* swimming

natais [na'tajʃ] *adj pl de* **natal**

Natal [na'taw] *m* Christmas; **Feliz ~!** Merry Christmas!

natal [na'taw] (*pl* **-ais**) *adj* (*relativo ao nascimento*) natal; (*país*) native; **cidade ~** home town

natalino, -a [nata'linu, a] *adj* Christmas *atr*

nativo, -a [na'tʃivu, a] *adj*, *m/f* native

natural [natu'raw] (*pl* **-ais**) *adj* natural; (*nativo*) native ♦ *m/f* native; **ao ~** (*CULIN*) fresh, uncooked; **naturalidade** [naturali'dadʒi] *f* naturalness; **de naturalidade paulista** *etc* born in São Paulo *etc*; **naturalizar** [naturali'za*] *vt* to naturalize; **naturalizar-se** *vr* to become naturalized; **naturalmente** [naturaw'mẽtʃi] *adv* naturally; **naturalmente!** of course!

natureza [natu'reza] *f* nature; (*espécie*) kind, type

nau [naw] *f* (*literário*) ship

naufrágio [naw'fraʒu] *m* shipwreck; **náufrago, -a** ['nawfragu, a] *m/f* castaway

náusea ['nawzea] *f* nausea; **dar ~s a alguém** to make sb feel sick; **sentir ~s** to feel sick

náutico, -a ['nawtʃiku, a] *adj*

nautical
naval [na'vaw] (pl **-ais**) adj naval;
construção ~ shipbuilding
navalha [na'vaʎa] f (de barba)
razor; (faca) knife
nave ['navi] f (de igreja) nave
navegação [navega'sãw] f navigation, sailing; **~ aérea** air traffic;
companhia de ~ shipping line
navegar [nave'ga*] vt to navigate;
(mares) to sail ♦ vi to sail; (dirigir o rumo) to navigate
navio [na'viu] m ship; **~ aeródromo/carguero/petroleiro** aircraft carrier/cargo ship/oil tanker; **~ de guerra** (BR) battleship
nazi [na'zi] (PT) adj, m/f = nazista
nazista [na'ziʃta] adj, m/f Nazi
NB abr (= note bem) NB
neblina [ne'blina] f fog, mist
nebuloso, -a [nebu'lozu, ɔza] adj foggy, misty; (céu) cloudy; (fig) vague
necessário, -a [nese'sarju, a] adj necessary ♦ m: **o ~** the necessities pl
necessidade [nesesi'dadʒi] f need, necessity; (o que se necessita) need; (pobreza) poverty, need; **ter ~ de** to need; **em caso de ~** if need be
necessitado, -a [nesesi'tadu, a] adj needy, poor; **~ de** in need of
necessitar [nesesi'ta*] vt to need, require ♦ vi: **~ de** to need
negativa [nega'tʃiva] f negative, (recusa) denial
negativo, -a [nega'tʃivu, a] adj negative ♦ m (TEC, FOTO) negative ♦ excl (col) nope!

negligência [negli'ʒẽsja] f negligence, carelessness; **negligente** [negli'ʒẽtʃi] adj negligent, careless
negociação [negosja'sãw] (pl -ões) f negotiation
negociante [nego'sjãtʃi] m/f businessman/woman
negociar [nego'sja*] vt to negotiate; (COM) to trade ♦ vi: **~ (com)** to trade ou deal (in); to negotiate (with)
negócio [ne'gɔsju] m (COM) business; (transação) deal; (questão) matter; (col: troço) thing; (assunto) affair, business; **homem de ~s** businessman; **a ~s** on business; **fechar um ~** to make a deal
negro, -a ['negru, a] adj black; (raça) Black; (fig: lúgubre) gloomy ♦ m/f Black man/woman
nele(s), -a(s) ['neli(ʃ), 'nela(ʃ)] = **em + ele(s), ela(s)**
nem [nẽj] conj nor, neither; **~ (sequer)** not even; **~ que** even if; **~ bem** hardly; **~ um só** not a single one; **~ estuda ~ trabalha** he neither studies nor works; **~ eu** nor me; **sem ~** without even; **~ todos** not all; **~ tanto** not so much; **~ sempre** not always
nenê [ne'ne] m/f baby
neném [ne'nẽj] (pl **-ns**) m/f = **nenê**
nenhum, a [ne'nũ, 'numa] adj no, not any ♦ pron (nem um só) none, not one; (de dois) neither; **~ lugar** nowhere
neozelandês, -esa [neozelã'deʃ, deza] adj New Zealand atr ♦ m/f New Zealander
nervo ['nexvu] m (ANAT) nerve; (fig) energy, strength; (em carne) sinew; **nervosismo** [nexvo'ziʒmu] m (nervosidade) nervousness; (irritabilidade) irritability; **nervoso, -a** [nex'vozu, ɔza] adj nervous; (irritável)

touchy, on edge; (*exaltado*) worked up; **ele me deixa nervoso** he gets on my nerves

nesse(s), -a(s) ['nesi(ʃ), 'nɛsa(ʃ)] = em + esse(s), -a(s)

neste(s), -a(s) ['neʃtʃi(ʃ), 'nɛʃta(ʃ)] = em + este(s), -a(s)

neto, -a ['nɛtu, a] m/f grandson/daughter; **~s** mpl grandchildren

neurose [new'rɔzi] f neurosis; **neurótico, -a** [new'rɔtʃiku, a] adj, m/f neurotic

neutralizar [newtrali'za*] vt to neutralize; (*anular*) to counteract

neutro, -a ['newtru, a] adj (LING) neuter; (*imparcial*) neutral

nevar [ne'va*] vi to snow; **nevasca** [ne'vaʃka] f snowstorm; **neve** ['nɛvi] f snow

névoa ['nɛvoa] f fog; **nevoeiro** [nevo'ejru] m thick fog

nexo ['nɛksu] m connection, link; **sem ~** disconnected, incoherent

Nicarágua [nika'ragwa] f: **a ~** Nicaragua

nicotina [niko'tʃina] f nicotine

Nigéria [ni'ʒerja] f: **a ~** Nigeria

Nilo ['nilu] m: **o ~** the Nile

ninguém [nĩ'gẽj] pron nobody, no-one

ninho ['niɲu] m nest; (*toca*) lair; (*lar*) home

nisso ['nisu] = em + isso

nisto ['niʃtu] = em + isto

nitidez [nitʃi'deʒ] f (*clareza*) clarity; (*brilho*) brightness; (*imagem*) sharpness

nítido, -a ['nitʃidu, a] adj clear, distinct; (*brilhante*) bright; (*imagem*) sharp, clear

nível ['nivew] (pl **-eis**) m level; (fig: *padrão*) standard; (: *ponto*) point, pitch; **~ de vida** standard of living

no [nu] = em + o

-no [nu] pron him; (*coisa*) it

n° abr (= *número*) no

nó [nɔ] m knot; (de uma *questão*) crux; **~s dos dedos** knuckles; **dar um ~** to tie a knot

nobre ['nɔbri] adj, m/f noble; **horário ~** prime time; **nobreza** [no'breza] f nobility

noção [no'sãw] (pl **-ões**) f notion; **noções** fpl (*rudimentos*) rudiments, basics; **~ vaga** inkling; **não ter a menor ~ de algo** not to have the slightest idea about sth

nocaute [no'kawtʃi] m knockout ♦ adv: **pôr alguém ~** to knock sb out

nocivo, -a [no'sivu, a] adj harmful

noções [no'sõjʃ] fpl de **noção**

nocturno, -a [no'tuxnu, a] (PT) adj = **noturno**

nódoa ['nɔdwa] f spot; (*mancha*) stain

nogueira [no'gejra] f (*árvore*) walnut tree; (*madeira*) walnut

noite ['nojtʃi] f night; **à** ou **de ~** at night, in the evening; **boa ~** good evening; (*despedida*) good night; **da ~ para o dia** overnight; **tarde da ~** late at night

noivado [noj'vadu] m engagement

noivo, -a ['nojvu, a] m/f (*prometido*) fiancé(e); (no *casamento*) bridegroom/bride; **os ~s** mpl the engaged couple; (no *casamento*) the bride and groom; (*recém-casados*) the newlyweds

nojento, -a [no'ʒẽtu, a] adj disgusting

nojo ['noʒu] m nausea; (*repulsão*) disgust, loathing; **ela é um ~** she's horrible; **este trabalho está um ~** this work is messy

no-la(s) = nos + a(s)

no-lo(s) = nos + o(s)

nome ['nɔmi] m name; (*fama*) fame; **de ~** by name; **escritor de ~** famous

writer; **um restaurante de ~ a**
restaurant with a good reputation;
em ~ de in the name of; **~ de
batismo** Christian name

nomeação [nomja'sãw] (pl **-ões**) f
nomination; (para um cargo) appointment

nomear [no'mja*] vt to nominate,
(conferir um cargo a) to appoint;
(dar nome a) to name

nominal [nomi'naw] (pl **-ais**) adj
nominal

nono, -a ['nonu, a] num ninth

nora ['nɔra] f daughter-in-law

nordeste [nox'dɛʃtʃi] m, adj northeast

norma ['nɔxma] f standard, norm;
(regra) rule; **como ~** as a rule

normal [nox'maw] (pl **-ais**) adj normal; (habitual) usual; **normalizar**
[noxmali'za*] vt to bring back to
normal; **normalizar-se** vr to
return to normal

noroeste [nor'wɛʃtʃi] adj northwest, northwestern ♦ m northwest

norte ['nɔxtʃi] adj northern, north;
(vento, direção) northerly ♦ m north;
norte-americano, -a adj, m/f
(North) American

Noruega [nor'wega] f Norway;
norueguês, -esa [norwe'geʃ,
geza] adj, m/f Norwegian ♦ m (LING)
Norwegian

nos [nuʃ] = **em** + **os** pron (direto) us;
(indireto) us, to us, for us; (reflexivo)
(to) ourselves; (recíproco) (to) each
other

-nos [nuʃ] pron them

nós [nɔʃ] pron we; (depois de prep)
us; **~ mesmos** we ourselves

nosso, -a ['nɔsu, a] adj our ♦ pron
ours; **um amigo ~** a friend of ours;
Nossa Senhora (REL) Our Lady

nostalgia [noʃtaw'ʒia] f nostalgia;
(saudades da pátria etc) homesick-

ness; **nostálgico, -a** [noʃ'tawʒiku,
a] adj nostalgic; homesick

nota ['nɔta] f note; (EDUC) mark;
(conta) bill; (cédula) banknote; **~
de venda** sales receipt; **~ fiscal** receipt

notar [no'ta*] vt to notice, note;
notar-se vr to be obvious; **fazer ~**
to call attention to; **notável**
[no'tavew] (pl **-eis**) adj notable,
remarkable

notícia [no'tʃisja] f (uma ~) piece of
news; (TV etc) news item; **~s** fpl
(informações) news sg; **pedir ~s de**
to inquire about; **ter ~s de** to hear
from; **noticiário** [notʃi'sjarju] m
(de jornal) news section; (CINEMA)
newsreel; (TV, RÁDIO) news bulletin

notoriedade [notorje'dadʒi] f renown, fame

notório, -a [no'tɔrju, a] adj wellknown

noturno, -a [no'tuxnu, a] adj nocturnal, nightly; (trabalho) night atr
♦ m (trem) night train

nova ['nɔva] f piece of news; **~s** fpl
(novidades) news sg

novamente [nova'mẽtʃi] adv again

novato, -a [no'vatu, a] adj inexperienced, raw ♦ m/f beginner, novice;
(EDUC) fresher

nove ['nɔvi] num nine

novela [no'vɛla] f short novel,
novella; (RÁDIO, TV) soap opera

novelo [no'velu] m ball of thread

novembro [no'vẽbru] (PT **N-**) m
November

noventa [no'vẽta] num ninety

novidade [novi'dadʒi] f novelty;
(notícia) piece of news; **~s** fpl (notícias) news sg

novilho, -a [no'viʎu, a] m/f young
bull/heifer

novo, -a ['novu, 'nɔva] adj new;
(jovem) young; (adicional) further;

de ~ again

noz [nɔʒ] f nut; (da nogueira) walnut; ~ **moscada** nutmeg

nu, a [nu, 'nua] adj naked; (arvore, sala, parede) bare ♦ m nude

nublado, -a [nu'bladu, a] adj cloudy, overcast

nuca ['nuka] f nape (of the neck)

nuclear [nu'klja*] adj nuclear

núcleo ['nuklju] m nucleus sg; (centro) centre (BRIT), center (US)

nudez [nu'deʒ] f nakedness, nudity; (de paredes etc) bareness

nudista [nu'dʒiʃta] adj, m/f nudist

nulo, -a ['nulu, a] adj (JUR) null, void; (nenhum) non-existent; (sem valor) worthless; (esforço) vain, useless

num [nũ] = em + um

numa(s) ['numa(ʃ)] = em + uma(s)

numeral [nume'raw] (pl -ais) m numeral

numerar [nume'ra*] vt to number

numérico, -a [nu'mɛriku, a] adj numerical

número ['numeru] m number; (de jornal) issue; (TEATRO etc) act; (de sapatos, roupa) size; **sem ~** countless; **~ de matrícula** registration (BRIT) ou license plate (US) number; **numeroso, -a** [nume'rozu, ɔza] adj numerous

nunca ['nũka] adv never; **~ mais** never again; **quase ~** hardly ever; **mais que ~** more than ever

nuns [nũʃ] = em + uns

núpcias ['nupsjaʃ] fpl nuptials, wedding sg

nutrição [nutri'sãw] f nutrition

nutritivo, -a [nutri'tʃivu, a] adj nourishing

nuvem ['nuvẽj] (pl -ns) f cloud; (de insetos) swarm

O

o, a [u, a] art def **1** the; **o livro/a mesa/os estudantes** the book/table/students

2 (com n abstrato: não se traduz): **o amor/a juventude** love/youth

3 (posse: traduz-se muitas vezes por adj possessivo): **quebrar o braço** to break one's arm; **ele levantou a mão** he put his hand up; **ela colocou o chapéu** she put her hat on

4 (valor descritivo): **ter a boca grande/os olhos azuis** to have a big mouth/blue eyes

♦ pron demostrativo: **meu livro e o seu** my book and yours; **as de Pedro são melhores** Pedro's are better; **não a(s) branca(s) mas a(s) cinza(s)** not the white one(s) but the grey one(s)

♦ pron relativo: **o que** etc **1** (indef): **o(s) que quiser(em) pode(m) sair** anyone who wants to can leave; **leve o que mais gustar** take the one you like best

2 (def): **o que comprei ontem** the one I bought yesterday; **os que sairam** those who left

3: **o que** what; **o que eu acho/mais gosto** what I think/like most

♦ pron pessoal **1** (pessoa: m): him; (: f) her; (: pl) them; **não posso vê-lo(s)** I can't see him/them; **vemo-los todas as semanas** we/them see her every week

2 (animal, coisa: sg) it; (: pl) them; **não posso vê-lo/s** I can't see it/them; **acharam-nos na praia** they found us on the beach

obedecer [obede'se*] vi: **~ a** to obey; **obediência** [obe'dʒēsja] f obedience; **obediente** [obe'dʒetʃi] *adj* obedient

óbito ['ɔbitu] *m* death; **atestado de ~** death certificate

objeção [obʒe'sãw] (*PT* -cç-; *pl* -ões) *f* objection; **fazer** *ou* **pôr objeções a** to object to

objetivo, -a [obʒe'tʃivu, a] (*PT* -ct-) *adj* objective ♦ *m* objective

objeto [ob'ʒetu] (*PT* -ct-) *m* object

oblíquo, -a [o'blikwu, a] *adj* oblique; (*olhar*) sidelong

obra ['ɔbra] *f* work; (*ARQ*) building, construction; (*TEATRO*) play; **em ~s** under repair; **ser ~ de alguém/algo** to be the work of sb/the result of sth; **~ de arte** work of art; **~s públicas** public works; **obra-prima** (*pl* **obras-primas**) *f* masterpiece

obrigação [obriga'sãw] (*pl* -ões) *f* obligation; (*COM*) bond

obrigado, -a [obri'gadu, a] *adj* obliged, compelled ♦ *excl* thank you; (*recusa*) no, thank you

obrigar [obri'ga*] *vt* to oblige, compel; **obrigar-se** *vr*: **~-se a fazer algo** to undertake to do sth; **obrigatório, -a** [obriga'tɔrju, a] *adj* compulsory, obligatory

obsceno, -a [obi'srnu, a] *adj* obscene

obscurecer [obiʃkure'se*] *vt* to darken; (*entendimento, verdade etc*) to obscure ♦ *vi* to get dark; **obscuro, -a** [obi'ʃkuru, a] *adj* dark; (*fig*) obscure

observação [obisexva'sãw] (*pl* -ões) *f* observation; (*comentário*) remark, comment; (*de leis, regras*) observance

observador, a [obisexva'do*, a] *m/f* observer

observar [obisex'va*] *vt* to observe; (*notar*) to notice; **~ algo a alguém** to point sth out to sb

observatório [obisexva'tɔrju] *m* observatory

obsessão [obise'sãw] (*pl* -ões) *f* obsession; **obsessivo, -a** [obise-'sivu, a] *adj* obsessive

obsoleto, -a [obiso'letu, a] *adj* obsolete

obstáculo [obi'ʃtakulu] *m* obstacle; (*dificuldade*) hindrance, drawback

obstinado, -a [obiʃtʃi'nadu, a] *adj* obstinate, stubborn

obstrução [obiʃtru'sãw] (*pl* -ões) *f* obstruction; **obstruir** [obi'ʃtrwi*] *vt* to obstruct; (*impedir*) to impede

obter [obi'te*] (*irreg: como* **ter**) *vt* to obtain, get; (*alcançar*) to gain

obturação [obitura'sãw] (*pl* -ões) *f* (*de dente*) filling

obtuso, -a [obi'tuzu, a] *adj* (*ger*) obtuse; (*fig: pessoa*) thick

óbvio, -a ['ɔbvju, a] *adj* obvious; **(é) ~!** of course!

ocasião [oka'zjãw] (*pl* -ões) *f* opportunity, chance; (*momento, tempo*) occasion; **ocasionar** [okazjo'na*] *vt* to cause, bring about

oceano [o'sjanu] *m* ocean

ocidental [osidẽ'taw] (*pl* -ais) *adj* western ♦ *m/f* westerner

ocidente [osi'dẽtʃi] *m* west

ócio ['ɔsju] *m* (*lazer*) leisure; (*inação*) idleness; **ocioso, -a** [o'sjozu, ɔza] *adj* idle; (*vaga*) unfilled

oco, -a ['oku, a] *adj* hollow, empty

ocorrência [oko'xẽsja] *f* incident, event; (*circunstância*) circumstance

ocorrer [oko'xe*] *vi* to happen, occur; (*vir ao pensamento*) to come to mind; **~ a alguém** to happen to sb; to occur to sb

oculista [oku'liʃta] *m/f* optician

óculo ['ɔkulu] *m* spyglass; **~s** *mpl* (*para ver melhor*) glasses, spectacles; **~s de proteção** goggles

ocultar [okuw'ta*] vt to hide, conceal; **oculto, -a** [o'kuwtu, a] adj hidden; (desconhecido) unknown; (secreto) secret; (sobrenatural) occult

ocupação [okupa'sãw] (pl **-ões**) f occupation

ocupado, -a [oku'padu, a] adj (pessoa) busy; (lugar) taken, occupied; (BR: telefone) engaged (BRIT), busy (US); **sinal de ~** (BR: TEL) engaged tone (BRIT), busy signal (US)

ocupar [oku'pa*] vt to occupy; (tempo) to take up; (pessoa) to keep busy; **ocupar-se** vr: **~-se com** ou **de** ou **em algo** (dedicar-se a) to deal with sth; (cuidar de) to look after sth; (passar seu tempo com) to occupy o.s. with sth

odiar [o'dʒja*] vt to hate; **ódio** ['ɔdʒju] m hate, hatred; **odioso, -a** [o'dʒjozu, ɔza] adj hateful

odor [o'do*] m smell

oeste ['wɛʃtʃi] m west ♦ adj inv (região) western; (direção, vento) westerly

ofegante [ofe'gãtʃi] adj breathless, panting

ofender [ofẽ'de*] vt to offend; **ofender-se** vr: **~-se (com)** to take offence (BRIT) ou offense (US) (at)

ofensa [o'fẽsa] f insult; (à lei, moral) offence (BRIT), offense (US); **ofensiva** [ofẽ'siva] f offensive; **ofensivo, -a** [ofẽ'sivu, a] adj offensive

oferecer [ofere'se*] vt to offer; (dar) to give; (jantar) to give; (propor) to propose; (dedicar) to dedicate; **oferecer-se** vr (pessoa) to offer o.s., volunteer; (oportunidade) to present itself, arise; **~-se para fazer** to offer to do; **oferecimento** [oferesi'mẽtu] m offer; **oferta** [o'fɛxta] f offer; (dádiva) gift; (COM)

bid; (em loja) special offer

oficial [ofi'sjaw] (pl **-ais**) adj official ♦ m/f official; (MIL) officer; **~ de justiça** bailiff

oficina [ofi'sina] f workshop; **~ mecânica** garage

ofício [o'fisju] m profession, trade; (REL) service; (carta) official letter; (função) function; (encargo) job, task

oitavo, -a [oj'tavu, a] num eighth

oitenta [oj'tẽta] num eighty

oito ['ojtu] num eight

olá [o'la] excl hello!

olaria [ola'ria] f (fábrica: de louças de barro) pottery; (: de tijolos) brickworks sg

óleo ['ɔlju] m (lubricante) oil; **~ diesel/de bronzear** diesel/suntan oil; **oleoso, -a** [o'ljozu, ɔza] adj oily; (gorduroso) greasy

olfato [ow'fatu] m sense of smell

olhada [o'ʎada] f glance, look; **dar uma ~** to have a look

olhadela [oʎa'dɛla] f peep

olhar [o'ʎa*] vt to look at; (observar) to watch; (ponderar) to consider; (cuidar de) to look after ♦ vi to look ♦ m look; **olhar-se** vr to look at o.s.; (duas pessoas) to look at each other; **~ fixamente** to stare at; **~ para** to look at; **~ por** to look after; **~ fixo** stare

olho ['oʎu] m (ANAT, de agulha) eye; (vista) eyesight; **~ nele!** watch him!; **~ vivo!** keep your eyes open!; **a ~** (medir, calcular etc) by eye; **~ mágico** (na porta) peephole; **~ roxo** black eye; **num abrir e fechar de ~s** in a flash

olimpíada [olĩ'piada] f: **as O~s** the Olympics

oliveira [oli'vejra] f olive tree

ombro [' õbru] m shoulder; **encolher os ~s, dar de ~s** to shrug one's shoulders

omeleta [ome'lɛta] (*PT*) f = **omelete**

omelete [ome'letʃi] (*BR*) f omelette (*BRIT*), omelet (*US*)

omissão [omi'sāw] (*pl* -**ões**) f omission; (*negligência*) negligence

omitir [omi'tʃiʀ*] vt to omit

omoplata [omo'plata] f shoulder blade

onça ['ōsa] f ounce; (*animal*) jaguar

onda ['ōda] f wave; (*moda*) fashion; ~ **curta/média/longa** short/medium/long wave; ~ **de calor** heat wave

onde ['ōdʒi] *adv* where ♦ *conj* where, in which; **de ~ você é?** where are you from?; **por** ~ through which; **por** ~? which way?; ~ **quer que** wherever

ondulado, -a [ōdu'ladu, a] *adj* wavy

ônibus ['onibuʃ] (*BR*) m *inv* bus; **ponto de** ~ bus-stop

ontem ['ōtē] *adv* yesterday; ~ **à noite** last night

ONU ['onu] *abr* f (= *Organização das Nações Unidas*) UNO

ônus ['onuʃ] m *inv* onus; (*obrigação*) obligation; (*COM*) charge; (*encargo desagradável*) burden

onze ['ōzi] *num* eleven

opaco, -a [o'paku, a] *adj* opaque; (*obscuro*) dark

opção [op'sãw] (*pl* -**ões**) f option, choice; (*preferência*) first claim, right

OPEP [o'pɛpi] *abr* f (= *Organização dos Países Exportadores de Petróleo*) OPEC

ópera ['ɔpera] f opera

operação [opera'sāw] (*pl* -**ões**) f operation; (*COM*) transaction

operador, a [opera'do*, a] m/f operator; (*cirurgião*) surgeon; (*num cinema*) projectionist

operar [ope'ra*] vt to operate; (*produzir*) to effect, bring about; (*MED*) to operate on ♦ vi to operate; (*agir*) to act, function; **operar-se** vr (*suceder*) to take place; (*MED*) to have an operation

operário, -a [ope'rarju, a] *adj* working ♦ m/f worker; **classe operária** working class

opinar [opi'na*] vt to think ♦ vi to give one's opinion

opinião [opi'njāw] (*pl* -**ões**) f opinion; **mudar de** ~ to change one's mind

oponente [opo'nētʃi] *adj* opposing ♦ m/f opponent

opor [o'po*] (*irreg: como* **pôr**) vt to oppose; (*resistência*) to put up, offer; (*objeção, dificuldade*) to raise; **opor-se** vr: ~-**se a** to object to; (*resistir*) to oppose

oportunidade [opoxtuni'dadʒi] f opportunity

oportunista [opoxtu'niʃta] *adj, m/f* opportunist

oportuno, -a [opox'tunu, a] *adj* (*momento*) opportune, right; (*oferta de ajuda*) well-timed; (*conveniente*) convenient, suitable

oposição [opozi'sāw] f opposition; **em** ~ **a** against; **fazer** ~ **a** to oppose

oposto, -a [o'poʃtu, 'pɔʃta] *adj* opposite; (*em frente*) facing; (*opiniões*) opposing ♦ m opposite

opressão [opre'sāw] (*pl* -**ões**) f oppression; **opressivo, -a** [opre'sivu, a] *adj* oppressive

oprimir [opri'mi*] vt to oppress; (*comprimir*) to press

optar [op'ta*] vi to choose; ~ **por** to opt for; ~ **por fazer** to opt to do

óptico, -a *etc* ['ɔtiku, a] (*PT*) = **ótico** *etc*

óptimo, -a *etc* ['ɔtimu, a] (*PT*) *adj* = **ótimo** *etc*

ora ['ɔra] *adv* now ♦ *conj* well; **por ~** for the time being; **por ~ ..., ~ ...** one moment ..., the next ...; **~ bem** now then

oração [ora'sãw] (*pl* **-ões**) *f* prayer; (*discurso*) speech; (*LING*) clause

oral [o'raw] (*pl* **-ais**) *adj* oral ♦ *f* oral (exam)

orar [o'ra*] *vi* (*REL*) to pray

órbita ['ɔxbita] *f* orbit; (*do olho*) socket

Órcades ['ɔxkadʒiʃ] *fpl*: **as ~** the Orkneys

orçamento [oxsa'mẽtu] *m* (*do estado etc*) budget; (*avaliação*) estimate

orçar [ox'sa*] *vt* to value, estimate ♦ *vi*: **~ em** (*gastos etc*) to be valued at, be put at

ordem ['ɔxdẽ] (*pl* **-ns**) *f* order; **até nova ~** until further notice; **de primeira ~** first-rate; **estar em ~** to be tidy; **por ~** in order, in turn; **~ do dia** agenda; **~ pública** public order, law and order

ordenado, -a [oxde'nadu, a] *adj* (*posto em ordem*) in order; (*metódico*) orderly ♦ *m* salary, wages *pl*

ordens ['ɔxdẽʃ] *fpl de* **ordem**

ordinário, -a [oxdʒi'narju, a] *adj* ordinary; (*comum*) usual; (*mediocre*) mediocre; (*grosseiro*) coarse, vulgar; (*de má qualidade*) inferior; **de ~** usually

orelha [o'reʎa] *f* ear; (*aba*) flap

órfã ['ɔxfã] *f de* **órfão**

órfão, -fã ['ɔxfãw, fã] (*pl* **~s**) *adj, m/f* orphan

orgânico, -a [ox'ganiku, a] *adj* organic

organismo [oxga'niʒmu] *m* organism; (*entidade*) organization

organização [oxganiza'sãw] (*pl* **-ões**) *f* organization; **organizar** [oxgani'za*] *vt* to organize

órgão ['ɔxgãw] (*pl* **~s**) *m* organ; (*governamental etc*) institution,

body

orgasmo [ox'gaʒmu] *m* orgasm

orgia [ox'ʒia] *f* orgy

orgulho [ox'guʎu] *m* pride; (*arrogância*) arrogance; **orgulhoso, -a** [oxgu'ʎozu, ɔza] *adj* proud; haughty

orientação [orjẽta'sãw] *f* direction; (*posição*) position; **~ educacional** training, guidance

oriental [orjẽ'taw] (*pl* **-ais**) *adj* eastern; (*do Extremo Oriente*) oriental

orientar [orjẽ'ta*] *vt* to orientate; (*indicar o rumo*) to direct; (*aconselhar*) to guide; **orientar-se** *vr* to get one's bearings; **~-se por algo** to follow sth

oriente [o'rjẽtʃi] *m*: **o O~** the East; **Extremo O~** Far East; **O~ Médio** Middle East

origem [o'riʒẽ] (*pl* **-ns**) *f* origin; (*ascendência*) lineage, descent; **lugar de ~** birthplace

original [oriʒi'naw] (*pl* **-ais**) *adj* original; (*estranho*) strange, odd ♦ *m* original; **originalidade** [oriʒinali'dadʒi] *f* originality; (*excentricidade*) eccentricity

originar [oriʒi'na*] *vt* to give rise to, start; **originar-se** *vr* to arise; **~-se de** to originate from

oriundo, -a [o'rjũdu, a] *adj*: **~ de** arising from; (*natural*) native of

orla ['ɔxla] *f*: **~ marítima** seafront

ornamento [oxna'mẽtu] *m* adornment, decoration

orquestra [ox'kɛʃtra] (*PT* **-esta**) *f* orchestra

orquídea [ox'kidʒja] *f* orchid

ortodoxo, -a [oxto'dɔksu, a] *adj* orthodox

ortografia [oxtogra'fia] *f* spelling

orvalho [ox'vaʎu] *m* dew

os [uʃ] *art def* V **o**

osso ['osu] *m* bone

ostensivo, -a [oʃtẽˈsivu, a] *adj* ostensible

ostentar [oʃtẽˈta*] *vt* to show; *(alardear)* to show off, flaunt

ostra [ˈoʃtra] *f* oyster

OTAN [ˈotã] *abr f* (= *Organização do Tratado do Atlântico Norte*) NATO

ótica [ˈɔtʃika] *f* optics *sg*; *(loja)* optician's; *(fig: ponto de vista)* viewpoint; *V tb* **ótico**

ótico, -a [ˈɔtʃiku, a] *adj* optical ♦ *m/f* optician

otimista [otʃiˈmiʃta] *adj* optimistic ♦ *m/f* optimist

ótimo, -a [ˈɔtʃimu, a] *adj* excellent, splendid ♦ *excl* great!, super!

ou [o] *conj* or; **~ este ~ aquele** either this one or that one; **~ seja** in other words

ouço *etc* [ˈosu] *vb* V **ouvir**

ouriço [oˈrisu] *m* (*europeu*) hedgehog; *(casca)* shell

ouro [ˈoru] *m* gold; **~s** *mpl* (CARTAS) diamonds

ousadia [ozaˈdʒia] *f* daring; **ousado, -a** [oˈzadu, a] *adj* daring, bold

ousar [oˈza*] *vt, vi* to dare

outono [oˈtonu] *m* autumn

PALAVRA CHAVE

outro, -a [ˈotru, a] *adj* **1** (*distinto: sg*) another; (: *pl*) other; **outra coisa** something else; **de ~ modo**, **de outra maneira** otherwise; **no ~ dia** the next day; **ela está outra** (*mudança*) she's changed

2 (*adicional*): **traga-me ~ café, por favor** can I have another coffee, please?; **outra vez** again

♦ *pron* **1** o **~** the other one; **(os) ~s** (the) others; **de ~** somebody else's

2 (*recíproco*): **odeiam-se uns aos ~s** they hate one another *ou* each other

3: **~ tanto** the same again; **comer ~**

---

tanto to eat the same *ou* as much again; **ele recebeu uma dezena de telegramas e outras tantas chamadas** he got about ten telegrams and as many calls

outubro [oˈtubru] (*PT* **O-**) *m* October

ouvido [oˈvidu] *m* (ANAT) ear; (*sentido*) hearing; **de ~** by ear; **dar ~s a** to listen to

ouvinte [oˈvĩtʃi] *m/f* listener; (*estudante*) auditor

ouvir [oˈvi*] *vt* to hear; (*com atenção*) to listen to; (*missa*) to attend ♦ *vi* to hear; to listen; **~ dizer que ...** to hear that ...; **~ falar de** to hear of

ova [ˈɔva] *f* roe

oval [oˈvaw] (*pl* **-ais**) *adj, f* oval

ovário [oˈvarju] *m* ovary

ovelha [oˈveʎa] *f* sheep

óvni [ˈɔvni] *m* UFO

ovo [ˈovu] *m* egg; **~s de granja** free-range eggs; **~ pochê** (BR) *ou* **escalfado** (PT) poached egg; **~ estrelado** *ou* **frito** fried egg; **~s mexidos** scrambled eggs; **~ quente/cozido duro** hard-boiled/soft-boiled egg

oxidar [oksiˈda*] *vt* to rust; **oxidar-se** *vr* to rust, go rusty

oxigenado, -a [oksiʒeˈnadu, a] *adj* (*cabelo*) bleached; **água oxigenada** peroxide

oxigênio [oksiˈʒenju] *m* oxygen

ozônio [oˈzonju] *m* ozone; **camada de ~** ozone layer

P

P. *abr* (= *Praça*) Sq.

p.a. *abr* (= *por ano*) p.a.

pá [pa] *f* shovel; (*de remo, hélice*) blade ♦ *m* (PT) pal, mate; **~ de lixo** dustpan

paca ['paka] f (ZOOL) paca

pacato, -a [pa'katu, a] adj (pessoa) quiet; (lugar) peaceful

paciência [pa'sjēsja] f patience; **paciente** [pa'sjētʃi] adj, m/f patient

pacífico, -a [pa'sifiku, a] adj (pessoa) peace-loving; (aceito sem discussão) undisputed; (sossegado) peaceful; **o (Oceano) P~** the Pacific (Ocean)

pacote [pa'kɔtʃi] m packet; (embrulho) parcel; (ECON, COMPUT, TURISMO) package

pacto ['paktu] m pact; (ajuste) agreement

padaria [pada'ria] f bakery, baker's (shop)

padeiro [pa'dejru] m baker

padíola [pa'dʒɔla] f stretcher

padrão [pa'drãw] (pl -ões) m standard; (medida) gauge; (desenho) pattern; (fig: modelo) model; **~ de vida** standard of living

padrasto [pa'draʃtu] m stepfather

padre ['padri] m priest

padrinho [pa'driɲu] m godfather; (de noivo) best man; (patrono) sponsor

padroeiro, -a [pa'drwejru, a] m/f patron; (santo) patron saint

padrões [pa'drõjʃ] mpl de **padrão**

pães [pãjʃ] mpl de **pão**

pagã [pa'gã] f de **pagão**

pagador, -a [paga'do*, a] adj paying ♦ m/f payer; (de salário) pay clerk; (de banco) teller

pagamento [paga'mētu] m payment; **~ a prazo** ou **em prestações** payment in instal(l)ments; **~ à vista** cash payment; **~ contra entrega** (COM) COD, cash on delivery

pagão, -gã [pa'gãw, gã] (pl -s, -s) adj, m/f pagan

pagar [pa'ga*] vt to pay; (compras, pecados) to pay for; (o que devia) to

pay back; (retribuir) to repay ♦ v to pay; **~ por algo** (tb fig) to pay for sth; **~ a prestações** to pay in instal(l)ments; **~ de contado** (PT) to pay cash

página ['paʒina] f page

pago, -a ['pagu, a] pp de **pagar** ♦ adj paid; (fig) even ♦ m pay

pai [paj] m father; **~s** mpl parents

painel [paj'nɛw] (pl -éis) m panel; (quadro) picture; (AUTO) dashboard; (de avião) instrument panel

país [pa'jiʃ] m country; (região) land; **~ natal** native land

paisagem [paj'zaʒē] (pl -ns) f scenery, landscape

paisano, -a [paj'zanu, a] adj civilian ♦ m/f (não militar) civilian; (compatriota) fellow countryman

Países Baixos mpl: **os ~** the Netherlands

paixão [paj'ʃãw] (pl -ões) f passion

palácio [pa'lasju] m palace; **~ da justiça** courthouse; **~ do Planalto** see boxed note

---

PALÁCIO DO PLANALTO

Palácio do Planalto is the seat of the Brazilian government, in Brasília. The name comes from the fact that the Brazilian capital is situated on a plateau. It has come to be a byword for central government.

---

paladar [pala'da*] m taste; (ANAT) palate

palafita [pala'fita] f (estacaria) stilts; pl; (habitação) stilt house

palavra [pa'lavra] f word; (fala) speech; (promessa) promise; (direito de falar) right to speak; **dar a ~ a alguém** to give sb the chance to speak; **ter ~** (pessoa) to be reliable; **~s cruzadas** crossword (puzzle) sg

palavrão [pala'vrãw] (pl -ões) m swearword

palco ['palku] m (TEATRO) stage; (fig: local) scene

Palestina [palef'tʃina] f: **a ~** Palestine; **palestino, -a** [palef'tʃinu, a] adj, m/f Palestinian

palestra [pa'lɛʃtra] f chat, talk; (conferência) lecture

paletó [pale'tɔ] m jacket

palha ['paʎa] f straw

palhaço [pa'ʎasu] m clown

pálido, -a ['palidu, a] adj pale

palito [pa'litu] m stick; (para os dentes) toothpick

palma ['pawma] f (folha) palm leaf; (da mão) palm; **bater ~s** to clap; **palmada** [paw'mada] f slap

palmeira [paw'mejra] f palm tree

palmo ['pawmu] m span; **~ a ~** inch by inch

palpável [paw'pavew] (pl -eis) adj tangible; (fig) obvious

pálpebra ['pawpebra] f eyelid

palpitação [pawpita'sãw] (pl -ões) f beating, throbbing; **palpitações** fpl (batimentos cardíacos) palpitations

palpitante [pawpi'tãtʃi] adj beating, throbbing; (fig: emocionante) thrilling; (: de interesse atual) sensational

palpitar [pawpi'ta*] vi (coração) to beat

palpite [paw'pitʃi] m (intuição) hunch; (JOGO, TURFE) tip; (opinião) opinion

pampa ['pãpa] f pampas

Panamá [pana'ma] m: **o ~** Panama, the Panama Canal

pancada [pã'kada] f (no corpo) blow, hit; (choque) knock; (de relógio) stroke; **dar ~ em alguém** to hit sb; **pancadaria** [pãkada'ria] f (surra) beating; (tumulto) fight

pandeiro [pã'dejru] m tambourine

pane ['pani] f breakdown

panela [pa'nɛla] f (de barro) pot; (de metal) pan; (de cozinhar) saucepan; (no dente) hole; **~ de pressão** pressure cooker

panfleto [pã'fletu] m pamphlet

pânico ['paniku] m panic; **entrar em ~** to panic

pano ['panu] m cloth; (TEATRO) curtain; (vela) sheet, sail; **~ de pratos** tea-towel; **~ de pó** duster; **~ de fundo** (tb fig) backdrop

panorama [pano'rama] m view

panqueca [pã'kɛka] f pancake

pantanal [pãta'naw] (pl -ais) m swampland

pântano ['pãtanu] m marsh, swamp

pantera [pã'tera] f panther

pão [pãw] (pl pães) m bread; **o P~ de Açúcar** (no Rio) Sugarloaf Mountain; **~ torrado** toast; **pãoduro** (pl pães-duros) (col) adj mean, stingy ♦ m/f miser; **pãozinho** [pãw'ziɲu] m roll

papa ['papa] m Pope; (mingau) porridge

papagaio [papa'gaju] m parrot; (pipa) kite

papai [pa'paj] m dad, daddy; **P~ Noel** Santa Claus, Father Christmas

papel [pa'pew] (pl -éis) m paper; (TEATRO, função) role; **~ de embrulho/de escrever/de alumínio** wrapping paper/writing paper/tinfoil; **~ higiênico/usado** toilet/waste paper; **~ de parede/de seda/transparente** wallpaper/tissue paper/tracing paper; **papelada** [pape-'lada] f pile of papers; (burocracia) paperwork, red tape; **papelão** [pape'lãw] m cardboard; (fig) fiasco; **papelaria** [papela'ria] f stationer's (shop); **papel-carbono** m carbon paper

papo ['papu] (col) m (conversa) chat; **bater** ou **levar um ~** (col) to have a chat; **ficar de ~ para o ar** (fig) to laze around

paquerar [pake'ra*] (col) vi to flirt ♦ vt to chat up

paquistanês, -esa [pakiʃta'neʃ, eza] adj, m/f Pakistani

Paquistão [pakiʃ'tãw] m: **o ~** Pakistan

par [pa*] adj (igual) equal; (número) even ♦ m pair; (casal) couple; (pessoa na dança) partner; **~ a ~** side by side, level; **sem ~** incomparable

para ['para] prep for; (direção) to, towards; **~ que** so that, in order that; **~ quê?** what for?, why?; **ir ~ casa** to go home; **~ com** (atitude) towards; **de lá ~ cá** since then; **~ a semana** next week; **estar ~** to be about to; **é ~ nós ficarmos aqui?** should we stay here?

parabéns [para'bẽjʃ] mpl congratulations; (no aniversário) happy birthday; **dar ~ a** to congratulate

pára-brisa ['para-] (pl **~s**) m windscreen (BRIT), windshield (US)

pára-choque ['para-] (pl **~s**) m (AUTO) bumper

parada [pa'rada] f stop; (COM) stoppage; (militar, colegial) parade

parado, -a [pa'radu, a] adj (imóvel) standing still; (sem vida) lifeless; (carro) stationary; (máquina) out of action; (olhar) fixed; (trabalhador, fábrica) idle

paradoxo [para'dɔksu] m paradox

parafuso [para'fuzu] m screw

paragem [pa'raʒẽ] (pl **-ns**) f stop; paragens pl (lugares) places, parts; **~ de eléctrico** (PT) tram (BRIT) ou streetcar (US) stop

parágrafo [pa'ragrafu] m paragraph

Paraguai [para'gwaj] m: **o ~** Paraguay; **paraguaio, -a** [para'gwaju, a] adj, m/f Paraguayan

paraíso [para'izu] m paradise

pára-lama ['para-] (pl **~s**) m wing (BRIT), fender (US); (de bicicleta) mudguard

paralelepípedo [paralele'pipedu] m paving stone

paralelo, -a [para'lɛlu, a] adj parallel

paralisar [parali'za*] vt to paralyse; (trabalho) to bring to a standstill; **paralisar-se** vr to become paralysed; (fig) to come to a standstill; **paralisia** [parali'zia] f paralysis

paranóico, -a [para'nɔjku, a] adj, m/f paranoid

parapeito [para'pejtu] m wall, parapet; (da janela) windowsill

pára-quedas ['para-] m inv parachute; **pára-quedista** [parake-'dʒiʃta] m/f parachutist ♦ m (MIL) paratrooper

parar [pa'ra*] vi to stop; (ficar) to stay ♦ vt to stop; **fazer ~** (deter) to stop; **~ na cadeia** to end up in jail; **~ de fazer** to stop doing

pára-raios ['para-] m inv lightning conductor

parasita [para'zita] m parasite

parceiro, -a [pax'sejru, a] adj, matching ♦ m/f partner

parcela [pax'sɛla] f piece, bit; (de pagamento) instalment (BRIT), installment (US); (de terra) plot; (de eleitorado etc) section; (MAT) item

parceria [paxse'ria] f partnership

parcial [pax'sjaw] (pl **-ais**) adj, partial; (feito por partes) in parts; (pessoa) bias(s)ed; (POL) partisan; **parcialidade** [paxsjali'dadʒi] f bias, partiality

pardal [pax'daw] (*pl* **-ais**) *m* sparrow

pardieiro [pax'dʒjejru] *m* ruin, heap

pardo, -a ['paxdu, a] *adj* (*cinzento*) grey (*BRIT*), gray (*US*); (*castanho*) brown; (*mulato*) mulatto

parecer [pare'se*] *m, vi* (*ter a aparência de*) to look, seem; **parecer-se** *vr*: ~**-se com alguém** to look like sb; ~ **(com)** (*ter semelhança com*) to look (like); **ao que parece** apparently; **parece-me que** I think that, it seems to me that; **que lhe parece?** what do you think?; **parece que** it looks as if

parecido, -a [pare'sidu, a] *adj* alike, similar; ~ **com** like

parede [pa'redʒi] *f* wall

parente, -a [pa'rẽtʃi] *m/f* relative, relation; **parentesco** [parẽ'teʃku] *m* relationship; (*fig*) connection

parêntese [pa'rẽtezi] *m* parenthesis; (*na escrita*) bracket; (*fig: digressão*) digression

páreo ['parju] *m* race; (*fig*) competition

parir [pa'ri*] *vt* to give birth to ♦ *vi* to give birth; (*mulher*) to have a baby

Paris [pa'riʃ] *n* Paris; **parisiense** [pari'zjẽsi] *adj*, *m/f* Parisian

parlamentar [paxlamẽ'ta*] *adj* parliamentary ♦ *m/f* member of parliament

parlamento [paxla'mẽtu] *m* parliament

paróquia [pa'rɔkja] *f* (*REL*) parish

parque ['paxki] *m* park; ~ **industrial/infantil** industrial estate/children's playground; ~ **nacional** national park

parte ['paxtʃi] *f* part; (*quinhão*) share; (*lado*) side; (*ponto*) point; (*JUR*) party; (*papel*) role; **a maior** ~ **de** most of; **à** ~ aside; (*separado*)

separate; (*separadamente*) separately; (*além de*) apart from; **da** ~ **de alguém** on sb's part; **em alguma/qualquer** ~ somewhere/anywhere; **em** ~ **alguma** nowhere; **por toda (a)** ~ everywhere; **pôr de** ~ to set aside; **tomar** ~ **em** to take part in; **dar** ~ **de alguém à polícia** to report sb to the police

participação [paxtʃisipa'sãw] *f* participation; (*COM*) stake, share; (*comunicação*) announcement, notification

participar [paxtʃisi'pa*] *vt* to announce, notify of ♦ *vi*: ~ **de** *ou* **em** to participate in, take part in; (*compartilhar*) to share in

particípio [paxtʃi'sipju] *m* participle

particular [paxtʃiku'la*] *adj* particular, special; (*privativo*, *pessoal*) private ♦ *m* particular; (*indivíduo*) individual; ~**es** *mpl* (*pormenores*) details; **em** ~ in private; **particularmente** [paxtʃikulax-'mẽtʃi] *adv* privately; (*especialmente*) particularly

partida [pax'tʃida] *f* (*saída*) departure; (*ESPORTE*) game, match

partidário, -a [paxtʃi'darju, a] *adj* supporting ♦ *m/f* supporter, follower

partido [pax'tʃidu] *m* (*POL*) party; **tirar** ~ **de** to profit from; **tomar o** ~ **de** to side with

partilhar [paxtʃi'ʎa*] *vt* to share; (*distribuir*) to share out

partir [pax'tʃi*] *vt* to break; (*dividir*) to divide, split ♦ *vi* (*pôr-se a caminho*) to set off, set out; (*ir-se embora*) to leave, depart; **partir-se** *vr* to break; **a** ~ **de** (starting) from

parto ['paxtu] *m* (child)birth; **estar em trabalho de** ~ to be in labour (*BRIT*) *ou* labor (*US*)

Páscoa ['paʃkwa] *f* Easter; (*dos judeus*) Passover

pasmo, -a ['paʒmu, a] *adj* astonished ♦ *m* amazement

passa ['pasa] *f* raisin

passadeira [pasa'dejra] *f* (*tapete*) stair carpet; (*mulher*) ironing lady; (*PT: para peões*) zebra crossing (*BRIT*), crosswalk (*US*)

passado, -a [pa'sadu, a] *adj* past; (*antiquado*) old-fashioned; (*fruta*) bad; (*peixe*) off ♦ *m* past; **o ano ~** last year; **bem/mal passado** (*carne*) well done/rare

passageiro, -a [pasa'ʒejru, a] *adj* passing ♦ *m/f* passenger

passagem [pa'saʒẽ] (*pl* **-ns**) *f* passage; (*preço de condução*) fare; (*bilhete*) ticket; **~ de ida e volta** return ticket, round trip ticket (*US*); **~ de nível** level (*BRIT*) *ou* grade (*US*) crossing; **~ de pedestres** pedestrian crossing (*BRIT*), crosswalk (*US*); **~ subterrânea** underpass, subway (*BRIT*)

passaporte [pasa'pɔxtʃi] *m* passport

passar [pa'sa*] *vt* to pass; (*exceder*) to go beyond, exceed; (*a ferro*) to iron; (*o tempo*) to spend; (*a outra pessoa*) to pass on; (*pomada*) to put on ♦ *vi* to pass; (*na rua*) to go past; (*tempo*) to go by; (*dor*) to wear off; (*terminar*) to be over; **passar-se** *vr* (*acontecer*) to go on, happen; **~ bem** (*de saúde*) to be well; **passava das dez horas** it was past ten o' clock; **~ alguém para trás** to con sb; (*cônjuge*) to cheat on sb; **~ por algo** (*sofrer*) to go through sth; (*transitar: estrada*) to go along sth; (*ser considerado como*) to be thought of as sth; **~ sem** to do without

passarela [pasa'rɛla] *f* footbridge

pássaro ['pasaru] *m* bird

passatempo [pasa'tẽpu] *m* pastime

passe ['pasi] *m* pass

passear [pa'sja*] *vt* to take for a walk ♦ *vi* (*a pé*) to go for a walk; (*sair*) to go out; **~ a cavalo** (*ou de carro*) to go for a ride; **passeata** [pa'sjata] *f* (*marcha coletiva*) protest march; **passeio** [pa'seju] *m* walk; (*de carro*) drive, ride; (*excursão*) outing; (*calçada*) pavement (*BRIT*), sidewalk (*US*); **dar um passeio** to go for a walk; (*de carro*) to go for a drive *ou* ride

passível [pa'sivew] (*pl* **-eis**) *adj*: **~ de** (*dor etc*) susceptible to; (*pena, multa*) subject to

passivo, -a [pa'sivu, a] *adj* passive ♦ *m* (*COM*) liabilities *pl*

passo ['pasu] *m* step; (*medida*) pace; (*modo de andar*) walk; (*ruído dos passos*) footstep; (*sinal de pé*) footprint; **ao ~ que** while; **ceder o ~** a to give way to

pasta ['paʃta] *f* paste; (*de couro*) briefcase; (*de cartolina*) folder; (*de ministro*) portfolio; **~ dentifrícia** *ou* **de dentes** toothpaste

pastar [paʃ'ta*] *vt* to graze ♦ *vi* to graze

pastel [paʃ'tɛw] (*pl* **-éis**) *adj inv* (*cor*) pastel ♦ *m* samosa

pastelão [paʃte'lãw] *m* slapstick

pastelaria [paʃtela'ria] *f* cake shop; (*comida*) pastry

pasteurizado, -a [paʃtewri'zadu, a] *adj* pasteurized

pastilha [paʃ'tʃiʎa] *f* (*MED*) tablet; (*doce*) pastille; (*COMPUT*) chip

pastor, a [paʃ'to*, a] *m/f* shepherd(ess) ♦ *m* (*REL*) clergyman, pastor

pata ['pata] *f* (*pé de animal*) foot, paw; (*ave*) duck; (*col: pé*) foot

patamar [pata'ma*] *m* (*de escada*)

landing; (fig) level

patente [pa'tẽtʃi] adj obvious, evident ♦ f (COM) patent

paternal [patex'naw] (pl **-ais**) adj paternal, fatherly; **paternidade** [patexni'dadʒi] f paternity; **paterno, -a** [pa'texnu, a] adj paternal, fatherly; **casa paterna** family home

pateta [pa'teta] adj stupid, daft ♦ m/f idiot

patético, -a [pa'tetʃiku, a] adj pathetic, moving

patife [pa'tʃifi] m scoundrel, rogue

patim [pa'tʃĩ] (pl **-ns**) m skate; **patins em linha** Rollerblades ®; **patins de roda** roller skates; **patinar** [patʃi'na*] vi to skate; (AUTO: derrapar) to skid

patins [pa'tʃĩʃ] mpl de **patim**

pátio ['patʃiu] m (de uma casa) patio, backyard; (espaço cercado de edifícios) courtyard; (tb: ~ de recreio) playground; (MIL) parade ground

pato [patu] m duck; (macho) drake

patologia [patolo'ʒia] f pathology; **patológico, -a** [pato'lɔʒiku, a] adj pathological

patrão [pa'trãw] (pl **-ões**) m (COM) boss; (dono de casa) master; (proprietário) landlord; (NÁUT) skipper

pátria ['patrja] f homeland

patrimônio [patri'monju] m (herança) inheritance; (fig) heritage; (bens) property

patriota [pa'trjɔta] m/f patriot

patrocinador, a [patrosina'do*, a] m/f sponsor, backer

patrocinar [patrosi'na*] vt to sponsor; (proteger) to support; **patrocínio** [patro'sinju] m sponsorship, backing; support

patrões [pa'trõjʃ] mpl de **patrão**

patrulha [pa'truʎa] f patrol; **patrulhar** [patru'ʎa*] vt, vi to patrol

pau [paw] m (madeira) wood; (vara) stick; **~s** mpl (CARTAS) clubs; **~ a ~** neck and neck; **~ de bandeira** flagpole

pausa ['pawza] f pause; (intervalo) break; (descanso) rest

pauta ['pawta] f (linha) (guide)line; (ordem do dia) agenda; (indicações) guidelines pl; **sem ~** (papel) plain; **em ~** on the agenda

pavão, -voa [pa'vãw, 'voa] (pl **-ões, ~s**) m/f peacock/peahen

pavilhão [pavi'ʎãw] (pl **-ões**) m tent; (de madeira) hut; (no jardim) summerhouse; (em exposição) pavilion; (bandeira) flag

pavimento [pavi'mẽtu] m (chão, andar) floor; (da rua) road surface

pavões [pa'võjʃ] mpl de **pavão**

pavor [pa'vo*] m dread, terror; **ter ~ de** to be terrified of; **pavoroso, -a** [pavo'rozu, ɔza] adj dreadful, terrible

paz [pajʃ] f peace; **fazer as ~es** to make up, be friends again

PC abr m = **personal computer**

Pça. abr (= **Praça**) Sq.

pé [pɛ] m foot; (da mesa) leg; (fig: base) footing; (de milho, café) plant; **ir a ~** to walk, go on foot; **ao ~ de** near, by; **ao ~ da letra** literally; **estar de ~** (festa etc) to be on; **em ou de ~** standing (up); **dar no ~** (col) to run away, take off; **não ter ~ nem cabeça** (fig) to make no sense

peão [pjãw] (PT: pl **-ões**) m pedestrian

peça ['pɛsa] f piece; (AUTO) part; (aposento) room; (TEATRO) play; **~ de reposição** spare part; **~ de roupa** garment

pecado [pe'kadu] m sin

pecar [pe'ka*] vi to sin; **~ por excesso de zelo** to be over-zealous

pechincha [pe'ʃĩʃa] f (vantagem) godsend; (coisa barata) bargain; **pechinchar** [peʃĩ'ʃa*] vi to bargain, haggle

peço etc ['pɛsu] vb V **pedir**

peculiar [peku'lja*] adj special, peculiar; (particular) particular; **peculiaridade** [pekuljari'dadʒi] f peculiarity

pedaço [pe'dasu] m piece; (fig: trecho) bit; **aos ~s** in pieces

pedágio [pe'daʒju] (BR) m (pagamento) toll

pedal [pe'daw] (pl -ais) m pedal; **pedalar** [peda'la*] vt, vi to pedal

pedante [pe'dãtʃi] adj pretentious ♦ m/f pseud

pedestre [pe'dɛʃtri] (BR) m pedestrian

pedicuro, -a [pedʒi'kuru, a] m/f chiropodist (BRIT), podiatrist (US)

pedido [pe'dʒidu] m request; (COM) order; ~ **de demissão** resignation; ~ **de desculpa** apology

pedinte [pe'dʒĩtʃi] m/f beggar

pedir [pe'dʒi*] vt to ask for; (COM, comida) to order; (exigir) to demand ♦ vi to ask; (num restaurante) to order; ~ **algo a alguém** to ask sb for sth; ~ **a alguém que faça** ... ~ **para alguém fazer** to ask sb to do

pedra ['pedra] f stone; (rochedo) rock; (de granizo) hailstone; (de açúcar) lump; (quadro-negro) slate; ~ **de gelo** ice cube; **pedreiro** [pe'drejru] m stonemason

pegada [pe'gada] f (de pé) footprint; (FUTEBOL) save

pegado, -a [pe'gadu, a] adj stuck; (unido) together

pegajoso, -a [pega'ʒozu, ɔza] adj sticky

pegar [pe'ga*] vt to catch; (selos) to stick (on); (segurar) to take hold of; (hábito, mania) to get into; (com-

preender) to take in; (trabalho) to take on; (estação de rádio) to pick up, get ♦ vi to stick; (planta) to take; (moda) to catch on; (doença) to be catching; (motor) to start; ~ **em** (segurar) to grab, pick up; **ir** ~ (buscar) to go and get; ~ **um emprego** to get a job; ~ **fogo a algo** to set fire to sth; ~ **no sono** to fall asleep

pego, -a ['pɛgu, a] pp de **pegar**

peito ['pejtu] m (ANAT) chest; (de ave, mulher) breast; (fig) courage

peitoril [pejto'riw] (pl -is) m windowsill

peixada [pej'ʃada] f fish cooked in a seafood sauce

peixaria [pejʃa'ria] f fish shop, fishmonger's (BRIT)

peixe ['pejʃi] m fish; **P~s** mpl (ASTROLOGIA) Pisces sg

pela ['pɛla] = **por** + **a**

pelada [pe'lada] f football game; see boxed note

PELADA

Pelada is an improvised, generally short, game of football, which in the past was played with a ball made out of socks, or an inflatable rubber ball. It is still played today on any piece of open land, or even in the street.

---

pelado, -a [pe'ladu, a] adj (sem pele) skinned; (sem pêlo, cabelo) shorn; (nu) naked, in the nude; (sem dinheiro) broke

pelar [pe'la*] vt (tirar a pele) to skin; (tirar o pêlo) to shear

pelas ['pɛlaʃ] = **por** + **as**

pele ['pɛli] f skin; (couro) leather; (como agasalho) fur; (de animal) hide

película [pe'likula] f film

pelo ['pelu] = **por** + **o**

pêlo ['pelu] m hair; (de animal) fur,

coat; **nu em ~** stark naked

pelos ['peluʃ] – **por + os**

peludo, -a [pe'ludu, a] *adj* hairy; (*animal*) furry

pena ['pena] *f* feather; (*de caneta*) nib; (*escrita*) writing; (*JUR*) penalty, punishment; (*sofrimento*) suffering; (*piedade*) pity; **que ~!** what a shame!; **dar ~** to be upsetting; **ter ~ de** to feel sorry for; **~ capital** capital punishment

penal [pe'naw] (*pl* **-ais**) *adj* penal; **penalidade** [penali'dadʒi] *f* (*JUR*) penalty; (*castigo*) punishment; **penalizar** [penali'za*] *vt* to trouble; (*castigar*) to penalize

pênalti ['penawtʃi] *m* (*FUTEBOL*) penalty (kick)

penar [pe'na*] *vt* to grieve ♦ *vi* to suffer

pendência [pe'dẽsja] *f* dispute, quarrel

pendente [pe'dẽtʃi] *adj* hanging; (*por decidir*) pending; (*inclinado*) sloping; (*dependent*): **~ (de)** dependent (on) ♦ *m* pendant

pêndulo ['pedulu] *m* pendulum

pendurar [pedu'ra*] *vt* to hang

penedo [pe'nedu] *m* rock, boulder

peneira [pe'nejra] *f* sieve; **peneirar** [penej'ra*] *vt* to sift, sieve ♦ *vi* (*chover*) to drizzle

penetrante [pene'trãtʃi] *adj* (*olhar*) searching; (*ferida*) deep; (*frio*) biting; (*som, análise*) penetrating, piercing; (*dor, arma*) sharp; (*inteligência, idéias*) incisive

penetrar [pene'tra*] *vt* to get into, penetrate; (*compreender*) to understand ♦ *vi*: **~ em** ou **por** ou **entre** to penetrate; **~ em** (*segredo*) to find out

penhasco [pe'naʃku] *m* cliff, crag

penhorar [peɲo'ra*] *vt* (*dar em penhor*) to pledge, pawn

penioilina [penisi'lina] *f* penicillin

península [pe'nĩsula] *f* peninsula

pênis ['peniʃ] *m inv* penis

penitência [peni'tẽsja] *f* penitence; (*expiação*) penance; **penitenciária** [penitẽ'sjarja] *f* prison

penoso, -a [pe'nozu, ɔza] *adj* (*assunto, tratamento*) painful; (*trabalho*) hard

pensamento [pẽsa'mẽtu] *m* thought; (*mente*) mind; (*opinião*) way of thinking; (*idéia*) idea

pensão [pẽ'sãw] (*pl* **-ões**) *f* (*tb:* **casa de ~**) boarding house; (*comida*) board; **~ completa** full board; **~ de aposentadoria** (retirement) pension

pensar [pẽ'sa*] *vi* to think; (*imaginar*) to imagine; **~ em** to think of ou about; **~ fazer** to intend to do; **pensativo, -a** [pẽsa'tʃivu, a] *adj* thoughtful, pensive

pensionista [pẽsjo'niʃta] *m/f* pensioner

pensões [pẽ'sõjʃ] *fpl de* **pensão**

pente ['pẽtʃi] *m* comb; **penteado, -a** [pẽ'tʃjadu, a] *adj* (*cabelo*) in place; (*pessoa*) smart ♦ *m* hairdo, hairstyle; **pentear** [pẽ'tʃja*] *vt* to comb; (*arranjar o cabelo*) to do, style; **pentear-se** *vr* to comb one's hair; to do one's hair

penúltimo, -a [pe'nuwtʃimu, a] *adj* last but one, penultimate

penumbra [pe'nũbra] *f* twilight, dusk; (*sombra*) shadow; (*meia-luz*) half-light

penúria [pe'nurja] *f* poverty

peões [pjõjʃ] *mpl de* **peão**

pepino [pe'pinu] *m* cucumber

pequeno, -a [pe'kenu, a] *adj* small; (*mesquinho*) petty ♦ *m* boy

pequerrucho [peke'xuʃu] *m* thimble

Pequim [pe'kĩ] *n* Peking, Beijing

pêra ['pera] f pear

perambular [perãbu'la*] vi to wander

perante [pe'rãtʃi] prep before, in the presence of

per capita [pex'kapita] adv, adj per capita

perceber [pexse'be*] vt to realize; (por meio dos sentidos) to perceive; (compreender) to understand; (ver) to see; (ouvir) to hear; (ver ao longe) to make out; (dinheiro: receber) to receive

percentagem [pexsẽ'taʒẽ] f percentage

percepção [pexsep'sãw] f perception; **perceptível** [pexsep'tʃivew] (pl -eis) adj perceptible, noticeable; (som) audible

percevejo [pexse'veʒu] m (inseto) bug; (prego) drawing pin (BRIT), thumbtack (US)

perco etc ['pexku] vb V **perder**

percorrer [pexko'xe*] vt (viajar por) to travel (across ou over); (passar por) to go through, traverse; (investigar) to search through

percurso [pex'kuxsu] m (espaço percorrido) distance (covered); (trajeto) route; (viagem) journey

percussão [pexku'sãw] f (MÚS) percussion

perda ['pexda] f loss; (desperdício) waste; ~s e danos damages, losses

perdão [pex'dãw] m pardon, forgiveness; ~! sorry!, I beg your pardon!

perder [pex'de*] vt to lose; (tempo) to waste; (trem, show, oportunidade) to miss ♦ vi to lose; **perder-se** vr to get lost; (arruinar-se) to be ruined; (desaparecer) to disappear; **~-se de alguém** to lose sb

perdição [pexdʒi'sãw] f perdition, ruin; (desonra) depravity

perdido, -a [pex'dʒidu, a] adj lost; **~s e achados** lost and found, lost property

perdiz [pex'dʒiʒ] f partridge

perdoar [pex'dwa*] vt to forgive

perdurar [pexdu'ra*] vi to last a long time; (continuar a existir) to still exist

perecível [pere'sivew] (pl -eis) adj perishable

peregrinação [peregrina'sãw] (pl -ões) f (viagem) travels pl; (REL) pilgrimage

peregrino, -a [pere'grinu, a] m/f pilgrim

peremptório, -a [perẽp'tɔrju, a] adj final; (decisivo) decisive

perene [pe'reni] adj everlasting; (BOT) perennial

perfeição [pexfej'sãw] f perfection

perfeitamente [pexfejta'mẽtʃi] adv perfectly ♦ excl exactly!

perfeito, -a [pex'fejtu, a] adj perfect ♦ m (LING) perfect

perfil [pex'fiw] (pl -is) m profile; (silhueta) silhouette, outline; (ARQ) (cross) section

perfume [pex'fumi] m perfume, scent

perfurar [pexfu'ra*] vt (o chão) to drill a hole in; (papel) to punch (a hole in)

pergunta [pex'gũta] f question; **fazer uma ~ a alguém** to ask sb a question; **perguntar** [pexgũ'ta*] vt to ask; (interrogar) to question ♦ vi: **perguntar por alguém** to ask after sb; **perguntar-se** vr to wonder; **perguntar algo a alguém** to ask sb sth

perícia [pe'risja] f expertise; (destreza) skill; (exame) investigation

periferia [perife'ria] f periphery; (da cidade) outskirts pl

perigo [pe'rigu] m danger; **peri-**

goso, -a [peri'gozu, ɔza] *adj* dangerous; *(arriscado)* risky

periódico, -a [pe'rjɔdʒiku, a] *adj* periodic ♦ *m (revista)* magazine, periodical; *(jornal)* (news)paper

período [pe'riodu] *m* period; *(estação)* season

peripécia [peri'pɛsja] *f (aventura)* adventure; *(incidente)* turn of events

periquito [peri'kitu] *m* parakeet

perito, -a [pe'ritu, a] *adj* expert ♦ *m/f* expert; *(quem faz perícia)* investigator

permanecer [pexmane'se*] *vi* to remain; *(num lugar)* to stay; *(continuar a ser)* to remain, keep; **~ parado** to keep still

permanência [pexma'nēsja] *f* permanence; *(estada)* stay; **permanente** [pexma'nētʃi] *adj (dor)* constant; *(cor)* fast; *(residência, pregas)* permanent ♦ *m (cartão)* pass ♦ *f* perm

permissão [pexmi'sāw] *f* permission, consent; **permissivo, -a** [pexmi'sivu, a] *adj* permissive

permitir [pexmi'tʃi*] *vt* to allow, permit

perna ['pɛxna] *f* leg; **~s tortas** bow legs

pernil [pex'niw] *(pl* **-is)** *m (de animal)* haunch; *(CULIN)* leg

pernilongo [pexni'lõgu] *m* mosquito

pernis [pex'niʃ] *mpl de* **pernil**

pernoitar [pexnoj'ta*] *vi* to spend the night

pérola ['pɛrola] *f* pearl

perpendicular [pexpēdʒiku'la*] *adj, f* perpendicular

perpetuar [pexpe'twa*] *vt* to perpetuate; **perpétuo, -a** [pex'pɛtwu, a] *adj* perpetual

perplexo, -a [pex'plɛksu, a] *adj* bewildered, puzzled; *(indeciso)* un-

certain; **ficar ~** to be taken aback

persa ['pɛxsa] *adj, m/f* Persian

perseguição [pexsegi'sāw] *f* pursuit; *(REL, POL)* persecution

perseguir [pexse'gi*] *vt* to pursue; *(correr atrás)* to chase (after); *(REL, POL)* to persecute; *(importunar)* to harass, pester

perseverante [pexseve'rātʃi] *adj* persistent

perseverar [pexseve'ra*] *vi*: **~ (em)** to persevere (in), persist (in)

Pérsia ['pɛxsja] *f*: **a ~** Persia

persiana [pex'sjana] *f* blind

Pérsico, -a ['pɛxsiku, a] *adj*: **o golfo ~** the Persian Gulf

persigo *etc* [pex'sigu] *vb V* **perseguir**

persistente [pexsiʃ'tētʃi] *adj* persistent

persistir [pexsiʃ'tʃi*] *vi*: **~ (em)** to persist (in)

personagem [pexso'naʒē] *(pl* **-ns)** *m/f* famous person, celebrity; *(num livro, filme)* character

personalidade [pexsonali'dadʒi] *f* personality

perspectiva [pexʃpek'tʃiva] *f* perspective; *(panorama)* view; *(probabilidade)* prospect

perspicácia [pexʃpi'kasja] *f* insight, perceptiveness; **perspicaz** [pexʃpi'kajʒ] *adj* observant; *(sagaz)* shrewd

persuadir [pexswa'dʒi*] *vt* to persuade; **persuadir-se** *vr* to convince o.s.; **persuasão** [pexswa'zāw] *f* persuasion; **persuasivo, -a** [pexswa'zivu, a] *adj* persuasive

pertencente [pextē'sētʃi] *adj*: **~ a** pertaining to

pertencer [pextē'se*] *vi*: **~ a** to belong to; *(referir-se)* to concern

pertences [pex'tēsiʃ] *mpl (de uma pessoa)* belongings

pertinência [pextʃi'nẽsja] f relevance; **pertinente** [pextʃi'nẽtʃi] adj relevant; (apropriado) appropriate

perto, -a ['pextu, a] adj nearby ♦ adv near; **~ de** near to; (em comparação com) next to; **de ~** closely; (ver) close up; (conhecer) very well

perturbar [pextux'ba*] vt to disturb; (abalar) to upset, trouble; (atrapalhar) to put off; (andamento, trânsito) to disrupt; (envergonhar) to embarrass; (alterar) to affect

Peru [pe'ru] m: **o ~** Peru

peru, a [pe'ru, a] m/f turkey

peruca [pe'ruka] f wig

perverso, -a [pex'vɛxsu, a] adj perverse; (malvado) wicked

perverter [pexvex'te*] vt to corrupt, pervert; **pervertido, -a** [pexvex'tʃidu, a] adj perverted ♦ m/f pervert

pesadelo [peza'delu] m nightmare

pesado, -a [pe'zadu, a] adj heavy; (ambiente) tense; (trabalho) hard; (estilo) dull, boring; (andar) slow; (piada) coarse; (comida) stodgy; (tempo) sultry ♦ adv heavily

pêsames ['pesamiʃ] mpl condolences, sympathy sg

pesar [pe'za*] vt to weigh; (fig) to weigh up ♦ vi to weigh; (ser pesado) to be heavy; (influir) to carry weight; (causar mágoa): **~ a** to hurt, grieve ♦ m grief; **~ sobre** (recair) to fall upon

pesaroso, -a [peza'rozu, ɔza] adj sorrowful, sad; (arrependido) regretful, sorry

pesca ['pɛʃka] f fishing; (os peixes) catch; **ir à ~** to go fishing

pescada [peʃ'kada] f whiting

pescado [peʃ'kadu] m fish

pescador, a [peʃka'do*, a] m/f fisherman/woman; **~ à linha** angler

pescar [peʃ'ka*] vt (peixe) to catch; (tentar apanhar) to fish for; (retirar da água) to fish out ♦ vi to fish

pescoço [peʃ'kosu] m neck

peso ['pezu] m weight; (fig: ônus) burden; (importância) importance; **~ bruto/líquido** gross/net weight

pesquisa [peʃ'kiza] f inquiry, investigation; (científica, de mercado) research; **pesquisar** [peʃki'za*] vt, vi to investigate; to research

pêssego ['pesegu] m peach

pessimista [pesi'miʃta] adj pessimistic ♦ m/f pessimist

péssimo, -a ['pɛsimu, a] adj very bad, awful

pessoa [pe'soa] f person; **~s** fp (gente) people; **pessoal** [pe'swaw] (pl **-is**) adj personal ♦ m person personnel pl, staff pl; (col) people pl, folks pl

pestana [peʃ'tana] f eyelash

peste ['pɛʃtʃi] f epidemic; (bubônica) plague; (fig) pest, nuisance

pétala ['petala] f petal

petição [petʃi'sãw] (pl **-ões**) f request; (documento) petition

petisco [pe'tʃiʃku] m savoury (BRIT); savory (US), titbit (BRIT), tidbit (US)

petróleo [pe'trɔlju] m oil, petroleum; **~ bruto** crude oil

petulância [petu'lãsja] f impudence; **petulante** [petu'lãtʃi] adj impudent

peúga ['pjuga] (PT) f sock

pevide [pe'vidʒi] f (PT) f (de melão) seed; (de maçã) pip

p. ex. abr (= por exemplo) e.g.

pia ['pia] f wash basin; (da cozinha) sink; **~ batismal** font

piada ['pjada] f joke

pianista [pja'niʃta] m/f pianist

piano ['pjanu] m piano

piar [pja*] vi (pinto) to cheep; (coruja) to hoot

picada [pi'kada] *f* (*de agulha etc*) prick; (*de abelha*) sting; (*de mosquito, cobra*) bite; (*de avião*) dive; (*de navalha*) stab; (*atalho*) path, trail

picante [pi'kãtʃi] *adj* (*tempero*) hot

pica-pau ['pika-] (*pl* **~s**) *m* woodpecker

picar [pi'ka*] *vt* to prick; (*suj: abelha*) to sting; (: *mosquito*) to bite; (: *pássaro*) to peck; (*um animal*) to goad; (*carne*) to mince; (*papel*) to shred; (*fruta*) to chop up ♦ *vi* (*comichar*) to prickle

picareta [pika'reta] *f* pickaxe (*BRIT*), pickax (*US*) ♦ *m/f* crook

pico ['piku] *m* (*cume*) peak; (*ponta aguda*) sharp point; (*PT: um pouco*) a bit; **mil e ~** just over a thousand

picolé [piko'lɛ] *m* lolly

picotar [piko'ta*] *vt* to perforate; (*bilhete*) to punch

piedade [pje'dadʒi] *f* piety; (*compaixão*) pity; **ter ~ de** to have pity on; **piedoso, -a** [pje'dozu, ɔza] *adj* pious; (*compassivo*) merciful

pifar [pi'fa*] (*col*) *vi* (*carro*) to break down; (*rádio etc*) to go wrong; (*plano, programa*) to fall through

pijama [pi'ʒama] *m ou f* pyjamas *pl* (*BRIT*), pajamas *pl* (*US*)

pilantra [pi'lãtɾa] (*col*) *m/f* crook

pilar [pi'la*] *vt* to pound, crush ♦ *m* pillar

pilha ['piʎa] *f* (*ELET*) battery; (*monte*) pile, heap

pilhagem [pi'ʎaʒẽ] *f* (*ato*) pillage; (*objetos*) plunder, booty

pilhar [pi'ʎa*] *vt* to plunder, pillage; (*roubar*) to rob; (*surpreender*) to catch

pilotar [pilo'ta*] *vt* (*avião*) to fly

piloto [pi'lotu] *m* pilot; (*motorista*) (*racing*) driver; (*bico de gás*) pilot light ♦ *adj inv* (*usina, plano*) pilot; (*peça*) sample *atr*

pílula ['pilula] *f* pill; **a ~** (*anticoncepcional*) the pill

pimenta [pi'mẽta] *f* (*CULIN*) pepper; **~ de Caiena** cayenne pepper; **pimenta-do-reino** *f* black pepper; **pimenta-malagueta** (*pl* **pimentas-malagueta**) *f* chilli ou chili (*US*) pepper; **pimentão** [pimẽ'tãw] (*pl* **-ões**) *m* (*BOT*) pepper

pinça ['pĩsa] *f* (*de sobrancelhas*) tweezers *pl*; (*de casa*) tongs *pl*; (*MED*) callipers *pl* (*BRIT*), calipers *pl* (*US*)

pincel [pĩ'sew] (*pl* **-éis**) *m* brush; (*para pintar*) paintbrush; **pincelar** [pĩse'la*] *vt* to paint

pinga ['pĩga] *f* (*cachaça*) rum; (*PT: trago*) drink

pingar [pĩ'ga*] *vi* to drip

pingo ['pĩgu] *m* (*gota*) drop

pingue-pongue [pĩgi-'põgi] ® *m* ping-pong ®

pingüim [pĩ'gwĩ] (*pl* **-ns**) *m* penguin

pinheiro [pi'ɲejru] *m* pine (tree)

pinho ['pĩɲu] *m* pine

pino ['pĩnu] *m* (*peça*) pin; (*AUTO: na porta*) lock; **a ~** upright

pinta ['pĩta] *f* (*mancha*) spot

pintar [pĩ'ta*] *vt* to paint; (*cabelo*) to dye; (*rosto*) to make up; (*descrever*) to describe; (*imaginar*) to picture ♦ *vi* to paint; **pintar-se** *vr* to make o.s. up

pintarroxo [pĩta'xoʃu] *m* (*BR*) linnet; (*PT*) robin

pinto ['pĩtu] *m* chick; (*col!*) prick (!)

pintor, a [pĩ'to*, a] *m/f* painter

pintura [pĩ'tura] *f* painting; (*maquiagem*) make-up

piolho [pi'oʎu] *m* louse

pioneiro, -a [pjo'nejru, a] *m/f* pioneer

pior [pi'pjɔ*] *adj, adv* (*compar*) worse; (*superl*) worst ♦ *m*: **o ~** worst of all;

piorar [pjo'ra*] vt to make worse, worsen ♦ vi to get worse

pipa ['pipa] f barrel, cask; (de papel) kite

pipi [pi'pi] (col) m pee; **fazer ~** to have a pee

pipoca [pi'pɔka] f popcorn

pipocar [pipo'ka*] vi to go pop, pop

pique etc vb V picar

piquenique [piki'niki] m picnic

pirâmide [pi'ramidʒi] f pyramid

piranha [pi'raɲa] f piranha (fish)

pirata [pi'rata] m pirate

pires ['piriʃ] m inv saucer

Pirineus [piri'newʃ] mpl: **os ~** the Pyrenees

pirulito [piru'litu] (BR) m lollipop

pisar [pi'za*] vt to tread on; (esmagar, subjugar) to crush ♦ vi to step, tread

pisca-pisca [piʃka-'piʃka] (pl **~s**) (AUTO) m indicator

piscar [piʃ'ka*] vt to blink; (dar sinal) to wink; (estrelas) to twinkle ♦ m: **num ~ de olhos** in a flash

piscina [pi'sina] f swimming pool

piso ['pizu] m floor

pisotear [pizo'tʃa*] vt to trample (on)

pista ['piʃta] f (vestígio) trace; (indicação) clue; (de corridas) track; (AVIAT) runway; (de estrada) lane; (de dança) (dance) floor

pistola [piʃ'tɔla] f pistol

pitada [pi'tada] f (porção) pinch

pivete [pi'vetʃi] m child thief

pivô [pi'vo] m pivot; (fig) central figure, prime mover

pizza ['pitsa] f pizza

placa ['plaka] f plate; (AUTO) number plate (BRIT), license plate (US); (comemorativa) plaque; (na pele) blotch; **~ de sinalização** roadsign

placar [pla'ka*] m scoreboard

plácido, -a ['plasidu, a] adj calm; (manso) placid

plágio [pla'ʒu] m plagiarism

planalto [pla'nawtu] m tableland, plateau

planar [pla'na*] vi to glide

planear [pla'nja*] (PT) vt = planejar

planejamento [planeʒa'mẽtu] m planning; **~ familiar** family planning

planejar [plane'ʒa*] (BR) vt to plan; (edifício) to design

planeta [pla'neta] m planet

planície [pla'nisi] f plain

plano, -a ['planu, a] adj flat, level; (liso) smooth ♦ m plan; **em primeiro/em último ~** in the foreground/background; **P~ Real** see boxed note

---

PLANO REAL

The **Plano Real**, launched in 1994, was a plan for the economic stabilization of Brazil. In an attempt to contain inflation without resorting to measures such as a price and wage freeze, the government changed the Brazilian currency from the cruzeiro to the real. In addition, it speeded up the privatization of state-owned companies, reduced state spending and raised interest rates to rein in consumer demand.

---

planta ['plãta] f plant; (de pé) sole; (ARQ) plan

plantação [plãta'sãw] f (ato) planting; (terreno) planted land; (plantio) crops pl

plantão [plã'tãw] (pl **-ões**) m duty; (noturno) night duty; (plantonista) person on duty; (MIL: serviço) sentry duty; (: pessoa) sentry; **estar de ~** to be on duty

plantar 539 pois

plantar [plã'ta*] vt to plant; (estaca) to drive in; (estubelecer) to set up

plantões [plã'tõjʃ] mpl de **plantão**

plástico, -a ['plaʃtʃiku, a] adj plastic ♦ m plastic

plataforma [plata'fɔxma] f platform; ~ **de exploração de petróleo** oil rig; ~ **de lançamento** launch pad

platéia [pla'teja] f (TEATRO etc) stalls pl (BRIT), orchestra (US); (espectadores) audience

platina [pla'tʃina] f platinum

platinados [platʃi'naduʃ] mpl (AUTO) points

plausível [plaw'zivew] (pl -**eis**) adj credible, plausible

playground [plej'grãwdʒi] (pl ~**s**) m (children's) playground

plenamente [plena'mẽtʃi] adv fully, completely

pleno, -a ['plenu, a] adj full; (completo) complete; **em ~ dla** in broad daylight; **em ~ inverno** in the middle ou depths of winter

plural [plu'raw] (pl -**ais**) adj, m plural

pneu ['pnew] m tyre (BRIT), tire (US)

pneumonia [pnewmo'nia] f pneumonia

pó [pɔ] m powder; (sujeira) dust; **sabão em ~** soap powder; **tirar o ~ (de algo)** to dust (sth)

pobre ['pɔbri] adj poor ♦ m/f poor person; **pobreza** [po'breza] f poverty

poça ['posa] f puddle, pool

poção [po'sãw] (pl -**ões**) m potion

poço ['posu] m well; (de mina, elevador) shaft

poções [po'sõjʃ] fpl de **poção**

pôde etc ['podʒi] vb V **poder**

pó-de-arroz m face powder

---

poder [po'de*] vi 1 (capacidade) can, be able to; **não posso fazê-lo** I can't do it, I'm unable to do it 2 (ter o direito de) can, may, be allowed to; **posso fumar aqui?** can I smoke here?; **pode entrar?** (posso?) can I come in? 3 (possibilidade) may, might, could; **pode ser** maybe; **pode ser que** it may be that; **ele ~á vir amanhã** he might come tomorrow 4: **não ~ com: não posso com ele** I cannot cope with him 5 (col: indignação): **pudera!** no wonder!; **como é que pode?** you're joking!
♦ m power; (autoridade) authority; ~ **aquisitivo** purchasing power; **estar no ~** to be in power; **em ~ de alguém** in sb's hands

poderoso, -a [pode'rozu, ɔza] adj mighty, powerful

podre ['pɔdri] adj rotten; **podridão** [podri'dãw] f decay, rottenness; (fig) corruption

põe etc [põj] vb V **pôr**

poeira ['pwejra] f dust; ~ **radioativa** fall-out; **poeirento, -a** [pwej'rẽtu, a] adj dusty

poema ['pwema] m poem

poesia [poe'zia] f poetry; (poema) poem

poeta ['pweta] m poet; **poético, -a** ['pwetʃiku, a] adj poetic; **poetisa** [pwe'tʃiza] f (woman) poet

pois [pojʃ] adv (portanto) so; (PT: assentimento) yes ♦ conj as, since; (mas) but; ~ **bem** well then; ~ **é** that's right; ~ **não!** (BR) of course!; ~ **não?** (BR: numa loja) what can I do for you?; (PT) isn't it?, aren't you?, didn't they? etc; ~ **sim!** certainly not!; ~ (**então**) then

polaco, -a [po'laku, a] *adj* Polish ♦ *m/f* Pole ♦ *m* (*LING*) Polish

polar [po'la*] *adj* polar

polegada [pole'gada] *f* inch

polegar [pole'ga*] *m* (*tb:* **dedo** ~) thumb

polêmica [po'lemika] *f* controversy; **polêmico, -a** [po'lemiku, a] *adj* controversial

pólen ['pɔlẽ] *m* pollen

polícia [po'lisja] *f* police, police force ♦ *m/f* policeman/woman; **policial** [poli'sjaw] (*pl* **-ais**) *adj* police *atr* ♦ *m/f* (*BR*) policeman/woman; **novela** *ou* **romance policial** detective novel; **policiar** [poli'sja*] *vt* to police; (*instintos, modos*) to control, keep in check

polidez [poli'deʒ] *f* good manners *pl*, politeness

polido, -a [po'lidu, a] *adj* polished, shiny; (*cortês*) well-mannered, polite

pólio ['pɔlju] *f* polio

polir [po'li*] *vt* to polish

política [po'litʃika] *f* politics *sg*; (*programa*) policy; **político, -a** [po'litʃiku, a] *adj* political ♦ *m/f* politician

pólo ['pɔlu] *m* pole; (*ESPORTE*) polo; **P~ Norte/Sul** North/South Pole

polonês, -esa [polo'neʃ, eza] *adj* Polish ♦ *m/f* Pole ♦ *m* (*LING*) Polish

Polônia [po'lonja] *f:* **a ~** Poland

polpa ['powpa] *f* pulp

poltrona [pow'trɔna] *f* armchair

poluição [polwi'sãw] *f* pollution; **poluir** [po'lwi*] *vt* to pollute

polvo ['powvu] *m* octopus

pólvora [po'vora] *f* gunpowder

pomada [po'mada] *f* ointment

pomar [po'ma*] *m* orchard

pomba ['põba] *f* dove

pombo ['põbu] *m* pigeon

pompa ['põpa] *f* pomp

pomposo, -a [põ'pozu, ɔza] *adj* pompous

ponderação [põdera'sãw] *f* consideration, meditation; (*prudência*) prudence

ponderado, -a [põde'radu, a] *adj* prudent

ponderar [põde'ra*] *vt* to consider, weigh up ♦ *vi* to meditate, muse

ponho *etc* ['poɲu] *vb* V **pôr**

ponta ['põta] *f* tip; (*de faca*) point; (*de sapato*) toe; (*extremidade*) end; (*FUTEBOL:* *posição*) wing; (*: jogador*) winger; **uma ~ de** (*um pouco*) a touch of; **~ do dedo** fingertip

pontada [põ'tada] *f* (*dor*) twinge

pontapé [põta'pɛ] *m* kick; **dar ~s em alguém** to kick sb

pontaria [põta'ria] *f* aim; **fazer ~** to take aim

ponte ['põtʃi] *f* bridge; **~ aérea** air shuttle, airlift; **~ de safena** (*heart*) bypass operation

ponteiro [põ'tejru] *m* (*indicador*) pointer; (*de relógio*) hand

pontiagudo, -a [põtʃja'gudu, a] *adj* sharp, pointed

ponto ['põtu] *m* point; (*MED, COSTURA, TRICÔ*) stitch; (*pequeno sinal, do i*) dot; (*na pontuação*) full stop (*BRIT*), period (*US*); (*na pele*) spot; (*de ônibus*) stop; (*de táxi*) rank (*BRIT*), stand (*US*); (*matéria escolar*) subject; **estar a ~ de fazer** to be on the point of doing; **às cinco em ~** at five o'clock on the dot; **dois ~s** colon *sg*; **~ de admiração** (*PT*) exclamation mark; **~ de exclamação/interrogação** exclamation/question mark; **~ de vista** point of view, viewpoint; **ponto-e-vírgula** (*pl* **ponto-e-vírgulas**) *m* semicolon

pontuação [põtwa'sãw] *f* punctuation

pontual [põ'twaw] (pl -ais) adj
punctual

pontudo, -a [põ'tudu, a] adj pointed

popa ['popa] f stern

população [popula'sãw] (pl -ões) f
population

popular [popu'la*] adj popular;
popularidade [populari'dadʒi] f
popularity

póquer ['poke*] m poker

PALAVRA CHAVE

por [po*] (por + o(s), a(s) = pelo(s),
pela(s)) prep 1 (objetivo) for; **lutar
pela pátria** to fight for one's country

2 (+ infin): **está ~ acontecer** it is
about to happen, it is yet to happen; **está ~ fazer** it is still to be
done

3 (causa) out of, because of; **~ falta
de fundos** through lack of funds; **~
hábito/natureza** out of habit/by
nature; **faço isso ~ ela** I do it for
her; **~ isso** therefore; **a razão pela
qual ...** the reason why ...; **pelo
amor de Deus!** for Heaven's sake!

4 (tempo): **pela manhã** in the morning; **~ volta das duas horas** at
about two o'clock; **ele vai ficar ~
uma semana** he's staying for a
week

5 (lugar): **~ aqui** this way; **viemos
pelo parque** we came through the
park; **passar ~ São Paulo** to pass
through São Paulo, **~ fora/dentro**
outside/inside

6 (troca, preço) for; **trocar o velho
pelo novo** to change old for new;
comprei o livro ~ dez libras I
bought the book for ten pounds

7 (valor proporcional): **~ cento** per
cent; **~ hora/dia/semana/mês/ano**
hourly/daily/weekly/monthly/year-
ly; **~ cabeça** a ou per head; **~ mais**

difícil etc que seja however difficult
etc it is

8 (modo, meio) by; **~ correio/avião**
by post/air; **~ si** by o.s.; **~ escrito** in
writing; **entrar pela entrada principal** to go in through the main
entrance

9: **~ que** (por causa) because (PT),
why (BR); **~ quê?** why?

10: **~ mim tudo bem** as far as I'm
concerned, that's OK

PALAVRA CHAVE

pôr [po*] vt 1 (colocar) to put;
(roupas) to put on; (objeções, dúvidas) to raise; (ovos, mesa) to lay;
(defeito) to find; **poe mais forte** turn
it up; **você põe açúcar?** do you take
sugar?; **~ de lado** to set aside

2 (+ adj) to make; **você está me
pondo nervoso** you're making me
nervous

♦ pôr-se vr 1 (sol) to set

2 (colocar-se): **~-se de pé** to stand
up; **ponha-se no meu lugar** put
yourself in my position

3: **~-se a** to start to; **ela pôs-se a
chorar** she started crying

♦ m: **o ~ do sol** sunset

porão [po'rãw] (pl -ões) m (de casa)
basement; (: armazém) cellar

porca ['pɔxka] f (animal) sow

porção [pox'sãw] (pl -ões) f portion, piece; **uma ~ de** a lot of

porcaria [poxka'ria] f filth; (dito sujo) obscenity; (coisa ruim) piece of junk

porcelana [poxse'lana] f porcelain

porcentagem [poxsẽ'tazẽ] (pl -ns)
f percentage

porco, -a ['pɔxku, 'pɔxka] adj filthy
♦ m (animal) pig; (carne) pork

porções [pox'sõjʃ] fpl de **porção**

porém [po'rẽ] conj however

pormenor [poxme'no*] m detail
pornografia [poxnogra'fia] f pornography
poro ['pɔru] m pore
porões [po'rõjs] mpl de **porão**
porque ['poxke] conj because; (interrogativo: PT) why?
porquê [pox'ke] adv why ♦ m reason, motive; ~ (PT) why?
porrete [po'xetʃi] m club
porta ['pɔxta] f door; (vão da ~) doorway; (de um jardim) gate
portador, a [poxta'do*, a] m/f bearer
portagem [pox'taʒẽ] (PT) (pl -ns) f toll
portal [pox'taw] (pl -ais) m doorway
porta-luvas m inv (AUTO) glove compartment
porta-malas m inv (AUTO) boot (BRIT), trunk (US)
porta-níqueis m inv purse
portanto [pox'tãtu] conj so, therefore
portão [pox'tãw] (pl -ões) m gate
portar [pox'ta*] vt to carry; **portar-se** vr to behave
portaria [poxta'ria] f (de um edifício) entrance hall; (recepção) reception desk; (do governo) edict, decree
portátil [pox'tatʃiw] (pl -eis) adj portable
porta-voz (pl ~es) m/f (pessoa) spokesman/woman
porte ['pɔxtʃi] m transport; (custo) freight charge, carriage; ~ **pago** post paid; **de grande ~** far-reaching, important
porteiro, -a [pox'tejru, a] m/f caretaker; ~ **eletrônico** entryphone
pórtico ['pɔxtʃiku] m porch, portico
porto ['pɔxtu] m (do mar) port, harbour (BRIT), harbor (US); (vinho) port;

o **P~** Oporto
portões [pox'tõjs] mpl de **portão**
Portugal [poxtu'gaw] m Portugal;
português, -guesa [poxtu'geʃ, 'geza] adj Portuguese ♦ m/f Portuguese inv ♦ m (LING) Portuguese
porventura [poxvẽ'tura] adj by chance; **se ~ você ...** if you happen to ...
pôs [poʃ] vb V **pôr**
posar [po'za*] vi (FOTO): ~ **(para)** to pose (for)
posição [pozi'sãw] (pl -ões) f position; (social) standing, status; **posicionar** [pozisjo'na*] vt to position
positivo, -a [pozi'tʃivu, a] adj positive
possante [po'sãtʃi] adj powerful, strong; (carro) flashy
posse ['pɔsi] f possession, ownership; ~**s** fpl (pertences) possessions, belongings; **tomar ~ de** to take possession of
possessão [pose'sãw] f possession;
possessivo, -a [pose'sivu, a] adj possessive
possibilidade [posibili'dadʒi] f possibility; ~**s** fpl (recursos) means
possibilitar [posibili'ta*] vt to make possible, permit
possível [po'sivew] (pl -eis) adj possible; **fazer todo o ~** to do one's best
posso etc ['posu] vb V **poder**
possuidor, a [poswi'do*, a] m/f owner
possuir [po'swi*] vt (casa, livro etc) to own; (dinheiro, talento) to possess
postal [poʃ'taw] (pl -ais) adj postal ♦ m postcard
poste ['pɔʃtʃi] m pole, post
posterior [poʃte'rjo*] adj (mais tarde) subsequent, later; (traseiro)

rear, back; **posteriormente** [poʃterjoꭓˈmẽtʃi] *adv* later, subsequently

postiço, -a [poʃˈtʃisu, a] *adj* false, artificial

posto, -a [ˈpoʃtu, ˈpɔʃta] *pp de pôr* ♦ *m* post, position; (*emprego*) job; ~ **de gasolina** service *ou* petrol station; ~ **que** although; ~ **de saúde** health centre *ou* center

póstumo, -a [ˈpɔʃtumu, -a] *adj* posthumous

postura [poʃˈtura] *f* posture; (*aspecto físico*) appearance

potável [poˈtavew] (*pl* -**eis**) *adj* drinkable; **água** ~ drinking water

pote [ˈpɔtʃi] *m* jug, pitcher; (*de geléia*) jar; (*de creme*) pot; **chover a** ~**s** (*PT*) to rain cats and dogs

potência [poˈtẽsja] *f* power

potencial [poteˈsjaw] (*pl* -**ais**) *adj, m* potential

potente [poˈtẽtʃi] *adj* powerful, potent

PALAVRA CHAVE

pouco, -a [ˈpoku, a] *adj* **1** (*sg*) little, not much; ~ **tempo** little *ou* not much time; **de** ~ **interesse** of little interest, not very interesting; **pouca coisa** not much
2 (*pl*) few, not many; **uns** ~**s** a few, some; **poucas vezes** rarely; **poucas crianças comem o que devem** few children eat what they should
♦ *adv* **1** little, not much; **custa** ~ it doesn't cost much; **dentro em** ~, **daqui a** ~ shortly; ~ **antes** shortly before
2 (+ *adj*: = *negativo*): **ela é** ~ **inteligente/simpática** she's not very bright/friendly
3: **por** ~ **eu não morri** I almost died
4: ~ **a** ~ little by little
5: **aos** ~**s** gradually

♦ *m*: **um** ~ a little, a bit; **nem um** ~ not at all

poupador, a [popaˈdo*, a] *adj* thrifty

poupança [poˈpãsa] *f* thrift; (*economias*) savings *pl*; (*tb*: **caderneta de** ~) savings bank

poupar [poˈpa*] *vt* to save; (*vida*) to spare

pouquinho [poˈkiɲu] *m*: **um** ~ (**de**) a little

pousada [poˈzada] *f* (*hospedagem*) lodging; (*hospedaria*) inn

pousar [poˈza*] *vt* to place; (*mão*) to rest ♦ *vi* (*avião, pássaro*) to land; (*pernoitar*) to spend the night

povo [ˈpovu] *m* people; (*raça*) people *pl*, race; (*plebe*) common people *pl*; (*multidão*) crowd

povoação [povwaˈsãw] (*pl* -**ões**) *f* (*aldeia*) village, settlement; (*habitantes*) population

povoado [poˈvwadu] *m* village

povoar [poˈvwa*] *vt* (*de habitantes*) to people, populate; (*de animais etc*) to stock

pra [pra] (*col*) *prep* = **para a**

praça [ˈprasa] *f* (*largo*) square; (*mercado*) marketplace; (*soldado*) soldier; ~ **de touros** bullring

praga [ˈpraga] *f* nuisance; (*maldição*) curse; (*desgraça*) misfortune; (*erva daninha*) weed

pragmático, -a [pragˈmatʃiku, a] *adj* pragmatic

praia [ˈpraja] *f* beach

prancha [ˈprãʃa] *f* plank; (*de surfe*) board

prata [ˈprata] *f* silver; (*col: cruzeiro*) ≈ quid (*BRIT*), ≈ buck (*US*)

prateado, -a [praˈtʃjadu, a] *adj* silver-plated; (*brilhante*) silvery; (*cor*) silver ♦ *m* (*cor*) silver; (*de um objeto*) silver-plating; **papel** ~ silver paper

prateleira [prate'lejra] f shelf

prática ['pratʃika] f practice; (experiência) experience, know-how; (costume) habit, custom; V tb **prático**

praticante [pratʃi'kãtʃi] adj practising (BRIT), practicing (US) ♦ m/f apprentice; (de esporte) practitioner

praticar [pratʃi'ka*] vt to practise (BRIT), practice (US); (roubo, operação) to carry out; **prático, -a** ['pratʃiku, a] adj practical ♦ m/f expert

prato ['pratu] m plate; (comida) dish; (de uma refeição) course; (de toca-discos) turntable; **~s** mpl (MÚS) cymbals

praxe ['praksi] f custom, usage; de ~ usually; **ser de ~** to be the norm; **código da ~** see boxed note

---

PRAXE

Student life in Portugal follows the traditions set out in a written set of rules known as the *código da praxe*. It begins in freshers' week, where freshers are jeered at by their seniors, and are subjected to a number of humiliating practical jokes, such as having their hair cut against their will and being made to walk around town in fancy dress.

---

prazer [pra'ze*] m pleasure; **muito ~ em conhecê-lo** pleased to meet you

prazo ['prazu] m term, period; (vencimento) expiry date, time limit; **a curto/médio/longo ~** in the short/medium/long term; **comprar a ~** to buy on hire purchase (BRIT) ou on the installment plan (US)

precário, -a [pre'karju, a] adj precarious; (escasso) failing

precaução [prekaw'sãw] (pl -ões) f precaution

precaver-se [preka'vexsi] vr: ~ (contra ou de) to be on one's guard (against); **precavido, -a** [preka-'vidu, a] adj cautious

prece ['presi] f prayer; (súplica) entreaty

precedente [prese'dẽtʃi] adj preceding ♦ m precedent

preceder [prese'de*] vt, vi to precede; ~ **a algo** to precede sth; (ter primazia) to take precedence over sth

precioso, -a [pre'sjozu, ɔza] adj precious

precipício [presi'pisju] m precipice; (fig) abyss

precipitação [presipita'sãw] f haste; (imprudência) rashness

precipitado, -a [presipi'tadu, a] adj hasty; (imprudente) rash

precisamente [presiza'mẽtʃi] adv precisely

precisar [presi'za*] vt to need; (especificar) to specify; **precisar-se** vr: **"precisa-se"** "needed"; ~ **de** to need; (uso impess): **não precisa você se preocupar** you needn't worry

preciso, -a [pre'sizu, a] adj precise, accurate; (necessário) necessary; (claro) concise; **é ~ você ir** you must go

preço ['presu] m price; (custo) cost; (valor) value; **a ~ de banana** (BR) ou **de chuva** (PT) dirt cheap

precoce [pre'kɔsi] adj precocious; (antecipado) early

preconceito [prekõ'sejtu] m prejudice

precursor, a [prekux'so*, a] m/f precursor, forerunner; (mensageiro) herald

predador [preda'do*] m predator

predileto, -a [predʒi'letu, a] (PT -ct-) adj favourite (BRIT), favorite (US)

prédio ['predʒju] m building; ~ **de**

apartamentos block of flats (BRIT), apartment house (US)

predispor [predʒiʃ'po*] (irreg: como pôr) vt: ~ **alguém contra** to prejudice sb against; **predispor-se** vr: ~**-se a/para** to get o.s. in the mood to/for

predominar [predomi'na*] vi to predominate, prevail

preencher [preẽ'ʃe*] vt (formulário) to fill in (BRIT) ou out, complete; (requisitos) to fulfil (BRIT), fulfill (US), meet; to fill

prefácio [pre'fasju] m preface

prefeito, -a [pre'fejtu, a] m/f mayor; **prefeitura** [prefej'tura] f town hall

preferência [prefe'rẽsja] f preference; (AUTO) priority; **de ~** preferably; **preferencial** [preferẽ'sjaw] (pl **ais**) adj (rua) main ♦ f main road (with priority)

preferido, -a [prefe'ridu, a] adj favourite (BRIT), favorite (US)

preferir [prefe'ri*] vt to prefer

prefiro etc [pre'firu] vb V **preferir**

prefixo [pre'fiksu] m (LING) prefix; (TEL) code

prega ['prega] f pleat, fold

pregar¹ [pre'ga*] vt, vi to preach

pregar² [pre'ga*] vt (com prego) to nail; (fixar) to pin, fasten; (cosendo) to sew on; ~ **uma peça** to play a trick; ~ **um susto em alguém** to give sb a fright

prego ['pregu] m nail; (col: casa de penhor) pawn shop

preguiça [pre'gisa] f laziness; (animal) sloth; **estar com ~** to feel lazy; **preguiçoso, -a** [pregi'sozu, ɔza] adj lazy

pré-histórico, -a [prɛ-] adj prehistoric

preia-mar (PT) f high tide

prejudicar [preʒudʒi'ka*] vt to

damage; (atrapalhar) to hinder; **prejudicial** [preʒudʒi'sjaw] (pl **-ais**) adj damaging; (à saúde) harmful

prejuízo [pre'ʒwizu] m damage, harm; (em dinheiro) loss; **em ~ de** to the detriment of

prematuro, -a [prema'turu, a] adj premature

premiado, -a [pre'mjadu, a] adj prize-winning; (bilhete) winning ♦ m/f prize-winner

premiar [pre'mja*] vt to award a prize to; (recompensar) to reward

prêmio ['premju] m prize; (recompensa) reward; (SEGUROS) premium

prenda ['prẽda] f gift, present; (em jogo) forfeit; ~**s domésticas** housework sq

prendedor [prẽde'do*] m fastener; (de cabelo, gravata) clip; ~ **de roupa** clothes peg; ~ **de papéis** paper clip

prender [prẽ'de*] vt to fasten, fix; (roupa) to pin; (cabelo) to put back; (capturar) to arrest; (atar, ligar) to tie; (atenção) to catch; (afetivamente) to tie, bind; (reter: doença, compromisso) to keep; (movimentos) to restrict; **prender-se** vr to get caught, stick; ~**-se a alguém** (por amizade) to be attached to sb

preocupação [preokupa'sãw] (pl **-ões**) f preoccupation; (inquietação) worry, concern

preocupar [preoku'pa*] vt to preoccupy; (inquietar) to worry; **preocupar-se** vr: ~**-se com** to worry about, be worried about

preparação [prepara'sãw] (pl **-ões**) f preparation

preparar [prepa'ra*] vt to prepare; **preparar-se** vr to get ready; **preparativos** [prepara'tʃivuʃ] mpl preparations, arrangements

preponderante [prepõde'ratʃi] adj

predominant

preposição [prepozi'sãw] (*pl* -ões) *f* preposition

prepotente [prepo'tẽtʃi] *adj* predominant; (*despótico*) despotic; (*atitude*) overbearing

presa ['preza] *f* (*na guerra*) spoils *pl*; (*vítima*) prey; (*dente de animal*) fang

prescrever [preʃkre've*] *vt* to prescribe; (*prazo*) to set

presença [pre'zẽsa] *f* presence; (*frequência*) attendance; **ter boa ~** to be presentable; **presenciar** [prezẽ'sja*] *vt* to be present at; (*testemunhar*) to witness

presente [pre'zẽtʃi] *adj* present; (*fig: interessado*) attentive; (: *evidente*) clear, obvious ♦ *m* present ♦ *f* (*COM: carta*): **a ~** this letter; **os ~s** *mpl* (*pessoas*) those present; **presentear** [prezẽ'tʃja*] *vt* to present **alguém (com algo)** to give sb (sth as) a present

preservação [prezexva'sãw] *f* preservation

preservar [prezex'va*] *vt* to preserve, protect; **preservativo** [prezexva'tʃivu] *m* preservative; (*anticoncepcional*) condom

presidente, -a [prezi'dẽtʃi, ta] *m/f* president

presidiário, -a [prezi'dʒjarju, a] *m/f* convict

presídio [pre'zidʒju] *m* prison

presidir [prezi'dʒi*] *vt, vi*: **~ (a)** to preside over; (*reunião*) to chair; (*suj: leis, critérios*) to govern

presilha [pre'ziʎa] *f* fastener; (*para o cabelo*) slide

preso, -a ['prezu, a] *adj* imprisoned; (*capturado*) under arrest; (*atado*) tied ♦ *m/f* prisoner; **estar ~ a alguém** to be attached to sb

pressa ['presa] *f* haste, hurry; (*rapi-*

dez) speed; (*urgência*) urgency; **às ~s** hurriedly; **estar com ~** to be in a hurry; **ter ~ de** *ou* **em fazer** to be in a hurry to do

presságio [pre'saʒu] *m* omen, sign; (*pressentimento*) premonition

pressão [pre'sãw] (*pl* -ões) *f* pressure; (**colchete de**) ~ press stud, popper

pressentimento [presẽtʃi'mẽtu] *m* premonition

pressentir [presẽ'tʃi*] *vt* to foresee; (*suspeitar*) to sense

pressionar [presjo'na*] *vt* (*botão*) to press; (*coagir*) to pressure ♦ *vi* to press, put on pressure

pressões [pre'sõjʃ] *fpl de* **pressão**

pressupor [presu'po*] (*irreg: como* **pôr**) *vt* to presuppose

prestação [preʃta'sãw] (*pl* -ões) *f* instalment (*BRIT*), installment (*US*); (*por uma casa*) repayment

prestar [preʃ'ta*] *vt* (*cuidados*) to give; (*favores, serviços*) to do; (*contas*) to render; (*informações*) to supply; (*uma qualidade a algo*) to lend ♦ *vi*: **~ a alguém para algo** to be of use to sb for sth; **prestar-se** *vr*: **~-se a** to be suitable for; (*admitir*) to lend o.s. to; (*dispor-se*) to be willing to; **~ atenção** to pay attention

prestativo, -a [preʃta'tʃivu, a] *adj* helpful, obliging

prestes ['preʃtʃiʃ] *adj inv* ready; (*a ponto de*): **~ a partir** about to leave

prestígio [preʃ'tʃiʒu] *m* prestige

presunção [prezũ'sãw] (*pl* -ões) *f* presumption; (*vaidade*) conceit, self-importance; **presunçoso, -a** [prezũ'sozu, ɔza] *adj* vain, self-important

presunto [pre'zũtu] *m* ham

pretendente [pretẽ'dẽtʃi] *m/f* claimant; (*candidato*) candidate, applicant ♦ *m* suitor

pretender [pretẽ'de*] vt to claim; (cargo, emprego) to go for; ~ fazer to intend to do

pretensão [pretẽ'sãw] (pl -ões) f claim; (vaidade) pretension; (propósito) aim; (aspiração) aspiration;

pretensioso, -a [pretẽ'sjozu, ɔza] adj pretentious

pretérito [pre'teritu] m (LING) preterite

pretexto [pre'teʃtu] m pretext

preto, -a ['pretu, a] adj black ♦ m/f Black (man/woman)

prevalecer [prevale'se*] vi to prevail; **prevalecer-se** vr: ~-se de (aproveitar-se) to take advantage of

prevenção [prevẽ'sãw] f prevention; (preconceito) prejudice; (cautela) caution; **estar de** ~ **com** ou **contra alguém** to be bias(s)ed against sb

prevenido, -a [preve'nidu, a] adj cautious, wary

prevenir [preve'ni*] vt to prevent; (avisar) to warn; (preparar) to prepare

prever [pre've*] (irreg: como **ver**) vt to predict, foresee; (pressupor) to presuppose

previdência [previ'dẽsja] f foresight; (precaução) precaution

previdente [previ'dẽtʃi] adj: **ser** ~ to show foresight

prévio, -a ['prɛvju, a] adj prior; (preliminar) preliminary

previsão [previ'zãw] (pl -ões) f foresight; (prognóstico) prediction, forecast; ~ **do tempo** weather forecast

previsível [previ'zivew] (pl -eis) adj predictable

previsões [previ'zõjʃ] fpl de **previsão**

prezado, -a [pre'zadu, a] adj esteemed; (numa carta) dear

prezar [pre'za*] vt (amigos) to value highly; (autoridade) to respect; (gostar de) to appreciate

primário, -a [pri'marju, a] adj primary; (elementar) basic, rudimentary; (primitivo) primitive ♦ m (curso) elementary education

primavera [prima'vera] f spring; (planta) primrose

primeira [pri'mejra] f (AUTO) first (gear)

primeiro, -a [pri'mejru, a] adj, adv first; **de primeira** first-class

primitivo, -a [primi'tʃivu, a] adj primitive; (original) original

primo, -a ['primu, a] m/f cousin; ~ **irmão** first cousin

princesa [prĩ'seza] f princess

principal [prĩsi'paw] (pl -ais) adj principal; (entrada, razão, rua) main ♦ m head, principal; (essencial, de dívida) principal

príncipe ['prĩsipi] m prince

principiante [prĩsi'pjãtʃi] m/f beginner

principiar [prĩsi'pja*] vt, vi to begin

princípio [prĩ'sipju] m beginning, start; (origem) origin; (legal, moral) principle; ~**s** mpl (de matéria) rudiments

prioridade [prjori'dadʒi] f priority

prisão [pri'zãw] (pl -ões) f imprisonment; (cadeia) prison, jail; (detenção) arrest; ~ **de ventre** constipation; **prisioneiro, -a** [prizjo'nejru, a] m/f prisoner

privação [priva'sãw] (pl -ões) f deprivation; **privações** fpl (penúria) hardship sg

privacidade [privasi'dadʒi] f privacy

privações [priva'sõjʃ] fpl de **privação**

privada [pri'vada] f toilet

privado 548 proeminente

privado, -a [pri'vadu, a] *adj* private; (*carente*) deprived
privar [pri'va*] *vt* to deprive
privativo, -a [priva'tʃivu, a] *adj* (*particular*) private; **~ de** peculiar to
privilegiado, -a [privile'ʒjadu, a] *adj* privileged; (*excepcional*) unique, exceptional
privilegiar [privile'ʒja*] *vt* to privilege; (*favorecer*) to favour (*BRIT*), favor (*US*)
privilégio [privi'leʒu] *m* privilege
pró [prɔ] *adv* for, in favour (*BRIT*) ou favor (*US*) ♦ *m* advantage; **os ~s e os contras** the pros and cons; **em ~ de** in favo(u)r of
pró- [prɔ] *prefixo* pro-
proa ['proa] *f* prow, bow
probabilidade [probabili'dadʒi] *f* probability; **~s** *fpl* (*chances*) odds
problema [prob'lema] *m* problem
procedência [prose'dẽsja] *f* origin, source; (*lugar de saída*) point of departure
proceder [prose'de*] *vi* to proceed; (*comportar-se*) to behave; (*agir*) to act ♦ *m* conduct; **procedimento** [prosedʒi'mẽtu] *m* conduct, behaviour (*BRIT*), behavior (*US*); (*processo*) procedure; (*JUR*) proceedings *pl*
processamento [prosesa'mẽtu] *m* processing; (*JUR*) prosecution; (*verificação*) verification; **~ de texto** word processing
processar [prose'sa*] *vt* (*JUR*) to take proceedings against, prosecute; (*requerimentos*, *COMPUT*) to process
processo [pro'sesu] *m* process; (*procedimento*) procedure; (*JUR*) lawsuit, legal proceedings *pl*; (: *autos*) record; (*conjunto de documentos*) documents *pl*
procissão [prosi'sãw] (*pl* -ões) *f* procession

proclamação [proklama'sãw] *f* proclamation; **P~ da República** (*BR*) *see boxed note*

PROCLAMAÇÃO DA REPÚBLICA

Commemorated on 15 November, which is a public holiday in Brazil, the proclamation of the republic in 1889 was a military coup, led by Marshal Deodoro da Fonseca. It brought down the empire which had been established after independence, and installed a federal republic in Brazil.

---

proclamar [prokla'ma*] *vt* to claim
procura [pro'kura] *f* search; (*COM*) demand
procuração [prokura'sãw] *f*: **por ~** by proxy
procurador, a [prokura'do*, a] *m/f* attorney; **P~ Geral da República** Attorney General
procurar [proku'ra*] *vt* to look for, seek; (*emprego*) to apply for; (*ir visitar*) to call on; (*contatar*) to get in touch with; **~ fazer** to try to do
prodígio [pro'dʒiʒu] *m* prodigy
produção [produ'sãw] (*pl* -ões) *f* production; (*volume de produção*) output; (*produto*) product; **~ em massa**, **~ em série** mass production
produtivo, -a [produ'tʃivu, a] *adj* productive; (*rendoso*) profitable
produto [pro'dutu] *m* product; (*renda*) proceeds *pl*, profit
produtor, a [produ'to*, a] *adj* producing ♦ *m/f* producer
produzir [produ'zi*] *vt* to produce; (*ocasionar*) to cause, bring about; (*render*) to bring in
proeminente [proemi'nẽtʃi] *adj* prominent

proeza [pro'eza] f achievement, feat

profanar [profa'na*] vt to desecrate, profane; **profano, -a** [pro-'fanu, a] adj profane ♦ m/f layman/woman

profecia [profe'sia] f prophecy

professor, a [profe'so*, a] m/f teacher, (universitário) lecturer

profeta, -isa [pro'feta, profe'tʃiza] m/f prophet; **profetizar** [profetʃi-'za*] vt, vi to prophesy, predict

profissão [profi'sãw] (pl -ões) f profession; **profissional** [profisjo-'naw] (pl -ais) adj, m/f professional; **profissionalizante** [profisjonali-'zãtʃi] adj (ensino) vocational

profundidade [profudʒi'dadʒi] f depth

profundo, -a [pro'fũdu, a] adj deep; (fig) profound

profusão [profu'zãw] f profusion, abundance

prognóstico [prog'nɔstʃiku] m prediction, forecast

programa [pro'grama] m programme (BRIT), program (US); (COMPUT) program; (plano) plan; (diversão) thing to do; (de um curso) syllabus; **programação** [programa-'sãw] f planning; (TV, RADIO, COMPUT) programming; **programador, a** [programa'do*, a] m/f programmer; **programar** [progra'ma*] vt to plan; (COMPUT) to program

progredir [progre'dʒi*] vi to progress; (avançar) to move forward; (infecção) to progress

progressista [progre'sifta] adj, m/f progressive

progressivo, -a [progre'sivu, a] adj progressive; (gradual) gradual

progresso [pro'gresu] m progress

progrido etc [pro'gridu] vb V progredir

proibição [proibi'sãw] (pl -ões) f prohibition, ban

proibir [proi'bi*] vt to prohibit; (livro, espetáculo) to ban; "é proibido fumar" "no smoking"; ~ alguém de fazer, ~ que alguém faça to forbid sb to do

projeção [proʒe'sãw] (PT -cç-; pl -ões) f projection

projetar [proʒe'ta*] (PT -ct-) vt to project

projétil [pro'ʒetfiw] (PT -ct-; pl -eis) m projectile, missile

projeto [pro'ʒetu] (PT -ct-) m project; (plano, ARQ) plan; (TEC) design; ~ de lei bill

projetor [proʒe'to*] (PT -ct-) m (CINEMA) projector

proliferar [prolife'ra*] vi to proliferate

prolongação [prolõga'sãw] f extension

prolongado, -a [prolõ'gadu, a] adj prolonged; (alongado) extended

prolongar [prolõ'ga*] vt to extend, lengthen; (decisão etc) to postpone; (vida) to prolong; **prolongar-se** vr to extend; (durar) to last

promessa [pro'mesa] f promise

prometer [prome'te*] vt, vi to promise

promíscuo, -a [pro'miʃkwu, a] adj disorderly, mixed up; (comportamento sexual) promiscuous

promissor, a [promi'so*, a] adj promising

promoção [promo'sãw] (pl -ões) f promotion; fazer ~ de alguém/algo to promote sb/sth

promotor, a [promo'to*, a] m/f promoter; (JUR) prosecutor

promover [promo've*] vt to promote; (causar) to cause, bring about

pronome [pro'nɔmi] m pronoun

pronto, -a [prõtu, a] adj ready;

(*rápido*) quick, speedy; (*imediato*) prompt ♦ *adv* promptly; **de ~** promptly; **estar ~ a** ... to be prepared *ou* willing to ...; **pronto-socorro** (*PT*) *m* prontos-socorros (*PT*) *m* towtruck

pronúncia [pro'nũsja] *f* pronunciation; (*JUR*) indictment

pronunciar [pronũ'sja*] *vt* to pronounce; (*discurso*) to make, deliver; (*JUR: réu*) to indict; (: *sentença*) to pass

propaganda [propa'gãda] *f* (*POL*) propaganda; (*COM*) advertising; (: *uma ~*) advert, advertisement; **fazer ~ de** to advertise

propagar [propa'ga*] *vt* to propagate; (*fig: difundir*) to disseminate

propensão [propẽ'sãw] (*pl -ões*) *f* inclination, tendency; **propenso, -a** [pro'pẽsu, a] *adj*: **propenso a** inclined to; **ser propenso a** to be inclined to, have a tendency to

propina [pro'pina] *f* (*gorjeta*) tip; (*PT: cota*) fee

propor [pro'po*] (*irreg: como pôr*) *vt* to propose; (*oferecer*) to offer; (*um problema*) to pose; **propor-se** *vr*: **~-se (a) fazer** (*pretender*) to intend to do; (*visar*) to aim to do; (*dispor-se*) to decide to do; (*oferecer-se*) to offer to do

proporção [propox'sãw] (*pl -ões*) *f* proportion; **proporções** *fpl* (*dimensões*) dimensions; **proporcional** [propoxsjo'naw] (*pl -ais*) *adj* proportional; **proporcionar** [propoxsjo'na*] *vt* to provide, give; (*adaptar*) to adjust, adapt

proposição [propozi'sãw] (*pl -ões*) *f* proposition, proposal

proposital [propozi'taw] (*pl -ais*) *adj* intentional

propósito [pro'pɔzitu] *m* (*intenção*) purpose; (*objetivo*) aim; **a ~** by the

way; **a ~ de** with regard to; **de ~** on purpose

proposta [pro'pɔʃta] *f* proposal; (*oferecimento*) offer

propriamente [proprja'mẽtʃi] *adv* properly, exactly; **~ falando** *ou* **dito** strictly speaking

propriedade [proprje'dadʒi] *f* property; (*direito de proprietário*) ownership; (*o que é apropriado*) propriety

proprietário, -a [proprje'tarju, a] *m/f* owner, proprietor

próprio, -a [a 'prɔprju, a] *adj* own, of one's own; (*mesmo*) very, selfsame; (*hora, momento*) opportune, right; (*nome*) proper; (*característico*) characteristic; (*sentido*) proper, true; (*depois de pronome*) -self; **~ (para)** suitable (for); **eu ~** I myself; **por si ~** of one's own accord; **ele é o ~ inglês** he's a typical Englishman; **é o ~** it's him himself

prorrogação [proxoga'sãw] (*pl -ões*) *f* extension

prosa ['prɔza] *f* prose; (*conversa*) chatter; (*fanfarrice*) boasting, bragging ♦ *adj* full of oneself

prospecto [proʃ'pɛktu] *m* leaflet; (*em forma de livro*) brochure

prosperar [proʃpe'ra*] *vi* to prosper, thrive; **prosperidade** [proʃperi'dadʒi] *f* prosperity; (*bom êxito*) success; **próspero, -a** ['prɔʃperu, a] *adj* prosperous; (*bem sucedido*) successful; (*favorável*) favourable (*BRIT*), favorable (*US*)

prosseguir [prose'gi*] *vt, vi* to continue; **~ em** to continue (with)

prostíbulo [proʃ'tʃibulu] *m* brothel

prostituta [proʃtʃi'tuta] *f* prostitute

prostrado, -a [proʃ'tradu, a] *adj* prostrate

protagonista [protago'niʃta] *m/f* protagonist

proteção [prote'sãw] (*PT* **-cç-**) *f* protection

protector, a [protek'to*, a] (*PT*) = **protetor, a**

proteger [prote'ʒe*] *vt* to protect; **protegido, -a** [prote'ʒidu, a] *m/f* protégé(e)

proteína [prote'ina] *f* protein

protejo *etc* [pro'teʒu] *vb V* **proteger**

protestante [protef'tãtʃi] *adj, m/f* Protestant

protestar [protef'ta*] *vt, vi* to protest; **protesto** [pro'teftu] *m* protest

protetor, a [prote'to*], *adj* protective ♦ *m/f* protector; **~ solar** sunscreen; **~ de tela** (*COMPUT*) screensaver

protuberância [protube'rãsja] *f* bump; **protuberante** [protube-'rãtʃi] *adj* sticking out

prova ['prɔva] *f* proof; (*TEC: teste*) test, trial; (*EDUC: exame*) examination, (*sinal*) sign; (*de comida, bebida*) taste; (*de roupa*) fitting; (*ESPORTE*) competition; (*TIP*) proof; **~(s)** *f(pl)* (*JUR*) evidence *sg*; **à ~ de bala/fogo/água** bulletproof/fireproof/waterproof; **pôr à ~** to put to the test

provar [pro'va*] *vt* to prove; (*comida*) to taste, try; (*roupa*) to try on ♦ *vi* to try

provável [pro'vavew] (*pl* **-eis**) *adj* probable, likely

provedor, a [prove'do*, a] *m/f* supplier; **~ de acesso à Internet** Internet service provider

proveito [pro'vejtu] *m* advantage; (*ganho*) profit; **em ~ de** for the benefit of; **fazer ~ de** to make use of; **proveitoso, -a** [provej'tozu, ɔza] *adj* profitable, advantageous; (*útil*) useful

proveniente [prove'njetʃi] *adj*: **proveniente de** originating from;

(*que resulta de*) arising from

prover [pro've*] (*irreg: como* **ver**) *vt* to provide, supply; (*vaga*) to fill ♦ *vi*: **~ a** to take care of, see to

provérbio [pro'vexbju] *m* proverb

providência [provi'dẽsja] *f* providence; **~s** *fpl* (*medidas*) measures, steps; **providencial** [providẽ'sjaw] (*pl* **-ais**) *adj* opportune; **providenciar** [providẽ'sja*] *vt* to provide; (*tomar providências*) to arrange ♦ *vi* to make arrangements, take steps; **providenciar para que** to see to it that

província [pro'vĩsja] *f* province; **provinciano, -a** [provĩ'sjanu, a] *adj* provincial

provisório, -a [provi'zɔrju, a] *adj* provisional, temporary

provocador, a [provoka'do*, a] *adj* provocative

provocante [provo'kãtʃi] *adj* provocative

provocar [provo'ka*] *vt* to provoke; (*ocasionar*) to cause; (*atrair*) to tempt, attract; (*estimular*) to rouse, stimulate

próximo, -a ['prɔsimu, a] *adj* (*no espaço*) near, close; (*no tempo*) close; (*seguinte*) next; (*amigo, parente*) close; (*vizinho*) neighbouring (*BRIT*), neighboring (*US*) ♦ *adv* near ♦ *m* fellow man; **~ a** *ou* **de** near, close to; **até a próxima!** see you again soon!

prudência [pru'dẽsja] *f* care, prudence; **prudente** [pru'dẽtʃi] *adj* prudent

prurido [pru'ridu] *m* itch

psicanálise [psika'nalizi] *f* psychoanalysis

psicologia [psikolo'ʒia] *f* psychology; **psicológico, -a** [psiko-'lɔʒiku, a] *adj* psychological; **psicólogo, -a** [psi'kɔlogu, a] *m/f* psychologist

psique ['psiki] f psyche

psiquiatra [psi'kjatra] m/f psychiatrist

psiquiatria [psikja'tria] f psychiatry

psíquico, -a ['psikiku, a] adj psychological

puberdade [pubex'dadʒi] f puberty

publicação [publika'sãw] f publication

publicar [publi'ka*] vt to publish; (divulgar) to divulge; (proclamar) to announce

publicidade [publisi'dadʒi] f publicity; (COM) advertising; **publicitário, -a** [publisi'tarju, a] adj publicity atr; advertising atr

público, -a ['publiku, a] adj public ♦ m public; (CINEMA, TEATRO etc) audience

pude etc ['pudʒi] vb V **poder**

pudera etc [pu'dera] vb V **poder**

pudim [pu'dʒĩ] (pl -ns) m pudding

pudor [pu'do*] m bashfulness, modesty; (moral) decency

pular [pu'la*] vi to jump; (no Carnaval) to celebrate ♦ vt to jump (over); (páginas, trechos) to skip; ~ Carnaval to celebrate Carnival; ~ corda to skip

pulga ['puwga] f flea

pulmão etc [puw'mãw] (pl -ões) m lung

pulo¹ ['pulu] m jump; **dar um ~ em** to stop off at

pulo² etc vb V **polir**

pulôver [pu'love*] (BR) m pullover

pulsação [puwsa'sãw] f pulsation, beating; (MED) pulse

pulseira [puw'sejra] f bracelet; (de sapato) strap

pulso ['puwsu] m (ANAT) wrist; (MED) pulse; (fig) vigour (BRIT), vigor (US), energy

punha etc ['puɲa] vb V **pôr**

punhado [pu'ɲadu] m handful

punhal [pu'ɲaw] (pl -ais) m dagger

punho ['puɲu] m fist; (de manga) cuff; (de espada) hilt

punição [puni'sãw] (pl -ões) f punishment

punir [pu'ni*] vt to punish

pupila [pu'pila] f (ANAT) pupil

purê [pu're] m purée; ~ **de batatas** mashed potatoes

pureza [pu'reza] f purity

purificar [purifi'ka*] vt to purify

puritano, -a [puri'tanu, a] adj puritanical; (seita) puritan ♦ m/f puritan

puro, -a ['puru, a] adj pure; (uísque etc) neat; (verdade) plain; (intenções) honourable (BRIT), honorable (US); (estilo) clear

pus¹ [puʃ] m pus

pus² etc [puʃ] vb V **pôr**

puser etc [pu'ze*] vb V **pôr**

puta ['puta] (col!) f whore; V tb **puto**

puto, -a ['putu, a] (col!) m/f (semvergonha) bastard ♦ adj (zangado) furious; (incrível): **um ~** ... a hell of a ...; **o ~ de** ... the bloody ...

pútrido, -a ['putridu, a] adj putrid, rotten

puxador [puʃa'do*] m handle, knob

puxão [pu'ʃãw] (pl -ões) m tug, jerk

puxar [pu'ʃa*] vt to pull; (sacar) to pull out; (assunto) to bring up; (conversa) to strike up; (briga) to pick ♦ vi: ~ **de uma perna** to limp; ~ **a** to take after

puxões [pu'ʃõjʃ] mpl de **puxão**

Q

QG abr m (= Quartel-General) HQ

QI abr m (= Quociente de Inteligência) IQ

quadra ['kwadra] f (quarteirão) block; (de tênis etc) court; (período) time, period

quadrado, -a [kwa'dradu, a] adj

square ♦ *m* square ♦ *m/f* (*col*) square

quadril [kwa'driw] (*pl* **-is**) *m* hip

quadrinho [kwa'driɲu] *m*: **história em ~s** (*BR*) cartoon, comic strip

quadris [kwa'driʃ] *mpl de* **quadril**

quadro ['kwadru] *m* painting; (*gravura, foto*) picture; (*lista*) list; (*tabela*) chart, table; (*TEC: painel*) panel; (*pessoal*) staff; (*time*) team; (*TEATRO, fig*) scene; **quadro-negro** (*pl* **quadros-negros**) *m* blackboard

quadruplicar [kwadrupli'ka*] *vt, vi* to quadruple

qual |kwaw] (*pl* **-ais**) *pron* which ♦ *conj* as, like ♦ *excl* what!; **o ~** which; (*pessoa: suj*) who; (: *objeto*) whom; **seja ~ for** whatever *ou* whichever it may be; **cada ~** each one

qualidade [kwali'dadʒi] *f* quality

qualificação [kwalifika'sãw] (*pl* **-ões**) *f* qualification

qualificado, -a [kwalifi'kadu, a] *adj* qualified

qualificar [kwalifi'ka*] *vt* to qualify; (*avaliar*) to evaluate; **qualificar-se** *vr* to qualify; **~ de** *ou* **como** to classify as

qualquer [kwaw'ke*] (*pl* **quaisquer**) *adj, pron* any; **~ pessoa** anyone, anybody; **~ um dos dois** either; **~ que seja** whichever it may be; **a ~ momento** at any moment

quando ['kwãdu] *adv* when ♦ *conj* when; (*interrogativo*) when?; (*ao passo que*) whilst; **~ muito** at most

quantia [kwã'tʃia] *f* sum, amount

quantidade [kwãtʃi'dadʒi] *f* quantity, amount

---

quanto, -a ['kwãtu, a] *adj* **1** (*interrogativo: sg*) how much?; (: *pl*) how many?; (: *pl*) how many?; **2** (*o (que for) necessário*) all that, as much as; **daremos ~s exemplares ele precisar** we'll give him as many copies as *ou* all the copies he needs

~ tanto/tantos ... ~ as much/many ... as

♦ *pron* **1** how much?; how many?; **~ custa?** how much?; **a ~ está o jogo?** what's the score?

2: **tudo ~** everything that, as much as

3: **tanto/tantos ... ~** as much/as many as ...

4: **um tanto ~** somewhat, rather

♦ *adv* **1**: **~ a** as regards; **~ a mim** as for me

2: **~ antes** as soon as possible

3: **~ mais** (*principalmente*) especially; (*muito menos*) let alone; **~ mais cedo melhor** the sooner the better

4: **~ tanto ~ possível** as much as possible; **tão ... ~ ... as ... as ...**

♦ *conj*: **~ mais trabalha, mais ele ganha** the more he works, the more he earns; **~ mais, (tanto) melhor** the more the better

---

quarenta [kwa'rēta] *num* forty

quarentena [kware'tena] *f* quarantine

quaresma [kwa'reʒma] *f* Lent

quarta ['kwaxta] *f* (*tb*: **~-feira**) Wednesday; (*parte*) quarter; (*AUTO*) fourth (gear); **quarta-feira** (*pl* **quartas-feiras**) *f* Wednesday; **quarta-feira de cinzas** Ash Wednesday

quarteirão [kwaxtej'rãw] (*pl* **-ões**) *m* (*de casas*) block

quartel [kwax'tew] (*pl* **-éis**) *m* barracks *sg*; **quartel-general** *m* headquarters *pl*

quarteto [kwax'tetu] *m* quartet(te)

quarto, -a ['kwaxtu, a] *num* fourth
♦ *m* quarter; (*aposento*) room; ~
de banho/dormir bathroom/bed-
room; **três ~s de hora** three quar-
ters of an hour

quase ['kwazi] *adv* almost, nearly; ~
nunca hardly ever

quatorze [kwa'toxzi] *num* fourteen

quatro ['kwatru] *num* four

PALAVRA CHAVE

que [ki] *conj* **1** (*com oração subordi-
nada: muitas vezes não se traduz*)
that; **ele disse ~ viria** he said (that)
he would come; **não há nada ~
fazer** there's nothing to be done;
espero ~ sim/não I hope so/not;
dizer ~ sim/não to say yes/no
2 (*consecutivo: muitas vezes não se
traduz*) that; **é tão pesado ~ não
consigo levantá-lo** it's so heavy
(that) I can't lift it
3 (*comparações*): **(do) ~** than; *V tb*
mais; menos; mesmo
♦ *pron* **1** (*coisa*) which, that; (+ *prep*)
which; **o chapéu ~ você comprou**
the hat (that ou which) you bought
2 (*pessoa: suj*) who, that; (: *complemento*) whom, that; **o amigo ~ me
levou ao museu** the friend who
took me to the museum; **a moça ~
eu convidei** the girl (that ou whom)
I invited
3 (*interrogativo*) what?; **o ~ você
disse?** what did you say?
4 (*exclamação*) what!; ~ **pena!** what
a pity!; ~ **lindo!** how lovely!

---

quê [ke] *m* (*col*) something ♦ *pron*
what; ~! what!; **não tem de ~** don't
mention it; **para ~?** what for?; **por
~?** why?

quebra ['kɛbra] *f* break, rupture; (*fa-

lência) bankruptcy; (*de energia elétrica*) cut; **de ~** in addition; **quebra-
cabeça** (*pl* quebra-cabeças) *m*
puzzle, problem; (*jogo*) jigsaw puzzle

quebrado, -a [ke'bradu, a] *adj* broken; (*cansado*) exhausted; (*falido*)
bankrupt; (*carro, máquina*) broken
down; (*telefone*) out of order

quebra-nozes *m inv* nutcrackers *pl*
(*BRIT*), nutcracker (*US*)

quebrar [ke'bra*] *vt* to break ♦ *vi* to
break; (*carro*) to break down; (*COM*)
to go bankrupt; (*ficar sem dinheiro*)
to go broke

queda ['kɛda] *f* fall; (*fig*) downfall;
ter ~ para algo to have a bent for
sth; ~ **de barreira** landslide; **queda-
d'água** (*pl* quedas-d'água) *f* waterfall

queijo ['kejʒu] *m* cheese

queimado, -a [kej'madu, a] *adj*
burnt; (*de sol: machucado*) sunburnt; (: *bronzeado*) brown, tanned;
(*plantas, folhas*) dried up

queimadura [kejma'dura] *f* burn;
(*de sol*) sunburn

queimar [kej'ma*] *vt* to burn;
(*roupa*) to scorch; (*com líquido*) to
scald; (*bronzear a pele*) to tan;
(*planta, folha*) to wither ♦ *vi* to burn;
queimar-se *vr* (*pessoa*) to burn
o.s.; (*de sol*) to tan

queima-roupa *f*: **à** ~ point-blank,
at point-blank range

queira *etc* ['kejra] *vb V* **querer**

queixa ['kejʃa] *f* complaint; (*lamen-
tação*) lament; **fazer ~ de alguém** to
complain about sb

queixar-se [kej'faxsi] *vr* to complain; ~ **de** to complain about;
(*dores etc*) to complain of

queixo ['kejʃu] *m* chin; (*maxilar*)
jaw; **bater o** ~ to shiver

quem [kẽj] *pron* who; (*como objeto*)

who(m); **de ~ é isto?** whose is this?; **~ diria!** who would have thought (it)!; **~ sabe** (*talvez*) perhaps

Quênia ['kenja] *m*: **o ~** Kenya

quente ['kẽtʃi] *adj* hot; (*roupa*) warm

quer [kɛ*] *vb V* querer ♦ *conj*: **~ ... ~ ...** whether ... or ...; **~ chova ~ não** whether it rains or not; **onde/quando/quem ~ que** wherever/whenever/whoever; **o que ~ que seja** whatever it is

---

PALAVRA CHAVE

---

querer [ke're*] *vt* **1** (*desejar*) to want; **quero mais dinheiro** I want more money; **queria um chá** I'd like a cup of tea; **quero ajudar/que lá** I want to help/you to go; **você vai ~ sair amanhã?** do you want to go out tomorrow?; **eu vou ~ uma cerveja** (*num bar etc*) I'd like a beer; **por/sem ~** intentionally/unintentionally; **como queira** as you wish

2 (*perguntas para pedir algo*): **você quer fechar a janela?** will you shut the window?; **quer me dar uma mão?** can you give me a hand?

3 (*amar*) to love

4 (*convite*): **quer entrar/sentar** do come in/sit down

5: **~ dizer** (*significar*) to mean; (*pretender dizer*) to mean to say; **quero dizer** I mean; **quer dizer** (*com outras palavras*) in other words

♦ *vi*: **~ bem a** to be fond of

♦ **querer-se** *vr* to love one another

♦ *m* (*vontade*) wish; (*afeto*) affection

---

querido, -a [ke'ridu, a] *adj* dear ♦ *m/f* darling; **Q~ João** Dear John

querosene [kero'zɛni] *m* kerosene

questão [keʃ'tãw] (*pl* -ões) *f* question, inquiry; (*problema*) matter, question; (*JUR*) case; (*contenda*) dis-

pute, quarrel; **fazer ~ (de)** to insist (on); **em ~** in question; **há ~ de um ano** about a year ago; **questionar** [keʃtʃjo'na*] *vi* to question ♦ *vt* to question, call into question; **questionário** [keʃtʃjo'narju] *m* questionnaire; **questionável** [keʃtʃjo'navew] (*pl* -eis) *adj* questionable

quicar [ki'ka*] *vt*, *vi* to bounce

quieto, -a ['kjetu, a] *adj* quiet; (*imóvel*) still; **quietude** [kje'tudʒi] *f* calm, tranquillity

quilate [ki'latʃi] *m* carat

quilo ['kilu] *m* kilo; **quilobyte** [kilo'bajtʃi] *m* kilobyte; **quilograma** [kilo'grama] *m* kilogram; **quilometragem** [kilome'traʒe] *f* number of kilometres *ou* kilometers travelled, ≈ mileage; **quilômetro** [ki'lometru] *m* kilometre (*BRIT*), kilometer (*US*); **quilowatt** [kilo'watʃi] *m* kilowatt

química ['kimika] *f* chemistry

químico, -a ['kimiku, a] *adj* chemical ♦ *m/f* chemist

quina ['kina] *f* corner; (*de mesa etc*) edge; **de ~** edgeways (*BRIT*), edgewise (*US*)

quindim [kĩ'dʒĩ] *m* sweet made of egg yolks, coconut and sugar

quinhão [ki'nãw] (*pl* -ões) *m* share, portion

quinhentos, -as [ki'ɲẽtuʃ, aʃ] *num* five hundred

quinhões [ki'nõjʃ] *mpl de* quinhão

quinquilharias [kĩkiʎa'riaʃ] *fpl* odds and ends; (*miudezas*) knick-knacks, trinkets

quinta ['kĩta] *f* (*tb*: **~-feira**) Thursday; (*propriedade*) estate; (*PT*) farm; **quinta-feira** ['kĩta'fejra] (*pl* **quintas-feiras**) *f* Thursday

quintal [kĩ'taw] (*pl* -ais) *m* back yard

quinteto [kĩ'tetu] *m* quintet(te)

quinto, -a ['kĩtu, a] *num* fifth

quinze ['kĩzi] *num* fifteen; **duas e ~ a quarter past** (BRIT) *ou* **after** (US) **two; ~ para as sete a quarter to** (BRIT) *ou* (US) **seven**

quinzena [kĩ'zɛna] *f* two weeks, fortnight (BRIT); **quinzenal** [kĩze'naw] (*pl* -**is**) *adj* fortnightly; **quinzenalmente** [kĩzenaw'mẽtʃi] *adv* fortnightly

quiosque ['kjɔʃki] *m* kiosk

quis *etc* [kiʒ] *vb* V **querer**

quiser *etc* [ki'ze*] *vb* V **querer**

quisto ['kiʃtu] *m* cyst

quitanda [ki'tãda] *f* grocer's (shop) (BRIT), grocery store (US)

quitar [ki'ta*] *vt* (*dívida: pagar*) to pay off; (: *perdoar*) to cancel; (*devedor*) to release

quite ['kitʃi] *adj* (*livre*) free; (*com um credor*) squared up; (*igualado*) even; **estar ~ (com alguém)** to be quits (with sb)

quitute [ki'tutʃi] *m* titbit (BRIT), tidbit (US)

quota ['kwota] *f* quota; (*porção*) share, portion

quotidiano, -a [kwotʃi'dʒjanu, a] *adj* everyday

R

R *abr* (= *rua*) St

R$ *abr* = **real**

rã [xã] *f* frog

rabanete [xaba'netʃi] *m* radish

rabiscar [xabiʃ'ka*] *vt* to scribble; (*papel*) to scribble on ♦ *vi* to scribble; (*desenhar*) to doodle; **rabisco** [xa'biʃku] *m* scribble

rabo ['xabu] *m* tail

rabugento, -a [xabu'ʒẽtu, a] *adj* grumpy

raça ['xasa] *f* breed; (*grupo étnico*) race; **cão/cavalo de ~** pedigree

dog/thoroughbred horse

racha ['xaʃa] *f* (*fenda*) split; (*greta*) crack; **rachadura** [xaʃa'dura] *f* crack; **rachar** [xa'ʃa*] *vt* to crack; (*objeto, despesas*) to split; (*lenha*) to chop ♦ *vi* to split; (*cristal*) to crack; **rachar-se** *vr* to split; to crack

racial [xa'sjaw] (*pl* -**ais**) *adj* racial

raciocínio [xasjo'sinju] *m* reasoning

racional [xasjo'naw] (*pl* -**ais**) *adj* rational; **racionalizar** [xasjonali-'za*] *vt* to rationalize

racionamento [xasjona'mẽtu] *m* rationing

racismo [xa'siʒmu] *m* racism; **racista** [xa'siʃta] *adj, m/f* racist

radar [xa'da*] *m* radar

radiação [xadʒja'sãw] *f* radiation

radiador [xadʒja'do*] *m* radiator

radiante [xa'dʒjãtʃi] *adj* radiant

radical [xadʒi'kaw] (*pl* -**ais**) *adj* radical

radicar-se [xadʒi'kaxsi] *vr* to take root; (*fixar residência*) to settle

rádio ['xadʒju] *m* radio; (QUÍM) radium; **radioativo, -a** [xadʒjua-'tʃivu, a] (PT -**act**-) *adj* radioactive; **radiodifusão** [xadʒjodʒifu'zãw] *f* broadcasting; **radiografar** [xadʒjogra'fa*] *vt* to X-ray; **radiografia** [xadʒjogra'fia] *f* X-ray

raia ['xaja] *f* (*risca*) line; (*fronteira*) boundary; (*limite*) limit; (*de corrida*) lane; (*peixe*) ray

raiar [xa'ja*] *vi* to shine

rainha [xa'iɲa] *f* queen

raio ['xaju] *m* (*de sol*) ray; (*de luz*) beam; (*de roda*) spoke; (*relâmpago*) flash of lightning; (*alcance*) range; (MAT) radius; **~s X** X-rays

raiva ['xajva] *f* rage, fury; (MED) rabies *sg*; **estar/ficar com ~ (de)** to be/get angry (with); **ter ~ a** to hate; **raivoso, -a** [xaj'vozu, ɔza] *adj* furious

raiz [xa'iʒ] f root; (*origem*) origin, source; **~ quadrada** square root

rajada [xa'ʒada] f (*vento*) gust

ralado, -a [xa'ladu, a] adj grated; **ralador** [xala'do*] m grater

ralar [xa'la*] vt to grate

ralhar [xa'ʎa*] vi to scold; **~ com alguém** to tell sb off

rali [xa'li] m rally

ralo, -a [xalu, a] adj (*cabelo*) thinning; (*tecido*) flimsy; (*vegetação*) sparse; (*sopa*) thin, watery; (*café*) weak ♦ m (*de regador*) rose, nozzle; (*de pia, banheiro*) drain

rama ['xama] f branches pl, foliage; **pela ~** superficially; **ramagem** [xa'maʒel] f branches pl, foliage; **ramal** [xa'maw] (pl **~is**) m (*FERRO*) branch line; (*TEL*) extension; (*AUTO*) side road

ramificar-se [xamifi'kaxsi] vr to branch out

ramo ['xamu] m branch; (*profissão, negócios*) line; (*de flores*) bunch; **Domingo de R~s** Palm Sunday

rampa ['xãpa] f ramp; (*ladeira*) slope

rancor [xã'ko*] m bitterness; (*ódio*) hatred; **rancoroso, -a** [xãko'rozu, ɔza] adj bitter, resentful; hateful

rançoso, -a [xã'sozu, ɔza] adj rancid; (*cheiro*) musty

ranger [xã'ʒe*] vi to creak ♦ vt: **~ os dentes** to grind one's teeth

ranhura [xa'ɲura] f groove; (*para moeda*) slot

rapar [xa'pa*] vt to scrape; (*a barba*) to shave; (*o cabelo*) to crop

rapariga [xapa'riga] f girl

rapaz [xa'pajʒ] m boy; (*col*) lad

rapidez [xapi'deʒ] f speed

rápido, -a [xapidu, a] adj fast, quick ♦ adv fast, quickly ♦ m (*trem*) express

rapina [xa'pina] f robbery; **ave de ~** bird of prey

raptar [xap'ta*] vt to kidnap; **rapto** ['xaptu] m kidnapping; **raptor** [xap'to*] m kidnapper

raquete [xa'ketʃi] f racquet

raquítico, -a [xa'kitʃiku, a] adj (*franzino*) puny; (*vegetação*) poor

raramente [xara'mẽtʃi] adv rarely, seldom

rarefeito, -a [xare'fejtu, a] adj rarefied; (*multidão, população*) sparse

raro, -a [xaru, a] adj rare ♦ adv rarely, seldom

rascunho [xaʃ'kuɲu] m draft, rough copy

rasgado, -a [xaʒ'gadu, a] adj (*roupa*) torn, ripped

rasgão [xaʒ'gãw] (pl **-ões**) m tear, rip

rasgar [xaʒ'ga*] vt to tear, rip; (*destruir*) to tear up, rip up; **rasgar-se** vr to split; **rasgo** [xaʒgu] m tear, rip

rasgões [xaʒ'gõjʃ] mpl de **rasgão**

raso, -a ['xazu, a] adj (*liso*) flat, level; (*não fundo*) shallow; (*baixo*) low; **soldado ~** private

raspa ['xaʃpa] f (*de madeira*) shaving; (*de metal*) filing

raspão [xaʃ'pãw] (pl **-ões**) m scratch, graze

raspar [xaʃ'pa*] vt to scrape; (*alisar*) to file; (*tocar de raspão*) to graze; (*arranhar*) to scratch; (*pêlos, cabeça*) to shave; (*apagar*) to rub out ♦ vi: **~ em** to scrape

raspões [xaʃ'põjʃ] mpl de **raspão**

rasteira [xaʃ'tejra] f: **dar uma ~ em alguém** to trip sb up

rasteiro, -a [xaʃ'tejru, a] adj crawling; (*planta*) creeping

rastejar [xaʃte'ʒa*] vi to crawl; (*furtivamente*) to creep; (*fig: rebaixar-se*) to grovel ♦ vt (*fugitivo etc*) to track

rasto ['xaʃtu] m (*pegada*) track; (*de

veículo) trail; (fig) sign, trace; **andar de ~s** to crawl

rastro ['xaʃtru] m = **rasto**

rata ['xata] f rat; (pequena) mouse

ratificar [xatʃifi'ka*] vt to ratify

rato ['xatu] m rat; (pequeno) mouse; **~ de hotel/praia** hotel/beach thief; **ratoeira** [xa'twejra] f rat trap; mousetrap

ravina [xa'vina] f ravine

razão [xa'zãw] (pl **-ões**) f reason; (argumento) reasoning; (MAT) ratio ♦ m (COM) ledger; **à ~ de** at the rate of; **em ~ de** on account of; **dar ~ a alguém** to support sb; **ter/não ter ~** to be right/wrong; **razoável** [xa'zwavew] (pl **-eis**) adj reasonable

r/c (PT) abr = **rés-do-chão**

RDSI abr f (= Rede Digital de Serviços Integrados) ISDN

ré [xɛ] f (JUR) reverse (gear); **dar (marcha à) ~** to reverse, back up; V tb **réu**

reabastecer [xeabaʃte'se*] vt (avião) to refuel; (carro) to fill up; **reabastecer-se** vr: **~-se de** to replenish one's supply of

reação [xea'sãw] (PT **-cç-**; pl **-ões**) f reaction

reagir [xea'ʒi*] vi to react; (doente, time perdedor) to fight back; **~ a** (resistir) to resist; (protestar) to rebel against

reais [xe'ajʃ] adj pl de **real**

reaja etc [xe'aʒa] vb V **reagir; reaver**

reajuste [xea'ʒuʃtʃi] m adjustment

real [xe'aw] (pl **-ais**) adj real; (relativo à realeza) royal ♦ m (moeda) real

realçar [xeaw'sa*] vt to highlight; **realce** [xe'awsi] m emphasis; (mais brilho) highlight; **dar realce a** to enhance

realeza [xea'leza] f royalty

realidade [xeali'dadʒi] f reality; **na ~** actually, in fact

realista [xea'liʃta] adj realistic ♦ m/f realist

realização [xealiza'sãw] f fulfilment (BRIT), fulfillment (US), realization; (de projeto) execution, carrying out

realizador, a [xealiza'do*, a] adj enterprising

realizar [xeali'za*] vt to achieve; (projeto) to carry out; (ambições, sonho) to fulfil (BRIT), fulfill (US), realize; (negócios) to transact; (perceber) to realize; **realizar-se** vr to take place; (ambições) to be realized; (sonhos) to come true

realmente [xeaw'mẽtʃi] adv really; (de fato) actually

reanimar [xeani'ma*] vt to revive; (encorajar) to encourage; **reanimar-se** vr to cheer up

reatar [xea'ta*] vt to resume, take up again

reaver [xea've*] vt to recover, get back

rebaixar [xebaj'ʃa*] vt to lower; (mercadorias) to lower the price of; (humilhar) to put down, humiliate ♦ vi to drop; **rebaixar-se** vr to demean o.s

rebanho [xe'baɲu] m (de carneiros, fig) flock; (de gado, elefantes) herd

rebelar-se [xebe'laxsi] vr to rebel; **rebelde** [xe'bewdʒi] adj rebellious; (indisciplinado) unruly, wild ♦ m/f rebel; **rebeldia** [xebew'dʒia] f rebelliousness; (fig: obstinação) stubbornness; (: oposição) defiance

rebelião [xebe'ljãw] (pl **-ões**) f rebellion

rebentar [xebẽ'ta*] vi (guerra) to break out; (louça) to smash; (corda) to snap; (represa) to burst; (ondas) to break ♦ vt to smash; to snap; (porta) to break down

rebocador [xeboka'do*] m tug(boat)

rebocar [xebo'ka*] vt (paredes) to

plaster; (veículo) to tow

rebolar [xebo'la*] vt to swing ♦ vi to sway

reboque¹ [xe'bɔki] m tow; (veículo: tb: **carro ~**) trailer; (cabo) towrope; (BR: de socorro) towtruck; **a ~** on ou in (US) tow

reboque² etc vb V **rebocar**

rebuçado [xebu'sadu] (PT) m sweet, candy (US)

recado [xe'kadu] m message; **deixar ~** to leave a message

recaída [xeka'ida] f relapse

recair [xeka'i*] vi (doente) to relapse

recalcar [xekaw'ka*] vt to repress

recalque etc [xe'kawki] vb V **recalcar**

recanto [xe'kãtu] m corner, nook

recapitular [xekapitu'la*] vt to sum up, recapitulate; (fatos) to review; (matéria escolar) to revise

recatado, -a [xeka'tadu, a] adj (modesto) modest; (reservado) reserved

recauchutado, -a [xekawʃu'tadu, a] adj: **pneu ~** (AUTO) retread, remould (BRIT)

recear [xe'sja*] vt to fear ♦ vi: **~ por** to fear for; **~ fazer/que** to be afraid to do/that

receber [xese'be*] vt to receive; (ganhar) to earn, get; (hóspedes) to take in; (convidados) to entertain; (acolher bem) to welcome ♦ vi (convidados) to entertain; **recebimento** [xesebi'mẽtu] (BR) m reception; (de uma carta) receipt; **acusar o recebimento de** to acknowledge receipt of

receio [xe'seju] m fear; **ter ~ de que** to fear that

receita [xe'sejta] f income; (do Estado) revenue; (MED) prescription; (CULIN) recipe; **R~ Federal** ≈ Inland Revenue (BRIT), ≈ IRS (US); **receitar** [xesej'ta*] vt to prescribe

recém [xe'sẽ] adv recently, newly; **recém-casado, -a** adj: **os recém-casados** the newlyweds; **recém-chegado, -a** m/f newcomer; **recém-nascido, -a** m/f newborn child

recente [xe'sẽtʃi] adj recent; (novo) new ♦ adv recently; **recentemente** [xesẽtʃi'mẽtʃi] adv recently

receoso, -a [xese'jozu, ɔza] adj frightened, fearful; **estar ~ de (fazer)** to be afraid of (doing)

recepção [xesep'sãw] (pl -ões) f reception; (PT: de uma carta) receipt; **acusar a ~ de** (PT) to acknowledge receipt of; **recepcionista** [xesepsjo'niʃta] m/f receptionist

receptivo, -a [xesep'tʃivu, a] adj receptive; (acolhedor) welcoming

receptor [xesep'to*] m receiver

recessão [xese'sãw] (pl -ões) f recession

recesso [xe'sɛsu] m recess

recessões [xese'sõjʃ] fpl de **recessão**

recheado, -a [xe'ʃjadu, a] adj (ave, carne) stuffed; (empada, bolo) filled; (cheio) full, crammed

rechear [xe'ʃja*] vt to fill; (ave, carne) to stuff; **recheio** [xe'ʃeju] m stuffing; (de empada, de bolo) filling; (o conteúdo) contents pl

rechonchudo, -a [xeʃõ'ʃudu, a] adj chubby, plump

recibo [xe'sibu] m receipt

reciclar [xesi'kla*] vt to recycle

recinto [xe'sĩtu] m enclosure; (lugar) area

recipiente [xesi'pjẽtʃi] m container, receptacle

recíproco, -a [xe'siproku, a] adj reciprocal

recitar [xesi'ta*] vt to recite

reclamação [xeklama'sãw] (pl

-ões) f complaint

reclamar [xekla'ma*] vt to demand; (herança) to claim ♦ vi to complain

reclinar [xekli'na*] vt to rest, lean; **reclinar-se** vr to lie back; (deitar-se) to lie down

recobrar [xeko'bra*] vt to recover, get back; **recobrar-se** vr to recover

recolher [xeko'ʎe*] vt to collect; (coisas dispersas) to pick up; (gado, roupa do varal) to bring in; (juntar) to gather together; **recolhido, -a** [xeko'ʎidu, a] adj (lugar) secluded; (pessoa) withdrawn; **recolhimento** [xekoʎi'mẽtu] m retirement; (arrecadação) collection; (ato de levar) taking

recomeçar [xekome'sa*] vt, vi to restart

recomendação [xekomẽda'sãw] (pl -ões) f recommendation; **recomendações** fpl (cumprimentos) regards

recomendar [xekomẽ'da*] vt to recommend; **recomendável** [xekomẽ'davew] (pl -eis) adj advisable

recompensa [xekõ'pẽsa] f reward; **recompensar** [xekõpẽ'sa*] vt to reward

recompor [xekõ'po*] (irreg: como pôr) vt to reorganize; (restabelecer) to restore

reconciliar [xekõsi'lja*] vt to reconcile

reconhecer [xekoɲe'se*] vt to recognize; (MIL) to reconnoitre (BRIT), reconnoiter (US); **reconhecido, -a** [xekoɲe'sidu, a] adj recognized; (agradecido) grateful, thankful; **reconhecimento** [xekoɲesi-'mẽtu] m recognition; (admissão) admission; (gratidão) gratitude; (MIL) reconnaissance; **reconhecí-**

vel [xekoɲe'sivew] (pl -eis) adj recognizable

reconstruir [xekõʃ'trwi*] vt to rebuild

recordação [xekoxda'sãw] (pl -ões) f (reminiscência) memory; (objeto) memento

recordar [xekox'da*] vt to remember; (parecer) to look like; (recapitular) to revise; **recordar-se** vr: ~-se de to remember; ~ algo a alguém to remind sb of sth

recorde [xe'kɔxdʒi] adj inv record atr ♦ m record

recorrer [xeko'xe*] vi: ~ a to turn to; (valer-se de) to resort to

recortar [xekox'ta*] vt to cut out; **recorte** [xe'kɔxtʃi] m (ato) cutting out; (de jornal) cutting, clipping

recreação [xekrja'sãw] f recreation

recreativo, -a [xekrja'tʃivu, a] adj recreational

recreio [xe'kreju] m recreation

recriminar [xekrimi'na*] vt to reproach, reprove

recrutamento [xekruta'mẽtu] m recruitment

recrutar [xekru'ta*] vt to recruit

rectângulo [xek'tãgulu] (PT) = retângulo

recto, -a etc ['xɛkto, a] (PT) = reto etc

recuar [xe'kwa*] vt to move back ♦ vi to move back; (exército) to retreat

recuperação [xekupera'sãw] f recovery

recuperar [xekupe'ra*] vt to recover; (tempo perdido) to make up for; (reabilitar) to rehabilitate; **recuperar-se** vr to recover

recurso [xe'kuxsu] m resource; (JUR) appeal; ~s mpl (financeiros) resources

recusa [xe'kuza] f refusal; (negação)

denial; **recusar** [xeku'za*] *vt* to refuse; to deny, **recusar-se** *vr*: **recusar-se** a to refuse

redação [xeda'sãw] (*PT* -**çç**-; *pl* -ões) *f* (*ato*) writing; (*EDUC*) composition, essay; (*redatores*) editorial staff

redator, a [xeda'to*, a] (*PT* -**act**-) *m/f* journalist; (*editor*) editor; (*quem redige*) writer

rede ['xedʒi] *f* net; (*de dormir*) hammock; (*cilada*) trap; (*FERRO, TEC, fig*) network; **a R~** (*a Internet*) the Net

rédea ['xedʒja] *f* rein

redentor, a [xedẽ'to*, a] *adj* redeeming

redigir [xedʒi'ʒi*] *vt, vi* to write

redobrar [xedo'bra*] *vt* (*aumentar*) to increase; (*esforços*) to redouble

redondamente [xedõda'mẽtʃi] *adv* (*completamente*) completely

redondezas [xedõ'dezaʃ] *fpl* surroundings

redondo, -a [xe'dõdu, a] *adj* round

redor [xe'do*] *m*: **ao** *ou* **em ~ (de)** around, round about

redução [xedu'sãw] (*pl* -ões) *f* reduction

redundância [xedũ'dãsja] *f* redundancy; **redundante** [xedũ'dãtʃi] *adj* redundant

reduzido, -a [xedu'zidu, a] *adj* reduced; (*limitado*) limited; (*pequeno*) small

reduzir [xedu'zi*] *vt* to reduce; **reduzir-se** *vr*: **~-se a** to be reduced to; (*fig: resumir-se em*) to come down to

reembolsar [xeẽbow'sa*] *vt* to recover; (*restituir*) to reimburse; (*depósito*) to refund; **reembolso** [xeẽ'bowsu] *m* (*de depósito*) refund; (*de despesa*) reimbursement

reencontro [xeẽ'kõtru] *m* reunion

refazer [xefa'ze*] (*irreg: como* fazer) *vt* to redo; (*consertar*) to repair;

refazer-se *vr* (*MED etc*) to recover

refeição [xefej'sãw] (*pl* -ões) *f* meal; **refeitório** [xefej'tɔrju] *m* refectory

refém [xe'fẽ] (*pl* -**ns**) *m* hostage

referência [xefe'rẽsja] *f* reference; **~s** *fpl* (*informaçoes para emprego*) references; **fazer ~ a** to make reference to, refer to

referente [xefe'rẽtʃi] *adj*: **~ a** concerning, regarding

referir [xefe'ri*] *vt* to relate, tell; **referir-se** *vr*: **~-se a** to refer to

REFESA *f* (= *Rede Ferroviária SA*) ≈ BR

refinamento [xefina'mẽtu] *m* refinement

refinaria [xefina'ria] *f* refinery

reflro *etc* [xe'firu] *vb V* referir

refletir [xefle'tʃi*] (*PT* -**ct**-) *vi* to reflect ♦ *vi*: **~ em** *ou* **sobre** to consider, think about

reflexão [xeflek'sãw] (*pl* -ões) *f* reflection

reflexo, -a [xe'fleksu, a] *adj* (*luz*) reflected; (*ação*) reflex ♦ *m* reflection; (*ANAT*) reflex; (*no cabelo*) highlight

reflexões [xeflek'sõjʃ] *fpl de* reflexão

reflito *etc* [xe'flitu] *vb V* refletir

reforçado, -a [xefox'sadu, a] *adj* reinforced; (*pessoa*) strong; (*café da manhã, jantar*) hearty

reforçar [xefox'sa*] *vt* to relnforce; (*revigorar*) to invigorate; **reforço** [xe'foxsu] *m* reinforcement

reforma [xe'fɔxma] *f* reform; (*ARQ*) renovation; **reformado, -a** [xefox'madu, a] *adj* reformed; renovated; (*MIL*) retired; **reformar** [xefox'ma*] *vt* to reform; to renovate; **reformar-se** *vr* to reform

refractário, -a [xefra'tarju, a] (*PT*) *adj* = **refratário/a**

refrão [xe'frãw] (pl -ãos ou -ães) m chorus, refrain; (provérbio) saying

refratário, -a [xefra'tarju, a] adj (TEC) heat-resistant; (CULIN) ovenproof

refrear [xefre'a*] vt (cavalo) to rein in; (inimigo) to contain, check; (paixões, raiva) to control; **refrear-se** vr to restrain o.s

refrescante [xefref'kãtʃi] adj refreshing

refrescar [xefref'ka*] vt (ar, ambiente) to cool; (pessoa) to refresh ♦ vi to cool down

refresco [xe'frefku] m cool fruit drink, squash; ~s mpl (refrigerantes) refreshments

refrigerador [xefriʒera'do*] m refrigerator, fridge (BRIT)

refrigerante [xefriʒe'rãtʃi] m soft drink

refugiado, -a [xefu'ʒjadu, a] adj, m/f refugee

refugiar-se [xefu'ʒjaxsi] vr to take refuge; **refúgio** [xe'fuʒju] m refuge

refugo [xe'fugu] m rubbish, garbage (US); (mercadoria) reject

refutar [xefu'ta*] vt to refute

rega ['xega] (PT) f irrigation

regador [xega'do*] m watering can

regalia [xega'lia] f privilege

regar [xe'ga*] vt (plantas, jardim) to water; (umedecer) to sprinkle

regatear [xega'tʃja*] vt (o preço) to haggle over, bargain for ♦ vi to haggle

regenerar [xeʒene'ra*] vt to regenerate

reger [xe'ʒe*] vt to govern; (orquestra) to conduct; (empresa) to run ♦ vi to rule; (maestro) to conduct

região [xe'ʒjãw] (pl -ões) f region, area

regime [xe'ʒimi] m (POL) regime;

(dieta) diet; (maneira) way; **estar de ~** to be on a diet

regimento [xeʒi'mẽtu] m regiment

regiões [xe'ʒõjʃ] fpl de região

regional [xeʒjo'naw] (pl -ais) adj regional

registrar [xeʒiʃ'tra*] (PT -ista-) vt to register; (anotar) to record

registro [xe'ʒiʃtru] (PT -to) m registration; (anotação) recording; (livro, LING) register; (histórico) record; **~ civil** registry office

regra ['xegra] f rule; **~s** fpl (MED) periods

regressar [xegre'sa*] vi to come (ou go) back, return; **regressivo, -a** [xegre'sivu, a] adj regressive; **contagem regressiva** countdown; **regresso** [xe'gresu] m return

régua ['xegwa] f ruler; **~ de calcular** slide rule

regulador [xegula'do*] m regulator

regulamento [xegula'mẽtu] m rules pl, regulations pl

regular [xegu'la*] adj regular; (estatura) average, medium; (tamanho) normal; (razoável) not bad ♦ vt to regulate; (reger) to govern; (máquina) to adjust; (carro, motor) to tune ♦ vi to work, function; **regularidade** [xegulari'dadʒi] f regularity

rei [xej] m king; **Dia de R~s** Epiphany; **R~ Momo** carnival king

reinado [xej'nadu] m reign

reinar [xej'na*] vi to reign

reino [xe'xejnu] m kingdom; (fig) realm; **o R~ Unido** the United Kingdom

reivindicação [xejvdʒika'sãw] (pl -ões) f claim, demand

reivindicar [xejvdʒi'ka*] vt to claim; (aumento salarial, direitos) to demand

rejeição [xeʒej'sãw] (*pl* -ões) *f* rejection

rejeitar [xeʒej'ta*] *vt* to reject; (*recusar*) to refuse

rejo *etc* [x'eʒu] *vb V* **reger**

rejuvenescer [xeʒuvene'se*] *vt* to rejuvenate

relação [xela'sãw] (*pl* -ões) *f* relation; (*conexão*) connection; (*relacionamento*) relationship; (MAT) ratio; (*lista*) list; **com** ou **em ~ a** regarding, with reference to; **relações públicas** public relations; **relacionamento** [xelasjona'mētu] *m* relationship; **relacionar** [xelasjo'na*] *vt* to make a list of; (*ligar*): **relacionar algo com algo** to connect sth with sth, relate sth to sth; **relacionar-se** *vr* to be connected ou related

relâmpago [xe'lãpagu] *m* flash of lightning; **~s** *mpl* (*clarões*) lightning *sg*

relance [xe'lãsi] *m* glance; **olhar de ~** to glance at

relapso, -a [xe'lapsu, a] *adj* (*negligente*) negligent

relatar [xela'ta*] *vt* to give an account of

relativo, -a [xela'tʃivu, a] *adj* relative

relato [xe'latu] *m* account

relatório [xela'tɔrju] *m* report

relaxado, -a [xela'ʃadu, a] *adj* relaxed; (*desleixado*) slovenly, sloppy; (*relapso*) negligent

relaxante [xela'ʃãtʃi] *adj* relaxing

relaxar [xela'ʃa*] *vt, vi* to relax

relegar [xele'ga*] *vt* to relegate

relembrar [xelē'bra*] *vt* to recall

relevante [xele'vãtʃi] *adj* relevant

relevo [xe'levu] *m* relief

religião [xeli'ʒãw] (*pl* -ões) *f* religion; **religioso, -a** [xeli'ʒozu, ɔza] *adj* religious ♦ *m/f* religious person; (*frade/freira*) monk/nun

relíquia [xe'likja] *f* relic; **~ de família** family heirloom

relógio [xe'lɔʒu] *m* clock; (*de gás*) meter; **~ (de pulso)** (wrist)watch; **~ de sol** sundial

relutante [xelu'tãtʃi] *adj* reluctant

relva ['xɛwva] *f* grass; (*terreno gramado*) lawn

relvado [xew'vadu] (PT) *m* lawn

remar [xe'ma*] *vt, vi* to row

rematar [xema'ta*] *vt* to finish off; **remate** [xe'matʃi] *m* (*fim*) end; (*acabamento*) finishing touch

remediar [xeme'dʒja*] *vt* to put right, remedy

remédio [xe'mɛdʒju] *m* (*medicamento*) medicine; (*recurso, solução*) remedy, (JUR) recourse; **não tem ~** there's no way

remendar [xemē'da*] *vt* to mend; (*com pano*) to patch; **remendo** [xe'mēdu] *m* repair; patch

remessa [xe'mesa] *f* shipment; (*de dinheiro*) remittance

remetente [xeme'tētʃi] *m/f* sender

remeter [xeme'te*] *vt* to send, dispatch; (*dinheiro*) to remit

remexer [xeme'ʃe*] *vt* (*papéis*) to shuffle; (*sacudir: braços*) to wave; (*folhas*) to shake; (*revolver: areia, lama*) to stir up ♦ *vi*: **~ em** to rummage through

reminiscência [xemini'sēsja] *f* reminiscence

remo ['xemu] *m* oar; (*ESPORTE*) rowing

remoção [xemo'sãw] *f* removal

remorso [xe'mɔxsu] *m* remorse

remoto, -a [xe'mɔtu, a] *adj* remote

remover [xemo've*] *vt* to move; (*transferir*) to transfer; (*demitir*) to dismiss; (*retirar, afastar*) to remove; (*terra*) to churn up

renal [xe'naw] (*pl* -ais) *adj* renal, kidney *atr*

Renascença [xena'sẽsa] f: **a ~** the Renaissance

renascer [xena'se*] vi to be reborn; (fig) to revive

renascimento [xenasi'mẽtu] m rebirth; (fig) revival; **o R~** the Renaissance

renda ['xẽda] f income; (nacional) revenue; (de aplicação, locação) yield; (tecido) lace

render [xẽ'de*] vt (lucro, dinheiro) to bring in, yield; (preço) to fetch; (homenagem) to pay; (graças) to give; (serviços) to render; (armas) to surrender; (guarda) to relieve; (causar) to bring ♦ vi (dar lucro) to pay; **render-se** vr to surrender; **rendição** [xẽdʒi'sãw] f surrender

rendimento [xẽdʒi'mẽtu] m income; (lucro) profit; (juro) yield, interest

renegar [xene'ga*] vt (crença) to renounce; (detestar) to hate; (trair) to betray; (negar) to deny; (desprezar) to reject

renomado, -a [xeno'madu, a] adj renowned

renome [xe'nɔmi] m renown

renovação [xenova'sãw] (pl -ões) f renewal; (ARQ) renovation

renovar [xeno'va*] vt to renew; (ARQ) to renovate

rentabilidade [xẽtabili'dadʒi] f profitability

rentável [xẽ'tavew] (pl -eis) adj profitable

renúncia [xe'nũsja] f resignation

renunciar [xenũ'sja*] vt to give up, renounce ♦ vi to resign; (abandonar): **~ a algo** to give sth up

reouve etc [xe'ovi] vb V **reaver**

reouver etc [xeo've*] vb V **reaver**

reparação [xepara'sãw] (pl -ões) f mending, repairing; (de mal, erros) remedying; (fig) amends pl, reparation

reparar [xepa'ra*] vt to repair; (forças) to restore; (mal, erros) to remedy; (prejuízo, danos, ofensa) to make amends for; (notar) to notice ♦ vi: **~ em** to notice; **reparo** [xe'paru] m repair; (crítica) criticism; (observação) observation

repartição [xepaxtʃi'sãw] (pl -ões) f distribution

repartir [xepax'tʃi*] vt (distribuir) to distribute; (dividir entre vários) to share out; (dividir em várias porções) to divide up

repelente [xepe'lẽtʃi] adj, m repellent

repelir [xepe'li*] vt to repel

repente [xe'pẽtʃi] m outburst; **de ~** suddenly; (col: talvez) maybe

repentino, -a [xepẽ'tʃinu, a] adj sudden

repercussão [xepexku'sãw] (pl -ões) f repercussion

repercutir [xepexku'tʃi*] vt to echo ♦ vi to reverberate, echo; (fig): **~ em** (sobre) to have repercussions (on)

repertório [xepex'tɔrju] m list; (coleção) collection; (MÚS) repertoire

repetidamente [xepetʃida'mẽtʃi] adv repeatedly

repetido, -a [xepe'tʃidu, a] adj: **repetidas vezes** repeatedly, again and again

repetir [xepe'tʃi*] vt to repeat ♦ vi (ao comer) to have seconds; **repetir-se** vr to happen again; (pessoa) to repeat o.s.; **repetitivo, -a** [xepetʃi'tʃivu, a] adj repetitive

repilo etc [xe'pilu] vb V **repelir**

repito etc [xe'pitu] vb V **repetir**

repleto, -a [xe'plɛtu, a] adj replete, full up

réplica ['xɛplika] f replica; (contestação) reply, retort

replicar [xepli'ka*] vt to answer,

reply to ♦ *vi* to reply, answer back

repolho [xe'poλu] *m* cabbage

repor [xe'po*] (*irreg: como* pôr) *vt* to put back, replace; (*restituir*) to return; **repor-se** *vr* to recover

reportagem [xepox'taʒẽ] (*pl* -ns) *f* reporting; (*notícia*) report

repórter [xe'pɔxte*] *m/f* reporter

repousar [xepo'za*] *vi* to rest; **repouso** [xe'pozu] *m* rest

repreender [xeprjẽ'de*] *vt* to reprimand; **repreensão** [xeprjẽ'sãw] (*pl* -ões) *f* reprimand

represália [xepre'zalja] *f* reprisal

representação [xeprezẽta'sãw] (*pl* -ões) *f* representation; (*TEATRO*) performance; **representante** [xeprezẽ'tãtʃi] *m/f* representative

representar [xepreze'ta*] *vt* to represent; (*TEATRO: papel*) to play; (. *peçu*) to put on ♦ *vi* to act; **representativo, -a** [xeprezẽta'tʃivu, a] *adj* representative

repressão [xepre'sãw] (*pl* -ões) *f* repression

reprimir [xepri'mi*] *vt* to repress

reprodução [xeprodu'sãw] (*pl* -ões) *f* reproduction

reproduzir [xeprodu'zi*] *vt* to reproduce; (*repetir*) to repeat; **reproduzir-se** *vr* to breed

reprovar [xepro'va*] *vt* to disapprove of; (*aluno*) to fail

réptil ['xɛptʃiw] (*pl* -eis) *m* reptile

república [xe'publika] *f* republic; **republicano, -a** [xerepubli'kanu, a] *adj, m/f* republican

repudiar [xepu'dʒja*] *vt* to repudiate; **repúdio** [xe'pudʒju] *m* repudiation

repugnância [xepug'nãsja] *f* repugnance; **repugnante** [xepug'nãtʃi] *adj* repugnant

repulsa [xe'puwsa] *f* (*ato*) rejection; (*sentimento*) repugnance; (*física*)

repulsion; **repulsivo, -a** [xepuw-'sivu, a] *adj* repulsive

reputação [xeputa'sãw] (*pl* -ões) *f* reputation

requeijão [xekej'ʒãw] *m* cheese spread

requerer [xeke're*] *vt* (*emprego*) to apply for; (*pedir*) to request; (*exigir*) to require; **requerimento** [xekeri'mẽtu] *m* application; request; (*petição*) petition

requintado, -a [xekĩ'tadu, a] *adj* refined, elegant

requinte [xe'kĩtʃi] *m* refinement, elegance; (*cúmulo*) height

requisito [xeki'zitu] *m* requirement

rés-do-chão [xɛʒ-] (*PT*) *m inv* ground floor (*BRIT*), first floor (*US*)

reserva [xe'zɛxva] *f* reserve; (*para hotel, fig*) reservation ♦ *m/f* (*ESPORTE*) reserve

reservado, -a [xezex'vadu, a] *adj* reserved

reservar [xczcx'va*] *vt* to reserve; (*guardar de reserva*) to keep; (*forças*) to conserve; **reservar-se** *vr* to save o.s

reservatório [xezexva'tɔrju] *m* reservoir

resfriado, -a [xeʃ'frjadu, a] (*BR*) *adj*: estar/ficar ~ to have a cold/catch (a) cold ♦ *m* cold, chill

resgatar [xeʒga'ta*] *vt* (*salvar*) to rescue; (*prisioneiro*) to ransom; (*retomar*) to get back, recover; **resgate** [xeʒ'gatʃi] *m* rescue; ransom; recovery

residência [xezi'dẽsja] *f* residence; **residencial** [xezidẽ'sjaw] (*pl* -ais) *adj* residential; (*computador, telefone etc*) home *atr*; **residente** [xezi'dẽtʃi] *adj, m/f* resident

residir [xezi'dʒi*] *vi* to live, reside

resíduo [xe'zidwu] *m* residue

resignação [xezigna'sãw] (*pl* -ões) *f*

f resignation

resignar-se [xezig'naxsi] vr: ~
com to resign o.s. to

resina [xe'zina] f resin

resistente [xezif'tētʃi] adj resistant; (material, objeto) hard-
wearing, strong

resistir [xezif'tʃi*] vi to hold; (pessoa) to hold out; ~ **a** to resist;
(sobreviver) to survive

resmungar [xeʒmũ'ga*] vt, vi to
mutter, mumble

resolução [xezolu'sāw] (pl -ões) f
resolution; (de um problema) solution; **resoluto, -a** [xezo'lutu, a] adj
decisive

resolver [xezow've*] vt to sort
out; (problema) to solve; (questão)
to resolve; (decidir) to decide;
resolver-se vr: ~**se (a fazer)** to
make up one's mind (to do), decide
(to do)

respectivo, -a [xeʃpek'tʃivu, a] adj
respective

respeitar [xeʃpej'ta*] vt to respect;
respeitável [xeʃpej'tavew] (pl -eis)
adj respectable; (considerável) considerable

respeito [xeʃ'pejtu] m: ~ **(a ou por)**
respect (for); ~**s** mpl (cumprimentos)
regards; **a ~ de, com ~ a** as to, as
regards; (sobre) about; **dizer ~ a** to
concern; **em ~ a** with respect to

respiração [xeʃpira'sāw] f breathing

respirar [xeʃpi'ra*] vt, vi to breathe

respiro [xeʃ'piru] m breath

resplandecente [xeʃplāde'sētʃi]
adj resplendent

responder [xeʃpő'de*] vt to answer
♦ vi to answer; (ser respondão) to
answer back; ~ **por** to be responsible for, answer for

responsabilidade [xeʃpősabili-
'dadʒi] f responsibility

responsabilizar [xeʃpősabili'za*]
vt: ~ **alguém (por algo)** to
hold sb responsible (for sth);
responsabilizar-se vr: ~**se por**
to take responsibility for

responsável [xeʃpő'savew] (pl
-eis) adj: ~ **(por)** responsible (for); ~
a answerable to, accountable to

resposta [xeʃ'pɔʃta] f answer, reply

resquício [xeʃ'kisju] m (vestígio)
trace

ressabiado, -a [xesa'bjadu, a] adj
wary; (ressentido) resentful

ressaca [xe'saka] f undertow; (mar
bravo) rough sea; (fig: de quem
bebeu) hangover

ressaltar [xesaw'ta*] vt to emphasize ♦ vi to stand out

ressalva [xe'sawva] f safeguard

ressentido, -a [xesē'tʃidu, a] adj
resentful

ressentimento [xesētʃi'mētu] m
resentment

ressentir-se [xesē'tʃixsi] vr: ~ **de**
(ofender-se) to resent; (magoar-se)
to be hurt by; (sofrer) to suffer from,
feel the effects of

ressurgimento [xesuxʒi'mētu] m
resurgence, revival

ressurreição [xesuxej'sāw] (pl
-ões) f resurrection

ressuscitar [xesusi'ta*] vt, vi to
revive

restabelecer [xeʃtabele'se*] vt to
re-establish, restore; **restabelecer-
se** vr to recover, recuperate; **restabelecimento** [xeʃtabelesi'mētu] m
re-establishment; restoration; recovery

restante [xeʃ'tātʃi] adj remaining
♦ m rest

restar [xeʃ'ta*] vi to remain, be left

restauração [xeʃtawra'sāw] (pl
-ões) f restoration; (de costumes,
usos) revival

restaurante [xeʃtaw'rãtʃi] *m* restaurant

restaurar [xeʃtaw'ra*] *vt* to restore

restituição [xeʃtʃitwi'sãw] (*pl -ões*) *f* restitution, return; (*de dinheiro*) repayment

restituir [xeʃtʃi'twi*] *vt* to return; (*dinheiro*) to repay; (*forças, saúde*) to restore; (*usos*) to revive; (*reempossar*) to reinstate

resto ['xeʃtu] *m* rest; (*MAT*) remainder; **~s** *mpl* (*sobras*) remains; (*de comida*) scraps

restrição [xeʃtri'sãw] (*pl -ões*) *f* restriction

restringir [xeʃtrī'ʒi*] *vt* to restrict

resultado [xezuw'tadu] *m* result

resultante [xezuw'tãtʃi] *adj* resultant; **~ de** resulting from

resultar [xezuw'ta*] *vi*: **~ (de/em)** to result (from/in) ♦ *vi* (*vir a ser*) to turn out to be

resumir [xezu'mi*] *vt* to summarize; (*livro*) to abridge; (*reduzir*) to reduce; (*conter em resumo*) to sum up; **resumo** [xe'zumu] *m* summary, résumé; **em resumo** in short, briefly

retaguarda [xeta'gwaxda] *f* rearguard; (*posição*) rear

retaliação [xetalja'sãw] (*pl -ões*) *f* retaliation

retângulo [xe'tãgulu] *m* rectangle

retardar [xetax'da*] *vt* to hold up, delay; (*adiar*) to postpone

reter [xe'te*] (*irreg: como* **ter**) *vt* (*guardar, manter*) to keep; (*deter*) to stop; (*segurar*) to hold; (*ladrão, suspeito*) to detain; (*na memória*) to retain; (*lágrimas, impulsos*) to hold back; (*impedir de sair*) to keep back

reticente [xetʃi'sẽtʃi] *adj* reticent

retificar [xetʃifi'ka*] *vt* to rectify

retirada [xetʃi'rada] *f* (*MIL*) retreat; (*salário, saque*) withdrawal

retirar [xetʃi'ra*] *vt* to withdraw; (*afastar*) to take away, remove; **retirar-se** *vr* to withdraw; (*de uma festa etc*) to leave; (*MIL*) to retreat

reto, -a ['xetu, a] *adj* straight; (*fig: justo*) fair; (*: honesto*) honest, upright ♦ *m* (*ANAT*) rectum

retorcer [xetox'se*] *vt* to twist; **retorcer-se** *vr* to wriggle, writhe

retornar [xetox'na*] *vi* to return, go back; **retorno** [xe'toxnu] *m* return; **dar retorno** to do a U-turn; **retorno (do carro)** (*COMPUT*) (carriage) return

retraído, -a [xetra'idu, a] *adj* (*tímido*) reserved, timid

retrair [xetra'i*] *vt* to withdraw; (*contrair*) to contract; (*pessoa*) to make reserved

retrato [xe'tratu] *m* portrait; (*FOTO*) photo; (*fig: efígie*) likeness; (*: representação*) portrayal; **~ falado** identikit ® picture

retribuir [xetri'bwi*] *vt* to reward, recompense; (*pagar*) to remunerate; (*hospitalidade, favor, sentimento, visita*) to return

retroceder [xetrose'de*] *vi* to retreat, fall back; **retrocesso** [xetro'sesu] *m* retreat; (*ao passado*) return

retrógrado, -a [xe'trɔgradu, a] *adj* retrograde; (*reacionário*) reactionary

retrospecto [xetro'ʃpεktu] *m*: **em ~** in retrospect

retrovisor [xetrovi'zo*] *adj, m*: (espelho) **~** (rear-view) mirror

réu, -ré [xew, xε] *m/f* defendant; (*culpado*) culprit, criminal

reumatismo [xewma'tʃiʒmu] *m* rheumatism

reunião [xeu'njãw] (*pl -ões*) *f* meeting; (*ato, reencontro*) reunion; (*festa*) get-together, party; **~ de cúpula** summit (meeting)

reunir [xeu'ni*] *vt* (*pessoas*) to

bring together; (*partes*) to join, unite; (*qualidades*) to combine; **reunir-se** *vr* to meet; **~-se a** to join

revanche [xe'vãʃi] *f* revenge

reveillon [xeve'jõ] *m* New Year's Eve

revelação [xevela'sãw] (*pl* -ões) *f* revelation

revelar [xeve'la*] *vt* to reveal; (*FOTO*) to develop; **revelar-se** *vr* to turn out to be

revelia [xeve'lia] *f* default; **à ~ by** default; **à ~ de** without the knowledge *ou* consent of

revendedor, a [xevẽde'do*, a] *m/f* dealer

rever [xe've*] (*irreg: como ver*) *vt* to see again; (*examinar*) to check; (*revisar*) to revise

reverência [xeve'rẽsja] *f* reverence, respect; (*ato*) bow; (: *de mulher*) curtsey; **fazer uma ~** to bow, to curtsey

reverenciar [xeverẽ'sja*] *vt* to revere

reverso [xe'vɛxsu] *m* reverse

reverter [xevex'te*] *vt* to revert

revés [xe'vɛʃ] *m* reverse; (*infortúnio*) setback, mishap; **ao ~** (*roupa*) inside out; **de ~** (*olhar*) askance

revestir [xeveʃ'tʃi*] *vt* (*paredes etc*) to cover; (*interior de uma caixa etc*) to line

revezar [xeve'za*] *vt, vi* to alternate; **revezar-se** *vr* to take turns, alternate

revidar [xevi'da*] *vt* (*soco, insulto*) to return; (*retrucar*) to answer; (*crítica*) to rise to, respond to ♦ *vi* to hit back; (*retrucar*) to respond

revirar [xevi'ra*] *vt* to turn round; (*gaveta*) to turn out, go through

revisão [xevi'zãw] (*pl* -ões) *f* revision; (*de máquina*) overhaul; (*de carro*) service; (*JUR*) appeal

revisar [xevi'za*] *vt* to revise

revisões [xevi'zõjʃ] *fpl de* **revisão**

revista [xe'viʃta] *f* (*busca*) search; (*MIL, exame*) inspection; (*publicação*) magazine; (: *profissional, erudita*) journal; (*TEATRO*) revue

revistar [xeviʃ'ta*] *vt* to search; (*tropa*) to review; (*examinar*) to examine

revisto *etc* [xe'viʃtu] *vb* V **revestir**

revogar [xevo'ga*] *vt* to revoke

revolta [xe'vɔwta] *f* revolt; (*fig: indignação*) disgust; **R~ da Vacina** *see boxed note*

REVOLTA DA VACINA

This was a popular movement of opposition to the government, which took place in Rio de Janeiro in 1904 following the passing of a law which made vaccination against smallpox compulsory. It was the culmination of general dissatisfaction with health reforms undertaken at that time by the scientist Osvaldo Cruz, and the relocation programme of the prefect Pereira Passos, as a result of which part of the population of Rio had been moved from the slums and shanty towns of the central region to suburbs much further out.

---

revoltado, -a [xevow'tadu, a] *adj* in revolt; (*indignado*) disgusted; (*amargo*) bitter

revoltante [xevow'tãtʃi] *adj* disgusting, revolting

revoltar [xevow'ta*] *vt* to disgust; **revoltar-se** *vr* to rebel, revolt; (*indignar-se*) to be disgusted

revolto, -a [xe'vowtu, a] *pp de* **revolver** ♦ *adj* (*década*) turbulent; (*mundo*) troubled; (*cabelo*) untidy, unkempt; (*mar*) rough; (*desarrumado*) untidy

revolução [xevolu'sãw] (*pl* -ões) *f* revolution; **revolucionar** [xevolusjo'na*] *vt* to revolutionize; **revolucionário, -a** [xevolusjo'narju, a] *adj, m/f* revolutionary

revolver [xevow've*] *vi* to revolve, rotate

revólver [xe'vɔwve*] *m* revolver

reza ['xeza] *f* prayer; **rezar** [xe'za*] *vi* to pray

riacho ['xjaʃu] *m* brook, stream

ribeiro [xi'bejru] *m* brook, stream

rico, -a ['xiku, a] *adj* rich; (*PT*: *lindo*) beautiful; (: *excelente*) splendid ♦ *m/f* rich man/woman

ridicularizar [xidʒikulari'za*] *vt* to ridicule

ridículo, -a [xi'dʒikulu, a] *adj* ridiculous

rifa ['xifa] *f* raffle

rifle ['xifli] *m* rifle

rigidez [xiʒi'deʒ] *f* rigidity, stiffness; (*austeridade*) severity, strictness

rígido, -a ['xiʒidu, a] *adj* rigid, stiff; (*fig*) strict

rigor [xi'go*] *m* rigidity; (*meticulosidade*) rigour (*BRIT*), rigor (*US*); (*severidade*) harshness, severity; (*exatidão*) precision; **ser de ~** to be essential *ou* obligatory; **rigoroso, -a** [xigo-'rozu, ɔza] *adj* rigorous; (*severo*) strict; (*exigente*) demanding; (*minucioso*) precise, accurate; (*inverno*) hard, harsh

rijo, -a ['xiʒu, a] *adj* tough, hard; (*severo*) harsh, severe

rim [xĩ] (*pl* -ns) *m* kidney; **rins** *mpl* (*parte inferior das costas*) small *sg* of the back

rima ['xima] *f* rhyme; (*poema*) verse, poem; **rimar** [xi'ma*] *vt, vi* to rhyme

rímel ['ximew] ® (*pl* -eis) *m* mascara

ringue ['xĩgɪ] *m* ring

rins [xĩʃ] *mpl de* **rim**

Rio ['xiu] *m*: **o ~ (de Janeiro)** Rio (de Janeiro)

rio ['xiu] *m* river

riqueza [xi'keza] *f* wealth, riches *pl*; (*qualidade*) richness

rir [xi*] *vi* to laugh; **~ de** to laugh at

risada [xi'zada] *f* laughter

risca ['xiʃka] *f* stroke; (*listra*) stripe; (*no cabelo*) parting

riscar [xiʃ'ka*] *vt* (*marcar*) to mark; (*apagar*) to cross out; (*desenhar*) to outline

risco ['xiʃku] *m* (*marca*) mark, scratch; (*traço*) stroke; (*desenho*) drawing, sketch; (*perigo*) risk; **correr o ~ de** to run the risk of

riso ['xizu] *m* laughter; **risonho, -a** [xi'zɔɲu, a] *adj* smiling; (*contente*) cheerful

ríspido, -a ['xiʃpidu, a] *adj* brusque; (*áspero*) harsh

ritmo ['xitʃmu] *m* rhythm

rito ['xitu] *m* rite

ritual [xi'twaw] (*pl* -ais) *adj, m* ritual

rival [xi'vaw] (*pl* -ais) *adj, m/f* rival; **rivalidade** [xivali'dadʒi] *f* rivalry; **rivalizar** [xivali'za*] *vt* to rival ♦ *vi*: **rivalizar com** to compete with, vie with

roa *etc* ['xoa] *vb V* **roer**

robô [xo'bo] *m* robot

robusto, -a [xo'buʃtu, a] *adj* strong, robust

roça ['xɔsa] *f* plantation; (*no mato*) clearing; (*campo*) country

rocha ['xɔʃa] *f* rock; (*penedo*) boulder

rochedo [xo'ʃedu] *m* crag, cliff

rock-and-roll [-â'xɔw] *m* rock and roll

roda ['xɔda] *f* wheel; (*círculo*) circle; **~ dentada** cog(wheel); **em** *ou* **à ~**

de round, around

rodada [xo'dada] f (de bebidas, ESPORTE) round

rodar [xo'da*] vt to turn, spin; (viajar por) to tour, travel round; (quilómetros) to do; (filme) to make; (imprimir) to print; (COMPUT: programa) to run ♦ vi to turn round; (AUTO) to drive around; **~ por** (a pé) to wander around; (de carro) to drive around

rodeio [xo'deju] m (em discurso) circumlocution; (subterfúgio) subterfuge; (de gado) round-up; **fazer ~s** to beat about the bush; **sem ~s** plainly, frankly

rodela [xo'dɛla] f (pedaço) slice

rodízio [xo'dʒizju] m rota; **em ~** on a rota basis

rodopiar [xodo'pja*] vi to whirl around, swirl

rodovia [xodo'via] f highway, ≈ motorway (BRIT), ≈ interstate (US)

rodoviária [xodo'vjarja] f (tb: estação ~) bus station; V tb rodoviário

rodoviário, -a [xodo'vjarju, a] adj road atr; (polícia) traffic atr

roer [xwe*] vt to gnaw, nibble; (enferrujar) to corrode; (afligir) to eat away

rogar [xo'ga*] vi to ask, request; **~ a alguém que faça (algo)** to beg sb to do (sth)

rói [xɔj] vb V roer

roía etc [xo'ia] vb V roer

rolar [xo'la*] vt, vi to roll

roleta [xo'leta] f roulette

rolha [ˈxoʎa] f cork

roliço, -a [xo'lisu, a] adj (pessoa) plump, chubby; (objeto) round, cylindrical

rolo [ˈxolu] m (de papel etc) roll; (para nivelar o solo, para pintura) roller; (para cabelo) curler; (de briga) brawl, fight; **cortina de ~** roller blind; **~ compressor** steamroller

Roma [ˈxoma] n Rome

romã [xo'mã] f pomegranate

romance [xo'mãsi] m novel; (caso amoroso) romance; **~ policial** detective story

romano, -a [xo'manu, a] adj, m/f Roman

romântico, -a [xo'mãtʃiku, a] adj romantic

rombo [ˈxõbu] m (buraco) hole; (fig: desfalque) embezzlement; (: prejuízo) loss, shortfall

Romênia [xo'menja] f: **a ~** Romania; **romeno, -a** [xo'menu, a] adj, m/f Rumanian ♦ m (LING) Rumanian

romper [xõ'pe*] vt to break; (rasgar) to tear; (relações) to break off ♦ vi (sol) to appear, emerge; (: surgir) to break through; (ano, dia) to start, begin; **~ em pranto ou lágrimas** to burst into tears; **rompimento** [xõpi'mẽtu] m breakage; (fenda) break; (de relações) breaking off

roncar [xõ'ka*] vi to snore; **ronco** [ˈxõku] m snore

ronda [ˈxõda] f patrol, beat; **fazer a ~ de** to go the rounds of, patrol; **rondar** [xõ'da*] vt to patrol; (espreitar) to prowl ♦ vi to prowl, lurk; (fazer a ronda) to patrol; **a inflação ronda os 30% ao mês** inflation is in the region of 30% a month

rosa [ˈxɔza] adj inv pink ♦ f rose; **rosado, -a** [xo'zadu, a] adj rosy, pink

rosário [xo'zarju] m rosary

rosbife [xoʒ'bifi] m roast beef

rosca [ˈxoʃka] f spiral, coil; (de parafuso) thread; (pão) ring-shaped *loaf*

roseira [xo'zejra] *f* rosebush

rosnar [xoʒ'na*] *vi* (*cão*) to growl, snarl; (*murmurar*) to mutter, mumble

rosto ['xoʃtu] *m* face

rota ['xɔta] *f* route, course

rotativo, -a [xota'tʃivu, a] *adj* rotary

roteiro [xo'tejru] *m* itinerary; (*ordem*) schedule; (*guia*) guidebook; (*de filme*) script

rotina [xo'tʃina] *f* routine; **rotineiro, -a** [xotʃi'nejru, a] *adj* routine

roto, -a ['xotu, a] *adj* broken; (*rasgado*) torn

rotular [xotu'la*] *vt* to label; **rótulo** ['xɔtulu] *m* label

roubar [xo'ba*] *vt* to steal; (*loja, casa, pessoa*) to rob ♦ *vi* to steal; (*em jogo, no preço*) to cheat; ~ **algo a alguém** to steal sth from sb; **roubo** ['xobu] *m* theft, robbery

rouco, -a ['roku, a] *adj* hoarse

round [xãwdʒi] (*pl* ~s) *m* (BOXE) round

roupa ['xopa] *f* clothes *pl*, clothing; ~ **de baixo** underwear; ~ **de cama** bedclothes *pl*, bed linen

roupão [xo'pãw] (*pl* -ões) *m* dressing gown

rouxinol [xoʃi'nɔw] (*pl* -óis) *m* nightingale

roxo, -a ['xoʃu, a] *adj* purple, violet

royalty ['xɔjawtʃi] (*pl* -ies) *m* royalty

rua ['xua] *f* street; ~ **principal** main street; ~ **sem saída** no through road, cul-de-sac

rubéola [xu'bɛola] *f* (MED) German measles *sg*

rubi [xu'bi] *m* ruby

rubor [xu'bo*] *m* blush; (*fig*) shyness, bashfulness; **ruborizar-se**

[xubori'axsi] *vr* to blush

rubrica [xu'brika] *f* (signed) initials *pl*

rubro, -a ['xubru, a] *adj* (*faces*) rosy, ruddy

ruço, -a ['xusu, a] *adj* grey (BRIT), gray (US), dun; (*desbotado*) faded

rude [xudʒi] *adj* (*ingênuo*) simple; (*grosseiro*) rude; **rudeza** [xu'deza] *f* simplicity; rudeness

rudimento [xudʒi'mētu] *m* rudiment

ruela ['xwela] *f* lane, alley

ruga ['xuga] *f* (*na pele*) wrinkle; (*na roupa*) crease

ruge ['xuʒi] *m* rouge

rugido [xu'ʒidu] *m* roar

rugir [xu'ʒi*] *vi* to roar

ruído ['xwidu] *m* noise; **ruidoso, -a** [xwi'dozu, ɔza] *adj* noisy

ruim [xu'ĩ] (*pl* -ns) *adj* bad; (*defeituoso*) defective

ruína ['xwina] *f* ruin; (*decadência*) downfall

ruins [xu'ĩʃ] *pl de* **ruim**

ruir ['xwi*] *vi* to collapse, go to ruin

ruivo, -a ['xwivu, a] *adj* red-haired ♦ *m/f* redhead

rum [xũ] *m* rum

rumo ['xumu] *m* course, bearing; (*fig*) course; ~ **a** bound for; **sem** ~ adrift

rumor [xu'mo*] *m* noise; (*notícia*) rumour (BRIT), rumor (US), report

ruptura [xup'tura] *f* break, rupture

rural [xu'raw] (*pl* -ais) *adj* rural

rush [xaʃ] *m* rush; (**a hora do**) ~ rush hour

Rússia ['xusja] *f*: **a** ~ Russia; **russo, -a** ['xusu, a] *adj*, *m/f* Russian ♦ *m* (LING) Russian

rústico, -a [xu'ʃtʃiku, a] *adj* rustic; (*pessoa*) simple; (*utensílio, objeto*) crude

S

S. *abr* (= *Santo, -a ou* São) St

SA *abr* (= *Sociedade Anônima*) Ltd (*BRIT*), Inc. (*US*)

sã [sã] *f de* **são**

Saara [sa'ara] *m*: **o ~** the Sahara

sábado ['sabadu] *m* Saturday

sabão [sa'bãw] (*pl -ões*) *m* soap

sabedoria [sabedo'ria] *f* wisdom; (*erudição*) learning

saber [sa'be*] *vt, vi* to know; (*descobrir*) to find out ♦ *m* knowledge; **a ~** namely; **~ fazer** to know how to do, be able to do; **que eu saiba** as far as I know

sabiá [sa'bja] *m/f* thrush

sabido, -a [sa'bidu, a] *adj* knowledgeable; (*esperto*) shrewd

sábio, -a ['sabju, a] *adj* wise; (*erudito*) learned ♦ *m/f* wise person; (*erudito*) scholar

sabões [sa'bõjʃ] *mpl de* **sabão**

sabonete [sabo'netʃi] *m* toilet soap

sabor [sa'bo*] *m* taste, flavour (*BRIT*), flavor (*US*); **saborear** [sabo'rja*] *vt* to taste, savour (*BRIT*), savor (*US*); **saboroso, -a** [sabo'rozu, ɔza] *adj* tasty, delicious

sabotagem [sabo'taʒẽ] *f* sabotage

sabotar [sabo'ta*] *vt* to sabotage

saca ['saka] *f* sack

sacar [sa'ka*] *vt* to take out; (*dinheiro*) to withdraw; (*arma, cheque*) to draw; (*ESPORTE*) to serve; (*col: entender*) to understand ♦ *vi* (*col: entender*) to understand; **~ sobre um devedor** to borrow money from sb

saca-rolhas *m inv* corkscrew

sacerdote [sasex'dɔtʃi] *m* priest

saciar [sa'sja*] *vt* (*fome, curiosidade*) to satisfy; (*sede*) to quench

saco ['saku] *m* bag; (*enseada*) inlet;

~ de café coffee filter; **~ de dormir** sleeping bag

sacode *etc* [sa'kɔdʒi] *vb V* **sacudir**

sacola [sa'kɔla] *f* bag

sacramento [sakra'mẽtu] *m* sacrament

sacrificar [sakrifi'ka*] *vt* to sacrifice; **sacrifício** [sakri'fisju] *m* sacrifice

sacrilégio [sakri'lɛʒju] *m* sacrilege

sacro, -a ['sakru, a] *adj* sacred

sacudida [saku'dʒida] *f* shake

sacudir [saku'dʒi*] *vt* to shake; **sacudir-se** *vr* to shake

sádico, -a ['sadʒiku, a] *adj* sadistic

sadio, -a [sa'dʒiu, a] *adj* healthy

safado, -a [sa'fadu, a] *adj* shameless; (*imoral*) dirty; (*travesso*) mischievous ♦ *m* rogue

safira [sa'fira] *f* sapphire

safra ['safra] *f* harvest

Sagitário [saʒi'tarju] *m* Sagittarius

sagrado, -a [sa'gradu, a] *adj* sacred, holy

saia ['saja] *f* skirt

saiba *etc* ['sajba] *vb V* **saber**

saída [sa'ida] *f* exit, way out; (*partida*) departure; (*ato: de pessoa*) going out; (*fig: solução*) way out; (*COMPUT: de programa*) exit; (: *de dados*) output; **~ de emergência** emergency exit

sair [sa'i*] *vi* to go (*ou* come) out; (*partir*) to leave; (*realizar-se*) to turn out; (*COMPUT*) to exit; **sair-se** *vr*: **~-se bem/mal de** to be successful/ unsuccessful in

sal [saw] (*pl* **sais**) *m* salt; **sem ~** (*comida*) salt-free; (*pessoa*) lacklustre (*BRIT*), lackluster (*US*)

sala ['sala] *f* room; (*num edifício público*) hall; (*classe, turma*) class; **~ (de aula)** classroom; **~ de espera/ (de estar)/de jantar** waiting/living/ dining room; **~ de operação** (*MED*) operating theatre (BRIT) ou theater (US)

salada [sa'lada] f salad; (fig) confusion, jumble

sala-e-quarto (pl ~s ou salas-e-quarto) m two-room flat (BRIT) ou apartment (US)

salão [sa'lãw] (pl -ões) m large room, hall; (exposição) show; ~ de beleza beauty salon

salário [sa'larju] m wages pl, salary

saldo ['sawdu] m balance; (sobra) surplus

saleiro [sa'lejru] m salt cellar

salgadinho [sawga'dʒiɲu] m savoury (BRIT), savory (US), snack

salgado, -a [saw'gadu, a] adj salty, salted

salgar [saw'ga*] vt to salt

salgueiro [saw'gejru] m willow; ~ chorão weeping willow

salientar [saljẽ'ta*] vt to point out; (acentuar) to stress, emphasize; (saliente) [sa'ljẽtʃi] adj prominent; (evidente) clear, conspicuous; (importante) outstanding; (assanhado) forward

saliva [sa'liva] f saliva

salmão [saw'mãw] (pl -ões) m salmon

salmoura [saw'mora] f brine

salões [sa'lõjʃ] mpl de salão

salsa ['sawsa] f parsley

salsicha [saw'sifa] f sausage; **salsichão** [sawsi'fãw] (pl -ões) m sausage

saltar [saw'ta*] vt to jump (over), leap (over); (omitir) to skip ♦ vi to jump, leap; (sangue) to spurt out; (de ônibus, cavalo): ~ de to get off

salto ['sawtu] m jump, leap; (de calçado) heel; ~ de vara/em altura/em distância pole vault/high jump/long jump

salubre [sa'lubri] adj healthy, salubrious

salvação [sawva'sãw] f salvation

salvador [sawva'do*] m saviour (BRIT), savior (US)

salvamento [sawva'mẽtu] m rescue; (de naufrágio) salvage

salvar [saw'va*] vt to save; (resgatar) to rescue; (objetos, de ruína) to salvage; (honra) to defend; **salvar-se** vr to escape

salva-vidas m inv (bóia) lifebuoy ♦ m/f inv (pessoa) lifeguard; barco ~ lifeboat

salvo, -a ['sawvu, a] adj safe ♦ prep except, save; a ~ in safety

samba ['sãba] m samba; see boxed note

SAMBA

The greatest form of musical expression of the Brazilian people, the **samba** is a type of music and dance of African origin. It embraces a number of rhythmic styles, such as *sumba de breque*, *samba-enredo*, *samba-canção* and *pagode*, among others. Officially, the first samba, entitled *Pelo telefone*, was written in Rio in 1917.

---

sanar [sa'na*] vt to cure; (remediar) to remedy

sanção [sã'sãw] (pl -ões) f sanction; **sancionar** [sãsjo'na*] vt to sanction

sandália [sã'dalja] f sandal

sandes ['sãdɛʃ] (PT) f inv sandwich

sanduíche [sãd'wifi] (BR) m sandwich

saneamento [sanja'mẽtu] m sanitation

sanear [sa'nja*] vt to clean up

sangrar [sã'gra*] vt, vi to bleed; **sangrento, -a** [sã'grẽtu, a] adj bloody; (CULIN: carne) rare

sangue ['sãgi] m blood

sanguessuga [sãgiˈsuga] f leech

sanguinário, -a [sãgiˈnarju, a] adj bloodthirsty

sanguíneo, -a [sãˈginju, a] adj: grupo ~ blood group; pressão sanguínea blood pressure; vaso ~ blood vessel

sanidade [saniˈdadʒi] f (saúde) health; (mental) sanity

sanita [saˈnita] (PT) f toilet, lavatory

sanitário, -a [saniˈtarju, a] adj sanitary; vaso ~ toilet, lavatory (bowl); **sanitários** [saniˈtarjuʃ] mpl toilets

santidade [sãtʃiˈdadʒi] f holiness, sanctity

santo, -a [ˈsãtu, a] adj holy ♦ m/f saint

santuário [sãˈtwarju] m shrine, sanctuary

São [sãw] m Saint

são, sã [sãw, sã] (pl ~s, ~s) adj healthy; (conselho) sound; (mentalmente) sane; ~ e salvo safe and sound

São Paulo [-ˈpawlu] n São Paulo

sapataria [sapataˈria] f shoe shop

sapateiro [sapaˈtejru] m shoemaker; (vendedor) shoe salesman; (que conserta) shoe repairer; (loja) shoe repairer's

sapatilha [sapaˈtʃiʎa] f (de balé) shoe; (sapato) pump; (de atleta) running shoe

sapato [saˈpatu] m shoe

sapo [ˈsapu] m toad

saque¹ [ˈsaki] m (de dinheiro) withdrawal; (COM) draft, bill; (ESPORTE) serve; (pilhagem) plunder, pillage; ~ **a descoberto** (COM) overdraft

saque² etc vb V **sacar**

saquear [saˈkja*] vt to pillage, plunder

sarampo [saˈrãpu] m measles sg

sarar [saˈra*] vt to cure; (ferida) to heal ♦ vi to recover

sarcasmo [saxˈkaʒmu] m sarcasm

sarda [ˈsaxda] f freckle

Sardenha [saxˈdeɲa] f: a ~ Sardinia

sardinha [saxˈdʒiɲa] f sardine

sargento [saxˈʒẽtu] m sergeant

sarjeta [saxˈʒeta] f gutter

Satã [saˈtã] m Satan

Satanás [sataˈnaʃ] m Satan

satélite [saˈtelitʃi] m satellite

sátira [ˈsatʃira] f satire

satisfação [satʃiʃfaˈsãw] (pl -ões) f satisfaction; (recompensa) reparation; **satisfatório, -a** [satʃiʃfaˈtɔrju, a] adj satisfactory

satisfazer [satʃiʃfaˈze*] (irreg: como fazer) vt to satisfy ♦ vi to be satisfactory; **satisfazer-se** vr to be satisfied; (saciar-se) to fill o.s. up; ~ a to satisfy; **satisfeito, -a** [satʃiʃˈfejtu, a] adj satisfied; (saciado) full; dar-se por satisfeito com algo to be content with sth

saudação [sawdaˈsãw] (pl -ões) f greeting

saudade [sawˈdadʒi] f longing, yearning; (lembrança nostálgica) nostalgia; deixar ~s to be greatly missed; ter ~(s) de (desejar) to long for; (sentir falta de) to miss; ~(s) de casa, ~(s) da pátria homesickness sg

saudar [sawˈda*] vt to greet; (dar as boas vindas) to welcome; (aclamar) to acclaim

saudável [sawˈdavew] (pl -eis) adj healthy; (moralmente) wholesome

saúde [saˈudʒi] f health; (brinde) toast; ~! (brindando) cheers!; (quando se espirra) bless you!; beber à ~ de to drink to, toast; estar bem/mal de ~ to be well/ill

saudosismo [sawdoˈziʒmu] m nostalgia

saudoso, -a [sawˈdozu, ɔza] adj (nostálgico) nostalgic; (da família ou *terra natal*) homesick; (*de uma pessoa*) longing; (*que causa saudades*) much-missed

sauna ['sawna] *f* sauna

saxofone [sakso'fɔni] *m* saxophone

sazonal [sazo'naw] (*pl* **-ais**) *adj* seasonal

scanner ['skane*] *m* scanner

PALAVRA CHAVE

se [si] *pron* 1 (*reflexivo: impess*) oneself; (: *m*) himself; (: *f*) herself; (: *coisa*) itself; (: *você*) yourself; (: *pl*) themselves; (: *vocês*) yourselves; **ela está ~ vestindo** she's getting dressed; (*usos léxicos del pron*) V o vb em questão p. ex. **arrepender-se**

2 (*uso recíproco*) each other, one another; **olharam ~** they looked at each other

3 (*impess*): **come~ bem aqui** you can eat well here; **sabe-~ que ... it** is known that ...; **vende(m)-~ jornais naquela loja** they sell newspapers in that shop

♦ *conj* if; (*em pergunta indireta*) whether; ~ **bem que** even though

---

sê [se] *vb* V **ser**

sebe ['sεbi] (*PT*) *f* fence; ~ **viva** hedge

sebo ['sebu] *m* tallow; **seboso, -a** [se'bozu, ɔza] *adj* greasy; (*sujo*) dirty

seca ['seka] *f* drought

secador [seka'do*] *m*: ~ **de cabelo/roupa** hairdryer/clothes horse

seção [se'sãw] (*pl* **-ões**) *f* section; (*em loja, repartição*) department

secar [se'ka*] *vt* to dry; (*planta*) to parch ♦ *vi* to dry; to wither; (*fonte*) to dry up

secção [sek'sãw] (*PT*) = **seção**

seco, -a ['seku, a] *adj* dry; (*ríspido*) curt, brusque; (*magro*) thin; (*pessoa: frio*) cold; (: *sério*) serious

seções [se'sõjʃ] *fpl de* **seção**

secretaria [sekreta'ria] *f* general office; (*de secretário*) secretary's office; (*ministério*) ministry

secretária [sekre'tarja] *f* writing desk; ~ **eletrônica** (telephone) answering machine, V tb **secretário**

secretário, -a [sekre'tarju, a] *m/f* secretary; **S~ de Estado de ...** Secretary of State for ...

secreto, -a [se'kretu, a] *adj* secret

sector [sek'to*] (*PT*) *m* = **setor**

século ['sεkulu] *m* century; (*época*) age

secundário, -a [sekũ'darju, a] *adj* secondary

seda ['seda] *f* silk

sedativo [seda'tʃivu] *m* sedative

sede¹ ['sεdʒi] *f* (*de empresa, instituição*) headquarters *sg*; (*de governo*) seat; (*REL*) see, diocese

sede² ['sedʒi] *f* thirst; **estar com** *ou* **ter ~** to be thirsty; **sedento, -a** [se'dētu, a] *adj* thirsty

sediar [se'dʒja*] *vt* to base

sedimento [sedʒi'mētu] *m* sediment

sedução [sedu'sãw] (*pl* **-ões**) *f* seduction

sedutor, a [sedu'to*, a] *adj* seductive; (*oferta etc*) tempting

seduzir [sedu'zi*] *vt* to seduce; (*fascinar*) to fascinate

segmento [seg'mētu] *m* segment

segredo [se'gredu] *m* secret, (*sigilo*) secrecy; (*de fechadura*) combination

segregar [segre'ga*] *vt* to segregate

seguidamente [segida'mētʃi] *adv* (*sem parar*) continuously; (*logo depois*) soon afterwards

seguido, -a [se'gidu, a] *adj* following; (*contínuo*) continuous, consecutive; ~ **de** *ou* **por** followed by; **três dias ~s** three days running; **horas seguidas** for hours on end;

em seguida next; (*logo depois*) soon afterwards; (*imediatamente*) immediately, right away

seguimento [segi'mẽtu] *m* continuation; **dar ~ a** to proceed with; **em ~ de** after

seguinte [se'gĩtʃi] *adj* following, next; **eu lhe disse o ~** this is what I said to him

seguir [se'gi*] *vt* to follow; (*continuar*) to continue ♦ *vi* to follow; to continue, carry on; (*ir*) to go; **seguir-se** *vr*: **~-se (a)** to follow; **logo a ~** next; **~-se (de)** to result (from)

segunda [se'gũda] *f* (*tb: ~-feira*) Monday; (*AUTO*) second (gear); **de ~** second-rate; **segunda-feira** (*pl* **segundas-feiras**) *f* Monday

segundo, -a [se'gũdu, a] *adj* second ♦ *prep* according to ♦ *conj* as, from what ♦ *adv* secondly ♦ *m* second; **de segunda mão** second-hand; **de segunda (classe)** second-class; **~ ele disse** according to what he said; **~ dizem** apparently; **~ me consta** as far as I know; **segundas intenções** ulterior motives

seguramente [segura'mẽtʃi] *adv* certainly; (*muito provavelmente*) surely

segurança [segu'rãsa] *f* security; (*ausência de perigo*) safety; (*confiança*) confidence ♦ *m/f* security guard; **com ~** assuredly

segurar [segu'ra*] *vt* to hold; (*amparar*) to hold up; (*COM: bens*) to insure ♦ *vi*: **~ em** to hold; **segurar-se** *vr*: **~-se em** to hold on to

seguro, -a [se'guru, a] *adj* safe; (*livre de risco, firme*) secure; (*certo*) certain, assured; (*confiável*) reliable; (*de si mesmo*) confident; (*certeza*) settled ♦ *adv* confidently ♦ *m* (*COM*) insurance; **estar ~ de/de que** to be

sure of/that; **fazer ~** to take out an insurance policy; **~ contra acidentes/incêndio** accident/fire insurance; **seguro-saúde** (*pl* **seguros-saúde**) *m* health insurance

sei [sej] *vb* V **saber**

seio ['seju] *m* breast, bosom; (*âmago*) heart; **~ paranasal** sinus

seis [sejʃ] *num* six

seita ['sejta] *f* sect

seixo ['sejʃu] *m* pebble

seja *etc* ['seʒa] *vb* V **ser**

sela ['sɛla] *f* saddle

selar [se'la*] *vt* (*carta*) to stamp; (*documento oficial, pacto*) to seal; (*cavalo*) to saddle

seleção [sele'sãw] (*PT* -**cç**-) (*pl* -**ões**) *f* selection; (*ESPORTE*) team

selecionar [selesjo'na*] (*PT* -**cc**-) *vt* to select

seleções [sele'sõjʃ] *fpl de* **seleção**

seleto, -a [se'lɛtu, a] (*PT* -**ct**-) *adj* select

selim [se'lĩ] (*pl* -**ns**) *m* saddle

selo ['sɛlu] *m* stamp; (*carimbo, sinete*) seal

selva ['sɛwva] *f* jungle

selvagem [sew'vaʒẽ] (*pl* -**ns**) *adj* wild; (*feroz*) fierce; (*povo*) savage; **selvageria** [sewvaʒe'ria] *f* savagery

sem [sẽ] *prep* without ♦ *conj*: **~ que eu peça** without my asking; **estar/ficar ~ dinheiro/gasolina** to have no/have run out of money/petrol

semáforo [se'maforu] *m* (*AUTO*) traffic lights *pl*; (*FERRO*) signal

semana [se'mana] *f* week; **semanal** [sema'naw] (*pl* -**is**) *adj* weekly; **semanário** [sema'narju] *m* weekly (publication)

semear [se'mja*] *vt* to sow

semelhança [seme'ʎãsa] *f* similarity, resemblance; **semelhante** [seme'ʎãtʃi] *adj* similar; (*tal*) such ♦ *m* fellow creature

êmen ['eʃmẽ] *m* semen

emente [se'mẽtʃi] *f* seed

emestral [semeʃ'traw] (*pl* **-ais**) *adj* half-yearly, bi-annual

emestre [se'meʃtri] *m* six months; (*EDUC*) semester

emi... [semi] *prefixo* semi..., half...;

semioírculo [semi'sixkulu] *m* semicircle; **semifinal** [semi'finaw] (*pl* **semifinais**) *f* semi-final

eminário [semi'narju] *m* seminar; (*REL*) seminary

em-número *m*: **um ~ de coisas** loads of things

empre ['sẽpri] *adv* always; **você ~ vai?** (*PT*) are you still going?; **~ que** whenever; **como ~** as usual; **a comida/hora** *etc* **de ~** the usual food/time *etc*

em-terra *m/f inv* landless labourer (*BRIT*) ou laborer (*US*)

em-teto *m/f inv*: **os ~** the homeless

em-vergonha *adj inv* shameless ♦ *m/f inv* (*pessoa*) rogue

senado [se'nadu] *m* senate; **senador, a** [sena'do*, a] *m/f* senator

senão [se'nãw] (*pl* **-ões**) *conj* otherwise; (*mas sim*) but, but rather ♦ *prep* except ♦ *m* flaw, defect

senha ['seɲa] *f* sign; (*palavra de passe*) password; (*de calxa automáti-co*) PIN number; (*recibo*) receipt; (*passe*) pass

senhor, a [se'ɲo*, a] *m* (*homem*) man; (*formal*) gentleman; (*homem idoso*) elderly man; (*REL*) lord; (*dono*) owner; (*tratamento*) Mr(.); (*tratamento respeitoso*) sir ♦ *f* (*mulher*) lady; (*esposa*) wife; (*mulher idosa*) elderly lady; (*dona*) owner; (*tratamento*) Mrs(.), Ms(.); (*tratamento respeitoso*) madam; **o ~, a ~a** (*você*) you; **nossa ~a!** (*col*) gosh!; **sim, ~(a)!** yes indeed!

senhorita [seɲo'rita] *f* young lady; (*tratamento*) Miss, Ms(.); **a ~** (*você*) you

senil [se'niw] (*pl* **-is**) *adj* senile

senões [se'nõjʃ] *mpl de* **senão**

sensação [sẽsa'sãw] (*pl* **-ões**) *f* sensation; **oonoacional** [sẽsasjo'naw] (*pl* **-ais**) *adj* sensational

sensato, -a [sẽ'satu, a] *adj* sensible

sensível [sẽ'sivew] (*pl* **-eis**) *adj* sensitive; (*visível*) noticeable; (*considerável*) considerable; (*dolorido*) tender

senso ['sẽsu] *m* sense; (*juízo*) judgement

sensual [sẽ'swaw] (*pl* **-ais**) *adj* sensual

sentado, -a [sẽ'tadu, a] *adj* sitting

sentar [se'ta*] *vt* to seat ♦ *vi* to sit; **sentar-se** *vr* to sit down

sentença [sẽ'tẽsa] *f* (*JUR*) sentence; **sentenciar** [sẽtẽ'sja*] *vt* (*julgar*) to pass judgement on; (*condenar por sentença*) to sentence

sentido, -a [sẽ'tʃidu, a] *adj* (*magoado*) hurt; (*choro, queixa*) heartfelt ♦ *m* sense; (*direção*) direction; (*atenção*) attention; (*aspecto*) respect; **~!** (*MIL*) attention!; **em certo ~** in a sense; (*não*) **ter ~** (not) to be acceptable; **"~ único"** (*PT: sinal*) "one-way"

sentimental [sẽtʃimẽ'taw] (*pl* **-ais**) *adj* sentimental; **vida ~** love life

sentimento [sẽtʃi'mẽtu] *m* feeling; (*senso*) sense; **~s** *mpl* (*pêsames*) condolences

sentinela [sẽtʃi'nɛla] *f* sentry, guard

sentir [sẽ'tʃi*] *vt* to feel; (*perceber, pressentir*) to sense; (*ser afetado por*) to be affected by; (*magoar-se*) to be upset by ♦ *vi* (*sofrer*) to suffer; **sentir-se** *vr* to feel; (*julgar-se*) to consider o.s. (to be); **~ (a) falta**

de to miss; **~ cheiro/gosto (de)** to smell/taste; **~ vontade de** to feel like; **sinto muito** I am very sorry

separação [separa'sãw] (pl **-ões**) f separation

separado, -a [sepa'radu, a] adj separate; **em ~** separately, apart

separar [sepa'ra*] vt to separate; (dividir) to divide; (pôr de lado) to put aside; **separar-se** vr to separate; to be divided

sepultamento [sepuwta'mẽtu] m burial

sepultar [sepuw'ta*] vt to bury; **sepultura** [sepuw'tura] f grave, tomb

seqüência [se'kwẽsja] f sequence

sequer [se'kɛ*] adv at least; **(nem) ~** not even

seqüestrador, a [sekweʃtra'do*, a] m/f kidnapper; (de avião etc) hijacker

seqüestrar [sekweʃ'tra*] vt (bens) to seize, confiscate; (raptar) to kidnap; (avião etc) to hijack; **seqüestro** [se'kwɛʃtru] m seizure; abduction, kidnapping; hijack

┌─────────────────────┐
│ PALAVRA CHAVE   │
└─────────────────────┘

ser [se*] vi 1 (descrição) to be; **ela é médica/muito alta** she's a doctor/ very tall; **é Ana** (TEL) Ana speaking ou here; **ela é de uma bondade incrível** she's incredibly kind; **ele está é danado** he's really angry; **~ de mentir/briga** to be the sort to lie/fight

2 (horas, datas, números): **é uma hora** it's one o'clock; **são seis e meia** it's half past six; **é dia 1° de junho** it's the first of June; **somos/ são seis** there are six of us/them

3 (origem, material): **~ de** to be ou come from; (feito de) to be made of; (pertencer) to belong to; **sua**

família é da Bahia his (ou her etc) family is from Bahia; **a mesa é de mármore** the table is made of marble; **é de Pedro** it's Pedro's, it belongs to Pedro

4 (em orações passivas): **já foi descoberto** it had already been discovered

5 (locuções com subjun): **ou seja** that is to say; **seja quem for** whoever it may be; **se eu fosse você** if I were you; **se não fosse você,** ... if it hadn't been for you, ...

6 (locuções): **a não ~** except; **a não ~ que** unless; é (resposta afirmativa) yes; ..., **não é?**..., isn't it?, ..., don't you? etc; **ah, é?** really?; **que foi?** (o que aconteceu?) what happened?; (qual é o problema?) what's the problem?; **~á que ...?** I wonder if ...?

♦ m being; **~es** mpl (criaturas) creatures

sereia [se'reja] f mermaid

sereno, -a [se'rɛnu, a] adj calm; (tempo) fine, clear

série [ˈsɛri] f series; (seqüência) sequence, succession; (EDUC) grade; (categoria) category; **fora de ~** out of order; (fig) extraordinary

seriedade [serje'dadʒi] f seriousness; (honestidade) honesty

seringa [se'rĩga] f syringe

sério, -a [ˈsɛrju, a] adj serious; (honesto) honest, decent; (responsável) responsible; (confiável) reliable; (roupa) sober ♦ adv seriously; **a ~** seriously; **~? really?**

sermão [sex'mãw] (pl **-ões**) m sermon; (fig) telling-off

serpente [sex'pẽtʃi] f snake

serpentina [sexpẽ'tʃina] f streamer

serra [ˈsɛxa] f (montanhas) mountain range; (TEC) saw

serralheiro, -a [sexa'ʌejru, a] *m/f* locksmith

serrano, -a [se'xanu, a] *adj* highland *atr* ♦ *m/f* highlander

serrar [se'xa*] *vt* to saw

sertanejo, -a [sexta'neʒu, a] *adj* rustic, country ♦ *m/f* inhabitant of the *sertão*

sertão [sex'tãw] (*pl* **-ões**) *m* backwoods *pl*, bush (country)

servente [sex'vẽtʃi] *m/f* servant; (*operário*) labourer (*BRIT*), laborer (*US*)

serviçal [sexvi'saw] (*pl* **-ais**) *adj* obliging, helpful ♦ *m/f* servant; (*trabalhador*) wage earner

serviço [sex'visu] *m* service; (*de chá etc*) set; **estar de ~** to be on duty; **prestar ~** to help

servidor, a [sexvi'do*, a] *m/f* servant; (*funcionário*) employee; **~ público** civil servant

servil [sex'viw] (*pl* **-is**) *adj* servile

servir [sex'vi*] *vt* to serve ♦ *vi* to serve; (*ser útil*) to be useful; (*ajudar*) to help to; (*roupa: caber*) to fit; **servir-se** *vr*: **~-se (de)** (*comida, café*) to help o.s. (to); (*meios*): **~-se de** to use, make use of; **~ de** (*prover*) to supply with, provide with; **você está servido?** (*num bar*) are you all right for a drink?; **~ de algo** to serve as sth; **qualquer ônibus serve** any bus will do

servis [sex'viʃ] *adj pl de* **servil**

sessão [se'sãw] (*pl* **-ões**) *f* (*do parlamento etc*) session; (*reunião*) meeting; (*de cinema*) showing

sessenta [se'sẽta] *num* sixty

sessões [se'sõjʃ] *fpl de* **sessão**

sesta [ˈseʃta] *f* siesta, nap

seta [ˈseta] *f* arrow

sete [ˈsetʃi] *num* seven

setembro [se'tẽbru] (*PT* **S-**) *m* September; **7 de setembro** *see*

boxed note

---

7 DE SETEMBRO

Brazil's independence from Portugal is commemorated on 7 September. Independence was declared in 1822 by the Portuguese prince regent, Dom Pedro, who rebelled against several orders from the Portuguese crown, among them the order to swear loyalty to the Portuguese constitution. It is a national holiday and the occasion for processions and military parades through the main cities.

---

setenta [se'tẽta] *num* seventy

sétimo, -a [ˈsɛtʃimu, a] *num* seventh

setor [sẽ'to*] *m* sector

seu, sua [sew, 'sua] *adj* (*dele*) his; (*dela*) her; (*de coisa*) its; (*deles, delas*) their; (*de você, vocês*) your ♦ *pron*: **(o) ~, (a) sua** his; hers; its; theirs; yours ♦ *m* (*senhor*) Mr(.)

severidade [severi'dadʒi] *f* severity

severo, -a [se'veru, a] *adj* severe

sexo [ˈseksu] *m* sex

sexta [ˈseʃta] *f* (*tb*: **~-feira**) Friday; **sexta-feira** (*pl* **sextas-feiras**) *f* Friday; **Sexta-feira Santa** Good Friday

sexto, -a [ˈseʃtu, a] *num* sixth

sexual [se'kswaw] (*pl* **-ais**) *adj* sexual; (*vida, ato*) sex *atr*

sexy [ˈsɛksi] (*pl* **~s**) *adj* sexy

s.f.f. (*PT*) *abr* = **se faz favor**

short [ˈʃɔxtʃi] *m* (pair of) shorts *pl*

si [si] *pron* oneself; (*ele*) himself; (*ela*) herself; (*coisa*) itself; (*PT: você*) yourself, you; (: *vocês*) yourselves; (*eles, elas*) themselves

SIDA [ˈsida] (*PT*) *abr f* (= *síndrome de deficiência imunológica adquirida*) **a ~** AIDS

siderúrgica [side'ruxʒika] f steel industry

sigilo [si'ʒilu] m secrecy

sigla ['sigla] f acronym; (abreviação) abbreviation

significado [signifi'kadu] m meaning

significar [signifi'ka*] vt to mean, signify; **significativo, -a** [signifika'tʃivu, a] adj significant

signo [signu] m sign

sigo etc ['sigu] vb V **seguir**

sílaba ['silaba] f syllable

silenciar [silẽ'sja*] vt to silence

silêncio [si'lẽsju] m silence, quiet; **silencioso, -a** [silẽ'sjozu, ɔza] adj silent, quiet ♦ m (AUTO) silencer (BRIT), muffler (US)

silhueta [si'ʎweta] f silhouette

silvestre [siw'vɛʃtri] adj wild

sim [sĩ] adv yes; **creio que ~** I think so

símbolo ['sĩbolu] m symbol

simetria [sime'tria] f symmetry

similar [simi'la*] adj similar

simpatia [sĩpa'tʃia] f liking; (afeto) affection; (afinidade, solidariedade) sympathy; **~s** fpl (inclinações) sympathies; **simpático, -a** [sĩ'patʃiku, a] adj (pessoa, decoração etc) nice; (lugar) pleasant, nice; (amável) kind; **simpatizante** [sĩpatʃi'zãtʃi] adj sympathetic ♦ m/f sympathizer; **simpatizar** [sĩpatʃi'za*] vi: **simpatizar com** (pessoa) to like; (causa) to sympathize with

simples ['sĩpliʃ] adj inv simple; (único) single; (fácil) easy; (mero) mere; (ingênuo) naïve ♦ adv simply; **simplicidade** [sĩplisi'dadʒi] f simplicity; **simplificar** [sĩplifi'ka*] vt to simplify

simular [simu'la*] vt to simulate

simultaneamente [simuwtanja-'mẽtʃi] adv simultaneously

simultâneo, -a [simuw'tanju, a] adj simultaneous

sinagoga [sina'gɔga] f synagogue

sinal [si'naw] (pl **-ais**) m sign; (gesto, TEL) signal; (na pele) mole; (: de nascença) birthmark; (depósito) deposit; (tb: **~ de tráfego, ~ luminoso**) traffic light; **por ~** (por falar nisso) by the way; (aliás) as a matter of fact; **~ de chamada** (TEL) ringing tone; **~ de discar** (BR) ou **de marcar** (PT) dialling tone (BRIT), dial tone (US); **~ de ocupado** (BR) ou **de impedido** (PT) engaged tone (BRIT), busy signal (US); **sinalização** [sinaliza-'sãw] f (ato) signalling; (para motoristas) traffic signs pl

sinceridade [sĩseri'dadʒi] f sincerity

sincero, -a [sĩ'seru, a] adj sincere

sindicalista [sĩdʒika'liʃta] m/f trade unionist

sindicato [sĩdʒi'katu] m trade union; (financeiro) syndicate

síndrome ['sĩdromi] f syndrome; **~ de Down** Down's syndrome

sinfonia [sĩfo'nia] f symphony

singular [sĩgu'la*] adj singular; (extraordinário) exceptional; (bizarro) odd, peculiar

sino ['sinu] m bell

sintaxe [sĩ'tasi] f syntax

síntese ['sĩtezi] f synthesis; **sintético, -a** [sĩ'tetʃiku, a] adj synthetic; **sintetizar** [sĩtetʃi'za*] vt to synthesize

sinto etc ['sĩtu] vb V **sentir**

sintoma [sĩ'tɔma] m symptom

sinuca [si'nuka] f snooker

sinuoso, -a [si'nwozu, ɔza] adj (caminho) winding; (linha) wavy

siri [si'ri] m crab

Síria ['sirja] f: a **~** Syria; **sírio, -a** ['sirju, a] adj, m/f Syrian

sirvo etc ['sixvu] vb V **servir**

sistema [siʃ'tɛma] *m* system; (*método*) method

site ['sajtʃi] *m* (*na Internet*) website

sitiar [si'tʃja*] *vt* to besiege

sítio ['sitʃju] *m* (MIL) siege; (*propriedade rural*) small farm; (PT: *lugar*) place

situação [sitwa'sãw] (*pl* -ões) *f* situation; (*posição*) position

situado, -a [si'twadu, a] *adj* situated

situar [si'twa*] *vt* to place, put; (*edifício*) to situate, locate; **situar-se** *vr* to position o.s.; (*estar situado*) to be situated

slogan [iʃ'lɔgã] (*pl* ~s) *m* slogan

SME *abr m* (= *Sistema Monetário Europeu*) ERM

smoking [iʒ'mokiʃ] (*pl* ~s) *m* dinner jacket (BRIT), tuxedo (US)

só [sɔ] *adj* alone; (*único*) single; (*solitário*) solitary ♦ *adv* only; **a ~s** alone

soar [swa*] *vi* to sound ♦ *vt* (*horas*) to strike; (*instrumento*) to play; **~ a** to sound like; (*fig*) to go down well/badly

sob [sob] *prep* under; **~ juramento** on oath; **~ medida** (*roupa*) made to measure

sobe *etc* ['sɔbi] *vb* V **subir**

soberano, -a [sobe'ranu, a] *adj* sovereign; (*fig: supremo*) supreme ♦ *m/f* sovereign

sobra ['sɔbra] *f* surplus, remnant; **~s** *fpl* (*restos*) remains; (*de tecido*) remnants; (*de comida*) leftovers; **ter algo de ~** to have sth extra; (*tempo, comida, motivos*) to have plenty of sth; **ficar de ~** to be left over

sobrado [so'bradu] *m* (*andar*) floor; (*casa*) house (*of two or more storeys*)

sobrancelha [sobrã'seʎa] *f* eyebrow

sobrar [so'bra*] *vi* to be left; (*dúvidas*) to remain

sobre ['sobri] *prep* on; (*por cima de*) over; (*acima de*) above; (*a respeito de*) about

sobrecarregar [sobrikaxe'ga*] *vt* to overload

sobremesa [sobri'meza] *f* dessert

sobrenatural [sobrinatu'raw] (*pl* -ais) *adj* supernatural

sobrenome [sobri'nɔmi] (BR) *m* surname, family name

sobrepor [sobri'po*] (*irreg: como* pôr) *vt*: **~ algo a algo** to put sth on top of sth

sobressair [sobrisa'i*] *vi* to stand out; **sobressair-se** *vr* to stand out

sobressalente [sobrisa'letʃi] *adj*, *m* spare

sobressalto [sobri'sawtu] *m* start; (*temor*) trepidation; **de ~** suddenly

sobretaxa [sobri'taʃa] *f* surcharge

sobretudo [sobri'tudu] *m* overcoat ♦ *adv* above all, especially

sobrevivência [sobrivi'vẽsja] *f* survival; **sobrevivente** [sobrivi'vẽtʃi] *adj* surviving ♦ *m/f* survivor

sobreviver [sobrivi've*] *vi*: **~ (a)** to survive

sobrinho, -a [so'briɲu, a] *m/f* nephew/niece

sóbrio, -a ['sɔbrju, a] *adj* sober; (*moderado*) moderate, restrained

socar [so'ka*] *vt* to hit, strike; (*calcar*) to crush, pound; (*massa de pão*) to knead

social [so'sjaw] (*pl* -ais) *adj* social; **socialista** [sosja'liʃta] *adj*, *m/f* socialist

sociedade [sosje'dadʒi] *f* society; (COM: *empresa*) company; (*associação*) association; **~ anônima** limited company (BRIT), incorporated company (US)

sócio, -a ['sɔsju, a] *m/f* (COM) part-

soco 582 **som**

ner; *(de clube)* member

soco ['soku] *m* punch; **dar um ~ em** to punch

socorrer [soko'xe*] *vt* to help, assist; *(salvar)* to rescue; **socorrer-se** *vr*: **~-se de** to resort to, have recourse to; **socorro** [so'koxu] *m* help, assistance; *(reboque)* breakdown *(BRIT)* ou tow *(US)* truck; **socorro!** help!; **primeiros socorros** first aid *sg*

soda ['sɔda] *f* soda (water)

sofá [so'fa] *m* sofa, settee; **sofá-cama** *(pl* **sofás-camas)** *m* sofa-bed

sofisticado, -a [sofiʃtʃi'kadu, a] *adj* sophisticated; *(afetado)* pretentious

sofrer [so'fre*] *vt* to suffer; *(acidente)* to have; *(agüentar)* to bear, put up with; *(experimentar)* to undergo ♦ *vi* to suffer; **sofrido, -a** [so'fridu, a] *adj* long-suffering; **sofrimento** [sofri'mẽtu] *m* suffering

software [sof'twe*] *m* *(COMPUT)* software

sogro, -a ['sogru, 'sɔgra] *m/f* father-in-law/mother-in-law

sóis [sɔjʃ] *mpl de* **sol**

soja ['sɔʒa] *f* soya *(BRIT)*, soy *(US)*

sol [sɔw] *(pl* **sóis)** *m* sun; *(luz)* sunshine, sunlight; **fazer ~** to be sunny; **tomar ~** to sunbathe

sola ['sɔla] *f* sole

solar [so'la*] *adj* solar; **energia/painel ~** solar energy/panel

soldado [sow'dadu] *m* soldier

soldar [sow'da*] *vt* to weld

soleira [so'lejra] *f* doorstep

solene [so'lɛni] *adj* solemn; **solenidade** [soleni'dadʒi] *f* solemnity; *(cerimônia)* ceremony

soletrar [sole'tra*] *vt* to spell

solicitar [solisi'ta*] *vt* to ask for; *(emprego etc)* to apply for; *(ami-*

zade, atenção) to seek; **~ algo a alguém** to ask sb for sth

solícito, -a [so'lisitu, a] *adj* helpful

solidão [soli'dãw] *f* solitude; *(sensação)* loneliness

solidariedade [solidarje'dadʒi] *f* solidarity

solidário, -a [soli'darju, a] *adj*: **ser ~ a** ou **com** *(pessoa)* to stand by; *(causa)* to be sympathetic to, sympathize with

sólido, -a ['sɔlidu, a] *adj* solid

solitário, -a [soli'tarju, a] *adj* lonely; *(isolado)* solitary ♦ *m* hermit

solo ['sɔlu] *m* ground, earth; *(MÚS)* solo

soltar [sow'ta*] *vt* to set free; *(desatar)* to loosen; *(largar)* to let go of; *(emitir)* to emit; *(grito)* to let out; *(cabelo)* to let down; *(freio)* to release; **soltar-se** *vr* to come loose; *(desinibir-se)* to let o.s. go

solteirão, -ona [sowtej'rãw, rɔna] *(pl* **-ões, ~s)** *adj* unmarried, single ♦ *m/f* confirmed bachelor/spinster

solteiro, -a [sow'tejru, a] *adj* unmarried, single ♦ *m/f* bachelor/single woman

solteirões [sowtej'rõjʃ] *mpl de* **solteirão**

solteirona [sowtej'rɔna] *f de* **solteirão**

solto, -a ['sowtu, a] *pp de* **soltar** ♦ *adj* loose; *(livre)* free; *(sozinho)* alone

solução [solu'sãw] *(pl* **-ões)** *f* solution

soluçar [solu'sa*] *vi (chorar)* to sob; *(MED)* to hiccup

solucionar [solusjo'na*] *vt* to solve; *(decidir)* to resolve

soluço [so'lusu] *m* sob; *(MED)* hiccup

soluções [solu'sõjʃ] *fpl de* **solução**

som [sõ] *(pl* **-ns)** *m* sound; **~ cd**

compact disc player

soma ['sɔma] f sum; **somar** [so'ma*] vt (adicionar) to add (up); (chegar a) to add up to, amount to ♦ vi to add up

sombra ['sõbra] f shadow; (proteção) shade; (indício) trace, sign

sombrinha [sõ'briɲa] f parasol, sunshade

sombrio, -a [sõ'briu, a] adj shady, dark; (triste) gloomy

some etc ['sɔmi] vb V **sumir**

somente [sɔ'mẽtʃi] adv only

somos ['somoʃ] vb V **ser**

sonâmbulo, -a [so'nãbulu, a] m/f sleepwalker

sondar [sõ'da*] vt to probe; (opinião etc) to sound out

soneca [so'nɛka] f nap, snooze

sonegar [sone'ga*] vt (dinheiro, valores) to conceal, withhold; (furtar) to steal, pilfer; (impostos) to dodge, evade; (informações, dados) to withhold

soneto [so'netu] m sonnet

sonhador, a [soɲa'do*, a] adj dreamy ♦ m/f dreamer

sonhar [so'ɲa*] vt, vi to dream; ~ **com** to dream about; **sonho** ['sɔɲu] m dream; (CULIN) doughnut

sono ['sɔnu] m sleep; **estar com** ou **ter ~** to be sleepy

sonolento, -a [sono'lẽtu, a] adj sleepy, drowsy

sonoro, -a [so'nɔru, a] adj resonant

sons [sõʃ] mpl de **som**

sonso, -a ['sõsu, a] adj sly, artful

sopa ['sɔpa] f soup

soporífero [sopo'riferu], **soporífico** [sopo'rifiku] m sleeping drug

soprar [so'pra*] vt to blow; (balão) to blow up; (vela) to blow out; (dizer em voz baixa) to whisper ♦ vi to blow; **sopro** ['sɔpru] m blow, puff; (de vento) gust

sórdido, -a ['sɔxdʒidu, a] adj sordid; (imundo) squalid

soro ['soru] m (MED) serum

sorridente [soxi'dẽtʃi] adj smiling

sorrir [so'xi*] vi to smile; **sorriso** [so'xizu] m smile

sorte ['sɔxtʃi] f luck; (casualidade) chance; (destino) fate, destiny; (condição) lot; (espécie) sort, kind; **de ~ que** so that; **dar ~** (trazer sorte) to bring good luck; (ter sorte) to be lucky; **estar com** ou **ter ~** to be lucky

sortear [sox'tʃja*] vt to draw lots for; (rifar) to raffle; (MIL) to draft; **sorteio** [sox'teju] m draw; raffle; draft

sortido, -a [sox'tʃidu, a] adj (abastecido) supplied, stocked; (variado) assorted; (loja) well-stocked

sortudo, -a [sox'tudu, a] (col) adj lucky

sorvete [sox'vetʃi] (BR) m ice cream

SOS abr SOS

sossegado, -a [sose'gadu, a] adj peaceful, calm

sossegar [sose'ga*] vt to calm, quieten ♦ vi to quieten down

sossego [so'segu] m peace (and quiet)

sótão ['sɔtãw] (pl ~s) m attic, loft

sotaque [so'taki] m accent

sotavento [sota'vẽtu] m (NÁUT) lee

soterrar [sote'xa*] vt to bury

sou [so] vb V **ser**

soube etc ['sobi] vb V **saber**

soutien [su'tʃjã] (PT) m = **sutiã**

sova ['sɔva] f beating, thrashing

sovaco [so'vaku] m armpit

soviético, -a [so'vjetʃiku, a] adj, m/f Soviet

sovina [so'vina] adj mean, stingy ♦ m/f miser

sozinho, -a [sɔ'ziɲu, a] adj (all)

alone, by oneself; (*por si mesmo*) by oneself

squash [iʃ'kweʃ] *m* squash

Sr. *abr* (= *senhor*) Mr(.)

Sr.ᵃ *abr* (= *senhora*) Mrs(.)

Sr.ᵗᵃ *abr* (= *senhorita*) Miss

status [iʃ'tatus] *m* status

sua ['sua] *f de* **seu**

suar [swa*] *vt, vi* to sweat

suástica ['swaʃtʃika] *f* swastika

suave ['swavi] *adj* gentle; (*música, voz*) soft; (*sabor, vinho*) smooth; (*cheiro*) delicate; (*dor*) mild; (*trabalho*) light; **suavidade** [suavi'dadʒi] *f* gentleness; softness

subalterno, -a [subaw'texnu, a] *adj, m/f* subordinate

subconsciente [subkõ'sjẽtʃi] *adj, m* subconscious

subdesenvolvido, -a [subdʒizẽvõw'vidu, a] *adj* underdeveloped

subentender [subẽtẽ'de*] *vt* to understand, assume; **subentendido, -a** [subẽtẽ'dʒidu, a] *adj* implied ♦ *m* implication

subestimar [subeʃtʃi'ma*] *vt* to underestimate

subida [su'bida] *f* ascent, climb; (*ladeira*) slope; (*de preços*) rise

subir [su'bi*] *vi* to go up; (*preço, de posto etc*) to rise ♦ *vt* to raise; (*ladeira, escada, rio*) to climb, go up; ~ **em** to climb, go up; (*cadeira, palanque*) to climb onto, get up onto; (*ônibus*) to get on

súbito, -a ['subitu, a] *adj* sudden ♦ *adv* (*tb:* **de ~**) suddenly

subjetivo, -a [subʒe'tʃivu, a] (*PT* **-ct-**) *adj* subjective

subjuntivo, -a [subʒũ'tʃivu, a] *adj* subjunctive ♦ *m* subjunctive

sublime [su'blimi] *adj* sublime

sublinhar [subli'ɲa*] *vt* to underline; (*destacar*) to emphasize, stress

sublocar [sublo'ka*] *vt, vi* to sublet

submarino, -a [subma'rinu, a] *adj* underwater ♦ *m* submarine

submergir [submex'ʒi*] *vt* to submerge; **submergir-se** *vr* to submerge

submeter [subme'te*] *vt* to subdue; (*plano*) to submit; (*sujeitar*): ~ **a** to subject to; **submeter-se** *vr*: **~-se a** to submit to; (*operação*) to undergo

submirjo *etc* [sub'mixʒu] *vb V* **submergir**

submisso, -a [sub'misu, a] *adj* submissive

subnutrição [subnutri'sãw] *f* malnutrition

subornar [subox'na*] *vt* to bribe; **suborno** [su'boxnu] *m* bribery

subseqüente [subse'kwẽtʃi] *adj* subsequent

subserviente [subsex'vjẽtʃi] *adj* obsequious, servile

subsidiária [subsi'dʒjarja] *f* (*COM*) subsidiary (company)

subsidiário, -a [subsi'dʒjarju, a] *adj* subsidiary

subsídio [sub'sidʒu] *m* subsidy; (*ajuda*) aid

subsistência [subsiʃ'tẽsja] *f* subsistence

subsistir [subsiʃ'tʃi*] *vi* to exist; (*viver*) to subsist

subsolo [sub'sɔlu] *m* (*de prédio*) basement

substância [sub'ʃtãsja] *f* substance

substancial [subʃtã'sjaw] (*pl* **-ais**) *adj* substantial

substantivo [subʃtã'tʃivu] *m* noun

substituir [subʃtʃi'twi*] *vt* to substitute; **substituto, -a** [subʃti'tutu, a] *adj, m/f* substitute

subterrâneo, -a [subite'xanju, a] *adj* subterranean, underground

subtil *etc* [sub'tiw] (*PT*) = **sutil** *etc*

subtrair [subtra'i*] *vt* to steal;
(*deduzir*) to subtract ♦ *vi* to subtract

subumano, -a [subu'manu, a] *adj*
subhuman; (*desumano*) inhuman

suburbano, -a [subux'banu, a] *adj*
suburban

subúrbio [su'buxbju] *m* suburb

subvenção [subvẽ'sãw] (*pl* -ões) *f*
subsidy, grant

subversivo, -a [subvex'sivu, a]
adj, m/f subversive

sucata [su'kata] *f* scrap metal

sucção [suk'sãw] *f* suction

suceder [suse'de*] *vi* to happen ♦ *vt*
to succeed; ~ **a** (*num cargo*) to succeed; (*seguir*) to follow

sucessão [suse'sãw] (*pl* -ões) *f* succession; **sucessivo, -a** [suse'sivu,
a] *adj* successive

sucesso [su'sesu] *m* success; (*música, filme*) hit; **fazer** *ou* **ter ~** to be
successful

sucinto, -a [su'sĩtu, a] *adj* succinct

suco ['suku] (*BR*) *m* juice

suculento, -a [suku'lẽtu, a] *adj*
succulent

sucumbir [sukũ'bi*] *vi* to succumb;
(*morrer*) to die, perish

sucursal [sukux'saw] (*pl* -ais) *f*
(*COM*) branch

Sudão [su'dãw] *m*: **o ~** (the) Sudan

sudeste [su'dɛʃtʃi] *m* south-east

súdito ['suditu] *m* (*de rei etc*) subject

sudoeste [sud'weʃtʃi] *m* south-west

Suécia ['swɛsja] *f*: **a ~** Sweden;
sueco, -a ['sweku, a] *adj* Swedish
♦ *m/f* Swede ♦ *m* (*LING*) Swedish

suéter ['swete*] (*BR*) *m ou f* sweater

suficiente [sufi'sjẽtʃi] *adj* sufficient, enough

sufixo [su'fiksu] *m* suffix

sufocante [sufo'kãtʃi] *adj* suffocat-
ing; (*calor*) sweltering, oppressive

sufocar [sufo'ka*] *vt, vi* to suffocate

sugar [su'ga*] *vt* to suck

sugerir [suʒe'ri*] *vt* to suggest

sugestão [suʒeʃ'tãw] (*pl* -ões) *f*
suggestion; **dar uma ~** to make a
suggestion; **sugestivo, -a** [suʒeʃ-
'tʃivu, a] *adj* suggestive

sugiro *etc* [su'ʒiru] *vb V* **sugerir**

Suíça ['swisa] *f*: **a ~** Switzerland

suíças ['swisaʃ] *fpl* sideburns; *V tb*
suíço

suicida [swi'sida] *adj* suicidal ♦ *m/f*
suicidal person; (*morto*) suicide;
suicidar-se [swisi'daxsi] *vr* to
commit suicide; **suicídio** [swi-
'sidʒju] *m* suicide

suíço, -a ['swisu, a] *adj, m/f* Swiss

suíte ['switʃi] *f* (*MÚS, em hotel*) suite

sujar [su'ʒa*] *vt* to dirty ♦ *vi* to make
a mess; **sujar-se** *vr* to get dirty

sujeira [su'ʒejra] *f* dirt; (*estado*)
dirtiness; (*col*) dirty trick

sujeito, -a [su'ʒejtu, a] *adj*: ~ **a** subject to ♦ *m* (*LING*) subject ♦ *m/f* man/
woman

sujo, -a ['suʒu, a] *adj* dirty; (*fig: desonesto*) dishonest ♦ *m* dirt

sul [suw] *adj inv* south, southern
♦ *m*: **o ~** the south; **sul-africano,
-a** *adj, m/f* South African; **sul-
americano, -a** *adj, m/f* South
American

sulco [suw'ku] *m* furrow

suma ['suma] *f*: **em ~** in short

sumário, -a [su'marju, a] *adj* (*breve*) brief, concise; (*JUR*) summary;
(*biquíni*) skimpy ♦ *m* summary

sumiço [su'misu] *m* disappearance

sumir [su'mi*] *vi* to disappear, vanish

sumo, -a ['sumu, a] *adj* (*importância*) extreme; (*qualidade*) supreme
♦ *m* (*PT*) juice

sunga ['sũga] *f* swimming trunks *pl*

suor [swɔ*] *m* sweat

super- [supe*-] *prefixo* super-

superado, -a [supe'radu, a] *adj*

(idéias) outmoded

superar [supe'ra*] vt (rival) to surpass; (inimigo, dificuldade) to overcome; (expectativa) to exceed

superficial [supexfi'sjaw] (pl -ais) adj superficial

superfície [supex'fisi] f surface; (extensão) area; (fig: aparência) appearance

supérfluo, -a [su'pεxflwu, a] adj superfluous

superior [supe'rjo*] adj superior; (mais elevado) higher; (quantidade) greater; (mais acima) upper ♦ m superior; **superioridade** [superjori'dadʒi] f superiority

superlotado, -a [supexlo'tadu, a] adj crowded; (excessivamente cheio) overcrowded

supermercado [supexmex'kadu] m supermarket

superpotência [supexpo'tẽsja] f superpower

superstição [supexʃtʃi'sãw] (pl -ões) f superstition; **supersticioso, -a** [supexʃtʃi'sjozu, ɔza] adj superstitious

supervisão [supexvi'zãw] f supervision; **supervisionar** [supexvizjo'na*] vt to supervise; **supervisor, a** [supexvi'zo*, a] m/f supervisor

suplementar [suplemẽ'ta*] adj supplementary ♦ vt to supplement

suplemento [suple'mẽtu] m supplement

súplica ['suplika] f supplication, plea; **suplicar** [supli'ka*] vt, vi to plead, beg

suplício [su'plisju] m torture

supor [su'po*] (irreg: como pôr) vt to suppose; (julgar) to think

suportar [supox'ta*] vt to hold up, support; (tolerar) to bear, tolerate; **suportável** [supox'tavew] (pl -eis) adj bearable; **suporte** [su'pɔxtʃi] m

support

suposto, -a [su'poʃtu, 'pɔʃta] adj supposed ♦ m assumption, supposition

supremo, -a [su'prεmu, a] adj supreme

suprimir [supri'mi*] vt to suppress

surdez [sux'deʒ] f: aparelho para a ~ hearing aid

surdo, -a ['suxdu, a] adj deaf; (som) muffled, dull ♦ m/f deaf person; **surdo-mudo, surda-muda** adj deaf and dumb ♦ m/f deaf-mute

surfe ['suxfi] m surfing

surgir [sux'ʒi*] vi to appear; (problema, oportunidade) to arise

surjo etc ['suxju] vb V surgir

surpreendente [suxprjẽ'dẽtʃi] adj surprising

surpreender [suxprjẽ'de*] vt to surprise; **surpreender-se** vr: ~-se (de) to be surprised (at); **surpresa** [sux'preza] f surprise; **surpreso, -a** [sux'prezu, a] pp de surpreender ♦ adj surprised

surra ['suxa] f (ger, ESPORTE): dar uma ~ em to thrash; levar uma ~ (de) to get thrashed (by); **surrar** [su'xa*] vt to beat, thrash

surtir [sux'tʃi*] vt to produce, bring about

surto ['suxtu] m outbreak

suscetível [suse'tʃivew] (pl -eis) adj susceptible; ~ de liable to

suspeita [suʃ'pejta] f suspicion; **suspeitar** [suʃpej'ta*] vt to suspect ♦ vi: **suspeitar de algo** to suspect sth; **suspeito, -a** [suʃ'pejtu, a] adj, m/f suspect

suspender [suʃpẽ'de*] vt (levantar) to lift; (pendurar) to hang; (trabalho, funcionário etc) to suspend; (encomenda) to cancel; (sessão) to adjourn, defer; (viagem) to put off; **suspensão** [suʃpẽ'sãw] (pl -ões) f (ger, AUTO) suspension; (de trabalho, pagamento) stoppage; (de viagem, sessão) deferment; (de encomenda) cancellation; **suspense** [suʃˈpɛsi] m suspense; **filme de suspense** thriller; **suspenso, -a** [suʃˈpẽsu, a] pp de **suspender**

suspensórios [suʃpẽˈsɔrjuʃ] mpl braces (BRIT), suspenders (US)

suspirar [suʃpiˈra*] vi to sigh; **suspiro** [suʃˈpiru] m sigh; (doce) meringue

sussurrar [susuˈxa*] vt, vi to whisper; **sussurro** [suˈsuxu] m whisper

sustentar [suʃtẽˈta*] vt to sustain; (prédio) to hold up; (padrão) to maintain; (financeiramente, acusação) to support; **sustentável** [suʃtẽˈtavew] (pl -eis) adj sustainable; **sustento** [suʃˈtẽtu] m sustenance; (subsistência) livelihood; (amparo) support

susto [ˈsuʃtu] m fright, scare

sutiã [suˈtʃjã] m bra(ssiere)

sutil [suˈtʃiw] (pl -is) adj subtle; **sutileza** [sutʃiˈleza] f subtlety

---

T

ta [ta] = te + a

tabacaria [tabakaˈria] f tobacconist's (shop)

tabaco [taˈbaku] m tobacco

tabela [taˈbela] f table, chart; (lista) list; **por ~** indirectly

taberna [taˈbɛxna] f tavern, bar

tablete [taˈbletʃi] m (de chocolate) bar

tabu [taˈbu] adj, m taboo

tábua [ˈtabwa] f plank, board; (MAT) table; **~ de passar roupa** ironing board

tabuleiro [tabuˈlejru] m tray;

(XADREZ) board

tabuleta [tabuˈleta] f (letreiro) sign, signboard

taça [ˈtasa] f cup

tacha [ˈtaʃa] f tack

tachinha [taˈʃiɲa] f drawing pin (BRIT), thumb tack (US)

tácito, -a [ˈtasitu, a] adj tacit

taco [ˈtaku] m (BILHAR) cue; (GOLFE) club

táctico, -a etc [ˈtatiku, a] (PT) = **tático** etc

tacto [ˈtatu] (PT) m = **tato**

tagarela [tagaˈrɛla] adj talkative
♦ m/f chatterbox; **tagarelar** [tagareˈla*] vi to chatter

Tailândia [tajˈlãdʒia] f: **a ~** Thailand

tal [taw] (pl **tais**) adj such; **~ e coisa** this and that; **um ~ de Sr. X** a certain Mr. X; **que ~?** what do you think?; (PT) how are things?; **que ~ um cafezinho?** what about a coffee?; **que ~ nós irmos ao cinema?** what about (us) going to the cinema?; **~ pai, ~ filho** like father, like son; **~ como** such as; (da maneira que) just as; **~ qual** just like; **o ~ professor** that teacher; **a ~ ponto** to such an extent; **de ~ maneira** in such a way; **e ~** and so on; **o ~, a ~** (col) the greatest; **o Pedro de ~** Peter what's-his-name; **na rua ~** in such and such a street; **foi um ~ de gente ligar lá para casa** there were people ringing home non-stop

tala [ˈtala] f (MED) splint

talão [taˈlãw] (pl **-ões**) m (de recibo) stub; **~ de cheques** cheque book (BRIT), check book (US)

talco [ˈtawku] m talcum powder; **pó de ~** (PT) talcum powder

talento [taˈlẽtu] m talent; (aptidão) ability

talha [ˈtaʎa] f carving; (vaso) pitcher; (NÁUT) tackle

talher [ta'ʎe*] m set of cutlery; **~es** mpl cutlery sg

talho ['taʎu] m (corte) cutting, slicing; (PT: açougue) butcher's (shop)

talo ['talu] m stalk, stem

talões [ta'lõjʃ] mpl de **talão**

talvez [taw'veʒ] adv perhaps, maybe

tamanco [ta'mãku] m clog, wooden shoe

tamanduá [tamã'dwa] m anteater

tamanho, -a [ta'maɲu, a] adj such (a) great ♦ m size

tâmara ['tamara] f date

também [tã'bẽj] adv also, too, as well; (além disso) besides; **~ não** not ... either, nor

tambor [tã'bo*] m drum

tamborim [tãbo'rĩ] (pl **-ns**) m tambourine

Tâmisa ['tamiza] m: **o ~** the Thames

tampa ['tãpa] f lid; (de garrafa) cap

tampão [tã'pãw] (pl **-ões**) m tampon; (de olho) (eye) patch

tampar [tã'pa*] vt (lata, garrafa) to put the lid on; (cobrir) to cover

tampinha [tã'piɲa] f lid, top

tampo ['tãpu] m lid

tampões [tã'põjʃ] mpl de **tampão**

tampouco [tã'poku] adv nor, neither

tangente [tã'ʒẽtʃi] f tangent

tangerina [tãʒe'rina] f tangerine

tanque ['tãki] m tank; (de lavar roupa) sink

tanto, -a ['tãtu, a] adj, pron (sg) so much; (: + interrogativa/negativa) as much; (pl) so many; (: + interrogativa/negativa) as many ♦ adv so much; **~ ... como ...** both ... and ...; **~ ... quanto ...** as much ... as ...; **~ tempo** so long; **quarenta e ~s anos** forty-odd years; **~ faz** it's all the same to me, I don't mind; **um ~ (quanto)** (como adv) rather, some-

what; **~ (assim) que** so much so that

tão [tãw] adv so; **~ rico quanto** as rich as; **tão-só** adv only

tapa ['tapa] m ou f slap

tapar [ta'pa*] vt to cover; (garrafa) to cork; (caixa) to put the lid on; (orifício) to block up; (encobrir) to block out

tapear [ta'pja*] vt, vi to cheat

tapeçaria [tapesa'ria] f tapestry

tapete [ta'petʃi] m carpet, rug

tardar [tax'da*] vi to delay; (chegar tarde) to be late ♦ vt to delay; **sem mais ~** without delay; **~ a** ou **em fazer** to take a long time to do; **o mais ~** at the latest

tarde ['taxdʒi] f afternoon ♦ adv late; **mais cedo ou mais ~** sooner or later; **antes ~ do que nunca** better late than never; **boa ~!** good afternoon!; **à** ou **de ~** in the afternoon

tardio, -a [tax'dʒiu, a] adj late

tarefa [ta'refa] f task, job; (faina) chore

tarifa [ta'rifa] f tariff; (para transportes) fare; (lista de preços) price list; **~ alfandegária** customs duty

tartaruga [taxta'ruga] f turtle

tasca ['taʃka] (PT) f cheap eating place

tática ['tatʃika] f tactics pl

tático, -a ['tatʃiku, a] adj tactical

tato ['tatu] m touch; (fig: diplomacia) tact

tatu [ta'tu] m armadillo

tatuagem [ta'twaʒẽ] (pl **-ns**) f tattoo

taxa ['taʃa] f (imposto) tax; (preço) fee; (índice) rate; **~ de câmbio/juros** exchange/interest rate; **taxação** [taʃa'sãw] f taxation; **taxar** [ta'ʃa*] vt (fixar o preço de) to fix the price of; (lançar impostos sobre) to tax

táxi ['taksi] m taxi

chau [tʃaw] *excl* bye!

checo, -a [ˈtʃɛku, a] *adj, m/f* Czech

Checo-Eslováquia [tʃɛkuiʒloˈvakja] *f* = **Tchecoslováquia**

Checoslováquia [tʃɛkoʒloˈvakja] *f:* **a ~** Czechoslovakia

che [tʃi] *pron* you; (*para você*) (to) you

é [tɛ] *prep abr de* **até**

tear [tʃjaˈ*] *m* loom

teatral [tʃjaˈtraw] (*pl* **-ais**) *adj* theatrical; (*grupo*) theatre *atr* (BRIT), theater *atr* (US); (*obra, arte*) dramatic

teatro [ˈtʃjatru] *m* theatre (BRIT), theater (US); (*obras*) plays *pl*, dramatic works *pl*; (*gênero, curso*) drama; **peça de ~** play

tecer [teˈse*] *vt, vi* to weave, **tecido** [teˈsidu] *m* cloth, material; (ANAT) tissue

tecla [ˈtɛkla] *f* key; **teclado** [tekˈladu] *m* keyboard

técnica [ˈtɛknika] *f* technique; *V tb* **técnico**

técnico, -a [ˈtɛkniku, a] *adj* technical ♦ *m/f* technician; (*especialista*) expert

tecnologia [teknoloˈʒia] *f* technology; **tecnológico, -a** [teknoˈlɔʒiku, a] *adj* technological

tecto [ˈtɛktu] (PT) *m* = **teto**

tédio [ˈtɛdʒju] *m* tedium, boredom; **tedioso, -a** [teˈdʒjozu, ɔza] *adj* tedious, boring

teia [ˈteja] *f* web; **~ de aranha** cobweb

teimar [tejˈma*] *vi* to insist, keep on; **~ em** to insist on

teimosia [tejmoˈzia] *f* stubbornness; **~ em fazer** insistence on doing

teimoso, -a [tejˈmozu, ɔza] *adj* obstinate; (*criança*) wilful (BRIT), willful (US)

Tejo [ˈteʒu] *m:* **o (rio) ~** the (River) Tagus

tela [ˈtɛla] *f* fabric, material; (*de pintar*) canvas; (CINEMA, TV) screen

tele... [ˈtɛle] *prefixo* **tele...**; **telecomunicações** [telekomunikaˈsõjʃ] *fpl* telecommunications; **teleconferência** [telekõfeˈrẽsja] *f* teleconference

teleférico [teleˈferiku] *m* cable car

telefonar [telefoˈna*] *vi:* **~ para alguém** to (tele)phone sb

telefone [teleˈfɔni] *m* phone, telephone; (*número*) (tele)phone number; (*telefonema*) phone call; **~ celular** cellphone, mobile phone; **~ de carro** carphone; **telefonema** [telefoˈnema] *m* phone call; **dar um telefonema** to make a phone call; **telefônico, -a** [teleˈfoniku, a] *adj* telephone *atr*; **telefonista** [telefoˈniʃta] *m/f* telephonist; (*na companhia telefônica*) operator

telégrafo [teˈlɛgrafu] *m* telegraph

telegrama [teleˈgrama] *m* telegram, cable; **passar um ~** to send a telegram

tele...: telejornal [teleʒorˈnaw] (*pl* **~jornais**) *m* television news *sg*; **telenovela** [telenoˈvela] *f* (TV) soap opera; **telescópio** [teleˈskɔpju] *m* telescope; **telespectador, a** [teleʃpektaˈdo*, a] *m/f* viewer

teletrabalho [teletraˈbaʎu] *m* teleworking

televendas [teleˈvẽdaʃ] *fpl* telesales

televisão [televiˈzãw] *f* television; **~ por assinatura** pay television; **~ a cabo** cable television; **~ a cores** colo(u)r television; **~ digital** digital television; **~ via satélite** satellite television; **aparelho de ~** television set; **televisionar** [televizjoˈna*] *vt* to televise; **televisivo, -a** [televiˈzivu, a] *adj* television *atr*

televisor [televi'zo*] m (aparelho) television (set), TV (set)

telex [te'lɛks] m telex; **enviar por ~** to telex

telha ['teʎa] f tile; (col: cabeça) head; **ter uma ~ de menos** to have a screw loose

telhado [te'ʎadu] m roof

tema ['tɛma] m theme; (assunto) subject; **temática** [te'matʃika] f theme

temer [te'me*] vt to fear, be afraid of ♦ vi to be afraid

temeroso, -a [teme'rozu, ɔza] adj fearful, afraid; (pavoroso) dreadful

temido, -a [te'midu, a] adj fearsome, frightening

temível [te'mivew] (pl -eis) adj = temido

temor [te'mo*] m fear

temperado, -a [tẽpe'radu, a] adj (clima) temperate; (comida) seasoned

temperamento [tẽpera'mẽtu] m temperament, nature

temperar [tẽpe'ra*] vt to season

temperatura [tẽpera'tura] f temperature

tempero [tẽ'peru] m seasoning, flavouring (BRIT), flavoring (US)

tempestade [tẽpeʃ'tadʒi] f storm; **tempestuoso, -a** [tẽpeʃ'twozu, ɔza] adj stormy

templo ['tẽplu] m temple; (igreja) church

tempo ['tẽpu] m time; (meteorológico) weather; (LING) tense; **o ~ todo** the whole time; **a ~** on time; **ao mesmo ~** at the same time; **a um ~** at once; **com ~** in good time; **de ~ em ~** from time to time; **nesse meio ~** in the meantime; **quanto ~?** how long?; **mais** ~ longer; **há ~s** for ages; (atrás) ages ago; **~ livre** spare time; **primeiro/segundo ~** (ESPORTE)

first/second half

temporada [tẽpo'rada] f season; (tempo) spell

temporal [tẽpo'raw] (pl -ais) m storm, gale

temporário, -a [tẽpo'rarju, a] adj temporary, provisional

tenacidade [tenasi'dadʒi] f tenacity

tenaz [te'najʒ] adj tenacious

tencionar [tẽsjo'na*] vt to intend, plan

tenda ['tẽda] f tent

tendão [tẽ'dãw] (pl -ões) m tendon

tendência [tẽ'dẽsja] f tendency; (da moda etc) trend; **a ~ de** ou **em ou a fazer** the tendency to do; **tendencioso, -a** [tẽdẽ'sjozu, ɔza] adj tendentious, bias(s)ed

tendões [tẽ'dõjʃ] mpl de **tendão**

tenebroso, -a [tene'brozu, ɔza] adj dark, gloomy; (fig) horrible

tenho etc ['tɛɲu] vb V **ter**

tênis ['tenif] m inv tennis; (sapatos) training shoes pl; (um sapato) training shoe; **~ de mesa** table tennis

tenista [te'niʃta] m/f tennis player

tenor [te'no*] m (MÚS) tenor

tenro, -a ['tẽxu, a] adj tender; (macio) soft; (delicado) delicate; (novo) young

tensão [tẽ'sãw] f tension; (pressão) pressure, strain; (rigidez) tightness; (ELET: voltagem) voltage

tenso, -a ['tẽsu, a] adj tense; (sob pressão) under stress, strained

tentação [tẽta'sãw] f temptation

tentáculo [tẽ'takulu] m tentacle

tentador, a [tẽta'do*, a] adj tempting

tentar [tẽ'ta*] vt to try; (seduzir) to tempt ♦ vi to try; **tentativa** de [tẽta'tʃiva] f attempt; **tentativa de homicídio/suicídio/roubo** attempted murder/suicide/robbery; **por**

tentativas by trial and error

tênue ['tenwi] adj tenuous; (fino) thin; (delicado) delicate; (luz, voz) faint; (pequeníssimo) minute

teor [te'o*] m (conteúdo) tenor; (sentido) meaning, drift

teoria [teo'ria] f theory; **teoricamente** [teorika'mẽtʃi] adv theoretically, in theory; **teórico, -a** [te-'ɔriku, a] adj theoretical ♦ m/f theoretician

tépido, -a ['tepidu, a] adj tepid

PALAVRA CHAVE
---

ter [te*] vt **1** (possuir, ger) to have; (na mão) to hold; **você tem uma caneta?** have you got a pen?; **ela vai ~ neném** she is going to have a baby
2 (idade, medidas, estado) to be; **ela tem 7 anos** she's 7 (years old); **a mesa tem 1 metro de comprimento** the table is 1 metre long; ~ **fome/sorte** to be hungry/lucky; ~ **frio/calor** to be cold/hot
3 (conter) to hold, contain; **a caixa tem um quilo de chocolates** the box holds one kilo of chocolates
4: ~ **que** ou **de fazer** to have to do
5: ~ **a ver com** to have to do with
6: ir ~ **com** to (go and) meet
♦ vb impess **1**: **tem** (sg) there is; (pl) there are; **tem 3 dias que não saio de casa** I haven't been out for 3 days
2: **não tem de quê** don't mention it

terapeuta [tera'pewta] m/f therapist

terapia [tera'pia] f therapy

terça ['texsa] f (tb: ~-feira) Tuesday; **terça-feira** (pl **terças-feiras**) f Tuesday; **terça-feira gorda** Shrove Tuesday

terceiro, -a [tex'sejru, a] num third; ~**s** mpl (os outros) outsiders

terço ['texsu] m third (part)

termas ['texmaʃ] fpl bathhouse sg

térmico, -a ['texmiku, a] adj thermal; **garrafa térmica** (Thermos ®) flask

terminal [texmi'naw] (pl -ais) adj terminal ♦ m (de rede, ELET, COMPUT) terminal ♦ f terminal; ~ (de vídeo) monitor, visual display unit

terminar [texmi'na*] vt to finish ♦ vi (pessoa) to finish; (coisa) to end; ~ **de fazer** to finish doing; (ter feito há pouco) to have just done; ~ **por fazer algo** to end up doing sth

término ['texminu] m end, termination

termo ['texmu] m term; (fim) end, termination; (limite) limit, boundary; (prazo) period; (PT: garrafa) (Thermos ®) flask; **meio ~** compromise; **em ~s (de)** in terms (of)

termômetro [tex'mometru] m thermometer

terno, -a ['texnu, a] adj gentle, tender ♦ m (BR: roupa) suit; **ternura** [tex'nura] f gentleness, tenderness

terra ['texa] f earth, world; (AGR, propriedade) land; (pátria) country; (chão) ground; (GEO) soil; (pó) dirt

terraço [te'xasu] m terrace

terramoto [texa'mɔtu] (PT) m = terremoto

terreiro [te'xejru] m yard, square

terremoto [texe'mɔtu] m earthquake

terreno, -a [te'xenu, a] adj m ground, land; (porção de terra) plot of land ♦ adj earthly

térreo, -a ['texju, a] adj: **andar** ~ (BR) ground floor (BRIT), first floor (US)

terrestre [te'xeʃtri] adj land atr

terrina [te'xina] f tureen

território [texi'tɔrju] m territory

terrível [te'xivew] (*pl* -**eis**) *adj* terrible, dreadful

terror [te'xo*] *m* terror, dread; **terrorista** [texo'riʃta] *adj*, *m/f* terrorist

tese ['tɛzi] *f* proposition, theory; (*EDUC*) thesis; **em ~** in theory

teso, -a ['tezu, a] *adj* (*cabo*) taut; (*rígido*) stiff

tesoura [te'zora] *f* scissors *pl*; **uma ~** a pair of scissors

tesouraria [tezora'ria] *f* treasury

tesouro [te'zoru] *m* treasure; (*erário*) treasury, exchequer; (*livro*) thesaurus

testa ['tɛʃta] *f* brow, forehead

testamento [teʃta'mẽtu] *m* will, testament; (*REL*): **Velho/Novo T~** Old/New Testament

testar [teʃ'ta*] *vt* to test; (*deixar em testamento*) to bequeath

teste ['tɛʃtʃi] *m* test

testemunha [teʃte'muɲa] *f* witness; **testemunhar** [teʃtemu'ɲa*] *vi* to testify ♦ *vt* to give evidence about; (*presenciar*) to witness; (*confirmar*) to demonstrate; **testemunho** [teʃte'muɲu] *m* evidence

testículo [teʃ'tʃikulu] *m* testicle

teta ['teta] *f* teat, nipple

tétano ['tetanu] *m* tetanus

teto ['tɛtu] *m* ceiling; (*telhado*) roof; (*habitação*) home

teu, tua [tew, 'tua] *adj* your ♦ *pron* yours

teve ['tevi] *vb* V **ter**

têxtil ['teʃtʃiw] (*pl* -**eis**) *m* textile

texto ['tɛʃtu] *m* text

textura [teʃ'tura] *f* texture

thriller ['srila*] (*pl* ~**s**) *m* thriller

ti [tʃi] *pron* you

tia ['tʃia] *f* aunt

Tibete [tʃi'betʃi] *m*: **o ~** Tibet

tido, -a [t'tʃidu, a] *pp de* **ter** ♦ *adj*: **~ como** *ou* **por** considered to be

tigela [tʃi'ʒɛla] *f* bowl

tigre ['tʃigri] *m* tiger

tijolo [tʃi'ʒolu] *m* brick

til [tʃiw] (*pl* **tis**) *m* tilde

timbre ['tʃibri] *m* insignia, emblem; (*selo*) stamp; (*MÚS*) tone, timbre; (*da voz*) tone; (*em papel de carta*) heading

time ['tʃimi] (*BR*) *m* team; **de segundo ~** (*fig*) second-rate

tímido, -a ['tʃimidu, a] *adj* shy, timid

tímpano ['tʃĩpanu] *m* eardrum; (*MÚS*) kettledrum

tina ['tʃina] *f* vat

tingir [tʃĩ'ʒi*] *vt* to dye; (*fig*) to tinge

tinha *etc* ['tʃiɲa] *vb* V **ter**

tinjo *etc* ['tʃiʒu] *vb* V **tingir**

tinta ['tʃĩta] *f* (*de pintar*) paint; (*de escrever*) ink; (*para tingir*) dye; (*fig*: *vestígio*) shade, tinge

tinto, -a ['tʃĩtu, a] *adj* dyed; (*fig*) stained; **vinho ~** red wine

tintura [tʃĩ'tura] *f* dye; (*ato*) dyeing; (*fig*) tinge, hint

tinturaria [tʃĩtura'ria] *f* drycleaner's

tio ['tʃiu] *m* uncle

típico, -a ['tʃipiku, a] *adj* typical

tipo ['tʃipu] *m* type; (*de imprensa*) print; (*de impressora*) typeface; (*col*: *sujeito*) guy, chap; (*pessoa*) person

tipografia [tʃipogra'fia] *f* printing; (*estabelecimento*) printer's

tíquete [tʃi'ketʃi] *m* ticket

tira ['tʃira] *f* strip ♦ *m* (*BR*: *col*) cop

tira-gosto (*pl* ~**s**) *m* snack, savoury

tirano, -a [tʃi'ranu, a] *adj* tyrannical ♦ *m/f* tyrant

tirar [tʃi'ra*] *vt* to take away; (*de dentro*) to take out; (*de cima*) to take off; (*roupa, sapatos*) to take off; (*arrancar*) to pull out; (*férias*) to take, have; (*boas notas*) to get; (*salário*) to earn; (*curso*) to do, take;

(*mancha*) to remove; (*foto, cópia*) to take; (*mesa*) to clear; **~ algo a alguém** to take sth from sb

tiritar [tʃiri'ta*] *vi* to shiver

tiro ['tʃiru] *m* shot; (*ato de disparar*) shooting; **~ ao alvo** target practice; **trocar ~s** to fire at one another

tiroteio [tʃiro'teju] *m* shooting, exchange of shots

tis [tʃiʃ] *mpl de* **til**

titular [tʃitu'la*] *adj* titular ♦ *m/f* holder

título ['tʃitulu] *m* title; (*COM*) bond; (*universitário*) degree; **~ de propriedade** title deed

tive *etc* ['tʃivi] *vb V* **ter**

to [tu] = **te + o**

toa ['toa] *f* towrope; **à ~** at random; (*sem motivo*) for no reason; (*inutilmente*) in vain, for nothing

toalete [twa'letʃi] *m* (*banheiro*) toilet; (*traje*) outfit ♦ *f*: **fazer a ~** to have a wash

toalha [to'aʎa] *f* towel

toca ['tɔka] *f* burrow, hole

toca-discos (*BR*) *m inv* recordplayer

toca-fitas *m inv* cassette player

tocaia [to'kaja] *f* ambush

tocante [to'kãtʃi] *adj* moving, touching; **no ~ a** regarding, concerning

tocar [to'ka*] *vt* to touch; (*MÚS*) to play ♦ *vi* to touch; to play; (*campainha, sino, telefone*) to ring; **tocar-se** *vr* to touch (each other); **~ a** (*dizer respeito a*) to concern, affect; (*ser a vez de*) to be up to; **~ em** to touch; (*assunto*) to touch upon; **~ para alguém** (*telefonar*) to ring sb (up), call sb (up); **pelo que me toca** as far as I am concerned

tocha ['tɔʃa] *f* torch

todavia [toda'via] *adv* yet, still, however

todo, -a ['todu, 'tɔda] *adj* **1** (*com artigo sg*) all; **toda a carne** all the meat; **toda a noite** all night, the whole night; (*o Brasil* (*BR*)) all of Brazil; **a toda (velocidade)** at full speed; **~ o mundo** (*BR*), **toda a gente** (*PT*) everybody, everyone; **em toda (a) parte** everywhere

2 (*com artigo pl*) all; (: *cada*) every; **~s os livros** all the books; **~s os dias/todas as noites** every day/night; **~s os que querem sair** all those who want to leave; **~s nós** all of us

♦ *adv*: **ao ~** altogether; (*no total*) in all; **de ~** completely

♦ *pron*: **~s** *mpl* everybody *sg*, everyone *sg*

todo-poderoso, -a *adj* allpowerful ♦ *m*: **o T~** the Almighty

toicinho [toj'siɲu] *m* bacon fat

toldo ['towdu] *m* awning, sun blind

tolerância [tole'rãsja] *f* tolerance; **tolerante** [tole'rãtʃi] *adj* tolerant

tolerar [tole'ra*] *vt* to tolerate; **tolerável** [tole'ravew] (*pl* **-eis**) *adj* tolerable, bearable; (*satisfatório*) passable; (*falta*) excusable

tolice [to'lisi] *f* stupidity, foolishness; (*ato, dito*) stupid thing

tolo, -a ['tolu, a] *adj* foolish, silly, stupid ♦ *m/f* fool

tom [tõ] (*pl* **-ns**) *m* tone; (*MÚS*: *altura*) pitch; (: *escala*) key; (*cor*) shade

tomada [to'mada] *f* capture; (*ELET*) socket

tomar [to'ma*] *vt* to take; (*capturar*) to capture, seize; (*decisão*) to make; (*bebida*) to drink; **~ café** (*de manhã*) to have breakfast

tomara [to'mara] *excl*: **~!** if only!; **~**

que venha hoje I hope he comes today

tomate [to'matʃi] *m* tomato

tombadilho [tõba'dʒiʎu] *m* deck

tombar [tõ'ba*] *vi* to fall down, tumble down ♦ *vt* to knock down, knock over; **tombo** [tõbu] *m* tumble, fall

tomilho [to'miʎu] *m* thyme

tona ['tɔna] *f* surface; **vir à ~** to come to the surface; (*fig*) to emerge; **trazer à ~** to bring up; (*recordações*) to bring back

tonalidade [tonali'dadʒi] *f* (*de cor*) shade; (*MÚS: tom*) key

tonelada [tone'lada] *f* ton

tônica ['tonika] *f* (*água*) tonic (water); (*fig*) keynote

tônico ['toniku] *m* tonic; **acento ~** stress

tons [tõʃ] *mpl de* tom

tonteira [tõ'tejra] *f* dizziness

tonto, -a ['tõtu, a] *adj* stupid, silly; (*zonzo*) dizzy, lightheaded; (*atarantado*) flustered

topar [to'pa*] *vt* to agree to ♦ *vi*: **~ com** to come across; **topar-se** *vr* (*duas pessoas*) to run into one another; **~ em** (*tropeçar*) to stub one's toe on; (*esbarrar*) to run into; (*tocar*) to touch

tópico, -a ['tɔpiku, a] *adj* topical ♦ *m* topic

topless [tɔp'lɛs] *adj inv* topless

topo ['topu] *m* top; (*extremidade*) end, extremity

toque¹ ['tɔki] *m* touch; (*de instrumento musical*) playing; (*de campainha*) ring; (*retoque*) finishing touch

toque² *etc vb V* tocar

Tóquio ['tɔkju] *n* Tokyo

tora ['tɔra] *f* (*pedaço*) piece; (*de madeira*) log; (*sesta*) nap

toranja [to'rãʒa] *f* grapefruit

torção [tox'sãw] (*pl* -ões) *m* twist; (*MED*) sprain

torcedor, a [toxse'do*, a] *m/f* supporter, fan

torcer [tox'se*] *vt* to twist; (*MED*) to sprain; (*desvirtuar*) to distort, misconstrue; (*roupa: espremer*) to wring; (: *na máquina*) to spin; (*vergar*) to bend ♦ *vi*: **~ por** (*time*) to support; **torcer-se** *vr* to squirm, writhe

torcicolo [toxsi'kɔlu] *m* stiff neck

torcida [tox'sida] *f* (*pavio*) wick; (*ESPORTE: ato de torcer*) cheering; (: *torcedores*) supporters *pl*

torções [tox'sõjʃ] *mpl de* torção

tormenta [tox'mẽta] *f* storm

tormento [tox'mẽtu] *m* torment; (*angústia*) anguish

tornar [tox'na*] *vi* to return, go back ♦ *vt*: **~ algo em algo** to turn ou make sth into sth; **tornar-se** *vr* to become; **~ a fazer algo** to do sth again

torneio [tox'neju] *m* tournament

torneira [tox'nejra] *f* tap (*BRIT*), faucet (*US*)

torno ['toxnu] *m* lathe; (*CERÂMICA*) wheel; **em ~ de** (*ao redor de*) around; (*sobre*) about

tornozelo [toxno'zelu] *m* ankle

torpe ['toxpi] *adj* vile

torrada [to'xada] *f* toast; **uma ~** a piece of toast; **torradeira** [toxa-'dejra] *f* toaster

torrão [to'xãw] (*pl* -ões) *m* turf, sod; (*terra*) soil, land; (*de açúcar*) lump

torrar [to'xa*] *vt* to toast; (*café*) to roast

torre ['toxi] *f* tower; (*XADREZ*) castle, rook; (*ELET*) pylon; **~ de controle** (*AER*) control tower

tórrido, -a ['tɔxidu, a] *adj* torrid

torrões [to'xõjʃ] *mpl de* torrão

torso ['toxsu] *m* torso

torta ['txta] *f* pie, tart

torto, -a ['toxtu, 'txta] *adj* twisted, crooked; **a ~ e a direito** indiscriminately

tortuoso, -a [tox'twozu, ɔza] *adj* winding

tortura [tox'tura] *f* torture; (*fig*) anguish; **torturar** [toxtu'ra*] *vt* to torture; to torment

tos [tuʃ] = **te** + **os**

tosco, -a ['toʃku, a] *adj* rough, unpolished; (*grosseiro*) coarse, crude

tosse ['tɔsi] *f* cough; **~ de cachorro** whooping cough; **tossir** [to'si*] *vi* to cough

tosta ['tɔʃta] (*PT*) *f* toast; **~ mista** toasted cheese and ham sandwich

tostão [toʃ'tãw] *m* cash

tostar [toʃ'ta*] *vt* to toast; (*pele, pessoa*) to tan; **tostar-se** *vr* to get tanned

total [to'taw] (*pl* -**ais**) *adj, m* total

totalitário, -a [totali'tarju, a] *adj* totalitarian

totalmente [totaw'mẽtʃi] *adv* totally

touca ['toka] *f* bonnet; **~ de banho** bathing cap

toupeira [to'pejra] *f* mole; (*fig*) numbskull, idiot

tourada [to'rada] *f* bullfight; **toureiro** [to'rejru] *m* bullfighter

touro ['toru] *m* bull; **T~** (*ASTROLOGIA*) Taurus

tóxico, -a ['tɔksiku, a] *adj* toxic ♦ *m* poison; (*droga*) drug; **toxicômano, -a** [toksi'komanu, a] *m/f* drug addict

TPM *abr f* (= *tensão pré-menstrual*) PMT

trabalhadeira [trabaʎa'dejra] *f*: **ela é ~** she's a hard worker

trabalhador, a [trabaʎa'do*, a] *adj*

hard-working, industrious; (*POL: classe*) working ♦ *m/f* worker

trabalhar [traba'ʎa*] *vi* to work ♦ *vt* (*terra*) to till; (*madeira, metal*) to work; (*texto*) to work on; **~ com** (*comerciar*) to deal in; **~ de** *ou* **como** to work as; **trabalhista** [traba'ʎiʃta] *adj* labour *atr* (*BRIT*), labor *atr* (*US*); **trabalho** [tra'baʎu] *m* work; (*emprego, tarefa*) job; (*ECON*) labo(u)r; **trabalho braçal** manual work; **trabalho doméstico** housework; **trabalhoso, -a** [traba-'ʎozu, ɔza] *adj* laborious, arduous

traça ['trasa] *f* moth

traçado [tra'sadu] *m* sketch, plan

tração [tra'sãw] *f* traction

traçar [tra'sa*] *vt* to draw, (*determinar*) to set out, outline; (*planos*) to draw up; (*escrever*) to compose

tracção [tra'sãw] (*PT*) *f* = **tração**

traço ['trasu] *m* line, dash; (*vestígio*) trace, vestige; (*aspecto*) feature, trait; **~s** *mpl* (*do rosto*) features; **~ (de união)** hyphen; (*entre frases*) dash

tractor [tra'to*] (*PT*) *m* = **trator**

tradição [tradʒi'sãw] (*pl* -**ões**) *f* tradition; **tradicional** [tradʒisjo'naw] (*pl* -**ais**) *adj* traditional

tradução [tradu'sãw] (*pl* -**ões**) *f* translation

tradutor, a [tradu'to*, a] *m/f* translator

traduzir [tradu'zi*] *vt* to translate

trafegar [trafe'ga*] *vi* to move, go

tráfego ['trafegu] *m* traffic

traficante [trafi'kãtʃi] *m/f* trafficker, dealer

traficar [trafi'ka*] *vi*: **~ (com)** to deal (in)

tráfico ['trafiku] *m* traffic

tragar [tra'ga*] *vt* to swallow; (*fumaça*) to inhale; (*suportar*) to tolerate ♦ *vi* to inhale

tragédia [tra'ʒɛdʒja] *f* tragedy;
　trágico, -a ['traʒiku, a] *adj* tragic

trago¹ ['tragu] *m* mouthful

trago² *etc vb* V **trazer**

traição [traj'sãw] (*pl* -**ões**) *f* treason,
　treachery; (*deslealdade*) disloyalty;
　(*infidelidade*) infidelity; **traiçoeiro,
　-a** [traj'swejru, a] *adj* treacherous;
　disloyal

traidor, a [traj'do*, a] *m/f* traitor

trailer ['trejla*] (*pl* ~**s**) *m* trailer;
　(*tipo casa*) caravan (*BRIT*), trailer (*US*)

traineira [traj'nejra] *f* trawler

trair [tra'i*] *vt* to betray; (*mulher,
　marido*) to be unfaithful to; (*espe-
　ranças*) not to live up to; **trair-se** *vr*
　to give o.s. away

trajar [tra'ʒa*] *vt* to wear

traje ['traʒi] *m* dress, clothes *pl*; ~ **de
　banho** swimsuit

trajeto [tra'ʒɛtu] (*PT* -**ct-**) *m* course,
　path

trajetória [traʒe'tɔrja] (*PT* -**ct-**) *f* tra-
　jectory; path; (*fig*) course

tralha ['traʎa] *f* fishing net

trama ['trama] *f* (*tecido*) weft (*BRIT*),
　woof (*US*); (*enredo, conspiração*) plot

tramar [tra'ma*] *vt* (*tecer*) to weave;
　(*maquinar*) to plot ♦ *vi*: ~ **contra** to
　conspire against

trâmites ['tramitʃiʃ] *mpl* procedure
　sg, channels

trampolim [trãpo'lĩ] (*pl* -**ns**) *m*
　trampoline; (*de piscina*) diving
　board; (*fig*) springboard

tranca ['trãka] *f* (*de porta*) bolt; (*de
　carro*) lock

trança ['trãsa] *f* (*cabelo*) plait;
　(*galão*) braid

trancar [trã'ka*] *vt* to lock

tranqüilidade [trãkwili'dadʒi] *f*
　tranquillity; (*paz*) peace

tranqüilizante [trãkwili'zãtʃi] *m*
　(*MED*) tranquillizer

tranqüilizar [trãkwili'za*] *vt* to
　calm, quieten; (*despreocupar*): ~
　alguém to reassure sb, put sb's
　mind at rest; **tranqüilizar-se** *vr* to
　calm down

tranqüilo, -a [trã'kwilu, a] *adj*
　peaceful; (*mar, pessoa*) calm; (*crian-
　ça*) quiet; (*consciência*) clear; (*se-
　guro*) sure, certain

transação [trãza'sãw] (*PT* -**cç-**) (*pl*
　-**ões**) *f* transaction

transbordar [trãʒbox'da*] *vi* to
　overflow

transbordo [trãʒ'boxdu] *m* (*de via-
　jantes*) change, transfer

transe ['trãzi] *m* ordeal; (*lance*)
　plight; (*hipnótico*) trance

transeunte [trã'zjũtʃi] *m/f* passer-
　by

transferência [trãʃfe'rẽsja] *f* trans-
　fer

transferir [trãʃfe'ri*] *vt* to transfer;
　(*adiar*) to postpone

transformação [trãʃfoxma'sãw]
　(*pl* -**ões**) *f* transformation

transformador [trãʃfoxma'do*] *m*
　(*ELET*) transformer

transformar [trãʃfox'ma*] *vt* to
　transform; **transformar-se** *vr* to
　turn

transfusão [trãʃfu'zãw] (*pl* -**ões**) *f*
　transfusion

transição [trãzi'sãw] (*pl* -**ões**) *f*
　transition

transistor [trãziʃ'to*] *m* transistor

transitar [trãzi'ta*] *vi*: ~ **por** to
　move through; (*rua*) to go along

transitivo, -a [trãzi'tʃivu, a] *adj*
　(*LING*) transitive

trânsito ['trãzitu] *m* transit, pas-
　sage; (*na rua: veículos*) traffic; (: *pes-
　soas*) flow; **transitório, -a** [trãzi-
　'tɔrju, a] *adj* transitory; (*período*)
　transitional

transmissão [trãʒmi'sãw] (*pl* -**ões**

f transmission; (*transferência*) transfer; ~ **ao vivo** live broadcast

transmissor [trãʒmi'so*] *m* transmitter

transmitir [trãʒmi'tʃi*] *vt* to transmit; (*RÁDIO, TV*) to broadcast; (*transferir*) to transfer; (*recado, notícia*) to pass on

transparência [trãʃpa'rēsja] *f* transparency; (*de água*) clarity; **transparente** [trãʃpa'rētʃi] *adj* transparent; (*roupa*) see-through; (*água*) clear

transpirar [trãʃpi'ra*] *vi* to perspire; (*divulgar-se*) to become known; (*verdade*) to come out ♦ *vt* to exude

transplante [trãʃ'plãtʃi] *m* transplant

transportar [trãʃpox'ta*] *vt* to transport; (*levar*) to carry; (*enlevar*) to entrance, enrapture

transporte [trãʃ'pɔxtʃi] *m* transport; (*COM*) haulage

transtorno [trãʃ'toxnu] *m* upset, disruption

trapaça [tra'pasa] *f* swindle, fraud; **trapacear** [trapa'sja*] *vt, vi* to swindle; **trapaceiro, -a** [trapa'sejru, a] *adj* crooked, cheating ♦ *m/f* swindler, cheat

trapalhão, -lhona [trapa'ʎãw, 'ʎɔna] (*pl* -ões, ~s) *m/f* bungler, blunderer

trapo ['trapu] *m* rag

traquéia [tra'kɛja] *f* windpipe

trarei *etc* [tra'rej] *vb V* **trazer**

trás [trajʃ] *prep, adv:* **para** ~ backwards; **por** ~ **de** behind; **de** ~ from behind

traseira [tra'zejra] *f* rear; (*ANAT*) bottom

traseiro, -a [tra'zejru, a] *adj* back, rear ♦ *m* (*ANAT*) bottom

traste ['traʃtʃi] *m* thing; (*coisa sem valor*) piece of junk

tratado [tra'tadu] *m* treaty

tratamento [trata'mētu] *m* treatment

tratar [tra'ta*] *vt* to treat; (*tema*) to deal with; (*combinar*) to agree ♦ *vi:* ~ **com** to deal with; (*combinar*) to agree with; ~ **de** to deal with; **de que se trata?** what is it about?

trato ['tratu] *m* treatment; (*contrato*) agreement, contract; ~**s** *mpl* (*relações*) dealings

trator [tra'to*] *m* tractor

trauma ['trawma] *m* trauma

travão [tra'vãw] (*PT: pl* -ões) *m* brake

travar [tra'va*] *vt* (*roda*) to lock; (*iniciar*) to engage in; (*conversa*) to strike up; (*luta*) to wage; (*carro*) to stop; (*passagem*) to block; (*movimentos*) to hinder ♦ *vi* (*PT*) to brake

trave ['travi] *f* beam; (*ESPORTE*) crossbar

través [tra'vɛʃ] *m* slant, incline; **de** ~ across, sideways

travessa [tra'vesa] *f* crossbeam, crossbar; (*rua*) lane, alley; (*prato*) dish; (*para o cabelo*) comb, slide

travessão [trave'sãw] (*pl* -ões) *m* (*de balança*) bar, beam; (*pontuação*) dash

travesseiro [trave'sejru] *m* pillow

travessia [trave'sia] *f* (*viagem*) journey, crossing

travesso, -a [tra'vesu, a] *adj* mischievous, naughty

travessões [trave'sõjʃ] *mpl* de **travessão**

travessura [trave'sura] *f* mischief, prank

travões [tra'võjʃ] *mpl* de **travão**

trazer [tra'ze*] *vt* to bring

trecho ['treʃu] *m* passage; (*de rua, caminho*) stretch; (*espaço*) space

trégua ['trɛgwa] *f* truce; (*descanso*) respite

treinador, a [trejna'do*, a] m/f
trainer

treinamento [trejna'mẽtu] m training

treinar [trej'na*] vt to train;
treinar-se vr to train; **treino**
['trejnu] m training

trejeito [tre'ʒejtu] m gesture; (careta) grimace, face

trela ['trɛla] f lead, leash

trem [trẽj] (pl -ns) m train; ~ de
aterrissagem (avião) landing gear

tremendo, -a [tre'mẽdu, a] adj
tremendous; (terrível) terrible, awful

tremer [tre'me*] vi to shudder,
quake; (terra) to shake; (de frio,
medo) to shiver

tremor [tre'mo*] m tremor; ~ de
terra (earth) tremor

trêmulo, -a ['tremulu, a] adj shaky,
trembling

trenó [tre'nɔ] m sledge, sleigh (BRIT),
sled (US)

trens [trẽjʃ] mpl de **trem**

trepadeira [trepa'dejra] f (BOT)
creeper

trepar [tre'pa*] vt to climb ♦ vi: ~
em to climb

trepidar [trepi'da*] vi to tremble,
shake

três [treʃ] num three

trevas ['trevaʃ] fpl darkness sg

trevo ['trevu] m clover; (de vias)
intersection

treze ['trezi] num thirteen

triângulo ['trjãgulu] m triangle

tribal [tri'baw] (pl -ais) adj tribal

tribo ['tribu] f tribe

tribuna [tri'buna] f platform, rostrum; (REL) pulpit

tribunal [tribu'naw] (pl -ais) m
court; (comissão) tribunal

tributar [tribu'ta*] vt to tax; (pagar)
to pay

tributo [tri'butu] m tribute; (imposto) tax

tricô [tri'ko] m knitting; **tricotar**
[triko'ta*] vt, vi to knit

trigo ['trigu] m wheat

trilha ['triʎa] f (caminho) path;
(rasto) track, trail; ~ sonora soundtrack

trilhão [tri'ʎãw] (pl -ões) m billion
(BRIT), trillion (US)

trilho ['triʎu] m (BR: FERRO) rail; (vereda) path, track

trilhões [tri'ʎõjʃ] mpl de **trilhão**

trimestral [trimeʃ'traw] (pl -ais)
adj quarterly; **trimestralmente**
[trimeʃtraw'mẽtʃi] adv quarterly

trimestre [tri'mɛʃtri] m (EDUC) term;
(COM) quarter

trincar [trĩ'ka*] vt to crunch;
(morder) to bite; (dentes) to grit ♦ vi
to crunch

trinco ['trĩku] m latch

trinta ['trĩta] num thirty

trio ['triu] m trio; ~ elétrico music
float; see boxed note

TRIO ELÉTRICO

Trios elétricos are lorries, carrying
floats equipped for sound and/or
live music, which parade through
the streets during carnaval, especially in Bahia. Bands and popular
performers on the floats draw
crowds by giving frenzied performances of various types of
music.

---

tripa ['tripa] f gut, intestine; ~s fpl
(intestinos) bowels; (vísceras) guts;
(CULIN) tripe sg

tripé [tri'pɛ] m tripod

triplicar [tripli'ka*] vt, vi to treble;
triplicar-se vr to treble

tripulação [tripula'sãw] (pl -ões) f
crew

tripulante [tripu'lãtʃi] m/f crew

member

triste ['triʃtʃi] adj sad; (lugar) depressing; **tristeza** [triʃ'teza] f sadness; gloominess

triturar [tritu'ra*] vt to grind

triunfar [trjũ'fa*] vi to triumph; **triunfo** ['trjũfu] m triumph

trivial [tri'vjaw] (pl -ais) adj common(place), ordinary; (insignificante) trivial

triz [triȝ] m: **por um ~** by a hair's breadth

troca ['trɔka] f exchange, swap

trocadilho [troka'dȝiʎu] m pun, play on words

trocado [tro'kadu] m: **~(s)** (small) change

trocador, a [troka'do*, a] m/f (em ônibus) conductor

trocar [tro'ka*] vt to exchange, swap; (mudar) to change; (inverter) to change ou swap round; (confundir) to mix up; **trocar-se** vr to change; **~ dinheiro** to change money

troco ['trɔku] m (dinheiro) change; (revide) retort, rejoinder

troféu [tro'fɛw] m trophy

tromba ['trõba] f (do elefante) trunk; (de outro animal) snout

trombeta [trõ'beta] f trumpet

trombone [trõ'bɔni] m trombone

trombose [trõ'bɔzi] f thrombosis

tronco ['trõku] m trunk; (ramo) branch; (de corpo) torso, trunk

trono ['trɔnu] m throne

tropa ['trɔpa] f troop; (exército) army; **ir para a ~** (PT) to join the army

tropeçar [trope'sa*] vi to stumble, trip; (fig) to blunder

tropical [tropi'kaw] (pl -ais) adj tropical

trópico ['trɔpiku] m tropic

trotar [tro'ta*] vi to trot; **trote** ['trɔtʃi] m trot; (por telefone etc) hoax call

trouxe etc ['trosi] vb V trazer

trovão [tro'vãw] (pl -ões) m clap of thunder; (trovoada) thunder; **trovejar** [trove'ȝa*] vi to thunder; **trovoada** [tro'vwada] f thunderstorm

trufa ['trufa] f truffle

trunfo ['trũfu] m trump (card)

truque ['truki] m trick; (publicitário) gimmick

truta ['truta] f trout

tu [tu] (PT) pron you

tua ['tua] f de teu

tuba ['tuba] f tuba

tubarão [tuba'rãw] (pl -ões) m shark

tuberculose [tuberku'lɔzi] f tuberculosis

tubo ['tubu] m tube, pipe; **~ de ensaio** test tube

tucano [tu'kanu] m toucan

tudo ['tudu] pron everything; **~ quanto** everything that; **antes de ~** first of all; **acima de ~** above all

tufão [tu'fãw] (pl -ões) m typhoon

tulipa [tu'lipa] f tulip

tumba ['tũba] f tomb; (lápide) tombstone

tumor [tu'mo*] m tumour (BRIT), tumor (US)

túmulo ['tumulu] m tomb; (sepultura) burial

tumulto [tu'muwtu] m uproar, trouble; (grande movimento) bustle; (balbúrdia) hubbub; (motim) riot; **tumultuado, -a** [tumuw'twadu, a] adj riotous, heated; **tumultuar** [tumuw'twa*] vt to disrupt; (amotinar) to rouse, incite

túnel ['tunew] (pl -eis) m tunnel

túnica ['tunika] f tunic

Tunísia [tu'nizja] f: **a ~** Tunisia

tupi [tu'pi] m Tupi (tribe); (LING) Tupi

U

♦ *m/f* Tupi Indian

tupi-guarani [-gwara'ni] *m* (*LING*)
see boxed note

TUPI-GUARANI

This is an important branch of
indigenous languages from the
tropical region of South America.
It takes in thirty indigenous peoples and includes Tupi, Guarani,
and other languages. Before
Brazil was discovered by the
Portuguese, it had 1,300 indigenous languages, 87% of which
are now extinct due to the exter-
mination of indigenous peoples
and the loss of territory.

---

tupiniquim [tupini'kĩ] (*pej*) (*pl*
-ns) *adj* Brazilian (Indian)
turbilhão [tuxbi'ʎãw] (*pl* -ões) *m* (*de
vento*) whirlwind; (*de água*) whirlpool
turbulência [tuxbu'lẽsja] *f* turbulence; **turbulento, -a** [tuxbu'lẽtu,
a] *adj* turbulent
turco, -a [ˈtuxku, a] *adj* Turkish
♦ *m/f* Turk ♦ *m* (*LING*) Turkish
turismo [tu'riʒmu] *m* tourism; **turista** [tu'riʃta] *m/f* tourist ♦ *adj*
(*classe*) tourist *atr*
turma [ˈtuxma] *f* group; (*EDUC*) class
turno [ˈtuxnu] *m* shift; (*vez*) turn;
(*ESPORTE, de eleição*) round; **por ~ s**
alternately, by turns, in turn
turquesa [tux'keza] *adj inv* turquoise
Turquia [tux'kia] *f*: **a ~** Turkey
tusso *etc* ['tusu] *vb* V **tossir**
tutela [tu'tɛla] *f* protection; (*JUR*)
guardianship
tutor, a [tu'to*, a] *m/f* guardian
tutu [tu'tu] *m* (*CULIN*) beans, bacon
and manioc flour
TV [te've] *abr f* (= *televisão*) TV

UE *abr f* (= *União Européia*) EU
UEM *abr f* (= *União Econômica e
Monetária*) EMU
Uganda [u'gãda] *m* Uganda
uísque ['wiʃki] *m* whisky (*BRIT*),
whiskey (*US*)
uivar [wi'va*] *vi* to howl; (*berrar*) to
yell; **uivo** [ˈwivu] *m* howl; (*fig*)
yell
úlcera ['uwsera] *f* ulcer
ultimamente [uwtʃima'mẽtʃi] *adv*
lately
ultimato [uwtʃi'matu] *m* ultimatum
último, -a [ˈuwtʃimu, a] *adj* last;
(*mais recente*) latest; (*qualidade*)
lowest; (*fig*) final; **por ~** finally; **nos
~s anos** in recent years; **a última**
(*notícia*) the latest (news)
ultra- [uwtra-] *prefixo* ultra-
ultrajar [uwtra'ʒa*] *vt* to outrage;
(*insultar*) to insult, offend; **ultraje**
[uw'traʒi] *m* outrage; (*insulto*) insult, offence (*BRIT*), offense (*US*)
ultramar [uwtra'ma*] *m* overseas
ultrapassado, -a [uwtrapa'sadu,
a] *adj* (*idéias etc*) outmoded
ultrapassar [uwtrapa'sa*] *vt* (*atravessar*) to cross, go beyond; (*ir além
de*) to exceed; (*transgredir*) to
overstep; (*AUTO*) to overtake (*BRIT*),
pass (*US*); (*ser superior a*) to surpass
♦ *vi* (*AUTO*) to overtake (*BRIT*), pass
(*US*)
ultra-som *m* ultrasound
ultravioleta [uwtravjo'leta] *adj*
ultraviolet

PALAVRA CHAVE

um, uma [ũ, 'uma] (*pl* **uns, umas**)
num one; **~ e outro** both; **~ a ~** one
by one; **à ~a (hora)** at one (o'clock)
♦ *adj*: **uns cinco** about five; **uns
poucos** a few

♦ *art indef* **1** (*sg*) a; (: *antes de vogal ou 'h' mudo*) an; (*pl*) some; **ela é de ~ beleza incrível** she's incredibly beautiful
2 (*dando ênfase*): **estou com ~ a fome!** I'm so hungry!
3: ~ ao outro one another; (*entre dois*) each other

umbigo [u'bigu] *m* navel
umbilical [ũbili'kaw] (*pl* -ais) *adj*: **cordão ~** umbilical cord
umedecer [umede'se*] *vt* to moisten, wet; **umedecer-se** *vr* to get wet
umidade [umi'dadʒi] *f* dampness; (*clima*) humidity
úmido, -a ['umidu, a] *adj* wet, moist; (*roupa*) damp; (*clima*) humid
unânime [u'nanimi] *adj* unanimous
unha ['uɲa] *f* nail; (*garra*) claw; **unhada** [u'ɲada] *f* scratch
união [u'njãw] (*pl* -ões) *f* union; (*ato*) joining; (*unidade, solidariedade*) unity; (*casamento*) marriage; (*TEC*) joint; **a U~ Européia** the European Union
unicamente [unika'mẽtʃi] *adv* only
único, -a ['uniku, a] *adj* only; (*sem igual*) unique; (*um só*) single
unidade [uni'dadʒi] *f* unity; (*TEC, COM*) unit; **~ central de processamento** (*COMPUT*) central processing unit; **~ de disco** (*COMPUT*) disk drive
unido, -a [u'nidu, a] *adj* joined, linked; (*fig*) united
unificar [unifi'ka*] *vt* to unite; **unificar-se** *vr* to join together
uniforme [uni'fɔxmi] *adj* uniform; (*semelhante*) alike, similar; (*superfície*) even ♦ *m* uniform; **uniformizado, -a** [unifoxmi'zadu, a] *adj*

uniform, standardized; (*vestido de uniforme*) in uniform; **uniformizar** [unifoxmi'za*] *vt* to standardize
uniões [u'njõjʃ] *fpl de* **união**
unir [u'ni*] *vt* to join together; (*ligar*) to link; (*pessoas, fig*) to unite; (*misturar*) to mix together; **unir-se** *vr* to come together; (*povos etc*) to unite
uníssono [u'nisonu] *m*: **em ~** in unison
universal [univex'saw] (*pl* -ais) *adj* universal; (*mundial*) worldwide
universidade [univexsi'dadʒi] *f* university; **universitário, -a** [univexsi'tarju, a] *adj* university *atr* ♦ *m/f* (*professor*) lecturer; (*aluno*) university student
universo [uni'vexsu] *m* universe; (*mundo*) world
uns [ũʃ] *mpl de* **um**
untar [ũ'ta*] *vt* (*esfregar*) to rub; (*com óleo, manteiga*) to grease
urbanismo [uxba'niʒmu] *m* town planning
urbano, -a [ux'banu, a] *adj* (*da cidade*) urban; (*fig*) urbane
urgência [ux'ʒẽsja] *f* urgency; **com toda ~** as quickly as possible; **urgente** [ux'ʒẽtʃi] *adj* urgent
urina [u'rina] *f* urine; **urinar** [uri'na*] *vi* to urinate ♦ *vt* (*sangue*) to pass; (*cama*) to wet; **urinar-se** *vr* to wet o.s.; **urinol** [uri'nɔw] (*pl* -óis) *m* chamber pot
urna ['uxna] *f* urn; **~ eleitoral** ballot box
urrar [u'xa*] *vt, vi* to roar; (*de dor*) to yell
urso ['uxsu, a] *m/f* bear
URSS *abr f* (= *União das Repúblicas Socialistas Soviéticas*): **a ~** the USSR
urtiga [ux'tʃiga] *f* nettle
Uruguai [uru'gwaj] *m*: **o ~** Uruguay
urze ['uxzi] *m* heather

usado, -a [u'zadu, a] *adj* used; (*comum*) common; (*roupa*) worn; (*gasto*) worn out; (*de segunda mão*) second-hand

usar [u'za*] *vt* (*servir-se de*) to use; (*vestir*) to wear; (*gastar com o uso*) to wear out; (*barba, cabelo curto*) to have, wear ♦ *vi:* **~ de** to use; **modo de ~** directions *pl*

usina [u'zina] *f* (*fábrica*) factory; (*de energia*) plant

uso ['uzu] *m* use; (*utilização*) usage; (*prática*) practice

usual [u'zwaw] (*pl* **-ais**) *adj* usual; (*comum*) common

usuário, -a [u'zwarju, a] *m/f* user

usufruir [uzu'frwi*] *vt* to enjoy ♦ *vi:* **~ de** to enjoy

úteis ['utejʃ] *pl de* **útil**

utensílio [utẽ'silju] *m* utensil

útero ['uteru] *m* womb, uterus

útil ['utʃiw] (*pl* **-eis**) *adj* useful; (*vantajoso*) profitable, worthwhile; **utilidade** [utʃili'dadʒi] *f* usefulness; **utilização** [utʃiliza'sãw] *f* use; **utilizar** [utʃili'za*] *vt* to use; **utilizar-se** *vr:* **utilizar-se de** to make use of

uva ['uva] *f* grape

V

v *abr* (= *volt*) v

vá *etc* [va] *vb* V **ir**

vã [vã] *f de* **vão**

vaca ['vaka] *f* cow; **carne de ~** beef

vacilar [vasi'la*] *vi* to hesitate; (*balançar*) to sway; (*cambalear*) to stagger; (*luz*) to flicker; (*col*) to slip up

vacina [va'sina] *f* vaccine; **vacinar** [vasi'na*] *vt* to vaccinate

vácuo ['vakwu] *m* vacuum; (*fig*) void; (*espaço*) space

vadiar [va'dʒja*] *vi* to lounge about; (*não trabalhar*) to idle about; (*pe-*

rambular) to wander

vadio, -a [va'dʒiu, a] *adj* (*ocioso*) idle, lazy; (*vagabundo*) vagrant ♦ *m/f* idler; vagabond, vagrant

vaga ['vaga] *f* wave; (*em hotel, trabalho*) vacancy

vagabundo, -a [vaga'būdu, a] *adj* vagrant; (*vadio*) lazy, idle; (*de má qualidade*) shoddy ♦ *m/f* tramp

vagão [va'gãw] (*pl* **-ões**) *m* (*de passageiros*) carriage; (*de cargas*) wagon; **vagão-leito** (*pl* **vagões-leitos**) (*PT*) *m* sleeping car; **vagão-restaurante** (*pl* **vagões-restaurantes**) *m* buffet car

vagar [va'ga*] *vi* to wander about; (*barco*) to drift; (*ficar vago*) to be vacant

vagaroso, -a [vaga'rozu, ɔza] *adj* slow

vagina [va'ʒina] *f* vagina

vago, -a ['vagu, a] *adj* vague; (*desocupado*) vacant, free

vagões [va'gõjʃ] *mpl de* **vagão**

vai *etc* [vaj] *vb* V **ir**

vaia ['vaja] *f* booing; **vaiar** [va'ja*] *vt*, *vi* to boo, hiss

vaidade [vaj'dadʒi] *f* vanity; (*futilidade*) futility

vaidoso, -a [vaj'dozu, ɔza] *adj* vain

vaivém [vaj'vẽj] *m* to-ing and fro-ing

vala ['vala] *f* ditch

vale ['vali] *m* valley; (*escrito*) voucher; **~ postal** postal order

valente [va'lẽtʃi] *adj* brave; **valentia** [valẽ'tʃia] *f* courage, bravery; (*proeza*) feat

valer [va'le*] *vi* to be worth; (*ser válido*) to be valid; (*ter influência*) to carry weight; (*servir*) to serve; (*ser proveitoso*) to be useful; **valer-se** *vr:* **~se de** to use, make use of; **a pena** to be worthwhile; **~ por** (*equivaler*) to be worth the same as;

para ~ (*muito*) very much, a lot; (*realmente*) for real, properly; **vale dizer** in other words; **mais vale ...** (**do que ...**) it would be better to ... (than ...)

valeta [va'leta] *f* gutter

valha *etc* ['vaʎa] *vb V* **valer**

validade [vali'dadʒi] *f* validity

validar [vali'da*] *vt* to validate; **válido, -a** ['validu, a] *adj* valid

valioso, -a [va'ljozu, ɔza] *adj* valuable

valor [va'lo*] *m* value; (*mérito*) merit; (*coragem*) courage; (*preço*) price; (*importância*) importance; **~es** *mpl* (*morais*) values; (*num exame*) marks; (*COM*) securities; **dar ~ a** to value; **valorizar** [valori'za*] *vt* to value

valsa ['vawsa] *f* waltz

válvula ['vawvula] *f* valve

vampiro, -a [vã'piru, a] *m/f* vampire

vandalismo [vãda'liʒmu] *m* vandalism

vândalo, -a ['vãdalu, a] *m/f* vandal

vangloriar-se [vãglo'rjaxsi] *vr*: **~ de** to boast of *ou* about

vanguarda [vã'gwaxda] *f* vanguard; (*arte*) avant-garde

vantagem [vã'taʒẽ] (*pl* **-ns**) *f* advantage; (*ganho*) profit, benefit; **tirar ~ de** to take advantage of; **vantajoso, -a** [vãta'ʒozu, ɔza] *adj* advantageous; (*lucrativo*) profitable; (*proveitoso*) beneficial

vão¹, vã [vãw, vã] (*pl* **~s, ~s**) *adj* vain; (*fútil*) futile ♦ *m* (*intervalo*) space; (*de porta etc*) opening

vão² *vb V* **ir**

vapor [va'po*] *m* steam; (*navio*) steamer; (*de gas*) vapour (*BRIT*), vapor (*US*); **vaporizador** [vaporiza'do*] *m* (*de perfume*) spray

vaqueiro [va'kejru] *m* cowboy

vara ['vara] *f* stick; (*TEC*) rod; (*JUR*) jurisdiction; (*de porcos*) herd; **salto de ~** pole vault; **~ de condão** magic wand

varal [va'raw] (*pl* **-ais**) *m* clothes line

varanda [va'rãda] *f* verandah; (*balcão*) balcony

varar [va'ra*] *vt* to pierce; (*passar*) to cross

varejista [vare'ʒista] (*BR*) *m/f* retailer ♦ *adj* (*mercado*) retail

varejo [va'reʒu] (*BR*) *m* (*COM*) retail trade; **a ~** retail

variação [varja'sãw] (*pl* **-ões**) *f* variation

variado, -a [va'rjadu, a] *adj* varied; (*sortido*) assorted

variar [va'rja*] *vt, vi* to vary; **variável** [va'rjavew] (*pl* **-eis**) *adj* variable; (*tempo, humor*) changeable

varicela [vari'sɛla] *f* chickenpox

variedade [varje'dadʒi] *f* variety

varinha [va'riɲa] *f* wand; **~ de condão** magic wand

vário, -a ['varju, a] *adj* (*diverso*) varied; (*pl*) various, several; (*COM*) sundry

varíola [va'riola] *f* smallpox

varizes [va'riziʃ] *fpl* varicose veins

varrer [va'xe*] *vt* to sweep; (*fig*) to sweep away

vascular [vaʃku'ʎa*] *vt* (*pesquisar*) to research; (*remexer*) to rummage through

vaselina [vaze'lina] ® *f* vaseline ®

vasilha [va'ziʎa] *f* (*para líquidos*) jug; (*para alimentos*) dish; (*barril*) barrel

vaso ['vazu] *m* pot; (*para flores*) vase

vassoura [va'sora] *f* broom

vasto, -a ['vaʃtu, a] *adj* vast

vatapá [vata'pa] *m* fish or chicken with coconut milk, shrimps, peanuts, palm oil and spices

Vaticano [vatʃi'kanu] *m*: **o ~** the Vatican

vazamento [vaza'mẽtu] *m* leak

vazão [va'zãw] (*pl* **-ões**) *f* flow; (*venda*) sale; **dar ~ a** (*expressar*) to give vent to; (*atender*) to deal with; (*resolver*) to attend to

vazar [va'za*] *vt* to empty; (*derramar*) to spill; (*verter*) to pour out ♦ *vi* to leak

vazio, -a [va'ziu, a] *adj* empty; (*pessoa*) empty-headed, frivolous; (*cidade*) deserted ♦ *m* emptiness; (*deixado por alguém/algo*) void

vazões [va'zõjʃ] *fpl de* **vazão**

vê *etc* [ve] *vb V* **ver**

veado ['vjadua] *m* deer; **carne de ~** venison

vedado, -a [ve'dadu, a] *adj* (*proibido*) forbidden; (*fechado*) enclosed

vedar [ve'da*] *vt* to ban, prohibit; (*buraco*) to stop up; (*entrada, passagem*) to block; (*terreno*) to close off

veemente [vje'mẽtʃi] *adj* vehement

vegetação [veʒeta'sãw] *f* vegetation

vegetal [veʒe'taw] (*pl* **-ais**) *adj* vegetable *atr*; (*reino, vida*) plant *atr* ♦ *m* vegetable

vegetalista [veʒeta'liʃta] *adj, m/f* vegan

vegetariano, -a [veʒeta'rjanu, a] *adj, m/f* vegetarian

veia ['veja] *f* vein

veículo [ve'ikulu] *m* vehicle; (*fig: meio*) means *sg*

veio ['veju] *vb V* **vir** ♦ *m* (*de rocha*) vein; (*na mina*) seam; (*de madeira*) grain

vejo *etc* ['veʒu] *vb V* **ver**

vela ['vɛla] *f* candle; (*AUTO*) spark plug; (*NÁUT*) sail; **barco à ~** sailing boat

velar [ve'la*] *vt* to veil; (*ocultar*) to hide; (*vigiar*) to keep watch over; (*um doente*) to sit up with ♦ *vi* (*não dormir*) to stay up; (*vigiar*) to keep watch; **~ por** to look after

veleiro [ve'lejru] *m* sailing boat (*BRIT*), sailboat (*US*)

velejar [vele'ʒa*] *vi* to sail

velhaco, -a [ve'ʎaku, a] *adj* crooked ♦ *m/f* crook

velhice [ve'ʎisi] *f* old age

velho, -a ['vɛʎu, a] *adj* old ♦ *m/f* old man/woman

velocidade [velosi'dadʒi] *f* speed, velocity; (*PT: AUTO*) gear

velório [ve'lɔrju] *m* wake

veloz [ve'lɔʒ] *adj* fast

vem [vẽj] *vb V* **vir**

vêm [vẽj] *vb V* **vir**

vencedor, a [vẽse'do*, a] *adj* winning ♦ *m/f* winner

vencer [vẽ'se*] *vt* (*num jogo*) to beat; (*competição*) to win; (*inimigo*) to defeat; (*exceder*) to surpass; (*obstáculos*) to overcome; (*percorrer*) to pass ♦ *vi* (*num jogo*) to win; **vencido, -a** [vẽ'sidu, a] *adj*: **dar-se por vencido** to give in; **vencimento** [vẽsi'mẽtu] *m* (*COM*) expiry; (*data*) expiry date; (*salário*) salary; (*de gêneros alimentícios etc*) sell-by date; **vencimentos** *mpl* (*ganhos*) earnings

venda ['vẽda] *f* sale; (*pano*) blindfold; (*mercearia*) general store; **à ~** on sale, for sale

vendaval [vẽda'vaw] (*pl* **-ais**) *m* gale

vendedor, a [vẽde'do*, a] *m/f* seller; (*em loja*) sales assistant; **~ ambulante** street vendor

vender [vẽ'de*] *vt, vi* to sell; **~ por atacado/a varejo** to sell wholesale/retail

veneno [ve'nɛnu] *m* poison; **vene-**

noso, -a [vene'nozu, ɔza] *adj* poisonous

venerar [vene'ra*] *vt* to revere; (REL) to worship

venéreo, -a [ve'nɛrju, a] *adj*: **doença venérea** venereal disease

Venezuela [vene'zwela] *f*: **a ~** Venezuela

venha *etc* ['vɛɲa] *vb V* **vir**

ventania [vẽta'nia] *f* gale

ventar [vẽ'ta*] *vi*: **está ventando** it is windy

ventilação [vẽtʃila'sãw] *f* ventilation

ventilador [vẽtʃila'do*] *m* ventilator; (*elétrico*) fan

ventilar [vẽtʃi'la*] *vt* to ventilate; (*roupa, sala*) to air

vento ['vẽtu] *m* wind; (*brisa*) breeze; **ventoinha** [vẽ'twiɲa] *f* weathercock, weather vane; (*PT: AUTO*) fan

ventre ['vẽtri] *m* belly

ver [ve*] *vt* to see; (*olhar para, examinar*) to look at; (*televisão*) to watch ♦ *vi* to see ♦ *m*: **a meu ~** in my opinion; **vai ~ que** ... maybe ...; **não tem nada a ~ (com)** it has nothing to do (with)

veracidade [verasi'dadʒi] *f* truthfulness

veraneio [vera'neju] *m* summer holidays *pl* (*BRIT*) ou vacation (*US*)

verão [ve'rãw] (*pl* -**ões**) *m* summer

verba ['vɛxba] *f* allowance; **~(s)** *f(pl)* (*recursos*) funds *pl*

verbal [vex'baw] (*pl* -**ais**) *adj* verbal

verbete [vex'betʃi] *m* (*num dicionário*) entry

verbo ['vɛxbu] *m* verb

verdade [vex'dadʒi] *f* truth; **de ~** (*falar*) truthfully; (*ameaçar etc*) really; **na ~** in fact; **para falar a ~** to tell the truth; **verdadeiro, -a** [vexda'dejru, a] *adj* true; (*genuíno*) real; (*pessoa*) truthful

verde ['vexdʒi] *adj* green; (*fruta*) unripe ♦ *m* green; (*plantas etc*) greenery

verdura [vex'dura] *f* (*hortaliça*) greens *pl*; (*BOT*) greenery; (*cor verde*) greenness

verdureiro, -a [vexdu'rejru, a] *m/f* greengrocer (*BRIT*), produce dealer (*US*)

vereador, a [verja'do*, a] *m/f* councillor (*BRIT*), councilor (*US*)

veredicto [vere'dʒiktu] *m* verdict

verga ['vexga] *f* (*vara*) stick; (*de metal*) rod

vergonha [vex'goɲa] *f* shame; (*timidez*) embarrassment; (*humilhação*) humiliation; (*ato indecoroso*) indecency; (*brio*) self-respect; **ter ~** to be ashamed; (*tímido*) to be shy; **vergonhoso, -a** [vexgo'nozu, ɔza] *adj* shameful; (*indecoroso*) disgraceful

verídico, -a [ve'ridʒiku, a] *adj* true, truthful

verificar [verifi'ka*] *vt* to check; (*confirmar*) to verify

verme ['vexmi] *m* worm

vermelho, -a [vex'meʎu, a] *adj* red ♦ *m* red

vermute [vex'mutʃi] *m* vermouth

verniz [vex'niʃ] *m* varnish; (*couro*) patent leather

verões [ve'rõjʃ] *mpl de* **verão**

verossímil [vero'simiw] (*PT* -**osí-**) (*pl* -**eis**) *adj* likely, probable; (*crível*) credible

verruga [ve'xuga] *f* wart

versão [vex'sãw] (*pl* -**ões**) *f* version; (*tradução*) translation

versátil [vex'satʃiw] (*pl* -**eis**) *adj* versatile

verso ['vexsu] *m* verse; (*linha*) line of poetry

versões [vex'sõjʃ] *fpl de* **versão**

verter [vex'te*] *vt* to pour; (*por*

acaso) to spill; (*traduzir*) to translate; (*lágrimas, sangue*) to shed ♦ *vi*: **~ de** to spring from; **~ em** (*rio*) to flow into

vertical [vertʃi'kaw] (*pl* **-ais**) *adj* vertical; (*de pé*) upright, standing ♦ *f* vertical

vertigem [vex'tʃiʒẽ] *f* (*medo de altura*) vertigo; (*tonteira*) dizziness; **vertiginoso, -a** [vertʃiʒi'nozu, ɔza] *adj* dizzy, giddy; (*velocidade*) frenetic

vesgo, -a ['veʒgu, a] *adj* cross-eyed

vesícula [ve'zikula] *f:* **~ (biliar)** gall bladder

vespa ['veʃpa] *f* wasp

véspera ['veʃpera] *f:* **a ~ de** the day before; **a ~ de Natal** Christmas Eve

vestiário [veʃ'tʃiarju] *m* (*em casa, teatro*) cloakroom; (*ESPORTE*) changing room; (*de atar*) dressing room

vestíbulo [veʃ'tʃibulu] *m* hall (way), vestibule; (*TEATRO*) foyer

vestido, -a [veʃ'tʃidu, a] *adj:* **~ de branco** *etc* dressed in white *etc* ♦ *m* dress

vestígio [veʃ'tʃiʒju] *m* (*rastro*) track; (*fig*) sign, trace

vestimenta [veʃtʃi'mẽta] *f* garment

vestir [veʃ'tʃi*] *vt* (*uma criança*) to dress; (*pôr sobre si*) to put on; (*trajar*) to wear; (*comprar, dar roupa para*) to clothe; (*fazer roupa para*) to make clothes for; **vestir-se** *vr* to get dressed

vestuário [veʃ'twarju] *m* clothing

vetar [ve'ta*] *vt* to veto

veterano, -a [vete'ranu, a] *adj, m/f* veteran

veterinário, -a [veteri'narju, a] *m/f* vet(erinary surgeon)

veto ['vetu] *m* veto

véu [vɛw] *m* veil

vexame [ve'ʃami] *f* shame, dis-

grace; (*tormento*) affliction; (*humilhação*) humiliation; (*afronta*) insult

vez [veʒ] *f* time; (*turno*) turn; **uma ~** once; **algumas ~es, às ~es** sometimes; **~ por outra** sometimes; **cada ~ (que)** every time; **de ~ em quando** from time to time; **em ~ de** instead of; **uma ~ que** since; **3 ~es 6** 3 times 6; **de uma ~** for good; **de uma ~ por todas** once and for all; **muitas ~es** many times; (*freqüentemente*) often; **toda ~ que** every time; **um de cada ~** one at a time; **uma ~ ou outra** once in a while

vi [vi] *vb* V **ver**

via¹ ['via] *f* road, route; (*meio*) way; (*documento*) copy; (*conduto*) channel ♦ *prep* via, by way of; **em ~s de** about to; **por ~ terrestre/marítima** by land/sea

via² *etc vb* V **ver**

viaduto [via'dutu] *m* viaduct

viagem ['vjaʒẽ] (*pl* **-ns**) *f* journey, trip; (*o viajar*) travel; (*NÁUT*) voyage; **viagens** *fpl* (*jornadas*) travels; **~ de ida e volta** return trip, round trip

viajante [vja'ʒãtʃi] *adj* travelling (*BRIT*), traveling (*US*) ♦ *m* traveller (*BRIT*), traveler (*US*)

viajar [vja'ʒa*] *vi* to travel

viável ['vjavew] (*pl* **-eis**) *adj* feasible, viable

víbora ['vibora] *f* viper

vibração [vibra'sãw] (*pl* **-ões**) *f* vibration; (*fig*) thrill

vibrante [vi'brãtʃi] *adj* vibrant; (*discurso*) stirring

vibrar [vi'bra*] *vt* to brandish; (*fazer estremecer*) to vibrate; (*cordas*) to strike ♦ *vi* to vibrate; (*som*) to echo

vice ['visi] *m/f* deputy

vice- [visi-] *prefixo* vice-; **vice-presidente, -a** *m/f* vice president; **vice-versa** [-'vexsa] *adv* vice-versa

viciado, -a [vi'sjadu, a] *adj* addicted; (ar) foul ♦ m/f addict; ~ **em algo** addicted to sth

viciar [vi'sja*] vt (falsificar) to falsify; **viciar-se** vr: ~**se em algo** to become addicted to sth

vício ['visju] m vice; (defeito) failing; (costume) bad habit; (em entorpecentes) addiction

viço ['visu] m vigour (BRIT), vigor (US); (da pele) freshness

vida ['vida] f life; (duração) lifetime; (fig) vitality; **com** ~ alive; **ganhar a** ~ to earn one's living; **modo de** ~ way of life; **dar a** ~ **por algo/por fazer algo** to give one's right arm for sth/ to do sth; **estar bem de** ~ to be well off

vide ['vidʒi] vt see; ~ **verso** see over

videira [vi'dejra] f grapevine

vidente [vi'dẽtʃi] m/f clairvoyant

vídeo ['vidʒju] m video; **videocassete** [vidʒjuka'setʃi] m video cassette ou tape; (aparelho) video (recorder); **videoteipe** [vidʒju'tejpi] m video tape

vidraça [vi'drasa] f window pane

vidrado, -a [vi'dradu, a] adj glazed; (porta) glass atr; (olhos) glassy

vidro ['vidru] m glass; (frasco) bottle; **fibra de** ~ fibreglass (BRIT), fiberglass (US); ~ **de aumento** magnifying glass

vier etc [vje*] vb V **vir**

viés [vjɛʃ] m slant; **ao** ou **de** ~ diagonally

vieste [vi'jɛʃtʃi] vb V **vir**

Vietnã [vjet'nã] m: **o** ~ Vietnam; **vietnamita** [vjetna'mita] adj, m/f Vietnamese

viga ['viga] f beam; (de ferro) girder

viger [vi'ʒe*] vi to be in force

vigia [vi'ʒia] f watching; (NÁUT) porthole ♦ m night watchman; **vigiar** [vi'ʒja*] vt to watch; (ocultamente) to spy on; (presos, fronteira) to

guard ♦ vi to be on the lookout

vigilância [viʒi'lãsja] f vigilance; **vigilante** [viʒi'lãtʃi] adj vigilant; (atento) alert

vigor [vi'go*] m energy, vigour (BRIT), vigor (US); **em** ~ in force; **entrar/pôr em** ~ to take effect/put into effect; **vigoroso, -a** [vigo'rozu, ɔza] adj vigorous

vil [viw] (pl **vis**) adj vile

vila ['vila] f town; (casa) villa

vilão, -lã [vi'lãw, 'lã] (pl ~**s**, ~**s**) m/f villain

vilarejo [vila'reʒu] m village

vim [vĩ] vb V **vir**

vime ['vimi] m wicker vine

vinagre [vi'nagri] m vinegar

vinco ['vĩku] m crease; (sulco) furrow; (no rosto) line

vincular [vĩku'la*] vt to link, tie, **vínculo** ['vĩkulu] m bond, tie; (relação) link

vinda ['vĩda] f arrival; (regresso) return; **dar as boas ~s a** to welcome

vingança [vĩ'gãsa] f vengeance, revenge; **vingar** [vĩ'ga*] vt to avenge; **vingar-se** vr: **vingar-se de** to take revenge on; **vingativo, -a** [vĩga'tʃivu, a] adj vindictive

vinha¹ ['viɲa] f vineyard; (planta) vine

vinha² etc vb V **vir**

vinho ['viɲu] m wine; ~ **branco/ rosado/tinto** white/rosé/red wine; ~ **seco/doce** dry/sweet wine; → **do Porto** port

vinte ['vĩtʃi] num twenty

viola ['vjɔla] f viola

violação [vjola'sãw] (pl -**ões**) f violation; ~ **de domicílio** housebreaking

violão [vjo'lãw] (pl -**ões**) m guitar

violar [vjo'la*] vt to violate; (a lei) to break

violência [vjo'lẽsja] f violence; **vio-**

lentar [vjolẽ'ta*] vt to force; (*mulher*) to rape; **violento, -a** [vjo'lẽtu, a] adj violent

violeta [vjo'leta] f violet

violino [vjo'linu] m violin

violões [vjo'lõjʃ] mpl de **violão**

violoncelo [vjolõ'sɛlu] m cello

vir¹ [vi*] vi to come; **~ a ser** to turn out to be; **a semana que vem** next week

vir² etc vb V **ver**

vira-lata ['vira-] (pl **~s**) m (*cão*) mongrel

virar [vi'ra*] vt to turn; (*página, disco, barco*) to turn over; (*copo*) to empty; (*transformar-se em*) to become ♦ vi to turn; (*barco*) to capsize; (*mudar*) to change; **virar-se** vr to turn; (*voltar-se*) to turn round; (*defender-se*) to fend for o.s

virgem ['vixʒẽ] (pl **-ns**) f virgin; **V~** (ASTROLOGIA) Virgo

vírgula ['vixgula] f comma; (*decimal*) point

viril [vi'riw] (pl **-is**) adj virile

virilha [vi'riʎa] f groin

viris [vi'riʃ] adj pl de **viril**

virtual [vix'twaw] (pl **-ais**) adj virtual; (*potencial*) potential

virtude [vix'tudʒi] f virtue; **em ~ de** owing to, because of; **virtuoso, -a** [vix'twozu, ɔza] adj virtuous

virulento, -a [viru'lẽtu, a] adj virulent

vírus ['viruʃ] m inv virus

vis [viʃ] adj pl de **vil**

visão [vi'zãw] (pl **-ões**) f vision; (ANAT) eyesight; (*vista*) sight; (*maneira de perceber*) view

visar [vi'za*] vt (*alvo*) to aim at; (*ter em vista*) to have in view; (*ter como objetivo*) to aim for

vísceras ['viseraʃ] fpl innards, bowels

viseira [vi'zejra] f visor

visita [vi'zita] f visit, call; (*pessoa*) visitor; **fazer uma ~ a** to visit; **visitante** [vizi'tãtʃi] adj visiting ♦ m/f visitor; **visitar** [vizi'ta*] vt to visit

visível [vi'zivew] (pl **-eis**) adj visible

vislumbrar [viʒlũ'bra*] vt to glimpse, catch a glimpse of; **vislumbre** [viʒ'lũbri] m glimpse

visões [vi'zõjʃ] fpl de **visão**

visor [vi'zo*] m (FOTO) viewfinder

visse etc [visi] vb V **ver**

vista [viʃta] f sight; (MED) eyesight; (*panorama*) view; **à** ou **em ~ de** in view of; **dar na ~** to attract attention; **dar uma ~ de olhos em** to glance at; **fazer ~ grossa (a)** to turn a blind eye (to); **ter em ~** to have in mind; **à ~** visible, showing; (COM) in cash; **até a ~!** see you!

visto, -a [viʃtu, a] pp de **ver** ♦ adj seen ♦ m (em passaporte) visa; (em documento) stamp; **pelo ~** by the looks of things

visto etc vb V **vestir**

vistoria [viʃto'ria] f inspection

vistoso, -a [viʃ'tozu, ɔza] adj eye-catching

visual [vi'zwaw] (pl **-ais**) adj visual; **visualizar** [vizwali'za*] vt to visualize

vital [vi'taw] (pl **-ais**) adj vital; **vitalício, -a** [vita'lisju, a] adj for life

vitamina [vita'mina] f vitamin; (*para beber*) fruit crush

vitela [vi'tɛla] f calf; (*carne*) veal

vítima ['vitʃima] f victim

vitória [vi'tɔria] f victory; **vitorioso, -a** [vito'rjozu, ɔza] adj victorious

vitrina [vi'trina] f = **vitrine**

vitrine [vi'trini] f shop window; (*armário*) display case

viúvo, -a [vi'juvu, a] m/f widower/widow

viva ['viva] m cheer; ~! hurray!

vivaz [vi'vajʒ] adj lively

viveiro [vi'vejru] m nursery

vivência [vi'vēsja] f existence; (experiência) experience

vivenda [vi'vēda] f (casa) residence

viver [vi've*] vt, vi to live ♦ m life; ~ **de** to live on

víveres ['viverɛʃ] mpl provisions

vívido, -a ['vividu, a] adj vivid

vivo, -a ['vivu, a] adj living; (esperto) clever; (cor) bright; (criança, debate) lively ♦ m: **os** ~**s** the living

vizinhança [vizi'nãsa] f neighbourhood (BRIT), neighborhood (US)

vizinho, -a [vi'ziɲu, a] adj neighbouring (BRIT), neighboring (US); (perto) nearby ♦ m/f neighbour (BRIT), neighbor (US)

voar [vo'a*] vi to fly; (explodir) to blow up, explode

vocabulário [vokabu'larju] m vocabulary

vocábulo [vo'kabulu] m word

vocação [voka'sãw] (pl -ões) f vocation; **vocacional** [vokasjo'naw] (pl -ais) adj vocational; (orientação) careers atr

vocal [vo'kaw] (pl -ais) adj vocal

você, s [vo'se(ʃ)] pron (pl) you

vodca ['vɔdʒka] f vodka

vogal [vo'gaw] (pl -ais) f (LING) vowel

vol. abr (= volume) vol.

volante [vo'lãtʃi] m steering wheel

vôlei ['volej] m volleyball

voleibol [volej'bɔw] m = **vôlei**

volt ['vɔwtʃi] (pl -s) m volt

volta ['vɔwta] f turn; (regresso) return; (curva) bend, curve; (circuito) lap; (resposta) retort; **dar uma ~** (a pé) to go for a walk; (de carro) to go for a drive; **estar de ~** to be back; **na ~ do correio** by return (post); **por ~ de** about, around; **à**

ou **em ~ de** around; **na ~** (no caminho de ~) on the way back

voltagem [vow'taʒẽ] f voltage

voltar [vow'ta*] vt to turn ♦ vi to return, go (ou come) back; **voltar-se** vr to turn round; ~ **a fazer** to do again; ~ **a si** to come to; ~**-se para** to turn to; ~**-se contra** to turn against

volume [vo'lumi] m volume; (pacote) package; **volumoso, -a** [volu'mozu, ɔza] adj bulky, big

voluntário, -a [volũ'tarju, a] adj voluntary ♦ m/f volunteer

volúpia [vo'lupja] f pleasure, ecstasy

volúvel [vo'luvew] (pl -eis) adj fickle

vomitar [vomi'ta*] vt, vi to vomit; **vômito** ['vomitu] m (ato) vomiting; (efeito) vomit

vontade [võ'tadʒi] f will; (desejo) wish; **com** ~ (com prazer) with pleasure; (com gana) with gusto; **estar com** ou **ter** ~ **de fazer** to feel like doing

vôo ['vou] (PT **voo**) m flight; **levantar** ~ to take off; ~ **livre** (ESPORTE) hang-gliding

voraz [vo'rajʒ] adj voracious

vos [vuʃ] pron you; (indireto) to you

vós [vɔʃ] pron you

vosso, -a ['vɔsu, a] adj your ♦ pron: **(o)** ~ yours

votação [vota'sãw] (pl -ões) f vote, ballot; (ato) voting

votar [vo'ta*] vt (eleger) to vote for; (aprovar) to pass; (submeter a votação) to vote on ♦ vi to vote; **voto** ['votu] m vote; (promessa) vow; **votos** mpl (desejos) wishes

vou [vo] vb V **ir**

vovó [vo'vɔ] f grandma

vovô [vo'vo] m grandad

voz [vɔʒ] f voice; (clamor) cry; a

meia ~ in a whisper; **de viva ~** orally; **ter ~ ativa** to have a say; **em ~ alta/baixa** aloud/in a low voice; **~ de comando** command

vulcão [vuw'kãw] (*pl* **~s** *ou* **~ões**) *m* volcano

vulgar [vuw'ga*] *adj* common; (*pej: pessoa etc*) vulgar; **vulgaridade** [vuwgari'dadʒi] *f* commonness; vulgarity

vulgo ['vuwgu] *m* common people *pl* ♦ *adv* commonly known as

vulnerável [vuwne'ravew] (*pl* **-eis**) *adj* vulnerable

vulto ['vuwtu] *m* figure; (*volume*) mass; (*fig*) importance; (*pessoa importante*) important person

Xingu [ʃĩ'gu] *m*: **Parque Indígena do ~** *see boxed note*

XINGU

The Xingu National Park was created in 1961 by the federal government and directed by the brothers Orlando and Cláudio Vilasboas, who were known internationally for their efforts to preserve Brazil's indigenous people. Situated in the north of the state of Mato Grosso, it aims to preserve indigenous culture. It brings together sixteen communities, a total of two thousand Indians.

W

walkie-talkie [wɔki'tɔki] (*pl* **~s**) *m* walkie-talkie

watt ['wɔtʃi] (*pl* **~s**) *m* watt

X

xadrez [ʃa'dreʒ] *m* chess; (*tabuleiro*) chessboard; (*tecido*) checked cloth

xampu [ʃã'pu] *m* shampoo

xarope [ʃa'rɔpi] *m* syrup; (*para a tosse*) cough syrup

xeque [ʃeki] *m* (*soberano*) sheikh; **pôr em ~** (*fig*) to call into question; **xeque-mate** (*pl* **xeques-mate**) *m* checkmate

xerife [ʃe'rifi] *m* sheriff

xerocar [ʃero'ka*] *vt* to photocopy, Xerox ®

xerox [ʃe'rɔks] ® *m* (*cópia*) photocopy; (*máquina*) photocopier

xícara ['ʃikara] (*BR*) *f* cup

xingar [ʃĩ'ga*] *vt* to swear at ♦ *vi* to swear

Z

zagueiro [za'gejru] *m* (*FUTEBOL*) fullback

Zâmbia ['zãbja] *f* Zambia

zangado, -a [zã'gadu, a] *adj* angry; annoyed; (*irritadiço*) bad-tempered

zangar [zã'ga*] *vt* to annoy, irritate ♦ *vi* to get angry; **zangar-se** *vr* (*aborrecer-se*) to get annoyed; **~-se com** to get cross with

zarpar [zax'pa*] *vi* (*navio*) to set sail; (*ir-se*) to set off; (*fugir*) to run away

zebra ['zebra] *f* zebra

zelador, a [zela'do*, a] *m/f* caretaker

zelar [ze'la*] *vt*, *vi*: **~ (por)** to look after

zelo ['zelu] *m* devotion, zeal; **zeloso, -a** [ze'lozu, ɔza] *adj* zealous; (*diligente*) hard-working

zerar [ze'ra*] *vt* (*conta, inflação*) to reduce to zero; (*déficit*) to pay off, wipe out

zero ['zeru] *m* zero; (*ESPORTE*) nil; **zero-quilômetro** *adj inv* brand new

ziguezague [ziɣiˈzaɣi] *m* zigzag

Zimbábue [ziˈbabwi] *m*: **o ~** Zimbabwe

zinco [ˈzĩku] *m* zinc

-zinho, -a [ˈzĩɲu, a] *sufixo* little; **florzinha** little flower

zíper [ˈzipe*] *m* zip (*BRIT*), zipper (*US*)

zodíaco [zoˈdʒiaku] *m* zodiac

zoeira [ˈzwejra] *f* din

zombar [zõˈba*] *vi* to mock; **~ de** to make fun of; **zombaria** [zõbaˈria] *f* mockery, ridicule

zona [ˈzɔna] *f* area; (*de cidade*) district; (*GEO*) zone; (*col: local de meretrício*) red-light district; (: *confusão*) mess; (: *tumulto*) free-for-all; **~ eleitoral** electoral district, constituency

zonzo, -a [ˈzõzu, a] *adj* dizzy

zôo [ˈzou] *m* zoo

zoológico, -a [zoˈlɔʒiku, a] *adj* zoological; **jardim ~** zoo

zumbido [zũˈbidu] *m* buzz(ing); (*de tráfego*) hum

zumbir [zũˈbi*] *vi* to buzz; (*ouvido*) to ring ♦ *m* buzzing; ringing

zunzum [zũˈzũ] *m* buzz(ing)

zurrar [zuˈxa*] *vi* to bray

PORTUGUESE VERB FORMS

1 Gerund. 2 Imperative. 3 Present. 4 Imperfect. 5 Preterite. 6 Future. 7 Present subjunctive. 8 Imperfect subjunctive. 9 Future subjunctive. 10 Past participle. 11 Pluperfect. 12 Personal infinitive.

etc indicates that the irregular root is used for all persons of the tense, e.g. **ouvir 7** ouça ouça, ouças, ouça, ouçamos, ouçais, ouçam.

abrir 10 aberto

acudir 2 acode **3** acudo, acodes, acode, acodem

aderir 3 adiro **7** adira

advertir 3 advirto **7** advirta *etc*

agir 3 ajo **7** aja *etc*

agradecer 3 agradeço **7** agradeça *etc*

agredir 2 agride **3** agrido, agrides, agride, agridem **7** agrida *etc*

AMAR 1 amando **2** ama, amai **3** amo, amas, ama, amamos, amais, amam **4** amava, amavas, amava, amávamos, amáveis, amavam **5** amei, amaste, amou, amamos (*PT*: amámos), amastes, amaram **6** amarei, amarás, amará, amaremos, amareis, amarão **7** ame, ames, ame, amemos, ameis, amem **8** amasse, amasses, amasse, amássemos, amásseis, amassem **9** amar, amares, amar, amarmos, amardes, amarem **10** amado **11** amara, amaras, amara, amáramos, amáreis, amaram **12** amar, amares, amar, amarmos, amardes, amarem

ansiar 2 anseia **3** anseio, anseias, anseia, anseiam **7** anseie *etc*

apreçar 7 aprece *etc*

arrancar 7 arranque *etc*

arruinar 2 arruína **3** arruíno,

arruínas, arruína, arruínam **7** arruíne, arruínes, arruíne, arruínem

aspergir 3 aspirjo **7** aspirja *etc*

atribuir 3 atribuo, atribuis, atribui, atribuímos, atribuís, atribuem

averiguar 7 averigúe, averigúes, averigúe, averigúem

boiar 2 bóia, bóias, bóia, bóiam **7** bóie, bóies, bóie, bóiem

bulir 2 bole **3** bulo, boles, bole, bolem

caber 3 caibo **5** coube *etc* **7** caiba *etc* **8** coubesse *etc* **9** couber *etc*

cair 2 cai **3** caio, cais, cai, caímos, caís, caem **4** caía *etc* **5** caí, caíste **7** caia *etc* **8** caísse *etc*

cobrir 3 cubro **7** cubra *etc* **10** coberto

colorir 3 coluro **7** colura *etc*

compelir 3 compilo **7** compila *etc*

crer 2 crê **3** creio, crês, crê, cremos, credes, crêem **5** cri, creste, creu, cremos, crestes, creram **7** creia *etc*

cuspir 2 cospe **3** cuspo, cospes, cospe, cospem

dar 3 dá **3** dou, dás, dá, damos, dais, dão **5** dei, deste, deu, demos, destes, deram **7** dê, dês,

613

dê, demos, deis, dêem
8 desse *etc* 9 der *etc* 11 dera *etc*

deduzir 2 deduz 3 deduzo, deduzes, deduz

denegrir 2 denigre 3 denigro, denigres, denigre, denigrem 7 denigre *etc*

despir 3 dispo 7 dispa *etc*

dizer 2 diz (dize) 3 digo, dizes, diz, dizemos, dizeis, dizem 5 disse *etc* 6 direi *etc* 7 diga *etc* 8 dissesse *etc* 9 disser *etc* 10 dito

doer 3 dói 3 dôe (*BR*), doo (*PT*), dóis, dói

dormir 3 durmo 7 durma *etc*

escrever 10 escrito

ESTAR 2 está 3 estou, estás, está, estamos, estais, estão 4 estava *etc* 5 estive, estiveste, esteve, estivemos, estivestes, estiveram 7 esteja *etc* 8 estivesse *etc* 9 estiver *etc* 11 estivera *etc*

extorquir 3 exturco 7 exturca *etc*

FAZER 2 faço 3 faço, fiz, fizeste, fez, fizemos, fizestes, fizeram 6 farei *etc* 7 faça *etc* 8 fizesse *etc* 9 fizer *etc* 10 feito 11 fizera *etc*

ferir 3 firo 7 fira *etc*

fluir 3 fluo, fluis, flui, fluímos, fluís, fluem

fugir 2 foge 3 fujo, foges, foge, fogem 7 fuja *etc*

ganhar 10 ganho

gastar 10 gasto

gerir 3 giro 7 gira *etc*

haver 2 há 3 hei, hás, há, havemos, haveis, hão 4 havia *etc* 5 houve, houveste, houve, houvemos, houvestes, houveram 7 haja *etc* 8 houvesse *etc* 9 houver *etc* 11 houvera *etc*

ir 2 indo 2 vai, vais, vai, vamos, ides, vão 4 ia *etc* 5 fui, foste, foi, fomos, fostes, foram

7 vá, vás, vá, vamos, vades, vão 8 fosse, fosses, fosse, fôssemos, fôsseis, fossem 9 for *etc* 10 ido 11 fora *etc*

ler 2 lê 3 leio, lês, lê, lemos, ledes, lêem 5 li, leste, leu, lemos, lestes, leram 7 leia *etc*

medir 3 meço 7 meça *etc*

mentir 3 minto 7 minta *etc*

ouvir 3 ouço 7 ouça *etc*

pagar 10 pago

parar 2 pára 3 paro, paras, pára *etc*

parir 3 pairo 7 paira *etc*

pecar 7 peque *etc*

pedir 3 peço 7 peça *etc*

perder 3 perco 7 perca *etc*

poder 3 posso 5 pude, pudeste, pôde, pudemos, pudestes, puderam 7 possa *etc* 8 pudesse *etc* 9 puder *etc* 11 pudera *etc*

polir 2 pule 3 pulo, pules, pule, pulem 7 pula *etc*

pôr 1 pondo 2 põe 3 ponho, pões, põe, pomos, pondes, põem 4 punha *etc* 5 pus, puseste, pôs, pusemos, pusestes, puseram 6 porei *etc* 7 ponha *etc* 8 pusesse *etc* 9 puser *etc* 10 posto 11 pusera *etc*

preferir 3 prefiro 7 prefire *etc*

pervenir 3 previne 3 previno, prevines, previne, previnem 7 previna *etc*

prover 3 provê 3 provejo, provês, provê, provemos, provedes, provêem 5 provi, proveste, proveu, provemos, provestes, proveram 7 proveja *etc* 8 provesse *etc* 9 prover *etc*

querer 3 quero, queres, quer 5 quis, quiseste, quis, quisemos, quisestes, quiseram 7 queira *etc* 8 quisesse *etc* 9 quiser *etc*

614

11 quisera *etc*

refletir 3 reflito 7 reflita *etc*

repetir 3 repito 7 repita *etc*

requerer 3 requeiro, requeres, requer 7 requeira *etc*

reunir 2 reúne 3 reúno, reúnes, reúne, reúnem 7 reúna *etc*

rir 2 ri 3 rio, ris, ri, rimos, rides, ridem 5 ri, riste, riu, rimos, ristes, riram 7 ria *etc*

saber 3 sei, sabes, sabe, sabemos, sabeis, sabem 5 soube, soubeste, soube, soubemos, soubestes, souberam 7 saiba *etc* 8 soubesse *etc* 9 souber *etc* 11 soubera *etc*

seguir 3 sigo 7 siga *etc*

sentir 3 sinto 7 sinta *etc*

ser 2 sê 3 sou, és, é, somos, sois, são 4 era *etc* 5 fui, foste, foi, fomos, fostes, foram 7 seja *etc* 8 fosse *etc* 9 for *etc* 11 fora *etc*

servir 3 sirvo 7 sirva *etc*

subir 2 sobe 3 subo, sobes, sobe, sobem

suster 2 sustém 3 sustenho, sustens, sustém, sustendes, sustêm 5 sustive, sustiveste, susteve, sustivemos, sustivestes, sustiveram 7 sustenha *etc*

ter 2 tem 3 tenho, tens, tem, temos, tendes, têm 4 tinha *etc* 5 tive, tiveste, teve, tivemos, tivestes, tiveram 6 terei *etc* 7 tenha *etc* 8 tivesse *etc* 9 tiver *etc* 11 tivera *etc*

torcer 3 torço 7 torça *etc*

tossir 3 tusso 7 tussa *etc*

trair 2 trai 3 traio, trais, trai, traímos, traís, traem 7 traia *etc*

trazer 2 (traze) traz 3 trago, trazes, traz, 5 trouxe, trouxeste, trouxe, trouxemos, trouxestes, trouxeram 6 trarei *etc* 7 traga *etc*

8 trouxesse *etc* **9** trouxer *etc* **11** trouxera *etc*

UNIR 1 unindo 2 une, uni 3 uno, unes, une, unimos, unis, unem 4 unia, unias, uníamos, uníeis, uniam 5 uni, uniste, uniu, unimos, unistes, uniram 6 unirei, unirás, unirá, uniremos, unireis, unirão 7 una, unas, una, unamos, unais, unam 8 unisse, unisses, unissemos, unísseis, unissem 9 unir, unires, unir, unirmos, unirdes, unirem 10 unido 11 unira, uniras, unira, uníramos, uníreis, uniram 12 unir, unires, unir, unirmos, unirdes, unirem

valer 3 valho 7 valha *etc*

ver 3 vê vejo, vês, vê, vemos, vedes, vêem 4 via *etc* 5 vi, viste, viu, vimos, vistes, viram 7 veja *etc* 8 visse *etc* 9 vir *etc* 10 visto 11 vira

vir 1 vindo, 2 vem 3 venho, vens, vem, vimos, vindes, vêm 4 vinha *etc* 5 vim, vieste, veio, viemos, viestes, vieram 7 venha *etc* 8 viesse *etc* 9 vier *etc* 10 vindo 11 viera *etc*

VIVER 1 vivendo 2 vive, vivei 3 vivo, vives, vive, vivemos, viveis, vivem 4 vivia, vivias, vivia, vivíamos, vivíeis, viviam 5 vivi, viveste, viveu, vivemos, vivestes, viveram 6 viverei, viverás, viverá, viveremos, vivereis, viverão 7 viva, vivas, viva, vivamos, vivais, vivam 8 vivesse, vivesses, vivêssemos, vivêsseis, vivessem 9 viver, viveres, viver, vivermos, viverdes, viverem 10 vivido 11 vivera, viveras, vivera, vivêramos, vivêreis, viveram 12 viver, viveres, viver, vivermos, viverdes, viverem

VERBOS IRREGULARES EM INGLÊS

present	pt	pp	present	pt	pp
arise	arose	arisen	fall	fell	fallen
awake	awoke	awoken	feed	fed	fed
be	was, were	been	feel	felt	felt
(am, is,			fight	fought	fought
are;			find	found	found
being)			fling	flung	flung
bear	bore	born(e)	fly	flew	flown
beat	beat	beaten	forbid	forbad(e)	forbidden
begin	began	begun	forecast	forecast	forecast
bend	bent	bent	forget	forgot	forgotten
bet	bet,	bet,	forgive	forgave	forgiven
	betted	betted	freeze	froze	frozen
bid (at	bid	bid	get	got	got,
auction)					(US) gotten
bind	bound	bound	give	gave	given
bite	bit	bitten	go (goes)	went	gone
bleed	bled	bled	grind	ground	ground
blow	blew	blown	grow	grew	grown
break	broke	broken	hang	hung	hung
breed	bred	bred	hang	hanged	hanged
bring	brought	brought	(execute)		
build	built	built	have	had	had
burn	burnt,	burnt,	hear	heard	heard
	burned	burned	hide	hid	hidden
burst	burst	burst	hit	hit	hit
buy	bought	bought	hold	held	held
can	could	(been able)	hurt	hurt	hurt
cast	cast	cast	keep	kept	kept
catch	caught	caught	kneel	knelt,	knelt,
choose	chose	chosen		kneeled	kneeled
cling	clung	clung	know	knew	known
come	came	come	lay	laid	laid
cost	cost	cost	lead	led	led
creep	crept	crept	lean	leant,	leant,
cut	cut	cut		leaned	leaned
deal	dealt	dealt	leap	leapt,	leapt,
dig	dug	dug		leaped	leaped
do (does)	did	done	learn	learnt,	learnt,
draw	drew	drawn		learned	learned
dream	dreamed,	dreamed,	leave	left	left
	dreamt	dreamt	lend	lent	lent
drink	drank	drunk	let	let	let
drive	drove	driven	lie (lying)	lay	lain
eat	ate	eaten			

616

present	pt	pp	present	pt	pp
light	lit, lighted	lit, lighted	**sow**	sowed	sown, sowed
lose	lost	lost	**speak**	spoke	spoken
make	made	made	**speed**	sped, speeded	sped, speeded
may	might	–	**spell**	spelt, spelled	spelt, spelled
mean	meant	meant			
meet	met	met			
mistake	mistook	mistaken	**spend**	spent	spent
mow	mowed	mown, mowed	**spill**	spilt, spilled	spilt, spilled
must	(had to)	(had to)	**spin**	spun	spun
pay	paid	paid	**spit**	spat	spat
put	put	put	**spoil**	spoiled, spoilt	spoiled, spoilt
quit	quit, quitted	quit, quitted	**spread**	spread	spread
read	read	read	**spring**	sprang	sprung
rid	rid	rid	**stand**	stood	stood
ride	rode	ridden	**steal**	stole	stolen
ring	rang	rung	**stick**	stuck	stuck
rise	rose	risen	**sting**	stung	stung
run	ran	run	**stink**	stank	stunk
saw	sawed	sawed, sawn	**stride**	strode	stridden
			strike	struck	struck
say	said	said			
see	saw	seen	**swear**	swore	sworn
sell	sold	sold	**sweep**	swept	swept
send	sent	sent	**swell**	swelled	swollen, swelled
set	set	set			
sew	sewed	sewn	**swim**	swam	swum
shake	shook	shaken	**swing**	swung	swung
shear	sheared	shorn, sheared	**take**	took	taken
			teach	taught	taught
shed	shed	shed	**tear**	tore	torn
shine	shone	shone	**tell**	told	told
shoot	shot	shot	**think**	thought	thought
show	showed	shown	**throw**	threw	thrown
shrink	shrank	shrunk	**thrust**	thrust	thrust
shut	shut	shut	**tread**	trod	trodden
sing	sang	sung	**wake**	woke, waked	woken, waked
sink	sank	sunk			
sit	sat	sat	**wear**	wore	worn
sleep	slept	slept	**weave**	wove	woven
slide	slid	slid	**weep**	wept	wept
sling	slung	slung	**win**	won	won
slit	slit	slit	**wind**	wound	wound
smell	smelt, smelled	smelt, smelled	**wring**	wrung	wrung
			write	wrote	written

DATAS   DATES

▶ Dias da semana
segunda(-feira)
terça(-feira)
quarta(-feira)
quinta(-feira)
sexta(-feira)
sábado
domingo

▶ Days of the week
Monday
Tuesday
Wednesday
Thursday
Friday
Saturday
Sunday

▶ Meses
janeiro
fevereiro
março
abril
maio
junho
julho
agosto
setembro
outubro
novembro
dezembro

▶ Months
January
February
March
April
May
June
July
August
September
October
November
December

Note that the days of the week and the months start with a capital letter in Portugal and a small letter in Brazil.

▶ Vocabulário útil
Que dia é hoje?
Hoje é dia 28.
Quando?
hoje
amanhã
ontem
hoje de manhã/à tarde
em duas semanas
daqui a uma semana
o mês passado/que vem

▶ Useful vocabulary
What day is it today?
Today is the 28th.
When?
today
tomorrow
yesterday
this morning/afternoon
in two weeks *ou* a fortnight
in a week's time
last/next month

▶ **Que horas são?**   ▶ **What time is it?**

É meio-dia/meia-noite.
_____

It's midday/midnight.

É uma e quinze.
É uma e um quarto (*PT*).
_____

It's one fifteen.

Faltam dez para as duas.
São duas menos dez (*PT*).
_____

It's ten to two.

São três e meia.
_____

It's half past three.

Faltam vinte para as oito.
São oito menos vinte (*PT*).
_____

It's twenty to eight.

São nove (horas) da
manhã/da noite.
_____

It's nine o'clock in the
morning/at night.

NÚMEROS		NUMBERS

▶ Números cardinais		▶ Cardinal numbers
um (uma)	1	one
dois (duas)	2	two
três	3	three
quatro	4	four
cinco	5	five
seis	6	six
sete	7	seven
oito	8	eight
nove	9	nine
dez	10	ten
onze	11	eleven
doze	12	twelve
treze	13	thirteen
catorze	14	fourteen
quinze	15	fifteen
dezesseis (BR), dezasseis (PT)	16	sixteen
dezessete (BR), dezassete (PT)	17	seventeen
dezoito	18	eighteen
dezenove (BR), dezanove (PT)	19	nineteen
vinte	20	twenty
vinte e um (uma)	21	twenty-one
trinta	30	thirty
quarenta	40	forty
cinqüenta (BR), cinquenta (PT)	50	fifty
sessenta	60	sixty
setenta	70	seventy
oitenta	80	eighty
noventa	90	ninety

cem	100	a hundred
cento e um (uma)	101	a hundred and one
duzentos(-as)	200	two hundred
trezentos(-as)	300	three hundred
quinhentos(-as)	500	five hundred
mil	1.000/1,000	a thousand
um milhão	1.000.000/1,000,000	a million

▶ **Frações etc**   ▶ **Fractions etc**

zero vírgula cinco	0,5/0.5	zero point five
três vírgula quatro	3,4/3.4	three point four
dez por cento	10%	ten per cent
cem por cento	100%	a hundred per cent

▶ **Números ordinais**   ▶ **Ordinal numbers**

primeiro	1º/1st	first
segundo	2º/2nd	second
terceiro	3º/3rd	third
quarto	4º/4th	fourth
quinto	5º/5th	fifth
sexto	6º/6th	sixth
sétimo	7º/7th	seventh
oitavo	8º/8th	eighth
nono	9º/9th	ninth
décimo	10º/10th	tenth
décimo primeiro	11º/11th	eleventh
vigésimo	20º/20th	twentieth
trigésimo	30º/30th	thirtieth
quadragésimo	40º/40th	fortieth
qüinquagésimo (*BR*), quinquagésimo (*PT*)	50º/50th	fiftieth
centésimo	100º/100th	hundredth
centésimo primeiro	101º/101st	hundred-and-first
milésimo	1000º/1000th	thousandth

FRASES ÚTEIS

USEFUL PHRASES

▶ **Saudações**

Oi! (*BR*), Olá! (*PT*)
Adeus!
Tchau!
Bom dia.
Boa tarde.
Boa noite. *(para saudar)*
  (para despedir-se)
Bem-vindo!
Como está?
Bem, obrigado.
Prazer em conhecê-lo.
Tudo bem?
Até amanhã!
Até logo!
Boa sorte!
Felicidades!
Divirta-se!
Saúde! *(brinde)*
Saúde! *(ao espirrar)* (*BR*),
  Santinho! (*PT*)
Cuide-se!
Bom apetite!
Parabéns!
Feliz Natal!
Feliz Ano Novo!

▶ **Greetings**

Hello!
Goodbye!
Bye!
Good morning.
Good afternoon.
Good evening.
Good night.
Welcome!
How are you?
I'm fine, thank you.
Pleased to meet you.
How's life?
See you tomorrow!
See you later!
Good luck!
Congratulations!
Have fun!
Cheers!
Bless you!

Take care!
Enjoy your meal!
Happy Birthday!
Merry Christmas!
Happy New Year!

▶ **Ao telefone**

Alô? (*BR*), Estou? (*PT*)
Quem fala?
Aqui fala a Laura.
Posso falar com ...?
O meu (número de) telefone
  é ...
Está ocupado.
Ninguém atende.

▶ **On the telephone**

Hello?
Who's speaking?
It's Laura speaking.
Could I speak to ..., please?
My phone number is ...

It's engaged.
There's no reply.

Fala português/inglês?	Do you speak Portuguese/English?
Não desligue, por favor.	Please hold the line.
Eu gostaria de falar com o ramal 3395.	Could you put me through to extension 3395?
Quer deixar recado?	Would you like to leave a message?
Pode dizer que eu liguei?	Could you tell him that I called?
Volto a ligar mais tarde.	I'll call back later.
Acho que você ligou para o número errado.	I'm afraid you have the wrong number.

▶ **Cartas**

▶ **Letter Writing**

Exmo(-a). Senhor(a)	Dear Sir/Madam
Atenciosamente	Yours faithfully
Caro Sr. Fontes	Dear Mr. Fontes
Atenciosamente	Yours sincerely
Cordialmente	Best wishes
Cumprimentos	Kind regards
Cara Carlota	Dear Carlota
Um abraço	All the best
Um beijo	With love from ...
Envio anexo ...	Please find enclosed ...
Obrigado(-a) pela sua carta.	Thank you for your letter.

▶ **Correio eletrônico**

▶ **E-mail**

Você tem e-mail/correio eletrônico?	Do you have e-mail?
Qual é o seu endereço de e-mail/correio eletrônico?	What's your e-mail address?
Meu endereço de e-mail/correio eletrônico é ...	My e-mail address is ...
emma@coolmail.com = "emma arroba coolmail ponto com"	emma@coolmail.com = "emma at coolmail dot com"
Mandarei os detalhes para você por e-mail/correio eletrônico.	I'll e-mail you the details.